DATE DUE

SEP 2 3 2004	
OCT 1 8 2005	

BRODART   Cat. No. 23-221

Jung

ALSO BY DEIRDRE BAIR

Samuel Beckett: A Biography
Simone de Beauvoir: A Biography
Anaïs Nin: A Biography

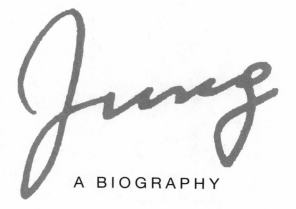

A BIOGRAPHY

DEIRDRE BAIR

LITTLE, BROWN AND COMPANY
Boston New York London

First Edition

Library of Congress Cataloging-in-Publication Data

Bair, Deirdre.
  Jung : a biography / Deirdre Bair. — 1st ed.
    p. cm.
  Includes bibliographical references and index.
  ISBN 0-316-07665-1
  1. Jung, C. G. (Carl Gustav), 1875–1961. 2. Psychoanalysts — Switzerland — Biography. I. Title.

BF109.J8B35 2003
150.19'9'54'092 — dc21   2003047472

10 9 8 7 6 5 4 3 2 1

Q-FF

Designed by NK Graphics/Diane Luopa-Filimonov

Printed in the United States of America

For
Isabel Anna Courtelis

Contents

Author's Note

By his own definition, Carl Gustav Jung would have been a "somewhat complicated phenomenon" for all the aspiring biographers who approached him in the last years of his long and eventful life. The thought of writing about it himself left him "at a total loss," even though he recognized the need for some record of his life and work. He thought the best way to approach it might be through a committee of biographers, specialists who would concentrate on specific areas where his life and work intersected. To him, the most important were medicine, religion, philosophy, mythology, literature, and art. Should the need for others arise, he was amenable to adding them later.

The biography by committee never came into being because Jung was persuaded instead to write his own version of his life. It became *Memories, Dreams, Reflections*, the book by which most people know the Swiss psychologist who was one of the two towering figures in the history of twentieth-century psychoanalysis. The other is Sigmund Freud, with whom Jung's name is most frequently linked, usually in a secondary if not derogatory position. Within the fractious history of psychoanalysis, Jung's association with Freud has routinely been the starting point for the popular perception of his role in the discipline's development. In a field whose history is inflamed by the quasi-religious status of its pioneers, partisans have been vocal, fiercely attacking or defending every issue in which they figured. As with so many other iconic figures, the controversy that swirled about Jung during his lifetime has suffused it since his death.

In a postmodern world where the concept of truth is subject to many differing variations and interpretations, perhaps an objective compilation of the facts and events is the best a biographer of Jung can hope to achieve. Anyone who undertakes to write about him is confronted by the many charges against him. Founded or unfounded, they began to mount after Jung rejected a key point in Freud's theory. But what was the truth about why he did it and what happened to him afterward? Was he anti-Semitic, as Freud charged? Was his theory a new form of religion with himself as its god?

Other charges emerged after Jung took a mistress. He treated her as a second wife and insisted upon a discreet triangular relationship that lasted their entire lifetimes. Did this make him the unmitigated womanizer so many have branded him?

Opprobrium smeared Jung's reputation when he accepted the presidency of a professional society in Germany during the Nazi regime, which he did not resign until well after World War II was under way. Did this make him a Nazi collaborator? If so, why then did U.S. intelligence operatives recruit him as an OSS agent to serve the Allied cause?

All the charges against him gained even more momentum with the accusation that Jung stole a cornerstone of his psychology, the idea of the collective unconscious, from a medical student whose work he supervised.

I entered into the biographical fray surrounding Jung through what he might have called "synchronicity," a term he coined to describe events related by their significance rather than by their cause. As he explained it, synchronicity has been in existence since the beginning of time, but it has no unifying origin, only appears sporadically, and does not progress logically. In other words, nothing comes about because of any one thing; nor does one thing lead directly to any other. It is probably the best way to describe the happenstance that resulted in this biography.

A writer-psychologist told me of a conference where historians of psychoanalysis representing different analytic persuasions took an informal vote and agreed that the one book their discipline needed most was an objective biography of Jung. He thought I should write it. Another writer told me she had just returned from a Swiss research trip and had arrived independently at the same conclusion. Suddenly, quite a lot of people who didn't know each other, and in several cases didn't know me either, were asking what my next book might be, and had I ever thought of writing about Jung?

I was slightly uneasy by the way Jung's name kept cropping up. I told my agent that his biography was one of the more novel suggestions repeatedly coming my way, and she said she thought I should pursue it. I reminded her that I had already written three biographies and was fearful of becoming typecast. She said I should think seriously about a life of Jung before I moved on to other kinds of writing, for he was exactly the sort of person whose life and work excited me. I was still hesitant.

And so it went in the mid-1990s, when almost every week brought an encounter with someone who suggested Jung as a subject, or who, in several instances, insisted forcefully and emotionally that I should go to Zürich and talk to the *Erbengemeinschaft C. G. Jung*, the committee of his heirs.

Before I did this, I read what others had written about Jung. Thus, when I did go to Zürich to meet Jung's heirs for the first time, I understood why they were reluctant to give any scholar free access to their archives. With the exception of a respectful biography by the German writer Gerhard Wehr and a fond memoir by Jung's English advocate Barbara Hannah, all other books about his life ranged from the supercilious, smug, and condescending to the scathingly negative.

For my own amusement, I did an informal survey of prominent persons who have been the subject of more than one biography, and the biographies almost all seem to follow a pattern. The first ones are usually hagiography, the life of a saint, respectful and discreet. The next ones expose the great person's "warts and all." After that, Oscar Wilde's dictum applies, that every great person has disciples, but Judas usually writes the biography. This seems to be where Jung landed from the beginning, bypassing the first two stages and going directly to hearsay, allegation, and innuendo. What was there about Jung that inspired such strong negative feelings? How could so many writers spend so many years in the company of a subject they so clearly despised? I think it was the entire question of Jung's sullied reputation that finally convinced me to write about him.

I started my official research in Zürich sometime in 1995, at the Swiss Federal Institute of Technology, the Eidgenössische Technische Hochschule (ETH). Even though most of Jung's archives have been deposited there, his heirs retain control of them. Access is rigidly monitored, and no document can be read by a scholar unless a member of the family has read it first. Also, I had to know which files I wanted to see — such as whose correspondence I needed to read, or which published essays had earlier, variant versions — because even the card catalogue was tightly restricted, and what was listed was not always useful.

The Jung heirs gave me permission to work in the ETH and agreed to the conditions under which I wrote my previous biographies: they would grant me access to the materials I believed I needed, but they would not try to influence the content of my book or read it before publication. This allowed me to protect the objectivity and integrity of my work, but it also ensured that any mistakes of fact or interpretation would be solely mine and not theirs.

I spent months on end in the ETH, reading letters and manuscripts. In an institution that represents the cutting edge in technology, where one must navigate through new and not yet unpacked stacks of computers piled in the hallways that lead to the reading room, I sat there scribbling painfully in pencil, for in this state-of-the-art environment, researchers are not permitted to use laptops or other electronic equipment.

To do the research, I lived in Zürich for one to four months a year as a way of integrating myself into the life of the community. I brought my German up to speed, but, fortunately, everyone I encountered spoke better English than I, so I used my German mainly for reading and relied on an excellent translator to make sure I got it right. Through friends in the United States, I was introduced in Switzerland to persons both within the Jungian community and far outside it. I talked to those who knew Jung or who trained at the Jung Institute in Küsnacht during his lifetime, and to those who practiced analytical psychology in Switzerland after his 1961 death. They granted me repeated interviews, provided me with much needed documentation, and answered all my questions with grace and patience, no matter how superficial or repetitive they might have seemed. Those I befriended outside Jungian psychology helped me, a foreigner, to give Jung the necessary grounding in his own Swiss culture and society. The information all these persons imparted and the investigatory work they did on my behalf have allowed me to present a nuanced portrait of the man and his culture and society, which would have been otherwise impossible.

Why did I spend so much time in Zürich? people asked. I learned to shrug and say something about what a nice place it was (which it is), for how otherwise could I describe the fallow times I spent twiddling my fingers, waiting for one of the Jung heirs to read the ETH archives before I could see them? And as they all have busy lives of their own, this sometimes took a while.

But waiting in my apartment had other compensations. If the phone rang before 8 A.M. or after 10 P.M., I knew it was not the ETH calling. It was someone who had been told by someone else who had observed me socially or professionally that they trusted me and approved of the book I intended to write. My callers thus felt comfortable in sharing information about, for example, what their parents and grandparents had said of Jung. It was hearsay, but it was also background, so of course I agreed to meet them. The first time this happened, I was convinced it would be a waste of time, and indeed it was. But that night at 11 P.M., the telephone rang and the same person asked me to come again, to receive an analytic diary kept by a parent. This person then told another to contact me and to give me a different kind of journal kept by an ancestor, and so it went. Letters, diaries — all sorts of documentation — came to me through "private sources, private archives."

The Swiss reverence for privacy takes some getting used to for an American brought up on a steady diet of celebrity or political gossip, when no matter how sordid, nothing is private. At first I told these persons I could not promise anonymity; all my previous biographies named my sources, and with Jung, because of the allegations and rumors that swirled about his life, I felt an even greater need to document every statement I made. They became so frightened that their privacy would be breached that they immediately withdrew their testimony and the materials they had offered. In some cases (two that ultimately did not matter) I never got them back; in most, I am happy to say that I did, but only after acceding to their wishes. I first asked if I could make a list of those who were my "private sources, private archives" and deposit it in a library where it would be restricted for at least twenty-five to fifty years. Even this possibility — that they and their ancestors would be identified only long after everyone involved was dead — so offended their sense of decorum that I had to agree never to reveal who these sources were.

People asked as I was writing it what my book would be about. Conscious of the debate that raged every time Jung's name came up in casual conversation, I joked that there would be something on practically every page to offend at least somebody, if not everybody. Now that I've written it, I say it seriously. Jung was that kind of person; his advocates are many and his detractors are just as numerous.

Did you like him? is the question every biographer is asked. My response is simple: Liking really doesn't enter into it for me. This is my chosen form of intellectual inquiry: I am intrigued by how the individual influenced the society in which he or she lived, and Jung was certainly among the most influential. He gave us word associations that we use in everything from children's games to serious personality tests; he taught us to talk about the complex, the archetype, the introvert and extravert; he gave us the phrases "New Age" and "the age of Aquarius"; and he gave us the concept of synchronicity that propelled me to write this book.

I could not have spent so many years in the daily company of someone's life unless I was absorbed by the person at hand. I was fortunate to find Jung's life and work fascinating, frustrating, contradictory, and intriguing, but ultimately of importance and value. I hope all those who read this book have at least some of the same experiences.

Deirdre Bair
February 17, 2003

Jung

INTRODUCTION

Faint Clews and Indirections

And so will some one when I am dead and gone write my life?
(As if any man really knew aught of my life,
Why even I myself I often think know little or nothing of my real life,
Only a few hints, a few diffused faint clews and indirections.
I seek for my own use to trace out here.)

WALT WHITMAN, *Leaves of Grass*

I regret that my biography . . . is in many respects unlike other biographies. . . . For me, life was something that had to be lived and not talked about. . . . I am what I am — a thankless autobiographer!

C. G. JUNG to Kurt Wolff, June 17, 1958[1]

In the last decade of his long life (1875–1961), Carl Gustav Jung thought a great deal about what it had been and whether it deserved to be reexamined, let alone preserved for posterity in written form.[2] He described himself as a "somewhat complicated phenomenon"[3] whose memories were such a "jungle" that he wondered why an "average reader" would want to wade through them. As for the factual events of his life, they had inspired so much controversy that he was "rather scared to tell the truth"[4] as he remembered it. How could he possibly commit such a morass to paper?

It took three decades of biographical trial and error before Jung arrived at *Memories, Dreams, Reflections,* his justly famous autobiography. Of all his writings — published in more than twenty volumes to date — Jung's story of himself is the work that has resonated most deeply with the "average reader" he despaired of ever reaching. From its first sentence to the last, this curious hybrid of reflected memory touches a chord that most readers agree cannot be defined or explained in any terms other than the personal and the individual.

"My life is a story of the self-realization of the unconscious" is his famous first sentence, written when he was in his eighties, several years before his death. He intended to tell his "personal myth" as he remembered it. Whether "true" or not was the reader's problem, not his, for it was his own "fable," his own "truth."⁵ He began with some of his earliest tactile memories, of the smell of milk, the color of sunset, and the vastness of water observed by a small child standing on a lakeshore. By the time he arrived at the concluding pages, his book offered a remarkable summation of his extraordinary life. Creativity's "daimon . . . ruthlessly had its way" with him, bringing conflict in his profession (with Freud, for example), moral ambiguity in his behavior (in the very public trio he formed with his wife and mistress), and praise and opprobrium in equal part throughout the world (for his psychological theory and political activity). In retrospect and from the vantage point of old age, he was mostly satisfied with the many "unexpected things" he had experienced. He was "astonished, disappointed, pleased," with his life even as he was "distressed, depressed, rapturous." He was the sum of all these emotions at one and the same time.

One of the pleasures of reliving his life by writing about it was the new and "unexpected unfamiliarity" it gave Jung with all those persons he had been: the lonely, desperately poor son of a Swiss country parson; the young medical doctor whose career began more in search of financial security than professional success; and the young husband who found both in a love match with the second-richest heiress in Switzerland; the handsome, charismatic thirty-year-old who had no experience with women before his marriage, even though he attracted them in droves; and the young psychoanalyst who had the courage of his convictions to separate his theory from Sigmund Freud's despite the banishment and disgrace he knew would result.

Throughout his book, Jung addressed the "alienation" that followed the decisions listed above and many others as well and described how they conspired to throw him into his own "inner world." There is scant detail of his daily life or work experience, for to him, "outward happenings" were "hollow and insubstantial." External realities became subsumed in a recapitulation of his inner experiences, for they were what defined him and what ultimately mattered most:

> I regret that my biography, or what I take to be it, is unlike other biographies in many respects. Without wanting to pass value judgments, it is completely impossible for me to remember the millions of personal details and to overestimate them so greatly after the fact as to seriously tell them all once more. I know there are people who already live in their own biography during their life-time and who act as though they were already part of a book. For me, life was something that had to be lived and not spoken. Moreover, my interest was always in the grip of a few, but crucial things, which I couldn't speak of anyhow, which I had to carry around with me for a long time before they were ready to be spoken of. I have also

been so consistently misunderstood that I've lost the desire to remember "important conversations" at all.

"God help me," Jung concluded: "I am as I am, an ungrateful autobiographer to be exact!"[6]

Jung was a psychoanalyst who never underwent formal analysis but used instead his "personal myth" as the starting point to formulate what he believed were enduring objective truths. He juxtaposed his personal myth against the myths of many disparate cultures, eventually adding new terms to the common vocabulary and new ways of thinking about ideas. Jung was responsible for so many terms we now consider common parlance, such as the "archetype," the "unconscious," and the "collective unconscious," all important components of the "individuation" process, of coming to terms with oneself and one's life.[7] Because of his research, we speak easily and casually of the "introvert" and "extravert," the two main divisions of his "personality types." So, too, do we bandy the terms "anima" and "animus," the female and male principles Jung believed are present in both sexes. His idea of a "complex" is still acquiring new interpretations and definitions, while "synchronicity" has become the catchword to explain so many contemporary ways of being. And in an era where "New Age" stands for whatever one wants it to, Jung's name and the adjective "Jungian" are often found preceding or following the term.

On a more serious level, his message about the necessity of connecting with one's unconscious through psychoanalysis is receiving new attention in a world recently obsessed with the quick fix offered by pharmacology, which he identified in the 1940s as an important avenue of future research. Today, scientists are discovering that many of Jung's notions of how the unconscious operates mirror actual changes in the physiology of the brain, and some of his more esoteric theorizing can be mapped objectively by modern medical machinery.

Jung began his career as a young medical doctor engaged in research science, seemingly destined for a life of laboratory analysis. With his refinement of the association test, which became the international standard in the early years of the twentieth century, he was praised for his application of meticulous, mathematical scholarship to the uncharted areas of the mind. This respect gave way to puzzlement, as his writings veered from the clinically precise to the densely ephemeral, resulting in a prose so prolix that multiple meanings abound and opposing interpretations can be culled from any single text. The medical Doctor Jung gave way in midlife to the philosophical Professor Jung, even though he insisted — often in high dudgeon — that he was an empirical scientist and should be regarded as such.

These contradictions and so many others in the life of Carl Jung have long intrigued both scholars and Jung's own average reader as they peruse his autobiography-memoir for clues about the facts and events of his life. Two early applicants for the position of Jung's authorized biographer found themselves stymied by his insistence that no one person could write comprehensively about him because that "specifical [*sic*] psychological synthesis would demand somebody equally at home in primitive psychology, mythology, history, parapsychology and science — and even in the field of artistic expression."[8] He held the "subjective fantasy" that a committee of experts would agree to write his life by agreeing entirely to his version of how he lived it. When this did not happen and he tried to write it himself, he discovered a "most peculiar and . . . unexpected fact," that he was "continuously disturbed" by the "subjective material" that colored his early memories.[9]

He thought of a way to resolve the dilemma by entitling his book *Improvised Memories*[10] and by making the conscious decision not to perceive every moment from the vantage point of age and wisdom but, rather, from the perspective of the age he was when the event occurred. He believed his obligation to his readers was to capture and record whatever emotion he had felt at these times of his life, no matter how unpleasant or embarrassing.

He proceeded with this plan but selected only those he believed were "moments of illumination,"[11] not only for himself but also for those who would read about him. Jung did not want these moments filtered through the acquired wisdom, knowledge, and refracted memories of his eighty-plus years. Retrospection and honest reflection became his preferred devices for sifting through his past in search of moments of universal resonance. Painful though many memories were, he still wanted to begin at his beginning, as the fourth-born and first-surviving child of a poor country parson and his unhappy and troubled wife.

It is here, too, that any biography of Carl Gustav Jung must begin.

CHAPTER 1

How the Jungs Became Swiss

The child who became the world-renowned psychologist C. G. Jung was christened Karl Gustav II Jung, after his illustrious grandfather Carl Gustav I Jung, but with the spelling of his first name modernized. His parents did observe the old Swiss custom of indicating that he was the second to bear it by placing the Roman numeral between his given and family names. Born on July 26, 1875, in the vicarage of Kesswil, he was the fourth-born but first-surviving child of Paul Achilles Jung, a poor country parson in the Swiss Reformed Church, and Emilie Preiswerk, his unhappy and unstable wife.

Each was a thirteenth child of well-known parents, so the union of a thirteenth Preiswerk daughter to a thirteenth Jung son was regarded as highly auspicious in a socially conscious Swiss culture imbued with equal parts of respect and fear for omens of any kind. On both sides there were so many prominent ministers and doctors that if families could be said to own professions, these two could lay claim to religion and medicine. And yet, even though each family enjoyed high social standing in the city of Basel, their personal eccentricities and unorthodox genealogies were more talked about than their professional successes.

Jung's mother, Emilie Preiswerk, was twenty-one on her wedding day, April 8, 1869, and by the standards of the time, a spinster on the verge of old-maidhood. The ceremony took place in the hallowed Basel Cathedral, the Münster, because the bride's father, Samuel Preiswerk, was the Antistes of Basel, the president of the company of pastors in the local Swiss Reformed Church.[1] Emilie's groom, Johann Paul Achilles Jung, was twenty-seven, a good age for a man to embark upon marriage in the last quarter of the nineteenth century. His father, Dr. Med. Carl Gustav I Jung,[2] was a physician and dean of the University of Basel's Faculty of Medicine. Even though both fathers held respected positions, there were degrees of difference in their social standing that were exacerbated by their scant financial resources. They had little to bolster their youngest children as they began married life, so the wedding party was modestly dressed, and the luncheon afterward frugal. Differences both overt and subtle were present at the beginning of the marriage and caused problems for as long as it lasted. They had an enduring effect on Paul and Emilie's son, known in maturity as C. G., influencing many aspects of his life and work.

In the last quarter of the nineteenth century, the Basel into which C. G. Jung was born was the most conservative of all the cities in the Swiss confederation of twenty-six cantons (states). Society was so rigidly stratified that even though the Antistes Preiswerk was pleased with his daughter's marriage, everyone knew that Emilie had, in a very real sense, married beneath her station. Paul Jung may have been well educated, but he was still a poor country parson barely able to provide for a wife. Social standing, however, was not Emilie's first consideration, as there had been no other suitors for her hand.

The Preiswerks were Swiss citizens with an impeccably conservative lineage, of the *vom Tieg*, the oldest patrician families in Basel. The Jungs were newcomers who became accidentally Swiss when their German patriarch, Dr. Med. Carl Gustav I Jung, was exiled for political agitation. He became notorious among the good burghers of Basel, not only for his liberal political views but also for the story he so enjoyed telling, that he was an illegitimate son of the poet Goethe.[3] His reputation in Protestant Basel was further blemished when nosy citizens traced his family history and found that the German Jungs were Roman Catholics, which in Basel was almost as damaging as being the descendant of a poet.

Paul and Emilie gave their son the modern spelling of his name, Karl, but he changed it to the original family form when he was a university student. As far back as the Jung family's history and genealogy can be traced, to approximately 1650, in Mainz, Germany, Carl was a popular name. Sometime before 1654, the earliest town records describe the esteemed Dr. Med. Dr. Jur. Carl Jung as a Catholic physician, lawyer, and rector (president) of the university.[4] His grandson, Franz Ignaz (1759–1831), became C. G. Jung's great-grandfather and was responsible for moving the Jung family to Mannheim when he became a physician in charge of a field hospital during the Napoleonic wars. His wife, Sophie Jung-Ziegler,[5] is alleged to have had the liaison with Goethe that led to the rumor of his fathering Carl Gustav I (1794–1864), Jung's grandfather and the first of the family's Swiss citizens.[6]

Carl Gustav I was a larger-than-life figure around whom legends abounded.[7] He attended the University of Heidelberg from 1813 to 1816, graduating summa cum laude with a doctorate in medicine and the natural sciences, awarded for a dissertation entitled "De evolutione corporis humani." A man "of tall, strong build with beautiful, almost girlishly soft features,"[8] he had many moods and talents. As a student he kept a small, exceedingly pink pig as a pet, shocking the good people of Heidelberg by cooing affectionately as he walked it on a leash like a dog.[9] He was a talented writer of poems and songs, some of which were published in the *Teutsche Liederbuch* (German Book of Songs). Leading literary figures urged him to give up medicine and concentrate on poetry, advice he did not follow, although he continued to publish anonymously. Very few people knew that he loved crime fiction (as did his grandson and namesake) so much that as Mathias Nusser he wrote a popular comedy, *Die Verdächtigen* (The Suspect). He was also Demius, the author of a play bearing the incendiary title *Die Revolution*.[10]

The medical career of Carl Gustav I blossomed from the start: when only twenty-four, he was called to Berlin to become surgical assistant to the legendary Charité Hospital ophthalmologist, Johann Nepomuk Rust, and to hold a joint appointment as lecturer in chemistry at the Königlich-Preussischen Kriegsschule (the Royal Prussian War College).

In Berlin, Carl Gustav I lived in the home of the publisher Georg Andreas Reimer and his wife, both of whom treated him as a son. Through the Reimers, he became part of a group of intellectuals that included leaders of the Romantic movement, Ludwig Tieck and the brothers Schlegel. Of greater influence, however, was Friedrich D. E. Schleiermacher, the most important Protestant theologian of the Romantic movement, instrumental in the founding of Berlin University and the first professor of theology.[11] He was also pastor of the Dreifaltigkeitskirche (Trinity Church), where crowds flocked to hear his sermons, "esteemed for their sincerity and religious fervour as well as, at this time of national depression, for their patriotism."[12]

Ties between the Jung and Schleiermacher families had been strengthened when Schleiermacher's sister married Carl Gustav I's elder brother, Sigismund, and converted to the Jung family's Catholicism.[13] Carl Gustav I's deeply religious Catholic parents were distressed when he weakened those ties by converting to Schleiermacher's firebrand Reformed Protestantism, best described as political activism based on the democratic ideas of German Romanticism.

On October 18, 1817, Carl Gustav I was among a large gathering of students at the University of Jena to celebrate the tercentenary of the Protestant Reformation. As a member of the nationalistic gymnastic corps headed by Frederich Ludwig Jahn (1778–1852),[14] he made the pilgrimage to the Wartburgfest at Wartburg, where Luther had earlier posted his Ninety-five Theses. Like most of the students, he paid greater homage to politics than to religion, commemorating the fourth anniversary of the Battle of Leipzig, which ended Napoleon's empire in Germany. The Wartburgfest sparked widespread student protest over the government's despotic policies, resulting in further severe restrictions on general civil liberties. When Carl Gustav I's friend Karl Ludwig Sand killed the reactionary poet August von Kotzebue on March 23, 1819,[15] all student fraternities and clubs were banned, and many professors who championed liberal views were arrested. Among them was Carl Gustav I, whose crime was mere possession of the kind of hammer used in mineralogical research, a gift to him from Sand.[16] The "demagogue" Jung was sentenced to thirteen months in the Hansvogtai prison and, when released, was unemployable in Germany.

He went to Paris to seek a career in medical research, and at this point his life becomes a mélange of "fiction and truth."[17] The only constant in the several legends of how Carl Gustav I Jung became Swiss and a citizen of Basel is the eminent natural scientist Alexander von Humboldt (1769–1859).[18] The present-day Jung family tells the same story favored by their grandfather C. G. II, but they do so with a healthy dose of skepticism, while he allegedly considered it fact.[19] In this version, Carl Gustav I is a "starving,"[20] down-at-heel German political refugee who sat shivering on a Parisian park bench, when a stranger (von Humboldt) engaged him in conversation. Von Humboldt was so dismayed by this casual acquaintance's desperate circumstances and so impressed with his scientific knowledge that he nominated him for a low-level medical position at the Swiss Berner Akademie, which he had been asked to fill. Bern did not hire Carl Gustav I, so von Humboldt (by this time his friend) made a second and successful nomination, to the more prestigious medical school at Basel University.[21]

Another version of how the Jungs became Swiss is more grandiose, with Carl Gustav seeking employment in Paris, armed with a letter of introduction from Dr. Rust of the Berlin Charité Hospital to the French surgeon Guillaume Dupuytren. Dupuytren is supposed to have invited Carl Gustav I to a banquet being given in his honor and seated him next to a distinguished middle-aged man whom he so dazzled that he was offered the professorship in anatomy, surgery, and obstetrics at the University of Basel. Only after Carl Gustav I accepted, so this version goes, did he learn that his benefactor was Alexander von Humboldt.

A third version is the most mundane but probably closest to the truth: Carl Gustav I lived in the Berlin home of the publisher Georg Andreas Reimer,[22] who was a friend and frequent correspondent of von Humboldt. Carl Gustav probably went to Paris highly recommended by Reimer and, quite possibly, Schleiermacher, who also knew von Humboldt. He also went with financial backing from his own father, which allowed him to live comfortably and marry the first of his three wives, Virginie de Lassaulx (1804–30).[23] Without parental assistance, he could not have supported himself, let alone a wife, on the salary of the poorly paid position he held until he went to Basel. The only verifiable fact in the three stories, however, is that von Humboldt did write one of several letters to Bürgermeister Wieland of Basel recommending Carl Gustav I for the professorship.[24]

On March 18, 1822, Carl Gustav I arrived in his new homeland,[25] and the following decade of his life was dominated by his heroic efforts to reorganize the medical school. When he and Virginie arrived, Basel was a community of fewer than twenty-five thousand people, a "viable anachronism" with a "patrician dominated social structure,"[26] smug in the worship of commerce and the practice of a rigid, restrictive, and conventional Protestant religion. For the most part, the cultural climate was so intellectually barren that even the canton's bureaucratic officials realized something had to be done about the sorry state of the university, which then enrolled fewer than twenty-eight students.[27] In 1818 they enacted broad laws that specified its total reorganization, but when Carl Gustav was appointed four years later, most had not yet been implemented. He used the stagnation to his own advantage: the medical school had appointments for four full professorships, but only three were filled; after one semester as a lecturer, he persuaded his colleagues to appoint him to the last vacancy. They took the lazy way out as an act of expediency, but he seized the initiative to become first among equals. In a city known as "the sulking corner of Europe," he enlisted other radical refugee professors who shared his vision of "national regeneration through the study of the classical languages and culture" to help restructure the curriculum.[28]

Despite sweeping transformations throughout the world in procedure and theory, medical instruction in Basel had not changed since the end of the eighteenth century, when the only professor, the great Johann Jacob Burckhardt, taught one full-time student and several barbers' apprentices. The other instructors taught no medical students and were totally occupied with their private practices. No wonder that between 1806 and 1814 not a single medical degree was granted. This was the situation facing Carl Gustav I in 1823, when he became chairman by default.[29] He exerted the full force of his brash personality to turn the medical curriculum into the most rigorous in the university, instituting new courses in anatomy and pathology and conceiving a related curriculum in *Therapie*, a combination of the latest medical technique and philosophy that was used to treat mental conditions.[30] He also appointed himself *Oberarzt* (senior physician) at the affiliated hospital, the Bürgerspital, where he enlarged the facilities and improved the quality of care. Six short years later, in 1828, he was appointed *Rektor*, the chief official of the entire university. A groundbreaker in medical affairs all his life, he founded a home for mentally deficient children in 1857, the Anstalt zur Hoffnung (Institution for Hope), which became a model of its kind and which he called his happiest achievement.

Carl Gustav I made few friends among the leading citizens, who took pride only "in writing six zeros after their names."[31] He was grudgingly respected but not much liked, for he agitated publicly about his two major bones of contention: German politics (about which the good burghers of Basel thought he should mind his own Swiss business) and Basel's highly restrictive civil rights, which caused sporadic armed warfare between residents of the city and those of the outlying lands.[32] Even though he obtained Swiss citizenship in 1824, in a surprisingly short period of time,[33] he was still known disparagingly as the *deutscher Demokrat und Liberaler* (German democrat and liberal). Not until 1830[34] was he granted a temporary respite from criticism and a modicum of sympathy, but only because his wife, Virginie, after having given birth to three (or four) daughters, died at the age of twenty-four, leaving him to raise the only one who survived.[35]

Shortly after, he began to court Sophie Frey, a member of one of the city's leading families and the daughter of the mayor of Basel, Johann Rudolf Frey. Despite Carl Gustav I's growing prestige, Mayor Frey was not pleased. According to their contemporary Jacob Burckhardt, Basel was still "a little hole," where "not a word is ever forgotten or forgiven [and] scandalmongering such as exists nowhere else spreads poison over everything."[36] The sweeping changes Carl Gustav I instigated in the medical school were added to the stigma of his revolutionary student activities and his prison record. Mayor Frey had personal concerns as well: Carl Gustav I was eighteen years older than Sophie and already had a daughter. The mayor was ready to refuse his suit, but the matter became moot when Sophie rejected the proposal first.[37]

Family legend has it that Carl Gustav I stormed into the nearest student pub and proposed marriage to the first woman he saw, the waitress Elisabeth Catherine Reyenthaler, a plain, tired, working-class woman several years older than he.[38] She accepted, to the amusement of the current generation of Jungs but to the chagrin of their grandfather C. G., who thought it fortunate that she conveniently "soon died of tuberculosis, and so did her children."[39] Jung was mistaken, as only one of Elisabeth Catherine's three children died; she did, too, three years after her marriage. Carl Gustav I garnered sympathy yet again, this time as the widower father of the three small surviving children by two wives. Finally, he became a truly respected figure, albeit grudgingly. Now he was described in Basel as "a man of irresistible charm, kind-hearted, tactful, and humorous."[40] It helped that he also had a lot more money from his thriving private practice. His many publications on anatomy and physiology enhanced his reputation, as word spread of the new curriculum, bringing students and physician-observers to Basel from other countries. By 1838 he was a member of the city council and in 1841 became chair of the academic guild. In 1850, he was so prominent throughout Switzerland that he was elected Grand Master of the United Swiss Freemason societies.[41]

Carl Gustav I was a prolific writer in these years, including one anonymously printed article that curiously prefigured his grandson's abiding passion. In it he observed that physicians had begun to concentrate on the "psychological aspect of medicine" and noted the proliferation of special journals dealing exclusively with developments in this field. He proposed — indirectly and discreetly, for Basel remained conservative in the extreme — that a separate section or department dealing with this discipline would make an excellent addition to any medical university. "I am not thinking of a lunatic asylum of the usual sort," he wrote, "but of an institute that would admit ill people of all kinds, whose cure could be attempted by means of psychological treatment."[42] When an asylum was created, he did, indeed, insist upon treatment rather than custodial care for the patients.

The last several decades of his life were domestically content, because Sophie Frey changed her mind and became Carl Gustav's third wife immediately after Elisabeth Catherine's death and stepmother to his three surviving children from the first two marriages. Between 1836 and 1852, Sophie gave birth to five sons and a daughter, bringing the total number of children, living or dead, fathered by Carl Gustav I to thirteen.[43]

At home, he was indeed the patriarch, a booming, commanding presence who was an object of fear more than love within his large family. The public may have excused his "quick temper" because "at the bottom of his heart he was kind," but according to his son Ernst (by Sophie), he was "severe, a ruthless disciplinarian" whose children were eager to leave his house.[44] Anna (Virginie's daughter) married young and moved to Germany. Elisabeth Catherine's two surviving children were in such conflict with their father that Karoline went to live with relatives in Darmstadt, where she died shortly after of typhus, and Karl, called by his father "undisciplinable," exiled himself to America and vanished from the history of the Jung family. No one ever heard from him again.[45]

Johann Paul Achilles, called Paul, the thirteenth child and father of C. G., was born on December 21, 1842, when his father was forty-eight, a venerable age in those days. Paul Jung's strongest memory of his father, one that he passed along to his son, was of having to sit with the rest of the family in total silence after each luncheon while Carl Gustav retired to take a short nap. No one dared leave the table, to move or talk, until he awakened.[46] He also remembered a father who grew more "melancholy" with each passing year, who kept meticulous diaries about the state of his health and records of persistent coughing, frequent fever, nausea, indigestion, and depression.[47]

In such a father's household, Paul learned as a child to be self-effacing and quiet. As he grew older, a natural affinity developed between them because both were happiest when engrossed in one of the scholarly tomes that filled Carl Gustav's study. Paul saw firsthand how classical languages, reading, and writing were valued, as he watched his father retreat every afternoon and evening to the solitary pursuit of scholarship. The difference between them, however, was that Paul lacked his father's tremendous ego and self-confidence. Although their fellow Basler the historian Jacob Burckhardt preached that individual "personality is the highest thing there is,"[48] conformity was Paul Jung's guiding principle. He appeared complacent and compliant in public, but when alone he was often engulfed in quiet rages and seething fury. He held these emotions in check when around others, for he was extremely shy and would have been horrified to show untoward demeanor in a city where he was known to everyone and closely observed by all.

In what the citizens of Basel deemed a decidedly un-Swiss gesture but one that Carl Gustav I believed represented international sophistication rather than his true view of the humanities at Basel University, he sent Paul to Germany to study Oriental languages at Göttingen University. There, he specialized in Arabic and wrote a dissertation on the tenth-century scholar Jephet Ben Eli's Hebrew commentary on Solomon's Song of Songs.[49] Paul seemed destined for a brilliant career as a scholar and teacher, but to everyone's surprise, he rejected a life of learning and announced his intention to become a priest in the Swiss Reformed Church Evangelical. He was careful to give the impression that he wanted to be ordained, but in reality he had no other choice: Carl Gustav I's financial situation, long in dire straits, now seemed beyond hope or salvation.

Like Paul's future father-in-law, the Antistes Preiswerk, Carl Gustav I enjoyed great professional respect that did not bring significant fortune with it. The academic profession, then as now, was poorly paid, and lecturers whose families were not rich had to count on gifts from patrons to be able to support themselves. In Basel, for example, the best families (among them the Bachofens, Burckhardts, and Bernoullis) usually had at least one member of every generation who followed a university career, but always in considerable comfort because of family money. Unfortunately for Paul, Carl Gustav I knew as early as March 20, 1849, that the bad investments of his father-in-law, Mayor Frey, meant "no prospect of an inheritance" for him and thus no help for his sons. He had already borrowed more than 6,000 Swiss francs from Sophie's "old upper crust family," so he was grateful when his wealthy patron, Susanna Vischer, persuaded her brother, Colonel Benedikt Vischer-Preiswerk, to give him this sum to pay off his relatives and his mortgage, and to contribute a bit more toward the education of his sons.[50] When his friend and fellow refugee the theologian Wilhelm de Wette[51] reproached him for ignoring his "present and future sad economic situation," Carl Gustav I retorted sharply: "It is true that I have spent much on book[s], but . . . I have sons and hoped that one of them would aspire to follow in my footsteps . . . and now my father-in-law has lost his fortune and my sons are only of average intelligence and worrying me." He despaired of how "to ensure their physical well-being," concluding that they would have to fare for themselves. Shortly after Carl Gustav I wrote this, Colonel Vischer-Preiswerk died, leaving a small legacy "to be used for the education of a family member who had the desire to become a minister."[52] Paul reluctantly gave up his dream of a life of scholarship and was ordained.

At the time of his marriage, he was pastor of the Swiss Reformed Church Evangelical in the remote village of Kesswil, Canton Thurgau, near the shore of Lake Constance. He had become the model example of what Karl Barth, the famed theologian and Basel native, described a century later as "the Basel theologian . . . from the start and in all essentials conservative, a basically shy man . . . of mild humanistic skepticism" and "practical wisdom" that prevented him from "diverging too much to the left or to the right." Barth's theologian may have enjoyed "a little free thinking" or "a little pious enthusiasm," but outwardly and at all times, Paul strove for "nothing impractical" and left "opening and closing statements to others."[53]

PAUL MET his future wife when he became a student of her father, Samuel Preiswerk (1799–1871). The scholarly interests of the two pastors were similar, but their personalities and the trajectory of their careers were not. Samuel Preiswerk was considered quite a character, with an outgoing personality, great joie de vivre, and curiously varied interests. "I have always suspected that my blessed grandfather laid a very strange egg into my mixture," his grandson C. G. believed.[54]

Like Paul, the Antistes Samuel also began his career as a student of languages, in his case Hebrew, and Old Testament theology. His grandson C. G. wrote that Samuel Preiswerk originally learned Hebrew because he believed it was the language spoken in Heaven and he wanted to be able to read the celestial newspapers once he got there.[55] Antistes Preiswerk is regarded today as a Zionist precursor, for he believed that Palestine should be ceded to the Jews to become their homeland and a Jewish nation. In Basel, a city noted for its underlying opposition to all things Jewish and for a deeply ingrained cultural anti-Semitism, Antistes Preiswerk openly defied the status quo by defending this unpopular idea. He chastised Swiss Jews for what he perceived as their lack of interest in a Palestinian homeland in *Das Morgenland*,[56] a monthly journal he published, despite the opprobrium of his fellow Gentiles.

Antistes Preiswerk's career progressed haphazardly in the extreme. Originally pastor of a small church in Muttenz, an industrial suburb of Basel, he moved into the city, hoping to find a better-paying parish when the city and its surrounding lands were divided into two separate cantons, Basel-Stadt (city) and Basel-Land (suburbs). The move proved unsuccessful, so he took his ever growing family to Geneva, where he became a professor of Old Testament exegesis and Oriental languages at the Theologenschule der Evangelischen Gesellschaft (Evangelical Theological Institute).[57] During this time, he wrote a highly respected grammar of the Hebrew language that was reprinted many times over throughout the Germanic countries. His teaching earned him many encomia and was responsible for his being called back to Basel as pastor of St. Leonard's parish, with a permanent appointment to the university as a professor of Hebrew languages and literature.

He married twice, first to Magdalena Hopf, who bore him one son, Samuel Gottlob, before she died in 1825.[58] By the time Antistes Samuel was ensconced in Basel, his wife was Augusta Faber (1805–62), another pastor's daughter who had reluctantly consigned herself to spinsterhood and was relieved to find a husband, much like her daughter Emilie a generation later.

Augusta Faber's family came originally from Nürtingen in Württemberg, descendants of French Alsatian Protestants who moved to Germany in 1685 after the revocation of the Edict of Nantes.[59] Called Gustele within the family, she became the mother of the Antistes Samuel's other twelve children and a well-known character in her own right. She was credited with bringing "the occult strain" into the family, and was the first to speak of "No. 1 and No. 2 personalities." Jung later described No. 1 as conscious or conventional, that is, "innocuous and human"; and No. 2 as unconscious, that is, "uncanny . . . unexpected and frightening."[60] In Gustele's case, her two personalities were represented by two monks she called the Good Monk and the Bad, who, she insisted, accompanied her everywhere. She also prefigured her grandson C. G.'s conception of the collective unconscious, that portion of the unconscious that is not "personal" and particular but, rather, an "omnipresent, unchanging and everywhere identical quality or substrate of the psyche per se."[61] Gustele earned her husband's respect when she described various incidents that befell her when in the monks' company in past lives and he verified them in various historical accounts that she could not have read. Jung remembered this when he began his own investigations into the collective unconscious.

Outspoken, feisty, and determined not to be suffocated by the overwhelming personality of Antistes Samuel, Gustele did not hesitate to tell anyone in Basel who came into her house that she was not happy about the special chair he kept in his study, where no one could sit but the ghost of his dear dead first wife. To Gustele's chagrin, Antistes Samuel retired to his study each week at a specific hour to have "an intimate conversation" with Magdalena's ghost. Even more bothersome was his habit of taking each of his four daughters away from household chores, training each in turn to sit behind him while he studied or wrote his sermons. Their task was to make occasional swatting motions to chase away the ghosts who, he insisted, tried annoyingly to scramble his thoughts.[62] Emilie, who became C. G.'s mother, regaled her son with tales of this and of her parents' other eccentricities. She was ten years younger than her next eldest sister, who married young to get away from home, so it was Emilie who spent the most years sitting behind her father, hating every boring minute of it.

One of the reasons Antistes Samuel was first attracted to Gustele Faber was her "second sight." Perhaps because of it, Gustele's mother chose her from among her many siblings to be the disposable daughter and sacrificial nurse for an elder brother who had scarlet fever, a highly contagious disease and at the time nearly always fatal. As the brother's illness ran its course, the eighteen-year-old Gustele fell into a trance of unknown origin, leading the doctor to pronounce her dead as well. For the next several days, even though she was actually laid in her coffin and the funeral was imminent, Gustele's mother refused to believe her daughter had died. As the family story goes, by holding a hot iron to the nape of Gustele's neck, her mother brought her back to life.[63] This became one of Emilie's favorite stories to tell her son, each time in ever more dramatic tones.

From the moment Gustele returned to life, she became a seeress whose prognostications astonished everyone. It made her the perfect mate for the Antistes Samuel, who also had "waking hallucinations (mostly visions, often whole dramatic scenes with dialogues, etc.)." Gustele's visions usually occurred after a fainting fit that was brought on by something that aroused her emotions and was almost always followed by "a brief somnambulism during which she uttered prophecies." Antistes Samuel actually encouraged his wife's emotional episodes and subsequent visions. He was quite used to such behavior, for his brother Alexander (1801–72), whom the family deemed "feeble-minded," had visions of extraordinary clarity and insight in which Samuel invested great conviction, and his sister Dorothea (1798–1881) was also a visionary, but mostly "a peculiar, odd character."[64]

Thus, Emilie Preiswerk (1848–1923), the youngest of the couple's thirteen children, grew up thinking that visionary experiences were an ordinary part of everyday family life. At a young age, she began to keep a daily diary in which she usually wrote about something oracular that happened in the Preiswerk household, frequently to her.[65] Her childhood was a curious combination of solitude and frenzied family activity. Although most of her siblings were gone to homes of their own when she was still young, there were frequent family gatherings among the Preiswerk clan, and she had many nieces, nephews, and cousins for playmates. Many of them had similar visions and believed in ghosts and visits from various spirits, and some even talked in tongues. Still, despite the collegiality of such shared experiences and beliefs, Emilie's disposition was solitary. She was more content when by herself, alone with her thoughts and her diary.

By the time she and Paul Jung decided to marry, she was a silent, self-contained young woman, large in size, awkward in mien, indifferent to her appearance and, it appears, to her suitor as well. The courtship was instigated by Paul, who first met Emilie when she was sixteen and he was twenty-two. He had recently given his first sermon at Easter, in 1864 in St. Jakob's Church, where the Antistes Samuel heard it in his official capacity as the chief pastor in Basel. Paul's own father attended, although seriously weakened by the heart problems that took his life several months later, on June 12. The two fathers had known each other professionally at the university, but there had been no other contact between them. After Carl Gustav I died, the Antistes Samuel took the orphaned Paul under his pastoral wing, and the two men began the mutually enjoyable custom of spending long hours reading Hebrew texts in his study at the Preiswerk home.

Paul probably noticed Emilie in these years, but as he could not support a wife, he did not consider her, or anyone else for that matter, a serious candidate for marriage. Now that he was twenty-six and in charge of a country parish, his need for a helpmate became serious. He probably mistook Emilie's stillness and seeming acquiescence for indications of a placid and agreeable personality; also in her favor, she was the daughter of a pastor and accustomed to a spartan way of life. As no other suitor had come along before Paul, and as Antistes Samuel enjoyed his company and conversation, he and Gustele eagerly received Paul Jung's proposal and encouraged Emilie to accept it. Emilie noted in her diary that Paul had proposed, but with little of the blushingly effusive commentary engaged girls usually employed to record such occasions. If there was a courtship, it consisted of waiting for the wedding, which took place all in due time, on April 8, 1869.

Immediately after, the young couple went to Kesswil and took up residence in the parish house. Paul was well liked by his parishioners, and Emilie was initially regarded as a most suitable bride who was certain to become an even more proper matron, a good "Frau Dr. Pfarrer"[66] who would work hard alongside her husband. Actually, her life soon became dreary and sad. She elicited much sympathy from the other women as one difficult pregnancy followed another, all culminating in dead babies. A daughter was stillborn on July 19, 1870; so, too, was a second daughter on April 3, 1872. On August 18, 1873, she gave birth to a son named Paul after his father. The baby died five days later, on August 23. Emilie withdrew, taking refuge in the private interior visions of the spirits she much preferred over the bustling activity of the small village community. If circumstances forced her to participate in parish life, she usually sat alone, directing her caustic wit and sharp tongue at anyone who tried to penetrate the shell she had constructed around herself. Soon everyone found it easier to leave her quite alone. Her husband seemed bewildered by the ill fortune that plagued them. Though still kind and concerned, he could not bear her acerbic barbs and found it easier to leave her alone as well.

Emilie grew even more careless about her personal appearance and became grossly fat, remaining so for the rest of her life.[67] Her contemporaries described her as "a capable and sociable lady" but also as "fat, ugly, authoritarian" or "haughty," and "afflicted with depressive moods."[68] Paul seemed shrunken and dazed before Emilie's towering anger, yet despite their escalating mutual indifference and separate bedrooms, Emilie became pregnant again.

This time it was different. On July 26, 1875, she delivered a robust son in the Kesswil vicarage.[69] Paul insisted the boy be named not for himself and his dead son (as Emilie wished), but after his father. Emilie was so surprised that the child was born alive that she did not care what he was called. All that mattered was that he should live.

CHAPTER 2

⟨⟨⟨⟨⟨⟩⟩⟩⟩⟩

"Pastor's Carl"

The fourth child thrived from the beginning, a large-boned blond boy who was the image of his father. Curiously, once they were sure that baby Carl* would live, his parents grew relaxed to the point of indifference about him and reverted to their previous apathy toward each other. Emilie seemed to make occasional, haphazard attempts to be a good mother, according to the precepts of proper behavior in the rural village. Everything, especially demonstrations of affection, came second to discipline and order. For the first several years of Carl's life, Emilie alternated between trying to cope with daily duties and retreating to her room for increasingly long periods of time. She seemed truly happy only when telling some of the parish women about the ghosts and spirits who roamed the parsonage halls at night or when she listened to their tales of those who haunted the pathways between the village and the lake. Meanwhile, Paul attended to the child with the same kindness and concern he gave his parishioners. He was gentle with but somewhat puzzled by the strapping boy who toddled through the parish house, so Carl was frequently left to play alone or in the company of their one harried housemaid, as Paul took refuge in the stillness of his private study.

When Carl was six months old, Paul secured an appointment to a better parish at scenic Laufen, where the church and vicarage were perched just above the castle of Schloss Laufen on the Rheinfall, the highest point of the Rhine rapids and one of "the most impressive of the natural sites of Europe."[1] The three-story vicar's manse plus all the attendant outbuildings provided an idyllic playground for a little boy fascinated by architecture and water.[2]

Paul sought this better position,[3] hoping that a change of scenery would banish the lethargy that had enveloped Emilie since Carl's birth. Instead, the move

---

*Because he used this spelling as an adult, it will be used for consistency throughout this biography.

19

made her profoundly depressed. By Carl's second birthday, she was more with-drawn from the life of her family than ever. The maid took care of Carl for weeks on end while Emilie shut herself in her bedroom. Paul moved in with Carl and shared his sleeping quarters for the three years they lived in Laufen. The family situation became critical when Carl was between three and four. Villagers gossiped openly about the pastor's unhappy marriage, and Paul's seething boyhood rages returned. He tried to hide them from his parishioners but not from his wife. Carl heard everything, as his father's anger resonated throughout the house. Conversations, such as they were, usually consisted of Paul's invective and Emilie's muffled response, followed by long periods of her silence.

The scenery[4] in which the vicarage was set was as dramatic as its inhabitants' quarrels, and so, too, was the daily drama of parish life. The roar of the falls was a constant background noise within the vicarage, and quite a few lifeless bodies, both from suicides and accidents, swept over them during Paul's tenure. Several of the drowned corpses were fished out and stored in the vicarage's laundry house until they were identified and buried. The precocious little boy was warned not to go there, but he went anyway, prowling around the outside of the locked shed until he found a drain where blood and water seeped slowly down. Fascinated, he stared. Later, he saw big men wearing black coats, tall hats, and shiny boots, all standing around a hole in the ground while his gentle Papa boomed orations in a voice he never used at home. When the maid took the lit-tle boy for a walk on the suspension bridge, he was mesmerized by the water be-low and sat with one leg dangling beneath the rickety railing. The maid told the story first, and later the boy's parents repeated it endlessly, of how she caught him just as he was about to slip through and drown. As an old man revisiting these memories for his autobiography, Carl Jung wondered if his behavior as a three- to four-year-old might have been "an unconscious suicidal urge" or per-haps "a fatal resistance to life in this world."[5] He did not add that as a small child he was familiar with the local fairy tales, of the boy swept over the falls in a boat, only to come out safely further down the river, and of the people who passed through the rapids unharmed.[6]

Jung remembered being "restive, feverish, unable to sleep," and how his fa-ther carried him as he paced up and down, singing old songs from his student days, his voice wafting gently through the soft country night. The little boy be-gan to have nebulous apprehensions, perhaps because he overheard his mother telling the other women of the village of the mysterious spirits who prowled about her house at night. His mother had always spoken matter-of-factly about such things, but now she began each day full of gusto, giving detailed descrip-tions of all the nighttime apparitions and repeating their conversations. As the day wound down, so, too, did she, and the boy's qualms increased. But in the evening, this same gleefully ghoulish mother became gentle and soothing, as she taught him a prayer that provided "a sense of comfort in the face of the vague uncertainties of the night." He was vexed because he could not understand how she could exhibit two such vastly different personalities. Meanwhile, the tension between his parents increased, and he was felled by "repulsive eczema." He suspected that everything was related to his parents' marriage, which "wasn't working."[7]

Then Emilie abruptly left the vicarage for the first of several long stays in a rest home near Basel.[8] Paul told his parishioners that she required hospitalization for a vague physical ailment, hinting that it was linked to unspecified complications at Carl's birth. Carl overheard and felt guilt and responsibility for her absence.[9] Both emotions were heightened by a sense of banishment, when Paul took him to live with Emilie's sister, his aunt Gusteli, twenty years older than his mother and a spinster living in the old Preiswerk home in Basel.[10] On the way, Paul told him repeatedly that his mother "love[d] him" and would return soon. But from that time on, whenever the word "love" was used in connection with Emilie, young Carl became anxious that another desertion would soon follow, that another separation was in the offing. For him, the "feeling of the feminine" became one of "natural unreliability, one can never rely on it." He called it the "handicap" from which his attitudes toward women were formed.

Paul missed his son during Emilie's first absence, so he rescued the child from Aunt Gusteli's kind ministrations and brought him back to the vicarage, where they lived alone until Emilie returned several months later. Even though she had other absences of varying duration, there were no further separations between father and son, and in those years they were quietly, affectionately close. For the boy Carl, "father" became synonymous with two emotions: "reliability and powerlessness."[11]

Two women were responsible for Carl's care during Emilie's hospitalizations while they lived in Laufen. One was the small, dark, olive-complected maid, whom the child associated with "other mysterious things"[12] he could not understand. The maid seems to have loved the boy, for he remembered being picked up and held quietly for long periods of time, and putting his head against her shoulder to breathe in the fragrance of her neck. Later, he used this type of woman as a component of what he called the "anima," his term for the "personification of the feminine nature of a man's unconscious."[13] The other woman was Bertha Schenk, a pretty blond, blue-eyed girl from nearby Uhwiesen who came regularly to the vicarage to play games with Carl and take him for walks along the banks of the Rhine. As an elderly man, he remembered how he associated everything about Bertha with a dazzling yellow light and bright sunshine. He loved this young woman who later became his mother-in-law, but he was aware that she "admired" his father, and that was deeply troubling to the little boy.[14]

He became clumsy and began to have accidents and injure himself, once tumbling headlong down the stairs, another time hitting his head against the sharp angle of a stove leg. Blood flowed — alluring, fascinating blood — and this time from his own head. The doctor stitched him up, but the scar remained faintly visible when he was an adult, turning angry red when he was excited. He told his mother quite matter-of-factly that, like the dead corpse whose blood oozed down the drain of the washhouse, his own blood was simply a matter of interest to him and that he felt no other emotion. He thought he was four when this happened. He never forgot it.[15]

Carl usually played alone in Laufen, for parents of the village children deliberately kept them away from the odd little boy whose parents were so peculiar.[16] He had other solitary powerful images that took him years to sort through, and to which he sometimes referred throughout his later life when he mined his memories for examples to use in writing and teaching.[17] One occurred when he was immersed in creating tiny kingdoms in the sand that lined the roadside leading from the vicarage up a steep hill. He looked up, straight into the sun, and saw what appeared to be a man wearing a woman's black dress. He was deeply frightened, and the thought shot through his mind that this was one of those dangerous Jesuits he had overheard his father discussing with a colleague. Paul's discussion was neither a single idle conversation nor a simple Protestant prejudice against Catholics, for the Jesuit order had been at the center of Swiss political dispute since 1844, when the canton of Luzern gave control of its higher-education facilities to the order. Sentiment against the power and influence of Jesuit teaching rose to such a pitch that Jesuits were declared "a national peril."[18] Even though the Society of Jesus was permanently banned from working in Switzerland four years later, in 1848, people still imagined the worst about their "dark machinations."[19] In the years that followed, widespread resistance against the Society of Jesus strengthened and deepened, so that by Carl's boyhood a quarter century later, the Jesuits were indeed a most frightening and fearful entity to most Swiss.

For some time, Carl connected the word "Jesuit" with the historical personage of Jesus,[20] of whom he had become leery. One of the hymns his mother sang at night was about a "Lord Jesus mild," who was entreated to protect "thy chick, thy child." Thus, even if Satan were to "devour" the child, no harm would "overpower" him. The adult Jung thought it probable that the child Carl mistook the High German *Küchlein* (chick) for the *Schwizertütsch* dialect *Chüchli* (cookies), and that he believed his mother was asking the Lord Jesus to eat him before Satan could do so. Still, when he was an old man, Jung could not rid himself of thinking the hymn was a "sinister analogy"[21] that linked Christ inextricably to the gloomy rituals of Protestant funerals and soutane-clad Catholic priests.

Left to himself so much of the time in the house and lacking playmates outside, the little boy depended upon his imagination for entertainment, frequently using both dreams and daydreams to create secret games and rituals that only he could play. Paul tried to make up for Carl's loneliness by reading to him and telling stories. These were mostly from the Old Testament and concentrated on heroes, action, and adventure. Initially the little boy was enthralled by quests and battles over demonstrations of faith, but he questioned them deeply several years later. Sometimes when Carl was playing outside, Paul would try to engage him in conversations about nature, but as he knew little and cared less about flora and fauna,[22] these chats did not last long. Paul's world consisted of the books and papers in his tidy study, so young Carl was usually left to his own devices. Village children were put to work on family farms as soon as they were able to perform the simplest tasks, so theirs was an abbreviated childhood, which contributed to Carl's isolation. The only occasions when he could play with another boy came when one or another of Paul's old school friends brought his family to visit. Among them was the father of Albert Oeri,[23] the boy who became Jung's lifelong friend. Some fifty-five years later, Albert Oeri recalled how Carl sat alone at their first meeting, playing a bowling game and ignoring him. "I had never come across such an asocial monster before," he marveled.[24]

All these experiences combined to promote the boy's self-reliance and, even more, his intense concentration on the inner life. The elderly Jung thought it was in Laufen, when he was nearly four, that he had the first dream he could remember. It became one of several about which he obsessed for the rest of his life, but one he kept secret until he was sixty-five and revealed it to his wife.[25] He thought it may have been related to his fear of the Jesuit priest, but he was never able to explain it to his satisfaction. The dream began in the meadow that extended from the rear of the vicarage to the sexton's house. While playing there, he found a hole that he had never seen before descending deep into the ground. The hole was rectangular and lined with brick, rather like a well, but inside was a stone stairway about one meter wide. He remembered feeling an equal mixture of fear and curiosity as he descended and found at the bottom an arch covered by a lush green brocade curtain. He pushed it aside and saw a rectangular chamber of about five or six meters, with an arched ceiling made of stone. Although he could not determine the source of light, there was just enough for him to see that the floor was also stone, covered partially by a red carpet that ran from the entrance to the other end, where a low platform held a "wonderfully rich" golden throne. He thought there might have been a red cushion on it, but there was also "a curious composition" that at first seemed a large tree trunk that almost reached the ceiling. On top was "an eye," but not "one that gazed." Rather, it resembled "an indistinct head."[26] Although the grotesque object was unmoving, Carl was still terrified that it might crawl wormlike toward him and attack.[27] Suddenly, in his dream he heard his mother's voice coming from outside the chamber and above the ground. "Yes," he heard her say, "just look at him. That is the man-eater."

Her comment was the most frightening part of the dream, and for a long time afterward, he was afraid to go to sleep for fear he would dream it again. Not until several years later did he realize that the sinuous worm of his dream was a phallus, and not until decades after that did he realize that it was a "ritual phallus."

As he matured, what puzzled him most about the dream was his mother's comment. Where had her emphasis been? Did she say "*That* is the man-eater," or "That is the *man-eater*"? If it was the former, the elderly Jung reasoned, she meant that neither Christ nor the Jesuits ate little children; only the phallus did so. If it was the latter, he was convinced she meant that all three were the "man-eater." He never explained how he came to this conclusion. He did, however, equate the fear he felt at the sight of the ritual phallus in his dream with the same fear he felt at the sight of the actual Jesuit in his real life. This, too, he could never explain, except to say that anything associated with Catholicism and/or Catholics was "completely other." Several years later, when he was between six and seven, his parents took him to Arlesheim on a vacation that included a tour of the ornate baroque church dominating the town's cathedral square. It was the first Catholic church the boy had ever seen, and as he rushed to go inside, he stumbled and fell, cut his chin, and bled heavily. He took it as an omen and considered it punishment for being so curious about the "other." For the rest of his life, he could not enter a Catholic church without "being afraid of Jesuits and falling, of blood and falling and Jesuits."

Throughout his long life, the dream of the phallus preoccupied him. He could not understand why he had had such a dream at so young an age,[28] or how a three- to four-year-old could visualize such an anatomically correct phallus.[29] In all his ruminations, he never considered that the priest, Jesuit or otherwise, might have exposed himself; nor did he ever seem to contemplate that he had shared his father's bedroom for as long as he could remember, and that toilet and bathing facilities in the Laufen house were such that he might well have seen his father in various states of undress.

Frightening as it was, he did not tell either parent about the dream. When he talked or wrote about it throughout his adult life, he preferred a symbolic interpretation, even though as an analyst he had frequently linked an "undervaluation of sexuality" with the self "symbolized as a phallus."[30] Several years before his death, he spoke of this dream within the context of what he called his "initial life"[31] and said he had never recovered from it. When he was an old man, he remembered that as a small boy he believed something both wonderful and terrible had happened to him: "A message to the world had come to me with an overwhelming power ... and from this emerged my scientific work. ... It's amazing that it didn't destroy me."[32]

AFTER THREE years in Laufen, Paul Jung realized "that his marriage was not all that he had imagined it to be," and there was no possibility it would change for the better as long as he remained there. He requested a transfer to any parish in the canton of Basel and in 1879 was elated by a call to Kleinhüningen.[33]

Carl was four when the family moved to the largest house in what was then a tiny rural village housing mostly fishermen and farmers. From time to time, several wealthy families had lived in the town, among them the Iselins, whose country house the vicarage had originally been and whose coat of arms was carved above a door.[34] Built in 1745 and still standing, the house consists of three stone stories with a full attic topped by a mansard roof. It has a curious half basement, which to this day has a dirt floor and several windows but no means of egress. During the Jung family's residence, the property also contained stables and outbuildings overlooking a large and formerly grand garden. The entire setting was in an "aristocratic style" far beyond "the means of a country pastor in those times."[35] Because the parish budget provided only one housemaid several days each week,[36] and because Emilie took so little interest in the life of her husband's parish, one of her first decisions was to close off many of the rooms. Curiously, these included the large formal parlor, where a pastor would usually receive parishioners before taking them into his study. Emilie's gesture was perceived as a hostile snub rather than as the work-saving device she intended. The parlor became one of Carl's favorite hiding places, where he liked to while away hours on end, sitting on the shrouded furniture and staring at the pictures on the wall.[37] Emilie also decreed that he would continue to share his father's bedroom, as he had done in Laufen.

Nevertheless, the move to Kleinhüningen did cause a great improvement in her disposition, mainly because it brought her back into the fold of the ever growing Preiswerk family. She became very *recht vom Teig*, a woman who thought highly of herself, especially when boasting of her siblings to her husband's parishioners.[38] Her brother Rudolf had married Celestine Allenspach, daughter of a wealthy farmer, who gave her a large dowry. Rudolf became even richer when he used part of it to buy a shop selling exotic spices and expensive cheese in the well-to-do St. Alban district and the rest to subsidize another career, as a successful dealer in cast iron and artisanal metalwork. He also bought a large estate called Margareten, where he and Celestine lived with their fifteen children and assorted relatives, including the increasingly odd brother of the Antistes Samuel, Great-Uncle Alexander.

Emilie loved Margareten and visited as often as possible, taking Carl to play with the nine children then born. There were other cousins as well, for Emilie's brother Gustav Adolph fathered eleven children, Samuel Gottlob had six, and Eduard also had several. All the relatives congregated at Margareten, where Celestine presided over a relaxed and pedagogically progressive household. "One child more or less won't make a difference," she was fond of saying, as she made the older siblings responsible for taking care of the younger ones. She treated her daughters the same as her sons, thus raising some family eyebrows — especially Emilie's — when she let the girls sleep outside in tents alongside the boys.[39]

All the family spoke of Rudolf and Celestine's son Wilhelm (1876–1946) as Carl's "closest" friend until they were fifteen, but this must be taken advisedly.

Carl really thought of Wilhelm as a "sissy" and enjoyed playing pranks on him.[40] In the midst of the noisy, frenetic household, Carl was often a silent and disapproving observer who wandered alone about the grounds. He saw his uncle Rudolf as a "very preoccupied businessman [who] could not devote much time to his children" and, anyway, died when they were very young.[41] He disdained the adults as "artisans and business people with very limited interests" and thought the fifteen children "suffered a great deal from the inconsequent, vulgar, and often brutal treatment they received from their mother."

WHILE EMILIE was taking comfort in the bosom of her family, Paul was retreating into "a sort of sentimental idealism" that left him prone to protracted reminiscences of the student days he now remembered as "golden." He adopted outdated student mannerisms and slang and smoked the long clay pipe favored by students. Parishioners who originally described him as "a big firm gentleman and a priest who was very good at spiritual welfare" now tried to conduct business outside his study, so they would not be trapped into listening to his oft-repeated stories. They thought him a great bore, best to be avoided if possible.[42] "I heard indirectly very much later that he was pushed aside by his wife, and, in consequence, both became neurotic," wrote his son many years later. But at the time, the couple were not only bewildered by each other, they were puzzled as well by their strange little boy.

Shortly after they moved to Kleinhüningen, the river Wiese, which normally flowed circumspectly into the Rhine, broke its dam and flooded the countryside. At least fifteen people drowned, and their bodies floated past the village or became stuck in the sand, deposited by the receding waters.[43] His parents were unable to control young Carl, then about five, as he went gleefully searching for bodies. He actually found one, a man in his churchgoing black frock coat, half covered by sand, his arm frozen in rigor mortis and shielding his eyes. Carl was mesmerized, but his mother "almost died of horror."[44]

The frequently absent Emilie was at home on the day one of the villagers slaughtered a fat pink pig opposite the vicarage. Carl threw a tantrum when she tried to snatch him away, and he insisted upon watching the entire procedure, entranced by the blood and entrails that were disgorged when the hapless pig's underside was slit open. He responded to his mother's horror by insisting once again that, like the two drowned men he had seen thus far in his young life and whose bodies and blood had so fascinated him, the pig's disembowelment was "simply a matter of interest."[45] Emilie thought his behavior was "an evil thing."

By the time he was six and sent to the village school in 1881, Carl was somewhat used to being called "Pastor's Carl." At first he thought it a special mark of distinction and was pleased to be so singled out from his classmates. Paul began to give him private Latin lessons when he was four, and the six-year-old liked to spout Latin expressions in school. He was naturally the best student, since all the others were children of barely literate farmers. He excelled in everything but mathematics, blaming his failure there on a "too vivid imagination." His best friends in the village school were the girls, of whom a great gaggle followed him about. They played their games on the village streets, avoiding the boys whom Pastor's Carl thought were "too clumsy . . . too awkward." At the age of eight, he was quite pleased with himself and his life, describing Emilie now as "a very good mother to me." He could not help adding that she had become "[very fat] rather stout."[46]

Carl was shocked when his mother gave birth to a daughter, Johanna Gertrud, on July 17, 1884. At the age of nine, he was embarrassed by a baby sister who represented a living advertisement of carnality in his own home, where his mother "had once again done something [he] was supposed not to know about."[47] Everything about his mother's new baby suffused him with shame, even though from his earliest years, village life had exposed him to various expressions of sexuality, and he had seen everything from mild flirtations in humans to copulation and birth among animals. Also, despite his trying to keep himself aloof from the vulgar jocularities of his classmates, he could not help witnessing their rough play. He did have an almost obsessional fixation on biology and botany, but his primary interest was in observation and stopped far short of curiosity about reproduction.[48] Years later, he admitted that he might have been "afraid of sexuality." His attitude toward all things sexual was properly Zwinglian in the sense of vaguely spiritual rather than rooted in concrete reality. This was all in keeping with his father's religious teachings, for in the years he attended the village school, he adored his father and wanted nothing more than to please him, even if it meant ignoring the schoolboy raunchiness that surrounded him.

Trudi, as his sister was called, was a frail, thin, red-haired baby with translucent skin that turned blotchy when she whimpered. Emilie feared the baby could not actually cry because she was so weak she might die. For the first year of Trudi's life, Emilie was so overprotective that others were kept away from the baby, especially Carl. He became sharply observant of everything that happened concerning Trudi, and he confused Emilie's "odd reactions" with his "suspicions that something regrettable was connected with this birth."[49] It was not until Trudi became a plump and robust toddler that Emilie relaxed enough to encourage Carl to play with his sister, but by then it was too late for closeness. Throughout their lives, their relationship was always cordial, but its most prominent characteristics were distance and detachment on his part, shy hero worship and an eagerness to please on hers.[50]

Emilie's disposition improved greatly after Trudi's birth. She passed her time contentedly caring for her daughter and visiting her Preiswerk relatives, and she awaited with relish the fascinating apparitions she claimed came to her bedroom every night. To Carl, she became "strange and mysterious," and he was frightened both by the way she acted and by what he thought he himself saw.[51] Sometimes at night, he thought he saw heads, one following the other and detaching from the same indefinite body. There were also tiny, far-distant balls that hovered closer and grew into large objects he feared would suffocate him. He dreamed of monstrous telegraph wires heavily laden with birds and awoke in terror, again feeling suffocated. His adult interpretation of his boyhood self was that the house's "atmosphere" was "unbreathable." He attributed these dreams to "overtures to the physiological changes of puberty."[52]

Between the ages of seven and nine, he became fascinated with fire and often used to light little fires in the crevices of the stone wall in the vicarage garden. Immediately in front of the wall, there was a slight slope from which a large stone projected. Carl liked to sit there and play a game in which he imagined that he and the stone interacted: first it was he who sat upon the stone; then he would mentally exchange places with the stone and ask himself whether he was the one who sat on the stone, or whether an unspecified "he," perhaps the personification of the stone, sat there. He never resolved the question, but whenever he played this game, he was left with a "feeling of curious and fascinating darkness."[53] In his tenth year, his "disunion" with himself and his "uncertainty in the world at large" became so severe that he did something he could not understand for many years to come. Like many other Swiss schoolchildren of his generation, he had a standard wooden pencil case, yellow and varnished to a high sheen and fitted with a ruler and eraser as well as pencils.[54] Carl carved a tiny manikin into the end of the ruler, the figure of a little man about two inches long. He dressed his little man like his father and the elders of the village, in a top hat, frock coat, and boots that he colored a gleaming black. The little man on the ruler lived in the pencil case with a talismanic stone he had picked up from a bank of the Rhine. As a special gift for the little man, Carl painted the stone with watercolors, so that it looked like it was divided into two halves, an upper and a lower. Quite pleased with himself, he rejoiced over "his" stone and believed that he and the little man shared a "great secret."

There were certain parts of the vicarage that were forbidden territory to the young boy, especially the attic, where the floorboards were dangerous to walk on because they were rotted by worms. Nevertheless, he stole up there and placed the pencil box on one of the highest beams. From time to time, he sneaked up to bring little presents for the manikin. These usually consisted of tiny scrolls of paper upon which he had written "letters" in "a secret language of [his] own invention," letters that the elderly Jung believed were probably sayings that he liked. He called them the manikin's private library.

At the time, he never wondered how he would explain his behavior if his parents were to catch him on one of his attic forays. He felt the euphoria of "newly won security" and believed that he possessed something no one else knew about or could have. He guarded his secret as he would have guarded his life, for he truly believed that "the safety of life depended on it." He never asked himself why this was so; he simply believed that it was true.[55] When the elderly Jung wrote about this in the autobiographical memoir *Memories, Dreams, Reflections,* he never revealed what happened to the little wooden manikin. As with all the meaningful possessions of childhood, its importance seems to have diminished gradually over time, and for all anyone knows, it remains still in its pencil box, entombed in dirt on the rafter where he abandoned it a century ago.[56]

Years after Jung created the little man and his world, when he was in his thirties and preparing to write *Psychology of the Unconscious*,[57] he read about the totems of native peoples, among them the soul-stones of Arlesheim, Australian churingas, and the Telesphoros of Asklepios. He did not remember his father's library containing books on any of these subjects, nor, to the best of his recollection, had his father ever spoken of any of them. He credits his association of these entities with his little man as the first time he thought "archaic psychic components" might have entered "the individual psyche without any direct line of tradition." Later, it supplied him with the starting point for his view of "dementia praecox and for the archetypes in general." It was one of his first attempts to define what he later called the collective unconscious. Several years afterward, in 1920 in England, he carved the manikin's figure in stone, called it "Atmavictu, the breath of life," and equated it with "the creative impulse."[58] After he formulated these views, he marveled at how the collective unconscious influenced his behavior as a child in ways similar to those he observed among African natives: "They do it first and don't even know it. Only much later do they think about it [and give it a name]."

ALL THESE events coincided with another major change when, at the age of eleven, Carl matriculated in the Humanistisches Gymnasium, Basel.[59] In Kleinhüningen, "Pastor's Carl" had been the star pupil, the burly boy who knew Latin as well as he knew his Bible and could recite long passages in both. All that changed in the city, as the Humanistisches Gymnasium was the school to which the best families of Basel sent their sons. Most arrived each day in the family carriage, wearing fine little suits and escorted by servants; Carl rose early to walk the several miles to school, because it took at least an hour and a half each way. The first part of his journey was on country lanes that meandered through thick woodland, and the latter part took him through the raucous industrial quarters of Basel and then onto the magisterial streets surrounding the cathedral on the *Münsterplatz*. He found this contrast extremely disconcerting and believed it contributed to the division within himself that he associated with so many other aspects of his school days. The other boys spoke excellent French and German, while he knew no French, stumbled in German, and mumbled the thick, clumsy *Baslertütsch* dialect of his village. He was a sturdy, thickset boy, taller than many of his classmates and already brawny; he was always bedraggled and usually wet and odorous when the weather was inclement; his clothes were shabby, and sometimes he had no socks to wear with his run-down shoes.[60] He was always ready to fight and frequently engaged in everything from roughhousing to outright brawls. His teachers constantly scolded or

punished him for aggressive behavior. As an old man, he thought his boyish behavior stemmed "unwarrantedly" from "a bad conscience." He thought it was
all due to the "bad atmosphere" between his parents and that he was probably
"depressed." He remembered how he sometimes misbehaved so badly that he
"even took notes for alibis and excuses" to his teachers.

To the other boys he was an oddity who stood out, not only because of his
appearance and bad behavior but also because of his avidity for learning and his
eagerness to show off what he knew. After one such incident, when he was accused by his German teacher of plagiarizing an essay (which was entirely his
own work), his classmates began to tease him with names such as "Father Abraham."[61] There were certain boys with whom he felt a natural intellectual affinity, but when he tried to play with them, he was embarrassed by his "unusualness"
and shamed by their rejection. Except for Albert Oeri (and even he was often
embarrassed by Carl's behavior) and their mutual friend Andreas Vischer,[62] Carl
was accepted only by boys from other poor families, by those whose disposi-
tions were placid and indifferent, or by those who were not very bright. These
were not the friends he wanted, and he was ashamed to be relegated to their
company. It did not help when he was frequently ridiculed by his teachers for
being "frankly, an idiot in mathematics."[63] In class, his "fear of failure and . . .
sense of smallness" left him in "silent despair."[64] Ironically, for as an adult he
became a gifted artist, his teachers removed him from drawing classes because
of his "utter incapacity."[65] He was happy with the decision to remove him from
gymnastics, which he hated because of "certain physical timidity." He linked his
aversion to his overwhelming need to know "to what and to whom" he was "entrusting" himself. Could it be, the adult Jung asked himself, that this was because of his mother's periodic abandonment throughout his infancy? His first
year at the Gymnasium was "completely ruined" because of his "disagreeable,
rather uncanny feeling" that he possessed "repulsive traits." He was convinced
that both teachers and pupils shunned him.

So many different things had happened in his young life to contribute to this
view of himself as unworthy, undeserving, and unlikable. To compensate, he
acted withdrawn and distant, as if nothing mattered, when in reality he was consumed with anger and rage. To himself, it seemed as if he were someone else, a
coolly detached observer of his own distress. As an old man trying to recapture
his most important and formative boyhood experiences, he recalled several that
he had puzzled about and pondered throughout his life and that he had used as
examples at various times in his writings and seminars, even though he often did
not have answers for the questions he raised.

THE MOST "fateful" event of Carl's school years coincided with his father's appointment as the pastor/counselor of the Basel Psychiatrische Universitäts-
klinik, the university's mental hospital/asylum known as the Friedmatt, a

position he held for the rest of his life.[66] It was expected that pastors in the Swiss Reformed Church would perform adjunct duty in hospitals or mental homes, but Paul fulfilled his obligation with excessive dedication, and it became one of his few pleasures. Perhaps it was because the appointment was to the very same division of the university hospital that his own father had revitalized, but he quickly became known as a pastor who specialized in psychiatric disorders and mental impairment. He liked conversing with doctors and ministering to patients, and his clinical duties soon took prominence over his religious ones. Although Jung never mentioned his father's affiliation with the Friedmatt in his memoirs, it did mark the first time he was privy to discussions about disorders and illnesses of the mind.[67] No doubt Paul Jung's interest in psychiatric literature and practice also had something to do with the crises of faith with which he struggled during these years, but in light of what happened to Carl at approximately the same time as Paul assumed these duties, there is always the thought that the father's interest in mental disorders was personal as well as professional.

Just before the end of his first year at the Gymnasium, Carl was standing on the *Münsterplatz*, waiting for a classmate who usually walked home with him, when another boy gave him an unexpected shove that toppled him to the curbstone. He struck his head so hard that he was momentarily semi-conscious. Jung later remembered clearly what he thought at that exact moment: "Now you won't have to go to school any more."[68] Bystanders quickly carried him to the nearby home of two Preiswerk aunts, Emilie's elderly spinster sisters, and his parents fetched him home to the rectory. From then on, the mere thought of having to return to school was enough to make him faint. Even so, he did return for a few brief weeks, and nearly every day between eleven and noon he fainted. As an adult he thought it ironic that no one ever considered that his fainting spells might be due to simple hunger, for he left home each day at 7 A.M. with only a cup of milk in his stomach, and sometimes not even that.

His teachers removed him from school when his classmates became more engrossed in waiting for Carl to faint than in doing their lessons. For the next six months, he stayed at home contentedly playing solitary games, daydreaming, and reading books in his father's library. He described himself as being closest to his mother during this time, but said, "She wasn't enough for me in conversation. She mostly admired me, and that wasn't good for me." So he was alone, and he "liked that best" because he was free to dream for endless hours. His games were mostly violent, filled with images of war and pillage, devastation and plunder. These generally took place in the woods, where he would spend entire days communing secretly with nature. He became even more introspective and silent, picking at his evening meal before retreating to the bedroom he still shared with his father. Paul was worried in the extreme, perhaps because of what he saw during his rounds of the hospital's psychiatric wards. Even Emilie, who had recently taken to confiding her specific marital problems and general unhappiness to Carl — as if he were an adult who could set things right for her, rather than her troubled twelve-year-old son — abandoned her self-centeredness long enough to agree with Paul's decision to send the boy away.

Carl spent the summer at Paul's brother Ernst's home in Winterthur, a visit he enjoyed enormously and one that seemed to have excellent benefits for his health. But despite his cousins and their many other playmates who lived nearby, he spent his days alone at the train station, sitting quietly on a bench, observing the thrilling hustle and bustle. When he returned to Kleinhüningen, everyone believed he was well and would return to school, but the fainting spells began as soon as the subject was mentioned. Paul took him to the doctors at the Friedmatt, who were all stymied. After all possibilities were exhausted, one suggested that Carl might have become epileptic and that his fainting spells were a manifestation of fits. The boy laughed when he overheard his parents discussing this, for he had acquired a surprising amount of medical knowledge from his father; he knew what epileptic fits were and that he did not have them. The knowledge left him with a feeling of superiority, of having bested his elders. It also left him with a "subtle feeling of bad conscience," but as he was "more and more detached from the world," he didn't really care.

Desperate to cure his son, Paul arranged for Carl to go to Entlebuch, a farming valley in the Bernese Oberland some twenty kilometers from Luzern. There, he boarded for the better part of a year with a Catholic priest who took him in for the cost of his food.[69] If being in the company of a priest raised any anxieties or fears similar to those of his phallus dream or the sighting of the Jesuit priest, Carl never mentioned it. He spent his days under the supervision of a country doctor who catered mostly to adults convalescing from one illness or another, and the boy fit in easily among them.

The high point of the stay occurred at the end, when Paul came to fetch him home and they took a steamship to Luzern. They went together as far as Vitznau, but then Paul, not having enough money for two tickets, sent Carl alone up the Rigi on the cogwheel railway. It was a journey he never made again but one that he never forgot. Throughout his adult life, whenever he was exhausted from overwork or stress, he would conjure up the image of himself at the peak of this mountain.[70]

Once back at the vicarage, he assumed his idle life would continue, but he was worried enough about what his parents thought that he began to eavesdrop. On one such occasion, when Paul and a friend were chatting in the garden and Carl was hiding in the shrubbery, he overheard his father say how distressed he was that his son's condition seemed likely to be permanent, for he had no money to provide for an adult unable to earn a living. The remark hit Carl like a thunderclap, and his innate pride, coupled with his basic unwillingness to be dependent on anyone, rose to the fore.

He strode into his father's study and began to read his Latin grammar with a vengeance, but to his distress, he felt light-headed and faint and thought he would fall off the chair. He, who believed he could control all aspects of himself, physical as well as mental, worried that perhaps this time it was too late and he would not be able to gain control over the fainting. He willed himself to resist, and the attack passed, even though another came shortly after. Again he told himself he would not give in, and again it passed. It happened several more times, and each time he triumphed. Several weeks later, he returned to school and never fainted again.

The adult Jung related this experience in his memoirs as an example of how he learned about neuroses. He felt rage and shame for what he believed was a situation he had helped to cause, that is, his being shoved to the ground. He vowed that never again would he permit circumstances to occur in which anyone could best or pity him. He became obsessed with his schoolwork, sometimes rising at 3 A.M., but never later than five, to pore over his lessons meticulously until it was time to leave. He did this, not for the sake of appearances, but because he wanted to "amount to something" for his own sake. His popularity rose to match his grades when he abandoned his solitary pursuit of nature and became a hearty fellow who joined in his schoolmates' games and pranks.[71] His bête noire was still mathematics, but "in those days, happily and sensibly, failing marks were ignored when the partially untalented student was known to be otherwise intelligent."[72]

Jacob Burckhardt was still teaching at the Gymnasium and was inadvertently responsible for Jung's intellectual interest in the writings of another great Basler personality, J. J. Bachofen, the cultural historian and sociologist.[73] In the classroom, Burckhardt made "derisive remarks" about Bachofen, which drew Jung to the writings of both men. Even as a schoolboy, he thought Burckhardt's perceptions of cultural history were "limited," whereas Bachofen's *Mutterrecht*, or theories of matrilineal descent, became a much consulted reference for the rest of his life.[74] Burckhardt also made "spiteful" remarks about Nietzsche (who had already left Basel, so Jung never actually saw him), and this piqued Jung's later interest in the philosopher.[75]

With his mind intellectually engaged in his studies and his popularity secure among his classmates, the remainder of Jung's Gymnasium years passed in harmony and tranquillity. It was a blessing, because his life outside school did not provide the same stability. As he walked to school one morning in his thirteenth year, he had an experience that he deemed "the end of his childhood."[76] He felt as if he were emerging from cloud and fog and heard himself proclaiming, "I am *myself!*" It was as if everything before this moment had happened to him without his conscious volition, whereas now he possessed "authority" and "value," and he knew he was truly in charge of himself. At the same time, he experienced a version of his mother's personalities No. 1 and No. 2 within himself.[77] On the one hand, he was a clumsy, awkward, mathematical dunce of a boy living in real time at the end of the nineteenth century; on the other, he was an old man living in the eighteenth century who dressed in high-buckled shoes, wore a powdered wig, and drove a fine carriage. Personality No. 1 was as powerless and ineffective as No. 2 was powerful and influential. This may have been an ordinary adolescent fantasy, ignoring one's shortcomings to favor power and importance, but it left Jung "confused" and "full to the brim with heavy reflections." The episode became one he reflected upon for the rest of his life.

At the same time, an upsetting daydream began to recur, one that he would try to command himself not to have, usually without success. It came anyway, always when he walked through the cathedral square and looked up to see the cathedral, bathed in sunshine and silhouetted against the sky. No matter how hard he tried to blot the image from his mind, he could see God, sitting on his throne in Heaven and "shitting" on the cathedral, so that "from under the throne an enormous turd falls," so big that the roof collapses under this load.[78]

What makes me think that God destroys his Church in this abominable manner? he asked himself. The "symbolism" of the childhood dream of the "man-eater" phallus and the "violence" of the imagery of God shitting on his own cathedral "upset me terribly," the elderly Jung wrote. Nevertheless, the youthful Carl was powerless to stop thinking about it. Emilie knew intuitively that something was troubling him, but she made the mistake of asking if anything had happened at school. Carl replied truthfully that nothing had happened there, so she let the matter lie. For several nights, he was tormented by the image of the shitting God until he hit upon the idea of roaming back through his ancestry to find some progenitor to blame for his wicked thoughts. Eventually he came to Adam and Eve and concluded that an omniscient God intended all along for the first humans to sin. He felt absolved from his misery but, pastor's son that he was, could not sleep until he puzzled out what it was that God specifically wanted from him.[79] When the image continued, unbidden, to come, he let it proceed even further, visualizing how "from under the throne an enormous turd falls upon the sparkling new roof, shatters it, and breaks the walls of the Cathedral asunder."

Carl believed it was God's will for him to think these things, for he was abiding by God's command that nothing truly evil will happen to one who survives tests of courage. He gave himself credit for original thinking here, disdaining his father's blind belief in Scripture and the rituals and social behavior of their Swiss forebears. He thought Paul did not understand or know how to honor the "immediate living God, who stands, omnipotent and free, above his Bible and His Church." When Paul prepared him for his confirmation, Carl was eager for what he hoped would be a real discussion of this and other differences. It was disappointing that Paul's usual response was "We'll skip that [for now]," even though he always followed it with the admission "I don't really know what one should make of it." Carl admired his father's honesty, but from that moment on, "all religious talk bored [him] to death."[80]

These different ways of responding to religious theory marked the beginning of the worst years of dissension within the strife-ridden household. Carl, at fifteen, had reached his full height and appeared much older than his actual years. Emilie treated him as her equal in age and outlook, assuming that he shared her derision for Paul. Carl did not, but he wanted to avoid open conflict with either parent, so he refused to be drawn into her marital debates. Emilie mistook his unwillingness for depression, and throughout the last years of his teens, she badgered him constantly to learn why he was so depressed, but he kept his own counsel and was silent.

To get away from his parents' constant bickering, Carl began to spend long hours in the pastor's study while Paul was ministering to the inmates of the Friedmatt. At first and because he thought he might have missed something, he pored over his father's Bible in search of answers to his religious questions. The family also owned a philosophical encyclopedia edited by Wilhelm T. Krug, and Carl studied the articles about "God, The Trinity, Spirit, and Consciousness."[81] He did not know what to make of them, so, between the ages of thirteen and fourteen, he began to read philosophy. One of the earliest works he read was A. E. Biedermann's study of Christian dogmatism,[82] which led directly to Schopenhauer, whose "somber picture of the world" received his "undivided approval," even as his "solution to the problem" of life did not.[83]

He gave no explanation for why Meister Eckhart entranced him or why he "despised" St. Thomas Aquinas and Hegel. He appreciated Kant for what he described as the philosopher's "painstaking work of distinguishing what belongs to me, what is within my reach, and what lies beyond, and where we cannot reach without being harmed." Nietzsche "touched" him most, particularly *Thus Spake Zarathustra*. What happened to Nietzsche there? he asked himself rhetorically in the *Protocols*, the working drafts of *Memories, Dreams, Reflections*. All of Nietzsche's writings carried intellectual meaning, but *Zarathustra* touched him on "a human level." He placed it "on the same level" as Goethe's *Faust* and considered the two to be "the starting points for my own work." His intense reading of philosophy resulted in his "marked resistance to theology." It led to lively discussions with his father, but only as long as philosophy never touched upon theology: Paul would say, "You have to believe, not think," and the discussion was over.

For years, he had gone into his father's library to read the Grail legends over and over, until he could quote them by heart. He considered them his first great literary experience, one that was not equaled until he read Goethe's *Faust*, which was his mother's favorite and soon became his. He read poetry with passion and pleasure, and among his favorite poets were Hölderlin, from whose "Patmos" he quoted long passages when an old man; Mörike, whose "Orplid" he found utterly amazing, especially since the rest of his poems were so "mediocre"; and Hugo Wolf, because he set Mörike's poems to beautiful music. He liked F. T. von Vischer's *Auch Einer* (Also One).[84]

He also read Shakespeare in translation, preferring the dramas (unspecified) and the sonnets, even though he dismissed some of these (unnamed) as "typically literary." He esteemed Schiller's "ethical pathos" and took great pleasure in reading Johann Peter Eckermann's conversations with Goethe. He appreciated Heraclitus, had a lesser interest in Pythagoras and Empedocles, and felt no interest in Plato.[85] He had a passing attraction to Greek drama but was captivated by *The Odyssey*. Myth in any form, about any country or culture, became a favorite subject. At school, he "openly" read the adventure novels of Gerstäcker[86] and German translations of classic English novels, especially Sir Walter Scott's swashbucklers. He described these as the assertion of personality No. 1 (the oafish, dull boy) over the more introspective and scholarly No. 2 (the discerning eighteenth-century aristocrat).

He had eight hours of Latin each week with a "complete fool" of a teacher who "had a stomach neurosis and was a first-class neurotic," but he enjoyed *The Aeneid*, Caesar, and Cicero and "quite a bit of lively Latin," including Baco of Verulam.[87] He also studied Greek, but the teacher was "an old hypochondriac with a nice diagonally cut beard" from whom he learned very little. As for religion, his teacher was an expert on Reformation history. "I can't tell you what agonies I suffered there," he recalled. "This terrible boredom!"

BY THE time he was fifteen, the question of Carl's future was often the main topic of conversation, not only between Emilie and Paul but also among members of their extended families. Emilie had six brothers who were ministers, and, like himself, Paul had two brothers who were ordained. Unlike Paul, however, all eight men were pastors of prosperous parishes, and many had married wealthy women whose dowries enhanced their standard of living even further. All the Preiswerk and Jung siblings who remained in Switzerland, not just the ministers, lived lives of great comfort and in some cases obvious wealth. This did not escape the ever-observant Carl.

Each Thursday he was expected to lunch at his uncle Samuel Gottlob Preiswerk's table in the posh rectory of St. Alban's. Called Isemännli (little iron man) by his brothers and sisters, he was the eldest son and de facto head of the Preiswerk clan since the death of Antistes Samuel. All his sons were ministers, and as he had significant influence over his many nephews' choice of professions, he took it for granted that Carl would become a minister. In the beginning, Carl enjoyed these luncheons because the men engaged in intellectual conversations. Granted, they were mostly about points of theology, but occasionally names such as Kant or Burckhardt were mentioned, if only to be dismissed as too liberal or too difficult to understand. Another name much mentioned in other quarters of Basel — Nietzsche — was never heard at the Isemännli's table. Carl, who regretted that such conversations seldom occurred in his own home because they always resulted in disagreements of intellect versus belief, soon realized that his uncle and cousins were only more agreeable versions of his own father. Blind faith ruled in the Reverend Samuel Gottlob Preiswerk's house, just as it did in the Reverend Paul Jung's. In Carl's view, both pastors used the hardened formalities and rituals of the creed they shared as buffer or protection against any possibility that they might have to encounter the uncertainties found in an individual's own life experience of a God. No matter how much Carl tried to steer it there, discourse in both households stopped short of veering from the safety of accepted dogma into the realm of religious questioning. It was not until many years later that Carl understood the reason for his father's unwillingness to engage in intellectual religious discourse, that he, like his son, was "consumed by inward doubts."[88]

Both the Preiswerks and the Jungs stopped talking about the priesthood as a possible profession for Carl when they realized his unsuitability. Yet, the question of what he was to do remained. In his adulthood, Jung frequently alluded to a desire to be a historian or philologist, but especially an archeologist. Those who knew him best wondered if this was true, for at the time, he seemed quite content to follow his illustrious grandfather and namesake into the medical profession.[89] When he wrote his memoirs, he created a complicated series of circumstances that led to his eventual career decision, but when an interviewer asked the then-eighty-four-year-old Jung why he became a doctor, Jung replied with one word: "opportunism."[90]

Of all his relatives, his grandfather Carl Gustav I was certainly the most prominent and respected in Basel society, even though his financial peccadilloes were generally known. During his Gymnasium years, Carl was never "Pastor's Carl," but always "Dr. Med. Jung's grandson." Despite his insistence that his peers and teachers looked down upon him, Dr. Jung's grandson garnered more approving glances and comments on the *Münsterplatz* than he was willing to admit, either then or when he was an old man.

Jung's friend and colleague Marie-Louise von Franz thought he was talking about his own experience in selecting a profession when he wrote of decision making in *Psychology and Alchemy*.[91] Jung wrote of all the "hesitations, timid shrinkings . . . petty complications and meticulous excuses" that an individual resorts to, concluding that "the personal psyche is running round this central point like a shy animal, at once fascinated and frightened, always in flight and yet steadily drawing nearer."

In Carl's case, the decision to become a doctor hinged on other criteria than the simple desire to be one. Foremost was the question of money, for Paul would have to struggle just to pay his tuition to the university, never mind the several years of medical training that came afterward. And he would have to go to Basel University because his family could not afford the fees elsewhere, let alone the transportation and housing. To ensure that Carl could attend even Basel, Paul had to petition officials for a sizeable stipend that would be in effect for each year as long as Carl maintained proper grades and suitable deportment. He did not tell Carl until it was granted, and then the young man was shamed by his father's action, because he thought it exposed their dire poverty to the encapsulated segment of Basel society in which they were known.[92]

Once Carl's future was decided, he was relieved that he would soon be spending long days in the city and would thus be away from the vicarage. In the last year or so before he began his university studies, home life had deteriorated alarmingly. Emilie's No. 2 personality dominated, as she saw an increasing number of ever stranger visions and many of her uncanny psychic predictions proved true. She was now dragging little Trudi along for lengthy visits to her sister, the Aunt Gusteli who had taken care of the baby Carl, now married late in life to the "Widower Weiss." Gusteli lived in the curious structure known as the Bottmingermühle, formerly an operating mill and now simply a building owned by Emilie's favorite brother, Eduard Preiswerk. It was a gathering place for many of the Preiswerks, but no one talked much about why they gathered there or what they did. When Emilie came home from the mill, she was strangely preoccupied, humming little snatches of song under her breath, occasionally breaking into private, cackling laughter.

As if this were not disconcerting enough, Paul underwent decided changes. Physically, he seemed to shrink before Carl's eyes, so that the robust Emilie now seemed enormous and he himself a giant in comparison to his father. Paul's gentle demeanor changed to an attitude of combative condescension, and he let no opportunity pass to berate his wife and belittle his son. Only the silent, ethereal Trudi escaped his venom. Paul was fifty-four years old, a shrunken, bitter man who grew silent during the autumn of 1895, Carl's first semester at the university. Still sharing a bedroom, the young university student usually left so early and came home so late that he did not realize how ill his father was until several months before his death, when Paul diminished to "a sack full of bones."[93] Until then, Carl had mainly been grateful for his father's silence and thus managed to avoid the realization that he was terminally ill.

Johann Paul Achilles Jung died on January 28, 1896, from an unspecified abdominal cancer, probably of the pancreas.[94] He was buried in the Kleinhüningen churchyard next to the vicarage, with most of the Preiswerk and Jung relatives and all of his parishioners in attendance.[95] That night, after everyone had gone home, Emilie sat alone in the darkened parlor. When her son came in, she turned and said eerily in what he thought of as her No. 2 voice, "He died in time for you."[96] For years afterward, he wondered what she meant.

CHAPTER 3

—⚬⚬⚬—

Unconventional Possibilities

From his first semester in the Faculty of Natural Sciences at the University of Basel, Carl Gustav II Jung flourished. Intellectually, he felt as if "golden gates"[1] had opened wide before him. Emotionally, he was exuberantly happy, more gregarious and sociable than he had ever been.

For the first two years, 1895 to 1897, he followed the set program for students who wished to go on to medical training, concentrating on courses in anatomy and physiology and their variants. He was especially fascinated by those that dealt with diseases in humans and the history of human physical development. If choosing medicine for his career had been a compromise, he showed no sign of regret; nor was there any yearning glance toward another profession. He simply taught himself how to incorporate knowledge from other disciplines into his medical education — mythology, cultural anthropology, and comparative religion being just several among many examples.

Socially, Carl enjoyed a rousingly successful student life. He had been invited to join Zofingia, the same fraternity to which his father had belonged. It was a genuine honor, for only the best and most popular students from the four different faculties of the university were tapped for membership.

Shortly before Paul's death, Zofingia provided a mutually happy occasion for father and son to enjoy each other's company without the rancor that characterized their usual daily interaction. Carl invited his father to don his own colorful cap and hoist his clay pipe (both of which he had cherished all his life) on a student outing to a south German village in the Markgrafen district that was noted for inexpensive but decent wine. After much imbibing, Paul gave an impromptu speech about his own student days that earned resounding applause from his son's classmates. Carl was of two minds about his father's tipsy oration: happy, because Paul had not embarrassed him before his fellow students but had, on the contrary, raised his popularity several notches; and sad, because he realized yet again how Paul's student days must have been the happiest of his life. Carl wondered if his own life would diminish to such a sorry pass.

———

THERE WERE major changes in the Jung household after Paul's death. Emilie became calm and stable, a solid, constant presence for both her children. With Carl, she adopted a polite and deferential manner, for in the tradition of Swiss culture he had become the man of the family and head of the household. Ever since he was twelve or thirteen, Emilie had treated him as a combination of colleague and co-conspirator; now, strong woman that she was, she became deferential to the twenty-year-old as the household's savior. It was taken for granted that he would occupy the bedroom, study, and library that would have been Paul's, and that he would be in charge of the household finances.

The most urgent matter to settle was where to live. They had to vacate the vicarage for the new pastor within the week after Paul's funeral, so a hasty relocation was necessary. Paul's salary ended with his death, and there was no pension for his widow. They had no savings, and if Carl remained a student, they would have no income.

As head of the Preiswerk family, the Isemännli Samuel Gottlob was in charge of deciding his sister's fate, but he was in one of the deepest of his many recurring depressions and incapable of making any decision, let alone this one.[2] Eduard, Emilie's favorite brother and childhood confidant (two years older than she), solved the problem by letting her live rent-free in part of the ground floor of the Bottmingermühle in Binningen, a formerly working mill that had come to him through the dowry of his wealthy wife, Emma Friedrich. The rest of the ground floor was occupied by Aunt Gusteli, who had become a bride at age fifty-eight when she married the spectral "Widower Weiss."[3] For Emilie and her children, the move was happy, despite the fact that the ramshackle mill was in a decrepit section of Basel surrounded by overgrown and unkempt grounds and abutting a busy railroad crossing.[4]

Thus, one of the Jung family's pressing problems was solved, but an even more serious one remained: how they were to exist without income. On this issue, the well-off men of the Preiswerk family were curiously silent. Only Maria-Sophia, Emilie's elderly sister, offered limited help. She was the widow of a minister, Edmund Fröhlich, who left her a small but excellent collection of family antiques. Frau Fröhlich-Preiswerk needed money, too, so she charged Carl with selling the antiques to Basel's better dealers. Shrewdly, he educated himself to learn what they were worth and then disposed of them individually rather than collectively, thus garnering a larger sum. Through an agreement with his aunt, he kept a good percentage of the profit.

That money, however, was not enough to see him through to the end of his university studies, let alone medical school. His Preiswerk uncles held a family conference at which Emilie's brother Gustav Adolph, the family "quack and dentist" and father of eleven children,[5] told the assemblage that it was foolish hubris for Carl to stay in school. They all agreed that he should lower his sights and find a job as a clerk in some sort of firm where, if he worked diligently, he might eventually earn a salary good enough to support his mother and sister.

Carl was furious. In desperation, he asked his paternal uncle Ernst Jung[6] of Winterthur for a loan to be paid in regular increments until he graduated, when he would then be able to provide for his mother and sister himself. Ernst Jung agreed to these terms and supported his sister-in-law and her children until Carl completed his studies.[7] Carl took charge of the money, doling out household expenses each week and keeping careful accounts of everything that the household spent.[8] In this way, and with various tasks he performed at school to earn money, they managed well enough.[9]

IN HIS first two academic years, Carl Jung was enrolled in the Propädeuticum 1 and 2, the set preparatory courses for medical school.[10] The curriculum centered around the usual courses in biology[11] and anatomy, which he enjoyed not for their corporeality but for their theory. He enjoyed reading about comparative anatomy and evolutionary theory, and he excelled in abstract, conjectural discussions. He spoke freely in the classroom and expressed his views more creatively than clinically.

His professor Frederich von Müller had the same sort of mind-set and soon selected the outspoken pupil for his junior assistant.[12] There was a true meeting of the minds between teacher and pupil, for when von Müller left for a brief lecture trip to Munich, he chose Carl to act as substitute instructor in the next segment of the course, histology. When von Müller returned, he told Carl that he was leaving Basel to accept a professorship in Munich and that a junior appointment there might well be his if he would specialize in internal medicine. The young doctor-to-be thought he would, not because he wanted to, but because he could not afford the long training necessary to become a surgeon, which was then his first professional choice.

His belief that he was well suited for a career in either surgery or internal medicine did not last much longer, however, for he soon learned something crucial about himself: that the child who had relished the sight of blood was now a man who detested physiology. He could not bear his classes in vivisection and hated having to observe experiments that were done on animals. Dissection of cadavers was so unsettling that he cut as many classes as he could, stopping just short of failing the course. In fact, although he enjoyed everything that had to do with reading, talking, or learning about the many different and sometimes monstrous things that could go wrong within a human body, he did not like anything that required him to touch a person, living or dead.

When the time did come for him to choose a specialty, psychiatry was not as surprising or late a choice as he tried to paint it in his memoir.[13] He had been flirting with an interest in psychiatry for years, ever since Paul had become affiliated with the Friedmatt. Even before he entered the university, Carl saw and at least glanced at, if he did not actually read, the books Paul brought home from the Friedmatt's psychiatric library.[14] In many of their quarrels about religious faith, Paul had used references from these texts to bolster his religious views. All too frequently, however, psychiatric examples had the opposite effect, only pointing out his many questing uncertainties. As far as Carl was concerned, during these disagreements with his father, psychiatry as it was then practiced did not provide useful answers to human concerns.

As an elderly man, Jung gave the credit for his decision to specialize in psychiatry to Richard von Krafft-Ebing, best known for his *Psychopathia sexualis*. Jung cited his *Lehrbuch der Psychiatrie* as the last textbook he read before the required state examination for his degree, which he took and passed on September 28, 1900.[15] He did not elaborate on the reasons that he saved this particular subject until last, but in fact, his interest in psychiatry as a specialty dated from his first semester in medical school, when two unexplainable events occurred in the Bottmingermühle that led him to read widely about spiritualism, then considered a related adjunct of psychiatry.

He was studying in his room one summer afternoon, when he heard a loud crack, much like a pistol going off, in the dining room. He ran in and discovered that the seventy-year-old walnut dining table, an heirloom from Sophie Jung-Frey's dowry, had split from center to rim in a way that had nothing to do with its construction or the natural grain of the wood. Also, the weather was unlikely, a hot, humid day as opposed to a dry one in winter, when such mishaps might be expected. Carl was disconcerted when Emilie, in her No. 2 voice, said, "Yes, yes, that means something."[16]

Several weeks later, there was another untoward event. Carl returned home early one evening to find his mother, sister, and the maid[17] all visibly upset. There had been another noise, this one coming from the sideboard, a solid piece of Swiss nineteenth-century furniture.[18] The women had been too frightened to look for the cause, so Carl searched for it by opening the various drawers until he came to the side cupboard, where the bread was usually kept. There lay the bread knife, its blade neatly severed in several places in a manner that could not have occurred naturally.[19] It could only have broken in such a manner if the blade had been snapped deliberately several times, but there had been only one resounding noise, and no one had touched the knife since the previous meal. Seeking an explanation, Carl took the knife to a cutler, who insisted that it must have been broken in an act of mischief, as it was made of very good metal and could not have shattered naturally. When Carl told Emilie this, she looked at him "meaningfully," and once again he had nothing to say in reply. He kept the broken knife for the rest of his life.[20]

In one of the several coincidences that Jung later called "synchronicity," or "repeated experiences that indicated events do not always obey the rules of time, space and causality,"[21] he chanced upon a book in the library of Albert Oeri's father that dealt with a phenomenon of spiritualism, a now-esoteric text dealing with the case of one Gottliebin Dittus, as described in *Blumhardts Kampf*.[22] Jung credited this book with relieving many of his doubts about the power of the mind and classified it as belonging to a subcategory of the literature of psychiatry. Reading it led him to other books on the subject of spiritualism, and the more he read, the more he was convinced that there had to be something to the worldwide coincidences, where the same seemingly unexplainable phenomena kept being reported over and over. He did not surrender entirely to the primacy or total authenticity of these views, for some of the observations of the spiritualists seemed "weird and questionable," but they were, nevertheless, the first sustained accounts he read of "objective psychic phenomena."[23]

He began to read widely in this field. Kant's *Dreams of a Spirit-Seer* came "at just the right moment." Names of other nineteenth-century writers who were associated with spiritualism, such as Zöllner, Crookes, Eschenmayer, Passavant, Justinus Kerner, Görres, and Swedenborg, became an active part of his vocabulary.[24] In her No. 2 demeanor, his mother nodded happily when she saw him reading these works, for she thoroughly approved of his interest and usually read the books after him. Carl was not so sure that her approval was a good thing, for people other than Emilie, Trudi, and some of the Preiswerk relatives were "distinctly discouraging" about this strange interest of his. He himself felt "pushed to the brink of the world" by such utterly "unconventional possibilities."

These experiences occurred during his second year at the university, when he was still in the Propädeuticum. Psychiatry was a relatively new required subject for medical students, having started in 1888.[25] Jung enrolled in courses a decade later, in 1898, the same year he chose psychiatry as his specialty. During the winter semester of 1898–99 and the summer semester of 1900, he studied primarily under the psychiatrist Professor Ludwig Wille (1834–1912), an adjunct professor at the university and director of the curriculum in psychiatry who enjoyed great fame and respect throughout Basel for being the founder and director of the St. Urban Cantonal Mental Asylum, the city's "lunatic asylum."[26]

Jung knew that Wille believed psychoses were due to physical causes, most notably physical degeneration of the brain, and that he believed in incarceration rather than treatment. Knowing Wille's outlook, and given Jung's aversion to aspects of medicine that required him to touch actual bodies, he still chose psychiatry, because it was the discipline that most closely allowed him to pursue his primary interests: spiritualism and religious theory.

In the first semester of 1900 he moved on to classroom training, general clinical observation, and practice on patients while under the observation of other professors and doctors, a program not much different from internship as it is practiced today.[27] On September 28, 1900, he took and passed the final examinations to become a medical doctor, the *Medizinische Fachprüfung*, or *Staatsexa-*

men. He was not, however, allowed to use the title of Doctor of Medicine. That would come only after he wrote a dissertation and had it approved by the medical faculty of a university.[28]

For the rest of that year, Jung was a general practitioner, meaning he took whatever paid work he could find, and he scrambled to find it. He received a pittance for his work with patients in the mental hospital, so he needed something else. An opportunity came in late summer 1900, when a Zofingia brother told him that a Dr. Heinrich Pestalozzi of Männedorf needed someone to look after his practice during his vacation.[29] Männedorf, a village on the northern shore of Lake Zürich, marked Jung's first experience of the countryside where he would live and work for the rest of his life.

FINANCIAL NECESSITY had forced Carl Gustav II Jung to race through university studies and medical training in five years. He had motivation, certainly, for the sooner he graduated, the sooner he would begin to earn money. He was, after all, responsible for two other persons as well as himself. Yet, all the while he was doing the many things poor medical students do to make money, he was also having a very good time. Despite his insistence throughout his memoir that he was unlikable and unliked in his youth and that nothing good ever came his way, the historical record proves otherwise.

He was rarely drunk, but "if he was, was loudly so,"[30] which is probably why his Zofingia brothers called him "the Barrel" and elected him their president in 1897–98. Albert Oeri called him "the Steam Roller" and remembered how he dominated "an unruly chorus of fifty or sixty students from different branches of learning" and lured them "into highly speculative areas of thought" with the papers he read at their meetings. He was always ready to rebel against the *Tugenbund* (the virtuous bunch) and was "by choice an outsider," but one who was still able to "keep everyone under his intellectual thumb."

This was due in large part to Jung's profound knowledge of theology, philosophy, and literature. "All of us had benefited by a classical education and a cultured intellectual tradition," Jung remembered. "We argued over Schopenhauer and Kant, we knew all about the stylistic niceties of Cicero, and were interested in theology and philosophy."[31]

However, his ability to preside over "animated discussions, and not always about medical questions only,"[32] came about because of what his friends deemed the courage to express his convictions about the validity of occult literature, spiritualistic phenomena, and parapsychological experiments, and his insistence that there was a place within scientific discourse for their objective, dispassionate consideration. While the other students dismissed spiritualists such as Zöllner and Crookes, Jung insisted they were "martyrs of science"[33] and incorporated their findings into his arguments.

Jung gave his first talk to the Zofingia, entitled "The Border Zones of Exact Science,"[34] in November 1896. He began by introducing himself to his classmates, saying that on both sides his family was famous in Basel for being "peculiarly given to offending well-meaning citizens because it is not our custom to mince words." Of himself, he said it seemed that he had been born "in an evil hour, for I always speak and behave just as my black heart prompts me to do."[35]

This first lecture, C. G. Jung's earliest published writing, was couched in the language and form of what constituted proper academic discourse of the time. Coupled with the occasional facetious remarks of a student wiseacre is a clear indication of the division of interests that would dominate his mature professional writing and thinking: science and (in an all-inclusive and nonparticular sense) spiritualism. Here, and indeed throughout the four other papers Jung presented to the Zofingia, he questions why those who practice science should be so rigidly determined not even to consider, let alone include, aspects of spiritualism. He rebelled against the solidly entrenched foundation of materialism that dominated university teachings at the turn of the century, basically the devotion to material rather than spiritual objects, needs, and considerations. He urged his fellow students to ponder the possibilities of reasoned, objective inquiry into spiritual matters.[36]

He bemoaned the fact that in both Switzerland and Germany (to which Swiss academicians looked constantly for guidance and approval),[37] "there seems to be no sign that men like Kant, Schopenhauer or Zöllner have ever lived. Gone and forgotten!"[38] Nor were people willing to listen to the philosopher Eduard von Hartmann, or (again) Baron DuPrel, "who deserves closer study." He chastised the people of Basel for blind acceptance of the miracles found in the Old and New Testaments while turning a blind eye toward "identical or similar events" that were being reported by various spiritualists in the present day.

Jung devoted his final lecture to a consideration of the theory of the German Protestant theologian Albrecht Ritschl (1822–89), who denied the mystical element in religion. Jung admitted that theologians could well deride him for "sketchy" or "overhasty" appraisals of theological matters, and that Zofingians could well express surprise over a medical student choosing to speak about theological issues, but "truth" was the reason he chose to abandon "the solid ground under [his] feet." However, "as a human being," he expected "hospitality even from adversaries."

How could Ritschl, he asked, call himself a "committed Christian, when his God is compelled to go through official channels whenever he wishes to do something good for man?" Jung said he had been an attentive listener to theologians for the past several years, "vainly hoping to gain a clue to their mysterious concept of human personality." He had listened in vain, because he had yet to discover "where human personality gets its motivational force."

He chose, in this essay, to ask a question that he asked repeatedly throughout the remainder of his long life. His question was most likely based on his reading of Ernest Renan's *Life of Jesus;* namely, how to understand the historical actuality of Jesus Christ the man rather than the God-man that organized religions had imposed upon the world. There had been little progress in understanding "the person of Christ," Jung argued, saying also that Christ was "not a 'normal man,'" but one who should be regarded as he saw himself: "namely, as a prophet, a man sent by God." Jung argued for the reinstatement of "the mystery of a metaphysical world, a metaphysical order" to the center of the Christian religion. He posited the unpopular view that Christ came to Earth with a sword rather than in peace, "for he unleashes the conflict of the dualistic, divided will." In Jung's view, Christian religion had been in decline for almost the two thousand years of its existence, but it was not yet fully extinguished. He expected that mankind had "not yet seen the last lightning bolt flare up out of its dark reaches." Many had perished, he concluded, citing a Latin proverb, but "manifold shall be knowledge."

IN HIS published writings, Jung never mentioned by name the few Zofingians who may have shared some or all of his beliefs, but they and he had been participating in regularly scheduled séances and keeping notes about them ever since he was invited to the home of one known only as Walze, on March 19, 1897.[39] In his notes, he calls the other participants by surnames that may also have been nicknames: Fex, Icarus, and Stengel participated in the March 19 session; they were joined on March 22 by Kneippe, Joseph, Bebbi, and Elsi. The medium was called Weiss, but Jung gave no identifying characteristics as to age or sex. The students used a primitive, homemade Ouija board and a glass that moved over the letters to spell out answers to questions. The spirit invoked by the medium moved the glass and tilted a table with three legs, but it would permit nothing else to be known about it, not even its initials.

In the March 22 session, again in Walze's apartment, the participants tried to duplicate some of Crookes's experiments, but the spirit again proved uncooperative. These failures lasted until someone asked if the assembled group needed a "stronger medium." By tilting the three-legged table, the spirit indicated that it did and then agreed to give its own name: the observation "it is *n i u gg k*" appears in the manuscript, followed by "(K. G. Jung)."[40] That particular part of the session then ended without further written comment, and the participants turned to "experiments on long-distance effects," namely, asking the spirit to tell them the whereabouts of someone in another place.

No notes exist for the next scheduled séance, on March 26, and the next time details were recorded was August 18, 1897, when Carl invited some of his classmates to the Bottmingermühle. This time correct identifications listed the participants as the medical students R. Glauser, A. Müller, and K. G. Jung; E[rnst] Preiswerk, student of philosophy; and C. R. Staehelin, a medical school candidate. Here, the medium was identified as Carl's young cousin and Ernst's sister, Hélène Preiswerk.

These séances differed from those in the Walze apartment because they had been ongoing since June 1895 (six months before Paul's death), when Emilie Jung organized three of them in the Kleinhüningen rectory.[41] Emilie's brother Rudolf died the same year as Paul, and while the two men lay on their sickbeds, Emilie found herself gravitating to Margareten to commiserate with her sister-in-law Celestine, not only about their husbands but also about the unexplainable happenings in both their households. These included the routine nighttime visitations by spirits and poltergeists, as well as the two women's own uncanny predictions. Also, both women believed that some of the upcoming generation had inherited their gift of second sight.

Trudi Jung made some occasional startling pronouncements, but Celestine's eleventh child, Hélène, who was then fourteen and in her second year of classes at the Lyceum (a school for girls), was considered the family's phenomenon. Called Helly, she was commended by her teachers for her "sensitive nature" and her fascination with the vivid stories that comprised lessons in history and geography for young ladies of good family. Helly was especially fond of the Italian Renaissance and began to imagine that she had lived a previous life as a princess engaged to a nobleman she named Ludwig Sforza.[42] On a summer vacation to the Swiss Alps to visit an older married sister, Helly began to sign her letters home with her own name and Sforza's and to include information about what she had done in this earlier life. Throughout 1894 and 1895, Celestine and Emilie heard Helly volunteer accounts, frequently in a trance, of what she had done as Sforza's betrothed. She also spoke of events within the family that seemed bizarre until subsequent information proved them true. In one such trance, she told her family to pray for her sister Bertha, who had immigrated to Brazil to work for wealthy landowners, because she had just given birth to a "Negro" child. Several weeks later, the Preiswerk family received a letter from Bertha saying she had been married for two years to a "Mestizo" and had just given birth to a son.

Emilie and Celestine had kept these occasions secret from their husbands, as both men were "skeptical when it came to spirits" and "despised all devilish haunts." Supposedly, neither man ever knew of the "games" that became full-fledged séances in 1895. That spring, Helly completed her courses in languages and accounting at the Lyceum and was granted a degree in commerce. She spent the summer at Kleinhüningen working once again as Emilie's maid and coming into daily close contact with both her cousins, but especially with Carl.[43]

He was almost six years older than Helly, who was the most "unprepossessing" of the Antistes Samuel's sixty-four grandchildren. Although "unnoticed by everyone [else]," she was Samuel's favorite, which is probably why she selected him to be her guide when she became a medium.[44] She had been in Carl's company on many previous occasions, particularly when her older sister Louise (called Luggy) led the cousins on expeditions to various places in Basel.[45] Helly probably had a schoolgirl crush on Carl, but it was Luggy whom Carl considered his "first love."[46] He was shy and bewildered and a little in awe of her. In 1894 she took him and several of her brothers and sisters to the newly opened historical museum in the Barfüsserkirche, where she pointed proudly to the coat of arms of the Preiswerk family, hanging among those of the oldest merchant families. Then she took her charges into the Bischofshof, the bishop's court portrait gallery, where the face of Antistes Samuel peered from among the other dignitaries. This emphasis on the Preiswerk relatives did not sit well with Carl, who led the group to the Augustinergasse near the *Münsterplatz*, where the citizens of Basel had erected a statue of Carl Gustav I Jung. Carl Gustav II is reported to have directed his cousins to observe the revered grandfather's features closely and to note his resemblance to Goethe. The Preiswerk cousins were suitably impressed, for being Goethe's great-grandson was "an even more distinguished and at the same time mysterious origin, more impressive" than their own. The family dated Helly's crush on Carl to this event, when his own claim of a romantic poetic ancestor now matched her own claim of romantic poetic past lives.

Carl told his cousins that "the man with the buckled shoes who often came riding in his old-fashioned carriage from the Schwarzwald to him in Klein-hüningen"[47] was his illustrious ancestor Goethe. He also claimed Goethe's friend Marianne Jung-Willemer as the matriarch from whom his branch of the Jung family descended, and his gullible cousins believed him.[48]

Shortly after this excursion and for the next three years (1895–98), Helly began her trancelike speaking in the deep, resonant voice of the Antistes Samuel, which many of the Preiswerk descendants believe was a direct response to Carl's claims of exalted ancestry. By the time she came to work for her aunt Emilie in the summer of 1898, she claimed she had already taken several fabulous spiritist "journeys" at his behest, over the North Pole and to North and South America. When Carl checked the date of the journey during which Helly revealed the birth of Bertha's "Negro" child, he learned that it had occurred on the baby's actual birthday. "Very strange," said Emilie in her No. 2 voice when he told her.

Later, Helly told her sister and a friend, Emily (Emmy) Zinsstag,[49] that Antistes Samuel had been visiting her for years, ever since the birth of her sister Esther in 1887, when Helly was five. Seemingly in a trance when she said this, Helly "spoke in a dignified manner as though she were an adult" and announced that ever since her childhood, "good spirits" had been preparing her for life as a medium who would bring "messages from Grandfather" to the family. She did not tell the family that her grandmother Gustele, wife of the Antistes Samuel, had kept a diary of her "medial experiences" in which there was a long discussion of an "article" called "The Poltergeist Man," and that she had been reading it surreptitiously.[50] Then the fourteen-year-old girl added the remark that clinched her authority: "Carl wants to explore the soul and the hereafter. I'm chosen to help him in this exploration. That's my destiny, which makes me happy."

In June 1895, the summer between the Gymnasium and the university, Carl studied experiments on table tilting.[51] Helly wanted to participate, so Emilie agreed to let them try. Five persons participated in what is generally believed to be the first séance: Aunt Gusteli, Helly and Luggy Preiswerk, and Emilie and Carl Jung (the eleven-year-old Trudi had been sent to bed against her wishes, with the promise that she could participate when a few years older). Ottilie, another of Helly's sisters, was there, seated slightly behind the table, for her job was not to participate, but to "write down everything during the occult games."[52]

It became the custom to hold the séances on Saturday nights, and it would seem that they became a fairly regular entertainment much anticipated by the participants. As the first séance was so successful, a second was planned for several weeks later, when Carl used a homemade Ouija board, writing the letters of the alphabet on cardboard and employing an overturned glass to roam among them. This time, when Helly entered her trance, the Antistes Samuel had someone with him: Professor Carl Gustav I Jung. "We'll watch over you together," Helly proclaimed in the deep voice of the Antistes.

Carl noted ironically that the two men had not really known or liked each other in their lifetimes. Helly, who could not bear to hear unpleasant remarks made about any of her relatives, "twitched imperceptibly" and continued to speak in her own voice about various other spirits who wore elegant robes and handed her bouquets of beautiful flowers. Someone had ripped the flowers from her hand, she said angrily as soon as she awakened. "It was Carl. He has to leave. He doesn't deserve the flowers."

She also insisted that Carl leave a third séance, held a week later, but he hid outside the room and listened to what she said. Helly told the group that another sister, Dini,[53] would soon give birth to a deformed child who would not live. Her prediction came true two months later in August, and Helly was in despair, believing that she had caused the stillbirth. Emilie decided that Helly's "talent" as a clairvoyant was too painful for them to continue. "We have to stop this," Emilie said, "or she will get sick."

There were no séances at the Bottmingermühle until the autumn of 1896, when Dini gave birth to a second stillborn child and supposedly asked Helly to use her supernatural powers to remove the curse she believed haunted her. Carl was seated at his desk studying when he found a scrap of paper with curious scribbles on it. When he got up to take a book from a shelf, another scrap fell to the ground. Now that he was looking for them, he spotted others, and when he looked in the other rooms of the mill, he found many more. All had a curious script that he thought might be a variation of Latin, and all said such things as "Conventi, go! Ivenes vent. Go, gen Palus." The following Saturday, when Helly and Luggy were taking tea with Carl, Emilie, and Trudi, he asked who had written the notes. Helly blushed and admitted that they were an exorcism, not only for Dini but for the mill as well, which she believed was haunted by the poltergeist Conventi.

He was, she told them, an Italian murderer who had been the miller's servant and who had been caught grinding up bodies between the millstones. Ivenes was "the pure, white one," a female who played a special role among the spirits and who only appeared every several hundred years. Astaf was "Lucifer's friend" who erred and fell but was subsequently redeemed. Carl was "sarcastic," but Helly "was truly convinced that she had been given the power to exorcise evil spirits with the help of God."

For her fifteenth birthday in March 1896, Carl presented Helly with a copy of Justinus Kerner's *The Seer of Prevorst*.[54] Literally at that moment, she fell into a trance and sang a song that she said was given to her by the Antistes as a birthday present, one she was supposed to teach the others.[55] Helly continued, speaking in her own voice as well as in the voice of the Antistes Samuel, in High German (as opposed to *Schwizertütsch*), and then launched into Hebrew. Emilie was convinced that the Antistes was teaching her the language.

There were no actual séances for the better part of a year, until 1897, because Helly and Luggy were being prepared for their confirmation by the Isemännli Samuel Gottlob, who disapproved of the sessions. The medium did not dare confess to her uncle that they were holding séances against his wishes, so the participants thought it best not to hold any until both girls' religious instruction ended. Helly carried the secret heavily but she kept it. In the meantime, Carl invited Luggy to several of the dances given by his Zofingia fraternity and was much admired by his brothers when the pretty Luggy wore the traditional dress of the Unterwalden, loaned by Emilie, who had cherished the costume since her own girlhood.[56] He did not like dancing, calling it "absolutely senseless to hop around a ballroom with some female until one was covered with sweat." But Luggy liked dancing and parties, and as she was his "first love," he was eager to please her.[57] Following Helly's confirmation, she became infected with such religious zeal that she lost weight and took on the ascetic qualities of one preparing for sainthood. Even so, she kept Carl in mind as she studied Kerner's book and read Camille Flammarion's *Astronomie Populaire*,[58] a book he also enjoyed on his visits to Margareten. On her own, she devoured the popular romantic novels for impressionable young girls written by a distant relative, Ottilie Wildermuth.[59]

By this time Carl was deeply engrossed in the literature of psychiatry and eager to observe what Helly might do in controlled circumstances, so he urged her to begin the séances again. He hoped to conduct experiments that might shed some light on the connection between spiritualism and psychiatry. There was a sixth person at the table when the séances resumed, for Trudi was now deemed old enough to participate.

In August 1897, the First Zionist Congress took place in Basel. When Theodor Herzl praised the Antistes Samuel as a precursor of the movement, it had an enormous emotional effect on Helly. In the first session after the Zionist Congress, she described "Ivenes, her somnambulantself" as a woman with Jewish features who spoke Hebrew. Helly-Ivenes said the Antistes Samuel had charged her to complete his work of leading the Jews back to their homeland and then "reforming" them so they could "share in the blessings of Christ."[60]

The attendees were unsettled by the séances that followed, when Helly invoked various spirits who seemed to come directly from the novels of Ottilie Wildermuth and saw landscapes (such as that of Mars) straight from the pages of the Flammarion astronomy book. The sessions continued sporadically until June 1898, when Helly told Carl she dreamed of trying to save him from drowning, but he was "a different man, dead and pale," under the water.[61] A month later, her brother Friedrich (called Fritzi) drowned in the Rhine. The Jung family went to Margareten to pay condolences, and Trudi fell into a trance, speaking in the voice of her late father. Trudi told Carl that Paul wanted him to know he had been spared only because someone else paid for his (Carl's) sins.

Helly was deeply upset by her cousin's vision, and the Preiswerk women took her on a vacation to recover from Fritzi's death and to remove her from the place where the séances were held. Trudi took over as the medium, but she was "a weak and somewhat uninspired imitation of Helly," and her dreams held little interest for her brother.[62]

It was in August 1898 that the Jungs' table cracked and the knife shattered, both at the same time as the Preiswerk women were returning to Basel from their vacation. Everyone was convinced that it was a sign the séances should resume, and so they did. The usual participants all noted the high level of maturity and talent that Helly was now exhibiting. They were especially amazed at her moving rendition of songs, for she was known to be totally lacking in any musical ability. She also composed poetry, mostly ballads in the style of Robert Burns, who was then quite popular in Switzerland.[63]

Carl was studying Nietzsche that summer and, every now and again, he would discuss various points with some of his male cousins. Apparently Helly overheard some of these conversations, for in the voice of the Antistes, she warned Carl to beware of the "Antichrist," as the Isemännli Samuel Gottlob always called Nietzsche. In several subsequent séances, she warned him to believe his grandfather, who told her that Nietzsche's doctrine was filled with errors "when it comes to God," and that he had "made a deal with the devil! He's arrogant!"[64]

It would seem that Helly was not achieving any of her desired effects on her cousin. In the autumn of 1898, she reverted to Ivenes, who she claimed had led a privileged existence over the ages, including many marriages to great men. The content of her visions became increasingly sexual, until eventually, Helly/Ivenes gave passionate depictions of herself as Goethe's lover, as the mother of Carl's "illegitimately born grandfather," and as the lover of Carl, who took shape in her trances as both Goethe and his grandfather.

Rather than being alarmed or dismayed by Helly's pronouncements, Jung began to brag about the phenomenal talents of his medium-cousin to his Zofingia brothers. Both Albert Oeri and Gustav Steiner recalled how he tried to persuade them to attend a séance and how he urged them to borrow his personal copies of books on spiritualism. They were busy with their own interests and declined both offers.[65] Carl eventually persuaded two other classmates to join him at a session, but to his extreme annoyance and embarrassment, Helly refused to perform before strangers.[66] Carl tried to substitute Trudi, but her visions disappointed everyone, especially her brother. Helly's refusal led to discontinuing the sessions until August 1899, when Dini delivered a third stillborn baby and begged for her sister's help.

Sessions followed in which Helly claimed to be exorcising spirits from various centuries who were spreading bacilli and casting spells on Dini. On some evenings Helly became so disoriented and debilitated after her "journeys" that Carl had to walk her home, supporting her all the way. Her mother had long worried that Helly was infatuated with Carl and was inventing situations to court his attention. She suspected this was happening routinely, but she did not become alarmed until one Sunday morning after the usual Saturday night séance, when Helly was delirious and Celestine could not waken her.[67]

Celestine hurried to ask Emilie Jung to stop the séances forever, but Emilie refused. With great trepidation because the entire family feared his wrath, Celestine decided there was no alternative but to tell Samuel Gottlob everything and ask him to intercede. He ordered Emilie and Carl to stop the séances at once and forbade Helly and Luggy to go to the Bottmingermühle without an older male being present, especially on Saturday nights. The actual séances ended finally and abruptly in the early autumn of 1899, when Helly Preiswerk's mother sent her to Montpelier, France, to begin an apprenticeship with a ladies' dressmaker. Jung had no contact with Helly for the next two years, but he thought of her often as he re-created the séances for his dissertation, "On the Psychology and Pathology of So-Called Occult Phenomena."[68]

He broke with tradition by submitting his dissertation to the medical faculty of the University of Zürich rather than to his own university in Basel. By Swiss law, medical dissertations could be submitted to a different university than the one from which the candidate graduated. There were any number of reasons for Carl's decision, starting with the desire to keep it away from his Preiswerk relatives until such a time as it might fade from their purview.[69] More important, however, was his decision to leave Basel — temporarily, or so he thought — as he cast his lot with Zürich for the next several years to work under Dr. Eugen Bleuler at the Burghölzli Mental Hospital. His friends could not understand why he would do this and thought he would soon return to Basel, even though Jung hedged his bets and said it was probably "out of the question."[70]

He told no one the real reason he had applied for the job in Zürich: that his professor Dr. Wille, with whom Carl had disagreed openly about the treatment of mental patients, had told him he would not be recommended for an assistantship and that he should look elsewhere for employment. However, Wille conveyed this news in a manner that gave Jung the hope he might relent if he distinguished himself at the Burghölzli. As he was working in Zürich when it came time to publish his dissertation, he thought it made sense for him to offer the first example of his psychological writing to the doctors who would, in one way or another, be the possible guides and determinants of his future career.

By December 1900, he was ensconced in Zürich. He had left Nietzsche's "breeding ground of all my ills" and Jacob Burckhardt's "little hole . . . so turned in on itself,"[71] to accept a low-level and decidedly unprestigious appointment to the Burghölzli Mental Hospital. Burckhardt longed most of his life to be "out of Here! Out of [Basel]!"[72] Jung was young and eager for adventure, but he only partially echoed Burckhardt's sentiments. He did not imagine he would be the Basler to make good the escape his predecessor never managed, but "the pressure of [Basel] tradition"[73] had become too heavy for a young and ambitious doctor to carry. On the one hand, he wanted to stay in Basel, but on the other, he believed that if he began his career there, no matter how high the level of his future accomplishments, he would be known for the rest of his days as the poor boy called Pastor's Carl, the grandson of the eccentric Carl Gustav I. His life would be an echo of Burckhardt's: "[one of] extreme reserve and politeness; there will be no one I can trust fully, no one I can talk to without constraint . . . you have no idea how grotesque and all-pervasive the Basel reverence for wealth is."[74]

Zürich reminded Jung of a "village," because the people there related to the world "by commerce" rather than through the life of the mind, but he still believed they were more receptive than Baslers to newcomers and their ideas. He knew he would miss Basel's "rich background of culture," but he could not face a life "weighed down by [its] brown fog of the centuries."[75] Nevertheless, there was one highly significant way in which he ensured that his Basel lineage would always be known to anyone aware of what constituted status and respect in that city: he changed the spelling of his first name to Carl, thus officially claiming, finally and firmly, an elective affinity with his illustrious ancestor.

Emilie was vocal in her distress at his decision to leave Basel, but in several hastily called family conferences, she and Carl's Preiswerk uncles were unable to sway him once he made up his mind. Even though he would receive a salary (if only a pittance), and even though he was required by the terms of his contract with the Burghölzli to live in hospital quarters, many chose to believe the worst of him. Like the Preiswerk relatives, many Baslers were aghast, believing that he had abandoned his mother and sister by leaving them behind. In truth,

Emilie and Trudi continued to live rent-free in the Bottmingermühle, while Carl remained faithful to his responsibilities and paid their household expenses until 1904, when he married and could afford to move them to Zürich.

Before he took up his duties at the Burghölzli, however, he wanted to have sheer fun for the first time in his life. Wanting to experience "longed for" luxuries, he financed them with a bit of money scrupulously hoarded from the sale of his aunt's antiques.[76] His first indulgences were the local theater and his first opera (Bizet's *Carmen*). Then, feeling "terribly cosmopolitan," he divided the days of December 1 through 9, 1900, between Munich, where he visited art museums, and Stuttgart, where he visited his great-aunt Frau Anna Reimer-Jung (daughter of Virginie de Lassaulx). Inwardly, he was "intoxicated and overwhelmed" as arias from *Carmen* resonated in his ears while the train crossed the border into Germany and "the wider world." But despite the pleasures of traveling, it was still "a dismal week."

The young doctor had not yet discovered the kinds of leisure activity that would give him pleasure, and, for the rest of his life, attending performances and visiting art galleries were never high on that list. For the time being, he was comfortable only with what he had known all his life, the routine patterns imposed by unending work. He felt much better as soon as he entered the Burghölzli in December 1900, because it offered "an undivided reality — all intention, consciousness, duty, and responsibility." Henceforth, his satisfaction would come entirely through the "subjective experiment" from which his "objective life" followed.[77]

CHAPTER 4

Unadmitted Doubt,
Unadmitted Worry

On December 10, 1900, ten days after he passed the *Staatsexamen* granting medical certification, Carl Jung crossed the threshold of the Cantonal Psychiatric University Hospital and Clinic of Zürich, more commonly known as the Burghölzli Mental Hospital. Waiting for him in the doorway, as was his custom, was the distinguished director, Dr. Med. Eugen Bleuler. To Jung's shock, Dr. Bleuler insisted upon performing another customary courtesy by carrying Jung's modest suitcase all the way to his quarters on the topmost floor of the main building, despite the fact that Jung, whose robust physical appearance would earn him the name "Our Siegfried" in the following years, was half a foot taller and many pounds heavier than his intense, slim, and bearded superior.

Then, without pausing, Bleuler personally escorted Jung on a tour of the hospital, introduced him to the other doctors and some patients at tea, and sat next to him at dinner at a table that again included patients as well as lower-level hospital staff and several doctors.[1] Bleuler's unconventional treatment stemmed from nineteenth-century *Anstaltspsychiatrie*, institutionalized treatment characterized most notably by close interaction between doctors and patients.[2] Bleuler included inmates whenever possible, not only in planning the course of their therapy but also in the daily governance of the hospital. He also broke with accepted custom by having women, both staff and patients, interspersed at every table, and he encouraged them to participate actively in the many clinical discussions and meetings that punctuated the daily schedule.

Jung, whose mind was whirling in the face of more clinical unorthodoxy than he had hitherto encountered, slept badly that night. The next day, December 11, he began to work as "second level assistant physician" in what he described without exaggeration as "the monastery of the world."[3] Bleuler asked nothing of his doctors that he himself was not prepared to give, and from this day forward, he expected young Dr. Jung to dedicate every aspect of his life to serving the needs of the patients.

Bleuler (1857–1939)[4] was a genuinely modest man whose ascetic sensibilities were both innate, due to his family background, and learned, due to the tutelage of his mentor and the former director of the Burghölzli, Auguste Forel. Jung described Bleuler as "motivated solely by a truly Christian ambition not to stand in the way of others, [with] a youthful eagerness to learn."[5]

Bleuler was of peasant stock and the first member of his family to be educated beyond elementary school. Born in what was then the "socially inferior" (by legal decree) farming village of Zollikon, which is now a stylish suburb abutting the corner of Zürich where the Burghölzli stands,[6] Bleuler's father left the family farm to become keeper of a small shop in the village and administrator of the local school. Both Bleuler's father and grandfather were active in the political struggles that culminated in the reforms of the Zürich liberals in the 1830s, among them the right for farmers to join trades, practice professions, and have access to higher education in the brand-new University of Zürich, founded at the peak of the reforms in 1833.[7] It was accepted without comment that Bleuler would reap the fruits of his family's political struggle and attend the university. It was also taken for granted that he would study medicine and specialize in psychiatry, for his sister had a severe case of catatonic schizophrenia, and several other family members reportedly suffered from variants of the same disease.

Zollikon was a tiny cluster of houses surrounding an ever diminishing amount of open farmland, so many of the residents supplemented their incomes by working full- or part-time at the Burghölzli. Bleuler grew up hearing them grumble about the first directors, the distinguished German doctors Wilhelm Griesinger, Bernard von Gudden, and Eduard Hitzig,[8] complaining that they spent more time with their research than with their patients. And even if they had taken an interest in people rather than statistics, they could not have done much, for they spoke only High German, whereas their patients spoke a variety of Swiss dialects. The Burghölzli under these men was simply a warehouse where mentally ill patients languished while its directors conducted research that gained an international reputation for them and, by extension, for the hospital.

When Bleuler became director, he was determined that his primary responsibility would be to his patients, to whom he would talk in their own dialects. He believed that by listening to the incoherent delusions of schizophrenic patients, he could establish contact and even rapport with them; if the therapist could succeed in engaging the patient in a human relationship, schizophrenia could be successfully treated and diminished, if not completely halted. For Bleuler, this meant keeping the patient slightly off guard through an absence of routine and order in daily life and a degree of the unexpected in treatment.

To the surprise and dismay of his assistants, Bleuler would suddenly and for no apparent reason transfer a patient from one ward to another; at other times, he would discharge a patient whose treatment seemed far from finished. Above all, he would not permit any single assistant to speak of "my" patient, for every doctor (all male during Jung's first years) was supposed to know every detail of every single patient's history and to behave toward each as if he and he alone were in charge of treatment. Each doctor was expected to be prepared to act as each patient's primary physician at a moment's notice.[9]

All this required extraordinary amounts of work, especially the writing of daily reports about whichever patients the doctors treated on any given day. The reports were supposed to be thorough and detailed, which meant lengthy as well, and this was at a time when typewriters were only just being introduced and everything had to be painstakingly written by hand.[10] However, Bleuler's primary insistence was that his doctors had to learn the many different dialects the inmates spoke, to speak to them in theirs and behave as if they were co-equal in sanity and social standing. This policy led to many complaints by his assistants and associates at the Burghölzli — Jung among them — that Bleuler was, in manner and bearing, little more than a gross peasant. In truth, he was merely the champion of an unorthodox collegiality and the soul of ascetic re-finement.

Jung, from the beginning, thought of the Burghölzli as a temporary stopover on his way to a probable career in academic medicine in Basel. It was easy for Jung to think of Bleuler as "the cross-breeding of a peasant and a school-teacher," because, being from Basel, he had a "terribly snooty" attitude: "There I belonged, so to speak, to the aristocracy, and also [the aristocracy] of the mind. [In Basel] there existed a very well-tended tradition that one could sense as ed-ucation in the conversations of people and as their background. With Bleuler all that was missing."[11]

Bleuler's excessive devotion to his patients began during his first residency in Bern and intensified in the years following, when he studied with Jean-Martin Charcot and Emile Magnan in Paris and with Bernard von Gudden in Munich. For a brief period, he observed psychiatric practices in London, where he is generally believed to have first preached his fairly unorthodox attitude of *affek-tiver Rapport*, or emotional connection to the schizophrenic patient.[12] But the true formulation of his clinical methodology took place in the years following, when he returned to Zürich to become first assistant to Auguste Forel at the Burghölzli, who was also known for his unorthodox treatment of mental illness.

Under Forel's direction, the Burghölzli achieved world renown, on the level of Jean-Martin Charcot's Salpêtrière school in Paris and Emil Kraepelin's clini-cal research in Munich. Forel had studied under Hippolyte Bernheim in Nancy, where he settled on using hypnotism to cure mental patients. Forel's rate of suc-cess was high, not only with hospital inmates but also with sufferers of rheuma-tism and other physical ailments who consulted him in an outpatient clinic he founded. His biggest success, however, and the one that influenced Bleuler the most, was his treatment of alcoholics. Forel claimed that his excellent results were due to his own abstinence, and he persuaded Bleuler to follow him. Bleuler became a teetotaler with a vengeance, and Forel was so pleased that he helped his protégé to secure an appointment as the medical director of the Klinik Rheinau in 1886 at the youthful age of twenty-nine.[13] During his tenure at the Rheinau, Bleuler lived among his patients and shared their chores, meals, and other aspects of their daily lives so closely that it was sometimes difficult to tell the director from the inmates. When it came time for his Burghölzli successor to be named in 1898, Forel supported his senior assistant, A. Delbrück, rather than Bleuler. He resented that cantonal officials chose Bleuler instead, because he had rehabilitated what was then the most backward psychiatric facility in all of Switzerland by replacing mere incarceration with his own unorthodox treatment.[14] It is ironic that Forel resented Bleuler's appointment, because it ensured the continuity of his ideas and methods. Forel was only fifty when he retired, and Jung quickly became annoyed with how he puttered about the hospital for years afterward, nattering and meddling in every aspect of hospital business.[15] Jung thought Bleuler's indifference to Forel was only another of his many faults; nevertheless, Jung was well aware that Bleuler was a force to be reckoned with, and for the first several years he was on staff, he managed to keep his hostile feelings to himself.

Bleuler was so highly regarded throughout Germany and Switzerland that his practices and procedures were discussed formally in medical school courses (Jung's among them) and informally and respectfully among the students outside their classrooms, many of whom thought it would be an honor far beyond their abilities even to think of working with him. Jung claimed he was not impressed by Bleuler's reputation in the larger world and had applied to work with him only because "in Basel, nothing was going on."[16] He applied at the beginning of the 1899 school year, but Bleuler's reply was so perfunctory that Jung thought his chances were nil and began to look for a job in "another lunatic asylum." He had forgotten all about the Burghölzli and was surprised when Bleuler wrote again in late October 1900, telling him to appear, ready to work, that December. Bleuler was notorious for overworking his assistants, which may have been why he carefully omitted mentioning that Jung's was the only application he received.

Jung appeared as ordered and for the next six months did not leave the asylum grounds. He called this period the end of his "entire youth," when "everything was gone." He felt guilty for having rushed away from his family and missed his friends, who had all dispersed to begin their own careers. His ostensible reason for leading such a restricted life was that he had to learn "to adapt" to Bleuler's system, because nothing he had learned in medical school had prepared him for it. He was "deeply humiliated" to see how Bleuler and his only other assistant doctor moved so confidently about their duties, while he was "all the time more and more baffled" and plagued by such "feelings of inferiority that [he] could not bear to go out of the hospital."[17] Another equally important reason was that he had only one pair of pants and two shirts and was too poor to socialize because he sent his entire salary to support his mother and sister.

His old resentments toward both parents smoldered during these months of self-imposed isolation. He held them both responsible for "an enormous spiritual tension and burden." Only with "the utmost concentration on the essential" could he keep himself from "exploding." He blamed his family's poverty for the shame he felt about his lack of experience in life. He could not help remembering over and over again that the first time he went to the theater was at the age of twenty, and even then, guilt was his primary emotion because he could not really afford it. Now the need to send his small salary to his mother dictated that he had to keep himself "away from all trivialities," as he deemed any form of pleasure. It left him with no alternative but to "concentrate excessively" on hospital work, which provided the excuse he gave for not leaving the grounds during his first six months on the staff.

More than fifty years later, he remained shocked and saddened by something his friend Ludwig (called Ruedi) von Muralt (then Bleuler's chief assistant)[18] told him, that the other doctors often discussed — not as gossip but as a clinical possibility — that because he lived "like a hermit, like a monk," he might be "psychologically abnormal." Jung countered that living like one who obeyed "the rule of a religious order" was his only means of protecting himself "from the intense tension and burden" bequeathed by his parents: "If one also still has the fate of father and mother on one's shoulders, one simply has too much. Then one can only keep oneself 'whole' through the utmost concentration on a goal." His was to read every single volume of the *Allgemeine Zeitschrift für Psychiatrie*, the most prestigious German psychiatric journal, starting with 1836, when the series began.

He may have arrived at the Burghölzli believing himself "inadequate" to do the work, but he soon hit his stride during this "reclusive" six months, and after that his confidence never deserted him. There were never fewer than four hundred patients in the Burghölzli during the years Jung worked there, and frequently there were more. In the beginning, besides himself and Bleuler, there was only one other doctor (von Muralt). Later, there were four others, and in 1904, six more were added to the staff.[19] Jung thought of von Muralt as "an aristocrat . . . [of his own] caliber," but the others seemed to him like everyone else in Zürich he had met thus far, "a conglomeration of the peasant population." But he was quick to add, "Back then I mostly seemed very unfriendly to people. Some admired me, the others hated me." His self-imposed isolation and boundless zest for work conspired to make him appear conceited and antisocial to his associates, so they were polite even as they distanced themselves from genuine conversation. In the few moments of a typical day when he was not actually working with patients, his only outlet was to closet himself in the hospital library, reading old psychiatric journals in search of an idea for his dissertation.[20]

Jung's day began around 6 A.M. and sometimes earlier with a hurried breakfast followed by detailed rounds of every ward to observe how the approximately four hundred patients had passed the night.[21] A daily staff meeting took place between 8 and 8:30 A.M., and he had to be prepared to report the history of any patients Bleuler might ask about or, if not called upon to narrate specifically, to add his observations to those of the other doctors. There were *Gemeinsame*, or general meetings, at least three mornings each week to discuss treatment of new patients, and all the doctors were expected to contribute their thoughts and ideas. This sort of meeting was held on several evenings as well, when the doctors were also charged with discussing their own research and what they had read of the newest developments in the field. Here Jung heard Franz Riklin Sr. talk about Wilhelm Wundt's association experiment, and he himself reported on Freud's newly published *The Interpretation of Dreams*.[22] He merely summarized the book's contents, for it did not acquire particular resonance until later, when he read it a second time.

The doctors ate with patients, so observation and supervision continued even during meals. Bleuler believed in occupational therapy, and he put patients to work on the hospital grounds, either tending the plant nurseries and gardens or working in the dairy that provided milk and cheese for the hospital. Although staff members were directly responsible for supervising these activities, doctors were often sent to oversee them by participating in the work. Even Bleuler did so, and an oft-told story passed into hospital legend of how, wanting to earn a dangerously disturbed patient's trust, he collected two sharp axes and took the man out for an afternoon of chopping wood.

Not wanting a wasted minute in anyone's day, Bleuler organized leisure activity as well. Patients took part in musical occasions, such as concerts and recitals, and were expected to attend (and sometimes to participate in) dances, lectures, and dramatic presentations of various kinds. To Jung's chagrin, he was appointed social director of the program for his first two years at the Burghölzli.

Evening rounds took place between 5 and 7 P.M., and doctors ate the evening meal hurriedly, because a long night's work was still ahead of them. Bleuler wanted daily patient reports and case histories, so the doctors sometimes worked until midnight writing them by hand. As there were neither secretaries nor typewriters, those who were married usually enlisted their wives as scribes.

Bleuler expected strict abstinence from his doctors, and they had to sign a pledge that they would not drink alcoholic beverages. Jung, who had grown fond of wine and beer in his student years, did not touch alcohol all the while he worked at the Burghölzli. Also, the doors to the outside world were locked by 10 P.M., and sometimes earlier, so that any second-assistant doctor who wished to leave the hospital grounds in the evening not only had to secure specific permission from Bleuler or von Muralt but also had to get a key from one of these men and be prepared to justify his reason for leaving.

The assistant doctors may have chafed privately at their workload, but as Bleuler carried the same and did more, they made no public comment. One of the assistant doctors who worked under his direction described the Burghölzli as "a kind of factory where you worked very much and were poorly paid. . . . Bleuler was kind to all and never played the role of chief."[23]

Still, Jung did not seek Bleuler's counsel, finding what little friendship he had during his early Burghölzli years in von Muralt. In the *Protocols* that later became *Memories, Dreams, Reflections*, Jung said several times that what interested him most about medicine was not its actual practice but rather the possibility of conducting research within the profession. When Jung wrote his letter of application to Bleuler, it was partly in the hope of doing the kind of research that he could not do in Basel. He knew that Bleuler conducted experiments with mediums and was interested in the same kinds of spiritualist activity that he had engaged in with Helly Preiswerk's séances. He hoped for the possibility of cooperative research in these areas, but he knew almost as soon as he entered the Burghölzli that it would not happen. He confided these regrets to von Muralt, saying he wanted to write about Helly Preiswerk but was afraid of Bleuler's reaction. Von Muralt encouraged him to speak to Bleuler, and when Jung did, he was surprised that Bleuler approved the idea at once.

Throughout the year it took Jung to write the dissertation, Bleuler remained interested in the project and often discussed various sections of it with him. He also demonstrated his interest by inviting a male medium to the Burghölzli on a fairly routine basis, but despite their mutual interest in observing séances,[24] no friendship jelled between Bleuler and Jung. To Jung, there was just some indefinable quality lacking in Bleuler. The closest he came to expressing it was when he talked about the daily grind Bleuler imposed upon the Burghölzli staff, which Jung called the absence of an "educated and intellectually interesting environment." He thought it simply "didn't exist in Zürich." To his dismay, he found none of the excitement of his medical school days in Basel, when he and his classmates, all products of the same classical education, "argued about Schopenhauer, about Kant and the theological views." In Zürich, Jung was convinced "they had never heard of theological arguments"; nor could they understand his Basler sense of humor or appreciate his "bloody jokes."

Only von Muralt seemed exempt from this categorization. Jung's friendship with him began during a research project in which brain sections taken from cadavers were observed microscopically in search of lesions that might show damage caused by psychotic disorders.[25] Von Muralt initiated the project, which Jung described as a form of "histology" based on the research of the Spanish physician Santiago Ramón y Cajal.[26] His task was to make and color "brain cuts" by using different compounds under the microscope. For a time, Jung thought his findings would become the subject of his dissertation, but von Muralt grew bored with the project and turned to photography, which did not interest Jung.

By early 1900, Jung was beginning to re-create the séances with Helly Preiswerk as the basic material for his doctoral dissertation. It was, of necessity, "a mode of fictionalizing required by the new field [of psychology] . . . a new form of writing about psychological persons."[27] In short, it was a case study, the ultimate fiction. In a field where confidentiality is the paramount tenet that seals the patient's testimony beyond the grave, the analyst had to tell the truth in a form the professional community could put to use, but through every possible form of disguise. Names, places, sometimes even the gender of the individual had to be camouflaged beyond any possibility of recognition.[28] Jung followed these precepts, and his dissertation was received positively by his superiors and respected by the general psychiatric community, but it caused outrage and scandal within the Preiswerk family and did them real social harm in Basel.

Entitled "On the Psychology and Pathology of So-Called Occult Phenomena,"[29] it began with an introductory section in which Jung summarized the existing research, drawing on case histories by (among others) Charcot, William James, Théodore Flournoy, and Bleuler. He presented a carefully reasoned, logical progression through the existing literature about the many variations inherent in altered states of consciousness. A model of objectivity and detachment, it was exactly what was required in a medical dissertation of the time.

Then he turned to Helly and her visions in a section whose very title was bound to raise hackles (at least among the Preiswerks): "A Case of Somnambulism in *a Girl with Poor Inheritance* (Spiritualistic Medium)" (author's emphasis). By the time the dissertation was published in 1902, Helly was a gifted needlewoman who had moved to Paris, where she supported herself as a seamstress and designer of fine women's clothing. Jung disguised her as S. W., the initials of a person (or amalgam of persons) whose symptoms served as one of the best-known case studies in Krafft-Ebing's widely used textbook on insanity — and who just happened to be a seamstress.[30] When word filtered through to the Preiswerk relatives, they condemned him for violating the entire family's privacy.

Jung telescoped the time during which he had observed Helly's "case"[31] into only two years, 1899 and 1900. He stated truthfully that during the time of the séances he had not examined her physically because she was not his patient, and he added another factual statement, that he had kept a "detailed diary" immediately after each séance.[32] Out of "regard" for Helly/S. W. and her family, Jung stated that he "altered" or "omitted" various parts of her "romances" (he himself put the word in quotation marks). In this written version of her visions, he made Helly/S. W. fifteen and a half when the séances began.

Several paragraphs followed in which Jung described everyone from Antistes Samuel to Aunt Gusteli and Helly's parents as, at the very least, odd or, at most, clinically unstable. Helly's mother "had a congenital psychopathic inferiority often bordering on psychosis," while one of her sisters was "an hysteric and visionary" and another had "nervous heart attacks." He deemed Helly "rachitic though not noticeably hydrocephalic," that is, she had rickets, but her head was not enlarged. As this was a good description of Helly's physical appearance, the Preiswerks added it to their list of Jung's invasions of their privacy.

Describing the family as "artisans or business people with very limited interests," he added the false statement that "books of a mystical nature were never allowed in the family." Curiously, none of the readers of his dissertation seem to have been concerned with the possible contradictions inherent in this statement, especially after he compared Helly's trances to those of Kerner's seeress of Prevorst, from the book of the same name, which she studied and to which her own trances bore an uncanny resemblance. Jung also belittled Helly's education as "deficient," when in truth it was the best possible for a young woman of her social class and station.

His entire presentation of Helly and her family, when seen from their point of view, is both derogatory and derisive, and his attempts to disguise her identity are indeed fairly clumsy. However, they can also be read as the natural caution of a medical student who was preparing a dissertation for a basically conservative audience, which required prudence in intellectualizing the ideas about spiritualism and occult phenomena that he embraced so emotionally in his earlier Zofingia lectures.[33] In the dissertation, his intention was to make the point that psychic powers emerge from psychological states of mind and have nothing to do with the so-called supernatural. In the original German version, in a concluding paragraph that he omitted from the English (canny degree candidate that he was), Jung wrote with great restraint a statement that would dominate his research from that time forward: that he hoped to demonstrate the "manifold connections" between "so-called occult phenomena" and the subjects usually considered appropriate for research and debate by the medical and psychological professions. Here, he couched what would become his credo as a straightforward belief that it would be a "rich harvest for experiential psychology" and hoped it would lead toward "the progressive elucidation and assimilation of the as yet extremely controversial psychology of the unconscious."[34]

In the concluding portions, Jung's "curtain fell" on Helly, as he wrote that she went to France and became "pleasanter and more stable." He kept her in the text obliquely, as he listed the sources that may have been the inspiration for her different manifestations. As one example, he offered Nietzsche's possible cryptomnesia, or, how he unconsciously remembered something that had supposedly been forgotten and then dredged it up later to reproduce as his own. The reference seems to verge on the gratuitous, but it did allow Jung to show off a correspondence he had initiated with Nietzsche's sister, Elisabeth Förster-Nietzsche, whose own version of her brother's history influenced Jung's writing and subsequent thinking for many years to come.[35]

Having "exhaust[ed]" his knowledge of where Helly may have found the sources for her visions, Jung added rather casually that "naturally" he "waded through the occult literature so far as it pertained" to his subject. With either a backhanded salute toward Helly or a justified caution for his medical readers, he concluded that, given her "youth and mentality" and the intelligence she expended on constructing her alternative worlds and personalities, what actually transpired in the séances should be considered "something quite out of the ordinary."[36]

The dissertation was accepted by the medical faculty of the University of Zürich in early 1901, where it rested without comment until it was published in 1902[37] and read by his relatives in Basel. Some of the "Preiswerkeri" erupted angrily,[38] and others were deeply hurt to learn they were now the object of local gossip. Considerable importance was laid upon heredity in those years, and rumors spread that the entire Preiswerk family was tainted by differing degrees and kinds of insanity. Later generations held Jung's dissertation directly responsible for the fact that many of the younger Preiswerk daughters in Helly's generation did not marry.

IF JUNG had any awareness of the repercussions his dissertation caused, he spent no time trying to assuage them. By the time he submitted the dissertation to the University of Zürich, he had hit his stride at the Burghölzli. Among the other doctors, those who liked him from the beginning liked him more and looked to him for leadership, while the rest despised him, probably for a combination of reasons: first, because he was bursting with self-confidence, evident from the moment he learned how to provide for his own interests within his grueling daily schedule; then, because he was physically so big, so handsome, full of energy and enthusiasm, his voice and laugh so booming that he seemed to fill every room he entered. As he barreled his way through the Burghölzli's hushed monastic chambers, his colleagues, modest in both size and demeanor, seemed diminished by comparison.

Another reason for those who already disliked Jung to resent him further was Bleuler's continuing interest in his research, which resulted in the work that brought his first sustained recognition, the association experiments.[39] His interest in this topic began when von Muralt grew bored with examining brain lesions, and Jung lost the impetus to go forward on his own. Bleuler wanted Jung to continue with brain lesions, so he suggested that Jung deputize Franz Riklin Sr.,[40] who had just returned reluctantly from Germany because of his father's financial difficulties. Needing to earn money, Riklin became an assistant physician at the Burghölzli while preparing for the *Staatsexamen*. His research in Germany was done under Gustav Aschaffenburg,[41] where he worked on a variation of Francis Galton's word association experiment, as Wilhelm Wundt later refined it. Riklin thought there might be a way to produce a system capable of identifying disease-inducing lesions through the use of word association tests, so he had used Wundt's version of a test in conjunction with his own series of "brain cut" slides that showed how diseases progressed. Bleuler encouraged his two assistants to cooperate in an effort to nudge Jung into a continuation of his previous brain-lesion work with von Muralt but with a concrete research goal in mind.[42]

Because Riklin's arrival in Zürich was late at night, the ever courteous Bleuler went to the train station to bring him to the Burghölzli.[43] On the way back, he spoke so enthusiastically of Jung that the two men decided not to wait until morning, and Bleuler roused him from his quarters. All three then talked through the night about how best to continue Riklin's research while putting it to immediate practical use. Jung instantly took control of the project as primary researcher and radically changed its direction, conducting tests mainly with Riklin under the ostensible supervision of Bleuler.[44] Initially they followed Freud's research on free association, in which the investigator merely offered words to the subject-patient, who responded or not in any given time. They changed the procedure to one of rigorous, controlled empirical investigation in which a subject was presented with a list of one hundred words[45] selected for the possible associations they might raise and then instructed to respond with the first word that came to mind. Their refinement was to concentrate instead on the disturbances the subject exhibited in response to certain words said by the investigator and to measure the degree of distress by the amount of time it took the subject to formulate a reply. In most cases, these disturbing words could be grouped into a related cluster that Jung called "stimulus-words,"[46] which had much to do with either something in the patient's conscious knowledge or with information unconsciously repressed. In the former, the patient was embarrassed by or ashamed of circumstances or experiences that produced emotions ranging from fear to self-loathing; in the latter, the task was to make the patient aware of behavior or experiences that had been unconsciously buried within his or her memory.

Jung found that patients differed in the amount of time they took to formulate responses to the stimulus-words, usually hesitating before those that had something to do with distressing personal information. Together with Riklin, he coined the term "complex" to stand for "personal matter" that was "always a collection of various ideas, held together by an emotional tone common to all."[47]

The investigators measured precisely the time it took the subject to answer, which they believed determined the underlying complex,[48] or, the root cause of the patient's distress. As Jung later elaborated in an essay on the analysis of dreams, the investigator's task was "to establish the context [of the association] with minute care."[49] Words such as "marriage" or "mother," for example, often provided striking insights into the subject's mind.

Besides the actual time it took the subject to answer, they measured other factors, which included prolonged delay or an outright inability to respond. They sought reasons that might possibly underlie superficial or spurious reactions and paid careful attention to the reasons that the subject expressed some responses in highly charged and emotional language. Jung adapted and encapsulated Theodor Ziehen's term *gefühlsbetonter Vorstellungskomplex* (usually translated and explained as an emotionally charged complex of representations,[50] of which the patient was probably unaware) into the single word: "complex."[51] In his terminology, he used the word to designate detached fragments of personality that maintained an independent, autonomous function within the unconscious, and from which they (i.e., one or more complexes) were capable of exerting an influence upon the conscious mind.[52] Jung described the complex as an "agglomeration of associations" that were "rather difficult to handle."[53]

From the beginning of his medical training, Jung's interest was the individual patient rather than a group suffering similar manifestations of the same illness. Instead of seeking physical evidence from which to generalize, he concentrated on the "possibility of demonstrating the presence, the influence and the structure of those 'partial souls' which he now called 'feeling-toned complexes.'"[54] Although his language was vague and his intentions not yet clearly defined, hindsight shows that he was taking another step toward a recognition of the unconscious, one he began with his dissertation. In this case, it was clearly the personal unconscious, for the collective unconscious was still to be formulated.

Bleuler was involved in the early stages of the experiment, and he composed a list of 156 stimulus-words for experimentation on "all types of psychosis."[55] Jung noted that Bleuler immediately encountered the problem of how to qualify and quantify responses, particularly how to separate the normal from the abnormal. His initial variation upon Bleuler's work was to shorten the list to one hundred words, to select thirty-eight "normal" subjects to participate in the first round of experimentation, and to note that "the concept of normality must be very elastic." As the tests progressed during the years 1901 to 1904, the list was expanded to four hundred words, and subjects were broadened to include epileptics, schizophrenics, and hysterics, among others. To quantify reaction time accurately, Jung invented a variation of a "galvanometer" (later called a psychogalvanometer),[56] which measured the subject's response to stimulus-words through a "psychogalvanic effect," that is, by measuring breath rate, pulse, and perspiration.

All these techniques were formulated and refined during Jung's first three years at the Burghölzli, and he remembered both the experiments and the time as a period of personal psychological upheavals. The experiments were the main focus of his life, and he covered the walls of his rooms with graphs, charts, and lists, so thickly that his mother, visiting one day from Basel, looked at his "wallpaper" and asked what it was all about. Jung told her proudly that it was the experiment he was working on, when, in her deepest oracular No. 2 voice, Emilie, "standing there like a judge . . . the Delphic oracle," said, "Well, do you think that's something." Jung was stunned. He was unsure if Emilie meant that he assessed his work too highly, or perhaps not highly enough. As she reverted back to her ordinary No. 1 voice and spoke of ordinary everyday things, he was unable to elicit her true meaning. Basically, he knew his mother had intuited his own "unadmitted doubt," his "unadmitted worry" that what he was doing might not really have much of a purpose. Jung was usually so full of self-confidence that in this instance, as throughout his life, he had difficulty admitting his judgment could be faulty. There were very few people capable of instilling self-doubt in him, but Emilie topped this minuscule list. For the next three weeks, her remark rendered him incapable of working on the experiment.

Jung expressed in other ways as well the doubts Emilie's remark caused. When he was able to work again and began to test hysterics, he compared them to her, for as with the patients, "one could only find [Emilie's] real truth through endless divisions and subtractions." With schizophrenic subjects, his frustrations took yet another form based on something Emilie told him. One day, apropos of nothing, she said he did not know enough women. Now he found himself so frustrated by his inability to "know" female schizophrenic patients, to penetrate into their delusional world and reach them through his lists of words, that he was suddenly blasted by the thought that he must have sex with such a woman in order to see if that might bring about the experimental reality that was otherwise so elusive. Quickly horrified, he abandoned the thought, realizing that he "detested the traces of hysteria" in Emilie, and that such women who were impossible for men to control had always been those he most "timidly avoided."

By the beginning of 1902, Jung was both stalled and stymied, personally and professionally. He was bored by the routine of the association experiments, for he related the necessary exactitude and collation they required to the hated mathematics of his school days. Riklin was better able to handle these aspects of the procedure, and Jung willingly surrendered them. Also, he had been at the hospital for two years and was tired of the routine of his duties. He was still pleased that he had chosen psychiatry but not with the direction in which his career seemed headed. He would be twenty-seven in July, but he knew little of life other than work, so any attempt he made to effect change would have to come through some aspect of his profession.

He was also unsettled by a new degree of uncertainty in the social life of the hospital when Bleuler married a woman who worked there. Hedwig Bleuler-Waser (1869–1940)[57] was a formidable woman, well educated and later one of the leading feminists in Switzerland. She held degrees from the University of Zürich in literature and history and had been a lecturer there before becoming the German teacher in the Höheren Töchterschule Zürich, the most rigorous school for young women of the highest social classes. In 1901, she embraced Forel's doctrines of alcoholic abstinence, resigned her teaching position, and went to work with patients in the Burghölzli. Given that she was twelve years younger than her husband, the marriage seemed to outsiders to be one dominated by mutual intellectual views rather than personal passion. Like all the women of her time, Frau Bleuler-Waser surrendered her individual interests and put herself to work entirely for her husband in whatever capacity he required. Nevertheless, despite her self-effacement, she was the wife of the chief physician, and attention had to be paid to Hedwig Bleuler-Waser. Jung wasn't quite sure how he was supposed to do this.

In frustration, he thought of two things that might allow him to withdraw temporarily from the new tensions within the Burghölzli: a sabbatical from hospital routine and a new avenue of research. He began with the latter because he was excited by the work Théodore Flournoy was doing in Geneva on somnambulism, which Jung read about in *Des Indes à la Planète Mars* during his first year at the Burghölzli.[58] He was so taken with it that he wrote to ask Flournoy if he could translate it into German. More than six months passed before Flournoy replied, saying another translator was already at work.

On several of his days off, Jung traveled to Geneva to visit the older doctor (1854–1920), who became his "revered and fatherly friend."[59] In a sense limited by time and occasion, Flournoy became Jung's mentor. "I still needed support," he wrote in the *Protocols*:

> I had the feeling then that I was still much too young to be [professionally] independent. I needed someone I could talk to, also, about the problems that he and I were dealing with in our scientific work. . . . His views were exactly along my lines and they helped me a lot. I had no one [at the Burghölzli] who shared my interests in this regard.[60]

Because of these conversations with Flournoy, and at his instigation, Jung decided to approach Bleuler about the possibility of a sabbatical in Paris to meet Alfred Binet, who was about to publish his method of measuring children's intelligence,[61] and to attend Pierre Janet's weekly lectures at the Collège de France. Jung was not sure how much time he would devote to observing Binet, for his interests paralleled Janet's more closely. Janet was originally a philosophy teacher, but he gained his reputation for highly regarded research on neuroses and "somnambulic influence" and had just formed the Institut Psychologique International.[62] Jung hoped to work with him several days each week in the experimental psychology laboratory on theoretical psychopathology that Janet directed at the Hôpital Salpêtrière.[63]

Initially, in an incident to this day still unexplained, Bleuler refused permission for Jung's leave. On July 23, Jung submitted his resignation in writing, and canton officials told Bleuler they would accept it.[64] Bleuler had been aware of Jung's unsettled state but was still puzzled by his drastic action, for he knew Jung needed a salary and had no other job in the offing. He valued Jung's work at the Burghölzli and wanted to keep him, which may have been why he did not grant the request for leave. On the other hand, Bleuler was always eager to further the Burghölzli's international reputation, and Jung's presence in Paris would certainly lead to ties being strengthened and formal exchanges effected between French and Swiss psychologists. Bleuler knew that Jung shared many of Janet's research interests and was sure that his intelligence and buoyant personality would capture the professor's attention. He was correct in these assumptions, for throughout his life, Jung credited Janet with strongly influencing his career. Still, Bleuler did not rescind his refusal, and Jung did not withdraw his resignation. Others were left to ponder questions for which Bleuler and Jung refused to provide answers.

Jung went to Paris upon his release from hospital duties on October 1, 1902, but before he left, he had a number of other obligations to discharge. The first was his annual duty with the Swiss Citizens' Army, into which he had been inducted as a soldier when he was a university student in 1895 and in which, like all Swiss men, he served annually until 1923, when he was nearing fifty.[65] In 1901, he became a lieutenant in the medical corps and was sent to Basel for training. There, he renewed his family ties, seeing his mother and sister frequently and occasionally his disapproving Preiswerk relatives, who were still angry with him for leaving Basel but not for his dissertation, which they had not yet read.

Helly and her friend Emmy Zinsstag[66] had finished an apprenticeship with Emmy's aunt in Montpellier, France, and were now working in a designer's dressmaking shop in Paris. Despite the ill will the family harbored toward cousin Carl for his so-called abandonment, they were willing to forgive his "youthful misdeeds" and "spiritist transgressions." They trusted him to act as chaperone for Helly's younger sister Vally,[67] whom etiquette could not permit to take the train alone to Paris.

In October 1902, the cousins departed together, with Carl keeping a deep secret from everyone in the family but his mother. He was engaged to be married, and the wedding date was already set, Valentine's Day 1903. His wife-to-be was an heiress, the second richest in Switzerland, which may have been why, not wanting to become the target of common hospital gossip, he kept the real reason for his willingness to resign from the Burghölzli so secret. Paris represented professional opportunity and personal freedom, both of which he sorely needed. If he could survive financially until the marriage, money would never be an issue again.

CHAPTER 5

———⊸⊰⊱⊶———

"Timidly Proper with Women"

Until he wed Emma Rauschenbach when he was almost twenty-eight, Carl Jung was always so "timidly proper with women" that he had not had "an adventure before marriage, so to speak."[1] His romantic history with women (girls, really) was scant. He took special care to hide his feelings for Luggy Preiswerk from her, but more especially from his canny mother, whose scorn he feared. When he was a medical student, he was attracted to an upper-class Basel girl with the right social pedigree whom he met at a friend's house, but "an inner warning" led him to avoid her. He believed his intuition was vindicated when she committed suicide some months later.

Earlier, on a fraternity excursion to Zofingen, he joined a celebration on the main square and danced with a girl from French Switzerland with whom he pronounced himself hopelessly in love. Several days later, without having consulted this otherwise anonymous young lady, he went into a jewelry store and tried to buy two gold wedding rings for the equivalent of an American quarter. When the shocked owner told him their true cost, Carl threw the rings onto the counter and left the store, angry not only with the jeweler but also with the girl, whom he never saw again.[2]

Even earlier, during his high school years when he was on a brief visit to Sachseln,[3] he encountered a girl from the village while out walking and was immediately smitten. As he knew no girls at the time other than his cousins, he was awkward and embarrassed around her. His excuse for not pursuing her was that, since Sachseln was in a predominantly Catholic canton, she probably would not be interested in a Protestant pastor's son.

He gave this incident a great deal of importance when he used it in his memoir to delineate aspects of his No. 1 and No. 2 personalities, but since it is the only such romantic encounter throughout the entire book that he discusses in some detail, it takes on other resonances than he intended. Jung occasionally digressed into personal aspects of his life at various times in the writings that form his *Collected Works* and in the *Seminars* published afterward. He sometimes related biographical material to illustrate theoretical points he wished to make, but he used it so sparingly that it is often tantalizing in its opacity. Also, any incidents pertaining to his life generally concerned patients, and he seldom discussed contacts with women who were not.

Throughout his life he was curiously reticent when issues of sexuality arose, but never more so than when young. One of the most stunning admissions he made came in a letter to Freud, whose work he knew as early as 1900 but whom he did not meet personally until March 1907. He made an offhand admission on October 28, 1907, just months after their first meeting, when he was still trying to build Freud's confidence in him; quite possibly, he offered this facet of his personal experience as another way of doing so.

Comparing his "veneration" of Freud to a "religious" crush, Jung confessed that as a boy he had been "the victim of a sexual assault" by a man he once "worshiped."[4] He said his feelings "hampered" him considerably ever since. Any man, Jung wrote — be he friend, colleague, or even his superior, Bleuler — any man who tried to become a close friend, who offered an "intimate relationship" (in the platonic sense), always became "downright disgusting." Jung told Freud that he found Bleuler's increasing regard for him, as well as his attempts to move their working relationship onto a more personal, friendly level, particularly "offensive." With this admission, Jung outlined the route most of his friendships with men would follow throughout the rest of his life: all would begin positively, but most would end badly, in bitterness, rejection, and recrimination. Jung told Freud that he just wanted him to know this, but it was almost as if he were issuing a warning prefiguring the outcome of their own friendship.

The identity of the man who assaulted Jung has long been a mystery, as has the truth of what actually happened between them. In Jung's later life, a few members of his inner circle claimed to have heard him say (but more claim to have heard that he said it to someone else, who then repeated it to them, and so on)[5] that the man was a close friend of his father's. Some of Jung's descendants agree that this is true, and some have described the man as "a distant uncle,"[6] but most claim they know nothing about the man or any of the circumstances pertaining to the incident. All, however, agree that the most likely suspect was the Catholic priest who became Paul Jung's best friend during Carl's boyhood and in whose house Paul often spent "regular" vacations away from his family.[7]

Carl thought his father's friendship with a Catholic priest was "an act of extraordinary boldness."[8] Initially, he was fascinated by the man and thrilled when Emilie occasionally permitted him to visit his father overnight at the priest's house in Sachseln. Once before, at the age of fourteen, Carl had been in the presence of a Catholic priest, when he was sent to live in a rectory in Entlebuch that routinely housed patients taking health cures. He described the visit to Entlebuch in his published memoirs with a single sentence: "Nothing in the least menacing happened to me."[9] Many interpretations are possible for a remark such as this, but why Jung believed he needed to express it remains a mat-

ter of speculation. When, as an old man, he wrote these passages about his boyhood in the unpublished *Protocols*, he usually wrote about both in tandem. He
described the visits to Sachseln casually as "the collision with the priest," which
may be why he felt compelled to state that nothing untoward happened in
Entlebuch.[10]

Whoever was the perpetrator of the alleged "collision," it is a matter for
speculation of another kind, too, because of the discrepancy in the physical appearance of the Sachseln priest and the boy. At the age of fourteen, Carl was
almost six feet tall, burly, brawny, and able to hold his own in any of the
schoolboy fistfights he so proudly boasted of winning. The Sachseln priest, on
the other hand, was a "slight" man of "medium" height and build, and probably
not strong enough to overwhelm the boy by physical force. Still, the boy was
ashamed of what happened, so the question remains whether or not he was a
willing participant — up to a point or entirely — in what appears to have been
a single encounter.

Years later, Jung told the story of how he stopped overnight in Naples before
boarding a ship bound for the United States, and of how his guide offered to
take him to a bordello. When he declined, the guide offered to procure beautiful boys for him. "I'm even less interested in that," Jung replied, to which the
ever helpful guide responded by offering to bring him some beautiful goats.[11]
Jung equated this episode with all things Romish and popery, and with the animal spirit of antiquity that he believed pervaded the Catholic Church, a spirit
he held responsible for instilling such fear that he could never bring himself to
go to Rome. Whatever contributed to the totality of his reasons, Catholicism
and Catholic priests induced a certain degree of terror throughout his life.

These few episodes comprise the known accounts of Carl Jung's sexual fantasies and experiences before marriage. Although other biographers have speculated about possible visits to brothels in Paris, no evidence exists to support or
deny it. And, as he boasted in the *Protocols* of how he was so poor he lived on 1
franc per day in the Hotel des Balcons, Rue Casimir Delavigne, it is unlikely
that he had enough money to patronize such establishments more than once, if
at all.

CARL JUNG had, in a sense, known Emma Rauschenbach all her life.[12] Emma's
mother was Bertha Schenk, the "auntie" who was Paul Jung's parishioner and
friend in Uhwiesen, one of the three villages comprising the parish of Laufen,
and who figured in some of the baby Carl's earliest memories. Bertha was the
golden blond who took him for walks along the Rhine riverbank in a haze of
glittering autumn leaves, the one who instilled vague fears in the child because
she was there and his mother was not and, most of all, because his father liked
her so much.

Rosina Bertha Schenk (October 10, 1856–March 16, 1932) was the daughter
of the owner of the Gasthof zum Hirschen, a comfortable old country inn in

Uhwiesen that had been in her family for more than a century. She was a very pretty girl who married above her social station on June 2, 1881, when she wed Johannes Rauschenbach Jr. (November 21, 1856–March 2, 1905). He was the only son and principal heir to the considerable fortune of Johannes Rauschenbach Sr., whose own parents were proprietors of a lucrative spice shop in Schaffhausen called The Silver Snail. After a career as a journeyman apprentice to a locksmith master in Zürich, Bern, and Dijon, Johannes Sr. returned to Schaffhausen and set up a mechanic's repair shop nearby.[13] When it prospered, he moved into a larger factory building directly on the Rhine and began to manufacture wire pins and machines that processed cotton and wool. His real fortune began in 1846, with the manufacture of high-quality threshing machines; by 1867, those bearing the Rauschenbach name were valued as the best in the world. He became even wealthier after he bought the Jones Watch Company, a bankrupt American firm that manufactured machine-made watches for English and American markets. Johannes Sr. renamed it the International Watch Company, or IWC, and it became a part of the growing Rauschenbach machine-manufacturing empire.[14]

Johannes Sr. became so wealthy that when the city of Schaffhausen was in financial difficulties, he simply wrote a check for a loan of 500,000 Swiss francs. He was responsible for the construction of the beautiful Mühlentorgrabenstrasse and a member of the commission that rechanneled the waters of the Rhine to make Schaffhausen more industrially profitable. A member of the town council for twenty-three years, he was a legend because of his civic beneficence, including the donation of the huge organ that still plays in the church of St. Johann. His wife, the former Maria Barbara Vogel, never became accustomed to the enormous wealth that allowed her husband to build the mansion on the Rhine known as the Haus zum Rosengarten.[15] "If you had only remained a mechanic," she frequently complained, "at least on payday we would always know how much we get!"[16]

Johannes Sr. died in 1881, the year before Emma was born to Johannes Jr. and Bertha, who lived with the widow Barbara in the Rosengarten. Emma Maria was their first child, born in their quarters on the upper floor on March 30, 1882. The following year, on July 7, 1883, their second and last child was born, Bertha Margaretha, known throughout her life by the nickname Gret. Despite their radically different personalities, the sisters were devoted to each other all their lives. Emma was a serious child who learned to read early and liked quiet, solitary pursuits. She was especially interested in nature and liked explorations and experiments in the natural sciences. Gret had a fiery temper and was prone to quick flashes of anger that alternated with a disposition as sunny as Emma's. Of the two, she was the musical child who played the piano and sang beautifully and the athlete who boasted of swimming year-round in the Rhine until she was well advanced in age.[17]

The Rosengarten was a magical house, where Grandmother Barbara kept an impressive collection of children's toys she allowed the girls to play with, but only if they let her join the games. This was also true of her many dolls, which she kept in a specially constructed closet converted from a huge *Bettkasten*, the equivalent of a Murphy bed. Her favorite pastime was reading, and she prepared for her pleasure by donning her favorite costume, "a mightily ribboned lace bonnet . . . with small lorgnon in hand."[18] She always sat in a massive armchair in front of a window that overlooked the Rhine and the transmission pillars with the huge wheels that carried water power to the various factories in the city, her late husband's prominent among them. She claimed the noise was soothing, a pleasant musical accompaniment to her reading. The two girls considered it an honor when Grandmother Barbara invited them to join her.

Grandmother Barbara also told Emma and Gret ghost stories about the house, claiming it was haunted by a drunken priest whose house formerly occupied the site. She claimed she could hear him at night, shuffling through the long corridors or trying to shove huge barrels of wine through the cellar windows. Gret was skeptical, but Emma claimed to hear him, too. Of her two granddaughters, Barbara believed Emma was her kindred spirit in regard to ghosts.

The gardens and stables were a children's paradise equal to the house. There were two prize Hungarian horses called Lori and Ceda, groomed by a man called Reeper, formerly the dashing orderly to a cavalry officer in Emperor Franz Joseph's Austro-Hungarian army. The girls adored Reeper, who often took them on daylong excursions to ruined castles along the Rhine, where they roamed at will among crumbling dungeons and towers.

Emma was in grade school when her father decided to buy thirty-five hectares in the countryside known as the Ölberg.[19] Family legend is that Johannes bought the land from two crazy sisters, and supposedly got it cheaply because people were hanged or beheaded there in the Middle Ages, so no one else wanted it. On the site was a famous ruined chapel dedicated to St. Wolfgang in 1477 and a place of pilgrimage ever since. A penurious farmer had built a ramshackle farmhouse that the Rauschenbach family used for several summers after it was connected to the chapel by a long hallway. The daughters slept in the chapel's choir loft, amusing themselves in the light of the long summer nights by peeling off bits of ancient frescoes from the walls. In 1897, Johannes Jr. had both buildings torn down and in their place built a house also called the Ölberg. It remains in the family today.

Even by the standards of the time, the Ölberg was exceptionally grand.[20] There were electric lighting and central heat, provided by an enormous coal furnace in the cellar. Full bathrooms were fitted with fine marble and brass fixtures, and there was indoor plumbing. Emma and Gret had rooms on the upper floor, where there was a tower that looked out over the hills to Germany beyond the river. Everything on their floor was pink, including the girls' dresses, for it was Emma's favorite color, and her mother allowed her to surround herself and her sister with it.

In the evenings, the little family gathered in one of the side parlors on the ground floor, where a small fireplace was always lit in the winter, more for aesthetics than for warmth. They used the grand reception room for many occasions entailed by Johannes Jr.'s business entertainments. This room seemed exceptionally gracious because it opened onto long south-facing terraces that traversed the rear of the house. The only room that no one really liked was the dining room, heavily paneled in dark wood and located on the north side, where it got scant light and where heat from the furnace never seemed enough to warm it.

Emma's girlhood could not have been more different from her fiancé's, and by her own admission, it was "magical." The magic ended in 1894, when her father went blind and a "hard time" followed. "The childhood was broken"[21] when everyone was enlisted to serve as Johannes's eyes and he became the center of the family's existence. Bertha took over the business, running it with the help of Johannes's only sister's husband. Because Emma was the elder daughter and the one most interested in scholarly pursuits, she was chosen to become her father's household eyes, reading aloud everything from adventure novels about explorers (those featuring Livingston and Stanley were his favorites) to detailed financial documents from his business, and several daily newspapers. In this way, she amassed an extraordinary knowledge of financial management and acquired a deep interest in the natural sciences, history, and politics.

Johannes had been blind in one eye since a boyhood accident. As an adult, he compensated for his partial vision by holding his head in a quirky, slanted manner that gave him an inquisitorial air and was frequently commented upon, usually in tones of fear and trepidation by those who did not know him well. His appearance was enhanced by his generally dour personality, which his colleagues attributed to the fact that he was the son of a highly successful self-made man and therefore depressed because he believed his own achievements were underestimated and undervalued. "He sought his revenge in a certain kind of contemptuous sarcasm,"[22] which he frequently directed toward his wife and daughters as well as his business associates.

His blindness in the second eye began even before he built the Ölberg house, but he still supervised every detail of its construction through plans that were drawn in relief, with raised surfaces denoting the various rooms and installations, over which he could move his fingers and thus visualize what the house would become. When it was built, he moved surely and securely from room to room, knowing instinctively where steps and doorways were located and where his favorite chairs were placed.

There was speculation in the family and the community that Johannes Rauschenbach's blindness was caused by syphilis and that his wife welcomed the doctor son of her deceased friend as a suitor for her daughter, since he could verify discreetly that she was free of infection.[23] Jung renewed his acquaintance with Bertha Rauschenbach-Schenk during a visit to a fraternity brother in Schaffhausen in 1899, when his mother reminded him of the beautiful blond girl who had looked after him in Laufen and asked him to pay a courtesy call on the now respected Frau Rauschenbach.

When Jung entered the house's imposing central hallway, he saw a young brown-haired girl halfway up the broad staircase. She halted long enough to appraise her mother's visitor and then turned and ran to the upper floors. From that moment on, Jung claimed that he was smitten and knew instinctively that this girl would become his wife. He told this to the friend who accompanied him to the Ölberg, who said it was impossible to understand how a twenty-four-year-old doctor could be so instantly smitten with a seventeen-year-old girl. Perhaps his first sight of Emma was simply another version of his previous history with women, but Jung knew from the start that she was the one. His friend laughed dismissively, saying, "Well, you've always been crazy."

In later years, Jung insisted that he first saw Emma when she was fourteen, but in fact, she was a poised young woman of seventeen who had just returned from a year in Paris. Emma's education had consisted of five years in the private elementary school for girls of elite society in Schaffhausen, the Mädchenele-mentarschule, followed by five more in the secondary Mädchenrealschule, from which she graduated first in her class.[24] As women had recently been granted permission to attend the University of Zürich, Emma wanted to enroll in the natural sciences, but her father would not hear of it. It was simply unthinkable for the daughter of a Rauschenbach even to contemplate mingling with the great variety of students who enrolled in the university. Swiss students were mostly men from many different social classes; the women were usually free-thinking foreigners, primarily from Germany and Russia.[25] Who could predict what ideas a girl like Emma would assimilate from being in such company, her father worried, or what her outlook on life would become. The only thing certain was that a university education would make her unfit for marriage to a social equal, for what man would want a woman whose interests were not entirely centered in the home.[26]

Instead, Emma was sent to Paris on May 1, 1898, to live for a year with the Lavater family, business friends of her parents. Until May 1, 1899, she was an upper-class au pair to their children, and in her spare time, she pursued such cultural interests as she and her parents thought would enhance her qualities as a marriage prospect. During this year, she learned to speak flawless French and to read Old French and Provençal because she had developed an interest in the legends of the Holy Grail and wanted to read them in the original languages.[27]

When Carl took tea with Emma for the first time in the summer of 1899, she was an elegantly poised young woman who contributed quietly to the conversation, but only when prompted by her mother and then mostly to offer an observation about Paris. Jung was charmed, and even more smitten than at his first sight of her, while Emma was merely polite. She believed herself "more or less betrothed" to a young man from Schaffhausen, the son of a business associate of her father's and highly approved of by him. They had walked unchaperoned (but with her father's approval) in the gardens several times, and Emma had boldly permitted the young man first to hold her hand and then to brush her cheek lightly with his lips. She believed this had "compromised" her and made her unfit for marriage to anyone else.

Jung never cited his attraction to Emma as one of the possible reasons he left Basel for Zürich, but train travel in those days between Zürich and Schaffhausen was relatively quicker, easier, and cheaper than the corresponding ride from Basel.[28] Jung made occasional visits to the Ölberg between their first meeting in the summer of 1899 and the formal betrothal on October 6, 1901, but these were usually for ceremonial occasions such as parties in the Rauschenbach house during the Christmas and Easter holidays, when the invitations were issued by Bertha and not Emma.

Carl Jung wooed and won Emma Rauschenbach through letters[29] and with a great deal of help from his future mother-in-law, who took care to keep the details of the long-distance courtship from her husband until she persuaded their daughter to take the young doctor's intentions seriously. When Jung was free for several hours on Sunday afternoons, he took the train to Schaffhausen as often as he could afford. Bertha made sure that Emma was always at home but could not persuade her to be in his company other than at teatime. Bertha learned the reason for Emma's reticence only after Jung asked her to walk in the garden and she refused. That evening she questioned Emma discreetly and learned that she considered herself betrothed to the other young man. Bertha assured Emma she had not compromised herself and was not betrothed and urged her at least to consider the young doctor as a possible marriage partner. Emma was confused by her mother's entreaties, for they were at great variance with her father's wishes for her future.

Carl Jung was a poor salaried doctor (he had not yet told her of his plan to resign), and not only that, an *Irrenarzt*, the old pejorative for a psychiatrist and at that time "the most despised branch of medicine"[30] in Switzerland. It was true that his ancestral pedigree placed him on a higher rung of society's ladder, but only in Basel, whereas hers was grounded in great wealth and made her far more influential in Schaffhausen. He had no status of any sort there or in Zürich. However, it helped greatly that Emma adored her mother, who was more like a confidante and older sister, and that she was afraid of her father's severe opinions and the sarcastic venom with which he expressed them.

From the beginning, Carl was aware of Emma's innate intelligence, which he respected and furthered. Among the topics in his letters were suggestions for books she might enjoy, both literary and psychological. She had begun to learn Latin and Greek as a means of understanding medical texts, and although she did not begin to study mathematics until after her marriage, she told him she intended to because it would give her an understanding of logical thought and "a greater sense of reality."³¹ A deep and lasting bond formed between them when Emma told him of her interest in the Grail legends, which had fascinated him for years.³² She wondered why he was not more interested in the French language, and he wondered how he could get her to share his increasing absorption in mythology. He also described his research and his psychological readings and told her amusing stories about the behavior of some of his patients, thus painting a rosy picture of daily life in the Burghölzli, for he knew that if she married him, their daily life would be centered around his career. He also painted the best possible word portraits of his mother and sister, because Emilie was suggesting that she and Trudi would have to move from the increasingly decrepit Bottmingermühle and hinting at the likelihood of their joining him in Zürich. He told Emma nothing of the uncertainties of his work and family responsibilities, as he was still hoping that some position might arise to let him return to Basel in a more elevated station than when he left.

As the correspondence progressed, Emma Rauschenbach found qualities in Carl Jung that she knew she would never find in any of the other young men who had begun to court her. He was certainly handsome, and she appreciated his good looks. He was poised and confident when with her, and she felt that he would be the protective buffer between her and the world that a good Swiss husband was supposed to be. But, most important of all his qualities, he also valued her intelligence and urged her to expand her mental horizons. She believed she could be more than just a housewife and mother of his children if she married him, and she dreamed of furthering her knowledge and education so she could be as much of a partner in his professional life as he would need. When he described the long hours he spent at the Burghölzli writing daily case reports about the patients, she practiced her handwriting in preparation for the secretarial duties she intended to perform for him.

By October 6, 1901, they were officially engaged. Bertha was overjoyed, and if Johannes Rauschenbach harbored objections, he kept most of them to himself. There was a small family celebration that included Emilie and Trudi, but the engagement was not officially announced or publicized within either extended family. The ostensible reason was that Carl was expecting to take his sabbatical to Paris, and he needed to try to save money before the marriage could take place; the unspoken reason was that Johannes Rauschenbach thought this was unlikely to happen, since the almost penniless doctor had abruptly resigned his salaried position. He wanted to keep his daughter's options open for marriage to someone more to his liking. Emma was certain Carl would manage to win her, and she explained the long courtship as due to her need to amass a considerable dowry, which for a bride of her station would certainly take time.

JUNG WENT to Paris with no choice but to live as cheaply as possible and with no chance to save money. He continued to write frequently to his fiancée and her mother, telling all the details of his daily life. In one letter, he spoke of the unseasonable heat and in another shortly after, the chilling cold that had fallen upon the city. Bertha was so distressed by thoughts of his discomfort that she sent him a warm winter coat and no doubt occasional gifts of money as well.

The young Dr. Jung concentrated on living a busy professional life in Paris because he was determined to make the most of his second "real" trip abroad. (His first was to Munich and Stuttgart in 1900. He did not count an earlier student walking tour to Belfort, France, or another to Lake Como.) In Paris, he took pride in the simple enjoyments that came his way during what was really a period of grim poverty, and he relished the occasional simple meal and modest cigar offered by friends or colleagues. He worked hard in Janet's laboratory, both as observer and experimenter, and attended every one of his lectures. Because he planned to spend two months in England at the end of his Paris sabbatical, Jung took daily lessons at Berlitz to perfect his English and spent time each day reading English books and newspapers to build his vocabulary.[33] Also, he never missed an opportunity to converse in French because he was ashamed of his heavy German accent and wanted to get rid of it. He later boasted that all his hard work paid off, as he acquired a Parisian accent.

Janet was known for his sociability and held regular "afternoons" in his large and gracious apartment on the Rue de Varennes, to which all his associates received open invitations. Jung always accepted but was shy and reserved on these occasions, usually speaking French softly and slowly, as if this would somehow mitigate his accent and lessen his imposing size amid such delicate drawing-room furniture and so many slim, short people.

But it was Paris itself that fascinated Jung, and not the lectures, lunatic asylums, and hospitals that he visited routinely as an observer.[34] He was preoccupied with two aspects of the city: the fine arts and the human misery he encountered on a daily basis. The combination threw him into a "terrible condition," because he had never encountered anything like it before. As a possible solace, he thought often of the Buddha, whom he knew of through reading Schopenhauer. Nevertheless, he could not keep himself away from the Morgue, Les Halles, and the slums in the northern districts of the city, where he liked to perfect his argot in the bistros and cafés. When all the poverty and misery blurred into one overwhelming sensation, he put medicine aside and went to art museums "to the point of exhaustion." As a university student, he had been so "crazy about Holbein and Böcklin[35] and the old Dutch painters" that he started his own collection of copperplate engravings. Now he browsed among the *bouquinistes* and was rewarded by finding one of Dürer's. He read French novels until he was completely "imbued"[36] with them. Every day he went to the Louvre to watch the copyists, with whom he liked to talk, especially those who painted the *Mona Lisa*.[37] He was a steady visitor to the Egyptian galleries, and he credited them for his initial interest in ancient Egypt's literature and art. Also, he took up painting himself, trying to duplicate the landscapes of northern France and painting from memory clouds, skies, and small city vignettes.

By the time he arrived in London, he considered his English "still very imperfect" and discovered that he was "affected" with an American accent, acquired from the American students and doctors who were coming to the Burghölzli in increasing numbers. He thanked God that by the time he arrived in Oxford, he had lost it. Oxford was the "high point" of his stay. He was overwhelmed with emotion by his first sight of the colleges, remarking, "Oh, the conversations there!" After dinner, a little silver horn with snuff was passed around, followed by black coffee, cigars, and liquor, and then "conversations in the style of the 18th century." He approved of the fact that only men were present, "because one wanted to talk exclusively at an intellectual level."

He did have occasional feminine company, but only in Paris, where he sought out his Preiswerk cousins, as if nothing untoward about the séances had ever interrupted their friendship.[38] By dining most nights on a single bag of roasted chestnuts, he saved enough money to invite Helly once each to the opera and theater and to dinner on her birthday, November 15. Mostly, he invited her and her sister Vally and their friend Emmy Zinsstag to walk in the Bois de Boulogne on Sunday afternoons, or he accepted invitations to tea at the house in Versailles where the three women lived. With them, he went to Fontainebleau, the palace at Versailles, and the Trianon.

Helly had matured to become a quiet, self-assured woman who supervised more than twenty-two other seamstresses in her dressmaking establishment. For the first time, she and Carl related to each other as friendly adults, and they never discussed the mediumistic experiences they had shared. Spiritualism may still have been an active component of Jung's professional life, but Helly had put those years behind her. Although she had other suitors, including Emmy Zinsstag's brother Dolph (whom she passed on to her sister Mathilde), Helly was passive and distant toward men, and eventually they all drifted away. With hindsight, her Preiswerk relatives believed that because of her ability as a seer, she knew that she had (or would have) the tuberculosis that eventually claimed her life on November 13, 1911.[39]

By December 1902, Carl was no longer keeping his engagement to Emma Rauschenbach a secret. Helly asked about Emma, and Carl told her about his fiancée in glowing detail. When Carl left Paris, the cousins parted on friendly terms, because Helly still knew nothing of his dissertation. She wished him well in his marriage and asked him to tell his bride she would be pleased one day to sew a dress for her.[40] In the last years of her life, before she died at the age of thirty, Helly returned to Basel, where she and Vally owned one of the best dressmaking establishments in the city, on the fashionable Aschenplatz. Emma visited, probably curious to see Helly, and ordered the lovely, soft gray dress that was her husband's favorite.

By the time the wedding date was set for February 14, 1903, Johannes Rauschenbach's health was failing fast.[41] Nevertheless, it was a grand wedding, with a large crowd of relatives and friends attending the ceremony in the Swiss Reformed Church of Schaffhausen. Two days later, on February 16, an elaborate wedding banquet followed at the Hotel Müller (today the Hotel Banhof), which featured among the twelve courses shrimp bisque, river trout, chicken breasts à la Périgord, foie gras, a cleansing sorbet followed by pheasant, artichoke hearts, salads of the season, and various puddings, cakes, sauces, and molded ice creams. All were served, naturally, with the appropriate wines, sherries, ports, and champagnes.[42] Both the bride and groom appreciated good food, and guests noted how heartily they ate. The next day, the couple left for Lake Como, where they spent several days before traveling on to Genoa to board a ship that took them to their honeymoon in Madeira and the Canary Islands.[43]

In early spring 1904, they moved into an apartment on the Zollikerstrasse, within walking distance of the Burghölzli. The Jungs seem to have concentrated more on married life than on his career until May, when he began to substitute at the Burghölzli for doctors on military duty. When von Muralt became ill and took several extended leaves, Jung rejoined the staff temporarily as Bleuler's deputy. All this while, he was quietly negotiating to return to Basel as a physician affiliated with the cantonal mental hospital and for an adjunct appointment to the medical faculty of the university. These hopes were dashed by a "Basel calamity," when the position went to a German "Dr. Wolff." Jung thought his chances of returning in triumph to his native city were "wrecked *forever*," and he resigned himself to sitting "under a millstone" at the Burghölzli.[44] When von Muralt resigned, Jung asked Bleuler to reappoint him to the staff. He returned officially in October 1904, and in December was named an adjunct lecturer at the University of Zürich. From that moment on, Jung cast his lot with Zürich and never made another attempt to return to Basel.

The Jungs moved into the hospital that October, to an apartment directly beneath the one occupied by Bleuler and his wife, who soon became a good friend and mentor to Emma. Hedwig was as determined to be a significant aide to her husband as Emma hoped to be to hers, so the wives formed an initial friendship based on this mutual desire. Later, when each discovered the wide-reaching intellectual interests of the other, the friendship flourished in other areas, too. There were, however, many visible differences not only between Emma and Hedwig but also between Jung and Bleuler, and between Jung and the other doctors as well. Emma decorated their apartment with her innate good taste, with the exquisite furnishings and fine antiques that comprised her dowry. The Bleulers, who both came from humble backgrounds, lived in exceedingly modest circumstances. Until their respective children were born, the Bleulers took all their meals in the hospital dining room, while the Jungs took theirs privately, cooked by the servant Emma engaged to help her care for the apartment. Now, the poor boy from Basel who arrived at the Burghölzli with one pair of trousers and two shirts wore the clothing of a prosperous physician, with a proper outfit for every occasion, while Emma dressed modestly, behaved circumspectly, and never gave a hint that she was the heiress to great wealth.

According to Swiss law at the time, Emma's money was now solely under her husband's control. She could certainly express her wishes about how it should be spent or saved, but he was the one who ultimately made the decisions.[45] Both parties were content with this arrangement, which, in the early years of their marriage at least, was never a major bone of contention, simply an underlying one on Jung's part.

The first year or so of their married life opened a wide new world for them both. With his usual boundless energy, Jung resumed the grueling rounds of hospital work. He told a friend that Bleuler had gone on leave and he was working as "director, senior physician and first assistant," losing "fourteen pounds" in the process. But he said he was happy: "For what satisfies us in life more than real work?"[46] True to her intention, Emma did help by transcribing his notes into the formal case reports Bleuler required. When they could, the Jungs dipped cautiously into the waters of Zürich's cultural life, going once or twice to the theater and opera. Jung soon made it clear that he did not enjoy attending performances,[47] so from then on, they usually left the hospital grounds only to dine in a fine restaurant, for they both enjoyed good food and wine.

They usually dined alone, for there was little opportunity to meet like-minded couples of Emma's social station in Zürich. Those their age were for the most part in business or professions other than medicine, and Jung did not want to spend his precious free time talking to men with whom he had little in common. Bertha Rauschenbach and Gret Homberger were frequent visitors, and a pattern evolved that held true for the rest of the Jungs' married life: when not socializing with people who were deeply interested in psychology, either from Zürich or elsewhere, they spent their intimate social occasions with family members, first Emma's and later their own children and grandchildren. In the midst of an outgoing, highly visible international life, they remained deeply private and somewhat cloistered within their own community.

By the early summer of 1904, their social visibility as a couple came to an end. Emma was pregnant and, in keeping with the customs of the time, seldom seen in public, except for her daily constitutional on the hospital grounds or infrequent, dutiful visits to her mother-in-law, who now lived nearby. Using some of Emma's money, Jung had moved Emilie and Trudi from Basel to a small house in the nearby village of Küsnacht, where he was also looking for a suitable lakefront plot of land on which to build his own house. Because of Emma's pregnancy, he groomed Trudi, then a shy woman of twenty who had never been apart from her mother, to replace Emma as his secretarial assistant. Trudi had previously had some training as a nurse in Basel, but it was not until the other doctors discovered her sympathetic rapport with patients that she was able to combine being her brother's occasional secretary with working as a nursing aide.[48] She loved the work, which she performed for several years, and thrived on the social contact.

By the time Emma gave birth to Agathe Regina on December 26, 1904, her intellectual ambitions were stymied by the exigencies of motherhood, even as her husband embarked on the whirlwind of work that would soon bring him to the attention of the international psychiatric community. The marriage had settled into a routine: he soared, while she, of necessity, took care of the mundane details so that he could.

CHAPTER 6

"Something Unconsciously Fateful ... Was Bound to Happen"

The last decade of Johannes Rauschenbach's "hermitlike life indoors" was one of "great suffering." On March 2, 1905, the "poor rich man" whose eyes "had long been extinguished" died in his sleep at the age of forty-eight.[1] Five persons comprised the *Erbengemeinschaft*, the committee of heirs who inherited his immense fortune: his widow, their two daughters, and their respective husbands. His firm became an *offene Handelsgesellschaft*, an open commercial company, henceforth known as the Uhrenfabrik of J. Rauschenbach's Erben, the watch manufacturing concern of the Rauschenbach heirs. Gret's husband, Ernst Jakob Homberger, became the managing director and sole authorized representative in charge of the family's financial dealings. Homberger was a quiet, serious, home-loving man twelve years older than his wife, whose greatest pleasure other than his business was to sit in his armchair in the Ölberg (where he and Gret lived with Bertha) dispensing bonbons from the huge silver goblet on the side table to his children and their Jung cousins.[2]

Bertha was the major shareholder, receiving half the total profits until her death in 1932. Her daughters, who had originally received one-fourth each, then became half owners. As Emma's husband and head of their family, Carl wrote the annual letters to the company's financial officers to express appreciation and respect for their successful annual increase in profits. On December 31, 1908, Carl and Emma held a 162,500 Swiss franc share of the total capital of Sfr650,000. The following year it rose to Sfr175,000. After a capital increase of Sfr50,000, their share of the profits was a dividend of Sfr15,210.70. Under Homberger's dedicated management, this figure increased yearly and carried other financial perquisites as well.[3]

Jung was suddenly a wealthy man because of his wife's inheritance, but like all good Swiss of their social class, he and Emma displayed few outward manifestations of wealth. Although Emma's dowry brought furnishings and household goods of excellent quality to their flat in the Burghölzli, envious gossip had long since ceased because she was so down-to-earth that everyone liked her. Carl's only possibly ostentatious sign of wealth was the large gold IWC pocket watch Emma gave him as a wedding gift, which he wore throughout his life with loving pride.[4]

If others commented about a visible display of their wealth, it was usually when Gret Homberger came to visit, for she greatly enjoyed her role as wife of a managing director and dressed the part in fine furs, leather, and couturier clothing. Although she always had a chauffeur, she liked to drive her large luxury sedans herself, parking imperiously wherever she pleased and thus receiving citations nearly every time she left home alone.[5] This certainly brought attention to the Jungs whenever she came to the hospital to visit.

What the money really did for Jung was provide professional independence. Unlike some of the other doctors who depended on their salaries and whose research was therefore often dictated by those above them in authority, Jung knew that as long as he fulfilled his many duties at the Burghölzli, he could pursue whatever interested him because he was free to resign when or if he no longer cared to be on staff. For the next three years, however, until 1908, he did not want to leave the Burghölzli, because the patients were so engrossing and his research was fully supported by Bleuler, allowing him to initiate what he later called the actual beginning of his professional life. His "true work," his "real creative work,"[6] had begun in 1903 with the association experiments, considered by many traditionalists to be his most important contribution to psychoanalysis because they followed scientific procedure and used rigorous experimentation to demonstrate the effects of the unconscious.[7]

For the remainder of his Burghölzli years, Jung's primary research centered on the study of complexes. He progressed from testing "mentally sound" persons to "neurotics and psychotics of the most varied kinds and of the most varied reaction types."[8] Although the work was engrossing, it was also, for a man of his temperament, limiting. His lifelong aversion to mathematics was well known, so throughout their collaboration, Riklin assumed responsibility for timing and calculations, particularly after they began to use a galvanometer[9] to measure the differing responses. Jung administered the tests and observed the physical reactions of a variety of subjects, both normal and abnormal. He investigated their social, cultural, and educational backgrounds in order to ascertain connections between even the most bizarrely expressed associations.[10] Riklin was more or less content to collate numerical results, especially after Jung enlisted Trudi to help ensure that every observation was precise.[11] As the testing progressed, Jung's interest moved beyond collective statistics to the individual as he sought "to catch the intruders in the mind" that caused "the blockage in libido flow."[12] He noted that Freud was concurrently "evolving his conception of the complex."[13]

UNTIL 1905, Jung seldom referred to Freud, and then mostly in passing. Although he read The Interpretation of Dreams for the first time in 1900, he realized when he returned to it in 1903 that he had not fully grasped its significance. However, two fleeting references he made to Dreams in his 1900 dissertation show that similar thinking by the two theoreticians had been present since Jung's first reading. In one, Jung pondered whether the "split" in a medium's personality during a séance "offers a parallel to the results of Freud's dream investigations"; in a second reference, he noted that autonomous personalities such as Helly Preiswerk's "Ivenes" were reminders of "the independent growth of repressed thoughts."14 When Jung discerned a pattern whereby subjects in the association experiments could not respond to stimulus-words, he reread Dreams for other possible correspondences. His subjects' patterns of "repressions"15 convinced him that, in essence, Freud's theory of the unconscious was true, although he differed with Freud's insistence that the root cause of every repression was "sexual trauma and shock."16 Jung had seen too many examples of hospital patients "in which sexual things were of quite secondary importance compared with the role played by social adaptation." Freud, who had no hospital affiliation and saw only private patients who were generally educated and well-to-do, did not have the same firsthand knowledge of the illnesses and diseases of the lower social orders. But at the time, Jung could easily overlook this profound difference because there were so many other exciting areas of agreement between him and Freud and he innocently thought each could benefit from the other's expertise.

Jung initiated the possibility of contact with Freud in a letter written on behalf of a patient on September 25, 1905, a half year before their true correspondence began.17 The letter itself was preceded by Jung's notation that it was a "Report on Fräulein Spielrein to Herr Professor Freud in Vienna," one he had given to the patient's mother "for possible use."18 Sabina Spielrein, the patient, was a young Russian woman previously hospitalized elsewhere. She came to Zürich in 1904, intending to enroll in the university's medical school, but several days later, on August 17, she was admitted to the Burghölzli after several attacks of acute hysteria. Jung supervised her treatment until June 1, 1905, when she left the hospital and moved into an apartment at Scheuchzerstrasse 62, near the medical school from which she received her degree in 1911.19 Throughout these seven years, her life was both professionally and personally entwined with Jung's, and their relationship has been a matter of intense speculation and wide-ranging disagreement ever since.20

In his initial "report" to Freud, Jung described Spielrein as she was when he first met her, a nineteen-year-old girl who had a considerable hereditary disposition toward hysteria because both parents suffered from the illness.21 Her father was a well-to-do Jewish merchant in Rostov-on-Don, Russia; her mother (also Jewish, the daughter of a rabbi) had been sent to Christian schools and the local university, where she trained as a dentist. The marriage was arranged and

her a note saying Sabina needed underwear, asking her "politely" to send her daughter's two suitcases "soon." Three days later, Bleuler wrote to Frau Spielrein about the *"Fräulein Doctor,"* as Sabina was known in the hospital: he and Jung wanted to see "everything that is written by hand," for she had informed them of the voluminous daily diary she kept, and they thought they could speed her treatment by reading it.[26]

Sabina was not an easy patient, and her demands escalated by the hour. Bleuler wrote to the cantonal officer who determined the patients' fees to ask that hers be set at the highest because of the trouble she caused, 10 francs per day plus supplements, even though most of her care was provided by a private nurse. The family, he added, "seems very rich."[27] Herr Spielrein, alarmed by his wife's cryptic communication and dissatisfied with Bleuler's direct reports, went to Zürich in September to see for himself what was wrong with his daughter and arrived just in time to witness a horrendous tantrum. Sabina decided she needed a new wardrobe to wear in the hospital, but her mother agreed to pay for only one dress, and only if the hospital seamstress made it. Bleuler, at a loss in such situations, was called to mediate and suggested that Herr Spielrein engage "the couturier concerned," because the fit could not be guaranteed if the hospital's seamstress made it.[28] Unable to cope, Herr Spielrein evaded his wife and daughter and hurried home to Rostov.

Ten days later Bleuler wrote him a detailed assessment of Sabina's first month in the hospital.[29] He noted a slight improvement and expressed cautious optimism: the tantrums she threw and the sometimes vicious pranks she played on the staff had lessened in both frequency and intensity. As per his custom, Bleuler involved the patient in her own treatment, and he treated this particular one like the doctor she wished to become. Sabina's behavior stabilized when he allowed her to make morning rounds with the doctors, but Bleuler made sure her private nurse was with her. He also allowed Sabina to observe some of the doctors' research in the hope that she would become interested in a project and work regularly scheduled hours. This proved to be a tremendous enticement, for she eagerly agreed to help Riklin collate the results of the association tests. Her behavior improved further because she liked it even better when Jung allowed her to sit quietly and observe him giving the test. If Sabina had an outburst, it usually happened after lunch, when she was taken away from Jung's laboratory and made to walk the grounds with her nurse. No one seems to have noticed that her admiration of Jung was becoming hero worship.

Bleuler concluded his report to her father by telling him that although Sabina's fees were paid through the end of September, he wanted an advance payment of 1,250 Swiss francs to cover the next three months, wisely ensuring that Herr Spielrein would not remove her before she was cured. As part of her treatment, Bleuler forbade all contact with her father for an unspecified period of time, but on October 1, when Jung left for his annual three-week stint of military duty, Sabina disobeyed Bleuler and wrote to her father. On the twelfth, when he had not replied and Jung was still away, her agitation verged on the uncontrollable. Bleuler changed his mind and told Herr Spielrein to write in the hope of calming her. Herr Spielrein kept silent, so Bleuler wrote a second time, but to no avail. Seeking to stabilize her, Bleuler began to let Sabina walk alone on the hospital grounds, then to walk with her nurse outside the gates. On the basis of her behavior during the outings, Bleuler accepted Sabina's opinion that she — his patient — was ready to begin medical studies in the spring. He urged Herr Spielrein to let her enroll in Zürich and agreed with her demand that she live alone in her own apartment. Without naming Jung, Bleuler told Herr Spielrein that Sabina had begun to assist one of the doctors at the hospital on "scientific work that interests her very much," adding that it was the only activity in which she showed "pleasure and consistency."[30]

Jung's first surviving letter to Herr Spielrein is from November 28, 1904, after he returned from his annual military duty with the Swiss Army Medical Corps. He wrote in his capacity as Bleuler's chief assistant and as if he had only just become acquainted with Sabina's case, not mentioning that he had been treating her for some time and that she regularly assisted him with the association studies. He said he found her relatively stable but thought her recovery would be slow and prolonged. The sole activity that had a positive effect was attending the required evening gatherings where the doctors reported on new discoveries. She was always on her best behavior before these regularly scheduled meetings because otherwise she could not participate.

Although Bleuler was still her doctor of record, it was Jung who apologized to Herr Spielrein for Sabina's "unreflected way of acting" when she wrote the letters. He promised that she would not do it again now that he was back, and December did pass without incident. When the New Year 1905 brought regression as Sabina exhumed memories of her past and churned through the real or imagined offenses of both parents, Jung put her to work in his laboratory. He also assigned extracurricular scientific readings and required her to write reports. Jung firmly forbade any further letter writing and kept her too busy even to think of it.

At the end of January, Frau Spielrein left the Baur au Lac and went home to Rostov. Jung told her she could visit later that spring, but only if she came alone, as other family members would disrupt Sabina's fragile stability. He told Frau Spielrein he hoped to bring Sabina to the point where she could write her weekly progress report, because the doctors were too busy to do it. He was happy to report that Sabina could now dine alone in a restaurant and usually ate hospital meals at the assistant doctors' table. By February Jung pronounced Sabina "for the most part, liberated from the hysterical symptoms" and reasonably cured.[31]

On April 18, Jung sent a letter to officials at Zürich University, stating that Sabina Spielrein had been at the Burghölzli since August 17, 1904, and would "probably stay sometime longer," but she still intended to enroll. Bleuler followed with a medical certificate dated April 27, in which he attested that Fräulein Spielrein was "not mentally ill," but was being treated only "for nervosity and hysterical symptoms." He, too, recommended her for matriculation.

Sabina was attending classes when Herr and Frau Spielrein came to Zürich in early May, bringing two of their sons with them.[32] Jung implored Herr Spielrein to have them, particularly the older one, matriculate in another university far from Zürich, since his involvement in her financial affairs seemed to trigger Sabina's worst behavior yet. She especially did not want to have to receive her allowance from him, so Jung told Herr Spielrein that if he did not wish to give Sabina's allowance to her directly and if he still wanted "to have a certain control" over her, Jung "would like to be in [his] service and take the money for Miss S." Apparently, Herr Spielrein rejected the suggestion, for no documentation exists to show otherwise.

Jung saw Sabina several times weekly during the summer, when she came for sessions as an outpatient and when she assisted him and Riklin with the association experiments. She was always calm, formal, and professional, especially after Herr Spielrein removed one son from Zürich and set the other up in an apartment far from Sabina's. It was Frau Spielrein who created a problem of an altogether different sort.

The most curious aspect of Sabina's education was her mother's insistence that she be kept totally unaware of sexual congress. Frau Spielrein was so insistent that Sabina remain a tabula rasa about sex that she actually used her influence to have the science curriculum in the Gymnasium modified to eliminate all references to reproduction.[33] She was horrified and refused to believe it when Jung euphemistically informed her that the most important part of her daughter's complex was based on sexuality.[34] Whenever mother and daughter were together, terrible arguments ensued, with the inevitable return of Sabina's hysterical behavior, that is, until Sabina discovered the perfect form of retaliation, which she practiced with a vengeance. Jung summarized it noncommittally in his report to Freud: "During the treatment the patient had the misfortune of falling in love with me. Now she always raves ostentatiously to her mother about her love, [and takes] a secret spiteful joy in her mother's terror. . . . That's why her mother now . . . wants someone else to treat her."

He told Freud that "naturally" he agreed.[35] Nothing untoward had yet transpired between Jung and his patient when Sabina began to taunt her mother. Several years later he told Freud without specifying what his "relationship" was with Sabina that he had continued to see her after her discharge from the Burghölzli because he "knew from experience that she would immediately relapse" if he withdrew: "I prolonged the relationship over the years and in the end found myself morally obliged, as it were, to devote a large measure of friendship to her."[36] Be that as it may, Sabina Spielrein's initially unfounded taunts to her mother became firmly lodged in her mind, and she began to take them seriously, believing they were true.

JUNG WAS in one sense relieved that the patient Sabina Spielrein was well enough recovered to begin an independent life in Zürich; in another, he was intrigued by her as a woman because she was unlike any he had known thus far in his emotionally restricted life. Chronologically she was three years younger than Emma, but she was light-years beyond her in worldliness and sophistication. Emma was docile and domestic, while Sabina represented the wildness of all that was foreign; as a Russian visitor to Switzerland she was allowed more kinds of freedom than any Swiss woman could even dream about, for even though Swiss universities had recently admitted women, none of the better classes matriculated.[37] When Sabina entered medical school, the only women were German, Russian, and a few Americans,[38] all generally disrespected and subjected to marginalization, exclusion, and harassment. Unlike Emma, who was shyly retiring and deferential with Carl's colleagues and professional acquaintances, Sabina was fearlessly outgoing and never hesitated to express her views as if she were their equal.[39] Although not really a natural beauty, she was dark and sultry, whereas Emma's natural serenity was frequently mistaken for bland dullness. While she was a patient, Sabina believed she was unattractive, paying such scant attention to her appearance that she wore a long pigtail and dressed in peasantlike creations, but these only gave her an air of exoticism. Emma, in contrast, was always modestly coifed, and no one noticed anything about her clothing but its suitability. Sabina's tantrums gave the impression that she whirled rather than walked; Emma lumbered, hugely pregnant with her second child as her first clung to her skirts.

Since the birth of Agathe Regina ("Aggi") on December 26, 1904, Emma had taken what she thought was a temporary respite from helping Carl to write his patient reports every night.[40] After the birth of Anna Margaretha ("Gret") on February 8, 1906, she was too tired to do more than listen to whatever Carl talked about in their few moments alone at the end of his long workdays. She and Hedwig Bleuler-Wasser commiserated over their lack of time for scholarly pursuits as they sat in the gardens, each with her two children, on pleasant afternoons. Sometimes they saw Sabina, now smartly dressed, as she came and went from her university classes to keep appointments with both their husbands. Emma and Hedwig were secure in their marriages, although "certain unkind remarks [about Sabina] passed between them," but they had no doubt that she was "certainly a force of nature, one to be reckoned with."[41]

There was another reason that Emma and Carl had so little time to converse in late 1905, when Sabina was officially his patient. He had taken on many new responsibilities after Riklin took Bleuler's former position as director of the Klinik Rheinau in October 1904. Jung was promoted to *Oberarzt*, Bleuler's first assistant, and in addition to his normal duties, he was put in charge of a newly created outpatient department, where former patients as well as new ones were treated without being hospitalized. With Riklin gone, Jung needed research assistance from others on the staff, so he initially enlisted Drs. Karl Abraham, Hans Maier, and Emma Fürst.[42] The director of the Burghölzli always held the chair in psychiatry at the University of Zürich, and Bleuler continued to teach; as his newly promoted first assistant, Jung was entitled to become the lecturer if his credentials warranted it. It was quite an honor, and Jung wanted it very much. Foremost among his new duties was preparation of the *Habilitationsschrift*, the research paper qualifying him to teach.

Emma was thrilled when Carl enlisted her to help Trudi with his burgeoning secretarial needs. In the spring of 1905, shortly before he assumed the new responsibilities, he took Emma to Berlin for what was supposed to be a holiday. To her dismay, he spent most of his days either in medical bookstores or visiting various hospital laboratories to observe comparative procedures and techniques.[43] Within a month of their return, the trip took on embarrassing and depressing associations for Emma, when she learned she was pregnant again. Just as her daughters were reaching the age where she was finding a bit of time to put her talents to use by helping her husband, another child was on the way to curtail her freedom. Her mood was only partly improved when Jung insisted that he still needed her help on the *Habilitationsschrift*, but instead of allowing her to participate in the research process, he made her one of his subjects.

Granted, psychoanalysis, the study of the mind and its mysteries, was in its earliest days, when none of the clearly delineated boundaries that govern the profession today had been established. Husbands analyzed wives, and analysts and patients engaged freely in social as well as sexual relationships. Analysts did not hesitate to hurl various clinical terms at other analysts, using their "science" as a pejorative weapon to wound or disable the opposition. In this battle, ethics and objectivity often took a backseat to an analyst's use of a personal theory to enhance his professional vision of what psychoanalysis was, or what it should become. Freud and Jung certainly exemplified many of these boundary-blurring positions throughout their long careers, and certainly one of Jung's earliest occurred when he made Emma take the association test.

Emma became "Subject No. 1," the "married woman who placed herself at [his] disposal in a most cooperative manner and gave [him] all the information [he] could possibly need."[44] Speaking as her doctor and not her husband, Jung said her primary "disturbance" was a "pregnancy-complex" and the fear it might cause her "to lose her husband's regard . . . in particular, [to cause] her husband's estrangement."[45]

Most of Jung's research, especially Emma's test, was done in late autumn of 1905 and coincided with his analysis of Sabina Spielrein. It was the first work assignment he gave Sabina as part of her treatment, and some years later, in 1909, she wrote her version of the event to Freud.[46] Here, the former patient was assuming the role of an analyst, as Spielrein told Freud that she could comment on Jung's "intellectual growth" because she had been "in a position to follow his development step by step" and had learned much "not only from him but also from observing him." She said Jung told her time and again to become a psychiatrist, saying, "Minds such as yours help advance science." She interpreted this to mean that theirs "was not just the usual doctor-patient relationship."

Sabina had had no direct or private contact with Emma until the time of her test, but she told Jung she had "dreamed" about how Emma complained that he was "so terribly dictatorial and that life with him was difficult." Sabina claimed he "did not respond to this like a doctor," but only made a vague remark that "living together was difficult." In fact, his remark was impeccably appropriate because it answered her question without revealing anything personal about his marriage, which both he and Emma, as befitting their conservative upper-class background, would never have discussed with anyone, let alone a patient who was in a crucial period of treatment and exhibiting severely presumptive behavior.

Spielrein told Freud that she had discussed women's "equality or intellectual independence" with Jung, but she did not add that the perfectly representative Swiss Dr. Jung responded in the only way a man of his culture and society could, that she was the "exception" to the rule because she was Russian and a foreigner, whereas Emma was "an ordinary [i.e., Swiss] woman and accordingly only interested in what interested her husband." The importance of Jung's comment should not be underestimated, for this profound cultural belief influenced much of his later thinking, writing, and analytic treatment of women, especially his attitude toward the upbringing and education of his own daughters.

Jung's research treatise was accepted by the university, and he received the appointment as lecturer in psychiatry. On October 21, 1905, he gave his first class, speaking on "The Psychopathological Significance of the Association Experiment."[47] He described how the field of psychopathology was finally becoming free of the "rigid schematic anatomical notions" that had dominated it, thanks mostly to investigations by Kraepelin, Wundt, Robert Sommer, and Aschaffenburg. Then he discussed findings and techniques for administering word association tests, finally settling on the question of subjects. He concluded that "analysis will not be difficult" with a man, especially a man who is of "excellent education, intellectually unbiased, and able to think objectively about his own feelings."[48] Jung thought that analysis of a "sensitive woman . . . would be considerably more difficult." He expressed the duality of his attitude toward women several paragraphs later, when he divided "normal" subjects into two groups: "men and women."[49] He began with women, whose complex he believed was "in essence, usually of an erotic nature." His explanation of the difference was vague; he said that he used "'erotic' in the noble literary sense, as opposed to the medical," perhaps differentiating between a woman's mind and body, for he singled out "apparently intellectual women" to express his contention that "no woman who thinks scientifically will take [it] amiss." Jung considered the "erotic complex" in men to be "on the same level as that of ambition, or striving for physical, intellectual, or financial power. Money usually plays the leading part." He allowed that there were men in whom the "erotic complex is all pervasive," but he insisted that "the exception . . . proves the rule."

Jung's interest in psychopathology led him to experiment with legal evidence, "that most unpredictable element in legal proceedings."[50] Building on William Stern's "Contributions to the Psychology of Evidence," which he called a "real treasure-house," he investigated "the 'diagnosis' of a criminal case by the study of the psychological make-up of the witness." He believed such findings could be used "for practical purposes" in several ways: to identify complexes that held "individual significance"; to help identify the one important factor in the completely disturbed mental life of an hysteric; and (although he did not explain further) to illuminate complexes present in dementia praecox (as schizophrenia was then called).

He also cited another application of an experiment by two pupils of the famed criminal psychologist Hans Gross (whose son, Otto, would become one of his most controversial cases several years later), that is, that a criminal who knows the facts of the case in which he is involved will "unconsciously" betray his involvement. Jung had one "powerful objection to the practical forensic application of the method," offering "blushing, which so often occurs as a result of baseless accusations, [and] has before now been interpreted as a symptom of guilt."

Even as he admitted that "the truth of this experiment is not obvious, it has to be tested," Jung was applying it in a real case. An elderly gentleman contacted him in September 1905 because he noticed that various sums of money were missing from his house during the previous several weeks. He suspected "a young man of eighteen, his protégé," with whom he lived, but he did not want to embarrass the young man or his family. Rather than go to the police, he asked Jung to examine the protégé for psychological evidence of his guilt under the pretext of a consultation about other ailments. When Jung collated the test results, he found so much evidence of the young man's guilt that he accused him directly, and after some protestation, the young man confessed. Jung concluded that "the experiment was a complete success" but in the next sentence added that such success must still be "examined critically."

Officers of the Zürich courts were not so hesitant, however, to apply his findings. They called Jung frequently during the next several years to testify in various proceedings and gave his testimony the highest regard, no matter that verdicts rendered were often at variance with his recommendations. Such forays into the city during the bustling daylight business hours provided a stimulating change from the unending sameness and cloistered isolation of the hospital. Frequently Jung took lunch in one of the restaurants or paused for late-afternoon refreshment before boarding the tram in which he and it both turned their backs on the city to mosey up the long hill that led to the hospital. The ride usually left him with a vague indefinable malaise. Years later, when trying to re-call the exact feelings of his young adulthood, Jung speculated about those times when he knew that "something fateful will happen here."[51]

One of those moments was his first sight of Emma, halfway up the staircase at the Ölberg; the other concerned the months, even years, leading up to his first meeting with Sigmund Freud. There was a "knowledge" inside him, the elderly Jung remembered, that "something unconsciously fateful . . . was bound to happen." It belonged somewhere in his future, and he already knew about it "without knowing it."

CHAPTER 7

"Who Is the Boss in This Hospital?"

The year 1906 marked Jung's sixth in the Burghölzli and the beginning of his international reputation. Each year he was on staff brought an incremental increase through two arenas: his writings about the association experiments, and the opinions he expressed about the state of psychiatry in general that appeared in a variety of periodicals. The Burghölzli's reputation as one of the world's most important research hospitals drew doctors from throughout Europe and America who came to observe Jung and returned to their homelands touting his successes.[1] He had the personal satisfaction of learning of their praise when their colleagues, who had not been to Zürich, contacted him to learn more about his work.[2]

Jung's reputation was so sterling that even the controversial professor of psychology at Harvard Dr. Hugo Munsterberg was not above using the association test courtroom experiments as if they were his own.[3] In a notorious murder trial in Boise, Idaho, Munsterberg boasted that his expertise was based on having administered "nearly one hundred [association] tests and experiments" to the chief suspect, omitting all references to Jung (and Riklin, Bleuler, and the other doctors whose prior research had made these tests so highly regarded in courtroom procedure).

When Munsterberg's remarks were reported in the three newspapers Jung read each day, the *Neue Zürcher Zeitung* (Zürich), *Le Matin* (Paris), and the *Daily Telegraph* (London), he wrote to Harvard's President Eliot, imploring him to reprimand the professor, who "does not mention who the discoverer of this method is, so that some journals have taken for granted that he is the sole originator of all this."[4] By doing so, Jung continued, Munsterberg "violates all customs of international literary etiquette." Munsterberg dismissed Jung's allegations, saying "everybody knew where the technique had been developed, and moreover such attributions were not appropriate in popular journals."[5] Emma tried to persuade Carl that even backhanded compliments carried recognition, albeit grudging, but he was still angered by such blatant usurpation.[6]

Jung thrived under his growing renown, considering it the natural, expected result of his hard work and intellectual acumen. Others, however, had a different perspective. Much negative commentary arose from those who accused him of so needing adulation that he would stoop to various unpleasantries to get it, and their remarks influenced what many others thought of or wrote about him from that time onward. Such vituperative talk may have been started for any number of reasons, from those who envied him for having married an heiress to those who could not match his robust health and appetite for hard work. Some called him vain and self-centered; others said he was an opportunistic bully. Remarks about his arrogance multiplied, and he was accused of running roughshod over those who dared to question his methods let alone disagree with his results. There is a modicum of truth in every one of these opinions, but as in so many instances throughout Jung's life, the part cannot be made to stand for the whole. Individual judgments such as these should be noted and compiled; final judgments should be held in abeyance until the conclusion of the long and complex life he actually lived.

But in these particular years, Jung's brash behavior earned more enmity than friendship. A remark the Burghölzli's former director Auguste Forel allegedly made during Jung's first year at the hospital was now being repeated by the newer colleagues who had not been there to hear it firsthand. "Who is the boss in this hospital," Forel is supposed to have demanded, "Dr. Bleuler or Herr Jung?"[7] Forel's question was really an insult, for he deliberately addressed Jung as Mr. rather than Dr.

This period marked the start of twenty years of active enmity between Bleuler and Jung that, while both were still at the Burghölzli, varied from the occasional veiled remark to openly hostile invective, often before shocked doctors or frightened patients.[8] The situation between the two had greatly deteriorated since 1902, when Bleuler, as supervisor of Jung's dissertation, declared himself convinced of his protégé's "high scientific qualities."[9] Now Bleuler damned with faint praise Jung's "cold intellectual insight."[10] There were many professional reasons for the mounting tension between the chief doctor and his first assistant, as their research led them in different directions toward opposing conclusions, but the personal were at play as well. And, in one particular and widely commented upon instance, the two were combined.

Jung enjoyed teaching at the University of Zürich and took his lectures seriously. He was always well prepared and, unlike most other professors (especially Bleuler), never waited until the last moment to appear. Rather, he went early to sit quietly on one of the benches in the corridor, where anyone who was interested in his subject could talk to him or ask questions. He "kept his students spellbound by his temperament and the wealth of his ideas," was communicative and open, and relished how his ideas were being discussed by the community at large.[11]

Jung's lectures became so popular that they had to be moved to the largest room in the building, and as they were considered an open forum, anyone interested in the topic, whether affiliated with the university or not, could attend. The wealthy women of Zürich who had the time and leisure to further their interests in history, culture, and ideas began to frequent Jung's lectures because they touched on so many more engaging points than Bleuler's coldly clinical explanations of laboratory technique and statistical figures. Jung incorporated into his lectures remarks about everything from hysteria to hypnotism in case studies of individuals, many of them women, that his audience could relate to their own lives. He introduced ideas ranging from family dynamics to the thought processes of writers (Conrad Ferdinand Meyer being one example) or musicians (Robert Schumann being another). There was a general intellectual caliber to his lectures that made these women eager for further enlightenment, and they began to form small study groups that met afterward in their homes to read and discuss the many sources he cited. Jung soon acquired a devoted, highly visible female following who marched with poise and self-assurance into his every lecture, commandeering the best seats and thereby earning the enmity of the students, who had to stand at the rear of the auditorium.[12] These women were dubbed the *Zürichberg Pelzmäntel*, the "fur-coat ladies" from the richest part of the city, dismissed by those who scorned both them and Jung as — in the contemporary language of the daughter of one — little more than "sex-starved groupies or postmenopausal hysterics."[13] Even though Jung would have been hard-pressed to find a spare moment to be unfaithful to his wife, his reputation as a ladies' man was well along toward acceptance as gospel truth, furthered on two fronts: first, by the wealthy women who built his "local fame as a wizard,"[14] and second, by Sabina Spielrein's wanton tale to anyone within earshot of her "love," which was now common gossip among medical students who were happy to interpret it as an affair, even though there was no proof.

As his lectures increased in popularity, Jung began to think that, because of his divergences from Bleuler on both subject matter and theoretical outlook, the university should create two separate chairs in psychology. Everyone knew he "chafe[d]" under Bleuler's direction, but the reason most frequently given was also the most negative and the one most repeated by those searching for a reason to dislike him: that Jung believed "clinical psychology should be rather in the background and the teaching of his doctrines should be more important."[15] Jung's version was more to the point and reflected their growing differences: Jung was interested in what the individual patient could tell him about the illness and its symptoms, while for doctors such as Bleuler, "the psychology of the mental patient played no role whatsoever." Jung accused him of preferring to make diagnoses by comparing symptoms and compiling statistics.[16] He was not entirely fair to Bleuler, who was in charge of a large publicly funded teaching hospital where the research he conducted was exactly what cantonal authorities expected.

Still, Jung was criticized for his attitude toward the Burghölzli's patients. As

Oberarzt, Bleuler's chief deputy, his primary duty was administration. He was expected to know the history of every patient and to match each one with the appropriate assistant doctors, whose work and treatment schedules he was supposed to set and coordinate. His detractors also accused him of supreme indifference, of wanting to know only the patient's "unconscious content, dreams, or hallucinations," to the neglect of the often tedious work amassing the "personal biography [as found in] the case history."[17] No one discerned that his interest was already moving far beyond the clinical treatment of specific psychotic cases and into the general study of the neurotic, where his insights and observations about the human condition coalesced to become the work of his entire lifetime. And that, too, depending on his reader, is either praised or reviled.

But while he was *Oberarzt*, the assistant doctors united in claiming that Jung was such a lax and disorganized administrator that they had to rely on their mutual goodwill and collegiality to apportion the work fairly. For their own amusement, they mimicked Jung's routine when he made the obligatory afternoon patient rounds: They alleged that he bellowed up to the wards from the bottom of the stairwell, "Is there anything interesting going on up there among you?,"[18] not even bothering to go up to see for himself. As his shouts took the patients by surprise, no one ever answered the disembodied voice, so Jung used their silence as the excuse to head back to his laboratory with all due speed.

His local hospital reputation became that of the doctor who did not pull his weight, even as his international reputation mounted steadily. Requests for private consultations and lectures multiplied, and as this was the direction in which Jung's intellectual interest veered, he began to ask for repeated leaves without pay, some as short as several weeks, others as long as a semester. That he could follow his personal bent was naturally resented by most of the other doctors, who depended on their salaries and were severely impeded by a lack of free time for their own research pursuits. Bleuler's output remained particularly scant, which many scholars attribute to the press of his hospital duties. He did approve every leave Jung requested but became increasingly critical as the number increased.[19] What exacerbated their differences most, however, was Jung's decision to contact Sigmund Freud in the spring of 1906.

Bleuler had been corresponding with Freud for several years[20] and frequently expressed to the staff his admiration for the Viennese neurologist. In a 1904 review of Leopold Löwenfeld's *Psychic Obsessions*, Bleuler singled out Freud for special praise, writing that his studies on hysteria and dreams revealed "part of a new world, though by no means all of it," and that while "consciousness" allows one to see "in its theater only the puppets," Freud's research showed "many of the strings that move the figures."[21] Such regard could not help but make a strong impression on Jung, who subsequently turned his theoretical affinities from Zürich (Bleuler) and Paris (Charcot, Janet) to Vienna (and Freud). Since 1903, he had been paying more attention not only to Freud's writings but also to the writings of others who wrote about him,[22] which at the time were mostly negative. No matter what others such as Ziehen (who called everything Freud wrote nonsense) or Hoch (who said psychoanalysis was merely another name for religion) may have thought, Jung believed attention still had to be paid to Freud.[23] When he published the now-classic *Interpretation of Dreams* in 1900, Freud left behind forever his reputation as a little-known neurologist who held eccentric and unorthodox views and cemented his standing as the founder of a new theory. In the words of the great historian of psychoanalysis Henri Ellenberger, "Freud had become a celebrity and a much sought after therapist" who "received signs of acknowledgement and devotion from everywhere."[24]

Nonetheless, Jung's "task of getting [Freud] properly placed"[25] within his own work took a certain degree of courage. "When I started with Freud, I knew that I was risking my career,"[26] he wrote many years later when he tried to explain that he had already done so much independent research on the same subject that no one could have faulted him for presenting it without acknowledging that Freud had covered much of the same territory. He said it was "far from pleasant" to discover how much his association studies agreed with Freud's theorizing about the mechanisms of repression, but intellectual honesty demanded that he say so when he published.[27]

Also, there was a distinct difference in their stations in life: Jung was on the verge of what then seemed a brilliant academic career as a university lecturer and private consultant, whereas Freud was an independent theorist, "*persona non grata* in the academic world" and isolated within a self-imposed "scientific Calvary."[28] There was no question that for Jung to espouse Freud's work openly in the international scientific community "would have been damaging." Nevertheless, when Jung published the *Diagnostic Association Studies* in 1906, his citations increased beyond the casual references that had dotted his earlier writings to become an integral part of the text, clearly demonstrating the high regard in which Jung and, by extension, Bleuler and the other researchers at the Burghölzli held Freud. In short, Jung was preparing to jump into the intellectually unknown, with all its risks and possible rewards, in order to follow Freud.

Jung drew extensively on Freud's "Fragment of an Analysis of a Case of Hysteria" for the last essay in the book, one that dealt with a case of obsessional neurosis that he treated by first administering the association test and then following it with several weeks of intense and frequent psychoanalysis. The treatment took place mostly in June 1905, after which the patient was dismissed from the hospital. In November she returned to the Burghölzli in high spirits to thank Jung and tell him she considered herself cured. With such verification, Jung thought the time was right to send his book to Freud, and he did so in early spring 1906, without first clearing it with Bleuler. Bleuler was miffed but kept his counsel and said nothing, even though he resented what he described privately as an affront to his authority.[29]

A correspondence and, later, a personal relationship began between Jung and

Freud that lasted until 1914. Despite its brevity, it arguably overshadowed the rest of their lives. Even as an old man, Jung became emotional whenever he spoke of Freud; Freud evidently thought Jung's letters and books important enough that he included them among the limited number of possessions he was permitted to take to England when he fled the Nazis in 1938. At various times and in various ways throughout their writings, lectures, and conversations, the two men tried to analyze what happened or what went wrong between them, but in the years since their friendship ended, the amount of writing devoted to it and its subsequent rupture has grown exponentially, as partisans for each man and his theory have sought to assign either praise or blame to the other party. The known facts are few, public, and distinct; the interpretations are many, partisan, and often "single-minded and humorless."[30]

Jung's first letter to Freud appears to be lost, so Freud's reply on April 11, 1906, begins the extant published correspondence.[31] Freud thanked Jung for sending the *Diagnostic Association Studies* but said that in his "impatience" he had already bought and read the book. He immediately established his primacy in research, expressing delight that Jung's independent experimentation proved "everything *I* have said about . . . our discipline" (author's emphasis).[32] Freud had been so thrilled by Bleuler's comments in the review of Löwenfeld's book that he described it to his friend Wilhelm Fliess as "the absolutely stunning recognition of my point of view . . . by an official psychiatrist, Bleuler, in Zürich. Just imagine, a full professor of psychiatry."[33] Only the exclamation point was missing. Now along came Jung, the esteemed Zürich lecturer in psychiatry, to put the glorious frosting on Freud's already delectable cake. Switzerland, with its many private clinics and fine public hospitals attached to universities in Basel, Geneva, and Zürich, was regarded as the leading center of academic psychoanalysis in the world. Now two of its most important figures, Bleuler and Jung, were openly espousing Freud's ideas and methodologies.

When Jung sent his book to Freud, the association tests and the writings that followed arguably made him an equal in research and only slightly inferior in reputation, so their standings in the psychological community were almost on a par. Doctors throughout the world studied and adopted Jung's results, which the general public became aware of through the likes of Munsterberg and the popular press. Freud was slowly emerging from a period of self-enforced privacy, but he was nevertheless a researcher whose ideas everyone in the field had to take note of, even if only to dismiss them.[34] The main difference between them was their respective ages: Freud, born in 1856, was almost fifty; Jung, born in 1875, was almost thirty-one.

It was Freud, however, who dictated in his very first letter how the relationship would unfold. Jung's role was to corroborate rather than compete: "I am confident that *you* will often be in a position to back *me* up," he wrote (author's emphasis). The phrase, most likely written to assure collegiality, becomes ironic in light of the father/son, leader/disciple relationship both men were so eager to establish and accept in the beginning. Freud wrote that he would "also gladly accept correction,"[35] but as their history unfolded, he was incapable of doing so and it became a sore bone of contention between them.

SIX WEEKS after Jung received Freud's letter, he was off on another of his unpaid leaves, this time to attend the Congress of Southwest German Neurologists and Psychiatrists at Baden-Baden. Emma, as she usually did during his absences, took Agathe and the infant Gret to her family home in Schaffhausen. Relieved by the absence of "the whirlwind" Jung, the assistant doctors "drew breath and conducted [their] affairs in tranquillity."[36]

Jung made his first public defense of Freud at the Baden-Baden congress when he rebutted Gustav Aschaffenburg, the pioneer of association testing who called Freud's method "wrong in most cases, objectionable in many and super-fluous in all."[37] Jung initiated "a lively correspondence"[38] with Aschaffenburg that was not persuasive in changing his views, so he wrote a rebuttal that was published in the same journal the month after Aschaffenburg's paper.[39] Jung wrote his rebuttal with "honest conviction,"[40] but Ernest Jones, Freud's most partisan biographer, described it as ineffective,[41] probably because Jung expressed too much hesitation about Freud's insistence that "all hysteria is re-ducible to sexuality." Jung told Freud he hoped he had not "misrepresented" his belief, but he had nevertheless "tailored it a bit to [his own] subjective stand-point."[42] He added that he was willing to concede that not all but only an "in-definitely large number of cases of hysteria derive from sexual roots."[43]

Jung's second surviving letter to Freud is dated October 5, 1906, and in it he again expressed reservations about the primacy of sex. With all due tact and diplomacy, he told Freud he agreed that the "genesis of hysteria" was "predom-inantly" but "not exclusively" sexual. Freud replied the same day he received the letter, saying Jung's writings made it clear that his "appreciation" of Freud's pronouncements on sexuality was not total and complete. He chided Jung, stat-ing that because of his research into obsessional neurosis, he should know "how consummately the sexual factor hides."[44]

The dates of the two letters above are as important as their content in pro-viding an illustration of how the correspondence developed: Freud replied the very day he received a letter from Jung; Jung, as his next letter, dated October 23, shows, did not normally reply until considerable time had elapsed. There was no ulterior reason; it was merely that Jung was so busy with his many and varied responsibilities that to fix a time for daily correspondence was impossi-ble. Often he postponed his increasingly voluminous mail until he could no longer put it off and then stayed up half the night dashing off hasty, apologetic letters. He had no secretarial help other than what his sister could spare from the nursing duties that paid her salary, so he usually scribbled brief replies by hand. In contrast, Freud's life was enviably smooth, for everyone in his house-hold, from his wife, Martha, and their children to his sister-in-law Minna, loveless, and each partner brooded for years over lost first loves. Sabina's father was moody and tyrannical, frequently taking to his bed or threatening suicide when even his slightest wish was thwarted. Her mother was exceedingly vain and compensated for her unhappiness by buying great quantities of clothing and jewelry as she traipsed throughout Europe with the child Sabina in tow.

Sabina was the eldest of five children, followed by a sister who died in infancy and three brothers who were left at home with their father and with whom she was in constant conflict. Sabina's intelligence was recognized early by her parents, and her mother sent her to an elementary school in Warsaw run on the then-experimental Fröbel model.[22] In the five years she was enrolled, she added French and German to her native Russian and Polish. By the age of seven, she was fluent in all these languages, and she later added English, in which she was passably good. She returned to Rostov for her Gymnasium studies, there learning Latin, Greek, and ancient Hebrew. By her last year at the Gymnasium, she was known as a formidable intellect, but the various conflicts at home were so intense and the symptoms she exhibited in response so alarming that her parents had her admitted to a sanatorium in Interlaken, Switzerland, run by a Dr. Heller.

Jung explained her symptoms in his report to Freud. When Sabina was between the ages of four and seven, Herr Spielrein vented his rages and dissatisfactions with his wife upon his daughter, beating her repeatedly on the buttocks. The little girl became sexually aroused by the beatings and began to masturbate by pressing her thighs together.[23] Eventually, no beatings were necessary for arousal, only threats, curses, or even a menacing motion of her father's hands. As an adolescent, she could not look at his hands without becoming sexually aroused.[24] According to Sabina, at this time one of her brothers became involved in her bizarre behavior, either when he was punished by their father or when he himself became abusive toward her; whatever the context, the mere sight of him aroused violent fantasies and she could not bear to be near him.[25] By the time Sabina was brought to Switzerland when she was almost eighteen, she could not meet anyone's gaze directly, could not eat in company because of an irrational fear that she would immediately defecate, and when not prone to violent outbursts, usually made faces and stuck out her tongue in derision.

She was so unruly in the Heller sanatorium that after a few short weeks in which she "tortured the caretakers to the quick," they dismissed her. The Spielreins approached Constantin von Monakow, a Swiss neurologist (1853–1930) of Russian origin who also directed a private sanatorium, but he received a warning letter from Heller and refused to admit her. Although well able to afford a private sanatorium, Sabina thus came by default to the Zürich public asylum. Frau Spielrein literally dumped her embarrassing daughter at the Burghölzli and then ensconced herself in the luxury of the finest hotel in Zürich, the Baur au Lac, and proceeded to enjoy life. A week later, on August 24, 1904, Jung sent obeyed a daily routine that permitted him to concentrate on "the single-minded pursuit of his mission." Freud described himself to Jung as a member of "the class 'obsessive,' each member of which lives in a world shut off from the rest."[45] "His heroic effort at self-mastery in the service of concentrated work had chained him to a most precise timetable," and "he lived . . . by the clock."[46]

Throughout their letters, Jung's apologies for his prolonged delays frequently crossed with Freud's expressions of impatience, anxious hopes, and blatant entreaties for Jung to write to him. Freud's eagerness for contact was especially apparent at the time of Jung's December 1906 publication, *The Psychology of Dementia Praecox*.[47] He was elated to find that his name appeared throughout but surprised to find it usually connected with equivocation or disclaimer, especially because Jung had just taken his side a second time against fierce vocal opposition during a conference of psychiatrists in Tübingen.[48]

Jung's equivocation began in the introduction. Although he stated that even the most superficial glance at his work would show how deeply he was indebted to Freud's "brilliant discoveries," he still insisted upon the scholarly necessity of defining and explaining his own views in relation to them. His stated intention throughout was to be scrupulously fair to Freud's dogma while nevertheless maintaining "independent judgement." In his next several sentences, Jung spelled out what would become the ultimate difference between him and Freud: he acknowledged "the complex mechanisms of dreams and hysteria" but was unwilling to grant "the psychological universality which Freud, it seems, postulates . . . [to] infantile sexual trauma."

It took two letters from Freud to reassure Jung that he had not overstepped the bounds of acceptable criticism and that his independent thinking would be tolerated — at least for the time being.[49] Freud told Jung that even if he had been really distressed, he would have found proper diplomatic language to hide his true feelings, for it would not be prudent to alienate the "ablest helper" who had thus far embraced his theory.[50] It was his most direct statement about how important "the Zürich School" was to him.

Jung, however, could not let the matter drop there. Determined to make Freud understand why they "did not see eye to eye on certain points," he took the time to cite five different instances, showing how and where their differences originated.[51] These five points also indicated how great were the contrasts between them, but again they were unnoticed and regarded as unimportant until hindsight came into play. Jung's five points began with his patients, who were, for the most part, uneducated schizophrenics (although he was still using the term "dementia praecox"), whereas most of Freud's theorizing came from self-examination and was based on his own experiences. Jung cited his upbringing and the influence of his social and cultural background on the formation of his character; left unsaid were the vast differences between the Swiss cities of Basel and Zürich and Vienna, and between the Christian Jung and Jewish Freud. Jung spoke of how his scientific training differed from Freud's and modestly claimed that it meant his clinical experience, in comparison, was smaller. In obeisance to the older man's longer experience, Jung claimed his own talent for psychoanalysis was lesser, "both in quantity and quality." As a further sop, he also regretted his "lack of personal contact" with Freud and the "regrettable defect" in his training that compromised his ability to explicate Freud's ideas in any other than an introductory or provisional manner. Jung admitted that Freud had his "finger on the weak points" of dream analysis in his book and then made a startling confession that moved the correspondence from professional equality to a level of personal affinity. He admitted that he was the "friend" whose dream he had analyzed and whose "personal and family circumstances" he knew well.[52] Admitting that "the analysis and use of one's own dreams is a ticklish business at best," Jung used the neutral pronoun to say that, no matter how objective "one" tried to be, there were "inhibitions emanating from the dream" that were impossible to avoid.[53]

"My wife is rich," Jung confided, apropos of nothing, telling Freud that Emma rejected his first proposal "for various reasons" before finally accepting him. "I am happy with my wife in every way," he wrote; there was no "sexual failure" between them, but "more likely a social one." Jung described his dream succinctly in the book: He saw horses being raised to great heights by thick cables and was particularly impressed by a powerful brown stallion, all strapped up and being lifted like a package. The cables supporting this particular horse broke suddenly, and it crashed to the street. The dreamer feared the horse was dead, but it leaped up and galloped off. The dreamer then noted that the stallion was dragging a heavy log and wondered how it could move so quickly while carrying such a weight; he feared it might cause an accident. Then a small horse bearing a rider appeared and moved slowly in front of the large brown one, thus modulating its pace. While the dreamer was still worrying that the smaller horse might be run over by the stallion, a cab appeared and drove in front of both, thus causing an even slower pace. The dreamer relaxed, thinking "now all is well; the danger is over."[54]

In the text, Jung had the dreamer describe to the doctor and writer how he had recently seen a periodical in which skyscrapers were being built, and how he was particularly struck by *"work* at such a dizzy height." In the dream, the horses were secured by the same sort of sling-straps as those who were being lowered into the mines for "labour, toil, etc." Jung/doctor asked Jung/dreamer whether the heights and depths represented by skyscrapers and mines might be bringing work and toil together. Jung/dreamer replied that he was an ardent mountaineer and had recently wanted to climb a particularly dangerous one, but his wife, who was pregnant, would not let him do it. Also, because of her pregnancy, they had had to forgo a planned trip to the United States to which both had very much looked forward. This was "particularly disagreeable" to the dreamer, for he already had "business dealings" there and hoped that a personal visit would help him in his quest to "establish new and important connections."

On the prospect of this voyage, the dreamer had "built vague plans for the future" that were "rather lofty and flattering to his ambition." Jung/doctor wrote that further analysis of Jung/dreamer revealed that he saw himself as the large brown stallion, and the log it dragged might well have corresponded to his own youthful Zofingian nickname, "the Barrel." The dreamer thought the rider of the smaller horse may well have been his wife, and that the cab that slowed her down was filled with "a whole cartload of children."

The dream's ultimate meaning, according to the doctor, was that the dreamer feared too many constraints upon his career by the advent of too many children. The dream's "top layer" expressed "clearly enough the hopes and disappointments of an upwardly striving career," but beneath it was hidden "an extremely personal matter which may well have been accompanied by painful feelings." In his letter to Freud, Jung alluded to his increasing attraction to Sabina Spielrein by admitting that marital satisfaction did not prevent dreams of illegitimate sexual desires "that had better not see the light of day."[55] Perhaps, he posited, the "little rider" was Bleuler, who already had two sons,[56] and perhaps the dreamer was envious because he had merely fathered two daughters.

Freud saw through the hesitations and equivocations of Jung's self-analysis but did not respond to them until New Year's Day 1907.[57] Whether true or not, he told Jung he had already guessed the dreamer's identity and had prepared a response even before Jung sent his self-interpretation. Jung replied eight days later, apologizing for the delay by saying he was "rather embarrassed at having played hide-and-seek." He told Freud there was a very good reason for his not having made the obvious connection that the "log" the stallion dragged equaled a "penis": he confessed that he had dictated this portion of the book to Emma, and he found himself incapable of speaking "impersonally" while she wrote.[58]

EMMA WAS indeed rich, as Jung had disclosed to Freud, and even though Swiss law granted him legal control of her money, she managed the household budget and decided how much he could spend. Emma liked to travel, and the trip to America had been her idea. She thought they should accept the invitations proffered by doctors who wanted to reciprocate for their own sojourns at the Burghölzli and had been chagrined when her second pregnancy prevented the journey. From the beginning of their marriage, Emma's money paid for household help, which now included a nanny for the two girls as well as a daily maid and twice-weekly laundress. She wanted freedom from all housewifely duties, not only because a woman of her social class did not do them but also because she was intelligent and wanted to continue her self-education. In the early "Burghölzli years" of their marriage, Emma and Carl shared a mutuality of interests that led her to serve when he allowed as an excellent editor and critic of his writings, as well as his general amanuensis. Even before he began his correspondence with and public defense of Freud, Emma realized that Carl needed secretarial help. She wanted to provide all of it, but he resisted, mostly for reasons having to do with her social standing. She wanted to attend his lectures, but all too often he found reasons why she should not. He knew that her sharp eye missed none of the adulation that came from the many women who surrounded him before and after each lecture, and he was uneasy about how she would react to it.

Now that Jung and Bleuler's relationship was becoming increasingly formal and prickly, Emma and Hedwig reflected it by aping their husbands' behavior, even though they still were subject to each other's company because their children were playmates. Hedwig was known for her "terribly wounding honesty," and it was common hospital gossip that she had told Emma "the Spielrein girl was throwing herself at Carl."[59] It was, for Emma, the last straw.

Living in the hospital may have suited the Bleulers, who both lived for their work, but Emma was tired of the lack of privacy and wanted a house of her own. She was as aware of the dazzling speed of Carl's professional ascent as he was, and her ambitions matched his: she was the first to suggest that he should think about the proper moment to leave the restrictive life of the Burghölzli to engage in his own research and build his own practice. Emma also shared Carl's desire for a son, and as the trappings of their two daughters gave her claustrophobia in the apartment that had once seemed so grand and gracious, she wanted to look for a suitable house or land on which to build one.

Thus, it seemed that all things personal and professional were coalescing at the end of 1906 to produce the "social" crisis Jung had described to Freud. The dream of the brown stallion was a major embodiment, albeit only one. Emma was indeed "rich," in the many different ways already enumerated, but she shared every one of her husband's visions and desires and was ready to put every aspect, from her fortune to the potentialities inherent in her social standing, at his disposal. Emma offered unlimited possibilities to Carl, and although he was self-confident enough to embrace and accept them as nothing less than his due, the sheer volume of activity in his daily life was so overwhelming that, for the first time ever, he needed to stand back and take stock of everything that had happened to "Pastor's Carl" since his arrival in Zürich seven years earlier. Self-reflection had not been his strong suit during these years, but now he found himself badly in need of introspection.

He started with the personal. Holidays and special occasions were usually celebrated in Schaffhausen with Emma's family and their friends. Bertha Rauschenbach was infinitely respectful of her doctor son-in-law and treated him as the godlike dispenser of all wisdom, but the Hombergers tended to ignore him. Gret had become an imperious woman who never hesitated to express an opinion, no matter how scathing, and in these years she had scant respect for Carl's professional stature and future prospects. Ernst, her husband, was a company director who had risen to the pinnacle of his profession, was secure in every aspect of his professional life, and felt content with his elegant wife and growing family. As chief investor of the Rauschenbach family fortune, he was a supremely confident man who would not brook the most tentative question about his investment strategies. An otherwise gentle man, Ernst interpreted even the most polite request for financial information as criticism or interference, so everyone, including Carl, learned not to ask. It was frustrating for a man of his temperament not to know how much money would come each year until the official statements and dividend checks arrived.

And professionally there was his growing antagonism with Bleuler, who suddenly seemed eager to undermine Jung's thriving but still fragile rapport with Freud. Seemingly out of the blue, Bleuler dispatched Max Eitingon, one of the volunteer doctors at the hospital, to go to Vienna to meet Freud and report on what psychiatry might gain from the study of his psychoanalysis.[60] Heir of a wealthy Orthodox Jewish family of Russian origin who had settled in Germany, where he was educated, Eitingon worked as a "volunteer" rather than as a staff doctor. Suave, sophisticated, and ironic, he enjoyed making thinly veiled allusions to the difference between his money and "Jung's wife's money."[61] Jung disliked him intensely, calling him "a totally impotent gasbag," but one whom he nonetheless envied for his "polygamous instinct."[62]

Jung was even more envious when Eitingon returned from Vienna and boasted of having attended several meetings of the Vienna Psychoanalytic Society in January 1907.[63] He had also met privately with Freud and was full of anecdotes about the intimacy of their personal meetings, long walks, and the intense conversations that later came to be known as the first training analysis.[64] The two men spent enough time together that when Eitingon returned to Zürich, he could hardly talk of anyone or anything else. His "personal devotion" to Freud "came to know no bounds, and he was second to none in his hero-worship and total dedication."[65] "You were the first to come to the lonely one," Freud wrote to Eitingon, not once but several times, a remark guaranteed to increase Jung's inquietude and sense of displacement.[66]

Eitingon's visit to Freud was the catalyst for two crucial decisions Jung made in early January 1907. Still unwilling to surrender his intellectual independence, he hedged by swearing to Freud that he would never forsake any part of Freud's theory that he considered "essential," because he was "far too committed to it." Also, he decided that the time had come for "the long-desired pleasure of a personal conversation." He wrote that he was "firmly resolved" to devote his entire spring vacation to travel to Vienna to meet Freud.[67] He would make the pilgrimage and pay the homage at his earliest opportunity.

CHAPTER 8

⸺

Divorce/Force, Choice/Pain

On October 23, 1906, "at the risk of boring" Freud, Jung described a "difficult" case he was treating with Freud's "method," "an hysteric" Russian girl, aged twenty, who had been ill for six years.[1] Jung condensed Sabina Spielrein's patient history into one succinct paragraph culled from the longer version he had written in 1905 when her mother dismissed him. Jung said he would be grateful for advice from Freud that would help him treat the patient, a remark since interpreted as "the first known request for analytic supervision."[2] As usual, Freud replied immediately, pleased that the Russian girl was a student, because persons without education made unsuitable subjects.[3]

Neither spent much time discussing Spielrein's case. This single clinical, impersonal exchange was the only time either mentioned her until the following July.[4] What makes it interesting is that Jung presented the case with such dispassionate detachment. The professionalism with which he wrote about Spielrein, coupled with Freud's totally impersonal response, validate Jung's claim that she was still nothing more than an interesting patient. He neither hinted at nor asked Freud if, by chance, her mother had contacted him earlier; nor did he make any reference to Sabina's proclamations to all and sundry that she and Jung were lovers. Though some at the Burghölzli could not resist such titillating gossip, most considered it harmless because Emma dismissed it so brusquely, even though Jung was seeing Spielrein privately. She was not a paying patient, but for the previous six or eight months, they had fallen into a routine whereby she came to the Burghölzli several times each week for confidential talks that might have been deemed therapeutic sessions had she paid for them. These meetings almost always took place in Jung's laboratory or office, where others came and went freely. Sometimes when the weather was pleasant, they took long walks on the grounds, where everyone could see them. Here, too, there was no privacy.

A new wrinkle appeared in the fabric of rumors about Jung's alleged "womanizing" when some of the *Zürichberg Pelzmäntel* began to invite the Herr Professor to join them in discussion groups at their homes. At the university, clusters of these women formed a phalanx around him before and after each of his lectures; privately, several competed to see who could lure him to their homes for private consultations. No one at the hospital dared joke about this with Emma, nor about the constantly changing progression of Russian and German women medical students who sought the same tête-à-têtes as Spielrein and then proclaimed the same sort of attraction between the married doctor and themselves. Jung seemed even more frazzled and distracted by his burgeoning clientele these days, and Emma's usually sunny visage now had an uncharacteristically grim set.

In such a fraught personal climate, Jung agreed in January 1907 to be the subject of several association tests that Ludwig Binswanger needed to administer as part of the research for his medical dissertation.[5] There was nothing untoward about Jung's participation: most of the hospital patients were so severely traumatized and mentally incapacitated that they were not suitable subjects; when medical students from the university were in short supply, it was fairly usual for the staff doctors to volunteer as subjects for each other's research. And because it seemed that everyone in the hospital knew something of everyone else's "inner politics,"[6] the test subjects frequently revealed, even if inadvertently, a great deal of biographical information about themselves. In Jung's case, both his reactions and Binswanger's comments about them were assuredly "(auto)biographical *prima materia.*"[7]

Ludwig Binswanger had come to the Burghölzli in 1906 from his family home (which was also his family's occupation), the Bellevue Kuranstalt (asylum) in Kreuzlingen.[8] In the years when the Burghölzli staff included doctors who later became psychoanalytic luminaries (among them Karl Abraham, Hans Maier, and Max Eitingon), Binswanger's pedigree placed him one rank higher than the rest. He and Jung soon became friends because both shared the view that Freud introduced "the psychological question into psychiatry."[9] They were cooperating on how to adapt Freud's theorizing into a treatment based primarily on careful attention and response to a patient's case history. Until Jung became familiar with Freud's writing, his experience was based on what he learned in psychiatry classes, of "abstracting from the experience with the patient to the statistic . . . labelling the patients and putting them aside with a diagnosis. One never asked *why* does this patient have this idea and someone else another." Freud became "crucial" to Jung because he offered "a way toward the further examination of the individual cases."[10] And as Jung's career progressed, it was the individual who attracted and dominated his most sustained research.

Binswanger and Jung built a close friendship based on shared ideas, so Jung entered into Binswanger's testing with a relaxed openness that he might not have had if another doctor had been the administrator. Moreover, because Binswanger was privy to so much of Jung's personal life before the two separate tests (the first in January, the second in February), his analysis was more nuanced and incisive than a relative stranger's might have been. Their rapport led to a curious "doubling" factor within the text of Binswanger's written commentary, as Jung was both the subject of his experiment and the supervisor and authority whose research he used to prove his conclusions.

Binswanger first described Jung/subject as "a married doctor well acquainted with the association experiment," and then as the supervisor whose previous writings provided authoritative documentation and support for his conclusions.[11] Speaking of test subjects in general, Binswanger wrote that "the relationship of the subject to the experimenter has a particular influence which produces its effect throughout the whole experiment." He then cited Jung as the authority who "has brought this out very clearly [in *The Psychology of Dementia Praecox*]."[12] What is most remarkable about the tests is how precisely they depicted Jung's life at the time. In one telling instance, Binswanger noted that "the action word *have* . . . only occurs in definite complex places," and Jung/subject gave it as his reply to five different key words: manners, money, fame, salary, and child. Binswanger also noted that Jung/supervisor called "such stereotyped reaction-words *complex representatives*," then added that for Jung/subject "the complex is quite unconscious here."[13]

Jung/subject did indeed "have" — in the sense of possessing — all five of the test words, but each in its way contributed to something he was worried about. In connection with the test word "child," he feared that his youngest, Gret, might be "slightly unwell" because she was so different from Agathe, her older sister. Agathe was a large, sunny blond child, independent, outgoing, and easy to raise; Gret was dark and thin, cranky, irritable, and obstreperous. Even when she was an infant, Emma and Carl were struck by how much her looks and personality were like her namesake aunt's, Gret Homberger, a resemblance they thought grew stronger as their daughter grew older.[14]

The Hombergers were also connected with the test words "manners," "money," and "salary," albeit obliquely. Jung had been trying to arrange for another of his frequent leaves without pay to visit several London hospitals but had not been able to do so because of his Burghölzli duties. He envied Ernst Homberger, who went regularly to London on business and came home each time with the finest representations of English culture, from bespoke clothing and fine tobacco to exquisite household objects and gifts for his wife. Gret, who had already given birth to two sons, was smugly pregnant again, arousing competitive feelings in Emma, who did not hide them from Carl.

As for "salary," that, too, produced irritations connected with the Hombergers. They were too well mannered to be openly disdainful of how slight Carl's salary was in comparison to Emma's annual income, but he was hypersensitive and aware of their true feelings. His personal pride required him to contribute to his family's income, so he needed to earn money. His wages tied him to the Burghölzli, thus limiting his travel and perhaps keeping him from greater "fame." Binswanger noted with tactful restraint that these responses brought the subject "only a vague feeling of hindrance."[15]

He also noted that Jung/subject had "a strongly pronounced striving for knowledge, work, and recognition." Binswanger said it was connected with frequent accusations by "family" that he was "too proud," in the sense of wanting public approval far more aggressively than a man of his social standing should. This response reflected a source of conflict between husband and wife, especially when Emma was too long in Gret's company, for the younger sister had a unique ability to make the older dissatisfied with her lot in life. For the most part, Emma not only supported her husband's work but also shared his interests. However, there were moments when life in the Burghölzli fishbowl became too much for the heiress from Schaffhausen, especially when her elegant younger sister was quick to point out the discrepancies between their husbands' professional standings. Binswanger noted a significant rise in Jung/subject's emotional level when he responded to a stimulus word with "Ölberg," the name of Emma's family home.[16] Binswanger commented that Jung had, "in general, a strongly developed conscience," again associated with his family, who he believed had "reproached" him in another association as "being too proud." Jung/subject always associated "ambition" with the "thirst for knowledge." In his mind, he thought he was seeking professional respect, but to Emma's family, he wanted to thrust himself into the public limelight.

Binswanger noted Jung's reaction "to an extreme degree" about "the period when he was engaged with philosophy," when he was on his Paris sabbatical and free to follow his intellectual interests wherever they led. Jung said he was thinking during this part of the test that it had been one of the happiest times of his life.[17] He was now yearning for days of pure intellectual inquiry such as those, for he chafed at the monotony of his work and worried that if he did not soon find a way to change it, his personal responsibilities might turn his professional life into an unending succession of administering and refining the association tests.[18] Throughout Binswanger's testing, Jung's strongest response was connected with these fears and "strongly marked" by them. Binswanger defined such reactions as "the will to power" and a "money" complex, correctly discerning that both were closely related to Jung's "love of traveling, his salary at the asylum, and his future way of living." No wonder Binswanger observed a distinct tone of "unpleasure" connected to the related word "asylum."

Other aspects of varying degrees of importance in Jung's daily life intruded into the test, such as when he gave in to Emma's wishes and became "annoyed at having to go to a ball next day," or regretted that work coupled with family responsibilities left him little time for the simple pleasure of hiking in the mountains. Images of water produced a much stronger response, showing his longing to go to sea for "the promised journey to England" that figured large in his imagination. Several other times, Binswanger noted that "England is here again" or "the journey to England is involved."

Then came the first of two segments of the test in which Jung/subject showed "distinct excitation." The first concerned the word "*Kröte,*" whose primary meaning in German is "toad," secondarily, "a cheeky little minx" or "spiteful creature." Binswanger misrecorded Jung's response word as *"spöte,"* which is not German but a corruption of the *Schwizertütsch "spoeti,"* from the expression *"Ich bin i einere spoeti,"* or "I am very late." In Jung's time, word-association parlor games that punned on dialect words or phrases from well-known literature were popular in bourgeois families, and it is likely that he played them with his wife and children.[19] Thus, his pronounced and visible emotional response to this pair of words, with their connotations of a flirtatious young girl and the flight of time making whatever he envisioned "too late," was striking. Binswanger chose to gloss over it in his interpretation, ascribing the words to a "thought of the well-known verse to these rhymes to the name of Goethe."[20] Further emphasizing the association of sounds, Binswanger casually alluded to Goethe's name as setting up "a strong emotional tone" that "cannot be gone into here." From this point on, however, Binswanger did observe "distinct excitation" in Jung's responses, especially to the next word, "divorce," to which Jung replied "force."

Jung took the second portion of the test several weeks later, in February, and produced answers that Binswanger judged to be "much more 'nervous,' labile," and "sexually" charged. The word "love" produced "a strong emotional" response, and the word "belly" meant "something very antagonistic to the subject, especially in scientific matters." When Binswanger said "sex," Jung's response became "extreme." Binswanger stated that he analyzed Jung's responses immediately after the test, causing Jung to admit how much he feared he had "exposed" all his complexes. He told Binswanger he remembered thinking during the analysis, "Now everything will come out." Either Binswanger did not see any indication of intense marital dissatisfaction or was too tactful to discuss it fully in his written analysis. To the combination of "repent/spent," for example, he only noted that "for personal reasons this complex was not analyzed more thoroughly." The remark appears to be characteristic of much of his commentary about other similar associations, such as "divorce/force" and "choice/pain."[21] Throughout his analysis, Binswanger opted for a positive gloss wherever he could impose one. He chose, for example, to see Jung's reactions toward matters of sexuality as related primarily to his desire for a son, even though Jung/subject's response to his wife's most recent pregnancy had been dismay. "Notice how the complexes increase," Binswanger observed, "and that they are not new ones."

Later in the second test, a cluster of responses produced what Binswanger called an extremely "unpleasant" sex-related complex associated with "certain sounds," particularly the "sch" that occurred prominently throughout some test words. Binswanger interpreted these as having to do with "a former female patient, whose name begins with this sound" and who had earlier "slandered" Jung. Of all the *Zürichberg Pelzmäntel* and the Russian and German women students in Zürich with whom Jung had any sort of contact at that time, only Sabina Spielrein's name contained such a sound.[22]

Jung's reaction to the "sch" words was so highly agitated that Binswanger directed him to remain seated and relax once this part of the test was concluded. Jung fell asleep and dreamed, and when he awakened, he told Binswanger that he had "had a dream in which this ["sch"] lady plays the chief part." In his written report, Binswanger tactfully attributed it to Jung's "Goethe complex" but again said he was unable to comment further for "personal" reasons. Almost apologetically, Binswanger noted that Jung exhibited "great embarrassment . . . at revealing this complex to the experimenter."

Probably because Binswanger was such a good friend, the discreet experimenter dropped the matter without further commentary. Had he proceeded he might have written about how the marriage of Carl and Emma Jung had veered precipitously toward divorce in the few short weeks between the two experiments.[23] The gossip about Carl's possible infidelity coupled with her life in the Burghölzli fishbowl had finally become too much for the Schaffhausen heiress. Emma, at the provocation of her sister, Gret, who railed against the supposed humiliation and social embarrassment Carl had heaped upon the Rauschenbach family, but against her mother Bertha's wishes (for she adored her son-in-law), had presented Carl with an ultimatum: he was to find a house for them or else have one built, and he was to find a way to disassociate himself (she stopped short of ordering him to resign) from his position in the Burghölzli as soon as possible. Emma thought a private home for her and a private practice for Carl was the only answer to her dilemma, but he was reluctant to give up the prestige of lecturing at the university, which he would lose if he resigned from the staff.

The most important question, however, concerned money, and he had to consider it seriously. If Emma divorced him, the money she brought to the marriage would return to her control — or, more accurately, to Ernst Homberger's, for he was the family head, which was galling to Jung's pride. The children were another matter, for under Swiss law, the father had primary claim to custody. Emma knew it was unlikely that Carl would exercise an option that would saddle him with raising two daughters, but the possibility of his doing it to spite her was a prospect she could not ignore.

The problem for Carl was that he truly loved Emma, and although he had not yet taken advantage of what her money could buy, except for the sabbaticals that permitted his independent research, he also loved the possibilities it offered for the future life he wanted them to live together. But he was also, as Binswanger noted, thirty-one and eager for change, which exacerbated their differing views.

Life itself, that is, the idea of the life he had not yet lived, was something Jung brooded about increasingly during these days. In the progression of his years, "Pastor's Carl" had become the hearty and popular Zofingian "Barrel," who in turn had become a dedicated medical researcher who married a gentle-born woman and was subsequently expected to assume the proper mantle of contented husband and exemplary father. But Jung thought that along the way he might have left out several intriguing stops at life's way stations. Two were important among them: that of being a lover to women other than the one he married, and experiencing the satisfaction that supposedly came to a patriarch who was the principal financial provider for his family.

Jung seems always to have taken his good looks and good health for granted, but now, with so many women eager to fall at his feet, he became conscious of the power over others, particularly women, his handsome physical appearance gave him. As the women fluttered before him, his numerous flirtations grew increasingly dangerous and, by extension, increasingly exciting. And, as he could not hope to achieve satisfaction from being the principal provider in his current situation because Emma's fortune was simply too vast, it was easier as well as more interesting and more personally satisfying to find power through approval and affection elsewhere. His problem was that the strong-willed Emma was ready to put the damper to his flame with her flat-out assertion that she would divorce him rather than suffer further, deeper humiliation. He knew she meant it.

Whether Jung ever confided any of this to Binswanger remains in the realm of speculation, for Binswanger chose to hide behind the "Goethe complex" and offer no explanation other than to attribute Jung's concerns about sexuality to his suppressed "propagation complex" and his need to find new work that engaged him. This, according to Binswanger, was connected with "the question of [Jung's] future" and occurred most prominently when he spontaneously inserted the word "Vienna" into the test. "Paris," Jung replied promptly, remembering once again those happy days of free intellectual inquiry. "He can hardly wait," Binswanger said of Jung's plan to spend his Easter vacation in Vienna. Binswanger's next spontaneously substituted test word was "soon." Jung's reply was "yes."

Jung made such "strong deviation" during this part of the test that Binswanger said it could only be attributed to "the subject's great need of new 'sensations.'" He was correct to write that Jung had "a general feeling that 'something is soon going to happen.'" It was the same sensation that led him to Zürich in 1900; now, in 1907, it would take him to Vienna and Freud.

THERE WERE several minor frustrations and schedule changes before Jung could fix firmly the date of his first meeting with Freud, finally set for Sunday, March 3, 1907. These delays were mostly due to Emma's insistence that they should celebrate the Easter holidays with her family and after that take the vacation she believed her husband owed her. Jung had to factor everything into consideration without revealing any of it to Freud. A compromise was effected: Emma would allow him total freedom to do whatever he liked in Vienna if he would take her to Budapest afterward. Although she lived there only briefly while her father oversaw a branch of his business when she was two years old, Emma remained fascinated by the Hungarian capital.

All these negotiations and compromises created a definite tension from the time they began to plan the trip. At the last moment, hoping to alleviate it, Jung spontaneously invited Binswanger to travel with them as far as Vienna. Ostensibly, he wanted his young protégé to meet Freud, but he also knew Binswanger's presence would soothe Emma because they got along so well. Jung took special care with his initial presentation of Binswanger to Freud, casually mentioning that he and his wife would be traveling with a pupil who just happened to be the nephew of the sitting professor of psychiatry at the University of Jena. He left unstated the possibility that this might help further academic dissemination of Freud's doctrine.[24] Jung knew how much Freud lusted for academic recognition, and with his interest thus piqued, he agreed eagerly to meet the younger Binswanger. They got on so well that Binswanger stayed an extra week after the Jungs departed for Budapest, his time with Freud laying the groundwork for what became a lifelong friendship that, through their correspondence, offered important insights into Freud's theoretical camp long after Jung had bolted.[25]

"Young" and "Younger," Freud dubbed the two doctors, punning on the meaning of Jung's name,[26] but it was Jung, not Binswanger, upon whom Freud trained his sights. Having described "the impression of greatness and dignity that emanated from [Freud]," Binswanger noted his own "somewhat skeptical" response to "the enthusiasm and confidence" with which Freud concentrated on Jung. "Immediately," Binswanger wrote, Freud anointed Jung as his "scientific 'son and heir.'"[27]

Freud believed Jung's "appearance on the scene" was an extraordinary stroke of good fortune: to have "a Christian and a Pastor's son" embrace his theory was his first guarantee that psychoanalysis would not become "a Jewish national affair."[28] Jung's first response to Freud was quite different. Unlike Freud, who had spent the last decade away from the academic and medical communities, Jung was an established scholar of international repute. Freud's writings and teachings brought scholars, doctors, and patients to Vienna, but they and others also went to Zürich to study Jung's medical procedures as well as his psychological techniques. Jung went to Vienna more impressed than most with the importance of Freud's work, and he certainly did want to learn all he could from the older man, but still, he went there as separate and equal.

On the first visit, Jung agreed with Binswanger that Freud was "certainly a striking personality," but privately he thought him "rather hard, although he did have the Viennese charm." He was wary of Freud's "very many light and dark sides" and wanted to proceed slowly with such "a very complex phenomenon."[29] Freud, however, exuded such warmth that Jung capitulated to his graciousness and charm. Many years later, in 1953, Jung was still scarcely able to describe his emotions when Freud showered such affection upon him. "I mean," the elderly Jung said, stumbling for words, "I was, of course, I mean, of course, if one is confronted with such a man, then one is simply also included, you know, and is part of the party, you know, and all that, you know."[30] He was more circumspect in the heavily edited *Memories, Dreams, Reflections*. His first impressions "remained somewhat tangled." His final impression of their first meeting remained the most lasting: "I could not make him out."[31]

JUNG ENTERED Freud's apartment at Berggasse 19 for lunch at 1 P.M., stayed through dinner, and left at 2 A.M., after a thirteen-hour marathon of nonstop talking. There are many different versions of what transpired between the two, and because most have been given by partisans of one man or the other, they vary greatly. Freud's son Martin, after admitting that "[Freud's] children's contacts with the learned men who came to see him to discuss his theories were naturally of the slightest," gave a negative portrayal of Jung.[32] Unlike many of the other "learned men," Jung was described by Martin Freud as an exception who never even tried to make social conversation with Frau Martha Freud or any of the six Freud children, or with Martha's sister, Minna Bernays, who was an integral part of the household. Instead, he simply continued "the debate which had been interrupted by the call to dinner." Martin Freud added that Jung did all the talking and his father, "with unconcealed delight," all the listening.

What makes Martin Freud's account especially interesting is that it contradicts what every other biographer or friend of Freud has written about mealtimes in the Freud household.[33] Freud never permitted any conversation other than family news at the midday table (he usually took his evening meal alone, long after the family had consumed its light supper). Even when "learned men" were present, Freud expected them to make polite conversation with his family. If they tried not to, he led them back into generalities with such explicit force that they knew better than to cross him. So it seems unlikely that Jung behaved badly (at least at their first luncheon; perhaps he did transgress later), especially since Emma was with him, and in those days he was always exceedingly deferential to her in public. Also, Binswanger's memory of the luncheon was that "the flock of children" behaved well, and "a completely unconstrained tone dominated."[34]

Emma and Binswanger excused themselves after lunch, and Jung was finally admitted to the inner sanctum of Freud's office, where professional conversation began in earnest. According to Ernest Jones, Jung had so much to tell Freud that "with intense animation, he poured forth in a spate for three whole hours,"[35] leading the bemused Freud to suggest they group the subjects under discussion into systematic categories and proceed accordingly. Jung wanted to know what Freud thought about parapsychological phenomena and precognitions. In Jung's old age, when he was writing *Memories, Dreams, Reflections*, he attempted repeatedly to explain what happened between him and Freud at their first meeting.[36] Freud never offered a sustained account, but in Jung's version, he "absolutely rejected" both, which caused Jung to accuse him of "materialistic bias" and to persist stubbornly in describing his own personal experiences. When he told of the knife that shattered, Freud "expressed such a flat positivism" that Jung found it difficult "not to respond in a way that would have been a bit too biting." Jung found "such an absence of philosophical consciousness" in Freud's comments that "it actually turned [his] stomach." Freud continued to talk, and Jung's stomach felt as if it were "made of iron and would be turning red hot, a red hot diaphragm vault."

Suddenly, there occurred such a noise from the glass-fronted bookcase in front of which they were sitting that both jumped, fearing it would fall on them. "Now this is a so-called catalytic exteriorization phenomenon," Jung insisted. "Oh, no, that is complete nonsense," Freud replied. To prove his point, Jung insisted there would be another noise, and immediately there was "an indescribably terrible noise in the cabinet!"

"Freud looked at me with horror then," Jung remembered. "This raised a distrust of me in him, for you see, something like that isn't possible, something like that doesn't exist in his world view. Consequently, for him, I had to be absolutely out of kilter somewhere. Later I had the definite feeling that I had done something to upset him." They never spoke of this incident again and the conversation moved to other subjects chosen by Freud. From here on, he was in charge of the agenda.

At 1 A.M., both men looked at the clock and were astonished to discover how much time had passed since they began to talk. "A world happened then," Jung told the distinguished Freudian Dr. Kurt Eissler many years later during an interview. Jung compared his day with Freud to the act of giving birth: "At birth everything is already there! In reality there is no time! Time is, is nothing! That's what one realizes on such occasions. Those are, there are moments, that are completely timeless."

"Yes," he replied in agreement with Dr. Eissler, "that was really an intense encounter." It impressed him most of all because it showed "what depth [Freud] had!" "God," Jung added poignantly, "if he had only gotten over himself, you know! But there was this neurotic element. If he had gotten over *that*, yes, that — it would have been crazy you know, to ever want anything other than to work with him."

BUT THE red flag of danger was there from their first extant exchange of letters, when Jung expressed his reservations about the primacy of sexuality in Freud's theory and Freud replied with the hope that Jung would accept its significance. In their first meeting, Jung expressed his continuing reservations, arguing that Freud had substituted sexuality for what he loosely termed "the mystical." In a tone Jung described as spoken "very passionately," Freud implored him, "Promise me one thing: look after sexuality!" Jung was struck by Freud's tone, which seemed the same as if he were saying "'and promise me one thing, my dear son: go to mass every day!,' or 'make sure that the Eucharist is always being celebrated.'" Jung later consigned Freud's view to "scientific materialism," which he said "always amounted to the game of cats and dogs," Jung's editors' English translation of the German idiom for comparing apples with oranges.

Nevertheless, "*everything!*"[37] about the day was such an incredible, stimulating experience that Jung believed he had finally found what he had been looking for ever since his first six months at the Burghölzli, when he studied the *Allgemeine Zeitschrift für Psychiatrie* to learn how best to conduct his profession. Now here was Freud, offering so much collegiality that Jung was willing, indeed eager, to suspend his disbelief and substitute instead a modest degree of doubt. Freud wanted to be the kind of father Jung had always wanted, so why not become his "son and heir" and enjoy the opening of the professional doors that such a relationship would bring?

The first was the door to the weekly gathering of Freud's small band of followers, then known as the Vienna Group, later called the Wednesday Psychological Society, and finally the Vienna Psychoanalytic Society.[38] Jung's admiration for Freud did not extend to the group, which then had about seventeen members, all of whom were elected by unanimous consent. A paid secretary, Otto Rank, took detailed minutes of the talks, which on Jung's visit included one by Alfred Adler on anal masochism.[39] Jung and Binswanger attended and sat quietly, as neither was impressed. Jung "deplored" the "medley of artists, decadents and mediocrities" who surrounded Freud.[40] Binswanger was more circumspect, citing Freud's "keen" dismissive assessment of his followers rather than quoting his observation: "Well, now you have seen the gang."[41]

EVERYTHING JUNG experienced on the Vienna trip, but especially the Wednesday evening gathering, coalesced into an admission he made to Freud that had far-reaching consequences for his lifelong views of politics and culture. Vienna was a "reasonably small" city but one so "rich in culture and creativity" that the "intelligentsia produced innovations that became identified throughout the European culture sphere."[42] It was as different from Zürich as the proverbial night from day, and everything about Vienna melded into a barrage of overwhelming sensations. He was a man in his thirties who had no experience with the kinds of conversation one had in the cultural salon or the coffeehouse, and he wanted to describe his impressions of Viennese public social life to Freud. On several occasions during this first visit, Freud analyzed Jung's dreams (and occasionally Binswanger's). In a session that followed the Wednesday meeting, Jung offered an interpretation for his dream of the previous night. He told Freud he thought it represented the "trouble" he had adapting to life in Vienna.[43] "I felt so foreign before this Jewish intellectual society," he said. "That was something completely new to me. I had never experienced that before . . . I found it very difficult to adjust, to adopt the right tone." The coffeehouse atmosphere was "so foreign," the conversations all contained "a certain cynicism," and Jung felt like a country bumpkin in the face of such sophisticated banter.

"You wouldn't be an anti-Semite now, would you?" Freud asked.

"No, no!" Jung replied. "Anti-Semitism is out of the question."

Not for Freud, however, who continued to level such charges in subsequent meetings and throughout the several years of their collaboration. Jung countered the first accusation by saying that if Freud insisted on branding him as such, he would call him "anti-Christian," because his "every second word was always a quote from Voltaire." Freud dismissed it, preferring his own interpretation of Jung as an "anti-Semite."[44] He turned the conversation to the Wednesday group and began to "rant," calling them "those damn Jews." Jung felt "independent" enough to contradict Freud, praising the "virtues" of the Jews, who he said were famous for their sense of family unity. "There you are mistaken," Freud insisted. "They only stick together by their common hatred."[45]

DESPITE JUNG'S declaration that Emma had given him carte blanche to do whatever he wanted in Vienna, the Freud family had other ideas. Martha remained at home to prepare the midday meals that Carl and Emma took with the family on several occasions. Freud's sister-in-law Minna Bernays and the Freud daughters took Emma shopping and sight-seeing. Jung joined them on one occasion, when a military parade passed along the Ringstrasse, and he pushed through the crowd like a young boy eager to see it. Minna Bernays, her tone somewhere between amusement and disapproval, told Freud, who chose to see Jung's behavior as yet another expression of his "vitality, liveliness, [and] unrestrained imagination."[46]

Both Jungs were keenly observant, and both were struck by what they called "certain oddities" in the Freud family's dynamic.[47] Upon their arrival in Vienna, Freud came to the hotel to greet them, offering Emma a lavish bouquet of flowers and apologizing that he could not invite them to his apartment, for he "had nothing to offer but a modest house and a rather elderly housewife."[48] Emma was shocked by his comment, especially since he then proffered an invitation to lunch for that very day. Afterward, Emma told Carl that Frau Freud was "a very nice lady." He agreed, although he thought her "completely extinguished."

Martha Freud's role appeared to be that of a super-housekeeper. She oversaw every aspect of the family's daily life, but her primary responsibility was to safeguard her husband from anything that might interfere with his work. Freud and their children accorded her every homage and deference, and as mistress of the household, she sat in a place of honor at the table, directly opposite him. But all this politeness did not hide the fact that she was spoken to only on matters relating to schedules or appointments or (in the case of the children) various permissions they needed.

The person who acted as Freud's companion and intellectual counterpart was his sister-in-law Minna Bernays.[49] She was the one who knew every aspect of his work and the only one who dared to mention it at mealtime; she knew when patients were coming or going, and she was the only member of the family who dared to tease Freud or make innocent jokes or puns based on his writings. Emma was more puzzled by Minna's ambivalent status within the family than Carl was, who seems to have kept his views to himself and urged his wife to do the same. All he was willing to say was that "[Minna] had a great transference and Freud *was not insensible.*"[50] But privately he was intrigued by how many times Freud, then aged fifty, would remark, apropos of nothing in their conversations, that he was "an old man now and . . . yes, if one had a young woman, then one could rejuvenate oneself again!"[51]

BEFORE THEY left Zürich, Jung reluctantly agreed to take Emma's sentimental journey to Budapest, but he did not tell her until they arrived that he would spend most of his time working. When Bleuler read their itinerary, he directed Jung to observe the work of psychiatrist Fülöp Stein and prepare a detailed report on the Hungarian anti-alcohol movement he had founded.[52] Emma did her sight-seeing alone, and she got her vacation only after Carl had had his fill of Stein's ideas and insisted they must flee from Budapest. They had always intended to finish their vacation at two Adriatic resorts, Fiume and Abbazia, where Carl could be entirely free of professional concerns, but as they arrived several days earlier than had been planned, there was more time for trouble to build between them.[53]

Tensions were exacerbated when Carl developed a "compulsive infatuation" in Abbazia with a "Jewess" who has never been identified who was staying in their hotel.[54] The woman, a Hungarian married to a wealthy Austrian with a vague connection to the Viennese medical profession, either knew something of Jung's research or else pretended that she did. She initiated several intense conversations in the hotel dining room, where they lingered long before moving on to a secluded corner of the lounge. Some conversations eventually ended in late-night walks on the hotel grounds. Emma was furious, but Carl persuaded her that his interest was professional: the woman and her husband had influence and could further both his and Freud's reputations. Emma didn't like it, but she tolerated the flirtation until their departure.

ONCE BACK in Zürich in April, Jung was barraged by a veritable frenzy of work. Bleuler, who possessed "the Swiss national virtues to a fault," showed a great deal of "resistance" and "negative shilly-shallying" to everything Jung told him about Vienna.[55] His remarks probably had as much to do with his general health as with his attitude toward Jung; overworked and underpaid as he had been for so many years, Bleuler finally had to admit that he needed time away from the hospital. In May, he left for a month at a sanatorium and had no option but to leave the hospital's direction to Jung, his chief assistant.[56]

Throughout this time, Freud wrote often and eagerly to Jung, saying he had come to regard their exchange of ideas as a "necessity."[57] Jung's replies were usually filled with apologies for not replying promptly, blaming the delay on hospital "overwork"[58] and a host of other activities. He was making plans for yet another departure from the Burghölzli, this time to interview Janet in Paris in order to determine what he thought of Freud, and perhaps even to firm up his own conclusions about the degree to which his allegiances should veer from Paris toward Vienna.[59] He planned to go on to England and the Bethlem Royal Hospital, where he wanted to consult the prior history of an intriguing patient in the Burghölzli.

This was Emile Schwyzer, who became Jung's most controversial patient, achieving fame as "The Solar Phallus Man," whose delusions led to Jung's formulation of the theory of the archetype. Jung presented Schwyzer's case history as a "case of paranoia" to Freud, who called him "The Paranoid" in his analysis.[60] But Freud was not interested in pursuing Schwyzer's case history beyond this single exchange, and Jung had too many other things on his mind in 1907 to concentrate on it.

Jung did not go to London: he was so disappointed by the general analytic situation in Paris and Janet's attitudes toward Freud that he went sight-seeing to the castles of the Loire Valley instead.[61] He did attend the Amsterdam conference in July, where he defended Freud by opposing Aschaffenburg. He had been in correspondence with Aschaffenburg, and the exchange convinced him that the German doctor was particularly obtuse and understood nothing of Freud's theory.[62] Jung told this to Freud but was rankled by his reply: Freud said he had been invited first to debate Aschaffenburg, but he had declined. When the conveners suggested Jung as his substitute, Freud said it verified that "the world at large" also "shared" his view of their "relationship."[63] It was the first of many times to come that Jung scorned Freud's "timidity before the world" and resented him for "never risking an appearance at a congress and never representing his case publicly."[64]

There was, however, another continuing motif woven into their correspondence, initiated and nudged along repeatedly by Freud: he wanted a journal dedicated to his work to be founded, and he wanted Jung to be its editor. Jung agreed that a journal was a good idea and agreed to "let the leaven work,"[65] for he was busy with a parade of distinguished visitors who came to the Burghölzli to observe the association tests. Among them were Théodore Flournoy and Edouard Claparède from Geneva, as well as six unnamed Americans, one Russian, one Italian, and one Hungarian (but "no Germans!").[66] That was all very fine, Freud replied, and he was pleased that Bleuler was back and Jung's period of overwork seemed to be ending, but he really wanted the first issue of a journal devoted to his work to be published, and no later than the autumn of 1908.[67] Jung wanted this to happen as much as Freud did, but he was unable even to think about it, let alone pursue his growing interest in what he loosely termed "experimental studies," or prepare a "systematic working up of Dementia praecox."[68]

He and Emma talked about how he might create the long stretches of time he would need to sit quietly and think in order to further his own research, and she was, as always, eager to put all her resources at his disposal. If he had to give up his small salary, he was still determined to salvage the high status of his current position, so he formulated a proposal that was later called many different things, among them "creative and original" and "daring and brash" but most often "arrogant and self-serving."[69]

He told Freud he presented a plan to Bleuler that had his "vigorous support," but in light of subsequent developments, it is more likely that Jung misread his superior's responses.[70] Jung wanted to create a private laboratory of psychology with himself as director that he would then affiliate to the Burghölzli as a "more or less independent institute." Such a plan was "daring" indeed, more likely a euphemism for a shockingly presumptuous proposal, but where Jung really ran into conflict with Bleuler was over his second proposition: that the chair of psychiatry at Zürich University be given to a researcher other than the director of the hospital — namely himself. Jung was after the best of both worlds: the independence of doing his own work coupled with the most prestigious university position in psychiatry in all of Switzerland. It seems improbable that he did not realize the arrogance of his attempt to unseat Bleuler, that he did not realize how much holding this chair meant to him. All the same, Jung blithely presented his proposal to Bleuler, who merely said he would need time to think about it.

Meanwhile, Emma was complaining about her loneliness and his lack of attention to their daughters. He assured her that his situation would soon change and then turned his concentration to hospital business. Foreign doctors continued to submit applications to work with Jung, and he had to read them and choose the ones he thought best and most interesting. Ernest Jones, later to become Freud's biographer, joined this parade of visiting observers in November. He pushed for a conference devoted to Freud's theory in Salzburg within the coming year, which Jung was to organize.[71] Binswanger, Jung's most loyal and hard-working assistant, had gone to Jena to study with his uncle, which meant that when Jung's current students clamored for his attention on their dissertations, there was no one he could delegate to do the work for him. Also, the cases of several of the patients had become so compelling that Jung found himself observing them for many more hours than was required. And he suddenly became aware that his ex-patient Sabina Spielrein was a very interesting woman, now that she had begun some engaging research of her own. On top of everything else, he had to spend most of the month of July on military service. Even his normally robust constitution rebelled: when he returned in August, he was felled by acute gastroenteritis and had to spend most of September in bed.[72]

In retrospect, Jung agreed that Freud was right to say that his ambition was the "agent provocateur" of the "fits of despair," which all his responsibilities imposed.[73] Defending his behavior, he insisted that everything he did was governed by "honest enthusiasm for the truth." His fervent desire was to use Freud's theories as the basis for a "breakthrough" to the world at large, "even though the element of self-interest could be denied only by the very obtuse." For the time being, he intended to keep on keeping on, and everyone else in his personal and professional sphere who wanted to remain there would simply have to run to keep up with him.

CHAPTER 9

※

Vocatus atque non vocatus, Deus aderit

Early in 1908 Emma Jung discovered she was pregnant for the third time. She issued a decree to her husband: he could remain at the Burghölzli as long as he wanted, but he must give her a home of her own.

Emma would get her house, but it would be exactly what Carl believed it should be, "none of that Art Deco, Art Nouveau, all the muddling of style that was just starting then." He wanted a solid and substantial house, in the traditional early baroque style built along the Zürichsee throughout the nineteenth century. Jung entrusted its design to his architect cousin, Ernst Fiechter of Munich,[1] charging him to create an enduring fortress that transcended time. Jung wanted it to be imposing, but in a manner that prized dignity, comfort, security, and continuity rather than fashion. Fiechter "made the plans," but Jung "put [his] whole weight into it, of course."

On a Sunday afternoon walk in nearby Küsnacht, the Jungs saw a plot of land for sale on the lakefront.[2] They liked the village, where they had already bought a small house for Emilie and Trudi, and they bought the land quickly. The plot was long and narrow, extending from the lake to the Seestrasse, the main road that still meanders through the shoreline communities from Zürich to Rapperswil.[3] The view was spectacular, on the lake's "gold coast," so called in Jung's time because it faced south and received the best light and sunshine in an often gloomy climate, and still called the same today, although its meaning has changed to "real gold," or the side of the lake where the wealthiest reside. There was easy access to deep water, and Jung planned to buy a sailboat as soon as they moved in, if not before.

Initially, the lake frontage was just enough for the house, but shortly after they purchased the land, an adjacent parcel became available, and they quickly bought it. Buying land was an "unforgettable event" for Jung. "To think that this was my earth!" he still marveled shortly before his death. "This was the earth where I will stay, my earth in which I am standing like a tree!" It gave him "pleasure beyond comparison." When his great fame brought offers of distinguished positions from foreign universities, he did not give them even passing consideration: "I could not be separated from my earth. And that was that."[4]

He was quite taken with creating a house and wanted to oversee every aspect of its development, but because of professional demands, he had to leave most of the details to Emma. It was fortunate they agreed about how the house should evolve, and their architect helped it become exactly what they envisioned.[5] They wanted a large entrance hall with a gracious, curving staircase leading to the upper floors. On the ground floor, to the right of the staircase, were the kitchen, pantries, and other areas where the business of running a household took place. To the left of the staircase and behind it was a large living-dining room, the grandest room in the house. The south wall had windows facing the lake. French doors at the east end opened onto a stone-floored solarium and terrace that led to the gardens. This imposing room was planned to be the heart of the home, with meals taken at a dining table built specifically to fit under ornate ceiling moldings that delineated its place. The north wall behind it held a huge buffet/china closet, again specially designed and built for this area. They situated comfortable furniture to face the large stone fireplace at the far end of the room and bought a piano for their daughters to learn to play.[6] There was also a large tiled stove, even though the house had central heating as well as up-to-date plumbing.

On the second floor, directly above the stairs and in the house's central core, was a gracious hallway. To the left, a frosted glass door led to the family's private quarters, and to the right were two small rooms: Jung's study and the patients' waiting room, the only one in the house "unsatisfactory from a household point of view."[7] It was lined with linen closets and meant for other household storage as well, but no one could use it during his consulting hours for fear of disturbing a patient. Jung's inner-sanctum study was directly behind it. There, he retreated to write and sometimes to hold analytic sessions beneath the frosted and stained-glass windows that glowed in the occasional sunlight. The largest and grandest room on that floor was Jung's library, where he saw most of his patients. Several sets of French doors overlooked the lake, and comfortable sofas and chairs were grouped invitingly so that patients could face the view or not, as they chose. Jung placed his worktable under a window, close to a large green-tiled stove that kept the room warm in winter; in summer, refreshing lake breezes cooled it.

The family's private quarters were separated from the professional part of the house by frosted-glass doors that opened into a hallway lined on either side with bedrooms. Emma's rooms were at the farthest corner of the house, public enough to receive visitors but private enough that she was not otherwise disturbed. There, she installed her personal library and dreamed of quietly studying mathematics, mythology, and psychology. She was planning to begin lessons in Latin and Greek as soon as they were settled. The third and top floor of the house held more bedrooms; some for servants, some for children and guests, and various storage rooms and closets. One attic room was used for drying herbs and fruits, and the basement contained a wine cellar.

The gardens were extensive, and at lakeside a boathouse was built for Jung's sailboat, rowboat, and dinghy. A small adjacent shed stored tools and summer garden furniture. Emma planned to make the small paved area in front of it her private domain, where she would sit and read and think in pleasant weather. There was a waterside terrace at the westernmost point of their land, and Jung intended to make it his private sanctuary, where he would meditate and see friends and patients in the warm summer months.

Leading from the street to the front of the house were a brick walkway and gravel driveway that gave onto an area sufficient for several cars to park or turn around. A garage was built at the southeast end, large enough to hold several vehicles and with a room above that became the workshop and private sanctuary of the employee who served as handyman, groundskeeper, and chauffeur. It became the fiefdom of "young Müller," who stayed with the Jung family for so many years that he retired as "old Müller." There was also an area in the garage that naturally evolved into a root cellar and drying room for the vegetables from the extensive gardens that Müller lovingly tended and both Jungs enjoyed supervising. Emma's household staff included a cook, two full-time housemaids, and a part-time cleaning woman as needed.

The most important aspect of the house, however, was an adage of Erasmus that Jung ordered to be carved into the stone over the towerlike entryway: *"Vocatus atque non vocatus, Deus aderit"* (Whether called or not, God will be present).[8] Jung first read it at the age of nineteen, when he was still the skeptic who envisioned God defecating on the Basel Cathedral. By the time he built his house at age thirty-three, the adage had grown in personal importance because of his experiences with patients and his own readings in psychology, mythology, and philosophy. Every day since he had first read it, it reminded him that the true beginning of wisdom lay in fear and awe of God, although he was not yet ready to define what he meant by the idea and concept of God. What mattered was to recognize the quest he must undertake to find out, and to be willing to make the journey that would lead to "a much more important road" wherein he could ponder the ultimate question of "God himself."[9]

It became the enduring quest of his lifetime, but it is nevertheless curious that the adage was so fraught with meaning when the house was being built, for he and Emma did not consider themselves particularly religious. Both were indifferent about attending services at the Swiss Reformed Church into which they had been baptized and confirmed, limiting their appearances to weddings, funerals, and other ceremonial occasions. But privately both were beginning to feel the terror and awe that Jung described, for they both became slightly uneasy whenever they thought of their many good fortunes. To whom or to what, they sometimes wondered, did they owe their good health and growing family, her wealth, and his burgeoning professional respect — just a few among so many other blessings they enjoyed. Many years later Jung described himself as a "Christian-minded agnostic" for whom God was a certainty as well as a mystery.[10] It was an apt description of how he and Emma felt at the time their new house was in construction.

PREGNANT, FULLY occupied with two daughters, and happy to daydream about her house, Emma let Carl pursue his professional responsibilities without the usual complaint that he was neglecting his family. It was good that she was so contentedly busy, for she saw little of him as the year unfolded and the house took shape. The fall term marked the start of an avalanche of work that gave Jung no respite until repeated illness made it impossible for him to keep to his hectic pace. He had to observe a new crop of students at the university and new doctors at the hospital in clinical settings, help them identify research topics, and then guide their endeavors. Binswanger, his mainstay, married and left for Kreuzlingen; Abraham, whom he did not like but who was a willing aide, departed for Berlin. Jung was left to deal with the new assistant doctors, all apt and eager pupils who were destined to play a role in the evolution of analytic psychiatry, among them Hans Meier, Abraham Brill, Alphons Maeder, and Hirsch Nunberg. Jung had university lectures to write and case reports to prepare each day. A continuing influx of visiting physicians, among them Fülöp Stein and Sandor Ferenczi of Hungary and Frederick W. Peterson of New York, all required differing degrees of professional cordiality after the day's work was done. The onslaught began in late summer shortly after Jung finished his month's medical service with the Swiss army. In September, he was felled again with "acute gastro-enteritis,"[11] but he was too busy to take the proper time to recover fully.

That same month, Jung was instrumental in setting up a meeting that brought together an initial group of twelve physicians who before the year ended numbered about twenty, all willing to declare themselves members of the Swiss Society for Freudian Researches. Jung considered it imperative to persuade Bleuler to accept the chairmanship because of his hesitation to accept Freudian doctrine. Wanting to mitigate his hesitation, Jung thought holding office might lead Bleuler to embrace Freud with the same exuberance as his own, and he urged Freud to come to Zürich during the Christmas holidays in the hope that his presence might entice Bleuler securely into their fold. Jung wrote truthfully that Bleuler would certainly charm Freud with his "grand display of dedicated, unassuming scientific interest," which always "bowls the uninitiated over." Unable to stem his sarcasm, Jung then described his "chief" as "a brilliantly successful pseudo-personality" and "a psychoanalytical curiosity."[12] Nevertheless, they needed him for Freud's cause.

In late October, the Swiss Cantonal Medical Society asked Jung, not Bleuler, to speak. Bleuler had never been keen about such activities, but even so, he thought it an affront. Jung's paper, "The Significance of Freud's Theory for Neurology and Psychiatry,"[13] was resoundingly delivered but not especially remarkable for its content. Shortly after, news of Jung's talk reached Geneva, and a group of French-Swiss doctors led by Edouard Claparède in "benevolent neutrality"[14] asked him to address them on the same topic. Both addresses were so convincingly delivered that several doctors who were not present wrote Bleuler to ask if they might come to the hospital to observe Jung in action.[15] This, too, enhanced Bleuler's feelings of usurpation.

Ernest Jones was among the doctors who heard about Jung's talks and came to observe him. Jones was then the medical registrar at the West End Hospital for Nervous Diseases in London and had met Jung the previous spring at the International Congress of Neurology in Amsterdam. Each found the other sympathetic because of their mutual interest in Freud, but the affinity between the two men was lopsided from the beginning. On his first afternoon in the Burghölzli, A. A. Brill, thinking Jones a novice, started to explain how the psychogalvanometer worked. Jung quickly interrupted, saying, "We didn't invite Dr. Jones here to teach him, but to consult him."[16] The remark was merely a courtesy, for Jung really thought of Jones as "an extremely gifted and active young man" who had only a superficial understanding of Freud, which Jung charitably ascribed as most likely due to Jones's "splendid isolation" in London. He hoped it would soon be remedied by his enthusiasm.[17]

Jones, who tended toward extremes, held a glowing opinion of Jung: "a formidable presence," "a restlessly active and quick brain," "forceful," and "domineering in temperament." Many years later when things had changed drastically, Jones still grudgingly admitted to his biographer that Jung was a major "focal point"[18] for the first ten years of their acquaintance. Arguably, Jung remained a focal point for the rest of Jones's life, albeit negative rather than positive.

Jung related news of Jones to Freud, who was not really interested in him as an individual but was delighted because a generic Englishman was embracing his views. Freud predicted rightly that once the English in general understood them, "they will never let them go."[19]

Like Freud, Jones was a small man of about five feet seven inches. He was filled with nervous energy and brimming with enthusiastic plans that he seldom concentrated on long enough to bring to fruition. In the early years of the psychoanalytic movement, he served as the catalyst who inspired others to do it for him. When he learned that Freud wanted a journal devoted to his views, Jones began to push for an immediate publication, no matter where or by whom, thus forcing Jung to pay close attention to yet another demand on his overcrowded agenda. Freud had been urging him to found a journal since their first meeting, but Jung always deterred him with pleas of overwork. Now that Jones was eager to become the follower who founded a journal dedicated to Freudian theory, Jung set to work. Just before Christmas, he told Freud he was negotiating for a journal that would be "international, since we must emancipate ourselves as much as possible from the German market."[20] He had been "contemplating the great hole in German psychiatry with unspeakable glee" and called most of the younger doctors "fog without form."[21] A journal under Swiss-Viennese control would give the Germans the necessary instruction to remedy this sorry situation.

Jones was brimming with other ideas. When he overheard that Drs. Stein and Ferenczi had suggested in passing that a meeting be organized to discuss Freud's work, Jones proposed one to follow the Congress for Experimental Psychology in Frankfurt on April 22–25. Unwilling to cede authority or pride of place, Jung started to plan one to be held at Freud's convenience somewhere in Austria. He enlisted Claparède in Geneva and Bleuler in Zürich as his first allies in both projects, thus deftly maneuvering Jones into a subordinate role.

Shortly thereafter, Jung contacted the American psychologist Morton Prince (who had also been an earlier observer at the Burghölzli), hoping to persuade him to amalgamate their proposed journal with *The Journal of Abnormal Psychology*, which he had founded in 1906. Prince was eager for contributions from Europeans, and Jung had just sent a paper, "On the Psychophysical Relations of the Association Experiment."[22] In the end, Prince preferred to keep control of his own separate fiefdom, so Jung's inquiries came to naught.

Jung began negotiations with a series of Swiss, German, and Austrian publishers and soon became initiated into the mysteries of press runs, paper costs, and postage, all of which he conveyed to Freud. He also told of his frustrations as an editor forced to deal with recalcitrant writers who missed deadlines or turned in unusable articles. On top of this, many of his patients left Zürich for Vienna and he had to write detailed reports of their cases for Freud. Conversely, he had to read almost as many from Freud when he sent his patients to Zürich to consult Jung.[23] These added to the burden of Jung's other correspondence, which included letters he wrote at Bleuler's peremptory request to the relatives of patients, cantonal authorities, other institutions, and miscellaneous inquirers.[24] Jung was actually relieved when Freud said he could not make a Christmas visit to Zürich.

From the end of November until late March, Jung was periodically bedridden, felled by recurring gastroenteritis or influenza (he described it as one or both, depending on his correspondent). He expended much energy trying to schedule time to go alone to the thermal baths in nearby Baden or to the Italian sunshine of Lago Maggiore.[25] In mid-February, he apologized to Freud yet again for not writing, saying he had been too weak to do anything other than the bare minimum at the Burghölzli: "All sorts of psychogenic complications insinuated themselves" and "a complex connected with my family played the very devil with me."

Emma naturally wanted him to spend time in Schaffhausen with her and the children during the holidays. He did, but both his mind and body were absent from the cheerful public rooms where the family gathered. Pleading illness, he pretended to be resting in bed while he chafed at his general inability to do any of his own scientific work. He had to give an important lecture at the university to inaugurate the new term in mid-January, and he wanted it to be a blazing account of his own work and a further paean to Freud.[26] But as he was surrounded by so many family members and children, his mind was a muddle and he was unable even to draft notes. It did not help matters when Emma and the girls got the flu. Servants took care of everyone's physical needs, but Emma was unable to provide even the minimum professional assistance he had come to take for granted, such as helping him with the notice he had to write and mail for the proposed First Congress for Freudian Psychology,[27] now set for Salzburg on April 26–28.

JUNG ORGANIZED the congress himself, which generated a barrage of tiny tempests in minuscule teapots. It started with Jones, who was "shocked" by the "pretentious title" and wanted the word "meeting" instead. By limiting the topic to "Freudian" psychology, Jung had "personalised what should remain objectively scientific."[28] Jung sent a second invitational letter, stressing the "*completely private nature* of the project,"[29] hoping it would soothe ruffled English and Viennese egos. Jones then accused him of an "attitude" of rigidity that would give Bleuler "a handle for criticism," which was a convenient excuse for his own.[30] A turf war erupted when the German Society for Psychiatry announced that it also planned to convene in Berlin on April 24–25, thus overlapping the Frankfurt meeting of the Congress for Experimental Psychology. Travel costs and time constraints created a dilemma for many of the doctors, who had to choose from among the three societies. Most decided initially that Jung's Salzburg congress would be superfluous. Others, such as Claparède and the Genevans and Jones and the London contingent, decided to go to the experimental psychology meetings in Frankfurt and then to Salzburg for Freudian theory. Bleuler cited financial constraints, saying he would go only to Berlin to deliver a paper and then return directly to Zürich. Fearing further defections, Jung begged Freud (who did not plan to attend either the Berlin or Frankfurt conference) to come to Salzburg and lecture on any subject he chose. He sent Freud twelve copies of the "impudent invitations"[31] (the initial announcement) in the hope that Freud would persuade a large contingent of his Viennese followers to attend. Freud told Jung he hoped most would not come, "because they are not all fit to exhibit."[32]

The German Karl Abraham, whom Jung never liked when he was at the Burghölzli, threatened to become an irritant from Berlin, where he had moved and established a practice. In December 1907, Abraham made his first pilgrimage to Vienna. Jung had already told Freud he disliked Abraham because he would listen attentively to anything Bleuler and Jung discussed and then rush something similar into publication. Jung added that patients disliked Abraham, other assistants disdained him, and his only virtue was his bureaucratic efficiency. Never mind, Freud replied, he liked Abraham because he attacked sexuality "head-on."[33] Freud reported to Jung every bit of gossip about others, so Jung naturally worried about what they said about him. Freud relayed the details with seeming guilelessness, creating feelings of rivalry in Jung, finding the situation advantageous to exploit.

Freud knew that Abraham was the more dependable of his two adherents — or three if he included Bleuler, whose reticence was becoming a major concern. Freud was "rather annoyed with Bleuler for his willingness to accept a psychology without sexuality, which leaves everything hanging in mid-air."[34] He knew that Bleuler was to speak about his research into dementia praecox at the Berlin conference and feared he might depart even further from Freudian orthodoxy by insisting (rather than hinting, as he had recently done) that organic abnormalities were the root cause of the illness.[35] Freud felt scant relief when Bleuler delayed taking sides by limiting his paper to a discussion of his own findings and omitting all references to Freud. The question of how to gain Bleuler's total allegiance loomed large.

For two days in a row Freud wrote letters urging Jung to offer the chairmanship of the Salzburg conference to Bleuler.[36] He called himself an "outlawed knight" and said it would make a much better impression on the world at large if the "oldest and most authoritative" of his defenders presided. He urged Jung's support, saying his "Viennese [would] be much better behaved with [Bleuler]." Freud asked Jung to consider this request "personal," and to sweeten his plea, Freud moved their relationship one step closer to the purely personal. In a society where letter writing was governed by extremes of etiquette, Freud changed his usual professional salutation of "Dear Friend and Colleague" to the intimate "Dear Friend." Jung noticed the change immediately. His next letter was still addressed to "Dear Professor Freud," whom he thanked "with all my heart" for "the undeserved gift" of friendship.[37] Jung, still cautious, asked to "enjoy" the friendship "not as one between equals but as that of father and son," which would "prevent misunderstandings and enable two hard-headed people to exist alongside one another in an easy and unstrained relationship."

Jung appreciated Freud's concern about Bleuler but asked him to stop insisting Bleuler be made chairman. With the most objectivity he had expressed toward his superior in years, Jung explained that Bleuler had "that magnificent Zürich open-mindedness," which he himself valued as one of the "highest virtues." He told Freud that Salzburg would be "a modest meeting" where they should avoid formalities, "as is customary at our more republican meetings in Switzerland."

Jung got his way on everything. Bleuler did go to Salzburg after Berlin, but he did not speak. When the "historic occasion" was convened on April 27, 1908, in the Hotel Bristol, there was "no Chairman, no Secretary, no Treasurer, no Council, no kind of sub-committee whatever, and — best of all — no business meeting!" To top it all off, the entire proceedings "occupied only one day."[38] They were as "international" as Freud and Jung had both hoped: forty-two persons listened to nine papers given by speakers from Austria (four); Switzerland (two); and England, Germany, and Hungary (one each). The group unanimously endorsed the new journal, and the *Jahrbuch für psychoanalytische und psychopathologische Forschungen* was officially founded, directed by Bleuler and Freud and edited by Jung.

The only hint of discord came from the Viennese delegation, who complained that not only had they not been consulted but they were not represented in the journal. With his usual haughty disdain for his closest followers, Freud had discussed the *Jahrbuch* in detail only with Jung, bringing in Abraham, Brill, Jones, and Ferenczi much later, when it was a fait accompli. Bleuler still evaded the full and total embrace of Freud's ideas, but he agreed to be the *Jahrbuch*'s co-director because he sincerely believed in the possibilities for open discourse that it was supposed to offer. Freud ignored Bleuler's intention, concentrating his delight on Bleuler's name on the masthead, which signified that the Zürich-Vienna axis was not only intact but also blessed by the imprimatur of the most highly regarded academic psychiatrist to embrace the newly founded psychoanalysis. For the time being, Freud thought it enough and returned to Vienna "pleased . . . refreshed . . . and with a pleasant aftertaste."[39] Jung thought differently, being "of two minds" about whether to apply a "business" or "emotional yardstick" to the proceedings.[40] Freud's lecture was "perfection itself," but everything else had been "simply padding, sterile twaddle in the darkness of inanity."

As soon as he returned to Zürich, Jung was confronted with the ongoing impediments of his daily life, starting with the seemingly unending negotiations with publishers over the *Jahrbuch*. The main frustration, however, was his inability to find time for his own research. "The chief obstacle is my pupils," he told Freud. "Training them and overseeing their papers consume my time. They get ahead at my expense, while I stand still." As he listened to the papers in Salzburg, he resented that others were presenting work on dementia praecox, while he had done no significant research to speak of for the previous nine months and saw little possibility of doing any in the future. He had read nothing new and had not had any discussions of substance with anyone in Zürich. He concluded his letter to Freud with another of his periodic gestures of independence, claiming his need to be more than "just a faithful follower." Freud had no shortage of those, he said, "but they do not advance the cause, for by faith alone nothing prospers in the long run."

Freud more or less ignored Jung's black mood, ascribing it to a temporary "negative oscillation." Jung could overcome it, he said blithely, as he tripped along to his chief interest, the *Jahrbuch*. He confided that Jones had been to see him twice, using the Englishman's name as he had earlier used Abraham's to goad and mollify Jung in equal part. Freud said Jones gave him a feeling of "racial strangeness" and asked Jung how he was able to get along with such a "fanatic [who] doesn't eat enough." Still, Freud intended to see Jones again at the next meeting of the Wednesday Society and ordered Jung to stop "the rift in the making" between himself and Abraham. He directed Jung to include Abraham's paper in the first *Jahrbuch*: "We mustn't quarrel when we are besieging Troy."[41]

On the same day Freud wrote this to Jung, he wrote to Abraham, instructing him that even though he was "in the right," he must defer to Jung on everything, and their "inevitable" rivalry had to stop. He told Abraham to discuss with Jung everything he intended to write before he put a word to paper, to listen to Jung's objections, and then to change his arguments accordingly. It was imperative that Jung "should find his way back to the views that he has now abandoned."[42] Just as he had played on Jung's emotions over Bleuler, Freud now played on Abraham's with the same words: such an "act of courtesy" would be "a great personal favor" and give him "great pleasure." Freud cheerfully concluded that this was only a "small self-sacrifice," and Abraham should not "make too heavy going" of it.

The last paragraph of Freud's letter has been debated by nearly everyone who has studied his brief alliance with Jung, for it gives one of the earliest examples of the Christian/Jewish undercurrent that plagued it. Freud said it was easier for Abraham to follow his ideas because of "racial kinship," whereas Jung, "a Christian and a pastor's son, finds his way to me only against great inner resistances." He needed Jung: "I nearly said that it was only by his appearance on the scene that psycho-analysis escaped the danger of becoming a Jewish national affair."

"I hope you will do as I ask," he concluded firmly. Six days later, when Abraham had not replied, Freud wrote again to "reinforce" his "request."[43] Abraham acceded to all his demands. Jung still felt "undisguised contempt" for Abraham's continuing appropriation of the ideas of others, but he accepted Freud's dictum that Abraham be entrusted with preparing abstracts and editing German submissions for the first *Jahrbuch*. Abraham was "simply not a gentleman" in Jung's view, which was "just about the worst thing that can happen to anyone."[44]

AND SO, with consciences salved, egos soothed, rivalries smoothed, and crises staved off, Freud's much desired journal limped into being, and none of his followers deserted. The cauldron containing his polyglot international stew bubbled merrily, and for the time being, flavors melded nicely and aromas were decidedly pleasant. There were one or two strong spices, but he expected that in time they would blend with the rest. Fülöp Stein in Budapest was more interested in anti-alcohol treatment than psychotherapy, but Sandor Ferenczi remained devoted; Bleuler was hesitant, but Jung kept the Zürich group loyal with the full force of his belief. Meanwhile, the curious Americans held fast to their vaunted independence while still wanting to be apprised of every detail, and Jones was successfully proselytizing in London. Neither Jung nor Freud concerned himself with the French, but both worried about how to convert the many warring German psychological factions, which considered themselves superior to each other and certainly to anything coming from Zürich or Vienna.

Freud's main worry, however, was Jung, but he couched his concern about allegiance in the question of how best to keep the Zürich group in close contact with the Vienna Psychoanalytic Society. To this end, he suggested that he and Jung exchange news and information on a weekly basis, adding smugly that he could always make the time to do so. He hoped Jung's "multifarious other occupations"[45] would not divert him, for the research into neuroses was the foundation of their entire enterprise.

CHAPTER 10

"... Like My Twin Brother"

Freud had no idea how many "multifarious other occupations"[1] were keeping Jung busy or how far-reaching were the changes they were instrumental in causing in his life.

"I have been dabbling in spookery again," he wrote offhandedly some months before the Salzburg congress, telling Freud he had been named an honorary fellow of the American Society for Psychical Research because of his "services as an occultist."[2] "Here, too," he added, as if to mollify an unbeliever, Freud's discoveries were "brilliantly confirmed." He asked Freud's opinion of this sort of research, but Freud didn't reply.

Zürich was a center for serious investigation into psychic phenomena in Jung's Burghölzli years,[3] and from time to time until the early 1930s, he attended séances or meetings either as an official participant or a private observer.[4] But while he worked at the Burghölzli, his observations took place almost entirely in the capacity of an assistant to Bleuler, whose interest in psychic phenomena and parapsychology was equal to his own.[5] Americans came to Zürich primarily to observe Bleuler's experiments, not Jung's, and once they returned to their homeland, they solicited Bleuler's advice about their own. Bleuler continued to shun every sort of honor or recognition, but he still took umbrage when the Americans honored his subordinate with membership in their society and did not offer it to him.

"Spookery" was just about the only kind of research Jung was able to observe with any consistency. He was eager to get on with observations concerning dementia praecox, especially in the patient Emile Schwyzer, the controversial "Solar Phallus Man" whose case he had first observed in 1901.[6] Jung wanted to expand his 1907 publication, using Schwyzer as the focal point of a larger study, and observe such symptoms of paranoia as fixed complexes, which he suspected probably could not be integrated into consciousness. He sent an abbreviated version of Schwyzer's case history to Freud on June 4, 1907,[7] but by early sum-

mer 1908 chafed that he had been unable to do more than write a detailed summary of the case as a "Patient History" for hospital records.[8]

Unfortunately, Jung got no further than conjecture, because a troublesome
new patient was admitted.

DR. OTTO Gross had been confined as Bleuler's patient in July 1902 and again
in 1904.[9] He was readmitted in May 1908, this time armed with a certificate
from Freud specifying that he was to be Jung's patient.[10] Gross's previous incarcerations were for addictions to morphine, cocaine, and opium, habits he acquired in 1900 while employed as a steamship doctor sailing between Germany
and South America.

Born March 17, 1877, in Gniebing, near Feldbach, Austria, Otto Gross was
the only child of Dr. Med. Hans Gross, professor of criminology and criminal
law in Graz and founder of the *Archiv für Kriminalanthropologie und Kriminalistik* in Leipzig.[11] Hans Gross was domineering and his wife subservient; in their
household Otto was sheltered and pampered, and discipline was erratic and
punitive.[12] Otto's earliest memory was of his sometimes fierce, sometimes in-
dulgent father warning a visitor that "he *bites!*"[13] Otto attended private schools
and took his medical degree in Graz in 1899. After the year as ship's doctor, he
became a psychiatric intern and resident in Munich during the academic year
1901–02. The hospital provided easy access to drugs, and the city offered a
highly politicized coffeehouse culture. Gross indulged in both and had periods
of such total dysfunction that he had to be hospitalized. Still, he managed to do
a minimal amount of research and writing. By 1907, his published articles and
books showed his penchant for political, cultural, and sexual revolution and a
flamboyant advocation of sex, drugs, and anarchy.[14] They were considered a serious threat to the established values of the German-speaking bourgeoisie and
earned opprobrium from the psychological establishments represented by
Freud, Jung, and diverse academic enclaves.[15]

Gross's notoriety stemmed also from the sheer force of his good looks, erratic behavior, and manic peregrinations in Austria, Germany, and Switzerland.
A comment from his original admission to the Burghölzli in 1902 aptly described him: "He had no sense of duty, could not subordinate himself anywhere,
absolutely had to have his own way, and was lacking in a sense of common
goals."[16] In his day, "analysts [did] not usually write about ecstasy, lust, orgy"[17]
as enthusiastically as Gross did, and he practiced what he wrote with gusto.
"Nichts verdraengen!" (repress nothing!)[18] was his credo, and he had the extraordinary ability to persuade others to do the same. Gross said his primary goal was
"not to be like other people." He also claimed to be asexual until 1901, when he
was twenty-four.[19]

Jung first met Otto Gross at the 1907 Amsterdam congress, for he had been
largely absent on sabbatical leaves during Gross's prior incarcerations at the
Burghölzli in 1902 and 1904.[20] In June 1907, Jung found "all sorts of oddities"

in Gross's latest book, even though he admitted grudgingly that Gross had "an excellent mind."[21] After hearing his Amsterdam paper, so full of energetic support for Freud, Jung regretted that a man with "a very intelligent head on him" could be "such a psychopath."[22]

Ernest Jones told Freud he was "a little uneasy" about Jung treating Gross "psychically" because of the "fundamental differences of opinion between them on moral questions."[23] Two weeks after Gross became his patient, Jung addressed some of Jones's concerns in several self-righteous passages to Freud.[24] Jung objected to Gross's comparison of Freud with Nietzsche, but more to his assertion that "the truly healthy state for the neurotic is sexual immorality." He lauded sexual repression (in the sense of monogamous self-control) as an "important and indispensable civilizing factor" and thought Gross was going too far "with the vogue for the sexual short-circuit." Gross's view, he concluded, was "neither intelligent, nor in good taste, but merely convenient, and therefore anything but a civilizing factor."

Gross was two years younger than Jung, and their social backgrounds and medical education were similar. Otherwise, they had nothing in common but their support of Freud.[25] Like Jung, Gross was also married, to the former Freida Schloffer, daughter of a poor lawyer in Graz.[26] Freida was so thrilled to have married above her social station and so besotted with her "Blond Dionysius" that she conveniently ignored the snowy cocaine that usually dusted the front of his jacket, as well as the parade of other women he bedded and children he fathered.[27] The usually bedraggled Freida Gross, "one of the few Teutonic women"[28] Freud ever liked, tagged along after Otto during his escapades, following him from Graz to Munich, Ascona, and now to Zürich. She agreed with Hans Gross, who spent much of his life taking legal action to have Otto declared incompetent to handle his own affairs,[29] that Otto should be committed to a mental hospital.[30]

Hans Gross first tried to get Otto into Kreuzlingen, but the Binswangers said they had no room (conveniently or otherwise is not known). By default, everyone agreed that he should be admitted to the Burghölzli. The problem was that Otto Gross disliked Bleuler so intensely he refused to be treated by him.[31] Hans contacted Freud, whether to mediate or to attend is not certain, but Freud did some fancy verbal footwork to avoid direct contact with the mercurial will-o'-the-wisp. Bleuler told Hans Gross that "the influence of Herr Prof. Freud, of which we expected most, proved to be completely impotent."[32] It may have been why Freud insisted to Jung that Otto "urgently needs your medical help,"[33] thus leaving the recalcitrant patient to him.

Throughout his life, Jung did indeed have a certain degree of difficulty maintaining objectivity with some of his patients, and Ernest Jones was correct to place Gross among them. To complicate the situation, Jung became moody and irritable in the weeks preceding the Salzburg congress, and his occasional outbursts had since deepened into black rages.[34] He had always resented daily administrative responsibilities, and the burden of details connected with the up-coming conference was particularly aggravating. Everything was exacerbated by Jones's "Chinese rigidity" and "remarkable political and organizational abili-ties." Jung secretly compared Jones to a little bulldozer, eager to bury him and take his place with Freud.[35] Adding to the pressures imposed by Bleuler and Freud during the conference were the several letters Hans wrote imploring Jung as a personal favor to take Otto back to Zürich and into the hospital.

"Of course [Otto] Gross will give me the slip," Jung noted morosely. And of course he did, rushing back to Munich, drugs, and dissipation as soon as the conference ended. When Bleuler heard the news, he wrote to Hans and urged him to "travel personally to Munich and with the help of the health police, take [his] son and bring him forcefully into an institution."[36] Freida Gross had trun-dled to Munich in Otto's wake, and Ernest Jones, who was "seriously smitten"[37] with her, followed them both. Jones told Freud he went to Munich to treat Freida only at Otto's behest, but Freud worried that his instruction to Jones to "gain influence" over Otto was being ignored because of his attraction to Freida.[38] Now it was Freud's turn to write morosely to Jung: "It looks as if this [is] going to end badly."

Freud became involved, however reluctantly, when Bleuler refused to accept Otto without a letter certifying his admission to the Burghölzli and Hans asked Freud to write it. "I confirm," Freud wrote, "that Dr. Otto Gross, private lec-turer of neuropathology, whom I have known personally for years, urgently needs to be admitted to a closed institution so that he may achieve his with-drawal from opium and cocaine under medical supervision; throughout the last years he has been taking these medications in a manner that threatens his phys-ical as well as psychological health."[39] On May 6, 1908, Freud enclosed the cer-tificate in a letter to Jung, imploring him to keep Gross firmly confined until "October, when I shall be able to take charge of him."[40]

Freud's letter raises two questions, particularly because Freud enjoyed the full trust of both Hans and Otto Gross: Why didn't Freud take Otto directly to Vienna when the Salzburg congress ended, as Hans begged him to do? Granted Freud wanted to take a summer vacation, but that was not until several months later. And what did Freud expect to become so changed in his highly regulated life in October that he could treat Otto then? The most common response from partisans of both Freud and Jung is that Freud wanted Jung to detoxify Otto, af-ter which he would step in to psychoanalyze and pronounce him cured. Jung's response to Freud's proposal was to complete Otto's detoxification and psycho-analyze him without Freud's assistance, and in an amazingly short time.

On May 11, five days after Freud wrote his certification letter, Otto Gross entered the Burghölzli, escorted by his wife alone. Jung began immediately to treat him.[41] He did not write to Freud until May 14, and then only to say he had no time to confide details because Gross was consuming his every minute, day and night. Jung's first step was to record Gross's medical history, incorporating every minute scrap of information he could glean during long talks with Freida.[42] Thus, Jung gave her opinions about her husband's behavior primacy and authority, as they comprise the beginning of the written record.[43] Freida told Jung that, even in Otto's youth and long before his addictions began, he was never able to adjust to the ordinary routines of life because he believed himself super-extraordinary. Otto's addiction to cocaine began when he was Kraepelin's assistant in psychiatry. An appointment at Kraepelin's Nervenklinik der Ludwig-Maximilians-Universität in Munich was extremely prestigious, so highly regarded that doctors throughout the world came to observe his procedures.[44] Otto's outlandish behavior stood out in such an atmosphere from the moment he insisted that all the other doctors regard him as a prophet and pay homage. When he awakened patients in the middle of the night to examine them and force them to engage in games and exercises for his amusement, Kraepelin confiscated Otto's hospital keys and dismissed him, but not before Otto managed to steal large quantities of drugs. At every step, Hans intervened to keep Otto from serious punishment, and because of the medical establishment's high respect for Hans Gross, Otto's serious medical infractions were repeatedly dismissed as boyish pranks.

Freida told Jung their happiest years were 1905 to 1907, when they lived in Munich and made their first trip to Ascona. In Munich, they lived in the Schwabing district, where avant-garde intellectual life flourished: Musicians like Bruno Walter played piano in cafés while Frank Wedekind and Erich Mühsam sang the songs of Hofmannsthal, Dehmel, and Thoma; anarchists like Kropotkin ranted and declaimed to anyone who listened. Mühsam invited them to Ascona, where a group of followers of Henri Oedenkoven, the son of a wealthy Amsterdam industrialist, had established a sort of commune called Monte Verità that was governed by anarchic principles and dedicated to natural healing, vegetarianism, and sexual liberation. Freida called Monte Verità an "erotic emancipation" for them both and repeated what Otto had told Jung in Amsterdam: "Sexual immorality was the most important step toward the liberation of the human being from societal constraints."[45] Jung was "astonished" by Freida Gross, the first woman he met who spoke about choosing sexual partners as casually as his own wife might have discussed shopping for vegetables.

When he began to treat Otto, Jung's primary observation was of delusions, mostly of grandeur. Gross refused to eat except for an occasional vegetable that had to be cooked to his exact specification.[46] Even though all Zürich was wilting in unusually hot weather, he insisted on taking off his underpants repeatedly "to warm them," and wore five or six undershirts at a time.[47] He never washed and was unshaven and unkempt; his room was filthy, and all his belongings were strewn chaotically. He had to have all the lights on all the time, and if he did not think they were bright enough, he became severely agitated. He was highly excitable and wandered through the wards scribbling on walls and floors, making "very odd drawings of people and other things." Jung studied them carefully, hoping they would offer a key to the workings of his unconscious thought processes.[48] Gross insisted on being allowed to wander at will, both inside the hospital and in the gardens, and if anyone forbade him to do so, he would take to his bed with a pillow over his head, lying in catatonic rigidity of long duration.

Throughout his confinement, Gross easily found someone, probably on the hospital staff, to provide him with extra drugs to buffer the ever diminishing dosage of powerful anaesthetics that Jung prescribed during his withdrawal. Gross mixed them freely with opium, his current drug of choice, and as Jung could always tell when he had done so, he responded by decreasing the medication correspondingly. Gross still tried everything to get Jung to give him larger quantities of drugs, from pleading to bribery to unspecific threats of blackmail, all of which led to naught. "He has no insight that this would be impossible in a psychoanalytic relationship," Jung wrote in his patient notes.

Gross wanted Jung at his beck and call, and if the doctor didn't come fast enough, the patient became violent. There were destructive outbursts during which he broke furniture and thrashed about so furiously that he had to be restrained. As the bouts were unpredictable and happened day and night, and as Jung held himself entirely responsible for curing Freud's wunderkind, he was exhausted. Each nighttime summons disturbed the pregnant Emma, so Jung slept in a residents' lounge. Emma disliked it because sometimes several days passed without their seeing each other. There were strain and stress on every front of Jung's life.

Everything deteriorated until the end of May, when Jung decided to try another tactic and told Otto about Freida's version of his illness. He listened calmly and then insisted that she be admitted as a patient so that he — her husband and the man who knew her best — could analyze her. Jung naturally refused, so Gross declared that he would have to analyze Jung instead. This was normal procedure for Gross, whose own psychoanalytic studies of patients frequently resembled the diagnoses his doctors made of him: "He was as often patient as doctor, and was widely recognized as a gifted analyst and theoretician as well as declared to be a dangerous lunatic."[49]

As soon as he assumed traces of medical bearing, Gross began to have longer stretches of calmness and lucidity. "The worst withdrawal symptoms often disappeared during conversation and without renewed [dosage]," Jung reported. For the first ten days of June, he reduced Gross's medication steadily, and even though Gross protested (which Jung noted carefully in his daily record), he improved. On June 12, Jung noted that he had stopped all medications and pronounced him free of drugs. As he was still prone to anger, subject to tears, and full of grandiose plans for his future, Jung's declaration might be questioned, especially as he added that Gross either spent his time pacing constantly or lying in bed for days on end, "avoiding the demands of reality."

Freida Gross visited on June 14, and Otto told her he wanted her to discharge him. She refused, provoking one of his most violent outbursts. When he was finally calm, Gross told Jung he was completely cured but threatened a relapse into "anxiety neurosis" if Jung did not discharge him at once. He added that he hated Freida and had just left her permanently, so she had no further authority over his case. Jung did not record whether he administered drugs to calm the patient during this time.

On June 16, Gross veered into manic happiness that included constant proclamations of undying love for Freida, the announcement that all was well between them, and an assurance that he had resigned himself to remaining in the hospital. June 17 saw other grandiose manic delusions, most concerning the important work he had to do immediately but could not begin until Jung discharged him. Gross raced around his room collecting dirty clothes, cigarette butts, and scraps of paper that were supposedly part of this "great work," all of which he insisted were needed for his career as a ship doctor on the long voyage he intended to take with an unidentified "female friend."

It was the last conversation between Jung and his patient, for that afternoon during an unsupervised walk around the grounds, Otto Gross escaped over the garden wall. "He had free access to the garden," Jung wrote succinctly. "He has no money with him." The next day Jung received a letter from Gross, saying he was in a Zürich hotel and asking for money to begin his long journey. Jung had already telegraphed Freida, who had returned to Munich on the fourteenth, asking her to come collect her husband. By the time she got to Zürich, Otto was gone. "Who knows where?" Jung wrote. "Probably Heidelberg."

Jung's last entry into Gross's patient history was written on June 19: "Whereabouts unknown." He never saw Otto Gross again.[50]

THE IMPACT on Jung's life and work of his brief interaction with Otto Gross has been a subject of debate and controversy, and in recent years some revisionism. The current "temptation" has been to "romanticize Gross as a forgotten genius/martyr of the analytic movement,"[51] which he certainly was, but it ignores everything else about him, especially his headlong rush to self-destruction. Jung realized Gross's personal complexity and recognized his intellectual contribution to psychoanalysis probably as much as Freud did, but for different reasons. Freud was cognizant of Gross's intellectual acumen, but he was more impressed with his stature as the brilliant son of a distinguished professor and especially with the fact that he was another Christian, a quality Freud actively sought among his followers. Jung's primary interest was in how the excesses of Gross's personal life could be brought under control, at least long enough to harness his intellectual ability in the hope it would permit him to do further important research.

When Jung tried to tell Freud what had transpired between him and Gross in May and June 1908, he wrote a subdued account, arguably aimed at putting the best possible perspective on a grim situation that ended badly and in embarrassment, but it was still an account filled with personal anguish. One wonders why, now that Gross was gone and Jung had the time, he did not relate the details of Gross's patient history to Freud in the same detail as he conveyed other patients' histories whenever he sought advice. Why, for example, did he not describe in his earlier letters some of Gross's more vivid delusions, his various ways of acting out his compulsions, his need for drugs? Why did he limit his remarks to his alleged successes in analytic sessions? Was it because his need to prove the efficacy of psychoanalysis according to Freud was overwhelmingly important? It would seem so, but then there were other aspects of the Jung-Gross encounter that Jung eliminated entirely from the patient history and only hinted at, especially his own participation in the analysis.

No detailed record exists to verify what the analysis consisted of apart from the notation of doctor-patient sessions or conversations. As early as May 25, Jung told Freud that his analysis was finished except for "minor obsessions of secondary importance."[52] Jung never specified what these were, stressing instead how mutually rewarding their encounters had been; whenever he faltered, he switched their roles and allowed Gross to analyze him — all to the benefit of Jung's own "psychic health." Granted, psychoanalysis was still a fledgling science with no code of conduct, no rules, and no fixed boundaries, which may be why Freud heartily approved of the doctor ceding medical authority to a clearly disturbed patient and then accepting the patient's diagnosis of what ailed him. Freud urged Jung to cultivate a friendship in the hope that a scientific collaboration between him and Gross would result. He admitted how "amazed" he was that Jung completed the analysis in just two weeks, saying it would have taken him "much longer."[53]

The date of Jung's next account of Gross's treatment, June 19, 1908, is telling, for it is the exact opposite of his earlier optimistic account and reflects the chaotic month just passed. It is also a clear account of how his treatment failed to affect the seriously ill patient and how deeply distressed he was by its failure. Ultimately, it is about how much the experience of knowing Otto Gross meant to him. With palpable sadness, Jung admitted that none of the "moments of profound empathy"[54] that passed between them would have any lasting effect; Otto Gross would never have a "psychological yesterday"; and he would go through life responding to everything that happened to him "like a six-year-old boy." He would remain locked forever into "heaven knows what monstrous possibilities." Despite his failure, Jung considered Gross a "friend, for at bottom he is a good and fine man with an unusual mind."

Jung told Freud he had also conducted a "partial psychoanalysis" of Freida in the hope it would help to cure Otto. When he saw that nothing was working, Jung said his diagnosis was one he had "long refused to believe" and now saw "with terrifying clarity: Dem. praec." The letter Otto sent after he escaped was "especially distressing" because he thanked Jung profusely for curing him: "In his ecstasy he has no inkling of the revenge which the reality he has never even glimpsed will wreck upon him. He is one of those whom life is *bound* to reject." Jung was equally saddened that he had been so ineffectual with Freida, who, he said, "sticks it out only because Gross represents for her the fruits of her own neurosis. I now understand her, too, but cannot forgive her on that account."[55]

Treating Otto Gross was "one of the harshest" experiences of Jung's life, but "in spite of the sorrow of it," he would "not have missed [it] for anything." Not only had it given him an insight into "the nethermost depths of Dementia pr.," but it also allowed him to discover much about himself he had not known. Jung told Freud that, except for the dementia praecox, Otto Gross "often seemed like my twin brother." That he had been unable to cure such a twin was indeed "tragic."

The experience was still vivid twenty-seven years later, but Jung changed it utterly when the analyst Dr. Fritz Wittels asked for biographical information about Otto Gross.[56] Jung told Wittels Gross was a megalomaniac who believed he had been hospitalized because his doctors needed treatment that only he could provide. Jung denigrated Gross's writings as spurious with one exception, the paper on secondary functions, which he freely admitted he had integrated into his book on psychological types.[57] Otherwise, he insisted that Gross showed no signs of creativity, unless Wittels wanted to consider relentless chatter and nonsensical joking as symptoms of genius. In contradiction, Jung said that now and then, despite the chaos, Gross exhibited flashes of brilliance, which was why he worked so hard to treat him. Bitterly, he conceded that he had had no success whatsoever.

Jung's hostility toward Gross had begun to intensify long before 1935. His correspondence with Freud shows the gradual hardening of negativity, as when he described Gross as "a complete nut."[58] In truth, Jung began to think of Gross as hopeless from the moment he leaped impetuously over the garden wall. His feelings were tinged with sadness, for he missed Gross's "wonderfully stimulating" conversation. He told Freud there had been only one "really intelligent man" to talk to for several months after Gross departed, Professor Adolf Meyer, who came from New York to observe hospital procedures.[59]

Jung's sadness quickly turned to anger, and much of the force that directed it toward Gross may have been an amalgam of feelings of betrayal that Gross could so easily have abandoned him. It could also have been a defensive feint to deflect or otherwise avoid having to confront a host of more authentic emotions that Gross caused to surface during their mutual analysis. Until Jung met Gross, the only time Jung the doctor had assumed the patient's mantle of introspection was in the association experiments and an occasional letter to Freud, wherein he related one of his dreams or confided something about himself that he wanted Freud to know. Most times, Freud provided only cursory comfort, as if he did not want to risk saying anything that might lead to a kind or degree of intimacy he could not control. Yes, yes, Freud's letters seem to say, here is a sop of comfort for your personal concern of the moment, but now let us return to the main business of our acquaintance, the furtherance of Freudian psycho-analysis.

It must have been breathtaking for Dr. Carl Jung to find that Dr. Otto Gross, someone as brilliant as himself, wanted to probe into his thoughts, challenge his every basic assumption, and pose the one simple question he had never had the time or given himself permission to ask: Why not?[60]

Why not?, on so many different levels, in regard to so many different aspects of his life. *Why not* question Bleuler's authority, and *why not* try to institute changes in hospital procedure and personal responsibilities? *Why not* stop being so deferential to Emma just because of her great fortune, and *why not* insist that she behave as a good Swiss wife rather than an intellectual partner in the marriage? And, most important of all, *why not* permit himself to enjoy the perquisites, if not the pleasures, of other female company?

One year after Otto Gross bolted, Jung told Freud that knowing him had been one of the two most "bitter experiences" in his psychoanalytic career to date: "To none of my patients have I extended so much friendship and from none have I reaped so much sorrow."[61]

CHAPTER 11

— ∞∞ —

Poetry

Besides Otto Gross, Jung had another cause of sorrow, his former patient Sabina Spielrein. Now in her first year of medical school, she occasionally participated in research projects of the Burghölzli doctors. She treated Jung with distanced politeness, was brusque with everyone else, and had nothing good to say about any of her colleagues, especially the women.[1] She decided to write her dissertation under Bleuler's supervision toward the end of 1907, thus removing herself further from Jung's aegis and granting him a respite on one front at least.

The situation between Jung and Bleuler was decidedly strained throughout 1908. It was exacerbated by Gross's departure, which Bleuler interpreted as Jung's unforgivable failure of treatment and hostile disregard of his rules for administrative procedure.[2] The year 1908 marked the beginning of Jung's last of eight years at the Burghölzli and a dramatic shift in his position vis à vis Bleuler. It had been a long time since he was Bleuler's "humble student" (as Bleuler scornfully addressed him in public). Now, because of the *Jahrbuch*, Bleuler spoke sarcastically of Jung as a "scientific giant" or a "triumphant rival."[3] Officially, Bleuler was co-director of the *Jahrbuch* and Jung was merely the editor, but Jung made all decisions without consulting him, confiding only in Freud. Such arrogant behavior increased Bleuler's doubts about lending his name to the whole Freudian enterprise. Bleuler was also convinced that Jung let no opportunity pass without mocking him, but what goaded most was how Jung ignored him in the hospital, going about his duties "as if he owned the place."[4] All the assistant doctors were aware of the tension between their superiors and either chose sides openly or cautiously avoided having to do so. Spielrein tried to have it both ways, with Bleuler as her dissertation director, and Jung as her particular confidant and friend — whenever she felt the need.

Several days after Gross clambered over the wall, she sent Jung a letter commiserating with his misfortune, giving her own forceful version of why Gross's treatment had gone wrong and asking if a meeting to discuss what happened might be useful. Her overture caught Jung by surprise, but he still replied the same day, telling her in a mixture of colloquial and psychoanalytic language that her rough, tough letter was right on target and had thoroughly grabbed his unconscious. "Of course something like this could only happen to me!"[5] he moaned, not specifying whether he meant Gross's departure or Spielrein's offer of friendship.

He did agree to meet her, but not at the hospital and not for the next several days. He had an appointment in the city on June 30 and suggested that they meet afterward at the Bahnhofstrasse boat landing, where they could take one of the ferries that plied the lake and be alone and speak uninterruptedly. He did not add the most important consideration, that the likelihood of anyone recognizing them would be slight. It is the ambiguous last sentence in this letter, however, that has become a subject of debate in the years since their letters were discovered: in the sun and out on the open water, Jung wrote, it would be easiest "to find clear direction amidst the emotional turmoil."[6] Again, he did not specify its cause.

Jung was so pleased with the boat-ride conversation that he completely changed his mind about Spielrein. She left him with the impression that they were kindred spirits who regarded "life and thought as one" and did not "abuse the power of their mind to devise shackles but rather liberties."[7] He concluded ecstatically that Spielrein would become an intellectual companion whom he could "love" but who would have no other expectations. He did not specify beyond this except to say that for him she would remain an independent spirit for whom the most important qualities of life were "personal freedom and independence."

Whatever Spielrein said to Jung that day, it struck exactly the right chord. They met again on July 3, and Jung left feeling "inwardly calmer and freer." Spielrein was taking a vacation the next week in eastern Switzerland, and he proposed that they travel independently to Rapperswil for another meeting beforehand. Apparently she could not arrange it, so he proposed they meet on the Zürich lakeshore after he finished testifying in a court case, to walk from the Utoquai to Zürichhorn and then back to the Burghölzli. In this letter, she became "My dear!," having progressed from "My dear young lady!" and "My dear friend."

JULY WAS a busy month for Jung. He had to appear as a witness in the district court at least once each week, and he had several private patients in the town. Bleuler went on holiday midmonth and did not return until the end of August, leaving Jung to work "endlessly."[8] Emma, now five months into her third pregnancy, went to Schaffhausen with their daughters in June and planned to stay for four months, until he returned from his month-long military service at the end of October. Even though the maid came to the Burghölzli apartment regularly, Jung still had to take care of the many daily details that ordinarily Emma handled silently and well. And she expected him to spend all his free time in Schaffhausen, especially the weekends. In all of July, he found time to write to Freud exactly once, and then in brevity and haste.

He began with his usual apology, complaining that he was "not a free agent" but, rather, at the beck and call of "half a dozen other people." He would have a "miserably short holiday" from September 1 to 15, which he planned to spend alone in an isolated cabin on Mt. Santis in eastern Switzerland.[9] After that, he hoped to persuade Freud to come to Zürich at the end of his long summer holiday[10] to stay for several days in the Burghölzli apartment. As Emma and the children would still be in Schaffhausen, Jung planned to ask Bleuler to relieve him of hospital duties so that he and Freud could speak uninterruptedly about psychoanalysis in general and the *Jahrbuch* in particular.

Freud accepted with alacrity for a number of reasons, most connected with the first issue. He was still dickering with the masthead, which would eventually list him as Prof. Dr. S. Freud,[11] and wavering between the publishers Marburg and Deuticke (which was eventually chosen). He settled all questions of publication and content: the journal would appear biannually, with the first issue in early 1909. The content would consist of two parts: in the first, papers by Freud, Jung, Abraham, Binswanger, and Alphons Maeder (a French-Swiss doctor now working with Binswanger); in the second, a survey of all published psychoanalytic writings to date, arranged by country of original publication.[12] In short, Freud — not Jung — made every administrative and editorial decision and was ultimately responsible for the launch of the journal as well as its appearance and content.

Freud had two other equally important reasons for wanting to meet with Jung: to resolve the ongoing hostility between Jung and Abraham, and to see if what Abraham had told him about the Zürich group was true. Abraham had become a confidant who exchanged gossip and personal opinions freely with Freud, who felt they "understood" each other and was attracted to the younger man's "consanguineous Jewish traits."[13] Abraham held negative views of everything emanating from Zürich. He thought Bleuler could not be counted on to further Freudian theory, for he was "a mass of reaction formations" whose "external simplicity and often exaggerated modesty cover strong grandiose tendencies."[14] He blamed Jung for the falling attendance at the Zürich group meetings because of his reversion to "former spiritualistic inclinations." Even though Freud knew what Abraham said was basically true, he did not want to accept such an "unfavorable prognosis."[15] With a mixture of diplomacy and pressure, Freud tried to jolly him back in line. He agreed that Bleuler was lost to his cause but insisted that Jung was "a different matter." He said he liked Jung personally and counted on his interest in the *Jahrbuch* to form a bond that could not be broken. He hoped that Abraham's "competitiveness" was not clouding his judgment. "Why cannot I harness Jung and you together," he moaned, with "your precision and his élan?"

To Jung, Freud wrote that he had given up trying to keep Bleuler in check, because his professional interests mattered more to him than being counted among Freud's followers.[16] Then he added a sentence that Jung took to heart, one that had far-reaching consequences for his immediate future: "You would not have invited me if you did not know that Bleuler has no objection and will not interfere with us." Jung took it to mean that Freud did not even want to see Bleuler, let alone talk to him, and a dangerous snub was set in motion.

Freud arrived at the Burghölzli on September 18 and stayed until the twenty-first.[17] During that time, he and Jung spent all their waking hours together, walking, talking, and observing patients. Not once did Freud see Bleuler, not even to exchange greetings at arrival or departure.[18] When he returned to Vienna, he wrote to Abraham that his assessment of the Zürich situation was "only partly" correct: Bleuler's defection was "imminent," and his relations with Jung were "strained to the breaking point." As for Jung, Freud believed he had "overcome his vacillation" and "adheres unreservedly to the cause." He also believed he had healed the breach between Jung and Abraham and urged them to communicate directly as "befits colleagues who respect each other."

Freud left Zürich with an overly optimistic view of his visit, as there were several points on which he was entirely wrong. The first was to think Jung's adherence to his cause was unreserved, even though it may have appeared so in a letter he wrote to Spielrein, who was in Russia with her family.[19] He told her it was his first opportunity to see Freud in an environment other than his own, and it only deepened his impression of what a good and great man he was, so deeply knowledgeable about human nature. If earlier he had only admired Freud from a distance, now he said he sincerely liked him. They had made good use of their time together, and he saw so many things much more clearly.

Freud's visit did him "a world of good," Jung said, omitting how deeply troubled he was by Freud's responses to some of his patients, differences that intensified and hardened over the course of the next several years. The most upsetting was Freud's response to "Babette S.,"[20] an elderly woman psychotic who had been confined all her adult life. Jung thought she had "such lovely delusions,"[21] particularly when she called herself "the Lorelei" and quoted Heine's poetry. Studying her case left him convinced that what others dismissed as delusional ramblings had a certain coherence if only they were listened to intently and interpreted correctly. He described this process as locating the somewhat "normal" personality in the "background." Jung was circumspect about discussing such patients with the other doctors in the hospital, for Bleuler had decreed that schizophrenia was incurable, and therefore no disagreement was allowed. On the rare occasion when Jung did succeed in reaching a patient's somewhat normal background personality and restoring a semblance of normal functioning, Bleuler usually countered that the cure was false because the patient had not been a "real" schizophrenic.

Jung asked Freud to observe Babette S. and was disappointed when he pronounced her merely "interesting." His main reaction was to ask Jung how he tolerated "spending hours and days with this phenomenally ugly female." Jung was "dumbfounded"[22] by Freud's "lack of objectivity" and attributed his thoughtless remark to "how very little he knew of psychiatry."[23] When Jung was an old man, he was still bothered by Freud's disdain for Babette S.: "He was really a layman when it came to psychiatry. . . . He simply only knew *his* theory. And his theory did not suffice. It suffices for a certain area but not for the whole."

Jung wanted Freud to understand Babette S., so he took him into the Burghölzli library and asked him to read a memoir he had been studying since it appeared in 1903, Daniel Paul Schreber's *Memoirs of My Nervous Illness*.[24] Freud agreed to take it to his room but did not read it then, saying he was too tired at night to do more than glance through it. Jung entreated him to study the book, for he believed much could be learned from observing Freud's hypothetical treatment of a patient such as Schreber. "I thought, I would not be able to do it, but he would be!" he said. "I told him he would have to do it sometime!" Eventually Freud read the book, and "he did try it [a hypothetical analysis] then, and he went terribly wrong because he simply doesn't know the spirit of schizophrenia."[25]

Freud was also wrong about Bleuler and Jung's relationship. It was not "strained"; it was totally ruptured. Freud and Jung's "tête-à-tête"[26] had been the crowning insult Bleuler could not accept from his former "humble pupil," now behaving so blatantly as his "triumphant rival." In early October, he asked Jung for his resignation, effective as soon as possible.

Bleuler's request caught Jung off guard, and he responded with confusion. On the one hand, it was something he had long wanted to do, to leave onerous clinical responsibilities behind in order to concentrate on research and writing. He could resign easily because Emma's money was more than enough to support the family, and his own fees from private patients were building nicely.[27] But on the other hand, it came at an inopportune time. Emma was due to deliver her third child in late November, and the house in Küsnacht was still in the early stages of construction and would not be finished until the following spring. She could certainly remain in Schaffhausen until she gave birth, but she didn't want to; nor did she want to move to a temporary residence and then move again several months later.

Also, Jung had to work out the terms of his departure in a manner that would not cause unpleasant gossip and opprobrium toward both men, which neither wanted. Bleuler could not risk being seen as a failed administrator unable to instill order and discipline in his ranks; Jung could not risk adding to his existing reputation as a boisterous bully. He wanted to continue to lecture at the university, and he wanted access to patients, particularly those whose cases he had been following for some time, such as Emile Schwyzer and Babette S. Moreover, the current academic year had just started, and to announce a resignation so early would cause confusion in the petty world of Swiss academic politics.[28]

They arrived at a mutually satisfying agreement: Jung would not resign formally from the Burghölzli until the spring of 1909, when classes were ending at the university and he could move his family directly into the new house. He would give as his reason the desire to pursue his own research; Bleuler would publicly accept his resignation with dignified regret. He would grant Jung continued access to the hospital's laboratory, where he could work until the theses of all the students he was currently advising were completed, but once they were accepted, Jung would have to find his own patients and make his way alone. Jung could also continue to teach at the university, and although the question of duration was not broached in the autumn of 1908, Bleuler fully expected that he would bow out gracefully, probably sometime in early 1910. Jung had no intention of doing so, but he kept this news to himself.[29] In fact, neither man told anyone in October that Jung would be leaving the hospital as soon as the following April. They simply avoided each other whenever possible, and if they had to be together were coldly polite. Alphons Maeder, who observed it all, remembered "the two masters," locked in mortal combat, "fighting to the death."[30]

JUNG BEGAN immediately to tie up the many loose ends that needed his attention. One he had been working on for several months took precedence, a paper based in part on his analysis of Otto Gross that he wanted to publish in the first *Jahrbuch*. He called the essay "The Significance of the Father in the Destiny of the Individual,"[31] and like much of his earlier work, it gave expression to previous theoretical beliefs and hints of those to come. Starting with a brief explanation of the rightness of Freud's regression theory, Jung's thesis was that a father's influence, both hereditary and psychological, was far more lasting and had far more impact upon a family than a mother's. He supported his contention by citing the reaction-time experiments of his pupil Dr. Emma Fürst and, "more particularly, in an analysis carried out conjointly with Dr. Otto Gross."[32]

Jung offered case histories of three patients (a man and two women) to support his thesis before turning to Gross himself, his fourth and most extensively detailed case. In their mutual analysis, Gross had gone into great detail about his lifelong homosexual fixation on his father, which from his earliest childhood led him to masturbate obsessively.[33] He also told Jung how he adored his mother, feared his father, and resented his parents' sexual relationship (mutually satisfying, as Jung interpreted it). Jung included this information and Gross's reactions to it to demonstrate his contention that, whether male or female, the individual was never able to surmount the influence of the father and was shackled forever by what the relationship had been before the child became adult. He argued that neurotic sufferers struggled to free themselves from the imagined "demon" who guided their destiny, and that they chose to believe their "steps had been guided by a power foreign to us." He quoted Shakespeare as cited by Schopenhauer to support his contention that "fate," not God or the devil, was responsible for "our misfortunes and their consequences."[34] Throughout his life, Jung continued to believe this thesis had theoretical validity, and he revised the paper twice, in 1926 and 1948, both times to refine his argument and incorporate new thinking. In the last revision, the concept of fate had become "the archetype."[35] Clearly, in 1908 he was headed toward his theory of the collective unconscious.

By using biblical analogies and references in the essay, he was also making his first exploratory gestures toward mythology in general rather than (as he had done earlier) simply enlisting a particular myth to support the evaluation of a patient. He had been interested in myth ever since Riklin wrote about fairy tales, and now others were, too. Abraham announced that he was working on a new project to investigate the symbolism and numerous analogies between dreams and myths.[36] Freud joined in, telling Jung offhandedly that his thoughts had turned toward mythology, and he was starting to suspect that myth and neurosis had much in common.[37] Everyone, it seemed, would publish on the subject while Jung was still chafing at how to begin his own investigations.

EMMA RETURNED to the Burghölzli in October to await the birth of her third child. Even though the two Bleuler boys played every day with the Jung girls, it was an uncomfortable time, as Hedwig Bleuler treated Emma with the same coldness Bleuler exhibited toward Jung. Emma was lonely while Jung dithered with details surrounding the imminent publication of the *Jahrbuch*. Political machinations were frenzied, as all of Freud's followers jockeyed for position. Jung's response was "more authoritarian than Freud's . . . he would brook no exchanges with his collaborators, was short with them, and made all the decisions."[38]

On November 28, Emma gave birth to a son, Franz Karl Jung. The child was healthy and the mother ecstatic that he was male, but the father's "mood" was "torn to the very bottom."[39] "Now that I have a son I can depart in peace," he told Freud. "A great deal more could be said on this complex theme"[40] — and, although he did not mention them, on many other conflicting emotions. He did tell Freud that he was "inwardly detaching" himself from the Burghölzli and was suddenly aware of how "cramped" his intellectual freedom had been. Freud said the combination of leaving the hospital, the birth of a son, and the paper on the influence of the father suggested he was at a crossroads but headed in the right direction. He assured Jung that his own "fatherhood" would not be an additional burden, for he was "accustomed to giving what I have."[41] Jung agreed with Freud's analysis but added that he was separating from another father as well, Bleuler, on whose part "the tie . . . seems to be the stronger."[42]

He did not tell Freud that throughout these multiple extrications he was becoming entangled with Spielrein. Emma was too busy caring for her three children to listen to her husband's doubts and confusion, but it is unlikely that, as befitted a Swiss husband, he would have confessed any "weakness" to his wife.[43] Instead, he confided in Spielrein. He told her he was rife with fear: for his work, his goals in life, and for the new and mounting opportunities presented to him through his increasing recognition by the international community of analysts. His was a "sensitive soul," and he was troubled by his many weaknesses. Jung, who had always been the most private of men, told Spielrein about how his earliest childhood memories were coming to mind unbidden and he was unable to stop them. He told her about his frequent childhood injuries, and about how the maid saved him from falling off the bridge and into the Rheinfall. He asked her forgiveness for stepping outside the boundaries of a doctor-patient relationship and begged her never "to take revenge" upon him for telling her so many personal secrets. He veered into questions of love, about how he was searching for someone who knew how to love without "punishing, locking in, draining the other." He wanted a lover who could accept "that love will always be its own end and not always the means to an end." He called it his misfortune that he could not be without "passionate, ever changing love." Whenever he fell in love, his first inclination was to pity the woman for dreaming of "infinite faithfulness"; she was destined for a painful awakening because he was incapable of it. Therefore, he added, if a man was already married, it was better for him to commit such deception only once and then repent it that time only, rather than to lie and disappoint over and over again.[44]

He wanted to talk about this "at length" because he needed to "resolve this uncertainty." Would she be free the following Tuesday morning? Could he meet her in her apartment, as she might be "less inhibited" there? He wanted them to arrive at "certain agreements," wanted "to be calm" about her intentions. He wanted her to return some of the "love and patience and selflessness" that he claimed to have given her during her hospitalization. "Otherwise," he concluded, "my work suffers, and my work seems to be more important than the momentary problems and present suffering."

Spielrein told him he could come to the Scheuchzerstrasse. He had not "the slightest idea" where the street was and asked her to meet him at the Bellevue tram station and take him there. They had now known each other for four and a half years, during which Spielrein described Jung as having progressed from her doctor to her friend. Shortly after he asked for this meeting, he became her "'poet,' i.e., my beloved,"[45] no doubt her euphemism for lover, just as "poetry" was her euphemism for sex. She did not elaborate until later, when everything went sour: "Things went as they usually do with 'poetry.' He preached polygamy, his wife was supposed to have no objection, etc. etc."

ON DECEMBER 30, 1908, Freud wrote to thank Jung for the gift of a Christmas cheese, ending with the imperative that they "remain close" in 1909.[46] He also told Jung that G. Stanley Hall, president of Clark University, had invited him to give a series of lectures during ceremonies the first week of July celebrating the "twentieth (!)" anniversary of the university's founding. Freud could not resist European sarcasm toward the youthful American institution, but he was otherwise circumspect. He planned to refuse the invitation because the $400 honorarium was not enough to offset lost income. He told Abraham there was only one good thing about Hall's invitation: it "can be talked about here in Europe."[47] He was much more direct with Ferenczi: "America should bring money, not cost money."[48]

Jung urged Freud to consider the invitation seriously because it would boost his reputation in the United States. He cited Janet's recent trip, in which his American patients paid his travel expenses handsomely, and he mentioned Kraepelin, who was paid "a modest tip of 50,000 marks"[49] for one consultation in California. Clearly, Jung was both aware of and informed about burgeoning American interest in psychoanalysis, but, like Freud, he still considered Americans "a horse of a different colour."[50] When Morton Prince began to back away from the sexual underpinnings of Freudian theory, Jung mocked American prudishness, which he thought showed scant sign of diminishing. He decided he would have to "stomach it" but would no longer "water down the sexuality" for American consumption.

On January 18, 1909, Freud read the first fourteen pages of the *Jahrbuch* and was "delighted" with the "magnificent job" Jung had done.[51] He was still "meddling in editorial affairs," even as he insisted it was all "quite involuntary."[52] He blamed it on the publisher, Deuticke, who, supposedly in the interest of saving time, communicated with him rather than with Jung, "the man in charge." Jung said such meddling was quite all right, as he did not yet feel "too firm in the saddle."[53] Deuticke raised two further editorial questions: the first was about unsolicited contributions, which Freud quickly dismissed. The second was more worrisome: Freud thought Jung's preface seemed to create a division between what he called his "school" and the "Zürich clinic." He requested changes that Jung agreed to make without much thought, for he had other things to worry about.

Bleuler, "with an air of innocence" and "in passive connivance," appointed Riklin to a university lectureship, effectively bypassing Jung for the second time.[54] It was a serious snub, for unlike the Viennese, who freely bestowed the honorific "professor" (even on Freud), the Swiss did not dispense honorary titles. It meant that Jung's academic prospects were bad, because without Bleuler's recommendation he could well be denied the permanent teaching position he believed he needed for professional respectability in Switzerland. Jung blamed Bleuler, but he was unaware that Bleuler had many allies on the faculty who had their own "serious reservations" about Jung's reputation as a womanizer and had been looking for an excuse to oust him.[55] He gave Freud an oblique hint about why the faculty rejected him when, apropos of nothing, he told of a recent conversation between himself and an unnamed young lady. "One has to believe you," she said, "you look at people so *con*vincingly." Jung was actually boasting by saying she accented the syllable "con": in German, the word "*überzeugungsvoll*" is normally stressed on the third syllable to mean "convincing"; when stressed on the first, it means "over-full of procreative power."[56]

Whether or not such gossip trickled to Vienna, Freud quickly issued an invitation for both Jungs to visit in early spring, as soon as the academic term and Jung's position at the Burghölzli ended. There were, of course, many issues to discuss relating to the *Jahrbuch*, but the timing suggests other concerns as well. Freud said Jung's answers to questions about his personal life were evasive, and he hoped all was well.[57]

A week later Freud wrote that Arthur Muthmann paid him a visit and spoke of a woman who called herself Jung's mistress.[58] Freud explained it away as a transference, one of "the perils of our trade." He still expected the Jungs to dine with him and his family a week later. As if to divert further inquiry, two days before Freud wrote this letter, Jung broached the subject of "a woman patient"[59] who had just profaned their friendship "in the most mortifying way imaginable." According to Jung, the woman (later identified as Spielrein) was creating a scandal by telling everyone Jung refused to father her child. She had taken to calling him "Siegfried" and described to all and sundry the magnificent specimen of a child their combined hereditary features would produce. Jung discreetly omitted the details, only telling Freud he had "always acted the gentleman" toward Spielrein. Still, because of his "rather too sensitive conscience," he did not feel "clean" about what had happened. Because his "intentions were always honorable," that hurt him most. "But you know how it is," he entreated, "the devil can use even the best of things for the fabrication of filth."

Jung insisted that something good had come of this bad situation: even after all his self-analysis with Gross, he did not realize until Spielrein's scandal became public that he had "polygamous components." He was pleased that such self-knowledge helped him to "secure moral qualities" that would be advantageous in his later life. Also, and even more important, the emotional turmoil caused his relationship with Emma to grow "enormously in assurance and depth." He addressed Muthmann's charge directly in his next letter, saying he had erupted with "terrific moral reaction" because his heart was "on the whole — blameless." Muthmann's story was "Chinese" to him. He had "never really had a mistress." He was "the most innocent of spouses." This sort of gossip gave him "the horrors."[60]

The scandal in Zürich was much more extensive than Jung admitted to Freud. Small town that Zürich was, medical students as prone to gossip as they were, and with Sabina Spielrein openly proclaiming her feelings to anyone within earshot, everyone believed they were having an affair. She called it poetry, he insisted it was friendship gone awry, and no definitive proof has yet been found to prove one right and the other wrong. Whatever the truth of their relationship, people were talking.

Someone even sent an anonymous letter to Frau Spielrein, telling her to rescue her daughter before Dr. Jung "ruined" her.[61] "There is reason to suspect his wife," Spielrein told Freud, for she was now writing to him to express her side of the equation. Between May 30 and June 20, 1909, besides writing detailed diary entries about Jung, she sent eight rambling letters to Freud to define her version of the relationship.[62] She also included some excerpts and some entire letters that Jung wrote to her mother. According to Spielrein, when her mother received the anonymous missive, she wrote Jung "a moving letter," telling him he had earlier "saved" her daughter and should not "exceed the bounds of friendship" and "undo her now." In his reply Jung told Frau Spielrein that the relationship had progressed from doctor to friend, and because he had "never charged a fee," he did not feel "professionally obligated" to keep anything personal out of it. This is a curious remark, especially as he thanked Spielrein in an earlier letter for "money received," and as Burghölzli patient records show that her father paid him regularly for her Friday afternoon sessions. Money and payment figure perplexingly in the rest of his letter to Frau Spielrein.

"You do understand," Jung asked, "that a man and a girl cannot possibly continue indefinitely to have friendly dealings with one another without the likelihood that something more may enter the relationship? For what would restrain the two from drawing on the consequences of their love?" In answer to his own question, Jung said that only a doctor would know where boundaries lay and would never transgress them, because he was *"paid"* for his trouble (Jung's emphasis). He argued that money alone would impose "the necessary restraints" on his behavior. If Frau Spielrein expected him to "adhere strictly" to the role of a doctor, she should pay him "ten francs per consultation." This would be the "prosaic solution," he concluded, as well as "the more prudent one."

Sabina Spielrein sent this "insulting" letter to Freud, along with fulsome details of her meetings with Jung that described everything but actual sexual congress. On one occasion, she described how they came to physical blows. She grabbed a knife, he took it away, she "boxed his ears," and ran off to her classes. When other students noticed she "was covered with blood," she told them it was his, not hers. "Oh, Lord, what a mess!"

Freud wrote three short letters in reply to her eight or ten, but not until after he heard and accepted Jung's version as the more truthful of the two. Hindsight makes this as suspect as so many of Freud's other conclusions: he wanted to believe Jung's evasive, casuistic explanations even though there were actual witnesses to corroborate much (but not all) of what Spielrein told him. However, Freud did respect Spielrein enough to address her in each letter as "Dear colleague."[63] In his first, he told her not to come to Vienna for a personal consultation. Dr. Jung was his "friend and colleague," he wrote in the second, and therefore could not possibly have engaged in such "frivolous or ignoble behavior." He urged her to suppress and eradicate from her "psyche" whatever feelings she still had about her "close relationship" with Jung, and not try to involve a third person (himself) as mediator.

By the time he sent his third and most conciliatory letter, he had also sent Jung a telegram demanding an explanation. Jung complied by telegram and a long letter as well.[64] He admitted that Spielrein was the woman about whom he had spoken in previous letters and accused her of being the source of the rumor that he would soon divorce Emma and marry her. He said he had no idea what she would do next after having involved Freud as a go-between, but as far as he was concerned, he had made "a clean break" with her. Jung needed to find a way to disparage Spielrein's story and defuse the emotional intensity she had obviously conveyed to Freud, so he collected some experiences from his past and lumped them together, just enough to show that he might have behaved foolishly but had never been morally reprehensible. He spoke of his "compulsive infatuation" years before toward the unnamed woman in Abbazia and passed Spielrein off as someone similar, that is, a totally unthinkable mate for a Swiss Protestant, a "Jewess . . . in another form."

Not wanting to absolve himself completely and thus risk Freud's disbelief, he said that all the while he was trying to cure his "patient . . . gratissime (!)," Gross's "notions" about polygamy as a natural form of human sexuality "flitted about a bit too much" in his mind. His ultimate attempt to diminish Spielrein came in the concluding sentence of the same paragraph, when he changed the subject to Gross, who had not sent him a copy of his new book. Jung asked Freud to send the publisher's name so he could order it and then filled the rest of the letter with matters of business. His ploy was successful; Freud absolved him, calling his letter to Frau Spielrein "ever so wise and penetrating."[65]

"The way these women manage to charm us with every conceivable psychic perfection . . . is one of nature's greatest spectacles,"[66] Freud said as he turned to business, letting Jung assume the mantle of a sheepish "son and heir"[67] who had behaved foolishly and was embarrassed.

Jung put the matter of Sabina Spielrein temporarily to rest on June 21, when he told Freud he had "good news to report."[68] He explained that he had wrongly accused Spielrein of spreading the rumor that he would leave Emma and marry her, for someone unknown had done it. Spielrein had "freed herself from the transference in the best and nicest way." She had not contacted Freud to create "intrigue," but only to pave the way to talk with him about professional matters. Jung had not meant to insult Frau Spielrein, only to assure her that he was not "the gratifier of her daughter's sexual desires but merely her doctor." Still, he would not exonerate himself, for he had committed "sins" and was responsible "for the high-flying hopes" of his "former patient." Now that he had confessed everything to Freud, he begged his "pardon many times" and asked for "a great favor." Jung wanted Freud to convince Spielrein that he had explained everything with "perfect honesty." Freud accepted Jung's version because the "lapse" had to be "blamed on the man and not the woman." Freud asked Spielrein to receive his "entire sympathy for the dignified way in which [she] resolved the conflict."[69]

EVERYTHING THAT Jung described to Freud in the letter above happened during a meeting with Spielrein in his office in the new house, where he and Emma moved in early June.[70] Spielrein wrote in her diary that Jung invited her to the house because he wanted her to become Emma's friend, but "understandably" Emma "wanted no part of this business."[71]

Of the three separate times throughout her married life when Emma Jung seriously contemplated divorce, this was not one of them.[72] She was clearly angry and deeply hurt by the salacious gossip that spoiled what should have been one of the happiest times of her life. So many confusing things had happened since the scandal broke the previous spring, but Emma chose to look ahead rather than backward. She convinced herself she had left everything unpleasant behind when she walked off the Burghölzli grounds for the last time in late March.[73] Her new house was everything she wanted, the perfect setting for a family that now doted on the son and heir. Her husband did everything he could "to paint himself as lily white,"[74] and she chose to believe him.

They left the children in the Küsnacht house in care of Grandmother Emilie and Aunt Trudi[75] and celebrated Jung's resignation by making their second visit to Freud in Vienna, from March 25 to 30. Freud genuinely liked Emma, and he joined the women of his family to welcome her warmly, something he seldom did with other wives who made the pilgrimage to Berggasse 19.

Before they left for Vienna, on March 7 Jung submitted his letter of resignation to the director of public health, Canton of Zürich, asking to be released from his duties on April 15 so he could devote himself to private scientific activities.[76] At the same time, he asked to remain affiliated with the hospital as a volunteer doctor so he could continue to supervise doctoral theses and have access to patients. Bleuler sent an accompanying letter the same day, telling cantonal officials he had known of Jung's impending resignation for some time and had planned accordingly. He had no objection to Jung's continuing affiliation as a volunteer doctor.[77]

It was the end of an era, a farewell to everything that was "average, commonplace, barren of meaning," of "oppressively narrow horizons, and the unending desert of routine."[78] Jung had arrived at the Burghölzli as an unmarried, untested doctor of twenty-five. He left it almost a decade later as a thirty-four-year-old father of three and internationally known and respected research psychiatrist. He was almost at life's midpoint, which he placed at about thirty-five and considered a time of significant change.[79] He believed the tasks governing the first part of life — building a career, establishing a reputation, starting a family — should give way in the second half to something entirely different. Then, he believed, a person seriously searching for individual well-being should turn inward, replacing concentration on the outer with emphasis on the inner life. Jung planned to do this by devoting the second half of his life to research and writing in the sanctuary of his new home.

But on the same day that he resigned from the Burghölzli, "Fate, which evidently loves crazy games,"[80] intervened. It brought him a rich and powerful American patient, Joseph Medill McCormick, one of the heirs to a Chicago newspaper empire.[81] Known as Medill, he had just suffered his second alcoholic breakdown. He was ostensibly on a business trip to Berlin, but the real purpose of his journey was to be treated by Jung in Zürich. He spent two weeks in the Burghölzli as Jung's private patient, and no other doctor was permitted to examine him. Bleuler was furious because McCormick's disease stemmed from alcohol, his special interest, but there was nothing he could do if he wanted to keep the wealthy patient in his hospital. Jung diagnosed McCormick's illness as stemming from a disabling dependence on his powerful mother, "a power devil of the very first rate."[82] He would never recover unless he was somehow removed from her influence. To bring this about, Jung sent a certificate to officials at the *Chicago Tribune* declaring McCormick a hopeless alcoholic and permanently incapable of performing duties. Kate Medill McCormick, his mother, accepted the diagnosis reluctantly, but the others who ran the newspaper were relieved to see him leave. His life "was thus spared through an act of mercy for which Jung earned his patient's lasting resentment."[83] Still, Medill McCormick was Jung's first "so-called brilliant case," and the fact that he had been to Zürich and returned to Chicago "cured" was enough to bring a steady stream of Americans in his wake.[84]

AMERICA WAS in the air as, throughout the spring, Freud remained preoccupied with his invitation to lecture at Clark.[85] When President Hall informed him that the anniversary celebration had been postponed to September and the travel allowance increased to $750 — a very handsome sum indeed — Freud decided to accept. He invited Ferenczi to accompany him (at his own expense) and to make and pay for in advance all the travel arrangements (both his own and Freud's). Freud would reimburse him only after the money came from Clark. Correspondence between the two men became full of details pertaining to when they should travel, from which ports (Mediterranean or northern European), and on which ships.

Suddenly, on June 12, without giving any other details, Jung asked Freud, "Isn't it splendid about America?"[86] He, too, had been invited, but when, why, or by whom was "veiled in something of a mystery."[87] While Freud and Ferenczi continued their dithering over everything from their wardrobes to the prices of separate cabins on various other ships, Jung immediately booked passage on the *George Washington* in "a very expensive cabin."[88] After all their indecisive nattering, they, too, booked passage on the ship. Jung had "a complicated itinerary,"[89] so they arranged to meet in Bremen on August 21, the day the ship would sail.

When they boarded the *George Washington*, Freud saw that the passenger list corresponded to the incorrect identification card he had been issued in the name of Sigmund "Freund." The error was repeated when the ship docked and he and Jung were interviewed by the German-language newspaper the *New Yorker Staats-Zeitung*.[90] Worst of all, William Stern, professor of philosophy at the University of Breslau and also invited to Clark, received featured coverage in an otherwise general article that mentioned some distinguished "German" guests in passing, among them Dr. "Freund."[91]

LEGEND HAS it that Freud and Jung stood on the deck together as the ship sailed into New York Harbor. Freud is supposed to have looked at the skyline of New York City and said, "If they only knew what we are bringing to them."[92] Actually, he had put the matter much more succinctly to Ferenczi many months earlier, when he worried that as soon as the Americans discovered "the sexual underpinnings" of his psychology, "we could soon be 'up shit creek.'"[93]

He was right on both counts.

CHAPTER 12

⚬⚬⚬

America

Tensions lay just beneath the bonhomie from the moment Jung joined Freud and Ferenczi in Bremen. Jung had been responsible for introducing Ferenczi to Freud shortly after he and Fülöp Stein came from Budapest to observe procedures at the Burghölzli. Jung was impressed with Ferenczi's eagerness to learn about psychoanalysis and considered him one of his earliest pupils and first therapeutic analyses.[1] Their work together as "a teaching analysis in the Freudian spirit" so pleased Jung that he gave Ferenczi a glowing letter recommending him to Freud.[2]

Freud took to Ferenczi as he had earlier taken to Abraham, finding a kinship based in large part on their mutual Jewishness and Ferenczi's willingness to extend unquestioning intellectual homage. A friendship began that lasted many years, so close that Ferenczi, whose devotion and allegiance never wavered, was often invited to share the Freud family's holidays and vacations. By the time they got to Bremen, the friendship was already forged, and thus the interpersonal dynamics among the three men had already shifted. Years later, Jung insisted that he was always "the crown prince . . . on top," but he did face competition on this trip from Ferenczi, who behaved as if he were Freud's loyal, devoted servant and busied himself anticipating all of his master's needs. Freud quietly but firmly exploited the situation for all it was worth.

Freud and Ferenczi were both short, slight men, and both were riddled with masses of insecurities. Freud worried endlessly about everything, from not having the proper wardrobe for every possible occasion to the sheer size of the American continent. He feared American "prudery"[3] and particularly what he saw as the overweening crass commercialism of American culture and society. He was prepared to dislike and disapprove of everything even before he departed.

Freud was so timid that he never allowed himself to be in any situation where there was the slightest possibility that he might be confronted or bested. The moment he accepted his invitation to Clark, he insisted that someone he trusted had to accompany him as both buffer and amanuensis. Freud not only expected Ferenczi, a man of modest income who had to pay his own expenses, to go along to guard one of his flanks, but he also expected his brother Alexander to guard the other — and at his own expense as well. When Alexander Freud proved unable to make the trip,[4] Freud had to settle for his one true disciple, Ferenczi. He could not really count upon Jung to play a subservient role for a variety of reasons, especially because Jung had received his own invitation and at the age of thirty-four would be likely to receive a great deal of attention as the youngest scholar among the twenty-nine honored guests.

In Bremen, Ferenczi, with a worn-out Baedeker and a huge bundle of American money that Freud thought looked "dirty,"[5] played both host and tour guide until Jung appeared and rushed, "beaming as he always does," to greet the sardonic Freud. Exuding confidence and well-being, the big brash Swiss immediately took charge by hiring an expensive private car for a tour of the city and booking a table for lunch at Bremen's most famous and expensive restaurant, the Essighaus. Freud ordered wine, and to his surprise and "satisfaction," Jung drank copiously. It was Jung's first alcoholic beverage since he had entered the Burghölzli in 1901 and taken the vow of abstinence Bleuler (and before him, Forel) demanded of all the assistant doctors.

Whether it was the wine or the excitement of the journey, Freud became flushed with perspiration and felt faint. He stopped eating and said Jung would have to drink his share of the wine.[6] Freud blamed his feeling faint on the salmon and lack of sleep the previous night, but Jung thought it was directly related to the topic of their conversation, the *Moorleichen*, mummified corpses found in the swamps and peat bogs of northern Germany and Sweden.[7] When they toured the Bremen Cathedral, Jung confused them with corpses that had been mummified there by the sheets of lead under which they were buried in the *Bleikeller*, or lead cellar.

Jung thought he was making interesting mealtime conversation about what they had seen on their tour that morning, when Freud suddenly turned on him: "What is it with you and these corpses? Wouldn't it be better if you admitted that you wish I would drop dead?" And then he promptly fainted, for the first of two times on two separate occasions several years apart.[8] After each fainting spell, Freud blamed Jung for causing it through an "act of resistance against the father" and a "death wish" against him.[9]

Jung was stung by the accusation and denied the charge strongly, but he was ultimately frustrated when Freud was incapable of or unwilling to accept his explanation. He was distressed that Freud could even harbor the suspicion, an emotion that gradually hardened into anger. Jung was furious that despite all the work he had done for Freud's "cause,"[10] more than all his other "students" put together, Freud could still accuse him of "personal motives that did not exist at all." For the time being, he consoled himself that no matter what he did, Freud "always had to find something wrong," when there was never any factual basis for it: "In the years we were together, it was always pure projection."

Once they boarded ship, tensions simmered further. Freud caused a scene when he spotted Jung engaged in animated conversation with the philosophy professor William Stern, who relied heavily on Jung's use of word association tests in the courtroom and planned to incorporate it when he lectured at Clark about the uses of testimony. Freud brought their conversation to an abrupt end by shouting at Jung: "Sit down with me! Bad company ruins good manners!"[11] Later, and with evident satisfaction, Freud recorded in his travel diary that "the shabby Jew [the distinguished Professor Stern] . . . in embarrassment departed."[12]

THE SHIP docked at Hoboken, New Jersey, on August 29. The three travelers disembarked and proceeded directly to New York, where they checked into the Hotel Manhattan. The next day in a letter to his wife, Freud described America as "very expensive" and lacking in the "necessary comforts" to which their family was accustomed. He modified this view when he wrote the following day: "Gradually one gets used to this city. In a week one could get settled."[13]

For the next six days and despite each man's unremitting gastric distress, they went sight-seeing separately and together. Even though each took a turn fasting for a day in the hope of calming his raging digestive tract, they all kept a frenetic pace.[14] Dr. Abraham Arden Brill, an Austrian-born psychoanalyst practicing in New York, had been translating what became the first of Freud's work to appear in English,[15] and he volunteered to guide the party while they were in the city. He and his wife, Dr. Rose Owen Brill, escorted Freud, Jung, and Ferenczi from Harlem to Chinatown to Coney Island.

Jung was both surprised and discomfited that Mrs. Brill, "good American that she is,"[16] accompanied them everywhere, whereas a proper Swiss wife would have presided self-effacingly over the dinner table and then retired for the rest of the evening.[17] They dined several times at the Brill apartment on Central Park West, where Freud admired the location,[18] and Jung marveled at Rose Brill's "unbelievable, wildly imaginative dishes!" In a letter to Emma, he described the ingredients of his first Waldorf salad: "apples, head lettuce, celery root, nuts, etc., etc." "Otherwise," he added, "the meal was good."

Jung went alone to the Metropolitan Museum to study the Egyptian, Cypriot, and Cretan collections. He also spent solitary time in the Pierpont Morgan Library museum studying the tapestries, and in the American Museum of Natural History's paleontological collections. He even went to see the lobby of the Plaza Hotel because of its "columns and all the obligatory splendor," where, he wrote, "your knees go soft when you enter. Extreme worldliness on a grand scale in every way."

His opinion of the Plaza was typical of his general response to everything about New York, and it illustrated how he and Freud saw the United States from differing points of view. Jung was wildly enthusiastic about American culture and eager to experience every aspect of it in order to better understand its vastly diversified population. Freud had little interest in the American people or their country except to impose his theory on it. Still, Jung could not win: his zest for all things American was sometimes mistaken by those who observed the two men for overzealous boorishness, while Freud's masked disapproval was seen as a perfectly mannered example of European politeness.

While Freud rested, wrote letters, or worked on his lectures in his hotel room, Jung was busy making professional visits as well as sightseeing. He called upon Dr. Adolf Meyer, now working at Ward's Island in the New York State Pathological Institute and with whom he had enjoyed a professional friendship ever since Meyer's sojourn several years earlier at the Burghölzli. He was frustrated when conflicts in their schedules meant he could not visit Dr. Bronislav Onuf[19] at Ellis Island, where he worked as a neuropsychiatric consultant. He was joined, however, by Freud and Ferenczi when Brill gave a guided tour of the Columbia University Psychiatric Clinic, where he worked as a clinical assistant to supplement the income from his private practice. Afterward, because they disagreed over some "insignificant"[20] technique of Brill's and wanted to discuss it further, Jung and Freud left Ferenczi behind and walked to a vantage point that overlooked the Hudson River and the New Jersey Palisades.

Freud continued to be "extremely touchy" even after they arrived in New York, but, as usual, Jung gave him the benefit of the doubt: "He does not like other sorts of ideas to come up, and I might add, he is usually right."[21] A conversation during a walk in Central Park demonstrated their fundamental differences, but again, the persons to whom they expressed their views must be taken into consideration as much as what each man wrote. Freud wrote to his wife, and it is an acknowledged fact that he never discussed anything professional with her; Jung wrote to Emma, with whom he always discussed professional concerns with respect for her sophisticated grasp of his subject.

Freud told his wife about the sights he had seen, how there were so many Yiddish signs with Hebrew lettering all over New York, and how Central Park "swarms with Jewish children, large and small."[22] Jung told his wife that he and Freud spoke "a good deal about Jews and Aryans," adding that he recounted a recent dream that "offered a clear image of [their] difference." He did not explain either his dream or the conversation with Freud any further to Emma, saying they were unable to go into detail because of all the excitement and activity around them. Shortly after this a mishap occurred that even before they boarded the *George Washington* seemed destined to happen: Freud urinated in his trousers as they stood in disagreement overlooking the Hudson.[23]

Attempting to ease Freud's embarrassment, Jung bundled him into a cab and took him back to the hotel. He had been aware of Freud's "neurosis" since the previous autumn, when Freud wrote from London[24] about his propensity to urinate when he found himself in a public place where there was no toilet. The urge to relieve himself would become so severe that he could not control it. What, he asked in his letter to Jung, could cause such a neurosis? In the cab, Jung repeated what he had told Freud in his reply: that it was indeed "a real neurosis," that it probably occurred because Freud "obviously suppressed and devalued love and thus fell prey to power. The pursuit of power became pathological."[25] Long afterward Jung recollected: "I didn't comprehend it at the time, but [later] I saw it, when a systematic devaluation of the unconscious is carried out, then the unconscious doesn't quite work *with* the person anymore, but *against* him." But as the cab went down Broadway, Jung remembered their conversation as follows:

FREUD: Why should it be a neurosis? It is a paralysis!

JUNG: Professor, now let me tell you with the greatest respect . . . everyone knows after all that you are extremely ambitious.

FREUD: *Me?!* [Jung's emphasis]. Ambitious? Anything but that!

JUNG: Yes, and thus, blind! Terribly blind! This is a psychogenic neurosis because you, — you, — you have the wrong attitude! I will get around it, I will analyze you!

FREUD: I would be overjoyed! Good! So, do try it then!

They reached the hotel in high excitement. Freud changed his clothes, and they began at once to analyze his dreams. Jung's account continued: "I was able to do it because I was the crown prince after all, and I came from outside [Vienna], I was not a personal student of his. And then I analyzed him and the usual material was revealed, and there were very personal matters, very delicate things."

Because this was the first time in all their mutual analysis that Freud confessed so freely, Jung stopped it to advise him that he needed to decide whether he wanted to continue in such an intimate vein. He recalled how Freud sat silently for a very long time and then said, almost in a whisper, "My dear boy, I cannot risk my authority."[26]

The "delicate," "personal" material concerned Freud's alleged sexual relationship with his sister-in-law, which Jung claimed to have known about ever since Minna Bernays confided in him on his first visit to Vienna. However, he also insisted he had never, ever, discussed with Freud the details of what Minna told him, either in Vienna or in New York.[27] Jung was offended by Freud's response, first because he refused to go further just as they were approaching the most important part of the analysis, but mostly because Freud had addressed him as if he were a callow, presumptuous youth instead of according him the respect due to an analyst who had earned his well-deserved reputation. As far as Jung was concerned, by not being willing to risk his own personal authority, "at that very moment [Freud] lost it forever for [him]."

However, something good did come from the partial analysis: "We did bring out enough for [Freud's] symptom [the need to urinate] to disappear completely." For the remainder of the trip, "he was no longer tormented by it."

ON SATURDAY, September 4, Dr. Ernest Jones joined the trio, and that evening the foursome boarded the night boat for Fall River. The next morning they took the train to Worcester via Boston. The importance of Freud and Jung to President Hall's celebration was evident through their lodgings: the other twenty-seven honorees went to hotels, but Freud and Jung were houseguests of the Halls, who appeared to Jung as a "sort of power-hungry man with great airs,"[28] and his "plump, jolly, good-natured, and extremely ugly"[29] wife.

Jung told Emma the Halls were "a stiff and solemn New England family whose respectability was almost terrifying." Still, staying in their house was "almost like home, for there are very conservative and highly respectable people in Switzerland, too."[30] Inexplicable "solemnity brooded over" every occasion, especially meals, which made Jung feel as if he were "eating lunch in a circus." To dispel "the solemnity of great virtue," he told jokes, but the only persons who laughed were the black servants dressed in formal attire who waited on table. Jung particularly loved to make one "African brother" laugh, while Freud sat in dignified (perhaps mortified) silence with the Halls and their other, rotating guests invited from among the honorees.

All were distinguished scholars recognized internationally for their contributions to the physical, biological, and social sciences. Among them were two Nobel laureates, the physicist A. A. Michelson and Ernest Rutherford, who was honored for his investigations into the structure of the atom and radioactivity. Freud and Jung were lumped in with a diverse collection of eight scholars in the psychology and pedagogy group.[31] These included Franz Boas for anthropology,[32] William Stern for his work in personality and forensic psychology, and Adolf Meyer for studies in psychopathology. Freud thought being in this august company the realization of "an incredible daydream";[33] Jung simply accepted it as his due,[34] even though he was almost surely a last-minute substitute for Professor Ernst Meumann of the University of Münster, an expert in the emerging field of child development.[35]

Meumann was among eminent researchers who, for various reasons, had to decline Hall's invitation. These included philosophy professor John Dewey, biologist William Morton Wheeler, and Wilhelm Wundt, who established the first experimental laboratory in psychology. They, as well as those who accepted, were chosen as representatives of Hall's primary research interest: the development of children. At the time of the celebration, he was highly regarded as an expert in experimental psychology and as the founder of the first American laboratory dedicated to such research.[36] It was only natural that he chose others whose work complemented his to participate in what was essentially a symposium and that he assigned them topics related to his own interests.

From Hall's perspective, Freud was a developmental psychologist whose research contributed to understanding the role played by sexuality and the unconscious in the development of children. It is probably why Freud included among his five lectures[37] the now-famous "Little Hans" case history and why Jung presented as a kind of counterpoint the case of "Little Anna." Despite the fact that Jung owed his international reputation to the word association studies (which were of primary interest to the other participants, especially Stern and Meyer), Hall asked him to speak about mental hygiene as an aspect of child psychology. Jung interpreted Hall's directive with the utmost freedom, and as he (and Freud as well) spoke in German, it may be why the newspaper reporters who praised Jung either were not aware of or chose not to mention the fact that two of his three lectures had little bearing on his announced subject.

In the months between receiving Hall's invitation and his actual appearance at Clark, Jung had scant time to devote to his topic or produce something original. Although he introduced his first lecture on September 10 by saying that he would devote three separate talks to "the psychology of childhood,"[38] only the last came close to filling Hall's dictum.

The first lecture, "The Association Method," was a thorough summary and compendium of all that he had previously written on the subject, and in it he managed to hold the attention of his knowledgeable audience with anecdotes that illustrated how the tests could be used in criminal detection and crime solving. His second lecture was based primarily on work Dr. Emma Fürst did under his supervision at the Burghölzli.[39] His supplemental anecdotes again captivated the audience, as they included such cogent observations as how "the emotional environment constellated during infancy influences . . . the patient's destiny even down to its very details," among them "an unhappy choice of profession and disastrous marriage."[40] His third lecture was the only one of the three based entirely upon new material. Here, Jung complied with Hall's directive by turning some casual observations about his own children into "Little Anna," a thinly disguised account of his daughter Agathe's reactions to the birth of her brother, Franz. Jung's paper originated the previous January, when Freud asked some general questions about infant suckling and Jung responded by describing his elder daughter's reactions to her new baby brother.[41]

Freud and Jung lectured on the same day, with "Little Anna" following "Little Hans," to which Jung referred somewhat nervously for corroboration and verification. He spoke of the four-year-old girl's curious equation of the birth of a sibling with the devastating earthquake in Messina and of how both raised in her mind two fears: that her mother might die and that her mother might prefer the new baby boy to her and (only indirectly) her younger sister. Jung did not dwell on interpretations, and of the three lectures, this last and most original seems to have had the least impact on his audience.

It did not meet with Freud's wholehearted approval either. A year later, when a modified version was published in the *Jahrbuch*, he expressed regret that

Jung's research depended more on his paternal feelings than on correspondences with Little Hans. Freud accused him of forgetting that his reader was by "definition a simpleton [who] deserves to have his nose rubbed in these things."[42] Jung's reply reflects how the situation between the two was already cooling: "One must after all leave something to the reader's imagination."[43] Still, if measured by the distinguished scholars who sought him afterward for further, private conversations, his three and Freud's five lectures constituted a triumph for Freudian analysis.

WILLIAM JAMES was among the attendees at Clark, and he and Jung met privately to talk, primarily about a subject that had not been on the program: the importance of parapsychology in providing access to the unconscious.[44] They met twice, and their subject was the same on both occasions: parapsychology, spiritualism, faith healing, and other nonmedical applications of psychotherapy.[45] It was only natural that Jung began his initial evaluation of James's intellectual achievement by comparing him to Freud. Ultimately he contrasted both men with Théodore Flournoy and in a sense found both wanting. Class distinctions figured in Jung's perceptions of all three: Flournoy came from a "cultivated and distinguished" background, as did James, whereas Jung was "always aware of [Freud's] . . . uneducated and lower-class parents. He was certainly very smart, but only that."[46] Jung thought Flournoy provided a necessary and much needed "counterweight" to Freud, whose "devaluing ways, that sniffing out of the inferior and of sexuality" he increasingly "didn't enjoy at all." He credited Flournoy with teaching him "the loving contemplation of a case"[47] and to "see things correctly . . . as a whole." In public he continued to insist on his total fealty to Freud, but privately he worried that there was too much in his theory that "distorted many things for the sake of a bias," especially the primacy of sexuality. Jung described Freud's manner as "dynamic and penetrating" but ultimately flawed because "he wanted something from his cases." Flournoy, in Jung's view, did not: "He was a professor of philosophy" who analyzed his cases from "a truly objective *approach*."[48]

As soon as their first conversation began, Jung believed he had found in James a scholar who shared Flournoy's "objective and refined attitude." Also, as the conversation evolved, Jung and James "got along excellently with regard to the assessment of the religious factor in the psyche." He was gratified to find that both James and Flournoy "reinforced [Jung's] universalist view" because both "were rather observing men and much too sensitive to get in direct contact with the object." After his second conversation with James, Jung came to the realization — startling and troubling in equal parts — that Freud, "due to the narrowness of his intellectual horizon, let himself be overwhelmed by the object." Even further, Freud's psychology began to seem a female psychology, where sexuality is an enormous issue in the biological respect: "For a woman, sexuality has a social component, it is a socially important matter and can even be a business. It doesn't play such a big role for the man. For the man it is a physiological function that has absolutely no social significance, but *par réper-cussion* becomes a highly mystical affair that is usually denied."[49]

Jung believed Flournoy had "a warm understanding" of "the problems raised by the female," but also "a great conventional timidity which [Jung] had in common with him." Thus, when he met James, who was "a bit dry" and who "kept . . . [his] sexuality locked up in a darkroom," Jung felt a certain degree of kinship, despite his overall impression that James's "*participation*[50] in life was very slight." James, "physically long and thin," was "extremely kind, humane . . . but [he] was bloodless." Jung's interactions with Flournoy were "warmer on a human level."

Ultimately, however, William James was unable to provide some of the clear-cut theoretical positions and responses that Jung, to his increasing dismay, was beginning to realize he needed but would never get from Freud. With a certain degree of respectful regret, in the end Jung appraised James as "only a philosopher." Flournoy was "greatly impressed" with James's Pragmatism, but either Jung did not know enough about it to discuss it at their initial meeting, or, more likely, their shared interest in parapsychology was of greater conversational interest to them both. Unfortunately, their rapport had no opportunity to develop further, for James was already ill, and he died the next year, on August 26, 1910.

ON SEPTEMBER 11, Adolf Meyer planned what he thought would be a pleasant automobile excursion around the nearby Lake Quinsigamond, a suitable farewell to the American wilderness before the Europeans sailed for home. Jung robustly enjoyed the outing, Freud sourly did not, and Ferenczi tried gamely to mollify each of the principals into thinking he shared their respective views. Jung decided to ignore their mumbled natterings and revel in the spectacular autumn landscape.

That evening, while the others rested, Jung went alone by train to Boston, where he spent the evening and the next early-morning hours walking through the streets in search of some of the most historic sites in America. Just before noon, he took another train, this time to Gloucester on the North Shore, where he was a luncheon guest of Mrs. Frederick W. Peterson, wife of his former research collaborator at the Burghölzli and one of his earliest English translators.[51] Immediately afterward, his stamina intact, he took the late-afternoon train back to Worcester, where Freud, Ferenczi, and Brill got on board and joined him on an excursion to Buffalo and Niagara Falls. Then Brill returned to New York City, while the three Europeans went to the resort town of Lake Placid for an overnight stay. The next day, they were met by Dr. James J. Putnam, a neurology professor at Harvard Medical School.

Putnam, who would soon become one of Freud's most important American allies,[52] had been with them at Clark. When he learned they would have several days free before sailing, he spontaneously invited them to be his guests at a family compound in the Adirondack Mountains near the community of Keene Valley.[53] They made the last leg of their journey in "a curious two-horse conveyance over deeply rutted roads,"[54] and for Jung it was as if his boyhood impressions of the American West (gleaned from Friedrich Gerstäcker's German adventure novels) had come to life. He relished everything about the trip, including their lunch of thick slabs of bacon on bread and corn on the cob, which Freud nibbled while Ferenczi nervously fussed and clucked.

The Putnam camp had been in the family since 1876, when James and Charles Putnam joined William James and another distinguished Harvard Medical School professor, Dr. Henry Bowditch, to purchase a property that was originally known as The Shanty.[55] There were other Putnam and Bowditch family members in residence, both male and female, but they were housed according to sex and age in the ten or so cabins that came to dot the enclave over the years. There were also cabins for the various family servants who were brought from Boston. The main cabin was The Stoop, which doubled as a social center and mess hall; The Chatterbox cabin, with its one large sitting room dominated by a massive fireplace, housed the three Europeans.

Freud spent most of his time in The Chatterbox, nursing a so-called nervous appendix, so naturally Ferenczi remained in attendance. Jung hiked alone or with some of the Putnams along the various streams up into the "northern primeval forest," and to the top of 4,960-foot-tall Haystack Mountain. He told Emma that Freud wore a "philosophical smile" to scan "this richly varied world," but he himself "trot[ted] along and enjoy[ed] it."

There were so many things to see and do, not just in the Adirondacks but throughout this vast new country, that Jung regretted he would not have enough time to see it all. One day he was shivering on a bare mountain peak, the next he was in the midst of "metropolitan bustle,"[56] first in Albany, then in New York City. He could scarcely describe "the hundred thousand enormously deep impressions" he would take back to Zürich. Everything was "too big, too immeasurable."

Nevertheless, there were some immediate impressions he wanted to share with Emma. He thought Americans enjoyed the "ideal potentiality of life," while all of Europe lagged "miles behind" American "technological culture." American men enjoyed all the benefits of the cultural climate, but women were "badly off." Once back in Zürich, he viewed the men as "a flock of sheep," women as "ravening wolves — within the family circle, of course." He thought the world had never seen anything like it before.[57] This extreme difference was one Jung would become well aware of in the next two decades as American women flocked to Zürich to seek his counsel. For every aspect of life in the United States that inspired his "enthusiastic admiration," there were many others that made him "ponder social evolution deeply." Trying to understand such a fascinating culture would become one of his keen interests for the rest of his life. But still, he was deeply and profoundly Swiss, and he retained the opinion he had expressed to Emma in a letter written earlier from the Adirondacks: "It is good to leave while the going is still so great."

On September 22, after a farewell celebration with the Brills and some of their friends and colleagues, the three men boarded the *Kaiser Wilhelm der Gross* for the return journey. Jung said he did so with a "light heart and an aching head,"[58] because he liked champagne and was well along to becoming a connoisseur of fine wine, which he was for the rest of his life. He told Emma he was "honorably withdrawing" from his "various teetotal societies" and planned to become an "honest sinner" whose only attraction would be to "the forbidden." Therefore, he concluded, "I must not forbid myself too much."

He foresaw the eight-day sea voyage to Bremen as one that would force the three traveling companions "into the fruitful bottomlands of [their] own psyches." As for his own unconscious, Jung wrote, he would have "a lot of work to do, putting in order all the things America has churned up within us."

CHAPTER 13

The Solar Phallus Man

Shortly before he went to the United States, Jung thought he had finally found the perfect research assistant, a "very intelligent and subtle-minded" medical student, "the *studiosus* Honegger," who, he told Freud, would probably be writing to solicit his advice.[1]

Johann Jakob Honegger Jr. was called Johann to distinguish him from his father, Johann Jakob Honegger Sr. (1851–96), called Jakob. Born November 26, 1885, he was a prodigy noted as much for his good looks and engaging personal charm as his brilliance.[2] He received the *Matura* degree[3] with highest praise from a Zürich Gymnasium in 1904 and then blazed through the University of Zürich and its medical school in five years. A desire to specialize in psychiatry led him to the Burghölzli in search of a dissertation topic in the spring of 1909, when he was twenty-five and ten years Jung's junior.

Johann Honegger came by his interest naturally. His father was also a Burghölzli *Assistenzarzt*, from 1875 to 1879, when Eduard Hitzig was director. Jakob Honegger's dissertation on the brain's anatomy[4] led him to establish a research laboratory consisting mostly of brain slides similar to those Jung studied. He forged such a distinguished reputation that Forel appointed him acting director of the Burghölzli while he was away in 1891.[5] Unfortunately, the appointment coincided with the onset of a "severe organic brain disease"[6] that killed Jakob Honegger at the age of forty-five. In 1893, two years after its onset, the former director of the Burghölzli became a patient and died there in 1896.

The last five years of Jakob's life were traumatic for his wife and children (there was also an elder daughter). For the first two years, before the illness was diagnosed, Jakob's erratic behavior frightened patients, and his private practice declined. Desperate to maintain her family's middle-class standing, Frau Honegger turned their home into a pension known for the refinement of its clientele. She kept her husband at home until he became physically abusive toward her boarders and then, reluctantly, had him admitted to the Burghölzli.

She must have waited too long, for he was discreetly described by the admitting physician as in a severe "state of neglect."

Johann's formative years were marked by revulsion at his father's horrifying deterioration. Whether because of this alone or for other reasons as well, he developed an attachment to his mother that became both obsessive and compulsive. Friends were embarrassed by his excessive maternal affinity but excused it as an emotional reaction caused by the frequent hospital calls he made in her stead (for whatever reason, Frau Honegger did not[9] visit her husband). However, Johann was so popular with friends and classmates that they ascribed his manic outbursts, biting sarcasm, and vicious jibing to boyish high jinks rather than familial distress.

The boy learned early that the best way to cope with his father's disintegration and his mother's physical and financial plight was to throw himself into his studies. He became consumed with learning, thus deflecting the dreariness of daily life in both home and hospital. His teachers noted his rich imagination, frequently hysterical sense of humor, and a cynicism that he aimed witheringly at any scholastic competitor. He was determined to be the best, and if he thought it required exaggeration and scorn in equal parts, he did not hesitate to use them, but he always tempered his outbursts with charm and winning smiles.

Like Jung before him, he joined the Zofingia fraternity and, also like Jung, was much admired for his powers of persuasion and oratorical skills. But unlike Jung, he did not seem to know how to keep himself from crossing the line that separated socially acceptable behavior from unsound self-indulgence. In Zofingia, he began a lifelong friendship with Walter Gut, who later became the professor of theology and president of the University of Zürich. Gut was one of the few persons perceptive enough in their youth to realize the profound effect Johann's father's illness had on his son's mental stability. He found it unsettling when, shortly before Johann went to the Burghölzli, he began to sign his letters as "Jakob Honegger II."[7] This period marked Jung's first contact with Johann Honegger, not as his superior colleague but as his physician.

Honegger consulted Jung for treatment several days after "a loss of reality-sense . . . (Psychasthenia = libido introversion = Dem. praec.)."[8] During their several sessions, Honegger said he wanted to specialize in psychiatry, which alarmed Jung as much as his description of his experiences, not only during this most recent delusionary incident but also in several previous ones of shorter duration and intensity. Jung urged Honegger to enter analysis so he could "analyze himself *consciously*" as a possible method of at least delaying, if not averting altogether, "the automatic self-disintegration of Dem. Pr."

Even though Jung recognized from the start that he would be unlikely to stop Honegger's downward spiral of incurable mental illness, he so admired the young doctor's brilliance that he recruited him as a research assistant. Jung began to analyze Honegger sometime in spring 1909,[9] but no documentation has yet been found to show what the treatment embodied, except for the discovery of their mutual affinity for ancient history, symbolism, and mythology.[10] Jung asked Honegger to do several things during the autumn that he was in the United States: to familiarize himself with the existing literature on mythology and compile a bibliography, and to make systematic observations about two patients, a man and a woman.

Honegger first began to record the oral history of a "Frl. Pfenninger,"[11] but abandoned it in order to concentrate on the male patient whose case had fascinated Jung since his 1901 admission: Emile Schwyzer, who became known in subsequent Jungian history as "The Solar Phallus Man."[12] Jung had actually presented Schwyzer's case to the Burghölzli staff in 1906,[13] but his responsibilities permitted little more than a cursory summary in terms of Bleuler's theory of dementia praecox. Jung's charge to Honegger was to collect enough material on one or both of these patients to constitute a dissertation and have it ready by Jung's return from the United States. To his happy surprise, Honegger said he wanted to concentrate solely on Schwyzer and would most likely have not only a detailed outline but also much of the actual dissertation written by then.

Honegger's enthusiasm offered a welcome change for Jung, who constantly complained that supervising medical students kept him from his own research. Nevertheless, he attended to their interests as scrupulously as if they were his own and tried to discern where their interests and abilities lay. He then matched them with the appropriate patients, whose case histories they were to study before investigating the literature pertaining to the illness and preparing treatment proposals. In this way, Jung learned along with his students as they followed the cases, particularly when they became so engrossed in the histories of particular patients that they wrote their dissertations about them. Jung considered this kind of supervision the most important of his many clinical responsibilities.[14] Normal Burghölzli procedure required each of the seven to ten doctors on staff to be familiar with and fully involved in the treatment of all 350 to 400 patients at any given time. Those who were the objects of sustained research thus became the particular patient of both the supervisor and the investigating assistant physician (in Schwyzer's case, Jung and Honegger respectively). Although the assistant's name was usually the primary one on any written or published research, the supervisor's really belonged there as well, for he was at most the originator of the research, at the least its co-director.[15] One among the many possible examples of how Jung fulfilled the role of senior advisor was exemplified by Franz Riklin Sr., whose research about mythology had deeply absorbed Jung for the past several years. Although he cited Riklin's work in a number of his own writings, Jung was ultimately disappointed that he could not nudge him into original thinking and scholarship, and that Riklin remained content merely to be a compiler and categorizer. But until 1908, when Jung was giving serious thought to resigning from the Burghölzli, none of the assistant staff doctors was interested in Emile Schwyzer's case. Now to find that Honegger was as engrossed as he in ancient history, mythology, philology, and archeology seemed too good to be true — or more likely because of Honegger's instability, too good to be lasting. But there was no one else, so Jung urged his young associate onward.

THE PATIENT Emile Schwyzer (1862–1931) was admitted to the Burghölzli on October 27, 1901, when he was nearly forty and after he had been hospitalized for almost two decades in other institutions.[16] His delusions began in 1882, shortly after he went to England to work as a *commis*, or bank messenger. Six months later he was dismissed for unknown reasons, became delusionary, and attempted suicide by shooting himself on the left side of his head. He was committed to an unnamed London hospital in 1882, and in 1884 was transferred to the Bethlem Royal Hospital in West Wickham, Surrey, where he remained until 1887. His family then brought him home and had him confined in the private Mönchhof asylum until they could no longer afford the modest fee. On March 22, 1897, he was admitted to the Kantonale Irrenheilanstalt (cantonal insane asylum) at Münsterlingen. In 1901, he was transferred directly to the Burghölzli because the family members who were his external guardians moved to Zürich, and by Swiss law that canton became responsible for his care.[17]

There was a history of mental illness in the Schwyzer family: both his mother and sister were diagnosed with "strong neuropathic tendencies," a grandfather died of "senile imbecility," and a maternal uncle's untimely death was attributed to a "brain disease."[18] Initially, Schwyzer appeared free of his family's troubled history, for his Swiss neighbors remembered him as an ambitious young man, industrious and eager to better himself. No symptoms of illness appeared until after he learned English, made his way to London, and found a clerical position.[19]

As soon as he arrived, he had severe anxiety coupled with hallucinations that he was being followed. His family was concerned that he did not write but did nothing until they received an alarming letter from him, saying there was no need for letters because his entire family had followed him to England, where they were being tortured. No one would ever return to Switzerland because their many persecutors would probably kill them all. Shortly after, British hospital authorities notified Schwyzer's relatives of his first confinement, which coincided with an attempted suicide: when the imagined voices of his persecutors became too much to endure, he shot himself in the head.

He survived, but with a strabismus, the paralysis of all the muscles of the eye, in his case the left eye, with a pupil that did not react to light. Although the shooting left him with a ferocious visage, he was not considered dangerous, only "odd and suspicious." The London hospital authorities released him as stable enough to live on his own, which he did for several weeks, until another incident triggered more violent outbursts and he was confined again. He apparently harbored a secret infatuation for a young girl from Zürich whom he called "Marie," whose social class was far above his and who knew nothing of his feelings for her. When he heard that she was engaged, "pronounced megalomania joined his various notions of persecution," and he became "a danger to himself." This second hospitalization marked the beginning of his lifelong confinement.

By the time he was transferred to the Burghölzli twenty years later, Schwyzer's delusions alternated between megalomania and persecution. At times he thought of himself as a millionaire, the Savior of the world, owner of the asylum, and the object of interest to all sorts of fashionable ladies who came to see him but who, for some perverse reason known only to themselves, dressed in men's clothing in order to confuse him. According to the succession of Burghölzli doctors who took case notes over the next thirty-some years, Schwyzer's delusions were not particularly unusual except for the specifically grandiose one that sparked Jung's interest in 1901 and that Schwyzer frequently and freely repeated to all and sundry.[20]

Schwyzer "thought of himself as God," and because he was "the Lord," became particularly agitated by his "obligation to distribute his semen, since otherwise the world would perish." He would usually add, "That's simply the crazy thing!" and then burst into laughter as if it were a joke he and the doctors shared together. What made him unique for Jung was the clearly expressed delusion that always followed the semen/God outbursts, when Schwyzer insisted he was "capable of producing the weather."[21] If asked how he did this, he would reply that the sun had a gigantic phallus, and if he looked at it with eyes half shut and moved his head from side to side, he could make the phallus move, thus creating the wind and, by extension, the weather. He told this with gestures and embellishments and in a particularly archaic language that had no connection either to his life in Switzerland or to anything Jung could possibly connect to his sojourn in England. Jung was, to say the least, intrigued.

Schwyzer could perform mundane tasks and chores, and he was a thorough and dependable daily kitchen worker and "the mainstay" in keeping his ward clean, but he was unable to express "a trace of logical thinking" and could communicate only "in fragments." No one could engage him in sustained, sensible discussion, either about his delusions or his daily tasks. He could not converse, and he could neither understand nor process "new things." Jung wrote that he "no longer thinks, he forgets, judges wrongly . . . frequently produces a perfect verbal mess because he is so scatterbrained, and is absolutely under the spell of his hallucinations and delusions." When Jung wrote this last observation in 1908, Schwyzer was forty-six and ever since his early twenties had been "indifferent about anything that does not concern his complexes, his wishes." Jung diagnosed him as "suffer[ing] from an incurable mental illness (youthful imbecility),"[22] a disease of long duration that would necessitate his continuous institutionalization for the rest of his natural life. He saw no possibility for the patient's cure, but neither did he foresee further degeneration.

Jung's diagnosis may have been his unstated partial agreement with Bleuler's most recently published research, wherein he used the term "schizophrenia" for the first time.[23] Bleuler coined it as a way to distinguish a subcategory of mental illness from the previously accepted term, the catchall "dementia praecox," first used by Emil Kraepelin in 1893 to indicate psychotic disorders that were progressively degenerative and usually life-ending. Bleuler now believed there was a subgroup within this classification of clearly psychotic patients whose symptoms seemed to reach a stage beyond which no further degeneration would occur. He also believed that in some few cases, symptoms could actually be remitted and patients discharged as cured. Schwyzer's early patient history paralleled his theory up to a point, but there it seemed to end.[24] Nevertheless, Jung asked Honegger to keep Bleuler's investigations into schizophrenia in mind as he observed Schwyzer.[25]

From the beginning of his interest in Schwyzer's case, Jung wondered if the content of the patient's delusions had a connection to a myth he might have encountered before or even during his various hospitalizations. He thought the former unlikely because of the Schwyzer family's lack of education and impoverished circumstances. They were peasants who lived in one of the meanest sections of Zürich, isolated by poverty and so riddled with suspicion that they were convinced persecution and harm lay on every front. It was doubtful that any printed matter ever found its way past their hovel's door.[26]

Even so, despite his brief and incomplete grammar school education, Schwyzer must have possessed a certain degree of intelligence and ambition, for he did, after all, learn English and get himself to London. In his delusions, he appears to have had a sophisticated knowledge of geography (referring to, among other places, Monaco and Australia) and the global conflicts of his time (the Greek-Turkish war, the slaughter of Armenians, Russo-Japanese engagements). He was fascinated by European royalty and had fantasies concerning Queen Maud of Norway (that she was in love with him), Queen Victoria (that she was his mother), and the Duke of Clarence (who he thought he was).[27]

With the exception of his belief in the sun's gigantic phallus, none of Schwyzer's known experiences or his delusions indicated that he had even a rudimentary familiarity with literature or folklore. Jung checked his previous hospitalizations and ascertained that there had been no patients' library in any of them. Even if there had been printed matter, Schwyzer's inability to concentrate or speak coherently indicated that his reading would have been as haphazard as all his other behavior.[28] Nevertheless, it is this single aspect of Schwyzer's delusions — that he could create the weather by causing the sun to move a phallic appendage — that has caused controversy since Jung first cited the case in his 1912 book *Wandlungun und Symbole der Libido*.[29]

Jung does not name Schwyzer in his book, but he describes his perplexity that he could not interpret a schizophrenic patient's delusion: if he moved his head from side to side, he could make the sun's phallus move as well, and *"that was where the wind came from"* (Jung's emphasis).[30] Jung said the "bizarre notion" remained "unintelligible" until he read Albrecht Dieterich's 1903 book,

Eine Mithrasliturgie, shortly after it was published in a second edition in 1910 and, at about the same time, G. R. S. Mead's *A Mithraic Ritual*.[31] Dieterich described in the Mithraic liturgy "a so-called tube, the origin of the ministering wind . . . hanging down from the disc of the sun."[32] In related research, Jung uncovered a painting by an unnamed early German artist showing "a sort of tube or hose-pipe" descending from heaven, where the Holy Ghost, represented as a dove, flies down it and up beneath the robes of the Virgin Mary to impregnate her. Seeing these and "other experiences like them" convinced Jung that a "universally human characteristic" was involved, and that humankind possessed "a functional disposition to produce the same or very similar ideas." Later, he called it the "archetype" of the collective unconscious and said it was akin to "the pattern of behavior" in biology.[33]

These thoughts coalesced further in a dream that Jung had during the trip to the United States, which he tried to discuss with Freud during a walk in Central Park. It was important to Jung, who introduced it into several of their subsequent conversations. It eventually became a signpost for differences with Freud that Jung was trying to explain away, and later, when he assessed Honegger's case study of Schwyzer, he realized it was one of the most important dreams he would ever have, for it provided the basis for what he termed the "collective unconscious."[34]

In his dream, Jung was on the upper floor of a two-story house, in a living room filled with baroque and Renaissance furniture that was both beautiful and uncomfortable. He remembered thinking that the historical period when the furniture was made must have been sometime between 1650 and 1750. Then he looked at paintings hanging on the walls and realized suddenly and with astonishment that this was the contemporary house in which he lived. He was further astounded that he should be on the second floor with no knowledge of how he got there or what, if anything, was on the ground floor. He descended and found everything was Medieval: dark wood, no fabric, and heavy stone floors. He felt obliged to investigate the rest of the house and thus came upon an old door that led to a basement. The stairs were made of ancient stones that descended into a vaulted room whose walls were built of Roman brick. Jung's curiosity reached its peak when he found a huge metal ring embedded in the cellar's stone floor. He lifted the slab and saw another set of narrow stone steps that led to a low cave carved into rock. This was the true bottom of the house, and the cave's floor was encased with thick dust that covered bones, broken vessels, and several partially decayed human skulls without lower jaws, obviously the victims of violence, as the tops were forcibly bashed in. Jung certainly wanted to analyze this dream with Freud.

They spent much of the Atlantic crossing alone and in intense discussion, with Freud assuming the role of teacher and guide. Jung contentedly acquiesced to being the "pupil," because "after all, [he] did want to learn from him." He was exceedingly open about personal and potentially embarrassing aspects of himself, whereas Freud was always guarded and circumspect. On several occasions, when Jung pressed Freud to go further into self-analysis, he demurred, saying that he had taken a dream "far enough," and to go further was neither "appropriate" nor "relevant" to its full understanding. Jung, because he was bursting with so many other thoughts and ideas, accepted Freud's dicta and allowed him to move the conversation to other topics, but they were always vague and only those Freud deemed "suitable."

Still, the dream of the house dominated Jung's thoughts: "I was enormously interested in it. I did have some idea what the dream might mean, namely a sort of diagram of psychology. But I didn't tell Freud that, for I did not trust my own judgment back then." Jung noted that Freud was interested in only one aspect of it anyway: "He was always circling around those skulls. He thought I was supposed to harbor a wish there." Freud asked repeatedly: "Who do you wish were dead? Doesn't anyone come to mind?" His questions formed a pattern. Whose skulls were they? What did Jung want from them? What did he want to happen to them? Again and again, and above all, Freud hammered the point: whose death was it worth Jung's while to wish for?

Jung was befuddled: "He expected me to find a wish there, so I named my wife and my sister-in-law[35] because I thought that was in accordance with his theory. It wasn't true, but I followed his intention anyway because I wanted so much to learn from him. I thought he understood things better than I, so I kept thinking, What does he really want? What does he want me to say?"

Offering up his wife and sister-in-law must have been at least partially satisfying, for as soon as Jung said their names, Freud seemed "suddenly liberated." It disappointed Jung: "[Freud's] negative judgments could continuously hurt you without your noticing it. He had to regard everything, for example, my relationship to my family, from the negative side. For him the world couldn't continue to exist unless it were [negative]."[36]

Jung recalled Freud's prior "historical attempts" in other interpretations, such as the Oedipus complex, the Pompeiian fantasies of the Villa dei Misteri, and Jensen's *Gradiva*. He remembered how he thought that Freud, "when confronted with such dreams was completely helpless." With that realization he said to himself, "Now to hell with this! What does this dream really mean?"

He analyzed it many different times and for many years afterward, but in the beginning, he was sure of only one thing: it meant that Freud's view of dreams differed from his. He accepted this particular one *tel quel*, such as it is, despite Freud's insistence "that the dream pursued a tendency to deceive." Jung disagreed, arguing that "the unconscious appeared as something natural, as a natural function that is completely independent from consciousness."

Jung returned to the Burghölzli with the dream swirling in his thoughts and with Mithraic myths in mind. He instructed Honegger about how to proceed: to begin with the simple observation of Schwyzer's daily routine, to watch as he went about his cleanup chores on the ward, and to listen carefully and record everything he did or said. When Schwyzer was taking his "recreation," which he liked to do by sitting on a bench outdoors in all but the most inclement weather, Jung asked Honegger to sit beside him and write down his rambling diatribes in as much detail as he could. When bad weather confined Schwyzer to his ward, Jung asked Honegger to observe his restless peregrinations and to make copies of the "maps and charts" he drew, a fairly sophisticated albeit skewed rendition of the world as he saw it. Better yet: Jung asked Honegger to collect the actual drawings and scribblings for further study, but only if he could safely distract Schwyzer, who frequently erupted violently and unpredictably to imagined invasions of his person or property.[37]

Honegger did as Jung asked, dating his verbatim recordings of Schwyzer's testimony from December 31, 1909, until the end of February 1910. He amassed approximately 240 hand-written pages of Schwyzer's delusional ramblings that he then buttressed with his own marginal observations and interpretations. These were followed by what can best be described as early drafts of what Honegger probably intended to become his dissertation, all of which amount to another hundred or so pages of critical analysis.[38] Even before he read them, Jung was so convinced of Honegger's brilliance that he sang his praises to Freud, saying Honegger showed such "*great* understanding" of the Schwyzer project that Jung intended to "entrust to him everything I know so that something good may come of it."[39] He began to goad Honegger to work faster toward compiling "scientific observations" for presentation at the Second International Psychoanalytic Congress in Nuremberg March 30–31, 1910.

It was important for Honegger to present this material so Jung could stake his claim to preeminence in the sudden spurt of interest in mythology among other psychoanalysts.[40] All the attendees would assume that, as Jung's protégé, Honegger produced work that was the direct expression of Jung's views and, as such, an important indicator of his original thought and research. Jung wanted to be the first to present a direct connection between a specific patient and the mythology of other societies and cultures, but most of all, he wanted to be the first to identify and define what was still only the roughest formulation of the collective unconscious and stake his claim to it. He put tremendous pressure on Honegger to work harder and faster, even as the trajectory of both their lives from October 1909 through the summer of 1910 became filled with professional stress and personal strain.

"IT PROBABLY isn't nice of you to keep me waiting," Freud complained on November 11, when Jung finally wrote after twenty-five days.[41] "Pater peccavi," Jung replied, "it is indeed a scandal." His excuse was that he was "positively wallowing in people and social life," most of which Emma occasioned. Like her husband, she was not fond of the niceties and chatter of ordinary socializing, but as matron of such a grand new house, she had to observe certain Swiss conventions. Although they had been in the house since June, Carl's travels and other professional responsibilities forced them to delay until the autumn of 1909 the receptions they were expected to hold. They then had more people wandering through their house and gardens than they did until many years later, when public ceremonies celebrating Jung's achievement and old age made such gatherings necessary once again.

Jung's main excuse for not answering Freud's letters was the great amount of time he spent in daily interchange with the "so intelligent and subtle-minded" Honegger.[42] A month previously, he told Freud he was looking forward to an autumn of ease because he had "no crush of patients . . . only two thin ones." But between Emma's entertaining and Honegger's research, he became "so taken up with people and things" that it became "difficult to concentrate."[43]

Much of his distraction was due to Emma's increasing dissatisfaction with her personal circumstances. She had envisioned daily life in the new house as bringing her emotionally closer to her husband and permitting her to share his professional interests as well. Instead she found herself relegated to the sidelines on all fronts. Jung expected her to oversee everything connected with the household and when he needed her, to be available as general factotum to visitors and patients and occasional secretary to his many correspondents. He wanted Emma to be primarily a contented *Hausfrau* who would step out of that role only when he required her considerable charm and intelligence to ease professional situations. This was all well and good, and she was happy to comply, but she wanted to put her abilities to more consistent use.

Several years later, she described to Freud the plight that began when they moved into the Seestrasse house in 1909 and intensified greatly thereafter.[44] She told him she realized her good fortune to have married such a man as Carl Jung and said she was usually content with her lot. However, there were times when she was "tormented with conflict" about how best to carve out a separate role for herself: "I find I have no friends, all the people who associate with us really only want to see Carl, except for a few boring and to me quite uninteresting persons." When she tried to discuss this with her husband, he advised her to "stop concentrating on him and the children."

"What on earth am I to do?" she wailed to Freud. The women with whom they came in contact were "all in love with him," and the men instantly "cordoned" her off as an appendage of the great man, whom they regarded as their "father or friend." In social situations, the quietly poised Emma found herself uncharacteristically making conversation "extra stupidly" to get any sort of attention, and later suffering agonies of embarrassment that she had done so. She confessed, albeit offhandedly, that she had a "strong tendency to autoerotism" and said she would be grateful for any advice Freud could give. Coming from a woman as reserved as Emma Jung, the frankness of such a letter is astonishing, especially as no documentation has yet been found to show that she ever had a conversation with Freud or wrote him a letter that would have made such intimacy appropriate. And if Freud replied to her admission, it is unfortunate that his letter appears not to be extant either.

Jung's way of dealing with his wife's unhappiness was to psychoanalyze her. Again, it bears repeating that rules and boundaries were undefined in the early days of psychoanalysis, so whether he was the first and/or the only analyst to treat his spouse is open to speculation. Whether or not he intended it as sop or stopgap or whether he had more altruistic reasons is also not known, but as soon as he returned from the United States, he scheduled sessions with Emma as if she were just another patient. According to him, she was "bearing up splendidly . . . and everything is going à merveille."[45] In retrospect, these sessions had unintended but lasting consequences: Emma began to read and study the same literature as her husband, and to use much of it in her lifelong study of the legends of the Holy Grail. She not only became a gifted analyst in her own right but she also provided her husband with objectivity, balanced judgment, and occasional sharp criticism when she appraised his work.

Temporarily, at least as 1909 ended, Carl's analysis of Emma mollified her enough to end the jealous tirades that he insisted were groundless, even though he did tell Freud that "the prerequisite for a good marriage . . . is the license to be unfaithful." Emma must have wanted to believe him, for if Sabina Spielrein's diary for this period is truthful, it certainly attests to Jung's infidelity. The diaries of several of the Zürichberg Pelzmäntel hint at other liaisons, and in one specific case, the woman describes in fairly graphic detail several "treatment sessions" in her home that became sexual encounters. These women exchanged gossip, and Emma's sharp ear was attuned to it as well.[46]

In connection with his analysis of Emma, Carl decided she needed a vacation. As they often did, they left their three children in his mother and sister's care while they spent New Year's week in Unterwasser, Canton St. Gallen. Within the month, Jung told Freud that Emma was again pregnant, "by design and after mature reflection."[47] Otherwise, nothing changed outwardly in the Küsnacht household except that in addition to her regular duties, Emma assumed more of Carl's administrative needs because he was so often away from home.

Trudi Jung came fairly regularly to help with various other secretarial duties,[48] but she and Emma together were hard-pressed to keep up. So, too, was Jung, who spent most of Christmas Day answering his mail. A reply to Ferenczi was typical of much of what he wrote, that it was "impossible" to maintain a detailed exchange of analytic information through letters. He asked everyone to settle for "now and then . . . a sign of life and no diplomatics when we meet."[49]

The demands of his practice increased as well. Wealthy Americans who had heard of his successful treatment of Medill McCormick were consulting him; physicians, alone or in groups, who were intrigued by what they heard of his Clark lectures came to Zürich for lectures as well as private analysis. Jung asked

Freud what he would think if "things [were arranged] in such a way as to exploit the situation financially a bit." Freud thought the "idea of getting some profit" from those eager to observe ΨA was "quite justified." Besides the various "guests" (as Freud called the private students), Jung was also teaching "incessantly" at the University of Zürich for twelve hours weekly. He was "very much interested in the psychology of incurables" and pleased that his "ideas on the theory of Dem. praec." held "hopes of further progress."[50]

In conjunction with all his personal activity, the machinations of psychoanalytic politics also mounted. Details of various jousts and spats filled most of his letters to Freud, as individual doctors and newly formed societies throughout Europe contended for the prominence of their particular theories.[51] Jung entered each fray with alacrity: after a meeting of Swiss psychiatrists in Zürich,[52] he gloated, "Your (that is, our) cause is *winning all along the line.*"[53]

Although the cause was still one the two men shared, there were hints of disagreements to come that had not yet been brought into open contention. One in particular would have far-reaching consequences: "I am coming to attach more and more importance to the infantile theories of sexuality," Freud confided.[54] Jung made no direct reply.

In Jung's Christmas Day letter to Freud, interrupted and unfinished until the thirty-first, he attempted to clear up another potential misunderstanding. He was miffed that Freud yearned for scholars of mythology, linguistics, and the history of religions[55] to join their research, for it implied he thought Jung "unfit for such work."[56] Jung took pains to stake his claim that the key to decoding the conditions of neurosis and psychosis lay within the history of civilization and the study of mythology. He was confident that he and Honegger could contribute new ways of thinking to this enormous subject and alluded to "marvelous visions, glimpses of far-ranging interconnections" that he was still "incapable of grasping." Whether he believed Jung or not, Freud quickly replied that he agreed.

Honegger had already made "a splendid impression" with a curiously arrogant letter[57] in which he must have analyzed Freud without their ever having met. Freud saw nothing amiss with it and urged Jung to ensure that Honegger presented at the Nuremberg congress. This was precisely Jung's intention, even though he worried that Honegger would not perform as he wanted, because it was impossible to control what he might do or say. Interestingly, Jung did not recognize the elements in Honegger's relationship with him that were analogous to his own with Freud. Just as Freud was always trying to cajole, entice, interest, and even convert Jung into adopting his views and expressing them within a severely prescribed orthodoxy, so, too, did Jung try unsuccessfully to persuade Honegger of the correctness of his perspective and to work solely within it. "I do have opinions in the matter of work discipline," Jung complained to Freud. "He [Honegger] reads too little and 'works' too much by flashes of genius." Jung thought he relied far too much on external "stimulation," which was merely a means of hiding his "lack of self-reliance." He objected to Honegger's procedures, which were erratic, unscientific, and undisciplined, and was "very much against such shiftlessness."[58] All of this Freud thought about Jung in varying degree, but when he replied, it was with a "grandfatherly" opinion that Honegger was of "a later generation" and built of "softer stuff" than Jung. "We would not want him to be a copy of yourself," he chided, urging Jung to "take him as he is and train him on the basis of his own nature, rather than try to mould him to an ideal that is alien to him."[59] Sound advice, which Freud could never heed, especially when it came to Jung.

Thus, Honegger's brilliant beginning in terms of how he collected data about Schwyzer seemed likely to end with nothing further than mere compilation to show for it. His initial attempts to analyze the information were superficial because he had not done the systematic reading about ancient mythologies that Jung set for him, particularly in Friedrich Creuzer, Richard Payne Knight, Mead, and Dieterich. Freud did not share Jung's chagrin about this, so it was especially distressing when he asked whether Jung was wise to let Honegger "plunge directly into the general problem of ancient mythology." He thought it would be better for them both to base their methodology on "a series of detailed studies"[60] that relied heavily on compilations by experts in individual fields, leaving unspecified the question of who would investigate which compilations if Honegger refused to do systematic research.

The situation became further complicated sometime between February and March 1910, when Honegger suddenly announced that he had become engaged to a young woman of good family, Helene Widmer. Jung was alarmed because Honegger's only previously known attachment to a woman had been to his mother, and in some quarters, its intensity provoked snide comments about his sexual preference. Jung chose to ignore the derisive gossip and instead put all the blame for what he considered a travesty on the unfortunate Miss Widmer. He had very little good to say about the quiet, patient, and well-mannered young woman, either to Honegger or anyone else who would listen to his complaints. Jung was vocal about how "unsuitable" she was, until he got himself into another "tight corner." He then engaged the intelligent Miss Widmer as his first paid secretary and stopped judging her "much too unfairly." Meanwhile, he told Freud, Honegger was continuing his independent ways while "win[ning] all hearts."[61]

THE DATES of the Nuremberg congress were finally set for March 30–31, when, from Freud's isolated viewpoint in far-off Vienna, a series of semi-catastrophes threatened to topple his needed supports. Bleuler announced that he would not attend; nor would the Reverend Oskar Pfister, who had become one of the stalwarts of the Zürich group. "What will happen if my Zürichers desert me?" Freud wailed, when it seemed that even Jung himself would not be there.[62]

Medill McCormick had suffered a catastrophic breakdown, and his mother begged Jung to attend to him personally in New York.[63] "Now don't get cross with me for my pranks!" Jung wrote to Freud, using much the same language as Honegger often used to placate him. The trip *"had"* to be made, Jung insisted, and he had arranged his "severe conflict of duties" to ensure he would *"be back in time for Nuremberg."*[64] Emma was as worried as Freud, but for a different reason: since Jung's return from Clark he had spoken many times about following other Swiss physicians — Brill, Hoch, and Meyer among them — to the professional opportunity and financial success offered by the new world. She knew her husband well enough to suspect that his offhand comments about emigrating might be more than idle speculation.

Jung went to New York and left Honegger to treat his patients and help Emma with the many unresolved details connected with the conference. Jung's "thin" roster of patients had suddenly grown so fat that, despite Honegger's will-'o-the-wisp flightiness, he was considering taking him on as a junior associate. He discussed it with Honegger but also set several nonnegotiable conditions: Honegger had to write a dissertation on Schwyzer's case and have his medical degree in hand; most important of all, he had to present his findings at the Nuremberg congress in a form that would bring credit to Jung. All this put pressure on Honegger while Jung was away, but he seemed to be meeting the challenges. Emma told Freud that without Honegger's help, she would "otherwise . . . be rather nervous about everything turning out all right."[65] She also told Freud that in retrospect this brief trip did have one important and lasting personal benefit: Carl assured her he was no longer attracted to the United States for anything other than visits, which had indeed "taken a stone from [her] heart."

JUNG'S WHIRLWIND voyage deposited him in Nuremberg at 5 A.M. the day the conference started. Honegger spoke "On the Formation of Paranoid Delusions,"[66] and Jung was as relieved as Freud was delighted with the presentation. Unfortunately, the congress triggered the downward spiral into which Honegger's behavior careened for the rest of his short life. A legitimate question is how much his presentation propelled it, for the paper itself was a morass of confusion and distress, at times an incoherent melding of the author's voice with the subject's visions. By the time he reached his conclusion, Honegger's assessments of Schwyzer's delusions tumbled out in garbled, lofty, omnipotent, and paranoid prose — so alarming that it raises several questions: Why did the abstract printed later in the *Jahrbuch* (probably written by Otto Rank, whose task it was to prepare them) give such pride of place to Honegger's incoherence, and why was it so succinct and respectful of his conclusions? And why were the attendees — Jung and Freud primarily — not alarmed by it? Why did they, in particular, consider his presentation a triumph? Honegger ended with the grandiose statement that he would offer convincing proof for everything he said "in a more detailed paper," but if he ever wrote one, it seems to have disappeared, as he did shortly after from Zürich. With Honegger's abrupt disappearance began the rumors that plagued Jung for the rest of his life: that at best, he misappropriated his pupil's research; at worst, he stole it and lied that it was his own.[67]

AFTER NUREMBERG, Honegger's colleagues at the Burghölzli were convinced he had become "psychotic" and were puzzled as to why Jung could not admit it. Several of the other doctors incorrectly assumed that it was Honegger and not Schwyzer who "had developed the delusional idea that the sun had a pendulum, and that its oscillations were responsible for the alternation of light and darkness."[68] The rumor gained credibility because Honegger was not there to refute it: immediately after his triumph at Nuremberg, he stunned his Zürich colleagues by announcing that he had accepted a position as an assistant in the private clinic of Dr. R. J. Löy, the Kurhaus de Territet et Sanatorium de l'Abri on the shores of Lake Geneva in Montreux-Territet. Honegger left without explanation or farewell at the very moment Jung was trying to arrange to monitor his deteriorating condition by persuading the famous diet doctor Maximilian Bircher-Benner (creator of the breakfast cereal Birchermüsli) to make him an assistant in his local clinic.

Honegger bolted in a manner reminiscent of Otto Gross's scaling the Burghölzli wall, so once again Jung tried to save face, this time by telling everyone (including Freud) that he had "reluctantly" consented to Honegger's taking the Territet appointment. In search of a surrogate assistant, he told Freud his "libido . . . was thrashing around for a suitable object" and he chose Riklin to "replace the temporary loss." All Jung's hopes for sustained cooperative research into how the delusions of patients could be interpreted through universal mythology were dashed, but he still could not "let go of Honegger." He vowed "to carry out his plan," to write about the Schwyzer case history himself.[69]

WITHIN A month, Honegger, fueled by manic energy, announced that he was returning to Zürich to enter into private practice with Jung. Jung learned of this when someone congratulated him on his new partnership, and he sprang to stop Honegger.[70] First of all, he had to stop Walter Gut, whom Honegger had deputized to assist Helene Widmer in finding "suitable quarters [in Zürich] for the firm of Jung-Honegger . . . three rooms, unfurnished, with telephone."[71] This was a complete surprise to Jung, who never intended to remove his practice from his home, even if an eventual partnership with Honegger did come to pass. He contacted Honegger in Territet, telling him firmly he must not leave until he wrote a dissertation, that there would be no professional association until he received a medical degree. Honegger ignored Jung, left Territet, and was back in Zürich by late June.

Little is known of his life throughout the rest of 1910, except that he probably lived with his mother, may have tried to set up an analytic practice, and most certainly tried repeatedly to break his engagement to Miss Widmer.[72] With her, he was in a no-win situation: marriage would have led to unhappiness for both parties, but an unchivalrous rupture would have resulted in professional disgrace and personal shunning for him and lifelong social opprobrium not only for the unfortunate woman but also for her family. Jung described the situation as "sickly and unendurable . . . dismal and depressing." Throughout the ongoing drama, he had "not had the least help" from Honegger and had "to pull the whole cart" alone.

On February 1, 1911, Honegger made another abrupt departure from Zürich, this time for a position in the cantonal psychiatric hospital, the Klinik Rheinau. Amazingly, Honegger was still perceived as "an up-and-coming psychiatrist," so this was "not the wisest move," because only chronic cases were lodged there, and the director was not "particularly outstanding."[73] Still, Honegger was much more stable and even "cheerful" during his first month at the Klinik Rheinau than he had been for the previous six months in Zürich.[74] His mood darkened, however, when he was ordered to begin his annual military service as a medical corps trainee. One of Honegger's junior colleagues at the Klinik Rheinau, Dr. Karl Gehry, remembered him as "at loose ends and morose," unable to assuage his unfocused anxiety. As Honegger had already fulfilled several prior military stints, Gehry thought his behavior seemed disproportionately irrational and his anxiety most likely based on something else he would not or could not address. Gehry suggested that he ask Jung, as his analyst of record, for a certificate of excuse. Honegger refused, alarmed at the prospect of once again subjecting himself to Jung's authority, a response that was especially perplexing: he was determined to keep himself free and clear of his former mentor even as he was equally determined to go into partnership with him.

Still, military service loomed in April, and on the night of March 28, Honegger carefully prepared and then knowingly "injected himself with a concentrated solution of morphine." He did not respond when the hospital porter tried to awaken him the next morning, and the other staff doctors who were quickly summoned were unable to revive him. He died without regaining consciousness and was buried on April 1.

Jung diagnosed Honegger's suicide as the desire to "avoid a psychosis" by one who could not live unless it was by the "pleasure principle."[75] When Freud sent condolences to Jung, he observed that something within Honegger made him unable to adjust to the social constraints of life. "I think we wear out quite a few men," he concluded.[76]

JUNG WENT to Berlin in early April to assist "The Berlin Group" in planning a congress proposed for Weimar in the fall.[77] He did not have time to digest the fact of Honegger's death until late April, when he dashed home for two days so

Emma could brief him about events in his practice and other professional affairs. He then rushed to Stuttgart for the annual meeting of the German Society for Psychiatry.[78] "Shades of Honegger" accompanied him on these trips.

"How wasteful children are," he told Freud, "with their own precious, irreplaceable lives!" Still, he thought Honegger's decision to terminate "the most brilliant gifts of the mind" was a better alternative than staying alive and succumbing to the "Moloch of neurosis and psychosis." He thought it "evil" that Honegger, "marked by the gods . . . so rare . . . should be the victim of madness or an early death." Jung thought Honegger "did it [suicide] well . . . without fuss, no sentimentalities like letters, etc."

As the physician who directed Honegger's research, Jung thought it his duty "to get hold of any manuscripts he may have left behind (?) so as to save for science anything that can be saved."

Thus began the next spate of rumors, concerning the information Honegger compiled at the Burghölzli and the other writing (or writings) he may (or may not) have left behind. Both Jung's admirers and detractors have related the question mark within his comment to a multitude of queries, the most lasting and divisive focusing on who — Honegger or Jung — was the originator of the concept of the collective unconscious. Some clues exist in the papers Jung collected.[79]

Most of Honegger's original writing appears to be lost, as only fair copies in a variety of hands are in the documents that have come to be called the "Honegger Papers." In these, Honegger acknowledges that Jung's May 1906 "clinical introduction" of the Schwyzer case to the Burghölzli physicians was his own point of departure for a study of the patient's delusions. Because various hands record them, it is impossible to determine who recorded Schwyzer's delusions, whether it was Honegger alone or whether he was one among several physicians (Jung included, whose handwriting is identifiable) who made the daily observations in the patient's official record. There is also no way to determine who among the doctors decided which of Schwyzer's statements were important enough to record, whose analytic theories the observations reflected, and whose scholarship (Jung's or other mythologists') led Honegger to his personal interpretations. In a rambling, incoherent attempt to summarize all the information that he may have intended for his dissertation, Honegger stated that the data did not add up to a coherent entity and did little if anything to further the cause of analytical psychology — except for the singular delusion of the sun and its solar phallus. "Scripsit Honegger!!" Jung's handwriting attests in the margin next to this observation.

There are other historical records besides the Honegger Papers, however, such as Jung's correspondence with Freud, that offer a possible means to assign some division of credit to Jung and Honegger. The *Jahrbuch* abstract and Honegger's Nuremberg paper closely parallel Schwyzer's patient history dating back to 1901, which was compiled by Jung and the other Burghölzli doctors.

Also, Honegger's list of the varieties of mythological correspondences Schwyzer exhibited parallel those Jung described in his letters to Freud. These parallel Honegger's research from the beginning, when Jung complained of having to read all that his assistant was too "shiftless" to do.

It was Jung who read Herodotus, whose "prudery" in glossing over many things sexual "for reasons of decency" led him to wonder, "Where did the Greeks learn that from so early?"[80] He read with delight "the 4 volumes of old Creuzer."[81] He thought Richard Payne Knight's 1865 *Discourse on the Worship of Priapus, and Its Connection with the Mystic Theologie of the Ancients* was "capital," whereas Thomas Inman's 1874 *Ancient Pagan and Modern Christian Symbolism Exposed and Explained* was "unreliable." Jacob Burckhardt's *History of Greek Civilization* was too superficial for his taste, but it led him to Erwin Rohde's *Psyche,*[82] and from there to interpretations of Dionysian myths in light of (among others) Bachofen's *"Mutterrecht."* Traces of all these writings are in Honegger's abstract, and some appear in his paper as well, but who can say whether Honegger's general comments were gleaned from conversations with Jung or whether he actually read the same texts? Honegger certainly would have been able to pull off the feat without actually reading them, for he had been praised ever since his Zofingia days for "his vivacity and splendid oratory gift."[83]

The one text missing from this compilation is Albrecht Dieterich's *Eine Mithrasliturgie.* Dieterich's book was first published in 1903 and is generally considered to be the first discussion of the so-called Mithras Liturgy and the ur-description of a solar phallus vision corresponding to Schwyzer's delusion. Jung's personal copy in his library was the second edition, of 1910, so it is quite likely he did not read it until he owned it. To date, nothing has been found to suggest that Honegger read it, either independently or at Jung's urging. However, it is highly unlikely that Schwyzer ever had access to either edition, for he had been institutionalized for a decade prior to its first publication. Dieterich's book did not take on significance until long after Jung's death, when it became the text most often cited by contemporary critics as the primary reason to believe Jung stole Honegger's research and lied about his role in the Schwyzer case.[84]

There is, however, one document among the many Honegger papers that hints at how he arrived at the methodology he applied, a section of several brief pages that begins with "Introductory Remarks" and seems his most sustained and coherent attempt at a medical dissertation. Honegger wrote that he began his observations of Schwyzer by excerpting the medical histories compiled by the other doctors who treated him in his several institutionalizations before the Burghölzli. With these case histories, Honegger intended to "draw the borderline of the already known from which the analysis proceeded from different points [of view]." He intended to trace the course of Schwyzer's illness "chronologically," but first he listed obstacles he had encountered. He described Jung's earlier attempts with the association experiment and other free association techniques as having "failed" because "it was impossible to achieve in [Schwyzer] the attitude necessary for it." Honegger then described his own "analysis" of Schwyzer, saying it consisted of "very laborious questioning about the unclear points of medical history." Like Jung before him, he was constantly frustrated because Schwyzer rarely answered his questions; instead, he "usually produced a colorful hodgepodge of memories of his life and delusional ideas and indulged himself in ever new variations of the same thing."

"So much that I was searching for wasn't found," Honegger wrote, "some things that I hadn't searched for were discovered." At this point, Honegger's reason and coherence faltered and then veered into confusion between the patient's delusions and the doctor's ruminations. The writing reflects his dilemma: entire paragraphs are crossed out, either with straight lines or a series of circles; some words are completely blackened; other passages are heavily scored and underlined, as if the writer is frantic to show emphasis. Some of the most intriguing passages are those in which it is difficult to ascertain where the patient's history ends and the doctor's musings begin. In retrospect, Honegger's statement in his Nuremberg presentation, that no logical paper could ever be written about Emile Schwyzer, takes on special resonance and might well stand as the epitaph for why he ended his own short and tragic life: "There wasn't anything else left to do."

WHEN JUNG collected the papers after Honegger's death and tried to put them in order, he might well have come to the same conclusion: that the data Honegger collected did not add up to a coherent entity, and that the material in hand did little if anything to further the cause of analytical psychology — except for the singular delusion of the sun and its solar phallus.

The question of whether or not Jung stole Honegger's research and, by extension, the idea of collective unconscious preoccupies those who seek the true history of analytical psychology. Unfortunately, there is no firm documentation, so only supposition is possible. Because the Honegger Papers so clearly delineate the young doctor's mental illness, and because the research was compiled in a country and a culture obsessed with a reverence for privacy, Jung might well have ceased to mention Honegger's participation in the research simply to protect his family from the stigma of his publicized insanity and subsequent suicide. Or Jung may have decided that Honegger's role was a minor one; that he had amassed the Schwyzer delusions but was incapable of synthesizing them, and that in a number of instances he had mishandled the information by misinterpreting the patient's delusions as his own. Overall, Honegger's assessments seem to have confused the patient's with his own sad history, which is something Jung as his physician would have taken great care to protect and was obligated to keep private.

For whatever the reason, Jung stopped mentioning Honegger's role in the evolution of his thought early on, but for the rest of his life he insisted that the true "turning point of his thought"[85] was Schwyzer's solar phallus delusion. Long after the delusional patient Schwyzer died, long after all traces of Honegger's family disappeared from Swiss genealogical history and Helene Widmer became a sad footnote within it, the Honegger Papers remain hotly contested. Partisans continue to make charges and offer defenses; investigations are launched, but definitive answers remain elusive. Still, conclusions can be drawn: Honegger did not originate the study of the Solar Phallus Man, and his own words show him as too impaired to be capable of producing the coherent, powerful analysis that led to the eventual formulation of the theory of the collective unconscious. Jung originated the research when he recognized something universal in Schwyzer's solar phallus vision as early as 1901. Objectivity should allow him to take credit for its final formulation.

CHAPTER 14

❦

"The Family Philosopher"

Emma Jung was an exceedingly reserved woman who rarely spoke of herself or her marriage in her younger years, but in maturity she occasionally made a comment that stunned everyone who heard her say it.[1] Emma delivered the remark offhandedly, interjecting it in the midst of a discussion of someone else's marital woes or, as she did on several occasions, confiding it to her analysands during particularly emotional sessions. In every instance what she said was always the same: there were three separate occasions when she not only wanted to but actually tried to divorce her husband. Each time, he either became ill or incapacitated or had a serious accident that required her, as a dutiful wife, to take charge of their affairs and nurse him back to health and stability.

Her first attempt to begin divorce proceedings ended with her fourth pregnancy, which resulted in the birth of their third daughter, Marianne, on September 20, 1910. It began when Emma learned of Carl's involvement with Sabina Spielrein and lasted throughout the most heated moments of that relationship. It is widely believed, and most likely true, that Emma exposed her husband's nonprofessional alliance with his patient sometime in spring 1909 by writing an anonymous letter to Frau Spielrein.[2] It is true that Carl acquiesced to Emma's every demand from that time onward — from his Burghölzli resignation to the Küsnacht house, to accepting her administrative help with psychoanalytic politics, to the "deliberate" pregnancy that resulted in Marianne's birth. Emma's demands were unconditional and the only terms under which she would remain in the marriage.

By the time Marianne was born, there was a semblance of stasis in the household because Sabina became engrossed in her career and went to Munich to study art history and conduct further medical research.[3] "He is gone, and 'tis good thus," she wrote in Munich as she confided her feelings to her diary. When the term ended, she planned to go to Vienna for a semester of further study, but she was vague about whether she would try to meet Freud. She did, however, ask Jung for a letter of recommendation to use in both cities to introduce herself to psychiatric circles. Meanwhile, Jung was reading her manuscript, eventually published as "Destruction as a Cause of Coming into Being."[4] He gave it the same careful attention he had given previously to her dissertation[5] and urged her to begin her professional life by contacting Leonhard Seif in Munich, who would receive her more cordially than would the Viennese, who were reluctant to recognize women as colleagues. Only "Grandpa Freud," he thought, would be as "delighted" as he was with the "fruit of [her] mind."[6]

With Sabina gone from Zürich, Emma was relieved of a personal threat and free to concentrate on her husband's work with whatever attention she had left after caring for four children and a large house. Here, she found another possible threat, minor in comparison to Spielrein. Jung's practice was burgeoning, particularly with wealthy women from Zürichberg who passed the news among themselves of how much the glamorous doctor in the grand house by the lake had helped them. In their circle, "going to Jung" was "somehow very chic and modern, a *frisson* that made them *au courant* with everything new and exciting."[7] The attention was so flattering that Jung told Freud he had to "make heroic efforts" to keep his practice "at arm's length."[8] He did not tell Freud about his attraction to Maria Moltzer, the Dutch doctor he first met when she was an assistant at the Burghölzli and who was now setting up a private practice in Zürich, both on her own and in conjunction with Franz Riklin. Moltzer was an heiress to the Bols liquor fortune who chose to keep that information private by living an austere and frugal life. Reed-thin, she was usually called "Sister Moltzer" and described as nunlike, ascetic, virginal, and pure. She was intense, intellectual, and driven, and Jung was so physically attracted to her that he called her the first inspiration for his formulation of the anima, the inner female configuration within the male.[9] Whether he consummated this passion is not known, but his attraction was real and lasting throughout his life, even though at the time he took great pains to paint a self-portrait for Freud of a man too busy for any form of dalliance. He explained that he had one day each week to devote to scientific research because the rest of his time was taken up with seminars, correspondence, lecture courses, and "the perennial visitors." The crush of people whose needs he had to meet in one way or another was such that he could not relax on Sundays with sailing or hiking, the physical activities he so much enjoyed, because he needed to spend the time alone in his library, resting and restoring himself. It was a "deplorable state of affairs," especially for Emma, who had to keep four children out of his sight and hearing.

In August, his many activities in and around Zürich were punctuated by a week in Brussels, where he spoke at the first Congrès International de Pédagogie.[10] His vacation was a week in September, when he and Emma went to the nearby Bernese Oberland. The stay was brief because Freud was to be their houseguest from September 16 to 19, and the next day they were to entrain together for Weimar and the Third Psychoanalytic Congress, held September 21–22.

Freud was alarmed by the frenzy of Jung's peripatetic itinerary and urged him to guard against "the dragon" of so many professional demands. He urged Jung to let his "charming, clever, and ambitious wife" free him from "the business of moneymaking."[11] As if to soften the crassness of his statement, he added that his own wife had often expressed the wish to be able to do the same for him. Freud couched his dislike of the United States and all things American in a concern about Jung's "taste for moneymaking," especially as so many rich Americans were now passing through Zürich to seek his counsel.[12] He advised that it would be "good business" to "forgo ordinary pursuits," for it was the only way to be sure of "extraordinary rewards."

Jung took this to heart and responded fully in his next letter with an openness that was uncharacteristic in their relationship at this moment. Because of various misinterpretations as well as actual misunderstandings during the past half year, Jung was now careful not only of what he said to Freud, but also of how he said it, no matter what the topic. The tone of this particular letter harkens back to earlier days, when Jung's role was of supplicant before Freud's patriarchal authority. His moneymaking wasn't "all that bad," Jung insisted, even as he granted that Freud was correct to say he was overextended. It was just that he was often overcome by "a feeling of inferiority" when he measured himself against Freud, and he compensated by increasing his "emulation." Freud's large practice was a necessity because his wife had no private income and he had to support six children and a sister-in-law, whereas Jung saw his own full practice in two lights: first, as a way to "gain experience," for he did not think he possessed the same foundation of knowledge as Freud; and second, because he needed to earn goodly sums of money "to rid myself of the thought that I am non-viable." Emma's fortune was thus a double-edged sword, and his feelings, he admitted, were a collection of "frightful stupidities" that could only be overcome by "acting them out." He promised to "be merciless" with himself and to structure the coming winter semester in a way that would leave time for research, but his assessment of the situation was almost gloomy: "It is, as you know, no light matter to suffer financial success. I have never thrived on it. Scientific work does me far more good."

THE WEIMAR Congress is generally considered the "outstanding event of [Freud's 1911] year," and the "high-water mark of the early psychoanalytic movement."[13] Ernest Jones was delighted that "no Viennese opposition obtruded itself,"[14] and pleased that it re-created the "friendly atmosphere" of the first congress in Nuremberg in 1910, when the International Psychoanalytic Association was founded and Jung was elected the first president. Indeed, both Freud and Jung had had a fractious psychoanalytic year, punctuated by the hesitations of other doctors to join the new society (Bleuler, and, consequently, the entire Burghölzli staff, to give but one example);[15] defections (Adler's); rehabilitations (Wilhelm Stekel's);[16] and new alliances (James Jackson Putnam and a growing band of Americans). Fifty-five persons came to Weimar, among them members of the press who were invited visitors. They were henceforth banned when one newspaper reported that "interesting papers were read on nudity and other current topics."[17]

Emma Jung was as personally delighted with the occasion as her husband was professionally satisfied. During the days when Freud was in her home, Emma listened attentively to his conversations with their other houseguests, Leonhard Seif and James Jackson Putnam. In private, using language, incident, and theory gleaned from her husband's writings and conversations, she spoke about herself so freely to Seif that he boasted later to his (then) good friend Ernest Jones that he was her analyst. Jones lost no time in telling Freud, who had himself spent six hours analyzing Putnam, at the end declaring the American a "potential murderer."[18]

For Emma it was all heady stuff, even though in reality she was more observer than participant. She joined her husband and their houseguests on the train, highly anticipating the role she was sure she could fashion for herself within the growing federation, encouraged in this thinking because seven other women were registered among the attendees. She was not even dismayed by the possibility that even though Sabina Spielrein said she would not attend, she might arrive as a late registrant.

A month earlier, Jung had replied to a letter from the miffed Spielrein, saying that, as usual, she was "getting angry too early."[19] She was neither snubbed nor ignored: he had simply not yet mailed invitations to the congress. She vacillated until just before the starting date, when she told Jung she could not attend because there was "something organically wrong" with her foot.[20] He doubted it, he told her, in a tone bidding fond but final farewell to their earlier relationship. He told her he had rid himself of "all the bitterness in my heart that I still harbored against you." His ill will derived not from her work, which he had always respected and tried to further, "but from earlier times and all the inner agony that I suffered because of you — and you suffered because of me." Hereafter, he wanted only the best for her, and he urged her to overcome any ill feelings she may have harbored against him, from "selfishness" to "pride" or "defiance." Now that she was his colleague, he insisted none of these emotions should keep her from the congress. In his capacity as president and as a public gesture of his professional respect, he personally distributed copies of her dissertation to all the attendees. As a further indication of the high professional standing in which he held her, he said she did not need a letter of recommendation from him in order to contact Freud, for her dissertation had made such a positive impression he would proffer a warm welcome in Vienna. "Meet him as the great master and rabbi, and everything will be fine," Jung urged.[21]

EMMA WAS not well acquainted with the other women who composed what her husband called "the feminine element . . . from Zurich."[22] She had heard Maria Moltzer speak and had read some of her papers based on the research she conducted under Jung's supervision. But if Emma also heard the rumors of Carl's possible liaison with "Sister Moltzer," she gave no indication and always treated her with cordiality and respect.[23] Emma treated Martha Böddinghaus of Munich the same way, even though she knew of her professional rivalry with Moltzer, and may have also heard the rumor that it began because both women were contesting for Carl's attention, if not his affection.[24] Emma liked the American medical doctor Beatrice Moses Hinkle and agreed with her husband that she was indeed "an American charmer."[25] A woman slightly older than Jung, Hinkle was then married to a wealthy American and comfortable with her profession and social position. Emma enjoyed her company, and for a brief time Hinkle became her role model. Of the final member of the Zürich contingent, Emma had little to say because she thought she had absolutely nothing to fear from her. But in this regard, her usual astute judgment was dead wrong.

Toni[26] Anna Wolff met Carl Jung as his patient, brought to him by her mother in mid-1910 shortly after the death of her father. Her Zürichberg friends told Frau Wolff of Jung's success with disturbed young people, and she thought her daughter could benefit from talking to him. Toni Wolff was twenty-two, sheltered, pampered, and seeming much younger than her years when she had her first session with Jung.

Born in Zürich on September 18, 1888, into one of the city's oldest and most distinguished families,[27] Toni was the eldest of three daughters. Her father, Konrad Arnold Wolff (known as Arnold), was born in Zofingen on April 9, 1846, and died in Zürich on December 24, 1909. He represented a Swiss company that specialized in importing silk fabrics from the Far East, and between the ages of twenty and forty-two he lived in Yokohama and served as Switzerland's consul to Japan. He was fond of all things Japanese and proud of the title of honorary consul, given when he returned to Zürich in middle age to find a wife.

Their families arranged his introduction to the twenty-year-old Anna Elisabetha Sutz of nearby Meilen, whom he married after a brief courtship. Ostensibly the marriage was arranged, but Arnold was a compassionate, considerate man, and his young wife adored him. Theirs was a blissful union cut short by his death at age sixty-three, when she was forty-two. Arnold respected Anna's intelligence and, as if he knew he would die long before her, trained her throughout their marriage to understand all his financial dealings. When he died, she moved easily into the role of head of the household and combined his financial acumen with her own considerable personal skills in raising three daughters. She was a "quiet woman but very lovable, a fixed mark, very safe and solid in the life of her family."[28]

After Toni, Frau Wolff gave birth to two more daughters: Erna Maria, born in Alstätten, Canton St. Gallen, in 1890; and Susanna Christine, born in Aarau, Canton Argau, in 1892. The family lived briefly in both places before settling

permanently in a grand *Jugendstil* mansion at Freiestrasse 9, surrounded by exquisite gardens on extensive grounds.²⁹ Their life was affluent and cultured,
amid paintings, books, and music provided by their talented daughters. One
room was furnished with Japanese furniture and antiques that Arnold brought
back with him, and throughout the rest of the house, there were pieces with a
decided Oriental flair, bought by Anna, who shared her husband's love of the
Far East. She completed the house's decoration with lush silks, brocades, and
velvets and the finest rugs and tapestries. The three Wolff daughters enjoyed a
privileged upbringing and were encouraged by loving parents to excel in intellectual and creative interests.

Toni showed a studious bent when she became interested in philosophy,
comparative religion, and mythology, and she began to collect books, photographs, and objects dealing with these subjects. Susi, the youngest, had artistic
inclinations and became a skilled goldsmith and jewelry designer. Erna, the
middle daughter, was teased as "the family's bourgeoise," for her main concern
was to do all that was expected of a young girl of good family to prepare for a
good marriage. Of the three, it was Erna who concerned herself with the Wolff
family's illustrious social history and its standing in the community and who
voiced occasional regret that no son had been born to carry on their father's
name. Toni and Susi "became freer of those traditions," and a certain tension
was created between them and their mother and sister. Frequently, there were
"lively discussions at meals," but Anna Wolff seldom allowed her "genuine concerns" to surface and strove to be "quite impartial." In this she succeeded, as her
children and grandchildren considered her their "enduring safe haven."³⁰

As the eldest, Toni filled the role of her father's son and heir. She was the
closest daughter and the one who spent long relaxed afternoons or evenings in
the *Herrenzimmer*, his private study, where no other woman in the family did
more than pause in the doorway to deliver messages or announce visitors.

All three daughters were given the best education for women of their class
and station. After private elementary and secondary girls' schools in Zürich,
they were sent to French Switzerland to learn the language and be "finished,"
with all the appropriate attributes they would need as mistresses of their own
gracious homes. They were also given gymnastics training and were expected to
be graceful in dance and sports. All three had musical ability and took lessons
on various instruments, but Toni and Susi had the most talent and played piano
best. They played and Susi sang during the many "balls" they had at home,
where never fewer than twenty young people in evening clothes danced,
supped, and paired off under the watchful eyes of parental chaperones. With
their many cousins, the Wolff sisters wrote their own plays and performed them
for all those who enjoyed the generous Wolff hospitality.

In short, the daughters were given so many social privileges and so much intellectual freedom that Toni was shocked when she asked her father, who was
supporting a young girl cousin's education at the University of Zürich, if she

could attend as well, and he refused. It was all right for her cousin, Arnold Wolff said, because the cousin's father had no money for a dowry and she would have to "get a foundation for her living" in order to support herself in years to come.[31] A university education would not be necessary for Arnold Wolff's daughters; in fact, it might well impede their chances for brilliant marriages, and he had plenty of money to settle on them to make sure they married well.

To compensate for not sending Toni to the university, he sent her back to Geneva for more courses in fine homemaking. On her seventeenth birthday, filled with more than the usual amount of adolescent angst, the precocious girl poured out her deepest feelings in a letter to her father, as she wondered what was to become of her — what had she done with her young life, and what, if anything, had she achieved thus far?[32]

Arnold Wolff replied on behalf of himself and his wife, respectfully and thoughtfully. They were pleased to know that Toni was thinking so seriously about her future, but they did not want her to "brood" about it. Rather, they urged her to take "delight" in the pleasure of being young:

> The serious side of life will come your way soon enough. It was always Mama's and my goal to make your youth as happy and sunny as possible, for no matter what the future may later bring, and it will not be absolute sunshine for you either, a carefree and happy youth is the most beautiful and best memory one can give a person for her journey through life, which will help her get through many a bitter hour in her later career.

He urged her not to torment herself with thoughts of nonaccomplishments. The only thing they wanted from her was "joy, and we are happy to attest that you have given it to us." She was not to worry that the end of her time in Geneva might also signal the end of her educational opportunities:

> Upon your return you will first have to familiarize yourself with the practical work of an inner household, which is as absolutely necessary for an educated "feminine woman," as you say, as her outward refinement, because a woman who does not have the household completely under control and in all details is a failed creature; yet her whole life does not have to revolve around it. It is self-evident that in addition to this you are free to pursue more serious intellectual and aesthetic studies, but not to the exclusion of practical ones.

It was Arnold's hope that Toni would go to England for a minimum stay of six months, "not because that is fashionable now," but because he was convinced that an understanding of English language, history, and tradition, so different from the Swiss, would benefit her greatly in later life.[33]

He urged her to pursue her studies "with seriousness and diligence," for this would be the greatest service to herself as well as the most pleasing to her parents. He said he hoped he would live long enough for her "to carry out all this in all leisureliness," and that she would return home to give "comfort and support" to her parents and sisters, adding "especially to your dear Mama when I will no longer be here one day." His concluding advice was surprisingly enlightened for a man of his time and station:

> For since the male element is so weakly represented in our family, you, my daughters, will have to make up for it and be able to act independently and to follow your own judgment so that you will not become dependent on third uninterested parties. To help you do so to my best knowledge and capability, that will be my serious ambition as long as I can pursue it.

When she came back from England, Toni did study at the University of Zürich, but not as an officially enrolled degree candidate. Her father could not be budged from thinking that an "official education" was "not becoming" for a wealthy woman, but he was proud of her "unofficial education."[34] During the several years she took courses in religion, philosophy, and mythology, her father praised her "creative, artistic mind" and called her "the family philosopher." He was especially pleased when she asked to have two portraits of Wolff ancestors who had been professors of theology hung in her room.[35] At the university, Toni broadened her friendships to include all sorts of persons she would not otherwise have met socially. She was accepted by groups that included students rich and poor, Swiss and foreign, because she was "very intelligent, independent, extremely cultured."[36] But although she was welcomed in their apartments, coffeehouses, and other university meeting places, she never invited them to her home. And despite her exposure to them, she remained unsophisticated and somewhat naïve.

She had numerous flirtations and several semi-serious infatuations during her university days. One, more serious than the rest, caused her deep distress when it did not develop as she hoped. She met William Wolfensberger in a course in comparative religion at the university. A young man whose background was similar to hers, he was also the eldest child of another well-to-do Zürich businessman but slightly younger than she (b. June 17, 1889). When they met, William was already writing poems and short stories and seemed destined for a promising career as a writer that was already earning his father's opprobrium. When he declared his intention to be ordained as a Protestant minister, the senior Wolfensberger withdrew financial support and all but disowned him. Toni met William after he made a public declaration to side with the liberal socialist element in the Swiss Reformed Church and took an activist role in preaching equality to peasant farmers. This so enraged his father that he had to live austerely, barely supporting himself by tutoring dull rich students who could not otherwise pass their examinations. Undeterred, Toni found this life exceedingly romantic and hoped to share it, but William was an ascetic with a mission, and he preferred to go alone to Fuldera, then an isolated parish in the most remote part of the Graubunden.[37] Even though the attraction had been stronger on her part than on his, Toni was still astonished by William's rejection.

William's departure coincided with a most unfortunate time, the final months of Arnold Wolff's terminal illness.[38] Toni was the closest daughter and also "the most impressionable of the three sisters." Even before her father became ill, her university friends deemed her "the most serious, the one who hardly ever laughed"; afterward, her family and friends observed that in point of fact, she "never laughed."[39] When Arnold died on Christmas Eve 1909, Toni became "severely disturbed, clinically depressed." By mid-1910, her condition was so grave that her mother, feeling she had nowhere else to go, listened to her friends' advice and brought her to Jung.[40]

In the beginning, Toni resisted all his attempts to address her inconsolable grief. She was glum and recalcitrant in their first several sessions until, searching for a way of getting her to talk, he compared her grief to several episodes in Greek mythology. She chided him for telling the tales with sloppy informality and gave her own precisely detailed version of each myth. He was delighted with her spunkiness, and his face brightened to think that he had found so much depth in such a child, for that was his initial impression of her. Basking in his obvious approval, she became alert and involved in the conversation that ensued. With an offhanded ease that was nevertheless a kind of flirtatious showing off, she let him know that she was well read in classical mythology. From then on, their sessions concentrated on shared intellectual interests and were as much about what she learned in her university classes and her own independent reading as they were about her depression. Soon it lightened, although it did not lift entirely. Jung's main concern at this point was how best to keep her in treatment long enough to effect a total cure. His own research in mythology provided the answer, and Toni Wolff became the first in a long line of women who gravitated to Jung because he allowed them to use their intellectual interests and abilities in the service of analytical psychology. She willingly did research in the university library, something for which Emma did not have either time or liberty, and that Trudi, still providing occasional secretarial help, was intellectually incapable of doing.

Jung was thirty-five when he met the twenty-two-year-old Toni Wolff. Emma was twenty-eight, not much older than Toni in physical years but light-years older in terms of life experience. Emma was an independent matron running a complicated household and responsible for the upbringing of four children; Toni had always lived in her mother's house and depended (as she did for the rest of her life) on her mother and a retinue of servants to take care of her. Emma regarded Toni only as a prize patient of the right sort, a young girl treated so successfully by her husband that his professional reputation could only be further burnished in the best social class in Zürich. This mattered greatly to a young mother with an eye on how four growing children would be received there in the future. Emma was pleased when Toni showed such an interest in psychoanalysis that she asked for and was granted permission by her mother to attend the Weimar conference as a guest of Herr Jung and his dependable young wife, who would ensure that she was properly chaperoned.

Jung introduced Toni to Freud as his "new discovery," praising her "excellent feeling for religion and philosophy." He listed Emma "last, but not least" among the feminine contingent of female attendees, but she rated only the briefest description as "my wife."[41] Freud's reply, alluding to Emma on quite another matter, praised her for being a "solver of riddles."[42] In many ways, it was an uncannily accurate estimation of the role she would play for the rest of her life in the triangular relationship composed of herself, her husband, and Toni Wolff.

CHAPTER 15

"Unsuited to the Position"

F reud called Emma Jung a "solver of riddles" because she was trying to mediate the growing tension over theoretical differences between him and her
husband. Emma's instincts told her Freud was investigating the same subject as
Jung, the origin of religion. Freud grudgingly admitted that he had not planned
to discuss it for fear of "confusing" Jung,[1] but not until after he read the
Jahrbuch article that became the first part of Jung's *Wandlungen und Symbole der
Libido*, originally entitled in English *Psychology of the Unconscious* and later renamed *Symbols of Transformation*.[2] Jung's book began as a long article about how
classical myths and universal legends could be used to express and explain basic
psychological concepts. By the time he published the second part of what became the book, he realized that he could no longer accept Freud's original definition of the libido in its entirety, namely, that sexual energy was the root of all
mental dysfunction, and he offered his own modification. Jung believed that the
sex drive was not the primary influence upon human behavior because there
were other equally complex influences, among them the universal archetypes
that emerge from the collective unconscious. Jung's first part, in which he used
historical materials (i.e., the myths, legends, and other representations of symbolic information), appeared in print before Freud's *Totem and Taboo*, but that
did not deter Freud from claiming that, as Jung's article was merely the expression of his (Freud's) own findings, he would no longer need to keep his research
secret. In short, Freud was claiming ultimate authority for all things pertaining
to psychoanalysis by insisting that no matter who expressed an idea, he was its
originator.

Freud's ongoing silence about Jung's article bothered Emma and prompted
her to act. Even though she knew Freud had enormous respect for her acumen
and held her in affectionate esteem, she was afraid to approach him directly. Instead, she wrote to Ferenczi to ask if he had noticed any "resistance"[3] from
Freud toward her husband. She asked him not to tell Freud of her letter but, astute as she was, knew he would disregard her instruction and may even have

201

wanted him to do so. Ferenczi did just that. Under the guise of asking Freud for advice on how best to reply, he sent Emma's letter along with his own. He told Freud he planned to compose a "calming" letter to assure her that he sensed no antagonism on Freud's part and to tell her not to be afraid to contact Freud directly and ask for his response. Ferenczi thought that Emma, who "really thinks and writes in a kind and at the same time perceptive manner," might well have sensed the same sort of "dissatisfaction with the *incomplete*[4] intimacy with [Jung's] teacher (father)" that he himself previously experienced with Freud. He thought Emma was "partly right" to assert that Freud had an "antipathy" toward full and open friendship, no matter with whom, but that she was wrong to think it was a tactic he used to protect his "authority."

"Obviously," Ferenczi concluded, as if to sound out Freud's true feelings, "Frau Jung may have discerned something of your disapproval of Zürich occultism and perhaps also your not total satisfaction with Jung's paper on libido."

Freud's need for "authority" surfaced in his reply to Ferenczi. He understood how much Ferenczi wanted to "triumph" but would, he said, "see to it that you will not succeed."[5] He saw nothing in Emma's letter to give any proof "that Jung himself has this impression." Nevertheless, he did admit to the "possibility" that Emma could be expressing her husband's feelings. He told Ferenczi that his proposed reply to her was fine, except that he should strike "the reference to astrology [i.e., "Zürich occultism"]." And besides, his objections to Jung's paper on libido were "very slight and very clear."

Freud could have put the matter to rest simply by writing this to Jung. For reasons he never explained, he was mostly silent for three months, from the article's publication in August until the following November. He volunteered an opinion only after he exchanged several more letters with Emma, but by then his reply was too much, too coyly effusive, and, worst of all, too late. In the meantime, the theoretical differences and real or imagined slights between him and Jung festered.

Immediately after the Weimar conference, Jung departed for St. Gallen and his annual month of military duty. Emma took the children to her mother's in Schaffhausen, so Freud was most likely correct when he told Ferenczi "the couple probably haven't spoken to each other for weeks." They did exchange daily letters, however, so Emma had ample opportunity not only to hear about Freud's lack of enthusiasm but also to correspond in her husband's absence without his knowledge, first with Ferenczi, then with Freud.

She was well aware of Freud's two previous offhand comments to Jung: the first on August 20, saying that he had received the *Jahrbuch* but had had time only to cut the pages and not to read them; and his equally evasive remark on September 1, that he would have to reread the article but could not do so at the moment because Ferenczi took his copy.[6] Neither remark was the sort to calm Jung's uneasiness or, by extension, Emma's. Ferenczi, inadvertently or not, added to it.

When Freud read Emma's letter, he told Ferenczi that when he replied, he should strike (i.e., *streichen* [to strike out, eliminate]) any mention of tendencies toward occultism in Zürich and his objections to the *Jahrbuch* article. Ferenczi did just the opposite: he misread *streichen* as *streifen* (to touch upon), and because he did not want Emma to know that he had sent her letter to Freud, discussed both topics as if they were his own independent views on the matter. When Ferenczi reread Freud's letter, he realized his mistake and told Freud at once, admitting, "The matter doesn't exactly look like a triumph for me!"[7] Freud's comment on Ferenczi's "act of false obedience" was simply "the matter is becoming very interesting."[8]

Emma in the meantime had written directly to Freud, who told Ferenczi disingenuously that it was "only just now dawning" on him that "the only incriminating evidence" for her uneasiness was his "failure to mention the 'Wandlungen,'" adding that he might have "aroused mistrust through some idiosyncrasies that have to do with the roots of my work." He went on to say: "I will in any case very carefully conceal the signs of wanting-to-find-everything-alone and hand over what is permissible. My 'Postscript,' which seems suspicious in this light, was finished in Klobenstein *before* the arrival of the *Jahrbuch*."[9] Freud thus not only justified the originality and primacy of his ideas but also assuaged any misgivings about his overweening need for "authority."

Freud believed he had satisfied Emma's qualms, so he put an end to their correspondence. What he wrote is not known, for his side of the exchange is presumed lost.[10] What is known, however, is that the dauntless Emma was not satisfied and wrote again. If one takes Freud's commanding need for "authority" into consideration when reading her letter, what she wrote can only be described as falling somewhere between spunky and suicidal.

Emma began by thanking him for relieving her "stupid" doubts and for the "goodwill" he showed "to all of [them]."[11] Nevertheless, she still had some thoughts of her own, and with all due deference and respect, she listed them. First was her concern about what he thought of Jung's article. She emphasized that the concern was truly hers, not Jung's: "Actually Carl, if he holds something to be right, would have no need to worry about anybody else's opinion." She was willing to concede that Freud had perhaps done the right thing by withholding his views, because, by doing so, he permitted Jung a semblance of independence that did not "reinforce this father-son relationship."

Her second reason was deeply personal and showed just how much Freud liked and trusted her. He may have been reluctant to discuss anything with his male colleagues that would risk his "authority," but he told Emma more personal and biographical information about himself than he ever told anyone else.[12] On the morning after Freud arrived in Küsnacht en route to the Weimar conference, he and Emma had had a private conversation in which he talked at length about his family. He told her that his children remained his "only true joy," even though they became "a real worry" as they grew to adulthood. As for his marriage, it had long been "amortized," and now nothing remained to him "except — die." Emma was puzzled; Freud's remark was astonishing, and she thought about every possible aspect of its meaning. She concluded that he intended the remark to refer to her situation, specifically to her marriage. There is the possibility that Freud confided in Emma because of some rift he discerned between her and Jung due to the other women who flocked around him, and that his example was intended to sustain her. But if so, he must not have divulged any details that would cause her to compare her situation with his.

She moved on to a topic that probably infuriated him, when she asked if he was really sure that his children "would not be helped by analysis." When even children of ordinary fathers had trouble asserting their independence, she asked, did he not think the problem might be magnified for children of a "distinguished father," especially one who "also has a streak of paternalism in him, as [he himself] said?" They had discussed this in their Küsnacht conversation, when Freud told her he had no time to analyze his own children because he "had to earn money so that they could go on dreaming." "Do you think this attitude is right?" she asked.

She offered Freud a comparison of their marriages as a sop to the harshness of her questions. Her perception of her own husband's behavior was astute and, despite her deep emotional commitment to him, almost infallibly objective. She referred obliquely to the close bond she yearned to forge, one based on sexual passion and common intellectual interests, but said it eluded her because Jung substituted "the imperative 'earn money'" as "an evasion of something else to which he has resistance."

She asked forgiveness for her "brazen candor" but said she still had "another thing" she wanted to express. Freud was then fifty-six years old, certainly an elderly man by the standards of his time, but to Emma, an admirable man in the prime of professional life. She was obviously proud that he chose her husband as his principal spokesman, but why, she asked, was Freud looking at Jung "with a father's feeling: 'He will grow, but I must dwindle.'" She thought Freud was wrong to see in Jung "the follower and fulfiller more than you need. Doesn't one often give much because one wants to keep much?" Why was he behaving like such an old man, so eager to pass on the reins of succession instead of basking in "well-earned fame and success"? Why didn't he "rejoice and drink to the full the happiness" of receiving personal homage as psychoanalysis gained increasing professional respect and allegiance from physicians and scientists throughout the world? Perhaps Emma thought she had gone far enough. "Don't be angry with me," she concluded, signing her letter "with warm love and veneration."

SHORTLY AFTER, Jung's military service fulfilled for another year, he returned to Küsnacht, his practice, and the overwhelming dual burden of being president of the International Psychoanalytical Association and editor of the *Jahrbuch*. A further complication had been generated at the Weimar conference when a new publication was created: the *Zentralblatt*, meant to serve as the official publication of the International Psychoanalytic Association and to supersede the *Correspondenzblatt*, or *Bulletin*, a hodgepodge of reviews, abstracts, minutes of meetings, and announcements of forthcoming events and publications. Freud intended for it to report on society meetings and give abstracts of minutes but also to provide a forum for articles that were, for any number of reasons, not sufficiently "scientific" for the more formal and prestigious *Jahrbuch*.

To the consternation of the Viennese, Jung had been reelected president of the IPA, and Franz Riklin Sr. (now his cousin by marriage) had been reelected secretary. The *Jahrbuch* would continue to originate in Zürich, and they would decide what belonged in it and what should go in the *Zentralblatt*. Freud told Jung he would retain "budgetary prerogative" as one method of controlling the new journal; he retained the ultimate control of its content when he decreed that it would be printed in Vienna.[13] The possibilities inherent for many different kinds of power struggles were thus present at the new journal's birth, and Jung did not let them pass unnoticed. As he began the arduous task of deciding the relative content of the two journals, he asked Freud if he did not worry that the *Zentralblatt* might compete unnecessarily with the *Jahrbuch*.[14]

Everything was a bone of contention with the *Zentralblatt*, even its appearance. The size of its print caused an uproar, as the Vienna group thought it should be smaller than the *Jahrbuch*'s to indicate the *Zentralblatt*'s secondary status. Jung thought the typefaces in both journals should be the same, as both represented the organization; Freud, seemingly eager to please at this stage, agreed. He blamed the controversy on those around him: "You see how petty one becomes when one is reduced to such company as I am here in the Vienna Society."[15]

Freud succeeded in obtaining the resignations of "the whole Adler gang (six of them),"[16] but Stekel, at various times in and then out, continued to "interfere."[17] Freud begged Jung to believe that he had nothing to do with Stekel's machinations, adding only that he had "decided to get along with him."

Two days later, Freud was delighted to tell Jung that another journal had been launched in Vienna: *Imago*,[18] with Hanns Sachs[19] and Otto Rank as editors and Hugo Heller (already publishing the *Zentralblatt*) as publisher. Freud included himself, without assigning a specific function or title. He counted on Jung's "benevolence towards the new-born child," calling it "another of the possessions" he intended Jung to inherit.[20] He instructed Jung to think of the journals as "three organs of a single biological unit."[21]

In other words, Jung was to muddle and mediate his way through the various dissensions and still produce a first-rate "scientific" publication in the *Jahrbuch*, turn the *Zentralblatt* into a first-rate compendium of administrative news and announcements, and pass along to the newly created third journal, *Imago*, the many "literary" submissions with which he was increasingly inundated that did not fit under the rubric of the first two. All this, plus the demands of his correspondence with Freud and the many letters generated by his IPA presidency, left little time for his wife, children, practice, and research.

"THE OMENS are favorable,"[22] Freud wrote happily in late November from his serene vantage point in Vienna. While others scurried to do his bidding with the new journals, still others wrote of plans to form new societies devoted to his theoretical teachings. Many made the pilgrimage to consult the master of Berggasse 19, both individuals who wanted to be analyzed and groups who wanted to learn in order to go forth and teach. There were defections, of course, Adler being the most prominent to date, with Magnus Hirschfeld[23] of Berlin almost as prominent. All in all, the reception of psychoanalysis throughout the world was increasingly positive, even in France, where Freud was surprised to receive an apology "in the name of French psychiatry for its neglect of psycho-analysis."[24] Despite all the cheering news, he still told Jung he did not have "any great expectations; gloomy times lie ahead."

In Zürich, complications of every sort multiplied. From scandals to defections, Jung was involved in varying degrees. The Zürich society was fractious and riven with jealousy over Jung's favored status with Freud. Of the group, the person most loyal to both was Pfarrer Oskar Pfister, a Protestant minister who wanted to use psychoanalysis in his religious practice, specifically the education of children.[25] He had been a mediating influence between Jung and Bleuler as well as a frequent writer and lecturer to local and international groups. He and Freud were on such good terms that their correspondence lasted throughout their lives.[26]

Now Pfister had fallen in love with a widowed cousin, Martha Zuppinger-Urner, and wanted to divorce his wife, Erika Pfister-Wunderli.[27] When his wife refused, Pfister was convinced Jung could change her mind through analysis.[28] Freud thought analysis for such a reason was "a bad sign," but it became moot when Erika Pfister refused to have anything to do with Jung. The scandal became public knowledge, and for a time Pfister was in danger of losing his parish. It took the better part of a year for the public to tire of it, and the scandal died down only because "the individual [Pfister]" decided not to "stand apart from the prevailing moral standards of the community" and agreed to postpone divorce action for eighteen months.[29]

Everything about the Pfister contretemps tainted Jung when it became linked with the Swiss public's general disapproval of "the wickedness coming from Vienna." During the past several years, a spate of articles had proliferated in newspapers, urging "the pure-minded Swiss" not to become corrupted by Freud's sexual theories, and Swiss analysts "had a very unhappy time" of it. From his lofty perch in the Burghölzli, Bleuler managed to stand aloof from most of the criticism, but when the public outcry over Pfister's personal dilemma became too strident, he took compensatory action by "requesting" that Pfister refrain from any further analysis in the hospital. Jung took it personally: "Once again Bleuler has allowed himself to be worked up because of his everlasting opposition to me. . . . He just *doesn't want* to see it my way."[30] Jung was only slightly exaggerating Bleuler's general caution, but Pfister's situation did offer a convenient "pretext" for Bleuler to send his letter of resignation to Freud, who told Jung he did not know or care what Bleuler would do in the future: "ΨA will manage without him."[31]

WHETHER SUCH things as Pfister's desire for a divorce and Bleuler's defection were responsible or not, Jung's practice had "dwindled to a trickle." It was "fine" with him, for he could always count on Emma's support, and he enjoyed being free to do his own research. But so, too, had Riklin's practice declined, and as he had no other income, that was "not so fine." Jung noted glumly that his own caseload was almost entirely divorce cases. "To hell with them!" he told Freud.[32]

A cast of gloom permeated the grand house after Carl discovered Emma's correspondence with Freud when he saw an envelope in the familiar hand that was not addressed to him. Freud was chastising Emma for the audacity of her previous letter,[33] but she managed to keep from telling Carl what had already passed between her and Freud and to keep him from reading it. He was not pleased that she had initiated the exchange, so Emma implored Freud not to discuss it with Jung: "Things are going badly enough with me as it is." She tried to placate Freud but still had the gumption to justify her earlier remarks, which he dismissed as her "amiable carpings." She had not meant to imply that Jung did not value Freud's opinion of his work, for "it goes without saying that one recognizes an authority." But she had been wrong to think that Jung was unable to continue with the second part of the *Wandlungen* because Freud had not yet pronounced his opinion of the first; rather, Jung was using the possibility of Freud's disapproval as an excuse to avoid the "self-analysis" the writing required.

She followed her semi-apology with a spirited defense of what Freud deemed her "admittedly uncalled-for meddling" in his family matters and thanked him again for discussing his "most personal affairs" with her. His arguments were persuasive, even though she continued to "struggle . . . against it." If he recognized a streak of independence in both Jungs when he read Emma's letter, Freud did not address it. Nor, it seems, did he worry about it.

THINGS WERE indeed "going badly enough" for Emma. There was no rhythm to the household's daily life because Carl was never at home for very long. After his military duty there were trips both long and short — to Munich on business for the society or to Geneva, Basel, and other Swiss cities to attend local meetings or to meet with such luminaries as Théodore Flournoy, on whose counsel he was becoming increasingly reliant.

Whenever he could, that is, when there were not patient appointments or professional engagements, he dined with the family, but most of the time he was preoccupied and expected Emma to keep the children silent while he ruminated privately. Immediately after, he locked himself away in his second-floor study while his wife turned the children over to the maids, who got them ready for bed.[34] Then Emma usually went into the library to sit unnoticed while Carl fussed with his pipe and chafed and growled at the pile of papers on his desk that never seemed to diminish.

Now even hushed evenings in the library were often off-limits to Emma, for Toni Wolff had begun to frequent it. Toni was never like Emma or Trudi, content to take dictation or perform other secretarial tasks. From the start, she behaved as an intellectual equal who wanted to do the same work as Jung. She did go to the various Zürich libraries to search for references he wanted, but most of the time she brought back her own contributions more than the specific sources he asked for, and often hers presented strikingly different interpretations from what he first envisioned. From the beginning, she contributed an independent perspective to his work, and her part of their conversation was peppered more frequently with remarks such as "yes, but . . ." than with the simple "yes." All this took place under the guise of Toni's continuing analysis, and in Emma's house.

Toni, elegantly prim, self-contained, and seemingly asexual, was not perceived by Emma as a rival or as the usurper of her personal life. Emma's primary emotion was frustration that her husband found in another woman the intellectual stimulation and camaraderie she so wanted to provide.

IT IS ironic in retrospect that the most partisan of Freud's biographers, Ernest Jones, should have been the one to describe most objectively the darkening situation between Jung and Freud as 1911 ended and the final year of their collaboration began. According to Jones, the reason for the rift and what upset Freud most was not the one given by so many other commentators — the increasing differences in how the two scholars interpreted the concept of libido; rather, it was "Jung's intense absorption in his researches [that] was gravely interfering with the presidential duties [Freud] had assigned to him."[35] In Freud's mind, Jung's primary role was "direct successor to himself . . . acting as a central focus for all psychoanalytical activities." Jung was to be merely

the liaison officer between the various societies, advising and helping wherever necessary, and supervising the various administrative work of Congresses, editorial work and so on. Freud would thus in his way be relieved from the active central position for which he had no taste.

"Unfortunately," Jones rightly discerned, "neither had Jung," whose faults included the fact that he worked best alone and had none of the special talent needed for cooperative or supervisory work with other colleagues. Nor had he much taste for business details, including regular correspondence. In short he was unsuited to the position Freud had planned for him as President of the Association and leader of the movement.

Jones seemed to think Jung was guilty of an even more egregious sin, that of not gratifying "Freud's more personal wishes," because he was "at all times a somewhat erratic correspondent; his absorption in his researches made him increasingly remiss in this respect." Absorption in independent research also made Jung an increasingly formidable threat to Freud, but Jones either carefully avoided making any such observation or was not astute enough to see it.

It did not seem to matter to Freud, nor did Jones acknowledge it when he wrote about Freud's life, that Jung had become internationally known and respected as a leading figure in experimental psychiatry when he was in his early thirties. The word association test brought him initial renown, but his important book *The Psychology of Dementia Praecox* brought scholars and scientists to the Burghölzli because they specifically wanted to observe him at work. They came in the same numbers long after he left the Burghölzli, so that as much of his time was taken by private lectures and seminars as it was by Freud's administrative demands. The years Jung served as Freud's crown prince and heir apparent can well be described as an administrative detour that kept him from his real work.

As early as 1907, when he published the studies on dementia praecox, Jung realized that psychosexuality could not be held accountable for all psychoses, and that there had to be another cause, perhaps an organic genetic factor, which he called "anomalies in the metabolism — toxins, perhaps" and which he believed were responsible for psychotic states.[36] It was a belief he had been expressing in greater or lesser degree ever since but had little research time to pursue. His frustration frequently made him curt and abrupt with other doctors, and he often addressed them in terms that earned him a reputation for behaving with the overbearing disposition of a bully.

Alphons Maeder, who had known Jung and worked with him ever since he became an assistant at the Burghölzli in 1906 and who also knew and had corresponded with Freud since 1909, had ample time to observe the unfolding dynamics between the two men: "Jung was, in his own way, as authoritarian as Freud; he had no understanding of nor taste for exchanging points of view with collaborators. He was very short with them."[37] And as Freud increasingly sought to plug Jung firmly into a tight little slot of his devising, he did not hesitate to display short temper and irritation.

When Freud finally got around to telling Jung what he thought of part one of *Wandlungen*, he referred to it coyly: "[It is] one of the nicest works I have read (again) [by] a well known author."[38] Nonetheless, he had reservations, that Jung's approach had been "too narrowed by Christianity"[39] and seemed more "above the material than in it." He damned it with faint praise as Jung's best work to date, "though he will do still better." Freud again claimed primacy, pleased that Jung agreed with "things [he had] already said or would *like* to say."[40]

Freud abandoned obliquity to make the direct admission that he was worried he might inadvertently appropriate an idea Jung originated, or vice versa. His plaint was genuine, as was his explanation of how their research was likely to proceed: "Probably my tunnels will be far more subterranean than your shafts and we shall pass each other by."

Recognizing the possibility of serious conflict, Jung did not let this letter sit for several weeks but answered it immediately. He told Freud that if he continued his investigations into the "psychology of religion," he would become "a dangerous rival — if one has to speak of rivalry."[41] Freud was well along with *Totem and Taboo*[42] and had no intention of putting it aside, which Jung foresaw as an inevitable clash. Successful resolution of the dilemma would come only through the "personal differences" that distinguished each man's thinking. Jung explained that Freud unearthed "precious stones," while he worked by "degree[s] of extension . . . the whole to the part."[43] Freud criticized Jung for relying too heavily on outside sources. Using them gave Jung's writing an air of learned authority but detracted from the purity of his thought. Jung countered that it was "too upsetting to let large tracts of human knowledge lie there neglected." Freud insisted the differences in how they researched would no doubt cause them to "meet from time to time in unexpected places."[44] Whether Jung believed this or whether he was being conciliatory, he conceded that Freud would remain the leader because he had "anticipated by far the greater part already." Jung found it "difficult only at first to accustom oneself to this thought. Later one comes to accept it."

Jung claimed to be working "diligently" on the second part of his article, but the rest of the letter belies the statement, filled as it is with a gloomy recitation of time-consuming psychoanalytic politics. He ended on a "note of imprecation," to which he was emotionally incapable of adding a "heart-felt," as Freud had done in his previous letter. Curtly, he bid Freud "adieu" with the cool "best regards" instead of his usual "most sincerely yours."

JUNG WAS a prolific writer to whom ideas came easily. Words flowed from his pen, and the only time he was ever at a loss was when he found himself blocked and unable to complete part two of the *Wandlungen*. When he first began to write, he stumbled upon the technique that best suited his temperament and used it from then on, despite the confusion it sometimes inspired in his readers and the many criticisms it garnered from scholars. As an old man in his eighties, he felt the need to explain it, trying repeatedly in every extant version of the interviews and rough drafts that were eventually refined and edited to become

Memories, Dreams, Reflections. In each of these *Protocols* (as the early drafts are called), he begins with an apology to his readers similar to this one:

> I am sorry that I repeat certain things. I always did that in my books. I regarded certain things again and again, and always from a new "angle" because my thinking is circular. I circle around the same question again and again. That is the method that appeals to me. In a way it's a new kind of peripatetic [word missing]. It just works best for me to write this way.

This circularity compounds the difficulty of reading not only any particular work but also Jung's oeuvre in its entirety. Often he revisited an original text to modify or add to it, or he elaborated upon the initial point while introducing other related points to support his original contention. These points may have required separate discussion within the same work or, if they raised issues too large to be dealt with there, in a future work yet to be formulated. There were times, for example in his last decade of life, the 1950s, when he was still refining ideas developed as early as 1912.[45] Traces of earlier work are always present, for not only did he expand and develop ideas, he sometimes contradicted them. "That is what I thought then," he would respond when asked about a discrepancy, "but this is how I think about it now."[46]

In large part, this was how he approached his differences with Freud over the theory of the libido. He circled around the material, trying to perceive it from every angle, trying to make his thesis conform to Freud's and finding in the end that he simply could not reconcile himself to a monocausal point of view. A prime example was Freud's insistence that a definition of libido began with the primacy of a sex drive that dated from an individual's infancy, and Jung's contention that the definition had to be broadened to include universal patterns of behavior common to many different historical cultures throughout historically different times.[47] Freud described Jung's definition as a "demonstration of unconscious heredity in symbolism" that proved "the existence of 'innate ideas.'" He admitted it merited further investigation, even though it was outside "the original limits of ΨA,"[48] limits Freud insisted upon because of the neatly empirical manner in which they supported his theory and proved it true.[49]

All his life, Jung remembered how passionately Freud implored him, "promise me one thing: look after sexuality!" He never forgot the expression on Freud's face, or his tone of voice as he said it.[50] It convinced him that Freud was a "scientific materialist"[51] and that was what "made his view so unwieldy, namely the biological mode of expression. . . . The man simply had a biological attitude." When Freud criticized his divergence, Jung responded that it was "a good thing to make occasional incursions into other territories and to look at our subject through a different pair of spectacles."[52] This exchange occurred after Sabina Spielrein read a paper to the Vienna Psychoanalytic Society called

"On Transformation." In a discussion with "the little girl," Freud found her idea "to subordinate the psychological material to *bio*logical considerations" (his emphasis) as wrongheaded as Jung's reliance on "philosophy, physiology, or brain anatomy."[53] Then he launched a stinging critique of Jung, saying he showed no discernment when he used mythology indiscriminately. He chastised his use of derivatives rather than originals, saying that only the originals could be subjected to "psychoanalytic elucidation," using the Book of Genesis as a prime example of distortion through variant renderings of the same information.[54]

Freud penned this when he was writing *Totem and Taboo* and was beset with metaphorical "rapids, waterfalls, sandbanks, etc." Even as he decried his disagreement with Jung, he remained doggedly insistent that his original position was correct and offered no possibility of compromise. As far as he was concerned, there were "two basic drives," and only "the sexual drive can be termed libido."[55]

Jung was equally firm about the "booming reverberations"[56] that beset him after he read Freud's study of the German jurist Daniel Paul Schreber. Freud, who never met Schreber, wrote an analysis based entirely on Schreber's autobiography, *Memoirs of My Nervous Illness*,[57] which Jung had urged him to read during his stay in the Burghölzli. Freud maintained that this book alone was proof that the single cause of Schreber's psychosis was his sexuality, a conclusion he then used to vindicate and support his general theory of the libido. Jung had been the first to use Schreber's autobiography, in his 1907 study of dementia praecox. He disagreed with Freud then and had continued to do so ever since. Now he knew he could no longer offer lip service to Freud's theory: "The loss of reality function in D. pr. cannot be reduced to repression of libido (defined as sexual hunger). Not by me at any rate."

Something in these dissenting exchanges lifted the writer's block that had kept Jung from finishing part two of the *Wandlungen*. Using his typical roundabout, all-inclusive technique, he was able to "put together all the thoughts on the libido concept that have come to me over the years," and to structure them into a separate, complete chapter. Wary of discussing his conclusions by mail, Jung did disclose his "essential point . . . that I try to replace the descriptive concept of libido by a *genetic* one" (Jung's emphasis). His concept would include "all those forms [of libido] which have long since split off . . . a wee bit of biology was unavoidable here."[58] And he, too, closed on a note of insistence, that Freud had to consider everything within his thesis, and to "feel its full impact. Mere fragments are barely intelligible."

Freud soft-pedaled in his reply, choosing to concentrate on Bleuler's "opposition" as the necessary force that kept their common ties strong. His note was all conciliation, as he was entirely in favor of Jung's addressing the libido concept. He expected "much light" from Jung's conclusions.[59]

ONE OF the most interesting aspects of *Wandlungen und Symbole der Libido* (Symbols of Transformation) is how similar its structure is to Freud's Schreber analysis. To repeat, Freud never actually met Schreber, whose memoir he used as proof of his theory of sexual libido. With *Symbols*, Jung also used the case study of an actual person he never met, an American woman whose real name was Miss Frank Miller.[60] He first heard about her through Théodore Flournoy, who had become something of a mentor[61] to him since he "began to notice where the limitations lay in Freud."[62] Unlike Freud, who "distorted things for the sake of his bias," Jung believed Flournoy was different:

> [He] saw things objectively, as a whole. He approached a case carefully and comprehensively, always looking at the broad horizon. He was a well-educated man, intellectually balanced, and that was very beneficial for me. . . . [His views were] exactly along my lines and they helped me a lot. I was still interested in somnambulism, in spiritualism, and I got from him the term "Imagination créatrice." I also got the case of Miss Miller.

Their intellectual exchange began in earnest when Jung read Flournoy's book *From India to the Planet Mars: A Study of a Case of Somnambulism with Glossolalia.*[63] He expressed interest in translating it from French into German, but Flournoy had already engaged someone else. The book was about a medium called Hélène Smith, who sued Flournoy for royalties when the book was published and barred him from attending her séances.[64] Whether because he believed himself too old and tired to take on another set of fantasies,[65] Flournoy gave Jung his own French translation of the original English version of Miss Miller's fantasies as well as thoughts and ideas he gleaned from later conversations and correspondence.[66]

Frank Miller was not a pseudonym, as Jung originally described the name.[67] She was an American woman born in Alabama in 1878 and christened with her father's first name. She went to Europe around the turn of the century to study; beginning in 1899 she was enrolled for a semester each in the universities of Lausanne, Berlin, and Geneva. She met Flournoy in 1900, just after his brouhaha began with Hélène Smith, and offered her own fantasies as a means for him to rebut his critics. When her semester in Geneva ended, the attractive Miss Miller returned to the United States and fashioned a successful career giving lectures about European cultures, in which she wore Russian, Greek, or Scandinavian costumes. By 1907, she suffered some sort of distress or upheaval diagnosed as "psychopathy" and was admitted to the Danvers State Hospital in Massachusetts. The admitting physician was Charles Ricksher, who had been Jung's colleague and research associate at the Burghölzli and whom he met again during his sojourn at Clark University.[68] Miss Miller stayed at Danvers for one week before she was released to the care of an aunt, who promised to take her to a private hospital. There is no record that this happened, and Miss

Miller seems to have disappeared into a subsequent private life about which little is known. To date no evidence has been found that she was ever aware of Jung's book or that she contacted him about it.

Miss Miller's diagnosis, "psychopathy," has come under scrutiny by feminist scholars,[69] who note that it was frequently a catchall term at the beginning of the twentieth century applied to independent young women who chose not to marry, to live apart from their families, and to try to construct if not careers, then certainly self-supporting jobs. This was enough to brand them with terms ranging from immoral to indecent to insane. Many of their families leaped at the opportunity to have them institutionalized if they showed the least sign of faltering, be it from fatigue, financial difficulty, or emotional distress. Miss Miller's history fit this stereotype, but Jung did not know this when he wrote about her in early 1910.

Up to this point in his career, his primary research interest was the direct observation of patients with psychotic delusions, or supervising the research of colleagues who investigated the same (Honegger[70] being the prime example). Jung believed the study of involuntary delusions was the necessary pathway toward successful treatment of psychosis, and when he wrote about Miss Miller, he believed she fit into this category. What he did not know then and seems not ever to have known is that all her fantasies were voluntary. Jung described them as "poetical unconsciously formed phantasies,"[71] but Miss Miller had actually created them from within a normal, novelistic imagination. She had invented her appealing fictions to support her beloved teacher Flournoy, who was under merciless attack from critics who derided his earlier book.

Miss Miller's fantasies had a strong underpinning of her American heritage, showing influences ranging from such poetry as Longfellow's "Hiawatha" and Poe's "The Raven" to an Aztec legend of a god she called Chiwantopel. They also reflected American secondary education of the time, with references to (among others) Shakespeare, Milton, and Samuel Johnson. In part one of *Symbols*, to support his theory of a collective unconscious, Jung superimposed his own vast readings upon hers to provide additional support. He drew from many sources, from classical mythology to Goethe's poetry, to the writings of colleagues from Riklin to Rank, and made frequent references to Freud. Of the two parts of this work, it is by far the most cohesive, for Jung's theorizing proceeds directly from and corresponds in almost every instance to Miss Miller's initial fantasizing. Nevertheless, it was this method of piling on external references rather than drawing from within his own experience that earned criticism from Freud,[72] who thought "everything essential . . . is right," but that part one still lacked "ultimate clarity." Freud's two sharpest criticisms attacked Jung's statement that "sexuality destroys itself" and his too-facile connection between one of Miss Miller's visions and a Mithraic image (i.e., pertaining to Mithras, the Persian god of light and truth, and later of the sun).[73] "The analogy is not overwhelming," Freud decreed.

Freud could well have applied his comment to the entirety of part two, which is much longer than the first, more convoluted in form, and much more reflective of Jung's vast mythological erudition. Miss Miller's actual fantasies lie buried here not only beneath Jung's circular methodology but also under a framework gleaned during his university education, one in which the nineteenth-century German approach to understanding and interpreting science determined the written expression of ideas. It is, in many ways, a clumsy text, "nothing more or less than the record of Jung's own fantasy life, recklessly projected onto ancient symbols and myths."[74] It is also arguably the first time Jung tried to decode his own personal symbolic system through his scientific (i.e., in the sense of Germanic *Wissenschaftlich*) writing.

Freud's differences with the interpretations in part one were minor, but when part two was published in 1912, he claimed to know exactly "the very page where Jung went wrong":[75]

P. 174 . . . he is simply begging the question and misunderstanding me. I never obliterated or changed the meaning of libido, but stuck to my first definition all over. I threw up the problem whether paranoia can be explained by the traction of the libidinous components, left it unsolved, but pointed to a certain way of solving it. He is proclaiming without further proofs, that libido theory is unable to answer for the loss of reality, as if it was *Selbstverständlichkeit* [a foregone conclusion]. . . . The fact is he stumbled a first time in the application of libido theory on Paraphrenia* and now he is stumbling again in the opposite direction. . . . I must confess, the paper did not interest me enough after this discovery to finish it.[76]

By the time Freud wrote this letter to Ernest Jones in September 1912, the final break between him and Jung had occurred, even though neither man was willing to admit or accept that it had happened. Despite Jung's perceived heresy, Freud was willing to let pass what he wrote in part two. He agreed to "make no difficulties" if Jones "and the Zürich people" wanted to effect "a formal reconciliation," but it would, however, be a mere "formality." Freud was not certain that his "former feelings" could ever be restored because "[Jung] wanted a dissension and he produced it." Freud would never be able to move beyond his belief; Jung would never be able to retract the independence of his thinking. A stalemate ensued.

Meanwhile, as Jones was busy stoking the fires of Freud's smoldering resentment toward Jung by assassinating his character,[77] Bleuler, the most unlikely of moderators, offered a temperate view that no one heeded:

---

*With the word "paraphrenia," Freud is intending to coin a substitute term for Bleuler's word "schizophrenia."

Jung's new concept of libido resembles the one Freud had a number of years ago, which he has modified somewhat since then. As you know, in my opinion, this whole libido theory, as developed now, still lacks clarity. I therefore have no judgement that I would like to pass on. On the other hand, I consider Jung's work, subjective though it is, to be very important. It is remarkable how much material the man has been able to amass in a few years. Even in matters of secondary importance there are many clever and certainly to a large extent also good ideas. But, as I say, for now and perhaps even for the next ten years no one will be competent to give a definite judgement about the work as a whole.[78]

Bleuler's willingness to give Jung and Freud ten years to sort out their differences was wishful thinking. A mere six months later, it was already too late.

CHAPTER 16

⁓

The Kreuzlingen Gesture

The Freud-Jung "duet" in the service of psychoanalysis became a "duel" as 1912 began.[1] Rather than address their theoretical differences directly, each combatant resorted to evasion or indirection, choosing to level accusations or assign blame for matters of minor consequence. The first misunderstanding involved a patient of Freud and Pfister who consulted Jung briefly before returning to Freud in December 1911. Elfriede Hirschfeld (called Frau C. in the Freud/Jung letters)[2] was born in Frankfurt in 1873 and described by Freud as a woman of "high moral feelings [and] a narrowly limited intelligence."[3] She became a teacher and married a much older man, a "foreigner" who took her to Moscow, where he conducted a successful business. Wanting children and unable to conceive, she consulted a specialist who said she needed corrective surgery. On the eve of the operation, her husband confessed that the fault was his, that disease had left him sterile. Following the disclosure, "she fell seriously ill of a neurosis," an "anxiety hysteria." Afterward "a never-ending sequence of therapies ensued, all failures even though some of the very best psychiatrists, psychotherapists, and psychoanalysts of the time did their best to help her."[4] She spent seven years in analysis with Freud, beginning in October 1908. In May 1911, although "it is not quite clear who had actually taken the initiative,"[5] Freud asked Pfister if he would take Frau Hirschfeld's case during his summer vacation. When Freud learned that the two had established a rapport and begun a full analysis, he suggested that Pfister keep her in Zürich and do everything in his power to prevent her from returning to Vienna. Pfister was unsuccessful, and she disappeared from Zürich for several weeks, arriving at Freud's office just before Christmas. She was confined in a sanatorium for at least part of the time until summer 1912, when Freud sent a telegram to Pfister asking him to come to Vienna and help her learn "to do without custody."

At this point, Frau Hirschfeld entered into the personal conflict between Freud and Jung, as she "triggered" a debate over "the question of how to react to a patient demanding sympathy and concern." Freud wrote three increasingly hostile letters about her treatment before Jung replied with a single one. In part the delay was due to the fact that a neighbor's dog had bitten him while playing, and his hand was too swollen to write. Mostly, it was because he could not control his anger at how Freud chastised him as if he were a misbehaving adolescent rather than a respected clinician.

In the first of the three letters, written on December 17, Freud thought Frau C. incapable of benefiting from therapy, but he was still so eager to treat her that he planned to turn some of his other patients over to his Viennese cohorts to make room on his schedule.[6] When he saw her on December 28, he bluntly contradicted Jung's prior analysis, saying she and Pfister had no other choice but to consult him.[7] On New Year's Eve, he leveled a full blast, sayiing if Jung harbored any offense toward him, he did not need to use Frau C. as an excuse to express it.[8] Freud apparently believed her version of events, that Jung and Pfister (but primarily Jung) were in some sort of unspecified collusion against him.[9]

His letters are notable for two other admissions as well. In the first, he chides both Jung and Pfister for how they conducted treatment, "giving a good deal of yourselves and expecting the patient to give something in return." He was objecting to one of the most distinct differences in their therapies: Freud's patients lay on a daybed draped with a Persian carpet and covered with velvet cushions in muted earth tones, while he sat behind them silently, out of sight in a forest-green velvet armchair. Jung and his patients sat on chairs placed close, faced each other directly, and engaged in an interactive dialogue. One of his patients described a typical session: "He sat at one side of the window and the person interviewed sat on the other. The window was alongside you, the light being full on his face and full on your face so that you *saw* him. . . . You didn't lose anything of the facial expressions or the feelings that he had."[10] Freud thought Jung's technique "ill-advised. . . . We must never let our poor neurotics drive us crazy."[11]

Freud's second notable admission was yet another example of his need for ultimate authority. He hinted at it by telling of a recent disagreement with Ferenczi, who accused him on more than one occasion of distancing himself and withholding affection from colleagues as well as patients. Ferenczi had since admitted he was wrong and Freud had been "well advised."

"I don't deny that I like to be right," Freud continued, calling it a "sad privilege" of old age and accusing "younger men" of not knowing how to cope with their "father complexes."[12] Jung replied to all three letters on January 2, interrupting a vacation in St. Moritz, where he and Emma had gone without the children. In a calm and patient tone, he gave a detailed explanation of what had happened between him and Frau C. He closed on a note meant to assuage Freud, that his only intention had been "to get her back to Vienna" and "on the right track again."[13]

Jung returned to Zürich long enough to deposit Emma and then went to

Munich, where he spent several days "rather breathlessly . . . improving [his] education," touring various art galleries, museums, and monuments. He did not tell Freud that his main purpose was to gather new material and confirm existing hunches about mythology for part two. On January 9, in a cloud of distraction, he tried to go back to work.

His concentration had been interrupted since December by a debate in one of the city's leading newspapers, the *Neue Zürcher Zeitung*. A noted local neurologist, Dr. Max Kesselring, had given a public lecture in which he attacked psychoanalysis and called Jung one of the most vulgar of the Swiss Freudians.[14] Kesselring spoke under the auspices of the *Keplerbund*, a group founded in Germany whose aim was to defeat pseudoscientific speculations (i.e., psychoanalysis) and reconcile the true natural sciences with the Christian faith.[15] He gave several lectures on psychoanalysis as a "materialistic and atheistic doctrine that taught fantastic speculations as if they were scientific truth."[16] In each, Kesselring aimed sharp gibes at Jung that were repeated in print and enhanced each time in the telling by a reporter known only as "F. M." (later identified as Fritz Marti). By mid-January, Jung thought he had no alternative but to reply.

Jung's first response was a letter in which he accused Kesselring of unprofessional behavior by discussing technical subjects before an uninformed lay audience. He left himself open to a sharp retort by using gynecology as his unfortunate example when he asked rhetorically if Kesselring intended to discuss other branches of medicine in detail as well. Kesselring pounced, saying that was exactly *his* point: that the Freudians had no qualms about discussing intimate details of sexuality that were unfit for public consumption, and that the moral Swiss wanted no part of such immoral revelations. Jung thought the matter was ended when he retorted that Kesselring had proven *his* point precisely: a vulgar public discussion of sexual matters could not in any way correspond to an informed, intelligent appraisal of the concept of libido as psychoanalysis defined it.

Instead of ending the debate, Jung broadened it. Describing the ongoing articles as "blackmail,"[17] he consulted a lawyer about suing for libel. He settled for issuing a formal protest on behalf of the IPA and the Zürich Psychoanalytic Association, published on January 27, which provoked another attack by "F. M." The debate woke August Forel from his somnambulant retirement near Lake Geneva long enough to write an amorphous letter intended to denounce Kesselring and support Jung. It only confused matters more, especially after "F. M." began to argue in print with Forel.

All this occurred during the time Jung's hand was so swollen by the dog bite that writing was painful. Emma stepped in eagerly as his secretary, and it was she who mailed the various press clippings to Freud. He thought Jung handled the matter well and asked him to thank Emma for sending the "fine article."[18]

THE KESSELRING debate also occurred while Jung was scheduled to give a lecture on psychoanalysis to a Swiss teachers' group. The audience's attitude was typical of the Swiss approach to psychoanalysis, which was to put its precepts to practical, positive use and employ them as the means to solve religious and/or educational problems.[19] Because of the press ruckus, six hundred teachers assembled to hear Jung "thunder out ΨA like Roland sounding his horn."[20]

Everything, it seemed, was conspiring to happen at the "most inopportune" time. Jung was "overwhelmed with the work" connected with editing the next *Jahrbuch*, even as he was "grappling with the endless proliferation of mythological fantasies [for *Symbols*, Part II]." He was working "unceasingly" and was "intellectually drained." Typically, an article submitted to the *Jahrbuch* required Jung to exchange several letters with the author before it arrived at a satisfactory form. The author almost always disagreed with Jung, so the author would turn to Freud as the ultimate authority, whose decision was always final. Jung then took care of all the technical details connected with printing. Sometimes he asked others to evaluate submissions, especially Otto Rank, whose literary acumen he valued; sometimes he asked the writers to consult Rank directly on how best to present their argument or how to make their submissions conform to *Jahrbuch* standards.[21] As submissions for each issue usually hovered at thirty or more, this part of Jung's professional life alone created a staggering amount of work.

There was also the complication of how to refuse articles that were clearly not up to the standards he had set for the publication, but despite his attempts to be tactful, rejections garnered ill will and bad feelings toward him. The "abrasiveness," "arrogance," and even "anti-Semitism" of the "rough Swiss peasant" were charges that others hinted about but did not level directly at him. Still, they reached his ears and they smarted.[22]

Sometimes, even with articles he accepted, further letters were necessary because misunderstandings still arose. Sabina Spielrein provides one example among many. When he first glanced at her article "Destruction as the Origin of Becoming,"[23] he mistook the first word of the title for "Distinction." When she inquired about publication, Jung made a passing reference to the title in what he thought was a friendly note of praise for her work. He explained how puzzled he was until he reread it carefully and realized the correct word, for it showed how her theory had considerable parallels to his: "Your wish for destruction is certainly correct. One does not only want the ascent, but also the descent and the end." He thought he was praising the originality of her ideas; she thought he was taking "priority"[24] for them.

"You're getting unnecessarily upset again," he wrote in yet another letter engendered by the misunderstanding. "When I was speaking of 'mysterious similarities,' you took this much too literally again. I meant it as a compliment to you." He gave her credit for first recognizing the death wish, and to further mollify her, he assured her not only that she would publish first but also, that no one should even suspect that you borrowed from me, so to speak. That's out of the question. Matters of secret penetration of thoughts are higher questions that can't be considered in our public existence, for we know far too little about them to take them seriously into account. Maybe it was I who borrowed from you: I'm sure that unwittingly I have swallowed a piece of your soul, as well as you of mine. What matters is what one makes of it.

"And," he concluded, "you have made something good of it!" Then he ended on a note of personal gloom concerning part two of *Symbols:* "[My] new work will *most likely* be misunderstood" (Jung's emphasis). He hoped she would be able to support it. He knew even before it was published that he would need allies.

JUNG'S BRIEF "lull in the feud" with Kesselring ended when Forel threatened Kesselring's "total annihilation."[25] Forel's "confounded" International Psychotherapeutic Society was to hold its annual meeting in Zürich the following autumn, and the city was already "seething." Psychoanalysis was "the talk of the town"; even the "carnival newspapers"[26] were writing about it. In late February, Jung lectured before a large group of local clinicians who were "eager to taste the poison." He followed it with an address to students at a teachers' college in Bern on the uses of psychoanalysis in pedagogy.[27] Although "opponents" of psychoanalysis had trained their sights firmly on the unfortunate Pfister and his marital problems as the symbol of everything wrong about the discipline, a lay organization in its favor sprang up in Zürich called the "Society for Psychoanalytic Endeavors." On balance, there was more good news to report to Freud than bad.

Jung made time for his writing despite the barrage of distractions. In his first communication to Freud in a month, he described his "grisly fights with the hydra of mythological fantasy." He told Freud he hoped to finish part two within the coming month, but he told Spielrein a different story, that his progress was slow because he was simultaneously correcting both style and language as he went along, and it took an enormous amount of time.[28] He was getting help from Emma, who worked "consciously at etymology,"[29] but he was also getting a great deal more from Toni Wolff.

Whether it was because Toni Wolff finally found something to engage her intellect or because her regard for Jung had gone beyond the professional to the personal, the skinny, twitchy chain-smoker with fingernails bitten to the quick, messy hair, and unkempt clothes had transformed herself. She was now a poised, articulate woman whose polished fingers held her cigarettes in an ebony holder. Her carefully coiffed hair was usually hidden beneath a stylish cloche hat, and her thin figure showed her dark, tailored clothing to best advantage. She used her mother's couturier now and began to dress in the style she would effect for the rest of her life, in lush fabrics that gave an air of foreign mystery, slightly hinting of the Orient, though she never wore anything that would deliberately suggest she was anything other than an elegant, upper-class Swiss woman. Several times each week she came to Küsnacht, loaded down with books, illustrations, and objects, some very expensive and rare that she gave to Jung as gifts — all with not the slightest hint of inappropriate behavior on either side. Emma was grateful for the library research Toni did, which she, as the mother of four rambunctious children, could not do outside her home.

JUNG'S HASTY and long-delayed replies to Freud's ongoing stream were brief and tense. His workload lifted slightly as February ended, so he tried to explain and apologize for his silence. He did not tell Freud the primary reason he could not write long letters, too much of the hated administrative work. Instead, he blamed himself for spending all his libido on his own writing. Dreading a rash of questions, Jung described it in the briefest possible analytic language as "an elaboration of all the problems that arise out of the mother-incest libido, or rather the libido cathected mother-imago." He asked Freud not to worry about his "protracted and invisible sojourn in the 'religious-libidinal cloud.'"[30]

Freud went on the alert when he read this, but rather than regard it as two scholars involved in the same basic research who were airing their differences, he chose to lecture Jung about how the association was "not functioning properly" under his presidency. Curtly admitting that he was a "demanding correspondent," he said he had taken himself "in hand," conquered his "excess libido," and was now "undemanding and not to be feared." Then he thundered on about Jung's failures as president: none of the groups within the organization had contact with the others; the times between the issuance of each *Bulletin* and *Jahrbuch* compounded the problem because there were no timely reports or announcements to assist members. And, Jung had done nothing about arranging the annual congress for the coming autumn.

A further problem was presented by Franz Riklin Sr.,[31] who had even less liking for administration than Jung and who neglected his secretarial duties to the extent that he did not even send postcards to acknowledge manuscripts received. He was so careless about details that he became a standing joke within the profession for such mistakes as sending a letter intended for his banker about the status of his accounts to a patient, and then sending the banker the letter intended for the patient, in which he offered medical advice.[32]

Jung had other information about Riklin that he was keeping from Freud because he knew it would upset him and cause another flurry of anxious letters, and it was more trouble than it was worth to try to explain. Riklin was married to Jung's cousin Sophie Fiechter,[33] whose family in Basel was of the *vom Tieg*, the small select group that directed most aspects of life in that city. Although the Fiechter family prospered through sound business acumen, Sophie's branch was considered the most cultured and artistic; her brother Ernst was the architect who designed Jung's house, and she herself was praised for her talent in several arts and crafts.[34] With Sophie's support, Franz Beda Riklin was trying to decide if he wanted to remain a psychiatrist or turn his hobby of painting into a profession. He was a gifted amateur artist who became one of the group who congregated in Zürich during the First World War and called themselves *Das Neue Leben*. Hans Arp and his then-wife, Sophie Tauber Arp, were among them, and, for a short time, Paul Klee. Riklin was taken up by Augusto Giacometti, a painter of lesser stature than his talented brother Giovanni, father of Alberto and Diego. Augusto Giacometti won a competition to paint frescoes at the *Hauptwache*, the main police station opposite the *Rathaus*,[35] and invited Riklin and the artists Giuseppe Remigio Scartezzini and Jakob Gubler to assist him.[36] It was an impressive invitation, and Riklin's work began attracting praise from knowledgeable collectors in Zürich who said they wanted to buy his canvases but had not actually done so. As he had no private income, Riklin needed to be sure he could support his family on an artist's salary, so he dawdled on every front, seriously neglecting his practice as well as his myriad secretarial duties. At first Jung tried to cover for him, but as Riklin was so careless about records and files, it was virtually impossible.

Jung took great care when he responded to Freud's charges of mismanagement.[37] He admitted, without giving details, that Riklin was negligent and agreed that he would have to be removed from office if he continued to be so. He explained that he had not been remiss about arrangements for the congress but could not set a definite date because, despite his repeated entreaties, the Swiss army had not notified him about his annual service. He defended his decision for not playing an "active part" in any of the three publications by saying it took all his energy to keep the *Jahrbuch* up to the mark and left little time for his own manuscript, which now amounted to more than three hundred pages. He thought it more important to complete a major work than to dissipate his energies on short articles of fleeting import.

As for his personal failings, Jung said he hoped his efforts to promote Freud's version of psychoanalysis counted for more than "[his] personal awkwardness and nastiness." He added, "I have my work cut out to put up with my own personality without wishing to foist it on you and add to your burdens." He said he had made the deliberate decision not to write letters unless he needed to relay necessary information so he could concentrate on his own work, and this was not "a demonstration of ostentatious neglect [of Freud]."

"Or," Jung asked, "can it be that you mistrust me?" He answered his own questions by calling such a thought "groundless."

"I would never have sided with you in the first place had not heresy run in my blood," he said, quoting Nietzsche to enforce his point, one that Freud was ultimately unable to accept, let alone respect: "One repays a teacher badly if one remains only a pupil."

Freud's reply resembled a neglected spouse's plaintive cry more than it did one colleague's asking another to clarify their working relationship. If Jung insisted that he needed "greater freedom," Freud would turn his "unemployed libido elsewhere" and wait patiently until Jung realized that he could "tolerate greater intimacy." When that happened, "you will find me willing," said Freud.[38]

Even though Freud sensed the need to placate Jung, he could not resist couching it in terms of his own superiority: "You seem to recognize that I am right," because "otherwise we agree about everything." There matters rested for the next several months as Jung attended to work and duty.

BY THE end of March, Jung was so "fagged out" that he planned to take a short vacation alone until Emma persuaded him to extend it to one with her in northern Italy. He agreed but insisted on first going alone to Lugano for several days to work on his manuscript. When she joined him, they continued on to Genoa, Pisa, and Florence.[39] The dates for his military service were set for August 22 to September 6, and a possible conflict arose when Fordham University in New York invited him to lecture, beginning September 10. He told Freud he felt obliged to accept because it would be good for the reception of psychoanalysis in America and proposed they set the conference dates for August 19–20 in Munich, as it was centrally located for most of the members.[40] Freud gave lukewarm congratulations to Jung's invitation but postponed the conference until the following spring. An August meeting would interrupt his annual vacation, and he thought not enough had happened since the last congress to justify meeting so soon.

Jung kept his resolution not to write except about business, so their letters dealt mostly with contretemps among the various societies until late April, when Jung finished part two. He was reeling from the frenzy of finishing, which may have been why he sent the manuscript to the publisher without first submitting it to Freud's scrutiny. He may not have considered how offensive Freud would find such a gesture, or perhaps he was simply postponing the inevitable, knowing what Freud's reaction would be, no matter when he read it.

"What have you written, what is this now?" Jung scrawled in large letters at the bottom of his copy of the manuscript.[41] If he could not fathom fully what his imagination had brought forth, how could he fathom how Freud would receive it?

ALTHOUGH HE told no one at the time, the terror and trauma of writing part two were so great that he began to practice yoga to gain the courage necessary even to approach it, let alone write it. Years later, he tried to describe what happened to him throughout the final months, but even with distance and time he could not express it in a logical and coherent manner. He said part two, in which he categorically denied the primacy of sex in the libido theory, poured out in a language that he thought must have corresponded to how the archetypes spoke. It was the first time it happened to him. The doctrine it made him espouse was quite literally earth-shattering, but he chose to describe it with a curious term: he said it "embarrassed" him because it went against his grain, referring to all his medical training and the previous writings that his peers considered models of scientific objectivity. But he had no choice and was compelled to write it down as he heard it spoken inside himself, so he listened to the inner voices. It was as if, beneath the threshold of his consciousness, emotions and images rose spontaneously and refused to bow to his outward, conscious control. He was afraid the voices he obeyed would cause an involuntary slide into neurosis: "They would have torn me up, or I could have been split off. . . . After all, I lived in a quiet world then and there were no personal entanglements."

He did not know from what place within his creative consciousness this work originated — that would take further research into the concept of the collective unconscious. He only knew that he believed in the correctness of what he wrote, that he would have to publish it, that he would have to stand behind it. And that by choosing the role of truth seeker rather than defender of Freud's faith, he would be in for a rocky time.

He admitted to Freud that he had finished the book only when Freud sent him an article he wrote to be published in *Imago*. Jung said offhandedly that it was "a pity" part two was already with his publisher, because he could have used it to make "a number of improvements" in Freud's essay. He stayed calm when Freud raged at his effrontery and demanded that he clarify his remarks. Jung explained that he interpreted "the incest problem . . . primarily as a fantasy problem."[42] His explanation was unsuccessful, and a week later he wrote a second letter.[43] Freud made "three observations . . . not refutations" that reflected his doubt about Jung's "conception of incest."[44] Jung tried to explain a third time.[45] At last Freud saw how Jung's conception of libido differed from his, but he still could not accept it. He harbored "strong antipathy" for two reasons: first because it was "regressive," and second because it carried a "disastrous similarity to a theorem of Adler's," though he quickly added that he was not condemning "all Adler's inventions." No further letters were required, and he would await Jung's manuscript itself. He appreciated Jung's advance "warning" about what it would say.[46]

Freud ended with the simple direct statement that he planned to visit Ludwig Binswanger in Kreuzlingen, Lake Constance, arriving on the evening of Friday, May 24, and departing the following Monday. He did not invite Jung to join him, nor did he express any form of regret or apology that he could not continue on to Zürich afterward, as time would be too short.

The reason for Freud's visit concerned Binswanger's recent appendectomy, during which the surgeon discovered and removed a malignant abdominal tumor. At that time, the prognosis for surviving such tumors was poor, and Binswanger fully expected to die.[47] He told Freud but asked him not to tell anyone else. Freud thus arranged what he thought would be their farewell meeting for the Whitsun holiday weekend in late May. Ostensibly they were to discuss the paper Binswanger wanted to complete during what he thought would be his last months alive, "The Significance of Freud for Clinical Psychiatry." As it was to be a study of the relations between Freud's psychoanalytic method and its bearing on the general practice of psychiatry, Freud wanted to make sure that Binswanger finished it. He thought of Binswanger as "one of those who were supposed to continue [Freud's] own life"[48] and wanted to make sure Binswanger expressed his theory exactly as he wanted.

FREUD'S DECISION to visit Binswanger and bypass Jung has entered the history of psychoanalysis as "the Kreuzlingen gesture." The passage of time has inflated it to mythic proportion, as partisans for Jung and Freud argue the rightness of each combatant's version of events and subsequent behavior. Throughout, one fact stands out clearly: all their theoretical differences were initially subsumed in an argument about manners, about who snubbed whom in an exchange of letters.

Freud insisted that he mailed two letters on the same day, Thursday, May 23: one to give Binswanger his travel itinerary; the other to tell Jung of his impending visit. But Binswanger wrote a memoir interspersed with partial quotations from and many paraphrases of his correspondence with Freud, and he gave Thursday, May 16, as the date of Freud's letter to him. He said Freud told him they would discuss all that was "close to [their] hearts, about Bleuler, Jung, and the general world situation." If he intended to discuss Jung at the same time as the disobedient and disloyal (according to Freud) Bleuler, it certainly reinforces the interpretation that he had no intention of seeing Jung. When he wrote to Jung one week later, it appears that he wanted Jung to know he was being snubbed.

At that time, a letter mailed from Vienna one day was delivered in Zürich the next, and everyone knew it. Jung should have received Freud's Thursday, May 23, letter on Friday, May 24. He wrote to Freud on Saturday, May 25, hoping that Freud's uncustomary delay in replying to his previous letter of May 17 was not due to anything "untoward" and that "no weightier reasons" lay behind his silence.[49] There is no indication in the published *Freud/Jung Letters* that Freud responded to either of Jung's two letters, and the next extant letter is from Jung to Freud on June 8, 1912.

Jung said nothing about how he spent his time over the Whitsun holiday weekend, but a mixed air of acceptance coupled with sadness and regret pervades. Jung was hurt that Freud "felt no need" to see him during the Kreuzlingen visit, accepting that it was probably because of the libido theory. He remained committed to what he wrote even as he tried to soften it with a joke: "You know how obstinate we Swiss are." He took special care to offer Freud a face-saving exit from the impasse by saying he had just been in the mountains on military exercises and thought some of his mail might have been lost. He hoped letters from Freud were not among them.

However, from the metaphors of war with which he began the letter, Jung

THE KREUZLINGEN GESTURE · 227

probably knew he had already lost the battle and been cast out of Freud's army. Although he never addressed the Kreuzlingen gesture directly in either the *Protocols* or *Memories, Dreams, Reflections*, he did describe Freud at this time as "terribly merciless! As soon as someone varied just a little bit, then he was finished."[50] Jung was well aware of how ruthlessly Fliess, Adler, and now Stekel had been cast out and shunned. With Adler specifically, Freud was already "dispos[ing] conclusively of Adler's case against him," and he kept on doing it "week after week, for years."[51] Jung knew it could happen to him.

But the question of when Jung received and when he actually read Freud's May 23 letter remains clouded by the passage of time. May 24, the day it should have been delivered, was a Friday. If Jung had received and read it then, he would have been able to go to Kreuzlingen that day or the next, or even on Sunday, the twenty-sixth, to see Freud briefly before his departure. This would have been seen by Freud as an acolyte paying proper homage to the master, but it might also have been seen by Binswanger and his wife as an impolite or even arrogant intrusion upon a private visit. Freud left everything so vague in his letter that even the scrupulously polite Emma might well not have known what to tell her husband to do. The only certainty is that if the letter had been delivered, Emma would have recognized Freud's handwriting and moved the world if it were necessary in order to bring it to Jung's attention.

Also, Kreuzlingen was only forty miles from Zürich, and daily trains were fast and frequent, as was direct service from Zürich to Vienna. Freud seems never to have considered this when he made the convoluted arrangements for round-about travel that took longer than the forty-eight hours he spent at his destination. Telephone service throughout Switzerland was also reliable in 1912, and either he or Jung could have soothed the other's ruffled feathers with a courtesy call, which neither made.

Thus, in the letters the two men exchanged between June 8 and the end of November 1912, there is only bitterness, allegation, recrimination, and retaliation. Freud, who "when it came to intellectual rough and tumble . . . was well able to look after himself and the cause, and to defend both without paying too much attention to Queensbury Rules,"[52] began the exchange with a casuistic and self-serving explanation. His technique throughout was first to put Jung on the defensive, then to offer a soothing sop. In one example, he said he heard rumors as early as 1908 that Jung and the Burghölzli contingent had supplanted his views, but he found them false as soon as he visited Zürich.[53] Therefore, Freud decreed, he could not accept Jung's accusation that he had not returned to Vienna via Zürich because of their differing libido theories. A particularly meandering explanation followed of why, how, and when he traveled as he did. He admitted that he did not ask Jung to join him in Kreuzlingen, but said he would have been pleased if Jung had thought of doing so on his own. Rubbing salt into Jung's wound, he added that Binswanger would not have minded, because while Freud was there, he phoned Paul Häberlin (with whom Jung had long-standing theoretical differences) and invited him and his wife to join them.[54] Jung knew a snub when he saw one: Freud (and/or Binswanger) had not extended the same invitation to him and Emma as he had to the Häberlins. Freud then jousted to the offensive by declaring himself "pain[ed]" because Jung "did not feel sure" of him. It was just the sort of groveling remark that grated on Jung and in the past, when similar instances required him to write soothing replies declaring undying fealty, had resulted instead in truculent declarations of loyalty.

On this occasion, he did not address Freud's plaint directly but may have done so obliquely. In a three-sentence letter, Jung wrote that he now understood "the Kreuzlingen gesture," but his curtness and brevity makes one wonder what exactly he meant. His second sentence said only that future public reception would determine whether his or Freud's "policy" was correct. In the third, he said he had "always kept [his] distance" and would "guard against any limitation of Adler's disloyalty."[55]

In the letters that followed, both men concentrated on matters of business even as each insisted upon the correctness of his personal behavior and theoretical position. Emma stepped in quietly one more time, but in a way that required neither to become involved. She told Freud he must allow them to honor him as the first person to receive an offprint of part two.[56] Chatting on as if nothing were amiss, she extended cordial greetings to his wife and children and said her own four had given her a dismal summer, with whooping cough followed by measles. Carl had been away most of the time, and now he was in New York. She had so much to do that she could not send "too much libido" (probably using the word to imply her respectful affection for him), as "it might so easily get lost on the way." It was a warm and friendly letter, but Freud did not give the courtesy of an answer to the woman he supposedly liked and respected and in whom he had earlier confided.

Sorting out conflicting details can go only so far, for there are gaps in the surviving written evidence (primarily the correspondence), and the chronology of events can be only partially traced. Freud admittedly had a score to settle when he castigated Jung in his 1914 history of the psychoanalytic movement,[57] but Jung never addressed that work directly, either in his seminars, writings, or autobiography. The honest Binswanger, the third party who was directly involved, admitted that he had no documentation and depended entirely on memory for his memoir when he recounted the details of Freud's visit many years after it happened (for he survived the tumor and lived into old age). But there were so many other interested parties whom Freud involved (Ferenczi and Pfister, to cite just two), and still others who then went on to speak or write about it (Jones, for example), that much of what began as hearsay entered into the realm of fact early in the history of psychoanalysis simply because others reported it as such (each man's many partisan biographers are among them).

Throughout, it seems that scant attention has been paid to the astute observation of Ferenczi's executor, Michael Balint:

> It has never been asked whether something in Freud has or has not contributed to a critical increase of tension during the period preceding a crisis. Still less has any analyst bothered to find out what happened in the minds of those who came into conflict with Freud and what in their relationship to him and to psychoanalysis led to the exacerbation. We have been content to describe them as the villains of the piece.[58]

JUNG WAS at home for little more than a day between military exercises and his departure for New York. He left Küsnacht on September 9, not to return until early November. Emma took charge of all his affairs, especially the soothing of patients who fretted at canceled appointments and came repeatedly to the house, even though they knew Jung was not there. She answered all his professional correspondence and made the many immediate decisions required by much of it without consulting Riklin, who still vacillated between two careers and neglected both equally. She even liaised with Bleuler, who had agreed to act as editor of the *Jahrbuch* in Jung's absence.[59] It was a staggering burden on top of managing a complicated household and caring for four children, but Emma not only did it well, she also found time to write to her husband about everything, in minute detail, and usually every day.[60]

Dr. Smith Ely Jelliffe and his co-director of the New York conference, Dr. William Alanson White,[61] invited Jung to join a group of "eminent specialists from London, Madrid, Montreal, Albany and Washington"[62] to give the inaugural lectures for an annual "International Extension Course." The audience, however, was distinctly American, as eighty-eight psychiatrists and neurologists representing twenty-one states convened to hear lectures on topics concerning all aspects of "management of diseases of the nervous system." Jung noticed an "extreme *eagerness*"[63] among them to learn how his particular "technique" differed from Freud's. He formed a lifelong, lasting impression of American clinicians during this visit. They had "less theoretical understanding" than their European counterparts because they were not interested: "They only want to know how it is done, not what it means."[64]

A select few of the speakers were granted honorary Doctorates of Law, and Jung was among them. His degree was conferred in absentia on September 11, as he was in transit and could not attend the convocation. The citation noted that although he was not yet forty, he had "attracted the attention of the world by his contributions to psychoanalysis." The works specifically mentioned were the word association test and the study of dementia praecox, called "one of the best known of recent publications." Of all the speakers and honorees, the *New York Times* singled out Jung for a lengthy interview published in the Sunday magazine along with a studio portrait photo taken by one of the city's most stylish studios.[65] The article reached a large audience, including some who later went to Zürich because of what they read.

Jung arrived on September 18, and was met by Smith Ely Jelliffe, whose happy houseguest he was because "life in hotels in New York is somewhat disagreeable."[66] Jelliffe, co-planner of the program with White, made good use of Jung's time. Over the next ten days, Jung gave nine lectures, had individual conferences with doctors, addressed others in small discussion groups, and held clinical demonstrations for larger audiences. The venues included daily two-hour seminars for two weeks at Fordham, clinical lectures at Bellevue Hospital and the New York Psychiatric Institute on Ward's Island, and a formal address to the New York Academy of Medicine.[67]

Jung's nine lectures were grouped under the general heading "The Theory of Psychoanalysis."[68] One of their more remarkable aspects is their composition, for he wrote them swiftly and easily in the several weeks after finishing *Symbols*. The nine lectures employ the same writing pattern and exhibit the same scientific precision as the writings on word association and dementia praecox that established his international reputation. They are more "Freudian" than "Jungian" in style, for each begins with a thesis, develops it with logical consistency, and ends with a convincing summation. They are classical in the Freudian sense, with none of the Jungian circularity that pervades most of his other writing.

Jung used the nine essays to explain clearly and succinctly how his views differed from Freud's. At all times he was respectful of Freud; in every instance where he was mentioned, Jung praised Freud's achievement and his theoretical contribution to the point under discussion. Proceeding in the same calm and reasoned vein, he outlined the degrees of difference in their respective positions. In the third lecture, for example, "The Concept of Libido," Jung explained that Freud's definition of the term "connotes an exclusively sexual need, hence everything that Freud means by libido must be understood as sexual need or sexual desire."[69] Jung granted that the medical term was "certainly used for sexual desire and specifically for sexual lust." He had encountered the term in classical writers such as Cicero and Sallust and in others who used it "in the more general sense of passionate desire." He told his audience the concept of libido would be an important component of his lectures; he would try to retain Freud's sexual meaning for the time being, but he would show that the word "really has a much wider range of meaning" than it had either in medical terms or in Freud's. By the time he arrived at his sixth lecture, "The Oedipus Complex,"[70] he was ready to proclaim a manifesto of his independence.

He began by referring to the fantasy material of the adult mind, in which are found many variations of ideas that he believed sprang from religion and mythology and were what he called "the forerunners of religious and mythological ideas." He made a "passing reference" to *Symbols* and defined his version of "sacrifice" as it differed from the ambiguously named "castration complex," which he said represented "the special attitude of the Viennese school towards the question of sexuality." Of Freud's term "Oedipus complex," Jung said it "seems the most unsuitable one possible," as it was too "narrow[ly] restricted" to be truly inclusive.

He made his break with Freudian theory most apparent in the section subtitled "The Problem of Incest." Still discussing "sacrifice," he pointed out its "parallels in the history of religion" and said it was "not surprising that this problem plays an important role in religion, for religion is one of the greatest helps in the psychological process of adaptation." Immediately following this heretical (in the Freudian sense) statement, Jung, in effect, nailed his articles to the door: "The chief obstacle to new modes of psychological adaptation is conservative adherence to the earlier attitude."

"It is possible that I am not expressing myself correctly," Jung said when trying to explain how his view differed from Freud's "special conception of the incest complex." For Freud, it was "an absolutely concrete sexual wish . . . the root-complex, or nucleus, of the neuroses." Jung believed that Freud "reduce[d] practically the whole psychology of the neuroses, as well as many other phenomena in the realm of the mind, to this one complex." Shrewdly, he did not elaborate upon his own theory here, that there were factors other than the sexual that had to be considered. By contenting himself with giving his version of Freud's theory, he was not only enlarging his theoretical territory but also consigning Freud to such a neat and tidy box that, as soon as he knew where Jung put him, he would have to burst out.

By the end of his ninth and final lecture, when Jung had finished explaining how his approach differed from Freud's, his writing reads as if a great weight had been lifted and he is floating on air. He concluded the series with the confident assertion that the "insights and working hypotheses" of his "present and future work" deviated from Freud's "not as contrary assertions but as illustrations of the organic development" of theoretical positions.[71] He insisted that his thoughts had not materialized "out of thin air," but "hundreds of experiences" had convinced him of the rightness of his stance. His fervent hope was that his lectures would "clear up various misunderstandings and remove a number of obstacles which bar the way to a better comprehension of psychoanalysis."

LIGHTNESS OF spirit and quickness of travel dominated the rest of Jung's American sojourn. After New York, he went to Chicago to see Medill McCormick and to treat several others who knew of McCormick's "successful" analysis and were eager to consult him. They subsequently became his patients, not only in Chicago, but also in Zürich, where some lived for protracted periods of time.[72] Then he went to Baltimore to see his former colleague Trigant Burrow, and afterward visited White at St. Elizabeths in Washington, D.C. Jung was particularly attentive to "Negro" patients and claimed to have analyzed at least fifteen of them in the short time he was there.

Thanks to a letter of introduction from Medill McCormick, then vice chair-man of the Progressive National Committee, Jung met former President Theodore Roosevelt. McCormick wrote:

> Busy as you are, I have ventured to give to Dr. C. G. Jung, of Zürich, a let-ter of introduction to you, because he is now not only the most distin-guished psychiatrist in Europe but a remarkable, earnest, brilliant, honest savant, for whom I have a lively affection.[73]

Jung described the meeting:

> And then I once shook hands with Roosevelt. A senator introduced me to him. But that wasn't a special experience. . . . I wasn't a politician, so he didn't know what to make of me, and I didn't know what to make of him ei-ther.[74]

JUNG WANTED to travel through the American South after he left Washington, end his trip somewhere in the West Indies, and sail home from there. But time did not permit, and he returned directly to New York, from whence he sailed on October 26.

Meanwhile, Jones had been busy stirring a pot of rue. He wrote "three times to Brill to put him on his guard against Jung,"[75] but Brill was still struggling hard to remain impartial and did not reply. Jones reported that others told him Jung's lectures caused "quite a furore" and that he was "very happy over his suc-cess." But, said Jones several weeks later, he had news of Jung via a letter from James J. Putnam, in response to and "possibly aided by [Jones's prior] warning letters."[76] Jones then gave a long excerpt allegedly from a Putnam letter that has never been seen since.[77] Jones claimed that Putnam wrote of Jung's "breaking off" from Freud, saying he (Putnam) did not agree with such an action even though it would "go far (although possibly in an unfortunate way) toward gain-ing adherents for the ΨA method."

To further enflame Freud, Jones described the American loyalties as follows:

> [Adolf] Meyer's hostility to Jung, which is even greater than that to you, may help us, and if so Hoch will follow him. Burrow I am sure I can con-trol, in spite of his devotion to Jung, and no doubt Brill is safe. So alto-gether I am hopeful that we shall prevent any serious inroads being made on the theory in America. [L.] Pierce Clark is made of weaker stuff.

Several weeks later, Jones sent what he called a "curious" letter to Freud that Jung had allegedly mailed to Jones's father's home in Wales.[78] There is only Jones's word that this is true, as only the letter is extant and not the envelope.[79] It is highly unlikely Jung would have sent a letter to Wales, because he knew that Jones had just stopped in Küsnacht to pay a formal call on Emma before continuing on to an Italian vacation. She immediately related their conversation to Jung, who was in the mountains for a few days of relaxation after the rigors of the American trip.[80]

Jung's so-called curious letter is hardly that, but rather more a letter to a friend, for that is how Jung thought of Jones until mid-1913. It begins with Jung eager to end the dispute with Freud by telling this mutual friend his side of the story. As Emma had relayed some of Jones's "mistakes or doubts about [Jung's] attitude toward [Jones]," Jung wanted to explain that his lack of correspondence was not a snub; nor was it intended as such to Freud and their other colleagues, whom he had also neglected during the past year. His "neglect" was due to the need to reserve what little free time he had for his own work. "I never had any personal resistance toward you," he implored Jones. "I was simply too much 'introverted' and devoted to my work." Even as he made this decision, he knew that *Symbols* was "destined to destroy [his] friendship with Freud":

> I knew that Freud never will agree with any change in his doctrine. And this is really the case. He is convinced that I am thinking under the domination of a father complex against him and this is all complete nonsense. It would break me, if I were not prepared to see it through, the struggle of the past year where I liberated myself from the regard for the father. If I will go on in science, I have to go on through my own path. He already ceased being my friend, understanding my whole work as a personal resistance against himself and sexuality. Against this insinuation I am completely helpless. I only can regret that I am not able to express myself so clearly that Freud can understand it.

When Jones described this letter to Freud, the roiling emotionalism he attributed to Jung bore no relation to what Jung actually wrote. Jones ended his impassioned account, created out of whole cloth, by telling Freud he now understood a remark Jung made to him three years previously, of how Freud would eventually destroy his own work by his extremism, but how he, Jung, "would save it (or words to that effect)."[81] If this were true, one wonders why the faithful Jones waited three years to alert Freud to Jung's alleged double-dealing.[82]

Jones used innuendo, gossip, and slander — all the intrigue fostered by the minor characters who surrounded the two major players — to his own lasting advantage. Earlier that summer, he began to build on a casual remark of Ferenczi's, that a select group of Freud's followers should submit to being analyzed by him so they could be sure of representing his theory in all its purity. To do this would have been impossible as they were so geographically dispersed, so Jones proposed instead that "a small group of trustworthy analysts" agree to form "a sort of 'Old Guard' around Freud."[83] Jones's conception of the group originated in "stories of Charlemagne's paladins from boyhood, and many secret societies from literature." Through their loyalty, these men would give Freud "the assurance that only a stable body of firm friends could."

Freud accepted with alacrity and enhanced the notion of the chosen by giving each of the members of his "secret committee — Jones, Ferenczi, Abraham, and Hanns Sachs — an antique intaglio that each then had set into a gold ring."[84] Even within this group, Freud needed to assert "authority." He told Jones that neither he nor Ferenczi should take full credit for the idea, for it had been his "in better times, when I hoped Jung would collect such a circle around him." Now this was not to be, for as early as August 1912, Jung was firmly excluded.

NEITHER MAN was willing to address the Kreuzlingen gesture (as both now called it) directly, or to make any other attempt to end the stalemate. On November 24, they met in Munich, the stated reason being an emergency meeting convened by Jung of all the European society presidents of the IPA "for the common deliberation about the general outlook."[85] They were to discuss the recent political machinations in Vienna, most particularly Freud's conflict with the dissident Stekel, who had resigned from the group but would not relinquish control of the *Zentralblatt*. Freud had been forced out when the publisher, Deuticke, took Stekel's side in the dispute. Now Freud planned to leave the journal to them and found a new publication in its place, the *Internationale Zeitschrift*. He expected the presidents to ratify his decision and thus affirm their allegiance. Those who were in Munich did, but they also represented divided loyalties: Jones and Abraham were there to support Freud unequivocally, while others supported Freud but were also loyal to Jung. These included Seif from Munich and Riklin and a Dutch colleague working at the Burghölzli, J. H. W. van Ophuijsen (standing in for Alphons Maeder). Harmony prevailed as they all affirmed Freud in the Stekel contest and agreed both on the venue of the next convention (Munich in September 1913) and the subject, "The Function of the Dream." Power would once again be shared between Zürich and Vienna, as Alphons Maeder and Otto Rank were to be co-speakers.

The unstated reason for the Munich gathering was the opportunity it gave Jung to meet Freud face-to-face in yet another attempt to settle their differences. Jung knew, however, even before he arrived that a break was inevitable. In the so-called curious letter to Jones, Jung (who had no idea of Jones's machinations against him) said Freud had created a difficult quandary and he doubted whether or not he would be invited to contribute to the new journal. As Freud intended it to supplant the *Jahrbuch* as the official written organ, and as he was the president of the international association, Jung knew such a rebuff would give the members a very bad impression of his standing. He already believed that Freud was maneuvering to force his resignation not only from the presidency but also from the society. Nevertheless, he declared that he would be "content" to continue to edit the *Jahrbuch* as well as possible, "even if [Freud] misunderstands me."[86]

THERE IS only Freud's version of what transpired in Munich, for Jung never wrote or spoke of the specifics of their conversation. Freud told Ferenczi,[87] Jones,[88] and Abraham of Jung's alleged betrayal, and soon Freud's version became another hardened fact in the contested history of psychoanalysis. Freud claimed that during their "appointed walk" after the meeting, he asked Jung why he kept "harping" on the Kreuzlingen gesture. He said Jung accused him of going to his "enemies, Binswanger and Häberlin," a remark that, even if Jung did say it, was only partially true: Binswanger did not enter Jung's ken long enough to merit such distinctive status but was merely considered a minor practitioner within the same field; Häberlin, too, was someone with whom Jung differed but who was unlikely to merit the energy one would expend on an enemy.[89]

Freud insisted that Jung considered the Kreuzlingen visit as much of an insult as if he (Jung) had gone to Wiener Neustadt, a suburb of Vienna, and not paid a call. Freud defended himself by saying his May 23 letter had given Jung ample time to do something if he felt like it, but Jung firmly denied receiving the letter until Monday, the twenty-seventh. According to Freud, at that point "something quite unbelievable and unexpected happened." Jung made the spontaneous admission that he had been away sailing over the weekend and did not return until Monday morning, when he found Freud's letter waiting for him. Freud seized the initiative: "Now the ball was in my court, and I made proper use of it":

I asked him whether it didn't occur to look at the postmark on the card or to ask his wife[90] before he raised the objection that I had purposely let him know too late? . . . He was absolutely crushed, ashamed, and then admitted everything: that he had already feared for a long time that intimacy with me or with others would damage his independence, and for that reason he had decided to withdraw; that he had certainly construed me according to his father complex and had been afraid about what I would say about his modifications, about his particular manner of expressing himself; that he was certainly wrong in being mistrustful; that it hurt him to be judged a complex fool, etc. I spared him nothing at all, told him calmly that a friendship with him couldn't be maintained, that he himself gave rise to the intimacy which he then so cruelly broke off; that things were not at all in order in his relations with men, not just with me but with others as well. He repels them all after a while. All those who are now with me have turned away from him because he threw them out.

Freud admitted to "deceiv[ing] himself on one point" only, that he had once believed Jung to be "a born leader." Now he thought Jung "immature himself and in need of supervision." According to Freud, Jung allegedly "totally ceased contradicting me and admitted everything. I think it did him good." Freud did not believe their conversation would lead to any "lasting change," because "there is a kernel of dishonesty in [Jung's] being." To support his contention he cited his own personal paragon of ethical probity, Ernest Jones, who corroborated Freud's allegation that Jung was a liar by repeating his own, that he had overheard Jung maligning Freud several years earlier at the Salzburg congress.

Freud closed his account of Jung's alleged confession with the single statement in the entire letter that Jung most likely did utter: "You will find me completely with the cause," for he truly meant it. No matter how he and Freud differed in interpretation of individual points, what mattered most was psychoanalysis and how best to further its reception in the wider world.

AFTER THEIR walk, Freud and Jung joined the others for luncheon in a private dining room in the Parkhotel, where the meetings had taken place. Jung remembered many years later that the name of Amenophis IV, who allegedly had a father complex, was introduced into the conversation.[91] No doubt whoever brought it up did so deliberately, for Freud had broadcast his belief far and wide that Jung had one and held it against him. The unnamed person insisted that the pharaoh had destroyed all his father's regal cartouches, that is, his name wherever it appeared on the stelae, as part of his "death wish" toward his father. Jung, "irritated to the extreme," immediately interjected that the pharaoh had done so "not as an act of resistance against his father but because he was a creative man." And at that moment, just as he had done several years earlier, Freud fainted.

Everyone stood aghast and unable to move. Jung, saying, "My God, something has to be done!," swooped Freud up and carried him into the next room, where there was a sofa. Freud came "half way to his senses" in Jung's arms. Jung never forgot Freud's look, "as if I were his father, or his mother." He was aware of Freud's "helplessness," which he thought "terribly odd." Years later, he insisted, "That's how it was, and if other people say something different, then they're lying."[92]

Freud gave varying accounts of the fainting incident to numerous others, especially his three faithful correspondents, Jones, Ferenczi, and Binswanger. He told Jones it was an unfortunate event because it made him lose "a portion of [his] authority."[93] He attributed the faint to fatigue, lack of sleep, and too much smoking before he alluded to the first one in 1909 and another one much earlier, years before in Munich with Wilhelm Fliess. He believed the city fostered "some psychic element," in him and that there was, especially with Jung, "an unruly homosexual feeling at the root of the matter."

He told Ferenczi the last attack was similar to the first, which he said took place in the Essighaus Restaurant in Bremen (rather than the Parkhotel in Munich, as he told Jones).[94] He called it an "anxiety attack," which he attributed to fatigue after a long day, a trying week, and a sleepless night in a railway car.

He felt faint "for a moment" but said he stood up under his own power and felt nauseated for a while and better in the evening. He ended this truncated account by saying he slept well on the overnight train and felt fine ever since.

Freud told Binswanger that the second Munich fainting attack was "surely provoked by psychogenic elements" and "strong somatic reinforcements."[95] Freud admitted that his main reason was "repressed feelings, this time directed against Jung, as previously against a predecessor of his [Fliess]."

"The agreement reached in Munich will hardly hold for long," Freud wrote. "His attitude precludes this." Still, he implored Binswanger, "Slow down the process by remaining utterly discreet about everything concerning him and me."

TRUE TO his desire, Freud began to "renounce any kind of personal relations [with Jung] and merely preserve the official connection." The year 1912 ended with an exchange of letters mostly about legal and publishing matters concerning the new journal, now known as the *Internationale Zeitschrift für therapeutische Psychoanalyse*.[96] But each man still managed a well-aimed dig at the other in what became a metaphorical game of psychoanalytic chess, as they moved mutually insulting knights and sarcastic bishops across the board. Freud approved of Jung's critical review of Adler's book, because it would end the rumors that he was taking Adler's side.[97] Jung replied that even "Adler's cronies" did not regard him as "one of theirs," and it was "deplorable" that Freud insisted upon treating the science of psychology "as a profession of faith."[98] Unfortunately, when Jung described himself as not one of "theirs," he used the pronoun *"Ihrigen"* (yours) instead of *"ihrigen"* (theirs). Thrusting for check, Freud seized upon it, asking if "Dear Dr. Jung" (as he now addressed him) was " 'objective' enough to consider [the slip] without anger."

Jung parried with the honest Swiss bluntness that was so often turned into a negative personality trait by those who strove to disparage him. He admitted his "ambivalence" toward Freud, saying he wanted to take "an honest and absolutely straightforward view" of their differences, and if Freud doubted his word, "so much the worse" for him.[99] Freud's customary way of treating pupils as if they were patients was a *"blunder"* that produced "either slavish sons or impudent puppies" (Jung's emphasis): "You go around sniffing out all the symptomatic actions in your vicinity, thus reducing everyone to the level of sons and daughters who blushingly admit the existence of their faults. Meanwhile you remain on top as the father, sitting pretty." Jung added that "nobody dares to pluck the prophet by the beard" and "so long as you hand out this stuff I don't give a damn for my symptomatic actions; they shrink to nothing in comparison with the formidable beam in my *brother* Freud's eye."[100]

But then Jung's anger gave Freud exactly the gambit he wanted. "I am not in the least neurotic," he insisted as he accused Freud of being so himself. He ended the letter by saying he would stand by Freud in public but would maintain his own views in private. In letters, he would "start telling . . . what I really think of you," as it was the "only decent" way to go on. "No doubt you will be outraged by this peculiar token of friendship, but it may do you good all the same."

Jung's response was "out of proportion to the occasion," Freud replied in a letter filled with serenity and self-control.[101] He may have gained his admirable self-discipline by venting his emotion to Jones and Ferenczi before writing to Jung. He told each man the same thing — that Jung was crazy and that his letters veered between "tenderness and arrogant presumption."[102] He served the checkmate in his next letter to Jung: "One who while behaving abnormally keeps shouting that he is normal gives ground for the suspicion that he lacks insight into his illness."

Freud proposed total rupture, an end to anything personal between them. He himself would "lose nothing," for his sole "emotional tie" with Jung had "long been a thin thread — the lingering effect of past disappointments."[103]

"Take your full freedom," Freud wrote in this letter of January 3, 1913, "and spare me your supposed 'tokens of friendship.'"

On that same day, Jung wrote to Freud, offering greetings for the new year and the wish that psychoanalysis would continue to gain adherents, "its vitality unimpaired and indeed heightened by internal conflicts and cross currents. Without them there is no life."[104] Jung thought his "honorable intentions" were "perfectly clear," and he left "the rest" up to Freud.

When he wrote next on January 6, he had Freud's stunning rebuff in hand, the letter of the third.[105] On a typed postcard, Jung agreed to honor Freud's wish to abandon personal relations. Saying he would never "thrust" his friendship on anyone, he would leave it to Freud to be the "best judge" of what this rupture would mean in years to come. The friendship officially ended when Jung made one of the most famous and oft-quoted remarks of their seven years of correspondence: "The rest is silence."

THE PERSONAL diatribes were mostly over, but the correspondence continued throughout 1913 with a studied, self-conscious formality dominated by discussions of content and contracts for the journals, criticisms by and of members of the various societies, and defections and allegiances. Things were too quiet for Jones, so he stirred them a bit by accusing Jung of conspiring with Bleuler to keep his article out of the *Jahrbuch*.[106] Jung explained that it was Bleuler's decision, an editorial judgment made while he was speaking at Fordham, but his first letter did not appease Jones, and he had to write another. In the second, Jung seemed to resign himself to Jones's continuing accusation that he had conspired to exclude the article, and also to Jones's "inability" to follow Jung's "somewhat altered views." He explained that he himself was "not in love" with them: "I just consider them as working hypotheses and not as eternal truths." He offered those who liked his views the freedom to adopt them, but he acknowledged that many of his friends would not be able to accept them. If his ideas were valid, he concluded, they would "find their way."

HE INTRODUCED them to the world fully and succinctly in August 1913, at the International Congress of Medicine in London, where he gave a series of lectures in which for the first time he defined his theoretical overview as "analytical psychology" rather than as Freud's "psychoanalysis" or even what he called Bleuler's "depth psychology."[107] In his warmly received lectures, Jung "suggested" that psychoanalysis be freed from "the purely sexual standpoint" and enlarged to include "an energic viewpoint" that he formulated after reading authors as varied as Sallust and his own French contemporary Henri Bergson.[108] By the time Jung arrived at his final summation, he made the flat-out declaration that he could not "see the real aetiology of neurosis in the various manifestations of infantile sexual development and the fantasies to which they give rise."[109]

Jones attended the London meetings and lost no time giving Freud his own version of events. He told Freud that he personally "squashed" Janet[110] and ignored Jung's "few courteous generalities"; he was only "in the background." Freud read Jung's paper and deemed it "innocuous, beyond my expectation."[111] From his distant perch in Vienna, he thought he had "very much overestimated the danger" Jung posed.

Jung, however, was fortified by the positive reception for his ideas in London and largely unaware of the machinations going on behind his back. He went to Munich for the Fourth Private Psychoanalytic Meeting, held on September 7–8.[112] He was determined to show Freud that their personal differences were immaterial and that they needed to work together for the greater good of the movement. Many years later, Jung remembered their first encounter:

I greeted him warmly and asked about his family. That's when he looked at me in utter astonishment and asked why I was working up this humanity. But I welcomed him warmly on purpose, to show that I had no personal resistances but merely represented another scientific opinion. He, on the other hand, thought that I wished for his death . . . he always accused me of personal motives that didn't exist at all. Something always had to be wrong, but that was pure projection on his part.

Abraham persuaded Freud that it was important for him to speak at the congress.[113] Freud agreed, and spoke on "The Disposition to Obsessional Neurosis: A Contribution to the Problem of Choice of Neurosis."[114] Once again he stated his theory of the primacy of sex but this time in a manner Jung called "the psychology of the nothing but."[115] He kept his frustrations to himself over Freud's inability to permit discussion of any view that disagreed with his own, and then delivered a paper that marked another of his so-called radical departures, "A Contribution to the Study of Psychological Types."[116]

Eighty-seven members and guests gathered to watch each man — Freud as patriarch and founder, Jung as president — seated at a separate table surrounded by his supporters and facing the other with his minions clustered behind and around. Freud feigned boredom during the proceedings, but his supporters were more vocal. Among them was Lou Andreas-Salomé, who criticized Jung's "pure aggression, ambition, and intellectual brutality."[117] She objected "not so much" to Jung's divergences from Freud but rather "that he does it in such a way as if he had taken it on himself to rescue Freud and his cause *by* these divergences."

"One glance at the two of them tells which is the more dogmatic, the more in love with power," Frau Lou (as she was called) wrote, expressing the criticism leveled against Jung by all Freud's faction. As president, Jung decided who would speak and how much time would be allotted for each presentation. When Freud wrote about it in his *History of Psychoanalysis*, he complained of Jung's "disagreeable and incorrect manner . . . the discussions overwhelmed the papers."[118]

In this fractious atmosphere, voting for a president to serve for the next two years took place. At least twenty-two of the fifty-two persons eligible to vote submitted blank cards rather than support Jung, but the thirty votes in his favor returned him to office. Ferenczi told Jung angrily that his arrogance, the "quite one-sided and partial comments" he made as the papers were read, and the "personal behavior" of his supporters were what "caused us to protest by voting with blank cards."[119] Charges and countercharges were hurled: Jones accused Jung of making anti-Semitic remarks; Freud told Maeder that Jung was an anti-Semite;[120] Jung allegedly muttered that the Jewish participants had voted against him en bloc because he was a Christian.[121] Freud suggested that the international organization be dissolved and the Vienna, Budapest, and Berlin societies regroup to form a new one excluding the "Zürichers [who] have lost the gift of making themselves intelligible."[122] Jones and Abraham pointed out that this would leave Jung in control of the original "International" body, so Freud agreed to let things stand for the time being.

There were other ways to isolate Jung, to sidetrack, stymie, and ignore him, and Freud moved swiftly to instigate them all. "We are mostly dependent on him for helping us by his foolish ways," Freud told Jones. "If he were clever, there would be no chance."[123]

CHAPTER 17

<hr/>

"My Self/Myself"

One of Freud's earliest letters to Jung, offering both advice and warning about how their professional relationship should develop, became an uncanny prediction of why it would end. On New Year's Day 1907, Freud told Jung not to "deviate too far," when they were really so close, because if he did, the day might come when they would be "played off against one another." He also begged Jung not to hide his true thoughts behind a curtain of collegiality, for "utmost frankness is the best diplomacy."[1] Unfortunately, by 1914 he was unable to heed his own counsel and wanted nothing less than "an end to all compromises" and a "desired rupture."[2] Jung had to be cast into an oblivion from which there would be no grant of "clemency."[3] When Freud rushed his version of the *History of Psychoanalysis* into print, he decreed emphatically, "Psychoanalysis is my creation. I consider myself justified in maintaining that . . . no one can know better than I do what psychoanalysis is."[4]

By the time this polemic appeared, Jung was resigned to Freud's censure, but Jones, still worried about a possible reprieve, orchestrated events to guarantee that Freud's sights would remain firmly focused on Jung's alleged heresy.[5] In one instance, Jones invited Jung to contribute an article explaining his "deviate" views to the same issue of the *Zeitschrift* as Freud's polemic against him.[6] The ostracized Jung refused, believing he had explained his position as well as he could in *Symbols* and the subsequent lectures he gave about the book. He saw no use in writing an article when "Munich has shown what the attitude of the Vienna school is." He told Jones he so disliked "advertising, even in science," that "if people don't understand what I have said, they may work until they begin to understand, if not — *tant pis pour eux*."[7] Too bad for them.

It was a courageous sentiment, but in truth he was racked by feelings of loss, trepidation over the magnitude of what had transpired, and fear for his immediate professional future: "After all, I knew nothing beyond Freud, and yet, I dared to take the step into darkness." When Jung was an old man, during a discussion that still reverberated with the pain and confusion he felt years before, he remembered the sensation of complete disorientation, of "falling out into that which is not known." The feeling was so overwhelming that he thought he must be "experiencing a psychological disorder."

This eerie sensation marked the beginning of a period that began in the autumn of 1913 and lasted to the end of 1917. He described it as a time when he "devoted attention to the unconscious," and became "conscious of my *Self/myself* through my occupation."[8]

He credited the beginning of this "occupation" to 1912, at the very moment when he drew the line at the end of the manuscript of *Symbols* and wrote the curious sentence he could not understand: *"What have you written, what is this now?"* (his emphasis). At first, he thought the sentence referred to his book, and that it concerned what he believed the book was all about: "the myth in which the human being has always lived." Because he was a Swiss citizen of the twentieth century, he assumed his personal myth was Christian. He pondered his initial question to himself and then followed it with a further series in which he both questioned his possible meaning and offered possible answers to it:

Do you live in that [i.e., the Christian myth]?
If I have to be honest, no; I could not say that I live in the Christian myth.
So then we no longer have a myth?
Yes, apparently we do not have a myth anymore.
Yes, but what is your myth in which you live?

From the vantage point of old age and much wisdom, he remembered how this question made him "too uncomfortable" to go on, and how he forced himself to "stop thinking." He felt as if he had "fallen into an immense hole — that is the fact." Looking back on himself at this moment, he believed that if he could name the single most important achievement in his life, it was that he "saved [his] life from that hole" and "didn't drown in it." Some of the answers to his questions of what personal "myth" he should adopt and how he should cope with the abyss created by the professional rupture with Freud did not begin to coalesce until a year later, and then they came through visions and dreams that even then he could not fathom.

There were three major episodic groups in all. The first occurred in October 1913, just after the momentous Munich conference, when its full consequences were unfolding. Jung was riding the train to Schaffhausen to bring his family back to Küsnacht from their extended summer vacation in Emma's mother's house. He had what he described as "two visions,"[9] one after the other, of all the countries of Northern Europe being covered by a "monstrous flood." When it approached the Swiss border, the Alps rose to block it from inundating Swiss territory. Jung saw horrendous waves of urine-yellow water bearing garbage, detritus, and decayed corpses that slammed into the Alps and piled up against them, when suddenly the water changed to blood, carrying still greater amounts of its ghastly cargo. The vision lasted until the train came into the station, an he disembarked feeling "perplexed and nauseated, ashamed of [his] weakness." Several weeks later, in a casual conversation about European politics, he recalled the vision but decided it had less to do with the possibility of war and more to do with himself. He thought he was being "menaced by a psychosis."

The second was a dream he had at Christmastime 1913. In it, he was in a beautiful Italian loggia that reminded him of the Palazzo Vecchio in Florence and was seated in a golden Renaissance chair facing a table made of green stone that resembled an emerald. He knew that his children were somewhere about, but he sat staring into space, when a white bird, a small gull or dove,[10] flew down onto the table. He gestured to his children to be silent and unmoving, but just then, the bird turned into a golden-haired little girl who ran away to play with them. He was thinking about the metamorphosis, when the little girl/dove returned and gently put her arms around his neck. Just as suddenly, she was metamorphosed into the dove, which spoke in a human voice and said she was allowed to become human only "in the first hours of the night, while the male dove is busy with the twelve dead." The dove flew away, and Jung woke up. His first thought was that the girl/dove had used a "peculiar" word not often used in German to describe the male dove, *Tauber*.[11] His first emotion was alarm, for "what should a male pigeon be doing with twelve dead?" — whoever or whatever they may have been.

He spent the rest of the night thinking of aspects of the number twelve as it related to the apostles, the months of the year, and the zodiac, about which he had written in *Symbols*. He tried to connect it to the *tabula smaragdina*, the emerald tablet in the alchemical text of Hermes Trismegistus, the "Thrice Greates [*sic*] Hermes,"[12] wherein only the truth was told and the wisdom of all the ages was engraved upon it in Greek: "Ether above, Ether below, Heaven above, Heaven below, all this above, all this below, take it and be happy." For some time afterward, he had a "tremendous animation of the unconscious" but could not develop a theoretical overview that let him order his impressions or make sense of them. Finally he gave up, telling himself "just to wait, keep on living and watch the fantasies."

The third crucial vision/dream came between April and June 1914, when he had repeated dreams of the onset of polar cold, yellow flood, and dark red blood. He persuaded himself that this time the dreams were a "true precognition of the war," and tried not to worry about them in a personal sense, even though the dream of the white bird continued to tantalize.

Then he remembered that as a small boy, he had heard one of his Preiswerk uncles use the word *"Tauber."* He thought a possible way to establish an interpretive "technique" would be to make a conscious analysis of his infantile memories and see what correspondences arose. He could make neither order nor sense of them, but he still thought early childhood memory must contain the key. He decided to try to "live through" his boyhood experiences again, "to recover the emotional tone of childhood."

As soon as he began, he was beset by an unending torrent of fantasies that he feared would overwhelm him. He recognized the danger the phantasms presented because of his psychiatric training, and he knew he was taking a tremendous risk by abandoning himself to the flood of bizarre images that rose from his unconscious. He also knew that he had to follow them wherever they led, and he hoped he possessed enough willpower to analyze them and put them to positive use, rather than to let himself succumb to their siren song and be dragged under. Shortly after he made the decision to follow the images no matter where they led, he had a powerful dream about wanting to kill the mythological hero Siegfried. When he began to analyze the dream, he equated it with the political situation in Germany. Just as the German government wanted to impose its will and have its own way within Europe, Jung realized that he had wanted to do the same in both his personal and professional circumstances. His subsequent analysis of the dream showed him that his course of behavior was the wrong one for him and that killing Siegfried equated to the need to change his ways. He gave credit to this dream for allowing him to bring what he called his "experiment with the unconscious" to a satisfying conclusion.[13]

In later years, he insisted that reverting to the games of his childhood and childlike behavior was one of the few things he could do, for he claimed that throughout 1914, he was incapable of most other "adult" activity or behavior. The evidence, however, is contradictory.

First of all, he said he was unable to read since he finished *Symbols*. Whenever he tried to concentrate on the burgeoning literature of psychoanalysis or any other "scientific" writing, he comprehended it only as so much gibberish that made no sense in any of the four languages in which he was fluent. His inability to absorb what he read so frightened him that he became convinced he was "locked off completely from the world." His distress was so intense between 1914 and 1917 that he insisted he did not read "a single book," especially scientific literature, although the writings he published during this period indicate otherwise.[14] Describing himself as "completely devastated, with all pleasure in conscious work lost," he claimed he could read only an occasional Swiss newspaper, and then only to glance at the headlines concerning the onset of World War I. Nevertheless, he had such a fear that his sorry condition would be evident to others that he resigned from his teaching lectureship at the University of Zürich, the position he had earlier taken such pains to keep. The gesture left him isolated from professional circles and almost all intellectual exchange.

He knew he needed a "counterweight" to "this terrible inner world," so he turned to his family for verification that he was "a normal human being." Afraid the unconscious would drive him "wild," he clung to external realities:

the fact that I have a Swiss diploma as a physician, a wife and five children,[15] and live at 228 Seestrasse in Küsnacht; those were facts, that was my concreteness that always proved to me again: I really do exist, I am not just an empty sheet tumbled about by a spirit like Nietzsche, who completely lost his identity along with himself because he had nothing but the inner world.

To work his way through the morass in which he found himself, the distinguished Dr. Med. Jung began the well-thought-out, conscious occupation of setting aside time each day for children's play. Remembering how much he liked building blocks when he was a child of ten, he tried to re-create the activity, this time with sticks, stones, and other detritus that washed up on the lakeshore in front of his house. He may have been in the grip of a psychosis, but he was cognizant enough to slot his play into a full, fixed schedule, and he did it only as part of an organized daily routine, every day after lunch.

He could not play in the morning because he spent the early hours in his study writing about his dreams. Before the break with Freud and the onset of his crisis, he attended to his correspondence haphazardly, even though Emma nagged him to be more organized. Often he bundled letters into his pockets intending to make notes on the envelopes toward eventual replies, but usually he just jotted notes about anything that came to mind. If he answered letters at all, he usually dashed off quick replies on trains or trams and frequently forgot to mail them.[16] Now, when he was supposedly in the midst of a psychotic episode, he wrote letters on a fixed daily schedule, usually replying by hand and carefully posting them himself. Then he either saw a few patients or, more likely, spent the rest of the morning talking about himself with his foremost confidante and associate, Toni Wolff.

Like his children, who were also eager to get in some play before their afternoon activities, Jung began to bolt his noontime lunch so that he could build his little villages until sometime between 2 and 3 P.M., when the first of the steady stream of afternoon patients arrived.[17] If he finished seeing them early enough that it was still daylight, he rushed outside to build even more intricate structures.

"Building! This is what I'll do," he said, elated, as he formed little villages. Churches, houses, and castles surrounded stone squares; little roads and rivulets of water became rivers and canals. One day quite by chance he spied a red pebble in the water, a rectangular pyramid that became the stone altar within his little church. At first he thought it "a product of pure coincidence," but then the dream of the underground phallus came into his conscious mind, the dream of the monstrous appendage that had frightened him so when he was a small child. It sparked him to meditate: "I asked myself: what are you doing there? . . . you are doing that like a real ritual. And then I had the feeling — this is mythology! . . . Building! that was the beginning. Building! And that's when I started *The Black Book*."

Playing the building game resulted in his filling the first of the six small notebooks that have collectively come to be called *The Black Book*.[18] Jung described each entry as an "ur-experience" about himself, an "experiment of personal confrontation with [his] soul," one of the earliest examples of his using the word in this manner.[19] In devoting himself to explorations of himself, he "both loved it and hated it; it taught [him] and [he] taught it." Playing with his little villages soothed his frazzled thoughts, and as he proceeded, he was able to bring a certain degree of self-regard to his play and observed that it "cleared" his rational thoughts, leaving "a fantasy" inside him. He duly recorded all these cleared thoughts into the black notebooks every evening and soon discovered that the descriptions required drawings to accompany and enhance them, both of representational objects and of symbols. In the process of performing this evening ritual, a "mythology" (as he called it for want of a better word at the time) was emerging. He began to use it on his patients, to "listen for the personal mythology" when he treated them, but it was not until many years later that he realized it was the first concrete step he took toward establishing his own "technique" as distinct from Freud's. When he spoke earlier to the British medical groups in London and Aberdeen, he had used Freud's term "psychoanalysis" but had offered as an alternative "analytical psychology." Now, for the first time, he began to think about a name for his theoretical system, once even offering the phrase "prospective [as in the sense of digging deep] psychology."[20]

In the years between 1914 and 1917, when he was working toward what eventually became his next published book, *Psychological Types*[21] (which many scholars consider to be his most important contribution to the literature of psychoanalysis), he felt it would be dishonest to continue to apply Freudian constructs when he could not accept Freud's system in its totality. Furthermore, he believed that Freud had onerously branded him a charlatan when the 1914 *Jahrbuch* appeared with his one-sided version of theory and event, "On the History of the Psychoanalytic Movement."[22] There Freud castigated Jung for devoting himself to "the unscrupulous pursuit of his own interests" and for his "misconceptions of psychoanalysis and his deviations from it." Jung realized his credibility would be nil if he continued to use Freudian technique, especially after Freud further attempted to discredit him by printing a letter from a former patient who claimed he was "forced to experience" an analysis with Jung.[23] Jung made no formal written reply to Freud's invective because his distress and confusion were too acute to do otherwise. By his relative silence, he left what seemed to be the last and final word to Freud, the "superb controversialist."[24]

Still, Jung had patients to treat, so he made the conscious decision that if people sought his clinical expertise, he had the obligation at least to listen to them. He would offer no interpretations that were based on his own earlier scientific writings because in his current condition he was unsure of their worth. More important, he would make no diagnosis based on his interpretation of the writings of others, especially of Freud.

Suddenly, he "noticed" that his patients were bringing dreams and visions "of their own accord" to their sessions because his method of treatment had become one of asking simple, direct questions: "What do you mean by that? Where does that [interpretation] come from? What do you think about it?" Just as suddenly, he noticed that his "interpretation came to light all by itself. I looked at nothing but the material and didn't bring any theoretical prerequisites to it." In the beginning, this method truly frightened him because he thought it so unorthodox, but as time passed, it became still another of the ways that helped him to achieve a kind of "self-healing" or an "integration" of the self, even as he observed in fascination how it helped his patients to achieve the same result.

If, as he believed, the break with Freud deprived him of the legitimate right to continue to use Freudian psychology in his own practice, it had one beneficial side effect: there was no more of the hated administrative work connected with the *Jahrbuch*. Even the distraction of dealing with political machinations was eased when the Zürich contingent decided that Freud's attack in the *Jahrbuch* was intolerable, as it crushed all possibility for independent writing and research. On July 18, rejecting the unacceptable "papal policies of the Viennese" and Freud's "principle of authority," fifteen of the sixteen Swiss members voted to resign from the International Psychoanalytic Association, with only one dissension.[25]

It was exactly what Freud wanted. Throughout the spring, he had been writing to Abraham, anxiously anticipating the Zürich withdrawal he had done everything to provoke in the hope that it would come before the Dresden congress in September.[26] Now he gloated that his "bombshell" had done its work, that he had finally rid himself of "the brutal sanctimonious Jung and his disciples."[27] Jones, too, did not mind letting the "Zürich people go to hell," but despite their "stupid foolishness," he had hoped to avoid the break until the *Zeitschrift* was on firmer footing. Deeming its preservation "all important," he worried that without Jung and the Zürichers, the subscription list of one hundred would dwindle even further, leading publisher Heller to declare it unprofitable to continue.[28]

Among the fifteen Zürich members who resigned were Riklin[29] and Maeder, both of whom had previously taken an active part in the society's politics.[30] Now they and the others deferred to Jung as the natural leader who would steer them toward reconstitution as a separate professional entity. Fortunately for Jung, the Zürich withdrawal happened just as his August vacation was about to begin, and he did not have to worry about it until late autumn. It also happened during the anxious interregnum between the assassination of Archduke Franz Ferdinand in Sarajevo on June 28 and the onset of world war in September.

The international preoccupation with war provided Jung with time to reconnoiter. He was invited to England and Scotland at the end of July to address the British Psycho-Medical Society in London and the British Medical Association at its annual meeting in Aberdeen. The invitation was probably issued because of a detailed account of the Freud-Jung rupture written by Dr. M. David Eder and published in the January 1914 issue of the *British Medical Journal* that concluded with praise for Jung's "return to a saner view of life."[31]

Jung's invitation provoked Jones to a frenzy.[32] He told Freud he planned to follow Jung from lecture to lecture and "contradict him on the spot." Freud urged Jones not to show "too great anxiety," but to contradict Jung "on a single occasion, which [he might] choose to [his] pleasure." He thought it would be even better if Jones were to attack Jung afterward, "in print, drily and mercilessly." Freud had just read a new introduction to a reissue of "On the Content of the Psychoses" and sneered at what he perceived as Jung's newfound adherence to the views of Henri Bergson: "He has found another Jew for his father complex. I am no more jealous."

THE TRIP to England was one of many escapes from Küsnacht Jung made after Freud began maneuvering to marginalize him. He lectured in Bern, attended meetings in Munich, and visited several other German cities, ostensibly on the International Society's business and to further the cause of Freudian psychoanalysis. There were also the voyages to the United States, his annual month of military duty, and numerous short hiking and biking vacations through the Swiss Alps, the Ticino, and northern Italy. In short, he was away from Küsnacht more than he was at home. He never commented directly about his eager, almost frenetic, travels, but several possibilities suggest themselves.[33]

In June 1913, Emma became pregnant with their fifth and last child: a fourth daughter, Emma Helene, born March 18, 1914. Sometime before or during Emma's pregnancy, Jung and Toni Wolff recognized how deeply they were attracted to each other, and an unorthodox emotional triangle began that endured for the remainder of their lives. Two short weeks after Emma gave birth to "Lil" (as the child was known in the family), Jung and Toni took a vacation in Ravenna, leaving Emma and the baby to be cared for by her mother, and the older children by his.[34] Ravenna took on a special meaning for Jung, and although no documentation exists to prove it one way or the other, the city is generally believed to be the setting for his and Toni Wolff's first sexual intimacy.[35]

Jung described his adulterous behavior during this period at varying times throughout his life in a variety of ways. Referring to his theory that an element of the feminine exists in every man (just as an animus is found within every woman), Jung was dismissive about taking responsibility for his actions: "Back then I was in the midst of the anima problem." At other times he was sheepish and apologetic, making comments such as, "What could you expect from me? — the Anima bit me on the forehead and would not let go."[36] But most often he was filled with anguish over being caught in a situation he felt he could not control and made no attempt to offer either rational or self-serving explanations. He merely kept on doing what he felt he had to do in order to explain himself to himself.

Toni Wolff was the only person besides his six-year-old son, Franz, whom Jung permitted to sit with him as he played his lakeside games.[37] Usually she sat quietly smoking some distance away, trying to seek shelter from the sun that hurt her eyes and burned her fair skin, speaking only when he initiated conversation. Sometimes, when she knew that Jung did not have morning patients, she would come to the Seestrasse house and spend the time before lunch sitting with him in his library. The maid would let her in, for Emma chose not to see her. Toni usually sat in a corner of the sofa facing the windows that looked out on the lake, away from even the most indirect contact with a light that hurt her eyes. Even in cloudy Zürich, she was prone to eyestrain and headaches if she did not wear dark glasses outdoors. Jung, if he sat at all, was usually at his worktable directly under the window, where any sun that shone through the usually overcast climate fell directly upon him. He could never get enough of the sun, to which he would expose himself on all but the most inclement days.[38]

Usually he paced and talked as Toni hunched forward listening intently. She interrupted often, and he used the pauses to tamp fresh tobacco into his ubiquitous pipe as she gave her interpretations of his visions, dreams, and ur-experiences. He could hardly wait for her to finish before he broke in, and their exchanges sometimes became a raucous jumble as each interrupted to tell the other his or her thoughts and impressions.

Toni Wolff was the only person during early 1914 to read *The Black Book*,[39] and if Jung ever had any sort of formal (or informal) psychoanalysis, she gave it to him then. When the maid knocked on the closed door to announce lunch, he and Toni usually took time to finish their discussion before descending the regal staircase slowly, still engrossed in conversation. He saw her to the front door most courteously, for she was never invited to lunch, and Emma always made sure that she and the children were in the dining room, safely seated. On some days, when Jung and Toni had not finished talking, he left her alone in the library, telling the maid to bring her tea before he hurried into the dining room to join Emma and the children. Afterward, when Toni saw him from the window, she tiptoed down to join his lakeshore games.

None of Emma's pregnancies was difficult, but she used the last one as an excuse to avoid having to meet anyone she did not care to see. Toni certainly fell into this category, especially after her vacation with Jung in Ravenna, when Emma could no longer avoid the obvious. However, not inviting Toni to lunch was not taken as the snub Emma actually intended, because the pregnancy and subsequent convalescence were valid excuses in their stratum of Swiss society. Emma undoubtedly resented Toni's personal relationship with Carl, but she equally resented his growing intellectual dependence on her because family demands severely limited her own time with her husband. By the time he came down to breakfast, Emma was seeing the children off to school. He gulped his meal and left for his own private pursuits, where she knew better than to follow unless invited. The family pattern at lunch was much the same.

It was not until after the evening meal that she had any time alone with him. He ate in silence unless something was on his mind, and then he conducted a monologue that no one dared interrupt. Emma had trained the children not to speak unless he spoke to them first, but as their upbringing was her responsibility and as he had little interest in children per se, he had no need for their conversation.[40] Often, he rose abruptly to go to his study. Emma followed after giving directives to the children, who remained seated at the table to wait for the maids, who saw to their bedtime. There were no kisses or hugs from Emma, just instructions for them to behave.

Her children believed that Emma had "warm feelings," but she never showed them.[41] When they were young, they excused her for never kissing them, because they thought their father probably forbade such displays, but when they became adults, they used Jung's terms and attributed her undemonstrative behavior to Emma's typology, a "sensation-thinking introvert." She was "not at all a feeling type," said her only son. "She loved us, and only later did we know and understand this. She was so much warmer with her grandchildren, but she was never open or spontaneous with us. We were only kissed on birthdays or other ceremonial occasions."[42]

And so Emma waited eagerly for the evening, when she could join her husband in his study. She sat on the same sofa that earlier bore Toni Wolff, reading in silence while he wrote or drew in the Black Books she was forbidden to read and that he never discussed with her.[43] After several hours, she said good night just as quietly as she had sat and went off to her own bedroom at the far end of the house,[44] leaving him still engrossed in self-scrutiny of one sort or another.

Whenever Emma did express deep emotion, it came through eruptions of such withering anger that it frightened those who were the object of her rage. But she was so controlled that she seldom lost her temper, and rarely in front of her children when they were young. Others have described Emma's "unfocused rages" during her last pregnancy, when she "seethed with an anger" she would neither discuss nor explain.[45] As the Jung children matured, they realized just how strong their mother's personality was, and how, in many different ways, she "held her own" against their father. But the one instance where she failed utterly was her inability to persuade Jung to let her be the confidante he so obviously needed and wanted but thought he could find only in another woman, outside his marriage.

Sadly for Emma now that Jung had broken with Freud, there was no one with whom she could discuss her plight, no one to whom she could confide whatever anxieties and fears she felt. There was no male authority she could risk consulting, for she would not have dreamed of discussing her husband with the likes of Riklin, Maeder, or a fairly recent acquaintance, the Reverend Adolf

Keller, whose own wife's dissatisfaction with her marriage was becoming common knowledge in the "Zürich school."[46] Emma did not yet know Tina Keller well enough to do more than greet her with the polite expressions a woman of her social class would be expected to make, and these did not include — under any circumstance — an airing of marital problems. Also, Riklin, Maeder, and Keller were her husband's subordinates in terms of their psychoanalytic standing in Zürich. Ironically, Emma believed her husband's situation was similar to Freud's when he refused to risk his authority through self-revelation; Jung was foremost among his Swiss colleagues and she could not risk damaging her husband's authority by discussing her humiliating situation with any of them. Jung had no genuine male friends at the time, but the man who came closest was Hermann Sigg-Böddinghaus, a local businessman with whom Jung often hiked or biked. Emma could not risk confiding in Hermann in the hope that he would relay her anguish to Jung, because Hermann's wife was the analyst Martha, who Emma feared might convey her distress to the rest of the analytic community.

Franz Jung, who for many complex reasons always took his mother's side within the family dynamic, described her plight: "Can you imagine living with a man who left you with full responsibility for his house and his children while he passed the time playing their games or being in that same house with another woman?"[47] Franz also told the poignant story of a rare occasion when Jung took his four older children sailing and bought them sweets when they docked at a village on the lake: "When we got home, Marianne ran across the lawn to Mother and cried, 'Just look! Franz's father bought me a little cake.' Of course Mother immediately said, 'Now, look, Marianne, you must understand that Franz's father is *your* father, too!' "[48]

The anecdote points out the general loneliness Emma felt in Zürich. Because she was heiress to a great fortune, the Jungs were admitted to the highest social class, but his profession set them apart from the businessmen and professional men who composed it. Emma made few women friends because most of their wives were more interested in Jung's professional services than in inviting him and Emma to dinners where their husbands would have nothing to say to "the quack mind doctor."[49] Carl's profession was a barrier that did set him and Emma apart from couples she would normally have gravitated to for friendship, but she found them as boring as he did. He spoke for them both when he told how he "recoiled from these people who are not supported by a main work. . . . I could never linger with others' stupid stories. I stormed right over them because I had before me the vision others didn't see. I might have offended countless people [as] I stormed on."[50] So Emma only entertained those who interested "C. G." (as nearly everyone now addressed him, both English and German speakers pronouncing it in German, as "say gay"). She never visited friends of her parents or their grown children who might have become her friends. All her entertaining at home was for persons who would never have crossed the doorstep of her family's house in Schaffhausen.

Emma learned to be a gracious hostess to all sorts of people. These included the likes of Albert Einstein, to whom she served several dinners that he ate mostly in silence.[51] Jung thought Einstein "was not a man whose thoughts radiated from him. . . . [He was] like a musician who can be a listless guy, but then — when he makes music, you can see that he himself is the music and therein lies his greatness!" Although they had empathy for each other, it was not of a sort that invited camaraderie: "Einstein was his thoughts; his thoughts were Einstein. He rode off into his mathematical reflections like in Noah's Ark, and that's what happened with me, too."[52]

Otherwise, Emma and Carl's socializing became limited to the small group of people who were interested in psychology and analytic theory and technique, and who usually met weekly in the Jung home. These included the Maeders, Riklins, Kellers, Sigg-Böddinghauses, Maria Moltzer, Oskar Pfister, and a changing group of doctors who were on staff or associated with the Burghölzli. Sometime around 1910, Bleuler began to hold meetings of what was loosely referred to as the "study group for doctors interested in Freudian ideas." By 1912 his original hesitations became so strong that he withdrew and Jung took over by default. By mid-1913, those named above formed the nucleus of a changing group that included a fair contingent of women who ranged from "a Zürichberg woman obsessed with Jung"[53] to practicing analysts, such as Moltzer and Sigg-Böddinghaus, unmarried working women, such as the young refugee journalist Aline Valangin,[54] and dissatisfied wives, such as Tina Keller, who was about to begin medical studies to qualify as a doctor. In the early years of these group meetings, Emma always sat quietly on the fringe, but the women remembered how closely she observed them as they contributed their opinions or contradicted the men's. Tina Keller thought Emma had "a great heart and a fine intuition" and made a silent prediction to herself that she would someday become an excellent analyst. As for Jung, Frau Keller was frequently "repelled" by him because when others offered their views, "he could be so sarcastic. He made fun of people in an unfeeling way."[55]

BEFORE THE advent of Toni Wolff into her husband's and, by extension, her own life, Emma welcomed her mother and sister to Küsnacht on a fairly regular basis. Now, because she never knew when Toni would be there, Emma tried to limit them to ceremonial occasions such as special Sunday luncheons or birthday celebrations. She still took her children for long summer vacations in Schaffhausen, but as of 1914 even these visits were causes for anxiety and embarrassment.

Jung usually joined his family on long weekends, sometimes for an entire week or two before and after his military service. He began to play his games at the Ölberg as well, but they were different from the lakeside building games. Instead, he oversaw his and the Homberger children in games of "Indians against the English," wearing a souvenir Royal Canadian Mounted Policeman's hat and cowboy boots bought in the United States.[56] Frau Rauschenbach still kept a carriage and several horses, so each side recruited one of the big placid animals to stand guard outside the tents, which they pretended were teepees. The side that first stole the other side's horse was declared the winner, and when his side won, Jung whooped and roared to the consternation of his wife, her mother, and her disapproving sister and brother-in-law. Frau Rauschenbach was probably the only person who dared to challenge Jung, so when he showed the children how to dig tunnels large enough for them to crawl through, she called a firm halt to the games for fear that someone would be buried alive. The children went on to other amusements, but the chastised and miffed Jung retreated to a bedroom to sulk.

When the Jung children were of the age to begin their own socializing, they were somewhat set apart from others like them. Little girls were allowed to invite the Jung daughters to their homes after school, but they were not allowed to go to the Jung house, except for special occasions such as birthday parties. If the daughters were invited to parties, balls, and other formal or semi-formal functions, it was usually out of respect for Emma's fortune. Other parents did not encourage further closeness, because they were leery of Jung's profession. "All those foreigners, those strange American zombies staying in the [Hotel] Sonne, wandering the lakefront; that rich woman in the [Hotel] Baur au Lac; that club where they all practiced strange rituals — well, we just stayed away from all that," said one parent, speaking for them all.[57] As late as the 1960s, a grandson in graduate study at the University of Zürich recalled how a young woman from a good family was forbidden by her parents to invite him to Sunday lunch because of his recently deceased grandfather's "reputation" in the town.[58] Socially, Emma Jung had to deal with this sort of opprobrium all her life, but she conveyed such a sense of self-confidence that her children and grandchildren copied it and exuded it as well. Jung laughed when he overheard the five-year-old Marianne playing with dolls in the garden congratulate them for living with the "majesty Jungs"; and when he learned that his daughter Gret's son Dieter Baumann (also at the age of five) told his great-grandmother Rauschenbach she could not scold him because "you can't scold God[s] — that is child psychology!"[59] Like their grandparents, the children and grandchildren lived their lives on their own terms in the encapsulated bubble that still is Zürich today.

C. G. AND Emma Jung were better off financially in 1914 than they had been at any previous time in their marriage. The money caused another shift in their relationship because the balance of power became more equally shared. Despite his insistence that he was incapable of adult activity, Jung's practice grew to the point where he was earning a substantial income from patients. Many still came from Zürich, but clients from the United States and the British Isles were arriving as well. After Medill McCormick, his next American patient was the prominent American journalist and writer Elizabeth Shepley Sergeant, who had first been hospitalized briefly at the Burghölzli in 1904.[60] Thanks to her praise and McCormick's, other wealthy Americans followed and became regular annual clients. Analysands who came from England were initially recommended by David and Edith Eder, the medical doctor and his wife who were among Jung's earliest translators.[61] Edith went to Zürich for analysis, and Dr. Constance Long followed her example.[62] Others made the trek when they heard the distinguished British physician Dr. William McDougall make a public pronouncement that he was so impressed with Jung's psychology that he planned to be analyzed by him.

Ever since he married Emma, Jung had never had to think about money, so when he began to make a significant amount on his own, he had little interest except for the security it gave to know that he was, if not an equal partner, at least a solid contributor. Emma continued to pay for all the household expenses, but she kept Jung's bank accounts healthy by letting her own financial managers oversee their steady growth.

AND SO, on the one hand, the break with Freud had actually produced public and professional stability and a firm personal foundation that should have been deeply satisfying to a man of C. G. Jung's age and station. He had the "perfect" wife, as Emma was described by everyone who knew her; five healthy and beautiful children, all in awe of him; a substantial house that attested to his professional success; and a practice that was growing faster than he could keep up with it. On the other hand, he was riven by deep private uncertainty.

Many years later, reflecting on the period from 1913 to 1915, Jung described these years in which he pursued "the inner images" as the most important time of his life. "Everything else can be derived from it," he insisted. "My whole life consisted of reappraising what had broken free of the unconscious back then and flooded me like a mysterious stream and threatened to destroy me." The problem now was how to integrate all this amorphous "material," which he knew even then was "more than enough for just one lifetime."

The "outward classification, the scientific processing, and the integration into life" were certainly rewarding; they soothed and comforted the tortured man who needed a mantra of the facts of his life to keep himself rooted to reality — that he was a medical doctor who lived at 228 Seestrasse, was married, and had fathered five children. He recognized even as he was living these years that they were the "numinous beginning" that "contained everything." He had a premonition that there was enough raw material in them to engage if not consume him for the rest of his life.

———∞∞∞———

CHAPTER 18

"Psychologically Minded" Persons

In 1925, Jung gave a series of talks with an overtly biographical content that were published many years later as the book *Analytical Psychology*. His talks, often extemporaneous and highly personal,[1] told of the years of creative foment that followed the publication of *Symbols* and the break with Freud. He recalled "a particularly lucid moment"[2] sometime around 1915, when he perceived that he did indeed have the answer to the questions he had scrawled at the end of the manuscript. Writing the book gave him the "key" to comparative mythology, and henceforth he could use its "power to unlock all doors" in psychoanalysis.

But at that point he remembered stopping short and asking himself, what would be the point, what would he really accomplish? He had already written a book about the myth of the hero and, by extension, the myths of past societies and cultures. He had already questioned whether or not his own had its particular myth and decided it did not. Most of all, by writing that book he was forced to admit that neither he nor anyone else truly understood the workings of the unconscious. "Around these reflections," he wrote, "as around a central core, grew all the ideas that came to partial expression in the book on types."

The research eventually coalesced into the 1921 book *Psychological Types*,[3] an examination of personality as an attempt to explain how consciousness operates within different people. Jung's starting point was with insights gleaned from his own patients that he applied to all of history, beginning with classical thought, ranging through medieval society to romanticism, and ending with what was for him the contemporary era, as exemplified by the philosophy of William James and works by Carl Spitteler, Friedrich Schiller, and Goethe. Jung divided personality into two basic groups, coining the terms "introvert" and "extravert" to describe them. According to his system, the introvert sees the world in terms of his own situation within it, whereas the extravert defines himself in terms of what is happening in the world around him. To these two basic ways of perceiving the world, Jung added four basic functions that can be found in differing combinations within both types: thinking, feeling, sensation, and intuition. He added a further division within the four functions, the rational pair of thinking and feeling, and the irrational pair of sensation and intuition. Such divisions and pairings gave Jung the model for how an individual both situated and adjusted himself or herself toward both the inner self and the external world. The book shows his extraordinary erudition, as he ranged through detailed analyses of — to name only some — comparative religion, philosophy, educational theory, literature, biography, and psychology.

Jung's interest in how one's personality type affects one's being in the world was but one of many ideas that grew to expression around 1915, when Zürich became the fixed center where he formulated and disseminated the "technique"[4] he now referred to more and more frequently as "analytical" psychology. Zürich had become the destination for all manner of people interested in his psychology, and these were the years when the confluence of people with place occasioned the historical moment in which it became both founded and grounded, as the book on *Types* so clearly demonstrated. This period of Jung's personal history has become the subject of both contradictory and controversial analysis, as critics and partisans have used the same generally available biographical information to interpret it in widely differing ways.[5]

To take but one example, descriptions of Jung's mental state veer from the oxymoronic "creative illness"[6] to the vague "'fallow,' inactive, empty" to the stridently dogmatic "years of psychic disturbance, even psychosis."[7] Both the inner workings of Jung's mind and his external life have been described as "deep introversion and disorientation,"[8] or, at the opposite end of the emotional spectrum, as "constructively engaged and surely in [self-]control." Varying degrees of absolute truth lie in all these depictions, but like most explanations of character and personality, fact and event, some have more validity than others.

One way to assess these persistent criticisms is to consider several areas of Jung's professional activity: first, his roster of patients, that is, the stature and situation of those who sought his counsel; then, his own speaking and writing, both its quantity and quality; and lastly, how everything coalesced in the founding of that curious entity — anomaly, perhaps — the Psychological Club of Zürich, which from this time onward played such a large role in Jung's life.

IF FREUD expected (or even hoped) that the Zürich Psychoanalytical Association would dissolve into fractious fragments after he denounced Jung, he was mistaken. If anything, the Swiss contingent became stronger, better organized, and more determined to follow the original bent of analytic inquiry that they believed Freud had forbidden. When they read his *History of Psychoanalysis*, they could not accept his decree that he was the sole originator and final authority for all doctrinal pronouncements in the field. These independent-minded psychiatrists could trace their group's origin to late 1911, when Bleuler called an informal gathering in the Burghölzli and they began to meet on a fairly regular basis to study all theory, not just Freud's. The Zürich Psychoanalytical Association was formed in early 1912, when they demonstrated their independence by separating not only from the Burghölzli but also from the University of Zürich. By the time they rejected Freud's authority in 1914, they were, in a sense, removing themselves from the possibility of having to accept Jung's leadership as well.

Freud, who kept a sharp eye and keen ear attuned to news from Zürich, found his own work "at a standstill" in 1915 mainly because of worry about his sons in the Austrian army. His own private war against Jung consisted of exchanging news of Swiss allegiances and defections with his several devoted correspondents. With his usual droll humor, Freud shared Abraham's view that the war had brought one real benefit to his life, no "unpleasant discussions with the Swiss."[9] He told Ernest Jones that he was "in no mood to accommodate the vacillators and half-hearted," and he denounced the Swiss reputation for financial acumen by saying that, Jung excepted, as soon as they realized there was no money to be made in psychoanalysis during wartime, they would "direct their work elsewhere."[10] Several months later, Pfister brought temporary solace to Freud's otherwise gloomy isolation by "drawing closer to [him]" when he enlisted into Freud's ranks another analyst disgruntled with Jung, Dr. Max Nachmannsohn.[11]

Overall however, Freud remained pessimistic, telling Jones, "What Jung and Adler left intact of the movement is now perishing in the strife among nations."[12] Jones continued to try to cheer Freud, bombarding him with letters written "tirelessly in his old tone." When he learned that Dr. Constance Long, one of Jung's most fervent English supporters, was to write a section of a forthcoming textbook, he wangled an assignment for himself in the same volume, intending "to discredit [Dr. Long] successfully."[13] When Brill began to express differences with other "Jungians," Freud told Abraham that Brill "hopes we shall win."[14] It seems to have been a one-sided war, with Freud aiming fusillades while Jung was hunkered down behind the neutral barricade of Swiss isolation, with neither allies in Zürich nor correspondents elsewhere to give him news of Freud — should he have wanted any.

PSYCHOTHERAPY IN early 1916 in Vienna may have been "perishing in the strife among nations," but that was hardly the case in Zürich.[15] For the past several years, a group of psychiatrists who were members of the IPA but who had also organized themselves into a loosely affiliated association had met independently of the IPA on Wednesday evenings in rotating Küsnacht homes, frequently Jung's. If this group had a real leader, it was Franz Beda Riklin, who was instrumental in convening it. Jung attended not only because he wanted a sounding board for his own ideas but also because he wanted to know what the others were thinking. Even though he did much to keep the group alive, neither he nor Riklin had formal leadership status, as the other doctors took their own ideas quite seriously and wanted equal time to debate them. Theoretical differences resulted in a fluctuating membership, and there was some intermingling with and occasional desertion to another *Verein* (association) that began to meet on Thursday evenings sometime in early 1912 in Zürich's restaurant Seidenhof.[16] Eventually, through an informal osmosis, these two groups melded into one, even though the psychologists who lived in or near Küsnacht continued to hold the Wednesday meetings awhile longer. On January 30, 1914, all the doctors consented to form a single group that would allow selected laypersons to join as "associated members." The first deemed worthy were Toni Wolff and Maria Moltzer.

Interestingly, the impetus to form this *Verein* came not from the medical doctors but from former patients who wanted a forum in which to air their own concerns as well as to become better educated about psychoanalysis. The doctors decided that the only criterion for admission of laypersons would be prior analysis, so the initial membership soon comprised three categories: about twenty or so physicians, the two lay analysts, and laypersons who had been or were still patients of the first two. Jung, who did not attend this group's meetings until October, thought it "interesting from the standpoint of the question of the social application of ΨA education."[17] Thus, the group seems to have adhered to the primary role originally defined for psychoanalysis in Switzerland: to educate people to lead more fulfilling lives. The emphasis was not on curing various forms of mental illness but rather on helping ordinary persons to function at a higher level of adaptation to and contentment with their lives — what Jung would eventually call the process of individuation.[18]

That January, Franz Beda Riklin was named the first chairperson, and formal meetings were held every two weeks. On October 30, 1914, following the Zürich chapter's withdrawal from the IPA because of Freud's dictatorial policies, Professor O. Messmer suggested that the combined "Küsnacht-Seidenhof" group should constitute itself formally under a more accurately descriptive name, the *Verein für analytische Psychologie* (Association for Analytical Psychology). At first glance, it seems curious that a group that insisted upon freedom from dogmatically imposed leadership should elect Jung the first president, but he had not yet defined a theory or technique that threatened the other independent thinkers.[19] He may have been considered first among equals in Zürich because of his earlier association with Freud, but like the other doctors, he was also searching for more theoretical sustenance and satisfaction than Freud had given to any of them.

BESIDES MARIA Moltzer and Toni Wolff, both of whom were now seriously engaged in their own private analytic practices, the persons who congregated to this new group were an interesting lot who came to figure in Jung's life in varying degrees and times from then on. One of Toni Wolff's first analysands was her sister Susanna, called Susi, a dynamic, outspoken woman who considered herself a "liberated feminist"[20] years before the term was defined. Toni introduced her sister to Hans Trüb, a young doctor from Aarau who analyzed with both her and Jung and became an analyst because of the experience. He and Susi married in 1915, following his graduation from the University of Zürich medical school. Trüb chose the Burghölzli for dissertation research he wished to base on Jung's association tests, but more specifically because he wanted to work under Jung's direct supervision. Even though Jung had no official status in the Burghölzli, he collaborated frequently with staff doctors or visiting physicians, even participating in some of their experimental studies (yet another indication that the years 1914 to 1919 were more productive than he admitted later in life). Susi and Hans Trüb soon became fixtures in Jung's psychological firmament and close friends of Emma's as well. When the five Trüb children were born, both Jungs became godparents to several.

The prim, ascetic Maria Moltzer had a private practice in the tidy Zürich apartment where she lived, still exhibiting nothing in her demeanor or surroundings to suggest that she was a principal heiress to the Bols liquor fortune. Most persons in her professional circle were totally unaware of the great wealth she could have commanded, because she also supervised Burghölzli students for pay and worked for Jung from time to time, which people thought she did because she needed the money.[21] By this time in their lives, their relationship was strictly professional and often prickly. Moltzer was a shadowy figure about whom not much is known[22] but who was often heard complaining about how difficult it was for a woman "to get a grounding as an analyst in Zürich" and how her particular difficulty was compounded because she was Dutch, and the Swiss were reluctant to consult a foreigner.[23] Moltzer's feeling of not being fully accepted was one of several festering resentments in her life and work that erupted a decade later. She eventually found it impossible to remain in Zürich and returned to Holland to live and practice for the remainder of her life.

Moltzer usually worked for Jung when he was away from home, answering his correspondence and taking sessions with his patients.[24] One whom he turned over to her around 1913 who remained for years and became her most devoted client and close friend was the thirty-nine-year-old American Fanny Bowditch (later Katz, after her marriage at the age of forty-two to the Dutch psychologist Rudolph Katz). Rudy Katz was younger than his virginal wife, sexually sophisticated, and wildly promiscuous, and his subsequent behavior ensured that the marriage became the prime topic of their therapy with Moltzer (for both husband and wife were her patients).

Bowditch Katz (as she is usually called) was the daughter of Henry Pickering Bowditch, the respected physiologist and great friend of William James.[25] Fanny was thirty-nine when her father died in 1911. She became suicidal, obsessed by fear that her girlhood was ended, and diagnosed as suffering from anxiety and depression.[26] Her "Cousin Jim,"[27] Jung's American ally James Jackson Putnam, sent her to Zürich. Jung thought he "aroused [negative] resistances"[28] and passed Fanny Bowditch along to Moltzer, who he thought did not.

The change was successful, for Bowditch Katz basked in the attention Moltzer gave, convinced that she "had never given [it to] any other patient."[29] From time to time, Bowditch Katz still consulted Jung, but always with a sharply critical eye for his foibles and failings. The diaries she kept of their meetings (as well as of hers with Moltzer) provide fascinating insights into the actions and interactions of those who participated in the formulation of analytical psychology in its early years.

No boundaries had yet been defined; there were no rules, no standards of behavior. Therapists were often teachers, friends, or lovers of their patients;[30] socializing and entertainment often existed in tandem with therapeutic treatment; massive egos frequently collided, as theoreticians sought dominance for pet theories and sometimes even pet analysands. It was a heady time, with everything new and in flux for those involved in trying to make order and sense of the new mind doctors and their talking cures. Zürich may have been "the tense and often claustrophobic dead center of the war in Europe . . . a virtual container, neatly sealed off and protected from all the turmoil,"[31] but everyone felt so very modern, and it was, indeed, a grand time to be alive.

OF THE Zürich contingent that had earlier followed Freud, most clustered loyally around Jung during this period. Among the better known were Riklin, still vacillating between art and psychoanalysis but until 1920 tending more toward the latter than the former. After the Zürich chapter resigned from the IPA, he actually became better organized as an administrator than he had ever been during his years as secretary. Alphons Maeder, one of Jung's staunchest supporters when he broke with Freud, became one of the new association's most respected members; "revered by his patients . . . radiating a warmth nearly unheard of for a psychiatrist . . . [he] thawed even Jung."[32] Several couples joined the initial stalwarts: Pastor Adolf Keller and his wife, Tina,[33] who was about to begin medical studies to prepare for a career in psychoanalysis, and Hermann Sigg-Böddinghaus, a wealthy businessman and personal friend of the Jungs, as was his new wife, the analyst Martha Sigg-Böddinghaus. Fräulein Ida Teuscher,[34] a young woman barely twenty who had already had several years of analysis, became such a willing and indispensable worker that she moved quickly into the small inner circle of the governing committee that included Emma Jung and Toni Wolff but — noticeably — not Maria Moltzer, who resented it. With her feelings of exclusion on other fronts already festering, Moltzer thought this was yet another in the long line of rebuffs she claimed were her lot in Switzerland.

There was a glut of doctors in Zürich, a greater number proportionally than in other Swiss cities, because many who were educated at the superb medical faculty of the university and trained in the internationally renowned Burghölzli remained afterward to establish practices. Hans Trüb was one, as was the Hungarian Herbert Oczeret, whose wife, Irma, also practiced sporadically as an analyst. Through them both, a fairly large contingent of patients entered Jung's sphere.

Among Oczeret's was Aline Valangin,[35] a young Alsatian woman who had come to Zürich shortly before the war as governess to a wealthy widowed factory owner's two small daughters. Once fighting began, she was unable to return to her homeland and stayed on as a refugee. The widower fell in love and, after first proposing an affair she rebuffed, offered marriage. But Valangin had met someone closer to her own age whom she liked better, the Jewish refugee Vladimir Rosenbaum, whose father had fled Russian pogroms and who was just beginning what seemed destined to be a brilliant legal career. Valangin consulted Oczeret because of indecision over whether to choose the older man of great wealth or the young pauper to whom she was attracted. Thus, she became another of Oczeret's "harem" patients, for he was "an interesting and handsome man" who surrounded himself with "a bevy of women," some of whom knew him "not only as their teacher but also as their lover."[36]

Some of his patients who were active in the avant-garde art scene in Zürich were initially attracted to Jung and the newly formed analytic association. These included Suzanne Perrottet, the director of Rudolf von Laban's dance school, and Max Pfister, who later became famous as master dancer with the Berlin Opera under the name of Max Terpis. But like many other members of Zürich's artistic community,[37] they soon came to the conclusion that, although Jung's ideas were interesting, other interpretations, particularly of sexuality, were more relevant to their lives. Ironically in light of how subsequent generations of the artistic world were attracted to Jung's psychology, many in Zürich's artistic community drifted away during the early years because they found the lectures given by him and others boring and incomprehensible, and because they were put off by the stolid bourgeois burghers who attended the *Verein* meetings in glum and dour silence.

LIKE VLADIMIR Rosenbaum, Emilii Medtner[38] (1872–1936) was a Russian émigré, but for psychological reasons rather than religious persecution. His wealthy family was originally of German origin but had been in Russia for several generations. His businessman father, director of the best Moscow lace factory, regretted that he had not pursued an artistic career; his mother was descended from a musical family active in the German Court Theater of St. Petersburg and the Moscow Conservatory. All the Medtner children inherited musical talent. Emilii's younger brother was the composer Nicolai Medtner, on whom he had a lifelong "fixation," claiming that he "sacrificed" his own dreams of becoming a conductor in order to manage his brother's career.[39] As a young man, Emilii Medtner developed symptoms of "pseudo-Ménière's disease in the form of nausea, vertigo, and noise in the ears," which kept him in and out of therapy from then on.

By 1914, when he was forty-two and consulting Jung, besides being the erstwhile manager of his brother's musical career, he was a central figure in the early-twentieth-century Russian symbolist movement, which he attempted to align with the German legacy of Kant, Goethe, Nietzsche, and Wagner. He was a founder of the respected Moscow publishing firm Musagetes; the author of a study of Goethe; a follower of Rudolf Steiner; and a devotee of the Russian novelist Andrei Bely. For a brief period, he was a patient of Freud's, because in each of his incarnations, he had exhibited varying degrees of psychological distress that often left him physically incapacitated.

Even while declaring himself profoundly Russian, Medtner was deeply attached to all things German. He was in Munich when World War I began and was deported three days later "under circumstances that were extremely humiliating for such a Germanophile."[40] As he was unable to return to Russia, he went to neutral Switzerland, intending to live in Zürich. The Munich expulsion so unhinged him that he sought psychiatric attention from Eugen Bleuler, who gave him a list of names headed by Jung's.

Jung accepted Medtner with alacrity, and from that time on, many people, including his wife, Emma, made a recurring observation: that the ideas a patient brought to Jung were far more interesting than the actual person.[41] Medtner seems to prove their contention, as Jung saw him eagerly every weekday and often invited him for tea or dinner on the weekend. The patient was equally delighted with their rapport, finding in his analyst "a kindred Symbolist current of thought."[42] Medtner was also convinced that Jung shared the rabid anti-Semitic sentiments he expressed during sessions when he guided their discussions into what he euphemistically called the "racial question," but his is the only version of what they said, and much of what he ascribes to Jung is without substance.[43]

By early October the camaraderie was such that Medtner considered their sessions a "joint research project." What convinced him that his status was special was the difference between the way Jung and Freud analyzed (as has been discussed earlier): in Medtner's sessions with Freud, Freud sat out of sight, quietly listening; in those with Jung, they faced each other in "a non-authoritarian, give-and-take relationship."[44] Much of their discussion centered around concepts of the typologies Jung was formulating at the time. Words such as "introvert" and "extravert," and "functions" such as "thinking" and "feeling" dot the detailed journals Medtner kept. According to the conversational exchanges he recorded, Medtner does not seem to have contributed any original ideas but merely recorded Jung's developing thoughts as they pertained to his (Medtner's) specific personal trauma. Medtner reports Jung's diagnosis, that he shared a "national conflict" similar to that of many Americans who were of English descent; that is, that Medtner's German heritage kept him from being able to assume a totally Russian identity.

Medtner gave himself high praise, however, when he wrote that Jung was so impressed by his "experience of the identity between inner and external reality" that Jung declared him "the most modern person" he had ever met.[45] Medtner so ingratiated himself with Carl and Emma Jung that he became one of the few persons this exceedingly formal couple permitted to address them with the familiar *du*. The "Russian Mephisto," as his biographer later dubbed him, soon became a constant, important presence in the Zürich analytic community and an intimate among the men who formed Jung's inner circle and were for varying periods of time his devoted friends as well as followers.

Among the men Jung saw during these years was his school friend Albert Oeri, mostly when Oeri came to Zürich from Basel, where he was now one of Switzerland's most distinguished and respected journalists. They liked to sail alone together in Jung's boat, taking turns reading passages aloud from the *Odyssey*, particularly the "Nekyia," when Odysseus sojourns in Hades, the land of the dead. As old friends of long standing, they found it easier to center their conversations around literature rather than around the two topics that interested each man most and the other not much at all and that made for awkward pauses: politics for Oeri, particularly the war and how it affected Switzerland's moral and economic position in Europe; psychological typologies for Jung and how they determined an individual's relationship to society. Medtner yearned to join them on the lake, but his severe vertigo induced seasickness, so he had to be content with reports furnished by the several other companions who shared Jung's analytic interests and were sometimes invited to sail. These included Jung's new friend, his dentist and analysand, Siegmund Hurwitz,[46] who was also an authority on Jewish mysticism; and, a few years later, the chemistry professor at the ETH, Hans Eduard Fierz. Medtner stayed on land and became not only a personal friend of Emma Jung but an analysand of Maria Moltzer, for by this time Jung had formulated the view that it was useful for a patient to be analyzed concurrently by both a man and a woman.[47] Later, Medtner was analyzed briefly by Toni Wolff, but despite his insistence that an "erotic current" flowed through their relationship, she was not impressed, and their sessions ended by mutual consent.[48]

THERE WAS a growing group of "psychologically minded"[49] persons who began to gather socially around Carl and Emma Jung, many of whom had been or were still his patients. It was not unusual for someone who had been in Jung's office during the afternoon to return to his drawing room for one of the evening receptions he and Emma now held several times each month. Medtner dubbed this group a "psychological sect" and thought its informality was "much more 'reasonable'" than Rudolf Steiner's tightly organized and rigidly defined anthroposophy, which Medtner had observed in the *Goetheanum*, the remarkable wooden building that Steiner designed and built in Dornach, Switzerland.[50]

In retrospect, the interpersonal dynamics of the attendees at the Jungs' home become fascinating. Only Carl, Emma, and Toni knew that theirs had become a triangular relationship, so when the three were together in the company of others, they were careful to behave like a happily married couple and their most trusted professional associate. But there were other triangular relationships in this group, some better known than others, and all were received more with curiosity than condemnation. Jung had two male patients who remained with him for years because they wanted to discuss their (in one instance) "single long-lasting extramarital relationship" and (in the other) "multiple meaningful infidelities."[51] In the course of time, when Carl's true relationship with Toni became a matter of public speculation and gossip, the main topics these two men introduced into their therapeutic sessions became their lovers and tips on how to cope with their unhappy and exasperated wives. Both men were perplexed because they told everything to Jung and he said next to nothing.

Women, too, were not immune to extramarital entanglements. Susi Trüb-Wolff did not hide an affair with Medtner that lasted for several years; nor did she make much effort to control speculation about her other numerous "friendships."[52] Linda Fierz-David, the wife of Jung's "witty, charming, and handsome friend" Hans Fierz,[53] originally entered therapy because her husband's cousin was "something like a second husband to her."[54] But as soon as she consulted Jung, the cousin "faded into the background" and Jung became the object of her admiration.[55] The entire Fierz family became closely aligned with the Jung family for the rest of their lives, but Linda started the process by training to become an analyst.

She was a remarkable woman, much like Toni Wolff, who became her fast friend.[56] Born Linda David in Basel in 1891, she was the first woman admitted to the university there. Her father was a politician who thought he was a poet, and her mother's background was as exotic as her interests: the daughter of a Galician Jew from Cracow and a Croatian countess, she loved Tarot, fine clothing, and expensive jewelry in equal part. Linda was very much like her mother, an elegant dresser who favored exotic fabrics and colors not usually worn by the good gray matrons of Zürich. She surrounded herself in her well-appointed home with beautiful objects, read extensively about mythology, collected rare and obscure books and manuscripts, and shared the pervading local interest in the histories of other cultures and societies.

Toni and Linda were representative of most of the women who came to the Jung receptions. The primary status of most may have been as adjuncts of their husbands, but they all were intelligent and in the course of time found ways to use that intelligence. Lena Hurwitz-Eisner, for example, the wife of the Jung family's dentist, Dr. Siegmund Hurwitz, became one of the editors of the German edition of Jung's *Collected Works*. Even the flighty Susi Trüb, who had begun analysis with Maria Moltzer, switched to Riklin, whom she felt gave her better instruction in psychology and encouraged her "intellectual affinities."[57]

All these women liked Emma Jung and showed her great respect and deference, mostly because of her husband but increasingly because they valued her comments in their conversations. Gradually, their main topic became the historical situation of woman, her problems and circumstances. A "small circle of seven"[58] gradually evolved, one that lasted for the better part of the next decade. The women had no official leader, but they assigned topics of mutual interest, did research, and made formal reports. In the beginning the circle consisted of Emma Jung, Toni Wolff, Susi Trüb, Lena Hurwitz-Eisner, Tina Keller, and Martha Sigg-Böddinghaus. Linda Fierz-David was the last to join when she moved to Zürich several years later. Maria Moltzer knew about this informal group and probably could have become part of it, but whether her shyness or her preference for the company of the male analysts who surrounded Jung kept her from doing so remains a matter of conjecture. However, in her mind, exclusion from the group became yet another of the real or imagined snubs and insults that she steadily accreted.

Despite Leonhard Seif's contention that he analyzed her earlier, Emma began her first real analysis with Hans Trüb. She and Trüb discovered they had many interests in common besides psychology, and a deep platonic and intellectual friendship formed between them. From accounts left by the principals,[59] it seems to have been centered more around Emma's literary and philosophical education than around her mental health or psychological attitudes. In those years, Trüb was one of Jung's brightest and most devoted students, and Emma certainly used him as explicator of and sounding board for her husband's ideas. Trüb was also her guide into the Grail legends and her fleeting interest in modern European literature. He urged her to read Tolstoi, Pushkin, and Dostoyevsky, but after a brief foray into *Anna Karenina*, Emma admitted that she preferred mythology. She was working hard to educate herself in her husband's interests, not only because of her genuine interest but also because she was deeply confused about Toni Wolff and the central role she was assuming in the life of the entire Jung family.

In short, Toni was "always there"[60] — in Emma's house and in her life. She came to all the receptions and the smaller informal gatherings, which usually consisted of a talk followed by a casual supper. Each Sunday she was the only guest at luncheons which had hitherto been sacrosanct family occasions. The children were taught to call her "Tante Toni," which they did innocently enough at first, but as they grew older, with sarcasm and derision. They resented how, after the meal ended, Toni would take coffee with C. G. (as he was now always addressed)[61] and Emma and then go off to walk about the grounds alone with him in pleasant weather or to his study on inclement days. Emma, her cheeks suffused with anger or shame, tried to appear busy about the household. If there was a lecture or reception elsewhere, it was taken for granted that C. G., Emma, and Toni would arrive and depart together and that the two women would be seated in positions and places that — if anyone was judging — could be deemed equal.

"It was hard for Emma in the beginning," Susi Trüb remembered.[62] "She tried very hard to accept and understand it, but it was so bewildering, so impossible really." It was difficult for everyone, C. G. included. His confusion about how to ensure that each woman received the same degree of respect and that they were treated equally was so overwhelming that one day while swimming in the lake, he thought the only solution was to stop trying to stay afloat and let himself drown. When he confessed this to Tina Keller, she was horrified and urged him never to consider suicide again because of the damage he would do to all those he left behind.[63]

Eventually, he told Emma that he could not treat Toni as anything less respectful than "his other wife."[64] He had known from the first moment Toni entered his consulting room that there was some frisson between them,[65] and he described how he tried to send her away permanently after a brief period of analysis because he did not want to involve her in a relationship that would preclude her having a satisfying personal life. But Toni refused to go away completely; she came to every public occasion where Jung was present, always with "a dark and sad impression" about her. Soon, her natural untrained affinity for Jung's emerging vision of psychoanalysis became apparent to them both, and soon after that, they were constantly together.[66]

Citing the Wolff family's distinguished history and Toni's widowed mother's high social position, Jung told Emma he would not inflict opprobrium or humiliation on her or her family. Despite Emma's emotional distress, it all made sense to the practical-minded Rauschenbach heiress from Schaffhausen. She did not like her husband's decree that she must allow him to give Toni the same status and respect as he gave to her, but she had a horror of any private matter becoming public, so she agreed to keep her primary feelings of anger and disgust to herself for the time being, hoping his infatuation would soon end.[67] If this was the third time Emma tried to divorce Carl, she seems to have written about it only once and never to have spoken of it afterward. Shortly before her death, Emma told one of her analysands something she might well have accepted when she first attempted to cope with her husband's decree: "There are egos and egos and egos. The problem is to find the right one."[68]

As for Toni, there is no question that her mother colluded in her unorthodox affair, albeit with regret and resignation. "Did our mother know?" Susi Trüb asked herself. "Yes. Did it trouble her? Yes. But I think she was more troubled for Emma. She may have thought it was good for Toni to have a 'friend,' but I know how she felt about poor Emma. [There was] no easy answer for anyone!"

Because Toni lived in the relative protection of her mother's house, Carl was able to go there as a friend of the entire family without causing undue gossip. Soon he began to spend every Wednesday afternoon in the big house on the Freiestrasse. In the years when cars were still rare enough on Zürich streets that one could park almost anywhere, Jung parked his in plain sight directly in front of the house, for he was an invited guest for Frau Wolff's grand midweek luncheon, almost always staying on for a small private supper with her and Toni.[69] Frau Wolff employed an excellent cook, and the midweek meal was festive, an open house to which she invited her children and grandchildren as well as any friends who wished to join them. After lunch, Jung and Toni would spend the afternoon in her private rooms, later to join Frau Wolff for an aperitif before sharing the simple evening meal.

One of the grandchildren remembered how Jung held court during these meals: "[He] dominat[ed] the occasions by the authority of his presence, but not in any rude or domineering manner. He was, in a way, part of the family because he had friendships with the entire Wolff family."[70] Indeed, there was such an air of propriety connected with Jung's presence in the Wolff household that this same grandson was a medical student in the university before he realized what Toni and C. G.'s true relationship had been for many years. Reflecting the social attitude of the 1930s and 1940s, which was when he became aware of it, he said, "We would not have understood her relationship to Jung if we had known of it earlier, and if we had known, we could not possibly have approved of it. I think that is why they were so very respectful of their circumstances. No one ever spoke of it, so we could not compare it with anything, nor could we discuss it with anyone."

Meanwhile, Emma took all meals with her children, saw that they were settled after dinner, and then retreated to her rooms at the far end of the house to submerge herself in an intensive study of higher mathematics, philosophy, and Latin. It was at this time that everyone who met her remarked about her "quiet dignity" and how unsettling her "direct, unflinching gaze" could be.[71] One of Jung's unfaithful male patients confided to his journal that he went out of his way to avoid Emma when he went to the house because "she can see everything, that woman can. I would not want to be her husband."[72]

And so the three stumbled toward some sort of coexistence, constrained by a combination of their own needs and desires within the conjunction of their rigid social circumstances. Tina Keller, who had gone to Toni Wolff for analysis and became her close friend and admirer in the process, was aware of these tripartite "special circumstances," even though Toni never discussed it. Keller believed the "exceptional relationship" among the three developed only because of "the quality of the three persons involved . . . it was very different from an 'affair.' . . . There was responsibility, and a common task which was beyond but which included a love relationship."[73]

How long C. G., Emma, and Toni might have continued to stumble along in their private misery remains in the realm of conjecture, but with the founding of the Psychological Club, all three were provided with a public setting where they found a safe emotional outlet and an intellectual forum for their "common task,"[74] the formulation of analytical psychology.

EDITH ROCKEFELLER McCormick was the daughter of one of the richest men in the world and the wife of another, and Jung allegedly said "she thought she could buy everything."[75] She certainly tried as far as he was concerned, for she was a woman of strong principles, and if she wanted something or believed in someone, money was no object. Jung met Mrs. McCormick through her cousin by marriage Medill McCormick, who had been his patient in the Burghölzli in 1909 and whom he had treated occasionally for several years afterward.[76] Edith Rockefeller, the "Princess of Standard Oil" and daughter of John D. Sr., was married to Harold McCormick, the "Prince of International Harvester" and scion of the Chicago farm machinery family. Their marriage was "close but tumultuous . . . in many ways, a classic mismatch."[77] Harold was sociable and outgoing, a "peacemaker, a placator, a surface skimmer,"[78] very much a man's man, a Princeton graduate who thrived on competitive sport, physical activity, and male camaraderie. By 1915 he had had one year of intense analysis with Jung. They socialized just as intensely, sharing frequent motorcar excursions, hearty meals, and rigorous walking trips in the Swiss Alps.[79]

While Harold possessed a "first-class temperament and a second-rate intellect,"[80] Edith was exactly the opposite. Although she could be a gracious and extravagant society hostess when necessary, she preferred to be at home alone, immersed in the serious study of literature and philosophy. She became even more solitary and withdrawn after two of her five children died in infancy and shortly after she was diagnosed with tuberculosis of the kidney. Her recovery period was protracted and isolated, and she became depressed, reclusive, rigid, and afflicted with severe agoraphobia. She managed nonetheless to accompany her husband on a two-month tour of Hungary in the summer of 1910, as he sought new sites for his International Harvester factories. The strain of the trip left her exhausted, and her behavior was so erratic when she returned to Chicago that rumors circulated that she was in the midst of a serious mental breakdown. By 1912, she had broken with the Rockefeller family's staunch adherence to their fundamental Baptist faith and was frequenting spas and clinics in search of a cure for the many symptoms that her doctors, quacks or otherwise, generally lumped together under the catchall term "depression." Harold, who had grown up with two insane siblings,[81] knew Edith needed better medical attention than she was getting and asked Medill for help.

Jung was in and out of the McCormick family's lives during these years, mostly on his American trips, but he did not meet Edith until after the Fordham conference in 1912, when Medill asked him to evaluate her. Jung thought her "very much on the edge" and a "latent sch[izophrenic]." He considered his diagnosis confirmed when she presented one of her dreams, about a tree struck by lightning and split down the middle. Cautiously skirting Edith's emotional fragility, Jung suggested that she return to Zürich and begin treatment with him. In her typical flamboyant manner, albeit one complicated by genuine agoraphobia, she offered instead to buy him a large house near hers in Chicago, to pay whatever it cost to move his entire family there, and to support them all until he established his practice.[82] Actually, this was not such an unusual counteroffer when one considers that Edith wore a two-million-dollar pearl necklace to dine alone and built a forty-four-room mansion on Chicago's lakeshore, filled with a staggering number of priceless furnishings that were never unpacked and left to molder in a house she never occupied. Her grandiose offer was initially fascinating to C. G. but so frightening to Emma that she worried about it in letters to Freud. The plan never progressed beyond the realm of speculation and daydream during the brief period when Jung was enthralled by all things American.

Edith still considered Jung to be a professional whose services she engaged and who would therefore do her bidding. To impress this upon him, she took him to meet her father and see firsthand the wealth she commanded. Jung met John D. Rockefeller Sr. on October 20, 1912, at Kykuit, the family's Hudson Valley home. Jung did not like the old patriarch: lumping the Standard Oil Trust together with the Catholic Church, he decried the "thousands of decent human beings" who were "destroyed" by the former and "wiped out" by the latter.[83]

And so Edith remained in the United States and had several short periods of analysis with Jung until 1913, when he himself escorted her, some of her children, a retinue of retainers, and massive amounts of luggage on the journey from New York to Zürich.[84] He helped her settle into a suite at the Hotel Baur au Lac and introduced her to members of the local analytic milieu. By 1915, the rest of her family had joined her for various periods and also entered into different kinds of analysis. Her son, Fowler, was enrolled at Groton (and later at Princeton) and came for vacations. He had a few sessions with Maria Moltzer but mostly was "studying a little analysis and taking [short] walking trips" with Jung.[85] At Jung's suggestion, Edith engaged an Englishwoman who later became a founding member of the Psychological Club, Miss A. M. Richards, as governess to her sickly daughter Mathilde, who lived in a Davos sanatorium. At the time, Miss Richards and her sister Marguerit (who also lived in Zürich and was another founding member of the club) favored Riklin's approach, so Edith engaged Maria Moltzer (also at Jung's suggestion) to analyze her other daughter, Muriel, who stayed with her in the hotel when not in a Swiss boarding school.[86]

Edith, meanwhile, remained sequestered in her hotel suite, emerging only when she could not avoid her husband's entreaties for brief walks on the hotel grounds.[87] Knowing that Harold chafed at the lack of physical activity, Jung invited him on frequent short excursions, and in late August they took a long walking tour of the Engadine, covering ten to twenty miles each day. They were joined midway by Emma ("lovely and sympathetic and deeply in support of the Dr. and his work") and "Miss Wolff, an analyst who has been analyzed by him." Harold thought Jung "as nearly perfect to my mind as a man can be."[88] He appears to have been, as was Edith, entirely unaware of the true relationship among the three.

———

THE NATURALLY secretive Edith was fairly guarded about what happened within the analytic encounter when she wrote to her father, who seems to have had a genuine curiosity about the process equal to his unstated concern that his daughter and son-in-law might have fallen into the hands of a charlatan. John D. Sr. frequently inquired about what actually took place between analyst and patient, but Edith told him very little. The brash, outgoing Harold, however, confided details of the process to the man he always addressed in writing as "Dear Father." Although Harold's comments range from a vague grasp of analytical psychology to the impulsive praise of a proselytizer, his letters offer a window into Jung's analytical psychology as he was formulating it in the teens and early twenties.

On October 31, 1915, Harold wrote a twenty-six-page letter with a two-page addendum, trying to explain what exactly Jung was teaching him about himself. He began by saying analysis was difficult to talk or write about because it was "so strictly personal."[89] His own few experiences had made him aware of how easily the subject could be misunderstood or misinterpreted by those who had no experience of it or were prone to doubt its efficacy. Referring to Jung as "a visionary spirit," he said only when a person was keenly interested in the visionary's subject — as he was — could the principles of analytical psychology be grasped. Harold thought "so much of it has to be felt not in the way of 'faith,' but in the way of 'need.'"

Reflecting Jung's emerging thought about personality types, Harold noted "two general aspects" worth mention. The first was "scientific . . . the knowledge and observance of certain laws of life, of human nature, etc." His term for the other was "metaphysical or spiritual." The first aspect would be helpful in the daily life of a businessman or "an average socially healthy man." The second could be compared to a "'religious attitude' — entirely different in precept from 'religion' but of the same character" and of benefit to "the tired soul." He admitted that his two categories were "*very vague* and perhaps not even correct," but for him, they "really merge[d] into an attitude . . . towards life and things, and this attitude when *found* directs one's daily life in almost everything" (his emphasis). Two decades later, one of Jung's most perceptive commentators, Jolande Jacobi, would sum it up more succinctly by saying, "Apart from its medical aspect, Jungian psychotherapy is thus a system of education and spiritual guidance, an aid in the forming of the personality."[90]

Before analysis, Harold classified himself as among those businessmen who had been "more or less 'at one with themselves,'" and not among the "poor tired soul[s]" who "don't know themselves at all." He had not been particularly unhappy with his former self but thought his experience proved how much analysis "would *help* everyone."

Six months later, on June 15, 1916, and still proselytizing in a letter to his mother, Harold told the dour and disapproving Nettie Fowler McCormick that "analytical psychology *is* wonderful for Edith and me, and that is all we can or do say. *It works!*"[91] He did not mention the Psychological Club, which Edith had "founded and endowed on January 26, 1916." And Edith did not tell the formidable matriarch about it until she sent New Year's greetings for 1917.[92] Edith told Nettie she intended the "Psychological Club" to serve as a meeting place for "analyzed people." She sent a photograph of the impressive building she leased for two and a half years and, as if to forestall Nettie's disapproval, cautioned that "any new movement has a slow growth but [the club] assures lasting quality."

Edith McCormick was the sole financial contributor to the founding of the Psychological Club. In January, just before she signed the lease, she asked her father to increase her allowance because he had not done so since 1910.[93] As a forty-three-year-old woman who gave most of her money away and spent only a "sixth or seventh" on herself, she believed she needed more than the $3,250 she received each month. By July, he had not responded, so she sent a detailed letter outlining her annual expenditures. Her three major interests were the Memorial Institute for Infectious Diseases ($25,000), the Chicago Opera Company ($125,000), and the Psychological Club, to which she had just contributed $120,000 of her own money and $80,000 in bank loans.[94] The last left her deeply in debt, but for "a cause" such as the club, she had no qualms about "willingly" making further loans should they be needed: "The bankers are very nice with me and I expect no difficulties in paying off my debt in time." On August 15, 1916, a month after receiving this letter, Rockefeller instructed his lawyers to increase Edith's allowance by $500, for a total of $3,750 a month.

Freud heard the news from Oskar Pfister, whose allegiance was now so firmly his that he never joined the club. Freud told Ferenczi, "not without bitterness," that "Swiss ethics" had finally achieved its "sought-after contact with American money."[95]

ON FEBRUARY 11, 1916, the *Verein* members who had been meeting in the restaurant Seidenhof moved a little further down the street toward the *Hauptbahnhof* (the main railway station), into the first home of the Psychological Club, a grand house at Löwenstrasse 1.[96] Edith McCormick intended the imposing three-story stone building to "tend and promote Analytical Psychology as pure psychology, as well as for medical and educational purposes, and for the entire sphere of the sciences of the mind." Because she also wanted members to give each other "mutual support,"[97] she patterned the club along the lines of the better Anglo-American social clubs, where members could rent rooms, take meals, and have their needs met by a concierge and various supporting servants. There was no model for such a club in Zürich, and disagreements over what the Psychological Club should become were rife from the beginning.

Because she was a foreigner, Mrs. McCormick had to register the club with authorities of the Swiss government and make an official *Schenkungsurkunde*, or deed of gift, to a Swiss citizen, who could be held legally accountable.[98] She naturally chose Jung, whose name thus appeared on the official document that registered the transaction and who read it officially to the twenty-four women and sixteen men comprising the founding members.[99] At the next monthly meeting on March 11, they were joined by an additional fifteen persons, bringing the founding membership to fifty-five, where it hovered for the next several years.

Jung deliberately chose not to be a member of the *Vorstand* (governing committee), but Emma became the *Vorsitzende* (chairwoman) when Alphons Maeder refused. "All the strings will be in your [Jung's] hand," Maeder said. "Only what *you* want will be done; only what *you* say will be accepted."[100] The businessman Hermann Sigg-Böddinghaus was named treasurer, and Irma Oczeret secretary. Fräulein Ida Teuscher was made overseer of the clubhouse, a kind of housemother to the cook, three servants, and several workmen. Edith McCormick was a board member but without a more specific title than "owner." Neither Maria Moltzer nor Franz Riklin was chosen to hold office, which their many devoted followers saw as both a snub and a grab for power by Jung and his minions.

Grumbling about leadership was muted at first, but membership was contested from the beginning. A committee was formed to define eligibility that included medical doctors, medically trained analysts, lay analysts, and former patients of all three. Pfarrer Adolf Keller was named adjudicator because disagreement was so strong. At first, there were three categories: full members, hospitants (auditors), and statutory associates. The first two were limited to medical and lay analysts; the last was a category of guests who could not attend the annual meeting, vote on any motion, peruse the club's accounts, or attend the Christmas dinner. They were permitted to attend only selected lectures, functions, and excursions, and they paid a lesser fee than regular members. Prior analysis was always necessary. Eventually the by-laws were amended to admit those who had "a certain psychological attitude, which in principle [could] only be acquired through an analysis based on complex psychology." In other words, membership was largely ad hoc and decided on the basis of the applicant's perceived compatibility with current members, mostly a deeply introverted group forced by the physical setting of the club into unavoidable and often highly resented conviviality.

There were several large reception rooms in the grand old house, which was torn down several years later and replaced with a nondescript office building. Private rooms on the top floor were rented to some of the members who were in intense analysis and who flitted about in shadowy seclusion. On the floors below were a dining room, library, a billiard and games room, several smaller sitting rooms, and some even smaller rooms that were used by various analysts for therapy sessions. The large kitchen staff prepared and served three meals each day to club members who initially came to dine out of novelty but returned as regulars. Jung usually held Saturday morning therapy sessions in the club and often took meals or had tea with his patients afterward. He and Emilii Medtner, for example, often spent a weekend afternoon in a therapy room and followed it with late-afternoon tea.

Very soon the members rejected conviviality and reverted to their true introspection. Meals went uneaten, library publications unread, and the billiard table unused. Few came to the club on weekdays unless Jung was scheduled to give a seminar or read from his work in progress, the book on typologies. The committee planned parties, raffles, and other social events, all in the hope of attracting a steady stream of users of the facilities, but to little avail. By July 1916, only six months after Edith had endowed the club, it was in severe financial distress and an "extraordinary" meeting of the membership was convened to discuss how to save it. Edith again importuned her father, and the club was able to lurch along until October, when the membership was petitioned in writing to suggest ways to involve members in more frequent use of the facilities. About thirty replied, and they were almost equally divided into two groups.

The first wanted greater emphasis on intellectual activity, namely, more lectures, study groups, and opportunities to conduct what can only be described as group therapy sessions. They wanted to share their ideas about readings, discuss their dreams, and talk about approaches to the analytic encounter in so-called general terms but in reality to offer thinly disguised accounts of their own therapeutic process.

The second group wanted entertainment: more dances, especially masked balls; pantomimes; and other ways of acting out therapeutic experiences that were loosely based on rhythm and dance. They wanted music, both to perform and experience. They approved of the piano Edith rented and wanted her to provide even more musical instruments.

Some of what each group wanted was worked into the general program, but the club continued to show a deficit. Edith continued to meet it, to her father's horror and her bankers' chagrin. In June 1917, the house was sold to a new owner, who made it clear he had no intention of renewing the lease when it expired a year later. After much searching, a less expensive property was found in the quietly residential Hottingen section of Zürich, at Gemeindestrasse 27. Although it was purchased in October 1918, the club could not occupy it until September 1919 because a doctor who rented apartments on two floors refused to move until her lease expired. The club had to make do with a shabby five-room apartment at Bleicherweg 44 for a year, during which its lasting entity and identity were formed.

It became what Edith McCormick had intended all along: a meeting place for the dissemination of ideas and information about analytical psychology, and especially — and quite soon only — the ideas of C. G. Jung.

CHAPTER 19

"The Work of a Snob and a Mystic"

From the day the Psychological Club opened its door, the membership was enveloped in controversy. Minor rifts became major fractures, most notably over the constant financial crisis and differing views of how to solve it. Deep theoretical differences surfaced when analysts who held opposing views began to clamor for a greater share of the spoils because it meant enhancing their sphere of influence. Some jousted for mere consideration of their theories, while others were determined to settle for nothing less than supremacy. Friendships floundered while others dissolved in acrimony. Social divisions arose as well when most members found they could not afford to use the club because the restaurant and rooms were too expensive.[1]

Something had to be done to keep the members from resigning en masse, so the ever astute Emma used her influence as chairwoman to set the club on an even keel. She sent a *Rundbrief*, a circulating letter, asking all members for thoughts about how to save the club. Harold McCormick was the first to reply. On November 13, 1916, he read a position paper to the entire membership, all of whom had been directed to attend the meeting but had not been told why. Harold's views were so blunt that members demanded copies so they could study his paper privately before responding. Many shared his views, but as they were all but submerged by his rambling and discursive text, a clearer statement seemed to be needed.

Never one for brevity, Harold devoted most of the thirteen typed pages (whittled down from countless hand-written originals) of "The Welfare of the Psychology Club"[2] to urging support for a "community of idea[s]" over "individual" interests. To encourage members to use the facilities, he suggested four kinds of programs that would put aside "personal equation[s]" or "particular proclivities." He called them "intellectual, social, formal, and informal" and wanted them to include everything from "debates on current and vital general questions" to costume balls, billiards competitions, group sing-alongs, and charades.

All of this was window dressing, for hidden within the paper was his real assessment of why the club was roiling: "Unconsciously there is too much of an atmosphere of rank." Harold wanted members to lay aside "the mantle of 'caste'" at the doorway, a losing proposition as the shadows of Jung and Riklin loomed large across it. Even larger was the triangular shadow composed of C. G., Emma Jung, and Toni Wolff.[3]

Some of the members were stunned and intimidated by the way the three principals strode into the club in "a phalanx of power, as if everyone should bow to Their Majesties."[4] In the lecture room, three comfortable armchairs were reserved for the triumvirate in the front row, while the membership sat behind in a motley collection of wooden chairs. If they did not attend, their armchairs remained empty and by their emptiness "signaled a presence that was as large as if they were there in life."[5] Jung's chair was in the middle, Emma's and Toni's at opposite sides of the room. If Emma spoke in her capacity as chairwoman, a small vase of flowers was usually placed on the podium; if Toni spoke later in the program, Fräulein Teuscher or another of the female deputies would jump up and whisk the flowers away. Everyone noticed the snub and, sadly, most approved of it. At one point, Alphons Maeder, who liked and respected Toni, took Jung aside and urged him to find a way to lessen the blatant insults. Jung was furious and told Maeder to tell the other members he would "take her on my knee and hold her there throughout every meeting until they stop hounding her."[6] When Maeder tried to explain how inflammatory such remarks were, Jung "grew florid, red-faced, angry. He became defensive, and quite insulting." It may have been the reason why Jung began to carp, quibble with, or make an insulting aside to every comment Maeder offered, whether social or theoretical. At one point, Maeder lost his temper and accused Jung of lying about something a lecturer said that was "totally innocuous and now long forgotten."

"Here blood will flow!" Jung thundered as he left the room. Maeder entreated him to come back the next evening to discuss it and try to diffuse their growing animosity. Jung did, but all through their dinner, Maeder said, they "talked about everything but our differences."

The incident concerning Jung's anger toward Maeder was typical of too many others for the general membership to ignore. Fault lines formed as they took sides, with Jung loyalists on one and "The Riklin Circle"[7] on the other. Jung's group included Pfister (who never became a formal member and whose primary allegiance was to Freud but nevertheless attended most meetings), Dr. Oscar Rothenhäusler, Hans Schmid, the Siggs, and the Kellers. Riklin's circle openly included Maria Moltzer, Dr. J. B. Lang, Dr. Rudolph Pestalozzi,[8] and, more discreetly, Maeder and Hans Trüb. Thus, when Harold subtitled his paper "The School of Zürich" and used the term "school" throughout, whether he meant to or not he was conflating Jung's psychology with the club's raison d'être. In so doing, he was ceding dominance to Jung both in the club and in the larger Swiss analytic community.

Harold's title was coming into general parlance and being bandied about with increasing frequency in both the club and the community. It was due partly to the unrelenting isolation imposed on neutral Switzerland by the war and partly to Jung's prior history as a major player in the international analytic community. But in independent-minded Zürich, groups of acolytes had also formed around (to name only the most obvious) Franz Beda Riklin, Eugen Bleuler, Adolf Keller, Alphons Maeder, and Hans Schmid.[9] To align them with Jung into a "school" was a misnomer, for they were a disparate group of individuals who happened to find themselves lumped together collectively just because a rich American woman thought it would be beneficial for all to air their differences within a setting that aped an elite English gentlemen's club. What happened instead was that her club became one reeking with unresolved competitive neuroses, or worse. The contretemps within the club was a very small tempest in the tiny little teapot of an isolated country, but it consumed the lives of fifty or sixty people who became the principal sounding board for C. G. Jung's developing ideas.

MOST OF the members responded to Emma's *Rundbrief*, but Harold McCormick's essay seems to have sparked the most debate, and it became the one to which all others, especially Jung and Maria Moltzer, directed their replies.[10] Harold's paper (which Moltzer, representing those who objected to Jung's primacy of place, disdainfully called a "letter"[11]) began with the premise that "The School of Zürich and the Psychology Club are in one way two separate propositions, but in another sense they are identical in interest," for "what affects the club affects the School and vice versa." He waxed metaphorical when calling the club "the Citadel of the School [of Zürich] . . . the Visible Church, the Workshop of which the school is the Laboratory."

The main problem as he saw it was the disturbing issue of "rank," but ever the convivial Ivy Leaguer, he believed he had the answer: "Club Spirit is the most important thing to develop." He submitted eighteen "Conclusions," intended to persuade the mostly Swiss-German members to "accept the principle of the need for the Club and its success." But suspicion was a natural attitude for the Swiss, who were bewildered by the alien concept of collegiality. Only one of Harold's eighteen conclusions penetrated their inherent reserve: "Do not expect too much at the start."

JUNG AND Maria Moltzer were Harold's first two respondents. She was expressing not only her own ideas but also, without specific attribution, some of Riklin's,[12] whose ally she had become. Moltzer now worked as an independent analyst, seeing Jung's patients only during his annual military obligation or some other extended absence, and then only if her schedule permitted.[13] Her office was near Riklin's, and as they both experienced feelings of marginalization and exclusion, they gravitated into a professional kinship. Now Riklin took over the role that Jung had previously played for Moltzer, as teacher, leader, and sometimes devil's advocate. Together they compared patient histories, evolving techniques, and emerging theories. Both claimed they had never been able to do this on an equal footing with Jung, who always imposed his views without listening to what either had to say. Together, their remarks were meant more to stake out their own particular turf than to rebut Jung, who read his paper on "Individuation and Collectivity"[14] to the club in October 1916.

Jung used Emma's *Rundbrief* more than Harold's paper as the platform for his thesis to contrast the need for privacy within the analytic session with the club's potential value as a public forum.[15] He described the analytic session as the "personal-collective" or "individual function," because only the analyst and analysand were present at the occasion. He wanted the club to become an "establishment of analytical collectivity," a forum that permitted two separate inclinations to surface among the members. Jung defined the first as a haven for those who wanted a "rigorous conception of the principles of analysis"; the second for those wanting "ordinary familiarity . . . a social gathering." He approved of both and thought they should coexist equally even as they operated separately. He cautioned that the separation should not be strictly delineated, because members would, from time to time, want to move from one group to participate in the other.

Jung thought the majority would want "simple conviviality." The rest, a much smaller group, would consist of members in the midst of analysis who would live in the club and consider it both refuge and home. He wanted the living facilities far removed from the meeting rooms, preferably on a separate floor where residents could enjoy a modicum of privacy, thus ensuring both "mutual independence" and "mutual relationship."

Moltzer disagreed, and Jung's letter coupled with Harold's provided her with ammunition for further fusillades. She thought Jung's ideas were mostly spurious, but she had withering scorn for everyone. Even as she conceded that "one does not look a gift-horse in the mouth," Moltzer proceeded to mock "Mr. McCormick's fantasy" and deride Edith for paying all the bills, including each member's dues, all of whom "should be ashamed to be such parasites."[16] Moltzer had some degree of disagreement with every one of Jung's proposals, but, either resigning herself to a fait accompli or because she believed it, she conceded Harold's most important point: "Mr. McCormick's fantasy" should prevail, and the club should adopt the precepts of the "Zürich School." Almost grudgingly she admitted that if a way could be found for the "collective-principle" to function equally with the "individual-principle," the club might eventually mature into "a real analytical collectivity." Throughout her attack, Moltzer had an underlying reason she barely touched upon: her genuine theoretical differences with Jung.

At this point, speculation enters the argument because of an untitled, undated, and unsigned essay that may have been circulated in the club during this time and that may or may not have begun as another letter to the members. Of no import in and of itself, the essay has provoked controversy among scholars who hold differing views about whether Moltzer or Jung wrote it, as it reflects portions of the developing theory of each in regard to psychological types.[17] The likelihood is that Moltzer wrote it, as the only known copy was found among the Fanny Bowditch Katz archives at Harvard. However, because so much of the content also reflects the divergent views Riklin expressed in his few tentative essays, which never progressed beyond outline or draft, his name must be factored into the equation, and the question of authorship must include him.[18]

JUNG'S THEORY of psychological types evolved during the early years of the Psychological Club's existence. It was often the main topic of lectures and discussions, and in one particular instance, it provoked sustained dialogue and correspondence that almost resulted in a collaborative book with Hans Schmid, a Basel analyst who was investigating the same topic.[19] The friendship between Jung and Schmid began sometime in 1911, after their wives became friends at a medical meeting of the Swiss Society for Psychiatry in Lausanne. By 1914, the two men were boon companions who made several bicycle tours of northern Italy and spent weekends camping and sailing along the Zürichsee. Schmid became such a close friend of Jung's and so deeply integrated into the analytic life of Zürich that, even though he lived and practiced in Basel, he asked Jung to be godfather to his last-born daughter in a baptism celebrated by Pfarrer Keller in Zürich's Peterkirche.[20]

Both analysts were investigating the psychology of types, and beginning in late 1916 and continuing throughout most of the next year, Jung gave informal seminars at the club, most of which Schmid attended. Tensions and disagreements surfaced among the members during Jung's discursive, extemporaneous talks, where he seemed to create a new idea in every sentence, contradicting everything he said before. The most sustained verbal criticism came from Moltzer and Riklin (as expected) but also from Keller and Dr. J. B. Lang, the Luzern analyst. Jung's most sustained written dialogue was with Schmid, who was conducting his own independent research on the subject. Their letters,[21] a series of meandering, sometimes garbled, sometimes inconsistent theorizing, provide insights into the evolution of Jung's final formulation.

Initially, they intended their correspondence to become a small book, perhaps a pamphlet meant only for the club membership and selected patients. Thus Jung began by referring to their earlier "talks" for the record, reminding Schmid that for the past several years he had been preoccupied with "the interesting but difficult problem of psychological types." His interest did not stem from "intellectual grounds," but rather it sprang, he wrote, "from the real difficulties of my daily analytical work with my patients, as well as from the experiences I have had in my personal relations with other people." Jung recalled how "certain controversial points in analytical psychology" illuminated two distinct but "diametrically opposed types," and how their mutual efforts revealed "the extraordinary importance for the psychology of human relationships in general."

Both men agreed on one point, "the problem of the *existence of two kinds of truth*,"[22] but they disagreed about naming them. Jung wanted "two kinds of truth"; Schmid preferred "two ideals"[23] and gave them an entirely different meaning. At this point in their letters and conversations, they still strove more for agreement than for intellectual superiority.

Their separate research toward the definition of psychological types led them to posit two major categories: the "introvert" (represented by Jung) and the "extravert" (represented by Schmid). They agreed to append a further refinement to each: the designation of "thinking" (Jung) and "feeling" (Schmid). In these early letters, neither man had yet identified what eventually became the two other functions that brought Jung's total to four: "intuition" and "sensation."[24] At this point, their differences intensified. Jung accused Schmid of nineteenth-century romanticism, of "simply going ahead with relationships." Pronouncing himself a rationalist, Jung said he was "the sort of person who must always have an a priori conception before [he] can engross [himself] in anything." The *"pragmatic tendency"* of modern philosophy caused him "worries." He made "no secret" of his "unbounded admiration for Schiller and William James" but still confessed "that Pragmatism leaves me with a rather bleak feeling." It was simply "too business-like." Jung devoted a large part of his book to the subject, having expressed gratitude to Schmid in their letters for freeing him from "the bleakness of Pragmatism" and also for leading him to Henri Bergson's "two intimately connected principles which mutually condition one another: the *rational* and the *irrational*." Jung took "pleasure" in thinking of them as "hypostatized, for then I can admit their existence morally as well." He urged Schmid to consider these observations not as "philosophizing" but rather as "psychological confessions which could not offend even the specialist, since in psychology thoughts are duty-free, being themselves the stuff of psychology." He devoted the rest of the letter to hypothetical case studies that were intended to support his thesis but that contradicted or subverted it on every front.

In his reply, Schmid took issue with everything Jung posited, especially his views of Bergson. Schmid quoted other, dissenting passages from Bergson at length and with great authority, but always with politeness and tact. Although seven years younger than Jung and not nearly as well known in the analytic profession, Schmid still expressed his views with a maturity that made Jung, by contrast, seem juvenile, aggressive, and unfair.[25]

"I think it is absolutely necessary that we should give each other credit for not wishing to react personally against the other," Schmid implored. If they were to exchange "spontaneous reactions," he thought they needed to "avoid futile and . . . dangerous misunderstandings."[26]

Jung's reply was sarcastic. He "admire[d] the capacity of the extravert to feel his way forwards out of the difficulty," but he dismissed Schmid's queries like a master chastising a novice who could not fathom "different levels"[27] of discourse. Each still sought to diffuse the situation, but the next exchange became a protracted disagreement over the "two truths" (Jung) and "two ideals" (Schmid). The argument originated with a casual remark Moltzer made during a sailing excursion on the lake, comparing the introvert to a motorboat and the extravert to a sailboat: when the sailboat lacks wind or the motorboat runs out of gas and each needs a tow from the other, each feels a "violation" when the other asks for assistance. Or, as Jung put it, if they wanted to make trips together, they would have to learn from the experience: "All his thinking no longer helps the introvert and he has to feel, and empathy no longer helps the extravert and he has to think."

Still seeking to belittle Schmid's "two ideals" and determined to enfold them into his "types," he ventured into a line of reasoning that only confused the matter more, that for each of the two types there are two types of realities, the "inner" and the "outer." Schmid disagreed and cited Goethe as an "extravert [who] repeatedly expressed mistrust of a self-knowledge and personality development that are carried too far."

Jung's response focused on the impossibility of language to convey a single meaning:

> When the type problem is discussed by two opposed types, the greater part of the discussion consists in misunderstanding and talking at cross purposes. Language here reveals its incredible incapacity to give the finer shadings which are indispensable for understanding. Every verbal sign can designate meaning and counter-meaning as soon as it has to cover psychological views.[28]

His letter continued to hector and admonish, but Schmid gave no ground even as he verified Jung's allegation that different types interpret language differently:

> You have read a mistrust into my last letter (and therefore speak of mutual mistrust) which wasn't there. I gave credit where credit was due, as postulated in your letter, and therefore my first reaction on reading it was a great astonishment that you have taken most of my remarks so personally and have adopted the attitude of one who is defending himself against mistrust. . . . It was far from my intention to "instruct" you, let alone "better" you; I was simply explaining what I feel to be my truth.[29]

Their disagreements expanded to the concepts of "value" and "utility," which Schmid believed they interpreted "at cross purposes." He did not want to consider the "utility" of such matters as religion, love, or art but rather to "inquire into the *values* which these three manifestations of life have for life." The highest values of such concepts, Schmid believed, could never be known by "cognition" but rather by "a transcendent value beyond utility and knowledge, a value, he said, he could "only estimate by feeling, which . . . cannot be known by any cognition however deep, since it is beyond cognition."

Their arguments moved to the respective values of "analysis" and "life," mostly in connection with how individuation might develop within the analytic process. Jung thought "thinking is life." Schmid believed "feeling is life and life for me can also be a realization of thinking." Jung thought "the highest value of analysis [lies] in knowledge." Schmid believed "life can take the place of analysis despite [Jung's] assertion to the contrary, without 'doing a grave wrong to the spirit of analysis.'"

The uses of analysis and the concise definition of "individuation" became a major impasse. Schmid begged Jung to consider that, if they went on "counter-asserting like this without listening to the other's argument, we shall very soon come to an unedifying dispute about competence." And that is exactly what happened.

Jung now allowed his side of the correspondence to dwindle, as if by failing to persuade Schmid of the rightness of his views, he accepted their agreement to disagree and decided there was nothing to write about. Schmid refused to let it end and sent four last long letters to Jung's two or three brief notes.[30] As he was "compelled" to defend his views in the "confrontation," Schmid conceded that he held "a completely different set of premises."[31] Jung refused to acknowledge any of them.

Schmid accepted that the correspondence could "never be published in this form," but he still wanted his theories aired, for he thought club members could benefit from "a certain confusion." Schmid intended to write his own book on personality types but agreed to defer temporarily to Jung, saying he would not make a "counter-presentation" before Jung had the opportunity to address the entire membership.

Jung brushed off all Schmid's proposals; undeterred, Schmid pressed harder. For the first time, he abandoned politeness and struck a powerful blow, accusing Jung of not being able to understand "the most valuable attribute of the e.v. [extravert] . . . his ability to love."[32] Prefiguring some of Jung's later arguments about the nature of God[33] Schmid accused Jung of a failure to be able to love in three important ways, the first being:

1. From your work: the problem of love, for example, is hardly mentioned in the work on libido. Spontaneous love is infantile. Love only seems to make sense as a manifestation of the pleasure principle *[Lust-Unlustprincip]*. Love amounts to playing saviour and missionary, etc. etc.

The second was personal, based on Schmid's direct observation of Emma's emotional pain, Toni's humiliation, and the general gossip expressed by outraged club members who witnessed the former and caused the latter:

> 2. From your reactions to other people close to you as I have observed them. I will, by God, never bring out this evidence, for it is up to these people themselves, once they have become independent individuals who also acknowledge their own emotional lives, to react to your reactions.

The third was most personal of all, and of course Jung used it to denigrate the qualities of the feeling extravert:

> 3. Your reactions to me.

Schmid's first two criticisms hit their mark, for Jung was furious and denied them. With the third, he verified Schmid's appraisal of the "strangely affective, often almost ironically spiteful tone" that he used to denigrate Schmid's extravert's concept of love. Schmid was saddened that their entire exchange strengthened his view that Jung was unable "to emotionally acknowledge the e.v.'s [extravert's] empathy, his sympathy, his love and friendship." He also pointed out a secondary aspect within their letters that in one sense paralleled Jung's earlier break with Freud. Jung, as Freud had earlier done with him, warned Schmid several times, "[You had] better look at the resistances against me that you are filled with." But these warnings illustrate a major difference in how he and Freud handled deviations from orthodoxy: Freud would not tolerate it — be it from Fliess, Joseph Breuer, Adler, Jung, Rank, or Ferenczi (to name only the most prominent defectors); anyone who dared to refine, let alone question, his theory or technique was humiliated, discredited, ostracized, and banished.[34] Jung did indeed try to bulldoze Schmid out of the way by insisting that his ideas were the only correct ones; he did continue to barrel away on his own individual path, as if no one but he had formulated the concept of psychological types. But despite the unresolved theoretical differences between them, which lasted until Schmid's early death in 1932, the two men remained good enough friends that they could still hold theoretical conversations and enjoy social occasions. Schmid was even able to stick Jung with an occasional barb, such as reminding him how he actually admitted several times that Maria Moltzer was better able "to convey thoughts that [Jung] had told her, in a more acceptable and vivid form." Jung accepted the charge even as he resented the truth of it.

The major exchanges of the Schmid-Jung correspondence ended in 1915, but they continued sporadically for the better part of the next decade. One letter, misdated December 17–18, 1915, refers to Jung's Bollingen Tower on the upper part of Lake Zürich, a beloved retreat that he did not build until 1923. In it, Schmid accurately describes Jung's regard for the external world and his construction of a way of life that required the world to respond to him just as he wanted. Schmid compared Jung's "'wonderful' Viennese idyll" (i.e., his years as Freud's appointed heir) to his current life, which he described as a "'bitterly true' Zürich Lake Idyll":

> In a tower at the Obersee you . . . have adopted the heritage of Nietzsche, a father to no one, a friend to no one, completely self-sufficient, fulfilled by yourself. Across the way, here and there, live a few other male and female introverts, each in his own tower, loving humanity in those "farthest away," thus protecting themselves from the devilish love of their "neighbors."

Convinced that he would never penetrate the powerful exterior shell Jung had constructed to support his innermost beliefs, Schmid recalled Moltzer's analogy of the motorboat: "And now and then they [the neighbors] meet each other on the lake, each is his/her motorboat, and prove to each other the existence of human dignity."

THROUGHOUT THE period he exchanged letters with Schmid, Jung was also corresponding with Sabina Spielrein. This interchange also caused certain refinements of the *Types* but was mostly centered around concepts that led to three essays concerning the individuation process and the transcendent function. The book and the three essays, four works in all, formed the "core process" of Jung's so-called fallow period and provide insight into "the narrative, processive, and developmental character"[35] that distinguishes his system of analytical psychology.

By 1916, when this second phase of correspondence with Spielrein began, she had married Paul Scheftel, given birth to a daughter, and was living and working in Geneva, where one of her later patients was the famed child psychologist Jean Piaget.[36] Even though Spielrein first wrote to Jung for personal reasons, and despite her having become a devoted follower of Freud, the letters soon concentrated on an impartial exchange of analytic theory. They offer an indication of how Jung used the experiences of his own life to seek a coherent overview that might be generally applied to all those who sought psychoanalysis.

In the beginning, the letters dealt in large part with his typologies, among them what he was then calling inductive and deductive methods.[37] Jung insisted that the introvert used both, whereas the extravert could do so only "insofar as he is capable of thinking." At this stage of his theorizing, Jung believed the extravert, when compared to the introvert, was "lacking because his principle is feeling not thinking." In what seems an obvious move to preempt Spielrein from rekindling their personal past, he ended his first letter with "best wishes among colleagues." It may have stopped her from replying immediately, but it set the tone for the exchange that followed a year later.

In September 1917, when Jung was fulfilling his military service as commander of the camp that interned British prisoners at Château D'Oex, the correspondence became constant rather than sporadic.[38] It began with Spielrein's request that Jung interpret some of her dreams, but for the next two years it ranged over a broad spectrum of the works he was trawling for similarities to his own and for examples to support it. These moved from the philosophy of Nietzsche to the differing systems of Adler and Freud, with Jung's emerging theory of typologies underlying every exchange.[39] Spielrein pressed Jung repeatedly to define his concepts more precisely, so that she might better understand their differences. She equated introversion with the "will to power" and extraversion with "the need for *self-surrender*."[40] Jung's response was a perfect example of what Schmid earlier called the "strangely affective, often almost ironically spiteful tone" with which he rebutted any question, comment, or criticism: he dismissed Spielrein as an "intuitive-extraverted type" who was being too "arbitrary." He resented her constant comparisons of his theory with Adler's and Freud's, and when she insisted that he needed to work them into his "equation," he dismissed her plea with the simple remark that she did "injustice"[41] to both other theoreticians. Jung was so determined to follow his own personal quest toward theory that even though he was willing to listen to others, his mind was so focused on his own vision that he could not allow anyone else's to interfere with it.

Like his letters to Schmid, Jung's to Spielrein disintegrated into hectoring, chastising, and correcting. At one point, Jung asked her to review Emilii Medtner's translations of his work into Russian, all of which she found "poorly translated, both in style and in content." Jung told Medtner, who retaliated by accusing Spielrein of being unnecessarily "pedantic to the point of insulting him." Jung ignored her entreaty that he should wait to publish until the political climate stabilized and they could create a "Russian terminology" that truly expressed the meaning of his concepts.[42] Medtner, who had persuaded Edith McCormick to pay all the expenses connected with translation and publication, continued to work unimpeded and unsupervised in his uniquely idiosyncratic manner.[43]

Undeterred, Spielrein continued to press Jung to refine some of the generalities he had brusquely insisted upon retaining, even after Schmid questioned them. If she drew a diagram, the better to explain her distinctions, Jung drew two, each more detailed than hers.[44] But just as the letters with Schmid degenerated into personal animosity, so too did those with Spielrein, with echoes of her dismay over his handling of the "Siegfried . . . Aryan-Semitic"[45] fantasy, her wish that he father her child. "At times one has to be undignified, simply to be able to live," Jung admonished,[46] arguably validating Schmid's criticism of his brusque behavior in personal relationships.

A month later, Jung told Spielrein he could not answer any more questions about typology: "I would have to write a book to do so. It is, however, already written. In it your questions are answered in detail."[47] Without expressing gratitude for her suggestions, he said he had to "revoke the original identity of extraversion and feeling, as well as that of introversion and thinking." He had made the original connection because these were the two types that stood out most, at least in his exchanges with Schmid. Now he simply distinguished between "a general introverted or extraverted attitude" and gave examples: Bleuler was an extravert whose most differentiated function was thinking; he was not sure about Freud, whom he knew "too little on a personal level," but his "neurotic predisposition" fit into Jung's general theory of extraversion. Jung classified himself with Nietzsche as introverts, Goethe as an intuitive and extravert, and Schiller as intuitive and introvert.

As for Spielrein: "You probably used to be much more extraverted than you are now." Like a teacher dismissing a pupil's persistent questioning, Jung ended the correspondence with the hope that his diagrams would "make some sense" to her.[48]

SPIELREIN MADE no attempt then or ever to return to Zürich, so she was not present at any of the talks on typologies that Jung gave to the Psychological Club. Schmid did attend the informal presentations, but he sat quietly in the audience and spoke only if Jung addressed him directly. He did not once offer his own dissenting views.[49] The only questions from members were requests for clarification, for Jung became biting and sarcastic if anyone dared to differ and frequently held the unfortunate person up to ridicule.[50]

Jung generally announced his topic well in advance, ostensibly to alert his audience to what would follow. Later, these talks became more formally designated as "seminars" dedicated to a specific topic presented in weekly sessions throughout an academic semester or year. Between 1916 and 1918, they were mainly presentations of "work in progress" about *Psychological Types*. He usually strode to the lectern brandishing a sheaf of notes that he seldom referred to, preferring an extemporaneous, rapid-fire delivery that permitted frequent digressions and asides. Sometimes he abandoned his stated topic altogether when an illustration from his own experience, especially one of his dreams, proved too enticing not to pursue.

His audience was hard-pressed to follow the breadth of his knowledge and the depth of his ideas. Many took notes and afterward compared them with others' to be sure they not only understood what Jung said but had written it down correctly.[51] The members had not yet hit upon the idea of designating one or more of their group to be in charge of preparing a semi-official transcript — that did not happen until several years later — but some who attended the early sessions kept journals, while others wrote letters to their friends and families about what Jung said.[52]

Harold McCormick was among them, sending a twenty-eight-page letter to his father-in-law on October 31, 1915, to assuage Rockefeller Sr.'s increasingly insistent demand to know what "propaganda" of Jung's kept them in Zürich and why they did not come home.[53] Harold explained how he and Edith represented Jung's two types: "the Introvert (Edith's type) who *thinks* and . . . the Extravert (my type) who *feels*." But Jung, perhaps because of the dialogues with Schmid and Spielrein, was unsure of the accuracy of "introvert" and had begun to substitute the term "stoic type" interchangeably. Harold's letter hints at other refinements that were similar to those Jung told Spielrein and Schmid but that he had still not formulated to his satisfaction. Jung said the two types led naturally to an examination of "traits of character" that caused the formation of specific "groups as represented by individuals." Knowing this, a person could identify the type to which he or she belonged. If it occurred during the analytic process, the individual could "ascertain how best to approach himself for development as well as how best to approach and understand the other person." Neither extreme was good, Jung insisted; "a balance is better." Harold was among the members who agreed that balance was certainly good. But how, they puzzled, was it to be acquired?

Harold returned to the United States shortly after, while Edith remained ensconced in her suite at the Baur au Lac, at first to continue her analysis, later to conduct her own analytical practice. Despite all their work toward resolving their differences, they still divorced in 1921. C. G. and Emma remained friends with both McCormicks and their son, Fowler, who became C. G.'s boon companion in his last several decades of life. Both Jungs agreed that Edith had successfully completed her treatment and had become a competent analyst, so their meetings now were nearly always social occasions arranged by Emma. Emma's interests were now concentrated on the Grail legends; Edith's were wider ranging and paralleled Jung's, especially Gnosticism, comparative religion, and mythology. If they did discuss analysis when they met, Edith was usually seeking Jung's advice about her own techniques and practices.[54]

WHEN JUNG published *Psychological Types* in 1921, Freud was among the first to read it — and to dismiss it as "the work of a snob and a mystic, no new idea in it. . . . No great harm to be expected from this quarter." The book is, as Freud also noted, "of enormous size 700 pages thick."[55] His main objection was that Jung was still insisting, as he had done since he published *Symbols* in 1913, that there could be no "objective truth" in psychology because of "personal differences in the observer's constitution," or, as Jung now defined it, "typology." Jung wrote *Types* with Freud's primacy of sex and Adler's power firmly in mind and eagerly expressed his differences with both.

In a very real sense, the book's genesis occurred around 1913, when Jung separated from Freudian orthodoxy; arguably, his entire oeuvre leading to the 1921 publication can be read as notes toward a gradually emerging unified theory of typology. Freud's shadow looms over this work, as Freud's extraversion and Jung's own introversion provide a convenient explanation for why they were unable to harness their differences. Extrapolating from himself and Freud and seeking to explain how individuals perceived the world and related to it, Jung offered other famous historical feuds that originated in intellectual disagreement. His examples were religio-philosophical, among them St. Augustine and Pelagius, Tertullian and Origen, and Luther and Zwingli. From philosophy and literature he employed Nietzsche's distinctions of Apollonian and Dionysian; Wilhelm Ostwald's classical and romantic attitudes;[56] Carl Spitteler's differentiations of Prometheus and Epimetheus; and Goethe's diastole and systole, terms coined to indicate expansion and contraction.

The book is a stunning compilation of Jung's extensive reading, but there are no references to anything he had not read before he wrote *Symbols*. He simply examines the type problem as it occurs in the many writings that would serve as his workhorses for many years to come, the standard references he would trot out repeatedly to support theoretical positions. Fortunately, he chose well, for he culled works that are the finest in (among others) poetry, psychopathology, aesthetics, modern philosophy, and biography. He devoted a chapter to William James's types, particularly the characteristic pairs of "tough" and "tender-minded" opposites, which he examined in many different ways. He acknowledged that the type problem had fascinated humankind forever, from ancient astrology to palmistry, phrenology, physiognomy, and graphology, and to those most recently as Wilhelm Ostwald and Otto Weininger. Jung admitted that he had chosen to write only of those theories that supported his own but did not insist that his was "the only true or possible type-theory."[57] Admitting this allowed him to fault James's typology as "almost exclusively concerned with the thinking qualities of the types."[58] His criticism of James drew heavily on the views he had expressed in his earliest letters to Schmid and that he continued to hold: of Pragmatism, "which restricts the value of 'truth' "; of Bergson and the "intuitive method," "élan vital," and "durée créatrice"; of Nietzsche's *Zarathustra*; and of Schopenhauer and Hegel, who since his school days had provided Jung with corroboration for whatever idea he sought to prove.[59]

Jung saved his own typology for the last chapter, which comprised the final 150 or so pages of his text. To the "attitudes" of introvert and extravert, he added four further differentiations called functions. To "feeling" and "thinking," he now adopted Schmid's and Toni Wolff's suggestions and gave equal status to "intuition" and "sensation."[60] Feeling and thinking he grouped under the rubric of "rational," while sensation and intuition became "nonrational." He now acknowledged the importance of nonrational functions to the development of the psyche, because they allowed for a priori knowledge, something he had stabbed at but could not spear in the dialogue with Schmid. "A type theory must be more subtle,"[61] he believed, and in his schema, the two attitudes and the four functions thus permitted a grand total of eight possible psychological types.

In the years following the 1921 publication, Jung was asked repeatedly why he had proposed a system composed of two types, four functions, and eight possible types. "That there are exactly four is a matter of empirical fact," was his consistent response:

> The four functions are somewhat like the four points of the compass; they are just as arbitrary and just as indispensable. Nothing prevents our shifting the cardinal points as many degrees as we like in one direction or the other, nor are we precluded from giving them different names. It is merely a question of convention and comprehensibility.[62]

But few persons, it seemed, read the book as Jung intended. By the time it had gone through multiple printings in many languages, he felt compelled to address the "regrettable misunderstanding[s]" that had turned the book into "nothing but a childish parlour game."[63] He complained that even within the medical profession his typology was used to slot patients into his system and give them corresponding "advice." He insisted that his "typology is . . . not in any sense to stick labels on people on first sight: It is not a physiognomy and not an anthropological system, but a critical psychology dealing with the organization and delimitation of psychic processes that can be shown to be typical."

He believed the primary value of his book was "not merely for the obvious, all too human reason that everyone is in love with his own ideas," but rather "for the objective reason that it offers a system of comparison and orientation which makes possible something that has long been lacking: a critical psychology."

IT HAD been a long trek from Freud's 1913 ostracism to the 1921 publication of the book that signaled Jung's formulation of his own "unique system of psychological thought." He now had his own vocabulary to describe and his own method to treat the "inner processes of the lives of all men and women."[64] Jung had survived professional exile and, through formulating analytical psychology, had prevailed if not triumphed. He was forty-six years old, and "the unbearable age" of youth and young manhood had given way to "the period of maturity" wherein "a man in middle life still feels young, and age and death lie far ahead of him."[65] Jung made these observations many years later, when the fullness of life was mostly behind him, and old age and the idea of death were daily companions. But in the years when World War I and the isolation it imposed upon him were ending, several of his writings besides *Psychological Types* were piquing interest and gaining the attention of the larger world.

Having bested all local rivals, he emerged within his own community as the leading representative of psychoanalysis. Internationally, he was deemed the only theorist worthy to be seen as Freud's rival. "All these moments in the individual's life, when the universal laws of human fate break in upon the purposes, expectations, and opinions of the personal consciousness, are stations along the road of the individuation process," was another passage Jung wrote late in life.

He called these moments the "process" through which "the spontaneous realization of the whole man" would evolve.

The publication of *Psychological Types* signaled Jung's new attitude toward the world, that of "the whole man." His admirers would call this "confidence" or "charisma"; his detractors would see it as the "unbridled arrogance" of a "great big bully."[66] Jung became everything from "the wisest man I have ever known" to the man who "saved my life." He was also "a perfect fool"; and even the allegedly self-proclaimed "god known to us as Aion."[67]

In truth, throughout the last half of his life, he was a little of them all.

CHAPTER 20

A Prelude and Starting Points

D uring the years Jung was conceiving his analytic system, he also wrote an intensely personal text, so baffling and obscure that he kept it secret from all but a few trusted friends until the end of his life. The *Seven Sermons to the Dead* (or, in his original Latin, *Septem Sermones ad Mortuos*) sprang from his imagination suddenly, spontaneously, out of nowhere. The process through which it evolved began in 1913 and ended in late 1916. He hid this "prelude," as he always referred to the *Seven Sermons*, until the last year of his life, when, "hesitantly and only 'for the sake of honesty,'"[1] did he agree to let it be printed as an appendix to *Memories, Dreams, Reflections*.[2] Even then, he was unable to formulate a precise definition of the curiously elusive text. He settled for calling it "conversations with the dead . . . a sort of prelude to what I had to tell the world."

His perplexity over how the *Seven Sermons* originated was lifelong, for he returned to the subject time and again in the conversations that formed the *Protocols* and later became the *Memories*. Because he spoke of them so much and so often, his editors persuaded him that it no longer made sense to keep them from his readers. In one of the many sections of the *Protocols* pertaining to the *Seven Sermons*, he described the work as akin to "phenomena that taught me there are things that I don't make, but that make themselves."[3] Trying to remember the first experience that may have culminated in the *Seven Sermons*, he traced it to his first psychotic vision, the October 1913 train journey to Schaffhausen.[4] The vision occurred after he decided it would be dishonest to continue treating patients using "Freudian theoretical assumptions." It was also when war was imminent and he was beset by so many other dreams and fantasies in "a vast multitude of aspects" that he was led to formulate the theory of active imagination, the process of concentrating on a single image or event long enough to allow it to develop of its own volition.[5] As soon as he accepted the diverse products that arose from these visionary experiences as "facts," they became the "starting point" from which "everything else is imagination," and this was what he committed to paper.

Trying to determine how best to use dreams, fantasies, and imagination in treating patients, Jung found a partial answer during another train journey, when he went to Aberdeen in 1914 to lecture on schizophrenia and realized that the only way to define a system separate from Freud's would be to treat himself as if he were his own patient. Recalling the detailed daily journals he had kept until 1900, he thought that reviving the habit might provide a useful entrée to self-observation, meditation upon the unconscious, and what he was then calling inner states and later called individuation. Most of these journals comprise the *Black Books* discussed earlier, but now he thought he needed something separate and different from them.

Instead of writing down the random thoughts, daily happenings, and jottings from readings that had filled the earlier journals, he planned to confine himself to "language metaphors." For example, if he dreamt that he was lying in a desert exposed to the burning sun, he would begin with "sun = consciousness" and permit "long visions" to flow unguided and undirected by his conscious mind. The first time he sat down to write, he remembered hearing a distinctly female voice speaking quietly, but with authority. "That is art," she said, which made him angry because he thought he was constructing an empirical science. The voice he heard was irritatingly familiar, and the words she spoke had actually been sent to him in a letter. Jung disguised the letter writer as an "esthetic lady," and the speaker's voice became that of "a female patient who had a crazy animus, and who, without fail, lured out the anima in me." Only in the *Protocols* that eventually became *Memories, Dreams, Reflections* did he identify them both as Maria Moltzer, for the dialogue had actually happened between them years before, when their emotional involvement was at its height.[6]

Even though he was alone in his study as he wrote this vision down, he could not free himself from the belief that the patient was "inside of [him], a very vivid figure inside of [him]." He said he was not comfortable listening to this female voice and did not want to dignify it with a name. He was actually relieved when, quite early in his musings, she was preempted by a male. Jung named him Elias,[7] but he, too, did not stay. A third separate male voice evolved whom Jung called Philemon[8] and who remained. When the female returned from time to time, he named her Salome. She was always secondary to Philemon, who dominated Jung's visions.

Jung described Philemon as the pagan voice of an old man of "simply superior knowledge." He believed Philemon was teaching him:

> psychological objectivity, the reality of the soul. He represented the dissociation between me and my imaginary object. Earlier, it used to be what *I* say, then it became a thing apart from me, and he personified this thing. He formulated this thing that was not me and expressed everything that I had not thought. . . . Until the *Septem Sermones*, it was only said by him. Then it was demanded of me that I say it myself. . . . The *Septem Ser-*

mones, that was when Philemon simply lost his absolute autonomy and I had to say it myself.

Until he wrote the *Seven Sermons*, Jung recorded what Philemon told him in a handsome new journal that he dubbed *The Red Book*, a folio volume of manuscript vellum bound in red leather.⁹ In it, he labored over lavishly illustrated drawings of his fantasies accompanied by interpretive texts in fine black ink and a script of his own devising that resembled a cross between Middle High German and Irish Insular, a "monkish, black-letter script that recorded his most important dreams since 1913," all illustrated with "disturbing, really mad drawings."¹⁰

Jung chose to abandon the *Black Books* for the *Red* because he believed a very special journal was required for the "language metaphors" that evolved whenever Philemon spoke within his visions. Philemon's speech created an "Egyptian-Gnostic-Hellenistic mood" with "a clearly Gnostic tinge because he really was a pagan." It marked the beginning of Jung's sustained interest in Gnosticism and was the dominant mood he sought to convey in the musings he confided to the *Red Book*.

Philemon initially appeared in a dream, so Jung painted him that way, as a winged creature suspended in the midst of a brilliant blue sky. The sky itself moved as if it were an ocean, beneath heavy clouds that alternated between breaking apart like ice floes and covering it entirely in darkest blue. Philemon was also a very old man who wore the horns of a steer on his head, carried a heavy key chain in his hand, and had wings like a kingfisher's extending out from his back.¹¹ The day after his dream, as Jung was painting the picture, he found a dead kingfisher on the shore in front of his house. He insisted it was an omen, for such birds were seldom seen in his part of the lake. He took the dead bird to a taxidermist, had it preserved, and placed it in a prominent place in his library. He did not use the word "synchronicity" until many years later, but when he found the bird, he described his first sight of it as similar to being struck by lightning, a "Kha-soul," or "stone-soul" experience. He therefore drew his Philemon standing on a "stone or metal" object that was meant to signify that his soul came from beneath the earth. Jung's Philemon bore wings and floated like an angel, but his visage was nevertheless "something demonic . . . something Mephisthophelean." The Philemon of Jung's dream confided, "I am the one who buries the gods in gold and jewels," for not only was he "the natural power . . . who makes everything real," but he was also "the one who robs it of meaning." Gradually over a period of years, Jung filled *The Red Book* with variants of the Salome-Elias-Philemon fantasies, until all the elements melded and the figures became "real and integrated."

Many years later, Jung permitted his translator and trusted friend R. F. C. Hull to read *The Red Book*. Having worked on Jung's texts for almost two decades, Hull was uniquely positioned to evaluate the text, which he did with his usual acerbic perspicacity: "Talk of Freud's self-analysis — Jung was a walking asylum in himself, as well as its head physician."[12] Reading *The Red Book* raised Hull's admiration for Jung because of what he had been strong enough to put himself through. He thought *The Red Book* offered "the most convincing proof that Jung's whole system is based on psychotic fantasies — which of course it is — and therefore the work of a lunatic." But he was also aware that "only the wounded physician heals" and that Jung was a "medicine man" in a long line of "shamans" who understood "madness, and can heal it, because at periods they are half-mad themselves":

> He went through everything an insane person goes through . . . had it not been for his astounding capacity to stand off from those experiences, to observe and to understand what was happening, he would have been overwhelmed by the psychotic material that came through the "dividing-wall." His achievement lay in hammering that material into a system of psychotherapy that worked.

The ultimate merger of fantasy with system happened when Jung realized he could never publish *The Red Book*, "as it lets the cat right out of the bag." By mid-1916, he could no longer avoid speaking "the meaning" of what he had gone through in his own voice: "The dead came to me then. I didn't want to write that at all. I had no idea what was expected of me. But there was a great restlessness in my house, and then we started to be haunted."

No DOUBT his children perceived the parental anxiety engendered by Jung's relationship with Toni Wolff. Their collaboration, both erotic and professional, was at the zenith of its intensity, and Toni was a constant presence in the household. It was she who listened to all Jung's visions, dreams, and fantasies, serving his every need from sounding board to devil's advocate, and who was his unacknowledged personal analyst. She helped him to identify, define, and even name some of the concepts within his analytic system — the "sensation" function in the *Types* book, the "anima" and "animus," and "persona." The Jung children were now old enough to resent her. They saw their father little enough; now he seemed always sequestered with Toni behind the study's closed door, where not even Emma dared to interrupt their privacy. The atmosphere in the big house on the Seestrasse was loaded with marital tension, and it percolated down to the children. The older three overheard whispers and mutterings about their father's behavior, especially about how Toni was always on one of his arms when he strode into the Psychological Club with the subdued Emma on the other.

Something had to give, and it did, on a stifling Sunday evening in summer.[13] Toni had just departed after eating the noonday meal with the family and spending the rest of the afternoon alone with C. G. by the lake. A thunderstorm threatened, and everyone hoped it would come to break the oppressive heat and tension that had been gathering all weekend. At breakfast that morning, Gret, then ten, had told how she was awakened three times Saturday night by "someone" pulling the blanket off her bed. Agathe, then twelve, told how she, too, had been bothered repeatedly by a "white figure" walking through the bedroom she and Gret shared.

The previous night, Friday, Franz, almost eight,[14] had had a nightmare that required both parents to calm him. He was still upset the next morning, so Jung asked him to draw the visions that so frightened him. It took Franz the better part of the weekend, but he created a surprisingly sophisticated picture for a child who, until then, had never shown a talent for drawing. He entitled it "the picture of the fisherman," whom he depicted as standing on the bank of a river with a fish on the end of a pole. Upon his head was a large chimney that belched fire and smoke, and on the other riverbank a devil cursed him for allowing so many other fish to get away. Above the fisherman was an angel, who admonished the devil not to do harm, for this fisherman "only catches the wicked fishes!" Jung had not yet discussed the content of *The Red Book* with anyone but Toni, not even Emma, so he was astonished by the similarities between the child's fisherman and his own Philemon.

It took Franz two days to draw his picture, which he presented to his father on Sunday afternoon as soon as Toni departed. Suddenly, the doorbell began to ring steadily and "like mad." The two older girls, who were in the kitchen, sprang to answer it.[15] No one was there, and they could not catch anyone outside who might have been playing tricks, for as they stood before the open door, the bell went on ringing again and again.

"The air was thick, I'm telling you," Jung remembered many years later. "All I said was: 'Something has to happen now.'" It seemed to him that the house was "thickly filled with ghosts."

"For God's sake, what is this?" he demanded aloud. In his mind he heard a chorus reply: "We are returning from Jerusalem, where we didn't find what we were looking for."

And that, he said, was how he began to write the *Seven Sermons*. He did not say how his wife and children reacted to his rhetorical questioning of the chorus of voices, or what, if anything, he did to comfort them. Apparently, he left them to their own devices, ran into his study, and slammed the door. "That's when it started to flow out of me," he said. "Within three evenings it was written."

He worked in a frenzy, writing steadily into the night without stopping. When he finally set down his pen, "the entire gathering of ghosts collapsed," the house was quiet, the atmosphere "pure." Around him, his family slept deeply. Next morning, when they gathered at the breakfast table, there was a sense of contentment, if not happiness, that had been missing for many months. But as the day progressed, the atmosphere thickened until, by nightfall, he was compelled to write again in order to disperse the ghosts. On the last day, when he had nothing left to write, the ghosts left forever.

Seeking to understand what had constrained him to write the *Seven Sermons*, he decided that it was supposed to be a conscious offering stemming from his unconscious, and that it was perhaps nothing more than a gift he was supposed to present to Edith McCormick for her birthday[16] in gratitude for her endowment of the Psychological Club. But as soon as he started to copy the text onto some of the vellum paper similar to that in *The Red Book*, he could not stop himself from reading it with the critical eye of the editor rather than with the writer's loving approval of his own words.

In a sense, what he read horrified even as it fascinated him. He knew that he could not show such a text to the skittery Edith, and perhaps wisely — considering the historical time and his personal circumstances — he decided not to let anyone else read it either except for the few persons he trusted implicitly. Emma saw it, as did Alphons Maeder, Herman Sigg, and Adolf and Tina Keller, and there is some evidence that Toni told Hans and Susi Trüb that Jung had written a provocative new "fiction."[17]

"THAT PHILEMON," Jung recalled years afterward, "he was a terribly mysterious figure. At times he almost seemed to be real. He was fantastical." Even so, Jung abandoned the visionary figure that served as the raison d'être for *The Red Book*, as well as *The Red Book* itself, for he stopped writing in it until the last year of his life. He left the inner world of Philemon and went on to other, more active involvement in the outer world when he realized he could never show the world the "raw material" of the *Seven Sermons:* "That would be like prophesying and that goes completely against my grain." He put the *Seven Sermons* into the category of "raw material that flows forth, but that just does not contain the entire person. One must not overestimate the unconscious." Jung used Nietzsche as an illustration of his meaning, saying the philosopher went insane because he "believed in his entire spontaneous creation," whereas he (Jung) "always had a critical stance" when it came to exposing inner visions to the world. "I always said: there is this talk, but it isn't I who is talking. I only hear it, and I perceive it as regrettably poor. I was simply swept up by this stream and felt as if I were in it. But throughout that process I always preserved my critical view. I gnashed my teeth, so to speak, because I didn't agree with it at all."

Jung made the conscious decision not to "let any of this out into the world. Except for, eventually, the *Seven Sermons*. They were something finished."

The entire text comprises a neat little totality, well organized and proceeding from one of his recently defined analytic concepts to another with an inner logic and natural progression. Revelatory in technique, the sermons have a seerlike prophetic quality that Jung reinforces at the outset with a prefatory note announcing their writer as "Basilides in Alexandria, the city where the East toucheth the West."[18] Jung was actually following the rhetorical style of G. R. S. Mead, whose "some 16 or 18" volumes of mystical and Gnostic writings he was then studying. Mead's guide in his musings was Valentinus, whose "fantastically convoluted speculations" were equaled by those of Basilides, a second-century

Christian eventually denounced as a heretic. In many ways, Mead's style and subject matter thus became Jung's.[19]

In Jung's first sermon, the dead return from Jerusalem without having found the salvation and peace of mind they sought, and they ask the narrator to instruct them. He begins with the concept of nothingness and expands it into a discussion of the "pleroma," by which he means the totality of all the qualities found in a supreme being. The essay becomes a meditation upon "individuation," the process by which the individual's personality becomes integrated and whole, which Basilides/Jung describes as "the essence of the creature." Jung veiled the use of newly defined psychoanalytic concepts behind a scrim of archaic language, but the technique of active imagination is evident, as are the personal and "collective" unconscious (or "suprapersonal," as he sometimes still called it).

The second sermon continues with the question of personal individuation as it begins with the question of whether God is dead. This allows the narrator to introduce remarks that prefigure Jung's later views of the *privatio boni*, the privation of good and the possibility of evil in God. Here he speaks of the Gnostic god Abraxas,[20] who is described in the third sermon as "hard to know." Indeed, the qualities Jung ascribes to him are many and varied, and at the end of Sermon III, "the dead howled and raged, for they were unperfected." Sermons IV and V veer from the introduction of Eros[21] to multiple gods, the Tree of Life, and the one god who gives unity through communion. All these contain aspects of "anima" and "animus," which he was trying to define elsewhere in empirical terms. But in Sermon VI, the "daemon of sexuality approacheth" from the underlying shadows, where it has lurked in the previous three sermons, for the real subject here is the unveiled animus and anima.

In the final sermon, "man," or all of humankind, is coalesced into an entity united in its quest for salvation (in all the many forms and meanings of this concept). A "Star" provides light, which is magnified by "prayer." The final image is of humankind's rejection of the "flaming spectacle of Abraxas" and the embrace of a single god who will lead to ultimate redemption. In the *Protocols*, Jung uses the examples of pagan Pompeii and Christian Rome to give a partial explanation of what he intends here. Writing *Symbols* had given him a "relationship to the spirit of antiquity, the ur-beginning," but he did not "yet understand the transition to Christianity." He still needed "to bring it into consciousness."

When all seven of the sermons are considered as a whole, they become much more than a simplistic monotheistic rejection of multiple gods. The *Seven Sermons* in toto reads as a highly stylized, carefully delineated guidebook, a kind of self-help textbook (albeit in archaic language) for successful individuation and peaceful acceptance of the collective unconscious — as Jung had thus far envisioned what he meant by the latter. With hindsight, the clues are there to show how Gnosticism would ultimately be found lacking and how research into other systems of belief, from mythology to alchemy, would provide more meaningful answers.

Still, Jung questioned when, how, and even if he should present it to his primary audience, the members of the Psychological Club and those persons in the rest of the world who were interested in his work. He debated what to do with it until the end of 1917, when he decided to suppress it, at least for the indefinite future. But he always thought the text had value, and sometime in the mid-1920s, when his interest in Gnosticism was becoming more focused on alchemy, he realized that this curious little work served as a precursor to themes with which he was grappling. Still, it remained a secret pamphlet, a very special gift given only to his most trusted associates.

In one of the last instances when he discussed the *Seven Sermons* in the *Protocols*, he equated it with the unfinished *Red Book* and compared them both with a metaphorical house, wondering what it would mean if such a house were encountered in a dream. "A house depicts a situation in life," he concluded. "One is in it as one is in a situation."

He noted that, when patients brought him dreams of houses, or even when he himself dreamed of them, they were always unfinished, always in need of another room, or there was always a mysterious corridor attached to one's actual residence that led to rooms that were not there in reality. And when the dreamer awakened, there was always the conscious feeling that one should "solve the question of this house, to do something with it."

The analogy to *The Red Book* "clicks!"[22] Jung realized. Like the unpublished *Seven Sermons*, he decided to leave *The Red Book* "unfinished": "[I] saw right away that the things I am saying in it would still have to be brought into a shape in which one can bring them into the world."

Writing *The Red Book* and the *Seven Sermons* had served two important purposes in Jung's life. First, it dispelled the household ghosts and provided harmony and stasis within his family, as his children and Emma grudgingly accepted Toni Wolff's presence in their lives. But probably more important, these two writings brought about Jung's decision to end the years of concentration on his personal unconscious and involve himself in the larger world. Switzerland's borders were open now that the war had ended, and Jung's self-imposed creative isolation was arriving at its own natural ending as well. His life took a new and public turn, as his main project now became how to get his theories into a shape that would make them accessible to the world.

CHAPTER 21

—∞∞∞—

The Second Half of Life

The chaotic years of creative illness that began with Freud's ostracism brought closure to the first half of Jung's eighty-six-year life. Sometime between 1920 and 1922, when he was about forty-five, years of competition and upheaval gave way to years of satisfying professional routine and personal comfort, punctuated by interruptions only when Jung chose to initiate or accept them. The sole imposed obligation was his military service, the annual bout of "odious corporeality," in which he released "a lot of aggression" even as he maintained that "the only satisfactory role is that of general."[1]

He did much professional traveling to explain his psychology to eager audiences in many countries, England and Germany primary among them. Personally, and often impulsively, he was a tourist in fairly exotic places such as North and East Africa and the Grand Canyon of the United States.

His analytic calendar was generally filled months in advance, so those who sought his therapy often had to wait as long as a year for an appointment.[2] He counted on Emma, Toni, and even his sister, Trudi, to insulate him from the demanding supplicants who filled a therapeutic day that usually began around 7:30 A.M. and ended between 6 and 7 P.M. By the mid-1920s his schedule vaguely paralleled the academic calendar: from July to October he was on vacation; from mid-October to Christmas he saw patients and gave seminars unless he was traveling; he took another vacation from mid-January until mid-March, when he resumed the professional schedule; he usually took a three-week vacation to coincide with Easter celebrations; and he resumed professional life from sometime in April until the end of June. Other local analysts knew "these very long holidays were possible only because he had a very rich wife. He could not have done it otherwise."[3]

Whenever he felt too pressed, he withdrew impulsively for periods ranging from several days to as long as several months, claiming the need to concentrate on the many writings inspired by his surfeit of ideas. At first, he closeted himself in the small study adjacent to his library, but increasingly he thought about a hideaway, a secret place where no one could go but himself. It eventually resulted in the building of his beloved tower at Bollingen, but that did not happen until several years later.

Often he changed his itinerary with callous disregard for the financial constraints suffered by those patients who traveled long distances or from foreign countries for long-anticipated sessions only to be told that he was away indefinitely and they would simply have to wait for his return if they wished to see him at all.[4] Many of these frustrated, unhappy persons checked into the Hotel Sonne for two reasons: it was as close as they could get to Jung's house, and it was very cheap. People in the neighborhood grew used to the "gray shadows" who passed their days walking aimlessly down the Hornweg to the Theodor Brunner-Weg, then up to the Seestrasse, past the house and back to the hotel.[5] As they all took meals in the communal dining room, they soon intuited the shared purpose that brought them there, and some of the less shy (or "introverted") began polite and reserved friendships that lasted long after they returned to their homelands.[6]

Many persons who appeared throughout the second half of Jung's life came to Zürich in the 1920s. Some stayed permanently, while others, even though they departed after sojourns of varying length, remained on the periphery of his professional life in one sense or another. This influx began slowly, as Harold McCormick observed, because few "outsiders" could afford to live in Zürich in the five to seven years after the war because of the unfavorable exchange rate for most currencies. He did note wryly that many of the "hoboes" who filled the grand hotels were often heard asking each other "which ex-King they may be!"[7]

Many wealthy refugees and expatriates sought Jung's counsel, but there were also increasing numbers of ordinary citizens of modest means who looked to him for advice. The war spawned a disillusioned generation eager to say "goodbye to all that,"[8] by which they meant the rigid status quo of the long Edwardian afternoon that followed the oppressive Victorian social code, and to replace it with the hitherto unimaginable freedoms that were now theirs for the taking. But such freedoms also meant having to learn how to cope with the upheavals foisted upon them by the swift and sometimes overwhelming social change that confronted them. Jung believed these questing souls represented "the general neurosis of our age" and thought they suffered "not . . . from any clinically definable neurosis, but from the senselessness and aimlessness of their lives."[9]

His practice had evolved naturally, so that a majority of those who consulted him were mature adults in what he called "the second half of life."[10] Many had already tried other forms of psychotherapy with varying degrees of success or satisfaction, thus presenting Jung with a special set of problems. From the very beginning of his postwar, or mature, practice, he observed only occasional schizophrenic or paranoid patients and was seldom responsible for their sustained treatment. For the most part, his patients fell under the rubric of the neurotic. Most were intelligent, well educated, independent in their outlook on the world, and generally from the middle and upper classes. "Most of my patients are socially well-adapted individuals, often of outstanding ability, to whom normalization means nothing," Jung observed, probably referring to the artists and writers, the so-called "bohemians,"[11] who came to him for treatment. The analysands whose careers were in business, industry, and government, the "so-called normal people," presented him with another set of problems altogether: "There I am really in a fix, for I have no ready-made philosophy of life to hand out to them" — which was exactly what most captains of industry wanted him to provide.

His philosophy for treating everyone was as blunt and basic as he himself: "The shoe that fits one person pinches another; there is no universal recipe for living." With each new patient, he felt required to invent, adjust, or change his therapeutic technique, and as he was writing at the same time as he was formulating theory, there are many seeming discrepancies in what he wrote. One of the major and most lasting criticisms of Jung's oeuvre arose during these years; namely, that it is inconsistent and contradictory, with so many conflicting ideas that a reader can find something within it to support whatever contention he or she wishes to put forth. Jung responded by defending the circularity of his thinking and his belief that coherence and consistency were best served by requiring readers to think of all possibilities and then to select those that met the individual's need.

By the time most persons sought his guidance, they were frequently at loose ends, having exhausted "the resources of the conscious mind." In an essay he wrote in German, Jung used "ordinary English" to describe how they seemed at their first session: "stuck."[12] When they pressed him for definite answers, asking, "What do you advise? What shall I do?," Jung could only shrug them off with an "I don't know either." He told them there was only one sure thing: they would have to learn to listen to their "unconscious psyche" if they really wanted to move beyond "the unbearable standstill" in which they found themselves.

AMONG THE earliest artists and writers who were drawn to Jung was Hermann Hesse, introduced in 1916 by Jung's former pupil and Hesse's analyst, Dr. J. B. Lang, then directing the Sanatorium Sonnmat near Luzern.[13] Lang, according to Jung, was "a very curious, though extremely learned, man, who had studied oriental languages (Hebrew, Arabic, and Syrian) and was particularly interested in Gnostic speculation." Jung said Lang "got from me a considerable amount of knowledge concerning gnosticism which he also transmitted to Hesse."[14] Jung and Hesse stayed in fairly frequent contact for the next several years, even though Dr. Lang was Hesse's primary analyst. Jung felt such a strong rapport with the writer that he was one of the few to whom he entrusted a copy of the *Seven Sermons*. Around 1919, when Hesse moved to Montagnola, Ticino, and was on the verge of a serious breakdown, he began to consult Jung as well as

Lang. Hesse saw Jung weekly between 1921 and 1922, when his personal life was in turmoil, his condition exacerbated by the lasting stress of conflicts generated by his outspoken pacifism during the war. Hesse and Lang had become close friends during therapy, so ostensibly he remained Lang's patient, but during his most troubled time, Jung really became his primary analyst.[15]

Like Emilii Medtner's before him, Jung enjoyed Hesse's analytic sessions because the two men shared so many intellectual interests. Hesse's writings, copiously self-illustrated, not only reflect his own psychoanalytic preoccupations but also are complementary to the evolution and development of Jung's. Jung told a scholar of Hesse's writing that he gave the novelist many "hints and implications" during their analytic encounters but was unable to estimate how "conscious[ly]" Hesse responded to them.[16] Still, the time line of Hesse's writing between 1919 and 1925 reflects Jung's developing views on Gnosticism, mythology, Eastern religions and philosophies, and, increasingly, themes and ideas that were certainly related to these fields but that Jung expressed most clearly in the later alchemical writings, where he was only just beginning to concentrate his scholarly inquiry.

Hesse also shared Jung's interest in Goethe, which he incorporated into his own system of individualization, one that had strong underpinnings to Jung's theory of individuation. As the son of Christian missionaries to India, Hesse shared similar boyhood experiences with Jung, the pastor's son, but Hesse expressed his beliefs in what he called *Weltglaube*, a worldview that combined a vague, nonspecific Christian faith with a spiritual belief in an imprecise striving toward goodness. These were similarities he shared with Jung, but Hesse's most fundamental belief was in pacifism, which he superimposed upon everything he wrote, and it was here that he and Jung parted company.[17]

Hesse, awarded the Nobel Prize in 1946, was among the many writers who consulted Jung and whose subsequent writings most reflected their mutual interests and concerns.[18] With another great writer whose life intersected Jung's at several crucial instances even though he himself was never Jung's patient, there was only perplexity and bafflement on both sides and never a point of agreement.

JAMES JOYCE came to Zürich at the end of June 1915, an expatriate from his native Ireland and a refugee from war internment in Trieste, where he had been living with his wife and two children. Switzerland, particularly Zürich, offered him "artistic detachment, *au dessus de la mêlée*,"[19] and there he composed what most people consider his greatest work, *Ulysses*. Always on the verge of penury, Joyce came to Edith McCormick's attention in early 1918. Without first consulting Jung or seeking his approval, she decided to add Joyce to the list of artists, writers, and musicians whom she deemed worthy of anonymous benefaction and whom she supported independently. She arranged for an annual stipend of 12,000 Swiss francs to be deposited in Joyce's name at a local bank, payable in monthly installments of Sfr1,000. It was easy enough in such a small town for Joyce to learn his patron's identity, and when he did, he sent Mrs. McCormick a letter of thanks, although he did not meet her in person then or ever. Joyce depended upon the monthly stipend's steady arrival but did not change his habits, which appeared to outsiders as little more than seemingly dissolute perambulations to his favorite cafés and restaurants. His wife's extravagant spending, especially her recent obsession with couturier clothes, no doubt enhanced their family image as one of daily debauchery and self-indulgence. Nor did Joyce's physical being merit the approval of the stolid burghers of Zürich, with the pointy black goatee he sported, his thick glasses, mismatched jackets and trousers, and shabby shoes. Also, his walking stick, large feminine-looking ring, and broad-brimmed black hat all contributed to a slightly sinister appearance. His clothes were due to one thing, his general lack of concern, but the hat, stick, and glasses were quite another: defenses against a severe eye disorder and a weapon to gird against his pathological fear of dogs and thunderstorms.

Joyce was a major curiosity even in a city where the likes of Tristan Tzara and Hans Arp had recently proclaimed the doctrine of dadaism in the *Aldstadt*'s Café Voltaire, where Lenin spent much of each day scribbling in solitude in the Odeon Café until the sealed train took him back to Russia (to the indifference of the entire Swiss populace), and where by accident of war, Zürich had become the center of the best theater in Europe, as so many companies who fled there en masse when conflict began liked it so much they stayed on when it ended.

Joyce was unsure of what the "numerous (and useless) people" he encountered thought of him, but he was certain their views had to be "conflicting":

> A batch of people in Zürich persuaded themselves that I was gradually going mad and actually endeavoured to induce me to enter a sanatorium where a certain Doctor Jung (the Swiss Tweedledum who is not to be confused with the Viennese Tweedledee, Dr. Freud) amuses himself at the expense (in every sense of the word) of ladies and gentlemen who are troubled with bees in their bonnets.[20]

Without specifying who, Joyce spoke of a woman who circulated the rumor that he was "extremely lazy and will never do or finish anything." The rumor was especially galling because, by his own estimate, he had by then spent twenty thousand hours writing *Ulysses*. The woman in question was probably Mrs. McCormick, who, just as abruptly as she had started it, ended his stipend. Joyce blamed a host of people but eventually settled on Jung, whom he had not then met but who years later agreed that he was probably responsible "in an indirect way."[21]

Among others supported by Edith McCormick was the composer Ermanno Wolf-Ferrari, who found himself blocked and temporarily unable to write music. Wolf-Ferrari made a serious financial mistake when he engaged Jung as his analyst and confessed in one of their sessions that he dreamed recurrently of bleeding to death. Jung thought the dream represented an intolerable situation from which the composer was begging to be released, namely, dependence on Edith's money. As confidentiality had not yet become the sacrosanct rule governing the analytic session, Jung discussed Wolf-Ferrari's case with her, saying he thought the composer's block could only be caused by the pressure her stipend instilled. He advised her to terminate it, and she did. Shortly after, Wolf-Ferrari completed several major works, and Jung took this as proof of the rightness of his diagnosis.

Mrs. McCormick did not tell Jung that she planned to take a similar action with Joyce, but Jung thought she must have perceived a parallel to Wolf-Ferrari's situation and so acted without knowing just how hard Joyce worked each day before he began his late-night peregrinations to Zürich's watering holes. The angry Joyce used the episode the same way as he did everyone and everything that touched his life: Mrs. Mervyn Talboys, the whip-cracking sadist dominatrix in the Circe episode of *Ulysses*, owes much to Edith McCormick, and Jung's "psoakoonaloose" is ridiculed in *Finnegans Wake*. Joyce left Zürich without meeting Jung and would have nothing good to say about him until a decade later, when he had no option but to entrust Lucia, his "yung" daughter so "easily freudened,"[22] to the ministrations of the "grisly old Sykos."

JUNG DID not treat Vaslav Nijinsky personally, but their names have also been linked since Nijinsky's several periods of treatment in Zürich between 1919 and 1921.[23] Romola Nijinsky, the dancer's wife, was alarmed by the monthlong bout of furious scribbling in which Nijinsky filled four notebooks intended to be his "final words addressed to the world."[24] She brought him to Binswanger's Bellevue Kuranstalt in Kreuzlingen from their home in St. Moritz, and Binswanger consulted Bleuler, who asked to read the notebooks before seeing the patient. As soon as he read them, Bleuler took two actions: he ordered Nijinsky to be committed to the Burghölzli, and (perhaps remembering the Schwyzer case and Honegger papers) he asked Jung to read the notebooks and evaluate the case.[25] Jung probably did not read Nijinsky's notebooks then, and he never saw the patient in person.[26] What makes their near-encounter most interesting is that as late as 1920–21, Bleuler still valued Jung's views on schizophrenia so much that he solicited them for the most difficult cases in the Burghölzli.

So, TOO, did the British medical establishment seek to hear what Jung had to offer. One of the first and "most intellectually gifted"[27] among Jung's British advocates was Dr. Constance Long, who had known him since 1913, when his presentation to the British Psycho-Medical Society[28] so impressed her that she followed her friends (and Jung's translators) Dr. Montague David Eder and his wife, Edith, to Zürich for her own analysis. Although Long was one of the original members of Ernest Jones's London Psychoanalytic Society, by 1916 her orientation had diverged sufficiently from Freud and toward Jung that she became chiefly responsible for overseeing the English translation of his *Collected Papers on Analytical Psychology*.[29] This led to close friendships with other women physicians who were interested in Jung's evolving theory, among them the American Dr. Beatrice Moses Hinkle, whose professional acumen Jung had respected since the Weimar conference and who had just translated *Symbols* for publication in the United States as *Psychology of the Unconscious*.[30]

Long was one of only three distinguished British doctors invited to participate in one of the twentieth century's earliest landmark gatherings of feminist women, the International Conference of Women Physicians, held at the New York YWCA September 15–October 24, 1919.[31] Long and Hinkle[32] tried to persuade Jung to address the "YWCA gathering,"[33] but when he went to England in July of that year, he told Long he had too many other commitments and could not find time to go to New York.

His infatuation with the United States appears to have been temporarily supplanted by one of more lasting duration, with England and all things English. From this time on, there was always "something oddly English about his appearance,"[34] as Jung sported the clothes he affected for the rest of his life: Harris-tweed jackets, tiny-checked woolen sport shirts, paisley ties, corduroy trousers, and comfortable cardigan sweaters. His favorite pipe tobacco came from England, as did the brown brogans and other English footwear that he custom ordered. He liked to pepper his German lectures and writings with examples of current English slang and was proud of the colloquialisms in his spoken English. In later years, Sir Laurens van der Post would note perceptively that Jung had a "profound love of the Englishness of the English as opposed to the British in them." The novelist Hugh Walpole put it more succinctly: "He looked like some genial English cricketer."

These qualities endeared Jung to his first British followers before the war, and his first invitation to lecture outside Switzerland came from them as soon as the war ended: the Royal Society of Medicine and the Society for Psychical Research invited him to give three lectures in July 1919.[35] He lavished much more care and attention on the preparation of these British lectures than he did for those in Switzerland, where he lectured frequently during the war.

All these talks fall into two loose groupings: for the Psychological Club he described his developing system as it evolved, first of "complex" psychology, then of "psycho-analysis" (as the word was then written), and occasionally of "analytical" psychology, which he eventually chose as the lasting title of his theoretical system.[36] If his language was rough, his thought unclear, his terminology contradictory, it was because he was working it through as he went along, and he expected the club members to accept it without question. For the second group, the associations, or *Vereine*, he used the same developing themes and topics but tailored them to cover the specific interests of each audience. However, the few examples that survive[37] must be lumped into the category of tentative, evolving, and nonfinal writing. Throughout these years and until 1927, Jung said at the beginning of all these talks that he would not give formal lectures until he devised to his personal satisfaction his own analytic system and a psychology as well. But by 1919, even though he had attracted a significant following in England, he knew better than to take lightly invitations to speak there, so he prepared carefully. Jones was still in control of a psychoanalytic society openly dedicated to the furtherance of Freudian doctrine — and to the personal and professional denigration of Jung and anyone with the temerity to follow him. As there was yet no formal British society for the furtherance of Jung's psychology, much hinged upon these lectures, not only how his adversaries would criticize them but also how his advocates would receive them.

One of the advocates who attended the lectures and later wrote her own interpretation of Jung's system was the journalist and early popularizer of "psychoanalysis"[38] M. K. Bradby, who became the object of Constance Long's deep and mostly unrequited affection.[39] Bradby had gone to Zürich to analyze with Jung in the mid-teens and had also had either actual sessions or individual conversations with Toni Wolff and Maria Moltzer.[40] Bradby also attended informal gatherings at the Psychological Club, so she heard Jung use some new terms, such as "persona," "shadow," "anima," and "animus." She later explained them all to Long, but she gave her own personal slant to everything Jung said. What makes Long's relationship with Bradby a point of interest in the evolution of Jung's psychology is that by June 1919, one month before his British lectures, Long had already confided the latest developments concerning his *Personality Types* to her diary in the terms Bradby had heard him employ earlier in Zürich, terms that had not yet gone beyond the club's membership to reach a wider audience.

But at the same time as Long was giving her diary details and definitions of Jung's terminology — that is, Bradby's interpretation of it — she was also confiding "MKB's anger" at her refusal to (in Bradby's words) "'accept anything or any authority but J[ung].'"[41] Long worried that her "resistance" to MKB's authority was due to her resentment that Bradby could write so easily and fluently about Jung's ideas, while she, one of his most devoted English followers, did not have "a single original idea"[42] worthy of a book. She never did write a book, but she produced several papers that still serve today as fine illustrations of Jung's evolving theory.[43]

Long, Hinkle, and Bradby were among the first of the many remarkable women[44] who were profoundly influenced by Jungian psychology and who would later be clustered under the belittling appellation of the *"Jungfrauen"* or the "Valkyries." Although these terms did not come into common parlance until later in the decade, the denigrating and dismissive status accorded to the women who followed Jung was already in effect by the time these three were working on his behalf. Their ranks were enhanced by three others at the International Conference of Women Physicians who became the major proponents of Jungian psychology in the United States: the Americans Kristine Mann and Eleanor Bertine, later to form a triumvirate with the British Dr. M. (Mary) Esther Harding, when she relocated to New York.[45]

Mann and Bertine were at the forefront of a band of committed adherents in the United States who stuck by Jung despite Freud's banishment; thanks to Hinkle's translation of *Symbols*, their rank was growing exponentially. Reviews such as Aleister Crowley's in the chic *Vanity Fair*[46] increased interest in Jung, especially Crowley's approval of how he "balk[ed] at some of Freud's conclusions":

> Instead of relating will to sex, [Jung] related sex to will. Thus, all unconsciously, he has paved the way for a revival of the old magical idea of the will as the dynamic aspect of the self. . . . So, once more, we see Science gracefully bowing her maiden brows before her old father, Magic.

Unwittingly, Crowley identified precisely what it was about Jung that made him so attractive to Americans when he wrote that "Jung's great work has been to analyze the race myths, and to find in them the expression of the unconscious longings of humanity." The Americans who flocked to Zürich seemed to represent Crowley's view rather than Walter Lippmann's, who dismissed Jung's book in *The New Republic* as "a personal adventure in search of a philosophy far more than a contribution to psychoanalytic understanding . . . a series of grandiose generalizations about human destiny."[47] Lippmann's opinion, however, remains to the present day one shared by many of Jung's critics and denigrators.

EVEN THOUGH many women were staunch proponents of Jung's psychoanalysis in both the United States and England, they have always been relegated to secondary status, as little more than helpmates to the men who were the most visible champions of his theory. This is especially true in England, where Dr. Esther Harding provides an example. She decided a society dedicated to the study of Jung's theory needed to be organized, and on September 24, 1922, she called the first meeting in her home of what became the London Psychological Club, later known officially as the London Psychoanalytic Club, forerunner of the several British societies established later. She invited three women physicians to join her as founding members, Drs. Mary Bell, Helen Shaw, and Adela Wharton, and one man, Dr. Helton Godwin Baynes. All three women had analyzed with Jung and also had supplementary sessions with Toni Wolff.[48] Baynes, a big, brash, and booming personality who was always called Peter, was, in Jungian parlance, an "extraverted feeling man."[49] Baynes went to Zürich around 1920 to consult Jung about his second wife's depression (he had a total of four wives) and stayed long enough to become "Jung's first assistant."[50] By all accounts, he was Jung's most trusted associate simply because he was a foreigner and not allied with any of the feuding theoretical factions in Zürich. His duties, if any, seem to have consisted of providing a nonspecific liaison between CGJ and the members of the Psychological Club, listening to the latter's complaints and soothing ruffled feelings, neither of which he did very well. Baynes's German was good enough for him to become the English translator of Jung's *Psychological Types, Contributions to Analytical Psychology*, and *Two Essays on Analytical Psychology*, and these remained Jung's principal English-language publications for many years afterward.[51]

Although Harding's idea generated the club, Baynes became its first chairman, while she was elected secretary. The club flourished steadily from its inception, primarily because of Baynes's enthusiasm and organizational talents. By October 5, when the first official meeting was held (again at Harding's home), Baynes was already recruiting new members, their number growing steadily to the eventual core of twenty-five who kept it going.[52] Baynes wrote the society's ground rules, as simple and straightforward as the requirements for membership.[53] The club would hew to the "fundamental psychological principles" established by Jung; membership would be awarded to anyone "who has been analyzed by Dr. Jung himself,"[54] and there would also be "a medical section consisting of qualified practitioners who are practicing analysis." In his brief statement of incorporation and purpose, Baynes urged "all who have worked with Dr. Jung in Küsnacht" to "appreciate the need for solidarity at home." He encouraged all members to "give their personal efforts in the furtherance of the goal."

WHEN BAYNES returned from Zürich to London, and the club there began to operate, he made sure that "the navel string attaching it to Zürich" remained taut, and that the club's "output and general character were very largely contingent upon inspiration derived from its parental source."[55] The London Psychoanalytic Club was specifically designed to emulate the Zürich model but with one notable difference. Both clubs agreed that their major focus would be group relations and the individuation process, with the furthering of Jungian precepts through lectures, discussion groups, and individual use of both clubs' excellent libraries. But the London club was both different from Zürich and divided within its own membership over whether or not the social and political issues of the day should be explored alongside the major topic: the emphasis on archetypal concerns. Eventually, this question became one of several that resulted in divergences and the formation of other groups, both based upon and separate from Jungian orientation.[56] But throughout most of the 1920s, there was no major dissension, and topical discussion occurred where and when the members deemed it appropriate.

There was serious dissension, however, within the Zürich club when Hans Trüb was elected chairman in 1921.[57] After four years, 1916 to 1920, Emma

Jung decided to step down. Eugen Schlegel, a local lawyer, became interim president for a year, a compromise candidate chosen to mollify competing theoretical factions. Schlegel and his wife, Erika, were friends of the Jungs but did not openly side with him. Schlegel was regarded as a man of high community standing who joined the club because he and his wife were intellectually curious about psychology and had had some intermittent sessions with an unnamed analyst, most likely Jung. It was soon evident that Schlegel was no match for the conflicting egos of the major theoreticians, and his chairmanship was indeed a year of caretaking; or, as one member recalled, "his finger was in the dike, and, miraculously, it held back the waters."[58]

Even though Hans Trüb, as Toni Wolff's brother-in-law, was a fairly obvious candidate, his selection as chairman came after a relatively complex set of interpersonal circumstances. Jung first befriended Trüb when he was a young medical student who came from the small town of Aarau and a family of modest means. In the years since, Trüb had studied Jung's evolving theory with painstaking thoroughness but constant objectivity. He was intelligent enough to be able to question every theory and concept, and while Jung was merciless, biting, and cruel with other doubters, he always responded to Trüb patiently and carefully. However, when Trüb was analyzed, he did not go to Jung, but selected Maria Moltzer as his primary analyst, and after her Riklin. Trüb's wife, Susi, took her analysis in exactly the opposite sequence: Riklin first, then Moltzer. Neither of the Trübs thought of engaging Toni Wolff, because they did not consider her "officially qualified" at the time.[59] Nor did they ever seek formal analysis with Jung, although Susi did consult him briefly in 1920. He told her then that he was "too strong" for her and said she should consult her sister. Susi was very much against it because, as the youngest of three sisters, she believed "Toni owned the intellect in the family" and her own role was to be "dumb. Dumb, but very competent at living."

Hans Trüb's relationship with Toni Wolff was equally complicated. Susi described his entry into the life of her family when he was a medical student and Jung's trusted junior colleague. Jung introduced Hans to Toni, and he was immediately attracted to her. Susi wondered if Jung was aware of it or even if he might have deliberately encouraged it. All she really knew for certain was that "somehow it didn't work. Toni was too complicated." Shortly after, Hans married Susi.

Jung continued to like and trust Toni's "open, simple, and spontaneous" brother-in-law, and when Edith McCormick wanted a tutor to help her become an analyst, Jung chose Trüb as the one who could best teach his psychology. Hans was Edith's primary instructor for several years, until she left Zürich permanently in 1921 to return to the United States. Even though he and Edith were divorcing, Harold was so grateful to Trüb that he gave him a parting gift as a bonus for helping Edith, enough money to rent a large house in the Ticino, where he intended to establish a community similar to what he wanted the Psychological Club to become, before circumstances forced his resignation in 1924.[60]

Since the club was founded in 1916, its membership had been fragmented for a variety of reasons. First and foremost were the various splits due to ideological differences, best exemplified by the opposition of Riklin and Moltzer to Jung, even though both had resigned from the club by the time Trüb became president. These were two of the most prominent resignations, and over the years, various reasons have been offered for each. The most frequently cited is the sheer force of Jung's overwhelming presence and personality, which supposedly became too much for Riklin. Depending on who evaluates Riklin's reason for leaving, he either grew tired of the infighting and the constant jockeying for position; he was despondent over his inability to attract a following for his version of psychology; or, quite simply, he wanted to concentrate on a career as an artist.[61] Whether one reason or all figured in his decision, Riklin resigned quietly and left the forum to his cousin-adversary.

Maria Moltzer resigned too, feisty as ever and in high dudgeon, complaining that she had to "work in the dark, and alone" and did not "get the recognition or the appreciation" for what she did "for the development of the whole analytic movement."[62] Fanny Bowditch Katz soon followed her.

Oskar Pfister, never a formal member, became so distressed with the cult of personality he saw forming around Jung that he withdrew from any activity that might have brought him into contact with Jung, not only within the club but also within the larger analytic community. In so doing, he disappeared from the narrative of Jung's life.

Alphons Maeder, who was the first candidate suggested to succeed Schlegel as club chairperson, and whom Jung had also nominated to be the first president of the Schweizer Gesellschaft für Psychoanalyse, refused to be considered for either position for the same reason: "You nominate me," he told Jung, "but in the background all the strings are in your hand. Only what you want will be done; only what you say will be accepted. I would be president only from the outside. And that I cannot accept."[63] Maeder withdrew from active participation in the club, although his wife attended meetings for a few years longer and even served one term as chair from 1926 to 1928, as much an interim caretaker as Schlegel had been.

Adolf and Tina Keller were also put off by Jung's behavior, but like the Maeders and Heinrich Steiger, another Zürich resident, they kept their membership and stayed quietly on the fringes of the club until the Oxford Moral Rearmament Movement was formed several years later. As they believed strongly in its precepts, it gave them a convenient excuse to withdraw from the club, which they all did together.

Into this strained atmosphere of "introverts against the extraverts," of "too many power struggles, the disagreements, and, always later, the reconciliations" that kept Jung firmly in control of the club's focus and purpose, came the "revolutionary spirit" Hans Trüb, with his private vision of a "revolutionary presidency."[64] Jung and the board of directors settled for Trüb as the next compromise candidate when Maeder refused the position. Toni Wolff had serious reservations, which Susi attributed to Toni's fear that Hans would become "competition"[65] and usurp the intellectual closeness she shared with Jung. Toni was also worried because Emma had begun analysis with Trüb midway through her chairmanship and several years later was still consulting him, although less regularly. Hans Trüb became one of Emma's closest and long-lasting friends, and such harmony raised qualms in Toni. She told Jung he could not count on Trüb's unswerving allegiance, but Jung insisted Trüb was "a trusted disciple"[66] and paid no attention to any of her concerns. In this instance, she was — as usual — more intuitive than he.

From the beginning, Trüb's goal was to change the club from "a place where only one side [Jung's] was presented" into "a community . . . of common ground and common interest."[67] He believed that the club was an institution:

> created too much by the artificial gesture of a few people from one day to the next. It didn't originate from a small beginning, didn't grow, but was suddenly put up as a finished institution through the initiative of a few people. It was a homunculus, an artificially created being.[68]

Trüb wrote this in 1924, after he resigned from the club, but he had believed it since at least 1920, the year before he was elected chairman. At that time, he began to write his observations of the dynamics of the club as a way of clarifying his own ideas about why it was not the ideally functioning entity he envisioned. His observations resulted in a curious document entitled "Notes on the Reflections of the Happenings of 1920–23," which he never intended for publication or public consumption.[69] Mainly, it consists of brief sketches of club personalities and descriptions of events, both with many cross-outs, corrections, and addenda. Trüb had an excellent opportunity to observe members' behavior on these occasions, for he served several years as chair of the Welcoming and Entertainment Committee, in charge of everything from billiards contests to costume balls.[70] Long passages present his version of how the members interacted with Jung, but even longer ones are devoted to trying to understand the theoretical differences between them and him, primary among them Maeder, Moltzer, and Riklin. Trüb tried not to "name the problems by name"; he strove "to be loyal to Jung"; and in most passages, after scrupulously acknowledging Jung's "founding position within the Club," he constructed a painstaking chronology of unfolding arguments and theoretical differences to help himself "make sense of them."

But Trüb believed himself to be in "an early stage" of "revolutionary youth," which was his euphemism for his inability to accept Jung's theory in its entirety or to subdue his disapproval of how the club was hardening into the unquestioning acceptance of Jungian doctrine. He believed it was his responsibility as chairman to see that the club functioned not merely as "an experimental field for Jung but for the views of others as well." Even before he became chairman, he described the club by the German term *"Das Kollectiv,"* the collective, or the collaboration. Toni Wolff saw the term as a warning signal of inevitable conflict, but Jung was either too secure, too preoccupied, or too unconcerned (or, more likely, a combination of all three) to pay attention.

Around 1922, just after Trüb was elected chairman, he met Martin Buber, who became one of the most important influences on his life and thought and who thus became an indirect participant in Trüb's eventual clash with Jung. Trüb's route to Buber was roundabout: he first heard of the Austrian-born Jewish philosopher sometime after 1914, most likely through Poul Bjerre, the Swedish psychotherapist who had been among Freud's earliest adherents but had ultimately chosen to align himself with Jung.[71] Bjerre was often in Zürich and a frequent attendee at the Psychological Club's programs, and, like Buber, was connected with the Swiss group of writers, editors, and philosophers who preached a new social order loosely described as Protestant religious socialism.[72] Among them were Leonhard Ragaz, with his magazine, *Neue Wege;* Emil Brunner, the prominent theologian who was professor of systematic theology at the University of Zürich; and Théophile Spöeri, professor of literature at the same university. Jung knew of these men but had no contact whatsoever with any of them or, indeed, with any of the significant number of intellectuals who were resident in Zürich in those years. In fairness and to give but one example, neither did Bleuler, for psychology was still considered an adjunct to medicine; with the exception of Pfister, the most prominent theologians and philosophers mostly ignored the discipline.

Of all the intellectuals Trüb met during this time, the most important in the life of his entire family was Ernst Michel. The prominent Roman Catholic socialist was lecturing at Frankfurt's Academy of Labor and the University of Frankfurt and was a frequent houseguest of the Trüb family.[73] It was Michel who introduced Trüb to Martin Buber, when Buber was formulating the view that around 1920, "Jewish and Christian philosophers and theologians independently of one another overcame the egocentricity of idealistic thought." It was the beginning of Buber's "dialectical theology" and the doctrine of the "I and Thou."[74] To the deeply religious and idealistic Trüb, it pinpointed exactly the source of his hesitation with Jung and gave him the necessary counterbalance he sought between religion and psychology. For Trüb, successful individuation would not suffice; it was the analyst's Christian duty to instill a responsibility in the patient that would lead naturally to participation and interaction within the community.

Eventually, he would call this mode of therapy psychosynthesis,[75] but between 1921 and 1923, he was mainly trying to acquaint club members with ideas other than Jung's, and those of Buber and the Swiss intellectuals named above were paramount. Trüb read Russian well, and he also tried to introduce ideas gleaned from Russian literature, particularly the novels of Andrei Bely, an appreciation he shared with Medtner and that intensified their friendship until Jung made his disapproval known and Medtner withdrew it.[76] When Trüb spoke of Brunner, Spöeri, and the others, most of the club members responded blankly, as if they were either unable to comprehend these outside ideas or did not want to risk appreciating them for fear they might offend Jung, whose behavior at club events was increasingly outrageous.[77]

Many members were offended by the way he strode into the club flanked by Toni and Emma, "a phalanx of power with an air of invincibility about him."[78] One member who "saw things" said "it became routine to see an aura of flames, an almost solid halo, hovering over the women's heads and surrounding Jung." The tension was palpable.

Jung invented a game he called Alleluia, in which he made all the members stand in a circle and throw a large handkerchief tied in heavy knots at each other, all the while shouting personal confessions or disclosing something embarrassing or accusatory about the member at whom they aimed the object. Anyone who missed catching it or was not fast enough in thinking of some charge to hurl before throwing the handkerchief was out. The mostly introverted members hated the game but dared not refuse to play. Instead of getting the evening off to a good start, it had quite the opposite effect, as participants were too embarrassed or ashamed to risk eye contact or other communication afterward. But Jung liked the game, and so they endured.[79]

When Jung did not like a speaker, he would sit throughout the lecture talking loudly to Toni Wolff, sometimes harrumphing and guffawing, to the discomfiture of the speaker and chagrin of the audience. Emma took no part in such impoliteness but sat quietly in her big armchair at the opposite side of the room. This continued for well over a year, as no one dared to chastise Jung. No one asked Trüb to intercede, but he still had the temerity to suggest that the membership present Jung with a "motion to censure." No one joined him but Maeder, who seconded the motion.

Once again black with fury at Maeder, Jung hurled another of his "heads will roll over this" diatribes and left the club. Jung, Emma, and Toni resigned their memberships and did not set foot on the premises again until Trüb resigned in 1924. Trüb was astonished at the severity of Jung's action, but he was somewhat naïve to think that Jung would accept such comeuppance from the likes of him after having disposed of so many other competing theorists. Still, for Jung to have willingly walked away from his most powerful forum, two qualities must have been in force: first, his towering anger that a mere lad (as he thought of Trüb) would chastise him, and second, the even higher tower of his belief in the rightness of his position. *"Tant pis!"* he had told Ernest Jones in regard to how

Symbols would be received. *"Tant pis!"* he was now, in effect, telling the Psychological Club.

In the final year of his chairmanship, Trüb lost his moorings and floundered in a depression that was exacerbated by his lifelong affliction with frequent migraine headaches. In December 1923, Trüb invited Buber to address the club on the topic "The Psychologizing of the World."[80] Jung used his influence to keep members away, and the audience was embarrassingly small. Shortly after, in deep despair, Trüb resigned, and he and Susi left the club. Buber became Trüb's spiritual advisor and mentor and was responsible for persuading him to write what have since been regarded as two articles that form the cornerstone of his psychosynthesis, "A Scene in the Doctor's Consulting Room," and "From a Corner of My Consulting Room."[81] He continued to see patients, and to believe that a major part of the therapeutic process was to ensure that his analysands learned not only to individuate (Jung) but also to relate to the world and to feel social responsibility for their participation in it (Buber). Gradually, the latter became so important for Trüb that the former became merely the first step in the process.

Emma Jung, godmother to the Trübs' daughter, still consulted Hans professionally but only rarely. She saw Susi frequently, mostly when she entertained the other women with whom she discussed the situation of women. For the next decade, Emma remained a good friend to both Trübs, visiting them at their home in Zürich and spending long vacations in their Ticino home without her husband and children. If someone special came to lecture at the club, she invited the Trübs to be her guests, but they did not accept until the mid-1930s, and then only to hear Emma speak about her research on the Grail. Emma made it clear to C. G. that her friendship with the Trübs would continue despite him, but she also made it clear to the Trübs that she would always align herself publicly with her husband.

C. G., godfather to two of the Trüb children, saw no one in the family, despite Susi's imploring letters asking him to lift her husband's banishment and lessen his depression. C. G. always replied to Susi's letters, but only to give her his news of the moment: he never mentioned Hans or responded to her many entreaties for a reconciliation.[82] When they came to the club to hear Emma speak, he pointedly ignored them.

The predicament between the Trübs and the Jungs created a problem for Toni Wolff, but no outside observer would have been aware of it. Susi and Hans retreated into their large house on the Schmerzbergstrasse, where Susi saw to it that they lived in "the Zürich Old Style":[83] he saw his patients, and she entertained and raised their five children. They stopped going to Frau Wolff's Wednesday lunches because Jung was always there, and Toni never went to their house. On the surface, nothing seemed changed, but Susi never forgave Toni for "interfering." For the rest of her life, she thought Toni was partly to blame for the separation. . . . It was a very deep violation, but I can also understand my sister's position. She was afraid. She was a very lonely person, and in Jung she surely had found the man, the partner, the someone who corresponded to her intellectual, her spiritual nature. He calmed her down. She could not afford to lose him.[84]

When Jung built his tower at Bollingen, Toni sometimes invited Susi to join them for Sunday lunch, and Susi often accepted. On the surface, Toni tried to make it appear that nothing was different, but for Susi, Toni was only "the god-mother of one of our children. It was never again close, just congenial."

AFTER JUNG returned to the Psychological Club of Zürich in 1924, it became an organization whose sole reason for being was to provide a forum for his evolving psychology. In retrospect, all the other members who thought the club had been established to provide a forum for the objective appraisal of theory in general had never assessed the situation clearly. No matter how inclusive their statements at the time of incorporation, Edith and Harold McCormick were devoted proselytizers of Jung's technique and method, and from the beginning their primary intention was to provide him with a forum for the research, practice, and demonstration of his ideas. No doubt the enforced conviviality that was written into the club's statutes slowed the process of its becoming a platform for Jung, but like a naval "shake-down cruise," the eight years from the club's founding to Jung's being in complete control were probably necessary to bring it into the fighting trim in which it operated from that time onward. All those who came to the club came to hear Jung, and the two were synonymous from that time onward.

Cementing control of the club enhanced the seeming tranquillity and serenity of Jung's life. He commanded his professional environment in Switzerland and was highly regarded in other national arenas that mattered to him, particularly England and Germany. He returned several times to England, taking both Emma and Toni. He met Graf (Count) Hermann Keyserling and was invited frequently to his School of Wisdom at Darmstadt, sometimes taking Emma, sometimes Toni, sometimes both. Wealthy Americans were flocking to Zürich, among them many Midwesterners and Californians who heard of his successes from their Eastern counterparts who had already been there. Jung's practice was so full that he now began to see patients as early as 7 A.M., six days a week, to fit them all in.

His children were growing nicely and had reached ages when he enjoyed their company and conversation. His wife was ever loyal and had accepted his mistress with grace and dignity beyond description. His mistress retained the poise and discretion typical of her class while still placing his every need at the forefront of her life and fulfilling them all — this despite the snide remarks and slights aimed her way by those who knew they could get away with them because she was too discreet to call attention to the reality of her situation.

Jung should have been in the catbird seat, satisfied to let the world come to him, pay him homage, sit at his feet, and let him pontificate, content to assume the mantle that settled around his shoulders. He was on the verge of becoming "the wise old man of Küsnacht," the appellation so many ascribed to him in the latter part of his life, but for the moment he was "the sage of Zürich"[85] and practically an icon. Still, there is an inner contradiction to these serene outward appearances. For much of the next decade, he traveled constantly, spending almost as much time away as at home. In an undated passage in his *Protocols*, Jung attributed his peregrinations to a "Syndrome Ambulatoire."

"In such cases," he wrote, "people are seized by something like an urge to travel, have an amnesia concerning the past and just travel or run away." The question, of course, is why?

CHAPTER 22

Bollingen

The Jung children were growing up, their ages in 1923 and 1924 ranging from twenty (Agathe) to ten (Helene). Emma rigorously supervised her daughters' education, preparing them to be sheltered in the privacy and comfort of advantageous marriages. Emma thought Agathe "had too much interest in boys"[1] and, as the Freies Gymnasium was co-ed, sent her and Gret to the private girls' secondary school in Zürich. Afterward, she enrolled them in a finishing school in the French section to learn cooking, fancy needlework, and housekeeping.

Agathe grew up acting as her siblings' second mother, because Emma "worked with father and had not much time for us." Family life revolved around Jung's "regular eight-hour workday,"[2] and weekends and vacations, when he wrote. The parents still spent the evenings alone, when Jung "smoked his pipe . . . read detective novels, or, for a change, Latin tomes." Now he added a new activity that included Emma: they "played pool," while the children were relegated to "sweaty Ping Pong tournaments on the porch" or "hardly less passionate card games." If they made too much noise, Jung rang the bell in his study three times, the signal for quiet.

If Emma "was not always there," Grandmother Emilie Jung-Preiswerk was.[3] Each day after school, the children gravitated to Grandmother's, which was on their way home. Emilie never left the house, even to go to church. She excused herself by saying the pews were not comfortable, but in reality, she was too fat to sit on them. Neither would she board a train, for she was so large she could barely squeeze through the door. Her girth provided reason for not going out, but in fact, "they were simply excuses, because she lived in a world of fantasy, and the real world disturbed her." The world came to her, however, as all her Basel relatives frequently visited the elderly woman who was "so much fun to be around."

Of all the Jung children, Agathe had the closest affinity with Emilie, who listened carefully as the young girl described the spirits who came to her bedroom at night or told of the long-dead relatives who confided to her in dreams and visions. Emilie nodded approvingly, for clearly Agathe had inherited the Preiswerk family's psychic abilities.[4] Emilie told such horrific ghost stories that Agathe was often too frightened to walk home unless Trudi escorted her. Jung tried to diffuse the girl's anxiety by drawing many *Drudenfüsse*, Druid's feet hexagrams, to paste on Emilie's windows and doors to "prevent the witches from coming in." Agathe noted quietly that Grandmother Emilie "never laughed at these stories; she believed them. She could laugh about anything and had a great sense of humor, but not about ghosts, who were to be feared. They were terribly real for her."

Her sense of humor was a welcome contrast from the strictness of the children's home. All remembered how unusual it was in those days to be "so free with one's grandmother," but Emilie encouraged them, laughing at their pranks even as she called them "you horrible children!" The only time she left her house was in the summer's worst heat, because she loved to swim in the lake. The children called her "the stranded whale," as she floated in an enormous pair of trousers that served as her bathing suit. Agathe and Gret stole the trousers one day, and each jumped into a leg, then into the lake, where they nearly drowned because there was not room enough to paddle in such a costume. Jung fished them out with the boat hook, but he was not amused.

Grandmother Emilie and Aunt Trudi were always busy with some kind of needlework that they wanted to teach the mostly uninterested girls, who preferred to join brother Franz in eating the cakes and cookies the two women baked each day in anticipation of their arrival. Trudi had a collection of toys, but the children especially liked the small glass dog that "was colored and shiny, and you could look through it."[5]

Agathe, sunny and unruffled and "not occupied with the psyche, as the others were," knew from childhood that all she wanted in life was to be a good wife and mother. Ever since she was sixteen Agathe's beau had been Kurt Niehus, an engineer educated at the ETH, from a good family in the Bernese Oberland. They married when she was almost twenty.[6]

Gret, almost eighteen, "did not play with the other children, but always went on her own." As an adult describing herself and Agathe, Gret said, "My sister and I experienced our parents completely differently, and partly heard opposite facts."[7] They received the same education (so, too, did Marianne and Helene in turn), but Gret was not a willing student of household skills. A loner who resented that she "was not taken notice of,"[8] Gret was dark and stormy, highstrung, and prone to moods and outbursts. Everyone thought it uncanny how much she resembled her namesake aunt, Gret Homberger, in everything from name to behavior. Gret Jung threw tantrums, but only before her mother and never her father, for whom she had "a father complex."[9]

Unfortunately Gret was the butt of most of the jokes and "nasty tricks" Jung liked to play on his children. Once he threw a lighted firecracker between Gret's legs that went off and made her deaf in one ear. She told her children it was one of the two main reasons she grew up *"verbittern"* (embittered).[10] The other was wanting to go to university and study psychology, which Emma would not allow. Instead, she ordered Gret to abandon her serious study of astrology and follow Agathe to the same French finishing school.[11]

Interestingly, Emma was making such conservative decisions about Gret's future just at the time she and her women friends were investigating feminist issues through a detailed study of Jung's concepts of anima and animus. She had also engaged a tutor from the university to teach her Latin and Greek and, encouraged by her husband and Hans Trüb, was giving serious thought to beginning her own analytic practice. In short, Emma was bent on establishing the professional life she emphatically denied to Gret, seemingly contradictory behavior that is easily explained by considering her Swiss social origins.[12] She was a securely married mother who had already raised her children and fulfilled most of her familial responsibilities; therefore, as a mature woman, she was free to develop her intellect. As a good Swiss mother, she could not permit her highly intelligent daughter to do anything but follow the chronological path of her own example. Her highest duty was to ensure that all her daughters would make good marriages to men with social standing and sound prospects. Only after they were secure mistresses of their own households would they be free to do whatever they wanted. And so, at the age of twenty, Gret married Frederick O. A. "Fritz" Baumann, subsequently gave birth to five sons, never made a formal study of psychology, and did not become famous and honored for her astrological abilities until her later adult life.[13]

Marianne (called Nannerl) was fourteen and still too young to have ambitions, although she showed early musical ability. Even though the children were really young adults, they were still expected to eat their meals in silence, but as Marianne loved the piano and was always humming and drumming scales at the dinner table, the other children learned not to flinch when Jung peered sternly over his glasses at almost every meal to roar at Nannerl, "Don't sing!"[14]

Lil (Emma Helene) was only ten, and she and Marianne were so much younger than their sisters that they formed their own little coterie, counting on Agathe to braid their hair, tell them stories, and keep them out of harm's (i.e., Gret's) way. Agathe was closest to Marianne of all her sisters, while Franz, even though six years older than her, was closest to Lil.[15]

Jung described Franz, then sixteen and his only son, as "a very different type from me [who] took after his mother's family more than mine."[16] Franz enjoyed special status with his mother, for as a male, he was more privileged than the sisters who complied instinctively with his directives and acceded to his wishes. Still, the leader among the children and the one whose word was their law was not Franz, but Agathe. She was tall, blond, and bursting with health and energy, while he was "a thin, bony boy in a not very strong body, and not tall until he was a man."[17] Such a pallid son was mostly tolerated by his robust father simply because he was male, but otherwise Jung ignored him. Franz was devoted to his mother and worshiped her with something close to reverence, which meant that he despised Toni Wolff and was her chief tormentor when she was with the family.

The girls were coldly polite to Toni, but Franz was openly hostile and rude. Toni endured silently, refusing to cause enmity within the household. The sharp-eyed Emma knew everything that happened under her roof, and as Franz grew increasingly bold with his insults and practical jokes, all the girls joined him because they sensed their mother was giving indirect approval by not stopping them.

They thought Toni "one of the silliest women in existence" and often laughed uproariously in her face over the mostly innocent tricks they played on her. Toni had no interest in anything but working with Jung, so these tricks usually centered around her attempts to help Emma in the Küsnacht kitchen or, later, to participate in the housekeeping rituals at the Bollingen Tower. The children were delighted when Jung joined their laughter, especially when "he laughed the loudest and the most."[18] Emma never joined in taunting her rival, because she was "more centered" than her husband of "so many different sides: intelligent, spiritual, centered, and very earthy and very rude."[19]

Jung's earthiness was off-putting to everyone; from Toni and Emma to his children and grandchildren, all were repulsed by much of his behavior, especially his eating habits and especially at breakfast. He ate soft-boiled eggs every day, breaking them into a bowl of bread and smacking his lips, slurping them up without benefit of napkin. Emma averted her eyes and ignored him, while the children wanted to but never dared to ask him to remove the dripping yellow crusts that formed on his moustache or around his chin.[20]

With such a formidable father, it was not unusual that the son should fade into the background, and Franz was somewhat blurred in his family's collective memory of these years. Unlike Jung, whose childhood was financially and emotionally impoverished, Franz grew up in the comfort of Emma's money and the security of her regard, which may have been why his ambitions were not as sharp as his father's. He just assumed that when the time came, he would enroll in the University of Zürich and study medicine, becoming some sort of physician and not necessarily a psychoanalyst. Because Jung was largely absent from the children's daily upbringing and discipline,[21] Franz felt no competitive drive and no excessive need for his father's approval. He was content to be who he was, the special only son of a doting mother and the only brother to four sisters who gave him pride of place.

Franz did begin medical school at the University of Zürich, but he had no aptitude and failed his courses. The son was humiliated, but the father was enraged by what he considered a personal disgrace. Jung gave Franz a small amount of money and told him to leave the family home and Zürich as well, and not to come back until he had made his own way in the world. Somehow, Franz ended up in Stuttgart in the home of his cousin Ernst Fiechter, the architect who designed the Seestrasse house. Whether by avocation or default, Franz qualified as an architect under his cousin's supervision. He returned to Küsnacht and became respected throughout Canton Zürich for designing substantial but unimaginative bourgeois houses in the nineteenth-century style.

As YOUNG adults, the Jung children were growing into interesting company for their father, who had enjoyed playing raucous children's games with them and their Homberger cousins. Emma was not an outdoorswoman, and she seldom joined her robust brood. She suffered from vertigo and did not like to climb mountains or sail. She enjoyed being in the garden but did not like to do more than cut flowers or pick vegetables; she did not cook or do any kind of handwork, even though she insisted her daughters become proficient in all these tasks and crafts. She preferred to stay at home quietly reading and studying and began what became a lifelong hobby, painting with watercolors over the etchings and engravings in old books.[22] If she did consent to join her family, she placed her chair in some quiet area far removed from their antics and tended to her meticulous painting. On the several occasions when she had no choice but to camp out with them, she provided them with anecdotes they told with gusto for the rest of their lives, such as the time she was very proud of putting up flypaper in the ladies' tent. She forgot it was there, and the next morning when she sat up, her hair became so entangled that the girls had to cut it off in clumps to extricate her.[23]

Now that the children were free of Emma's sharp-eyed supervision, they and the Homberger cousins became Jung's boon companions on his outings. He treated them all alike, taking any of the girls who wanted to go on "North Pole journeys,"[24] no matter how fierce the weather, either hiking up a mountain on winter Sunday afternoons or sailing up the lake. Jung's sailboats were built expressly to his specifications and were difficult for everyone but him to handle.[25] He would sit in "the admiral's seat"[26] and then bark orders and curse his crew in several languages as they cleared the boathouse. His sons-in-law generally ignored him, but his son never sailed in the same boat, always taking the second smaller one instead, even if he had to sail it alone.[27] Everyone dreaded the process of getting under way, and no one relaxed until they were well out on the lake and Jung had lit his pipe, the signal that his mood was changing for the better.

They usually headed for the upper reaches of the lake, the Obersee, where they camped out and slept in tents, dug trenches for latrines, and cooked their food over open fires. In the wilderness, the children were "allowed to behave as you wanted, the louder the better." Jung sometimes joined them (and later his grandchildren) in "trying to light farts," which they "loved, because in the Seestrasse, you had to behave yourself."[28] One night after a very young Franz smoked five cigarettes, he threw up all over his father, who was sleeping next to him. Jung patiently cleaned both himself and the boy, got back into the tent, and told Franz that if he had to be sick again, to "turn the other way, away from me."[29]

Yet despite their father's peasant vitality and the fact that he always kept dogs and seldom had them neutered or spayed, the Jung girls grew to adulthood so sheltered that they knew nothing of sex. Emma never discussed it, so Agathe learned how to deal with menstruation from the housemaid, and she, in turn, instructed her sisters. They all learned about sex from their husbands.[30] Emma let her daughters "just grow up." She had no concern for the details of daily living, which their grandmother Bertha Rauschenbach instilled in them. They called her Granny Beispiel, the example. They may have had lessons in how to manage a home at their French finishing school, but it was Grandmother Bertha who really taught them how to manage servants, entertain guests, and "how to have the house just so, and how to make it nice. At home, everything was left to you to puzzle out."[31]

It was the same with religion. All the Jungs considered themselves members of the Swiss Reformed Church, but Jung never attended Sunday services, and Emma stopped going as soon as the children were old enough to be sent alone. When the time came for the ceremony of confirmation, they were sensitive to their father's coldness and their mother's disdain, so none of the five was ever confirmed. Shortly after, they all drifted away from the practice of organized religion. In later life, they insisted they did so because they sensed it was what their father wanted.[32]

EMMA HAD settled into the second half of a life dominated by compromise and adjustment. Besides Toni Wolff, there were other "affairs"[33] that she accepted because "she knew if she left him, he would fall apart."[34] And in another sense, when Emma used the word "affairs," she was often alluding to one of her husband's sarcastic descriptions of the many women who settled in Zürich to devote themselves to his psychology, the "eleven thousand virgins."[35] Others may have called them the *Jungfrauen* or the Valkyries, but Jung never used these terms.

More than a decade after these women began to flock to Zürich, Emma made one of her rare comments about her marital situation to a confidante. At a professional gathering, she pointed scornfully to the many women who hovered around Jung and said, "Look at all these women here, blooming like flowers." Pointing to Toni Wolff on the other side of the room, Emma added scornfully, "*She* got what they all wanted to get."[36] Interestingly, by the time Emma heaped such scorn upon Toni, the physical passion between her and Jung had been extinguished for years, and Emma was well aware of it.

Toni Wolff told Marie-Louise von Franz, one of the *Jungfrauen* and one of the most respected and revered of the scholars who worked closely with Jung from around 1930 until his death, that "she never really liked sex," and that the enduring strength of her relationship with Jung came through "the likeness of their minds."[37] This was really what Emma could not bear: to know that another woman was able not only to follow but sometimes to lead *her* husband into verbal virtuosities and intellectual gymnastics that she, bright as she was, was incapable of initiating or following. All Emma could do was to listen, support, succor, and sustain. In the end, it was enough, but at that time, it was deeply wounding and humiliating.

Circumstances were teaching Emma that in order to survive intact within her marriage, she had to perfect the public persona she learned to present to the world throughout the last half of her life and from which she never departed, that of the "grand dame," "the serene lady." As her children and then later her grandchildren explained it, "To be in her presence was a little bit like being invited to meet the queen. There was this distance; she always kept somewhat of a distance. She was quite nice, but from then on [the 1920s], she didn't talk much." As the years passed, she became ever more "*zurückhaltend*,"[38] cool, reserved, restrained. "Father was her chief interest. She was not really neglecting us, but her chief interest was Father. She was only here for Father. She lived in his work, and it took all her time and her interest."

Her descendants believe the inscription Jung carved on a stone at the Bollingen Tower after his wife's death was the most accurate description of how she lived her life: *O vas insigne devotione et obedientia* (O vase, sign of exceptional devotion and obedience).[39]

FOR THE better part of the decade that had passed since his break with Freud, Jung had been trying to buy land on the sparsely populated upper lakefront. First he tried to buy an island opposite the village of Schmerikon, but he withdrew after a series of frustrating political negotiations with the local community. The island, rich in medieval history, originally belonged to the cloister of the monastery of St. Gallen and was the site of the hermitage of St. Meinrad, which local people revered as a shrine. They did not want "the mind doctor from Zürich" to own such sacred land, and whenever he and his family camped there, they rowed around the island every Sunday staring as if to intimidate "the crazy Jung family."[40] They did not object, however, when he wanted to buy a parcel on the mainland that had also been a part of the monastery's holdings but held lesser religious significance. Jung's friend the crafty businessman Hermann Sigg told him to compromise with the villagers and buy the lakeside plot between Schmerikon and the village of Bollingen, which Jung did in late 1922.

From the moment he bought it, he began to think of what to build, and the process of imagining how the structure should evolve became intricately connected in his mind with the evolution of his writing.[41] As he waxed philosophical about both writing and building, he became the "philosopher" of towers, "or, more accurately perhaps, its psychographer."[42] His original vision was of a wide, single-story tower, with a cooking hearth in the middle and sleeping cots along the outer edges. Then, as he began to reflect upon the course of his "true work," that is, his research since 1903, the tower assumed a different shape in his imagination. It became less wide and much higher, with two stories instead of one.

He made a drawing of what he wanted the tower to be and showed it to Walther Niehus, the younger brother of his new son-in-law, Agathe's husband, Kurt. Walther was then an eighteen-year-old architecture student whose interest in the family was directed toward the "extraordinary" father[43] and who would marry the then-eleven-year-old Marianne a decade later. He was flattered when Jung showed him his drawings and asked for a formal design based upon a tower that was round with a cooking hearth in the middle and, to get the process started, was to be only a single story. Throughout the cold of winter, Jung, Franz, Kurt, and Walther sailed to Bollingen every weekend and started to build this version by themselves, even though their construction experience was little to none, especially with stone. They camped out in tents commandeered by Jung from Château D'Oex that had once belonged to English internees.[44]

An unexpected event soon changed the original conception. In February 1923, Emilie Jung-Prieswerk, seventy-five and with no obvious sign of ill health, died after complaining for several days of not feeling well. The news came as a shock to Jung, who was away in a village on Lake Lugano, where he had gone to be alone to write.[45] He took the night train back to Zürich but sat awake, hearing festive music in his head and strangely unable to grieve. During the next several months, thinking about his mother led to thoughts about his writing, and both led to a major revision in plans for the tower. Symbolically, it had become "a place of maturation, a mother's womb," within which Jung could revert to a simpler time: "I could be myself again, could be in my most personal essence that corresponded to me. [word deleted in mss] the tower was as if I had been reincarnated in stone. Like . . . a depiction of individuation . . . this had a therapeutic effect."

The revised structure became too complex for the four men to build, so workmen were engaged to complete it. Jung stayed in it mostly alone until 1927, when he wanted more enclosed space so the family would no longer have to sleep outside in the threadbare English tents. He did have a horizontal space built onto the original structure and divided it into several areas he named the foyer, the lower study, and the guestroom. It took until 1931 for the building to attain its next-to-final form, when he added a second tower at the end of the horizontal space to balance the original. In 1935, he built what he called "an outer structure," with a smaller room. On one matter he remained adamant despite the protests of his family: he refused to install indoor plumbing or electricity, and to this day visitors use the outhouse, pump cold water from a well and boil it in the fireplace, and get their light from candles or kerosene lanterns.[46]

Jung always called the compound by the name of the village, Bollingen, and others learned to do so as well. Because too many curiosity seekers and pilgrims found their way there, as well as his own patients or other disturbed persons who felt the need to see him, Jung had a wall built around the tower. Inside one portion of the wall, he added a stone-and-concrete loggia, an outdoor room with table, banquettes, and fireplace, where the family gathered during pleasant weather. Between it and the main dwelling the masons laid a stone courtyard. On the loggia's ceiling Jung and other family members painted the Jung and Rauschenbach family crests as well as the crests of his children's spouses.

Even so, Bollingen did not fully satisfy him. It was still "too primitive . . . too simple and chthonic." There was no "spiritual peculiarity," so he turned to stonecutting as one of the ways in which to acquire it. He began to carve some of the external stones on the tower itself and then worked on rectangular tablets delineating his family genealogy, which he hung over the fireplace mantel.[47] When workmen delivered a massive square block by mistake, he urged them to leave it, saying he had not known how much he needed it until it was delivered. All these carvings are visible, known, and much photographed; others he kept secret, known only to himself. One of the hidden inscriptions reads in Latin *Philemonis sacrum Fausti poenetentia* [*sic*], a homage to both the Philemon of his *Red Book* and the marriage of Philemon and Baucis, the "simple old loving couple, close to the earth and aware of the gods."[48]

There were various other connections for Jung as well: Emma was represented by the original tower, where he had his first bedroom and kitchen put into one unified space; the second tower represented Toni and was a "self-containedly spiritual" place. Still, he fretted that something was missing, but he did nothing until after Emma's death, when he added a second story to the horizontal, central portion. He had it built because he wanted to overcome the feeling of "disappear[ing] between the two towers" and to "start emphasizing myself now."[49] Jung called this final area "the chapel," a room where only he could go and "a selected few" were occasionally permitted to enter. On the walls he painted

> . . . everything that leads me into seclusion. There is a nice corner in the park of the Castle Arlesheim, there's an 18th-century country house, there's a bench in a romantic spot, and right there it says, *o beata solitudo, o sola solitudo.* — That expresses it! Everything is in [this room] that takes me out of time, out of the present.

He compared the sensation of being in this room with "a sort of strange rapture" that he felt for the first time when he was a student on a pilgrimage to the crypt of Oberzell on the Reichenau. He called it "my place" and returned every year during student vacations, even though it "displaced" him because it conjured images of "a grave — from the world, into the nontemporal, into eternity."

"That was what I had in mind when I built the 'chapel,'" he said. "It was also supposed to be a sort of a grave."

Decorating the walls was an ongoing process for the rest of his life. He sometimes added sayings or pictorial representations that seemed appropriate or passages from books he was reading. This room, located at the highest center portion of the dwelling, became his private bedroom and study, and he placed his desk directly under the windows so he could look out over the lake as he wrote.[50] He kept the room locked and always carried the only key in his pocket, like a talisman. "There is nothing in there for curious eyes," he said, "and I always carry the key on me. No one else gets in there."[51]

BUILDING THE tower at Bollingen coincided with the years when Jung was an almost frenetic traveler, away from home as much as he was there. Between 1919 and 1925, his principal professional journeys included at least three trips to England, many short overnight or weekend trips throughout Switzerland, several each to France and Holland, and slightly longer periodic stays in Germany. In the *Protocols*, he referred to this period as the time when he "began to give a lot of smaller lectures in a great many places and to write smaller papers."[52]

As a tourist he went twice to Africa, throughout the northern countries on the first trip and to East Africa on the second. He visited the United States twice, once going as far as the Grand Canyon of the Colorado River and to the Hopi Pueblo of the Southwest.

There are many reasons for so many voyages, the main one being his fervor to advance both knowledge and acceptance of his analytic system in an era when the adjective "Freudian" was highly popular and a trip to Vienna was becoming de rigueur among the cognoscenti. An equally important reason, as his spur-of-the-moment acceptance of several of the invitations for tourist travel attest, was his simple zest for and natural curiosity about places and things unknown. There was also another equally important reason: although these years may have seemed stable and tranquil to those who did not live in Zürich, they were fraught with major changes in his personal life. For someone like Jung, who had hitherto been in command and control of everything and everyone in his native environment, these were years of settling into an accommodation that would characterize the last half of his life.

His eldest daughter, Agathe, was married, and in 1925 she made him a grandfather. If Emma's attitude about becoming a grandmother is any indication of his feelings, too, he was not enthusiastic. Emma

did not behave like a grandmother, because she was too preoccupied with her own life. It was not until later, when there were so many grandchildren, that she took an interest, but it was not until she became a great-grandmother that she became excited. Still, she did not like being a great-grandmother and paid no more attention to these children than she did to her children or grandchildren.[53]

Jung seemed more befuddled than excited by what became a steady stream of new additions to his family. There was a certain softening in his disposition when he was around the new arrivals, but his mood usually changed abruptly to one of irritation, a sign recognized by the young mothers that they should remove their babies at once.

Another family upheaval occurred when Franz left Zürich under what Jung considered a humiliating cloud of failure. A further quandary arose when the truculent Gret, "the family problem," decided to marry a perfectly decent man whom she dominated to such a degree that both parents feared for the outcome before the marriage even took place. Gret "exasperated [Jung] so terribly" that he would beg the others not to let her near him, as "she puts such pressure on one" that he could not sleep after their daily battles.[54] Gret's fury started building months before her wedding because Emma would not let her marry on the astrologically fortuitous day she wanted in March 1926 and insisted that she wait until April, when Jung would return from East Africa. There was no doubt in anyone's mind that Jung and Gret would "cross swords" as soon as he set foot in the house. Looming on the horizon was the grumpy (for him) likelihood that she would probably make him a grandfather a second time. Emma was still upset that Agathe and Kurt had christened Sybille, the first grandchild, while Jung was away; no one could predict what Gret would do if provoked.

The two youngest daughters had a much easier time growing up, because Emma was preoccupied with her new career as a therapist and left them much to their own devices. On the rare occasion when Jung took notice of them, it was to scold Emma for not maintaining stricter control, which would lead to yet another of her ongoing imposition of "regimes,"[55] rules and regulations that she set down sternly and promptly lost interest in enforcing.

Now that Emilie was gone, Emma could not count on Trudi to come and care for the house and children whenever she needed. Trudi was starting a new career as a home health aide in the nursing profession she loved but had given up when Jung left the Burghölzli. Trudi moved from her mother's house into a small apartment over the Küsnacht pharmacy that she shared with a good friend who worked with her. She seemed content and happy, finally over a much-earlier "crush" on a shadowy figure known in the family only as "the unsuitable man" or "the opera singer."[56]

Gertrud Jung was fast approaching forty when her mother died, but under Swiss law, as a parentless, single woman no matter what her age, she was legally subject to the authority and dictates of her closest male relative. In Trudi's case, her brother was entitled to direct all the terms of her existence, especially where and how she lived and whether or not she could work outside the home. The authorities in Canton Zürich looked askance at the full freedom Jung granted to Trudi, while those in his immediate circle saw it as a mark of his feminist enlightenment. In truth, he let her do as she pleased because of his general unwillingness to get involved in any forum of domestic politics.[57]

As Trudi lived separately from the Jung household, only the servants were left to oversee Nannerl and Lil, who ignored them all. Emma continued to be the ideal helpmate, but the private tension between her and Toni intensified to such a degree that both found it difficult to keep it under control in public. Emma became increasingly openly sarcastic to Toni, who responded in kind. Jung chose to ignore their gibes, but without any other buffer, the most convenient way to avoid unpleasant clashes was to absent himself.[58]

Another important buffer disappeared when the McCormicks left Zürich for separate lives in America. With their presence, club members were reminded whose money backed Jung, so when they departed, members felt freer at least to mutter their differences, if not to express them forcefully. Jung certainly contributed to the chaos in the club under Trüb's chairmanship, but without the McCormicks, the members' machinations forced another intrusion of psychoanalytic politics that he had hitherto avoided. Never politically savvy, he did not now relish the idea of involving himself in what he considered demeaning stratagems. Travel was a welcome diversion that allowed him to remain above the various frays. He shut his eyes to the resentment of those he left behind and let them sort things out as best they could while he forged ahead, doing exactly what he wanted.

Still, the traveling created a problem whenever he had to decide which of the two women should accompany him. If the occasion were a professional conference or seminar, the obvious answer was to take both, but that raised another question: how to keep their natural animosity from becoming apparent to others, since they all traveled together and were always in the same company. In the beginning, they were not successful: Jung "would get moody and uncomfortable; Toni would give him hell. Emma would look down at the ground, blush, and be embarrassed."[59] They only became successful some years later, for it was not until then that most of their acquaintances realized that Jung and Toni Wolff's relationship was far more encompassing than merely professional.

Perhaps Emma and Toni learned to cope with the situation by taking their cue from Jung's early formulation of the anima, for he wrote in the *Protocols:*

> It seems as though for the woman the emotional relationships are more important than for the man. For the man, it is the achievements and what he accomplishes in life that are important to him and through which he is free and unbound. When it comes to that [emotional relationships], no one is any better off than the other.[60]

Emma enjoyed most of these professional gatherings, even though her usual reserve kept her quietly in the background. Toni bloomed on these occasions, particularly in England. Whether it was in imitation of Jung's love of all things English, from language to culture or to the people themselves, Toni shared his affections.[61] She made many friends at the early professional meetings and for the rest of her life took many vacations with them and the wider circles to whom they introduced her. She traveled throughout the British Isles, often staying in homes that ranged from cozy cottages to grand estates. Her friends were struck by the contrast with the stern professional demeanor she showed when with the Jungs, for when alone, she had such zest for new experiences, took joy in simple daily pleasures, laughed easily, relaxed completely, and thoroughly enjoyed herself. She was as fluent and colloquial in the English language as Jung was, but she developed a fondness for English literature, particularly nineteenth-century novels, that he did not share.[62]

The first trip to England that both women made with Jung was in September 1920, when Constance Long organized a series of talks primarily for those who later became members of the society founded by Baynes and Harding. The dozen or so participants included a newcomer, Dr. Eleanor Bertine, who was so impressed with what she heard that she spent the following year in Zürich in analysis with Jung.[63] The setting for the 1920 talks was the idyllic Sennen Cove in Cornwall, an area dear to Emma, whose studies of the Grail were now focused on the role of Merlin within the Arthurian epic.[64] For two weeks, all the participants lived in the same boardinghouse and attended seminars that centered around the 1916 novel *Authentic Dreams of Peter Blobbs*.[65] They took their meals together and were alone with Jung for private analytic sessions only early in the morning or late at night, after the evening meal and the subsequent socializing. It made for long, exhausting days, so when the talks ended, Jung and Emma took a brief vacation to Glastonbury and Tintagel in search of historic Grail sites. Toni went to London for a few days before returning alone to Zürich.

Emma also returned to Zürich alone, while Jung went on to London for a monthlong lecture series arranged by Peter Baynes for the growing number of persons interested in analytical psychology. Weekdays were strenuous, as Jung followed a hectic schedule of speaking, teaching, and private sessions, as well as press interviews and much conviviality with the constantly expanding list of petitioners for his attention. To let him recuperate on weekends, Baynes rented a house in Buckinghamshire, "a charming cottage . . . at a ridiculously low price."[66]

There, four weekends in a row, while Baynes and the others in the party slept soundly, Jung was kept awake by an unexplainable presence. As he wanted someone else to observe the phenomenon, he urged Baynes to spend a weekend alone in the cottage after he returned to Zürich. Baynes had an upsetting experience as he, too, was visited by the apparition. He canceled his lease and a short time later told Jung that the cottage was destroyed by the owner, who could neither sell nor rent it because it was haunted by ghosts. Jung concluded that "parapsychology would do well to take account of the modern psychology of the unconscious." He certainly did, for throughout the 1920s and well into the 1930s, he spent a significant amount of time examining "spiritism" and attending séances.[67]

Hedwig and Eugen Bleuler were prominent among those in Zürich who studied parapsychology and investigated psychic phenomena.[68] Despite their nonparticipation in the Psychological Club, they remained in frequent contact with Jung and his former student the German Dr. Med. Gustav Richard Heyer, whom they often invited to attend. In the 1920s, Jung became more closely involved with them and with Dr. Phil. Rudolf Bernoulli, a professor of art history at the ETH, in whose apartment most of the séances were held.

The most thoroughly documented sessions featured the current phenomenon, the sixteen-year-old medium Rudi Schneider.[69] Jung attended four different sessions with Schneider, reportedly observing telekinesis as well as materialized hands. Mostly, he was a quiet witness whose only comment was to agree that he, too, had seen a disembodied hand pick up a bell and ring it, a hand that could not have belonged to Schneider.[70]

He attended sessions with a second medium, Oskar Schlag, that were far more controversial. While others denounced Schlag as a trickster and charlatan, Jung supported his ability. In one session, while Jung himself "held O. Sch. in such a tight grip," the medium "nevertheless took off his jacket, which would not have been possible at all with the help of a trick."[71]

Some years later, while attending a conference in Munich, Jung was invited to dine by the Baroness Gabriele von Schrenck-Notzing in her palace.[72] Afterward, he went to a café with Heyer and Dr. Gerda Walther, who had also attended some of the Schlag séances. Walther asked Jung why he would not express more public support for parapsychology "since he was after all convinced of the phenomenon's authenticity." Heyer asked if Jung's reticence was perhaps due to his fear of losing face in scientific circles. Jung said it was because he was "more afraid of propagating a subject matter that can very easily have dangerous effects in the hands of unprepared people."[73]

"People will first have to take in and digest the other things I have to offer in psychology, and only then will they be ready for parapsychology. Now, it is still too early."

CHAPTER 23

⚋

"This Analytical Powder Magazine"

The 1920 English talks were so well received that Jung was invited to give a second series in 1923, again in Cornwall but at Polzeath. These were Jung's "first *recorded* seminars," written in longhand by Drs. Esther Harding and Kristine Mann, who later melded their notes into a single cohesive document.[1] Jung's subject was Human Relationships in Relation to the Process of Individuation.

Jung returned to Zürich and a full analytic schedule throughout 1924, punctuated only by the "smaller" lectures that required brief stays away from home. Even though his schedule was full, he spent as much time at Bollingen as he wanted. Agathe, gifted with the keen psychic insight of the Preiswerk family, questioned why Jung insisted on building the tower where he did, because she knew that corpses were buried there. Sure enough, while digging the foundation, they unearthed a badly decomposed body. They deduced it was one of the Napoleonic French soldiers who drowned in the Linth River floods of 1799, whose bodies were swept downstream to the upper lake and subsequently washed ashore. They gave the corpse a proper burial, and Jung, now a skilled stone carver, chiseled a proper grave marker.[2]

Throughout the winter of 1924, Jung spent long periods alone at the tower, and he, too, experienced ghostly presences. He heard music, as if an orchestra were playing; he envisioned a host of young peasant men who seemed to be encircling the tower with much laughter, singing, and roughhousing. These experiences each happened once, but he never forgot them. Years later, he found a parallel in a seventeenth-century chronicle by Renward Cysat of Luzern, who wrote about the *sälig Lüt*, the Swiss dialect expression for "departed folk," who manifested themselves through such carousing. Jung compared them to "Wotan's army of departed souls," who were "in the habit of walking about and showing themselves."

IN AUTUMN 1924, at the behest of the McCormick family, Jung was forced to clear his schedule abruptly for another trip to the United States.[3] Fowler Mc-

330

Cormick, a graduating senior with the Princeton class of 1924, shocked his family by announcing his intention to marry Anne Urquhart Potter Stillman — the mother of his college roommate — just as soon as she divorced her husband, his roommate's father. Edith and Harold were divorced, but they temporarily reunited in their opposition to Mrs. Stillman's becoming the wife of their only surviving son. Fifi (as she was called) was almost twenty years older than Fowler, the mother of four children, and "a striking redhead with a flirtatious manner and volatile temper . . . a siren to young men."[4] They had summoned Jung earlier that year to come and caution the unlikely couple about the pitfalls of such a marriage, but his commitments did not permit even a brief trip to the United States. He asked them to accept Peter Baynes, who he thought would make an excellent substitute because of their close association. Baynes, eager to dodge his then-wife in his chain of unhappy marriages, was all but commuting between London and Zürich to avoid her. He was only too happy to go to Chicago.

Depending on which member of the McCormick family was solicited for an opinion, Baynes's counseling was successful or not. Fowler remained besotted with Fifi and adamant that they would marry as soon as possible. Harold and Edith were devastated and desperate to prevent the marriage. Fifi Stillman credited Baynes "with having enabled her to 'find' herself and with having 'really won . . . the victory in the case of Stillman vs. Stillman.'"[5] Her divorce was final in 1926, and Anne (as she was henceforth known) began a liaison with Fowler that lasted until their marriage five years later on June 4, 1931.[6]

But in 1924, Edith and Harold worried that Baynes's disintegrating second marriage was affecting his judgment and begged Jung to come to America and talk Fowler out of his (to them) embarrassing infatuation. They wanted to keep the real purpose of Jung's visit as quiet as possible, so it was to be "unannounced" and "his identity [kept] from becoming public because he wanted a rest."[7] Actually, his monthlong visit passed in a whirlwind that began on December 10, 1924, when he saw patients in his home until the last minute and then rushed to the train that whisked him to Bremen and the steamer *Columbus*, which sailed on December 13.[8] The crossing was so rough that the ship arrived a full day late in New York on December 22. Before he sailed home on the SS *France* on January 14, 1925, he went to Chicago, Santa Fe, Taos, the Grand Canyon, northwest Arizona, the border region between New Mexico and Texas known as "the land of the Endless Horizon,"[9] New Orleans, Washington, D.C., and New York. He went as far west as Williams, Arizona, which he passed through after the Grand Canyon, but he did not reach California, then or ever.[10] In contemporary times, flying would make such an itinerary easy, but Jung traveled mostly by local trains and a 1924 Chevrolet.

Although all these places figured in Jung's imagination from time to time after he saw them, and many gave rise to opinions and conclusions that helped shape his subsequent writing, the most important and lasting aspect of the trip centered around the people he met and the variety of roles they played in his later life.

Jung was met at dockside in New York by Fowler McCormick and his friend George Porter, both of whom were his companions throughout the journey. Dr. Frances Gillespy Wickes also met the boat, for she was eager to set several dates for Jung to address the New York group. He would not agree to a definite date, acceding only to try to allow time at the end of his trip, when he would be in New York briefly. The three men went to the University Club, and two days later, on Christmas Eve, took the train to Chicago, where Jung was Porter's houseguest.

George Porter was the McCormick family's friend and principal heir to the fortune of a wealthy Chicago family.[11] Jung was never told of Porter's role in bringing him to the United States, that Porter made and paid for all the arrangements because Edith was suffering a severe financial crisis and Harold's income was entirely dedicated to supporting the operatic aspirations of his new wife, Ganna Walska. Porter also paid Jung a handsome stipend for "professional services" to the McCormicks,[12] which were to consist of seemingly casual conversations throughout the trip advising Fowler not to marry Mrs. Stillman.

On December 27, the three men boarded the train of choice to the Southwest, the Santa Fe Railroad's *California Limited*. Their first destination was the Grand Canyon, and from there, "the Zunis and the Pueblos." The journey took three days, and they arrived at the Grand Canyon on New Year's Day 1925. There they were met by a group of Californians, some of whom Jung had previously analyzed in Zürich and were to become good friends as well as patients and proselytizers of his analytical psychology.

First among them was Jaime de Angulo, a Spaniard born in Paris and educated at Johns Hopkins University School of Medicine. There, he married a classmate who was one of the school's first "hen medics,"[13] Dr. Cary Fink (later known as Cary F. Baynes, when she became Peter Baynes's third wife). Jaime de Angulo and Cary Fink both had significant private incomes, so both studied medicine primarily as a means to gain insight into the human condition without ever intending to practice.[14] During their marriage, she took occasional courses at Stanford University in botany or psychology, but only for personal satisfaction, while he became closely involved with the first generation of the celebrated Berkeley anthropologists[15] and an authority on the languages of Northern and Central American Indians.

Cary and Jaime were married from 1910 to 1922.[16] In 1923, she "kidnapped" their young daughter, Ximena, and fled to Zürich to keep from having to share custody.[17] In the decade they were married, Cary lived in Carmel, where an eclectic group of people clustered around her in a salon frequented by "friends and tame college professors" prone to "pyrotechnics."[18] Jaime was a deeply spiritual man who lived mostly alone in an isolated area of Big Sur, where he tried to establish a cattle ranch and make his living from the land. Cary, who always dressed in riding clothes, spent her time "h[olding] forth . . . from a chaise longue . . . a 'Madame Recamier in Pants.'" Jaime dressed as a Vaquero, his costume completed with extravagantly colored capes and blue French berets, his neck and arms covered with flamboyant pieces of Indian silver jewelry. They were truly an exotic couple and as fascinating to members of San Francisco society as they were to the poets, writers, and Berkeley anthropologists who literally camped out on their respective doorsteps.

Jaime and Cary may have had an unorthodox and fractious marriage, but they remained dedicated confidants by mail throughout the remainder of the 1920s. Their meticulously detailed letters provide a revealing exchange about Jung's method of analysis throughout the decade. They went separately to Zürich, she in early 1923 and he some months after, their ostensible reason being the need to consult Jung about the custody and upbringing of their daughter. Cary, who became one of the most forthright and objective of all Jung's adherents, stated her position in her initial sessions with Jung and benefited from what was basically his corroboration of her sensible attitude toward the child's upbringing. But Jung did not find such a commonsensical woman a particularly interesting patient, so he turned her over to Toni Wolff, whom Cary did not like. When she described Jung's ostensible snub to Jaime, he laughed and said that "the Pontiff herself [Cary] had to go through an understudy! Rather humiliating."[19]

Jung reversed his decision abruptly when Toni relayed the tales Cary told her Jaime was sending in letters, of "the creation myth of the Achumawi." Jung took her back, and Cary became his Scheherazade, a go-between whose news of Jaime intrigued him. She told Jung that the woman who became Jaime's second wife, the anthropologist Lucy (Nancy) Freeland,[20] thought his theories of mythical and racial consciousness were "completely off course." Cary warned Jung that Jaime and Nancy were influential in certain American intellectual circles, and if they thought him "all wrong about the anthropological parts of his thesis . . . a man of his intelligence cannot afford to ignore that criticism."[21] Jung's interest was so piqued by such outspoken disagreement that he could hardly wait to meet Jaime and rebut his objections, especially those concerning the collective unconscious.

Initially, the differences between de Angulo and Jung resulted in a mutually respectful intellectual friendship. Jaime told Jung that both his *Psychology of the Unconscious* and Freud's *Totem and Taboo* were "wrong from beginning to end," but he conceded that the most important aspect of each book's thesis was that "it *might* have happened that way! That's the important point."[22] Jung's greatest impact on Jaime came through the theory of personality types. Jaime sent detailed letters to Cary to be relayed to Jung. Not aware that Jaime had his own income, Jung urged Cary to send money for Jaime to come to Zürich for analysis.[23]

Jaime did not manage to get there until the summer of 1923, accompanied by his new (and pregnant) wife, Nancy. No official record exists to document how many analytic hours he spent with Jung, but Jung's diaries show that they did go to Bollingen for several long stays. There they talked about Jaime's theory of primitive thought from an anthropological and linguistic point of view as contrasted with Jung's mythological and philosophical perspectives.

Jaime spent much of his life in search of an authority figure to compensate for his own distant and disapproving father. Early on, he confided his fear to Cary that it would be unwise to meet Jung, for he would turn him into a father figure.[24] Jaime was delighted when Jung treated him as an equal colleague rather than a younger son. Jung said he was grateful for intellectual argument because so few men were interested in his work. He explained that far too many of his disciples were merely admiring, unquestioning women, and he was weary of the "eleven thousand virgin types." Nancy Freeland was not among these *Jungfrauen;* nor was she swayed by her husband's enthusiasm for Jung; she was "disgusted by the crowds of patients, the waiting-room intrigue, the petty alliances and jealousies." Nor did Jung endear himself at their first meeting, when he ordered Nancy to remove her hat so he could examine her head phrenologically.[25]

Jaime's analysis with Jung resulted in sporadic but ongoing sessions throughout the next four to six years, both in person and by mail through an extensive if unorthodox exchange of letters. Jaime returned to California and wrote detailed letters to Cary in Zürich about his dreams. She scheduled regular sessions with Jung to discuss them. To save him from the chore of lengthy written diagnoses, she took careful notes of what he said, then mailed them to Jaime. Jung's interpretation of Jaime's analytic situation did indeed reach him only after being filtered through a third party, but because Cary Baynes was so rigorously objective in every aspect of her life, her letters should be considered reliable documentary evidence of Jung's thought and technique at that time.[26]

"Golly," Jaime wrote to Mabel Dodge Luhan (a flamboyant society hostess, patron of the writer D. H. Lawrence, and owner of vast land holdings near the Pueblo), "but we have to be careful with this analytical powder magazine!" As his epistolary self-examination progressed, Jaime focused on changing himself from a thinking type to one who needed to learn to feel: "Without knowing it I wanted black magic from [Jung]. He, not being a magician, quietly refused. He says, 'I have only spirituality to give you. Take it or leave it — but don't give me headaches.' Jung said all that to me, last summer, but I wasn't ripe to understand then."[27] Jaime became fixated on his anima, which gave him a "terrific drubbing." He described it to Mabel Dodge Luhan as "almost physical . . . I saw Jung that afternoon. I said I was game to go on. He said: perhaps you ought to go more slowly. . . . I was on the point of abandoning myself over to the irrational, in desperation, because its pull was so strong . . . Jung made me realize the paradoxical knife edge."[28]

So it was not really surprising that Jaime should receive a telegram in January 1925 from George Porter, directing him to meet Jung at the Grand Canyon, "no expense to you." Jaime went, telling Mabel Dodge Luhan he "recognized the generous hand of Mr. Porter (of Chicago)."[29]

When he was in Zürich, Jaime told Jung about how he had collected the creation myth of the California Achumawi Indians and how devastated he was to have lost his manuscript in a fire. Jung offered to finance a second expedition so that Jaime could collect it again, on site, and Jaime accepted. He hoped to persuade Jung to go with him, but he directed Jung's interest in quite another direction when he described his friendship with a Native American of the Taos Pueblo. Antonio Mirabal, also known as Ochwiay Biano and Mountain Lake,[30] was an elder or leader of his pueblo and the Hopi nation. Jaime's casual description of Mountain Lake (as Jung usually addressed him) sparked his interest because the cultures of the Hopi and Zuni tribes were those most frequently studied by anthropologists, and most of their findings had been filtered to him by some of his California patients, among them the anthropologist Elsie Clews Parsons and the ethnologist Margaret Schevill Link. Dr. Frances G. Wickes, who lived in New York, befriended Mountain Lake on her visits to the Pueblo, and she also encouraged Jung to seek him out.[31] Jung was struck by how these two tribes had managed to remain more intact than other Native American tribes, despite the encroachments and indignities forced upon them by subsequent Spanish and English settlements. As the Hopi and Zuni were the two groups whose religious and mythological systems were most familiar to Europeans, Jung decided to focus on them. He was undeterred by Jaime's insistence that the Pueblo tribes were "too civilized" and not worth serious research.

When Jung insisted, Jaime agreed to connect him to "that group of old men, the Keepers of the Faith."[32] These were men far removed from the daily governance of the tribes, who never participated in tribal councils, and who spent most of their time fasting. They were the ones whose lives were devoted to keeping "in touch with the 'Powers Above,'" and thus they were the most revered members of the tribe. If Jung's visit were to be worth his while, these were the men whose confidence he needed to gain. Hoping to earn their trust, Jaime worked through Tony Luhan, the Pueblo Indian whom Mabel Dodge married.[33]

Tony Luhan was an intelligent, dignified Native American who suffered many slights and humiliations for having married outside his tribe. His kinsmen shunned him, and his wife's friends tended to treat him as a domesticated pet, both of which may have contributed to his eventual descent into alcoholism.[34] Luhan was caught in a bind where Jaime was concerned, as he liked and trusted him and wanted to effect communication between their two peoples, even though doing so would brand him as an informer at best, a traitor at worst. Honoring tribal strictures, Luhan insisted he would never disclose "the explanation of how everything is" or the "many things the whites don't know." Jaime swore that he would never publicize anything Tony told him and that he would tell no one "except that man in Switzerland" who "can do good with it, he can do things with it." He promised that when he and Jung were in Taos, they would conduct themselves as Tony Luhan's "friends." They would ask him nothing and would be content just to soak up the atmosphere, whether or not the tribal elders confided in them. Jaime swore to himself, to Tony Luhan, and to anyone else who would listen, that if he got "any stuff" that might be useful to Jung, he would pass it along, but he would not "sacrifice the Pueblo of Taos for the sake of museum anthropology." At the same time, he made clear to Jung his general dislike of the Taos Pueblo culture: "Pueblo psychology is a nasty one, too full of intrigue, lying, suspicion, gossip — too far removed from the big open life. These Indians are petrified in an attitude of submissive obedience to a labyrinth of secret rules and orders." He much preferred the openness of the California Indians "and their oneness with nature."

From Jaime's account, it appears that he and Jung both tried to evolve a theory of how Pueblo psychology might fit into and contribute to Jung's personality types. They hoped to present a system showing how Jung's position differed from the standard anthropological view held by, among others, Lévy-Bruhl, who posited that primitive peoples did not find local and prelogical thought mutually exclusive. Jaime believed that the Pueblo exhibited behavior that showed balance among all four of Jung's functions, that "each man carries the whole burden equally balanced." He asked Cary to check with Jung to make sure his impression was accurate, and she replied that Jung "agreed with all his intuitions."

Cary also reported that when Jung was with Antonio Mirabal, he had "the extraordinary sensation that [he] was talking to an Egyptian priest of the fifteenth century before Christ."[35] Mirabal was a complex man, a hybrid who was at ease in both the general American and the Native American cultures, a sophisticated political impresario as well as a revered spiritual leader. Although he affected a quiet and seemingly indifferent manner, he manipulated officials of the Bureau of Indian Affairs on matters of tribal importance and rendered them all but helpless when he persuaded George Porter to harness his considerable political clout on behalf of the Pueblo nation.[36] Mountain Lake was also the only Hopi elder who listened to Jung's theories about the mythology of the sun and responded in intellectual kind by divulging various Hopi myths about the sun, the moon, and the state of the world in general. However, when all Mountain Lake's remarks are taken as a whole — and they can only be filtered through Jung's recall of what he said, because that is the only extant account — it is clear that what he told Jung was superficial and guarded, little more than pleasing generalities already known to the public at large.[37] When he invited Jung to attend celebrations within the Pueblo, they were on the level of the "Buffalo Dance," a public ceremonial occasion written about patronizingly by the local *Taos Valley News*.[38]

Years later, when Jaime de Angulo had long since broken with Jung and was dying of cancer, he ridiculed Jung's experience with Mountain Lake. In a letter to Ezra Pound affecting Pound's unique phonetics, Jaime wrote:

> ai introdyused him tu the Indians in Taos & the s-o-b queered things there for me thru his teutonic stupidity ... but all that is anudher stori. ... sumtime ai may find dhe taim and inklinashun to put on paper mai rekollekshuns of Mountebank Jung in Zurich & his belief in astrology ... YES, and PHRENOLOGY too!![39]

Jung's ultimate version of the Taos experience consists of several paragraphs on one page of the *Protocols*. He seems bored and irritated that he must talk about it yet again.[40] "What impressed me there?" he asked himself. "Well, exactly all those things that are mentioned in all the travel writings." For the account that he knew would reach posterity, he condensed his conversations with Mountain Lake into a criticism of "Americans," meaning non–Native Americans, for the Pueblo people always spoke of themselves as "the people who live on the roof of the world."

Jung reported that he and Mountain Lake had two separate conversations, the first concerning the sun: "If the Americans didn't stop disturbing them in their religious activities through their missions, then the sun would no longer rise in ten years. The sun is their father and they help him rise. The sun wasn't made by God. It is the God." The second concerned the inner death of the "Americans": "What is wrong with the Americans? They are crazy, they think with their head and not their heart."

Mountain Lake's "sorrow" about the situation of his people impressed Jung, especially when he talked about his "religious conviction and his fear that the Americans could take these things [tribal ceremonies] away from them." Having expressed such a sympathetic understanding of Mountain Lake, Jung's final description is somewhat puzzling: ultimately, he saw the distinguished elder as merely "a man of above-average intelligence, i.e., above-average in comparison to the [other] Indians," and, quite simply, a man with whom he had some "good conversations."

JUNG'S PARTY spent almost two weeks in and around Taos, and during that time they were joined by a fluctuating contingent of Californians, some who came at Jaime's instigation and some who had been to Zürich for analysis and were eager to see Jung again. These included the aforementioned Elsie Clews Parsons, who would publish a study of the Pueblo Indians several years later,[41] and Margaret Schevill Link, who would study the Navaho nation.[42] Parsons was Jaime's friend, and Schevill (as she was then known professionally) frequently collaborated with Chauncey Goodrich, a San Francisco attorney who shared her interest in the creation myths of Native American tribes. Goodrich was accompanied on this trip by his wife, the former Henriette de Saussure Blanding.[43] He and his wife went to Zürich for analysis in 1923 on the advice of one of his sisters, Dr. Elizabeth G. Whitney, who had already been there in 1920 with her husband, Dr. James Whitney.[44]

This group of highly placed and influential Californians remained among Jung's strongest lifelong American adherents. They went to New Mexico hoping to persuade him to change his itinerary and come to the San Francisco Bay area to meet others who were interested in analytical psychology. Their active proselytizing caused many of their friends to become some of his most illustrious as well as his most interesting patients. Among them were the Pulitzer Prize–winning poet and writer Leonard Bacon;[45] the anthropologist Daniel Schirra Gibb, whose second wife was Nancy Freeland's sister Helen; Margaret Schevill Link's then-husband, Ferdinand Schevill, professor of Spanish at Berkeley; Bacon's friend George Beckwith, also a friend of Peter Baynes and, later, Jung's companion on his African journey. The Goodrich-Whitney circle also included the journalist Elizabeth Shepley Sergeant, who had been Jung's first American patient in the Burghölzli in 1904–05, and who would travel frequently to Zürich in the next several decades not only for analysis but also to write articles promoting his system.[46]

Despite the many persons who sought his counsel and company, Jung kept to the strict schedule that either he alone or in conjunction with George Porter established before the trip began. Besides the Pueblo Indians, he wanted to talk to "the American Negro in a natural outdoor habitat instead of a large city."[47] They raced across the "endless horizon" between New Mexico and Texas by car, then took a train to New Orleans, where Fowler McCormick knew of a "place near[by] . . . where Negroes were cutting trees to make forest products and living a natural life in the open." Fowler regretted that "Jung's opinion of the Negro was [not] advanced materially by our visit."

From New Orleans, the trio entrained to Washington, D.C., where Porter scheduled a visit for January 12 with Dr. William Alanson White at St. Elizabeth's Hospital. Ostensibly, Jung wanted to study "Negro patients" upon whom White was conducting research, but it seems unlikely it happened, as White's only recollection is that Jung met briefly with members of his staff. Porter wanted Jung and White to rekindle their acquaintance, because he was planning a subsequent lecture tour for Jung, a "worthwhile mission" to the University of Chicago. Porter envisioned it as a triumphant tour of most of the United States, including St. Elizabeths.[48] White said Jung was welcome to speak in the hospital, but there would be no funds to pay him; the point was moot, as the tour never took place.

Jung left Washington in a hurry on the early morning of January 13 in order to sail on the SS *France* from New York on the fourteenth. He stayed overnight at the University Club courtesy of Porter and spent most of the day firing off notes and letters. He did not go to Frances Wickes's apartment that evening, as she had wanted, but after a hasty dinner in the club, went to Kristine Mann's to meet a small group who would eventually comprise the nucleus of the New York Jung Institute.[49] Mrs. Wickes assembled them after Jung agreed to speak informally only to give them "a chance to see [him]."[50] He did not endear himself to this group, for his remarks centered on "racial psychology" and consisted of little more than bashing Americans for their lack of reverence for ancestral values. Traces of his interest in phrenology also emerged, as he stressed "morphological changes in the skulls of people."

Mrs. Wickes could not let the matter lie, because the other New Yorkers demanded an explanation for Jung's outrageous remarks. She wrote a gentle letter that expressed both her and the group's puzzlement over his unsettling performance, but instead of criticizing him, she asked if their views were valid. He "confirmed" them, but defended himself for having said what he did. "Things had to be as they were," he insisted, for the entire evening had been little more than "a ceremonial for the dead." He praised her for her "perfectly splendid" attitude that night and concluded that no matter what negativity he sensed from others, he sensed "no bad feelings" from her.[51]

Early the next morning, the *New York Times* reported that Jung sailed that day on the *France* after an unannounced visit to the United States. He had been in the country "about a month" and "kept his identity from becoming public because he wanted a rest."[52]

JUNG STAYED close to home between February and June 1925, writing some of the "smaller papers" and tending to the clamoring patients who descended in droves from the Hotel Sonne. From mid-July to mid-August, again with both Emma and Toni in tow, he gave a third series of English seminars, this time in Swanage, Dorset. One hundred or more persons attended, "far more than Jung liked in such a group."[53] They filled the only hotel in Swanage and overwhelmed the surrounding villages, testimony to how quickly Jung's analytical psychology captured British interest.

During this and the previous British engagements, a pattern formed that Jung followed throughout the remainder of his professional travels: he stayed on at the conclusion of his lectures for several days of relaxation, but always in connection with something educational. This time he went to London, where he made repeated visits to the Wembley Exhibition, especially the tribal African section. On little more than the spur of the moment, he began to think seriously about going back to Africa, to see primitive peoples for himself.

He had already been to North Africa, in March 1920, when Hermann Sigg invited him to see the sights while he tended to his oil investments. They touched land in Algiers and went from there to Tunis, where they boarded a train for a twenty-hour journey through Tunisia to Sousse and then to Tozeur and the oasis of Nefta, returning by steamer to Marseilles and by train back to Zürich.

Jung had prepared for this journey by reading an Arabic dictionary as they were conveyed from place to place, and he spent much time sitting in cafés or wandering through the streets and markets listening to the language and observing the people. He had a difficult time with Arabic and was disappointed that it was the only language he was unable or unwilling to learn thoroughly. He was certain this failure was linked to his father, who knew it well and was a noted scholar of its cultural history.[54]

The North African journey gave Jung his first "*point de repère* outside his own civilization."[55] It provided his first chance to observe a culture different from his own and to make comparisons, but North Africa was so different from Switzerland as to be incomprehensible and thus of little lasting import. Despite his insistence that he could not "write coherently" about Africa, he still described it with lyrical beauty in a letter to Emma. He was not sure what Africa was "saying" to him, but he was sure that "it speaks."[56] It was not until his second trip in 1925 that he realized he had not really undertaken his initial journey to investigate "primitive psychology." Instead, the first brief foray had made it necessary for him to confront a question he had spent years trying "to evade," of "what is going to happen to Jung the psychologist in the wilds of Africa?" Only after the second trip was under way did Jung realize that his interest in how Europeans reacted to primitive societies was not really an objective scientific project but instead an intensely personal one. His attempts to explore the subject "touched every possible sore spot in [his] own psychology."[57]

The 1925 expedition to eastern Africa was his longest journey ever, primarily because the African continent was so vast that long periods of time were needed to traverse even the small area his party covered. Such an interval provided an opportunity for Jung to think about what exactly there was in his home "atmosphere" that had become "too highly charged to endure."

———∞∞∞———

CHAPTER 24

The Bugishu
Psychological Expedition

On July 18, 1925, the most prominent story on page one of the *Milwaukee Journal* featured news of an "Expedition to Interior Africa" to be convened by "Dr. Jung, noted Swiss psychoanalyst." The local angle centered around Fowler McCormick, "heir to millions," who was to quit his job as a day laborer in his father's Milwaukee factory to join Jung. "Having become accustomed to the heat of a foundry," Fowler, the newspaper declared, would soon be going in "for something even more strenuous."

Fowler was working in such lowly circumstances because Harold was decidedly upset by his son's continuing infatuation with Anne Stillman, despite Jung's attempts to end the relationship. Hoping to do so himself, Harold exiled Fowler to one of his International Harvester foundries. For more than four months, the Princeton graduate had been punching a time clock and working rotating shifts to build heavy farm machinery. Other laborers allegedly praised him for not being "a snob," because he "spurned hundreds of offers to avail himself of honorary club privileges and invitations to exclusive homes . . . preferring rather to visit the workers with whom he toiled for eight long, sweaty hours." His grandfather John D. Rockefeller supposedly "highly approved of the method by which his grandson chose to learn the business to which he will fall heir."

The article was filled with misinformation, most of which the unnamed reporter gleaned firsthand from Fowler, who instigated its publication in the hope of persuading Harold and Edith to let him go to Africa and to pay at least half the expedition's costs. Fowler told the reporter that it would include "a group of British scientists" who would "penetrate hitherto unexplored regions of the African interior." What he really meant was that George Porter would be their traveling companion so that if Harold would not pay, Porter would. According to the newspaper, Fowler declared Jung's intention was to spend six months studying "native tribes and customs in connection with an extensive research on the psychology of the savage peoples."

The reporter, hell-bent on inflaming Milwaukee's large working-class Catholic population, described Jung as a former "disciple of Freud" who allegedly "shocked the world by announcing that the psychoanalyst is a more capable confessor than a priest because he is better trained." He ascribed Jung's fame in America to "Mrs. Edith Rockefeller McCormick [who] . . . was a student in his psycho-analytical clinic in Zürich."

Unfortunately, the article's impact was exactly the opposite of the one Fowler intended: Harold not only refused to give money for the expedition, but he also ordered Fowler to stay in Milwaukee, to stop seeing Mrs. Stillman, and to keep on laboring in the foundry.[1] In addition, Porter withdrew from the expedition, but with reasons so veiled and evasive that Jung could not penetrate them. Porter did not tell him his real reason, that he was going to India to propose to Mina de Manziarly, a Russian-French refugee with whom he had been in love for the previous five years. He was so uncertain of his suit that he told no one except his friend Kermit Roosevelt, who helped him arrange steamship tickets to India via England.[2] Jung was shocked when he learned from newspapers that Porter had married Manziarly on June 8 and gone on an extended honeymoon to parts unknown.

Fortunately, George Beckwith, another rich Chicagoan with more than enough money to finance the expedition, volunteered as a replacement. Beckwith had been commuting to Zürich off and on for several years from his luxurious life in Paris.[3] In his analysis, Jung decided that the troubled man's dreams revealed he did not have long to live. Because he was uncomfortable with Beckwith in a therapeutic situation, Jung followed his usual custom when there was something about a patient he did not want to deal with directly: he dispatched him fairly quickly to one of his adherents. In this case it was Baynes, because Jung thought he was less astute at interpreting dreams than Toni Wolff was and therefore could adapt more easily to this particular patient's needs. Baynes became Beckwith's primary therapist throughout the early 1920s in a querulous mentor-student relationship. The outspoken Beckwith did not hesitate to criticize or ridicule Baynes in public as well as privately. The "Pucklike"[4] Beckwith also criticized Jung, one of very few who could get away with it, probably because everything he did was so tinged with reckless disregard for himself, for others, or for anything that stood in the way of what he wanted. "A more delightful lunatic never walked a planet not distinguished for sanity," said his friend Leonard Bacon, who also described Beckwith as "the only man I ever knew who said whatever came into his head with complete effrontery and perfect impunity." For the stolid, middle-aged Jung, such behavior was mesmerizing. Although he would not take the risk of treating Beckwith, he liked having him around to observe.[5]

Thus, when Beckwith volunteered to pay for the African trip, Jung accepted.

When Beckwith insisted that Baynes join them, Jung acquiesced reluctantly. He had misgivings about Baynes's behavior even before they departed, fearing that he was "already abnormal back then." He thought Baynes was developing "affectations," which, whatever they may have been, he did not define. Most likely, Jung's accusations were couched in embarrassment. He had totally disregarded the troubled state of mind of Hilda Baynes, Peter's second wife, even after she began to make suicidal threats. Hilda Baynes was originally Jung's patient in Zürich during 1920 and 1921, another of those patients that he did not want to treat himself.[6] He turned her over to Baynes, upon whom she developed "such a school-girl crush" that she followed him back to London after the breakup of his first marriage.[7] Shortly after, Baynes married his patient. Hilda's wealthy Scottish family was so embarrassed by her insistence that she had been "possessed" since childhood by "bogies" and other "tremendous fears" that they were happy to entrust her to Baynes in marriage.[8] Shortly after, she began a pattern of frequent breakdowns and confinements, and Peter began his frequent escapes, mostly to Zürich.

Whether because of Peter's lengthy absences or not, Hilda's fears became so exacerbated when he told her he was going to Africa that she threatened to kill herself if he left her alone again. Jung allegedly advised Baynes not to "capitulate to her fears, as this would not help her in the end." The unfortunate woman made good on her threat by throwing herself off the roof of a block of London flats.[9] She did not die immediately but lingered long enough in full consciousness to upbraid Baynes throughout the anguished hours he spent at her bedside. He begged Jung for "advice, comfort, support," but if Jung gave any, no written document exists to verify it. After he heard of Hilda's death, Jung went to Bollingen for a few days alone and then resumed his frantic last-minute preparations for the trip. He told only Emma and Toni of Hilda Baynes's suicide: Emma sent a letter of condolence to Peter; Toni did not mention Hilda's death when she wrote but said only that if Peter wanted to talk, she was available.[10]

Baynes "never blamed Jung for Hilda's suicide"[11] but he became even more depressed after her death, his behavior more scatterbrained and erratic than when she was alive. Because Jung offered no overt comfort or support, Baynes dealt with his tragedy the same way he thought Jung did: he ignored it and kept busy. Contacting various agencies in the British government, he persuaded the Foreign Office to authorize and support the expedition under a grandiose title, "The Bugishu Psychological Expedition," and to pay a small stipend and provide letters of introduction to various colonial functionaries. All their crates were stamped with an impressive blue government seal that said "BPE" in large letters, so, on the surface at least, everything seemed in good order.

The first of the "Bugishu threesome's" many differences arose over the logistics of travel.[12] With their initial destination Mombasa, Kenya, Beckwith and Jung sailed from Southampton, England, on October 15, 1925. Beckwith wanted to sail on an English vessel, but none was available and Jung would not delay the departure, so they booked passage on the German ship *Wangoni*. This produced the first of Beckwith's continuing sulks. Baynes was not with them, as he had gone to France to be alone, and he did not join them until the ship docked at Marseilles. By then, Beckwith was deeply hostile and had insulted everyone on board.

All the other passengers were festive and merry, especially the five young British women who were going to Africa to marry colonial officials. They and their traveling companions avoided the strange threesome who formed a party but spent most of their time avoiding each other as well as the other passengers. Beckwith, his "patrician nose in the air," was "not a good mixer." Baynes "was very sad because he had just lost his wife," as he announced angrily to anyone on board who made the mistake of trying to engage him in conversation. He was "grief stricken" and wanted to get Jung alone to talk about it and "get straight with himself," but when Jung left his cabin, it was to spend his time "learning Swahili from an old settler."[13] He retreated to his cabin in a huff if Baynes so much as mentioned Hilda's name.

The Bugishu threesome was initially an object of curiosity, but by the time they reached Mombasa, everyone had grown accustomed to ignoring them. There was one Englishwoman on board, however, who was a chaperone for her sister, one of the Kenyan-brides-to-be, and who spent most of her time watching them surreptitiously. Many years later, Ruth Bailey could not recall whether she "picked up CG or he picked me up"[14] at the fancy dress party in the Mombasa hotel the night the ship docked.

Ruth Bailey was then thirty-three, a plain, outspoken, and independent Englishwoman. She had worked as a nurse with war veterans and as a home companion to the chronically ill, but most of her adult life was devoted to caring for her mother and her other siblings. She was "a very practical Englishwoman from Cheshire, straightforward and with an excellent sense of humor," and a woman of "great warmth, wisdom and integrity . . . [deeply engaged with] the details of domestic life and human relationships."[15] Once, while taking her constitutional walk on board the ship, she encountered Jung walking in the opposite direction. He gave her a "piercing look," but they did not speak. She thought, "He saw right through me. Not that I minded that, but it was a bit of a shock."[16]

With the masquerade ball in full swing, Ruth Bailey wanted to evade the jollity of all the happy couples. She went into a small room off the main ballroom and saw Jung sitting alone, engrossed in a sheaf of papers. She sat quietly for the better part of an hour until he broke the silence by asking if she was interested in maps; if so, he would be pleased to show her those parts of Kenya where he planned to go. After a pleasant hour, Ruth's sister and future brother-in-law came looking for her and she left. "I had never heard of Freud," she recalled, "so of course I had no idea who this Doctor Jung was or what kind of work he did. I didn't begin to find out until we were on the way home [from Africa] and my job was to keep all these wealthy Americans away who wanted to talk to him."[17]

The next morning when Ruth came down to breakfast in the hotel dining room, to the consternation of the others, Jung invited her to spend the day shopping with his trio in the local bazaar. Baynes "went off on his own affairs and Beckwith was annoyed." Jung used her as a buffer between himself and them for the rest of their time in Mombasa. She was with Jung every day for a week, "just saying what I thought and making him roar with laughter all the time."[18]

She dreaded leaving Mombasa, for she knew that six months of British colonial life lay before her, but her party of brides had to take a specific train to Nairobi, and they had to leave on schedule. Even though the Bugishu group had not yet engaged porters or collected the still-incoming supplies for their safari, Jung decided suddenly to go with the women, leaving Beckwith and Baynes behind to deal with logistics and get to Nairobi on their own.[19] Eventually they did, and by then the entourage consisted of personal baggage, tents, assorted utensils, two guns and four hundred rounds of ammunition, four native servant-bearers and a cook, and a truck to carry everything.[20] There was also a clumsy, primitive movie camera with which Baynes planned to film Jung among the natives. In addition, he arranged that during each of the four weeks they were on Mt. Elgon, supplies would arrive from Lawn and Alder in London that included bacon, eggs, sausages, apple rings, and even "apple tart and scones."[21]

To get to the mountain, Jung and the others set off without native escort in "a large safari box-body car."[22] They intended to drive from Nairobi to Mt. Elgon, where they expected to find their truck waiting to be unloaded. Afterward, they planned to walk midway up the mountain to the foothills, where the native tribes Jung wanted to study were settled. Apparently, their maps were outdated, for they intended to follow the old road to Uganda, not knowing it had been left in disrepair some twenty-five years previously, when the railroads made an easier connection.

The assistant district commissioner at Kapsabet, F. D. Hislop, described the former main road as "an out of the way place in those days," and he was surprised late one afternoon when a safari car pulled into his driveway and the largest of three men (Baynes) asked for the best route to Mt. Elgon. The commissioner thought it strange to see Europeans "wandering about, . . . more or less lost," but he showed them how the main road disintegrated into "a neglected earth track" several hundred yards from his house. He suggested they check into a nearby hotel for the night, as they could not cover seventy miles or so of unpaved tracks in the remaining hours of daylight in such a vehicle, but first he invited them to tea.

Baynes (whose name Hislop never learned), "a reddish-faced man," did the initial talking; Beckwith, immersed in "gloom" and "bored by the proceedings," never said a word; Jung, "the burly man," was "surprised and pleased" when Hislop asked if he was *the* Doctor Jung "of Zürich."

Hislop was curious about what they would do once they got to the mountain. Jung told him he planned to collect the myths and dreams of two tribes, the Karamojong and the Sabei. Hislop tried discreetly to tell Jung something he obviously did not know, that these two tribes were not even in Kenya, but in a "closed district" within Uganda, where outsiders were forbidden. As they had no documents authorizing entry into restricted tribal lands, they would have to apply to a separate nation for a permit. When they seemed "disconcerted," he switched to what he thought was a safer topic: how they expected to communicate with the natives when and if they ever reached them.

Jung explained that he had spent six weeks learning Swahili, the lingua franca of East Africa. Hesitating to appear as a "prophet of doom," Hislop nevertheless felt the responsibility to point out that such primitive tribes were unlikely to know Swahili, which anyway was weak in the expression of abstract ideas and emotions, and the two native tribal languages were even less likely to include concepts. Undeterred, Jung replied that "they had their own methods of getting results." Shortly after, they took their leave.

Whether the story originated with Hislop or with reporters who observed the trio during their time in Nairobi, the *East African Standard*, the largest newspaper in the area, ran a long article ridiculing Jung for thinking he could do research without knowing the native languages and concluding that even if he did it, "the natives would not tell him anything."[23]

"It was a queer thing," Hislop recalled, but he never heard another word of the Bugishu expedition, even though he had been "on the look-out for news for many years. Unless they had resources and prepared lines of work about which they did not tell me, I cannot help thinking that their safari could hardly have produced any useful results."

WHILE THE Bugishu expedition was wending its way toward Mt. Elgon, six weeks elapsed since Jung had said farewell to Ruth Bailey in Nairobi.[24] Ruth had accepted that she would pass the remaining five months of her African sojourn in the boredom and monotony of colonial life in Turbo, when one day, she recalled, "a runner came down from Dr. Jung to say, would I like to go up to the camp with them for a bit?" She sent back a simple message: "Yes." Her brother-in-law and the other Englishmen in Turbo thought her "mad," for no proper Englishwoman would make such a trip. It was such "a dreadful thing to do" that they refused to help her. Everyone was further appalled when Jung sent a long letter with a list of supplies he instructed her to buy and bring to "Rest Camp Kimilili." There, bearers would meet her at a certain time on a certain day (she remembered November 30 but was not sure) and would take her up to the base camp in the foothills. The intrepid Ruth was undismayed by the Turbo opposition, so she bought the supplies and set off on the 250-mile journey, cadging rides with various railroad workers until they plunked her down in a sea of "monkey grass." The bearers were there waiting, and together they all trudged up 2,100 meters to the Bugishu encampment.[25] When they entered the compound, Ruth Bailey realized why Jung wanted her there. "I was the buffer," she recalled. "When I got home and was thinking about it, I thought I was the comic relief. . . . I had made them laugh. But Mrs. Jung said that they all said I had saved their lives."[26]

Tensions were strained to breaking between Baynes and Beckwith, who both had exceedingly "short tempers." Even though there had been "nothing violent," Jung made Baynes sleep alone in a tent a good distance from his in one direction and placed Beckwith's at an equal distance in the other. While still in Zürich, Beckwith had told Jung he dreamt about being attacked and killed by poisonous snakes. Now in the jungle, the natives called Beckwith "the dandy," because he would not wear the sturdy boots such terrain required but insisted on wearing stylish trousers, long silk socks, and shoes that did not cover his ankles. He also insisted on leading the party when they went into the bush, and by the time Ruth arrived, he had shot thirteen or so mamba snakes, among the most dangerous in that part of the world. Jung feared for the possible consequences of such recklessness, and Ruth was exactly the calming influence they needed. Once she joined them, "they didn't fall out as much, which was all to the good because it was very hard going in places and we just had to keep going."

She had her own tent and there were more than enough supplies, because Jung, sure that Fowler would find a way to join them, had ordered provisions for four from the start. With her usual brisk efficiency, Ruth took charge of everything, from telling the cook what they would eat to telling the others when she thought they needed to attend to their personal hygiene, especially their laundry. For her, "everything was fresh and interesting and I loved it and enjoyed every minute of it even though it was very hard work sometimes." She realized what a disaster it would have been without her, how the "friction" between the others would have prevented Jung from working. What made the trip successful, and what made Ruth Bailey a lifelong friend and integral part of the entire Jung family once the safari ended, was her initial and lasting reaction to Jung himself: "CG [as she always called him] did not make *me* adore *him*, like all those women at home did. I never did that, and that is where the success lay in the end. That is why my relationship with him lasted so long."[27]

Once Ruth joined the expedition, she became, in effect, one of the boys. There was never any sexual tension, even though she teased Beckwith mercilessly about all the women in his life. She endured the physical hardships as well as any of the men did, and she chopped bush and climbed better than they did. When she told them forthrightly to get over their sulks, piques, and black moods, they obeyed her. She was the best possible "buffer" between Jung and the others, for she left him free to concentrate on what he had come to Africa for, the study of native culture and society.

DESPITE THE misgivings of Commissioner Hislop and the *East African Standard*, Jung had dealt wisely with the language difficulty by engaging as his "head-man" a native who understood both his Swahili and a little English, and who could communicate with the native tribes in their own languages. Ephraim, or Ibrahim, as he was called interchangeably by everyone,[28] made it possible for Jung to go where no other European had been before him. He took Jung into the huts of tribal elders, into the adjacent huts of their wives and children, and into the remote flea-infested caves, where some of the most primitive of these primitive peoples lived alongside their prized cattle, utterly indifferent to the dung-covered floors. In one such cave, Jung saw a native using a rudimentary stone ax, which he offered to exchange for one made of wood and steel. The native was pleased to have the modern ax, and Jung was delighted to take the prehistoric one home to Küsnacht, where it hung alongside other ceremonial weapons, shields, and clothing for the remainder of his long life.[29]

"I can hardly express what I experienced in Africa," Jung said in one of the earliest extant dialogues that became the *Protocols*. "It touched me from the start, the thought of what an artist I would have to be to express it." He tried repeatedly to describe what the experience meant but always seemed frustrated that his words could not convey the depth of his emotion.[30] His "first encounter with the original timeless primitive" came when he looked out the window of the train that took him from Mombasa to Nairobi and saw

> a Negro with two javelins motionlessly and completely naked . . . like a part of the landscape. There were reddish rocks and a giant euphorbia was growing there, very dark and high up in these reddish rocks and a tropical sun was shining. . . . Now: describe that! One cannot describe these emotions at all, one was simply enchanted.

He felt this enchantment throughout Africa, but never more so than in the native huts on Mt. Elgon. They were so primitive they reminded everyone of "Biblical times,"[31] surrounded as they were by hedges of thorn to deter marauding lions. To be extra safe, the natives had fashioned a removable door, also made of sharp thorns. Inside, a small stench-filled antechamber where the calves and miniature goats lived opened onto another tiny circular room with a pit in the middle for a fire, the dirt floor around it littered haphazardly with bones the natives had carved into primitive spoons. Even to stand in these huts was dangerous for Europeans, as the natives were indifferent about cleanliness or sanitation, and it was hard to avoid touching the walls or the floor. The natives were tiny people who wore no clothes, except for an occasional loincloth for the men and a sort of shell belt for the women, who were also loaded down with heavy metal jewelry.[32]

When Jung was with ordinary natives, he took everything in such good stride that Ibrahim had no qualms about presenting him to Libone, the witch doctor and most powerful member of the tribe. Libone, who always wore a blue monkey-skin cape, told Jung about the dreams the villagers confided, of how their ancestors came to them at night with green faces. Jung was fascinated because he remembered photos of Egyptian tombs on which all the faces of the dead were painted green. He was certain it indicated that some Egyptians had made their way as far south as Mt. Elgon in their search for what surviving manuscripts called the Mountains of the Moon. He believed the local tribes had incorporated the Egyptian green faces of the dead into their culture, as well as their worship of the rising sun and the young moon and their fear and distrust of the full moon.[33] Jung was relaxed when the native children flocked around him and clambered over his reclining body. His easy laughter forged a bond with the elders, who soon treated him with the same inquisitive camaraderie. These were the first white persons the natives had seen, but their fascination with pale skin did not hinder their perceptiveness in distinguishing one European from another. They called Jung the *Bwana Doctari,* or "Boss Doctor."[34] Baynes was *Bwana Mecuba,* "Boss Tall," because he was at least 6 feet 4 inches. Beckwith was *Bwana Maridadi,* "the beautiful one," because of the elegant wardrobe he sometimes changed several times each day.

As for Ruth, they were convinced she had rubbed chalk into her skin to be so white, so they rubbed her face and arms to see if they could see her real color beneath it. "I was terribly afraid," she remembered. "They kept pinching me, pinching my arms, and they were all like little skeletons to look at." One old man offered to pay four cows for her, and the sarcastic Beckwith urged Jung to take it: "Oh yes, C. G., let's get rid of her. We can drive those cows down into Uganda and sell them there." But then the old man noticed that Ruth had no jewelry, no copper rings around her neck, no brass plates in her ears. Jung showed them a small gold tiepin in the shape of a riding crop and told them it was hers and worth "twelve pounds." Everyone in the village came to see it, and the matter of selling Ruth was put to rest, for all agreed she was far too wealthy for the old man, and four cows was not nearly enough to pay for her.

THESE WERE some of the ordinary, routine experiences of daily life on Mt. Elgon, experiences that provided Jung with "an unconscious identity with everyone." By his easy acceptance of the natives and his willingness to accompany them up the mountain into isolated caves, the bamboo belt, dense jungle, and upper forest, he gained insights that served as a point of departure for many trained anthropologists for the next several decades. The Baynes film of the journey, for example, lingers long on many different species of plant life, as he and Jung collected data about the medicinal uses to which the natives put them. Once they spotted rhinoceros spoor, and by watching the ceremonial observances the natives performed while on the animals' trail, they learned of their fears, customs, and what might even be described as religious obeisance toward animals. They followed the medicine man as he conducted ceremonies for the dead, and noted the autonomy that many of the women, who lived in their own separate huts, had over their economic well-being.

On many days, they would trek the seventeen or so miles that took them to the top of the mountain. On one occasion when they traversed a grueling horizontal switchback route, it took most of the day to go a relatively short distance, because they had to chop through a bamboo thicket at every step. Suddenly, they were rewarded by stumbling into a field of wild delphiniums and sweet peas that looked exactly like an English garden. It was an astonishing sight that flung Jung abruptly back into European "cultural consciousness" after his immersion in "the incredible unity . . . the unconscious identity with [Africa]."

In one of the most emotionally chaotic passages in the early *Protocols*, Jung tried to explain what he meant by his feeling of unity with all things African:

> Every time I found the trace of the white man, as for example when the women didn't carry clay pots on their heads but petrol cans, a rupture went through me, like a wild animal that suddenly comes across human traces. Goddammit, now we have stepped into a memory of civilized life and we get a splinter in the foot! All that sounds so exaggerated because that primeval time was real, and it was like a beautiful dream where suddenly the unharmonious blaring of a gramophone spoils everything, or something like that. That [African unity] wasn't a romantic mood or anything, there was also an enormous cruelty in it and a gigantic meaninglessness. . . . And that is a world at rest in itself, which is complete, of gigantic meaninglessness and endlessly beautiful cruelty. It was as if I had fallen out of any time at all.

And then, he added:

> Of course I had to return to myself and think about what we will eat and where we will buy provisions and that we should go to this place and that. And I suddenly heard my friends speaking English and all that was terribly irritating, that these white pigs are right in the middle of it who belong to a completely different time and I myself was [part of] that awful disturbance . . . all that is tremendously emotional.

THE "BLISSFUL stay"[35] on Mt. Elgon ended after almost two months, when they struck their tents and set off for Uganda.[36] This was where Ruth was supposed to leave them and return to Turbo. Jung realized how beneficial her presence had been and how useful she could be on the rest of the trip, so he asked her to continue with them across Uganda and up the Nile through Sudan and Egypt to Cairo. To convince her, he said the best thing she could do for herself would be to live her own life and let her sister do the same. Ruth was eager to be persuaded to go along, but there was the problem of what to do about all the luggage she had left behind in Turbo. "Well, I'll leave you to deal with that," Jung replied.

"That was so typical of Dr. Jung," Ruth remembered. "Never once did he arrange anything for you. That was part of your task — you had to arrange everything for yourself." And she did, finding her way alone back to Turbo, where she collected her luggage, and eventually rejoined them in Jinja, Uganda.[37]

THE TREK down Mt. Elgon was difficult, especially for the heavily burdened porters, as they crossed makeshift bridges over deep ravines and hacked their way through dense jungle. Throughout Uganda there was a strong British colonial presence at every stage of the journey that took them into Sudan. There were many welcome "rest stations," fairly civilized encampments with running water and toilet facilities, but Jung thought there were also far too many "district commissioners" who invited them to drink whiskey in homes that looked as if they had been transported directly from the London suburbs.

The natives throughout Uganda and Sudan were used to performing for white men, and there is an oft-told story, by Jung and others, of how he was invited to an *n'goma*, a drinking-and-dancing tribal ceremony, which got out of hand, and he dispersed the threat by cracking his whip and shouting curses in *Schwizertütsch*, frightening the natives, who ran away.[38] When they related the story later to British officials, they were told these same natives had killed several white men the week before, and they were chided for their reckless behavior. Ruth haughtily informed the officials, "You don't know Dr. Jung! He *towered* above them. It was his will! His personality somehow, but he got them in line!"[39] Not for the first time, the British thought them all "mad" and feared for their safety. Jung's party remained secure in the belief that the sheer force of Jung's personal magnetism would keep them from harm. "He just loomed colossal!" was Ruth's final word on the subject.

While awaiting their arrival in Jinja, Ruth was "having a great time with all the 'cotton wallahs,'" as the young unmarried British farmers in search of wives were called. The town housed a collection of eccentrics, especially the hotel keeper who raised her parasol against the hot equatorial sun, as she followed her turkeys around to see where they hid their eggs. The woman fell ill, so Ruth took over running the hotel, which made Jung "jealous. . . . He would stalk out of the dining room, but I patched things up and we left town."[40] A group of local dignitaries came to see them board the local train, not because of Jung's reputation but because they loved Ruth: "It was my entourage," she noted, and Jung was a bit miffed.

They set off on January 14, 1926, for a very short train ride.[41] None of the British officials came to bid farewell, because they were alarmed by Jung's insistence that he and his party were going to walk most of the way across Uganda. They were sure it would result in certain death, and they wanted to keep their distance. There were no railroads in most areas and also no roads, because the British did not want Uganda and Sudan to be opened to each other. Those who insisted on going by land had to walk a distance of approximately one hundred miles on faint trails before they reached the place where they could board a steamer taking them up the Nile and into Egypt. Most Europeans wisely retraced their steps back to Mombasa, where ships took them around the Horn, through the Red Sea, and eventually into Port Said.

Even Sir Alan Cobham, the British daredevil flyer and aviation pioneer whose plane had touched down briefly, thought they were "mad to walk up to Egypt." Still, Cobham entrusted Ruth with delivering letters to people who lived along the way. When they met again several years later in England, Cobham was surprised that Ruth was still alive. "Whatever did you want to walk for?" he asked.[42]

No one wanted to walk, but Jung was determined not to waste time backtracking to Mombasa and was convinced they could walk the distance in three or four days at most. He must have been thinking in terms of hiking in the Swiss mountains, for the African landscape, clearly visible even though he chose to ignore it, was quite another story. On the first day, they discovered they could not walk after 9 A.M. because of the intense heat.[43] On the second, Jung made them get up in the dark and walk/run for about twenty miles, when heat and exhaustion prevented them from going farther. They were all losing weight at an alarming rate, especially Jung, who lost twenty pounds in several days but still insisted they had to keep going because they could not make it if they turned back. "You can't die here," Beckwith told Ruth. "We would just have to leave you by the wayside, so you just have to come on!" She thought he was encouraging himself more than her, as she was the one who kept Jung's pace the best.

On the third day of crazed trudging through scrub, Jung inadvertently started a brushfire that raged for miles. They watched in dazed stupefaction as birds and small animals fled in terror. The fire blazed for miles, but the bearers assured them no harm had been done, as fires started spontaneously all the time and the animals were used to them. Most worrying, they were running low on the chlorinated water that made their tongues swell and produced white foaming froth in their mouths. On the morning of the fourth day, they were surprised to see an old truck lumbering south along the dirt track they were following in a northerly direction. Jung stopped it and learned it had been hired by a German naturalist and his crew, who had been driven into the wilds and were now ready to be driven back out. Jung bribed the driver with money and goods, so the truck turned around, the foursome and their bearers boarded it, and they were driven north to their destination.[44]

They boarded a ship that took them past Juba, Mongalla, Malakal, Khartoum, Omdurman, Wadi Halfa, and Aswan. They spent most of their time sitting quietly on deck, happy to relax and watch the landscape. No one carried books, as they were too heavy in a backpack, and Jung did not keep a diary or journal at any time. The only record was Baynes's occasional filming, especially of the crocodiles, which mesmerized them all. Near the Ripon Falls, they learned that crocodiles had eaten several women who were washing clothes. Jung asked a Ugandan passenger why women continued to go there, when they knew the massive crocs would simply "flick them in with their tails." He was told it made no difference where the women went, because "if it is your time to go to the crocodiles, nothing will prevent it." Jung put the behavior down to another example of African fatalism.[45]

They broke the journey in Khartoum because Jung had been invited to lecture at Gordon College.[46] Baynes went off alone, muttering, and Beckwith sat around, "collapsed as usual." Ruth took the opportunity to spend many happy days at the zoo, being guided by the director, Major Brocklehurst, who also came from Cheshire. She developed a slight case of malaria, the first real illness to strike any of the touring party, but Jung fed her massive doses of quinine, and she was over it within a week. Beckwith, who had taken risks at every phase of the journey, now refused to take any precaution against mosquitoes and had a much more serious attack between Port Said and their final African destination, Cairo. Jung was so exasperated that he told Ruth to nurse Beckwith through it but not to bother him with health bulletins.

Jung was so entranced by everything he saw in Cairo that he decided not to leave until he was satiated, so they stayed for three months. For the first two weeks, he and Ruth went to the museum every day it was open. One of the curators took a fancy to Jung, so he let them into a private collection amassed by an old German, which was not open to the general public. Ruth remembered how, when they came out of the private chambers, "CG looked as if he was drunk with all this wonderful beauty he had seen, so much so that he walked in the middle of the road." She had to take his arm to lead him back to the hotel and thought of herself as a little English girl leading her drunken father home from a pub.[47]

They rode camels through the desert to visit the pyramids. Jung wanted to go through a Coptic monastery, and he thought Ruth should go with him, even though women were forbidden. He told her to dress like a boy and keep her mouth shut. He told the monks "this boy" was his disciple, and they were shown through without incident. They went to Abu Simbel, where German engineers were reconstructing some of the monuments. Jung spent hours watching them move back into place the finger of a statue, which was more than nine feet long.

When they arrived at Saqqara, site of the oldest pyramid, Ruth said she was tired and wanted to swim rather than climb all over yet another one. Jung was furious and "cut [her] cold." He did not speak to her as they continued on to Luxor, where they rode camels to the Valley of the Kings. She "threw a little tantrum" and said she might as well go back to England. It was an impressive threat, for now that they had reentered civilization, Baynes was more determined than ever to discuss his personal situation, and Beckwith suddenly wanted Jung to spend the days analyzing his dreams.

Ruth's interpretation of the situation was that Jung "always tried to keep me with him because he didn't always want to be talking shop. He wanted to be just an ordinary human being sightseeing and taking things in his own way. He got no chance with the other two." It was important for Jung to make peace with Ruth Bailey, and he did so by telling her she rode her camel well.

Jung "seldom went off by himself anywhere in Africa, but especially in Cairo," so his experiences there were partially filtered through the nearness of others. One thing he insisted upon, however, was that he "could never really relate to Islam."[48] The Africa that had the most meaning for him was the primitive, where he could find "the cruel meaninglessness of an indescribable bliss." He talked about this to Ruth as they sat at Port Said for four days, waiting for the boat to take them to Genoa. Beckwith decided to stay by himself in the hotel and "get over malaria," while Baynes sullenly nursed a toothache and hovered over Jung to be sure he was aware of it.[49] To get away from them, Jung chartered a sailboat every day, and he and Ruth would grab a bag of oranges and stay out on the water until nightfall. There, Jung talked about "the mood of Africa, of Africa's loneliness," and of how the inner effect of the continent was far more important than any external "weapons and pots and heaven knows what else the ethnologist has to show."[50] He talked about how disappointed he had been in his dreams throughout the six months he was there, for they were always "on the side of the conscious ego and not on the side of *primeval darkness.* I would have expected that the unconscious would joyfully seize this opportunity, but no, not at all!"[51]

What he deduced from his dreams was that "in the soul there lives a longing for light and an indispensable urge to emerge from the initial darkness." He talked about how the Elgonyi, as he called the mountain tribes, would wait for "the birth of the sun in the morning." He thought they were capable of sophisticated abstract thought, because they told him "it was not the sun that is god, but the moment when the sun appears is God." When they told him they were "happy that the night comes to a close now that the spirits are about," he credited them with the ability to rationalize and to recognize a godlike force, no matter how amorphously they expressed it.

Still, such insights depressed him. Perhaps it was partly due to simple exhaustion, but the trip threatened to end more on the emotional downside than on the up. Many years later, he tried to express what he was feeling at the time, convinced he could never convey his meaning to others:

For me the trip was a drama. One could say the drama of the birth of light because that was most intimately linked to me, to my psychology. It was extremely enlightening to me, but on the other hand, I felt completely incapable of putting it into words. It wouldn't mean anything to other people anyway! . . . I also wouldn't have been able to bear that people might have thought I had made up the fact that the Elgonyi had this religion that God was the moment. No one knows that after all, and now it is already lost anyway.

THE PASSAGE from Port Said to Genoa was fraught with storms, so everyone found a solitary space in which to hunker down and ride them out. Ruth was sad because she thought she would never see Jung again. She and Beckwith were going as far as Marseilles, but Baynes was going to Zürich with Jung, who had cabled Emma to send Franz to meet him and act as yet another buffer. Franz came on board when the ship docked, "very curious" about Ruth, whom he studied carefully before telling his father in a loud aside, "She's a bit too old for me." She thought of him as a tall, skinny, and socially awkward boy on the verge of manhood, and later, when he was tending to the luggage, she asked Jung why he had not brought Franz to Africa. Jung told her Franz was "still a schoolboy" and he did not want to cause problems with his teachers, who all thought his (Jung's) psychology was "terrible. They didn't understand it and they didn't like it. And besides, Franz would have been bored with Africa." She kept her own counsel but thought Jung wrong: "Franz would probably have wanted to go with his father very much indeed."

Ruth also thought Emma had sent Franz to Genoa to report back about "this curious Englishwoman" who had surmounted the rigors of the trip. She wondered what he would tell Emma about her, but it was obviously positive. Shortly after returning to Cheshire, Emma sent a cordial letter to ask if Marianne, who was taking music and language lessons in London, could spend her vacations with Ruth. The visit initiated a lifelong exchange between Cheshire and Küsnacht, as Jung, Emma, and their children went to visit Ruth and she spent many vacations and ceremonial occasions with them. In fact, she and Emma became more intimate friends than she had ever been with C. G., especially in the years immediately after the African journey, when his relationship with Toni Wolff developed complexities the principals could not have imagined when it began.

Shortly after Marianne visited Cheshire, Emma invited Ruth to Küsnacht. Ruth's first impression of Emma was of "a woman with a deep sadness in her eyes."[52] Beckwith, as a gift to Jung, had arranged for the artist George Hoyningen-Huene to paint Emma's portrait.[53] He wanted Emma to pose informally on the bend in the staircase that led up to Jung's consulting room and his library, but she sat stiffly and seemed unhappy with the entire process. "Come, Miss Bailey," the painter urged. "Tell her funny stories to amuse her." Ruth obligingly dropped down on one of the lower steps and began to chatter up to Emma. Even though she laughed, her eyes "remained very sad."

"Tell her stories about Africa," the painter urged, and so Ruth began to talk about the crazed hotel keeper under her parasol chasing turkeys in the noonday equatorial sun; of the splendidly tall native mistress of a colonial farmer, all decked out in European finery, who kept repeating over and over to no one in particular the only English she knew: "How do you do? How *do* you *do?*" Emma began to giggle, and Hoyningen-Huene was pleased. "Keep talking, tell her more."

Ruth told of how she and Beckwith came out of their tents one night on Mt. Elgon to wish upon and bow to the "sickle moon seven times over for good luck," and of how they disturbed Jung's sleep, so he rushed out of his tent to roar at them in only "shirt, no shorts, boots and leggings." When he heard what they were doing, he joined them in bowing to the moon, as Ruth and Beckwith "collapsed in hysterics." As she continued to tell "hilarious stories about Jung's antics," she noticed that Emma's face was a study in incredulity:

> Of course all this was a revelation to her because Jung only told her about the work he had done in Africa. That family was so formal that they shook hands every time they met: no one ever kissed or hugged, there was no happy chatter at mealtimes, no funny stories. I think Emma could picture the things I told her but all the same, it must have been something unknown.

Even though Ruth had just met Emma, only one word seemed accurate to describe the Jung marriage — "sad":

> I think they must have had some awfully good fun when they were young because they both always had such a good sense of humor when they were alone with others, not when they were with each other and other people. Before they got into this three cornered affair, it must have been quite amusing to be with them because they could both see the funny side of things.

JUNG HAD undertaken this second African journey to find out what the continent was "really saying" to him.[54] To his "astonishment," he realized that he had gone because "the atmosphere had become too highly charged" at home.[55] The overwhelming emotion that had suffused him at the Wembley Exhibition was much more than the desire of a civilized westerner to study his own reactions to primitive cultures. Only after he returned did he realize that the entire undertaking "had been not so much an objective scientific project as an intensely personal one."

He did not realize until the trip was over just how "stubbornly" his dreams ignored African experiences and had been about "personal problems."[56] Now that he was at home, he wondered why he had bothered to go, as daily life resumed the same old pattern: an overwhelming patient load, plus dealing with all those who clamored to become new patients; fulfilling his military service during July 1926; a short annual August vacation alone with Emma in the Engadine, followed by the ritualistic necessity of sending her home alone and inviting Toni Wolff immediately afterward to Bollingen. There were invitations as well, to speak in the United States, England, Augsburg, Prague, and Darmstadt. The Psychological Club wanted another seminar based on his experiences, and every day brought requests for translations of his previous writings as well as requests for new ones.

After Africa, he did continue to travel as a means of escape, but throughout most of the next decade, his journeys were short and swift. What he did mostly was think about all the "smaller papers" and the "smaller talks" he had been churning out one after the other and consider what they meant in the larger scheme of analytical psychology. He wondered if there was a coherent message that might lie within them and lead him to new work or if he needed to seek other arenas and avenues of expression.

Again, the *Protocols* show an elderly man working toward a cohesive way to express what he thought at a much younger time. In various passages, he touched upon the "No. 1" and "No. 2" personalities of his childhood; in others, he tried to speak about the "I" and "the self." He abandoned this line of inquiry by saying "conscious understanding" would not suffice when he tried to "switch off the I and make way for what wanted to reach me from the outside." He discovered that he could not empty his consciousness in order to do this, because he was overcome by "an inner hearing . . . an activity from the inside." Sometimes he had to resort to yoga to make this "inner arousal subside," but the resulting thoughts were still not satisfactory.

Because he could not formulate these ideas coherently, he decided to revisit what he had written and spoken about up to the African journey. In looking through his manuscripts and publications, he noted that his primary "scientific question" was "what happens when I turn off consciousness. I noticed from dreams that something was in the background."

At some point it became clear that what he needed to do now was "give it all a fair chance to come out."

CHAPTER 25

"Professor" Jung

Jung was fifty in 1925. On his birthday, "there was a beautiful sunset, the waterfowl called to one another, a chill night wind came down from the mountains, and [he] drank an extra bottle of wine and smoked a birthday cigar." One of his friends thought the occasion should be celebrated with a Festschrift, and Jung thought it "touching."[1]

No volume commemorated the birthday, but in retrospect it was an important milestone. His fiftieth year divided his professional life almost too neatly in half, with the years before distinguished by the evolution and development of a theory, and the years after noted for its mature expression. In the first half, lasting roughly until the end of the 1920s, his professional activity shifted from the original emphasis on clinical research to an intense study of comparative histories, cultures, societies, and religions. In the last half, he replaced his attempts to interpret the human psyche through the analysis of individuals with other kinds of explorations toward defining the collective unconscious, primarily through his study of alchemy.

His personal life saw several dramatic shifts as well around 1925, when a new group of individuals came to Zürich to study his psychology. Some remained for the rest of their lives and became central figures in assisting him to develop it; others returned to their homelands to practice analytical psychology and make his theory truly international. All these persons came for therapy but also, and sometimes with greater eagerness, for admission to his English seminars at the Psychological Club. Because they considered him more a teacher than a physician, they were responsible for changing his title through a kind of informal osmosis: "Dr. Jung" became "Professor Jung" for the rest of his life.[2]

Although, technically speaking, he had been giving "seminars" since 1913,[3] he did not begin to follow the lecture format consistently until 1925, when he instituted a series of Wednesday morning talks in English that continued for the next fourteen years. The fact that he spoke in English attests to his growing international following, for despite the club's stated intention to keep itself

Swiss, there were more British and American than Swiss or other German-speaking members.

The 1925 seminar was the shortest, running from March 26 through July 6.[4] Entitled Analytical Psychology, it focused on Jung's personal history of how his psychology had developed to that date. He began with his own psychological beginning, his university studies in 1896. He then explained how his theory developed during the years with Freud and followed that with an incisive account of how his psychology evolved after their break.

It was the first seminar Jung gave at the new home of the Psychological Club on Gemeindestrasse, the imposing house bought by Edith McCormick and still its home today. Admission was free, but only those persons Jung personally approved could attend, and, generally, they had to have been analyzed. The 1925 seminar was also the first to be officially recorded.[5] Cary F. Baynes acted as stenographer and multigraphed copies for the participants, who paid a small fee.[6] Jung spoke all morning, from nine until noon, with only a short break for tea. Afterward, surrounded by a bevy of chattering women, he walked the short distance to the Wolff house on the Freiestrasse, where he ate lunch with the family and spent the afternoon alone with Toni. If Emma did not have a luncheon engagement of her own, some of the more thoughtful seminar members escorted her to the nearby tram stop that took her either to the train station or the ferry, from which she went home alone to Küsnacht.[7]

DESPITE JUNG'S insistence that they were not suited to each other and their marriage would not last, Cary Fink de Angulo and H. G. Baynes did marry.[8] She had been living in Zürich for the previous several years with her daughter, Ximena, and her sister, Henri F. Zinno.[9] Cary and Henri both had substantial private incomes, and their house in Kilchberg became a salon where friends (mostly American and English) gathered to talk about analytical psychology, and where many others lived while they consulted Jung.[10]

Jung liked and trusted Cary Baynes, and he was the first of many who urged her to practice as an analyst, especially as she was already a medical doctor and he considered medicine the necessary preparation.[11] She never did, however, preferring to live life at her own pace without constraints imposed by others. The only task she willingly shouldered was doing whatever Jung needed to help further his work.[12] Besides acting as his stenographer and sometimes secretary when correspondence became too heavy, Cary was a meticulous translator and diligent editor. She was also rare among Jung's friends, for she did not hesitate to speak her mind and tell the truth as she saw it, which all too frequently he did not want to hear. Cary and Peter Baynes together translated into English the essays that became the books *Contributions to Analytical Psychology* and *Two Essays on Analytical Psychology*.[13] Both sold well and increased Jung's English-language audience, as many readers found them "rather clearer than the earlier ones."[14]

Jung wanted Cary and Peter to stay in Zürich because they were such valued helpers, but they left, despite his wishes. Cary persuaded Peter to return with her to California and set up a practice in the Bay Area, where they could prose-lytize further among the Californians who had been some of the first Americans to seek Jungian analysis, among them members of the Goodrich and Whitney families. By 1927–28, the year Cary and Peter spent in California, many had al-ready spent a year or longer in Zürich; among the women, it was often to the dismay of their husbands and the resentment of their children.[15] One Cali-fornian who went to Zürich for an extended stay was Frances Goodrich Léon, who had been living in New York with her husband, Maurice Léon, a French national and wealthy Wall Street lawyer. Frances had three children, for whom she also sought Jung's therapy despite Maurice's insistence that she bring them back to New York. When she refused to leave Zürich, he continued to pay his family's therapy expenses even as he became Jung's unrelenting enemy.

Some other Californians who went to Zürich included persons who became major figures in analytical psychology: the young Joseph Henderson; Jo and Jane Hollister Wheelwright; still later, Sheila Moon and Elizabeth Howes; and after them, the anthropologist Maude Oakes.[16]

With Cary away, Jung needed a new stenographer in November 1928, when he began the long series of seminars on dream analysis that continued through June 1930.[17] He found one in Mary H. Foote,[18] a new patient he had previously refused until Robert Edmond Jones's passionate pleas on her behalf won him over. Jones, already famous as a Broadway stage designer,[19] went to Jung in 1926 at the urging of his New York analyst, Frances Gillespy Wickes.[20] Mary Foote told no one but her closest friends, Bobby Jones and Mabel Dodge Luhan, that she was on her way in 1927 from China via the *Trans-Siberian* and *Orient* expresses to see "the old devil at 228 Seestrasse."[21] She begged them not to tell anyone else that she was in the midst of a "nervous breakdown," because she "hated nervous women" and considered herself "a professional who ought not to be having one." She expected to be in Zürich for a year at most, but when she died in 1968, her obituary described her as Jung's "secretary," who had only recently returned from Zürich to live in her native Connecticut.[22]

Of all the women who congregated around Jung in those years, Mary Foote appears to have been the most self-effacing and humble, the "little brown shadow who flitted on the fringes of Jung's professorial life."[23] However, her ap-pearance belied her past achievements and her station in life. Born in 1871 to a prominent Connecticut family, she was a cousin of Harriet Beecher Stowe and a neighbor and friend of Samuel L. Clemens. She was educated at the Yale School of Fine Arts and was one of the first women admitted to Yale Graduate School.[24] Until she went to Zürich, she forged a career as a noted portrait painter. Among her friends was the artist John Singer Sargent, who painted a bucolic outdoor setting that featured himself and Foote working at their easels.[25]

Mary Foote's subjects included Jo Davidson (who called her "the virgin foot"), Ruth Draper (whose brother, Dr. George, analyzed with Jung), Malvina

Hoffman, Senator Hiram Bingham, the Countess Palfy, and Jung himself.[26] Her portrait of Master William Draper graced the cover of *Town and Country* magazine.[27] Her friendships were diverse and included Eugene O'Neill, Sir Harold Acton, Leo Stein (brother of Gertrude), Frieda and D. H. Lawrence, and the Bragiotti family of Florence, one of whose daughters married John Davis Lodge, the governor of Connecticut, and another the artist Emlen Etting.

Despite having more commissions than she could accept, Mary Foote still lived hand-to-mouth on a small private income and what she earned from her portraits. Her letters frequently describe how much she hated going to wealthy homes in the American Midwest to paint uncooperative children, but how necessary was the income to support her beloved studio at 3a North Washington Square in New York. Despite her often grinding poverty (some winters she could not afford coal to heat the studio), she was loathe to give it up, as it was the single dependable constant in her life. For some years, she shared it with the American beaux-arts sculptor Frederick W. MacMonnies, until the early 1920s, when "a quite possibly carnal as well as physical"[28] relationship between them soured and she fell into a deep depression. Initially, like Bobby Jones and Mabel Luhan before her, she was a patient of Smith Ely Jelliffe, but they all left him for other analysts (Jones for Mrs. Wickes and Luhan for A. A. Brill). Jones and Foote agreed that "Jung got right down the first days farther than Jelliffe ever got."[29]

It took a great deal of persuasion by Bobby Jones to get Mary Foote to Zürich. He told her, "All I say is *stick!* and again, *Stick!* Stay and do it, and the old Bastard, as we all used to call him (he knew it), will do the rest."[30] It took an even greater amount of Jones's persuasion before Jung accepted the drab little painter, but once he saw the portraits of some of the Native Americans she painted at Mabel Luhan's Taos ranch, he was impressed by how sensitively she captured their inner spirit and became intrigued by her case. She thought she might be too old for analysis, but Jung told her age was not important: "As long as you live, you have all the problems of the living, only different ones than [at] twenty."[31] To Foote, Jung seemed "the greatest case of a square Swiss gentleman, but of course with the extra fluid intuitive thing."[32]

Her friends pressed her to describe her analysis, but she found it "perfectly impossible . . . because I'm the type that *experiences*, with no mind worth mentioning to explain things." She said she was "not a darting intuitive extravert like Bobby," but as Jung was "the most reliable feeling creature," she was sure he would lead her eventually to "emerge" from her depression.[33] She expected to finish her analysis in several months, but the schedule Jung had established since returning from Africa precluded this. He "only worked with his patients part of the time" and then "sent them off for a month . . . in April, we have another month off and two or three months in the summer."[34] Also, he established an ironclad rule not to see patients before "the first of October."[35] After his annual month of military service, his travels for professional engagements, and his occasional pleasure trips were all factored into his yearly calendar, he saw patients only from four to six months, and that is a generous estimate.[36]

Mary Foote's first session with Jung took place in 1927, and shortly thereafter she told some of her American friends that she was abandoning her career as a painter because "Jung didn't want me to paint."[37] Whether true or not, one year later she told Mabel Luhan she had given up her New York studio, "the one warm thing I had in life," to become "a floating particle with no background living on the tiny income that I have amassed and with *no* idea about the future. Jung didn't make me do it but it came *about*, with much agony on my part."[38]

From 1928 on, her "work" — the word she used throughout her correspondence — was to attend Jung's seminars, then to type, mimeograph, collate, and send copies to the attendees, as well as to a select group of subscribers who were unable to be in Zürich to hear them. Jung refused to read the typescripts Foote prepared, insisting that "reading what you *said* is like eating your own vomit."[39] Because he even resented having to answer the few questions she asked only if she needed to clarify or refine his meaning, she became entirely responsible for all textual changes. Her original typescripts show many modifications, but they were always stylistic, to improve or elucidate Jung's language without changing the substance of what he actually said. Her most overt changes were the insertion of relatively harmless additions to make the text read more smoothly (such as an occasional "however") or to make his English phrasing less dependent on awkward German constructions.[40]

In some instances, as in the 1928 seminars on dream analysis, there is a special difficulty in assessing what Jung actually said, because Foote prepared a composite text based upon the notes taken by six members of the seminar, giving special credit to the "constant cooperation and the specially valiant help of Mrs. [Cary] Baynes and Dr. [Mary] Howells." Some volumes contained drawings of the materials Jung used to illustrate his lectures, copied "by Mrs. [Charlotte H.] Deady."[41]

Each volume could run to 150 pages or more, and there were from 90 to 140 names on the mailing list. As most of the attendees returned to their homes once the lectures ended, Mary Foote had to collate, pack, and mail their copies. All too frequently, she had to pay for postage, because many who were filed in her ledgers under the heading "bad debts" refused to pay for it or for the book.

Some unidentified person(s) paid her a small salary, and most people thought it was her only income.[42] By the end of 1928, she had moved out of her dreary room in the Hotel Sonne and was in the first of the small apartments she rented, first in Küsnacht, then in Zürich. Despite living what she called "the most utterly monastic hard-working life,"[43] she kept her subscription to the Social Register and paid her dues as a charter member of New York's elite Cosmopolitan Club.[44] Interestingly, she continued to paint in secret, even though most of those in Zürich who knew her swore she had no life other than preparing copies of the seminars. When her last apartment was cleared out, she left behind many canvases that were tossed out on the street.[45]

Those who knew her best said Foote "made a religion out of friendship."[46] She maintained a private social life, with a continuing procession of friends who came and went, among them the "California Whitneys" and the "Goodrich-Léons," Elizabeth Shepley ("Elsie") Sergeant, and Frances G. Wickes, who she thought was "rather a power devil, especially with other women."[47] When Ruth Draper came to Zürich to visit her brother, Mary Foote was the only other person who knew she was coming. Dr. George Draper told Jung, who chastised Foote for her inordinate discretion before inviting them to tea with him and Emma at Bollingen.[48] Foote was secretive about her personal affairs to such an extent that she kept a notorious love affair so hidden that no one in Zürich, including Jung, knew about it. Sometime in the early 1930s, she had a liaison with the Harvard-educated Nazi Ernst Hanfstängl, with whom she later exchanged "passionate, Teutonic love letters."[49]

Mary Foote's private life was far more complex and worthy of serious description than it is usually accorded by those who study the history of analytical psychology or write about the life of Jung. In that sense, she is representative of many other women who came to Zürich at this time and remained for the rest of their lives to become important players in Jung's. Foote's family ungraciously described them — and her — as most other commentators on Jung's *Jungfrauen* have done, as women "with female problems who, like a lot of other sentimental-mystical crones, got in over [their] head and relaxed by attaching to the Doctor."[50] Such descriptions admittedly touch upon some of the personal difficulties in these women's lives, but they totally ignore their intellectual abilities and achievements. Thornton Wilder, who sought Jung's counsel shortly after his novel *The Bridge of San Luis Rey* won the 1927 Pulitzer Prize, had a much kinder view of the women whose lives were centered around analytical psychology than is usually accorded them. He saw them as women "whose melancholy gentleness seems to allude to the fact that life has been unjust and unkind."[51]

Another who was often derided was the British Barbara Hannah (1891–1986), daughter of the dean of Chichester Cathedral who became a bishop of the Anglican Church.[52] Her appearance was off-putting, so many people did not look beyond the gawky woman with the bad teeth and sunken jaw, piercing nasal voice, and nervous bleat of a laugh to see the witty and talented woman within.[53] Hannah went to Zürich in 1928 because she read Jung's essay "Women in Europe" and thought it spoke to her condition. At the time, she was living in Paris and struggling unsuccessfully to become a painter, isolated and hungry in the proverbial unheated garret.

She arrived in Zürich without contacting Jung in advance, took a room at the Sonne, and literally rang his doorbell to ask for an appointment. Her aggressive "animus hound"[54] appearance must have alarmed the maid, for Jung came rushing down to see her. As they spoke, he recognized some quality that led him to confide in her from the first as frankly and colloquially as he did in those whom he had to know well before trusting them.

"I loathe the baby work," he told her, using his personal slang for the beginning sessions of analysis. "If possible, I always send my new people to someone else first." Thus, Peter Baynes became Hannah's first analyst, as Jung wanted her to have something in common (in this case language) at the beginning. When Baynes left for California, Hannah worked next with Toni Wolff and then with Emma Jung. In the same colloquial succinctness that Jung liked to use, she described her three analysts.

Baynes "had a heart like a hotel, but otherwise he was quite all right." In other words, his empathy with his patients sometimes got in the way of their treatment. Toni Wolff "played a great role [in Jungian analysis] but of course people were jealous of her and she had many enemies. Her whole motive in everything she did was to help Jung so that he could devote himself to his creative work. People complained sometimes when he sent them to her, but she always understood and was not blinded by their complaints." Hannah, a lesbian who later shared her life and home with Marie-Louise von Franz, did not disclose that she had fallen madly in love with Toni Wolff, who did not return any emotion beyond professional friendship. As a gift of her love, Hannah painted an evocative portrait of Wolff, but despite the personal nature of the gift, Wolff did not let the relationship progress beyond their shared admiration for Jung's psychology and their mutual adoration of dogs, Hannah's English bulldogs and Wolff's Pomeranians.

Even though Emma did not officially begin her analytic practice until 1930, she saw Hannah unofficially before then. About Emma, Hannah said, "It was all very much like going to tea with a lovely and gracious lady, and only afterward did one realize that she was an excellent analyst."

Hannah bragged often that Jung recognized at their first meeting that she had the temperament to become an analyst. She was probably correct, but in years to come, his faith in her was frequently tested. Hannah had a quick intelligence and could grasp complicated concepts easily, but she was stubborn and all too often insisted upon imposing *her* view onto *his* theory. There were repeated conflicts between her and Jung over various transcriptions of his seminars and translations of his writings that she prepared (only some at his instigation).

When Hannah finally got beyond the "baby work" of analysis and Jung accepted her as his patient, they spent most of her sessions discussing methods and procedures. During one of the many they devoted to a study of psychological types in general rather than to Hannah's in particular, Jung made two points she never forgot. The first concerned differences between the national characters of the English and Americans. The conversation came about when Hannah told Jung she was thinking of returning to England to build a career as a lecturer who would explain his psychology to her compatriots. Jung did not respond specifically to this possibility, but he used it to make the comparison of how different the English were from Americans:

> In England you have to be careful not to make educated mistakes. You must look up everything you are going to mention. . . . Don't ever make that kind of mistake in England, because they will catch you at once. Now, in the U.S., it won't matter. Don't worry about it, because they wouldn't know the difference, most of them. *But* — and this is important — Americans have a 6th sense for the genuine. Don't *ever, ever, ever* say anything for the effect of it if you are not absolutely certain, because they will catch you up on it.

Jung told her, "The American sixth sense for the something real is the reason they have discovered me, while Europeans have yet to do so."

The other point he wanted to make concerned the anima within men. He said men could not work with him or become his friends because "they have a harder time accepting their anima than women [do in accepting their animus]." He said he could only get along with men who had established solid and respectable careers in other fields, because other psychologists always became competitive.

One such nonpsychological friendship began in 1930 with the Nobel Prize–winning physicist Wolfgang Ernst Pauli (1900–58).[55] Pauli was the son of a distinguished professor of chemistry at the University of Vienna whose numerous extramarital affairs caused Pauli's mother to commit suicide by poisoning herself.[56] Pauli became unhinged, and shortly thereafter, he jumped into a brief and hasty marriage with a cabaret performer. He quickly fled both Vienna and his wife and went to Germany, where work and womanizing proceeded in tandem. Work won out, and from 1923 to 1929 his theoretical brilliance was acknowledged when he identified the exclusion principle; fame followed after his collaboration with Werner Heisenberg on general quantum field theory. In 1928, at the age of twenty-eight, Pauli was appointed Professor of Theoretical Physics at the Zürich ETH.

By 1930, he was as infamous as he was famous in Zürich because of the so-called Pauli effect, a joke coined by colleagues who claimed that his mere presence in a laboratory was enough to make accidents happen. He began to quarrel violently with people throughout the university, and his position was jeopardized, but his real notoriety stemmed from carousing around Zürich, where he became falling-down drunk and got into highly public brawls in local bars. All these factors were certainly cause enough for him to consult Jung, but Pauli's main reason was nightly dreams so disturbing they affected his waking life.

He went to Jung for therapy in 1931, but Jung did not accept him. After an initial conversation in which he determined that many of Pauli's dreams stemmed from his problems with women, and because of his "extraordinary personality,"[57] Jung sent Pauli to Erna Rosenbaum, a young woman on the growing list of analysts whom Jung analyzed and then authorized to treat patients using his therapy. Jung chose Rosenbaum deliberately: describing Pauli as "chock-full of archaic material" and Rosenbaum as "a woman doctor who was then just a beginner and who did not know much about archetypal material," Jung decided to experiment by "getting that material absolutely pure."[58] He decided not to see Pauli at all during his analysis with Rosenbaum, so that he might be kept "free of [Jung's] own personal influence." Jung did not meet Pauli again until eight months had passed. He was Rosenbaum's patient for the first five months, and for the next three he had no analysis. Pauli recorded his dreams over a period of years, amassing a grand total of more than thirteen hundred, but when he analyzed with Rosenbaum, she had only four hundred to study. Of these, Jung personally studied only forty-five, and he incorporated parts of them later when he wrote "Individual Dream Symbolism in Relation to Alchemy."[59]

After the three-month hiatus when he had no analysis, Pauli resumed therapy with Rosenbaum, seeing her from 1931 to 1934. In 1932, he began to meet Jung every Monday at noon to discuss his dreams in what was more of a far-ranging, informal conversation than a formal analysis. Over the next twenty-six years, in person and by mail, they worked through Pauli's dreams, in the process forging "an extraordinary intellectual conjunction not just between a physicist and a psychologist but between physics and psychology."

The friendship with Pauli the physicist, twenty-five years younger than Jung, always had a tinge of the mentor and pupil about it, but it was different from Jung's friendships with psychologists. Men in psychology, Jung reiterated, "always need to best other men." The one exception he offered was Baynes, whom he spoke of with a roar of laughter and great affection as "someone who never listens to me, he always goes his own way, and that's what makes him so charming, if irritating."[60] That friendship lasted probably because Baynes returned to England with his last wife, Ann, in the early 1930s, and for the rest of his life most of his contact with Jung was by correspondence.

Yet, despite Jung's insistence that he could not establish profound personal friendships with men who were in his own profession, he established quite a few with other psychologists that were long-lasting, their occasional and sometimes serious differences of opinion notwithstanding. Some were with Americans, but many more were with German Jews. Prominent among them was James Kirsch, who met Jung in 1928 and began analysis in 1929, traveling periodically to Zürich from his practice in Berlin. From Emma Jung's native Schaffhausen came Dr. Carl Alfred Meier to become the closest approximation of a disciple Jung ever had. "Fredy" Meier began to work with Jung in 1930 after completing medical studies at the University of Zürich and psychiatric studies at the Burghölzli. For the next three decades he filled the role of "crown prince"[61] that

Jung had previously played for Freud. They were staunch colleagues until, as Meier put it, "we had a big falling out and went our own ways."[62]

Most of the women who followed Jung were, according to his system of types, introverts. The one notable exception was the extravert Jolande Jacobi, who, despite her tiny stature and birdlike appearance, strode through their midst like a colossus and (if Jung's other followers are to be believed) caused uproar and havoc wherever she went.[63] Jolande Szejacs Jacobi (1890–1973) was born into a wealthy Jewish family that converted self-protectively to Catholicism in anti-Semitic Hungary. At age nineteen, she married a wealthy lawyer. They fled Budapest after the 1919 Communist upheavals to live in Vienna with their two sons, where the marriage was far from serene. In 1925, Andreas Jacobi returned to Budapest, leaving his wife and sons in Vienna, ostensibly for their education. By that time, Jolande was involved in an extramarital affair of long duration and through her lover had become an active practitioner of her hitherto de facto Catholicism. Jung thought her as refreshing as a "blast of mountain air";[64] others called her the "locomotive" or the "ice breaker," while even larger numbers called her names "unfit to print."[65]

Jacobi was vice president in charge of inviting speakers to the Viennese *Kulturbund* and was reputed to use her position to seek out celebrities. In 1928, Jung became one in a line of invited speakers that included the composer Béla Bartók, the poet Paul Valéry, and the Indologist Heinrich Zimmer (later Jung's friend and colleague).[66] Jung was Jacobi's houseguest, and she gave a grand Viennese luncheon in his honor. Sympathetic to his psychology before they met, she was mesmerized when afterward Jung wrote all sixty-four hexagrams of the *I Ching* from memory. She began the thorough study of his theory that culminated in her doctorate in psychology a decade later in 1938, when she was forty-nine.

Jacobi's association with the *Kulturbund* was a contributing factor to her second exile for political reasons: at the end of the 1930s, she fled Nazi persecution in Austria for Zürich, where she lived and practiced psychoanalysis for the rest of her life. The *Kulturbund* had been a suspect organization even before the Nazis annexed Austria, for it was dedicated to learning about all aspects of contemporary culture and society, and its invited speakers were often highly controversial figures. There was, however, a particular slant to this conservative organization in the sense that, long before the anti-Semitic stigma associated with the word "Aryan," the *Kulturbund* embraced such leanings. It was no wonder Freud was doubly outraged when news reached him that Jung was to make his first appearance in Vienna since they were no longer allies, and before such a group. Freud dismissed Jung's visit sarcastically as a *"Sturm im Wasserglas,"* a tempest in a teapot. He would not attend the lecture, he told Ernest Jones, preferring to "miss an excellent opportunity of hearing about the Structure of the Soul from a first-rate source."[67]

THE LAST of the most important women to take her place in Jung's professional life was Marie-Louise von Franz (1915–99), whom he met in July 1933 when she was an "eighteen-and-a-half-year-old student at the University of Zürich."[68] Born in Munich, Marlus (her nickname) was one of two daughters of an Austrian baron who moved his family to neutral Switzerland for political reasons when she was three. Although born elsewhere, von Franz considered herself "deeply, profoundly Swiss" and was proud of and pleased with her "Swissness," even when others used the term pejoratively to describe her as "one of those who fossilize theories by a strict adherence to them."[69]

At the university, most students steered clear of the socially awkward girl who did not hesitate to use her formidable knowledge to correct her professors when she thought she knew more about a subject than they did. Her ferocious intelligence and fearless outspokenness came to the attention of Paul "Pablo" Naeff, Toni Wolff's nephew.[70] Toni was worried about Jung's foray into alchemical studies and his seeming abandonment of orthodox medical and clinical psychology. She wanted to expose him to the latest, trendiest topics that university students talked about when they were outside the classroom, so she asked her nephew to be on the lookout for interesting young people who should be introduced to Jung. Toni hoped their thoughts and opinions might interest Jung enough that he would pursue them rather than the esoteric scholarship she believed alchemy represented. Pablo was a popular student with friends in many different departments, so Toni invited him to bring the most intelligent and amusing students he knew to Bollingen for Sunday lunch. Although Marie-Louise von Franz was not among his friends — nor was she anyone's friend actually, as her authoritative behavior was so off-putting to her contemporaries — Pablo Naeff invited her because he thought her strident brilliance and vast knowledge would amuse Jung. Thus, she became the only woman in a group of eight or ten young men.

Because von Franz was recovering from a broken ankle, Toni Wolff met them at the train station in her big black BMW sedan. It was her first car, bought in response to Jung's 1929 purchase of a red Chrysler convertible that he always called "the Red Darling" and parked prominently on the Freiestrasse every Wednesday afternoon when he visited the Wolff house.[71] Not wanting to be excluded, Emma bought a gray Dodge sedan. All three were taught to drive by Müller, the handyman and general factotum of the Küsnacht property. The members of the Psychological Club could not resist interpreting both the cars and the way their owners drove them as consistent with their personalities. Emma was considered the safest driver of the three, and her vehicle the most sedate and seemly for a proper Swiss matron; Jung's car mirrored his behavior as the most flamboyant of the trio, even though he boasted accurately that he was the only one among them who had never had an accident; Toni's "racy vehicle" and "erratic driving" were seen by all as "positively unsafe, a menace and a hazard."[72]

When Toni arrived at the tower with von Franz and the other students, Jung greeted them by popping up "suddenly out of the bushes . . . an enormous man with a dirty shirt, dirty trousers, and gold-rimmed spectacles."[73] The tiny von Franz was overwhelmed by the towering Jung, and many years later she recalled how she "fell for him, in a terrific transference and a big schoolgirl crush."[74] He told the students he had not finished cooking lunch, then sent the young men down to the lake and asked von Franz to sit in the kitchen and help him chop vegetables. Von Franz makes no mention of where Toni was but only recounts how she was so enthralled by Jung's stories that she sliced her finger as well as a cucumber.[75] Jung helped her bind it, all the while talking about a female patient who believed she lived on the moon. Von Franz, who was then a "communist materialist atheist," dismissed the delusion, because the moon was only a "dead satellite" and "nobody's been up there yet." Jung only smiled and poured more Burgundy wine.

The lunch was so successful that the students remained to drink and talk until well after midnight. Only then did von Franz realize that Jung meant his anecdote about the woman on the moon to illustrate that "what happens psychically is real, and what happens outwardly is only secondary." She thought it would take her ten years to digest what "this old man" talked about that day. In years to come, she liked to add that it had not taken ten years; it had taken all her life.

As they prepared the lunch, von Franz told Jung she was undecided about whether to specialize in mathematics, medicine, or classical languages. Jung knew as soon as he met her that she had a particular kind of intelligence he needed to put to work for him. Interestingly, he did not direct her to study medicine, as he insisted all the men who wanted to practice his theory should do; he followed his usual pattern with women and set her to investigate a specific area where he needed research assistance, in this case classical languages and literature.[76] Although her professors approved of her major, she had to keep secret from them the reason that she chose this concentration — that she was determined to forge a career as Jung's chief associate. She not only had to hide her work on his behalf, she also had to hide her attendance at his ETH lectures on the general theory of the unconscious.

Soon she began to analyze her own dreams, but she "got in a mess" and asked Jung to take her on as a patient.[77] He agreed to take her free of charge if she would prepare translations from Latin and Greek alchemical texts in exchange. Naturally, she accepted. Jung told her his interest in alchemy sprang from the realization that everything within his own fantasies that he thought was personal was really anchored in a long historical tradition. Mythology had not given him the answers he sought; nor had his forays into comparative religions such as Gnosticism, Manicheism, and others. He was convinced that a study of the historical development of alchemy would result in parallels with his own spiritual development, and if so, would provide a logical extension from which he could generalize to treat patients. Jung planned to study alchemical manuscripts not because he wanted to find the secret of how to create literal gold, but, rather, because he sensed that the search of the ancient alchemists for transformation paralleled his modern one for successful individuation.

Thus, von Franz the still-teenage girl became the recipient of confidences Jung had hitherto told no one but Toni Wolff. He told von Franz he had been collecting information about alchemy for the previous decade, independent of but coinciding with meeting the eminent Sinologist Richard Wilhelm and reading his translation of *The Secret of the Golden Flower.* Jung told von Franz that that book provided the bridge between the dead end of Gnosticism and the great unknown represented by alchemy. To explain further, he told her how puzzled he had been by the dream of an American analysand who dreamt he was an eagle that ate his own feathers and fell to death in the desert. On his next visit to the British Museum, his excitement was palpable when he found "the so-called Ripley Scroll," in which there is an alchemical representation of an eagle eating his own feathers. Von Franz insisted that this was the first time she heard Jung describe the process he later defined as "synchronicity."[78]

It was very exciting for the nineteen-year-old-girl to become Jung's privileged confidante. He made her "blush with pride" when he told her she had "a lucky hand for finding things," and she was proud to become "a kind of hunting dog down at the Central Library." Many years later, she trained a clinically detached eye on her "tremendous transference" to Jung, calling it "love" and describing how it affected her life:

> It made me isolated. I had no friends of my own generation. I was always alone, so therefore I could do his scholarship. I shed all other people. I suffered a lot for that, because I never knew what was wrong with me, why I could not get on with my people [i.e., those her own age]. I lived in another world than they did. So it gave me a lot of time to study and work for Jung.

No one, it seemed, saw the danger in the young girl's attachment to Jung, or, if anyone did, all contrived to ignore it. Von Franz recognized and approved of Jung's capacity for "pushing his own children out of the house" even as he kept her inside it: "They were already attached to the mother, and the house was wonderful and agreeable, and the most exciting things were always happening there. So Jung deliberately and very often quite nastily, really, pushed them out of the nest." She had little regard for Emma then or ever, except to defer respectfully to the wife's privileged position in her husband's life: "Emma was such an introvert she was probably happy to have it quiet with the five children out of the house."

Emilie Preiswerk and Paul Jung at the time of their marriage, April 8, 1869. (Familienarchiv C. G. Jung, hereafter FCGJ)

C. G. Jung, age six, on November 18, 1881.
(FCGJ)

C. G. Jung (right), age seventeen, with two friends on the Haltingermoos, near
Basel. (FCGJ)

C. G. Jung (seated, third from left) and Zofingia fraternity brothers, c. 1896. (FCGJ)

C. G. Jung as a young doctor, 1900. (FCGJ)

Eugen Bleuler. (Medizinhistorisches Institut und Museum der Universität Zürich)

Emile Schwyzer, the "Solar Phallus Man." (Burghölzli Hospital Archives)

*Emma Rauschenbach (seated, second from left) in a school photograph.
(Private Archive)*

Carl and Emma Jung at the time of their marriage, February 14, 1903. (FCGJ)

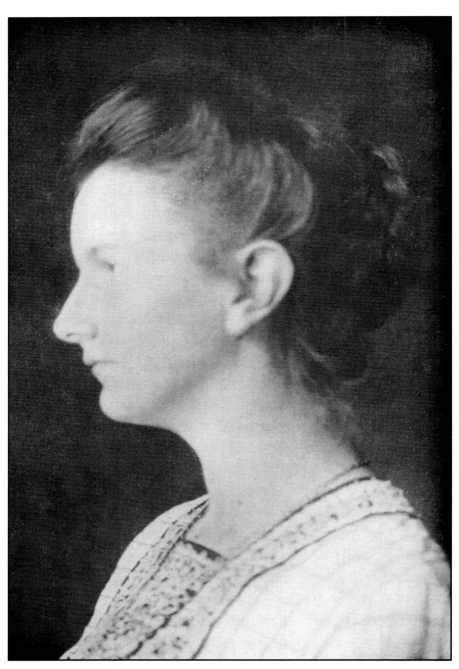

Gertrud Jung as a young woman, August 1904. (FCGJ)

Toni Wolff as a young woman. (Wolff Family Archives)

Clark University, 1909. Seated, left to right: Freud, G. Stanley Hall, and Jung. Standing: A. A. Brill, Ernest Jones, and Sandor Ferenczi. (Clark University Archives)

Persons connected with Jung who attended the Weimar Congress, 1912. Seated, left to right: Poul Bjerre, Eugen Bleuler, Maria Moltzer, Lou Andreas-Salomé (fifth from left), Beatrice Hinkle, Emma Jung, Toni Wolff (third from right), Martha Sigg-Böddinghaus, Franz Riklin. Second row, left to right: Otto Rank, Ludwig Binswanger, Oskar Pfister (fifth from left), Sandor Ferenczi, Sigmund Freud, C. G. Jung, James Putnam (third from right), Ernest Jones, Wilhelm Stekel. Third row, left to right: Jan Nelken, Max Eitingon (third from left), Leonhard Seif, Karl Abraham (fifth from right). Fourth row: Alphons Maeder (third from left), Adolf Keller (at right). (Wolff Family Archives)

The tower of the Jung house in Küsnacht. (Bollingen Foundation Archives)

Aerial view of 228 Seestrasse, Küsnacht. (Psychiatrische Universitäts-klinik Museum)

Emma and Carl Jung with four of their five children at Château d'Oex, 1917. From left: Franz, Gret (standing, rear), Marianne, and Agathe. (FCGJ)

Jung standing in his garden, c. 1935. (Margaret Nordfeldt, Kristine Mann Library Archives, C. G. Jung Center, New York, hereafter KML)

*Jung at the site of the future Bollingen Tower,
c. 1920. (FCGJ)*

*The Bollingen Tower from Lake Zürich. (Carl Jung, great-
grandson of CGJ)*

Jung at Bollingen, carving the square stone. (William McGuire)

Detail of Jung's carving on the square stone at Bollingen.
(William McGuire)

Atmavictu, stone figure carved by
Jung. (FCGJ)

Jung seated in the tower, c. 1950. (Bollingen Foundation Archives)

*Jung with Ruth Bailey and H. G. Baynes in East Africa, 1925.
(Ruth Bailey)*

Jung, c. 1928-1929. (Erna Wolff, Munich, KML)

Two of Jung's paintings on the walls of his private room in the Bollingen Tower. (KML)

"I knew about [Jung's relationship with] Toni Wolff almost at once," von Franz said, noting that Wolff's

> big mistake was in not being enthusiastic about alchemy. It was unfortunate that she refused to follow him there, because otherwise he would not have thrown her over to collaborate with me. He would have used me just for translating, and he would have confided in her. But she wasn't interested. She was too much a slightly conventional Christian, and she refused to follow him.

Von Franz was proud that "intellectually, I replaced Toni Wolff in Jung's life."

There were many power struggles among the women surrounding Jung as they jousted for intellectual supremacy, but von Franz agreed that they were all united where she was concerned: "No kidding, that older generation, they just didn't like me. I was rather brilliant, and I got a lot of jealousy. But I didn't care, because I am an introvert. I didn't want to be social with this group; I just wanted a collaboration with Jung."

The group she described was riddled with jealousy, primarily of Toni Wolff, who became the president of the Psychological Club in 1928 and ruled it with an iron hand for the next two decades. Linda Fierz was one of Wolff's closest friends and her strongest ally in changing the club's focus from social to intellectual. Fierz helped Wolff force the resignations of dissenting members who threatened their authority, among them the former club presidents the Schlegels.

Cary Baynes detached herself from club politics and remained aloof from jealousy. She detested all the women collectively but especially distrusted von Franz, calling her "obsequious and ingratiating."[79] Barbara Hannah, described by some as "a shrieking swan with wings spread for battle,"[80] tried to enlist Emma to mediate. Emma shared her husband's view that Hannah was "a bad dog, some days nice, mostly snappy,"[81] and refused to become engaged. She never participated in what she called the "women's politics"[82] of the club. She resented its collective "spirit," which she dismissed as *"grossewahn und selbstgerechtigkeit"* (inflated with their own importance and self-righteousness).[83] She never attended the Wednesday lunches at the Pfauen Restaurant,[84] where "the Zürich spinsters" congregated after Jung's lectures at the ETH or the club "to talk psychological jargon."[85] Emma chose instead to concentrate on her private studies and confined herself "only to helping these women cut through the universal transference to Jung."[86]

Jung was more sanguine about the club, comparing it to going to a good concert and hearing one member of the orchestra playing sour notes: as the rest of the performance was first-rate, one simply had to overlook the occasional wrong one.[87] Nevertheless, he did intervene periodically for the sake of harmony. He was indirectly responsible for ending one jealous intellectual rivalry — to see who could be his primary research assistant — when he suggested that

Hannah and von Franz set up housekeeping together. The two women established a happy personal relationship and were devoted to each other for the rest of their long life together.

More than a decade later, Jung complained that he had spent the previous thirty years treating "British and American spinsters." Obviously, he was forgetting such men as Pauli and Richard Wilhelm[88] when he complained, "I never seemed to have an interesting patient, some scientific mind, some man of quality who had achieved something at least. Just the eternal line of spinsters. They arrived in droves; it never seemed to end. I used to ask myself 'why am I cursed?' But I plodded along, looking after them the best I could, doing my research work on the side."[89]

He was also conveniently forgetting the respite from the strife of "eleven thousand virgins" that came through patients representing the German nobility. First there was Graf (Count) Hermann Keyserling in Darmstadt,[90] where Jung first went in late 1920 and where Richard Wilhelm introduced him to the *I Ching*. The count, an "intellectual aristocrat,"[91] convened a School of Wisdom to which artists and intellectuals were invited to discuss their current research. The count intended the school to offer an enriching cross-disciplinary experience, but in actuality it was "a series of lectures attended by some people with a genuine interest in the topics presented and a great many others who came because it was fashionable."[92] Jung attended his first School of Wisdom in 1920 because he was curious about what went on at the court of the "self-declared philosopher" with his "intensely emotional attitudes and alcoholic instability."[93]

He was pleasantly surprised to find Wilhelm there, for his reputation had preceded him to Zürich. The two men established a rapport based on true intellectual equality, which lasted until Wilhelm's untimely death in 1930. Jung said it was one of his most significant and influential friendships, but given the history of his others with men, one wonders how long it might have lasted had Wilhelm enjoyed a lengthier life. German by birth and deeply religious, Wilhelm went to China as a Christian missionary, and by the time he met Jung, he had been profoundly affected by Chinese culture and philosophy. The distinguished director of the China Institute in Frankfurt am Main, he was at work on a German translation of the ancient Chinese text *The Secret of the Golden Flower*. The two men recognized their many common interests, but their host's full and frenetic program made it difficult to explore them in Darmstadt.[94]

Even though Keyserling was "an aristocrat who peers at the world through a monocle," Jung thought he was "not to be taken as a joke."[95] His strongest memory of the count was "of a torrent. I was completely flooded. He talked incessantly and I basically never got to say a word. He talked and talked and talked me to exhaustion. I was snowed under."[96]

The Countess Keyserling, a granddaughter of Chancellor Otto von Bismarck, was her husband's exact counterpart. Another nonstop talker, she thought her rambling monologues were witty conversation, whereas Jung thought them closer to the schizophrenic divinations he heard from Burghölzli patients. Jung liked the countess's older sister better because she reminded him of a "true English lady: posture, aristocracy, very impressive." He thought the Keyserlings were closer to the local peasantry: "They possessed a clear undercurrent of brutality. The horse stables were right next door [to their main drawing rooms]. There was a violent streak in him and the lash could still be felt."

Horses figured largely in the Keyserling household, for the count had a mistress, Victoria Ocampo, who was an excellent rider and who struck Jung as a "very beautiful woman but a complete horse." Ocampo later became a notable Argentinean writer, translator, and publisher, but even though Jung admired her "distinguished personality," he still thought of her as "a mare — no, rather, she was a stallion."[97]

The count attracted an eclectic variety of people to his School of Wisdom, many of them wildly eccentric and fascinating to Jung, especially some of the titled members of the audience who flitted on the fringes of the groups of experts summoned to enlighten them. Jung prided himself on "getting along very well with these people [the aristocrats]. I knew how to deal with them — up to the point where the brashness began, which they all possessed." Through the Keyserlings, Jung and Emma met the Grossherzog (grand duke) of Hesse-Darmstadt, who invited them to be his houseguests while Jung gave lectures to his court. The grand duke was a simple man who spent his time hiding shyly behind the large embroidery frame his servants carried everywhere he went. He especially liked Emma because she sat quietly next to him, smiling her approval as he pulled his stitches through the frame. The grand duke had an "occultist" on his staff who reminded Jung of an eighteenth-century courtier: "a dark figure who just fit into the harmlessness of this royal court. Now he had culture — this dark count!"

Both the grand duke's and Keyserling's courts were "prickly with intellect and also a bit modish."[98] There Jung met the ethnologist Leo Frobenius, who often pranced around in his favorite trousers, made from a lion's skin complete with tail, which he "occasionally wagged" for emphasis. Jung had many conversations with the egotistical Frobenius and cited his writings fairly often from that time on, but Jung was wary of the friendship.[99] He appreciated Frobenius's "unbelievable vitality, such a smart man, but his ideas went overboard." Mainly, he disapproved of the ethnologist's "lack of culture" and "lack of proper upbringing," blaming them for his "lack of understanding of other people's ideas."

Jung held a snobbish idea of aristocracy, perhaps inherent in one born in Basel, that most snobbish city in the Swiss democracy. For the most part, he approved of aristocratic license and sided with the concept of noblesse oblige, especially among those who aped what he thought to be (without having had real firsthand observation) the behavior of the English aristocracy. He was "very impressed" when the brother of the German emperor, Prince Heinrich, entertained dinner guests with tales of how he personally punched "Reds" off the running boards of his car during the *"Spartakistenaufstand* of 1913," the German Rebel Socialists, precursors of the German Communist Party. He compared Prince Heinrich favorably with Keyserling, deciding that both were "aristocrats" merely trying to "assert themselves against the offences of that time."

Jung knew that Keyserling's court represented "the tail-end of the Aristocracy . . . an aristocracy at the end of its rope,"[100] but he remained sympathetic to the *"roi sans royaume"* whom he saw as a victim of "the trouble of the times . . . forced to deal with the *canaille* [riffraff]." Jung espoused this view to explain why he went so frequently during the 1920s to a School of Wisdom that was really little more than a setting for "tasteless vanity" — and one that certainly should have been anathema to a democratic Swiss citizen but that he enjoyed immensely.

Later, some of Keyserling's court and then various barons and counts from Germany and Austria came to Zürich with their spouses, all using their rank and station to remain above the fray of the Psychological Club's hoi polloi.[101] The most prominent among them, and the one for whom Jung had the most respect and deepest genuine affection, was Marie-Alix, the Princess von Hohenzollern-Sigmaringen, daughter of the last king of Saxony, descendant of the Wettin family, whose lineage could be traced back for more than a thousand years, and wife to Prince Franz Joseph Hohenzollern. Princess Alix offered Jung interesting speculation into how the unconscious operated in persons of distinguished ancestry. He thought her a woman of "exquisite simplicity" whose natural empathy inspired comfort and ease in anyone who came into contact with her.[102] Like many of Jung's German-speaking patients, she referred to him as *"Onkel,"* a term that irritated him when most others used it but made him smile when she said it. Jung thought the princess's simplicity was her greatest virtue, and because of it, he had no difficulty making her confront her insecurities during therapy.

"She has visible ancestry," he explained. "When *I* come to something dark I am immediately confronted with insecurity; not she, for she knows what is going to happen [because of] . . . her family that goes back a thousand years. . . . She, on the contrary, is quite certain of her position." He was less positively inclined toward other German nobility and the princess's good friends who were also his patients, the Baron Victor and Baroness Margaret Lüttichau.[103]

Jung tried to use the example of the princess's ancestry to help another of his patients, Catharine Rush Cabot, who considered herself American royalty, as she was born into Philadelphia's high society and married into Boston's highest. Jung often discussed European royalty with the charming and vivacious Katy Cabot, who saw him as "the court physician." As such, she added, he was "also the administrator of poison, . . . a dangerous position." In their conversations, Jung extrapolated from the princess to the subject of kings, queens, and contemporary politics. He feared modern England would tax its aristocracy out of existence and would then be "doomed to go to Hell." He thought a united Germany would be far better off "if it again became little kingdoms." Kings and queens provided value to society because they were so imbued with past tradition that they were unafraid of new situations. He compared royalty in general with his own genealogy:

> My sense of uncertainty has all the primitive factors in it as I only go back a short distance — then there is darkness — whereas she [Princess Alix] goes back a thousand years. . . . People who have history behind them have never met such a thing as me! I am an unheard-of novelty, a dangerous man, a sorcerer — only to be found in fairy tales.

When Jung told Princess Alix of his interest in alchemy, she said he "must be taken care of," as he was the "rare bird, the fellow we needed." He contrasted her easy acceptance of his controversial interest with the responses of ordinary people, who were greatly puzzled by it and everything else about him. "What do you do?" they often asked. He replied that he saw patients all day long. "Yes, yes," they usually responded, they knew all that, "but what do you *do?*" If Jung added that he was usually writing a book as well as treating patients, they still persisted, asking again, what did he "*really* do?"

Jung, the good Swiss democrat, believed that it took people like the princess and others from "old families" to exhibit "the right form. They may be decadent but their great asset is that they have history behind them which gives them the marvellous certainty about people and their behavior."[104] He thought it helped them cope with the inherent difficulties of analysis. The Anglican Bishop of Salisbury was representative of this tradition, Jung concluded, and that was why he was "not shocked by Jung's liberal ideas" but, rather, understood "that such a man must have such ideas."[105]

In the following decade, he wrote about "such ideas" as cultural expressions of national character, racial differences, the religious origins of social adaptation, and alchemy. The expression of such radical ideas inspired respect and rage in equal part, haunting, if not determining, his posthumous reputation.

CHAPTER 26

Unconventional Analytic Hours

By 1930, Jung's evolving system of analytical psychology still carried "the strong imprint of early psychoanalysis," but everything else about it was "in a state of flux and change."[1] Searching for a method to unify his "highly creative *mixtum compositum*," he made a slight but important refinement to the circular manner in which he expressed ideas. His new "peculiarity" was to "return to the basic problems in his [previous] writings, examine them from different points of view, think through old questions again, and give new and differentiated answers." Reading each new work as it emerged offered his readers "an exciting experience," but it also served to "complicate a thorough understanding of a particular problem."[2] Despite the many inconsistencies, there was one major constant: his work on typologies became the starting point for both his writing and practice. The first stage in therapy for anyone who made the pilgrimage to Zürich was to leave "no doubt about [the analysand's] personality type and function."[3]

These changes began immediately after Jung returned from Africa in 1926. He was yearning to "write much," not only about his impressions of Africa but also about himself as a Swiss psychologist who went there with a single external objective in mind but who returned with quite unexpected internal insights. Instead of being able to write, he found himself thwarted on every front, only able to prepare "some old papers" for publication because he had "no time to think."

"Patients eat me," he complained as his "resistances" toward them mounted "like thunderclouds."[4] Robert Edmond Jones warned Mabel Dodge Luhan not to come to Zürich as she had planned, because Jung "isn't very approachable this fall and doesn't seem to want to meet any new people." Jones told her Jung was "very much of a recluse, really, a solitary. Not at all a propagandist or a reformer, and feels himself most living when he is working entirely by himself."[5] When Luhan kept pressing Jung to take her on, he refused, with questions that became his criteria for accepting new patients: "Does she need to come? Is she sick? Then why should she come? I have far more work now than I can do!"[6]

Jung's irritation with the demands of his patients may have had something to do with how he became indirectly responsible for the foundation of Alcoholics Anonymous.[7] He saw the patient Roland H., an American alcoholic, in 1931, for either several weeks or as much as a year (accounts differ), but the therapy did not succeed in keeping Roland H. away from alcohol and binge drinking. He returned to Jung a year later to be told that it was unrealistic to seek a cure through psychiatry. Jung suggested that he join the Oxford Group, which conducted its meetings through strict, ritualistic procedures, hoping that such structure might lead Roland H. to undergo a conversion experience of a religious or spiritual nature that would give him the strength to stop drinking. Indeed he did, and soon after, Roland H. began to devote himself to helping other alcoholics. When he returned to the United States, he told his friend Bill W., another seemingly hopeless alcoholic, of his conversion experience. Shortly after, Bill W. had a similar religious event that was enhanced by the image of a group of alcoholics who would inspire each other to abandon alcohol. It was the foundation of the Society of Alcoholics Anonymous, as the group is officially known.

Jung's attitude marked the start of his turning away from using individual analysis to evolve theory and turning instead toward general psychic problems and historical correspondences. Rather than writing up patient histories as a means of establishing treatment models, he now wanted to concentrate on archetypes within the collective unconscious.[8]

To protect himself from the onslaught of both Swiss supplicants and international visitors, Jung devised an analytic technique that became a hallmark of his therapy, even though it was initially formulated to cater first to his personal needs and only secondarily to those of his patients. He wanted time to write and private space in which to think, which usually meant spending long periods in Bollingen. To distance himself from patients and their problems and ensure this degree of privacy, he began to rely on his closest associates to take over treatment and complete the therapy. Patients would see Jung for varying periods of time, some as short as a single visit or a week or two, some for as long as a year. In the latter case, Jung usually saw them for an hour one to four times each week, but he saw most patients twice a week. Often, and usually to suit his schedule rather than theirs, he would interrupt the therapy to accommodate his vacations or professional engagements, or to finish a lecture or meet a publication deadline.

When he turned the case over to one of his associates, he might see the patient occasionally but more often would rely on progress reports during the earliest version of what was later codified as training analysis.[9] With very few exceptions, this method worked well for all the participants.

Another convention that evolved during this time was that patients were analyzed not only by Jung but also by an associate whose sex was the opposite of theirs: men worked with women analysts, while women saw men. At first, his principal assistants were Toni Wolff and Peter Baynes (during periods when he resided in Zürich). Of lesser importance were Wolfgang M. Kranefeldt, who trained at the Burghölzli and was a close associate until he left Zürich to establish a practice in Berlin,[10] and Dr. John F. Rittmeister, a staff doctor at the Burghölzli from 1927 to 1935 and Jung's associate from 1927 to 1930. They fell out when Rittmeister became an outspoken Communist and political activist and could no longer tolerate the "vague, mystical and at the same time over-saturated atmosphere" surrounding Jung.[11]

Baynes, Kranefeldt, and Rittmeister were medical doctors; Toni Wolff had no formal education, but she was Jung's most trusted associate. Dr. Joseph Henderson, who later became one of the foremost American Jungian analysts, remembered being passed along to Toni Wolff, whom he called Jung's "complementary opposite."[12] Henderson described her sitting "with dignity in her high-backed chair, her long slender neck and neat coiffure and large dark eyes with a touch of sadness about them." Like many others, he perceived that "one could never feel close to her as one could with Jung. Hers was the method of placing distance between herself and her analysand."

Jung also sent an American woman who later became a respected lay analyst to Toni Wolff, Jane Hollister Wheelwright.[13] Although Wheelwright was married, she was not yet a mother, and she remembered how shocked she was when Jung declared at the beginning of their first session that he had spent "the past forty years listening to mothers and I can't bear it any more."[14] He sent her off to Toni Wolff, with whom she had an unsuccessful analysis: "I could never make the connection with her. She was cold as ice in life, which is how she was with all women. She went for the men. She thought they were what mattered. She was very aloof with women and as for me, she wouldn't give me any stable space anywhere." Jane Wheelwright's impression was in the minority, for despite the quality of reserve remembered by all of Toni Wolff's analysands, most of the women Jung sent to her or who sought her on their own remained devoted to her for life.[15]

Dr. Henderson and Mrs. Wheelwright were two of a number of persons in the formative years of analytical psychology who were analyzed concurrently by Jung and by one or more of the associates named above, and who either described their analytic experiences many years afterward or wrote about them during their therapy. All these accounts shed light on how Jung conducted their analytic encounters, almost every case of which differed from the others.

Dr. Henderson first went to Zürich in 1929.[16] His strongest memory of Jung was that, unlike Toni Wolff, "he could never be put into a frame," while she "was always most comfortable in a frame and had a particular talent for placing her analysands in their frames — at least for the duration of their analysis." Many people tried to "frame" Jung by creating categories into which they could pose him neatly, but he "always burst out of it, destroying the frame at the same time." Henderson found this equally true of Jung's analytic method:

During most interviews he paced back and forth, gesturing as he talked, and he talked of everything that came to his mind, whether about a human problem, a dream, a personal reminiscence, an allegorical story, or a joke. Yet he could become quiet, serious, and extremely personal, sitting down almost too close for comfort and delivering a pointed interpretation of one's miserable personal problem so its bitter truth would really sink in. And yet he made some of his best life-changing observations indirectly, offhand, as if they were to be accepted lightly — even joyously.

Henderson found "great immediacy" in how Jung related to people in general. For those who expressed genuine interest in the unconscious, he talked freely; for those who tried to "manipulate him in any way," he usually found something offensive to say to them. He told Henderson, "I am not taken in by intellectuals. You see, I am one myself."[17]

Henderson's sessions were held in Jung's study off the library. The room was small, barely large enough to hold an old wooden table-desk and two leather armchairs. Jung's dog of the moment was always present, sprawled on the floor and making the room seem even smaller. The study's one distinguishing feature was the window, three large stained-glass panels depicting scenes from the Passion of Christ: the flagellation, crucifixion, and deposition (burial in the tomb).[18] A curtain could be drawn across the west-facing window to protect it from the setting sun, and carefully hidden on the wall behind the curtain was a photograph Jung referred to as the *Linceul du Christ*, the Shroud of Turin.

Aniela Jaffé, later Jung's secretary, collaborator, and editor of the conversations that became *Memories, Dreams, Reflections*, remembered her own "unconventional analytic hours," which always took place in the large library adjacent to the study and overlooking the lake. She tried to explain Jung's "method" by recalling one of her first sessions. He did not wait for her to speak, but as soon as she entered, he took a "very precious" book about alchemy down from his shelves, "the *Mutus Liber*, a picture book with no text, published . . . in 1677." It was the first alchemical book Jaffé had ever seen, and as the hour ended, she realized they had passed it not talking about her concerns but only "looking at its pictures and talking about alchemy." Many years later, she credited this sort of hour with greater "lasting influence"[19] than those passed in more traditional therapy. As an example of Jung's ability to "find the truth in the face [of every analysand]," she described a session when she tried to tell him about her mother and he cut her off abruptly, saying, "Don't waste your time."[20]

Another man who was one of Jung's earliest patients and who saw him regularly for many years kept a detailed journal in which he recorded everything he could remember both of them saying during the analytic hour.[21] This man's extramarital affairs provided the substance of his conversations. He described himself as "an *unrepentant* adulterer, yes, but one who is nevertheless a *faithful* adulterer" (his emphasis). His reasoning was that, although he was unfaithful to his wife with an ongoing succession of individual mistresses — thirty-two at his last count — he was always faithful to one at a time in relationships that lasted from several weeks to several years.

His journal had a formulaic quality, as he usually began each entry with the setting (always the library and never the study), the time of day, the weather, and how he and Jung were dressed. He also noted that upon his arrival, Jung was almost always seated, relaxed and leaning back in his chair. The man wrote that Jung usually remained seated throughout the hour, fussed with one or more of his pipes, and often stared silently out the window at the lake. He then described what they talked about, followed by a ritualistic ending. Sometimes he wrote that he feared Jung had not listened to a word he said. His most frequent description of Jung was "morose," a doctor who neither criticized nor approved of his patient's liaisons and who seldom offered soothing examples from his own life.

This man knew Jung well enough to be aware of his relationship with Toni Wolff, whom he and his wife saw socially (as they did Emma and C. G. Jung). Sometimes he brought Toni's name into his analysis when he was searching for a comparison to something he thought he and Jung had in common. In one instance, he expressed surprise that Jung never introduced her name, and if the patient did, Jung was abruptly dismissive: "There can be no comparison in this matter."

Perhaps the reason Jung would not compare their situations lies in what he told another analysand about "auto-erotic people" who "only see themselves" in any given situation.[22] Using the example of the man who "had thirty-two women in his life," Jung said he "only experienced himself and never saw the women: He performed sexual intercourse with them to prove he had seen 'someone.' He only saw himself in that experience; to him a woman was merely an instrument for his vanity . . . the women did not exist for him."

Another man kept a diary of his analytic encounters, but in sporadic and haphazard accounts. He consulted Jung to talk about his problems with his wife and the single, long-term mistress he considered his "other" family. Most of what he wrote were complaints about how he paid Jung 50 francs an hour while Jung spent most of the hour complaining of his difficulties in navigating between Emma and Toni. Interestingly, these sessions always took place in the small study, rather than the library, to which Jung always took analysands who "caught him emotionally" and from whom he needed to "separate himself." There, as he later revealed, he was able mentally to "go up and sit on the window, on top of the window, and look down and watch myself, how I am acting, until I see what from the unconscious has caught me and I can deal with it."[23]

In still another instance, Jung had a patient who was an older woman of great wealth. Her life had been privileged and protected, but she suffered from a physical affliction that kept her in constant pain.[24] Even so, she had married, had children and grandchildren, and remained the bedrock upon which her entire family depended. She came to Jung because her daughter, approaching middle age and suffering from the same inherited physical condition, did not possess her mother's indomitable spirit and chose to blame her for a multitude of real or imagined wrongs. When this daughter's adolescent child was killed in an accident, she became depressed and committed suicide in a ghastly way, leaving behind a series of documents that blamed her mother. Jung's patient accepted her daughter's accusations and became deeply depressed. Her writings about Jung usually describe her sessions in language similar to this entry:

> I had nothing to say this day. I took my seat [in the library]. He pulled his chair close to mine. I did not want to meet his eyes, so we both stared ahead at the books on the wall. I could not speak, so neither did he. Occasionally he reached to stroke my arm or pat my hand. The hour passed and I became tranquil. I wish that peace would come with me when I leave, but it disappears without his presence.

Aniela Jaffé might well have been speaking of this woman when she described Jung's work with worried or depressed patients as a "demand for wholeness" and "not always easy to fathom": "He wanted to get them to integrate the necessary suffering into their lives, to accept and bear it as part of their wholeness — for without darkness and sorrow there is no life. To soothe it away or exclude it would rob them of a vital experience, while the core of the depression would remain and soon enough provoke new suffering."[25] He was advocating what some of his students later called "creative depression,"[26] meaning that the emotion should be examined rather than stifled or mitigated with medication.

After several years of thrice-weekly meetings that appear (from the troubled woman's perspective) to have passed mostly in silence, she told her diary that "a great cloud has lifted." She left Zürich and spent her remaining decade in prayer, fasting, and meditation; living in relative isolation in another part of the country; and sending an occasional greeting to tell Jung that she was well. Her friends remembered her as "beatific" and "at peace" until she died.

These reminiscences by patients were made either without his knowledge during Jung's lifetime or after his death.[27] But while he was still alive, one patient made what turned out to be a terrible mistake, temporarily shattering the bond she had hitherto forged. She told him that she kept a diary of their sessions, from the first one in the late 1920s to the last one in the 1940s. It was intended for her own private use, a document to consult periodically throughout her individuation. Now, almost thirty years after she began to keep it, she wanted to make it public.

Mary Briner-Ramsey was an American woman wealthy in her own right and married to an equally wealthy Swiss businessman. A Midwestern American and graduate of Smith College who went to Paris to live a life of culture and privilege, she married and moved to Zürich in 1928. She attended Jung's seminars, became his patient, and some years later established her own successful analytic practice.[28] Briner wrote a detailed record of each session immediately afterward, never intending to publish, until she learned that others were about to issue "autobiographical material of a Jungian analysis," purportedly a handbook for those who wished to practice analytical psychology. Briner was especially alarmed because the writers were two or three times removed from Jung: students of his psychology who had been analyzed by analysands of his analysands (literally, in some cases). Briner thought he would be better served if an actual account of his analytic sessions were published, one that described "what material came up and how it was treated in a way that differs from Freudian analysis," and the changes that took place throughout therapy "both in the unconscious and the conscious of the analysand."[29]

When she wrote to Jung about her plan and included a copy of her journal, his outrage was monumental. He said her description of how he worked gave him "such a headache"[30] that he could not read it in its entirety: "I was so deeply impressed by the abysmal stupidity of my 'method' that it would be suicidal if I put my 'placet'* to it." But he liked and respected Mary Briner, so he tried to explain what offended him most:

> It is absolutely impossible for you to know about the background to and the motivation of the things I say, no matter how accurate your report is. The over & undertones are inevitably lacking. The task you set to yourself is based on your own premice [sic]. You assume, as one generally does, that I follow a certain method. That is a great mistake. I have no method at all, when it comes to the individual case. When I am speaking or writing about what I do, then I abstract from all my individual experience of what happens in an analysis and I construct a method for the purpose of teaching.

Jung agreed that she had presented a "sufficient picture" of how she "experienced" his analytic action:

> But it would demand an almost superhuman genius who could paint a picture of what I am doing. . . . In your representation I am really absent, i.e., an insipid verbal cloud replaces the psychological fact: I am. The cloud does not even represent your total experience much less my part in the game. I may be wrong, but I did not even get a breath of all the nuances and subtleties of intonations and gesture, not to speak of the ever present and most influential unconscious background.

---

*placet: from the Latin placeo, -ere: "to be pleased with," "to agree with" or "accept."

He intended this to be more an observation than a reproach, for he knew she agreed that "all decisive moments in analysis have nothing to do with an intellectual method," but rather "originate in the indescribable human totality":

An encounter of two individuals, which analysis is, cannot be represented on principle, since it is a matter of the meeting of two totalities transcending the narrow confines of consciousness.

Jung tempered his tone further by telling Briner that his anger was directed not specifically against her version of what happened between them, but rather

against the general naiveté prevailing in the contemporary mind. The human individual is nothing comprehensible or classifiable when one takes into account the existence of the unconscious. But that is precisely the mistake of the contemporary mind, not to take into account the existence of the unconscious and to assume that we could give a complete picture of a human psyche. All our attempts at producing such records will be most fragmentary, incorrect, and unjust.

He conceded there could still be value in an account such as Briner's, but only if others would write and publish their versions of their analysis alongside hers. This could be a "very interesting task," Jung thought, if "somebody might try to reconstruct my personality from all the different individual experiences." He pondered the ways in which it might correspond to his own technique in writing and teaching.

If he had to describe his "so-called method," he believed it would consist of a "conceptual construction" based upon similar characteristics and patterns abstracted from individual patients and melded into a representative composite. Thus, in both his lectures and writings, he could observe confidentiality and protect each patient's individualism by subsuming them all within the ultimate fiction of the analytic process, the "case history." When Mary Briner asked Jung if she could publish her account of his method, he was in his eighties and to die shortly thereafter. His canon was complete and his psychology accepted as an established form of therapy throughout the world. Even so, he believed it imperative that the bond of confidentiality between himself and each patient remain inviolate. By this time in the development of psychoanalytic practice, the confidential imperative — that what happened in the analytic session was sacrosanct and never to be revealed, even after analyst and patient were both dead — had become an important tenet. In a sense, Briner was asking Jung's permission to break this bond by describing a single analysis, even though it was her own. But she was sensitive to Jung's wishes and respected them, so she never published her journal, and it has since vanished.

There are, however, two other analytic diaries that shed light upon Jung's analysis of women and the development of his anima theory: the analytic diary of Catharine Rush Cabot, published by her daughter in 2000 long after both analyst and analysand were dead; and Christiana Morgan's, still unpublished but widely quoted by biographers.[31] As both were emancipated American women, this aspect must also be factored into the analytic equation.

Cabot's diary is noteworthy because it offers a striking contrast to the impression Jung believed Mary Briner's would make. While Jung liked Briner personally and respected her analytic ability,[32] he still tended to place her loosely among women who he believed were dominated by their "intellectual animus" and could understand analysis only "in an intellectual way."[33] Cabot's diary is decidedly nonintellectual and chock-full of local gossip, as great parts of her analytic conversations with Jung centered around her opinions of persons in Zürich who were close to him. From what Cabot writes, Jung never volunteered comments but only responded to hers, and usually in ways that softened, mitigated, or explained positively the behavior of the persons about whom she spoke negatively. Cabot's diary shows a consistent portrait of Jung's "feeling" function predominating throughout her analysis, which was very different from the one he may have feared Briner's would show: a portrait of him as a hyperintellectual, highly theoretical "thinking" analyst.

Katy (as she was known) Cabot went to Zürich at the end of 1928, ironically at the indirect suggestion of Ernest Jones. One of her friends who consulted Jones spent so much time talking about Katy's problems that, for whatever reason, he told the woman to send her friend to Jung.[34] With her Philadelphia and Boston background, Catharine Rush Cabot had no education to speak of, for she was brought up to marry young and well and to be a proper ornament to her husband. When he died at the age of thirty-nine, leaving her with a small daughter, she developed what she called "the lump" and what others have described as a severe form of agoraphobia.[35]

She began analysis in 1929 and kept a record of her sessions until shortly before Jung's 1961 death, taking notes in swift longhand and expert shorthand throughout their sessions. Most of what she recorded is what Jung told her, particularly about his method. He said, for example, that an analyst could not just "sit there and analyze people in a cold-blooded way," even when his patients were "terribly boring people." He spoke of having to exert "tremendous effort" upon himself, to "bring out his unconscious so as to help them."[36] When she compared him to a "confessor," he countered by saying that his method was really about "teach[ing] people to agree and get along with themselves, and not make too much fuss."[37] When she asked him how he was able to continue to develop his analytic abilities year after year, Jung told her, "My patients forced me by their neurosis, otherwise I would never have lifted a finger."

Cabot's interest in how Jung treated patients stemmed from "the criss-cross of emotions"[38] she felt toward members of his seminars. From the early 1930s onward, she sensed that everything he told them was couched in an indefinable irritation he no longer cared to hide.[39] She thought his anger arose from the inability of participants to assimilate his ideas properly. He agreed: "I could just smash their heads when I come in [to lecture]. . . . It's as if you are talking to a flock of geese, that all scatter as soon as you begin to talk. You feel they can't any of them stand each other. In collectivity people get like that."

She asked how he felt, living and working in the relative isolation of Zürich, "with no one to carry on" his psychology. He told her it did not matter that he had no "crown prince," because he was leaving a vast body of writing for future generations. He included himself in a group with Nietzsche, Goethe, Schopenhauer, and Schiller, saying thinkers such as these did not "appear *en serie*, they only happen here and there." What irritated him most was that people who could not understand his theory accused him of being a "charlatan." He said this to Cabot in 1938, when he was sixty-three, but to emphasize his point, he used a childhood incident that still rankled: when the elementary school teacher read his essay and accused him of cheating because it was so polished. "People were astonished that I knew something!"

And so it remained more than six decades later. He told her about a group of "learned professors" with whom he tried to discuss psychological problems and who were astonished that his suggestions stemmed from "*research* work, *research!*" He thundered at what to do with people who dismissed psychology as nothing more than "mere talk," and who were astonished when he insisted that it had to be grounded in solid research and carefully reasoned theory. Far too many refused to see that both had to coalesce before written method could be constructed.

IF KATY Cabot's analytic diary was primarily about how she should relate to her immediate external world, Christiana Morgan's was quite the opposite. Cabot's therapy was centered around her relationships with her parents, in-laws, daughter, and lovers, but mostly with how she could learn to adapt and adjust to the fractious personalities who competed with her for Jung's attention. When Morgan first consulted Jung in the summer of 1926, her concerns were personal and internal, fixated entirely upon her inner self. A major concern was how to expand the dimensions of her personality through individuation; equally important was to learn how to develop satisfying ways to put her considerable intellect to constructive use. Most of all, however, she wanted to know what to do about the erotic attraction she shared with the psychologist Henry A. Murray.

The Jung-as-analyst who appears in Morgan's diary is not the father figure who mediates between abrasive personalities in Cabot's. Nor is he the objective scientist of the Pauli material, who adhered strictly to unbiased explication based on historical antecedents, who used his own personal history only when it was clearly germane. He is, rather, an analyst whose own triangular relationships with wife and mistress dominate the advice he gave Morgan about how to navigate in the similar situation she shared with Harry (as he was always called) and his wife, the Boston heiress Josephine Rantoul Murray. By extension, there was Morgan's husband, Will, whom she did love but in a most peculiar way. There was another dimension of Morgan's treatment that was totally absent from any of the analyses previously discussed: she was an artist of considerable ability, and Jung co-opted her paintings for his own uses and interpretations, particularly in The Vision Seminars he gave between 1930 and 1934.[40] In Morgan's case, it would seem that Jung was more interested in the material than the person, as he used her creative material to demonstrate how it expressed archetypal theory. What was unfortunate was that Morgan was so easily identifiable that Jung's intellectual attempt to assist others to understand this concept resulted in personal humiliation and suffering on her part.[41]

Morgan's analysis took place during the summer and autumn of 1926, but she remained "a living reality" for Jung long after his memory of most other patients had dissolved into "unreal shadows." A year and a half after they last met, she was still "just a bit of a marvel."[42] Christiana Drummond Councilman (1897–1967) was born into a comfortable Boston family that was accepted in Brahmin society, and her upbringing was like Cabot's in that it centered around preparation for a good marriage. As a "young postdebutante Boston girl," she married William Morgan, an "innocent and plucky Harvard lad"[43] who was badly scarred by his army service in World War I and returned home suffering from what today would be called post-traumatic stress syndrome.

In another parallel with Cabot, Morgan also had one child to whom she was a mostly absent parent, a son entrusted to a succession of caregivers until he was old enough for boarding schools. While Cabot became a young widow who moved to Europe and embarked on a series of affairs and liaisons of varying duration, Morgan moved to New York and became the bored young wife of an unhappy husband who abandoned in quick succession careers in journalism, banking, and stockbroking. Morgan remained in her marriage, but again like Cabot, she was a forthright woman who believed she was entitled to a straightforward, satisfying erotic life. Cabot's most-lasting liaison was with an Englishman, Major Oswald "Tommy" de Trafford, but when she began her analysis with Jung, she was involved with Ruth Draper's brother, Dr. George Draper (then also Jung's patient). Morgan took many lovers, among them the Zionist Chaim Weizmann, the philosopher Alfred North Whitehead, and the cultural critic Lewis Mumford. In the early years of her marriage, she was involved with Cecil Dunmore "Mike" Murray, the older brother of her longest-lasting relationship, Henry A. "Harry" Murray.

By 1923, the restless Will Morgan was taking courses at the New School for Social Research and in contact once again with both Murray brothers, whom he had known when they were all at Harvard. They and their wives soon became a couples' triumvirate who entertained each other socially, even as they were all aware that Mike was Christiana's lover and that she and Harry were erotically attracted. The attraction was intellectual as well as physical, and Christiana is generally credited with introducing Harry, then a physician engaged in bio-chemical research at the Rockefeller Institute, to Jung's writing. She urged him to read *Psychological Types*, the book generally cited as the basis of their lasting mutual interest in personality theory.[44]

By 1924, when the three men became dissatisfied with their individual ca-reers, they all agreed to move to England. The husbands enrolled in Cambridge University and expected their wives and the only child of each to provide com-pany for the others. Before they went, Harry told the group he intended to con-sult Jung about becoming a psychoanalyst, first doing so in the Easter recess of 1925. Murray did not write an analytic diary per se, but in a detailed interview many years later in 1968, he did discuss how Jung worked with him.[45] What Murray related about his sessions with Jung is of particular importance when assessing how Jung later analyzed Christiana because, in a very real sense, Mur-ray set the scene for how Jung would treat her.

When Murray arrived for his first session, he irritated Jung by trying to get him to explain some of his writing.[46] Realizing Jung was bored, Murray tried to save the session by describing a "mini-anima experience" he had just had in the lobby of his Fribourg hotel: he approached a woman whose looks intrigued him and told her he felt as if he had known her long before. The woman, Lady Winifred Gore, was on her way to another Swiss analyst, and after a friendly conversation, she and Murray parted, never to meet again.

Jung became engaged at this point, talking about Toni Wolff's place in his life in fulsome detail. He did not, however, speak of her concrete reality but only of her uncanny ability to bring to light material from his unconscious that had been "hidden back there under the crust of convention."[47] Murray asked Jung if morality and fidelity to one's wife were necessary for a successful and lasting marriage and was surprised by his answer. "Well maybe," Jung replied. "It [his relationship with Toni Wolff] isn't good in a moral sense, but it has to be."

Later, when Murray reflected upon his earliest sessions, he concluded that Jung's theory was autobiographical to an extraordinary degree. In particular, he cited the Two Essays on Analytical Psychology,[48] in which Jung formulated views about the concepts of animus and anima. Murray was convinced that everything Jung said about his emerging theory was really about himself and Toni Wolff, not as they were in life but as they appeared within his personal psychological processes. Because of how Jung analyzed him, Murray believed Jung's consuming interest was not in his patients but in "his own mental processes, in what you might say was his larger self."[49] Murray thought Jung "really wasn't too attentive to other people. . . . He does not present a person as you see him, or as you see him behave. He doesn't put him in any context. He talks about their dreams and how they reach this stage in their psychic develop-ment in terms of imagination, but you never see the person himself."

Murray also resented how Jung "could go on and on, like a steamroller"[50] during his sessions, but his criticism sheds light on Jung's process:

> He doesn't know how much he talks. He often writes that he lets the patient go on and on, then the patient arrives at what path he ought to take just by a sort of spontaneous process after going through alternative possibilities. He gives you a picture of taking a very listening part, not passive but not intervening. But he is intervening, every single minute. He tells you every minute what he thinks or very closely what he thinks, even though he may not say it explicitly in so many words.

If there was competition between them in the consulting room, Jung initially offered friendship outside it. Jung (then fifty) took Murray (thirty-two) sailing, to Bollingen, and to dine with his family. One of his first acts was to introduce Murray to both Emma and Toni. Murray sensed that Emma did not like Toni but grudgingly accepted her as part of Jung's ongoing self-analysis. He wondered if it was because Emma thought her husband was so disturbed that Toni was a necessary presence for his well-being.

Murray was convinced that Jung's idea of woman as the "contained" and man as the "container"[51] was based entirely on his personal situation. Jung assigned each woman to fulfill a man's special need: he expected Emma, as the "contained" entity, to play the role of wife and mother, and Toni that of *femme inspiratrice*, intellectual helpmate and erotic partner.[52] Murray quotes Jung describing himself as the "container," insisting that "the container is not contained." Rather, he is always invested with a certain amount of energy that permits him to look outward rather than inward at what is being contained, to keep an eye on "new developments elsewhere." Meanwhile, the "contained one" is expected to be "perfectly happy . . . securely surrounded" by the container.[53]

And so, Christiana Morgan was typecast even before she went to Zürich in the summer of 1926.[54] She had formed two primary intellectual interests in the few brief years of her marriage: psychology and art. When she lived in New York, she had taken courses at the Art Students League, and she was one of the first Americans to buy and study Jung's *Psychological Types* in the 1923 English-language edition. Now that they were living in Cambridge as part of the group that included the Murray brothers and their wives, she had long stretches of solitary time to fill. At the time she consulted Jung, she was described as "beautiful, witty and intuitive, but she cherished ideas, not feeling. She often related to men through ideas . . . but she was also sometimes cold and remote. . . . In hindsight, one can say she was lonely."[55]

One could also say she was depressed. She scoured libraries and bookstores for every publication she could find that dealt with psychology and psychoanalysis in an effort to try to understand her own unhappiness. To interpret it, she wrote about herself and drew some of the images that flitted through her mind.[56] When she arrived in Zürich, she appeared to Jung as "a woman of about thirty years of age . . . highly educated, very intelligent, a typical intellectual, with an almost mathematical mind. She is . . . exceedingly rational . . . has a great deal of intuition, which really ought to function but is repressed."[57]

Morgan went to Zürich with her husband, Will, and like her, he saw Toni Wolff as well as Jung. Christiana kept a thorough written record of her sessions, but Will wrote mostly sporadic, selective, and unenlightening snatches of dialogue.[58] In many of these, he and Jung discuss Christiana's drawings, and both are ill at ease. In one such, Will Morgan records Jung as follows: "She has gathered together her scattered self. . . . Aha ha — ho well well What did I tell you — you see there it is — she has achieved — this is marvelous. . . . Ah — all this is very wunderful [sic] . . ."

Jung had a tendency to project his idealized version of a woman's typology onto the actual person who sat before him. In Morgan's case, so much of her reality was eclipsed by his interpretation of what she represented, and her resemblance to Toni Wolff did not escape his notice.[59] Both women were of patrician background, both had developed their own personal sense of style, both showed flair in dress and deportment. Each woman had a luminous pale olive complexion and piercing dark eyes, usually enshrouded in a cloud of cigarette smoke. Each was also the "other woman" in a man's life, not the nurturing wife and mother but the hetaira (to use Toni Wolff's word) or "soror mystica" (Jung's). Before he ever saw Christiana Morgan, Jung had already told Harry Murray that it was possible and at times necessary for a man to divide the women in his life into categories formulated for his own masculine comfort and support. Murray added that Jung warned him that although such relationships were psychologically advantageous for certain men, they posed difficulties as well. Jung considered Harry one of these men and encouraged him to be honest and forthright with Josephine and Christiana about the role he expected each to play within his life, for such a personal arrangement was sure to enhance his professional creativity. Jung did not consider what such a relationship would inflict upon each woman, and from the documents Murray left behind, it appears that he did not consider it either.

Christiana Morgan went to Jung with a clearly delineated list of problems she wanted to resolve, the love-and-sex complications of her marriage and her lovers (particularly Harry) being but one. Other aspects of her life were equally troubling, such as her relationship with her father, whom she blamed for her attraction to older, powerful men whom she wanted to protect and cherish her. Another problem was her inability to channel her intelligence into a useful means of expression and, by extension, into satisfying work. Everything she tried to tell Jung about this last problem was complicated by one other factor: even though she was basically intelligent, she had not been given much more education than was necessary for a wealthy young woman who was expected to accept marriage as her only choice in life. Consequently, she believed that she lacked the language to describe her feelings and emotions and that she had scant knowledge of what possibilities for work might be available to her. Jung spent the least amount of time on this aspect of her therapy, dismissing it as just another example of her inability to express feelings. Instead, he spent their time together focusing almost entirely on her link to Harry Murray.

In Morgan's treatment as described by her biographer, the analyst Claire Douglas, Jung was "far more directive than an analyst would be today."[60] Still, Douglas credits him with helping Morgan "to make sense of herself and to understand her depressions and the meaning of her actions and fantasies. . . . Jung taught her to focus inward, allowing space for her feeling sense to develop . . . to trust herself."

The Morgans were in Zürich at the same time as Robert Edmond Jones, who lived in the same pension and with whom they soon became fast friends. Jung discovered that "Jonah," as he called the flamboyantly extraverted but deeply depressed stage designer, had a talent for active imagination. Jonah Jones did not hesitate to teach "trancing"* to the other residents, and Christiana became his star pupil.[61] With her artistic ability, Morgan was able to express what she saw while trancing in two forms: the verbal descriptions she recorded in analytic notebooks, and the paintings and drawings she made at Jung's request. She unleashed visions that Jung believed were allowing her "inferior function, feeling" to surface in ways that let her reach her "real self."[62] These consisted of more than one hundred fantasies she committed to paper during the summer of 1926. Four years later, Jung presented approximately forty-four of her visions in seminars at the Psychological Club.

He gave the seminars during a crucial turning point in his long relationship with Toni Wolff, at the moment when she was questioning why he insisted on concentrating his research upon alchemical literature, a field in which she refused to follow him. That she could even express such reservation was shocking, as was Jung's response to it. He told Murray, "All of a sudden Toni Wolff went out of my life just as fast as she came in. All of a sudden, that was the end."[63]

He fully expected Toni and Emma to continue to work peacefully on the two separate fronts where he needed them: helping to analyze patients and keeping the Psychological Club members under a semblance of control. But the two women were going through another of their recurrent periods of mutual resentment. In an effort to resolve their differences without involving Jung, they asked C. A. Meier to join them in what he later described as "the first group therapy session in analytic psychology."[64] As the only male, Meier assumed he would take charge of the sessions and direct the self-analysis of their dreams, but the women resisted. Nothing came of their two, possibly three, meetings.

---

*His term for the process of allowing a conscious image to determine the direction the active imagination would take.

The women ended them simply by not showing up at the time Meier appointed for the next one.

All three principals in this domestic drama — Jung, his wife, and his mistress — were engaged in thinking and writing about the anima and the animus during this crisis, which may have been why Jung decided to present Morgan's visions to the Psychological Club as the next in his ongoing series of seminars. It offered all the participants an opportunity to work out their differing theories on neutral territory and before an audience of supposedly unbiased respondents.

Although the analytic concept of confidentiality was not yet as firmly established as it has come to be, or even as it was at the end of Jung's life, when he berated Mary Briner for her willingness to breach it, he did, nevertheless, betray Morgan's privacy by sharing her visions with so many people to whom she was easily recognizable. However, Morgan was both female and American (and therefore not in Zürich), and most of the others who had been in Zürich when she was there had also dispersed, so Jung convinced himself that he could present it and still preserve an acceptable modicum of privacy. No one openly gossiped about whose visions they were during the entire four years of his lectures, so Jung was able to superimpose his own interpretation on Morgan's creative material before an unquestioning and receptive audience.[65]

His stated intention, to which he adhered throughout, was to show how Morgan's drawings contained symbolic and archetypal material that reflected the ways in which the collective unconscious revealed itself to one particular patient. As his lectures developed, Jung seems to have abandoned the woman who created them and substituted his own theoretical abstractions in her place. His lectures show his vacillation toward her material, as his remarks become dominated by frustration, indecision, irritation, and deprecation. In what appears to be boredom, he introduces analogies that are interesting but not vital to his point. There are long passages where he digresses into alchemy, Kundalini yoga, German folklore, or case histories of other patients. In a very real sense, his lectures paralleled his involvement with his patient outside the lecture hall, specifically, the strong attraction he felt toward Morgan that led him to belittle Murray and denigrate their (hers and Murray's) by-now consummated and well-established relationship.

The question of Jung's personal attraction to Morgan and the degree to which their involvement determined her analysis is cloudy. If the silliness of the remarks Will Morgan recorded are true, Christiana left Jung flustered. In the one published letter he wrote her, his language falters and his message flutters.[66] At the end of his life, Harry Murray made veiled comments suggesting that the doctor and his patient had much more than a therapeutic relationship.[67] "The spirit grows, tried by strange fires," Morgan wrote to Murray in October 1926 when she returned to Zürich for a brief second round of sessions with Jung in which he completely reversed himself:[68] instead of encouraging the feeling function he helped to unleash earlier, Jung told her to concentrate on her intellect and use her mind. He insisted that she fulfill her role as "anima woman and *femme inspiratrice*" because Murray needed her to hold a "positive attitude" if he was to be "free" and have "something to go ahead with."[69] Jung's response to an attraction between himself and Morgan, of the transference and countertransference in Jungian parlance, was far different from the way he handled the one between himself and Katy Cabot. He sent Cabot to Toni Wolff with instructions to put her "searchlight" on her feelings for him, but he did not do so with Christiana Morgan.[70]

JUNG'S VISION Seminars are a curious anomaly, a hodgepodge of Morgan's life and his theory, so biographical in content and interpretation that they puzzle scholars of both textual exegesis and analytic theory. He ended them abruptly, using the "growing political tension in Europe" as an excuse to turn to Nietzsche's *Zarathustra*.[71] Actually, the real reason he ended the Vision Seminars was Morgan's angry cable in the spring of 1934, ordering him to stop them at once.

Morgan and Murray had not been to Zürich since 1927. In 1934, Murray was director of the Harvard Psychological Clinic, and Morgan his noncredentialed general factotum. True, Morgan had originally given Jung permission to use the visions, but only under the condition that he guarantee her anonymity, which for four years she believed he was doing. Now Frances Gillespy Wickes, recently back from Zürich, told Morgan that other attendees had long ago guessed her identity and that allegations and rumors about her, Jung, and Murray were flourishing. Morgan's cable to Jung was so angry it resulted in a breach that was not healed until 1936, when he went to Cambridge to receive an honorary degree at Harvard's tercentenary. In her capacity as the Harvard Clinic's official hostess, Morgan invited Jung to a luncheon for the honorees, among them the aged Pierre Janet. Here again Jung devalued Morgan: despite the fact that she was acting in her professional capacity, he flaunted propriety and shocked the other guests by flirting outrageously. Whatever the reality of their relationship, his behavior fueled the fire of speculation forever.

JUNG TRAVELED extensively in the early 1930s, mostly on short trips connected with lecture engagements. Among them were his address to the Congrès international de Pédagogie in Montreux-Territet; the Literarische Gesellschaft of Augsburg; the Tagung des Verbandes für intellektuelle Zusammenarbeit in Prague; the IV. algemeinen ärztlichen Kongress für Psychotherapie in Bad Neuheim; and the Ärztlicher Verein and the Psychotherapeutische Gesellschaft in Munich. Most of his Swiss invitations came from groups that were not specifically medical but were concerned with public education, public health, literature, and philosophy. Most of what he told them consisted of material given elsewhere that he modified for each new audience.[72] His publications were also mostly revised and recycled versions of previously published work, several consisting of translations into which he incorporated refinements and changes. One of the most important that went through many of these phases was the essay "The Structure of the Unconscious."[73]

He also wrote a few new articles upon request, as if he were a journalist accepting assignments tailored for specific audiences. Two stemmed directly from his continued attendance at Count Keyserling's School of Wisdom. Even though their rapport was now dominated by rivalry,[74] Jung admired the count's "courage and sincerity" for declaring in a symposium before several hundred persons that all contemporary marriages were a "sham."[75] Discussion was heated, and a volume of essays dedicated to the debate seemed a logical endeavor, so Keyserling commissioned and edited a collection published as *The Book of Marriage.*[76] He asked Jung to write about "Marriage as a Psychological Relationship." At the same time, the *Europäische Revue* of Berlin asked for an essay about "Women in Europe." Jung called the latter "such a hazardous undertaking" that he insisted he would not have written it without the editor's "pressing invitation."[77]

Although both essays ostensibly dealt with the same subject, they were radically different in content. Jung disapproved of the theoretical underpinning upon which Keyserling constructed the philosophical premise of his school, comparing it to "a new house being built on the old shaky foundations. . . . Though the old damage is covered up, the new building does not stand firm."[78] There was also a personal element, for Keyserling irritated Jung on every front. He thought the count lived in a world of dreams, on the one hand totally unaware of the harsh realities of life in post–World War I Germany and on the other unable to withstand "the shock of glimpsing the face of his own shadow." Matters between them were further complicated when Keyserling insisted upon presenting his dreams to Jung in person and by mail, expecting a detailed — and free — analysis by swift return.[79] Despite the added friction of having to deal with the count's lordly treatment of him as if he were a vassal, Jung produced an essay that touched upon themes that were becoming a hallmark of his psychological philosophy. They are to be found in his writings from then onward and culminate in his last great work, the *Mysterium Coniunctionis.*

In the essay he wrote for the count's book, Jung dealt with the problem of opposites by referring to some of his conclusions in *Psychological Types.* He expanded further upon the animus and anima when he described marriage partners as container and contained, but now he assessed how a relationship differs in the first half of married life from the second. Although the specific subject of individuation is muted in this essay, it is very much woven into the fabric of Jung's idea of contemporary marriage, as he makes thoughtful references to the changes that occur in in the second half of life. In "Women in Europe," Jung noted how deeply World War I scarred "the psyche of the modern European." In the postwar decade, both men and women found it impossible to banish the war's trauma from conscious thought and were forced to search for a different sort of "psychic relationship": "Women are increasingly aware that love alone can give them full stature, just as men are beginning to divine that only the spirit can give life its highest meaning . . . love needs the spirit and the spirit love, for its completion."[80]

Jung held men responsible for creating the "alarming surplus of unmarried women" by waging war and the resulting attrition by death: "It is no longer a question of a few dozen voluntary or involuntary old maids here and there, but of millions." At this point, his essay becomes contradictory as he spills his ideas onto paper and leaves them to stand without the necessary editing that would have given it organizational coherence. Jung notes how women in the last half of the nineteenth century began to enter fields traditionally associated with men as they attended universities, established themselves in the professions, and stopped hiding "behind the mask of Mrs. So-and-so" to become "visible member[s] of society." He appears to favor this visibility but then declares that "mental masculinization of the woman has unwelcome results," one being that they overflow psychiatrists' consulting rooms. He proclaims this a theme that "would fill a large volume."

Women are "far more 'psychological'" than men, who are "usually satisfied with 'logic' alone." Men "find the discussion of personal relations painful and boring," whereas "women would find it equally boring to be examined on Kant's *Critique of Pure Reason*." Yet his underlying message is that women always benefit most from psychoanalysis, and therefore, as "the function of Eros," it is their responsibility to unify what man as "Logos has sundered." This "tremendous cultural task" might well signal "the dawn of a new era." Jung placed upon women the burden to force men to recognize the spiritual attributes of the self. He held men responsible for foisting an increasingly technocratic, scientific worldview upon humanity; therefore, women's task was to make men accept that Jung's unspecified spirituality was equally valid within that worldview.

The theme that begins to resonate throughout his writing is that middle age is a time of reflection as well as action. He wrote this essay "not for the young . . . but for the more mature man whose consciousness has been widened by the experience of life." What he expects of those "who have passed the meridian of life" is both the privilege and responsibility "to create culture."

With hindsight, it is easy to extract passages from both essays that might have had bearing upon Jung's personal circumstances, not only with Emma and Toni but also with Christiana. To do so would be casuistic, however, for one of the most interesting aspects of both essays is the absence of directly personal material. Up to this point in his writing, Jung relied upon two separate methods of illuminating his process and procedures. The first was the case study method, but the more successful one he used to keep his audience's attention or impress theoretical points upon his readers was to insert snippets of information about himself.

There is a clearly discernible trend in his writings from mid-decade onward, as he recounts fewer and fewer of his patients' personal problems and his own technical methods of dealing with them. More and more, he directs his attention toward the nonpersonal, the objective, the psychic, and all those concepts he would eventually gather under the rubric of the Archetypes of the Collective Unconscious.[81] Jung's writings reflected another major change: he diffused his primary identification as a medical doctor to embrace willingly the identity of a professor. To the end of his life, he insisted that he was an empirical scientist, but if his theory began with that mode of thinking, the work that ultimately emerged was far more philosophical than scientific. Dr. Joseph Henderson was among the first to recognize that by 1934

> his seminars no longer contained case material at all, but were concerned with analysis of the philosophy of Nietzsche and the study of Eastern religions, general mythology, and folklore. This change of interest was, of course, no sudden thing, nor did it take him away from his therapeutic tasks; he was still Dr. Jung to the many patients who came from all over the world to consult him. But in ten years time, the change had become very obvious to all who knew him.[82]

JUNG FELT free to shift the focus of his intellectual inquiry after he read Richard Wilhelm's 1929 German translation of the Chinese alchemical text *The Secret of the Golden Flower*. It was almost as if Wilhelm's book provided the imprimatur for him to make public something he had been keeping almost sheepishly hidden, his concentrated study of alchemy. Wilhelm's book offered a model for Jung to coalesce the particular combination of philosophy, medicine, and religion that eventually defined his canon. Jung reasoned that if a scholar of Wilhelm's standing could study esoteric texts and publish his findings, then he could turn a deaf ear to Toni Wolff's concern that the world would brand him a charlatan if he embraced alchemy, which she thought at best a pseudoscience, at worst sheer quackery.

In Jung's milieu, those unfamiliar with alchemy as it was practiced in the late Middle Ages generally ridiculed the process as a misguided chemical attempt to create gold from base metal or other dross and dismissed the alchemist's search for a universal elixir or a philosopher's stone as even greater foolishness. Toni Wolff worried that Jung would be lumped in with the worst practitioners of the so-called black magic or mumbo jumbo; Jung could not persuade her that the ancient alchemical texts dealt more with the internal, personal experiences of the alchemists — filled as they were with references to spiritual transformations — than with accounts of their laboratory procedures. When Jung read the ancient alchemical works, he found interesting parallels between their writers and many of the texts created by religious mystics, anchorites, and other visionaries, particularly within the Christian tradition. To him, alchemy was more about the process of internal growth that he called individuation, and as such, it became his metaphor for the process of transference within the analytic encounter as it evolved within his psychology.[83]

As always, the texts of the *Protocols*, blunt and earthy, do more to explain this evolution than does the polished account of *Memories, Dreams, Reflections*. While the published biographical text delineates fact and event in serene and orderly development, the interviews and conversations within the *Protocols* tell just how roundabout, haphazard, and lengthy was the questing and seeking that led to Jung's ultimate realization that alchemy was what had been missing all along from his study of archetypes and the collective unconscious.

In trying to explain how important *The Secret of the Golden Flower* was to his subsequent readings and writings, Jung went back to the origin of the *Red Book* and the dual question of why he had begun it and why he was unable to finish it. He realized as he was writing it that his thoughts had settled into what he dubbed a curious mix of fantasy and prophecy, both "completely against the grain" of a medical doctor. This in itself was upsetting, so he declared himself neither prophet nor poet, saying he saw no reason to finish a book that would be "regrettably poor." This was his ostensible reason for putting it aside, even though dreams still haunted him.

One in particular was a dream he had in 1913 that he referred to as "the Murder of Siegfried." He kept the dream fairly private, even though he interpreted it rigorously in 1913 and then expended much thought on reinterpreting it differently in the late 1920s.[84] Jung's original thought was that the attitudes of the hero were no longer appropriate for the life he needed to live, and therefore he had to kill him/them. When he returned to the dream, he thought it signified a "sort of intermediate realm . . . coming into a twilight" in which "I am this and still something else . . . something that I am, and something else that is different from me." Throughout the next twenty or so years, the meaning of this and other dreams either eluded him or changed with subsequent interpretation as he kept trying to "get to the bottom of . . . this stream of the unconscious [that] began with the dreams between 1912–14." Only when he read Wilhelm's *Golden Flower* did he realize that he had not reached his "foundation" until he studied alchemy.

The idea of Philemon as the wise old man and guide in the *Red Book* led Jung to study Gnostic writings and to conclude shortly before 1920 that "Philemon was a Gnostic," for like the practitioners of this early Christian sect, Philemon, too, possessed esoteric knowledge of spiritual things. Later that year, when he dreamt he was locked in the seventeenth century and could not get out, he realized that he could not find relevance in Gnosticism because it was "all still too far away,"[85] meaning he could find no intellectual satisfaction in the Gnostic idea that a "Godhead" was responsible for creating the world, because there was simply too much detail lacking or left unexplained. He reread scholars who wrote about early religions and various mythologies, among them Herbert Silberer, whom he had not consulted since his years with Freud. He found Silberer wanting because "he mainly . . . applied the Freudian interpretations." Then he turned to F. von Baader, who had "damned little to say," and afterward J. J. von Görres, who was "exactly the same." None of these writers touched upon "the dark substance . . . the dark side" to which Jung had always been attracted. "Just think of the experience of God shitting on the church," he offered as an analogy, and then he revealed another related dream of his student years that he had never spoken of until now:

> I was very insecure at the time and I always had the wish, if I only had a direct experience of the eternal, of a sighting of God. And then I had the dream in which I thought: now it is coming, now I will finally experience it! There was a door, and I understood that if I opened this door, the experience would happen and I would see. I opened this door and what was behind it — a big manure heap and on top of it there lay a big sow. Can you imagine what an awful impression that was for me? Not quite as bad as the experience at the Basler Münster, but still almost as bad.

He began to think of this dream repeatedly and concluded that he had to fit it and all the others into the intellectual mix that he hoped his forays into alchemical research would permit him to sort out.

"Alchemy called itself the 'black art' for a reason," he said in the *Protocols*, and this revelation offered "the bridge between past and present." For the first time, he felt he could "walk across it into the past," or into the collective unconscious. Alchemy was the bridge that led "from Gnosticism to Christianity" and that gave his psychology

> a historical ground: Otherwise it would have remained nothing but a phantasm. This comparative ground gives my psychology its substance. After all, I formulated my psychology from the knowledge of clinical experience and from my own experiences and I regarded alchemy within this context. This was important to me: to base my special experience on the ground of reality, and the historical ground is also part of that.

Jung made these reflections sometime after 1957, when he had fewer than five years of life remaining and his major work was all but complete. Despite forty-plus years of writing and thinking, the statement with which he concluded the reflection above is tinged with dismay and regret: "Otherwise, people would always have taken [analytical psychology] as a fantasy — which they still do today, by the way." But as the 1930s began, he saw his "main task" as one in which he needed to put the experiences he had gathered, of himself as well as of his patients, onto "firm ground." Hitherto, he had been "missing a piece," because he had always assumed that Gnosticism "had simply been finished, and one did not see that it was continued in the cabala and in alchemy." Jung had been reluctant to talk about, let alone to publish, such ideas, which he feared could be ridiculed and dismissed as "subjective fancy."[86] In Wilhelm's commentary on the text of the *Golden Flower*, Jung found a "fully confirmed . . . parallel" to what he saw happening in "the psychic development of my patients, none of whom is Chinese." It was a relief to find that the technique he had "unconsciously" developed before he knew of the existence of this text had been "the preoccupation of the best minds of the East for centuries." It gave him the courage to "depict in its full scope how my psychology is an exact equivalent of alchemy or vice versa in order to help analytical psychology stand firmly on the ground."[87]

But this would make all too evident what he thought was the main problem of "medical psychotherapy," that "people could always say my publication of medical case histories was arbitrariness on my part." It thus became his obligation, "given to me by fate to bring my knowledge of the unconscious into the reality of our spiritual tradition."

In years to come, Jung's writings expressed the development of how he integrated alchemy into analytical psychology. *Aion* permitted "a confrontation of analytical psychology with Christian views" and with "the central figure of Christ." *Answer to Job* allowed him to argue the case for God as both compassionate and punitive. *Mysterium Coniunctionis* demonstrated his ultimate intention, to make his "original idea . . . represent the whole scope of alchemy, a sort of psychology of alchemy or an alchemist foundation of psychology."

By placing analytical psychology within "reality," he would have a system in which "the whole thing is backed up. . . . Now it can stand on its own and with that my task was done." But having brought it to this "outermost border," Jung was forced to recognize "the transcendent, about which nothing can be said." And if nothing could be said, how, then, to say even that?

One of Jung's main concerns had always been to place his work within "the great cultural tradition," which for him meant the close of the nineteenth century, a period that coincided with the end of the reading he was required to do for his university studies. After that, he was by choice almost totally ignorant of twentieth-century arts and letters, for he seldom read contemporary fiction and never read biography or nonfiction unless it covered topical subjects that interested him. His favored form of recreational reading were *crimi*, the crime novels and murder mysteries of writers such as Agatha Christie (his favorite) or Simenon. He devoured them in the evenings, so friends in England and France made sure to send the latest as soon as they were published.[88] He never went to the theater, attended lectures only on psychological subjects, and avoided concerts like the plague: "I have to listen intently all day long, and I don't want to do it in my time off," he told patients, friends, and family. He even complained when his gifted daughter Marianne practiced her piano.

With his interests anchored in the late nineteenth century of his scholarly studies, he centered his idea of the ideal cultural tradition around the iconic figure of Faust. He first read Goethe's version when he was sixteen and even then thought the ending was "incorrect" and "should be done differently." When he started "working on the unconscious," he began by trying to read all the different interpretations of the Faust legend. It left him frustrated because "I cannot just look at things; I have to do something with them." Eventually, all his "inner figures" came from Goethe's *Faust*, especially Philemon, whom Goethe "mentioned only in passing." Jung thought Philemon was a "central figure . . . a recognition that Faust skipped over and didn't achieve." His personal interpretation became a way of "honoring the eternal human rights . . . the continuity of culture and spiritual history."

As decades passed and his theory developed, Jung became profoundly aware of his "need to integrate all the experiences of the unconscious into the historical frame in order to establish proof of it as a general human experience." He needed to prove he was not merely writing out of his own "subjective imagination" and thought it vital "to show the world that we have a meaningful unconscious and not just a messy concoction of perverse things." When he made this observation, he remembered how Freud's "depreciation" of this concept "always got on my nerves terribly."

From 1927 onward, Jung believed that his published work should include one other value: it should be read as a continuum dealing with "questions of world views" as they confronted but were also reflected within "religious questions."[89] He believed that "analytical psychology merges in a very peculiar way with alchemy" and that alchemy was the true "historical counterpart to the psychology of the unconscious." By 1930, he believed his contribution to the great cultural tradition would be to explain how alchemy had not only been depreciated but also maligned and misunderstood. Alchemy became for him a metaphor of inner spiritual growth and development and he planned to explain this through reading and commenting upon as many original texts as he could acquire, no matter what the ancient language in which they were written. His Latin was good enough that he could read it almost as easily as his native German; he was less fluent in Greek and required a dictionary; and for most other ancient languages he needed translations. He knew he would need help, but Zürich was filled with specialists, and he could always pay them for their professional services.

He counted, as always, on the dedicated Toni Wolff, his most trusted associate.[90] He presented her with a list of books he wanted and an outline for further alchemical research and was astonished that she was so aghast she would not even listen to his theories, let alone work with him. With more overt opposition than she had ever shown, she argued that to make such ideas public, let alone declare alchemy the foundation of his psychology, would marginalize him within the medical-psychological community and lead to ridicule and scorn in the world at large.

And so, with the exception of von Franz (who was then only doing translation and library research), Jung found himself for the first time mostly working alone, without a kindred spirit in whom to confide. There were plenty of people in Zürich who would have given up their work to help with his, but they did not have the necessary background or innate intelligence of Toni Wolff. He could not even count on correspondence with Wilhelm to exchange ideas, for he died on March 1, 1930, after a long battle with the amoebic dysentery that infected him years before in China.

Wilhelm was one of many male friends Jung lost in rapid succession. He had been extremely close socially and professionally to two men who lived in Zürich: Hermann Sigg, the businessman who introduced him to North Africa; and Jerome Schloss, also a businessman, who was first Jung's patient and then a dedicated supporter of his psychology. In the United States, George Beckwith, his recalcitrant companion in Africa, was killed in an auto accident in California, and George Porter committed suicide in Chicago. It was a curiously sad time. Jung felt the pressure of time passing and recognized that he was entering into old age. Perfecting his theory, getting it right and getting it written, became the force that drove him.

CHAPTER 27

"Dangerously Famous"

Ruth Bailey, beloved friend of the entire Jung family, hosted Emma and some of the daughters during the summer of 1932. That autumn, C. G. wrote to thank Ruth for her hospitality and to tell her he had not accepted her invitation himself because he had been busy becoming "dangerously famous." Even though the "Negro spiritual" recommended that one should "'steal away to Jesus,'" all he had managed was a brief respite in Bollingen.[1]

Jung was referring specifically to the commotion surrounding his latest honor, the first *Literaturpreis der Stadt Zürich*, a literature prize worth 8,000 francs bestowed by the city. There were howls of outrage among members of the city's artistic community, as many were offended that the prize went to a psychologist rather than to a creative writer.[2] Most of Jung's support came from the direct intervention of his publisher, Max Rascher, and Rascher's equally prestigious friend the physician and writer Charlot Strasser. Jung ignored allegations of favoritism and insisted the prize came "directly from the public." He took it as a sign that he was "no longer a prophet" without honor in his own country, and joked that winning left him with nothing local to complain about. He told Ruth it was "always sad when one has to look elsewhere for good causes."[3]

THE DECADE of the 1930s brought the famous and talented to Jung in ever increasing numbers. Some came for his counsel, but many more came because their curiosity was piqued by the publicity he generated. Many just wanted to say they had met the controversial "highly civilized modernist" who tooled around Zürich in his bright red Chrysler convertible, or "the primitive" whose "powerful arms" washed his own blue jeans in a tub at his medieval fortress.[4] Many were intrigued by articles describing Jung as a "force" possessing an "elephantine intelligence,"[5] and prominent among them were the British writers Hugh Walpole and H. G. Wells. Both came to Zürich to give lectures, and both specifically asked their hosts to invite Jung.

Jung actually went to hear Walpole speak, something he rarely did for anyone but a psychologist. He was invited to the dinner afterward and seated in the place of honor next to Walpole. Jung told him he had not read a single one of his books but changed his story shortly after by letter, saying he had "read a very decent number" of Walpole's novels and considered *The Prelude* a "psychological masterpiece."[6] A friendship did not develop, however, and the correspondence ended after a brief ritualistic exchange of mutual praise.

When H. G. Wells made a specific appointment to meet Jung in his study, the conversation was so engaging that Jung invited the writer to stay for dinner. They met on several other occasions when Wells came to lecture in Zürich, where he was exceedingly popular for his views on how developments in technology and science would mandate sweeping changes in contemporary society. Later, when Jung was in London, he dined at Wells's home. Their conversation, "with considerable elaboration," led Wells to feature Jung by name while turning him into a character in the novel *The World of William Clissold*.[7]

On two separate occasions, the British historian Arnold Toynbee asked Jung for appointments to discuss their respective views of mythology. Jung said it was a one-sided experience: "I told him some things about my ideas but he didn't offer anything about himself."[8]

F. Scott Fitzgerald watched Jung from afar during a January 1931 skiing vacation at Gstaad.[9] He had been living in Lausanne for the past five months while his wife, Zelda, was in Les Rives de Prangins, the Nyon sanatorium directed by Oscar Forel. Impatient with Forel's treatment, Fitzgerald took his daughter on vacation while he tried to decide whether to move Zelda to another facility, and if so, which psychologist to entrust with her treatment. Forel was amenable, even eager, that Zelda be taken either to Bleuler and the Burghölzli or to Jung. Fitzgerald was determined that whoever treated her had to direct a facility where she could be confined, and he was considering Ludwig Binswanger at Kreuzlingen.

Each night during his vacation, Fitzgerald sat at the same dinner table as Catharine Cabot, who by her own admission was a great snob. She stayed with him for long hours while he drank himself into depression and stupor, all the while berating her support of psychology in general and Jung in particular. To Forel's "relief," Fitzgerald eventually moved his wife to the Burghölzli, where she could be placed "under restraint." Complaining that both Jung and Bleuler charged "$500" for an initial consultation, Fitzgerald rejected Jung for dealing "primarily with neurosis" and accepted Bleuler because he treated "psychosis, which is to say one is a psychoanalyst and the other a specialist in insanity."[10]

JUNG SEEMED surprised that so many writers were eager to engage him in conversation because he never hid his opinion of contemporary literature: "I usually can't stand the typical literary writing. It bores me too much."[11] He may have been unread in current fiction, contemptuous of contemporary music, and indifferent to modern art, but he still did not hesitate to express his opinions in print. In 1932, the *Neue Zürcher Zeitung* asked him to write an article about Picasso to complement a *Kunsthaus* exhibition of more than 460 paintings.

Jung's disdain was evident from his first sentence: as a psychiatrist, he owed his readers an apology "for becoming involved in the excitement over Picasso," for the painter offered "too slight a theme" for so much public enthusiasm.[12] Taking oblique aim at James Joyce, Picasso's "literary brother" about whom he had also written, he responded to Picasso's "strange art" from the perspective of a psychologist. Still, he claimed artistic expertise because of his ongoing study of the art produced by his analysands, declaring emphatically that "Picasso's psychic problems, so far as they find expression in his work, are strictly analogous to those of my patients."

Jung divided his patients into two groups: neurotics and schizophrenics, slotting Picasso into the second because he "produces pictures which immediately reveal their alienation from feeling." Picasso was an artist "on the borderline," whose main characteristics were "so-called 'lines of fracture,' . . . a series of psychic 'faults'" that "disturbs one by [their] paradoxical, unfeeling, and grotesque unconcern for the beholder."[13]

When the article appeared, the editors were deluged with letters from outraged readers who ridiculed Jung's ignorance of contemporary art and resented that he dared to analyze an artist he had never met. Jung did not reply to any of the letters, but he acknowledged the barrage indirectly through a corrective footnote when he included the essay in his 1934 book, *Wirklichkeit der Seele*. He said he did not regard either Picasso or Joyce as actual psychotics but included them "among a large number of people whose habitus it is to react to a profound psychic disturbance not with an ordinary psychoneurosis but with a schizoid syndrome."[14] The public ridicule was humiliating and may well have been why Jung never again wrote about any modern artist in particular or contemporary art in general.[15]

THE PICASSO essay was Jung's second lambasting by press and public; the first followed his 1932 essay on Joyce's *Ulysses*.[16] Joyce had drifted back into Jung's ken sometime around 1930 through the esteemed Zürich publisher Dr. Daniel Brody of the Rhein-Verlag. As Joyce's publisher, he planned to launch a new literary review to coincide with the reprinting of the German-language edition of his novel.[17] Brody let Jung know that he had also supported him for the literature prize, which was his way of enticing Jung to contribute an inaugural essay to the review. That Brody was the instigator of Jung's essay has never been questioned, but the differing versions he gave later of why he asked Jung to write it and what actually happened between Jung and Joyce have been the subject of many contradictory interpretations.[18] Jung left behind at least three versions of what became the article he published, not in Brody's journal but in the *Europäische Revue*.[19] The most likely reason for Jung's multiple revisions and refinements were criticisms leveled by Carola Giedion-Welcker, one of Zürich's most formidable scholar-patrons of the avant-garde and Joyce's staunchest supporter. An art historian and critic, she was married to a distinguished professor at the University of Zürich who at one point in his career held the Charles Eliot Norton professorship at Harvard.[20] Both she and her husband had substantial private incomes, and their home on the Doldertal, filled as it was with the work of their friends, reflected what money could buy for persons of good taste. Represented were the artists László Moholy-Nagy, Hans Arp, and Kurt Schwitters, and the writers Tristan Tzara, Otto Nebel, and Alfred Jarry.

"I was always a great mixer," Carola Giedion-Welcker told an interviewer in the last years of her long and eventful life,[21] adding that it would not have been unusual to find Joyce and Le Corbusier conversing in her drawing room on any given evening when the two were in town. What she did not tell the interviewer was that Jung would never have crossed her threshold, for, although she respected his analytic ability, she thought he lacked the intelligence to appreciate culture. She shared Joyce's view that Jung was "stupid," one also expressed by his daughter, Lucia, who resented that her father entrusted her "soul" to "such a big fat material[istic] Swiss man."[22]

Carola Giedion-Welcker had read Jung's essay "Psychology and Poetry," published in 1930 in Eugene Jolas's *transition*;[23] prior to that, she had been in the audience of a local literary club when Jung gave the lecture from which he adapted the essay, then called *"Psychologie und Dichtung."*[24] Even though Jung used Goethe as his primary example of an artist, Giedion-Welcker inferred that his critical comments about writers of "the visionary mode" were really about Joyce. She was alerted by his comment that readers were "astonished, confused, bewildered, put on our guard or even repelled" by such writers, who reminded them of "nothing in everyday life, but rather of dreams, night-time fears, and the dark, uncanny recesses of the mind." She expressed her suspicions to Jung after his talk and believed he confirmed them when she read the note he added to the text of the published essay. In it, he described *Ulysses* as "a work of the greatest significance in spite of or perhaps because of its nihilistic tendencies."[25]

And so, when his essay on *Ulysses* was published, Giedion-Welcker was on the alert for possible inferences of Joyce's alleged pathological underpinnings. Even though Jung wrote that it would not occur to him to classify the novel "as a product of schizophrenia," he still expressed surprise that a work he found so boring could have been reprinted ten times since its original publication. He wondered how anyone could "go through the book from page 1 to page 735 . . . without fatal attacks of drowsiness."

Giedion-Welcker was outraged. She wrote to Jung, chastising his lack of appreciation for "the material from which today's art is derived."[26] Her letter instructed him on what he should have discussed had he but known enough to do so, then dismissed him as unworthy to have written about such a great writer. After giving Jung what might well be called a cram course in contemporary culture, she ended with the scathing remark that she deeply regretted his inability to understand literature, which was so much less than his evident analytic talent.

Joyce became aware of the brouhaha surrounding Jung's essay when Brody allegedly asked whether he should publish it in his review. Joyce dismissed it with a one-word response, *"Niedrigerhängen,"* which translates loosely as "publish it to show it up for what it is." As Brody had enormous respect for both Joyce and Jung, he gracefully evaded both writer and psychologist and let time pass while doing nothing. Thus, Jung published elsewhere, and there the matter rested until one year later, 1934.

Joyce was still smarting from the original contretemps when Edith McCormick ended his stipend, for which he blamed Jung. Having previously told Giedion-Welcker that he would never, under any circumstance, consult Jung, Joyce now felt he had no choice but to bring his daughter to Zürich and entrust her to "your friend, my enemy."[27] Lucia Joyce's behavior had been increasingly erratic for several years before her father, her self-appointed "psychiatric director,"[28] could accept that she needed treatment. He took her to Zürich in July 1933 to be examined by Dr. Hans W. Maier, professor of psychiatry at the university and a staff physician at the Burghölzli. Maier suggested she be sent to Forel at Prangins, and Joyce agreed. Six days later he withdrew Lucia when Forel diagnosed her as schizophrenic but with "pithiatric elements," that is, capable of being cured by persuasion or suggestion. Grasping at such slight hope, Joyce and his wife took Lucia back to Paris, where they spent the better part of the next year trying to cope with what was now dangerous behavior. They returned Lucia to Forel's care at Prangins, where she stayed for several months until she set several potentially deadly fires in her room. Forel told Joyce she had to be put under strict supervision in a facility such as the Burghölzli and that Maier should be put in charge. Lucia stayed one week, so infecting her father with her own panic that he had her removed, more for his sake than hers, to the private Brunner sanatorium in Küsnacht.[29]

At this point, Jung became the twentieth psychiatrist to supervise Lucia Joyce's treatment. It is curious that he accepted her, as, by his own admission, he was "out of touch" and "no longer interested" in the treatment of psychotic patients. For the past several years, he had limited his practice to neurosis, offering the excuse that his medical knowledge of psychosis was out-of-date.[30] He probably accepted Lucia's case from a combination of curiosity about her father and his own vanity, for there was a certain degree of satisfaction connected with knowing that the great Joyce had no recourse but to consult him. Another equally important reason was Cary Baynes's intervention and insistence.

For the previous several years, Maria Jolas, the American wife of *transition's* founding editor, Eugene Jolas, had been foremost among those who urged Joyce to overcome his animosity and take Lucia directly to Jung.[31] Maria had been Cary's friend since childhood, when they shared the same privileged up-

bringing in Louisville, Kentucky. They remained friends as adults and were often each other's houseguest in Zürich or Paris. Maria was well aware of Cary's
respect for analytical psychology and shared her firm belief that only Jung could
treat Lucia. But she also believed everyone surrounding Lucia would also need
Cary's help, for someone would have to take care of calming the distraught
Joyce and, to a lesser extent, his level-headed wife, Nora. Maria persuaded Cary
that if Jung accepted Lucia, she would have to take on the entire Joyce family as
her special project, because they would all need her soothing ministrations.

Once Lucia was established in Brunner's sanatorium, the Joyces checked into
the Hotel Carlton Elite and prepared to wait out what they assumed would be,
at most, one month's treatment, after which they fully expected Jung to dismiss
their daughter as well and cured. At the beginning, Jung did make scheduled
visits to Lucia, but they were decidedly unsuccessful, as he upset the girl's fragile equilibrium. At their first meeting, she insulted him; at their second, she
screamed, ranted, and threw things; at their third, she effected catatonia and refused to speak.[32] Jung gave up and stopped visiting entirely. He deputized Cary
to visit Lucia several times each week, to report to him immediately afterward
all that the young woman said or did. He then instructed Cary about what to do
on her next visit. It was the only time in their long friendship that he insisted
the reluctant Cary put both her medical education and study of psychology to
practical use on his behalf.

Cary took Lucia — always accompanied by a nurse who could subdue her if
necessary — on various outings, such as driving through the countryside or visiting the zoo. Lucia believed she was as talented as her father, but Cary determined that her artistic abilities were better suited to crafts than art. She took
Lucia shopping to find materials for sewing and other projects, even jigsaw puzzles, that the girl could do when she was alone in her room. At some of these
times Lucia was a delightful conversationalist, at others she was withdrawn to
the point of catatonia, at still others she was belligerent and threatening and the
nurse had to soothe her.

Cary usually had afternoon tea with the Joyces on the days she observed Lucia. Sometimes, when Lucia was being difficult or uncooperative, the frustrated
Cary took along her sister, Henri Zinno, in the hope that she could help persuade Joyce to face the reality of his daughter's condition. Nevertheless, Joyce
defeated all her efforts: "It was not possible to make even the smallest dent in
the wall he has erected against the understanding of [Lucia's illness]." As Joyce
always contradicted Cary's observations, she told Jung that the details he offered in rebuttal clearly showed "how much of an anima situation it is."[33]

At the end of October, Joyce went to Küsnacht in the late afternoon to meet
Jung in the quiet of his study and talk about what should be done with Lucia,
since there had been no change in her condition.[34] Jung thought it a privilege
and a "great good chance" to meet this writer whose work so perplexed him.
They talked as much about Joyce himself as about "his most important and sig-

nificant relation to his insane daughter."³⁵ The conversation confirmed Jung's impression of father and daughter as "two people going to the bottom of the river, one falling and the other diving."³⁶ Jung believed their conversation "justified all [his] suspicions as to the peculiar experiment Joyce represents in literary art."³⁷ He insisted it proved his contention that Lucia was her father's *femme inspiratrice*, which was the reason he so obstinately refused to admit she was mentally ill: "His own anima, i.e., unconscious psyche, was so solidly identified with her that to have her certified would have been as much as an admission that he himself had a latent psychosis."³⁸

Jung thought Lucia "was no genius like her father, but merely a victim of her disease." As for her father's "genius," he had not changed his opinion of *Ulysses:* "In any other time of the past Joyce's work would never have reached the printer, but in our blessed XX Century it is a message, though not yet understood."

For his part, Joyce decided that if "the Reverend Dr. Jung" (as he later disparagingly referred to him) could not understand *Ulysses*, he was therefore incapable of understanding Lucia, a mere girl, "yung and easily freudened."³⁹ Probably misconstruing what Jung really told him about his daughter, and thereby reinforcing Jung's view that he needed her as his *femme inspiratrice*, Joyce said with fatherly pride that "nobody could make any head of her but myself as she was a very exceptional case."⁴⁰

At the end of January 1935, Joyce dismissed Jung and took his daughter back to Paris, where the downward spiral of her disease eventually resulted in her permanent institutionalization. Before he left Zürich, Joyce inscribed Jung's copy of *Ulysses:* "To Dr. C. G. Jung, with grateful appreciation of his aid and counsel."⁴¹ Later, in *Finnegans Wake*, he asked the question he may well have first pondered in Zürich: "Is the Co-Education of Animus and Anima Wholly Desirable?" In a sense, he answered it himself: "anama anamaba anamabapa."⁴²

Still smarting in 1945, long after Joyce had taken Lucia from Zürich, Jung compared "the far reaching influence of Joyce's fathomless *Ulysses*" to "the germ" that had infected "political reality in Germany" during World War II.⁴³ His negative opinion never changed, but now he attributed novels like *Ulysses* to "the spirit of the age" rather than to "the perverse inventive gifts of the author." Ultimately, however, he agreed with Ernst R. Curtius that the novel was "a work of Anti-Christ."⁴⁴

JUNG FRETTED over what he wrote about Joyce and Picasso until the last year of his life, when he tried once again to define his views of modern art, this time for Sir Herbert Read, who was then one of the principal editors of his *Collected Works*.⁴⁵ Jung called Joyce and Picasso "two great initiators . . . masters of the fragmentation of aesthetical contents and accumulations of ingenious shards." Jung insisted that he could interpret one of Joyce's major symbols in *Ulysses*, that he knew "what that crumpled piece of paper meant, that went out down the

Liffey in spite of Joyce." He understood Joyce's "pain, which had strangled itself by its own strength." It was a tragedy he had seen time and again in his schizophrenic patients:

> In *Ulysses*, a world comes down in an almost endless, breathless stream of débris, a "catholic" world, i.e., a universe with moanings and outcries unheard and tears unshed, because suffering had extinguished itself and an immense field of shards began to reveal its aesthetic "values."

In the end, however, there was "no tongue" to tell what had happened to Joyce's "soul."

As for Picasso, "a very different man," it was his "ruthless strength" that instilled "dissolution" into his work. Picasso's art was "ingenious fragmentation: it shall go this way if it doesn't go the other way." He seized "the unconscious urge and voiced it resoundingly, even using it for monetary reasons." Jung insisted that he had "bestowed . . . honor" upon Picasso by comparing him to Joyce: "I could easily have done worse by emphasizing his falsity. He was just catering to the morbidity of his time, as he himself admits. I am far from diagnosing him as schizophrenic. I only emphasize the analogy to the schizophrenic process as I understand it."

When Jung wrote this to Herbert Read in September 1960, he could not help but extrapolate to what he believed the world in general had become:

> The great problem of our time is the fact that we don't understand what is happening to the world. We are confronted with the darkness of our soul, the unconscious. It sends up its dark and unrecognizable urges. It hollows out and hacks up the shapes of our culture and its historical dominants. We have no dominants any more, they are in the future. Our values are shifting, everything loses its certainty.

THE VIEWS Jung expressed in 1960 were those he held throughout the 1930s, when political realities were intruding into his placid Swiss existence and his professional responses were frequently confused. He spoke of "fear" in vague general terms, but his description of how others were behaving fit him as well: "They have not yet learned to be objective with their own psyche, i.e., between the thing which you do, and the thing that happens to you." Frenetic movement and activity came through constant travel and provided distraction from his personal disorganization. There was one major alleviation when, after four attempts to hire a full-time secretary, he finally found someone capable. Marie-Jeanne Schmid was the daughter of his former friend and colleague Hans Schmid, who died in 1931 at the age of forty-four. Marie-Jeanne was trilingual, an excellent typist, and swift with shorthand. She began work in the spring of 1932 and within weeks had organized Jung's office, library, appointment book, and correspondence. The entire family was ecstatic to have her, for she relieved them all of a great burden and ended the onerous process of trying to find a secretary for Jung.

His first attempt to find one failed when he insisted that his sister, Trudi, come to work for him after their mother died, for she "very much stood on her own two feet"[46] and had other ideas. Trudi may not have been "strong, but she was vivid," and "she liked to laugh" and make jokes. She had her own ploy for making her secretarial days brief: when Jung set her to typing the text that eventually became *Symbols of Transformation*, she slyly turned ordinary titles like *Fuss und Schuhsymbolik* (Foot and Shoe Symbolism) into the embarrassing *Fress and Schlucksymbolik* (Gluttony and Hiccup Symbolism). Jung was "livid" when he caught her deliberate mistakes, but Trudi had made her point, and "that was the end of her" as his secretary.

Trudi Jung died unexpectedly in 1935, when Jung was sixty, taking with her his last link to Basel. She had scheduled surgery for what was supposed to be a "simple routine procedure" but died during the operation.[47] Jung was convinced that she knew she would die, because she put her affairs into meticulous order before entering the hospital. "She was a very peculiar person," he observed. "I never had a very close relationship to her but I always had to admire her."[48]

Jung's next secretary was a professional typist whom Emma engaged through an agency, a bewildered woman who endured several days of his roaring at her incompetence before fleeing into anonymity. Then Marianne decided that only she could organize her father's affairs. Jung didn't want any of the daughters to become involved with psychology, but Marianne was his favorite, so she got her way. Her first offensive was to convert the former children's nursery into her own private office. Deciding that redecorating was needed, she summoned carpenters to install cupboards and shelves; painters and wallpaper hangers followed after. When the chaos subsided, Marianne's first secretarial act was to prepare a card index of the addresses of Jung's correspondents from his earliest days, but she gave it up because she couldn't read most of the handwriting, and besides, the letters were old and most of the writers dead. She decided to index the library, but the task was so daunting that she took a Paris vacation instead. Three days later, Jung bellowed from his study, demanding to know why she did not answer his calls. His ability to concentrate was so intense that, even though he had been told she was in Paris, he had quite forgotten.

At this point, Emma "put her foot down"[49] and told C. G. that Marianne would have to be replaced, as "she didn't know shorthand, could not type, and besides, was too preoccupied with getting married." Emma had just paid a condolence call on Schmid's widow and learned that her daughters needed to augment the family's income, so she asked Marie-Jeanne to come to work for Jung. She remained for the next twenty years, ostensibly the family friend who took lunch with him and Emma each day, but in reality the general factotum who came to work before 8 A.M. and often did not leave until eight or nine at night. In years to come, she was grateful she had not accepted Emma's invitation to live in the house, for her workday would never have ended.

To commemorate her first year on the job, Jung made a comment that she innocently repeated and that has since been frequently misconstrued: "You are playing the perfect secretary, and it is just sickening." She said if he had said such a thing earlier, she would not have understood what he meant and would have been deeply offended. Now she understood that it was his sincere compliment for the many different ways she freed him to concentrate on his writing, but it was also his way of telling her to claim time and space for a private life — even as his demands made it nearly impossible for her to do so.

Of all the tasks Marie-Jeanne performed, Jung was most grateful to her for freeing him from the arduous responsibility of his correspondence. She answered all his letters, having learned quickly which were highly confidential, which were merely urgent, and which required a decision from Jung before she could reply. She learned to separate them into those needing immediate "Küsnacht replies" and those that could go with him to Bollingen, to languish at the bottom of a pile on his worktable until she made her weekly visit by train and forced him to deal with them. She took dictation for his writings, typed his manuscripts, dealt with publishers and printers, and made him extremely happy because she actually enjoyed proofreading and did it so thoroughly. When Aniela Jaffé became his secretary in the 1940s, she complained that Jung read every letter she typed and was always on the lookout for typos; with Marie-Jeanne, he signed every letter and approved every typescript without more than a glance.[50]

Truly, Marie-Jeanne gave him a degree of freedom from professional responsibility he had never enjoyed before. She made possible two kinds of escape for Jung, into his writing and away from home, and he took frequent advantage of both.

—<small>∞</small>—

CHAPTER 28

A "Pretty Grueling Time"

On impulse in March 1933, Jung went to Palestine with Hans Edward Fierz-David, Linda Fierz-David's husband and professor of chemistry at the ETH.[1] Jung's feelings for the entire Fierz family ran the gamut from friendship to irritation. He was almost always testy with "Psyche-Linda," whom he mocked as a chariot-borne queen, the wheels formed by her four docile sons, and the whole shebang pulled by her husband, the draft horse.[2] Jung frequently cursed himself in the bluest *Schwizertütsch* for having sold the Fierz family land abutting his in Bollingen, as the four sons thought nothing of dropping in to chatter aimlessly for hours on end. One son, Heinrich, told Jung that after studying both law and architecture and not liking either, he had decided to become a psychologist, but not unless he could qualify without the medical training then required. Jung told him testily, "First please to learn the ABC's and then later on you can still become Jesus Christ."[3]

But Jung genuinely liked Professor Fierz, whose specialty was the chemistry of colors and who spent most of his professional life writing a history of chemistry that began with alchemy and ended with modern industrial research.[4] Fierz *père* described himself as "just an engineer," but he had a profound knowledge of the humanities and could recite vast passages of poetry and philosophy by heart. In short, he was a boon traveling companion for Jung.

The story goes that Fierz told Jung at one of his wife's dinner parties (either "pretentious with bad food" or "superb," depending on Jung's mood of the moment toward Linda[5]) that he was off on a cruise the following morning. He had booked first-class, and there were two beds in his stateroom, so he invited Jung to join him. Jung insisted it was impossible on such brief notice, but when Fierz arrived at the *Hauptbanhof* the next morning to take the train to Italy and his ship, Jung was there waiting, all decked out in a white suit and safari hat. The voyage took them through the Greek Islands to Athens, then through the Dardenelles and along the Turkish coastline to Palestine, then home via Egypt. Palestine made the most vivid impression on Jung because his friend James

Kirsch, who had fled Germany for London, was planning to move there later that year.[6] When Jung met some of the German Jews who were already settled in Palestine, he was curious about how they would practice psychology in an essentially alien culture and society. They who once considered themselves assimilated Germans now had to adapt to a second homeland, wherein they were exiles, unwanted by the native Arabs. When he asked these questions, it was not because of the current political reality in Germany but rather as a scholar who studied how individuals adapted when, for whatever the reason, they were uprooted from their native land.

THAT SUMMER, Jung attended his first Eranos *Tagung* (conference), sponsored by Olga Fröbe-Kapteyn at the Casa Gabriella, her home in southern Switzerland on Lago Maggiore near Ascona, Canton Ticino. Frau Fröbe, as she was generally known, was born to Dutch parents in 1881[7] in London, where her father was an inventor, engineer, and general manager of the British Westinghouse Brake and Signal Company. After 1906, he was sent to organize national divisions of his firm in Hungary, Austria, and Switzerland. Olga, already fluent in English and Dutch, learned German, French, and Italian.[8] Strong willed and independent, she was a champion skier who made one of the first ascents on the most dangerous face of Mt. Blanc, and a circus equestrienne who boasted all her life of her daredevil stunts.[9] She married Iwan Fröbe, an Austrian adventurer, flautist, flyer, and inventor. He crashed behind Russian lines in September 1915, rumored to be more interested in taking airborne photographs with a camera of his own invention than in flying the plane. He was either killed in the crash or executed as a spy,[10] leaving Olga penniless and responsible for twin daughters born in May. Her father bought the Casa Gabriella in 1926 with money from the inventions he patented, and Olga and her daughters lived with him until his death shortly after, when she inherited the property. Her father's patents were gradually replaced by newer technologies, thus leaving her in constantly straitened circumstances. In 1928, having no clear idea of how or when she would use it, she built a large rectangular structure beside the house, which eventually became the Eranos lecture hall. On the upper floor, she installed a fairly spartan apartment that no one used until the Jungs came along.[11]

Frau Fröbe always intended to make Casa Gabriella "A Meeting Place for East and West,"[12] for she had long been interested in Eastern and Western religions, anthroposophy, spiritual matters, and mythology. In 1928, she befriended Alice A. Bailey, who led a movement called the Arcane School in New York, and in August 1930, she invited Mrs. Bailey to co-sponsor a "School of Spiritual Research" at the Casa Gabriella.[13] The two strong-willed women parted ways two years later, and in August 1933, Olga convened the first Eranos *Tagung*, with Jung in attendance.

Olga Fröbe was a woman searching for something to believe in, but she was also looking for someone around whom to focus her quest. An early influence was Martin Buber, with whom she corresponded after attending a seminar he gave in 1924 at the nearby Monte Verità.[14] Then she became devoted to the eccentric poet Ludwig Derleth and friend to others in the Monte Verità group who clustered around the Baron von der Heydt, former banker to the German Kaiser. "Guests" of the baron, a flamboyant transvestite,[15] included the German crown prince and King Leopold of Belgium, the actor Emil Jannings, Chaim Weizmann, Thomas Mann, and assorted "Russian grand dukes, Parisian cocottes, and English Lords."[16] The effete baron fluttered among them, "more host than hotel keeper, in short white pants and open shirt, always with red umbrella unfurled." He was usually accompanied by his good friends "the international flaneur André Germain and the painter Marianne von Werefkin." When World War II began, he joined the Nazi Party but kept his membership and sympathies to himself until he dropped his wallet on the lakeshore, where it was found by Will Roelli (Ximena de Angulo Roelli's husband). He turned it in to the local police, who saw the membership cards.[17]

The formidable Frau Fröbe and the outrageous Baron von der Heydt, both *salonistes*, became intellectual rivals and competitors, but she did not best him until she persuaded Jung to become a permanent part of the Eranos *Tagung*. Jung replaced the baron, Derleth, Buber, and a host of theosophists and Eastern thinkers in "a long running relationship that was more a conflict than a harmonious accord," for "the headstrong Olga was not cut out to be student or adherent to anybody or anything."[18]

Frau Fröbe met Jung in Darmstadt at Count Keyserling's School of Wisdom sometime around 1930. From that time on, she considered Jung another important influence on her life, and he, in turn, valued her indomitable spiritual strength. The idea for Eranos did not come from Jung and did not crystallize until two years later, after Olga parted from Alice Bailey and paid a call on the eminent scholar of religion Rudolph Otto. Otto never attended a single *Tagung*, but he named it Eranos, stressing that it should always be a gathering place for psychologists, physicians, mythologists, theologians, and scientists to exchange ideas about their relative disciplines. This never really happened, for after Jung attended the first one, all other conferences, no matter what their ostensible theme, became a forum for analytical psychology, with him as its focal point.

In the years that followed, the strongest impression of Frau Fröbe among those who attended the meetings was "one of those people who always float through life an inch or two off the ground . . . dressed as always with large hat, loose garment too long to be fashionable and 'things' around her neck, chains or beads or things [of what she called] 'esoteric significance,' seemingly in possession of some mysterious talisman and yet enormously efficient."[19] They remember her and Jung "walking along the road to Ascona, she talking, talking, talking, and Jung clumping along beside her, smoking his pipe and *listening!* . . . Mrs. Fröbe always seemed to be in the business of merchandising Higher Things!"[20]

Twenty-five years after Jung attended the first Eranos *Tagung*, Olga Fröbe tried to explain how it became her life's work.[21] From its inception, it was her "personal enterprise," for she could not work with committees, boards, or even individuals. She admitted that her methods were "in part irrational and are thus no methods at all," but what she did "worked," and was "therefore valid." Planning for each meeting was her "inner way or quest," while the actual conference was merely its reflection as seen by the outer world. Eranos was Olga Fröbe's "way of individuation." In a "relationship" that was often a "battle," Jung was not only her inspiration and guide but also her drawing card for some of the world's most interesting scholars, thinkers, and theoreticians.[22]

By 1935, psychoanalysis in general was "all the rage"[23] in London, as it was throughout most of the world. Politicians were being psychoanalyzed by reporters in the daily newspapers, the literary world was entranced with the possibilities the new science offered for individual creativity, and critics in every field were busy applying and misapplying its doctrines to many disparate genres and disciplines. In the midst of the rush to embrace it, Ezra Pound happily declared himself the one remaining "non-believer" and boasted that he was "the only sane [i.e., nonanalyzed] writer left in Europe."[24]

In such a climate, Jung's theory of analytical psychology was of great interest to the British medical profession, and he was invited to explain it in a series of four lectures from September 30 to October 4 at London's Tavistock Clinic.[25] The invitation came from the Institute of Medical Psychology, and about two hundred persons were invited to attend, mainly medical professionals with an occasional journalist or writer scattered among them. One such was Samuel Beckett, later to win the Nobel Prize for literature but then a troubled writer in his late thirties who had yet to publish his first book.[26] Beckett was invited to hear Jung's third lecture by his analyst, W. R. Bion, later to become a noted authority on the psychology of groups but then a young doctor at the beginning of his career.[27]

Jung began his first lecture with the function of consciousness, which led naturally in his second to the existence of unconscious processes.[28] Lectures three and four centered around the analysis of dreams, which allowed him to explain a number of concepts that were central to his psychology, among them the autonomy of complexes, the collective unconscious, "big" dreams, and the continuing value of the association tests. Even though many now deemed the tests "old-fashioned" and Jung himself was not "particularly in love" with them, he still used them when he "must" as "the foundation of certain conceptions."[29]

It was not until the discussion following the fourth lecture, a continuation of dream analysis, that confrontation surfaced, albeit through a question couched in exquisite British politeness. Dr. David Yellowlees first expressed gratitude to Jung for explaining his own theories, "rather than spend[ing] time on controversial matters." But, as a significant portion of the audience practiced psychology "along lines not exclusively Freudian perhaps, but in accordance with certain fundamental principles with which Freud's name is associated," Yellowlees asked Jung to explain how his views differed from Freud's.[30]

In his long and reasoned reply, Jung judiciously avoided all direct criticism of Freud, even as he deflated Freud's authority. He did not allow Freud to be seen as his only rival, his polar opposite, or even his only equal; nor did he allow Freud's theory to stand inviolate and alone as the only opposition to his. Instead, he introduced Adler's psychology, thus placing both himself and Freud as two theoreticians merely numbered among others. Jung said his main contribution to psychology was his own "subjective confession," stemming from something "personal" and allowing him to express "psychological facts" in his own way.[31] He said Freud and Adler should also confess that their ideas originated within their own "subjective point of view" as well, because only when "we admit our personal prejudice" are we "really contributing towards an objective psychology." His purpose before this British audience was to "give you some interesting ideas and let you see how I tackle things."[32] He considered himself a "craftsman," with psychotherapy merely the craft he practiced in his own individual way, "a very humble way with nothing particular to show." He did not "believe for a moment" that his view was "absolutely right," because "nobody is absolutely right in psychological matters."[33]

For him, psychology was "not a religious creed but a point of view."[34] And the "problem" within his individual point of view was having to "wrestle with the big monster of the historical past, the great snake of the centuries, the burden of the human mind, the problem of Christianity." He admitted his task would be much simpler if he "knew nothing"; but because of his ancestry, his education, and his wide-ranging interests, he knew "too much," which made his responsibility toward his patients that much greater. Although he expressed the following sentiment in self-defense, it was an accurate description of his mood of the moment: "If the whole world disagrees with me, it is perfectly indifferent to me. I have a perfectly good place in Switzerland, I enjoy myself, and if nobody enjoys my books, I enjoy them. I know nothing better than being in my library, and if I make discoveries in my books, that is wonderful."[35]

In his fifth and last lecture, the audience asked Jung to depart from his theory of dream analysis and explain instead how to put the transference to "practical use" within the process.[36] Jung's explanation led to a discussion of the role religion served within various psychotherapeutic systems, particularly his own. He told the audience that throughout thirty-plus years of analytic practice, he had made an informal statistical count of his patients' religious affiliations: most were either Jewish or Protestant; practicing Catholics numbered "about six."[37] It proved to him that the Catholic Church's "rigorous system of confession" was indeed a "therapeutic institution," as were groups such as the Oxford Moral Rearmament Movement,[38] to which a number of his patients and followers had gravitated.

Jung concluded that archetypal images required "a suitable form for their projection," and that "the collective unconscious is really a serious factor in the human psyche."[39] He turned instinctively to Germany for his examples:

> In the collective unconscious of the individual, history prepares itself; and when the archetypes are activated in a number of individuals and come to the surface, we are in the midst of history, as we are at present. The archetypal image which the moment requires gets into life and everybody is seized by it.

"I saw it coming," Jung reminded his audience. "I said in 1918 that the 'blonde beast' is stirring in its sleep and that something will happen in Germany." Hitler in Germany, Mussolini in Italy — these were not "ideas" but rather archetypes: "Give an archetype to the people and the whole crowd moves like one man, there is no resisting it."

None of the persons who asked questions made any reference to Jung's view of contemporary politics, which was about to embroil him in a controversy that would taint him as a Nazi sympathizer or brand him as an active collaborator. His general political obtuseness, coupled with some of his writings, statements, and participation in suspect conferences, would create a dense cloud that hovers over his reputation long years after his life ended. All this was yet to come, but the rumbles were already there by the time of the Tavistock lectures. Still, with the innate politeness of the British, Jung's audience focused instead on the nuts and bolts of analytic practice. They neither commented on nor mentioned Jung's allusions to Nazi Germany but asked instead for the definitions of a neurosis and active imagination.

If the applause he received after the concluding lecture was any indication, the general impression his theory made upon this particular branch of British medicine was highly positive, for it was far more sustained than mere politeness required.[40] Jung turned what began as his audience's skeptical criticism into acceptance and appreciation, reminding Esther Harding of Oliver Goldsmith's village parson, "whose church was always open to the passers-by, and those who scoffed remained to pray."[41] Many of the former scoffers were members of the medical profession who sought Jung for private conversation, if not therapeutic consultation. Former patients and those who wished to become new ones arranged for sessions that began early in the morning and lasted throughout the day. Jung lectured at 5 P.M. for about an hour; discussion took another hour, and drinks and dinner followed. When he could not fit into the day all those who wanted appointments, he scheduled appointments after the evening activities when everyone else had gone to bed.[42]

Jung took Toni Wolff to London, while Emma stayed at home. He introduced Toni as his colleague, which indeed she was, as she had co-analyzed nearly all those in attendance who had gone to Zürich to consult Jung. She, too, conducted a busy professional life in the times surrounding Jung's lectures, but

England released the best in her, and she managed to charm everyone she met. Amazingly, many years afterward, more men than women commented on her radiant appearance, especially her stunning couture and the strikingly different hat she wore to each lecture.[43]

UNLIKE THE stylish Toni Wolff, Emma had matured into "the most comforting thing on earth . . . a really nice old woman."[44] Jung took her to the United States in 1936 when he was invited by Harvard to receive an honorary doctorate and deliver a lecture at the university's Tercentenary Conference of Arts and Sciences.[45] There was no thought of Toni going with them, even in her guise as his distinguished colleague and the analyst of many Americans. Nor would he permit his analysand Catharine Cabot to sail with him and Emma when she volunteered to act as their unofficial guide to Boston and New York society.

Jung was pleased that Harvard wanted to honor him, but he was not looking forward to what he would have to "endure,"[46] wishing instead that he could have spent the autumn in Bollingen, concentrating on a book that had "long been due."[47] When Cabot said that the voyage would no doubt be "ghastly," Jung agreed it would be "pretty bad."[48] If not for Emma, he would have booked passage on a tramp steamer, where he would have been unrecognized and left alone to read and think. Instead, her insistence on comfort meant sailing on an ocean liner, with his fame guaranteeing they would be seated at the captain's table and most likely pestered by passengers.

Jung planned to see a few persons in Boston privately, among them Christiana Morgan and Harry Murray, as well as some of the doctors who had earlier journeyed to Zürich to work with him. As soon as word got out that Jung would be in Cambridge, analysts and patients from as far away as California began to importune him directly or else entreated the secretary of the Tercentenary Committee to arrange appointments for analysis.[49] The American trio of Drs. Esther Harding, Eleanor Bertine, and Kristine Mann were insistent that Jung visit them at Bailey Island, Maine, where they spent their summers in Mann's ancestral homestead, "The Trident."[50] Despite the blurring of analytic boundaries, they always invited a select group of their analysands to spend one month each summer in a working vacation. Both Jung and Emma were eager to go to Maine, as the "bit of nature" it offered seemed "rather heaven-sent."[51] They wanted to "see nobody"[52] but the Americans had other plans and insisted upon a full-scale seminar.

Jung tried to delay responding until it would have been too late to organize one, but Bertine wrote that a hundred "analyzed people" wanted to hear him speak. She insisted that he set firm dates and name a subject. He gave in and offered a choice of topics, from which they selected the individuation process as traced through a series of dreams or fantasies.[53] Beatrice Hinkle, then living and working in Washington, Connecticut, joined the three New Yorkers on the organizing committee. All four thought the honorarium he suggested was too modest and insisted on paying $1,000.[54] They asked him to speak daily for five or six days beginning around September 19 and told him they would "head off" all those who wanted individual analytic hours, unless he told them otherwise. He said he would meet privately with anyone who wanted to talk to him.[55]

The Jungs set sail on the *Georgic* from Le Havre on August 21, arriving in New York on the thirtieth. As was customary in the age of transatlantic crossings, reporters who covered this beat were supplied with passenger lists so they could interview anyone newsworthy. Because he was aware of this, Jung prepared an advance statement of his political views in light of the now "profoundly upset Europe":

> I despise politics wholeheartedly: thus I am neither a Bolshevik, nor a National Socialist, nor an anti-Semite. I am a neutral Swiss and even in my own country I am uninterested in politics because I am convinced that 99% of politics are mere symptoms and anything but a cure for social evils. About 50% of politics is definitely obnoxious inasmuch as it poisons the utterly incompetent mind of the masses.[56]

He prepared this statement because he had written about topics that were highly suspect in the current "politically poisoned and overheated atmosphere," "the undeniable differences in national and racial psychology." No newspaper was interested in his *apologia*; not only was it never published, but no publication announced his arrival. A reporter for the *New York Times* came to Jung's hotel at the end of the trip when he was waiting to board ship for Europe, but that interview was mostly concerned with what Jung thought of American politics.

However, the rumbles about Jung's Nazi sympathies grew to a low roar, and there had been considerable debate among the Harvard Tercentenary Committee members before they decided to invite him.[57] There was even protest from a disgruntled husband of one of Jung's former analysands, but the committee managed to keep it from the public. Maurice Léon, husband of Frances Goodrich Léon, was still smarting from real or imagined situations concerning Jung's treatment of his wife and children when they were his patients in Zürich.

Léon wrote to Jerome D. Greene, Esq., of the Harvard Corporation, saying he had intimate personal knowledge that Jung was "not merely a Nazi sympathizer" but rather "The Mephistopheles in the Nazi drama" and "the destructive brain behind the scene." He was convinced that when "an ignoramus like Hitler . . . spouts pseudo-scientific racial theories [he] is echoing what he has been told." Léon accused Jung of "taking an amused interest" in Nazi treatment of "Freud's brethren" because of the "animosity which he bears his old teacher."[58]

Greene took Léon's accusations seriously enough to reply personally and confidentially. He told Léon that "a rather fully documented statement of the case against Dr. Jung" had been prepared for the Tercentenary Committee, which had studied it carefully.[59] Although it contained "unfavorable ethical implications," he was nevertheless bound to consider the arguments for or against Jung within the parameters of "scientific jealousies." Ultimately, the entire Tercentenary Committee accepted the decision of its faculty advisors: Jung was a distinguished scholar, and using that criterion only, they should invite him. Greene acknowledged that Jung may have "allowed his own prejudices to carry him away from a strict observance of scientific objectivity," but the Harvard officials considered such behavior "a characteristic of many of the most eminent scientists in Europe" who were currently defending their views "with a tenacity suggestive of religious polemics." Even though there may have been concerns at Harvard about Jung's "objectivity where the racial issue is involved," Greene concluded that the university was unwilling to subject him to "censorship" in a symposium for which participants were deliberately chosen because they represented differing points of view: "There is no such thing as orthodoxy in science, and Harvard is the last place to set up a criterion of that kind. Whatever Jung contributes will be subjected to the merciless criticism of his peers, and that is the object of a conference which embodies first, last, and all the time the search for truth."

Léon was undeterred by Greene's intellectual rationale; in a second letter filled with undisguised personal spite, he denounced Jung as "a man of great cleverness," which made him "all the more dangerous as a physician and as a promoter, sub rosa, of sadistic notions."[60] Greene did not reply to the second letter, and Léon was apparently content to drop his charges without making them public.

Franklin Delano Roosevelt, the thirty-second president of the United States and a Harvard graduate, was the featured speaker, and Jung had ample time to observe him. The headline of his interview in the *New York Times* read "'Roosevelt Great,' Is Jung's Analysis,"[61] but his true impressions were more complicated than what he told the reporter: before he came to the United States, he thought of Roosevelt as "an opportunist, perhaps even an erratic mind"; once he heard him speak at Harvard, he thought him a "strong man, a man who is really great." "Perhaps," he added suggestively, "that's why many people do not like him." Jung was certainly among them, although he did not say so in print. He thought Roosevelt "had the dictator stuff in him,"[62] and he disliked his wife even more, calling Eleanor "the nightmare on the way to being dreamt."[63] Jung thought America had been better off under Herbert Hoover, for he was "easy to see through."[64]

THE JUNGS went to Providence, Rhode Island, for the weekend of September 12 to 15. They were invited by the Anglican Bishop James De Wolf Perry to address an organization known as The American Way.[65] Bishop Perry sent his sixteen-year-old son, John Weir Perry, to meet their train and drive them to the episcopal residence. Young Perry credited his subsequent career as a Jungian analyst to Jung's conversation in the car, when he "talked a blue streak about what the psyche does, how it operates, of myth, ritual and history." He thought Jung was "absolutely dazzling."[66]

Jung spent two nights in Providence: on the first evening, he spoke of European politics in a lecture to The American Way; on the second, the Perrys gave a dinner in his honor. His audience on both occasions described him as "scornful" of Hitler, particularly when Jung insisted that he was "not a man, but a phenomenon, a nobody who expresses what the Germans want to hear." Some who heard Jung thanked him for "opening their eyes for the first time," while others thought he showed "extreme bad manners" for dominating the conversation and insisting upon such an unpleasant topic at the table.

On the fifteenth, the Jungs went directly to Milton, Massachusetts, where they were houseguests until the nineteenth of Elizabeth and G. Stanley Cobb. Jung found the Boston area greatly changed in the years since he had been there last, and not for the better. "All the decent people" had moved to the suburbs, leaving the city itself to be "invaded by the Irish," whom he deemed "irresponsible."[67]

Jung's official citation at the Tercentenary read in part as follows: "Doctor of Science. A philosopher who has examined the unconscious mind, a mental physician whose wisdom and understanding have brought relief to many in distress."[68] It was one of the few positive statements connected with his visit, for unflattering anecdotes about his conduct at Harvard followed for years afterward. Some were true, others not. One widely circulated but untrue story had him renting a theatrical costume for the official ceremonies because he neglected to bring academic robes. As the story goes, when it rained on the afternoon of September 18,[69] the hat ran black ink all down his face. Actually, the university provided proper academic robes for all its honorees, Jung included, but they were all asked to wear formal dress, top hat and morning coat, for the investiture. Mrs. Cobb remembered Jung "prancing in front of the hall mirror with his [rented] dress clothes on" the night before the ceremonies.[70]

Another unflattering but true story happened in the Cobb home. It is curious that the sharp-eyed Emma did not notice, but she was apparently as unaware as her husband that the Cobbs did not have live-in help. Each night, Jung followed European custom and put his shoes outside the bedroom door to be shined, and Emma did not stop him. Rather than embarrass his guest, Cobb (a man of elegant reserve whose ancestry dated from the *Mayflower* and who had been considered for the presidency of Harvard), shined them himself.[71]

As hosts, the Cobbs were responsible for ferrying the Jungs to the many functions and ceremonial occasions that filled their official schedule; when they could not, the Jungs took taxis and billed the Cobbs. Mrs. Cobb sent the Tercentenary Committee the "very large bill" of $26.50 for five separate trips to and from Cambridge and Boston and asked for reimbursement, calling it the "kind of service" she was sure the committee would wish to provide. Her thrifty

Yankee sensitivities were offended by how the Jungs kept taxis waiting with meters running while they ran errands or took tea in friends' homes.[72]

Even though Cobb stuttered badly, he introduced Jung when he lectured to the small group of Cobb's clinic members — not, as legend has it, when Jung faced a standing-room-only audience for his official Tercentenary lecture in the amphitheater of the Massachusetts General Hospital.[73] The members of Cobb's clinic never forgot his slip when he presented "Dr. Freud,"[74] and the audience of those who supposedly heard him say it grew with each retelling.

There was also the widely circulated rumor that Jung had been invited only as a substitute for Freud. Hearsay has it that the committee that was convened to select honorees voted unanimously to invite Freud but reversed their decision when Erik Erikson told them he was too old and ill to travel and would most likely refuse.[75] Actually, Professor Edwin G. Boring, chairman of the psychology department, nominated a list of six psychologists after long discussions with his entire department. Jung's name was on every preliminary version of the final list; Freud's was never among them, for he was deemed from the outset "too old to consider." Jung came second in the voting but was eventually chosen because the Harvard psychologists believed his presence would permit the university to "do credit to itself and make clear its liberal position as against the more orthodox academic fields."[76] Nevertheless, some reporters did raise the question after Jung's lecture of why, if he were only Freud's "pupil," the "master" himself had not been invited. There is no record of any reply.

Generally speaking, Jung did not make the most favorable impression at Harvard, first, because of his remarks about differences in the racial psychology of Germans and Jews and his earlier unfavorable articles about American women and American Negroes. On September 11, at a dinner in Lowell House in honor of the visiting scholars, Jung was seated with Janet, Cobb, and some of the most distinguished members of the Harvard faculty. Four persons at his table were invited to make informal after-dinner remarks, but Jung was not one of them.[77] Second, he did not comport himself with the dignity and seriousness expected of an honoree. There was, as has been mentioned, his outrageous flirtation with Christiana Morgan and his snubbing of the elderly Pierre Janet at the Harvard Psychological Clinic's luncheon for the degree recipients in psychology. The Cobbs told any number of stories about his rude manners as their houseguest, and members of the Tercentenary Committee were miffed that Jung insisted on abandoning their carefully set schedule to meet or dine privately with persons of his own choosing, Fowler McCormick paramount among them.[78]

Also, Harry Murray did not endear himself to his colleagues for spiriting Jung away from an official function to have dinner with him and, later, breakfast with him and his wife.[79] Murray's behavior was especially galling because he had earlier refused the committee's request to have Jung as his houseguest. Even though he described Jung as "a particular friend of mine," Murray declined on the grounds that his German was "very fragmentary."[80] He conveniently forgot to mention that all his dealings with Jung were always conducted in English.

Bailey Island, in contrast to Providence and Harvard, was an unqualified success. Jung lectured for two hours each of six mornings, beginning by answering written questions based on his previous lecture. After his talks, given in the local public library, he took a seat outside to answer an unending stream of questions. Although no one was aware of it, Jung's lectures concerning the "highly intellectual man of thirty-two who had gotten off his track" were based on Wolfgang Pauli's dreams and visions, most of which he had previously presented in the Tavistock lectures. Throughout the formal and informal presentations, Fowler McCormick (who followed Jung to Maine from Harvard) marveled at his ability to "focus enormous amounts of information and material as well as wisdom upon given points."[81]

Everyone wanted a record of his lectures, so four "note-takers" took down in shorthand everything he said during the morning lecture and question period and then collated their texts every afternoon, transcribing and typing them up to have ready in booklet form for the participants before their departure. Jung tried to avoid the note takers' questions, filling his day with work from early morning until late at night. He lectured to the entire group and talked to smaller gatherings and also saw individuals privately, for whom the four women physicians arranged consultations. Many took place after the evening meal, when Jung tore himself away from the dining room at the very last moment to hold late-evening analytic sessions.

In the midst of all the work, there were many parties and receptions where everyone wore a name tag, and committee members and staff workers were identified by function. Jung spotted one that read "Entertainment" and said, "Ah! That's what *I* want."[82] However, when Jung watched couples dancing the fox-trot, Fowler McCormick was sure the expression on his face lay somewhere between "this is so silly" and "why don't they really go to work and have an orgy out of it?"[83] There were many skits on various aspects of psychology and even one in which members of the audience took the parts of C. G. and Emma. The planning committee was relieved when the Jungs took the good-natured kidding in the spirit of "the rollicking fun of the occasion."[84] Despite the heavy fog that covered the island throughout their stay, they still managed brief excursions by boat, which were probably as close as they came to relaxation.

Even here, in the midst of overwhelming approval and affection, Jung was beset by questions about his German sympathies and anti-Semitic pronouncements. One of his lecture transcribers was an official court stenographer, and Jung put her to work on the enormous correspondence that followed him even to Maine. "I am no Nazi," he wrote to someone who questioned what he had written about the "differences between Jewish and Christian psychology since 1917." "I am no anti-Semite," he insisted firmly.[85]

A real vacation did not come until the Jungs returned to New York. His supporters wanted to fill his every moment with their psychological enlightenment, but he managed to escape long enough to visit several museums, and Emma was happy to shop or go sight-seeing alone. It was not all vacation, however, as Jung gave a lecture at the Plaza Hotel on October 2, followed by a dinner in his honor.[86] Among the guests were Paul and Mary Conover Mellon, who had been invited by their analysts, Ann and Erlo van Waveren.[87] The Mellons were disappointed that Jung had been unable to give them private analytic hours and vowed to get to Zürich as quickly as they could arrange their schedules.

THE JUNGS sailed for home via London, as he had agreed to give private sessions and several lectures at St. Bartholomew's Hospital.[88] They had been arranged by two of Jung's American analysands, Joseph Henderson and Joseph Wheelwright, who were now enrolled in medical school, honoring Jung's recent dictate that they had to become physicians first if they wished to be Jungian analysts later.[89] Peter Baynes served as Jung's éminence grise for the overall itinerary, but his most important work consisted of quietly arranging private meetings for him with analysts who became important British allies in Jung's ongoing jousts with the organization in Germany that had been "conformed" to Nazi ideology.[90]

In London, questions of Jung's political sympathies arose when he was interviewed by *The Observer*,[91] making such controversial comments that they were reprinted by *Time* and *The Living Age*.[92] Here for the first time he expressed his true feelings about Roosevelt publicly, lumping him in with Mussolini and Stalin. Jung called FDR "perfectly ruthless, a highly versatile mind which you cannot foresee . . . a most amazing power complex . . . the stuff of a dictator absolutely." Hitler was "a Sybil, the Delphic oracle," who ruled Germany "by revelation." He praised England for maintaining "the aristocratic ideal," without which there could be no "stability." He thought that Switzerland resembled England in that both were "tribal" cultures, but England had something the Swiss did not: the inherent decency of the English "gentleman," which permitted Britannia to "possess the world."

THE JUNGS returned to Zürich and the pressures of daily life in late October. Because the United States had been a "pretty grueling time," Jung wanted to cancel all his winter lectures and reduce his analytic hours to concentrate on the unnamed "long [over]due" book, most likely the study of alchemy for which he was deep into research.[93]

He declined Jolande Jacobi's invitation for a return lecture at the Viennese *Kulturbund* but received two others so prestigious he felt obliged to accept. The first was from Yale University, where he was invited to deliver the Dwight Harrington Terry Lectures in October 1937,[94] and the second was from the University of Calcutta, where he was invited to receive an honorary degree in early

1938 in connection with a celebration of the university's twenty-fifth anniversary of its founding. The universities of Allahabad and Benares also invited him to receive honorary degrees.[95]

In October 1937, Jung and Emma stopped briefly in New York before going on to New Haven. Harding, Bertine, and Mann arranged for him to give a "continuation of the Bailey Island Lectures," now entitled "The Individuation Process as Shown in Dreams," at the McDowell Club. He spoke on the evenings of October 15, 16, and 17 and then again on the twenty-fifth and twenty-sixth.[96] In the interval between lectures, the doctors spirited the Jungs to their Connecticut country house, "Faraway," for a brief respite, then on to the shoreline community of Madison, where they were weekend houseguests of the writer Philip Wylie. Other guests included the translator W. Stanley Dell and his wife; and Wylie's analyst, Dr. Archibald Strong, and his wife. Jung had known of Dell since the mid-1920s, when he assisted Cary and Peter Baynes with translations, but this was their first encounter.[97] He had met Strong on several occasions in Zürich when he was there to study analytical psychology. They became professional friends and had exchanged collegial letters, so their relationship was already cordial.[98]

Wylie had been a longtime patient of Strong's, and at his urging he was scheduled for a private session with Jung in New York.[99] Jung found Wylie a sympathetic and knowledgeable host, and the talk that weekend ranged widely over everyone's mutual interests, particularly ethics and moral behavior and a general discussion of dreams. When Jung and Wylie corresponded in years to come, Jung told Wylie that he would never forget their talks in his "interesting den with the big fireplace."[100] Wylie, however, remembered something quite different that remains undocumented and unverified to this day.

At some point during the weekend, Wylie alleged, Jung told him in strictest confidence that the Nazi minister of propaganda, Josef Goebbels, had summarily commanded him to go to Berlin, there to attend public events and private ceremonies where Hitler, Hermann Göring, Heinrich Himmler, and Goebbels himself would be together.[101] Goebbels wanted Jung to discern whether "all four of them, as Goebbels feared, evidently were mad." In Wylie's account, Jung obeyed the summons and went to Germany, where he "sat through enough of their show to know they were madmen." Jung "secretly, swiftly, got out of Germany for fear his very life would be in danger." Wylie said he never told this story to anyone because Jung confided to him in confidence "and *he* didn't make it public, then or ever."[102]

The account Wylie remembered has surfaced from time to time in other accounts,[103] but in differing versions from his. Usually they have Jung already in Germany on another matter, to attend a conference or give a lecture, accidentally encountering one or another of the highest-ranking Nazi officials. Wylie is correct to say that Jung never made his story public, for no member of Jung's family nor any of his closest associates heard him tell it. Jung was known for his scrupulously bruising honesty, no matter whom it hurt, himself as well as others, and for his utter indifference to self-promotion or self-aggrandizement; Wylie was one of his most fervent partisans, bent on clearing Jung from any charges of Nazi sympathy or moral turpitude. As no evidence exists to corroborate Wylie's tale of this secret trip to Germany, it must remain just one among many unsolved puzzles of Jung's political behavior.

JUNG DELIVERED the fifteenth series of the Terry Lectures in New Haven on the twentieth, twenty-first, and twenty-second, with a fourth at the United Church of Bridgeport on the twenty-fourth.[104] His topic fell under the general rubric of "Lectures on Religion in the Light of Science and Philosophy," which the University News Bureau abbreviated in press releases to "Applied Psychology and Religion."[105]

Each of the first three talks abounded with references to Christ and Christian symbolism, but all were mainly recycled versions of the Tavistock and Bailey Island lectures. The fourth was merely a compilation of ideas lifted from the other three and delivered extemporaneously.

After the final lecture in Bridgeport, Harding drove him and Emma back to New York, where he lectured twice at the McDowell Club. These lectures, like the four at Yale, were also drawn primarily from previous talks and, like all his oral and written presentations throughout the latter part of the 1930s, recycled from his earlier work. His research interests were far removed from what he said in lectures and were now firmly lodged in the realm of alchemical writing and research.

While they were in New Haven, the Jungs occupied the guest suite in one of Yale's residential dormitories, Jonathan Edwards College.[106] The college master, Professor Robert Dudley French, arranged for them to dine in hall and invited faculty fellows and students who he thought would be congenial company for Jung. One whose company he most enjoyed was the anthropologist Professor Ward Goodenough; another was Dr. Francis Braceland, later president of the American Psychiatric Association and director of the Institute of Living in Hartford. Dr. Walter Miles, a professor in the psychology department, took charge of the rest of Jung's schedule. Among the students were freshman John Weir Perry, whom the Jungs had met the previous year in Providence, and James Whitney, the son of Elizabeth Goodrich Whitney and James Whitney Sr., who were among Jung's earliest patients from California. Jung made a great impression on young Whitney, who later became a respected Jungian analyst, as well as on a third student, Robert Grinnell, who became a writer and professor strongly influenced by Jungian theory, particularly alchemy.[107]

Legend has it that Jung told the Yale officials to schedule his lectures in a small hall so that the few people he expected to attend would not find themselves uncomfortably scattered throughout a cavernous chamber. Instead, the president of Yale, Charles Seymour, honored him with an introduction in

Woolsey Hall, the largest auditorium on the campus.[108] Jung was fond of telling the story that his initial audience was small but grew larger each time he spoke, when actually it began with a full house of twenty-five hundred and remained steady throughout. The second tale he liked to tell concerned Mrs. French, whom he called "a simple woman, an elderly lady,"[109] and her reaction to his final lecture. He quotes her as having said, "I didn't understand a word you said, but it was wonderful." Jung thought she meant he had touched her unconscious. By having done so with one single woman, he believed his talks made an impression on all who heard them.

President Seymour was unable to host the Jungs officially, but they still had a full social calendar. They were guests of honor at one of the elegant formal teas for which the Elizabethan Club was famous. They dined at the home of Professor and Mrs. Irving Fisher, parents of the American divorcée Carol Baumann, who moved to Zürich when she married a cousin of Gret Baumann-Jung's husband. Carol Baumann became a pillar of the Psychological Club and later an ardent defender against the charges of anti-Semitism that dogged Jung.[110] Interestingly, no such charges and no discussion of his politics tarnished Jung's reception at Yale.[111]

JUNG RETURNED to Zürich at the end of October, and on December 4, 1937, he and Fowler McCormick set sail for India on a ship that left from Marseilles. Jung's invitation was spontaneously proffered when McCormick came to hear him speak at Yale, just as he had earlier gone to hear him at Harvard.[112] Despite both Toni's and Emma's imploring him to get inoculations, and even though he had seen firsthand in Africa the dangers that befell the unwary traveler, Jung did not get shots but instead counted on a case full of quinine and chlorine tablets to keep him healthy.[113]

The weather was pleasant, and Jung enjoyed the twelve days at sea contentedly reading alchemical texts.[114] His only frustration arose from his inability to incorporate all his prior reading into a long and thoughtful compilation, but the subject was so large and disparate that he could not organize the material. Happily, all the other passengers were British, and shipboard protocol dictated that as they had not been properly introduced, they could not engage Jung and McCormick in conversation. Both men were delighted, as it freed them from having to dress in the costumes and silly hats favored by the British for evening entertainments. The ship stopped briefly in Aden before docking finally in Bombay.[115] On the way to Calcutta, Jung and McCormick visited (among other cities) Delhi, Ellora, Ajanta, Sanchi, Agra, Allahabad, and Benares, the last two for Jung to receive honorary degrees. They went also to Konarak, Madras, Mysore, Trivandrum, and Madura. On the return voyage, they stopped in Ceylon (now Sri Lanka) long enough to tour Columbo and Kandy, the ancient capital.

"The trip to India constituted a decisive point in my life," Jung recalled twenty years later.[116] "In India it was mostly the question of Evil that occupied me . . . what I experienced there meant the conclusion of the Christian problem for me." His subsequent thoughts about religion are especially revealing because he filtered his experiences through the prism of Christianity, concentrating his thoughts around questions of good and evil. Train travel between internal destinations and sight-seeing in the cities exposed him to the sheer crush of humanity, the grinding poverty of the people, and the utter desperation of their circumstances. Jung thought all the religious images and monuments were imbued with an aura of sensuality that he found troubling, particularly the obscene sculptures that adorned the Temple of Konarak. They gave him ample opportunity to think about "the problem of evil, in how far it must be accepted since it is also a part of God's will."

He posed his thesis in two different ways, that "Indian Spirituality [contains] just as much of evil as of goodness, or to say it differently: lacks as much of evil as it lacks of goodness." What Western civilization called "the moral problem" did not play a role in Eastern societies because people felt themselves "apart" from any of the emotions Westerners equated with good and evil. Jung believed Easterners achieved the equilibrium of fatal acceptance through yoga, "the status of the Nirdvandva where they free themselves from these opposites." For Eastern cultures, "the goal is not moral perfection but . . . liberation from objects."

Reservations surfaced at this point in his thinking: how could a person be liberated from something he neither committed nor experienced? For him, "true liberation" was possible only if he acted "honestly" in some instances and knew when or even whether to act at all in others. Everything he encountered in India managed to contradict such reasoning. He thought it was because he had never before been "under the direct influence of a foreign culture." As if anticipating contradiction, he discounted his entire African experience: "You could say I passed through it as a tourist." The only Arab he spoke to in Africa was his interpreter, so he learned nothing of Muslim cultures, and when he spoke to the natives in Swahili, it was in "simple, primitive" language. He had not "encounter[ed] great minds or important personalities"; nor had he discussed with the natives any significant issues pertaining to the culture and society of Eastern Africa. Even in the civilized cities of Egypt, he remained "just as much of a foreigner."

India was different. For the first time ever he felt himself "under the direct influence of a foreign culture," and the only way to assess it was to compare it with his own. Everyone he spoke to in India was highly educated, many in some of the greatest universities of the West. Those he met ranged from "the guru of the Maharaja of Mysore" to the authors of sophisticated treatises on Kundalini yoga and the "cult of Kali Durga at the Kalighat in Calcutta."[117]

Jung found it "tremendously interesting to talk to people for whom the moral problem is not of foremost importance." It was not "single people or single places" who created confusion in his mind about how he should regard India in general; nor could he "put [his] finger on" what puzzled him specifically. Everything, he believed, turned on the question of good and evil. Fowler Mc-Cormick equated it with "the nature of evil as evidenced by the Goddess Kali, the great destroyer, associated with the color red."[118] McCormick recalled that "everywhere there was evidence of animal sacrifice, everything filthy, dried blood, betel nut. In Calcutta, Jung began to have dreams associated with red."

Jung's conversations with learned men did not suffice to "make the integration of evil acceptable," but they forced him for the first time to accept such concepts as "relative, so to speak. . . . Once they are made conscious, the good is no longer the good and the evil is no longer the evil, and the devil no longer has a tail."

Jung and McCormick had an unofficial guide between Benares, New Delhi, and Calcutta. Alfred Weifel had been suggested by a former patient of Jung's now living in New Delhi, the Swiss photographer Alice Boner.[119] Weifel left his native Germany for political reasons but was eager to hear news of what was happening there. In their conversations about India's political status as a British Commonwealth and Jung's near-veneration of all things British, Weifel became convinced that Jung had been "seduced by Fascism." The subject surfaced indirectly later in unflattering cartoons in newspapers in some of the cities Jung visited. He was furious to be depicted as an overweening peasant buffoon or a giant with an evil mien who hovered above a cowering Freud.[120]

By the time they arrived in Calcutta, Jung was "more and more annoyed" with the hordes of people, particularly students who "only knew their Freud"[121] and nothing of his psychology. McCormick thought Jung's increasingly sour disposition was due to irritation with such audiences and to troubled sleep with recurring dreams of red images. Jung knew it was more serious, that something was wrong with his health. His last coherent act for two weeks was to ask his hosts to take him to the British military hospital, where he was diagnosed with amoebic dysentery. He spent the next two weeks in a hospital, so weak that he missed all the festivities at the university, where his honorary doctorate was bestowed in absentia.

In the hospital, he slipped in and out of drugged sleep, having dreams he "could not understand at all." They all had one thing in common, and in his periods of lucidity, he realized that each centered around a different image of the Holy Grail. He was either on a quest to recover it for a group of unknown supplicants or charged by people he knew to bring it back to where they thought it belonged. In one of the dreams he was able to remember most completely, he described himself as being in India but high above the subcontinent and looking down on an island shaped like England. Where Cornwall should have been, there was a promontory with a medieval castle where he saw himself and various Psychological Club members, both men and women, "sight-seeing."[122] He entered the castle through the dungeon, where he could look skyward in an enormous tower. An iron gate and stone staircase led to a large hall, where a sign informed visitors that the Holy Grail would be celebrated. Jung was "impressed," but his companions were not.

The situation changed, and although he was still with club members, they were all men. The group began to march in a northerly direction, still intent on attending the Grail celebration. They were now out in the countryside and marched all day until, exhausted, they came to a body of water that cut the island in two. "How do we go on?" Jung asked himself in his dream. "Everything is deserted and bleak. Goodness, what to do?" As there was "no boat, no bridge, no street at all," he knew he had to swim across: "I knew one thing for sure: I have to reach that Grail." At that point he awakened, but the dream remained for the rest of his life one of his "most powerful dream impressions."

Ill and too weak to write on the voyage home, he spent much of his time in a deck chair reliving his Grail dreams and probing their meaning. He had always kept his research apart from anything connected to the Grail legend because he regarded it as Emma's special domain. They had discussed it from every conceivable point of view, and he knew "all the details" of the various legends surrounding it, so "the big question" for one already familiar with "the symbols of Christianity" was, what is the special significance of the Grail? Was it, he asked, simply "a variation of Communion . . . an infinitely precious gift one receives for having been a good knight?" If so, how then to reconcile those who belonged to "the [Arthurian] circle of the Grail [who] committed murder and slaughter." What remained and was therefore paramount in Jung's self-analysis was "the visibility of the Grail or the Grail's castle." Ultimately, "it is the secret of individuation, and that is a mystery and human comprehension simply ends there."

Jung described individuation as "a mystery one will never understand." To find it was "a lonely search" perhaps akin to the "process of dying," for one had to give oneself "over to the impersonal" in order to seek it. "Only few could bear such a search," he thought, attributing these curious, unfocused thoughts and images to "the distance from Europe, the completely different surroundings" in which he found himself in India. He thought he may have had such dreams there because his overall question was how and why the evil he encountered in India was "not a moral dimension," but rather "supported by an honest profession as a divine power."[123]

Another comparison/contrast with Christianity happened on the hill of Sanchi: "Buddhism dawned on me for the first time, but I could not yet put it into words." He was "deeply moved to the point of complete bewilderment," and for the first time understood what the life of Buddha stood for, "namely the realization of the self . . . that the self stands above all gods and really represents the mystery of the world and the human existence." For Jung, the Buddha was completely different from Christ, who was also a representation of the self: "The Buddha overcomes the world but out of insight. Christ does not overcome out of insight but as an event, for he is the victim." Jung had already read extensively about the Buddha's life and Buddhist philosophy, but the experience at Sanchi made both come alive for him. In Sanchi, he experienced "a historical human being, therefore ascertainable for people." Christ, by contrast, was

> not a complete human being but also a god, not ascertainable to people because he isn't even ascertainable to himself. He only knew he had to sacrifice himself. It was forced on him, happened to him, was his fate. With the Buddha, everything happened out of insight.

The Buddha represented "the enlightened *mind*, the chance if I am a Buddhist, to reach the same fulfillment, the same perfection."[124] But Jung was fundamentally a westerner and a Christian, so his dreams of the Grail signified what he had to attain: "The Grail is a symbol of enlightenment, in the Western sense, to be exact."

These thoughts, magnified no doubt by his weakened physical condition, were "so intense." He knew he had "reached beyond the Christian world" in India but could not bring himself to "cross over" to a larger, more frightening truth: "I saw what I had to subjugate myself to, but it was simply not acceptable to me. I wanted to keep my head above it and save myself from ethics by taking refuge in morals." He had to find another way to express his "new relationship to Christianity and what the Christian character is all about":

> I realized that I have to be one with myself, one with the human creature imposed on me, and that I have to say "yes" to the fact . . . that I am that way.

CHAPTER 29

Falling Afoul of History

When Jung told Ruth Bailey he must find good causes elsewhere now that he was an honored prophet in his own country, he chose one so controversial it has clouded his reputation ever since.[1] Jung remained affiliated with German psychoanalysis from the Nazi solidification of power in the 1930s through the first years of the war, insisting that his primary reason was to aid disenfranchised Jewish practitioners. He swore that his controversial decision was based on "idiotic altruism" and not "political sentiment,"[2] but debate still rages almost half a century after his death. A recent commentator astutely summarized all the charges leveled against Jung as "We have history. We have attack. We have defense."[3] Depending on the accuser's heat of rhetoric and point of view, the single constant accusation is that Jung had a misguided sympathy toward Nazi philosophy because of his ethnic identity as a native speaker of German.

Jung's detractors argue that he lost whatever honor and respect he commanded as an analytic pioneer because he cooperated with the "conformed"[4] German analytic society long after he should have resigned. They consider the unfortunate and untimely statements he made about Jewish character and culture even more damning. Jung's defenders have tried to downplay or rationalize these indictments by focusing on his many and varied efforts to assist Jewish physicians and psychologists whom the Nazis forbade to practice.

There is little doubt, however (as his Jewish friend James Kirsch put it), that Jung was "a man with his contradiction,"[5] or, as another commentator argued years later, that Jung was "— to put the best face on it — confused by the politics of his day."[6]

The historical record is unfortunately as cloudy as these and most other opinions, its opacity heightened by the particular slant scholars and critics impose upon documents they uncover piecemeal. The quest for historical truth is impeded by circumstances: many archives (both government and private) will not be opened until dates far in the future; others have been systematically plundered or destroyed by their partisans; still others have been selectively culled by persons who believe they have acted in the best interest of history. The facts are few compared with the many interpretations.

Jung's proven involvement in the field of psychoanalysis in Germany began shortly after 1926–27, when a group of German analysts led by Drs. Robert Sommer and Wladimir Eliasberg formed an organization in Berlin called the Allgemeine ärtzliche Gesellschaft für Psychotherapie, the International General Medical Society for Psychotherapy (hereafter, the International Society). The words "international" and "general" were chosen to distinguish this group from others already well established, especially the Deutsche Psychoanalytische Gesellschaft (DPG), strictly Freudian in orientation; and the world's foremost psychoanalytic training institute, the Berlin Psychoanalytic Institute (BPI), also largely Freudian.[7] The new "general" society aimed to create dialogue among practitioners whose allegiances were primarily to the three major theoreticians: Freud, Adler, and Jung; but also to provide a forum for those who followed others, Stekel prominent among them. As membership grew, divisions occurred between those who wanted to admit only medical doctors practicing psychoanalysis and those (Jung among them) who wanted to admit psychologists and lay practitioners who worked under the supervision of a physician.[8]

Jung was one of 399 "charter" members in 1928, when the society was formally incorporated; Adler was among the 344 who were German citizens. Jung took an active role from the start, but Freud remained above the fray, never joining it or any other society, preferring to advise those who administrated according to his wishes. Many who joined with Jung were known as independent thinkers, among them Frieda Fromm-Reichman, Karen Horney, Ernst Kretschmer, Viktor von Weizäcker, Wilhelm Reich, Felix Deutsch, Georg Groddeck, and Harald Schultz-Hencke. A lesser-known member was Matthias Heinrich Göring, an Adlerian who had been analyzed by Jung's old friend Leonhard Seif and who remained an unknown figure in the discipline's background until his cousin Hermann became *Reichsmarschall*, second in command to Hitler.

Such a disparate membership was regarded by the other societies as a conglomeration of "'wild psychoanalysts,' anathematized by Freud himself . . . proponents of other nonorthodox psychotherapeutic orientations whose tenets were not acceptable."[9] The organizers of the new group were unfazed by the charges and invited all and sundry to join in promoting constructive consensus for the advancement of the profession.[10] To further this intention, they founded a journal originally entitled *Allgemeine ärtzliche Zeitschrift für Psychotherapie und psychische Hygiene* (The General Medical Journal for Psychotherapy and Mental Health); changed when the society formally incorporated in 1928 to the more succinct *Zentralblatt für Psychotherapie*, the primary journal for the discipline. Sommer was the original editor, but Dr. Ernst Kretschmer joined him as coequal in 1928. Sommer was old, tired, and some said ill, and eager to cede authority to Kretschmer, professor of medicine at the University of Marburg and one of the most influential psychiatrists in Germany during the 1920s.[11] Under Kretschmer, the *Zentralblatt* became the most respected and widely read journal of its kind in Europe. Largely because of its success, he was chosen to succeed Sommer as president in 1930.

Throughout his career, Kretschmer was regarded as "politically suspicious,"[12] only later by the Nazis but originally by proponents of classical clinical psychiatry who disapproved of his desire to unite differing psychotherapeutic movements within one organization. This group was suspicious of Jung for the same reason, but even more for the alleged mystical, mythological, and religious underpinnings of his theory, which they thought had no place within the medical treatment of mental illness. These were the same qualities most of the "wild psychoanalysts" respected, and they were instrumental in electing Jung "2. *Vorsitzender*," the vice president. The society's statutes were so written that Jung would succeed Kretschmer automatically, either when his term ended or if he resigned beforehand.

By 1930, membership had grown to 575 representatives of diverse ethnic groups and religious persuasions, with congresses held throughout Europe. Jung spoke at most of them and published in the *Zentralblatt*, quickly becoming one of the most visible and quoted members, even though he was neither German nor residing in Berlin, where the society was headquartered. His prominence attracted a considerable German following, and on December 24, 1931, his advocates formally incorporated a C. G. Jung Gesellschaft in Berlin. Separate from the International Society and somewhat akin to the Zürich Psychological Club, its main purpose was the study and furtherance of analytical psychology. The Gesellschaft was active until war began, and after it ended, was reconstituted as a "committee."[13]

Through Jung's indefatigable participation in the International Society's activities, analytical psychology was elevated to a high pinnacle even before the Nazis assumed power. Jung's analytical psychology came to Nazi attention at a time when Freudian theory dominated psychoanalytic inquiry but before official policy decreed the obliteration of any system carrying a Jewish taint. In the prewar decade, Germany was generally regarded as the epitome of cultural and intellectual activity in Europe and, most particularly, the standard by which scientific inquiry throughout the world was conducted and evaluated. These were also the years when "*völkisch*"[14] (a term that carries much more meaning than the English equivalent, "folk") attitudes toward German life and culture were at their peak. The term as it was used throughout the Hitler years encompasses a reemergence of German national feeling and sentiment drawn from a combination of political history, folklore, legend, and mythology. Thus Jung, as a Germanic gentile, offered a more palatable political alternative than Freud.

In the summer of 1933, a great number of *völkisch* movements and societies were founded, but whether Jung was a "kindred spirit" remains "a complex question to which a conclusive answer may prove elusive."[15] Jung's only confirmed connection is his personal friendship with the indologist J. W. Hauer, but there is no record that he ever formally joined Hauer's Deutsche Glaubens-bewegung, the German Faith Movement, or that he ever participated informally in its activities or in those of any other *völkisch* group.[16]

Jung first met Hauer, the professor of Indian studies and comparative religion at Tübingen University, sometime in the late 1920s at Count Keyserling's School of Wisdom. They shared a similar interest in yoga, which Jung had practiced regularly for the previous twenty or so years, and he was interested in how Hauer thought it could be made useful within psychotherapeutic treatment. Jung attended Hauer's lecture on "Yoga in the Light of Psychotherapy" at the International Society's 1930 congress in Baden-Baden and invited him to repeat it for the Psychological Club in Zürich in 1931. Jung's interest intensified throughout 1932, when he interrupted his seminars on Christiana Morgan's visions to invite another indologist, Heinrich Zimmer, to present his findings, and in October and November he joined Hauer in a series of talks on Kundalini yoga.[17]

Six months later, with their professional paths already diverging, Jung accepted the presidency of the International Society, and Hauer founded the German Faith Movement, a loosely allied group of ten or so other groups, comprising a total membership of five to six thousand. Hauer's groups were both anti-Semitic and anti-Christian, rejecting all organized Christian religions and wanting to discredit the Old Testament because of its Semitic underpinnings. They emphasized a pagan vision anchored around the two great poles of Goethe and Nietzsche that was also grounded in mythology, the mysticism of Meister Eckhardt, and every nationalistic version of German romanticism hitherto expressed through poetry, art, and music. Hauer wanted the German Faith Movement, "an eruption from the biological and spiritual depths," to become the official religion of the Third Reich.[18] This was not to be, for Goebbels specifically derided Hauer and others who aimed to found new religions as "a conglomerate of prattlers, intriguers, vicious sanctimonious swindlers." Hitler dismissed them as "'those cretins' who made asses of themselves by worshiping Wotan and Odin and the ancient, but now obsolete, German mythology."[19] By 1934, Hauer was banned from Eranos[20] and Jung broke all ties with him; by 1936, the German Faith Movement, like most others, no longer existed.

Meanwhile, Jung's German star was in the ascendant. After years of relative physical isolation in Switzerland and with professional renown coming mainly from the United States and England — neither of which held the intellectual stature of Germany — it was, indeed, heady stuff to find his theory so respected there, and he relished it. But as his reputation grew, so, too, did murmurs that he owed his prominence to those who sought to distance themselves from the "Jewish science" of Freud and, by extension, his most prominent advocates in Berlin, Karl Abraham and Max Eitingon. Also, references to a 1918 essay in which Jung separated German Jews from ethnic Germans in his assessments of character and culture began to be bruited about. When the Nazis singled out some of these remarks in the early 1930s to validate anti-Semitic statements, alarms were raised and accusations of Jung's willing collaboration followed.

The 1918 essay, "Ueber das Unbewusste" (The Role of the Unconscious),[21] was published in a Swiss magazine with limited circulation and dedicated entirely to a parochial assessment of Swiss art and culture. Jung's essay was his attempt to explain to his compatriots why results were so different when theoreticians from various countries and cultures conducted research in primitive societies. He touched upon many differing concepts and constructs to make his point that a collective unconscious existed, among them theoretical divergences caused by the national characteristics of Germans and French, his own differences with Freudian theory, his views of the usefulness of Kantian philosophy, and how he believed the findings of biologists differed from those of, among others, psychologists.

But in 1930, only the political resonated. Readers in general were struck by the prescience of Jung's 1918 description of Germany as a "blonde beast . . . prowling about in its underground prison, ready at any moment to burst out with devastating consequences." The most controversial and most quoted portion of this otherwise straightforward essay (i.e., in terms of how it exemplified analytical psychology) were the several paragraphs wherein Jung held Christianity responsible for splitting "the Germanic barbarian into an upper and a lower half."[22] He focused on national identity by attributing such outbursts not only to individuals but also to a larger "social form." Such a "problem" did not exist for the Jew, who "already had the culture of the ancient world and on top of that has taken over the culture of the nations amongst whom he dwells. He has two cultures, paradoxical as that may sound."

Jung placed the Jew at an even farther remove from national identity: "He is domesticated to a higher degree than we are, but he is badly at a loss for that quality in man which roots him to the earth and draws new strength from below." He warned of the "chthonic quality," the reliance on the mythological underworld, that resided "in dangerous concentration in the Germanic peoples." Jung thought other "Aryan" Europeans were "perhaps . . . beginning to notice it in the present war [World War I]." By the 1930s, his prophetic conclusion was all but ignored: "And again, perhaps not."

What was remembered, however, was that Jung offered Jews as a facile example of a group that lacked "chthonic quality" because they had no homeland of their own, none of their "own earth underfoot." As further support, he invoked "Freud's and Adler's reduction of everything psychic to primitive sexual wishes and power-drives," calling such theory "beneficial and satisfying to the Jew, because it is a form of simplification." It allowed him to assert that Freud and Adler had created "specifically Jewish doctrines . . . thoroughly unsatisfying to the Germanic mentality." Ultimately, both within and apart from the context in which Jung intended it, this remark damaged his reputation most, as "conformed" German psychotherapists cited it time and again to justify their tactics of discredit and exclusion of the "Jewish" science propounded by Freud and Adler.

To put the remark back into Jung's context, the German he described was a "genuine barbarian" who should have, but did not, raise alarm signals among the post–World War I generation:

> Would that people could learn the lesson of this war! . . . The psychotherapist with a Jewish background awakens in the Germanic psyche not those wistful and whimsical residues from the time of David, but the barbarian of yesterday, a being for whom matters suddenly become *serious* in the most unpleasant way.

"It seems to me," Jung concluded, "that we should take the problem of the unconscious very seriously indeed." Unfortunately, by the 1930s and ever after, few people did, and the only part of the 1918 essay that resonated was what he wrote about the Jews.

JUNG'S ELECTION, first as vice president of the International Society in 1930 and then president in 1933, represented a significant personal coup. As a Swiss citizen he was imbued with the cultural cringe that regarded all things German as of higher intellectual caliber than those of the surrounding German-speaking nations. To define what this meant for him as an individual, he explained it in terms of the Swiss national character and the peculiar "crust" his countrymen developed as their "self-defense against the psychological influence" of Germany and Austria.[23] With his country divided among four language groups (French, German, Italian, and Romansch), Jung feared the Swiss would be subsumed if they were not "critical," "prejudiced," and on guard at all times. To maintain cultural autonomy they (particularly the German Swiss) had to overcome their natural sympathies to the cultures of the countries whose language they shared and whose borders abutted theirs. So, even though he was elated by his vice presidency, he had to restrain all feelings because, as a Swiss, it was important "never to show one is impressed . . . enjoying oneself too much with foreigners, or that one is being influenced."

Nevertheless, charges of hubris arose when Kretschmer resigned on April 6, 1933, and Jung automatically succeeded him. Kretschmer resigned primarily because he refused to help the Nazis subvert the discipline for propagandistic uses. He made many intemperate remarks, and these, too, were held against him. Jung privately described the old and infirm President Hindenburg to his friends as "the symbol of the 'Old Wise Man' to the German people, without the wisdom,"[24] but Kretschmer was publicly indiscreet. Early in 1933, he made a widely quoted comment alluding to Adolf Hitler after Hindenburg misguidedly appointed him chancellor on January 30: "There's something strange about psychopaths. In normal times we write expert evaluations on them; in times of political unrest they rule us."[25] After such indiscreet remarks, it was clearly only a matter of time until he would be forced to resign, so he began to prepare for an exit that would cause neither him nor the organization bodily or professional harm. He and Jung apparently discussed his resignation in letters that have never been found (and which may no longer be extant), for each man alluded to his thought processes in letters to others as Hitler solidified his hold on the country.[26]

The *Reichstag* was burned on February 27, and an edict was enacted on the twenty-eighth "for the protection of the people and the state." On March 21, the Enabling Act that proclaimed Hitler *oberster Rechtsherr* (supreme lawgiver) was rammed through by his supporters. Many other power seizures followed, among them the decree on the twenty-third boycotting all Jewish businesses and the April 7 decree in which "non-Aryans" (i.e., Jews) were stripped of all essential rights. On May 10, with forty thousand ordinary citizens cheering them on, five thousand swastika-carrying students burned more than two thousand books. Among them were Freud's, which the students consigned to the bonfire while shouting "against the soul-destroying overestimation of the sex life — and on behalf of the nobility of the human soul — I offer to the flames the writings of one Sigmund Freud."[27]

Hitler had been in office for six months by June 21, when Jung officially assumed the presidency. Already, the question of what to do about "life unworthy of life" had been officially sanctioned as "professional[izing] and medical[izing] the policy of 'positive eugenics,' " which was one euphemism for another: "the painless extermination of the miserable." Medical doctors were expected to implement this policy.[28]

Confronted with these events, many intellectuals who disagreed with Hitler were frightened into silence and withdrew from public life. Two separate groups that had been the most vocal, the Marxist-oriented Children's Seminar and the intellectuals within the Frankfurt Institute of Social Research, disbanded and emigrated. Jung's German-Jewish friend James Kirsch left Berlin for Palestine, and Julia and Erich Neumann, who became foremost practitioners of analytic psychology in Israel, followed shortly after. By August 1934, twenty-four of the thirty-six Jewish members of the DPG were gone, many fleeing to exile in England and the United States.[29]

Jung's comments about the situation in letters to various correspondents provide fuel for his critics. To one, he wrote, "German doctors are compelled only by the special circumstances of the time to make a political declaration of faith"; to another, *"Il y a des frontières politiques même en science* [there are political frontiers even in science]. In psychotherapy the last thing one should do is to tar everything with the same brush. Infinite nuances are needed if justice is to be done to human beings."[30]

Meanwhile, Kretschmer found it untenable to continue as the society's *gleich-geschaltet*, or conformed, president. He told a colleague that he was resigning because "a thing as complicated as the psychotherapeutic movement could only be pursued on a free and international basis, apart from all political influences."[31] He refused to comply with such absurdities as the *Gleichschaltung*, conforming decrees that allowed psychoanalytic treatment to continue, but only after the standard terminology (mainly Freudian in origin) was banned. The Jewish Eitingon, instrumental in gaining international respect for the DPG, was forced to resign the chairmanship, but the society was allowed to continue as a "conformed" entity under the direction of the self-serving Felix Boehm. The most respected institution of all, the BPI, was disbanded as a separate entity and incorporated into Boehm's DPG after it was cleansed of Freudian orientation and practice.[32]

As in so many other instances, the Nazis needed to mitigate the political aftereffects of Kretschmer's resignation or, in contemporary parlance, put a positive spin on it. Matthias Heinrich Göring moved closer to the center of power within German psychoanalysis, his favor (and, by extension, his powerful cousin's) openly courted by Ernst Cimbal, the general secretary. Cimbal was directed to offer Kretschmer the honorary chairmanship of an *überstaatliche Gesellschaft*, a new "supranational organization," one among other societies organized in different European countries under the umbrella of the International Society. It thus permitted the German group to function, but under Nazi conformity. Kretschmer refused to be co-opted.

Matthias Heinrich Göring, the formerly obscure psychoanalyst called Papi because of his long white beard and seemingly docile demeanor, was busy jockeying for the unconditional power he would shortly wield, thanks to his cousin Hermann. When Cimbal failed to bring Kretschmer back into "conformity," Papi Göring was assigned the task. Feelings were so strong about how to handle Kretschmer that on October 6, 1933, he was obliged to defend his resignation to Göring. He did it with as much diplomacy as he could muster,[33] writing that his refusal to cooperate was "due to the present structure" of the International Society, which was "trying too hard to embrace intellectual currents and special groups that were far too diverse." Although his interest in practicing psychotherapy "as a science and medical art" remained strong, he thought neither he nor anyone else could provide "strict and unified leadership" in the current political climate.[34]

That Kretschmer had to write this letter shows clearly how widespread were the tentacles of *Gleichschaltung*. The Nazis were determined not to let him get away or, if he insisted on going, to make him leave on their terms. In the several months that elapsed between Kretschmer's resignation and Jung's assumption of office, they discussed the predicament. Most of the society's German members assumed that, as a citizen of a neutral nation and one who was in sympathy with Kretschmer, Jung would refuse to succeed him. Many of the non-German members expected that all the elected officers (who were German) would resign as well.

Extant correspondence shows how aggressively Göring and Cimbal worked to forestall resignations, especially Jung's. Kretschmer also urged Jung to stay on, but not for the same reason: he thought Jung, as an independent Swiss, could withstand whatever pressures conformed Nazi officials might exert, thus ensuring a modicum of independence for the society. Jung shared this view and tried to convince "all those who have misgivings because of the political conditions in Germany" that he stood "on strictly neutral ground."[35] He mentioned the dilemma to one of his patients, a Swiss man who kept a detailed analytic diary of his sessions and was also an ardent Nazi sympathizer. This man wrote of his incomprehension on two occasions during May 1933, when he could not fathom why Jung was so reluctant "to be of service to such a glorious social movement" as National Socialism.[36] Several weeks before his presidency was announced publicly, Jung's equivocation was further evidenced in his letter to a fellow member of the society, Dr. Johann Heinrich Schultz. As "the Society is not being dissolved — the resignation of the Committee *en masse* is superfluous." The next phrase in his letter became a flashpoint for controversy: Kretschmer's resignation signified "it is now my [Jung's] turn."[37] Jung's detractors use the phrase as proof that he was greedy for power and eager to have it, no matter what the form; his defenders say it was merely his innocent comment on the nature of the succession. Actually, it was his response to the separate power struggle for the presidency that Schultz was then engaged in with Hans von Hattingberg. Both, as Germans, fully expected the Swiss Jung to resign and were busily competing for the right to succeed him.[38] Jung also told Schultz he had discussed with Cimbal the problems that might arise if the society's president lived in Zürich, while all those who carried out its daily work lived in Berlin. He said Cimbal assured him it would not be a problem, so he planned to serve "until the knotty problems that have arisen have been definitely straightened out."

Jung wisely intuited that he needed someone in Berlin to keep him informed of what was taking place under his ostensible command, so he asked Dr. Gustav Richard Heyer to serve as his deputy. He liked and trusted both Heyer and his wife, Lucy Heyer-Grote, long advocates of his psychology: in 1928, Richard founded a Jungian discussion group in Munich; Lucy, a gymnastics teacher, was one of the first to incorporate movement and dance into Jungian therapy.[39] In 1932, Jung praised Richard's "intuition and aggressive temperament." Unfortunately, he did not learn for several years that Heyer became an enthusiastic Nazi supporter in 1930 and was considered by many of his German colleagues a "politically dangerous and combative individual."[40] It also appears that Jung never learned how effectively Cimbal isolated Heyer from any direct involvement with those who really controlled power. A reading of the scant correspondence between Heyer and Jung shows how little useful information he unearthed.[41]

In retrospect, it appears that Jung's judgment of the people with whom he threw in his lot was wildly off the mark in every instance. He was wrong about Heyer, wrong to accept Cimbal's facile assurance that he would be the true leader of the society, wrong in his belief that he could keep M. H. Göring under control. Göring and Cimbal were undermining Jung's actions and limiting his authority even before he assumed office, for neither was certain that Jung's support of National Socialism was even lukewarm, let alone wholehearted. One of their reasons for questioning his allegiance stemmed from the lectures he gave in Köln and Essen that February, where he spoke of the relationship of the *Führer* (in the meaning nonspecific to Hitler, merely as "leader") to the masses. Axel von Muralt, who heard Jung speak and later became one of his most vocal critics, praised him for having "put the *Führer* firmly in his place"[42] when he said repeatedly that a true leader would not suffocate the individual. Another reason Cimbal and Göring doubted Jung concerned the annual meeting of the International Society, scheduled for October in Bad Nauheim. Cimbal told Göring they could not count on Jung to calm any disruptions provoked by Jewish members who had been officially banned from the governing board. Even though the conformed board wanted all Jewish members to resign completely, Cimbal was among those who argued that despite their "greatly elevated sense of self-worth," Jews should be allowed to retain general membership because Jung would refuse to "execute the standing order [to evict them] very strictly."[43] The subject became moot when the Nazis forbade the meeting to take place at all. Cimbal sent a *Rundschreiben*, a circular letter, blaming Jung for canceling it, saying he could not neglect his new duties as lecturer at the ETH.[44] Jung had indeed begun a professorship that would continue for years, but he never allowed teaching engagements to curtail other activities. Privately, Cimbal told Göring that, with the need to "liberate" the society from "Jewish influences . . . a long postponement of all important steps" would be to its "advantage . . . and its future." He warned that Jung's attitude signaled "immense difficulty" for their future efforts to impose conformity.

Even as he wrote this to Göring, Cimbal was writing soothingly to Jung that no restrictions would be placed upon his "scientific ability," that he could govern freely "once the political and business matters of the management are secured in the given [i.e., "conformed"] form."[45] Cimbal needed to placate Göring further, so he described Jung as little more than a puppet who was permitted to think he had free rein for two reasons: first, because the Nazis considered him "the most important Germanic researcher of *Tiefenpsychologie* in the Aryan–Anglo Saxon world," and second, because "all the other great masters of our science are unfortunately not Aryan."[46]

Cimbal realized how much the Nazis needed Jung, so he had to work hard to mollify Göring, who wanted to oust Jung and seize the presidency for himself. He assured Göring that Jung would have "no misgivings against your National Socialist management of the conventions," and swore that Jung had studied "the thought processes and probably also the literature of National Socialism very carefully and certainly agrees with them."[47] To date, no document has been found to verify Cimbal's contention, but Göring still wanted control. Cimbal told Göring there was no doubt that Jung would consent to his taking the leading "political" role in the "remodelling" of the society because "it was completely pointless for the individual to resist the so-to-speak meteorological conditions. . . . Give to the Emperor what is the Emperor's and to God what is God's."[48] Cimbal was certain that once Jung was confronted with the hard reality of *Gleichschaltung* politics, he would capitulate and support the party line.

WHILE CIMBAL was busy soothing and placating on all sides, Jung went to Berlin on several occasions during the summer of 1933. Well before Hitler came to power, he had accepted an invitation to give a seminar to the C. G. Jung Gesellschaft at their headquarters, Harnackhaus, in Dahlem. Since the Berlin group was loosely defined as the German equivalent of the Psychological Club, some Swiss members decided to go, not only to hear Jung lecture but also to meet their counterparts and see for themselves what was happening. Jung took Emma and Toni, and Barbara Hannah was among the contingent.[49] When she asked Jung if she would be safe driving alone in her car, he told her it would be "an interesting experience" and to "risk it!"[50]

Hannah found herself unable to connect with any of the German attendees on any level, either personal or intellectual. Even more troubling, most of the Swiss were openly Nazi sympathizers. Jung warned Hannah that she was "getting dangerously out of [her]self," because all Germany was "in a panic . . . scared stiff and [they] have no idea where this is heading." She noted his frustration at being powerless in the face of "inevitable disaster." He insisted there was still the necessity "of trying to help them [German Jews] as long as we can."[51]

The Nazis worked hard to maximize the publicity Jung's visit provided. In the month or so preceding it, articles were planted in newspapers and periodicals, typified by one in the *Berliner Börsenzeitung*. Entitled "Wider die Psychoanalyse" (Against Psychoanalysis),[52] it described Freud's *Sexualtheorie* as "unaesthetic and intellectually hardly satisfying" and Adler's *Machttheorie* as "distinctly poisonous." Jung was placed in opposition to them as "the reformer of *Tiefenpsychologie*." He was praised as "a real Swiss German conservative by nature," and celebrated for having linked "individuation" with "collective powers."

No document has yet been found to prove that Jung read this or any of the other articles about him, which is probably why he had no reason to be on guard during a June 26 interview on Radio Berlin with Adolf von Weizäcker, a former pupil and member of the executive committee of the C. G. Jung Gesellschaft. Von Weizäcker introduced Jung as "the most progressive psychologist of modern times" and founder of a theory that was "fundamentally constructive" in contrast to others such as Freud's that were "rightly . . . suspect nowadays."⁵³ He stressed how "important" was Jung's origin in "a Protestant parsonage in Basel" because it placed him on a "different footing" from Adler and Freud. Jung's approach to "the creative element . . . in the history of the German mind" stemmed from deep reverence that did not "devalue it," for his psychology was "not intellectual but . . . imbued with vision." Von Weizäcker's somewhat belittling but fairly innocuous interpretation was a prelude for questions he asked Jung to answer "as a Swiss, with a certain detachment."

He began with the "difference between the psychic situation of the Germans and . . . Western Europeans." Germany was "surrounded by the deepest misunderstandings," and von Weizäcker wanted Jung to explain what might have caused them. Jung attributed them to the relative newness of the German nation in comparison with the other countries of Western Europe. Only recently had Germany become a "nation building force," while older societies were imbued with a national chauvinism developed during many centuries of unity. Jung thought it natural that German youth led the drive for nationalism, because every generation of elders in every country was reluctant to accept new ideas. Von Weizäcker then asked Jung what the "task" of his psychology was "in such a time of activity." Jung said it should be used for "more consciousness and self-reflection." He emphasized the need for "inner meaning":

> If we do not succeed in getting this view, it may easily happen that we are as it were unconsciously swept along by events. For mass movements have the peculiarity of overpowering the individual by mass suggestion and making him unconscious. The political or social movement gains nothing by this when it has swarms of hypnotized camp followers.

What mattered, Jung stressed, was "for mass movements to possess adherents who follow not from unconscious compulsion but from conscious conviction."

In his next question, von Weizäcker spoke of psychology as being suspect in the new Germany because it was concerned "with the self-development of the so-called individual," whereas "the collective forces of the whole community" were now in charge of daily life. Jung stuck to his most basic contention, that the "self-development of the individual" was "the supreme goal of all psychological endeavor." Then he trained his sights on Hitler: "As Hitler said recently, the leader must be able to be alone and must have the courage to go his own way. But if he doesn't know himself, how is he to lead others?"

Von Weizäcker moved swiftly to safer ground by asking Jung to explain the difference between his psychology and Adler's and Freud's. Jung said Freud and Adler posited "a critique against the totality of the phenomenal world," which he could not accept, whereas the "German mind" recognized "the whole of creation." It was certainly his analogy for allowing the collective unconscious to be unlocked and do its necessary work, but within the context of the interview the comment could also be read as his approval of Nazi policies.

Von Weizäcker's last question concerned the "leading elite that is now acknowledged in Germany," which he asked Jung to compare with "elected government dependent on the opinion of the masses, as evolved in Western Europe." Jung's answer was tinged with resignation, if not dismay. He saw "barbarian invasions" unfolding "inwardly in the psyche of the [German] people." He equated "times of mass movement" with "times of leadership," for the triumphant leader was "an incarnation of the nation's psyche and its mouthpiece . . . the spearhead of the phalanx of the whole people in motion." Such a situation ensured that "Western Europe" would be incapable of comprehending "the special psychic emergency of the young German nation." Jung believed there could never be common ground between Germany and other European nations, "either historically or psychologically." But von Weizäcker needed an upbeat ending, so he commended Jung for being one among other "leaders . . . who really know something about the psyche, the German psyche, and whose psychology is not just intellectual chatter but a living knowledge of human beings." It was yet another indication of how important Jung's Swiss-German, non-Jewish psychology was to a regime determined to destroy the "wholly Jewish"[54] science of Freud and his followers.

Jung said that Freud once told him "the fate of psychotherapy will be decided in Germany," a belief he shared. He insisted that he was "not an opponent of the Jews," merely "an opponent of Freud's" because of

> his materialistic and intellectualistic and — last but not least — irreligious attitude and not because he is a Jew. In so far as his theory is based in certain respects on Jewish premises, it is not valid for non-Jews. Nor do I deny my Protestant prejudice. Had Freud been more tolerant of the ideas of others I would still be standing at his side today. I consider his intolerance — and it is this that repels me — a personal idiosyncrasy.[55]

All this was certainly true and grounded in historical evidence; nevertheless, for Jung to say it at such a dangerous moment sparked conflicting explications of what he really meant. There are several letters extant in which he tried to explain, but by trying to be scrupulously fair to both Germans and Jews, he succeeded only in adding fuel to an already dangerous fire.[56]

He believed that Freud's psychotherapy in Germany would have been "doomed to absolute perdition,"[57] had he not accepted the presidency: "I have broken this prejudice by my intervention and have made life possible not only for the so-called Aryan psychotherapists but for the Jewish ones as well." He accused his attackers of conveniently forgetting that most German psychotherapists were also Jewish and that he made many interventions on their behalf. He was angry that unnamed and unspecified "Jews" were "railing" at him, especially after his struggles to keep their memberships active and to maintain the neutrality of the *Zentralblatt*. "The Jews should be thankful to me for that," he insisted, blaming a "paranoid attitude" that kept others from acknowledging his work. Still determined to apportion blame and responsibility in equal part while holding himself neutral and therefore blameless, he concluded:

> During [World War I] people moaned that the Allies used the hunger blockade against Germany. The understandable opposition of the Jews to the Hitler regime now make it quits [i.e., moot]: everything German is outlawed, regardless of whether people are involved who are entirely innocent politically. I find that shortsighted, too.

He did not help his case after the war when he insisted:

> It is however difficult to mention the antichristianism of the Jews after the horrible things that have happened in Germany, but Jews are not so damned innocent after all — the role played by the intellectual Jews in pre-war Germany would be an interesting object of investigation.[58]

MATTERS CAME to an organizational head in September when M. H. Göring, using his cousin Hermann's influence and with the backing of a sizeable number of German members, was named president of a newly constituted entity, the German General Medical Society for Psychotherapy.[59] This seemed a logical move to supporters of National Socialism, for obviously they could not force branches of the International Society to "conform" to Nazi policy. Nor could other branches be forced to accept the new directive that all members had to read "thoroughly and conscientiously Adolf Hitler's basic book *Mein Kampf*," henceforth the "fundamental" text for anyone who wished to practice psychotherapy in Germany.[60]

Göring also declared not only that German practitioners must be conformed but also that the *Zentralblatt* had to "participate in the work of the people's chancellor in order to educate the German people for their heroic and self-sacrificing role." He named himself director of a new "special German issue" of the *Zentralblatt* in a "Preliminary Statement" justifying the new society:

> It became necessary to work out a plan for the Society (proper) and the psychotherapeutic movement within Germany which would express exactly the fundamental idea of the national government and would make it possible to adjust it completely to the national tasks of the German medical profession.[61]

When Jung read this, his response was succinct. He told Rudolf Allers, the Jewish editor of the "Reviews" section, whom he was fighting to keep, that the journal was now printing whatever "psychotherapy signifies under the present political conditions in Germany."[62] As the rules seemed to change daily, Jung was "still in the dark on this score." He knew the Germans would choose a specifically conformed "Reviews" editor for the special German issue, so he told Allers that as an "Austrian 'non-Aryan'"[63] he would be replaced: "The German government . . . seems to like having the editors of all periodicals appearing in Germany in safe and uncomfortable proximity." The new editor would need "the right nose for what one can say and what not. In any event it will be an egg-balancing dance." Allers refused to go quietly, however, and two years later Jung was still entreating Göring to take him back. Göring put it bluntly: "We cannot . . . since he is Jewish."[64]

Despite all Göring's machinations, Jung still thought he could influence this "very amiable and reasonable man."[65] Jung's one goal above all was that "psychotherapy must see to it that it maintains its position inside the German Reich and does not settle outside it, regardless of how difficult its living conditions there may be." He said this to Alphons Maeder, whom he tried unsuccessfully to enlist in founding a Swiss group; and to Poul Bjerre, the Swedish psychotherapist whom he had known since his days as Freud's "crown prince" and whom he was now urging to found a Swedish chapter.[66] Jung was also advising concerned non-Nazi Germans to "submit without hesitation," for what mattered "above all is that psychotherapy in Germany, now gravely threatened, should survive the adversities of the time." He wanted everyone to unite and "prevent the special political currents in the German group . . . from spilling over into the Society as a whole." His presidency was a "doubtful pleasure" he owed to German insistence on a "foreign" leader, but he stopped short of seeing himself as a figurehead for Nazi ambition. Because so many foreigners were "afraid" of the Hitler regime, he thought it necessary for "outside neutrals . . . to give [German science] an opportunity to make international connections."

Jung was not alone in working toward this goal, as all other groups and most individuals, no matter where their allegiance lay, joined in giving precedence to saving psychoanalysis in Germany over the moral or ethical considerations inherent in dealing with the Nazis. When Eitingon was forced to resign the directorship of the BPI, Freud told him that even though the Nazi faction had seized control, "it is also in the general interest [of psychoanalysis] that [the Institute] remain open, so that it may survive these unfavorable times."[67] Ernest Jones, whose behavior later earned him the sobriquet of "Freud's Rottweiler,"[68] revealed some of his "blatant, aggressive bigotry"[69] when he urged all Jewish members to resign and, in effect, disappear into the shadows to ensure they did not bring Nazi retaliation upon the organization. Jones actually sent a telegram to Therese Benedeck, one of the Jewish analysts who refused to go quietly, that read "urgently advise voluntary resignation."[70] A second reluctant analyst, Eva Rosenfeld, eerily prefigured later reality when she learned of Jones's edict, saying if Jews followed his advice, they were agreeing "to become their own executioners."[71] By 1936, the gentile Felix Boehm was still trying to keep the Freudian-oriented DPG licensed and operating, even though he knew it was to be merged within a new institute under the overall direction of Göring (to be known informally as the Göring Institute).[72] It, too, would operate under *Neue Deutsche Seelenheilkunde*, the new German psychotherapy.[73]

Freud was old and ill in the 1930s and had ceded most authority for the furtherance of his psychology in Germany to his daughter Anna and to Jones. She agreed wholeheartedly with her father's plan for keeping his theory viable by keeping the institute in operation, and she supported Jones in his effort to carry out Freud's intention. When the "few remaining Jews" were finally coerced into resigning from the BPI in December 1933, Jones was still negotiating to save "a little . . . something [of Freud's psychology]."[74] The only thing saved, however, was a single set of Freud's collected works, kept under lock and key until after the war in what was known as "the poison cabinet." Any psychoanalyst who applied for permission to read them risked much by merely asking.[75]

Hopes for co-existence were soon dashed on all fronts, but especially where Jung was concerned. When Göring took control of the newly constituted German chapter, he announced a new policy for the *Zentralblatt*: each country would be responsible for an issue describing how psychoanalysis functioned there, with the Germans going first. As soon as Jung heard this, he fired off a letter to Cimbal saying he wanted "no part in the German publication," either as editor or contributor.[76] He was already the victim of "awful harassment in Zürich" for his alleged "Germanophilia" and wanted to avoid charges of "editor's partisanship for the Nationalsocialist government." He insisted on having nothing further to do with *Deutsche Heft* and *Neue Deutsche Seelenheilkunde*. Jung insisted that Cimbal and Göring must publish the German special edition as a separate entity from all other issues of the *Zentralblatt*, and as the overall editor, he forbade any mention of "domestic [German] politics."

Cimbal was convinced they still needed the legitimacy Jung's neutral citizenship provided and told Göring they would have to humor him: "He does have to secure his own position, since he mostly makes his living off a foreign audience from mostly diverse countries."[77] Cimbal complained of sleepless nights imposed by the "very serious" dilemma of trying to keep Jung in line: "The foundations of sympathy which we hoped to have gained in Switzerland through Jung have at least partly been lost again." His concern makes it curious indeed that Cimbal and Göring risked losing Jung altogether with what they published in the German edition of the newly conformed *Zentralblatt*.

Göring wrote a "Founding Statement" of how *Neue Deutsche Seelenheilkunde* was henceforth to be conducted, a directive that was supposed to be printed only in Germany and distributed only to members of the German society. Whether by accident or intention, it was printed in every edition in every country that sponsored a branch of the International Society.[78] In it, Göring decreed that all German physicians had to "promote and practice psychomedical medicine that corresponded to the National Socialist worldview." To ensure this, they had to read *Mein Kampf* "conscientiously and thoroughly . . . [and] accept it as basic." He decreed further that "the *Zentralblatt* wishes to participate in the work of the people's chancellor in order to educate the German people for their heroic and self-sacrificing role."

Jung was personally compromised because the German edition, from which he had specifically asked Cimbal to remove his name as well as his editorial title, printed his official explanation of why he had accepted the presidency. His statement was not supposed to appear in the German edition, only in the other national printings, but because it was in the German as well, readers naturally inferred that he accepted anti-Semitic Nazi policy.[79] Jung wrote in part that, although psychotherapy "as a science has nothing to do with politics," circumstances required him to succeed Kretschmer during a time that "coincided with the great political transformation in Germany" and was "characterized by confusion of the teachings and points of view of psychotherapy." He viewed the basic task of the *Zentralblatt* as the society's founders did, to evaluate objectively the "concrete contributions" of the different theoretical schools in order to arrive at an "all inclusive viewpoint." By doing so, the journal would do "justice to the fundamental facts of the human soul in the highest possible measure." The unfortunate example he chose to illustrate this otherwise straightforward thesis was "the differences between the Germanic and the Jewish psychology which actually exist and which have been known to people of insight for a long time." Jung thought these differences should "no longer be wiped out," that is, ignored or unacknowledged. He believed that:

> In psychology more than any other science there exists a "personal equation" which, if it is neglected, will falsify results of practice and theory. In this connection, however, I wish specifically to emphasize the fact that no devaluation of Semitic psychology is implied here any more than it would constitute a devaluation of Chinese psychology if we were to speak of a specific and special psychology of the peoples of the Far East.[80]

To have expressed such a view in a Nazi-conformed journal at the end of 1933 was unbelievably naïve and politically misguided, but a central thesis of Jung's psychology was the differences that exist among nations, tribes, and other groupings, and so he stated it. His critics ignored his contention that he intended "no devaluation of Semitic psychology," and controversy intensified.[81]

That summer, when he was lecturing in Berlin, several "leading Nazis" whom he did not otherwise identify said they were so eager for him to relocate they were willing to arrest him to keep him in Germany.[82] "But why?" he asked. "I am no politician, I am a psychologist, what have I to do with your enterprise?" The Nazis replied, "Exactly, you are a psychologist, you are outside the whole thing, so you are the man who could tell us what we are doing." Jung was amazed: "You see, they don't know."

The firestorm over Jung's statement worried Cimbal and Göring, who feared his "inconsistent behavior" was making it difficult "to gain the sympathy of foreigners for National Socialism."[83] They worried that he was so angry about their deception that he would boycott the forthcoming Bad Nauheim conference, "which would mean that the entire *Überstaatlicher Verband* [the international chapters] including the *Zentralblatt* will be dissolved." Göring tried to ease the tension by telling Jung he understood "the problems facing foreigners who sympathize with us."[84] He blithely assumed that Jung supported his belief that theirs was an era requiring "the rejection of the individualistic-capitalist system" and said he was sure that border countries, particularly Switzerland, would soon "support" and "work hand in hand" with the Nazis:

> For this reason, we would like to ask you not to stay away from the *Nauheimer Kongress;* we will leave it up to you whether you will speak or not but we would appreciate it greatly if you announced the date, of course without commentary, in the *Zentralblatt.* There will certainly be quite a few among the foreign psychotherapists who will be interested in our view of psychotherapy.

Jung did go to Bad Nauheim, and his presence did provide a propaganda coup for Göring. He knew it would, but he went because the congress offered a possibility to protect the membership of German Jewish analysts. At first he thought he would have to resign and create a new organization separate from the International Society, an entity that would welcome a German chapter but would be governed from Switzerland or England and with "its own truly international journal."[85] Recognizing how much time, effort, and money would be required to start such a society, Jung decided on another tack.

ALINE VALANGIN had been Jung's patient since the mid-1920s, and he saw her with her husband, Vladimir Rosenbaum, at Eranos meetings.[86] Jung liked the idealistic, irreverent young lawyer, whom he occasionally consulted about translations of his writings; more frequently, he dropped into Rosenbaum's office just to chat when he was in Zürich. So it was not untoward when Jung wandered in one afternoon in 1934 for what became a "very peculiar consultation."[87] Rosenbaum recalled how puzzled his new secretary was by the "tall, important gentleman" she had never seen before who refused to give his name. Intrigued, he had the mysterious stranger ushered into his office. Without preliminary pleasantries, Jung said he had something to discuss that required absolute discretion. "Please, Herr Professor," Rosenbaum replied, "you are ensconced here in attorney's secrecy. You can speak as much in confidence here as I do with you in analysis."[88]

Jung described an ominous impending development. The Nazis were convening the upcoming Bad Nauheim conference for a specific purpose, the "Nazification of the statutes, i.e., the expulsion of the Jews." Jung knew it was "a resolution that cannot be avoided," but it put him in a dilemma: as president, he felt bound to attend "in the interest of his Jewish colleagues," and he was determined "to make a small contribution to try to save them." He then drew from his pocket a copy of the proposed statutes sent by Göring via Cimbal. He asked Rosenbaum to study the document carefully and write in any loopholes that might "mitigate the statute proposal and render the exclusion and extermination of Jewish colleagues as not so inevitable." Rosenbaum looked doubtful, but Jung kept insisting, "This is what I need to do!" Many years later, Rosenbaum recalled his feelings as he studied the document: "Now, I was very young then. The age difference between us was rather great and the relationship of respect was of course that of the patient toward his analyst. But all of that left me when I heard what he wanted me to do, and so I answered him as his lawyer." Rosenbaum tried to couch his thoughts politely by making a pun on Jung's name: "Pardon me, Herr Jung, but you really are *very young*." He wanted Jung to recognize his incredible naïveté in thinking he could hoodwink the Nazis. Jung turned on him "almost in a rage."

"How so?" he thundered. "Why do you say this?" Rosenbaum told Jung he was "caught in an illusion" and was powerless "to do anything that would help the Jews."[89] Jung was insistent: "I know this, but I want to! I must indeed try!" He entreated Rosenbaum to study the statutes and "revise them in the spirit of my intention." Rosenbaum acceded: "I considered whether to take on this assignment, then I said to myself, he'll go there anyway and if I don't do this for him someone else may do it badly. I thought I should at least try." So Rosenbaum "amused" himself as he created clauses to "fool the authors of these statutes in such a way that they would not notice it." He rewrote them until they were so ambiguous that multiple interpretations were possible for every single statement.

Rosenbaum wanted to straighten out something personal with Jung after he wrote the statutes, so he sent a letter thanking him for being a "gentle and wise guide" to him and his wife before he addressed his "one problem" with Jung.[90] Rosenbaum, imbued with the "hypertrophy of suspicion that a Jew can hardly shake . . . also suspected an 'anti-Semite'" in Jung. "This may be paradoxical," he continued, "but the misfortune that recently befell you in the outside world has taught me otherwise. For if you were an anti-Semite, you would precisely not have gotten yourself into a tight spot! . . . I am glad . . . that I can tell you this of all things at this very moment. Allow me kindly to shake your hand." He signed it "yours devotedly" and years afterward still chortled at the memory of how Jung went to Germany with statutes prepared "by me, the Jew Rosenbaum. I got that Nazi gathering to swallow statutes prepared by a Jew."[91]

Basically, the Rosenbaum document began with the premise that the German society should indeed function differently from all others because it had to comply with Nazi directives. It specified that Jewish members expelled from the German chapter could maintain individual membership in any international entity, whether they remained in Germany or relocated to the countries where they applied for membership.

Jung was delighted when he finessed his ruse at Bad Nauheim and all the statutes he proposed were adopted. The convention was otherwise politically uneventful, probably because Cimbal and Göring ordered their German colleagues not to wear Nazi decorations or give any "party character" to the proceedings.[92] The next issue of the *Zentralblatt* carried Jung's letter explaining that the organization would henceforth be constituted in national groups. Besides Germany, chapters had been or were in the process of being formed in Denmark, Holland, Sweden, and Switzerland. Requirements for membership varied "according to locally enforced statutes" and "political circumstances" in which "certain individuals are unable to join the corresponding groups."[93]

The next sentence contained the most important proviso, the one that Jung and Rosenbaum sneaked quietly into the statutes: "Therefore, the decision has been made that it is only optional to join a national group, i.e., it is possible to obtain an individual membership with the framework of the Überstaatliche allgemeine ärztliche Gesellschaft für Psychotherapie." This really meant that Jewish psychoanalysts could maintain professional status by joining the international organization as individual members. The Rosenbaum statutes had even wider resonance: when the DPG held its annual conference that summer in Luzern, Ernest Jones followed Jung's example and extended the same privilege to all Jewish members who had previously been forced to resign.[94]

Jung's gratitude toward Rosenbaum for his work on behalf of German Jews did not extend to helping Rosenbaum personally when he was in dire need.[95] In 1937, Rosenbaum was arrested and jailed for channeling money and munitions to anti-Franco forces in Spain, a violation of Swiss law. Freed after several months, he found himself penniless, disbarred, and divorced by Valangin. Needing to find his bearings, Rosenbaum went to Küsnacht to ask Jung if he could attend meetings of the Psychological Club. Jung was impressed with the individuation Rosenbaum recorded in his dreams and drawings while jailed, and he gave permission. Club members were furious and told Jung times were too perilous, that he must tell Rosenbaum to resign and never attend another meeting. Jung sent a letter asking Rosenbaum to come to Bollingen, where he greeted him at the gate but did not permit him to enter the compound. Without pleasantries, Jung said, "Even a mortally injured animal knows when to go off alone and die."[96] Rosenbaum reeled from Jung's venom but soon recovered his equanimity. He went to Ascona, where within several years, he was one of the most respected and important art and antique dealers in Switzerland. He owed his start to partial funding from Olga Fröbe, who so resented Jung's callousness that she always invited Rosenbaum to Eranos and seated him either next to Jung or in his direct line of vision. Jung never resumed cordial relations with Rosenbaum.

Those who strive for objectivity explain Jung's behavior as stemming from his "small bourgeois attitude" and "fear of the permanent threat of social discrimination within his community."[97] Rosenbaum became "the image of the socially discredited person," and therefore, at that time and in that place, Jung could not risk taking his side. His continued cooperation with Göring and company is thus all the more difficult to understand or explain, especially when negative attacks upon him intensified in Switzerland.

GUSTAV BALLY, a German psychoanalyst who fled when the Nazis branded him "hostile to the state,"[98] launched the first salvo in the *Neue Zürcher Zeitung* on February 27, 1934.[99] Bally argued that Jung's association with the International Society and his editorship of the conformed *Zentralblatt* legitimized the National Socialist view of "*deutschstämmige* [Germanic] psychology and psychiatry." Jung's distinction between German and Jewish traits contained no scientific value: his method of arriving at such a conclusion was muddled and the conclusion itself lacked any reasonable proof. Bally faulted Jung for not stating clearly that the discipline of psychotherapy had been created by both Jews and non-Jews and peoples of Roman as well as Germanic heritage. He warned Jung of the harm that would come from trying to cooperate with the Nazis: "The person who introduces himself with the racial question as the editor of a *gleichgeschaltete* [conformed] magazine has to be aware that his statements appear against a background of organized passion that will color the interpretation his words implicitly contain."

Several weeks later, the *Neue Zürcher Zeitung* published Jung's "Reply."[100] He explained that he was president "not of the *German* but of the *International* Society" (Jung's emphasis). He asked rhetorically whether he should have refused office and taken prudent refuge in Swiss neutrality and then answered that his personal moral code required him to "risk [his] skin and expose [himself] to the inevitable misunderstandings which no one escapes," saying that he was someone "who, from higher necessity, has to make a pact with the existing political powers in Germany." He concluded he had no choice "but to answer for [his] friends with the weight of [his] name and independent position."

Admitting that such a situation was probably difficult for citizens of the Swiss democracy to understand,[101] Jung described the German political situation, where "absolutely nothing can exist unless it has been *gleichgeschaltet* by the government." At this point, his rebuttal digressed into an amorphous comparison of various forms of totalitarianism, from Catholicism to Communism, with National Socialism the latest secular example. No person or group could exist under the Nazis without swearing allegiance to the state, "as any reasonable person will understand."

Jung explained that his editorial statement had been mistakenly printed in every edition of the *Zentralblatt*. He said he had given firm instructions to Cimbal that Göring's manifesto was to be printed for "exclusive circulation in Germany," but to his "great surprise and disappointment," it appeared in them all.

Jung did not doubt "there were inside political reasons for this," but he under-cut his own righteous indignation in his next sentence, dismissing the mix-up as "one of those lamentable tactical gaffes which were the bane of German foreign policy even in the Wilhelm era." He waffled further: because his name appeared "unexpectedly" in a journal that carried "so incriminating" an official Nazi manifesto, it put his editorship "in question." He hinted that he might have to resign, but no document has yet been found to suggest that he tried to do so at this time.

Jung admitted that he had been "incautious, so incautious as to the very thing most open to misunderstanding at the present moment . . . the Jewish question." He had a ready explanation for having done so:

> This I did deliberately. My esteemed critic appears to have forgotten that the first rule of psychotherapy is to talk in the greatest detail about all the things that are the most ticklish and dangerous, and the most misunder-stood. The Jewish problem is a regular complex, a festering wound, and no responsible doctor could bring himself to apply methods of medical hush-hush in this matter.

The puzzle is why Jung chose this critical moment to call attention "deliber-ately" to "the Jewish problem," for he knew the Nazis were using his psychol-ogy as fuel for their propaganda and fodder for their persecutions. Questions remain to this day: What made him think he could effect any change in Nazi at-titudes by bringing this "festering wound" into the open? Was it his belief that his international reputation was powerful enough to embarrass the Nazis into modifying their treatment of Jews if he merely proposed it? Was it political naïveté and a misguided belief that his personal moral sense was so overwhelm-ing that it would influence political zealots to reform? Or was it the simple hubris of his old schoolboy-self, "the Bull," "the Barrel," who always triumphed by riding roughshod over anyone or anything that stood in his way?

When Jung was trying to explain the Swiss national character in these same years, he described how his countrymen dealt with troubled situations, which he may have intended as a parallel for his own actions: "You must stand still and wait, as if you had to deal with animals. Just wait, and they will thaw."[102] Unfor-tunately for him, attacks hardened. The editors of the *Neue Zürcher Zeitung* prefaced the second part of Jung's rejoinder to Bally with a statement that they shared Bally's "astonishment" at Jung's view of the differences between "Christian-Germanic and Semitic psychology." Jung countered by insisting he did not "ac-knowledge racial psychology" and then reiterated the examples already cited, which, having previously inflamed his audience, now served to ignite it.

A Swiss Jewish periodical, the *Israelitisches Wochenblatt für die Schweiz*, took up the cudgels in March in the article "Ist C. G. Jung 'gleichgeschaltet'?"[103] Rather than risk legal action by accusations of outright collaboration with the

Nazis, the author provided a series of equivocations before he used Jung's own words to absolve him, that he was not an opponent of the Jews but merely an opponent of Freud and his theory, with its relentless insistence on sex as the root cause of all analytic problems.

Jung's friend James Kirsch, who had earlier warned him about thinking he could help Jews by cooperating with the Nazis, engaged in a dialogue with the analysts Erich Neumann and Gerhard Adler in the *Jüdische Rundschau*, a weekly newspaper with a large German Jewish circulation. Kirsch also wrote an article for the *Rundschau*, entitled "The Jewish Question in Psychotherapy," and asked Neumann to propose a dialogue with Jung on the same subject.[104] Jung agreed to cooperate, but the project was never realized.

The entire matter made him so angry that he wrote a long letter to Kirsch, explaining his actions.[105] He accused Kirsch of being "wide of the mark" when he interpreted Jung's general bad mood at the annual Eranos *Tagung* as anti-Semitism: "The objective results of the *Nauheimer Kongress* [i.e., the Rosenbaum statutes] prove beyond a doubt that I cannot be an anti-Semite." His next statement carried a barely veiled threat: if Kirsch did not accept his explanation, "then I will have to offer you witnesses and references who will confirm under oath the truthfulness of my statements." Jung used the word *"Beweisofferte,"* which translates as an "offer of evidence" and carries connotations of possible legal action.[106] That he would risk losing a friendship that meant so much to him by using this highly charged word shows how strongly he felt about the accusations.

By 1935, Jung's dilemma regarding Nazi Germany was shared by many other distinguished observers, among them Winston Churchill, who wrote that the verdict on how history would judge Hitler was still out:

> We cannot tell whether Hitler will be the man who will once again let loose upon the world another war in which civilisation will irretrievably succumb, or whether he will go down in history as the man who restored honour and peace of mind to the great Germanic nation and brought it back serene, helpful and strong, to the forefront of the European family circle.[107]

In the same year Churchill wrote this, Göring chose to tighten the screws that bound Jung to Nazi Germany. Cimbal and Göring, under the aegis of the German National Group, which really dictated how the International Society operated, suddenly became "most interested in the *Zentralblatt*."[108] All his professional life, Jung had been impatient with administrative responsibilities, and in this instance his lack of direct involvement permitted evasion, equivocation, and direct manipulation of his views to flourish.

To free himself from the detailed work that editing required, Jung forced the German group to accept his Zürich colleague C. A. "Fredy" Meier as the equivalent of a managing editor/secretary. For more than a year, Jung begged, threatened, and cajoled Göring to pay Meier an annual salary of Sfr120 (approximately $25 at the time) in compensation for the many hours he toiled to ensure that the publication remained as politically neutral as Jung could make it and still survive German censorship. Jung considered the "Reviews" section as important as the articles, for he used it to keep Germans apprised of new research being done elsewhere. As so much of it contradicted Nazi conformity, Göring was determined to get rid of the entire section, and when he found out that Jung secretly employed the Jewish Allers to write the reviews, he had the perfect excuse to eliminate the section entirely.[109]

The debate shifted to the national groups when the Dutch chapter, which had earlier agreed to host the 1936 congress, became alarmed at Nazi politics and withdrew the offer. At this point and for the first time, Jung did submit his resignation: "Since Holland disavows the true purpose of the *Internationale Gesellschaft* with this decision, and since the Dutch national group is the second largest . . . I am compelled to take my leave as the chairman . . . as it is hopeless to sustain an international organization under these circumstances."[110] He resigned because of the "fairly threadbare reasons" of the Dutch, which he interpreted as a stinging rebuke and signal of their belief he had "conformed." As he did in so many instances during these years,[111] he replied with a standard defense, blaming "a Freudian propaganda campaign [in Holland] against me personally."

He told Göring that resigning from the presidency would mean allowing the *Zentralblatt* to "revert to the German national group" with which the individual societies would henceforth have to negotiate. Some curious equivocation followed when he said his resignation "of course does not mean that I will break my ties to Germany," as he expressed hope to "at least succeed in maintaining the relationship between our Swiss group and Germany." Whether he wrote this as the polite discourse that brings a letter to a close, whether it was related to his ongoing efforts to ease the plight of German Jews, or even whether he hoped that Göring might persuade him to rescind his resignation, the comment is inscrutable.

Göring had a ready answer as 1936 dawned: he would cancel the congress entirely unless the Dutch agreed to the face-saving gesture of allowing it to be convened in conjunction with the Gesellschaft für innere Medizin, the Society for Internal Medicine, which planned to meet in a Swiss city.[112] To reel Jung back in, Göring invited him to Wiesbaden in March on society business, and Jung went, revoking his resignation in the process: "I will keep my post in this losing battle and hope for better times."[113]

WHILE JUNG was in Wiesbaden, "Wotan," his most controversial essay yet, was published in Zürich. Jung was continuing the argument with Bally that raged in the *Neue Zürcher Zeitung*, but he published instead in the *Neue Schweizer Rund-schau*, believing that if he defined his position once and for all, it would vindicate him of charges of anti-Semitism.[114] He used the methodology of psychoanalysis to explain to his democratic countrymen how contemporary political events were linked to a renewal of the spirit of the ancient Germanic god of war. He described the phenomenon as *Ergriffenheit*, the state of being seized or pos-sessed, and distinguished between the "*Ergriefer* (one who seizes) and the *Er-griffener* (one who is seized)."

Jung used the god Wotan as the *Ergriefer* to make a direct attack on Hitler as *Ergriffener.* Jung thought the most "impressive thing" about the current "*furor teutonicus*" was "that one man, who is obviously 'possessed,' has infected a whole nation to such an extent that everything is set in motion and has started rolling on its course to perdition."[115] He referred to a cartoon in *Punch* depicting Hitler as "a raving berserker tearing himself free from his bonds." To Jung's dis-may, Hitler had unleashed "a hurricane . . . in Germany while we [Swiss] still believe it is fine weather":[116]

> The Swiss do have their problems but they would not admit it for anything in the world, even though they see which way the wind is blowing. We thus pay our tribute to the time of storm and stress in Germany, but we never mention it, and this enables us to feel vastly superior.[117]

THROUGHOUT 1937, criticism of Jung and chicanery among the Germans con-tinued in equal parts. Criticism began with Axel von Muralt's assault upon "Wotan," which he continued verbally and in print throughout the next decade.[118] His main charge was that Jung was reducing the real danger of Na-tional Socialism by passing it off as just another ordinary religious movement. In 1946, with perfect hindsight, von Muralt declared Jung's ultimate failure to be his unwillingness to warn the world of Hitler's evil, and he damned the entire essay as little more than "a stab in the back from Switzerland" for those Ger-mans who did try to resist.

Chicanery consisted mainly of machinations connected with the *Zentralblatt*, most of them causing personal embarrassment to Jung. Articles from neutral countries that he accepted were either not published by the German editors or else so heavily rewritten that they contradicted the authors' intention. Authors were almost never allowed to read their galleys before publication, a precaution taken by the German editors who had "conformed" them. Naturally, the angry writers blamed Jung, furthering charges of his Nazi collusion. Hirzel, the jour-nal's publisher, was capricious at best, financially devious at worst. There were protracted delays on every front, which Hirzel always blamed on the printer, and he, too, was not above altering a text even more than the editors and pub-lisher. Several years after Göring agreed that Hirzel should pay Meier Sfr120 annually, Meier had yet to be paid, and no one knew what Hirzel had done with the money. When Meier threatened to resign, Jung threatened to do so as well.[119]

Cimbal had been succeeded as editor of the German *Zentralblatt* by Otto Curtius,[120] who Jung thought was more deceitful and disruptive than his predecessor, especially after he proposed tongue in cheek that *Rasse und Tiefenpsychologie* (Race and Depth Psychology) should be the topic of the next annual conference.[121] Curtius took malicious glee in taunting Jung, who he knew was weary of defending himself against the onslaught of attacks.[122]

Jung kept insisting, as he had done emphatically in the Bally exchange in the *Neue Zürcher Zeitung*, that he was not acknowledging the validity of "racial psychology" but merely defending a psychology of national identity and the collective and individual behavior that resulted from it. He well knew the subject was a political loaded cannon he would be wise not to fire, but he still considered it a topic of viable scientific interest. When a Swedish correspondent asked him why he opposed the study of racial psychology, Jung said what was required was "a very thorough formulation of the differences of national psychologies" to "challenge all the different political convictions that are actually raging in Europe." As far as he was concerned, any and all conference discussions of the topic were "absolutely out of the question."[123]

Still needing Jung's affiliation, Göring assured him the topic would never be chosen. He saw that Hirzel paid Meier, put Curtius on a tighter leash, and wrote repeatedly to both Meier and Jung that "[Jung] is indispensible to me."[124] Jung continued his presidency, probably because he was away from Europe throughout 1937 and had so few direct dealings with the Germans. However, he was in Berlin that September, when Mussolini came to meet Hitler. Although Jung did attend some of the public political ceremonies, including a parade to review troops and weapons that allowed him to observe the two dictators firsthand, he was there primarily to give private lectures to the C. G. Jung Gesellschaft.[125] "Out there, archetypes are already walking in the streets," he told the members.[126]

But as time passed, his ready excuse for ignoring his society responsibilities was the extensive travel connected with lecturing and receiving honorary degrees. Also, after the Indian trip, his health was weakened by amoebic dysentery, so his energy was finite.[127] In the little time he had at home, he wanted to concentrate on the alchemical writings that now consumed his interest, and he became angry if Meier even tried to discuss society business. Red-faced and shouting, Jung would yell, "You are being paid to look after this — you sort it out!," thus ending all discussion.[128]

As 1938 progressed, circumstances dictated that he could no longer remain aloof from the society's internal politics. Despite Göring's objections to a non-German holding the position, Jung persuaded Dr. Hugh Crichton-Miller[129] to accept the vice presidency of the International Society. He specifically invited

Crichton-Miller in the hope of strengthening British influence, and at the same time, he asked Peter Baynes to write something for the *Zentralblatt* with a two-fold purpose: to denote the international character of the journal, and to reinforce the strong presence of a British national group.[130] He hoped to counter Göring's insistence that the next conference be held somewhere in Germany, so he asked the newly formed British society (of which Crichton-Miller was a member) to host it in London. There followed a diplomatically phrased correspondence in which Peter Baynes, on behalf of the entire British group, asked for clarification: "These good conventional English people are searching for precedents. They want to know what standing the International Congress for Psychotherapy actually has."[131]

Göring disapproved, but when all the other societies approved a British venue, he could not impose his will.[132] Still, the British organizing committee refused to make a firm commitment until the German delegation offered specifics "with regard to the participation of non-Aryan lecturers."[133] Jung reminded Göring of the Rosenbaum statutes, in which "the umbrella organization is politically and religiously neutral" and all members "enjoy the same rights at international congresses." He personally advised the British that Aryan and non-Aryan guests were entitled to attend but both must avoid any allusion to political matters.[134] If they disobeyed, he said he would stop their lecture and personally eject them. The British gave assurance there would be no direct criticism of or insult to the German contingent; now Jung needed Göring's guarantee that the Germans would behave themselves and honor his directives. "The question of race," he concluded, "is an internal German affair which only has to be respected within German borders."

Negotiations were protracted,[135] but conciliations and concessions were agreed upon, and the congress was actually held in Oxford, July 29–August 2, to coincide with Jung's receiving an honorary doctorate from the university. Peter Baynes took an active role in coordinating Jung's schedule so he could participate in both university festivities and society meetings. Even though Baynes engaged a "professional secretary," Jung was still "rather over-organized," which was his way of saying Baynes had overly programmed every moment. Both Emma and Toni accompanied Jung, and Baynes took care of them as well by foisting them onto various wives who organized outings and chauffeured them to lectures.

Baynes conveyed the news that Freud had escaped to England, but all the details reached Jung filtered through a handful of people who had no firsthand knowledge of the circumstances. Baynes also reported on the "flood tide" in London of the "six or seven other analysts" who had recently escaped from Vienna after experiencing a similar "terrible time."[136] Gossip had it that Freud was about to open a practice, as was his daughter Anna.

There is a story that accompanies Freud's arrival in London during the Oxford ceremonies, parts of which are true, parts apocryphal. Allegedly, Franz

Riklin Jr. was sent to Vienna some months before Freud's departure by either (depending on who tells the story) Jung and Riklin Sr. (who each allegedly contributed $5,000) or rich Swiss Jewish businessmen (who raised the same amount). The money was to pay for Freud's move to Switzerland and support him after he settled there.[137] To date, no documentary evidence has been found to verify that this actually happened, and if it did, no evidence connects Jung with it.[138] But when Jung heard that Freud was safely in London, he immediately ordered a telegram to be sent welcoming him on behalf of the International Society. From that point, depending again on who tells the story, the greetings either did not arrive or were never sent at all. The mishap was blamed upon either Baynes's "professional secretary," one "Gibbs-Smith"; Curtius, as secretary of the International Society; or an unnamed secretary from somewhere within the Oxford University administration.[139] As time passed, the onus for this embarrassing episode was placed only on Jung, who was accused of deliberately snubbing his former mentor.

As GÖRING predicted, Jung was reelected president at the Oxford conference,[140] and he implored Jung to accept it: "At this time no one but you can represent our association. I am convinced that other psychotherapeutic movements would try to dominate our association if you do not remain its chairman. Also, for political reasons I think it best if the chairman comes from a small neutral state."[141]

Jung agreed to remain in office and was soon embroiled in other controversies. Göring's sixtieth birthday was April 5, 1939, and members of the German Society wanted the *Zentralblatt* to carry "some words of greeting."[142] "Baumann" (otherwise unidentified) asked Meier to secure "a few words [from] C. G.," attesting to the fact that Jung "agrees to the photo." He referred to one of Göring, on the back of which Göring himself had written, "Retouch to erase party badge," evidence that he was privy to the scheme and wanted a homage to appear in every edition. What followed is mired in controversy. By 1939, except for an occasional brief letter, Jung left all society correspondence to Meier, and no documentation has yet been found to confirm that he knew of the Göring tribute until Meier told him in late January.[143] Jung said he would "think about it" and let Meier know what, if anything, "the entire Swiss society" should contribute. On March 9, Curtius, who had not yet heard from either Meier or Jung, sent Meier a "requested draft about the activities of Professor Göring in Berlin."[144] No letter has yet been found to determine if Meier or Jung actually did "request" any such draft.

On March 10, 1939, Baumann sent a second document to Zürich detailing the development of a newly constituted Deutsches Institut für Psychologische Forschung und Psychotherapie, the German Institute for Psychological Research and Psychotherapy, another "conformed" institute that Göring created to engulf all previously nonconformed organizations, with himself as director.

Baumann praised Göring for combining psychiatry and *Erbforschungslehre*, loosely translated as the "study of hereditariness," and the latest euphemism for anti-Semitism. Jung and Meier ignored this document, so the March 9 statement the Zürichers had allegedly "requested" became the starting point for the text that eventually appeared in the *Zentralblatt*.

It consisted of two typed, single-spaced pages, similar to the one in the *Zentralblatt* under the signatures of Curtius, Jung, and Meier, but far more effusive than the printed version.[145] The original expresses "profound gratitude and admiration" to Göring for bringing German psychotherapy into "an entirely new stage, which one would not have dared to hope for just three years ago." The printed version merely states that German psychotherapy "has undoubtedly entered a new phase. Three years ago nobody could have hoped that this would come to pass." However, the printed statement ends with an effusive wish that seriously compromised the neutrality of the Swiss signers, that Göring might enjoy "a successful conclusion to the task he has undertaken to fulfill."

From the day it was published to the present time, Curtius and Meier were all but forgotten and Jung was reviled as the sole author. His critics ask how he could have consented to add his name to such a document in the spring of 1939, when he had several years of direct knowledge of Nazi atrocities. He knew that in 1937, Olga Fröbe's brain-damaged daughter was taken from the German institution where she lived and was murdered.[146] In October 1938, the Nazis "approved Swiss suggestions" for a "special passport stamp for Jews," a large "J" for *Jude*.[147] Jung read several Swiss newspapers daily, so he was aware of the articles praising customs officials who turned back "refugees" and other "hordes" at the borders every day, as well as the letters from indignant citizens who approved of such action.[148] He had many patients who thought this a fine policy and told him so. On the other hand, his defenders ask, what else could he have done but sign the greetings, as he was still working behind the scenes to help displaced Jews professionally as well as personally. Interestingly, no one on either side of the argument refers to the infamous *Kristallnacht* pogrom of November 9, 1938, after which it became frighteningly clear that nothing could be done within Nazi Germany to effect any change in the status of Jews who remained there.

Still, Jung's unpublished correspondence from 1934 onward contains many copies of official *Atteste*, notarized statements submitted to the *Fremdenpolizei*, the Swiss government agency responsible for admitting foreigners to the country. In many, Jung guaranteed that if for any reason these persons were unable to support themselves, he would assume all financial responsibility. These *Atteste* were signed on behalf of persons who range from those totally unknown today to those well known in the Jungian community, among them the French theorist Roland Cahan, and Jung's old friend Jolande Jacobi.[149] Jung treated many Jewish patients without charge once they managed to get into Switzerland, among them Aniela Jaffé, who later became his secretary and collaborator on his autobiography.[150]

Letters abound similar to one he wrote to Heinrich Zimmer on the eve of his immigration to the United States, telling him of persons he had contacted on Zimmer's behalf.[151] And he wrote many more to persons in England and the United States, often ordering them to *"help this Jew"* (his emphasis).[152] In December 1938, he replied to a deeply upsetting letter from Erich Neumann, who asked if Jung could possibly understand how difficult it was "to maintain an inner relationship with a man who naturally feels, at most, a superficial connection to the events that injure all of us Jews."[153] Jung asked how Neumann could ever think him "retired to the snow-covered heights, above world events." He reaffirmed how right he had been years ago when he predicted the "awful things" happening in Germany, even though they were still incomprehensible. Everyone in Switzerland, he insisted, was "deeply shocked" by events there. As for himself: "I have a lot to do with Jewish refugees and am permanently occupied with finding a place for all my Jewish acquaintances in England and in America. In this way I am in continuous connection with the events of our time."[154]

These personal efforts may not have brought extraordinary public result, but they gave Jung great satisfaction. Even as he was stymied by Göring on every front, he in turn tried all sorts of countermanding measures. Within the international group, Germany appeared isolated by an invisible barrier that no other society wanted to cross. Having bested Göring by holding the last congress in England, Jung thwarted him again when he persuaded the Dutch to host the next one in Utrecht (but war began, and it did not take place until 1951 in Leiden). Delegates from each national group were deciding when and where they should convene to plan the Utrecht program, and as everyone wanted to boycott German territory, Jung persuaded them to come to Switzerland. He was concerned that some of the national groups, particularly the British, did not realize how desperate the situation had become, so he begged Crichton-Miller to join the delegation as a needed "representative of higher reason." He told Crichton-Miller that he was tired of charges that he was a "secret Nazi agent" when, quite to the contrary, he was "no *persona grata* but rather a *persona suspecta*."[155] He did the same with Baynes, begging him to make a "flying visit" to Zürich to help wield counterinfluence against the Germans.[156]

Jung's main reason for convening the delegates away from Germany was that, after six years of trying to effect change, he was tired and wanted to quit. As his successor was unlikely to come from a neutral nation, he hoped to install a non-German. He had already offended the Germans by selecting Zürich as the meeting place; once there, they were outraged by the British delegate Eric Strauss, a German Jew now residing in England, who rejected the harsh dictates Göring was attempting to impose on all national groups to bring them into conformity with National Socialism.[157]

Now it was Meier's turn to cajole Göring. He urged him not to be upset by British suggestions "dictated by the prejudiced Jew Strauss." He guaranteed there would be no further "sharp attacks," because "for the most part *we* are sharply against it."[158] As secretary, Meier had been using the plural pronoun for years to convince others that he spoke for Jung. Many years later, when asked specifically about this letter and the possible anti-Semitism it contained, Meier explained that he and Jung agreed here on one primary point: there should be no attacks by any one national group upon any other; that above all, the society had to remain operational. If, Meier said, his language in this letter was "unfortunate with hindsight," it was nevertheless "necessary at the time to soothe Göring."[159]

Remarks such as these only strengthened contentions that Jung was a Nazi sympathizer. Delegates were further convinced he was in cahoots with the Nazis when he invited Göring and Curtius to a small private dinner in his home. When the delegates related this to their national groups, it was considered proof. A contingent loyal to the Dutch president, J. H. van der Hoop, charged him with telling Jung he had to resign.[160]

Jung could not have agreed more. He tendered his resignation for the second time at the July 1939 meeting, but the Nazi bureaucracy was so rigid and obfuscated that the paperwork to put it through dragged on for a year. Meier had to do the majority of it and was so overwhelmed that his *Zentralblatt* duties paled in comparison.[161] Göring still wanted to delay, if not prevent, Jung's resignation, which may have contributed to the paperwork delay. Göring dispatched Crichton-Miller in his capacity as international vice president to tell van der Hoop that "Jung is a convincing personality and is acknowledged in the world as no one else is, apart from Freud."[162]

Göring then told Jung he could not resign until he finished the paperwork admitting new groups in Italy, Hungary, and Japan. Jung knew these Axis societies would always vote with Germany, thus giving the Nazis enough votes to enforce *Gleichschaltung*. At the delegates' meeting in Zürich, several spoke angrily about Germany's "special position" and objected to admitting these groups. Jung replied that it was no longer his concern; he had just completed his second three-year term as president, and according to the statutes, he had to resign irrevocably. Göring immediately jumped in, saying no new election could take place among the delegates but must be held before a full convention; therefore, Jung must continue to serve until the next congress. Jung was anxious to distance himself from the Germans and suggested he be "honorary president." Göring was delighted with such a fiction: he would control the power and Jung would remain the figurehead. The delegates, whatever their impression of the true situation, unanimously accepted Jung's suggestion. Thus, between July 1939 and September 1940, when his resignation was officially accepted, Jung continued to be what he had always been, a figurehead but with a different title. For Göring and his cohorts it was business as usual.

However, the Germans once again needed a political spin. When Curtius wrote his account of the delegates' assembly for the *Zentralblatt*, he said no presidential election had taken place, nor had there even been any discussion of one. Without elaborating, he announced that henceforth all business concerning the International Society would be handled in Berlin. Again, Göring solidified full control, effectively neutering Jung. Not content to stop there, Curtius did Jung further damage in international eyes by writing that as honorary president, he was solely responsible for the admission of chapters from Italy, Hungary, and Japan, all of whom would help "determine" the next president. These two tasks were interconnected, "since the future president will also have to have the trust of the newly admitted national groups."[163]

War began in September 1939, and all the national societies operated in isolation until September 1940. Then, without consulting the other societies, Göring summoned delegates to a meeting in Vienna attended only by delegates from Axis countries and announced plans to admit chapters from Japan, Bulgaria, and Romania.[164] Göring's action created an irreparable breach between the International Society and the German chapter.

During the Vienna meeting, Göring got wind of Jung's Yale Terry Lectures and also of an interview he had given to the American journalist H. R. Knickerbocker, "Diagnosing the Dictators."[165] These writings may have been the convenient excuse Göring sought to discredit Jung, for it was he who placed Jung's name on the *Schwarze Liste* of authors whose work was banned in Germany, and, by extension, the *Otto Liste*, banning him in occupied France as well.[166]

Jung's third attempt to resign the presidency occurred with his official letter, dated July 12, 1940,[167] which Göring finally accepted. In it, Jung said all International Society activity should be suspended until the war ended. As the British Crichton-Miller could no longer serve as vice president, he asked Meier to take care of any necessary business until the next convention — if Göring should persist in calling one. Jung said his resignation as president meant that his name should disappear from the masthead of the *Zentralblatt* as well. He concluded with the hope that after his "seven not particularly easy years" as president, the society would be able to "reorient" itself for future viability without him. As for himself, he remained content with "the satisfaction of having supported my German friends at a difficult moment."

IN 1934, Jung received a letter from a woman inquiring about his typology. With hindsight, it provides a capsule description of the stain upon his reputation ever after. He told the woman his presidency had aroused a "terrific shindy" and that no one could have had "anything to do with Germany without becoming politically suspect on one side or the other."[168]

And yet, Jung brought upon himself much of the opprobrium that haunted him the rest of his life by choosing to explain — over and over again — aspects of his theory of cultural types in an era fraught with tension and peril. In less sensitive times, his remarks might have been perceived as relatively harmless, if not innocuous, but when set against official Nazi policy, they became charged with a meaning he swore he never intended to convey. Jung could have stopped talking, writing, or explaining, which might perhaps have allowed the controversies to die down, but he did not, which was quite in character for him. His professional life to this point had been one of staking independent positions (most notably against Freud's theory) simply because he believed them to be right and then holding on to them, no matter the consequence. Some saw this quality as sheer arrogance; others (who may not have agreed with his views) nevertheless respected his integrity. In this particular instance, his personality worked against him, especially his occasional coarseness of sensibility and his tendency to bully. For a man of such highly attuned sensitivity in the consulting room, within the larger world he was often insensitive to the feelings of others and did not recognize the damage his words could do. He was also a product of a particular moment in his Swiss culture, and he represented much that was not its finest, particularly the attitude of the time toward foreigners, refugees, and especially Jews.

All this must be factored into the equation of any future assessment of Jung's true role in German psychoanalysis throughout the 1930s. There is always the hope that new documentation will surface to provide conclusive answers, but until a definitive portrait can be painted, his 1934 summation of his plight remains tragic, true, and lasting: "I have fallen afoul of contemporary history."

CHAPTER 30

Rooted in Our Soil

Zürich was festive during the summer of 1939. The *Landesausstellung*, a national exhibition held once every twenty-five years, was so grand that it filled both sides of Lake Zürich. Large crowds from throughout the country and the rest of Europe came to see the showcase for Swiss technological achievement, industrial development, and the many foods and products for which the country was justly famous.[1] Exhibition halls ringed the lake's left bank, and restaurants and entertainment venues the right. The two shores were connected by a *Schwebebahn*, a cable car that crossed over a *Schifflibach*, an artificial stream that carried small boats ferrying those who did not want to walk through the exhibition's vast spaces. Jung loved everything, particularly the *Dörfli*, villagelike settings for the small restaurant chalets built in the style of the various cantons and serving regional specialties.[2] Emma went once and then stayed at home while the enthusiastic Jung and Toni Wolff made repeated visits, mostly to restaurants.[3]

This grandest of all *Landesaustellung* was specifically intended to represent general Swiss optimism — or, more accurately, wishful thinking — that Hitler would somehow be appeased and war avoided. Yet there was an ominous precedent: the last one, held in Bern in 1914, was interrupted by World War I. So when Germany invaded Poland on September 1, 1939, not only did another "great thing come to an end," but also "an epoch of life passed which could never be the same."[4] Optimism gave way to the fear that German-speaking Switzerland would be the next victim of Hitler's quest for *Lebensraum*. It was already widely known that German maps included Switzerland as part of the *Grossdeutsches Reich*, and in the context of Nazi racist ideology, the German-speaking Swiss were considered *Volksdeutsch*, or ethnic Germans.[5]

The German assumption that the Swiss would be eager for *Anschluss*, incorporation into the Reich, was encouraged throughout the 1930s by numerous groups that patterned themselves after similar Nazi organizations. Alarming photos had been appearing steadily in print since 1933, none more dramatic than that of the Zürich *Tonhalle* festooned with Nazi banners, the arms of the standing-room-only crowd thrust aloft in the Nazi salute.[6] The followers of Wilhelm Gustloff, known as the "Swiss Führer," grew steadily even after he was assassinated by a disgruntled Yugoslavian Jew in 1936. Many Swiss parents enrolled their children in Gustloff's youth groups, patterned after the *Hitler Jugend* and the *Bund deutscher Mädel*, until after the war was well under way. Jung told his children to tell everyone they knew to avoid such groups, and he denounced them in lectures and analytic sessions.[7]

The danger of invasion was greatest in early 1940, when Germany extracted harsh concessions from a vacillating national government.[8] The Swiss federal president, Marcel Pilet-Golaz, represented the mood of many when he declared it would be in Switzerland's best interest to adjust to the "New Europe,"[9] a euphemism for acceding to new Nazi demands. His faction had already passed a law in 1938 that marked passports of Jewish refugees with a large "J," which the Nazis eagerly adopted that same year. The Nazis took it one step further by exerting pressure on the Swiss to close their borders, and by 1942, the now-infamous declaration "the Boat is full"[10] was a Swiss commonplace. All through the war, though, the Swiss used a self-deprecating joke to describe their situation as a neutral country in a continent consumed by war: they may have worked for the Nazis during the week but they prayed for the Allies on Sunday.[11]

The Nazis were less successful in persuading the Swiss to enforce complete censorship upon publications. They did not take into consideration the fact that the majority of the four hundred or so Swiss newspapers as well as the citizens who read them were imbued with the rock-solid insistence upon neutrality that exemplified the national character.[12] Journalists such as Jung's schoolboy friend Albert Oeri, now a member of parliament and editor of the *Basler Nachrichten*, clashed perilously with Nazi-leaning censors who officially defamed him, sabotaged his presses, and threatened his life repeatedly.[13] Throughout all this, he and Jung became closer than they had been in years as they pondered together what responses Oeri should make to specific situations.[14]

With a total population of slightly over four million, the Swiss could mobilize an army of citizen soldiers of about 850,000, hardly enough to dent what appeared to be German invincibility. Knowing the Swiss could not resist attack, Pilet-Golaz preached appeasement even as the army commander-in-chief, General Henry Guisan, took another tack. Guisan called his officers to a meeting in the historic Rütli Meadow, where the *Ewiger Bund*, the everlasting bond of confederation, had been declared on August 1, 1291.[15] In a moment of symbolic importance, Guisan rejected accommodation (*Anpassung*) and instructed his officers not only to fight to the death (*Wiederstand*) but also, if defeat seemed imminent, to destroy the country's entire transportation system, its roads, tunnels, and railways. The line of defense was the *Limmatstellung*, a line loosely drawn near the Limmat River, which runs through Zürich: the fighting men assembled in mountain redoubts to the south of it, while the women, children, and aged were left to fend as best they could in the cantons bordering Germany, Zürich among them.[16]

JUNG WAS sixty-five in 1940, five years too old for active military duty and feeling like "a heap of scrap iron, rusty and deformed."[17] As every doctor under sixty was posted elsewhere, he was drafted as both psychiatrist and general practitioner for Zürich and the villages along the western bank of the lake. The relentless stream of needy patients was exhausting, especially after so many years of setting his daily schedule and following his own professional interests. Also, he still suffered from lingering effects of amoebic dysentery and seemed unlikely to regain his usual robust health. His doctor warned that the illness had damaged his heart and ordered protective measures. By February 1939, Jung tired so easily that he canceled his English seminars at the Psychological Club without warning, using the excuse that five years of interpreting Nietzsche's *Zarathustra* was quite enough. Those who knew him best could see how drastically he had aged, and they worried that the cancellation was due more to the exhaustion of his body than of his intellectual curiosity.[18] Still, he completed the more demanding lectures at the ETH in the spring term and resumed again in the autumn, this time addressing "The Exercitia Spiritualia of St. Ignatius of Loyola."[19]

Emma did not undertake any public responsibilities during the war, but Toni Wolff volunteered for the *Frauenhilfsdienst*, an auxiliary of women whose main duty consisted of learning to drive ambulances and other service vehicles on the off chance they would be needed.[20] Then in her fifties, Toni was excused from the rigorous two-week training school required of women between the ages of eighteen and forty. She was also in declining health, afflicted with hardening of the arteries and arthritis that deformed her hands and feet and made all movement painful. She was a lifelong chain-smoker, and her breathing was seriously impaired, but she insisted her damaged lungs resulted from medication, not from smoking. Despite her ailments, she put her own car into the service of the corps and proudly wore her uniform (which she had to buy herself), paying no heed to those who teased her that her bad driving was a more fearsome danger to public security than any wartime atrocity.[21]

As a physician, Jung was entitled to a ration of gasoline, which he used until he was relieved of most of his general practice early in 1941.[22] Emma had already put the family sedan up on blocks, and shortly after, he did the same with his Chrysler "Red Darling." When he lectured at the ETH, Jung walked the mile from his house to the Küsnacht station, descending at Stadelhofen station and walking to the Bellevue tram stop, then reversing the trek homeward at the end of the day. He brushed off his exhaustion as the necessary adjunct of walking for the exercise his doctor prescribed. He tried to dismiss his general physical weakness, as when he told Katy Cabot that his doctor said it was merely "an exhaustion of the heart muscle, caused by too much fat."[23] He was overweight and would have to diet, he added, which would not be difficult under wartime rationing.

In truth, photos from the time show how gaunt he was and how loosely his clothes hung upon his stooped frame. He also grumbled about the extra physical labor entailed by war, such as tending the old coal furnace, but no one took his complaints seriously, as Müller and the maids still took care of everything. Müller, the general handyman who had been with the family for years, now took on farming to comply with the "Wahlen Plan," which required anyone who had a bit of land to plant something on it.[24] On the long stretch of lawn that led from the front of the house to the street, Müller planted potatoes, onions, and other hardy vegetables. As war shortages intensified, most of the rest of the lawn surrounding the house was tilled for planting necessary staples for what had become a large household. With the agricultural battlefront of *Anbauschlacht* in full force, the government advised citizens to stockpile enough provisions to last a year. The Jungs estimated they had ample land to provide about three-quarters of the fresh fruits and vegetables they would need for little more than half a year. Many friends and former patients volunteered to help, and as long as mail came from the outside world, they received parcels of everything from Jung's favorite English tobacco to an occasional cheese or tinned meat.[25] When Mary Mellon wrote from Pittsburgh to ask what she could send, Jung said they really needed coal, which he well knew she could not provide. He told her there would be no shortage of milk and meat unless the Germans invaded the country and robbed it, and that Switzerland could be self-supporting if only people would eat one-fifth less of everything. Nevertheless, Jung was fearful: "Germany will destroy us. One does not quite see what good it would do to her. But we understand that reason is not just the criterium [*sic*] by which one should or could appreciate German mentality."

France had fallen when Jung wrote this, and he was in despair over the "complete moral crash" of the country's capitulation. "We are all in prison now," he added. "God save our souls! Which [are] more important than butter."[26]

FRANZ JUNG and the husbands of Agathe, Marianne, and Lil were called for military duty in autumn 1939. Gret, her husband, and their four sons were living in Paris, where he was manager of a Swiss business that required him to stay on post. Gret brought the little boys home, to live on the top floor of the Küsnacht house for the duration. Franz's wife, Lilly, was pregnant, and she, too, joined her in-laws. From September 1939 until May 1940, the Jung family lived much like the rest of Europe, "in a kind of suspended animation, waiting to be invaded."[27] Like many others in Zürich, they took the precaution of buying gas masks. In May, when France and the Low Countries fell, German troops were poised on the border, and news trickled out that invasion would come in June. Late that month, the entire family, some of their friends, and many of Jung's patients, took to the roads and joined the exodus toward the mountains. The Jungs, their daughters, their heavily pregnant daughter-in-law, and all the grandchildren settled in a pension Emma had prudently rented sometime earlier outside the village of Saanen in the Bernese Oberland. In early July, Lilly Jung gave birth there to her second son, Peter.

Emma had been urging family flight long before they actually went, but Jung would not abandon the medical practice he had been assigned. When they finally left, departure was abrupt and only because of a dramatic telephone call from a still-unidentified government official in Bern. The man warned Jung that his name was on the Nazi *Schwarze Liste* of persons who were to be arrested, incarcerated, or worse — he left other possibilities unsaid — as soon as the Germans occupied Switzerland. He urged Jung to go into hiding at once.[28]

At the time they went to Saanen, many of Jung's friends and former patients were imploring him to leave Switzerland and settle in the United States. Jung told them all much the same as he told Dr. Merrill Moore, a poet and physician he had met at Harvard: "I don't dream of leaving my country. We are pretty much rooted in our soil which we certainly wouldn't give up for our personal safety. Moreover I am . . . a patriarch of a whole clan of children and grandchildren which I'm not going to leave in the lurch."[29]

After several weeks in Saanen, Jung grew restless. The family stayed, but in late summer he began to commute to Küsnacht during the week. His general practice had been officially reduced, so he filled his analytic calendar with as many private patients as it could accommodate. On weekends he returned to Saanen, a routine he followed until winter was setting in and everyone was persuaded that it was safe to go home. They were all shocked when first Basel, then Zürich, were bombed by the Allies in December 1940. They only relaxed when the precision bombing "incapacitate[d]" specific industrial targets, and no further "accidental" bombings hit until the war was nearly over.[30] German invasion seemed indefinitely postponed, so everyone grew complacent, and daily life settled into the pattern it followed throughout the war. Marie-Louise von Franz remembered the war years as "a wonderful time, really," for all those confined to Switzerland: "All the foreigners couldn't come any more, so Jung was not overrun and had time for his writing. It was a quiet time and we who stayed saw much more of him."[31]

Those who stayed included many Americans married to Swiss citizens, among them Mary Rüfenacht-Bancroft, Mary Briner-Ramsey, and Carol Baumann-Sawyer. Those who had lived most of their lives abroad also stayed, including Mary Foote, Catharine Cabot, and her daughter, Jane Cabot Reid. Barbara Hannah was unique among Jung's "spinsters," for she chose to remain when all the other British citizens boarded "the English train" that took them home. Others, like Cary Baynes, her daughter, Ximena, and her sister, Henri Zinno, returned first to New York and, later, to a permanent home in Connecticut.

Mary and Paul Mellon stayed until Germany invaded Denmark and Holland in May 1940, when their advisors insisted they leave. They went reluctantly because, like so many others, they assumed Europe would adjust to forced occupation, and life would go on. Mary Mellon, in particular, had begun planning projects to publish Jung's work in English, and she fully intended to return once things "stabilized." As early as June 10, it was clear the Mellons could not return,[32] and she sent Jung numerous anxious and apologetic cables. He replied soothingly that it was "alright" [sic] for them to stay in the United States.[33]

The departure of so many trusted friends and associates resulted in Jung and Emma's more intense involvement with the Psychological Club and Frau Fröbe's Eranos meetings. Competitions accelerated, first between Toni Wolff and Linda Fierz to see who could command the most power in governing the club. The "horrid atmosphere"[34] was further infected by the sharp division within the membership among the minority, who were overt Nazi supporters, and the majority, whose political views ranged somewhere between neutrality and indifference. The division was apparent as early as 1938, when J. W. Hauer, Jung's former collaborator on the Kundalini yoga seminars, gave a series of lectures loosely based on Nazi ideology and his German Faith Movement. Jung took Hauer aside after his lectures and told him privately he would not be invited back anytime soon. "I am too 'German' for these people," Hauer wrote in his diary, angry at Jung's lack of sympathy.[35]

As the war years progressed, some members urged the club to institute programs dedicated to finding ways in which Swiss Germans could use psychology (not necessarily Jung's) to establish closer ties with their *Landsleute* (compatriots) in Germany. They were bitter about the club's general lack of enthusiasm toward their efforts to "conform" Swiss culture and society to "what is obviously best for us all."[36] Despite their pleas' falling on mostly indifferent ears, the executive committee made a secret rule so controversial that it has since dominated the club's entire history: in December 1944, it set a quota on the number of Jews who could hold membership.

No private diaries and no official club documents have yet been found to explain why the executive committee took such an action at that particular moment. The most logical reason is that the entire native Swiss membership became overtly hostile toward the large Jewish refugee presence, particularly to the number of physicians and analysts who were desperate to earn a living and remain permanently in Switzerland once the war ended. The secret quota on Jewish membership came in a closed session chaired by Toni Wolff, who raised the question and put forth the motion. It was seconded by Linda Fierz-David and approved unanimously by the committee (C. A. Meier among them). The motion decreed an "if possible" 10 percent quota on membership and a 25 percent limit on the special category of "guest" memberships.[37] The committee then took a second vote to make the ruling a formal appendix to the club's by-laws, but one that would remain secret and be withheld from the general membership. As the executive committee was also in charge of admissions, there was no problem with keeping this ruling secret for years afterward.[38]

Neither Emma nor C. G. Jung was a member of the executive committee, and no documentation has yet been found to show whether they knew of the quota before the vote, or when or even if they were informed of it afterward.[39] The likelihood is that they knew relatively early in the process, simply because they were so close to Wolff and Fierz-David, who both vied to tell full details of club business to the Jungs whether they wanted to hear it or not.[40]

Emma's negative opinion of the club's "spirit" had not changed since her earlier declaration that members were all puffed up with "*Grössenwahn*" (self-importance) and "*Selbstgerechtigkeit*" (self-righteousness) — indeed, her view grew stronger during the war.[41] Even though Jung insisted they had the obligation to attend club functions because these were times when civilization was clearly compromised and perhaps even endangered, Emma openly scorned having to associate with "Pharisees." Her phrase may have been another indication of what she thought of the secret quota.

But with Switzerland increasingly cut off from the outside world, Jung needed the forum the club provided. Without it, he had no access to persons eager to hear his ideas as they evolved. He needed an audience because it allowed him to express some of his most lasting theoretical insights through what may have seemed to others nothing more than extemporaneous commentary. Public expression was for Jung the necessary adjunct to refining his thought.[42]

He felt the same way about the Eranos meetings, especially because of the interaction and conversation with thinkers from diverse disciplines. So while others berated Frau Fröbe for her "power drive," her "inflation," and her "inability to accept the ideas of others," he defended her immense energy and organizational abilities and relished every *Tagung* encounter. He was particularly pleased when Mary Mellon agreed to pay for publication of an annual collection of Eranos essays, and for Frau Fröbe to travel to the United States in search of pictorial representations of symbols for what she intended would become an authoritative and all-inclusive archive.

Only those who lived in Switzerland attended the convocations of 1941 and 1942. Among them were the Swiss graphologist Max Pulver and Carl Kerényi, the Hungarian professor of philology and mythology who spent the war years in Ascona as a refugee. Pulver's and Kerényi's invitations were genuine, but those Frau Fröbe extended to several other Swiss professors were less enthusiastically proffered: they were only stopgaps, replacements for distinguished foreigners who could no longer enter the country. Jung kept his true feelings uncharacteristically hidden and always responded to their contributions with tactful reserve. They never knew how he ridiculed some of their ideas in private conversations with trusted friends.[43]

Another avenue of intellectual communication came through correspondence with Peter Baynes, who kept Jung abreast of events in England. Several years before the war, Baynes mentioned a friend surnamed Ashton-Gwatkin, a diplomat in the British Foreign Office who set much store in Jung's assessment of the German political situation.[44] Ashton-Gwatkin read Jung's "Wotan" in 1936 and was so impressed that he translated it into English and circulated it widely throughout the entire Foreign Office. When he became a member of the British diplomatic team sent that year to Berlin, he urged his countrymen to study Jung's essay to learn how to negotiate with the Nazis. Two years later, he was still asking Baynes to supply him with more copies of the original so he could give them to Germans whom he hoped to influence. When Jung learned of Ashton-Gwatkin's interest, he urged him to read his 1918 essay on "The Role of the Unconscious," which he still believed was an accurate prefiguration and valid appraisal of the "threatening events in Germany."[45]

Writing generally but with both essays in mind, Jung told Baynes that 1940 was the "fateful year" for which he had been waiting throughout the last twenty-five.[46] Although he had believed since 1918 that "a terrible fire would spread over Europe beginning in the North East," he did not foresee that it would lead to "such a disaster" and had "no vision beyond 1940 concerning the fate of Europe." Unaware that his terminology would result in two catchphrases that would define the end of the twentieth century, Jung told Baynes a new era was dawning, "the meridian of the first star in [the age of] Aquarius . . . the premonitory earthquake of the New Age" (author's emphasis).

Baynes wrote Jung from time to time of Ashton-Gwatkin's frustration over his inability to use Jung's writings to sway British policy toward Nazi Germany. His total failure is evident in the last cable sent from Berlin by the British ambassador Sir Neville Henderson on September 20, 1939, in which he still praised Hitler for his social achievements despite his "detestable" and "tyrannical methods."[47]

Throughout the early years of the war, Baynes was an important sounding board for Jung, as the two men exchanged detailed letters about their mutual projects. Baynes was preparing to publish a case study of Michael Fordham, a young medical doctor who was his patient and who later became an important analyst in his own right. All Jung knew of Fordham was that he was Baynes's most intriguing patient. He relished their dialogue by mail as they delved through Fordham's analytic history and studied the drawings he made as part of his treatment.[48] Baynes suggested that Fordham could benefit from sessions with Jung and urged him to go to Zürich. Jung agreed to meet Fordham but was either unaware that he wanted ongoing treatment or was unable or unwilling to take him on as a patient. When Jung's secretary replied to Fordham's initial letter, she simply confirmed a single appointment. On the strength of it, Fordham went to Zürich.

By the time Fordham arrived, he was already furious with Baynes for having published what he considered a too easily recognizable account of his analysis, so the situation was ripe for further misunderstanding with Jung. Fordham had not explained his personal situation but assumed that Jung would know he was a poor student who needed to find Swiss employment to earn a living and pay for analysis. He did not know until Jung broke the distressing news at their first meeting that, as of 1938, foreigners were no longer issued work visas. Unable to support himself, Fordham made the long trek back to England. He insisted for the rest of his life that he harbored no resentment toward Jung, but his true grudge equaled, if not surpassed, the one he held toward Baynes.[49]

Baynes was writing another book, which he envisioned as a "psychological study of war" but which actually became a specific psychological study of Nazi Germany based in large part on Jung's two essays. When Jung received *Germany Possessed*,[50] he was moved by the "almost overgenerous" introduction, "most unexpected, most unforeseen." He wondered how British readers would "swallow this mighty pill." Baynes's book became a bestseller and did much to further analytical psychology in England.

Jung's mind was crowded with ideas, many still unfocused; others existed in working drafts of essays, portions of which he later incorporated into book-length manuscripts. Baynes was among some of Jung's most devoted supporters and closest allies who, aware that he was approaching seventy and in deteriorating health, were so eager to read anything he wrote that they urged him to send work hither and yon for immediate publication, no matter how vague and rudimentary it might be. Baynes thought Jung should reserve some of the essays for a book but should send others directly to British journals.

In the United States, Mary Mellon was working to ensure that everything Jung wrote was translated into English, although she had not yet founded the Bollingen Foundation to publish Jung's *Collected Works* in a uniform edition. So eager was Mary Mellon to publish everything that she subsidized an annual volume of Eranos lectures for Olga Fröbe[51] because they always included Jung's contribution. Mary Mellon employed Cary Baynes as her unofficial editor and advisor because she was the only one whose views Jung and Frau Fröbe respected.[52] Cary called Frau Fröbe the "Great Mother . . . frightening everybody out of her way," and she was one of very few who could jolly her into choosing essays suitable for an international audience of intelligent general readers, especially an American one. Jung said selection did not matter much, as whatever the first volume included, it would be "more or less difficult chewing for Americans, unless they are highly educated people."[53] As for his own "poor" introduction to the volume, it was no matter, "because nobody reads [it]."[54] Cary would not approve his essay, saying it needed "much more of a build-up than [he] had time to give,"[55] but Jung did not revise it.

All these unconnected writings eventually saw print, most immediately in a book of disparate essays entitled *The Integration of the Personality*, published in England in 1940.[56] When Baynes read them, he wondered why "The Idea of

Redemption in Alchemy" (originally in the relatively esoteric Eranos collection) was "more accessible to the intelligent outsider" than "The Integration of Personality" (originally in the scientific journal *Nature*). Baynes was also puzzled why the subject of medieval alchemy would resonate more clearly to an ordinary reader than "Dream Symbols of the Process of Individuation," a topic of more contemporary interest. So, too, was Jung, who thought the general public largely consigned alchemical texts to "the dunghill of the past . . . a forgotten and despised field of investigation."[57]

Baynes's reaction was encouraging, for it verified Jung's thinking that the dreams of contemporary persons were replete with alchemical symbolism. Even so, he was not as certain as Baynes of the overall value of his recent writing, worried that it was "more and more [about] subjects just not suitable for public discussion." He offered only one example, his recent Eranos lecture on the Holy Trinity, but he believed most of what he was investigating could be included in this category.[58]

Jung seemed to be developing two major trains of thought concurrently, albeit independently. When he referred to them, it was usually under such broad rubrics as "the psychology of alchemy" and "the process of individuation." He thought the "general trend" of his research would lead to a "continuation" of *Psychology and Religion,* which was the only way he could see to connect them. He was not sure if he had enough for a book or just another collection of unrelated essays.

His health, as it did throughout the war years, dictated the development of his writing. Jung so overexerted himself during the 1941 Eranos *Tagung* that his doctor, worried about the strain on his heart, ordered complete rest and curtailment of all activity.[59] He later downgraded the diagnosis to exhaustion from overwork but still forbade Jung to give his ETH lectures that autumn.[60] Jung agreed but insisted on participating in ceremonies commemorating the four-hundredth anniversary of the death of Philippus Aureolus Theophrastus Bombastus von Hohenheim, called Paracelsus.[61] An alchemist known also as "the Luther of physicians," Paracelsus was as famous for his "revolutionary medicine" as for his "religious intensity," two qualities that initially intrigued Jung because he shared them as well.[62]

He presented his research in two lectures, the first in Basel on September 7 dealing with Paracelsus as a physician, the second on October 5 at the famed monastery in Einsiedeln (where Paracelsus was born and lived part of his life) focusing on him as a "Spiritual Phenomenon."[63] The content of the first lecture reflected the audience for whom it was tailored, two professional societies dedicated to the history of medicine and the development of the natural sciences, rather than what Jung really thought about the medieval alchemist and his esoteric ideas. He was content to publish it almost as extemporaneously as he spoke it, but the second was quite a different matter. He rewrote it extensively after an intense study of the "prolific medical, scientific, and theological writings" of "this contradictory and yet so significant personality." Aware of the difficulty of preparing a thorough synthesis of so many writings on such diverse subjects, Jung settled for "providing clues." These were to confer an understanding of "the roots and psychic background of his philosophy" — to which Jung added the cautionary phrase "if one could call it that."

There were interesting parallels between Jung's thinking and that of his subject's, and he tried to express those ideas that interested him most. Since his return from India, he had been studying the historical development of Protestantism and was intrigued by why such a straightforward rupture with Catholicism had evolved into so many diverse forms. His study convinced him that Protestantism had suffered an important loss when it eschewed the richness of Catholic ceremony and ritual, two important adjunct qualities for individuals who participated in the communal practices of organized religion. A lack of ceremony and ritual carried over into other forms of emptiness and longing that troubled individuals could neither express nor understand.

Jung saw something of himself in Paracelsus: while he explored the collective unconscious to gain insight into individuation, Paracelsus's forays into "alchemical 'philosoph[y]'" resulted in his own personalizing of religious practices to make them what he wished them to be, leading to "unconscious" conflict with the Christian beliefs of his time. Jung was convinced that both he and Paracelsus were investigating bodies of thought formed over time by communities or collectives and then passed down through succeeding generations that hardened them into ritual and doctrine. In the centuries after Paracelsus's death, many other observers formulated unconscious responses — dream symbolism one among many — to every sort of ritualistic practice, from yoga to the liturgy of the Catholic mass. Jung believed the central tenet and most important legacy of Paracelsus's life and work was "the authenticity of [his] own experience of nature against the authority of tradition." Such a belief "helped to emancipate natural science from the authority of tradition," but it also led to the ongoing "conflict between knowledge and faith" that dominated modern society.[64]

Jung ascribed similar qualities of "scepticism and rebelliousness" to Paracelsus that he himself used as he wended his way through the many works that resulted in the writings that followed this essay.[65] Between the years 1941 and 1954, Jung was working on what became the *Mysterium Coniunctionis*, generally considered his greatest work and the culmination of all his thinking, particularly of his research into alchemy. In the *Mysterium*, which includes so much of what he first posited in his studies of Paracelsus, he tried to explain how the inadequacies inherent in language hampered his efforts to explain his findings as precisely as he would have liked. Emphasizing that he did not "go in for either metaphysics or theology," and that his primary concern was "with psychological facts on the borderline of the knowable," he staked his turf:

Psychology is very definitely not a theology; it is a natural science that seeks to describe experienceable psychic phenomena. . . . But as empirical science it has neither the capacity nor the competence to decide on questions of truth and value, this being the prerogative of theology.[66]

With the *Mysterium* still embryonic, Jung returned to the writings of Paracelsus to develop theories he had expressed earlier in *Psychology and Religion*. Questions arose during his ETH lectures on St. Ignatius Loyola's *Exercitia Spiritualia*, wherein he referred frequently to the ritualistic exhortations of the monk Hugh of St. Victor.[67] One of his patients was a Catholic priest, the Rev. Dr. Gallus Jud,[68] whom Jung credited with making him fully cognizant of what he called "the Catholic mind" and with teaching him to appreciate "medieval mentality at its best."[69] Jung focused their sessions on a comparison of the writings of Hugh and Ignatius to show how "codified meditation" contained many of the same symbols that many patients who were entirely unaware of theology encountered on their road to individuation.[70]

Jung coupled his respect for medieval mentality with his mid-twentieth-century insistence that he was indeed a writer, but foremost he was an empirical scientist, becoming enraged if anyone questioned the scientific foundation of his research. His insistence upon scientific primacy led to a new development in his writing style and resulted in texts that were his most complex as well as his most perplexing.[71]

He could not have completed so much writing in so relatively few years without Marie-Louise von Franz, who became his most devoted collaborator in the last years of the war. An extraordinarily diligent researcher, she followed vague trails through all the libraries and antiquarian bookstores of Europe, unearthing rare alchemical texts that had languished unread for centuries. To place them in historical context, she investigated the history and biography of their authors, with her dedicated sleuthing leading to still more writers and texts that might otherwise have escaped Jung's purview. She trained herself to become expert in deciphering esoteric Medieval Latin handwritings and then translated the obscure texts into contemporary German, thus saving Jung literally years of labor. As a firsthand observer of his daily endeavor, she was uniquely positioned to describe what happened to his writing when alchemy became his paramount interest. Jung's usual method was "circularity," to roam around a subject, deviate into digressions, and jump from one seemingly unrelated topic to another before abruptly refocusing on his main theme. Readers charged that he was incapable of expressing his ideas with order, clarity, and precision, but von Franz argued that he did so "on purpose":

He writes with a double attitude, giving full justice to the paradoxes of the unconscious. He describes psychic phenomena from an empirical standpoint. The Buddha once said that all his sayings were to be understood on two levels and Jung's writings also have this double floor, these two levels.[72]

She compared Jung's technique to one adopted by nuclear physicists, wherein "facts are described in two complementary approaches which contradict each other but yet are needed in order that the whole thing may be grasped." Precise language became an "open problem" for readers of Jung's alchemical texts. "Words," von Franz concluded, "are only instruments and not the thing itself." She recalled how Jung was "frequently frustrated and never satisfied," feeling "that he was touching something which led still further, and he did not yet know where."[73]

Jung looked back at these writings almost two decades later from the vantage point of a complete canon, when he was collaborating on *Memories, Dreams, Reflections*. He called the alchemical texts "stations along my life's way . . . tasks imposed from within; their source a fateful compulsion." They were also extremely personal expressions, unguarded and revealing because, for the first time in his long life, he believed he had nothing left to gain from the outside world and no opprobrium left to fear. On the one hand, he found the manner in which the world at large responded to his ideas "truly astonishing," and for this he was delighted; on the other, the isolation imposed upon neutral Switzerland by wartime restriction left him lonely, depressed, and unappreciated. This period marked his first expression of what became a recurring theme: that his life's work had amounted to very little, and most of it was probably for naught.

This feeling of sending his work out into a void with no response or feedback changed in February 1942. Mary Mellon, fearing mail service between Switzerland and the outside world was about to be permanently canceled, rushed an air letter via the Pan Am Clipper to tell Jung the exciting news that her plan to publish his entire canon was successfully under way.[74] Originally, the Mellons approached Paul's alma mater, Yale, with the idea of a "Bollingen Press" that would become a special imprint under the auspices of its highly respected university press. Mary found that neither the university trustees nor the press's editorial board would give her the free rein she wanted; nor was either group enthusiastic about becoming the publisher of a psychologist whose reputation was still questionable in certain academic circles. Mary was upset that Yale wanted to put a "stuffy Professor of Psychology" in charge who would be "disastrous" and likely to "curtail perhaps just the books we thought good." When it appeared that the Mellons were about to take their press elsewhere, Yale offered a compromise: instead of arguing over what an imprint within its press might publish, there would be a separate "Bollingen Foundation, Inc.," giving the Mellons complete freedom to do whatever they wanted.

Mary's first business was to appoint the board of directors of the Bollingen Foundation, whose name she chose in homage to Jung's tower. In addition to herself, two of the Mellon family's lawyers, and a business associate, she named Heinrich Zimmer ("whom I now call Henry, if you please"), Edgar Wind, Stringfellow Barr, Cary Baynes, and Ximena de Angulo Roelli.[75] The foundation's official headquarters was Washington, Connecticut, where Cary Baynes now lived, but all decisions were "paternally overseen" in Washington, D.C., by Donald D. Shepard, the Mellon family's primary legal and tax advisor since 1927. It took almost two months for Mary Mellon's air letter to pass through the censorship of several countries before it reached Jung in early April in Bollingen, where he was on a working vacation. She outlined her plans for publishing the several writings she knew about, particularly the Eranos *Tagung* essays, but he had altogether different ideas. Jung took great care to explain not only what he had written and was currently writing but also his intentions for future publication, particularly the work about alchemy. His reply provides a useful summary for unraveling how his writing evolved during these years.

Referring to Mary's suggestion that "The Mass" (an early version of the essay "Transformation Symbolism in the Mass") appear as a separate monograph, Jung said he had a different plan, not only for that text but for others as well.[76] He wanted her to finance a "new edition" of the book just published in England containing "The Idea of Redemption in Alchemy" and "Dream Symbols." Because he had "augmented and improved both essays to a very large extent," he envisaged "a volume of about 300 pages." There was to be a second volume as well, containing some of the Eranos papers he described by short forms of their titles: "'Zosimos,' 'The Mass,' 'The Trinity,'" and "a paper by . . . von Franz about 'the Passio Perpetuae.'" He also wanted to reproduce the Latin text of the "Aurora Consurgens," deciphered by von Franz from a nearly illegible manuscript, as well as her translation of the first part.[77] He explained his reasoning in detail:

> In this setting [the proposed two volumes] the mass is in its proper place. The first paper of this series ["Dream Symbols"] is a demonstration of how symbols are spontaneously produced by the unconscious and how these are connected with medieval symbolism. The second paper ["Ideas of Redemption"] contains the demonstration of the symbolism in its connection with Christianity and Gnosticism. The third would be the Aurora Consurgens. The fourth the alchemistic transformation and its psychological interpretation ["Zosimos"]. The fifth essay would be the mass in which the Christian transubstantiation miracle is compared to the alchemistic transformation. The sixth contains the answer to the problem which has been often alluded to in the preceding papers, namely the problem of 3 & 4, or trinity and quaternity. The seventh [*"Passio Perpetuae"*] is a very impressive document about the visions of a young Christian martyr before her execution. Perpetua had visions and dreams in which there is a juxtaposition and a conflict of the Christian and the pagan view.

Mary Mellon also wanted to publish one other work as a monograph, *The Seven Sermons*, the privately printed edition Jung gave her as a gift on her only visit to Bollingen shortly before she left Switzerland. Jung did not rule out its publication but asked her to wait until he added "certain materials" about which he had "hesitated for years" and now thought he "might risk." But before *The Seven Sermons*, he wanted to publish a third volume in addition to the two proposed above: "papers on archetypes in general," for which he would supply "a general introduction." These could not be published separately and had to follow the two proposed volumes, as "they really belong together and make sense only in their proper surroundings."

All these plans introduced a host of related questions and created problems for Jung that required as much time and care to resolve as writing the actual works themselves. He had to put numerous persons to work on various forms of translation. Marie-Louise von Franz was in charge of Latin, Greek, and other ancient languages. Elizabeth Welsh and Barbara Hannah had been actively translating from German into English for a number of years; now they were joined by Dr. K. Bash, who worked specifically on the Greek myths Jung and Carl Kerényi[78] deemed important for their ongoing collaboration. Roland Cahan had worked sporadically on French translations before the war, but nothing he had done thus far met Jung's approval and no one else in France was interested.[79]

There were also questions of rights and permissions: even though Barbara Hannah was translating the new material for inclusion with the "Dream Symbols" and "Ideas of Redemption" essays, it was unlikely that Farrar and Rinehart would release the rights to Bollingen Press, since their edition had just been published and was still in print. Also, the British firm of Kegan Paul had been Jung's primary English-language publisher since 1916, so legal issues seemed bound to cloud Mary Mellon's desire to publish all of Jung's work "in a beautiful, substantial and uniform edition."[80]

Jung worked diligently for the next month, energized by the possibility of so much publication and in such fine form. So, too, did all his many helpers, who were equally thrilled at the prospect. No wonder all were stunned by Mary Mellon's next letter, with news so devastating that it threw Jung into what some called a "blue funk" and others bluntly called "severe depression."[81]

Mary had been sending foodstuffs through Macy's and the Red Cross to the Jung family and her other friends in Switzerland. Now she wanted to use some of the money she kept in Swiss bank accounts to dispense supplies in a more consistent manner. She asked Donald Shepard to investigate which relief agencies might act on her behalf, and he left the matter to the Mellon family lawyers in New York. One of them, Francis Carmody, became alarmed when he learned of the frequent letters and cables that had been flying between New York and Zürich since the Bollingen Foundation was started. As the United States was now at war, Carmody insisted that no one connected with any of the Mellon family's numerous foundations could risk running afoul of the Trading with the Enemy Act or incurring the severe penalties levied against those who dealt directly or indirectly with suspected enemy aliens.[82] He ordered Mary to cease communication with all other countries (England being the only possible exception) and not to touch any money she had in Switzerland *"for any purpose"* (Carmody's emphasis).

Meanwhile, Donald Shepard learned that the FBI had been officially investigating Olga Fröbe-Kapteyn since March 1941, when she entered the United States via the Pan Am *Dixie Clipper* from Bermuda. The Bureau had been aware of her since 1939, when she entered the country on the SS *Conte de Savoia*, holding a German passport and carrying several folders of "cryptic pictures."[83] On both occasions she said she had come to do "iconographic work," and as Paul Mellon was paying all her expenses, she gave his Pittsburgh address as hers. The FBI had another reason to be suspicious of Frau Fröbe, for she had written several letters to Eleanor Roosevelt, asking for her financial support and asking her to forward them to FDR for his.[84] In all innocence, Frau Fröbe also asked Mrs. Roosevelt to help decipher the symbolism of "The Great Seal [of the United States] at Washington." She requested a personal meeting to discuss how Mrs. Roosevelt might help her establish a postwar "Eranos USA" similar to the one at Ascona. As Frau Fröbe had just read that only those visitors who "are of some benefit to the country" would be readmitted for the duration of the war, she wanted Mrs. Roosevelt to persuade FDR to write "some official statement" on her behalf so she could enter and leave freely and frequently.

Mrs. Roosevelt probably never read the letter, for her secretary sent a polite generic reply thanking Frau Fröbe for her "interest" and "expressions of faith in the President."[85] Apparently, Frau Fröbe ran out of money before she could pursue Mrs. Roosevelt further. When Mary Mellon refused her request for an additional thousand dollars,[86] in swift succession she contacted the Rockefeller Foundation, the American Council of Learned Societies, and several individual professors at Princeton and Yale. She told everyone that she needed the money to help fund the proposed "Eranos USA," but she really needed it to pay for the many representations of symbols she was busily buying on credit and loading into cartons to ship back to Switzerland. As no one gave her funding, she had to curtail her buying and go home, but before she left, she did not hesitate to volunteer important references any time she thought it might cause others to open purses. Her list included everyone from Paul Mellon and Cary Baynes to Jung and the concierge at the Barbizon Hotel in New York (where she stayed). Eventually everyone but Jung was interrogated by FBI agents who wanted to know about the curious woman "who spent all her time in the Morgan Library gathering pictures for her collection."[87]

J. Edgar Hoover's first assistant at the FBI, Edward A. Tamm, shared the burgeoning file of the eccentric Olga Fröbe with the Mellon Foundation's Donald Shepard. Primarily because Olga Fröbe was suspected of being a German agent, Shepard urged the fledgling Bollingen Press to "cease all activities, correspondence, and financing of its work in Switzerland [that] might give aid and comfort to the enemy with serious results and untold embarrassment." Shepard wrote this to Paul Mellon, then in the army and stationed at Fort Riley, Kansas. When Paul inquired about Jung's role in the investigation, Shepard said he was "apparently, from what I hear . . . without question opposed to the Axis principles" and that the FBI would probably consider him "somewhat like a person exposed to some contagious disease, and who may be quarantined, even though he may not have the disease."[88] In other words, Jung was also off-limits.

The FBI also advised Shepard that Mary should write a letter of record to Jung that could be used as evidence if the government ever launched an investigation into the Bollingen Foundation. Paul concurred, and Shepard wrote a formal letter for Mary to sign, couched in legal language and addressing every possible situation that might have put the Mellons in breach of the Trading with the Enemy Act. He sent it to the disconsolate Mary, who was so despondent that she barely skimmed it before ordering it to be retyped on her personal stationery exactly as he wrote it. It was sent to Jung on May 25, with Mary's full formal signature and no other personal comment, a vast departure from her usual warm greetings but one necessitated by legalities.

On June 23, 1942, the lawyers advised further that the original Bollingen Foundation should be entirely dissolved and all its assets liquidated. Donald Shepard sent a second letter to inform Jung of what seemed a final and irrevocable act. This time, Mary substantially rewrote Shepard's letter, making it as cordial and diplomatic as legal language would allow. Still, it hit Jung as an even heavier blow. He broke the unfortunate news to Olga Fröbe with a single terse comment: "A message from Job, which was to be expected."[89]

CHAPTER 31

Agent 488

J ung thought Swiss privations after 1942 paled in comparison with occupied Europe's "misery . . . indescribable."[1] The Jung family was cognizant of restrictions, even though the country at large "clung to that ingenious interpretation [that life was] 'normal.'"[2] Little was rationed besides meat. The family cook occasionally went "tramping for one hour and a half" to find "two sausages" for dinner, but they had enough bread, vegetables, fruit, tobacco, and wine.[3] They complied fully with the Wahlen directive to cultivate every bit of land around the house and were rewarded with an ample harvest of root vegetables. Unfortunately, only the potatoes were salvageable, as most of it froze in the root cellar during the severe winter. The family compared the vile taste to sweet potatoes, which no one liked, but they were "grateful" to have them.

Even to leave the house in such cold weather put a strain on the elderly couple, as the train station was a mile away and they had to walk nearly everywhere. They seldom saw Toni Wolff, whose rheumatoid arthritis kept her confined to home after her two-week tour of active duty with the women's auxiliary. She had insisted on living in the barracks, and the primitive conditions exacerbated her ill health. Toni donated her car to the corps, so anyone who wanted to see her had to trek to the Freiestrasse, which was difficult for Jung. Katy Cabot offered him the bicycle of her recently deceased lover, Major de Trafford, but even though tempted, he refused, saying he was "too old for a new bicycle."[4]

WARMER SPRING weather and several forays to Bollingen were restorative, and Jung worked contentedly on the first sections of the *Mysterium Coniunctionis* he had earlier outlined for Mary Mellon. It was a welcome relief from writing a new introduction for yet another edition of a "tiresome little book" to explain the psychology of the unconscious to a lay audience.[5] This period of quiet introspection was interrupted from time to time by political involvement of several sorts, of plotting and spying, and all coming out of the blue, unannounced and uninvited. Jung thought these approaches "only natural, considering [his] line of work." As in the case of his presidency of the International Society, various rumors of his involvement colored much of the rest of his life, but he dismissed them all as quite "enough for [his] enemies" and of no concern to his friends.[6]

The first, and in many ways the most alarming, rumor blamed Jung for Hitler's persecution of the Jews. Mary Bancroft, an American who was married to a Swiss man and who lived in Zürich during the war, heard repeatedly that "it was Jung who gave Hitler the idea that the Jews were the best object on whom to 'project' evil."[7] She told Jung, who was convinced the rumor originated with "the Freudians," who always "had their knives out" for him. He thought it was probably an outgrowth of another rumor that had him flying routinely to Berchtesgaden to treat Hitler. That one may have started when the eminent Berlin surgeon Dr. Ferdinand Sauerbruch came to Switzerland several times during the war and asked to meet Jung. They had two brief conversations at the University of Zürich, little more than shaking hands and exchanging politenesses in full public view. After that, even though Sauerbruch remained in Germany and Jung had no further contact with him, there were rumors that they took turns commuting to Hitler to ensure that he kept Jewish persecution paramount on his agenda.[8]

The truth is that Jung's involvement with Hitler was peripheral: one of the Führer's physicians did telephone in early summer to ask Jung to go to Berchtesgaden and observe him.[9] When Jung proffered excuses, the physician put the case bluntly: a core of high-ranking German officers were concerned about Hitler's increasingly erratic behavior, particularly because he had begun to drink heavily.[10] They wanted him to be discreetly observed and evaluated, preferably by an analyst from a neutral country. The doctor did not, however, tell Jung the officers' primary reason: that, with such a report in hand, they hoped to persuade other concerned but still wavering government officials and military personnel to join in ousting the dictator and ending a war they knew they were losing. Jung was told only that he had been invited to consult in his professional capacity as a still respected psychologist in Germany, one whose theories Göring and his group trotted out when it helped their cause, albeit in their own *gleichgeschaltet* interpretations. Jung knew that by 1942 such status in Germany was nothing to brag about. He made his refusal firm by citing not only the difficulties of traveling across closed borders but also his health, weakened by wartime privation. His excuses were accepted, and he never heard from anyone that close to Hitler again. However, he was soon caught up in another unrelated plan to persuade Hitler to concede to peace.

Wilhelm Bitter, a German psychiatrist who practiced analytical psychology,[11] became a party to this particular plot and solicited Jung's participation. Bitter was a political economist and sociologist in 1934 when he recognized the danger Hitler represented, and he then changed his profession to medicine. He analyzed in Berlin with Käthe Bügler and Elizabeth Lambert[12] and did further work in Geneva with Max de Crinis, who sent him to Jung. In the year or so before war was declared, he and Jung often spoke of their mutual antipathies and problems with the Nazi government and its destructive effect on German psychoanalysis.

Bitter bought a vacation home in Switzerland in 1932, but he had not been able to go there since the war began and the Nazis restricted him to Berlin. He was working at the BPI and the Charité clinic when General Walter Schellenberg ("The Famous Number One of the Intelligence Service but [Bitter] didn't know it then")[13] asked him to investigate through his Swiss contacts what the outside world thought of Nazi policy. Just before the rout at Stalingrad, Schellenberg confessed that he thought National Socialism "completely wrong," and Bitter replied with the same honesty, saying only immediate unconditional surrender could save Germany from future occupation by Bolshevik Russia. The next day, a surprised Bitter became a go-between when Schellenberg phoned to say travel passes had been secured for him to go to Switzerland "for reasons of health." He charged Bitter with finding Swiss contacts who could help bring about Nazi surrender.

Schellenberg, the plot's chief instigator, was Himmler's chief of foreign intelligence and a close friend of de Crinis. When Jung refused to diagnose Hitler, Schellenberg asked de Crinis to do it, hoping he would find the dictator's unstable mental condition stemmed from a serious physical illness, as patriotic Germans would find it easier to remove an ill leader than support a possibly treasonous coup. The goal was to persuade potential conspirators that Hitler was fast becoming so disabled that their duty was to countermand his orders. With or without his consent, they hoped to bring about an armistice on the Western Front, thus freeing German troops to concentrate on defeating Russia. It was well known that Churchill feared the red tide of Communism might engulf Europe, so Schellenberg and the other conspirators thought their plan had a good chance because it would appeal to the British.

They decided to enlist Jung because of remarks he made about Russia in "Diagnosing the Dictators," his 1938 interview with the American journalist H. R. Knickerbocker.[14] Jung's views were well known in Germany because the article had been widely circulated in a *gleichgeschaltet* translation thoroughly vetted by Göring and Curtius. In the uncensored version, Jung told Knickerbocker that Hitler resembled certain of his patients who were so attuned to their own inner voices and visions that no one else's could penetrate. As Hitler was fixated on his personal fantasies, Jung believed the only way to save Western democracy was by influencing the direction in which he would inevitably seek further conquests: "I say let him go East. Turn his attention away from the West, or rather, encourage him to keep it turned away. Let him go to Russia. That is the logical *cure* for Hitler."[15]

Bitter was chosen to contact Jung because of his analysis and his participation in the 1939–40 ETH seminars and the seminars on fairy tales and children's dreams. With his travel permits, he moved frequently between Germany and Switzerland, ostensibly in pursuit of further study. The English contacts who worked with Schellenberg agreed that Bitter was the candidate most unlikely to arouse suspicion when he liaised with anyone Swiss, so Schellenberg persuaded Matthias Göring to issue a new pass, enabling Bitter to attend the bimonthly meetings of the Teaching Institute for Psychotherapy at the University of Zürich.[16] From 1943 to 1947, Bitter collaborated closely on psychoanalytic matters with Jung, even managing fairly regular attendance at the seminars Jung held in his home with Gustav Bally, Alphons Maeder, Medard Boss, and C. A. Meier.

When he was in Geneva, Max de Crinis helped Bitter to establish friendly contacts with British embassy workers there and in Bern whose real assignments were high-level undercover espionage. Schellenberg expected him to start with them, but Bitter went first to Jung. Jung said he was "interested" in Schellenberg's plan but first wanted to consult "two outstanding political friends." The first was Prof. Karl Burckhardt in Geneva, the former commissioner of Danzig under the League of Nations and an eminent international lawyer and historian; the second was Dr. Albert Oeri, editor of the *Basler Nachrichten* and a representative of Basel in the *Nationalrat*, the federal parliament, and his lifelong friend.[17] Jung also enlisted several Swiss physicians and businessmen to be part of the plot, but to this day they are unidentified.[18] From this secret group, several other wealthy and influential Swiss men who deplored their country's acquiescence with many of the Nazi dictates were delegated to ensure Jung's participation. They knew he had many prominent English acquaintances from his prewar trips to England, among them the Archbishop of Canterbury, William Temple, who they thought would be the person most likely to convince Churchill.[19] Jung knew they would need to work through an intermediary now that mail service was permanently severed and he had no way to contact anyone in England. Bitter gave him a series of codes to convey messages through a "Swedish connection," who sent them by letter and other couriers. Unfortunately, the Swedish agent was apprehended, and Bitter was warned to cease all activity on this front. For a brief time, there was talk "in the circles in which [Bitter] move[d] — and he [was] an extremely important person" that, instead of removing Hitler, they should concentrate on splitting off Prussia from the rest of Germany, because the southern regions were "fed up to the teeth with things as they [were]."

Where Jung was concerned, that plan went no further than talk, but it gave him an idea he believed "violently" for the remainder of the war, that "Germany must be split up."[20] He was convinced that "when a German feels his country is small, he has practically no faults," but "the moment he feels big and important, he is the most dangerous individual in the world." If the country were not partitioned, Jung said, "the whole story will start all over again and much sooner than anyone expects (and it will be much worse because of Russia)."

WITH THE Swedish courier inoperative, the conspirators needed to find another route to England. Jung thought they needed a British citizen in Switzerland who could use the excuse of wanting to return home. He turned to his faithful "bulldog" Barbara Hannah (who herself always kept an English bulldog), daughter of a dean in the Anglican Church, and his devoted acolyte who would sooner go to her death than betray or disappoint him. Jung invited her to Bollingen and swore her to secrecy, saying neither Emma nor Toni knew of his involvement in the plot. Hannah was happy in her adopted country and had no intention of deserting it, especially since once she was in England, there was no possibility of returning until the war ended. She still agreed to do whatever Jung asked. He explained that it would be relatively easy for a British spinster with no known political affiliation to ask for repatriation. For the time being, she was to do nothing but "nose it about" that she was thinking of leaving; as soon as he gave the signal, she was to apply to the British legation in Bern for travel permits.[21]

One month later, Hannah was still waiting anxiously for a signal that did not come, so she went again to Bollingen. There she found Jung as nervous as she. "Oh, damn it!" he asked. "Am I being too naïve?" He was afraid the Schellenberg plan would not amount to anything more than a "pipe dream," but he still felt he had to participate. In August, he told Hannah it had dissipated into an "Abraham's sacrifice," and the conspirators were forced to abandon the plot. Hitler's doctors became bold enough to suggest that de Crinis give him his routine physical examination, and Hitler became enraged and refused. As his ranting accusations grew in intensity, he concentrated his venom on the "defeatist" Bitter. Fearing for his life, Bitter fled to Geneva, where he spent the rest of the war in exile.[22]

WHILE THE Schellenberg plot was unraveling, Jung was trying to concentrate on the writings he had outlined earlier for Mary Mellon. He had told her how he dreaded the day when "all relations with America will be cut,"[23] so it was an enormous boost to be contacted by a young Swiss diplomat, Alphonse Hättenschwiler, who was her friend and also Kristine Mann's. Hättenschwiler told Jung that he routinely took the dangerous Stuttgart-Lisbon-Bermuda flight to Washington and volunteered to carry occasional letters in the diplomatic pouch. Jung tried not to abuse his kindness so he wrote infrequently and seldom received replies, as most of his correspondents did not have such privileged contacts. Still, it was a link to the outside world, no matter how tenuous. He was delighted to receive a letter from Mary Mellon, the first since the two letters dictated by the Mellon Foundation's lawyer, Donald Shepard, that had caused Jung such despair.[24] Her letter was filled with postwar plans for translating and publishing Jung's canon, and to receive it gave him a tremendous boost in productivity and energy, both of which he sorely needed.

Jung's daily wartime activity was filled with many irritating distractions from which Emma's money and Toni's psychological expertise could no longer insulate him. Now he worried about all sorts of family matters, primarily the constant pressure of the burgeoning household's most basic needs, enough to eat and wood and coal for minimum heating. He tried to concentrate on the new writing that was steadily flowing, but his involvement in the nerve-racking spy business began again when Allen W. Dulles, "the last American for a year and a half," entered Switzerland on November 8, 1942. Even though they did not meet personally for some time, Jung became Dulles's "sort of senior advisor on a weekly, if not almost daily, basis."[25]

Dulles's arrival coincided with the American landings in North Africa, after which the Nazis sealed Swiss borders and occupied all of France in retaliation.[26] He headed directly for the American Embassy in Bern to present his credentials to the "press attaché" Gerald Mayer, whose real job was "advance man" for the Office of Strategic Services (OSS), charged with laying the groundwork for "Agent 110," Allen Dulles.[27] William J. "Wild Bill" Donovan, head of the OSS, wanted a Swiss "listening post," and Dulles nominated himself for the position. His official title was "special assistant to the ambassador at Bern," a code name for the Central European representative of the OSS, who was expected to "mingle freely in intellectual and business spheres in Switzerland, who had previous contacts in European political circles, and a specific and superior background for the cover he would use." Dulles's cover was that of a senior partner in the prestigious international law firm of Sullivan and Cromwell, which he joined in 1926 after ten years in the State Department, primarily in Foreign Affairs. Charged by his firm with "promoting the firm's ability to serve special clients . . . [through] unusual and diversified means of obtaining information,"[28] Dulles was a natural for recruiting spies (later described as mostly "enthusiastic amateurs") to assist with "the subtle, delicate, often intuitive process of constructing a network against Nazi Germany."

Everyone in diplomatic circles was well aware of Dulles's real assignment, and most were engaged in the same activity, so no one paid him more than routine attention, even after local newspapers began describing him as "a confidential and well-connected 'personal representative of President Roosevelt.'"[29] Believing that "too much secrecy can be self-defeating,"[30] Dulles set himself up in a ground-floor apartment on the Herringgasse, a busy street in the city's center, in a former mansion house that dated back to the seventeenth century. As it was just off the busy Casinoplatz, the street was filled with foot traffic by day and was pitch-dark at night because of the blackout. Dulles's apartment's back door opened onto a garden that dropped sharply into a wooded conglomeration of grape arbors and garden allotments; visitors who had to beat a hasty retreat could disappear into densely wooded darkness all the way down to the river Aare. Dulles let it be known that he had plenty of money to pass around for information and anyone who wanted some of it was welcome to come and talk to him.

Gerry Mayer had been in Bern long enough to identify some of the best persons for Dulles to recruit. On the surface, Mayer seemed an unlikely intelligence gatherer, for people noticed him when he entered a room. An outgoing fellow and former newsman for NBC, Mayer had a hearty laugh and was given to effusive greetings and much backslapping. He deliberately gave the impression of drinking more than he should and therefore of talking too much as well. It was a carefully constructed public persona, for beneath the booming exterior, a steel-trap mind was hard at work taking in everything and forgetting nothing. Because there was a German legation in Zürich, he was often in transit between there and Bern, and because he was always on the lookout for recruits, it was only natural that he got to know many of the Americans who lived in both cities. After the war, when those who worked for him identified themselves, they all seemed the most unlikely spies, especially to all the others Mayer never approached (and who might have made miffed comments about them because he ruled them out from the beginning).[31] Of all the seemingly unsuitable candidates, Mary Bancroft was by far the most unlikely. She was then known as Mary B. Rüfenacht, divorced from the American father of her two children and remarried to a French-Swiss, Jean Rüfenacht.[32] Bancroft's second marriage was, for those days and that city (and as such marriages would be described at a later time), uncharacteristically and blatantly "open." She took lovers as she wished and had no qualms about describing the intimate details of her affairs to anyone within earshot. Katy Cabot was one of her many confidantes who pretended to be shocked and horrified but lost no time conveying all the salacious details to Jung, Mary Briner, and anyone else who would listen.[33]

When Dulles arrived in Switzerland, Bancroft was scandalizing the locals by her fairly public affair with a prominent married Swiss professor. The Jungian community, made more introverted and mutually dependent by war-induced isolation, was then centered entirely around the Psychological Club. There was little else for members to do but gossip about each other, and when Bancroft's romantic peccadilloes became general topics of conversation, they all tried unsuccessfully to snub her. First they tried to ban her from membership and prohibit her from attending meetings. However, Toni Wolff liked Bancroft and respected her considerable intelligence. Exercising her autocratic authority and defying her friend Linda Fierz-David (who detested Bancroft), Toni commissioned Bancroft to do research about Madame de Staël and her circle and present her findings in a series of lectures.[34] Shortly after, Toni saw to it that Bancroft became a member. So into this world of dour, retiring introverts came the big brash American extravert with the booming laugh. People could not help noticing Mary Bancroft in whatever setting she appeared, and afterward they were often unable to recall anyone else who had been there. "I used up all the oxygen," she boasted many years later.[35]

Most of the other Americans in Zurich's wartime Jungian community were women who had married wealthy Swiss men and took such care to fit so seamlessly into their husbands' worlds that they were often taken for Swiss themselves. They spoke the local dialect, affected the clothing, and learned not to display wealth or breeding in any way that made them different from the natives. Not so Mary Bancroft, with her bright slash of red lipstick and her fluent but heavily accented German and appalling *Schwizertütsch*, both of which she inflicted on anyone within earshot. She was tall, of imposing carriage, and wore her skirts shorter than other women did. Then thirty-nine, she described herself as "at the height of my sexual prowess and usually always on the prowl." And because she was known as a "blabber," most people tried to avoid telling her anything they did not want bruited about the town.

Gerry Mayer was aware of Bancroft's reputation but was canny enough to note that beneath her indiscriminate chatter lay a strong, calculating intelligence and an innate and deeply patriotic American sensibility. Her love of and respect for her country were never far from the surface of her conversation, and if anyone denigrated the United States, she would defend it vociferously. She had worked for Mayer before Dulles arrived, writing articles about Switzerland for American publications and articles about the United States for the Swiss press. He edited them to show both audiences that the Swiss concept of neutrality was only government policy and not necessarily a reflection of the pro-Allied sentiment of individual citizens.[36] Mayer also gave Bancroft an adjunct task: to read the speeches of Hitler, Göring, and Goebbels printed in German newspapers, and to use Jungian insights to analyze them.[37]

Bancroft was one of the first persons Mayer suggested Dulles should recruit, after a seemingly casual drink at the bar of the Hotel Baur au Lac in Zürich, where Bancroft basked in the attention of two attractive men. She and Dulles discovered that both were solidly entrenched in the same East Coast social and professional upper classes: she was the product of a Boston love marriage between a Brahmin and his Irish working-class wife, and her paternal step-grandfather founded the *Wall Street Journal*. Her mother had died within hours of giving birth to Mary, and although she was raised primarily by her father's family, she had frequent contact with her Irish relatives, whom she adored. Spending time with both families gave Bancroft knowledge of the mores and rituals of two different cultures, but her divided upbringing led her to question where her true identity lay (which was one of the reasons she sought analysis with Jung). It also made her a prime candidate for intelligence work because it gave her a solid grounding in what she termed "different, but equally real worlds," even though she was often flustered over when or how to integrate or keep them separate.

Dulles was born in rural upstate New York to a family of Protestant ministers who frowned upon any emotional display and embraced the Protestant work ethic and all that the phrase implied. A Princeton graduate who had prior intelligence training, his World War I career in the Diplomatic Service placed him in Europe during the worst fighting and its aftermath.[38] When he met Bancroft, Dulles was forty-nine to her thirty-nine and a connoisseur of beautiful women, even though he was committed to his marriage, devoted to his wife, and the father of three teenage children. He knew of Jung through his wife, the former Martha Clover Todd (always called Clover), who had long been interested in psychoanalytic theory and who went to Zürich after the war to train as a Jungian analyst.[39]

When Dulles and Bancroft met at the Baur au Lac, they were immediately attracted to each other, but neither gave any overt sign beyond the natural flirtation of two dynamic people. That night at dinner, when Bancroft told her husband she had met the "newly arrived special assistant to the American minister," he snorted at her naïveté, saying "everyone in Switzerland" knew that Dulles was head of the American intelligence service except all the other Americans. Bancroft (at least in her memoir) claims to have been surprised.[40]

Bern was a hotbed of espionage in 1943.[41] The social scene was frenetically active: multiple cocktail parties and receptions were held every day, and the possibilities for serious intelligence gathering in everything from harmless flirtation to outrageous philandering were limitless. Every Axis and Allied country kept a legation, all informally friendly on the surface but deeply serious about trying to ascertain what the others were doing. It was not uncommon to hear cocktail party chatter among allegedly friendly enemies as each tried to "turn" the other into divulging information. There were also a great many Allied prisoners of war in Bern who were supposedly interned for the duration but who talked their way out of detention centers and into diplomatic social circles. They, too, dispensed information as they came and went, many slipping quietly over the borders of several countries to make their way to Lisbon and eventually back to England to fly or fight again.

There was not much war-related activity of a visible, dramatic nature in Zürich, but constant traffic of a far more serious kind took place there. The Americans used Bern as their public center of diplomatic activity and kept their profile in Zürich lower than the Germans did, who maintained a large legation. Not only were vast sums of Axis money channeled through Zürich, but commodities, logistics, and serious diplomatic initiatives were all conducted in the Swiss banking capital. A related benefit for a German legation in Zürich was proximity to the German border at Schaffhausen, which allowed swift and frequent crossing between the two countries.

One of those quietly posted in Zürich was Hans-Bernd Gisevius, ostensibly a low-level vice consul in the German consulate; in reality, he was a senior agent in the Nazi *Abwehr*, the German military intelligence service.[42] Rear Admiral Wilhelm Canaris, who directed the *Abwehr*, had secretly turned against Hitler even before war was declared and had been systematically recruiting agents who shared his views, Gisevius prominent among them.[43] Canaris sent Gisevius to Switzerland, charged specifically with developing contacts with the Allies that would provide backup support for the most sensational plot to depose Hitler, the failed putsch of July 20, 1944.

Dulles knew he would have to tread carefully with Gisevius because he was deeply loyal to his own country and would cooperate only because he wished to end the suffering of the German people, not out of a desire to betray his government. Gisevius was secretly writing a book he wanted to publish simultaneously in English and German as soon as the war ended. It was both his personal memoir and an accurate historical account of the military and policy decisions he observed as a senior *Abwehr* intelligence officer.[44] Dulles learned of the book, thought it was the hook he needed, and at this point brought Bancroft into the story.

Bancroft already had her small but significant reputation as a journalist, and she was a decent typist. Dulles planned to pass her off as more highly skilled in secretarial skills than she really was and also to persuade Gisevius she was a gifted translator. Without telling her why, Dulles asked Bancroft to come to Bern, and she accepted happily because a train trip to the capital offered a pleasant break from the drab monotony of daily life in Zürich. Over drinks in his apartment, Dulles told Bancroft that he wanted her help in a secret undertaking that required absolute silence and discretion. Were she to speak of it, more than five thousand lives would be jeopardized, if not lost. Before she could reply to this stunning remark, he made another breathtaking statement: the work they did together would cover their "romance," and the "romance" could flourish while hidden by the work.[45] She thought it an interesting proposition, in every sense of the word.

Dulles told her to go home to Zürich and wait to be contacted by a German "Doctor Bernhard," not his real name, but she did not yet need to know it. Dulles said offhandedly that the work would require a modest amount of translation and typing, leaving Bancroft with the impression that whatever the task, it would be a relatively simple undertaking. Dulles ignored her protests that even so, she was not up to it. He said he was particularly interested in anything the "Doctor" might tell her that contradicted what he told him (Dulles). And he repeated the admonition about the need for secrecy or the resultant loss of many lives.

Bancroft, the self-proclaimed "blabber," the extravert among all the Zürich introverts, was worried about the five thousand otherwise unidentified lives she allegedly held in her hands. She knew she was an indiscriminate and tactless gossip and was well aware that no one told secrets to her if they wanted them kept. For the first time in her life, she was genuinely worried about the trouble she might cause, which brought her back to Jung in deep distress. Her previous analytic history had been one of conflict and competition, and she had broken off several times in high dudgeon. By her own admission, she was looking to Jung to provide her with the strong father figure her own absent, distant father had never been. She had other feelings toward Jung, too, for even though he was by now an old man, "stooped, slow, and a lot of the time ill," she found him "sexually attractive."[46] He was well aware of her mixed feelings and refused to respond to any or all, which led her to throw temper tantrums, send accusatory letters, and, eventually, to stomp out and end several incomplete analyses. She had not seen Jung for almost a year when Dulles so frightened her with his admonition that she phoned Jung's secretary to ask for an appointment. Bancroft was astonished when Marie-Jeanne told her that Dr. Jung had been expecting her call that very week and had left instructions that whatever amount of time she needed was to be left open for her. Bancroft was more confused than ever.

When she went to Jung, she told him exactly what she knew up to that point, which was indeed very little: that Dulles wanted her to engage in activity that would require total silence and discretion or else the five thousand mystery lives would be lost. Jung listened intently and then said he thought she was probably capable of keeping a secret, if only because she could not bear the thought of being responsible for five thousand corpses. It was exactly what she needed to hear, so she made two swift decisions: she arranged for regular appointments to talk to Jung and then went home to wait for the "Doctor" to get in touch with her. It was the beginning of her career as "Mrs. Pestalozzi," the code name Dulles assigned her.[47]

The next day, "Doctor Bernhard" telephoned to ask if he could bring his manuscript that afternoon. When he arrived, she paled at the sight: more than a thousand tightly filled pages either handwritten in minuscule script or typed in old German orthography, all of it in dense, complex, and scholarly German. She knew at once that her command of the language was insufficient and the sheer number of pages was staggering. This was not a casual, occasional project but a real job demanding daily slogging for hours on end, with a dedication she had never given to anything in her dilettantish life. Also, she was a proper Swiss housewife, and her husband's business and social standing required a great deal of her time. She had to run a bourgeois household, entertain on her husband's behalf, and be free to travel when his business affairs necessitated her presence. How to incorporate the massive amount of work to translate "Dr. Bernhard's" manuscript into her daily life was worrisome — especially because of the five thousand lives at stake.

Jung became an important and calming influence, and Bancroft came to depend on his wisdom and council. He convinced her that she was the perfect person for the job, and with his backing, she turned to the task with a dedication that had hitherto been absent from her life. Early on, she realized that in addition to her German not being good enough, the work was too much for one person. She needed help but was unsure about who could provide it. Without discussing her plight with Dulles, she asked Jung to verify her hunch that there was one American among all the others whose discretion was impeccable: Mary Briner.[48] He agreed, adding that he had urged Briner for years to open an analytic practice because she was so good at keeping secrets (later she did become a Jungian analyst).

Briner accepted, and as she was also consulting Jung, he was aware from the beginning of the hard daily work the two women undertook. Each frequently confided thoughts about material they had translated, asking Jung if he concurred with Gisevius's assessment of another person's character or behavior, asking him to confirm not only their translations but also their judgments of the text.[49]

Dulles and Jung had not yet met personally, but in the written "Reports" Bancroft submitted to Dulles on a routine basis, she made frequent references to Jung. Dulles was aware of the gossip about Jung's alleged sympathy for the Nazi cause as well as the allegations of his active collaboration. From his many different intelligence sources, he ordered a thorough appraisal which he believed proved such allegations unfounded and untrue. He began, at first indirectly and through Bancroft, to consult Jung himself. Jung was eager to meet Dulles because he had formed an opinion of his character through conversations with Bancroft. He told her Dulles was "quite a tough nut" and was "glad [she had] his ear." He explained that he did not expect ambitious men who held positions of great power necessarily to follow the advice women gave them, but he still wanted men to "listen" and "take it into consideration" in order to "exercise their best judgment and not go off the deep end."[50] Bancroft was "thrilled" to hear Jung say this because it gave her "so much self-confidence" that from then on, she had no qualms about standing up to Dulles if she thought he was "on the wrong track."[51]

By February 3, 1943, Dulles and Jung had met and were engaged in a "still-experimental marriage between espionage and psychology," the "psychological profile" of political and military leaders.[52] Dulles sent a telegram to David Bruce at the OSS, urging him to pay attention to Jung's analyses of how German leaders would act or react, "especially Hitler in view of his psychopathic characteristics." He wrote, "It is Jung's belief that Hitler will take recourse in any desperate measures up to the end, but he does not exclude the possibility of suicide in a desperate moment."[53]

Without specifying, Dulles told Bruce that Jung's opinion was based on "dependable information," most likely from Bitter and his Swiss cohorts and perhaps from unidentified patients.[54] Jung knew that Hitler was already living underground in his East Prussian bunker and that anyone who wished to see him had first to be disarmed and X-rayed. Guests invited to dine had to sit in silence as Hitler did all the talking, and the resulting "mental strain" had already "broken several officers." Jung said, but he was wrong (as the July 20, 1944, attempt on Hitler's life proved), that "the leaders of the Army were too disorganized" to arrange a coup, let alone carry one out.

FROM THAT moment on, Jung became "Agent 488" in Dulles's reports to OSS offices in Washington and London, and 488's dispatches were considered fact and figured importantly in the agency's operational policies. What really "hooked"[55] Dulles into consulting Jung on more than just the German situation was his analysis of Swiss politics. Jung told Dulles his life would be "simpler" if the pro-Nazi Swiss federal president, Marcel Pilet-Golaz, were removed from office. Jung thought recent critical articles in *Die Weltwoche* "might be able to do it, and the *Neue Zürcher Zeitung* [was] after him, too, but they [didn't have] the courage of the *Weltwoche*." Jung told him, "The press *can* do something in this country," and in any event, there was enough information "to hang" Pilet-Golaz.[56] Dulles investigated Jung's assertions about how the Swiss press limited and somewhat controlled the pro-Nazi actions of Pilet-Golaz and saw how much truth lay in his analysis. He told Bancroft, who was "surprised by his surprise: after all, Jung had been analyzing criminals since his days at the Burghölzli."[57]

Dulles credited Jung with helping him to understand the situation: "[He understood] the characteristics of the sinister leaders of Nazi Germany and Fascist Italy. His judgment on these leaders and on their likely reactions to passing events was of real help to me in gauging the political situation. His deep antipathy to what Nazism and Fascism stood for was clearly evidenced in these conversations."[58]

Jung was also a frequent subject of the private conversations between Dulles and Bancroft when they shared "the ritual cigarette after lovemaking."[59] He wanted her to "ask Jung" so many questions, supplying her with detailed questions she was to put to him, that their meetings (for by now they were no longer true analytic sessions) became devoted to them. Ever mindful of the five thousand lives (the phrase had by this time become their code for Allied operatives throughout Europe), she stored Jung's answers carefully in her memory, for even her particular American version of shorthand (a different script unreadable by the Swiss) would have been too dangerous to commit to paper. Jung's responses were based dually on his firsthand observations and his particular theory of Nazi psychology. Even though by now it was old news, Jung told Dulles everything about what he had observed in Germany throughout the 1930s. Many of Dulles's daily communiqués to Washington were based on Jung's prior observations of Nazi character and conduct, and in return, Jung became privy to much current top-secret Allied intelligence.

A related postwar encounter also describes how much Dulles valued Jung's observations. Jung had another friend who had been an army officer assigned to Information and Intelligence, William Kennedy. As a boy, Kennedy became Jung's ward in 1919 when he attended school in Vevey while his father, a cancer specialist, worked in Leipzig. Kennedy was a frequent visitor to the Jung family for the rest of his life, and after the war he was the editor at an American publishing house who asked Dulles to comment on a manuscript by a former high-level Nazi. When Jung's name occurred in the conversation, Dulles volunteered that "nobody will probably ever know how much Professor Jung contributed to the Allied Cause during the war, by seeing people who were connected somehow with the other side." Kennedy pressed for further detail, but Dulles said only that most of the documentation was "highly classified for the indefinite future," and "Jung's services would have to remain undocumented."[60]

By 1945, when the primary Allied objective was to convince the German population that surrender was inevitable, Jung's views on how best to get civilians to accept defeat were being read by the Supreme Allied Commander, General Dwight D. Eisenhower.[61] Jung's analysis of Nazi propaganda was that it tried "to hollow out a moral hole with the hope of eventual collapse." He believed the best propaganda of the war thus far was "General Eisenhower's proclamations to the German people," which, he said, "appeal *to the best* in the German people, to its belief in idealism, truth and decency. They fill up the hole of moral inferiority, which is infinitely better propaganda than destructive insinuations."[62]

ONCE GISEVIUS trusted Dulles (and Bancroft as his emissary), he, too, wanted to meet Jung. He had read "Wotan" in the late 1930s, not in the conformed German *gleichgeschaltet* version but in the English translation of the original text, and many of the observations and conclusions in his book were based on it. Bancroft asked Gisevius if she could show Jung some of the passages she translated, particularly the *Rückschau*, the review or summary of the book written expressly for potential English-language publishers.[63] Gisevius wanted Jung to comment on the *Rückschau* as a "psychological study," but Bancroft kept her real thoughts about what would interest Jung to herself: "As a psychological study it was really not worth bothering Jung about. The thing that would interest Jung would be Gisevius's own psychology." That was indeed the case. Jung read the book and offered a psychological profile before he met Gisevius. He thought the book was "saturated with Nazi ideology" and the *Rückschau* exactly what a German audience wanted to read, but he was not so sure Americans would accept such "declaiming." Jung concluded that Gisevius was most likely "an honest and a decent man," but one nevertheless "still drunk with revolution." Later, after Jung came to know Gisevius, he said he had "the most devious mind of anybody I have ever met."[64]

Gisevius wanted Bancroft to arrange an appointment with Jung because he could not risk doing so himself. Swiss police monitored every outgoing telephone call from diplomatic locations, and he could not use public call boxes too often, as even they were monitored. Also, German intelligence agents surveilled their own people, and although he had not identified "his tail,"[65] Gisevius was sure he had one. Unwilling to compromise her own phone line, Bancroft insisted that he make contact on his own. Gisevius countered that to risk seeing a psychiatrist during professional hours would surely lead to his permanent recall to Germany. Bancroft said she would tell Jung that a "Dr. Bernhard" would be phoning for an appointment; Jung said to add the sentence "The professor knows me." Bancroft told Gisevius all other arrangements were up to him. He said he could not risk going to Jung's house during the day, as both Swiss and German agents were undoubtedly watching his movements and were probably watching the homes of controversial persons such as Jung as well. Bancroft had an answer for everything: "I told him to make an evening appointment and to take a bottle of wine, as if it were a social occasion."

Jung teased Bancroft after his first meeting with Gisevius: "Isn't he a nice boy," he said, grinning. "Isn't he!"[66] He told Bancroft their work together would be "an interesting experience" because both were extraverted intuitives. He advised her never to ask a direct question that required a factual answer, for Gisevius's response would be just like her own: he would be "thrown off-balance," which would temporarily shut down the "freewheeling, associative way of communicating" through which she gleaned so much useful information.[67] Gisevius stood six foot four inches and was handsome in the image of Hitler's Aryan ideal; Jung advised Bancroft on how to handle him: "[If I] wanted him to spill stuff to me, I should play his vanity for all its worth and never in my dealings with him do anything to make him aware of what I am doing."[68] Jung became serious when Bancroft told how Gisevius had been *"kaput"* since hearing him expound on the *"Tier in Mensch"* (the animal in man). Jung said he did it "intentionally" because the best way "to get the feel of somebody is to punch 'em right through to the kidneys. . . . When I am doing that I can get my finger in." He assured her Gisevius was "all right. He's a nice boy but too naïve." Of his book, Jung thought, "The fellow has got something. He really has."[69] Bancroft remembered how Jung sat puffing on his pipe so quietly that she thought he must have forgotten she was there. "I wonder what he is really doing here in Switzerland," he said, as if to himself. "That would be really interesting to know!"

BECAUSE TELEPHONE communication was compromised, Bancroft and Gisevius phoned each other only under the most pressing circumstances. When she needed to speak to him because of some urgent request from Dulles, she would use mental telepathy, concentrating on willing him to phone. She told Jung that within the next ten minutes, he would call, usually asking, "Yes? What is it? I just got your message to call." Dulles thought this was "crazy," but Jung was fascinated and asked her to keep careful records of each time she communicated mentally, how long she spent doing so, and how long it took until Gisevius responded.[70] When Bancroft told Dulles about Jung's directive, he snapped, "I wish you'd stop this nonsense! I don't want to go down in history as a footnote to a case of Jung's!"

CHAPTER 32

The Visions of 1944

O n February 11, 1944, Jung set out for his afternoon walk.[1] At age sixty-nine, he followed the exercise regime his doctor prescribed when he was recuperating from amoebic dysentery, and every day he walked at least one mile, preferably two. On this day, instead of ambling along the level Seestrasse and the other lakeside streets that formed his usual course, he opted for a more strenuous uphill climb to the top of Küsnacht Almend.

There had been much snow during the winter, but the diligent Swiss house-holders kept their sidewalks clean, so Jung's climb progressed fairly swiftly. As he neared the top he was more interested in the view — the lake down below on his right, the countryside on his left — than in his footing, and he slipped on a patch of black ice and began to fall. Trying to catch himself before he hit the ground, Jung twisted his leg and realized he had suffered at the least a serious strain, at worst a broken bone. Fortunately the accident happened in front of a house, for the Almend was not then the heavily residential area it is today. He managed to limp to it and the householder phoned for a taxi to take him home.

The son of Jung's family physician, also a doctor, came at once and diagnosed a broken fibula.[2] An ambulance took him to Klinik Hirslanden, a private hospital in the vicinity of the Burghölzli, where the leg was set and he was put to bed totally immobilized. In retrospect, the treatment was exactly right for a broken leg but entirely wrong for an active man approaching his seventieth birthday. Ten days later, he suffered a myocardial infarct caused by embolisms that formed in the immobilized leg and broke loose; two lodged in his lungs, while one affected his heart.

Jung was attended by the eminent heart surgeon Dr. Theodor Haemmerli-Schindler,[3] who figured importantly in the "visions of 1944 . . . the most enormous experience [he] ever had." Their "vastness" convinced him that he was "very close to death," but when they ended, he was hard-pressed to describe what had happened. "Basically," he decided, "it isn't much." Upon reflection, he said, "It was only a lot when I experienced it. When it became conscious it seems scanty."

Jung lost consciousness when the embolisms dislodged and made their way through his body. He was treated with a combination of oxygen and camphor that induced a condition he called "the outermost border," somewhere between "a dream and an ecstasy."[4] More likely, he was drifting between delirium and coma. He experienced himself as floating in space high above the earth directly over the island of Ceylon (now Sri Lanka). Below he saw oceans, deep and blue, and the outlines of the Indian subcontinent.

He described his visions in detail in *Memories, Dreams, Reflections,* but he did not include "the other big caesura . . . and an enormously significant one" that he made much of in the *Protocol* manuscripts: his trip to India in 1938–39. He believed passionately that the two were the most important experiences of his life. India was his first exposure to a non-Western culture and provoked the initial reflections upon religion that served as the basis for all his writing on the subject from then on. The 1944 infarct affected him in ways resembling the amoebic dysentery, when he was engulfed with similar, but shorter, episodes of delirium.

In the longer-lasting visions induced by the 1944 infarct, he could not see the entire globe of earth, only its contours, but his most vivid impression was the intensity of color. The earth shimmered as if outlined in silver. The Red Sea lived up to its name, the desert of Saudi Arabia was red-yellow, and dotted on the rest of the land masses were various spots of "dark green . . . like oxidized silver, very colorful." When he gazed left, he saw the Mediterranean Sea, and when he turned right, he saw the snow-covered Himalayas. In his delirium, he thought how extraordinary and yet how "naïve" it was to use the expressions "left" and "right" when he was floating in space. He remembered thinking, "[I was] on my way of taking my leave from the Earth." The thought of impending death was not frightening because he was experiencing "the most wonderful and magical view" of his entire life. He was grateful for such a vision and concentrated on enjoying it.

Still, impressions from his Indian illness continued to interrupt, permeating these visions as if with an underlying imagery that determined their content. In one, he saw a dark block of stone as big as his Küsnacht house floating next to him in space. He remembered seeing such rocks off the coast of the Bay of Bengal, into which temples had been carved. Inside the visionary rock was a "completely black Indian in a white robe in lotus position," seated in such silent repose that Jung knew the man was waiting for him. To get to this figure, he had to climb a series of steps carved into the stone, similar to some he had seen at the temples in Kandy. They were framed by small oil lamps resembling a flaming wreath, a purifying essence through which he had to walk. He recognized the significance of what was happening:

I had a feeling as if I were shedding everything, or rather as if everything were being shed from me; everything that I believed or wished or thought was taken from me . . . it was an extremely painful process. I was aware of everything that I had experienced and done, everything that had happened around me. All that I *had*, it was with me now. I consisted of it, so to speak: I consisted of my story, I am this bunch of facts. It was a feeling of extreme poverty and at the same time of great contentment. . . . I was objective. I was what I had been.

He wanted to mount the steps, but they were made of air. He looked down to his "bottom right" and realized he had been drifting in space and was now over Europe. Floating toward him was his physician, Dr. Haemmerli, framed in a golden laurel wreath.[5] "Oh, that is my doctor who treated me," Jung thought. "He was delegated from the Earth. There have been protests against my leaving and I must return." He was suffused with "terrible disappointment" as the vision faded and he awakened. Disappointment gave way to depression, and it took more than three weeks until he could reconcile himself "to live again." During his waking hours, he was "always terribly depressed . . . miserably weak . . . hardly daring to move." He resented being called back from "the horizon of the cosmos" to a "grey world" where he would have to "delude" himself into resuming his place in one of the "little boxes" wherein every individual lived a life of tragic isolation. The idea of food disgusted him, and he could not eat. He could not rid himself of the idea that his body had been dismembered, and he did not want to go through the arduous task of putting it back together again. He thought he had become a fish, and when the nurses spoon-fed him soup, he feared the liquid would flow out through his gills and soil the bedding.[6]

He resisted all his doctor's instructions because he did not want to resume the life he had known. Suddenly it struck Jung that his own life was not at risk, it was Dr. Haemmerli's. He remembered having seen the doctor in one of the visions: "[He was] in his Ur-gestalt, and when someone has reached this gestalt, it means that he will have to die soon." Jung tried to explain what the vision meant, but the doctor would not listen. Tensions arose and Emma reproached her husband for "being so unfriendly." On April 4, almost two months after his accident, Jung was allowed to sit on the edge of his bed for the first time. He never forgot the date because it was also the day Dr. Haemmerli was put to bed with septicemia, the infection that caused his death several days later.

Jung recovered grudgingly, and he remained in the hospital until the end of June. D day, which he had longed for, came and went, but he took no interest in the Allied progression toward Germany.[7] He continued to refuse food during the day, but at night, while he hovered in and out of a delusional state, he consented to take nourishment. Generally he would sleep until midnight and then awaken "in a completely altered state." He felt as if he were "floating in space . . . protected in the womb of the universe in a vast void, but filled with the greatest possible bliss."

"Now that's eternal salvation!" he told himself. His hospital room seemed so "enchanted" that he was actually happy to be there.[8] He confused his night nurse with "an old Jewish woman" who he thought was preparing "ritual kosher meals" for him but who was, in reality, simply warming the evening meal he had refused to eat earlier.

On the day of his accident, he was reading an alchemical treatise from the sixteenth century, the *Pardes Rimmonim* of Moses Cordovero. In his semi-delirium, he assumed a role within the text, of the Rabbi Simon ben Jochai, who officiates at the wedding of Malchuth and Tifereth.[9] The wedding took place in a fragrant garden of pomegranates, and Jung could not determine if he had a role in it. He simply experienced the sensation: "I was it. I was the wedding." His euphoria was so great that he called it "the bliss of a blissful wedding." Suddenly, this vision was transformed into one of Christian symbolism: "the wedding of the lamb in festively decorated Jerusalem." It consisted of "angels and light and I don't know what else." Here, too, his role was central: "I am the wedding of the lamb." Then it disappeared as well, and his last vision replaced it.

Now he walked through a wide valley leading to a range of "gentle" mountains situated within a verdant landscape that funneled into a theater resembling outdoor amphitheaters of antiquity. Here, a "hierosgamos" was in progress, a "mystical wedding" that was the epitome of the "ancient notion" of all that the concept of symbolic union and mystical unity implied.[10] This wedding was pagan, to unite the Greek gods Zeus and Hera, but once again it gave way to Christian imagery. He was imbued with "the smell of the Holy Spirit," a "pneuma of unbelievable holiness." The thought came to him that this was the true "*mysterium coniunctionis*," and that it was the final outcome, the solution, the ending, the culmination — whatever he might ultimately decide to call it — of the alchemical research and writing he had been doing with such dogged but apologetic secrecy. More than a decade had to pass before Jung was able to describe how he transformed his studies of alchemy into his alchemical writings, and how they led to and culminated in the volume entitled *Mysterium Coniunctionis*.

When pressed to describe how the published works of the last third of his life originated, he said they came to him in many instances much earlier and stemmed from "biographical notes, dreams, fantasies, etc."[11] These became his "ur-materials," with the books that resulted providing the means of "somehow fitting this hot matter into a world." He compared his inner world of "imagination and dreams" to "fiery, liquid basalt which later turns to stone, from which one can form anything." The "passion" originated in "this fire," which then freed the "flow of lava," which then "forced the issue," that is, the writing of the books, into which "everything integrated itself very naturally."

Jung said of his process:

I am the damnedest dilettante who has ever lived. I wanted to achieve something in my science and then I came upon this lava flow, and only then was everything put into order. I say dilettantism because I live off borrowings, I constantly borrow knowledge from others.[12] What I have done about alchemy and in psychiatry is partly original work. Apart from that, I depend on taking the forming material from the outside and I call that dilettantism because I haven't created it myself. Everything that I could somehow elucidate was gathered together. That's also how I felt about alchemy. I gathered it together. Alchemy — that didn't come from the inside.

He said it was only after 1929–30, when his serious, sustained study of alchemical texts really began, that he was able to find "a sort of fabric in which to dress up this ur-revelation" that had hitherto eluded him. He realized, as he had many years before when he broke with Freud, that he was on the verge of "dangerous experiences, the material that also destroys people." He had written about this much earlier in *The Red Book*, where, unwilling to use himself, he used Nietzsche as his example of "a human being destroyed by images that contain the abundance of strength and imaginative possibility."[13] He had not then pursued this train of thought, because it was too terrifying; nor had he attempted to fathom where such images might lead during those first desperate years of his rupture with Freud. His struggle then was to attain wholeness and harmony in a life so violently changed.

But at the age of seventy, he had already lived two years past sixty-eight, the age he predicted he would be when he died, so he felt tremendous freedom to say or write exactly what he wanted.[14] Calling *The Red Book* "the vessel of my oeuvre," the point from which all else originated, he concluded that "it cost me forty-five years, so to say, to gather all the things I wrote back then." Now he had the courage to say them. With this courage, the "bliss" of the delusions ended and were replaced with "objective analysis" of what had befallen him: "The only thing that remains for the feeling is a sum, a brilliant whole that contains the expectancy of that which is beginning, the surprise for that which just happened, and the satisfaction about the result is already contained in it, too. That is complete objectivity . . . an indescribable whole." At the end of May, shortly before he was well enough to go home, he called "these visions of 1944 . . . the most enormous experiences" he had ever had, or would be likely to have in his remaining years of life.

EMMA WAS with Jung constantly while he was in the hospital. Because the Hirslanden was private, she was able to rent a room on the corridor leading to the intensive-care unit where Jung was treated. From February until May, she never left the building, not even to make the short journey down the hill to her house, relying on her children and servants to bring her what she needed. Everything

Emma did was based on love and concern for her husband's well-being, but her actions caused rumor and tension. Like a modern-day Cerberus, she was the formidable guardian of Jung's gate, and no information about his condition was dispensed unless she authorized it. As she was imbued with the social attitudes of her upper-class Swiss background, this meant no news at all, no bulletins of any sort.[15] Rumors about his health flew throughout Zürich and were exaggerated with each telling. No visitors were permitted unless Emma approved, and for several months she allowed none but her children. Everyone who knew her agreed she had not one vicious, jealous, or vindictive bone in her body, but still, no one suffered more from Emma's strictures than Toni Wolff.

Jung's illness struck the death knell for their long relationship, which had been imperiled since Toni refused to participate in alchemical research. Marie-Louise von Franz (and, to a lesser extent, Barbara Hannah) took Toni's place in the life of Jung's mind. Von Franz never doubted that Jung would make a complete recovery and had gone on diligently with her research. In May, when Emma permitted visitors, von Franz was one of the few whom she welcomed, hoping that Jung would become engaged with her findings, and indeed he was.[16] As for Toni, whether intentionally or not, Emma saw to it that there was no place left for her by permitting only one brief visit several days before Jung was discharged.

By the time Jung went home, he was as dependent upon Emma as a small child upon his mother. Emma had figured in some of his nighttime hospital visions, but if Toni did, he neither spoke of them nor recorded any.[17] His visionary dreams of Emma began with their courtship and took him through the years of her steadfastness throughout their long marriage. Like his visions of the "hierosgamos," he compared his dreams of Emma to "being confronted with [the same sort of] wholeness." From that time on, he revered her for all that she had brought to his life, and he sanctified their marriage as "an indescribable whole."

JUNG WAS released from the hospital at the end of June 1944, so weak that he could not mount the stairs to his second-floor bedroom. He spent the summer in the large central room on the ground floor, where a hospital bed was installed in a corner. To regain strength, he took little walks around the room, looking at the pictures on the walls and picking up objects, as if to reacquaint himself with his former life.

Emma took charge of everything. She told his secretary how to answer the barrage of mail from well-wishers, writing much of it herself.[18] She screened telephone calls and answered the doorbell, thus ensuring that few people got to see him, perhaps one every other day and then for strictly limited periods of fifteen minutes or less.[19] Every now and again, Jung would insist that Emma relax her strictures, and one of the few he managed to get by her was Mary Bancroft.

On a brilliantly clear Saturday morning, August 19, Emma told Bancroft she could stay for fifteen minutes, but Jung kept her there for well over an hour. Seeing him was "a great shock" to Bancroft, for he was much reduced by illness. His clothing hung from his rail-thin body, his shoulders were stooped, and he walked heavily and only with the aid of a cane. He insisted he was working steadily on a new book, the *Mysterium Coniunctionis*, but when Bancroft pressed for specifics, she sensed that the "grasping powers of his wonderful spirit had dimmed." She wondered what would become of the new book, for she was struck by "the definite impression that now it is a question with him of finishing up his life's work — nothing new will be undertaken."

Still, he retained an interest in world events. He told her he had been "absolutely dying of curiosity" to talk to her since "the *Attentat* of July 20," the failed plot to assassinate Hitler. He quizzed her "at white heat," as he had been following radio and newspaper accounts but did not have the inside information to which she and Dulles were privy. Jung told Bancroft he had not heard Admiral Canaris's name mentioned, nor his assistant's, Major General Hans Oster — names of Hitler's adversaries he knew from Gisevius's book and their conversations. He told Bancroft that as long as the two names were not in official reports, another assassination attempt had "every chance of being something tremendous." The failed putsch seemed further proof to Jung that Hitler had been spared yet again in order "to lead the German people to destruction." He told Bancroft to tell Dulles that he could not emphasize strongly enough how the Allies must partition Germany when the war ended, for if Germany were left united, "the whole story [i.e., another war] [would] start all over again and much sooner than anyone expect[ed]."

Then he asked her to walk with him down to the small pavilion beside his boathouse, several hundred yards from the back terrace of the house. He liked to sit there on summer days and listen to the water lapping, and he frequently invited his patients to take their analytic sessions in this secluded, tree-shaded setting. Emma found them there, deep in conversation, and insisted that Jung return to the full sunshine on the terrace and Bancroft take her leave. Jung made her promise to come again and sent regards to Dulles, saying he was welcome anytime, with or without an appointment.

As Bancroft took her farewell, she told Jung it was always comforting to talk to him, even though, she added, "I always know what you are going to say, but it is good to hear you say it."

"Oh sure," he replied with a smile. "Sure you always know what I am going to say! Sure you know!"

She left then, "feeling very sad to see one of the most remarkable spirits I have ever known getting so old and tired."

CHAPTER 33

⸺◈⸺

"Carl Jung, re: Subversive Activities"

The war in Europe ended in May 1945, but there was little outward change in Jung's daily life. He had no real contact with local public opinion until late October, when he realized how much he needed the outside world. It came through William Kennedy,[1] who had become the postwar officer in charge of films, theater, and music for Bavaria. He described Garson Kanin's new film, *The True Glory*, a documentary about the Allied D day landings, which Jung said he wanted to see. Kennedy sent it to Zürich and asked Lazar Wechsler, head of Praysans Film and renowned director of *The Last Chance*, to show it. Wechsler put his screening room and projectionist at Jung's disposal and told him to invite anyone he wanted to the showing.

"Word got out in Zürich," Kennedy remembered, and there was vehement protest. The loudest objection came from Dr. Emil Oprecht, director of the publishing house Europa Verlag and proprietor of the Europa bookstore on the Ramistrasse, a famous gathering place for Zürich intellectuals. Oprecht accused Jung of Nazi sympathies and urged a boycott if he attended. Jung was alerted to Oprecht's ill will, so he timed his arrival for one moment before the screening began. With him were Emma, several of his children, and a number of family friends and followers. Oprecht "ostentatiously got up and walked out" and a small coterie followed while Jung stayed and enjoyed the film. When Kennedy heard about Oprecht's snub, he tried to apologize, but Jung shrugged it off: "Well, obviously I have my detractors here in Zürich."

There were many, and they were encouraged by gossip filtering through the city about an *Attest* (testimony) Jung wrote for the German conductor Wilhelm Furtwängler, who fled Berlin before the war ended and now claimed he had never been a Nazi and should be permitted to remain in Switzerland for health reasons.[2] Furtwängler conducted the Berlin Philharmonic Orchestra throughout the war and was a highly visible and immensely valuable asset to Nazi propaganda. He lived sumptuously and was often photographed with leaders of the party on glittering occasions, which fueled rumors of his support for the regime.

Once he was in Switzerland, he insisted his wartime activity was because of his four children, whose "death sentence" he would have signed by acting otherwise.³

Furtwängler went to Switzerland ostensibly to give a series of concerts but really to go into exile. With the end of the war, public sentiment had become openly pro-Allied, and the concerts provoked outrage and led to demonstrations that were widely reported in the Swiss press. Reviled now in two countries, Furtwängler checked himself into the clinic La Prairie in Clarens-Montreux on February 24, 1945. Fearing the Swiss would deport him, he contacted Jung and went to Küsnacht to see him. Jung believed his story and diagnosed "a generalized depression with a basic mood of despair . . . psychogenic depression."⁴ Well aware of the cloud of suspicion of Nazi sympathizing that hung over his own head as well as Furtwängler's, Jung suggested they find someone whose reputation was impeccable and unsullied to make the ultimate diagnosis. He suggested a consultation with the eminent Dr. W. Löffler, dean of the University of Zürich Medical School, whose objectivity was unquestioned. Löffler agreed with Jung's diagnosis, adding that Furtwängler was also suffering from "a disease of the spine (spondylos deformans)" exacerbated by his depression. Jung thanked Löffler for taking over the case and asked him to meld into one the separate *"Atteste"* they each prepared. The individual documents have disappeared, but the blended one remains. In it, Jung and Löffler cite Furtwängler's "great personal courage" in keeping "Jews and half-Jews" in the orchestra "as long as they wished to stay, etc." Should the Swiss government deport him, they swore that he so "incense[d] the Party" (German and unspecified) that he would soon be "liquidated." Several months later, after repeated importuning by all three principals, the Swiss *Fremdenpolizei* granted Furtwängler asylum.⁵ Public opinion vilified Jung when it was over, and he hunkered down at home.

In his isolation, the resumption of mail service with the outside world became a momentous event. Jung groaned before the war at the volume of correspondence; now he regarded it a blessing rather than a curse as, spongelike, he soaked up news from his friends. Still mourning the death of Zimmer in 1943, he learned from Baynes's widow that his longtime British supporter had died of a brain tumor that same year.⁶ The paths of other colleagues had taken them far from Germany, and they were now adapting to new lives in new countries. Erna Rosenbaum (Pauli's analyst) joined Gerhard Adler to flee the Nazis and live and work in London; James and Hilde Kirsch were settled in Los Angeles, as were Max and Lore Zeller, German Jews who fled Berlin; Erich and Julia Neumann were in Palestine, eventually to become citizens of the State of Israel, where they lived for the rest of their lives.

Now that it was safe to do so, Mary Mellon reconstituted the Bollingen Foundation and was gearing up to translate and publish Jung's writings. She chafed at not being able to return to Zürich, but postwar travel restrictions and Paul's responsibilities to his family's foundations kept them in the United States. She delegated her close friend John D. Barrett to become the editor to liaise with Jung on her behalf and keep the project on a steady schedule.[7] Mary Mellon wanted Cary Baynes to commit to the project, either in New York or Zürich, but Cary "was generally content to stay where she happened to be."[8] Cary flirted with various proposals but was too dilatory to take concrete action to leave Washington, Connecticut, until the house she lived in was sold and she had no choice but to move. Even then, she went only as far as the next village, so Jung had to content himself with her letters rather than her presence.

Besides Cary, Ruth Bailey was one of the first persons to whom Jung wrote when mail service resumed, but because delivery was still difficult and slow, his letter went on "a very long journey" of several months before it finally reached her.[9] A local "witch" in her village who had been "remarkably accurate about the war" always predicted that Ruth's life would be entwined with Jung's and his family's, which Ruth thought "too fantastic to believe." She resumed her custom of sending newspaper clippings so Jung could see for himself "the mess" that England had to deal with after the war. When the printing of books and periodicals was suspended for lack of paper, she was as devastated that she could not send *Punch* as he was that he could not receive it.[10] He loved the "three [or] four trunks of stories" that she always had to tell, and he "longed to listen with open ears" to her meandering digressions.[11]

Years of total immersion in the infighting of the Psychological Club made Jung yearn for news of the outside world. The members' bickering, over which Toni Wolff had always managed a modicum of control, intensified when she announced her decision to resign the presidency. She had many reasons, most of them connected with age, infirmity, and awareness that some of her most important relationships were over. Her mother died early in the war, and now the three sisters were planning to tear down the grand old house on the Freiestrasse and replace it with two separate apartment buildings.[12] As the unmarried daughter, Toni received a significant financial settlement from her mother's estate, but the property itself was divided between Susi Trüb and Erna Naeff, whose children eventually inherited the title to half the land and one each of the two buildings. The sisters guaranteed an apartment of Toni's choice in whichever building she preferred. Alone now in the grand old house except for her mother's maid, Lina (who remained Toni's devoted servant for the rest of her life), she was now urging her sisters to act swiftly.

The government returned Toni's car, and even though gas rationing was still in effect, she would have had enough to visit Jung if either wanted to see the other. Emma remained cordial but was definitely cool. Marie-Louise von Franz took up so much of Jung's time that Emma lumped Toni in with all the others whose visits she still monitored and restricted. Toni did not resume her usual Sunday afternoons with the Jung family, and Jung was too ill to leave the house at all, let alone resume his Wednesday afternoons with her.

Toni kept up a full analytic schedule and was as deeply committed to the furtherance of analytical psychology as she had ever been, so others were surprised when she willingly surrendered the power and authority of the club presidency. Even though Linda Fierz-David was assumed to be her logical successor, Toni urged the board to appoint C. A. Meier. The board (of which Meier was a member) was as divided as the general membership. Many remembered how disorganized Meier had been when he was Jung's secretary in the International Association; they worried that his abrasive demeanor, coupled with his lackadaisical attitude toward administration, would not bode well for the club. There was, however, a sizeable contingent that regarded him as Jung's protégé and natural successor. Even though Jung himself never described him in those words, Meier did nothing to discourage such views. Jung did recommend Meier to succeed him as the ETH professor in psychology, and Meier was appointed largely because of the endorsement. The professorship was distinguished, so it helped keep murmurs of dissent few and muted, and thus, Meier succeeded Toni Wolff. One of her last official acts and one of the first Meier strongly supported was the formal expulsion of any member or statutory guest who had been an active Nazi or overt Nazi sympathizer during the war, among them Gustav Richard Heyer and Otto Curtius.[13]

Meier was a busy man with many other professional responsibilities, but club members soon felt he was neglecting their interests to an alarming degree. Months after she resigned from the presidency, Toni Wolff was urged to assume what Barbara Hannah called the "arduous and rather thankless post" of club secretary. Thus Toni became the éminence grise, a shadow president who worked harder than when she actually held the job. Despite Hannah's reverence for Jung and her knowledge that he acquiesced when Emma banished Toni, she still became Toni's close and trusted friend. Hannah observed that becoming secretary was "characteristic of Toni; she always did what she thought was best for the club and never bothered about her own prestige or power."[14]

JUNG'S SEVENTIETH birthday was July 26, 1945, and the club members wanted to celebrate it as grandly as possible. Some proposed a series of lectures in his honor;[15] others wanted to present him with a rare alchemical book or an expensive work of art that was illustrative of some aspect of his psychology; still others wanted a costume ball in all its old prewar splendor or, at the very least, an extravagant dinner at the Dolder Grand Hotel. One lone person held a different idea of how best to celebrate: Jolande Jacobi, who had been agitating for "a clinic" since 1939.[16]

Jacobi got the idea when she learned about the Menninger Clinic in Topeka, Kansas. She told Jung that, as Menninger was primarily Freudian, he needed to think about organizing "something like a Jungian university," where students could become qualified to teach and practice analytical psychology. Jung thought it a good idea and gave her 100 francs to go to Geneva and do research in "an institute . . . with the biggest library on education." He told her to prepare a report that covered two major areas: how therapeutic studies were taught within the major universities throughout Europe and North America, and how one would go about constituting such an "institute" in Zürich. It was the first time the word was used in connection with how best to further analytical psychology in a formal setting.

"We have no [medically trained] people," Jung said of the followers who surrounded him in Zürich. "We have all these old ladies here, all sick people . . . only cured or half-cured patients but no scientists." Jacobi insisted they could only overcome the parochialism of his followers by attracting an international student body and persuading distinguished scholars to join the faculty. For true viability, the curriculum had to be in both English and German. Jung agreed with all Jacobi's suggestions and directed her to study possible models, such as the Institute for Medical Therapeutic Study, founded in 1938 by Gustav Bally at the University of Zürich and of which he was a founding member.

The idea of a Jungian university was tabled for the duration of the war, but as soon as it ended, Jacobi wanted to resuscitate her dormant idea. She was hampered by Emma, who thought she excited Jung too much and restricted her access more than anyone else's, even Toni's. Because she could not see Jung, Jacobi felt she had no choice but to confide the details of her plan to Emma, who was appalled by the idea. Just as she considered the management of information about Jung's illness a private family affair, Emma considered birthdays and anniversaries private celebrations not suitable for public ceremonial commemoration. She and her children rigidly adhered to the upper-class Swiss belief that Jung was not a public figure but merely "her husband, [their] father, and now the grandfather of [their] children." It was a practice the children honored after their parents' deaths and for the rest of their lives, often to the impediment of scholarly inquiry.[17] Emma squelched the idea of an institute as a birthday tribute as soon as she heard it, which did not keep the miffed Jacobi from expressing her disappointment or confiding the tentative details of her plan to many others. Even though nothing was done at the time, the seed was planted and the idea grew. For Jung's birthday present, Jacobi had to content herself with telling him she was hard at work on the book *Psychological Reflections*, an anthology of excerpts from his writings.[18] The news made him angry rather than happy: "He told me that because I summarized everything, no one would read his books anymore. I felt terrible."

Emma's wishes prevailed, and the birthday celebration consisted of a private family dinner at home. The five children had by now produced eighteen grandchildren, so it was a large, noisy, and festive occasion that Jung thoroughly enjoyed. The gift he liked best came from Emma and their daughters, a black dachshund puppy named "Puck," who took up permanent residence on his lap, ignoring the basket intended as his bed. To assuage Jung's friends and followers, Emma invited them to a garden party on the afternoon preceding the dinner, and he enjoyed that as well. Everyone remarked about how well he had regained his vitality and zest for life.

One of the few public recognitions of his milestone birthday came via Mary Bancroft, who wrote a commemorative article for the Associated Press.[19] "Now what shall we write for the American public?" Bancroft asked. "Good heavens, I don't know!" Jung replied. They began at the beginning, as Jung spoke of his roots in Basel, where the city's "humanistic atmosphere" had exerted a powerful effect upon him. They spoke of Nietzsche, whom Jung called "a poet, but a morbid one, and . . . a marvelous psychologist." He told Bancroft that his initial intention had been to study languages (not archeology, as he often told others) before he settled on the natural sciences: "I don't like to say I did so because I felt in that way I could perhaps help humanity, but that was the real reason." Once again he cited Kant as "the real basis of my philosophical education," insisting that whoever did not understand Kant's theory of cognition "cannot understand my psychology." He despaired that people confused his psychology with metaphysics: "They think when I say God, I mean God rather than the idea of God." The distinction was important to him. Bancroft wrote that she was nonetheless "impressed anew, not only by the brilliance of his mind and the daring and originality of his ideas but also by the depth of his religious sense." To her, the words engraved over the front doorway, *Vocatus atque non vocatus, Deus aderit* (Whether called or not, God will be present), were "extraordinarily appropriate" for the theoretical canon that evolved during his long life. Bancroft asked Jung how many university degrees he had. "One real one," he replied, "and seven honorary ones." The latest had just been conferred by the University of Geneva in honor of his birthday, and Jean Piaget, the noted psychologist (and former student of Sabina Spielrein), came to Küsnacht to present it personally.[20] Once the conversational niceties were attended to, Bancroft turned to the major topics of the interview, "About humanity. About the world. Perhaps about Germany." He replied that he had said all he could possibly say in "After the Catastrophe," an article just published in the *Neue Schweizer Rundschau.*[21] He told Bancroft it was fitting that his first postwar commentary on the subject should appear in the same magazine that published "Wotan" in 1936. Jung said "Catastrophe" was the most difficult article he had ever written because it forced everyone, not only Germans but also all Europeans, Christian or not, to look deeply into themselves to assess "one's own share of responsibility." Bancroft wrote that "the fact that the crimes took place in Germany and were committed by Germans cannot be denied. But they also took place in Christian Europe and it is this fact which Dr. Jung feels must be faced before the moral work of reconstruction can begin."

To Bancroft's shock and Jung's distress, the Associated Press did not print the article she wrote. Whoever edited the piece substituted a pastiche of quotes taken out of context from some of Jung's other writings and a fabrication of comments attributed to him. None were his actual remarks; in every instance the passages were altered or rewritten to conform to what the editor(s) wanted

Jung to have said. When Bancroft received a copy of the printed text, so negative and damaging, she sent an annotated copy to Jung replete with the marginal notation "He never said it! M.B." She also sent a copy of her original
article, which proved she had not asked many of the questions in the printed
version, so he could not have given the answers attributed to him. The AP
quoted Jung as saying "one should be cold blooded and objective" about having
been drawn "much deeper into the German matter than we like to admit." In a
collection of nonsequiturs that make no sense, he is alleged to have said:

> We Swiss consider ourselves outside of the magical atmosphere of the
> German guilt. But that changes as soon as we as Europeans come in con-
> tact with another continent or another people. What would we say if a
> resident of India said to us "you want to bring us Christian culture! What
> did Europe do in Auschwitz and Buchenwald?" Will it help us to say that
> it did not happen among us, that it happened some hundreds of kilome-
> ters farther east; not in our own country but in a neighboring country?

The AP has Jung allegedly calling Hitler a *"Pseudologia phantastica"* and Hermann Göring a *"Bauernfaenger,"* which the editors translated as "a bamboozler,
literally a catcher of country yokels." He did say the former, but in "After the
Catastrophe" and not the Bancroft interview; he did not say the latter.[22] In the
opinion of "the Swiss savant" (as the AP dubbed Jung), Nazi criminals were
"only a manifestation of a general increase in criminality in the past half century." They alleged that Jung cast blame for this trend on "the general interest
in detective fiction."

THE AP article reached a vast print audience throughout the world and may
well have been the spark that ignited the controversy about Jung's alleged collaboration with the Nazis. It was fueled when he gave another interview to the
Zürich weekly *Die Weltwoche* that was mistranslated by the left-leaning New
York newspaper *PM*.[23] The first salvo was fired in September 1945 by S. S.
Feldman, M.D., in the *American Journal of Psychiatry*.[24] Feldman compared portions of Jung's 1934 essay in the *Zentralblatt*[25] with comments attributed to him
in *PM*. Using his own translation of the *Zentralblatt* text, Feldman quoted Jung
as having said the "Aryan unconscious has a higher potential than the Jewish,"
and when he "warned the world of this," he became tarred as an "antisemite."
In Feldman's most damaging passage, Jung is alleged to have said: "Freud is responsible for it. He and his Germanic followers could not understand the German
psyche. Have they been taught a better lesson by the powerful National-Socialism
at which the whole world looks with admiration — a movement which pervades
a whole people and is manifest in every German individual?"
Feldman's translation was always taken for fact by both critics and defenders,

as no one ever questioned its accuracy. It is unfortunate, because Jung made none of these comments in the printed text of the *Zentralblatt* essay. When he spoke of Freud or Adler, or any of those he deemed the other "forerunners" of psychotherapy, he did it courteously. His summary of Freud's contribution pays meticulous respect where he believes it is due, but he does conclude, "It does no good for a whole generation of physicians to go to sleep upon Freud's laurels. In matters of the soul we are far from knowing all there is, and what we need specifically today is the liberation from outdated viewpoints which have gravely restricted our vision of the whole."[26] Feldman used that statement to verify his accusation that Jung held Freud (and Adler) responsible for a "negative psychology because as Jews they could only see faults and not virtues."[27]

Well before the Feldman article was published, Bancroft urged Jung to make a rebuttal or ask AP for an apology, but he did not ponder how best to answer the mounting attacks until later. Rascher Verlag, his German-language publisher, seemed to have the best solution: a book to be entitled *Vor, Wahrend und Nach der Katastrophe* (Before, During, and After the Catastrophe). It would include the three essays "Wotan," "Die Psychotherapie in der Gegenwart" (Psychotherapy Today), and "Nach der Katastrophe" (After the Catastrophe). Jung agreed and began to collect notes toward a new preface.

When he told his friends and followers, disagreement flared. Hannah and von Franz, who at Jung's suggestion had just begun to live together in the same residence but had not yet declared their relationship as partners, disagreed on this, as they did about almost everything else in their daily lives.[28] Von Franz worried that it would distract Jung from writing the *Mysterium Coniunctionis*, while Hannah argued that he had a moral responsibility to make his position clear to the world. She might also have thought of the income and future work such a book would generate, as she had translated several of the articles and was eager to be named official translator of Jung's *Collected Works*.[29]

Hannah and von Franz represented the two poles upon which the disagreement hung, but with the directness of her extraverted intuition, Jolande Jacobi synthesized the major issues. When Jung asked what she thought of such a book, she argued forcefully against it and was convinced she had persuaded him not to allow Rascher to proceed. Several weeks later, she heard through the club grapevine that Jung was writing a new preface for the book. She begged him to reconsider in one of her longest and most impassioned letters ever (for she was as voluble with pen as she was in person). She urged him to read her letter as a sign of "sincerest devotion and not as unwanted meddling,"[30] knowing she was risking several decades of friendship by having the temerity to question his judgment.

Of course Rascher wanted to publish, she began. He would make a huge profit because the *Neue Schweizer Rundschau* worked for him and would charge next to nothing to set the text of work already printed. She accused Rascher of having no "intellectual understanding" of the delicacy of Jung's position, and of being interested only in the sales he stood to gain:

> Naturally your enemies will buy the booklet in order to attack it, the friends and enthusiasts will buy it to own it, and the greatest part will be those who are always curious and present whenever there's a smell of sensation in the air. . . . You don't have to convince those people who believe in you and are enthusiastic about you. But in no way will you win over or convert your enemies. . . . These works *don't have enough weight* for such a task [her emphasis].

She disparaged the essays as "more or less minor writings, carried by emotion, but not works of scientific research." To make them a book would appear to many readers merely as self-justification: "Why ask for such a reaction? Why pour oil onto the fire? Newspaper and magazine articles, no matter how inaccurate they may be, are never reviewed whereas a book such as this would be and would result in offering everyone the means of digging up things that should remain forgotten."

Jacobi thought Jung's critics could use these particular essays to do far greater damage to his reputation than if he left them to rest as separate articles buried in local journals with limited circulation. His writing style would cause further confusion because he circled around a subject from so many different perspectives and points of view that his many contradictory statements could easily be "lifted from their framework" and taken out of context. To make her point as strongly as possible, Jacobi selected random passages to show how easily it could be done: the 1934 *Zentralblatt* essay mistranslated by Feldman; some exchanges from the *Neue Zürcher Zeitung* dialogues with Gustav Bally; and a selection of letters written by readers highly critical of the most recent article in the *Neue Schweizer Rundschau*.

If he persisted, she posited several possibilities. He could — but only if he wished to waste his energies — rewrite these essays to give them "an objective, unaffected framework and background that elevates them from current political discussion." Even so, it would only result in "affective [negative] reactions." Another possibility was to write a preface and explain "in great detail *and honesty*" (her emphasis) what led him to insist upon airing his views about racial and national characteristics at a time when the Nazis could so easily use them for propaganda. This would appear to the public as his "confession and atonement" and would initially "cause a stir," but ultimately its "moral effect" would "rob all counter arguments . . . and strengthen [Jung's] position."

"I am telling you all this," Jacobi wrote, "because I have the feeling that you might not see the outside world clearly in your introversion." She urged him to heed the same advice he often gave her: "One should never argue with people whose resistance to oneself is based on projections, on irrational factors, etc." If Jung published this book, she believed he would do so at great risk because it would inflame "the deepest wounds of people" and make "objective discussion *impossible*" (her emphasis).

Following her sustained presentation of why Jung should not publish the book, Jacobi made two important points, the first an observation and the second a series of questions. In her observation, she spoke of the inadvisability of a psychologist repeatedly addressing such a highly charged subject:

> You are a psychologist, a scholar unique in his way, eminent and high above the confusion of everyday human issues. Your importance is undisputed, your research epoch-making, your works are acknowledged and respected all over the cultured world. If you speak on a political-ideological issue and do so in such a personal manner as it will appear in this book, then the entire developmental history of your path up to this point organically belongs in this place, too. Then you should speak openly about everything you feel and can answer to on this issue.

Then, like so many of Jung's admirers and detractors alike, she asked the questions that he never really answered:

> I myself do not quite understand why all this happened, why you didn't proceed aggressively against Nazism when it was still hidden to the world what kind of devils were at work in it. I understand you because I know you and because I know what it means to be deeply touched by the ambiguities of everything that is archetypal. I also understand the subtleties and the basic ideas which your statements concerning the race problem contained. But the audience does not understand them and cannot understand them, not only because they are too psychological but also because today these problems have the effect of a red rag to a bull, no matter how one approaches them.

Jacobi's thinking carried tremendous weight with Jung, as did his lawyer's, Dr. Jur. Hans Scharer, who agreed that the essays offered "too many targets for attack." But Jung eventually overruled them both and allowed Rascher to proceed with the book. The essays were published as he originally wrote them, unrevised and without an explanatory preface, in the book entitled *Aufsätze zur Zeitgeschichte* (Essays on Contemporary Events).[31] The book did not create the ruckus Jacobi feared. Swiss criticism remained mute even after several hostile articles by A. von Muralt in the *Winterthurer Tagblatt* (to which Jacobi wrote minutely detailed rebuttals).[32] It seemed to die down elsewhere as well. In Germany, an even more garbled version of the AP interview was printed in a manner Jung dismissed as "very misleading." The divided country was not yet ready to examine its recent past, so there especially, arguments faded from public purview.[33]

In the United States, the Bollingen Foundation was unsure of what to do with the book and ultimately decided it was best to do nothing for the immediate future. A decision had to be made when C. Halliwell Duell, of the firm Duell, Sloan & Pearce, heard of its existence and told Paul Mellon he would be interested in publishing it. Paul replied with a careful explanation of his two main reasons for refusing.[34] First, the book was "not up to the standard" of Jung's other writings, "either in conception, writing, or translations" and despite its "quality of timeliness," would "do more harm than good." Second, even as he insisted there was nothing in the essays to support the "ridiculous assumption that Jung is a Nazi sympathizer, or anti-Semitic," there was too great a risk that the book "might open the door to further vindictive attacks on Jung from the same sources as previously, by innuendo, tricks of quotation and omission, etc." Publication could only bring "irreparable harm" to the *Collected Works*. Duell concurred and let the project languish.

Still, it was only in the United States that controversy rolled on unabated for the remainder of the decade and in a very real sense ever after. Albert D. Parelhoff, one of Jung's most persistent critics, wrote a letter to the *New York Herald Tribune* that provoked a flurry of letters in support of Jung from (among others) Carol Baumann, Eleanor Bertine, and Esther Harding.[35] Parelhoff wrote again to rebut the rebuttals, as did Feldman and several others. Geoffrey Parsons, one of the paper's senior editors, told Allen Dulles in December 1945, "The Jewish campaign against Jung is in full cry, [but] its leaders have very little to go on."[36] Hoping to end an onslaught upon which he did not want to waste precious newsprint, Parsons told Dulles to "feel free to have the last word on the other side." Dulles telephoned Parsons to discuss how best to defuse the situation and then sent a letter intended for publication on December 28.[37] He admitted that he had no knowledge of Jung's "positions in writing or otherwise . . . prior to 1942" before pronouncing Jung "clean-cut and entirely anti-Nazi and anti-Fascist in his ideas and approach to world problems." As Dulles's wife, Clover, was in Zürich to analyze with Jolande Jacobi,[38] he told Parsons he would ask her to "scout around" for further information. He would also ask Mary Bancroft to try to persuade Jung to make a written statement in reply to his critics.

Jung did send Bancroft a written statement on January 25, 1946, a long *apologia pro vita sua* buttressed with footnotes referring to his own writings and those of some of his critics.[39] In an accompanying letter, he blamed Gerhard Adler for "starting this ridiculous avalanche." Why he blamed Adler, who was preparing to defend him in *The New Statesman* after attacks there by Feldman and Parelhoff, and what he expected Bancroft to do with his statement are equally unclear.[40] Three days later, on January 29, in reply to an impassioned plea from Cary Baynes, begging him to counter the attacks, Marie-Jeanne Schmid replied that Jung had decided not to respond "personally" because he was "convinced it would only make matters worse."[41] He had already prepared "a lot of material" for Adler, "as he felt that a Jew would be the best man to stand up against a Jew," and he would depend upon Adler's article to silence the critics. After it was published, Jung told Adler it was "very good indeed and corrects all the false accusations, bringing [out] all the real facts." He told everyone else the campaign against him was "so unspeakably idiotic that it [would] run itself dead after awhile because nobody gains . . . from such absurdities."[42] Jung was wrong, for Adler's article, based as it was on the *apologia* for Bancroft, silenced nobody. And, with the perfect hindsight of half a century, it was probably best that Bancroft and Dulles were unable to persuade anyone to publish the statement Jung wrote.

He began by blaming the attacks on "Prof. S. Freud and his followers," who, he said, "apparently have not grasped what may have induced me to represent a scientific view other than the teaching of their master."[43] He charged anyone who wanted to know why he rejected "FREUD" (his capitalization) to "make the effort of opening a book or two" of his writing. He held the belief that "Jewish psychology" differed from "Aryan-Germanic-Christian-European . . . long before the Hitler era," and he trotted out the usual examples to support his contention, among them his 1934 rebuttal to Bally in the *Neue Zürcher Zeitung* (complete with notes referencing himself). Jung offered Martin Luther as one who agreed with him when he said the Swiss had "a different spirit" than the Germans, for which no one ever charged Luther with being anti-Swiss. He argued that questions of racial and cultural difference could not be answered with scientific objectivity because of a single "fundamental fact" about psychology, wherein "the object of knowledge is also the organ of knowledge, which is the case in no other science." Thus, "every psychological theory [was] a subjective confession."

After several more pages of inconclusive examples and badly argued assertions, he addressed his own "position in the conflict of opinions" by saying only that he "worked with Germans a lot." His "exposed position naturally gave [his] ill-disposed critics new ammunition" but no critic took note of his many Jewish friends and students, none of whom had ever complained of his "so-called anti-Semitism."

Jung saved what he thought was his strongest defense until last: his version of the "particularly grave case" of Göring's 1934 *Zentralblatt* "declaration of loyalty" to the Nazis. Weakly, he termed it "very embarrassing," and said the reason he did not resign was that he felt "bound by a promise" to protect psychotherapy from being "suppressed entirely" in Germany. It was an "anything but easy" decision, but "any decent person would have done the same."

He dismissed his critics ultimately because they offered no "proof of the strength of their scientific position." They would neither gain from such attacks nor do him harm, but, conversely, they would cause "a good number of decent and responsible" persons to read his work and judge for themselves. Such attacks would only make "the slanderer's effort . . . come to naught." Once again, he was wrong.

ERNEST HARMS became Jung's apologist in an essay subtitled "Defender of Freud and the Jews."[44] It unleashed Albert D. Parelhoff yet again, who was now making "virtually a career of attacking Jung."[45] Parelhoff, instigator of the 1945 letter campaign in the *Herald Tribune*, became Jung's most sustained attacker with a three-part series in *The Protestant* subtitled "Nazi Collaborationist."[46] As both Harms and Parelhoff marshaled the same evidence to verify their opposing views, Jolande Jacobi's admonition rang true: supporters and critics could use the same writings to "counter these words you said with other words you said." No objective comment on such a charged subject seemed possible.

The debate cooled briefly at the end of 1946 but flared again in 1947 when Philip Wylie published a new book, *An Essay on Morals*, stating in the preface that his observations owed much to Jung's principles of analytical psychology. The single comment was enough to set off Parelhoff and like-minded cohorts. Wylie sent Jung a copy, but mail was still slow and sporadic and he had not received it when the attacks began. Concerned American friends told him Wylie's book provoked them, but they did not make it clear that Wylie championed his psychology. Jung jumped to the conclusion that the book was a diatribe, despite the positive impression he had formed of Wylie during their 1937 meetings. His negative conclusions were partly based on a series of wrong assumptions. Even though he had read and liked all of Wylie's previous books, he thought the publisher rather than the author had sent them, as no letter or personal message accompanied them.[47] During the war years, Wylie quoted Jung from time to time in his weekly syndicated column originating in the *New York Post*. Again, friends told Jung that his name was mentioned, but he never read the articles, and conflicting reports of their content filtered through from admirers and foes alike. Now there was mostly negative gossip about the *Morals* book, so Jung attacked Wylie on February 24, 1947.

"This rumour about me, that I am or was a Nazi, is an infamous lie," he roared. He was furious that Wylie had not asked him directly to respond to allegations before he published: "Talking of morals — I should prefer to inform myself before I am going to discredit a man by telling lies about him and I would not draw my information from irresponsible gossip based upon distortions and even downright falsifications and handed out to the public in a time where he could not defend himself." Now that the Nazis were deposed and Communism was the perceived threat of the time, Jung concluded that he would soon be painted red, as he had earlier been colored "a materialist, an atheist, a mystic, a Jew and what not."

The howl of wounded fury he dispatched to Wylie was stronger than the many other letters of protest and self-defense that he wrote to others during this time.[48] It is curious, however, that although he took the time to write so many private letters on the subject, he never felt the need to defend himself through an official letter to any editor of the many prestigious publications that would have printed his denial with alacrity. It seems he half-followed Jacobi's advice of not responding to his critics, of never explaining, never complaining. He only complained to his friends and may or may not have expected them to make explanations on his behalf.

A more likely explanation for his silence has to do with his family's overzealous concern for privacy and their policy of keeping themselves to themselves. The roles of father and son were shifting as Jung's only son, Franz, was moving into a position of paternalistic authority within his elderly father's life. Of the four sons-in-law, Walther Niehus was playing an increasingly commanding role in Jung's business affairs. Jung paid keen attention to Walther, husband of Marianne, the daughter who expressed the greatest interest in his professional life. They and his other children all advised silence and Jung complied.

Such a position might be more easily understood by a non-Swiss audience if considered in the light of an entry in the journal of one of Jung's analysands.[49] This person stubbornly clung to pro-Nazi sentiments even after severing all ties with Jung and analytical psychology. The diarist made some notations about impressions of "After the Catastrophe" and then justified personal behavior by comparing it to Jung's. The writer considered the Jung family's attitude typical of the false moral superiority that represented the entire country's perspective toward criticisms leveled by the rest of Europe and the world beyond. The Swiss, in this writer's view, believed that their wartime neutrality gave them the moral right to remain aloof from postwar comments, criticisms, and controversy and that the passage of time would show their hands to be clean and their behavior blameless. Until absolved by time, this diarist wrote that the Jung family in particular and the country in general believed silence was the appropriate Swiss response.

WHEN WYLIE received Jung's blast, he responded cautiously, writing four separate drafts of a letter, each approximately four single-spaced typed pages.[50] From the carefully prepared copies in Wylie's archives, it is not clear which he finally sent, but most likely it was the one in which he explained the "extent and nature" of his plan "to preach and teach Jung." His long-term intention was to write a series of books and use his syndicated column "which appeared once a week in twenty-five big city papers" to "create an audience" for Jung's psychology. "Since I am forty-five years old, the son of hardy stock," he wrote, "I think that in the course of my life I may make quite a few Americans aware that there is an architecture of the human spirit which they need to learn."

Wylie told Jung how difficult it was to write about his psychology because Freudian theory was dominant in the United States and its practitioners "do not understand your ideas because they wish not to." He spoke of "a considerable effort" to tar Jung as an anti-Semite and pro-Nazi "by quotations taken from context and by published inferences." Wylie described himself as "long a leading anti-Nazi writer" who tried "to allay these rumors of prejudice" in his book, which was garnering a "strange reception." An edition of fifty thousand copies was fast selling out because Jung's critics made it the "center of some of the most furious attack and equally perfervid defense." Jung thanked Wylie for his "brave courageous enterprise," and their intellectual friendship proceeded apace.[51]

Wylie was now the focus of a letter-writing campaign against Jung, so he defended him not only in his column but also in letters to various publications and in a long article as well. One column, entitled "A Dose of Jung Might Help Congress," led to an attack by psychoanalyst Clara Thompson, who charged Jung with promoting his own interests by serving the Nazi government as president of the International Society.[52] Thompson's argument energized other critics to write for and to other publications. Albert D. Parelhoff seized the opportunity to draw attention to his series of articles then appearing in *The Protestant* by sending letters to *The Saturday Review of Literature*, where Norman Cousins had just published one entitled "Bystanders Are Not Innocent."[53] Parelhoff called Wylie a "writing swashbuckler" who was trying to rehabilitate Jung's reputation because his own book's financial success depended on it.[54] When Jung heard about "that silly attack," he asked Wylie, "What in hell is it, that does ail them?" He was perplexed because none of his new writing had yet appeared in the United States: "Why should I be on their mind? Do I appear in their dreams?" From then on he ignored his critics and concentrated on analyzing Wylie's book.

Jung embraced Wylie's writing, much as Freud had embraced his own many decades before, conveying his joy in similar master-disciple terms at having finally found someone who understood him. Calling himself not flattered but "profoundly impressed" by Wylie's "seriousness of purpose," Jung said Wylie was the only person to date who "understood the basic principles of my psychology, as nobody else before."[55] Jung held this view for the next several years, during which he used uncharacteristically effusive language to express the importance of the relationship, as was evidenced in his attitude toward their correspondence.

Jung hated to write letters at any time but especially when he was at Bollingen. His secretaries described how resentful he was at having to deal with correspondence on the one day each week when they made the trek to his tower, carrying letters that had to be answered and the paraphernalia (particularly the heavy portable typewriter) they needed to do so.[56] But with Wylie, Jung was so eager to explain his theory and discuss his evolving ideas that he spent much of his time alone at Bollingen writing voluminous letters in longhand, imploring him to put up with his handwriting because he had "neither electricity nor typewriter"[57] and was too impatient to wait for his secretary.

The rapport lasted until 1949, when Wylie wrote an article meant to defend

Jung once more against the indefatigable Parelhoff, who attacked anew when the Library of Congress awarded the first annual Bollingen Foundation Prize in Poetry to Ezra Pound.[58] Jung had nothing to do with the award ("I don't know Ezra Pound, never read a word of him!"),[59] but Parelhoff managed to insert him directly into the controversy.

The Bollingen Foundation had been in full-scale operation since the waning days of the war, all according to Mary Mellon's plan to publish Jung's writings in a uniform edition in English translation. Her unexpected death from a fatal attack of asthma in October 1946 dealt heavy personal grief to Jung, Emma, and everyone else in Zürich who adored her,[60] but Paul Mellon honored all her commitments and even extended the foundation's mission in her memory. As both supporter and promoter of literature, the Bollingen Foundation frequently dispensed funds for individual scholarship and worthwhile competitions. One of the most important of these was a $10,000 contribution to support an annual prize in poetry that the Library of Congress wished to institute. In appreciation, the library named it the Bollingen Prize, and Ezra Pound was selected to receive the first, for his *Pisan Cantos*. The choice was controversial, as Pound had been imprisoned immediately after the war for pro-Fascist activity in Italy, and at the time of the award, he was confined to St. Elizabeths Hospital.

The Librarian of Congress, Luther Evans, was well aware of what would happen once the news of Pound's selection was made public: "The reaction would be, for the most part, emotional rather than intellectual; public conscience would be outraged." Evans sensed the award "possessed that bizarre quality that makes news," and the headline in the *New York Times* proved him right: "Pound, in Mental Clinic, Wins Prize for Poetry Penned in Treason Cell."[61]

Jung was drawn into the controversy because Parelhoff was determined that *The Saturday Review of Literature*, then one of the most respected literary publications in the United States, should enter the fray. He asked the editors of *The Saturday Review* if he could write an article attacking the prize — and Jung — but they decided to commission poet Robert Hillyer instead. Parelhoff made sure Hillyer was well supplied with information purporting to prove that Jung was a Nazi, that the Bollingen Foundation supported Jung, and ergo, everything about the award was political and an insult to American democracy.

Hillyer did possess notable credentials, as he was the current president of the Poetry Society of America and winner of the 1934 Pulitzer Prize for poetry.[62] He was, however, of the "Georgian, romantic-pastoral vein," an "isolated figure" better known for diatribes against modern poets such as T. S. Eliot and W. H. Auden, whom he had the temerity to regard as his chief rivals. His article began with the expected denunciation of Pound before he made the segue to Jung.[63] Asking rhetorically why the prize was named Bollingen and where the name originated, he answered that Jung lived there with his wife in an "idyllic cottage," where they received "the visits, adulation, and gifts of many, including such millionaires as Paul Mellon" (Hillyer then disposed neatly of possible legal action by saying there was "no implication" that Paul Mellon was aware of "Dr. Jung's former connection with Nazism.") Even though his subject was ostensibly Pound, Hillyer devoted the rest of the article to Parelhoff's "convincing proof" of Jung's "sympathies," which allegedly included "such Nazi flourishes as racism in general, the superman, anti-Semitism, and a weird metaphysics embracing occultism, alchemy, and the worship of Wotan." Hillyer based his knowledge on prior "personal contact" with Jung at the Harvard Tercentenary, claiming they were seated next to each other at an unspecified luncheon. He said Jung "introduced the subject of Hitler, developed it with alert warmth, and concluded . . . that Hitler's new order seemed to offer the one hope of Europe."

When Wylie sent a copy of the article, Jung responded to many of Hillyer's charges, but only because Wylie asked for documentation to prepare a rebuttal.[64] Jung said he might have told Hillyer that Hitler was "Germany's only chance," but he could not remember having done so: "At least I am sure that I often said so in conversations." He repeated his contention that "Germany, as she was and as I knew her (better than Mr. Hillyer), had indeed no other chance [i.e., choice]." He explained that whenever he expressed this view in the years prior to 1937, he did it because Hitler was in a "conservative phase" and there was "faint hope." Jung said he was not the only one deluded: "What about British statesmen with all the information of the Secret Service at their elbow and 'Peace for Our Time'?" He cited "Wotan" yet again, saying it took "supreme idiocy to misunderstand that paper." As for the Bollingen Foundation, "Hillyer's projections are incredibly ridiculous":

It is not my enterprise nor am I its instigator nor has it brought out a single book of mine nor am I financially benefitted by it. The late Mrs. Mary Mellon took a fancy to my tiny and most frugal country place, which she has seen just once. It is a little paradise, I admit, but it is chiefly the charm of the surrounding country. She took its name and I have not been paid for it even.

Wylie's article in *The Saturday Review of Literature* was entitled "What About Dr. Jung?," but his subtitle revealed that he had already answered his own question: "A Misunderstood Man."[65] He denounced the judges who awarded the poetry prize to Pound as morally irresponsible and intellectually incompetent, but the bulk of his article dealt with Jung as much as Hillyer's had. Wylie chastised Hillyer for veering from "the integrity of his good case against . . . Pound" into "a deluge of preposterous tirade against Jung."

There was a second article immediately following Wylie's, by Dr. Fredric Wertham and meant by *The Saturday Review* editors to be the last word on the subject. Wertham dismissed Wylie as Jung's "paladin," concluding that "his side has lost — at least for now." Wertham talked even less about Pound than all the previous writers. Mostly, he presented a factual recapitulation of Jung's cooperation with Nazi Germany during his years with the International Society, but he slanted chronological information and twisted it into an interpretation that allowed him to pronounce Jung a Fascist. He returned coyly to Pound only for his ending, saying he had no objection to Pound receiving the "Bollingen Prize"; he merely thought it should have been named "The Berchtesgaden Award," for no other American poet had lodged his art so firmly in the realm of Fascism.

The controversy moved beyond the pages of *The Saturday Review* when Leon Edel praised Hillyer in the *New York Daily Compass* for his "exemplary research," especially for finding out that the Bollingen Prize "was named after the Swiss estate of Jung, who himself shares Pound's pro-Axis beliefs."[66] In *The New Republic*, Malcolm Cowley concentrated his attack not on Pound or Jung, but upon "the Little American Republic of Letters." He denounced Hillyer as a Philistine for having "gone over to the enemy, like Pound in another war."[67]

The Pound fracas became political when Jacob K. Javits, the Republican senator from New York, read the Hillyer attack into the *Congressional Record* and called for an investigation. Other congressmen jumped on the Javits bandwagon, but instead of launching an investigation, they passed a resolution forbidding the Library of Congress to give any future prizes or awards.

Politics intruded in Switzerland as well. The Bollingen Foundation, concerned about the effect such accusations would have on the sale of Jung's books, was debating whether to ask him to prepare some sort of statement they could use to silence his critics. The editors consulted Jolande Jacobi for her opinion, and after much vacillation, she blurted out a tale that astonished them all. When Winston Churchill paid a highly symbolic visit to Switzerland in 1946, the Swiss government asked him whom he would like to meet. Churchill, through his daughter, Lady Mary Soames, put Jung first on the list. The Intelligence branch of the Swiss Foreign Office, well aware of the international controversy surrounding Jung, contacted Jacobi and ordered her to prepare a statement that would clarify Jung's position "in the face of certain attacks" not only there and in the United States but also in Germany, France, England, and other European nations.[68] Jacobi was astounded to learn that Jung and his close associates had been under surveillance by Swiss Intelligence for quite some time, as the government could not risk negative publicity compromising Churchill's highly symbolic visit.[69] She was warned to keep the inquiry confidential and was especially cautioned not to tell Jung (which she never did). She kept her silence until 1949, when she described the dossier she had prepared for the Bollingen Foundation editors in the hope that they could use something within it to quell the escalating rumors.

The Jacobi dossier consisted of a list of all the statements she had prepared to rebut past attacks throughout the world, such as her replies to von Muralt in Winterthur and a statement she thought she was sending in privacy through the mail to Adler in London. These, as well as her correspondence with Jung, had been intercepted, for the Intelligence agents had copies of everything, including her letters previously cited here. They also wanted a list of the statements she had culled from Jung's "speeches, articles, etc., which [were] indefensible taken out of context." Jacobi spent months preparing the dossier, collecting everything in which there was "allusion to, or accusation of, Jung's activities and point of view since the early thirties." She found clandestine wartime French newspaper articles reporting that his books were burned by the Nazis[70] and many wartime reports from other countries that represented a spectrum of differing views about his sympathies. She prepared a detailed curriculum vitae that documented Jung's every contact with Germans after 1933, his travels within Germany, and his participation (or refusal to participate) in German-sponsored activities or events, Nazi or otherwise. She also added a detailed list of the remarks "which, taken out of their context, are entirely indefensible, giving in each case either the proper context or his objective in making the statement."

It is almost inconceivable that a psychiatrist could have merited so much international attention, but the Swiss Foreign Office did send Jacobi's extensive dossier to "all its diplomatic and consular services throughout the world," where it surfaced intermittently throughout the next decade whenever Jung's wartime activity was questioned.[71]

HALF A century after the Bollingen Prize debacle, the dispute over Jung's wartime activity still remains an elusive event in American cultural history. When all the letters written to every publication involved in the Pound fracas are sorted into two piles, there is more debate about Jung than Pound and more pro-Jung letters than pro-Hillyer, Parelhoff, and others who shared their view. There are also fewer con-Jung letters than those against his attackers. When the few facts of his activity are analyzed within the subjective interpretations of both camps, the only true lasting judgment is Jacobi's, that words can be interpreted to mean just about anything.

Perhaps the best summation of what happened between 1946 and 1949 lies within a letter written by Malcolm Cowley to Allen Tate just as the controversy was fizzling out.[72] Cowley described a party he attended at which all the *Saturday Review of Literature* editors were present. One of them, Harrison Smith, told him: "Of course, we just printed the Hillyer articles and the editorial to start a controversy. It was a great success. We thought it would give us three exciting issues but it went on for six."

As THE controversy swirled in literary circles in the United States, the disgruntled husband of a former patient tried to take it further, not only to the United States Department of State and the FBI, but also to the British Foreign Office and the Nuremberg War Crimes Tribunal. Maurice Léon was by now divorced from Frances Goodrich Léon, Jung's patient between 1925 and 1935, but he had not overcome his still-festering resentment. At war's end, Léon was a part-ner in the prestigious Wall Street firm of Choate, Byrd, Léon and Garretson, with access to many highly placed officials in the United States government. As soon as the first letter defending Jung was printed in 1945 in the *New York Herald Tribune* (as it happened, by Carol Fisher Baumann, whom he knew from Zürich), Léon attacked. He wrote a fourteen- or fifteen-page "memorandum . . . con-cerning the case of Dr. Carl Gustav Jung," subtitled "Pseudo-scientist, Nazi Auxiliary."[73] Léon sent it to Benedict English at the State Department,[74] with copies to several others, among them Lieutenant Commander C. A. Horsky of the Office of United States Chief of Counsel for Prosecution of Axis Criminal-ity. Léon expected Horsky to send the memorandum to "the successor of Mr. Justice Jackson as Chief of Counsel for War Crimes," but Horsky left it to lan-guish on some State Department desk.

With a memorandum filled more with unbridled animosity and personal spite than actual charges, Léon sent a letter raising a specific question: "whether aiders and abettors of war crimes will be prosecuted, regardless of their nation-ality." Léon described Jung's followers as mainly "frustrated women." His home was a "stone house of rather forbidding mysterious exterior," and his wife "a woman of sad countenance who acted as an assistant to her husband, but in a ca-pacity secondary to that of Jung's principal assistant, Fräulein Toni Wolff." Jung himself cared only to be paid "fifty Swiss francs . . . whether the great man gave a 'treatment' or not"; Emma Jung "was on hand when the 'patient' or visitor left [to] collect the fee."

At this point, Léon's invective became a sad account of his personal history:

> The American women who have gone through the Jungian process may be divided roughly into two categories: those few who succeeded in get-ting their husbands to follow suit, and those who did not. Among the lat-ter divorces have been the rule. A man unwilling to drop all his normal activities in order to sit at Jung's feet for a year automatically proved his unfitness as a husband in the Jungian circle.

No one in Washington paid any attention to Léon, and a year passed during which he heard nothing. In frustration, he sent two copies to his friend in England, the diplomat and Germanophobe, Baron Robert G. Vansittart.[75] Lord Vansittart immediately contacted a colleague at the Foreign Office, F. F. Gar-ner, asking him to forward his by-now voluminous dossier to P. H. Dean, Esq. at the British War Crimes Executive, Nuremberg.[76] Vansittart thought little could be done to bring Jung to trial, "as he seem[ed] to be Swiss now," but wanted the British to use him to incriminate Matthias Göring, "just the sort of fellow who ought to be brought to book." Garner did as ordered and sent everything to Dean in Berlin, telling him "the best thing to do . . . is to put it straight into the waste paper basket and forget about it."[77]

LÉON'S NAME surfaced again during the *Saturday Review of Literature* controversy when he volunteered the same information to the FBI that he had earlier
given the State Department. The Bureau added it to a file begun in 1940 in
Pittsburgh entitled "Carl Jung, re: Subversive Activities."[78] Jung's name first
surfaced in the FBI's file on Olga Fröbe-Kapteyn, begun when she was innocently gathering materials for her collection on symbolism sponsored by Mary
and Paul Mellon. Both files originated in Pittsburgh because the Mellons lived
in Paul's ancestral home there after they left Zürich, and engaged in some of
their early, aborted efforts to set up the Bollingen Foundation. Jung's file languished until 1944, when Léon began to volunteer "confidential information"[79]
on a fairly routine basis, as did Hillyer and Parelhoff throughout the next several years.

Jung's file consists of fourteen to seventeen pages of mostly blacked-out areas, with only misinformation left intact.[80] One of the most amusing accounts
was recorded by an agent in New York sometime in 1945 or 1946, when someone notified the Bureau that Jung was "now in the United States" but the contact had "no definite information as to where." The report then quoted another
source who met a man who might have been Jung "on the bus line between
New Rochelle and Larchmont, NY." Mary Bancroft, aka the former "Mrs.
Pestalozzi" in her spying days, was responsible for this bit of falsehood, which
she gleefully passed along to Cary Baynes and Ximena de Angulo Roelli to warn
them the FBI would be questioning them soon.[81]

Just as they expected, Cary and Ximena were visited in Morris, Connecticut,
by a sweating young man in a dark suit, so wilted by the summer heat he could
hardly present his FBI credentials.[82] They invited him to drink lemonade and
cool off, but he spotted a copy of *Mein Kampf* on the bookshelf and beat a hasty
exit. Ximena worried that they would soon inspire their own FBI file and told
Cary she felt like "a character in a Hitchcock movie." Cary laughed off the entire episode, but unfortunately for Jung it was not that simple. Rumors of what
his FBI file contained were bandied about for the rest of his life, becoming a
major part of the mix of allegation and innuendo that dogged him long after
his death.[83]

Meanwhile, the editors at the Bollingen Foundation pondered whether the
Festschrift under preparation by Rhein-Verlag to celebrate Jung's seventy-fifth
birthday should be swiftly translated and published as an antidote to the negative press.[84] Echoing Harold Ross's famous phrase that *The New Yorker* was not
written for "the little old lady in Dubuque," they decided "not to bring Jung to
Peoria, let alone to defend him."[85] In this instance, as in every other, there was
no official comment. Jung kept silent, and so did everyone else.

CHAPTER 34

The Jungian University

In February 1947, Jung joked to Philip Wylie that even though serious illness delayed him from commenting on Wylie's *Generation of Vipers*, the novel certainly did not cause it.[1] Since November, Jung had been "slowly recovering"[2] from a second cardiac infarct that struck suddenly and unexpectedly. Unlike the first in 1944, he never lost consciousness or was hospitalized, although his doctor, the heart specialist Prof. Dr. Rohr, argued that he should be. Jung protested so violently that his racing pulse alarmed Dr. Rohr, who conceded if only to calm him. Dr. Rohr agreed to let Jung stay at home with round-the-clock professional nursing, but the Jung family never told him how difficult it was to arrange. The household situation was precarious because Emma had had six teeth pulled the day before Jung's attack and uncharacteristically had gone to bed with severe pain and swelling. The children were concerned because Emma had been generally "ailing" for some time, but they made her so nervous with their fluttering concern that she was adamant they could not stay in the house to minister to her or Jung. To complicate the situation, they could not find a nurse in Zürich because they all claimed to be superstitious about the "head doctor." Olga Fröbe finally found one in a village near Ascona who knew nothing about the old man's reputation, and she persuaded the woman to enlist another colleague. After a difficult few days, the two nurses agreed to go to Küsnacht, stay in the house, and divide the duty.

Several other related issues differentiated the two infarcts: unlike during his first, when Emma would not allow any information to be released, Jung directed Marie-Jeanne Schmid to send frequent bulletins to his correspondents and to inform anyone who phoned of the status of his health. Also unlike the first, an adjunct diagnosis of the second was tachycardia, a racing and irregular heartbeat, which Dr. Rohr attributed to extreme anxiety. As the infarct occurred during a period of intense creativity, the tachycardia was attributed to overwork, and medication was prescribed. No depression resulted from the second attack; nor was Jung sad to resume daily life, for he wanted to get back to work as quickly as possible. With that in mind, he insisted that the entire episode was psychosomatic, even as his doctor begged to differ.[3]

Jung was writing about "the historical counterpart to the psychology of the unconscious," about which he had been "up in the air until then."[4] He wanted to synthesize all his years of research on the workings of the unconscious mind into a method that would permit him to construct an objective science; by thus doing so, he hoped to create a cohesive system that others in the healing professions could apply to their own work. He started with examining how his research technique had evolved over the years into an amalgam of two distinctly different kinds. Since his break with Freud, he followed the custom of beginning with observations about himself, his ideas, intuitions, and dreams, which he buttressed with those his patients revealed during therapeutic sessions. By making such comparisons, he compiled empirical data and was able to assess more clearly not only what was shared and common but also what was uniquely individual. After collating the material, he looked for archetypal antecedents by reading widely and, in some instances, deeply through a variety of historical texts. The reading had a dual purpose: to search for further proof of his empirical observations as well as to look for new and possibly related areas of inquiry. Within this double-sided process, "the obscure, confused, and often grotesque statements of alchemy played the most important, indeed the decisive, role" in the final evolution of his mature theory.[5]

Jung explained his process in the opening pages of the essay "Introduction to the Religious and Psychological Problems of Alchemy."[6] He admitted that alchemy and the individuation process might seem "to lie very far apart," and the "uninitiated" might find it difficult "to conceive of any bridge between them," but those who understood the complexity of the human psyche would appreciate his contention that there was no end to what could be learned by studying it. In his own practice, he wrote, "hardly a day passes . . . but I come across something new and unexpected."

He was striving to identify that elusive something within the analytic process that he thought could best be compared to the ancient alchemists' search for the *lapis philosophorum*, the philosopher's stone. Jung believed this search was a metaphor for the alchemist's goal of self-realization, or, in his terms, individuation: "that is to say in the dialectical discussion between the conscious mind and the unconscious."[7] For Jung to pursue this quest meant making the conscious choice to become one of the "continuous chain of people, known in alchemy as the Golden or Homeric Chain, who from antiquity had undertaken the 'unpopular, ambiguous, and dangerous' venture of 'a voyage of discovery to the other pole of the world.'"[8]

The "perplexing nature" of such a line of inquiry had dominated Jung's intellectual life since 1928, when Richard Wilhelm gave him a copy of *The Secret of the Golden Flower.* The text became "the missing piece," or the "bridge,"[9] that allowed him to cross from Gnosticism through the cabala, which he studied cursorily before concentrating on alchemy. These readings ultimately revealed that the "central problem was of course the *coniunctio*," the alchemical symbol for the unification of opposites.[10] Until he came to alchemy, all his prior studies had been detours, or, as he was fond of saying, *"liber librum aperit"* (one book opens another).[11] The first offshoot of his research into alchemy was the 1946 publication *The Psychology of Transference*,[12] which was originally a separate and complete section of his final work, the *Mysterium Coniunctionis.* It took a decade to forge the *Mysterium* to his satisfaction, but when he did, it lodged his psychology securely "upon its historical foundations" and gave it "its place in reality."[13] Before this, however, he had to make several other detours into related byways.

The first was *Aion*, published in 1951. Jung dealt with the ramifications of Christianity found within the historical reality of Jesus Christ as well as with Christian symbolism and the idea of the Christ figure. He did not know what exactly he intended at various moments in the composition of *Aion* but felt "forced to write on blindly, not seeing at all what [he] was driving at."[14] Passages about "anima, animus, shadow and . . . self" soon accumulated into "about 25 pages in folio," leading him to realize that what he was after was "Christ — not the man but the divine being."

"If Christ means anything to me, it is only as a *symbol*. . . . I do not find the historical Jesus edifying at all, merely interesting because controversial."[15] This realization hit him like a "shock," and he "felt utterly unequal" to identifying, let alone explaining, what exactly he meant. The impetus to continue was the "beautiful material" he kept finding in his many readings.[16] *Aion* became an important milestone in the unfolding of his mature theory because in it Jung posited the idea that full self-realization was the only foundation for successful unity of being. Juxtaposing his concept of the self and the process of individuation against religious symbolism, particularly Christian, Jung concluded that religious symbols disappointed the contemporary person because both the historical and the symbolic Christ figures were incomplete symbols of the self. These religions, with their symbolic presentations, did not permit Christ to have a dark side, an "inferior" aspect of personality. The insistence upon the all-powerful and the all-good did not contain archetypes of the shadow, the anima, the animus, and thus resulted in an incomplete and unsatisfying symbol. In Jung's psychology, the archetype could not be whole and complete if it did not allow for the expression of both good and evil within the conscious and the unconscious.

Jung wrote about the number four, the idea of quaternity and many different expressions of the quaternion, including the four parts of the mandala; he created pairs of opposites that comprised both unity and opposition, such as good and evil, the spiritual and the material. For Jung, the ideas of good and bad were relative and only significant when both were present, for only then did he think psychic totality, the equilibrium of the self, was possible.

This question of a God who was both all-powerful and good but who also possessed a shadow and was capable of cruelty and evil became the subject of a text equally as important as *Aion*, his 1952 publication *Answer to Job*. "Finally many determinants came together," Jung said of *Job*, "and then one day it was ripe." In *Psychology and Alchemy* he had written of "the Christ" as a symbolic figure in order to explore what he called "the teaching of salvation."[17] This allowed him to question, criticize, and subsequently reject the Christian notion of God as "beautiful and good" and containing only "positive characteristics." He had questioned this doctrine briefly in the Vision Seminars of 1932 and more extensively in the 1940 Eranos *Tagung* essay "Toward a Psychology of the Idea of the Trinity."[18] Now, using the figure of the biblical Job, he took the position that to insist upon the absolute goodness of Christ in the traditional Christian scriptural sense would deny him "the shadow that properly belongs to [the Christian image of the self]."[19] Such a view did not permit the *privatio boni*, defined as the absence of or total lack of goodness that Jung believed the Christ figure had to contain in order to be whole. The next step in his research led to several unspecified alchemical texts that he lumped together loosely as "medieval nature philosophy." These he believed gave a more clearly defined "actual image of the God of this philosophy," or a *"complexio oppositorum."*[20]

He could not help thinking of these findings in relation to the character of Job. As Jung expressed it, "Job does expect that God shall in a way stand by him against God." He saw Job as "a prefiguration of Christ" because both were "connected by the idea of suffering." Christ had to suffer for the "sin of the world," but who, Jung wanted to know, "is to blame for this sin?" Melding the Trinity into one, he blamed "the God" for causing "the suffering," for having committed "this betrayal" and "who now has to suffer the human fate himself." The concept of evil became "a metaphysical reality, namely as contained within God himself." Where was it, he asked, if not in God? "Then it is in the human being and that doesn't explain it. After all, we didn't create the world. We ourselves are creatures of the world."

Jung eventually published *Answer to Job* for the same reason that *The Psychology of the Transference* (the first section of *Mysterium Coniunctionis*) appeared before the entire book was ready, because of the many questions that required him to explain his views on "the religious questions of modern man." With *Job* in particular, he hesitated for years, well aware of "the kind of tempest I would unleash." But as questions from patients intensified during and after World War II, and as audiences looked to him for answers in an existential world that many now considered to have no meaning or purpose, he could not help but be "moved by the urgency and difficulty of this problem."

He decided that the best way to present his theory was through his own "experience, sustained by subjective emotions." He hoped to "avoid giving the impression that [he] wanted to preach an eternal truth" and said he wanted *Answer to Job* to be "just the voice and the question of an individual who hopes for the thoughtfulness of the audience — or at least expects it."

IN THE last two decades of Jung's life, coinciding with the isolation and introspection imposed by the war, those who were close to him noticed changes in his attitude toward the world at large. In one of her succinct pronouncements, Jolande Jacobi described the major one: "He really wasn't interested in anyone's private life anymore. He was only interested in the 'Big Dreams,' in the collective archetypal world."[21] Using his two infarcts as his excuse, he curtailed public appearances and refused to meet most new people. He reduced his attendance at the Psychological Club and cut his analytic calendar drastically, seldom seeing more than four persons in any given day and then mostly for fifteen-minute conversations (a time limit Emma was happy to enforce) rather than full analytic hours.[22] Despite the many invitations that poured in, he chose not to travel, except for short trips within Switzerland. The only excursion he really looked forward to was the Eranos *Tagung* at Ascona, where he relished the intellectual contact.

True, he wanted to free as much time as possible for research and writing, but, as Jacobi put it, "in reality, he was no longer in contact with the pulsation of the outer world."[23] She explained his many inconsistencies by citing the two contradictory remarks he made most frequently and usually apropos of nothing, about the reception of his life's work. When he wanted to show how influential it was, he boasted that "the pope has my books on his night table." But almost in the same breath, he would complain morosely that "nobody reads my books. Nobody knows me."[24] Jacobi summed up everyone's concern: "When journalists came we were trembling and hoping that Müller the gardener gives the interviews because he is closer to reality. Jung lived now in another world."

There were more visible extremes in his behavior as well. During the three months he took to revise the original text of *Answer to Job*, he closeted himself away for long hours each day, writing to the point of exhaustion. Jacobi described him as "moody in a rude and crude way, like a peasant . . . furious all the time." The usually fastidious Jung sometimes went several days without shaving or (as some of his intimates inferred) bathing, but Emma was always there to see that he wore clean clothing.[25] Mixing analogies wildly, Jacobi described Jung's behavior as "like a woman giving birth to a child," or a man "who let himself go like an uneducated child." Everyone in his inner circle was concerned, and their worries coalesced into two categories: fear for the life of the man they revered; and serious concern for how best to preserve his heritage if he were no longer among them. Talk resumed about a "Jungian university," or some sort of formal "institute," and it soon became the primary topic of sustained discussion.

Besides concern for Jung's health, another reason the question of an institute became pressing was the influx of foreigners to the University of Zürich. To attract them, a general program of summer studies was offered in English, but quite a few liked the atmosphere and decided to enroll for a degree. Many were American veterans studying on the GI Bill; others were British or German, in flight from the postwar chaos of their homelands, happy to be in a country that offered sufficient food, heat, and shelter as well as a stable educational environment.

Jacobi was asked to teach a summer course in Jung's psychology. Twelve of the young American students asked for private lessons in Jungian theory and still others asked for Jungian analysis, so she told Jung the moment had come to act on her prewar plan of an institute for Jungian psychology akin to the Menninger Clinic in Kansas. At the same time, many of the older English and Americans who had been to Zürich before the war were returning in the hope of analyzing with Jung or, if not, of studying his psychology through some sort of formal program. As they usually made their initial inquiries at the Psychological Club, Linda Fierz-David lobbied to make it the official headquarters for any Jungian school that might come into being, with herself as the director. It put one headstrong, dynamic woman — Fierz-David — on a collision course with another — Jacobi.

Toni Wolff became involved in the dispute by merely listening to Fierz-David, with whom she would eventually side because she so disliked Jacobi. To bolster their case, Wolff enlisted C. A. Meier, who, because he was a man, she thought would carry more persuasive weight than all the women combined. Hannah and von Franz entered the fray, wanting an institute but not wanting either Fierz-David or Jacobi to have a leading role in it. They represented a united and vocal phalanx of two with special access to Jung: von Franz saw him every day to report her alchemical research; Hannah took her daily walk when Jung took his, so she had him to herself for at least an hour four or five times a week. Also, even though Müller still took care of the family cars and ran all the errands, Hannah elected herself Jung's chauffeur when he surrendered his driving license after the second infarct. She insisted on taking him and Emma to every meeting or function they wanted to attend, which gave her important access to the only person Jung really listened to — his wife.[26]

All these people harbored some sort of personal animosity toward both Fierz-David and Jacobi, but when pressed to take sides, they disliked Jacobi more. When this fractious group met to decide how to proceed, the Psychological Club became by default the venue, whether temporary or permanent to be decided upon later, where Jung's psychology would be explained to interested persons.

The beginning of the C. G. Jung Institute was that informal; the facts of how it became an organized entity are few and unclear. The personalities involved contested every statement hotly, in print and in public discourse; the feuds that raged at the time and the animosities that resulted were lifelong.[27] Throughout this entire contretemps, Jolande Jacobi was entirely absent. She was not invited to the executive committee meeting to present any of the information she had gathered so carefully for almost a decade about other clinics and foundations, about government rules and regulations that would have to be followed, or about faculty, curriculum, or finances. When she tried to speak at a general meeting to explore the idea of an institute, other members refused to give her the floor and demanded that she sit down and keep quiet.

Meier and Wolff then convened a private meeting of the club's executive committee to present their plan. They argued forcefully for a "bureau of lectures" designed primarily for the older English and American audience that already had some experience with Jung, knew something of his psychology, and was returning to Zürich for more detailed knowledge. They argued that some form of "social life" was needed, for the Swiss believed that the British and Americans could not digest an educational program unless it were interspersed with entertainment. Meier put Linda Fierz-David in charge of the program, even though she was "not trusted by the members."[28] There was such an outcry when he "sprang [the proposal] as a surprise" on the general membership that they rejected Fierz-David and petitioned to reconsider the entire matter, but only if Jung were present to make his wishes known. He agreed, and a second meeting was convened.

Barbara Hannah insisted that Jung should not discuss his intentions with anyone beforehand, so not even Emma or Toni knew what he would say. Everyone was shocked when he said he not only wanted an institute to be founded, but he wanted it to be organized "on quite a large scale." Hannah said he told her he changed his mind because all the controversy made him feel so powerless. He knew that his followers "would start one between [his] death and [his] funeral," so he wanted them to begin while he could "still have some influence on its form and perhaps stop some of the worst mistakes."[29] Jacobi gave a more cryptic account of why Jung changed his mind: "We will lose all our chances if we don't do this now," he told her.

Many years later, still bitter and smarting from the snub of exclusion, Jacobi described the meeting that set up the C. G. Jung Institute of Zürich: "The records of the Foundation [as the institute was then called] say that Mrs. Jacobi gave the idea, but the Club took over and founded it. I was not even invited. I was not even present." Jacobi was so completely ignored that none of those who set up the first programs deigned to consult the reams of documentation she amassed, even though she volunteered it repeatedly.[30] And yet, when the institute began, it followed exactly the pattern Jacobi envisioned in 1939, "along the lines of a European university, with many classes and non-compulsory attendance."[31]

But nothing could move forward without the approval of the Psychological Club members, a very real problem, as they were quite content to keep the dissemination of analytical psychology to themselves and for themselves only. Jung attributed their attitude to the extreme introversion of the membership, so he actively participated in forcing members to accept a more ambitious, extraverted

Jung in 1935, wearing his signature intaglio ring. (KML)

Jung at Eranos, Ascona, c. 1935. (Jane Cabot Reid)

C. G. and Emma Jung at Eranos, Ascona, c. 1935. (William McGuire)

C. G. Jung and Toni Wolff on his sailboat with her dog. (Wolff Family Archives)

Jung at Eranos, Ascona, c. 1935. (Photo by Catharine R. Cabot; courtesy of Jane Cabot Reid)

Jung with "my old darling," his red Chrysler convertible. (William McGuire)

Olga Fröbe-Kapteyn at Eranos, Ascona, c. 1935. (William McGuire)

Jolande Jacobi at Eranos, Ascona, c. 1935. (Ximena de Angulo Roelli)

Jung on the porch at Bailey Island, Maine, 1936. (KML)

Toni Wolff in her Women's Auxiliary uniform, c. 1940. (Wolff Family Archives)

Jung with Father Victor White at Bollingen. (Ruth Bailey)

Mary Conover Mellon. (William McGuire)

Frances Gillespy Wickes. (William McGuire)

Left to right: Barbara Hannah, M. Esther Harding, and Marie-Louise von Franz. (KML)

Toni Wolff in a rare smiling photo. (Wolff Family Archives)

Emma Jung in her last years. (Bollingen Foundation Archives)

Jung and Emma at Bollingen. (William McGuire)

The elderly Jung at Bollingen. (William McGuire)

R. F. C. Hull and Aniela Jaffé in Mallorca, 1962. (Birthe-Lena Hull)

Jung, holding a candle, in the last year of his life. (Photo by Aniela Jaffé; courtesy of Robert Hinshaw)

C. G. Jung: death mask. (Elsbeth Stoiber)

approach that would open his psychology to any interested person who wanted to learn about it.

The next step was how to organize the ambitious undertaking, starting with what to call it. Jung did not want his name in the title. He agreed with Toni Wolff on the title "Institut für complexe Psychologie," or simply the "Institute of Analytical Psychology."[32] Once again his followers won the day and voted to call it the C. G. Jung Institute.

Jung proposed a curatorium, a governing board independent of the Psychological Club, to be elected for life or at least for as long as members chose to serve. It was originally composed of five persons and later expanded to seven.[33] To keep the curatorium running on the track he wanted, Jung became the first board president but chose Meier to be its de facto director. Jung insisted also that Dr. Kurt Binswanger serve on the curatorium. Then director of his family's Kreuzlingen Sanatorium, he was an introverted, private man who had little interest in anything other than his work, but Jung wanted him because the Binswanger name carried a vestige of external esteem, and Kurt accepted as a gesture of respect toward Jung. For one of the two remaining members, Jung proposed Dr. Liliane Frey-Rohn, daughter of the president of the ETH and one of the younger analysts in Zürich who considered themselves Jungian in orientation. For the final member, he insisted on Jolande Jacobi. Cries of dismay resounded.

Both women were adjudged to be extraverted by the highly introverted (and disapproving) club members, but Frey was well liked because of her agreeable personality, whereas Jacobi was despised for her outspoken bluntness. In a second and highly visible snub, club members voted for Frey and against Jacobi. Jung called a special meeting in which he gave an impassioned speech, saying that the board needed Jacobi because she was the only person who knew how to operate in the world at large. Using Jacobi's research to plead his case, Jung held up the reams of official documents she had amassed and the detailed reports she had written. He begged the members to put her on the board because she knew how to liaise with — to give but one example — the Swiss government, with its avalanche of rules and regulations for every educational institution. Despite his insistence, they rejected Jacobi a second time, so Jung "pulled some very private strings" after the meeting to persuade several persons to change their vote. Without explanation or elaboration, Jacobi was pronounced a member of the curatorium.[34]

Allegedly, Linda Fierz-David never forgave Jung for not appointing her, but everyone was genuinely shocked when he did not select Toni Wolff. Barbara Hannah, who by this time considered herself Toni Wolff's closest friend, was more discreet than usual when she described Jung's decision coming as a "great surprise [to] many of her admirers and indeed [to] herself." She then quoted Toni's face-saving response that the new institute was not "her cup of tea."[35] Whether the rumor that arose was true or not, other club members were convinced that Emma was responsible for Toni's blatant omission; that, having moved to the center of her husband's life after his two illnesses, she was not about to jeopardize her status.

Just beneath the curatorium in rank, or equal to it in importance (depending on who made the assertion), were the "patrons," an international advisory board chosen because they represented important centers of Jungian activity. Although the Zürich institute became the acknowledged center for the study of analytical psychology when it opened in 1948, two centers had been operating earlier: in San Francisco and London.[36] Patrons who represented them included respectively Joseph Wheelwright and Joseph Henderson, and Gerhard Adler. Esther Harding was named to represent New York and James Kirsch Los Angeles. Membership was informal and personal, as Jung's casual invitation asking Father Victor White, the English Dominican, to join illustrates. Among the others were Wolfgang Pauli (described by Jung as "Nobel prize man") and Professor Adolf Vischer, who had been instrumental in his appointment to Basel University.[37]

As usual, Jolande Jacobi had something to say about both bodies: "The statutes make the *Curatorium* like Stalin, omnipotent! Dictators! Selected for a lifetime! It is impossible to do anything against them. Dispute is guaranteed between the Patrons and the Curatorium."[38] In a mixture of truth and exaggeration, she explained why Jung had to oversee the day-to-day operation of the fledgling institute: "No one wanted to do the work, only to quarrel." She might have explained it better by telling how everyone jumped to make individual decisions without consulting the others, which was the reason for all the communal quarreling.

Personalities soon revealed themselves: Emma and Toni lavished attention on the most minute administrative details; Barbara Hannah put herself, her car, and her outspoken opinions to work wherever she felt they were needed, becoming, in effect, the institute's first and most enduring "go-fer." Linda Fierz-David had a talent for defining curricula and syllabi, which put her in conflict with Marie-Louise von Franz, who thought she should be the final arbiter of both. Liliane Frey was the mediator whose cheerful mien soothed many a bruised ego. Meier was seen as a lackadaisical administrator who was "dictatorial, didn't give enough time or enough interest" and who "made scenes and didn't remember things, so there was often confusion."[39] He remained on the curatorium for the first decade of the institute's existence, but so many arguments, quarrels, and philosophic differences accumulated between him and Jung that he eventually resigned and severed all contact with the institute. Meier became the most visible of the many men who followed Jung at different times and who eventually parted with him on less than friendly terms. To the end of his life, he refused to comment on the ultimate reason for their break, but they seldom saw each other afterward.

THE ZÜRICH institute took its first students in 1948, and its "halcyon days"[40] lasted for the remainder of Jung's life. To name any of the students who went on to forge international reputations is to risk doing disservice to others not identified among them, but among the thirty or so students who enrolled yearly were the Americans James Hillman, Murray Stein, June Singer, Mary Ann Mattoon, and James Hall; the Canadian Marion Woodman; Luigi Zoja of Italy, Bou-Yong Rhi of South Korea, and Hayao Kawai of Japan.

Jung took an active role in the institute until 1950, when he decided that it was running smoothly, thanks to the administrators and faculty members who disseminated his theory. At the age of seventy-five, aware that his energies were finite and his canon not yet complete, he made the conscious decision to resign and try one more time to devote himself to writing. His family took over in his stead, with Emma becoming vice president of the curatorium and one other rotating member usually serving on the board or acting as patron. It thus became an informal custom for two members of the Jung family to serve at any given time.

The family's participation represented their varied interests. Only Agathe remained content in her chosen role of wife and mother, but her three children all contributed to the institute's governance in later years.[41] Jung's second daughter, Gret, found her métier as a respected astrologer and sometimes taught courses at the institute; his youngest, Helene, became an authority on icons, taught courses, and wrote several highly regarded books. Marianne took an administrative role within the family: overseeing all Jung's publications, becoming co-editor of the Swiss edition of his collected writings, and acting as liaison with the institute. As the only son, Franz was accorded a higher degree of deference by the curatorium, but his relationship to his father was undergoing many different shifts during these years and, depending on who tells the tale, his role in the institute is subject to many differing opinions.

ON APRIL 24, 1948, in his inaugural lecture to the C. G. Jung Institute of Zürich, Jung expressed his "particular pleasure and satisfaction" that an "Institute for Complex Psychology" would carry on his work.[42] The essay recapitulated his almost half century of research that began when "the broad fields of psychopathology and psychotherapy were so much wasteland." Giving credit to his forebears, he explained how the contributions of Freud, Janet, Flournoy, and Wundt had enriched his own work. He traced its development, citing how Richard Wilhelm and Heinrich Zimmer had led him in new directions. Mourning their early deaths, he also spoke of the more recent insights into the "phenomenon of the transference" he gleaned from the philologist Carl Kerényi. Jung then moved from past achievements into the realm of the future and the "unexpected and most promising connection . . . between complex psychology and physics, or, to be more accurate, microphysics." He gave credit to Meier for the concept of psychological "complementarity," and to Pascual Jordan for the "phenomenon of spatial relativity." He spoke of his former analysand and regular correspondent Wolfgang Pauli, with whom he was then collaborating on essays that would become the book *The Interpretation of Nature and the Psyche*.[43]

He dealt at some length with topics that were now engaging his interest, primary among them the *proportio sesquitertia*, or the ratio of 3 to 1. He called it "a fundamental problem in the psychology of the unconscious," and it became a subject he would investigate through its trinitarian and quaternian aspects in the *Mysterium Coniunctionis*. He mentioned the "space-time continuum" and the experiments into parapsychology of Dr. J. B. Rhine at Duke University[44] but did not mention the burgeoning interest in extraterrestrial phenomena that sparked his brief consideration of Rhine's work.

He paid brief homage to the writings of some of his pupils: Toni Wolff, Linda Fierz-David, Jolande Jacobi, Frances Wickes, H. G. Baynes, Gerhard Adler, Hedwig von Roques, Marie-Louise von Franz, and Erich Neumann. And he spoke of those who were not his immediate pupils or disciples but whose work demonstrated his significant influence on their thought: Hans Schär, W. P. Witcutt, Victor White, and Gebhard Frei.[45] Interestingly, he did not mention Hans Trüb, Philip Wylie, or the young American Ira Progoff, each of whom was a source of much intellectual ferment at the time.

Having given what he called a "picture of the past and present," he turned to "programmatic hints" for the future. In several paragraphs, he delineated what turned out to be an outline for research related to his interests in fields from psychology and medicine to religion and the humanities. Jung said he chose his topics "more or less at random," knowing they would be subject to the vagaries of "individual differences" and the "irrationality and unpredictability" of various disciplines. He made "no claim to completeness."

The essay is generally considered one of Jung's lesser works, published as it is in the last volume of his collected works, which bears the truthful if somewhat dismissive subtitle "Miscellaneous Writings." Nevertheless, it is worth serious scrutiny, not only for the summary of what Jung thought were his important and lasting contributions to his chosen field but also because it gives a capsule blueprint for the topics that engaged him for the remainder of his life. Here he was, at the age of seventy-two and in diminished health, setting out on a program of research that would have given pause to younger scholars at the beginning of their careers. It represented an overwhelming amount of work, but he completed it in a mere decade and a half.

He did not speak of any of his personal interests in his essay's conclusion or dwell on his current research. Rather, he ended on an upbeat note about what he hoped the C. G. Jung Institute would accomplish, citing one specific "prerogative" as its mission. Because it was an "institution with limited means, and not run by the state," the only way it would "survive" was through "work of high quality." He thought it had made a very good start.

CHAPTER 35

"Why Men Had to Quarrel and Leave"

Jung resigned as president of the curatorium in 1950, and Emma took his place on the board. He was pleased initially but grumbled later that she brought home too much news and gossip from their meetings and obliged him to listen. He seldom went to the institute during his last decade, but even so, his presence was strongly felt. All his disciples taught courses, and students were struck by how "everyone took a piece of him"[1] through unwitting (or perhaps conscious) imitation.[2] Meier wore a similar intaglio ring and twisted it when collecting his thoughts or fussing with his pipe, just like Jung. When von Franz wanted to emphasize a point, she clapped the edge of one hand on the palm of the other, timing her words to coincide with each rhythmic chop. Hannah tried to toss her head with the same lopsided shrug as Jung before breaking into a smile similar to his. Unfortunately, the students found her gestures alarming and awkward and were usually embarrassed. Only Jolande Jacobi seemed to be "her own person, centered and individuated." Students ranked her with von Franz as "the dominant influences at the Institute, exceptional women." Both, along with Toni Wolff, stood out because they concentrated on "the excellence of their lectures," but only Jacobi was praised for "furthering the business of the Institute."

Classes were held in the Gemeindestrasse house owned by the Psychological Club.[3] There, Toni Wolff moved through the hallways in spectral, dignified silence. Students thought she "lived a life of great pain," for she limped now and walked with a cane. Her anguish seemed more "spiritual" than physical, albeit for reasons they could not determine. Toni's complexion was haggard and gray, deeply lined from smoking. Students placed bets about how many cigarettes she could jam into her long ebony holder during class or how many times she would shrug in semi-apology as she did so, saying, "Everyone needs one vice, and I choose smoking for mine." Interestingly, there was no gossip about her past relationship with Jung, even among students native to Canton Zürich. If anyone knew of it, talking about it was "strictly taboo."

In contrast, Emma appeared to be "always there, floating in the background." When students asked questions during her lectures, she treated them as "potential peers," taking careful notes as they spoke before responding to each point raised. If Emma sensed that students were troubled, she found a graceful way to invite them to "come over to the house where [they could] talk." They thought her an exceptionally astute analyst.

A large photograph of Toni commemorating her long service as club president hung in the institute's main administrative office, and directly across from it hung one of Emma. Jung's was on the middle wall, between the two women's. No one thought anything of the placement until the American writer Lewis Mumford made much of it in an article written after all three were dead.[4] Even then, Toni's teaching was so respected that the primary response to Mumford's article was sadness that unwanted attention had been foisted upon such a great woman.

Others who studied at the institute in its first decade had a different explanation of the reason there was no gossip about Jung and Toni Wolff at that time: his followers "could permit no shadow on his image. This was the beginning of the 'cult,' the end of Jung the man as a physical reality and the beginning of Jung as an idea and an institution." In conjunction with this "routinization of [Jung's] personal charisma,"[5] the earliest students noted how too many classroom discussions ended with "but Jung said . . . ," as instructors cited his writing as ultimate authority to silence questions, disagreement, or even possible new applications of his theory. Students were promoted or failed according to "the guru system," in which their analyst made the highly personal decision of whether they were "trainable." Jealousies and animosities were common, and "the search for objective criteria was not yet there." The curriculum was "incredibly leisurely as compared to today." If students did not arrive with independent income or family backing, they were usually financially comfortable with such stipends as the GI Bill,[6] and the American dollar was high. There were "hours of talk and tennis playing in the afternoons, and nobody worked." In a short five years, everything changed, and it remains the same today: "Now they even have to clean houses in order to study here."

By 1955, the American presence remained large, but there were many more German-speaking students and a sizeable contingent from other foreign countries as far away as Australia.[7] The student body became a democratic group that represented different social and economic classes and insisted on bringing individual cultural experiences to bear on their studies. Most important of all, much of the classroom rigidity was replaced with a new and open professionalism. This was partly because new faculty had been recruited and the curricula broadened and enhanced, but it was also because of Jung's occasional contact with students.

He was an infrequent participant in seminars but gave "fireside chats" in his home several times yearly to answer questions submitted beforehand. Students remember that he did not really answer their questions; he merely used them as the starting point for thinking through his own ideas aloud.[8] When Jung was in his eighties, "when his voice was all but gone and he could hardly speak louder than a whisper," students marveled at his verbal virtuosities. In one instance he used the example of Sabina Spielrein to illustrate why he had to change his theory of intuition within the human psyche, and then he elaborated and expanded that theory anew as he spoke to them. Jung's overall point was the idea of "flux" and the need to be open to change, even if it meant contradicting one's earlier reasoning and writing. When he finished speaking, the mesmerized students realized he had given them important new theoretical insights they had been too busy absorbing to take notes upon, so there was no written record of anything he said. Unlike his seminars, where Mary Foote, Barbara Hannah, and a devoted band of stenographers took down his every word, this encounter ended like so many others, with nothing specific except his audience's impression of dazzling extemporaneous thought.

Several years after this incident, Jung tried to explain how his "system" evolved and why he so disliked both the word and the concept it implied. He said he dealt only with facts and attempted to construct hypotheses to cover them: "'System' sounds closed, dogmatic, rigid." He wanted to emphasize "the experimental, empirical, hypothetical nature of his work."[9] Jung created a dilemma for the students that became the most frequent topic of their informal "bull sessions," mainly, how an analyst should work:

> He had such radiance he was overwhelming. The man had so much charisma I could not help but think of how difficult it would be to have analysis with him. Jung taught us that the analyst must give the patient the space to be himself, must ask "but where are *you?*," but Jung was such an enormous personality that it was difficult to have one's own space when with him. He could not help it, it was just his personality. But I also believe it was the reason women fused with him and why men had to quarrel and leave.[10]

There were many intellectual disagreements with men in Jung's last decade and a half, so many that the nuances of each have been subsumed into a generalization that places the onus for their failure solely upon him. The most glib explanation is that Jung could not permit disagreement or deviation from full acceptance of his psychology; if any man questioned his authority, he was summarily banished by Jung and ostracized by his followers.[11] This was true in some instances; but in others it was far more subtle and complex, best illustrated through some of the most crucial broken friendships.

MEDARD BOSS was one of a select group of physicians and analysts Jung approached sometime around 1940, when wartime isolation made him yearn for professional conversation. He invited Boss and some others to join a workshop every fortnight in his home to discuss their cases and explain their methods. Through their different theoretical orientations, Jung hoped they could arrive at a consensus for a common form of treatment. The men he invited were seven of the nine curatorium members of the "Teaching Institute for Psychotherapy at the University of Zürich, founded in 1938 by Jung (president) and Bally (secretary), and in operation until 1948."[12] Among them were the medical doctors and psychiatrists Gustav Bally (Jung's attacker in the *Neue Zürcher Zeitung*), Hans Trüb (Toni Wolff's brother-in-law and former president of the Psychological Club), Kurt Binswanger (of the famous analytical family), Eric Katzenstein (a Zürich neurologist), and Hans Bänziger (a local psychiatrist and psychoanalyst). Alphons Maeder attended sporadically; C. A. Meier came regularly for a short time but pleaded the pressure of too many other duties and soon stopped attending.[13]

Boss believed that Jung formed the select group because he was unhappy that "he had no followers, no disciples or too few disciples among medical men."[14] He conceded that Jung's initial impetus stemmed from his genuine wish for "a kind of workshop . . . to present cases and refer to cases shown, practical cases," but he also believed that Jung's ultimate aim was "to point out his views about these cases" with the firm intention of having them adopted. After the meetings, Boss remembered that everyone was "a bit critical" of what transpired except Binswanger, who never commented. Boss was a younger member of the group, less hardened to a particular theory than the others, but he still believed his view represented theirs: "We didn't feel that the stories by Jung [i.e., from his current writings about alchemy] were proven or convincing but we still left it open. We thought we might understand [alchemy] more and better later." Still, they found the sessions rewarding: "We always had a good feeling after these meetings for we were most grateful to Jung that he sacrificed so much time and energy for us. But he never achieved turning us into followers or believers."[15]

One of the reasons for the group's collective hesitation may have stemmed from another of Boss's objections, a criticism he directed against Jung's writing: "Jung had a great disregard of the language of accurate formulation. He very much changes his formulations and switches from one saying to another." Boss exemplified one of the two general responses to Jung's writing style then current: students at the institute were dazzled by his brilliance and "flux," his ability to think on his feet; doctors in the workshop were irritated by "digressions" that impeded their search for system and order within medical treatment. The latter group was puzzled and dismayed, which may have been why they drifted off one by one until the group became so small (Boss, Katzenstein, Bänziger, and occasionally Meier) that Jung formally disbanded it in 1942.

After that, Boss had no further personal contact with Jung until 1947, when most of the group asked to reconvene informally, but only when a member wanted to present a case. Boss was particularly interested in soliciting everyone's opinion of his new theory of *Daseinsanalyse*, or existential psychoanalysis. He especially wanted Jung's commentary on the long thesis he needed to publish to secure his appointment as *Privatdozent* at the University of Zürich (where he later became professor of psychotherapy). Boss sent the manuscript, entitled *Sinn und Gehalt der sexuellen Perversionen* (The Meaning and Content of Sexual Perversion),[16] to Jung as a courtesy and asked for his comments and suggestions. In Boss's telling, Jung became "wild and cross" when he read it and raged that Boss was "betraying" him by "losing [himself] in philosophical fantastics."[17]

Afterward, when the dust from the dispute was mostly settled, Boss insisted he was "not critical" of Jung's analytical psychology but simply wanted to "replace it" with *Daseinanalyse* because "Jung's descriptions . . . were still loaded with the remnants of the old mechanistic exact-scientific way of thinking and with many outdated biological theories."[18] Boss insisted his work did not contain a single overt criticism of Jung, who "was not mentioned because he never worked on sexual perversion." Jung thought Boss was "going rather too far . . . to reproach [him] for a certain narrow-minded prejudice."[19] Boss insisted he was simply building on Jung's work on archetypes and extending it into existential analysis. Jung countered that Boss might believe he "discovered something entirely new and unknown to psychology." But in reality, he said, "You are describing exactly what I mean by the archetype." Jung extended the attack to the entire workshop group, saying they were responsible for creating an unfortunate situation where it seemed he wanted

> *à tout prix* to preach my doctrine (which isn't one) to unwilling listeners who later, in my absence, hold a discussion and eventually present their lack of understanding in writings and lectures to the public. As I always said, it was never my intention to promulgate my ideas, it was rather to collaborate. But when the other side does not participate and essential things are left outside, no fruitful discussion can develop.

Jung was so angry about meetings he believed they held behind his back that he told Bally it did no good if they met at his house and then convened elsewhere without him. He could not accept that Boss and the others were basically sympathetic to analytical psychology and merely felt the need for a neutral atmosphere away from his overwhelming "charisma," where they could decipher and digest what he told them before using it in the manner most appropriate for their needs. An impasse resulted.

Boss tried one last time to placate Jung,[20] who insisted he had been "maneuvered into a false position" that painted him as "the one with whom it is impossible to discuss any divergent opinion whatever."[21] He withdrew from the group with what he meant as a rebuff, suggesting that those who wished to continue to meet should begin with the "absolutely objective Katzenstein material" because he had played no part in its selection and it did not illustrate his "own concepts."

Boss regretted the lack of contact and in later years was one of the few members of the Zürich medical profession who participated — eagerly in his case — in celebrations honoring Jung, such as his eightieth birthday in 1955. Boss always expressed regret that "Jung was not accepted in Zürich medical circles. Very little so. But that is rather the fault of the medical people rather than of Jung."[22]

ONE OF Jung's quarrels of longest-running duration reached its climax during his dispute with Boss. Jung had been an adversary of Hans Trüb since the 1920s, when he forced Trüb's resignation from the Psychological Club presidency. The final rupture happened in the 1940s, when Trüb published a book entitled *Heilung aus der Begegnung* (Healing Through Meeting).[23] Sadly, the ramifications of their disagreement spread beyond the two men to have a profound impact on both families, ending a friendship so close that the two couples were godparents to some of each other's children. Toni's personal ties to Jung had diminished a decade before, but she chose to take his side despite her respect for Hans. Toni's always testy rapport with Susi became so strained that coldness and formality characterized their interactions for the final years of Toni's life.

The disagreement between Jung and Trüb had been brewing anew since 1936, when Toni and Emma, both hoping to resolve the widening theoretical gulf, worked uncharacteristically together to secure an invitation for Trüb to lecture at the club. As his method of treatment differed then only slightly from Jung's, they hoped his lectures would lead to dialogue and reconciliation.[24] By the time he spoke, Trüb had diverged even further from Jung by using some of the concepts and the term *"Psychosynthese"* as set forth by the Swiss psychologist Dumeng Bezzola.[25] Worse, as far as Jung was concerned, was Trüb's reliance on his close friend Martin Buber. Jung especially resented comparisons between his work and Buber's, so the disagreement deepened.

Basically, the dispute between Jung and Trüb hinged on a specific issue: how each man defined and differentiated the concepts of the *"Ich"* (I, ego) and *"Selbst"* (the self, or in Trüb's usage, *"Selbst-sein,"* self-being).[26] Trüb thought Jung's definitions were too theoretical in their reliance upon archetypal examples and, increasingly, upon alchemical correspondences. He did not see how they could be applied to what he called "practical psychology" and the treatment of seriously ill patients. To Trüb, Jung's psychology was useful only for patients with mild neurosis. It was not appropriate for the "suffering patient" who could not distinguish the *"doubleness"*[27] between *"Ich und Selbst."* As he considered himself a healing physician rather than a propounder of theory, Trüb felt a need to begin with Jung's psychology but a moral obligation to move beyond it.

To explain when and why he began to draw away from Jung and toward Buber, Trüb often referred to his 1930 article "Eine Szene im Sprechzimmer des Arztes" (A Scene in the Doctor's Consulting Room).[28] He joked that he wrote it during his "revolutionary youth, the early stage of [his] disagreement with Jung," but it was far more serious than that. The article marked the first time Trüb expressed the view that psychology could not be used alone but needed to be bolstered with concepts gleaned from disciplines that dealt with a broader external worldview, one example being how political actions and events effected the well-being of the individual person. Here, Trüb applied Viktor von Weizäcker's description of the doctor and patient as sharing "companionship," which he illustrated with the old German saying "He is only a doctor if he suffers [with] the patient."[29] Trüb thought Jung did not countenance such behavior because his primary interest was not in the individual patient but in the archetypal experience the patient presented. Trüb's theory was pessimistic, possibly stemming from his own recurring bouts of depression.[30] During one of the most severe in the early 1930s, his intellectual friendships were strongest with Ernst Michel, the Frankfurt intellectual and independent Roman Catholic thinker; Emil Brunner, the professor of systematic theology, and Théophile Spöeri, the professor of literature, both at the University of Zürich. These men disdained Jung, believing themselves his intellectual superiors, and Jung was well aware of their scorn. Emboldened by these friendships, Trüb openly challenged Jung's current research, saying he could not endorse the "exploration of this whole realm of the unconscious, the cultural, the myth." He was "more interested in personal relationships," to which Jung replied, "Personal relationships don't count very much for me."[31] Trüb found this remark so shocking that, as his archive shows, he spent the next twenty years, indeed the rest of his life, brooding about what Jung might have meant and trying to puzzle it out in various kinds of writing.

Again and again, he tried to explain why he rejected "purely intellectual efforts in general and especially in psychotherapy" and why he believed Jung took "the wrong direction" when he became "too intellectual about investigating what was wrong in a life." Some years later, when Trüb decided to publish *Healing Through Meeting*, he intended it to address his disagreement with Jung, to surmount Jung's psychology and offer a more reasonable replacement. Sensing the impending breach, Gustav Bally stepped in to heal it with a letter to Jung.[32] Bally tried to convince Jung that his distinction between "*Ich*" and "*Selbst*" was "completely clear" to Trüb and that he was neither disputing nor contradicting it, but merely trying "not to use either of these terms in a strictly defining sense, as one does and has to do in a scientific psychological reflection."

Bally sent a copy of the letter to Trüb, who made extensive marginal comments directly on it and wrote a detailed commentary as well:

I admire his [Jung's] life's work! But as a psychotherapist I am not only a psychologist, and here begins the disagreement. Already in 1934 I wrote about the "Limitation of Psychology."[33] Jung *never* took notice of this, looked right past it, let me know that it was "simply none of his concern" [his emphasis].

Trüb wanted to "bring about unity of *Ich und Selbst* into an encounter with the world." He accused Jung of concocting a mixture of the "self, God, and the soul" to the world's detriment, because it did not inform the patient how to act responsibly in the world. Jung dismissed Trüb's "dialectics" as "a monologue in which [he] couldn't get a word in edgeways."[34] Emma wanted to avoid a complete break because of all their personal ties, so Jung told her to mediate and bring Trüb back into line because he always listened to her. When she failed, Jung accused Trüb of sweeping Emma's "documented proofs . . . under the table without so much as a glance." The dialogue ended in a stalemate, with Jung calling Trüb's method "very much like that of a theologian [i.e., dictated by dogma], as was his gross misunderstanding."

Ironically, each theoretician pursued the same idea separately: if psychology in and of itself was no longer the sole means of achieving (in Trüb's words) "the unified commitment of the human being" to the world in which he or she lived, what were other, related areas where the psychologist should look for answers? In Jung's case, it led to the study of alchemy, mythology, and comparative religion. In Trüb's, it led to Martin Buber and adherence to his concept of the "I and Thou."[35]

In 1942, Hans Trüb fell into his deepest and most lasting depression at the same time as he was diagnosed with Buerger's disease, a narrowing of the arteries, which began in his legs and spread throughout his body, causing constant, debilitating pain. He brooded over his inability to express his theory in a way that would have retained Jung's friendship, and in frustration in 1947 he published *Vom Selbst zur Welt* (From the Self to the World). Although personal contact between the families was already curtailed, the book was interpreted by all as Trüb's "stark, outspoken" attack on Jung and "an attempt to break their every connection." A series of "endless" letters flew among the women[36] because they knew Hans was critically ill and were determined to prevent a complete rupture.

Emma began, urging Trüb to "soften his views" and Jung "to accept that others could still be loyal even as they disagreed." Trüb thanked her for her efforts, and then defended his position at length. Jung made no written comment. Susi asked Toni to intercede because she "always hew[ed] to Jung's position and the point of view in his teachings," even though she had effectively departed from it by refusing to follow him into alchemy. Susi said she understood her sister's allegiance but would, of course, side with her husband.

From 1947 on, despite the combination of Buerger's disease and depression, Trüb forced himself to write *Heilung aus der Begegnung*, which he intended to be his magnum opus and the theoretical statement that advanced his psychology far beyond Jung's.[37] He had a full but unrevised draft when he was felled by a coronary occlusion and died suddenly in October 1949. Susi was determined to see the book to publication despite Toni's entreaties that she should not.[38] When Susi persisted, Emma joined Toni, but Susi held firm. Emma broke their long friendship and never saw Susi again except at Toni's funeral some years later.

The book was published in 1951, with its central concept of the "ill doctor" who, recognizing "the knowledge of his own misery," strove to be "doctor and helper above all else . . . to suffering human beings." Toni was highly critical of the book and wrote to Susi to explain why:

> Basically, everything Hans says is only the introduction to the real thing, namely to the treatment and cure, because he writes as a doctor and this is about psychotherapy. Therefore the essential part would be the depiction of his method and his way of treating and curing patients. After all, psychotherapy is not philosophy, which is concerned with principles and terms, but rather the art of dealing with psychological facts.

Toni devoted the next three pages of her long letter to differences between Christian and Jewish interpretations of classical literature, mythology, and the Old Testament. Revealing what many long suspected was an inability to understand the Jewish perspective, and what many others considered her innate anti-Semitism, Toni complained that Hans's "relationships to all the Jewish writers," especially Martin Buber, kept him from truly understanding that the ultimate physician was "Jesus himself, who is wounded and killed as a healer and thus becomes the divine doctor and savior."

In her rebuttal, Susi tried to move the debate to another plane, explaining how difficult it had been for Hans, who had "practically grown up" with Jung's theories but needed to "stand fully by his own convictions." She was unable to accept Toni's "counterarguments" because their loyalties were so opposed. "Your" theories, she wrote (deliberately using the German plural pronoun to show that she really meant Jung's), seemed to her "questionable and dangerous in practical application," for "very few of the people who deal most intensively with complex psychology give the impression of being truly delivered and healed people." Susi knew this comment would wound Toni, as it dumped her among Jung's "eleven thousand virgins." Toni found Susi's stance "aggressive" and likely to isolate her. Cornelia Brunner, then the president of the Psychology Club, "suggested so gently" that Susi resign that she did, "because the spirit reigning there [was] too one-sided and narrow at a human level."

She asked Toni: "Can we two sisters, despite the great difference that now is lying between us, continue to have a real relationship with each other?" Each had become "the supporter of a cause, an ideology . . . two adult people who were led to this position by fate." Susi insisted that the respect she felt for Toni and for her "life's commitment" would remain strong "even if complete silence should come between [them]." The silence was not complete but close to it; the sisters exchanged birthday and holiday greetings and were polite to each other at family gatherings, but that was the extent of it.

JUNG'S RELATIONSHIP to the Dominican priest Father Victor White, O.P., has been described in terms ranging from a "dialogue" to a "dispute" that raised "a wall of misunderstandings" and caused "the failure of . . . a collaboration."[39]

They began a correspondence in August 1945, when Jung was seventy and White a forty-three-year-old professor of dogmatic theology at Blackfriars, Oxford. A scholar of St. Thomas Aquinas and translator of the *Summa Theologia*, White was investigating possible correspondences between Thomistic doctrine and Jungian psychology.[40] He was in analysis with John Layard,[41] at whose prompting he sent some of his writings to Gerhard Adler. Layard and Adler agreed that Jung would be "highly interested"[42] in how scholars and theologians who represented the official viewpoint of the Catholic Church regarded his work. Jung read them enthusiastically, thinking he found in White a scholar-theologian who recognized "the enormous implications" and "really understood something of what the problem of psychology in our present world means."[43] He wished that White lived in Zürich, so they could puzzle together the complexities of "patristic wisdom" in light of "modern psychological experience."

White brought a great deal of analytic knowledge to his initial exchanges with Jung. He had read Freud and Adler in depth (holding strong reservations about both), had been through extensive Jungian analysis with Layard, and had many friends in the British Jungian community.[44] During the war years, he spent much time thinking and writing about Jung's psychology, believing that it represented "the personification of the best 'new science.'" He hoped to glean insights to "create a modern Thomistic synthesis, recasting divine truth in modern psychological categories," with the ultimate aim of "recasting the true meaning of Christian faith" and making it more accessible to "the modern mind."[45]

Their friendship began with a flurry of long, intense letters, much the same as Jung's initial correspondence with Philip Wylie, with most letters written at Bollingen, where he could take the time to think through his arguments and define his positions vis à vis White's. His handwritten letters filled many pages, as he overflowed with enthusiasm to find a younger man who shared his interests. In a very short while their intimacy was such that White became one of the special few invited to share Jung's vacations at the tower.

They made an unlikely duo. Even with the diminishments inflicted upon his body by old age and illness, Jung towered over the frail and slight younger man. They talked nonstop as they chopped wood and prepared meals, "[White] like a butterfly fluttering around a bear [Jung]."[46] Invited visitors were few and far between when White was there, and the uninvited were rare, for they knew how brutally Jung would dismiss them so he could concentrate every moment on conversation with the priest. Although it is impossible to arrive at the total truth of any human relationship, the published correspondence between the two men does contain insights into the character of each.[47] Many have tried to explain the complexity of White's character and personality,[48] but he himself remains obscured by many different shadows, even as his shadow (in the Jungian definition, as the negative side of the personality) remains quietly hidden. There is a famous photo of White with Jung at the Bollingen tower in which Jung, wearing a white shirt, is illuminated by sunlight; behind him in full clerical garb stands White, only his face lit, his body obscured by darkness. Such was the tenor of their relationship, an interplay of light and shadow. Gleanings, however, can be surmised.

Theirs may not have been the traditional analyst-patient relationship, but there are overtones in the portions of the letters their literary executors have allowed to be published of a sage advisor who pontificates to an advisee seeking enlightenment to reconcile opposites. There are cryptic hints of dream analysis and vocational counseling (by Jung), and training analysis (of White).[49] There is also evidence that White was a man given to initial outpourings of tremendous enthusiasm for Jung's writing that soon changed to hesitation, equivocation, and, eventually, to disappointment and disagreement. In his own published writings, however, White shows a consistency of outlook and expression, so that where uneasiness exists, it seems to lie within his desire to compromise as far as he could in order to sustain the friendship with Jung that obviously meant so much to him.

Within five years, the friendship disintegrated into estrangement because of their inability to resolve theoretical differences centered around the *privatio boni*, the absence of good and the possibility of evil, which could no longer be evaded when Jung published *Answer to Job*. Their letters dwindled, as did personal contact. Jung delivered a painful snub when White (who had been invited by Jung to be a member of the institute's board of patrons) was asked by the curatorium to lecture in 1955. Jung said he would be at Bollingen but pointedly did not ask White to visit. He added a halfhearted invitation for White to stay in the Küsnacht house when he returned, but White did not contact Jung at all, and Jung made no effort to see him.[50] Both men regretted the strained situation but stubbornly held fast to their opposing viewpoints. Neither did anything to lessen the standoff that prevailed until White's early death from intestinal cancer on May 22, 1960.

Like Jung's relationship with Freud, his with Victor White followed a path preordained from the beginning, wide enough for one to lead but not for two to walk side by side. Both men's fervent desire was "to reconcile Jungian psychology and Christian theology,"[51] but neither theorist was willing to modify or surrender his beliefs even if it might bring closer the longed-for unity of their disciplines. Tracing their thought processes shows instead how each hardened his opposing viewpoint.

Jung may have "nursed the vain hope" that White would "carry on the *opus magnum*" of his psychology, but the hope was "apparently vain," for White never hinted at such a possibility.[52] As one critic put it succinctly if inelegantly, the two scholars were able to maintain a respectful and cordial tone to their disagreement until Jung "cornered God the Father, pinned him to the nearest couch and promptly set about psychoanalysing him."[53] Jung found God "guilty of being unconscious, having projected his shadow upon humanity, and of perpetuating a considerable amount of injustice and evil." When Jung concluded that Christian theology deprived God of the possibility of having a shadow, White was bound by the tenets of his faith to declare him wrong. As a priest, he had to adhere to his Church's traditional theological understanding of the *privatio boni* as the absence of goodness, with evil having no substance in and of itself. White was aware of the opprobrium he would suffer within his order and the irreparable damage it would do to their friendship if Jung published *Answer to Job*. Jung was undeterred, so White fired one last warning salvo in an attempt to stop him by reviewing his Eranos lecture "On the Self." White criticized Jung for his "somewhat confused and confusing pages," for his "quasi-Manichaean dualism," and, most wounding of all, for the "infelicitous excursion of a great scientist outside his orbit." He dismissed Jung's interpretation of Thomistic thought as "a brief and unhappy encounter."[54]

Jung realized White's delicate position vis à vis his order, so he did not respond in the attack mode he usually directed at critics. Instead, he mustered every possible argument to show White how he could remain a loyal Dominican while still expressing convictions based upon psychological self-understanding. Such reasoning was unlikely to satisfy White's superiors; nor were these views possible for a man whose religious vows bound him to uphold the doctrines of his faith. White's crisis of conscience deepened.

As the personal drama careened toward an inresolvable breach, White was enduring tremendous pressure from within his order simply for continuing to write about Jung's psychology.[55] He was hastily removed from his teaching position at Oxford and sent to California, where he discovered he had no defined responsibilities once he got there. White was overwhelmed by the culture and climate shock of the American West Coast, but when he wrote to Jung, his main concern was frank relief that the "cathartic outburst" of *Job* was not yet published in the United States, where it would have created further problems for him.[56] He worried that Jung would think his reservations "unforgivable," but he could not understand what was to be gained by publishing "such an outburst." White argued that it could only "harm" his efforts to "make analytical psychology acceptable to, and respected by, the Catholics and other Christians who need it so badly."[57]

White's time in California was short. He was recalled to England, where *Job* had been published, and it became incumbent upon him to declare his ultimate allegiance. He did so with a scathing review in his order's journal, *Blackfriars*.[58] White was convinced that the ostracism he experienced within his order was caused by his continuing study of Jung, and it made him "furious as well as profoundly hurt."[59] He told this to Jung, who said such criticisms were "certainly unjust and you know it," even as he insisted, "Nobody has more sympathy with your predicament than I have."[60] Nevertheless, White's splenetic review paid scant attention to the book's content and was instead a personal attack upon its author.

He began by asking why "the Emperor has appeared in public without his clothes" and then accused Jung of a "religious development . . . fixated at the kindergarten level."[61] White wrote that even after Jung became aware of "the ways of God" both in the Bible and contemporary life, he still chose to react like a "spoiled child." He saved the worst for his conclusion, that the book's "most distressing feature" was replete with "the typical paranoid system which rationalizes and conceals an even more unbearable grief and resentment."[62]

The importance of White's friendship to Jung is evident in his reply, with its uncharacteristically even-tempered moderation. In one of his most carefully constructed letters, Jung thanked White for his "interesting and illuminating" *"correctio fatuorum"* (correction of fools).[63] Then he worked through each of White's criticisms, defending his views with far more restraint than was usual.[64] He had indeed taken "a dive into St. Thomas" but was not "refreshed afterwards."[65] He found the *"privatio boni* business . . . odious on account of its dangerous consequences," and "the question of Good and Evil had no connection to metaphysics" but was "only a concern of psychology." He insisted he was not a "neo-Manichean," even though he found "dualism" lurking in "the shadows of the Christian doctrine." He agreed that "God" was "the mystery of all mysteries" but said that "Good and Evil are psychological relativities" and thus could not be projected onto "a transcendent being." He made one gentle accusation against White, that by avoiding any consideration of Manichean dualism he allowed for the rise of "other subterfuges" within doctrinal exegesis. "I guess I am a heretic," Jung concluded. "I am not on the winning side, but most unpopular right and left."

After his review was published, White wrote several letters of quasi-apology that disintegrated into flashes of attack, gave way to equivocation, and meandered into obfuscation. Jung did not reply until White wrote that he was returning to Zürich to lecture at the institute. Jung broke his silence by telling White not to bother with a "conventional call" because it would be meaningless, and "a straightforward talk may be painful and not desirable."[66] Jung invoked a hint of the crucified Christ when he said he was aware of White's "true situation" within his order and did not want to add to its "spikes and thorns." He left up to the priest the decision of whether to meet (they did not) and closed his short letter with "Needless to say, you can count upon my friend-ship."

Now that both men are dead, and with their complete correspondence un-available to scholars until an indefinite future time, one major question re-mains.[67] What would have led "a practiced writer" such as White to "abandon his usual rhetorical control for this degree of critical overkill"?[68] White's "lan-guage was dictated almost entirely by rage," but whether it was based upon per-sonal animosity or dogmatic belief remains enigmatic.

By the time White published his last book, *Soul and Psyche*,[69] his anger was somewhat palliated. The book contained the *Blackfriars* review but in a heavily revised version. White eliminated the most violent criticisms, such as the com-ments about the "Emperor" without clothing and the "paranoid system" with which the work was imbued. He also muted the language in the rest of his charges to the extent that many became mere declarative sentences, bland and harmless.

White's conflicted attitude toward Jung colored their every communication from that time onward. Jung took measures (always steeped in politeness to permit White to save face) not to see him when he came to Zürich. Throughout these exchanges White begged Jung to believe in his friendship, "wrong-headed and heartless though it sometimes is."[70] Yet after attempting to placate Jung, White could not keep from adding comments bound to upset, such as one about the tenor at the institute: "My dear C. G. has around him only syco-phants and flatterers: or people requiring audiences or transferences which no mortal can carry. I *hope* I am wrong: such a situation is *too* inhuman" (his em-phasis). He alternated attacks with apology. Several days before the letter above, he expressed regret at having published his review of *Job* "without any regard for your feelings or my own feelings for you."[71]

Their last letters disintegrated into accusation, defensiveness, and counter-accusation. While White lay dying, Jung apologized for being a *"petra scandali,"* saying the role of a stumbling block had been imposed upon him by "fate" and not by "choice."[72] White replied that he was not sure if Jung's self-characterization were true and added, "But to the extent that you may have been, I think I can honestly say that I am grateful for it."[73]

JUNG GUARDED his diminished energies as his seventieth decade moved inex-orably onward. He was plagued repeatedly by *"la grippe"* or "flu," complained about his liver and rheumatism, and fussily monitored himself for possible re-currences of tachycardia.[74] Fearing that his heart would be affected by changes in altitude on the journey to Ascona for the Eranos meetings, he decided to risk it only every other year. His last attendance was in 1953, his last lecture earlier, in 1951. He spoke on a concept that had intrigued him ever since he named it for the first time at Richard Wilhelm's memorial address on May 10, 1930: *"Über Synchronizität"* (On Synchronicity).[75]

According to Barbara Hannah, Jung's informal explanation of a synchronistic event was "the coincidence between an inner image or hunch breaking into one's mind, and the occurrence of an outer event conveying the same meaning at approximately the same time."[76] His interest in "acausal or synchronistic connective principle[s]"[77] came to the fore while he was writing *Aion*, wherein he made extensive use of fish symbolism and connections between the astrological age of Pisces and the beginning of Christianity. By extension, he wondered if astrology might provide an "intuitive technique" for "statistical evaluation" because it contained so much "meaningful coincidence."[78] Jung believed that astronomical data did "correspond to individual traits of character," and therefore could "serve as a basis for a character study or for an interpretation of a given situation." He planned to use astrology to measure "an absolutely certain and indubitable fact . . . the marriage connection between two persons."[79]

By 1950, he realized he would need a great deal of help from persons who knew much more about astrology than he had time to learn. He selected four women with significant expertise to join the unpaid army of other volunteer women who devoted their professional lives to his research (von Franz and Hannah primary among them). The newly recruited four were members of the Psychological Club who had long been interested in astrology through the Tarot: Frau Sabina Tauber, Fräulein Hanni Binder, and Miss Mary Elliot, a shadowy Englishwoman about whom "nobody knew nothing" except that she was an acquaintance of Barbara Hannah.[80] The fourth was his daughter, Gret Baumann-Jung, a respected authority and teacher of astrology who provided much of the initial impetus for Jung to select it as the best method for statistical evaluation of acausal correspondences, the felicitous conjunction of seemingly unrelated incidences that he was now calling quite simply "synchronicity."

Jung convened the four at his home, where he explained what he wanted, distributed assignments, and sent them off to do the work. Between 1950 and 1952, they met approximately a half dozen times as a group but more frequently with him individually: Binder and Tauber were his patients, Elliot was frequently in Hannah's company when she chauffeured the Jungs in her car, and Gret's visits were numerous and informal. For nine years, Gret and Hanni were students of a German Jewish refugee physician not licensed to practice in Switzerland and who made his living teaching astrology. They conveyed what they learned from him to Jung. He assimilated what they told him but preferred to trust his intuitions as he wrote and then submitted it (usually to Gret) for observations or corrections. Both Hanni and Gret used several different sets of cards when they taught him how to consult the Tarot before they settled on the Grimaud cards of Antoine Court de Gébelin, the *Ancien Tarot de Marseilles*. Jung thought it was the only deck that possessed the properties and fulfilled the requirements of metaphor that he gleaned from within the alchemical texts.[81]

Jung assigned different tasks to the four women. Gret Baumann-Jung prepared the astrological charts of the married couples who became part of the statistics. He sent Hanni Binder to various psychiatric clinics to test schizoid patients, but they made her so uneasy she "could not stand it anymore." He then gave the assignment to Sabina Tauber and sent Binder to hospitals to interview victims of accidents, particularly those caused by motor vehicles. Miss Elliot seemed to have no clearly defined responsibilities other than to collate and file what her colleagues reported. Jung believed their research corroborated "three active times during a person's year [i.e., when they could control the outcome of external events in which they participated] and two passive [i.e., when they could not]." The research confirmed that accidents always happened during the passive periods, when the victims reported that they often had premonitions that "something bad would happen" but "they did not listen to the unconscious." Jung also had the women measure two other groups who did not do well during passive times: students who could not postpone tests and often failed examinations, and patients who had difficult and slow recoveries after scheduled surgery.

After three years, Jung decided that Binder, Tauber, and Elliot had provided as much information as he was likely to get and what they had amassed was subject to differing analysis, so he terminated their work and kept only his daughter as a consultant. He unwittingly created tension when he made Liliane Frey check all Gret's findings and, if results differed, always used Frey's conclusions and not his daughter's. Professor Markus Fierz, then at the University of Basel, became Jung's overall consultant for mathematical assessments of astrology. Eventually Jung turned over all the findings of the four women researchers to Professor Fierz's mother, Linda Fierz-David, which created even more unhappiness and resentment.[82]

WHILE JUNG was at work on synchronicity, the Roman Catholic Church, independently to be sure, corroborated a thesis he had long held and championed. On November 1, 1950, Pope Pius XII officially promulgated the dogma of the Assumption of the Blessed Virgin Mary in the papal bull *Magnificentissimus Deus*. Jung considered it "the most important symbological event since the Reformation" and was overjoyed that within the Catholic Church, "the symbol . . . is alive and is nourished by the popular psyche and actually urged on by it."[83] It proved his contention that "the Catholic believes in continuing revelation," whereas "Protestantism" remained "way behind in the matter of dogmatic development."[84]

"The one joins the three as the fourth and thus produces the synthesis of the four in a unity," Jung wrote of the number four, which held so many important resonances for him. One of his earliest uses of the number came through his study of the mandala, which needed four sections to form a complete circle. Over the years, the concept of four came to represent the totality of the personality within the process of individuation. Within the Christian symbolism he began to question in *Aion*, and particularly in the Holy Trinity of Catholicism, he argued that completion could occur only when the element of the feminine was added to transform it into quaternity.[85] Now he was convinced he was "in possession of irrefutable and verifiable facts"[86] to make the leap to prove that the three categories of space, time, and causality, when combined, became the fourth or ultimate category within his concept of synchronicity. This was "no theory!!" but rather a "concept," Jung wrote to Philip Wylie. He insisted he did not propound "theories" but rather made "discoveries," such as "the world of the collective unconscious is a complete parallel to the mikrophysical [*sic*] world." It was the reason he was "now engaged in a lively discussion with mathematical physicists [i.e., Fierz and Pauli] about . . . synchronicity." He boasted "with all due modesty" that this concept was "one of the best ideas" he had ever had.

Even so, Jung's findings were immediately questioned by several of the scholars and writers he had elevated to the status of, if not disciple, then certainly primary explicators of his psychology. Jung was still envisioning what his essay on synchronicity would become when he explained some of his thinking to Philip Wylie. Wylie had no other data than Jung's letters to go on, but he still offered opinions and reservations. He also corrected some of Jung's fuzzy theorizing about physicists such as Einstein, Niels Bohr, Max Planck, and others, but he did so in a thoughtful, scholarly manner.[87] Hoping to persuade Jung that his comments were friendly, he concluded by recounting a 1937 conversation at his Connecticut home in which Jung gave "short shrift to mathematicians." Wylie, who was well educated in mathematics and the physical sciences, believed physicists had discovered "some formulations which the psychologist would eventually be obliged to consider." He praised Jung for "considering their concepts," as it proved "that the best living mind has turned its attention to an area I have always seen as fruitful."

Despite Wylie's 1949 letter of praise, Jung only recognized criticism and effectively ended their correspondence. He did not write again until 1957, and did so then only as a courtesy after Wylie's generous comments about *Answer to Job.* "Don't worry about my mathematics," Jung said in reference to the 1949 letter. He called himself "utterly 'amathematicós,'" and said his only "affiliation" with the discipline consisted of "the equation 3 + 1 = 4, which is a psychological fact indicating the fundamental relation between psychology and mathematics."[88]

Wylie continued to write to Jung from time to time, but Jung never wrote to him again.[89] Two decades after his 1949 letter, Wylie summarized what had made Jung so angry: "first my hunch about his excited intention, and second, the reasons that his logic and that of quantum math only seemed to be congruent, but actually were not even useful as illustrations of one process, or situation, or say, logical condition of being."[90]

IRA PROGOFF received a similar response when he read the essay in 1954 and made some of the same criticisms. Their first contact came when Progoff, the first social scientist to pay serious attention to Jung's psychology, was a doctoral candidate at the New School for Social Research in New York.[91] Progoff sent his thesis, an analysis of Jung's psychology and its significance for the social sciences, to the Bollingen Foundation, which subsequently awarded him a fellowship. Cary Baynes, then an advisor to the foundation, sent the thesis to Jung and asked for comments. Her daughter, Ximena de Angulo Roelli, was living in Zürich, and to ease Jung's reply, she wrote down his dictated comments and suggestions, most of which Progoff incorporated into his book.[92] Jung, thinking "the social point of view would be new to the Institute," invited Progoff to present a series of lectures on "The Social and Historical Significance of Jung's Psychology." When his book was published, Jung provided a blurb attesting that it correctly represented the main views of his psychology and covered its most significant aspects.

Jung thought so highly of Progoff's critical acumen that he sent him sections of the *Mysterium Coniunctionis* as he wrote them.[93] Progoff offered comments about Catholicism in the light of the recent papal bull and studied the synchronicity data rigorously in order to ensure that Jung used correct mathematical calculations. His mistake was to tell Jung there were two major "weaknesses" in the essay: his mathematical calculations were, quite simply, "wrong" and even worse was his use of astrology, which American readers would never take seriously.[94]

Jung did not reply until one year later, and then he never addressed Progoff's objections. Instead, he gave a scathing critique of the book Progoff was writing for his Bollingen fellowship, saying he would have to decide whether he wanted "to write a novel and be a writer" or present Jung's "'advanced ideas.'" If it were the latter, Jung wrote, "your tss [typescript] contributes very little. . . . You are obviously disinclined to submit to the mental discipline such a work demands."[95] Hinting that Progoff was "getting into trouble with Bollingen" for the originality of his work as it deviated from Jung's, Jung said he was "merely" offering suggestions for Progoff to follow or not. But it was "the condition I have to make, in case I am asked by Bollingen."

VICTOR WHITE, Philip Wylie, and Ira Progoff are typical of the men who began by wanting to boost Jung's reputation in the world at large but whose relationship with him generally ended in their ostracism or denunciation. They began by wanting to explain his psychology and to praise it, but they were original thinkers and creative writers themselves and could not help it if their attempts to enhance Jung's psychology were overwhelmed by their individual visions and the practical uses to which they put it. The most obvious comparison of Jung's intolerance toward these and other independent thinkers is with Freud's inability to permit Jung's earlier deviation from rigid adherence to his theory. The comparison stops short, however, because Freud seldom refined or departed from views he generally expressed once; he held them forever, whereas Jung maintained a lifelong openness to new ideas and new ways of thinking. To the end of his life, he possessed an almost childlike wonder as "one book opened another" within his consistently evolving system. Thus, his treatment of younger scholars who wanted to use his system to construct their own is a paradox: Jung welcomed the new, just as long as he originated it; he was unafraid to change or refine a position, or to admit he had been in error, but only if he made the admission first; he permitted dialogue and dissension, but only if he was the ultimate arbiter.

WHITE, WYLIE, and Progoff were not practicing psychologists, but their close association to the discipline made them likely candidates for Jung's ire.[96] Someone like the physicist Wolfgang Pauli, however, was not. Jung considered himself fortunate to have in his old age the "friendly interest" of Pauli, with whom he could "discuss these questions of principle" and who "could at the same time appreciate psychological arguments."[97] With Pauli, he could enter "the no-man's-land between Physics and the Psychology of the Unconscious . . . the most fascinating yet the darkest hunting ground of our times." Conflating physicists with "a few mythologists," Jung called them "the only scientific minds honestly interested in borderland phenomena and thoughts."[98]

Pauli returned to Zürich from the United States in 1946 (the year he became a U.S. citizen) to give lectures at the ETH during the summer term. He spent the war years at Princeton's Institute for Advanced Study but retained his 1928 appointment as professor of theoretical physics at the ETH, which he held sporadically until the end of his professional life. Pauli's intellectual friendship with Jung began the year after he won the 1945 Nobel Prize in Physics. Thus, even though Jung was twenty-five years Pauli's senior and the analyst to whom he had confided his dreams since 1932, Jung's role changed from Pauli's "spiritual father"[99] to that of an older, respected colleague with similar interests in science, philosophy, religion, and psychology.

The collaboration began in earnest when Pauli accepted Jung's invitation to become a patron of the institute in 1947.[100] In his acceptance letter, Pauli wrote that connections between Jung's research and alchemy presented "serious evidence that what is developing is indicative of a close fusion of psychology with the scientific experience of the processes in the material physical world." Pauli thought he and Jung were embarking on "probably a long journey" that would require "constant criticism of the space-time-concept." He hoped that between them they could "bring alive for the public the collision between the magic-alchemistic and the (new in the seventeenth century) scientific way of thinking."

Jung gave credit to Schopenhauer for being the "godfather" of his conception of synchronicity, which in one of his many definitions had become the "simultaneity of the causally unconnected, which we call chance."[101] He should have given credit to Pauli for bringing Schopenhauer's observation to his attention, for it was Pauli who provided both the source and the interpretation that Jung subsequently used as his own when he wrote his essay on the subject.[102] At other times, with no nod toward Pauli, Jung defined the concept as a "meaningful coincidence" or a "meaningful cross-connection."[103] Sometimes it was an "acausal connecting principle" for experiences or events that did not always "obey the rules of time, space, and causality."

Pauli did not use the word "synchronicity" himself, but he implied the concept when he told Jung how his attention was "focused strongly on the influence of the archetypal concepts . . . on scientific definitions." When Pauli was interested in a subject, his way of "making something clear" to himself was to announce publicly that he would give a lecture, thus forcing himself to do the research, so he scheduled two talks at the Psychological Club in late February and early March 1948 on "The Influence of Archetypal Ideas on the Scientific Theories of Kepler."[104] His talks encouraged Jung to break away from the *Mysterium Coniunctionis* and to write the essay on synchronicity as a companion piece.

Pauli was resident in Zürich throughout 1948, during which he and Jung met to exchange information. He used the term "synchronicity" for the first time in November, when he sent Jung a dream that dealt with "the relativity of the concept of space in relation to the psyche."[105] Conversations took place throughout the winter, and by the following June, Jung sent Pauli a working draft of his essay and asked him to "cast a critical eye over it."[106] A comparison of Pauli's suggestions with Jung's multiple drafts and revisions in the long and important letters that figure throughout the entire correspondence makes it clear that Jung followed every suggestion Pauli made. It is also interesting that Pauli duplicated many of the questions and criticisms raised by White, Wylie, and Progoff, but Jung quietly, unquestioningly, adopted his while dismissing theirs.[107]

PAULI OCCUPIED a unique position in Jung's mature intellectual life; he stood alone on the pinnacle of a Nobel Prize, whereas most other men were clustered together on several peaks of lower, even though still imposing, heights. Carl Kerényi, the Hungarian philologist and mythologist, came close to being ranked with Pauli, as he was so highly respected in his own field that (as he did with Pauli) Jung never questioned but only cooperated with Kerényi.

In the main, there were two major groups that figured in the last decade of Jung's life. There were those who came originally as acolytes interested in spreading his gospel; if they did not drift away, he severed communication with those who had the temerity to question his authority or to offer creative addenda or new insights into his method. The other group consisted of men who came to call on him at Bollingen and stayed, in effect, to sit at his feet, listen to his words, and collect and disseminate everything he said exactly as he said it.

This group includes a number of historiographers who produced books that rank today among the most frequently cited documents in the history of psychoanalysis and the biography of Jung. When they presented his views exactly as he wanted them, Jung tolerated some and befriended others; when they wanted to build upon his work or explain it for their own purposes, he either tolerated them with a certain degree of prickliness or else dismissed them outright.

Among the second group was Sir Laurens van der Post, who shared Jung's fascination with his native Africa and wrote of their friendship in books that are generally respected.[108] J. B. Priestley, H. G. Wells, and Philip Toynbee represented the English point of view in writings that satisfied Jung to varying degrees. The English clergyman H. L. Philps entered into extensive correspondence about Jung's views of religion. After submitting multiple drafts that Jung annotated and corrected, Philps produced a book that was more Jung's writing than his own, to which Jung gave his imprimatur as the best representation of his ideas on the subject.[109] In the last years of Jung's life, the American professor of psychology Richard I. Evans conducted a series of filmed interviews, and here also, Jung's unedited testimony was reproduced in book form.[110] Still among the second group and the most hagiographic of all was E. A. Bennet, who from the 1930s onward was one of Jung's staunchest proponents in England. The author of three books on Jung,[111] Bennet resumed his visits to Zürich in 1946 with the idea that he should write the official biography. Because Jung was grateful to Bennet for his lifelong support, he dissuaded him gently. Perhaps intending to write one anyway after Jung died, Bennet became a frequent guest both in Bollingen and the Küsnacht house.[112] He also became the closest Boswell to Jung's Johnson, the semi-official recorder of "what Jung really said" (also the title of one of his books), albeit mostly presented in Bennet's words and descriptions, with coy allusions to topics not covered in the text but perhaps reserved for further use.

All these writings, by all the men cited above and others not mentioned here, provide insight into the development of Jung's mature ideas and the manner in which he subsequently expressed them. The word "men" is used advisedly, for there was only one woman whose intellectual acumen Jung respected: Marie-Louise von Franz. He thought of Jolande Jacobi, author of a respected book first published in 1942 and still in print today, *The Psychology of C. G. Jung*, as merely the official explainer, the best explicator of his psychology. Toni Wolff seldom wrote, and Linda Fierz-David and Barbara Hannah were lesser talents merely because they did not possess von Franz's encyclopedic knowledge. She was a brilliant woman whose thinking and writing always began from her undeviating support of Jung's ideas; one who used her ferocious intelligence to position herself carefully as the official explicator of his psychology, which indeed she became after his death. In retrospect, all these relationships — failed or otherwise — enriched Jung's thinking and broadened his outlook, even as one fact remains clear: with the exception of Pauli, whose corrections Jung accepted only because he was not educated in quantum physics, Jung held steadfast to his "concepts," "ideas," and "discoveries" and never surrendered them to another's authority. Whatever "thesis," "system," or "theory" emerged in his writing, it was first and foremost his own.

—∞—

"The Memory of a Vanishing World"

Carl and Emma Jung celebrated their golden wedding anniversary on February 14, 1953. Typically, they told no one but a few close friends, and the only celebration was a sedate dinner at home with their family. The winter had passed quietly, Jung's "light grippe" their only concern.[1] Emma was tired all the time, but she blamed it on the demands of teaching at the institute and chairing the curatorium. No one worried about her seemingly invincible health, but everyone worried about his; the slightest sniffle or temper tantrum had her begging the doctor to come and monitor his lungs or racing heart. Both relied on their children for respite from the daily barrage of professional demands. Jung was in Franz's company more than ever before, using him as a buffer to avoid persons he did not want to see or things he did not want to do, and occasionally spending the night in Franz and Lilly's home. Marianne lived nearby but was almost always in her parents' home. Claiming that editing the German edition of his collective works was so time-consuming, she moved her things into her girlhood bedroom and slept there so often that her children were only half joking when they claimed they were raised by their father and the housekeeper.[2] But it was Agathe to whom the parents turned instinctively, and they went independently and together to stay at her home in Baden. Agathe remained the strong and sunny presence she had always been, and as she had "no interest in and no memory for anything psychological,"[3] being with her guaranteed Jung and Emma the ideal prescription for rest and recreation; she provided good food, company, and laughter as she cared for their physical needs and guarded their privacy. In Zürich, it was simply taken for granted that even though the persons close to Jung were afflicted with serious illnesses of various kinds, especially Toni with her arthritis, they would outlive him simply because he was older. The greatest shock to everyone's intimations of mortality came on March 21, 1953, when Toni Wolff's devoted maid brought the customary morning cup of tea to her bedroom and discovered she had died during the night.[4]

Lina had been in the Wolff family's service since her girlhood; now an elderly woman, she was the repository of much of the family's history. In recognition of their earlier closeness, Lina phoned Susi Trüb first, even though Toni had chosen to live in a flat in the building owned by Erna Naeff, who also resided there. Susi put aside her personal differences with the Jungs and telephoned them even before she ran to Toni's, wanting them to hear the sad news in privacy. How they handled their personal grief is known only to themselves, but their initial public response was as professional therapists. There was a spontaneous "open house" in Küsnacht that afternoon, as many others who were stunned by the suddenness of Toni Wolff's death gravitated to the Seestrasse as if they did not know what else to do. Emma gave them tea and cakes, and Jung hid his own feelings to comfort them.

No one, in Zürich at any rate, had any inkling that something was amiss with Toni. The last week of her life was typically busy, her analytic schedule fuller than usual. On the fourteenth, she was radiant as she presided for the first and last time at the Psychological Club in her new capacity as honorary president. She went to Küsnacht on Wednesday afternoon, the seventeenth, something she now did rarely rather than routinely, and instead of going in late afternoon for a brief tea, she had a long and relaxed lunch and spent the rest of the afternoon with both Jungs.

A gracious and generous accommodation had sprung up naturally between Toni and Emma sometime in the late 1940s, and it lasted for the remainder of Toni's life. Instead of Jung going off to see her separately, she came to Küsnacht, and the three spent time together. Emma was always kinder and more considerate, for Jung usually gulped down his tea and immersed himself in one of his crime novels. Visitors wondered why Toni put up with his rudeness and hostility and why she simply did not stay away.[5] On the infrequent occasions when Jung's doctors permitted him to go to Bollingen, both women sometimes went with him, and here again, Emma took care of Toni.

Toni was sixty-five, and at that time and in that culture, she was considered to be in old age. It certainly was painful for her, but there was no indication she was in life-threatening danger. However, two of her English analysands had such a strong sense that they should see her earlier than they were supposed to that they rescheduled appointments and went to Zürich shortly before her death. Gerhard Adler and Irene Champernowne were among the last to see Toni Wolff; later, both recorded memories of their final sessions and what they did when they learned of her death. The latter included spending part of the day with Jung and Emma, where Jung walked in the garden with some of the callers one at a time while Emma sat in the sunroom in companionable silence with others. As the afternoon drew to a close, they learned that Toni's death resulted from a cardiac infarct and, most likely, a stroke as well. They shared what medical knowledge they had gleaned, talking of how she had been taking regular shots of a new arthritis drug, and how her doctor had also been treating her hypertension with other medications. They speculated that the combination might have triggered a fatal reaction but quickly discounted the theory to tell how Toni scoffed at her doctor's "dire threats" of irreversible damage to her liver as she continued to abuse cigarettes and liquor.

That evening, Emma instructed the maid to tell callers that she and Jung were no longer available. They dined early and went to their separate bedrooms, where Emma recorded her emotions (as was her custom) in her diary. What Jung did is not known, although he still wrote sporadically in the latest *Black Book* when something crucial happened to him, and he had begun again to write and make illustrations in *The Red Book*.[6] Emma attended Toni's funeral service in the Peterkirche on March 25, but Jung did not. His absence was severely criticized, but he could not trust his emotions and did not wish to risk displaying them in public.[7] In the months to come, he presented a tranquil façade that many mistook for indifference, but inwardly he was in turmoil. Now it was his turn to take stronger medications to control the hypertension and tachycardia that Toni's death exacerbated.

On Easter Saturday, he dreamed that Toni visited him, garbed in a dress of many brilliant hues whose primary color was royal blue.[8] He remembered her carriage as regal and floating, majestic and like a bird, a kingfisher or a peacock. Although she said nothing in the dream, he awoke feeling comforted. Sometime that summer, he found a small stone whose shape seemed amenable to becoming a monument for Toni. He placed it within a grove of trees close to the Küsnacht house and, using Chinese characters, carved the following inscription: "Toni Wolff. Lotus. Nun. Mysterious."[9] Some months later, his feelings were aroused again when he chanced upon a young girl on a Zürich street who seemed to be Toni's reincarnation. He urged others to follow her, find out who she was, and observe her movements. When they demurred, he became so agitated that his caregivers feared he would suffer another infarct.

Seeking other ways to deal with Toni's death, he began to write again to Susi Trüb.[10] These were far different from the letters that predated his final rupture with Hans, when Jung crowed to Susi that having had no news from or about Toni was "all to the good" as far as he was concerned. After she died, he berated himself for having felt this way, and he wrote copious letters to Susi, even as he begged her not to tell anyone that he had initiated contact. His letters were filled with grief and, to a lesser extent, self-recrimination but overall with the compulsion to talk about Toni. He recounted some of her amusing foibles, personal experiences they had shared, and his pride in her public service during World War II. He talked about how disappointed he was when she stopped writing poetry and fiction shortly after she became interested in his psychology, and how much he regretted that she had not become the great literary writer he was sure she could have been. He spoke of the tremendous contribution she made to analytical psychology, but except for the relatively public details noted above, he did not speak of what she meant personally to him. The closest he came was to say that he mourned with the world the great loss imposed by her death.

Barbara Hannah was fond of repeating something she claimed Emma told her, that Toni provided certain qualities to her husband she could not, and therefore Emma would always be eternally grateful to her. Others wondered if such a generous remark could possibly be true, especially since no one else ever heard Emma say it or anything like it.[11] Fowler McCormick, whose lasting marriage to Anne had just ended with her death, was once again spending long periods of time in Zürich. He observed that, as much as was possible within a monogamous society, Jung had found a second wife in Toni and treated her with all the respect such status implied. He was fortunate to have in Emma a first wife who learned to accept such an arrangement. Dr. Joseph Henderson, agreeing with McCormick, added that having found two wives in these extraordinary women, Jung still did not provide a model for others to follow; his triangular relationship "depended on a form of consciousness that totally transcended the ordinary worldly model" of the married man and his mistress.[12]

Immediately after Toni's death, friends rallied to offer solace of many different kinds, but the Jungs refused them all. Jung declined Catharine Cabot's invitation to San Remo with the excuse that he had not left the house since his flu the previous winter and was weakened anew by the "fresh shock" of Toni's death.[13] Emma said she wasn't well enough to go anywhere except for short stays with Agathe in Baden. They decided not to go to Eranos and not to take a vacation in Ascona after everyone departed, which they sometimes did. By the autumn, both were still reeling from the "terrible blow" of "Toni's departure" and still struggling to accept it.[14]

The frail old couple's dependence on each other became total and touching. One night Jung was prowling in his wine cellar and found a forty-five-year-old bottle of Bordeaux. He decided to treat himself and Emma at dinner, but all he could think of to toast was "the memory of a vanishing world."[15]

"I HAVE to tell you something very important and serious," Jung wrote to Gerhard Adler on November 25, 1955. "Frau Professor Jung is not well, not well at all."[16] Emma Jung had cancer that began in her stomach and metastasized throughout her entire body. She was heavily medicated and was expected to die within days.

The disease began sometime in late 1952,[17] first manifesting itself as gastric distress. Emma's adult children teased that she was so stoic and private that they often didn't know when she had the flu because she never complained and never took to her bed. When the cancer started, no one suspected she was ill, because she treated herself with drugstore palliatives and did not consult a doctor for the better part of a year. By 1954, she had to admit something was wrong, as the

stomach discomfort had given way to severe back pain that often made it difficult for her to walk, let alone leave the house. Even though she did ask one of
her American analysands about how to import a recliner, she still managed to
hide her condition from everyone.[18]

Jung did not learn just how ill she was until the back pain became so crippling that a doctor had to be called. Tests revealed the possibility of tumors, surgery was performed, and cancer diagnosed. Not even her children were told;
only Jung. Everyone else was told she had been hospitalized for minor surgery
to correct back problems. In early 1955, again using back problems as the reason, she returned to the hospital for a second round of radiation and chemo-
therapy. Her recovery was so quick that for a few brief months she was convinced
the disease was in remission.

In July, Emma was well enough to participate in the extensive celebrations
for Jung's eightieth birthday. Unlike for the seventy-fifth, which she had succeeded in keeping a private affair for family and close friends, the international
Jungian community insisted upon participating in this one. Emma had to acqui-
esce because it is the Swiss custom to celebrate publicly every fifth-year anniversary after the seventy-fifth birthday.

Jung had serious doubts about whether he would "be able to decide" if he
should attend, let alone participate.[19] He was concerned about "a senile difficulty in finding words or terms" and could neither order nor stop the "continuous, quick movement of thoughts." He worried that his previous heart infarcts
were responsible for the tachycardia that, in turn, might be inducing the onset
of senility. He did not want to expose himself to others if this were apparent. In
early July, he described a visit to the hospital as "not so funny and matters are
not as right as they could be."[20]

But during the several days of festivities, Jung was in high spirits and in full
command of his faculties. A private family celebration was held on July 23 to
which only those closest to him were invited, including E. A. Bennet and Ruth
Bailey from England. She was always expected to be their houseguest, but as
every hotel in Zürich was filled with celebrants, Jung told Bennet for the first of
many times to follow, "so you got to stop at my house."[21] About forty family
members and friends boarded the *Stäfa* at the Strandbad pier near the Jung
house for a trip up the lake to the island of Ufenau.[22] They entertained themselves playing games such as "how much does *Gross Papa* weigh?" and "how
many windows did he build into his tower?" They disembarked to visit the little
Norman church belonging to the Einsiedeln monastery before reboarding the
boat to amble through the canal under the road from Rapperswil to Pfaffikon.
Eventually they disembarked at the Bad Hotel in Schmerikon to dine in a private room. A deeply emotional Jung told Bennet how pleased and proud he was
to have brought into being "the great body of healthy people who were his children, grandchildren, and great grandchildren." He was so happy to have them
all together.

The official celebrations took place on July 25 and 26, and there had been nothing in Zürich to compare since Winston Churchill's visit in 1946. In anticipation, Laurens van der Post made a long interview for the BBC in March,[23] and BBC Radio sent a second crew to record the actual celebration. Reporters came from French and German Switzerland, France, England, and the United States;[24] while various psychological publications planned articles or special issues. There were three gatherings, all at the Dolder Grand Hotel: a morning reception for anyone who had ever heard Jung lecture, either abroad or at the ETH, the Psychology Club, or Eranos; a large midday luncheon for civic leaders, psychologists, friends, and anyone else who had had scant personal contact but still wanted to attend (and there were many); and a smaller, select dinner for leaders of Jungian groups and institutes, all those who attended the institute, and anyone who had ever lectured there. Jung and Emma were at the head table for the dinner, with Bennet on his left and Michael Fordham, now a distinguished British analyst, on her right. Also seated there were Professor L. Michaud; Jung's cousin Elisabeth Riklin (the widow of Franz Jr.); Dr. A. L. Vischer, representing the Swiss Academy of Medical Sciences; Dr. Jur. Emil Landolt; Frances G. Wickes, who had come from New York; and the Jungs' eldest daughter, Agathe Niehus-Jung.

Jung made jokes in several languages and gave a gracious acceptance speech when the Rascher Verlag presented him with an elegantly bound advance copy of the first volume of *Mysterium Coniunctionis.*[25] He was deeply moved when the ETH awarded him an honorary degree and a number of professors made speeches that showed "not only deep appreciation of [his] work but an astounding understanding."[26] Jung roared with laughter when Elsie Attenhofer, the "Grand Old Lady of Swiss Cabarets," serenaded him.[27] He was less sanguine when the mayor of Zürich presented Emma with a large bouquet of flowers and said she, too, must be honored for having contributed five children to the Jung family.[28]

If there was any diminution of his faculties, no one noticed. No one suspected anything was wrong with Emma either, for she greeted everyone with her renowned graciousness. During the week following the official celebrations, the house was full of visitors as she welcomed all who came from a distance to honor her husband. Ruth Bailey was a helpful aide, but no one surmised that she visited so frequently because Emma was carefully preparing for Jung's life after her impending death.

Ruth Bailey was a lifelong resident of a Cheshire village in rural northern England. She stayed with the Jung family every summer until the war, and as soon as possible afterward, she resumed her holidays. There had always been reciprocal visits between the Jung household and hers, for even though Ruth's friendship began with Jung in Africa, it became deeper and more personal afterward with Emma. Ruth kept Emma laughing on the Wednesdays when Jung was with Toni by taking her to raucous British movies, and Ruth took care of each of the four daughters when they came to learn English on their long school vacations. Several years ago, Emma had asked Ruth to pledge that, no matter whether Emma or Carl died first, she would come to Küsnacht as their "professional looker-after" and care for the survivor.[29] Emma summoned Ruth for the first caregiving stay in 1949 when she tripped on a rug in the upstairs hallway and fell, fracturing her shoulder.[30] The bones were slow to set, and while Emma was in the Klinik Hirslanden, Ruth stayed in the house to look after Jung. Her life had been devoted to the service of her family, and now she lived alone and was free to travel since the death of her last surviving brother and her mother. Beginning with Emma's accident, Ruth made several visits yearly, each one lasting longer than the one before. The family found Ruth to be both refuge and respite, for like Agathe, she was more interested in persons than in the theory they propounded, so with her there was never any "shop talk."[31]

Ruth had a rollicking sense of humor, and they "never knew what was coming next," as she knew how "to make [them] laugh." A conversation she had with Jung in Africa illustrates the quality everyone treasured most.[32] Ruth recalled how she and Jung were "killing time" on the veranda of a hotel, when she spontaneously sang a silly ditty. "Really, Ruth," Jung said, "your brain is like a brawn, little bits hung together with jelly."

"That may be, but it entertains you."

"Yes, you are quite right, it does," he replied.

RUTH WAS in the house when Emma died. She had been bedridden for the last weeks but was still coherent and cognizant. She even managed to finish reading *Journey down a Rainbow*, dedicated to Jung by its joint authors, J. B. Priestley and his new wife, Jacquetta Hawkes.[33] There was a new cook, and Emma fussed because she could no longer plan meals and dictate menus, so Jung took over. He dictated menus detailed to the last spice or condiment to his new secretary, Aniela Jaffé, who typed them up and passed them along to the cook, who ignored them. Emma told her children they could visit but forbade them to sleep in the house or stage a vigil. She insisted that Jung keep up his professional schedule, so he was with a student from the institute on November 22 when he left the room to take a telephone call from Emma's doctor.[34] He was distraught when he finally reappeared, but he still bid the student a polite farewell.

The doctor told Jung the cancer had metastasized into Emma's upper spine and brain stem, she was uremic and her kidneys were failing, and she would slip into a coma from which she would not regain consciousness.[35] Jung repeated everything to Emma, telling his children he did so because "it was the right thing to do."[36] Until he heard the devastating prognosis, Jung clung to the hope that Emma would live for some months longer; he now had to accept that she would die within days.

Emma received the news with her usual stoicism and did not discuss her im-

minent demise with any of her children. Even though heavily medicated, she
defied the doctor's prognosis, drifting in and out of sleep but remaining mostly
conscious until her death five days later, November 27.[37] Her grandchildren
thought it "amazing" when she predicted the time she would die. On her last
day, in her last half hour of life, Emma told her daughters Gret and Marianne,
"I am going to die now. I am going to say good-bye to you right now." She
slipped into sleep and shortly after stopped breathing. Only Jung was at her
bedside, as her children had been asked to wait downstairs in the living room.
When he gained control of his emotions, he went down to tell them their
mother was dead.

Ruth Bailey remembered how he strode into the room, "very distressed —
all white and tense — and not speaking."[38] The family sat silently, the only
sound the click of needles as some of the women knitted nervously, "all afraid to
say a word to him." He walked into the enclosed sunporch adjacent to the living
room, and Ruth followed: "I got up and went after him and succeeded in getting him out of himself."

The funeral was held several days later in the Küsnacht Swiss Reformed
Church that none of the family attended but to which, by birth, they belonged.
Jung was supported by his son and sons-in-law, who formed the first phalanx
around him, and the remainder of the large family (which now included ten or
more great-grandchildren) circled behind the men to ensure that his grief
would not be exposed to the public. That afternoon, his family greeted callers
in the public rooms of the house while Jung remained secluded upstairs, first in
the library, then in his bedroom. Not even those in Jung's most immediate circle were allowed to offer their condolences in person because his grief was so
intense. Unfortunately, several persons alleged that they visited Jung in his
small study, and their account has since been taken as fact. Jung did indeed sob
for his late wife, and he did call her "a queen," but if those who told the story
did hear him say this, it was not on the day of her funeral.[39]

AFTER EMMA'S death, as he turned inward and was mostly silent, it was "touch
and go whether he would ever come back."[40] The man of force and vitality, whose
hands and mind were always occupied, now sat slumped and shuffling, staring
into a distance that only he could see. He even forgot to fuss with his many pipes,
which alarmed his children most of all. Generally, he kept his grief to himself,
only breaking down once in front of his daughters and Ruth Bailey, when the
daughters convened a meeting to decide what should be done about him.

All were gathered in the living room, trying to come to an agreement. Ruth
Bailey was not factored into their equation and had not been invited to participate in the discussion. Unaware of their purpose, she wandered into the room,
and shortly after, Jung came down from his study. Seeing the evasion and embarrassment on his daughters' faces made him realize why they were there. He
burst into tears and went through to the sunporch, where they could hear him

sobbing. Agathe asked Ruth what they should do. "Just love him a bit and show him affection," she said. They remained seated and Ruth went to sit silently with the old man until he recovered.

With the exception of Agathe, who was spontaneously affectionate with everyone, Jung's relationship with his daughters was exceedingly formal. The family decorum was such that they never kissed or hugged him, just as they had never kissed or hugged their mother. When they said hello or good-bye, they shook hands — if they touched at all. Each time Ruth saw them do this, she would shout, "Kiss your father, don't shake hands!" They were sheepish but could not change their lifelong behavior. They were appalled when Ruth punched his arm playfully or ruffled his thin hair; or when she teased him, calling him a pig for his bad table manners, or a cheat, which he certainly was with every game he played, particularly cards. To the daughters, their father was "an awesome person, distinguished, remote, and an object of respect." So when they talked about who would care for him, they thought of Ruth only as an embarrassment whom they could not possibly consider. Agathe never figured in these discussions, for she made it clear that her father was welcome to visit whenever he liked, but her life was in Baden with her husband and children. Gret wanted to move into the house, but because of the lifelong tension between her father and herself, she was the least likely candidate. Gret was a marvelous cook, but their relationship was so quarrelsome that each time she cooked one of her superb meals for him, he claimed she ruined his digestion. Lil's husband was ill with cancer, so that left Marianne, the one who wanted most to run her father's household and act as his official hostess. Of all the daughters, she was the one he could have tolerated most easily, but he was devastated at the thought of becoming dependent on any of his children in his own home. Eventually they all reached the sensible conclusion that Emma had indeed known best, and Ruth was asked to remain indefinitely, which she did.[41]

THE BEGINNING of Ruth's permanent residence in Küsnacht marked the beginning of Jung's renewed interest in life, but it also marked the beginning of his true old age. One of the first positive acts he engaged in was to carve the stone for Emma that he entitled *O vas insigne devotione et obedientia.* His loose translation of the carving was the same phrase he repeated to all those who offered condolences: "She was the foundation of my house." This time he placed it at the tower in Bollingen, where the sun would fall upon it for much of the day, and when the weather was just right, light was reflected upon it from the lake.[42] He had dreams about Emma as he had earlier had about Toni, but those of his wife were portraits "from the other side"[43] that left him peaceful and content. When one of his grandsons said Emma was coming to him repeatedly in dreams, Jung said to tell her to "disappear at once because she no longer belongs in the land of the living."[44] The next time she appeared, the boy did as Jung suggested, and he never dreamed of Emma again.

Emma had kept Jung's household running smoothly for more than fifty years, and in death, she left him consumed by an exaggerated degree of panic and anxiety, especially about money. Emma had followed Swiss law to the letter, which required her to leave a certain percentage of her great fortune to her surviving husband, but she left the bulk of her estate directly to her children.[45] Emma's wealth was enormous, but Jung had never concerned himself with it, even though from the moment of their marriage, all conjugal property became his and he was legally responsible for it. By law, he was the "head of the family" and Emma's fortune was subject to the *"union des biens,"* or the "union of property," which gave him this authority. If she had divorced him, her only recourse to what had been hers would have been *"une créance,"* a "claim for compensation," which he could have agreed to or not. Also as her husband, Jung was the sole administrator of Emma's fortune. Early and wisely, he realized his talents and interest lay elsewhere and ceded this responsibility to his brother-in-law, Ernst Homberger. Most of the time, Homberger simply carried out Emma's wishes, for she had a keen mind for financial analysis and presided carefully over the growth and disbursement of her money. It was she who paid all the household expenses for fifty years, set the modest fees Jung charged his patients, and took charge of all his billing and payments. It was also Emma who invested his earnings, amassing a substantial portfolio for him in his own right. Perhaps this was not entirely the favor she intended, for like royalty, Jung seldom carried money and never knew its value.

Speculation was immediate and has remained rampant as to why Emma chose largely to bypass her husband in favor of her children. As early as 1911, Emma was cognizant of her husband's attitude toward money when she told Freud that "with Carl . . . the imperative 'earn money' is only an evasion of something else to which he has resistances."[46] After her death, gossip fell into two categories: Jung's detractors thought she did it for "spite" and "wanted finally to get even for Toni and the other women"; her supporters claimed the opposite, that she was intelligent enough to realize that Jung had neither the interest in protecting her estate nor the acumen to make it grow, and direct disbursal was the only means to ensure her children's inheritance.

With Emma's death, Jung had to think about money for the first time since his impoverished boyhood.[47] Even though, between what she left him and what she had amassed for him privately in his own portfolio, he had enough money to continue to live comfortably, he could not stop worrying. His first concern was that he would lose his house (which he had owned outright for many years), so he insisted that the two architects in the family, Franz and Walther Niehus, prepare plans to divide it into separate apartments he could rent. They pretended to be busy with drawings they prudently never finished, and Jung eventually forgot about it. He scolded the maids for turning on the same lights they had always illuminated and ran behind them turning them off. When he saw a coal bill that was actually quite reasonable, he became agitated and cried, "This is just unbelievable! Where am I going to get this money?" He said they would have to resume wartime austerity with the heating and told Ruth he would henceforth examine every household expenditure. She merely laughed, and he soon forgot about that as well.

He was still so worried about money that he began again to hide cash, as he had done during the war. In wartime, he hid great wads of bills in his library and created a secret code to remind himself in which of his books he stashed it. Unfortunately he forgot the code, so most of the money remained in the books, found by his descendants after his death. It was the same with money he buried in the garden. He dug deep holes into which he put old vases and Chinese jars, which promptly shattered when covered with dirt. He forgot his marking system, so much of this disintegrating money remains in the ground today. After Emma's death he sought more secure hiding places and put "little gold *Münzen*" coins in the drawer of his bedside table and hid Swiss francs in the bathroom closet where he kept his special soap. Ruth would find and remove most of them periodically, but he never noticed.

When Emma was alive, there were four house servants; in an economy move, Jung dismissed two, keeping only the cook and a daily maid. It was taken for granted that Müller would remain as long as he wished to stay, but now, besides being gardener, general handyman, and chauffeur, he assumed an additional duty concerning Jung's health. In the last two years of Emma's life, Jung began to have prostate problems. To his great annoyance, ever since his 1944 heart infarct, Emma watched him obsessively for possible symptoms, immediately phoning the doctor at the slightest hint of one. In this instance, when he had a genuine medical condition and should have had surgery to correct it, Emma would not permit an operation for fear he would not survive it. Even though crystals formed periodically in his bladder and caused great pain, she preferred that he go discreetly into the hospital to have the blockage removed rather than allow it to be corrected surgically. Whatever his reason, he acquiesced to her wish. Before Emma died, whenever he needed a new catheter, she preferred to instruct Müller where to go and what to buy, and she inserted it herself. At first Jung tried to hide this condition from Ruth, but eventually she had to be told. Müller helped insert it after Emma's death, but when attacks were imminent and he was not there, Ruth had to do it. Hoping that his children would agree that he should have the condition corrected surgically, she tried to tell them, but "it was difficult to suggest that they do or get intimate personal things for him because they [were] so touchy." The condition dominated the remainder of his life, and he eventually became casual about letting Ruth know its status. She also helped him bathe, first guiding him to sit on an old wooden stool in the tub and then finding suction mats that permitted him to enter and exit safely.

He became casual about his person but remained exceedingly fussy about his clothing. He wore old-fashioned "butterfly" collars that attached to his shirts and required special antique irons to starch and smooth them. When there were no longer washerwomen who knew how to do this, Ruth found it simpler to throw the old ones away and buy new ones from the last remaining supplier in Zürich, but she never told Jung of this extravagance. Only at Bollingen did he wear the same pair of shorts for days on end, but he usually changed his shirt several times weekly.

Despite his attempts at frugality, he remained a gourmet and thought nothing of sending Müller into Zürich several times in a single day to collect expensive ingredients for the special sauces he delighted in preparing. Now he gave the detailed menus to Ruth, who cheerfully ignored them when the cook was off and generally slapped something together that he always ate with gusto. She never got used to the way he greeted all the utensils in the kitchen the first thing each morning, and how he would nudge her to make sure that she, too, went around the room saying "greetings to you" to the frying pans or "good morning to you" to the coffee pot.

After some violent initial conflicts, mostly about food, Jung and Ruth got along beautifully, like two old buddies who joshed and argued and generally forgot what they had been disagreeing about moments later. In the beginning, Jung insisted that Ruth never try to make herself indispensable or contradict him. He warned that he had a terrible temper, and she became its innocent victim when she put two hothouse tomatoes into a stew. He raged that he only ate tomatoes from his garden, and after a violent tirade, he swore he would never trust her again. That being the case, she said she would return to England in the morning. The next day he took her for a walk along the lake and promised never to lose his temper again (a promise he worked hard to keep but with only partial success).

Growing serious, he said, "What I want you to do is to see me out, will you? Will you stay with me and see me out?" Ruth promised that she would but to lighten the mood said she would try to remember "about the tomatoes."[48]

With Fowler McCormick, Ruth and Jung formed "ITCRA," the International Touring and Culinary Research Association. Fowler always drove his car, and Ruth and Jung took turns paying for the gas and the meal, which was the real reason they went off for excursions into the countryside to visit Roman ruins or small museums. Jung took great pleasure in finding small country restaurants where they could eat local specialties. Ruth kept him to a healthy diet at home, but he indulged on these occasions in fatty meats, heavy cheeses, and rich desserts.

He had been called "the sage of Küsnacht" as a mark of derision when he was younger, but in his old age term became one of respect. People came from all over the world to pay him homage, pick his brain, write something about him, record his voice, or film him.[49] In the main, these seekers seldom asked about *Aion* or *Mysterium Coniunctionis*, preferring to question him about *Answer to Job* or to talk about his new all-consuming interest, extraterrestrial beings. He was aided greatly in his research about flying saucers by his son-in-law Walther Niehus and by Fowler (who both shared his interest), and especially by his new secretary, Aniela Jaffé, who organized the masses of materials they and others provided into several bookshelves, file cabinet drawers, and multiple folders.[50]

Aniela (as everyone addressed her) was the last in the line of secretaries following Marie-Jeanne Schmid, who resigned to marry after twenty years with Jung. He first met Aniela in the 1930s when she was a German-Jewish refugee who came to him for analysis and whom he treated without charge, as he did so many displaced Jews in those days. Her interest in his psychology led to her becoming a respected participant in the analytic life of the local Jungian community. She was the institute's first secretary, a job she performed with competence and personal satisfaction and in which she expected to remain for the rest of her working life. Jung, meanwhile, spoiled by Marie-Jeanne's efficiency, had already endured one secretary who was a disaster and was now faced with losing another who had been barely satisfactory.

Barbara Hannah, "who could not accurately be called a meddler but who came damned close,"[51] installed her friend Una Thomas before either of the Jungs could object. Thomas was another of the shy, introverted Englishwomen who lived in the Hotel Sonne, went to the Psychological Club, and devoted their lives to interpreting "big dreams."[52] She lived in Zürich for forty years, but was always slightly different from the rest of the English who deferred to Hannah as their leader. Thomas held the firmly fixed idea that she was "generally always right" and that she "knew best about almost everything." She had never worked as a secretary and had no skills, not even typing, but Hannah persuaded the slightly desperate Jungs that Thomas could learn on the job. They most likely acquiesced because of Marianne, who was insisting she could handle secretarial duties along with editing the *Collected Works*. Her parents were already concerned that she was far too distracted from her family responsibilities. Thomas was Jung's secretary for one year, from September 1952 to October 1953, during which she was supposed to work each weekday afternoon. Jung greeted her after lunch but gave her few instructions and then napped until 4 P.M. As this was also the household staff's rest period, Thomas was expected to answer the telephone and the door and perform any other duty that needed to be done. Jung had tea at four, dictated until five, and saw visitors until six, after which he retired briefly until dinner. In and around this activity, Thomas was expected to prepare the correspondence he had dictated the previous day. He did not use a Dictaphone (which she could not have managed anyway), so she tried to write what he said in longhand but was frequently unable to take it all down. He wrote some of his longer, more theoretical letters himself, and she had to decipher his by now wavering handwriting and type them. She was also expected to type any manuscripts, but as she was a two-finger typist prone to mistakes, the process was slow and messy.

Thomas was stubborn, so she did things her way. When Jung told her to retype a letter, she simply signed her name as secretary on his behalf and mailed it. When she did not succeed in writing all he dictated, she invented what she thought he should have said. She even rewrote some of Jung's handwritten replies into what she considered better style and content, and she took the liberty of editing some of his manuscripts. All this took so much time she had no opportunity to file, so his important papers were often lost or misplaced. Jung had frequent temperamental outbursts and she broke down in sobs in response. The miracle is that she lasted as long as she did.

Doris Gautschy followed, a no-nonsense, competent middle-aged Swiss woman. She stayed for almost two years, until the summer before Emma's death in 1955. When Gautschy left for her annual vacation, she told Jung that the workload was so overwhelming she simply could not return. The bedridden Emma solved this dilemma as well: just as she had chosen Ruth Bailey to provide for her husband's personal needs, she now chose Aniela to take care of his professional life. At Emma's insistence, Jung asked her to become his private secretary. Aniela Jaffé stayed for the rest of his life and became not only "a sort of clearing house for . . . psychological ideas"[53] but also his collaborator for the texts and conversations that became *Memories, Dreams, Reflections*.

Aniela gave a terse and cryptic description of Jung's behavior when her secretarial career began: after "much chiseling in stone, he got interested in the world again." She, in turn, "stopped writing in his name."[54] Like Jolande Jacobi and Marie-Louise von Franz, Aniela Jaffé was a gifted interpreter of Jung's psychology and an author in her own right. Before joining the institute, she had worked for the art historian (and Jung's Joycean nemesis) Carola Giedion-Welcker and the sinologist professor Eduard Horst von Tscharner, so she brought much knowledge from this background to her study of analytical psychology. While she worked at the institute, she also did research on her own time for Jung, evaluating manuscripts on his behalf and then writing reports and frequently framing his replies to their authors. Although he checked everything she typed for possible mistakes (which she seldom made), something he had never done with Marie-Jeanne, he usually approved the content exactly as she wrote it. He thought so highly of her insights that he also incorporated her study of E. T. A. Hoffmann's fairy tale *Der goldene Topf* (The Golden Pot) into a volume of his essays.[55]

He trusted Jaffé and respected her acumen, but he told her the same thing he told Ruth: he was short-tempered and she was expected to put up with his outbursts or, better still, to behave in such a manner as not to provoke them. Under no circumstances was she to try to make herself "indispensable," for he saw this as typical female behavior, "a secret demand for power" and "the root of countless evils . . . in human relationships."[56] None of his admonitions about his "violent side" gave her pause, and Aniela accepted the job. Now that she worked for him full- and not part-time as she had done when employed by the institute, their relationship changed from "islands of peace in the flux of time" to become "more real and hence more complete."

EVER SINCE the second volume of *Mysterium Coniunctionis* was published in 1956, the general consensus has been that Jung produced very little in the last years of his life and what he wrote was minor. Even the briefest perusal of his *Collected Works* bibliography demonstrates that the first part of the contention is wrong and the second only partially correct. In the German section alone, there are more than sixty entries for writings published after 1957, and this does not take into account those still unpublished.[57] Granted, most of the published writings are introductions to the books of others, while others are his comments taken from interviews and conversations and revised for publication into other forms. These deal with his views on everything from how the Western world should treat the threat of Communist totalitarianism to UFOs. The often overlooked point, however, is that a man of eighty-plus years produced such a prodigious amount of writing in the last six years of his life, and that his thinking remained clear and uncompromised until the end.

Of his more sustained writings, two essays, one on schizophrenia and another dealing with a psychological view of the conscience, show the breadth and vitality of his interests, despite his advanced age.[58] In the former, he posited the theory, then quite new, that schizophrenia had "two aspects of paramount importance, biochemical and psychological," and that there might well be a *"toxic cause* traceable to an organic disintegration"[59] (Jung's emphasis). Jung believed that drug therapy was "an almost unexplored region awaiting pioneer research" because "the biological foundations of the psyche" were involved.[60]

Like the essay on schizophrenia, which was solidly grounded in recent scientific and medical research, the essay on conscience was equally grounded in moral philosophy. One of Jung's most overlooked writings, the essay is a model of clarity that proceeds logically from one point to the next in the classical essay style practiced by Freud rather than in the circular and digressive style Jung normally employed. It posits some of the moral dilemmas he thought were confronting postwar Western society. To reinforce his views, he reached into traditional theological doctrine and contemporary approaches to religion, all the while locating them firmly within his own psychology. The essay remains valid and vital more than fifty years after he wrote it.

Jung's book on unidentified flying objects reached the largest audience and generated the greatest response in his last years. He began to study the phenomenon as early as 1950,[61] and by the following year he had read the two books that sparked public interest: Donald Keyhoe's *Flying Saucers Are Real* and Gerald Heard's *Is Another World Watching? The Riddle of the Flying Saucers.*[62] Of the two, he initially thought Heard's the more authoritative but subsequently concluded that he "preach[ed] his cause a bit too much."[63] As for himself, he was "puzzled to death" about UFOs and not sure if they were "a rumour with concomitant singular and mass hallucination, or a downright fact." By 1954, his interest in UFOs was well enough known that a reporter for *Die Weltwoche* asked for an interview to discuss it. Jung declined but agreed to answer questions in writing for publication as a letter. He wrote that despite years of studying the phenomenon, he was unable "to establish an empirical basis sufficient to permit any conclusions to be drawn."[64] He was delighted that Edward J. Ruppelt's 1956 book, *Report on Unidentified Flying Objects*, supported his *Weltwoche* conclusion: "Something is seen, but nobody knows what."[65] He still held this view in 1958, the year his book was published in German, but his public was demanding that he take a position on one side or the other.[66] "It is not in my line to make statements about things that I cannot prove," he told one correspondent in 1958; in 1961 he told another that despite having studied UFOs "for about 12 years . . . I cannot even say whether they exist or not."[67]

Speaking of his 1958 experiences with German readers, Jung wrote in the 1959 preface to the English edition that "the moral of this story is rather interesting."[68] The worldwide press had subjected the book to "a sort of Gallup test," or poll of public opinion, to which Jung was responding through the English preface: "News affirming the existence of UFOs is welcome" even as "scepticism seems to be undesirable." Surely, he thought, one "remarkable fact" deserved the psychologist's attention. What were people looking for and what were they lacking that they needed to believe in the existence of extraterrestrial life? Why did people exhibit such "infantilism that they all want to jump at conclusions because they cannot stand it to leave something in suspension and they childishly think one could force an issue by belief?"[69] Citing his "conscience as a psychiatrist," Jung said he wrote the book because questions such as these imposed the duty upon him. By addressing such a controversial topic, he knew full well that he was jeopardizing his "hard-won reputation for truthfulness, reliability, and capacity for scientific judgment."[70] Nevertheless, he carried out this "thankless task in the expectation that [his] chisel [would] make no impression on the hard stone it encounter[ed]."

Shortly after the book appeared in the United States, the American publishers Helen and Kurt Wolff asked Jung to receive two of their closest friends at Bollingen, Charles and Anne Morrow Lindbergh. The weather was inclement, so they sat in the tower's small round room. Eventually, when the conversation turned to flying saucers, Lindbergh was astounded to hear Jung call them "factual."[71] He was further astonished because Jung did not seem "in the least interested in psychological aspects" or "in factual information relating to the investigation of flying-saucer reports."

Lindbergh told Jung of his investigations with the United States Air Force on "hundreds" of reported sightings, and of not finding "the slightest evidence of supernatural phenomena." Jung made it "obvious that he did not wish to pursue the subject farther." Undaunted, Lindbergh told Jung how the British "de

Havilland Comets," allegedly destroyed in midair by UFOs, had in reality disintegrated because of poor design and metal fatigue. He told Jung how the Pentagon disproved the many allegations by the writer (and author of the book Jung trusted) Donald Keyhoe about this and other incidents. In sadness, Lindbergh described how "mutual friends" told him that Keyhoe, whom he had "known intimately many years ago," recently experienced "several nervous breakdowns." Jung "showed not the slightest interest in these facts."

To place the conversation on less controversial footing, Lindbergh described a recent conversation with General Carl Spaatz, commander in chief of the air force. Spaatz, Lindbergh recounted, asked: "Slim, don't you suppose that if there was anything true about this flying-saucer business, you and I would have heard about it by this time?" Jung interrupted: "There are a great many things going on around this earth that you and General Spaatz don't know about."

"Thereafter," Lindbergh wrote, "I departed from the subject of flying saucers." But in retrospect, he wondered if there might have been other reasons why Jung did not want to discuss it. Anne Lindbergh thought Jung was "an Old Wizard," and Charles was "fascinated" by him: "One intuitively feels the elements of mysticism and greatness about him — even though they may have been mixed, at times, with charlatanism. . . . And in this instance, the 'Old Wizard' just didn't open his mind to me on the subject of flying saucers." Years later, Lindbergh's "admiration and respect" for Jung remained firm, and he still found "tremendous stimulation" in his writings. But he took everything concerning Jung "with even greater caution than in the past."

DESPITE THE popularity of the flying saucer book, the steady stream of distinguished worldwide visitors, and the sheer volume of daily correspondence, these indications of the high regard in which his work was held did not convince Jung of its lasting value. Nor did those who respected it, such as Pauli, who had been incorporating analytical psychology into his thinking since the 1930s; or Eugen Böhler, the professor of economics at the ETH who had been among his eulogizers at the birthday celebration and was about to publish a book incorporating analytical psychology into economic theory.[72] The respected Klinik am Zürichberg had been founded on the premise that it would offer students at the institute the opportunity to work in an inpatient facility that practiced analytical psychology.[73] In England, Anthony Storr and Anthony Stevens were writing books about Jung and his psychology that have since become standards. Henri Corbin, Giles Quispel, and Elie Humbert were championing his work in France to a public steeped in Freud and reluctant to receive it. In the United States, institutes had been founded in most of the major cities, and here, too, his work was the subject of discriminating writing and research. Interest was growing in Latin America and Australia, countries that had sent students to the Zürich institute. There was interest even in the Soviet Union, although it had to be hidden from the political system.

Cary Baynes told Jung she took special pride in all the honors he had been given, "because Switzerland, through you, has always stood in my mind for the growing point of consciousness in Europe and now in the free world."[74] But Jung was more likely to express the dour sentiment those closest to him remember: "Nobody reads my books anymore."[75]

He repeated this to E. A. Bennet, the English analyst he had known since the 1930s but to whom he became close only after the war. In this instance, he was speaking specifically of Ernest Jones's forthcoming biography of Freud, but he enlarged the comment to cover his entire life: "Nobody ever asks *me* how things really were; one only gives a one-sided and twisted representation of my relationship to him."[76]

It was this "one-sided and twisted representation" of so many things in his life and work that Jung brooded about until 1956, when he finally decided that all those who had been imploring him to write an autobiography — or, better still, to choose them as his authorized biographer — were probably right, and he had better do something about it.

⤜∞⤛

CHAPTER 37

Gathering Jung for the Future

The business of creating books and the related minutiae of turning them into a uniform edition dominated the last fifteen years of Jung's life, particularly the negotiations with publishers in two languages and three countries for what became his *Collected Works*. The person who most wanted this to happen besides Jung was the "rather unbusinesslike and naïve" Mary Conover Mellon, "a person of many plans" who did not live to see her dream come to fruition when she died suddenly of an asthma attack on October 11, 1946, at the age of forty-two. Her last words to her husband, Paul, were "And I had so much to do."[1]

During the war, when the Mellon family's lawyers directed Mary to disband the original Bollingen Foundation to avoid possible charges of dealing with enemy sympathizers, she began looking for ways to revive it as early as 1943, under the general rubric of the family's Old Dominion Foundation. She severed her ties with Yale University Press and was searching for another publisher when Heinrich Zimmer suggested another German refugee, who had just set up a publishing house, Kurt Wolff. At a meeting to determine if they were compatible, Wolff told Mellon how happy he was "to find an American so well versed in European thought" and, like himself, "nourished by the same roots."[2] A harmonious publishing relationship began that lasted twenty-five years and resulted in the Bollingen Series of scholarly publications, prominent among them Jung's *Collected Works* in English.[3]

Wolff (1887–1963) was "a singular presence in the literary world of the twentieth century" who had but one criterion for any book he published: "enthusiasm, enthusiasm, enthusiasm."[4] The vicissitudes of two wars and the politics of the publishing industry as well as of the government in his native Germany led to his launching seven publishing houses in a career that spanned six decades and two continents. Because Wolff's mother was Jewish, he left Germany before the outbreak of war to live in Italy; when that country became dangerous, he fled to France. After detention in refugee camps, Wolff made his way to New York with his second wife, Helen Mosel Wolff, also a distinguished editor and noted for her knowledge of art history and her gift for languages.[5]

The Wolffs entered the United States under observation by wartime security agencies and were investigated by the OSS, whose agents determined that Kurt Wolff operated Pantheon Books "in his apartment . . . on a shoe string." Although he was "definitely to the Left politically," he was "not Communistic" and was considered "entirely reliable and pro-United Nations in sentiment."[6] Financial backing for the new publishing venture consisted of $7,500 given to Wolff by another German refugee with the stipulation that he find an additional $7,500 to match it.[7] He did, and Kurt Wolff founded his seventh publishing imprint in 1942, Pantheon Books.

It was praised from its inception for writings of "unquestionable cultural value, or decided artistic significance, or a genuine attempt to contribute to the solution of the intellectual and spiritual dilemma of these difficult years."[8] His list included distinguished European writers, living and dead,[9] among them Jacob Burckhardt, Stefan George, and Charles Péguy; in later years, Boris Pasternak, Günter Grass, Julian Green, Albert Camus, and Giuseppe Lampedusa. The first American critical success came with the complete edition of *Grimm's Fairy Tales* in the James Stern translation. Anne Morrow Lindbergh added financial success to critical achievement in 1955, when *Gift from the Sea* became an international bestseller.

Mary Mellon's agreement with Wolff was for Pantheon Books to take charge of the manufacturing, production, and promotion of her books, with the Bollingen Foundation paying expenses as well as a decent royalty for each. With Jung, the beginning was rocky, a portent for things to come.[10] In 1944, when she was able to send letters via the Swiss diplomatic pouch, Mary told Jung of her plan to reconstitute the Bollingen Foundation and requested the rights to translate and publish his collected writings in English. On March 29, 1945, Jung denied her request: "After giving the matter careful thought and being mindful of experiences in the past years, I have come to the conclusion that I am unable to grant to Mrs. Mellon the publishing right for all of my works already published and to be published in the future."[11]

The shocked Mary Mellon could not accept that Jung had rebuffed her for the English firm of Routledge, later to be known as Routledge and Kegan Paul.[12] Even though the firm had been his English-language publisher for more than thirty years, she had hoped to forestall him from signing a contract for future work. She sent a cable on April 5 and another the next day, saying she needed to see him "badly" and would come in July. He replied by letter on the tenth, saying he had already settled with Routledge "when American communications [were] impossible and war issues uncertain."[13] On the thirteenth he wrote again, saying he would be "very busy" in July but would "try" to see her. After the warmth of their wartime exchanges, Mary was puzzled by Jung's harshness, because she thought she had explained and he had accepted that legal issues dictated her earlier coldness. She was unwilling to accept his snub and sprang into action.[14]

She began by trying to obtain the U.S. rights for *Psychology and Alchemy* from Kegan Paul, but she was given the erroneous information that another American publisher, Harcourt Brace, already had that option.[15] William McGuire, in his authoritative history of the Bollingen Foundation, described how Stanley Young (the first Bollingen editor) wrote to Cecil A. Franklin (the managing director of Kegan Paul), offering a $1,000 advance and mentioning that the Bollingen Series was endowed by the Mellon family. "A courteous letter came back, offering to negotiate."[16]

On January 1, 1946, the Bollingen Foundation began official operation. Mary Mellon was determined that the best of the Eranos lectures would become separate books within the Bollingen Series, and indeed many did, but her prime focus was on her long-delayed plan to "gather [Jung] up for the future."[17] By 1946, after negotiations both delicate and arduous with Routledge and Kegan Paul, the Bollingen Foundation secured the right to become his American publisher. Jung's writings were to be published first in Great Britain and later in the United States, but the order was reversed for the most practical of reasons: little was being printed in Great Britain because of the postwar shortage of paper.[18]

BEGINNING WITH the August 1946 Eranos conference, the Bollingen Press was represented by the new editor, John D. Barrett, in "the first paid employment of his life."[19] His bilingual (French-English) secretary, Vaun Gillmor, became the indispensable administrative link between Jung and his American, British, and German-language publishers. Barrett, armed with trenchant capsule biographies of all the participants that had been handwritten by Mary Mellon,[20] represented Bollingen on the August afternoon when the language of the U.S., British, and German contracts was hammered out in Olga Fröbe-Kapteyn's living room at the Casa Gabriella.[21] Among the others present were Cecil Franklin, the managing director of Routledge; and an editorial director of the firm, the poet and critic (and later Sir) Herbert Read. It was a confusing babble, with "everybody talking and all this throng . . . the lawyers all scribbling everything down, so as to make up this tri-partite thing."[22]

Jung sat quietly, listening to Cecil Franklin (who enjoyed pontificating) as he did "his whole Routledge business." Franklin droned on and on about Rascher (Jung's German-language publisher), of "the point with Rascher, the rights from Rascher," and so on, until a perplexed Jung turned to Barrett: "I never had any Russian rights. Does anyone here know [if] I ever gave any rights to Russia?" The situation threatened to disintegrate, as Jung grew agitated that Communists were stealing his work, until Read realized that he was misinterpreting Franklin's pronunciation of "Rascher." The mood lightened, the lawyers continued to "scribble," and contracts were agreed upon and eventually put into effect.[23]

When Jung made his original agreement with the firm that became Routledge and Kegan Paul, he dealt generally through his Zürich lawyer, Hans Karrer, who negotiated with Cecil Franklin. It was apparent that, with a publishing
venture of the magnitude of the *Collected Works*, someone in the publishing
house would have to be made coordinator of the project, and Herbert Read was
chosen. Jung liked Read, and a reserved friendship developed. It deepened to
one of trust after Jung read Read's only novel, *The Green Child*, which he believed would make "an old alchemist" weep for "sheer joy."[24]

Meanwhile in New York, Mary Mellon was jockeying to protect her own position. She wanted Dr. Violet de Laszlo,[25] a Swiss analyst then living and practicing there, to do the actual editing and Cary Baynes to be Jung's official
translator. Cary quickly declined for "a whole host of fears and misgivings," especially after having been "licked to a standstill by the *I Ging*" (the translation
of the *I Ching* that took her many years to complete).[26] The only point of operational procedure about which Mellon and Read agreed was the need for someone in Switzerland to represent Jung's point of view. They both wanted Toni
Wolff but did not even ask her, as they knew she would refuse. Jolande Jacobi's
name was also raised, but Mary Mellon "frankly . . . did not like her very much."[27]
Mary also raised the possibility of Michael Fordham to be "editor in chief."

Read had other ideas on every front. Still thinking first publication would be
in England, he wanted the staff to be London-based. Read suggested himself
for editor in chief and Michael Fordham for a lesser status as co-editor, with
R. F. C. Hull as translator.[28] Jung had reservations about Fordham because he
did not "know Dr. Fordham well enough to be absolutely sure that he would be
the right man."[29] Still hoping to convince Jung to accept her New York nomi-
nations, Mary said that as he was "unsure of [Fordham] as a choice," he should
consider "one or two other people," meaning her candidates, de Laszlo and
Toni Wolff. In the end, Read prevailed. Despite Jung's concern that Fordham
simply did not know enough German, Read allayed Jung's fear by agreeing to
appoint a third co-editor, the German Gerhard Adler, whom Jung had known
and trusted since 1930.[30] For himself, Read carved out a position where he became "the balance wheel and arbiter"[31] among the three co-equals, always the
conciliator between Fordham and Adler and the ultimate authority in any disagreement.

As for the translator, Richard Francis Carrington Hull was initially approached by Herbert Read because they were personal friends. All parties
agreed, however, that he was a superb choice even though he knew nothing of
Jung's psychology. Read soothed Hull's qualms by saying the editors specifically
wanted a translator and not a psychologist, "because most of them couldn't
write anyway."[32] Hull had lived in Munich's bohemian Schwabing district for
most of the 1930s and was already the translator of writers such as Alfred We-
ber, Martin Buber, and Georg Misch. When war began, he returned to England
and worked as a cryptographer in Bletchley Park, the British code center now

famed for deciphering the German "enigma." When Read selected him, Hull had just begun his postwar career as a professional translator. Hull was "tall, elegant, distinguished-looking" but afflicted with a "marked stammer." He also had "a remarkably quick mind and a capacity to grasp essentials,"[33] which made him perfect for the demanding task of translating Jung's often esoteric texts.

Although the initial negotiations with all those who became principals in the process began in August 1946, contracts were not officially signed until one year later, August 25, 1947. Part of the delay was due to Mary Mellon's untimely death, but it was mostly because Jung was such a "shrewd bargainer" who "asked for and received an unusually high royalty," and who stipulated that the first volume had to be translated and published within three years, by 1950.[34]

The three-year clause was beset by a series of mishaps that required three separate one-year extensions before *Psychology and Alchemy* finally appeared in 1953. The text had been previously translated into English for the 1939 British publication known as *The Integration of Personality*, but Jung never liked either the book or the translation. Hull had been engaged to prepare the official translation in 1946, but Jung was not informed until November 1947. Even then, he was only given partial information: Michael Fordham told him that Hull was working on *The Psychology of Transference* but not that a severe attack of poliomyelitis had paralyzed his arms and legs and was delaying its completion. Jung wrote angrily to Fordham that he did not approve of "such a manner of procedure. I should really like to be informed about the decisions you take concerning translations. I know nothing of Mr. Hull and his translations. . . . I sincerely hope that in future . . . a hearing is given to my opinion."[35]

Jung added news that was ominous to London and New York, that Barbara Hannah was already well along with a separate translation. Read, the conciliator, described carefully why they had chosen Hull: he was acclaimed for translations of Rilke and other German writers who required delicately nuanced texts. Jung retorted that Rilke was a "rather different" writer than himself, but he would reserve judgment until he read Hull's translation. Hull was working steadily even while he lay inert in his hospital bed and before he regained most of the movement in his arms and limited use of his legs. By April 1948, he was able to stand but did not have enough arm strength to operate a manual typewriter. The Bollingen Foundation bought him an electric IBM, but British customs impounded it until May 1949. He used it to edit his already finished translation, which he had been forced to dictate to his wife and then type himself with one hand.[36]

Meanwhile, to everyone's trepidation but Jung's, Barbara Hannah finished her translation. When Mary Mellon was still alive and involved in setting up a staff, Cary Baynes warned her to be "*very* cautious in dealing with the problem of Barbara Hannah." She said, "*All* of her ambition is locked up in this and a veritable hornet's nest will be released if she thinks we are trying to take it away from her."[37] Cary also warned that, as Hannah had obviously "won Jung's confidence," they would have to proceed tactfully, for "he has made mistakes before in his translators." Mary discussed the situation at length with her trusted editor, Jack Barrett, who asked her to give him "an angle on a mode of attack."[38] She told him to be "extremely nice" to Hannah, for "if not, you will have her against you and it will cause you a great deal more trouble than you can imagine."[39] Mary's "whole gorge" rose at the possibility of being forced by the British to print Hannah's "*terrible*" translation, but if they compelled her "to swallow Miss H." for *Psychology and Alchemy*, she said she would "wangle it so that we won't have to have another . . . by her in the future."[40]

Despite Cary Baynes's misgivings, Jung settled the dispute the moment he read and compared the two translations. After a single chapter, Jung declared Hull's work "remarkable" and praised his "natural gift" for a "better and more educated" text. Compared to it, Hannah's work was "*holperig*," clumsy and awkward.[41] The questions remained, however, how to mollify Hannah and what her future role, if any, might be. Jung told his publishers that she began her work expecting to be paid. They said they had already commissioned Hull and therefore could not be expected "to pay the same work twice over." Jung insisted they retain Hannah as a "consultant translator" to Hull.[42] The contradiction between his view of her abilities and the position he now wanted her to hold was apparent to all, but as Cary Baynes warned, tact and discretion were never more needed with Jung than here. Pointing out that Adler had been engaged specifically as "consultant translator," Read then changed the direction of the highly charged discussion by telling Jung how inadequate Hull's salary was; as he did all the work, it would be unseemly to divert funds for translation to Hannah rather than to him. Read succeeded in persuading Jung that whether or not Hannah should be involved in future translations was a decision best left to the future, when other works were under consideration.

Throughout the long and difficult publishing process, Hull was incredibly kind to all the women whose egos were bound up with working for Jung. Here, he did much to soften the blow to Hannah's by developing a genuine friendship with her. He told Barrett, "She has a deep understanding of Jung's latest work and the increasingly paradoxical turn it is taking. . . . Her help has been invaluable."[43] It appears there was no further discussion among the principals of whether to pay Hannah; nor is it known if Cecil Franklin invoked the clause in her contract "that if her translation is not up to standard, we shall bring it up to standard, charging her with the cost of doing so."[44]

WHILE NEGOTIATIONS for English-language staff were under way, a different sort was being assembled for the German *Gesammelte Werke*. The owners of Rascher Verlag had created an advantageous situation for their firm: Rascher would receive a subvention from the Bollingen Foundation to pay for printing costs and a royalty for books sold, while they would do no actual editorial work "in-house" and would not pay for others to do it on their behalf. Instead, a group of Jung's followers and associates was assembled to oversee the preparation of final manuscripts, none of whom had any direct experience either in textual scholarship or in publishing. Still, when Jung died, the Swiss editorial role became one of ultimate authority, causing many problems for the other firms involved.

The leader (and senior editor, although she never officially claimed the title) was Jung's third daughter, Marianne Niehus-Jung, who coordinated the activities of the others and had the last word about what constituted the final, definitive, and authorized text. Initially, she was assisted by two persons who died midway into the project: Franz Riklin Jr., the son of Jung's longtime associate and a distinguished analyst in his own right;[45] and Lena Hurwitz-Eisner, the wife of the Jung family's dentist and trusted friend, Dr. Sigmund Hurwitz.[46] Dr. Elisabeth Rüf, an analyst who lived and practiced nearby in Küsnacht, completed the original group.

Marianne Niehus was considered by all who knew her to be a "very impressive personality," but she was also regarded as a woman with such a "strong father complex that she could not separate herself."[47] She was a woman of enormous energy and willpower, both of which she needed during her tenure, for early on she was diagnosed with the same type of cancer that killed her mother. She worked despite its ravages until 1964, when she died at the age of fifty-four.[48] Lilly Jung-Merker, Franz Jung's wife, replaced Marianne until her own death from cancer shortly after.

Franz Riklin Jr. had other professional responsibilities, so his contribution differed from those of the other editors, all of whom were women. The work of Lena Hurwitz, as described by her son, was typical: "She screened manuscripts for the books, edited texts and copyedited them, made indices, corrected typos, et cetera. She worked full-time and never received a salary; she considered it an honor to do this work."[49]

Aniela Jaffé was never an official member of the editorial board, but she served as an important liaison between the German- and English-language contingents, particularly when trying to decide which textual variants should become the final manuscript. From time to time, when some writings could not be found within Jung's files or there were disputes among the editors about which version was definitive, Marie-Jeanne Boller-Schmid was called out of retirement to help Jaffé and the editors find the answer.

While Jung was alive, and with his health and interest fluctuating pretty much in tandem, he worked on the texts directly with Hull, the degree dependent on his health, stamina, and interest in the work at hand. Jung asked Hull how he wanted to proceed, even as he inadvertently described the major problem he created for all those trying to establish a definitive text:

I am keeping the mss of all my writings but the term "mss" is not clearly defined, inasmuch as I am usually writing a rough draft as the first thing, then that draft will be copied by machine, and then I am working over the copy until the mss. reaches its definite stage mature for printing. Now do you want the first handwritten draft, or do you want the first copy ready for printing? Please let me know.[50]

As so many rough handwritten drafts and edited typescript drafts existed for almost everything he wrote, establishing chronological development threatened to be impossible. While Jung was alive, he was often cranky and uncooperative when the editors tried to enlist his help; after he died, they had to presume which was his final version. However, many variant versions surfaced later that were not factored into their work, so the possibility that some texts might need modification or change remains today.

The editors worked as follows: Hull translated into English what the German editors gave him; then they read and compared his translation to the original German and commented upon it, which may or may not have influenced any revisions Hull then made; finally, they prepared a clean copy of the German manuscript for Rascher.[51] When the text had been set in print in both languages, there followed the arduous task of making the English correspond to the German and collating it by paragraph number, so that no matter what the language or which the edition, a reader is not dependent upon page numbers but has only to consult the paragraph number to locate a particular passage.

Jung was apprised of all these decisions and deliberations until the last months of his life and, for the most part, he was involved in them. A virtual round-robin of correspondence was in constant flight between him and the British and American editors whom he dubbed the "editorial Olympos,"[52] but the bulk of his exchanges were with Hull. All were in English, and they attest to Jung's superb command of the language.[53] The letters evolved over time, from short and specific replies to Hull's carefully phrased questions, to philosophical exchanges about what Jung intended when he conceived various fundamentals of his psychology, to what exactly he was attempting to explain when he cited the writings of others. Frequently they became exchanges of personal information, especially about unidentified flying objects, as both men were fascinated by the subject.

Hull sent Jung his translation of Georg Misch's *The Dawn of Philosophy* to illustrate why he chose the words he did to convey Jung's views of Eastern religions. Jung said he was concerned about the comparison, and his reply was lengthy, not only his opinion of the book itself but also his explanation of why his intellectual position differed from Misch's: "Don't forget: I am definitely no philosopher and my concepts are accordingly *empirical* and *not speculative*."[54] In the same letter, he asked Hull to ignore jokes he had made in the text for his own amusement ("cut it out, please!") and then wrote a long paragraph telling how he wanted his interpretation of Lucien Lévy-Bruhl's term *"participation mystique"* to be conveyed consistently throughout all his translations.[55]

Once the typescripts were approaching finality, the letters became even longer exchanges about the word-by-word, line-by-line editing. Hull sent Jung lists of questions that Jung answered in minute detail. He asked, for example, for possible alternatives for passages in the essay then in preparation on synchronicity.

"I realize this essay of mine represents a first-class difficulty when it comes to translation," Jung wrote repeatedly as he apologized throughout the many exchanges concerning the title eventually coined by Hull: "Synchronicity: An Acausal Connecting Principle." Jung thanked him for it and for understanding "how to transform the heavy German grammatical forms into English."[56]

In one exchange, Jung replied with a list of synonyms that would be English equivalents of the German word.[57] In another, he supplied interpretive paragraphs to explain how he and Wolfgang Pauli differed in their definitions of concepts such as correspondence. And in yet others, Jung dealt with appearance and typography: "The footnote is better left where it is now," he decided of one text; and he liked the English printing of *Psychology and Alchemy* better than "the coffin-like appearance of the American edition."[58]

Jung quickly put a stop to the idea suggested by a Mr. Hoppin, that he should retranslate the "Seminar Notes" transcribed and edited by Mary Foote and include them in the *Collected Works*. Jung entrusted Hull to present his case to the editors that all seminars were to be evaluated *"cum grano salis"* (with a grain of salt) because he had not revised them except for certain "isolated places."[59] He forbade Hoppin to "interfere with [his] style," of which he said, "Miss Foote has made a masterwork apparently. I myself think so."[60] And the seminars did not become part of the *Collected Works*.

Hull was a quick learner and soon became fluent in the language and concepts of analytical psychology. In the early years of their collaboration, he lived in Dorset, despite the cold British winters that aggravated his physical condition. Thinking Switzerland might provide a better climate as well as easier communication with Jung, Hull moved his family to Feldbach, a town midway between Zürich and Bollingen. The move did cement their reliance on each other, but winters were even more oppressive than in England, so Hull moved his family to Ascona and the dryer, sunnier Ticino in southern Switzerland, where Jung saw him during the Eranos meetings and on his winter vacations.

In 1955, Jung elevated Hull to a higher level of friendship when he began his letters with "Dear Hull."[61] With Hull, Jung probably had his most successful working relationship, in any field and on any level, with another man. Every extant comment Jung made about Hull's work is one of praise for his ability and gratitude for his devoted work; no evidence has been found to show that he ever questioned, had reservations about, or disapproved of any aspect of Hull's translations. They had been working together for almost ten years in 1958, when

Jung sent Christmas greetings that cemented the friendship. Thanking Hull for his "immense work," Jung offered his lasting view of Hull's contribution: "Your participation in your work is more than professional. It is alive."[62]

How much Jung liked and respected Hull came to light in his will: he left enough money for Hull to make a down payment on his final residence in Mallorca, where he finally found a climate that suited his physical condition.[63]

JUNG RELIED on Hull for much more than the texts of the *Collected Works*. Time and again, he asked if Hull might be "in a position to translate . . . as soon as possible" everything from his introductions to books written by others, to articles for newspapers and periodicals, to his own commissions, such as the "ms. of about 65 pages, not yet finished," which a "certain American foundation" asked him to write.[64] He told Hull what he basically wanted to say in reply to Philip Toynbee's review of *Answer to Job* and asked him to put it into good English;[65] when Upton Sinclair engaged him in a dialogue after the publication of his *A Personal Jesus*, Jung asked Hull to oversee his side of the correspondence.[66]

The house in Küsnacht became an office complex of sorts as it filled early every day with a bevy of people who were there to work, and Jung worked right along with them. He was remarkably vigorous and productive for an eighty-year-old man, despite the ever more frequent bouts of gastric distress, flu and "grippe," and minor episodes with his heart. He responded to the burgeoning requests for his thoughts, comments, and writings, and his correspondence took on a new depth and intensity. From psychology to religion to contemporary politics, he believed he had the obligation to reply to strangers with thoughtful disquisitions on his views.

And sometime around 1956, he also began to believe he had the obligation to take seriously that some form of writing about his personal life was necessary. The decision engulfed his last five years in "a good deal of legalistic squabble about the so-called biography," or, as he alternated almost indiscriminately, the "so-called autobiography."[67] Ultimately, he was convinced he had no other choice than to see it through.

CHAPTER 38

"I Am as I Am, an Ungrateful
Autobiographer!"

The idea of a biography had been percolating since the mid-1930s, but it came to a boil once the Bollingen Series was officially under way. There was a general feeling that Jung's life story was a logical adjunct, if not the necessary companion, to his *Collected Works*, but it remained in the realm of speculation until the early 1950s.

Jung was the first to recognize the need for a biography in the early 1930s, when he asked Cary Baynes to write one. She was his true *"trait d'union,"*[1] a trusted "first reader" and most stringent critic, a bilingual link between German and English publication. Cary was slangy, breezy, and blunt, forthright in the extreme, but when it came to writing Jung's biography, she couched her unwillingness behind his own reluctance "to put into it the time and effort it would require."[2] Actually, the reluctance was hers. Cary knew better than anyone the political intrigues and personal interferences Jung's biographer would face, from his family, with their fear that their privacy would be invaded, to those associates who considered themselves the keepers of his various flames and the only ones qualified to present his life story. Now that she was working for the Bollingen Press, she was privy to everything relating to the disputes about the accuracy of his translations and the contractual disagreements among his publishers. Cary knew that when these disputes were resolved, conflict over who had the right to publish the biography first would be inevitable. All this eventually happened just as she predicted, but in the mid-1930s, when the biographical impulse was beginning, she was prescient enough to recognize the problems and know she wanted no part of them.

THE IDEA of an outsider writing the official biography was first proposed around 1936 when Lucy Heyer-Grote nominated herself. Jung was in Berlin to address the Jung Gesellschaft when she surprised him with a one-page "Summary of Contents."³ Caught off guard, Jung begged Cary to resolve the dilemma. When she read Lucy's summary, Cary told him to consider her proposal. Jung knew Lucy well, for she was then married to Gustav Richard Heyer and both had been staunch practitioners of analytical psychology since the mid-1920s. Jung respected Lucy's analytic abilities and liked her personally but did not know her capability as a writer. His reservations were somewhat assuaged by the intelligent list of topics she proposed.

She planned to divide Jung's life into two parts, with the first and longest covering his growth and development. She would set the personal scene by discussing the influence of late-nineteenth-century culture on his native Basel as well as his immediate family, and trace how both affected his intellectual coming of age. Subsequent chapters were to follow his education, appointment to the Burghölzli, and marriage. This would lead naturally to the word association test and ensuing research. Then would come a chapter on the founding of the Psychological Club and other encounters, such as Keyserling's School of Wisdom. Part one would end with travels (Africa, the United States, and India), friendships (Richard Wilhelm and Heinrich Zimmer among them), his participation at Eranos, and his all-consuming interest in alchemy. Freud never figured in her outline, and for part two, she gave only a title without explanation: "Jung's Readings and Their Importance."

Jung did not need to make a decision about Lucy's proposal, for war intervened. When it ended, the Heyers divorced and Lucy settled in Basel, where she established a therapeutic practice and supplemented her income by writing articles on various psychological subjects for Swiss magazines.⁴ In 1953, she renewed her request to write Jung's biography and went to Küsnacht to formalize procedures. To support her credentials, she arrived with reams of documentation about the history and genealogy of the Jung and Preiswerk families. Jung was still apprehensive, but she so overwhelmed him with her doggedness that he gave her free run of his library and permission to take away whatever documentation she needed. She left loaded down with correspondence, manuscripts, and some of his books for which he had only a single copy.⁵ She quite naturally assumed his archival generosity meant full cooperation, so she pressed for a regular schedule of interviews. To Cary's incredulity, Jung agreed. But Lucy's questions in their first session so alarmed him that he spent most of the time he was with Cary (who was in Europe that summer) asking how he could extricate himself from a situation he had unwittingly created. Cary found his distress highly amusing: "There is something in the situation that makes me say 'it's as if the Little Red Hen were writing the biography of Fafnir [the dragon].'"⁶

On a more serious plane, Cary feared, as did Jung, that Heyer-Grote was insensitive to the nuances of his life. They both thought she was fixated upon superimposing a philosophical structure of her own conception onto a framework that, in many instances, had nothing to do with the actuality of his life and work. They were alarmed by her determination to fit contradictory facts and events into a neat and tidy composition where everything would conclude with preordained unity.

Beneath their obvious misgivings lay a different subtext to their many worried conversations about Heyer-Grote's biographical technique and the reason they were reluctant to dismiss her: "So few people under[stood]" Jung's psychology that Cary believed any attempt to explain it by a loyal follower was better than leaving it to a stranger. Cary told Jung she hoped that Lucy might "get out something valuable in mitigating the nonsense that [was] going to be written about [him]." At the same time, Cary was clinging "tenaciously" to another possibility, that Jung would trump both his supporters and detractors by writing an autobiography: "It is your psychological life curve that needs to be written, and you are the only person who can do it scientifically. For everyone else it is guesswork."

She ended her plea by recounting a recent conversation with biologist Adolf Portmann, which she claimed deserved serious attention simply because the man was not known for his "psychological imagination." According to Portmann, no single biography of Jung could provide an understanding of his life and work, for that would come only through "several works of volcanology." Cary asked Jung to think about how best to achieve this eruption.

HEYER-GROTE TRIED to stave off the rejection she intuited was coming by lying low in Basel and concentrating on "ancestry research."[7] When she returned to Küsnacht to resume the interview sessions, she determinedly ignored Jung's stubborn refusal to tell her anything. Curiously, Jung, who never hesitated to explode in wrath when anyone crossed him, found himself unable to speak firmly to the obstinate woman. Because he was angry with her, he lashed out instead at Cary, claiming she had "muscled Lucy Heyer into the situation" and then left him "holding the baby."[8]

Jung was bedridden with flu in August 1952, and Cary did not want to upset him, so she sent Emma a copy of a letter she had just received from Lucy, describing her "mandate" to write the book, either with Cary or alone. Cary blamed Dr. Daniel Brody of Rhein-Verlag for inspiring Lucy's letter. Brody was the printer of the Eranos *Jahrbuch* that Paul Mellon continued to subsidize after Mary's death, and Cary insisted that he was using his connection to the Mellons to make Heyer-Grote's biography a "fait accompli" so he could publish it. Cary told Emma it was up to her to tell "Brody and Lucy . . . where they got off the beam" and stop them at once. When Jung was well enough, she wrote a duplicate to him of her letter to Emma, insisting that he, too, had to tell Brody he did not want Lucy "to go it alone."

If such "direct word" ever reached Brody, he paid no attention to it. Nor did he convey it to his writer. "Happily thinking that her mandate held as she understood it," Lucy persuaded Paul Mellon to finance her project and pay her handsome stipends at regularly scheduled intervals.[9] Time passed, and as Cary heard nothing further, she concluded, like everyone else in the United States, that Jung had overcome his reservations and was cooperating with Lucy.

Eventually Jung apologized to Cary and told her he would not work with Lucy because her questions assured him she was incapable of "producing something that would look like an intelligent biography."[10] Politely and gently, he refused to grant further interviews by blaming himself for being "an utterly uninteresting case."[11] He begged Lucy to believe that his withdrawal sprang from his feeling that he was not a fit subject: "[It springs] solely from my insight that . . . the abyss between my common middle-class existence and that which I am under the damn obligation to work on, is virtually appalling." He said if he had to write his own life story, "it would discourage [him] completely."[12]

BUT PORTMANN's comment about the "several works of volcanology" needed to do justice to his life was intriguing enough to keep Jung mulling the possibility. The idea grew when the British theologian H. L. Philp, author of a book about "Freud's indictment of religion,"[13] asked Jung to discuss his views about the *privatio boni* in particular and religion in general. Their first exchange began sharply when Jung took umbrage at Philp's suggestion that he sought converts to "the new denomination 'Jungianism' or better 'Jungian Church.'" Jung called such charges "sheer defamation," and his written denial became so complex that it led to the same sort of detailed exchanges as his previous ones had been with Philip Wylie and Victor White. Eventually, his handwritten explanations became so intense and prolix that Jung declined to write further and asked Philp to come to Zürich for conversations.[14]

While cooperating with Philp, Jung conceived the idea that Portmann's proposed "volcanology" should be a collection of interrelated studies by different authors who would address specific aspects of his life and work. Philp was unaware that Jung lavished so much attention on his book because he wanted it to represent his views on religion, or that it had another éminence grise beside Jung, his friend (as well as Jung's) E. A. "Eddie" Bennet. When Philp asked Bennet to critique his manuscript, Bennet was so eager for the book to become exactly what Jung wanted that he sent the manuscript to Jung without telling Philp, who seems never to have known that many of the refinements and revisions Bennet suggested were actually Jung's.

Unlike his experience with Heyer-Grote, Jung was impressed with Philp's insights, enjoying both the intellectual repartee and the process of quasi-biographical inquiry. This worried Bennet, who was concerned that their working relationship was proceeding so smoothly it might interfere with his own ambition to become the "Jones" to Jung's "Freud."[15] Bennet, one of the rare men in the same profession who maintained a lifelong friendship with Jung, managed to do so by concentrating on enhancing Jung's reputation, so much so that his "obsequiousness" earned him the unflattering appellation of "Jung's dogsbody."[16]

When Bennet represented the English psychologists in the 1930s who were uniting to form a national group within the International Society, he did not inform the others that he was voting not as they directed but as Jung wanted.[17] After the war, Bennet wrote letters and articles to prominent British publications in defense of Jung, but most were deemed so effusive the editors declined to publish them.[18] Bennet liked to take credit for every English writer who wrote about Jung, claiming he sent everyone from Arnold Toynbee to Laurens van der Post to Zürich; he even took credit for having sent the BBC camera crew that filmed the eightieth birthday celebrations.[19] When Ernest Jones's three volumes of Freud's biography appeared, Bennet scrutinized every passage in which Jung's name figured, asked Jung for his version of the event, and then sent Jones "corrections" or "modifications" that he neither used nor acknowledged in subsequent printings.[20] Bennet was, however, sincere in his desire to further the growth of analytical psychology, as in his insistence that Jung receive Anthony Storr, with whom a friendship was forged as Storr became one of the most respected commentators on his psychology.[21]

In a sense, Philp forced Bennet's hand, but there were other forces fueling his desire to become Jung's authorized biographer. In January 1954, Cary Baynes asked Jung to receive her friends Helen and Kurt Wolff, who were taking a winter vacation in the Engadine. The Wolffs were preparing to publish a representative volume of J. J. Bachofen's writing. As Jung had often seen the revered Basel scholar during his university days, they wanted him to suggest texts to complement the book's centerpiece, *"Mutterrecht und Urreligion."*[22] Jung was hard-pressed to make a selection, saying, "Much of it is antiquated and wrong so that one has no heart to recommend it."[23] Still, the meeting was cordial and "meant a lot to the Wolffs."[24]

The idea of publishing Jung's biography under his own Pantheon imprint and not within the Bollingen Series had been in Kurt Wolff's mind since he first attended the Eranos conferences in 1951 in search of books to publish.[25] He followed the lead of John D. "Jack" Barrett, Mary Mellon's handpicked editor, who attended annually after 1946[26] and scheduled "conferences" before and after to bring Jung up to date on Bollingen Press activity. At every Eranos meeting, Kurt and Helen tried to ascertain if Jung might write an autobiography or, if not, authorize an official biography. The person they asked most often was Jolande Jacobi, who was not only the one most finely attuned to Zürich gossip but also the one who put it into the most objective perspective. They reasoned that *if* they could persuade Jung to write an autobiography, and *if* he should require help of any sort, Jacobi would be the best person for the job.[27] By their first meeting with Jung, they were feeling their way carefully over terrain made perilous by all the explosive egos involved.

Until they went to Küsnacht on February 4, 1954, Jung probably did not consider Helen and Kurt Wolff as anything other than personable publishers of other writers' books. As they conversed in Jung's home, the scope and variety of subjects revealed the immediate appreciation and respect each one had for the other's mind.[28] If the Wolffs wanted to publish the *"Mutterrecht,"* Jung advised them to start with Bachofen's own introduction, but he also suggested Carl Kerényi to write a new one. That way, they could justify publishing the now-outdated Bachofen by stressing his original thinking and the strong influence he exerted upon others, particularly Oswald Spengler and Frobenius. They noted Jung's succinct but apt descriptions and the wit with which he expressed them. With "a typical Jungian aside" and a deep "chuckle," Jung said the term "matriarchal law" as Bachofen used it was a misnomer, for matriarchy was "a society without law; 'law' being a specifically patriarchal creation." Jung reminisced over his memories of both Bachofen and Burckhardt as "a study in contrasts," the former "fastidiously elegant, but decidedly old-fashioned," the latter "shabbily dressed . . . stooped and giving the impression of an absent-minded half-wit." Burckhardt was a "historian and classicist, having no use for the romantic speculations of the visionary Bachofen."

Then Jung turned the conversation toward the "two subjects . . . in the immediate foreground of his actual preoccupations." The first was the Gnostic codex presented to him in November 1953 by the C. G. Jung Institute of Zürich and then being prepared for publication through their auspices.[29] Jung thought the gift giving a "disproportionate affair, to my taste, at least,"[30] but the codex itself enthralled him. He described it as a "Gospel of the Truth," a "Gnostic text by Valentinus" that was really a commentary to the gospels of the first century and a novel approach to "Christianity from a fascinating angle."

The second subject revolved around the research into parapsychological studies that arose at the institute in response to his and Pauli's essays on synchronicity. Jung was "quite wrapped up" in Pauli's proposal for some of the students to collect archetypal dreams and prepare mathematical analyses and for others to compare synchronistic experiments and possible correlations between oracular methods such as the *I Ching,* Tarot, astrology, and numerology.

What Jung wanted to talk about most was the public reaction to *Answer to Job.* Wolff said he thought Jung "rather enjoy[ed] the fray," and he described what he meant through an Old French proverb, that one of the advantages of old age was to *"mettre ses pieds dans tous les plats,"* to "put [one's] foot into everything." Jung roared with approval.

"All in all," Wolff concluded, "he was in an excellent mood." He cited as proof Jung's previous complaints to anyone within range that the Bollingen staff were taking far too long to publish his *Collected Works;* now when Wolff asked if he had a preferred sequence for forthcoming volumes, Jung said he was merely interested that they should appear at "fairly regular and brief intervals."[31] His good humor carried over into a letter he wrote to Jack Barrett about meeting the Wolffs, in which he expressed appreciation for the "cultural importance" of the Bollingen Foundation, "a small island in an infinite level of misunderstanding and flatness," a "shining beacon in the darkness of the atomic age," and a tribute to "the genius of Mrs. Mellon, who planned [it] with Paul

Mellon's generous aid." He pronounced himself "quite overwhelmed by the speed in which [his books were] turned out from the press."³² His satisfaction with the Bollingen Foundation from then on was genuine and lasting.³³

THROUGHOUT 1955, Jung's weakened health was a generally known topic of concern. Reports filtered back to Kurt Wolff, who worried that given Jung's advanced age coupled with illness, he would not have the stamina to write an autobiography alone. Well aware that Jung's other publishers would claim their contractual right to any new writing, Wolff trod carefully as he began his explorations. Because he appreciated Jolande Jacobi's expertise in explaining Jung's psychology, he asked if she would be *"Gebärmutter,"* or birth mother,³⁴ to a biography. She refused for two reasons: she had an imperative to continue to write independently because "all those others" who surrounded Jung in Zürich did not produce much objective commentary and therefore did little to explain or advance the case for analytical psychology; on a more personal level, she was well aware of how her extraverted intuitive personality would exacerbate "difficulties" with his followers.³⁵ Jacobi told Wolff to sound out Aniela Jaffé discreetly, but he waited almost a year to approach her directly, until after he had read her writings and observed her rapport with Jung. However, nothing was secret in Zürich, and gossip had it that Wolff was sending someone from the United States to conduct a series of interviews for an oral history, if not an actual autobiography. Jung alluded to such "a person" who was to begin interviewing him in early 1953, but if there was such a project, it was apparently stillborn.³⁶

Meanwhile, the idea of a biography was attracting all sorts of strangers who volunteered to write it. Trying to dissuade a Welsh professor of philosophy, Jung said he disliked the genre "because it is seldom true" and "only interesting when something has happened in the human life that people understand." As the general public did not understand his psychology, he saw "little use" in presenting the life of its creator. He could not write about himself "because quite apart from the lack of motive, [he] wouldn't know how to set about it." Nor could he envision anyone else "disentangl[ing] this monstrous Gordian knot of fatality, denseness, and aspirations and what-not!" that passed for his life.³⁷

BY 1956, Kurt Wolff persuaded Jung of the necessity for a biographical imperative, no matter what form it would take. It coincided with a time when Jung was not actually ill but neither was he in good health, so Wolff suggested that the best way to begin was casually: Jung should talk about any subject that struck his fancy while Aniela Jaffé wrote down what he said in shorthand. These informal interviews began in September 1956,³⁸ when Jung decided to talk about his personal concept and contemplation of God and how it differed from other cultures', societies', and religions'. Jaffé recorded one long paragraph — garbled, discursive, contradictory — that even with rigorous editing could not be turned into a coherent and cohesive passage. She did not record again until November 10,[39] this time taking down several passages purportedly from a conversation Jung had with a group of unidentified theologians. His remarks had little to do with his topic, "What a Psychologist Understands by the Term 'Numen,'" for he mostly recounted still another version of the dream about a Jewess that he had cited previously in other instances.[40]

There were no further transcriptions that year. One reason may have been Jaffé's normal workload for Jung or her own time spent checking proofs and preparing the index for a book.[41] The more likely reason was Jung's inability to organize his thoughts and focus on what he wanted to say. Ruth Bailey remembered how exhausted he was at the end of his first "biography hours"[42] with Jaffé, and how he resented them. Kurt Wolff sent twelve bottles of an excellent Burgundy wine, Côtes de Beaune, with the instruction to drink one after every such session. Jung thanked him for the "antidote."[43]

All this time, Jung was in close contact with Bennet, who knew of Wolff's plan to publish the informal talks with Jaffé. It prompted Bennet to suggest outright what he had long hinted at: that Jung should appoint him the "authorized" biographer.[44] Bennet made it seem as if this were a spontaneous new notion originating with Philp, who he said agreed it was a "good idea." Jung did not respond for almost a month, saying he needed time to reflect upon Bennet's "very interesting proposition."[45] When he did reply, perhaps alluding to Portmann's "volcanology," Jung described himself as "a somewhat complicated phenomenon" who could "hardly be covered by one biographer only." He suggested that Bennet consider the same proposition he had earlier put to Philp: based on their respective professions of physician and clergyman, each should submit lists of questions that Jung would try to answer:

> Being a doctor you would inquire into the anamnesis of your patient and you would ask the questions and I would answer as a patient would answer. Thus you would be . . . enabled to produce a picture of my personality understandable at least to more or less medical people (Philp certainly would produce a picture of my religious aspect, equally satisfactory).

Still, Jung hesitated to cast his lot with Bennet. Despite the "undeniable" fact that two of his "several aspects" were medical and theological, and specialists in these fields had "the best chance of being accurate," their writings would not present that "special psychological synthesis" of himself in his entirety. Jung believed he needed others "equally at home in primitive psychology, mythology, history, parapsychology and science — and even in the field of artistic impression." He told Bennet he didn't mean "to interfere at all" with his "plans and intentions," but he was still "playing with the idea" that Bennet and Philp would collaborate. He invited Bennet (as he had earlier invited Philp) to come to

Bollingen during his winter vacation of December–January 1957, when he would "submit willingly" to their questions.

Bennet's response was to proceed as if he were the sole official biographer. He sent Jung a list of questions entitled "Moments of Illumination"[46] that bore a striking resemblance to Lucy Heyer-Grote's, which he had read when Jung showed it to him. Jung avoided having to write detailed written responses by claiming that the topics were so "complicated and confusing," they required "voluminous argument."[47] He proposed another way for them to work, which became the method Bennet used for the two books he eventually wrote.[48] Jung was aware that "so many misunderstandings had been bruited about" concerning his life that he was "rather scared to tell the truth about [his] biography as [he saw] it." He preferred to speak spontaneously about what came to mind and told Bennet to "try to find your way through the jungle of my memories," and "pick out the relevant points." Jung was not then aware of it, but the method he proposed to Bennet was the one he eventually followed with Jaffé.

WHEN JUNG told Wolff and Jaffé of his agreement with Bennet, both were alarmed at the possible legal conflict it posed. As 1957 began, Wolff opened discussions with Bollingen and Routledge on the legal status of a Pantheon biography (Rascher was not yet involved in the negotiations).[49] Jung was adamant that, whether autobiography or biography, the book could not be part of his *Collected Works*. Nor could it be published in his lifetime; when it was published, it must appear first in an English translation and then in the German original. Wolff had no option but to accept Jung's decree. Wolff's main concern now was whether the publishers would succeed in making the book part of the *Collected Works* or whether he could publish it as a separate entity, as Jung insisted.[50] A secondary concern (which eventually became the major one) was authorship: if it was Jaffé, Jung's publishers had no claim to the book and Wolff was in the clear. Pantheon could also publish if it was either Jung's own "autobiography" but "ghost-written" with no mention of Jaffé, or if it was billed "as told to Aniela Jaffé," which still gave her "co-author" status.[51] Wolff asserted his right to sign contracts with the principals when he declared the book to be "interviews given by Dr. Jung to the author [Jaffé] during the past year and to be continued, and . . . supplemented by excerpts from autobiographical notes from various sources."[52] His description guaranteed Pantheon exclusive rights to publish either an autobiography or a biography; whichever, the book now had a tentative title: *Improvised Memories*.

Wolff was worried at this point about Bennet: if Jung gave him access to the same materials as Jaffé, Pantheon's book would be diminished in value and sales if Bennet published first. Wolff had a specific list of the "autobiographical notes from various sources" that he did not want Jung to discuss with Bennet: *The Red Book*, *The Black Book*, the *Septem Sermones*, Jung's "African Diary," and his

"Memories of a trip through India." In addition, he wanted to use the biographical references in the 1925 seminar notes on analytical psychology and dream symbolism.[53] Wolff worried also that Jung might change his mind and permit them to be included in the *Collected Works*, which would give exclusive rights to Bollingen or Routledge, excluding Pantheon completely.

Bennet had not made contractual overtures to publishers and was seemingly unaware of possible conflicts. He blithely ordered Jaffé to cover every category but "medicine," leaving himself to present Jung as a "natural scientist to the obscure material in the human mind,"[54] claiming, in effect, everything that mattered for a life of Jung. Jaffé and Wolff pleaded with Jung to make Bennet abandon his project, but Jung refused. Wolff turned to Cary Baynes for advice, as he would do frequently throughout his book's gestation.

Cary said Jung was not "doublecrossing" Wolff, because his behavior was, for him, "authentic and true."[55] To explain, she used the example of an unidentified "American theological student" to whom Jung gave copies of all the seminar notes and a handwritten letter authorizing him to use them as he wished. "Then the turn about-face took place," said Cary, and Jung entreated Jack Barrett "to help him off the hook," get back his letter, and prevent a possible lawsuit by Routledge and Rascher. Barrett did, "and so it goes, a long list," Cary concluded: "The injured party usually ends up by forgiving Jung because of his 'genius.'"

Cary's anecdote did little to calm Wolff; Bennet interpreted Jung's vagueness as "most cheering," and forged ahead. He went to Küsnacht periodically and took notes on conversations; when he returned to England, he wrote what he remembered, which may or may not have been "what Jung really said." To other observers, Bennet may have seemed a dilettante, but for the rest of Jung's life, Jaffé was looking over her shoulder, fearing his hot pursuit.[56]

ON OCTOBER 25, 1957, the language of a contract for the "tentatively entitled *C. G. Jung: Improvised Memories*" was approved by everyone.[57] Bollingen, Routledge, and Rascher agreed that Pantheon could publish it. Wolff, Jung, and Jaffé agreed to divide royalties fifty-fifty between Jaffé and "Dr. Jung and his heirs." He was to receive a lump sum of 10,000 Swiss francs upon signing, and she was paid Sfr500 per month for fifteen months, for a lesser advance of Sfr7,500. Following the official document was a supplemental agreement signed by Jung but composed by Wolff to circumvent future legal problems:

> Prof. Jung has been telling Frau Aniela Jaffé memories of his life, dreams and thoughts continuously beginning in the summer of 1956 until now, and has authorized Frau Jaffé, who has written down this information stenographically, on October 21, 1957, to give the copyright of these statements (supplemented by specifically referred-to additional material) to Pantheon Books Inc., New York.

By 1957, the "biographical hours" were in full swing every Friday afternoon between 5 and 7 P.M. In November, Wolff wrote a detailed "Memo" about content thus far.[58] He requested copies of "drawings by/of Jung" and a particular "chat" written into *The Black Book*. Jung described to Jaffé various dreams that seemed important; Wolff asked if they could be part of the book. Could she ask Jung which of his "many sessions" with Helly Preiswerk "stayed with him in particular"? When he spoke of "The 12 Dead," did he mean those in his *Septem Sermones?* Jung alluded several times to a letter Freud wrote on June 15, 1911; if he would not let it be reprinted entirely, Wolff wanted details: "[It] would be important."[59] Wolff made an astute observation about Jung's references, particularly those from literature: they all "seem to belong to the early years. . . . It would be nice and desirable, if occasionally important (negative or positive) impressions" from his adulthood were woven into the text.

Jaffé said she was sending "notes" containing "very personal passages" about Toni Wolff that were "important and valuable . . . since she was the companion of his early years with its enormous turbulences."[60] They were meant "only for [Kurt Wolff's] eyes," and for background information.[61] Whether she sent them is not known, for Kurt never commented and Toni's name rarely occurred throughout the protracted process of publishing the book.[62]

ON JANUARY 10, 1958, everything changed when Jaffé told Wolff that "something so wonderful and meaningful happened . . . *Jung himself is writing his autobiography all over again*" (Jaffé's emphasis).[63] He had begun to write early in November, but not until the end of the month did she allow herself to believe he would sustain the momentum. She told Wolff "so much had become clear to [Jung], and especially the meaning of his life which he had apparently not seen to its full extent." She pronounced what he wrote "splendid, simple and deep like a fairy tale." She offered Jung a transcript of their conversations to refer to, but he declined, wanting "to write it entirely new." He had begun at the beginning, with his birth, and was now into "his 9th year (before the experience with the Basel Cathedral)." Jung wanted their biography hours to continue, as he did not know "where all [his writing] will lead."

Wolff was thrilled that Jung was writing but worried that his other publishers would call it new work and claim the rights to it. On February 1, Jung explained what he was doing and how Wolff might resolve the situation.[64] As he talked to Jaffé about his memories, he realized he wanted to explain them "more thoroughly" and knew this would mean writing them himself. It also meant "colliding" with her book, but he felt sure his writing would make a "contribution." Jung blithely dismissed possible "publishing-related issues," for he did not know where his "preoccupation" with "early memories" would lead. He thought his original writing would probably end once he established "the connection to my scientific work." He assured Wolff that he would not "unnecessarily advertise" this new and original work: "As long as the thing is growing I forbid myself all speculations about the future of what I'm writing." Jung saw no need for "a definitive agreement," that is, a binding contract, and Wolff prepared none.

Jaffé was happy that Jung was writing himself: "The irrational element . . . has intervened creatively to an unexpected degree." But, she added, "the definitive . . . structuring of the two ms. [her writing and his] remains to be seen." Wolff underlined the next sentence in her letter with the thick red pencil he used to denote a possible crisis: "I told Jung that I would describe the coming-into-being of the book in my introduction and afterword, which he welcomed." Wolff kept silent, as it was too soon to worry about possible conflicts between authors, and Jaffé's next letter did include glowing appreciation of Jung's "unbelievably impressive . . . continuation."[65]

Jung was writing during his winter sojourn at Bollingen, his handwriting moving firmly and swiftly to cover page after page in a large black journal bought specifically for this purpose. "Jung can hardly let go of the ms.," Jaffé told Wolff, "it occupies him completely." But because he had begun to write, a second protective clause had to be attached to the October 1957 contract. If Jung were to publish these "written autobiographical notes as a whole or in part," they had to be "combined with the material told to Frau Aniela Jaffé in such a way that a unified book [was] created." The "editorial structuring" would be entirely "in the hands of Frau Jaffé," but she had to work "according to Prof. Jung's directives." In the meantime, she would continue to produce her own "autobiographical notes" based on the "biographical hours." All this legalese was to ensure that no matter who wrote which parts of Jung's life, it would remain firmly in Pantheon's control and could not be reclaimed by other publishers as part of the *Collected Works*. The document was subject to differing interpretations and did not stop Jung's other publishers from making the claim, but that was several years hence.[66]

The book's eventual final title was given for the first time in this document, but in German: *Erinnerungen, Träume, Gedanken*. The English translation, *Memories, Dreams, Reflections*, did not follow, which alarmed Wolff because he thought it meant Jung had changed his mind and planned to publish first in German.[67] Jaffé assured him Jung still wanted the book "*first in English* and then *later* in German (at Rascher)."[68] Wolff's antennae were raised anew when he read what Jaffé intended as reassurance, that Jung was in no hurry to settle any contractual matters. He pulled out his thick red pencil, made marginal notations, and underlined these passages. Two months later, his intuition proved correct. Beneath the two addenda to the contract, Wolff scrawled, not in the German of the document, but directly in English: "How was it possible, after the preceding passages, to call this book a work in which Prof. J. was not actively involved as a collaborator from the beginning, remains and will always remain a mystery to me."

Wolff's frustration reflected the latest of Jung's ongoing changes of mind caused by his poor health, fluctuating interest, and battles with outsiders. The latest began when Jung's children learned of "the 100 or so pages he wrote himself."[69] They united against any biographical revelation because of the family reverence for privacy but mostly because they thought his memories of childhood and youth showed him "in a bad light."[70] When they could not persuade Jung to stop writing and withdraw the text, they insisted that Wolff had to bill the book as Jaffe's creation, along with a disclaimer that Jung had nothing to do with its content. "The idea that their father belongs to the cosmos and not the family has never entered the heads of his children," Cary told Helen Wolff.

When his robust, middle-aged children began to importune him, Jung was eighty-three and in slowly but steadily declining health. His mental acuity remained strong, but his physical stamina was greatly diminished. He found it easier to let his children think he gave in than to quarrel with them, but he secretly kept on writing. Several weeks later, after filling many more pages, Jung had to defy his children openly, even as he recognized that theirs was the "normal [Swiss] attitude": "When my children say: the biography belongs in the family, I simply have to leave that aside. . . . The demon and the creative force have absolutely and recklessly gotten their way in me. . . . What I have is *amor fati*."[71]

He tried to explain why his writing was taking such an inward turn. Of his No. 1 self who lived in the outer world, there were only two events he considered "worth telling": the 1938 trip to India and the 1944 heart infarct.[72] Otherwise, all that mattered were events in which "the world of No. 2 [i.e., his inner world] broke into that of No. 1." He would write about his own individuation but would leave everything else for others to tell, from his travels and the people he met to his family and the environment in which he lived. He had forgotten most of the external details of his daily life, for they had a "different reality." The only things "imprinted" upon his memory were his writings, because they marked "stations" in his life, particularly in his mature years: "Each single one represents the attempt to bring the unsayable of the background into the objective world of science. All my works are commissions from the inside, so to speak."

Jung's primary objective was to write of his inner world of ideas while placing the research that resulted in "the objective world of science." Wolff seized on this to encourage Jung to write about his relationships with the great scientific figures who influenced his theory, such as Freud and Flournoy. Jung told him "medical discretion" did not permit him to use most of what he knew about Freud.[73] He was willing to say about Flournoy, "[He] was the only great mind with whom I could have an uncomplicated conversation. . . . I always tried to remember the model that he was for me." But he would write no more than that. Most of all, Wolff wanted Jung to write about someone who would appeal to an English-language (primarily American) audience. He urged Jung to write an entire chapter about William James, but Jung said that since he had already written about James's theory in *Psychological Types*, it would be "inexcusable superficiality" to write of him otherwise: "You have to consider that . . . I only saw him twice and talked to him for little more than an hour, and I didn't have any correspondence with him. Apart from the personal impression I had of him, I'm mostly indebted to him for his books."[74]

"God help me," Jung concluded: "I am as I am, an ungrateful autobiographer to be exact!" Wolff had no option but to bow gracefully before the force of the old man's resistance, to let him honor his own vision and continue at his own pace.

THE NEXT fracas over what the biography should include came in May 1958, when *The New Statesman* published "Jung and the Jews," an article rehashing all the old charges from the *Saturday Review* contretemps.[75] Wolff thought Jung should address the subject, and he readily complied with a letter he insisted should appear in the book exactly as he wrote it.[76] It contained his standard defense, that he wanted to help Jewish doctors practice their profession, and "as a man of honor," he had no choice but to succeed Kretschmer.

Jaffé was "very much against" including the letter,[77] so she showed it to Marianne Niehus-Jung. Even though the two women often differed, both were strongly united "against reviving the old political things." Kurt discussed it with his wife, Helen, who worked with him on every aspect of the book but had hitherto kept quietly in the background. Together they consulted Cary Baynes, who thought Jung was long overdue to explain himself and should therefore discuss his involvement with the Nazis. Cary thought the idea in principle a good one but the letter itself unlikely to quash further debate: "He has never made clear to himself just what he did and why . . . I think he looks on that controversy as a very insignificant temporal episode. . . . There is no answer that would be acceptable to the public, but I don't think that matters in the least to Jung."

Kurt thought Jung should not attempt to "whitewash" himself[78] but should say simply, "I made a mistake." He argued, "Nowhere would it fit better, be in fact, 'a natural,' not to say a must, than in an autobiography in which CGJ has never tried to appear as a saint or as *'unfehlbar'* [infallible]." Reluctantly, Kurt accepted everyone else's opinion: "*Impossible*, of course, for the book." Thus, everything Jung wanted to tell about his German activity in the 1930s was eliminated from his written life.

WHEN HELEN and Kurt went to Zürich for the summer of 1958 to work on what they believed was a nearly final manuscript, they learned that Jung was writing three concluding chapters to bracket the three he had written for the beginning. His tentative titles for the last three were "About Life After Death," "Late Thoughts," and "Reflections."[79] In addition, he proposed to write a separate chapter on Freud and to include the entire hundred-page journal of his African travels, which he refused to cut. He also insisted his remarks about alchemy during the "biographical hours" were vital, even though many were little more than unfocused ramblings. Kurt, whose imperious and dignified bearing intimidated the nervous and skittery Jaffé, had no luck convincing her of her duty to make Jung edit and cut. Helen assumed a new role, becoming Jaffé's soothing voice of reason, but she, too, could not persuade her.

Meanwhile, Kurt was hoping to persuade Jung to reinstate much of the external "concrete" material that, in his insistence upon the "inner" ("abstract") life, he had already excised. Wolff thought he had deleted too many "important excellent things." Primary among these were case histories that shed light on how his theory developed through his observation of patients. Encouraged that Jung wanted to write about Freud, Kurt pressed for his interactions with leading figures in the worlds of art, culture, and literature. Jung had already written and rejected "many amusing and malicious thumb sketches of personalities"[80] such as Thomas Mann, H. G. Wells, Hermann Hesse, and especially his old bugaboos, James Joyce and Pablo Picasso. Wolff wanted Aniela to convince Jung to put them back into the book.

During the year just past, she had truly become what Jung had earlier called her, "the clearing house for [his] psychological ideas," thus creating a blockade for Kurt and Helen and keeping them from direct contact with him. Jaffé answered the telephone and decided who could speak to Jung. She opened his mail and read it to him, and Kurt was sure she did so selectively, deciding what should reach his eyes or ears. Her behavior seemed a "gigantic inflation of the ego" for which Kurt was "absolutely unprepared."[81] But as time passed, he found that "in the face of Jung, she was a hypnotized bunny" who kept things from him if she thought they might upset him and "never dared to say the slightest critical word." Jung had no idea of Kurt's repeated insistence upon "the necessity of a certain balance between the various parts of his life," for Aniela never discussed it with him.

KURT STILL hoped that when summer ended, he would have a publishable manuscript, but the Wolffs returned to New York with the text no closer to finality than it had been four months earlier.[82] While they fidgeted in New York, Jaffé and Jung spent most of 1958 and 1959 changing the book's form as well as its content. The Wolffs learned of this newest stratagem and knew they needed a trusted outsider whom Jung respected to critique the book's content and structure. To mediate, Kurt asked Erich Neumann,[83] Jung's friend since the 1930s who was now a founder of the Israel Association of Analytic Psychology. Jaffé was "very grateful" to have Neumann, for Jung "had to be told this by a man after all, and a person who is not involved in the process."[84] Inadvertently, Kurt created another of the crises that threatened to scuttle the book.

Neumann read the entire manuscript and thought it should be revised as a "conversation" between two equals, himself and Jung. He thought Jaffé's "interventions" could be inserted where appropriate, by which he meant seldom if ever. Jaffé was unaware that Neumann wanted to marginalize her, so the Wolffs were stunned by her "tone of triumph" when she reported that she and Jung were in favor of this "new form." They groaned that the book's completion was relegated, as Helen put it, to somewhere in the "mythic distance."[85]

Added to this was a new worry about health, both Jung's and Kurt's. Kurt suffered two heart-related incidents in late 1957 and early 1958, from which he made a cautious recovery.[86] By 1958, Jung was beset by an unending succession of illnesses that ranged from gastric distress to severe influenza and to vaguely described episodes most likely related to his heart. He still insisted that the book could not be published in German during his lifetime, but relented about the English translation, which he now agreed to publish as soon as it was ready. The Wolffs were eager to bring it out while he was still alive and could enhance the publicity surrounding it. They complained about delays to Jaffé, but whatever she conveyed to Jung, he thought they were rushing to eliminate him from his own version of his life.[87] The tension was too much for the weakened Kurt, so Helen, always the soothing mediator, wrote to Jung on his behalf.

She told Jung that Kurt's only concern was to "present the reader purely and clearly and unobstructedly with your personality, your oeuvre, your thinking." Kurt wanted to reach not only the reader who knew something of Jung's psychology but also and "especially the one who only [knew his] work from the distorting mirror of an opinion disfigured by resentment." She believed that Kurt had a "keener eye" because he stood "outside the closest Jung circle," and she begged Jung to trust his objectivity. Jung appeared to be pacified, so the Wolffs assumed he would return the book quickly to its original version: his life as he wrote it or told it to Aniela Jaffé.

He did not, and thinking she was soothing them, Jaffé exacerbated the Wolffs' distress when she described yet another new procedure, how she "from time to time, if only very rarely, interven[ed] in the monologue with an explanation of a transition [that] has already proven helpful." What the Wolffs feared was true: her "transitions" overwhelmed Jung's story.

BY THE end of 1958, the Wolffs decided to leave New York permanently, not only for Kurt's health but also because they were convinced it was the only way they would ever see Jung's book in print in his lifetime. By early spring 1959, they were comfortably ensconced in the old-world gentility of the Hotel Esplanade in Locarno, prepared to work even though Jaffé had sent nothing to edit. To hurry things along, they established temporary summer quarters in the Dolder Grand Hotel in Zürich, thinking that if they could visit Jung daily, he would write more quickly. They had their first meeting with Jaffé — but not Jung — on May 29, when she refused to give them the newest version because it lacked Jung's "finishing touch."

Kurt wrote to Jung the next day, hinting obliquely at this latest barricade.[88] Jung replied, saying he was "perfectly aware that the biography is an urgent matter," and promised to do his "best" to finish as soon as possible, but he said Kurt must wait for "finished chapters" because he was inserting "some essential contributions" from his "many-layered life," all of which had just come to him in "a very impressive dream."[89]

Despite repeated delicate negotiation by the Wolffs and others on their behalf (Cary Baynes and Jolande Jacobi primary among them), Jung kept writing, and Jaffé used it as her excuse not to surrender the manuscript until August. In July, in her last attempt to stave off the increasingly frantic Wolffs, she dangled a list of intriguing materials she and Marianne Niehus-Jung allegedly uncovered, hinting she would not insert them into the book unless Kurt was patient.

Aniela had made Marianne her staunch ally ever since they stood together on the matter of excluding Jung's Nazi period. Whether or not Marianne agreed with her, Aniela made it seem they were on the same side whenever there was disagreement with the Wolffs, and she frequently invoked Marianne's or Walther Niehus's name as the reason that she could or could not comply with their requests. She used the same ploy with the editors at Bollingen, Routledge, and Rascher, telling each that the others — not she — were responsible for various delays and refusals.

In this instance, Aniela told Kurt that she and Marianne had found a cache of extraordinary documents while emptying drawers and closets in Emma's rooms.[90] Among these were Emilie Preiswerk-Jung's diary of her parapsychological experiences, and letters, photos, and other diaries (she did not state by whom) dating from Jung's childhood.[91] There were letters between Jung and various relatives, others between him and his father, and a single page he wrote about his sister Trudi's death.[92] There was also a cache of Jung's "pricelessly funny" letters to his mother from the Burghölzli. Kurt was not distracted by this tantalizing list and insisted he needed to see the entire manuscript. Early in August, Jaffé reluctantly sent it to him.

Kurt was in despair when he read it but knew he had to proceed with extreme caution. He began by telling Jung how "moved" he was by the "additional confessions," which presented him as "an entirely new pioneer who expands the borders of the mental and spiritual life."[93] He said his task as editor was "a modest thing," to "ensure the greatest possible atmospheric and artistic effectiveness for the book through some purely technical suggestions." After this cautious introduction, he arrived at his main point: "I have serious misgivings about its present form, as I have already hinted to you; the insertions of Frau Jaffé's commentary into your text disturbs, as you have sensed yourself, the great flow of meaning." With the "invasion" of her "second voice," Jaffé was interrupting and impairing Jung's "tone." Wolff had nothing against it, "merely against the place where it is used." Citing just one of her many "interpolations," Wolff said it told the reader "something that is already fully contained in your text, even in almost the same words." It was "redundant" and had "a weakening, even irritating effect. Less would be more, isn't this true?" There was a great deal at stake, he said: "namely to maintain the density, coherence, and uniqueness of your voice, your tone of voice, and thus the directness, intensity and purity of the effect on the reader overall." With definite intent, he added a clause that required Jung's direct response, thus ensuring that Jaffé would have to show him the letter: "That's why it is of greatest importance to me to make the suggested editorial changes with Aniela Jaffé — *once you have given your consent. . . .* At this point I need your advice on how to proceed and would be very grateful if you sent it to me in a short note" (author's emphasis).

Fortunately for the Wolffs, Jaffé was on vacation, so the letter went directly to Jung. His reply revealed that he was well aware of Aniela's many obfuscations but had allowed them because he believed everything she did was in his best interest. He refused to judge her harshly, excusing her for being "overwhelmed by the nature of the material." He did not want to write of external events himself, so when he told Aniela that his life "suggests such a way of looking at it," she tried to include them through her interventions. "I had to intervene and help her," he wrote. "The help has turned into a collaboration, in the process of which there unavoidably collected more and more weight on my side of the scale."

He also claimed responsibility for her interventions, because she did not write them until he insisted she had to pull "more weight" and strengthen her presence in the text: "*[Ask] critical or curious questions interfering with my propositions. This could loosen up my explanations* as well as liven them up, if done skillfully" (Jung's emphasis). As far as he was concerned, her interventions were a "service to the reader." He suggested integrating some but not all of them into his text, for he had full confidence in her as his book's "midwife." He refused to accept Wolff's view that every Jaffé insertion diluted his own moving and lyrical writing.

Jung then addressed the current holdup, the African travel diary. He swore he edited it, but Wolff knew he had not cut but expanded the original hundred pages. Jung maintained that he needed every word because it illustrated "how things simultaneously take two levels," that is, "the existence of a sympathetic undercurrent in the collectivity." Wolff wanted him to cut and combine it with India, but he refused: "I simply cannot summon the strength necessary for this anymore. I am too old."

His allusion to his age sparked further worries about his infirmity. Another holdup occurred when he refused to let Wolff read the newest manuscript until he reread it himself, but he kept postponing it because he was too weak and tired to do so. When Wolff asked if he could suggest cuts or changes, Jung prickled that he would "stand by Aniela Jaffé in her attempt to give the book a definitive shape." He would not follow Wolff's editorial comments, even though he accepted that Wolff had "incomparably greater experience in this regard."

Eventually, Jung improved and garnered enough energy to try to finesse Jaffé's circumventions. With the utmost diplomacy, Kurt told Jung it was "reassuring" to hear that he wanted "the problems" to be eliminated.[94] He began to communicate with Jung via Ruth Bailey, whom he, Helen, Cary Baynes, and Jolande Jacobi were now using as their go-between when they wanted to ensure that whatever it was, it reached him directly.[95]

Kurt also dispatched Helen to talk to Jaffé "quite openly" about her interventions.[96] Helen prepared a detailed "memorandum on the structure of the book"[97] and asked Aniela to study it in the hope that it would lead to regularly scheduled sessions when they could work together. By mid-September 1959, Aniela was still stalling and no meeting had taken place. In desperation, Kurt wrote to Cary, saying he had to talk to someone and she was "the poor victim — who else could [he] talk to?"[98]

He listed the many differences between the texts of 1958 and 1959 before getting to the "decisive negative factor: Aniela Jaffé has 'intervened'" and all her additions were "catastrophic." He had shown the 1958 version, which included a "prologue" written by Jung, to two of his writers who were also trusted friends, Anne Morrow Lindbergh and Iris Origo. Wolff said both found Jung's writing "the most beautiful and exciting introduction and seduction to reading the whole book." All were horrified when Jaffé excised every word of his prologue and substituted one of her own that was mundane and pedestrian. He then told how she circumvented everything they asked of her.[99] She was "certainly willing" to consider suggestions for cuts to her writing, but said: "In *principle*, however, [Jung] wants to keep — and he asked me to write you this — the present form of the book, including the AJ-interventions." Kurt was too angry to reply. She took his silence as an affirmation and wrote again a week later to say she was "particularly happy" that he agreed with her (and, by extension, Jung) about the ultimate form of the book: "Otherwise you certainly would have mentioned that important point of my letter." Kurt was flabbergasted.

Helen made him promise there would be no further "discussions" between him and Aniela, and he would neither write nor speak to her. "I rather tend to get on Aniela's nerves," he admitted ruefully to Cary,[100] so from this point on, only Helen dealt with Aniela. The book that Kurt hoped would "lead outsiders inside the work" of Jung was so "very far away from this goal" that he despaired of ever reaching it. "Oh, Cary," he concluded, "what can we do?"

It was one of the very few times in Cary's long friendship with Jung that she, too, was at a loss before "the strength of the Zürich transference."[101]

IN MID-NOVEMBER 1959, Helen Wolff finally persuaded Aniela Jaffé to sit down on a Sunday morning for the first work session.[102] It lasted nine hours. Helen suggested they work on the "Bollingen" chapter together because it was straightforward reportage and offered a nonthreatening way to demonstrate how "disruptive" were Aniela's interventions. In this sole instance, Helen succeeded in persuading Aniela: "[Your] explanations of the things that CGJ goes on to state spontaneously, naively, rousingly and convincingly are superfluous —

except for a headnote which (instead of the originally planned footnote) tells the reader what Bollingen is and how much time CGJ spends there — pure facts."

Then they turned to the "Freud chapter," where Helen used Jung's analytic vocabulary to describe how she aroused "great affective resistance"[103] in Aniela. Into Jung's writing about Freud, Aniela had inserted many effusive references to Erich Neumann, along with four pages of Neumann's own thoughts about Freud: "Here AJ as a Jewish woman makes it her task to clarify CGJ's relationship to Freud for the world; Neumann is also consulted as a Jew." Such sermonizing would irritate readers, Helen argued, and if it belonged anywhere in the book, it was as an appendix. Jaffé did not agree. As a compromise, Helen suggested she insert portions of several letters from Freud that Jung believed were important. Aniela's "highly revealing reaction" astonished her: She asked, "If Aniela goes in the appendix, then why should Freud be in the chapter?" It dawned on Helen that "a claim to power was announcing itself," and she would be up against it throughout their negotiations. Helen thought it "clearly legible between the lines of the conversation" that Jaffé believed the Wolffs wanted to "push her out of the main text" in order to make it "marketable" and a "best seller." She thought Aniela had become a "profoundly suspicious character who senses ulterior motives."

Actually, Aniela was a profoundly lonely woman who believed herself beset on all sides by hostile forces. As a German Jewish refugee, she was still an outsider in Zürich's tight little Jungian community. She had many analysands who respected her but few, if any, close friends. Even Jolande Jacobi, who first suggested her as Jung's co-author, now told everyone that Jaffé "detested" and was "suspicious" of her.[104] Jaffe's only means of support was what she earned; Jung was a very old man and her employment could end at any time. The anticipated royalties from the book were a lifeline she could not afford to lose. Jung's children resented that she was to share them equally, and she feared what eventually did come to pass, that they would bring legal action against her to claim them all.[105]

Helen still thought none of this excused Aniela's "defiance." When their nine-hour session ended in a stalemate, Helen said the only thing she could think of to describe Aniela was the title of a well-loved series of books for German girls, *Trotzköpfchens Zeitvertreib* (The Pastime of a Defiant Little Girl).

ALMOST A week passed with Helen fretting and Aniela believing all was well. Seeking to end the "hopeless situation,"[106] Helen composed a memo to Jung that she rewrote several times before she was satisfied it would not alarm him. Kurt could not write himself because he "was so depressed about the structural change . . . the didactic intervention, the interpolated interpretation."

Although Helen wrote to Jung, he replied to Kurt, but not until one month later.[107] Jung agreed that all "longer" comments by Jaffé should go into an appendix following each chapter; Kurt had no option but to allow it, but he insisted that her "special pleading" had to be excised and her only interjections could be "factual." He reminded Jung that Jaffé always agreed to whatever he asked "in principle," but added, "There are disagreements when it comes to the details." He suggested they appoint an arbiter: "[Someone] to have the final say: Cary Baynes to be exact, who you yourself wanted to be the first critical reader of the manuscript." Jung agreed.

THINKING THE details of structure were resolved at last, the Wolffs were now faced with a perilous problem raised by the publishers of the *Collected Works*. Cecil Franklin learned that Jung had been inspired to write his own chapters independently of Jaffé's interviews and invoked his general contractual agreement: Routledge was the official English-language publisher of anything Jung wrote, be it old or new. As Rascher had the same agreement for all German texts, that firm invoked the right to publish the Jung/Jaffé book as well.[108] Rascher struck first, informing Jung that he risked breach of contract. Jung reacted in panic, as he did whenever confronted with anything concerning legal action: he feared that if Rascher did not sue him, Kurt would. He told Kurt to remove all his original chapters and other writing from the book and to let Jaffé write whatever she wanted.

"Rascher?" Wolff soothed, "He will bark, not bite," and he told Jung why. Wolff said he had already given the German rights to Rascher: "[It was] as a gift, he shall not pay a penny for it, only the royalties directly to the authors." He begged Jung to believe that despite Rascher's collective greed, no one connected with the firm would jeopardize such a lucrative deal. Nevertheless, the tired, old, and ill Jung was irrationally convinced he would become the subject of a humiliating public lawsuit. Kurt was perplexed until Cary explained why: Ruth Bailey told her how Emma's will divided her estate among the children: "You can see how it makes it impossible for him to take any risks of a suit — that is, given his attitude toward money and his responsibility toward the children."[109] Cary's assessment was correct. Jung's panic intensified to the point where Marianne and Walther Niehus tried to bypass him by claiming he had diminished capacity, and they filed to become legal negotiators on his behalf. Just as Jaffé prevented Kurt from dealing directly with Jung, the Niehus couple now removed him a step further. The *"Ehepaar* [married couple] Niehus"[110] thus became a powerful force, and from this time onward, Kurt's primary task became responding to the complaints and concerns of Jung's children rather than assuaging Jung's fears. Although weakened by cancer, Marianne was still directing every aspect of the German *Gesammelte Werke*. Walther hired his own lawyer, ostensibly to help her oversee the series, but his main reason was to help the family gain legal control over the biography's content and the income it might generate.

A curious letter in Jung's published correspondence attests to the power the

Ehepaar Niehus now wielded.[111] Although it was not his custom to write New Year's greetings to his children, a befuddled Jung began 1960 by expressing gratitude to Walther and Marianne for all their help throughout 1959. Several months later in a move that surprised everyone (especially his other children), Jung appointed Walther his literary executor.[112] His letter of appointment used language dictated by the Schaffhausen lawyer Dr. Bernhard Peyer, whom Walther insisted he hired on behalf of all the Jung children. In it, Jung thanked Walther for his assistance with "my so-called autobiography."[113] Whether he thought of the book this way, or whether Walther dictated the term, Jung covered himself legally by emphasizing that the book was not his but "expressly . . . a book which Frau Jaffé has written." The chapters he wrote himself were merely "a contribution to [her] work." His final sentence was the clincher: "The book should appear under her name and not under mine, since it does not represent an autobiography that I myself have composed." This soon became general knowledge and the basis of all the scholarly squabbles about authorship that have plagued the book ever since.

From then on, Kurt was never permitted to discuss either practical or legal matters with Jung, but only with Walther, who was "very slow in reacting and acting," and, Kurt added, "knows as much about publishing and copyright as I know about designing houses or bridges."[114] Aniela continued her Pollyanna-ish peregrinations, interpreting Jung's letter to Walther as giving her total control of the book. Her obfuscations intensified as the publication date receded even further into Helen's "mythic distance."

Soon there were other cooks intent on stirring this muddled broth, and ill will and double-dealing became rampant. Jaffé the "hypnotized bunny" now became a scared "rabbit" in flight from a host of "boa constrictors."[115] She told most of her correspondents whatever they wanted to hear in the hope they would then leave her to do as she thought best. To enlist their sympathy, she often wrote that she was "telling things" only to them that she was "really not supposed to be telling."[116] A flurry of correspondence ensued, from the Wolffs to Cary Baynes, to Jack Barrett, to Wolfgang Sauerlander[117] at Bollingen, and vice versa; from Jaffé to everyone but Cary (who made her insecure and of whose acumen she was probably jealous); and occasionally from Jung (through Jaffé) to them all, which made everyone suspicious about whose views were actually expressed in the letters typed and often signed by her. Cary heard, "through the Zürich grapevine," that Marianne, "who used to have implicit confidence in Aniela, now believes her to be a liar."[118] Cary thought this was unfair, that "the trouble [lay] in her emotionality" about anything connected to Jung and the book. All misunderstandings, no matter who inspired them, "would have vanished like smoke in the wind" had Kurt been permitted direct access to Jung himself, but that never happened.

Kurt was aghast that no one consulted Jung's lawyer, Dr. Hans Karrer, whom he held partly "responsible for the endless delays and general legal mess."[119] Until Jaffé got wind of it, he did not know that Niehus had been moving to marginalize Karrer, even though he had represented Jung for years. Worried about protecting her status as co-author, Jaffé thought all she had to do was have Jung sign her outline and it would become a legally binding document. Niehus refused to let Jung comply, because he thought he could appease Routledge and Rascher by writing a letter saying it was Jaffé's book and Jung had merely "cooperated."[120] Kurt warned Jaffé that Niehus "cannot and must not be satisfied" with letters but must do "something drastic" to obtain binding agreements — "otherwise he asks for trouble."[121] He suggested they consult Dr. F. W. Beidler, director of the *Schweizerischer Schriftstellerverein*, the Swiss Writers' Organization, and ask him to tell Rascher "in the strongest possible language" that Pantheon's rights were "clear."[122] Walther ignored the suggestion, but he did agree to let Karrer draft his letters, which he then delayed sending until Peyer (not Karrer or Beidler) could negotiate a settlement.[123]

In a masterpiece of equivocation, Walther's letter told the publishers that both Jung and Jaffé had authorized him to speak on their behalf.[124] Actually, Jaffé had not, but she was too terrified to set him straight. He insisted that the book was Jaffé's invented text "as though Jung himself were speaking or writing," and he dismissed the chapters Jung wrote himself as "more or less a first draft . . . revised and completed by Mrs. Jaffé." Therefore, the book could not be called "a piece of writing of [Jung's own]"; nor was it "a scientific work" suitable for the *Collected Works*. And it was up to Kurt to decide which British firm could publish the Jaffé-Jung collaboration.

These machinations began in February 1960, during one of Jung's more serious heart-related episodes, this one coupled with a flu and/or virus that kept him mostly somnolent. In July, with nothing settled, Helen and Kurt arranged to meet with Marianne and Walther. "Mind you, we *like* the Niehuses," Helen told Cary as she described the Alice-in-Wonderland quality of the conversation.[125] "They were as pleasant as they could be," and did not contest Kurt's version of the book, that Jung was "the mouthpiece . . . Aniela the recorder." They were *perfectly familiar* with the facts," Helen emphasized, "but the amazing thing is that *in spite of this* they passed on the incredible statement that Aniela was 'die Verfasserin' [the writer] of the book." Helen was astonished by their attitude:

> [They were] really actually trying to hoodwink Rascher and Routledge, a bit like peasants who try to pass off a different kind of horse on the market. . . . [Walther] Niehus quite openly and candidly admitted to me that of course Aniela was *not* die Verfasserin, and that the book was obviously a faithful transcript of his father-in-law's actual words and formulations, opinion, and thoughts, and that Aniela had merely arranged them with an

occasional rewording as we all do in copyediting a mss — straighten out ungrammatical sentences or make obscurities clear. That still doesn't make her the *author!*

Walther and Marianne also told the Wolffs "quite candidly" that they were stalling for time until Rascher and Routledge "[would] make trouble for [the Wolffs] and not for them." When Kurt heard this, "he was literally trembling with suppressed indignation." Helen spent the rest of the evening "stuff[ing] Kurt with Kirschwasser and half a bottle of Swiss champagne." She told Cary there was only one thing left to say: "Wait till the Freudians hear about all this. They'll have a heyday!"

CECIL FRANKLIN, however, "was no fool." He told Niehus that "it appears that a good deal of this book will be by Professor Jung although it is masked as being written by Mrs. Jaffé."[126] By the end of October 1960, there was still no formal resolution, even though Jaffé, with her usual unfounded optimism, thought, "Next week something will start to move." Nothing moved until the end of November, when Walther Niehus and Bernhard Peyer went to Locarno to meet with the Wolffs.[127] Afterward, Kurt wrote acidly to Jack Barrett: "I am only surprised by how eager people are to harvest where they haven't sown."

All along, Kurt thought it would have been easier to give in to Franklin's veiled threats and let Routledge publish, but no one listened until Franklin threatened legal action.[128] Jung was emerging from a period of befuddlement most likely connected with irregularities in his heart, so his ordinary fear of lawsuits was heightened. With Franklin's latest intimidation, Jung was in an irrational frenzy, insisting that the biography had to be so separate from the *Collected Works* that it must bear the imprint of an entirely different publisher. Kurt found the solution: he invited the firm of William Collins to co-publish with Routledge,[129] reasoning that its founder, "Billy" Collins, was astute enough to recognize that an "autobiography" by Jung would be a bestseller for years to come, and profits would be considerable even if shared.[130] Cecil Franklin acquiesced because Collins had a "much more effective distribution in which [Routledge] hoped to share."[131]

JUST WHEN everyone thought the only remaining concern was to prepare the text for publication, Kurt Wolff delivered another bombshell: his resignation from Pantheon Books.[132] Even though Pantheon had been Kurt's creation, he decided that, with his heart increasingly problematic, "it was time to take a breather." He was not "forced out," as legend has since had it, and, sad as it was, "the decision to resign was his."[133] Wolff's departure left him totally without a say in Pantheon's operations, but he was so devoted to the book he had slaved over for five years that he agreed to oversee it to publication. He was also appointed to the Bollingen Foundation's board of directors, and he worked closely with the editors on the *Collected Works*, but his main concern was Jung's biography. His liaisons were complicated, ranging from Pantheon in New York to Jung and Jaffé in Zürich (actually Niehus, who assumed authority to speak for both); Collins and Routledge in London; Rascher in Zürich (publisher of the hardcover in German), and S. Fischer-Verlag in Germany (publisher of the German paperback at Jung's insistence);[134] the lawyers Karrer and Beidler in Zürich and Peyer in Schaffhausen; and, lastly, the Bollingen Foundation (whose only role at that time was *"amicus curiae,"* or friend of the project).

THE PROCESS of preparing the final manuscript that began in July 1958 was still off in Helen's "mythic distance" as 1960 ended and 1961 began. There was still no "ur-text" and "psycho-politics" threatened to swamp the project entirely.[135] The 1958 manuscript of the "tentatively entitled *Memories, Dreams, Reflections"* was the one Kurt wanted, approximately 180,000 words that he thought were a proper mix of Jung's "No. 1 and No. 2" personalities. It included a full chapter on Freud, with details of the 1909 trip to the United States and their personal relations until the 1913 break. But there were profiles of "other famous contemporaries" that were "practically unknown" to the American reader, and Kurt wanted them drastically cut if not eliminated entirely, among them Albert Einstein, H. G. Wells, Count Keyserling, Hugh Crichton-Miller, Richard Wilhelm, and Heinrich Zimmer.[136] There were also chapters about Jung's friends (all men, refuting the oft-leveled charge that he had none), including Albert Oeri, Andreas Vischer, some Zofingia brothers and Zürich businessmen, and some of his medical and analytic associates. Although Kurt thought them secondary, they did represent Jung's No. 1 personality, and he wanted to retain at least parts of them. Other chapters dealt with Jung's experiences among primitive tribes in Africa (extracts, not his entire journal), his exposure to Eastern thought in India, his experience as a psychotherapist in analytic sessions, his view of organized religions, and his personal religious experiences. Kurt was not convinced they needed the chapter on "parapsychological phenomena, etc." and "death and the beyond," but having gotten his way on what he wanted of the others, he gave in to Jung on these.

Kurt thought the only work left to do was to fill in noticeable chronological gaps and balance the existing text with references to the related materials Jung had consulted, or those that influenced his theory. When Kyrill Schabert, who succeeded Kurt at Pantheon, questioned why he was lavishing so much time on Jung's book, Kurt insisted it was not time wasted:

> Let's not forget: Freud wrote no autobiography. Dr. Jung's book will be the only one in which an explorer and pioneer of depth psychology, who has pushed the boundaries of human consciousness into new areas and af-

fected human thought and knowledge immeasurably and significantly, gives a summing up of his own experiences at the moment of its full ripeness.

As all the principles who had worked on the manuscript were bilingual, the question of who would make the English translation was raised but not settled. Wolff assumed it would be Hull because of the fluency and consistency he used to express Jung's concepts in the *Collected Works* and because Jung had the highest praise for his work. Kurt approached the Bollingen Foundation and was surprised when Jack Barrett refused, as did Cecil Franklin at Routledge, both saying they could not risk further delays to the *Collected Works*. Hull wanted to translate *MDR* (as everyone now abbreviated it), so he mounted a strenuous protest. He reminded Barrett that all delays were due to Franklin, who made him spend 1959 translating everyone but Jung.[137] Like everyone else, Hull believed *MDR* was in fairly final form and argued that the four to six months he envisioned for translation "would surely [be] a matter of no consequence."

Because Hull was offended at the mere suggestion of someone else being chosen to invade professional turf he rightfully claimed as his own, Barrett, "with his customary thoughtfulness and kindness," suggested a compromise.[138] Pantheon (i.e., Kurt) would engage another translator, and Hull would provide "final reading and checking for correctness." Pantheon's New York editors engaged Richard and Clara Winston, who lived in Connecticut, and trouble was there from the start.

The Winstons had a distinguished reputation and naturally assumed they were solely responsible for the definitive text; Hull thought they had been hired to do the general scut work, leaving final authority to him. It took all Kurt's diplomatic skills, on the one hand to convince the Winstons that Hull's only function was to ensure consistent translation of Jung's analytic terminology; and on the other to convince Hull that textual oversight did not mean retranslating an existing manuscript. In the midst of so much "ego inflation" (as Helen frequently put it), Hull and the Winstons cooperated so amicably that they were almost listed as co-translators. When the Winstons changed their minds at the end, Hull gracefully bowed out. He really shaped the text from 1961 to 1963, but he settled for Jaffé's expression of gratitude in the acknowledgments.

JUNG HAD been eerily removed from the machinations and negotiations that swirled around him in 1960 as his illnesses increased in frequency and duration. In January, he had a severe gall bladder attack that left him virtually paralyzed with pain.[139] In February, he suffered another "slight embolism" that left him "easily exhausted and intensely introverted."[140] It marked the start of his final decline and the real beginning of his lack of interest and loss of control over the written version of his life. He told Kurt he had done what he "intended to do for the biography" and refused to become involved with "matters of publication," as he had "other things to do."[141] Helen thought his decision was due as much to "the re-evocation of his past exhaust[ing] him" as it was to his age and poor health. Throughout his writing, she noted, "There were certain things which once he said, he wanted to take them back again. One sensed in him . . . that he had trouble with himself, and he also speaks about the fact that he was really two persons. One never quite knew which personality would be the uppermost."

THE WINTER had been extremely cold, so Jung wanted to take a February vacation in southern France, but he was bedridden and could not.[142] When he recovered, Fowler and Ruth took him on frequent short ITCRA[143] trips, not only in search of warmth but also to try to lift his spirits. He was depressed and preoccupied, which everyone thought was due to his illness. On leap-year day, February 29, when they were in Ascona, Jung had a sudden burst of energy and insisted that he had to spend the afternoon with Hull.

He was highly agitated when he arrived. "I want to talk to you," he said as he shooed Ruth and Fowler away and stomped into the house. Hull found Jung's "grimacing" over his "autobiography" (Jung's word) so alarming that he took him out into the garden, where Jung sat for more than an hour with his hat pushed back on his head as he leaned on his silver-tipped cane and talked. "She has written a lot of stuff about me which simply won't do," he repeated over and over.[144] What Jung told him so worried Hull that he made extensive notes as soon as Jung departed, thinking he needed a "historical record."[145] In July 1960, when all the principals were at loggerheads and the entire "Vita" (as the abbreviated *MDR* was called interchangeably) was jeopardized, Hull transposed his notes into a "Report" and sent it to Herbert Read at Routledge, who in turn sent a copy to Jack Barrett at the Bollingen Foundation.[146]

In his report, Hull described Jung as profoundly distressed by changes to his "authentic" text: "He impressed upon me, with the utmost emphasis, that he had said what he wanted to say in his own way, 'a bit blunt and crude sometimes,' and that he did not want his work to be '*tantifiziert*' [auntified]."[147] With "auntification," Jung coined a new expression that soon became an internal code word for Hull and the publishers. Hull first thought Jung meant the Wolffs because of various allusions to "big guns [that] will go off" if he protested against changes to his text.[148] It was not until one month later, when Hull read the first three chapters of Winston's English translation, that he realized the "auntifying" was not originating in Locarno (where the Wolffs lived) but in Küsnacht, and that Jaffé was the culprit. "Auntification" became shorthand for Jaffé, but the term was expanded shortly after to include Marianne and Walther Niehus. It was occasionally extended to Rascher and Milton Waldman, the Collins representative who did his share to confuse and confound with all sorts of issues that he instigated.

THE WINSTONS were entirely unaware that the constant barrage of revisions inundating them were from Jaffé rather than Jung, so they obligingly translated whatever she sent. The text thus became her auntified intervention. Hull praised the Winston translation of chapters I–III for its "dauntingly high standard"[149] and had no quarrel with it. His quarrel was with Aniela and the *Ehepaar* Niehus, who then reworked the Winston text to the point where it was unrecognizable as Jung's. Helen described what this unlikely trio of allies had done in a note to Hull: "Revealing for changes 'toning down' Jung original — *bowdlerized version!* Highly interesting for what was done to keep out Jung's frank and true statements about himself."[150]

In his original, Jung wrote that God sat on an enormous throne above the world, where he "shit" an "enormous turd" upon the Basel Cathedral. The trio excised these words. They changed Jung's boyhood dream from a "gigantic phallus" to a "fearful tree." The Niehuses deleted Jung's description of his parents as highly "neurotic," and toned down his description of their marriage to "not all [his father] had imagined it to be." They eliminated everything about his mother, especially that she was "grossly fat" and "hysterical." Hull wanted these remarks restored because he thought they "couldn't shock anyone, except the Swiss bourgeoisie."[151] He especially liked Jung's "highly dramatic use of the word 'shit,'" and wanted to reinstate an explanatory footnote about God and the Basel Cathedral deleted by the Niehuses: "This vision should not be understood only in terms of the twelve year old's experience; it signifies also, in the figurative sense, 'God shits on the Church,' the equivalent English idiom would be 'Does not give a shit for . . . [his church].'" Even though Jung himself told Hull that he "left the preparation of the German edition" to Jaffé, Hull was convinced he had no idea how she had "tampered with and emasculated" his writing.[152] Worse still was that she now submitted everything she auntified to Walther and Marianne, which they then revised, removing the text even further from what Jung actually wrote. Marianne refused to listen to Hull's arguments (sent to her via the Wolffs) that Jung wanted his text to be blunt and crude. She said she conferred with her siblings, who all agreed not to reinstate "shit" or "phallus," and to eliminate all depictions (no matter what) of Jung's parents. The "confounded *vertrackten*" of his mother's "hysteria" now had to be his mother's "invalidism."[153] They would not even let Jung describe some of his aunts as spinsters, or himself as a poor boy in tattered trousers whose feet were often wet in winter because his family was so poor that his shoes had holes and he had no socks.[154] They also forbade his memories of inspecting drowned corpses or of pigs being slaughtered.

"Oh, dear!" said Aniela, when she learned about this. Hull suggested that she and Kurt delete it from the galleys but let it "appear" in the book: "This not so flippant suggestion . . . would save a lot of trouble in the future if the Ehepaar Niehus found that their writ does not always run in New York." Helen thought it "quite incredible . . . amazing to see to what extent [Jung] was still under the spell of the Swiss bourgeoisie and to what extent his own children had no real sense of the importance and the grandeur of his personality."¹⁵⁵

Hull left the "auntifications" in abeyance to concentrate on passages he considered vital. He insisted that Jung needed the word "shit" and thought it imperative to describe Emilie Jung as "hysterical." Neither of these got past Walther and Marianne, and eventually they forced Hull to concede. He did try one last time, asking to substitute "nervous" for "hysterical," but that did not pass family censorship either.¹⁵⁶

There was one point, however, on which all those who meddled with Jung's text were united: that he must delete a long, rambling account of his two visits to Ravenna because they were factually incorrect. Jung could not be persuaded even by Cary, who told him that to include it would make him look "crazy."

"That settles it," Jung shouted. "The chapter stays in. I *want* the book to look crazy!"¹⁵⁷

Hull was doubly worried, first about the "full extent of the bowdlerizations perpetrated by Mrs. Jaffé" and then by the need "to play canny" with Walther Niehus. He thought Kurt had two options. The first was "to assemble the evidence of Mrs. Jaffe's sins of omission and commission in the German text" and present them to Jung at a meeting they would deliberately set for a time when she could not attend. The second option was to circumvent Walther Niehus by going "quietly ahead with the 'composite' translation," that is, one in which they had restored Jung's original writing, which they would send to him "via Miss Bailey" so he could read it before the meeting. Hull suggested that all questionable passages should be clearly marked. If Jung himself cut any or all, it would be "too bad," but at least Hull and Wolff would "know where we stand." Hull admitted that either procedure fell perilously close to a "conspiracy," but he said he knew "from dire experience that nothing can stop a *Jungfrau* on the warpath except a steamroller or a rather ruthless subterfuge."

Kurt agreed to let Hull send his amended Winston translation to Jung, via Ruth Bailey, with all the textual restorations clearly marked. Jung was too weak to read it himself, so Ruth read it aloud to him. She thus became a highly trusted and deeply secret go-between as they worked to restore the text, and she relished her role as Jung's "even more confidential 'confidential secretary'" than Aniela. "Personally," Ruth added, "I think it would be a pity to tone down his vivid passages and above all, to 'auntify' (lovely verb) the text."¹⁵⁸

THINGS REMAINED on hold for several months because Jung's energies were compromised and he went away often from the dismal Zürich summer in search of sun and warmth in western Switzerland or the southern Ticino. When he grew tired of waiting for better weather so he could go to Bollingen, he went in September, despite what seemed the early onset of winter. In October, he suffered another heart-related episode and had to be transported back to Küs-nacht. By late October, he was enough improved that he could walk the short distance from his house to a chair at the lakeshore.[159]

Kurt assumed that Jung approved of his working with Hull to restore the text and that Aniela would stop rewriting. Even so, she bypassed Kurt and Hull far too often by sending new changes directly to the Winstons. At first, and because they were not in the loop, Richard and Clara assumed she did it with Kurt's approval, so they made new translations and sent them directly to Hull. He was immediately aware of what Aniela was doing and alerted Kurt, who then engaged in a frantic round of correspondence with the Bollingen editors Sauerlander and Gerry Gross (who assumed responsibility after Kurt Wolff retired), the Winstons, and finally Aniela herself. She still did not obey Kurt's directive until everyone involved told her that the Winstons were henceforth forbidden to translate anything that was not sent to them either by Gerry Gross or Kurt Wolff. She still tried to circumvent everyone by saying there had not been time to consult them. Often, these apologetic letters gave Kurt his first inkling that she and/or the Niehuses had further "auntified" a text the unwitting Winstons had translated in good faith.

Aniela and the Niehuses were able to hide behind the excuse of time delays in 1960 because everything was done by mail. It took time for a manuscript that began in Zürich and went first to one part of Connecticut (where the Winstons lived), then to Ascona (Hull), Locarno (Wolff), and back to Zürich, and with possible detours to Cary in another part of Connecticut or to the London publishers, or even to Rascher, who now insisted on being apprised of the text, as he still claimed ownership of world rights.[160] The process was frequently punctuated by cables and telegrams that were confusing and enigmatic in their brevity. Letters reveal that attempts to speak by telephone were often thwarted by bad connections.

And there were all sorts of other interested parties who thought they were helping but who interfered when they added their own corrections and emendations as the manuscript passed by their desks. In London, for example, Michael Fordham, who knew little German, and his secretary, who claimed she was an expert on classical languages, added "subtleties" to Jung's comments on religion.[161] In Zürich, Mrs. Alice Lewisohn Crowley, a wealthy American who lived at the Dolder Grand for more than three decades and who had been in therapy with both Jung and Jaffé, decided that the book needed a better "Jung family tree."[162] Aniela allowed her to make one because she was too timid to say no to the formidable grande dame. But among the principals, it was often true that each person proceeded in what he or she thought was good faith simply because the time lag was so long that decisions had to be made without prior approval of the others.

Misunderstandings were rife, but there was no reason to think that any single problem was insurmountable until January 9, 1961, when Jung abruptly decided he no longer wanted Hull to supervise the English translation. Despite the fact that he held Hull in "high esteem" for his translations of analytic "terminology," Jung did not want the manuscript vetted "with special regard to technical terms," because in this particular book, he did not "attach great importance" to them. The Winstons had no prior experience with Jungian theory, so each time they explained a specific point, the words differed just enough to be confusing or contradictory. Jung claimed that he liked Richard and Clara's "descriptive way" (which Aniela called "blessed creativity"),[163] as it added to "the vividness of the entire depiction." Eventually, he admitted his real reason, that he was too old and too tired: "Hull will probably not fail to discover quite a few other divergences, and this entails a complication that I am not up to; it will generate too much work for me."

Even if Jung's demand had been reasonable, the process was too far along to bow suddenly to it. Kurt recognized the delicacy of the situation and wrote two letters, one to Jung and a second to Jaffé, but he mailed both to her.[164] He told Jung he could understand his not wanting to do more hard work on a book that had already cost "undue amounts of time and energy." He reminded Jung that he had only engaged Hull after "the urgent wish was expressed from Zürich [meaning Jung himself]" for Hull to become "the final responsible reader of the English version." He explained that Pantheon's policy was never to print a translation without having it checked by an independent expert on both language and subject matter, which was reason enough to retain Hull. However, if Jung still did not want him, "the Pantheon office in New York [would need] to find another qualified reader." That, too, would require "necessary grammatical and terminological corrections" to make the German and English texts correspond, so it made simple sense to keep Hull.

Kurt's seemingly inexhaustible patience had finally worn thin over Jung's insistence on excluding Hull, and he ended sharply: "May I ask you to tell him about the new decision — especially because of your last visit with him in the spring of 1960?" — an allusion to the *"tantifiziert"* episode. In the accompanying letter to Aniela, Kurt appealed to her to "think this problem through":

> Here is a book where CGJ speaks about his work, his psychiatric discoveries, insights, thoughts — if this happens in an imprecise, paraphrased form that will appear amateurish to the English reader, it will have terrible consequences. Jung isn't just any writer after all. His work is recognized worldwide, he personally created a terminology which has equivalents that are globally valid in all languages. . . . And now it's supposed to be the English version of this book that shall *not* use this terminology? . . . In the German edition the language is terminologically identical with that of the Jungian oeuvre and in the English one it's supposed to be different? That, dear Aniela, surpasses my comprehension.

He was puzzled about why she consented to supply "such cheap weapons" to Jung's "English critics and ideological opponents." He concluded with a stunning statement that had a profound effect on Aniela Jaffé and the book she eventually shepherded into being as he left the outcome squarely in her hands:

> Why are we still arguing if not for the sole sake of the book? Wouldn't it be much easier for me, who has left the publisher, who has no more materialistic advantages nor moral responsibilities for what Pantheon publishes in the future, to leave CGJ, you, and last but not least myself, alone? To spare myself rejections and rebukes and let it all take its course?

Jung stuck to his decision to remove Hull as textual overseer. Kurt broke the news to Hull, who was hurt and angry and who returned the advance Pantheon paid for work to come. With incredible understatement, Kurt told Cary that he was "a bit wearied of this battle between will and whim."[165] Then Jung changed his mind again, deciding it might be a good idea after all to permit Hull to oversee the Winston translation, "provided he confines himself to *spraechliche Korrecturen* [*sic*]," correcting his language.[166] It was exactly what Kurt had proposed in the first place, and it pointed out the futility of trying to deal rationally with the "Zürichers," as he now lumped them all together.

Jung's change of mind reached Kurt on January 18, 1961. On January 26, perhaps "a bit more wearied" than even he had realized, Kurt sent Jaffé a letter stating he would have "nothing more to do with the book."[167] He told his wife and son, "You can't deal rationally with these people. There can be no resolution. This is no longer about substance; it is all about power."[168]

EVEN THOUGH Aniela did not then realize it, Kurt's resignation meant that she had just lost her most patient ally. For the first time, she was hurled into the vortex of professional publishing from which he had shielded her. Wolfgang Sauerlander in New York and Milton Waldman in London confronted her with rigorous production schedules and made appointments for personal conferences, both of which she and the Niehuses found ways to avoid or ignore, thus further postponing publication.[169] Gerry Gross, inheritor of Kurt's role, tried to mediate between Aniela and the two translators. Sauerlander and Gross supervised the book long-distance until the manuscript was finally complete in late 1962, but Hull became the linchpin in all they did.[170] Both men relied on him to bring them up to date on the situation as he saw it, for even after he left Switzerland to live in Mallorca he fought the good fight on Jung's behalf.

Still searching for a better climate, Hull was moving to Palma. In March 1961, he went to Zürich to say good-bye to Jung on the "hunch" they would never meet again.[171] He found Jung "aged and rather tottery" but still "like a force of nature. The daimon drove him right to the end." Hull thought leaving Switzerland meant the translation was finished. He was unaware that the manuscript was still more than a year away from its final form and happily presented a copy to Jung, thinking it would soon be in print. Jung returned the favor by inviting him to read "the 'famous' Red Book."

Hull studied the "monkish, black-letter script" in which Jung recorded "his most important dreams ever since 1913, illustrating them with disturbing, really mad drawings. No wonder he kept it under lock and key! Talk of Freud's self-analysis — Jung was a walking asylum in himself, as well as its head physician." Because he had worked for the past fifteen years on Jung's writings, Hull understood *The Red Book*'s importance to the entire canon, and it made him doubly insistent that, no matter how much Jung wanted to distance *MDR* from the *Collected Works*, it was imperative to safeguard his "ur-text" and see that it became the published autobiography.

Reading *The Red Book* in the light of Jung's original biographical writing reminded Hull of a quotation from Coleridge's *Notebooks*. Later, he proposed it as "a motto" for Aniela's introduction, and she used it:

He looked at his own Soul with a Telescope. What seemed all irregular, he saw and shewed to be beautiful Constellations; and he added to the Consciousness hidden worlds within worlds.

Hull left for Mallorca, happy to have spent such a pleasant afternoon with Jung, even happier at the misguided thought that the autobiography would soon be published. Several months later, when news reached him of Jung's death, his reaction was one shared by so many others: "I felt as if the bottom of my world — and of the world of so many people I know — had dropped out."

———∞∞———

CHAPTER 39

"The Icy Stillness of Death"

Jung had been more ill than well since the embolism in February 1960. Everyone, his children included, decided to celebrate his eighty-fifth birthday on July 26 with more than the usual festivities. At a dinner in the nearby Hotel Sonne, he was made an *Ehrenbürger*, an honored citizen, and presented with keys to the city of Küsnacht. When all the celebrations ended, Jung was exhausted, but before he could recuperate, the daughter of one of his housemaids fell into the lake near his boathouse and drowned. The combination of events induced serious shock and tachycardia, but Jung insisted he was well enough to take an ITCRA trip to the Jura with Fowler and Ruth. He became sick along the way but would not let them turn back. No sooner had they arrived in the town of Onnens than Jung was felled by crippling gastric distress, the presenting symptom of recurring liver and gall bladder attacks.[1] His pain was so severe that Ruth summoned a doctor, who spent the night at his bedside. The next morning when Jung was stabilized, Ruth telephoned Marianne, whose cancer had so weakened her that she was living in her girlhood bedroom to continue supervising the *Gesammelte Werke*. Marianne wanted to charter a helicopter, but Walther persuaded her to let him drive to Onnens, hire an ambulance, and transport Jung home. From that time on, Jung was forbidden to travel.

In October, an especially severe combination of gall bladder, liver, and gastric upset left him even further debilitated. He did not express a desire to travel again until March 1961, when Cary Baynes was visiting her daughter in the Ticino and Jung wanted Fowler and Ruth to drive him to Locarno to see her. His doctor would not let him risk the altitude changes incurred in crossing the mountains, so he "condemned" Jung to "four weeks of imprisonment at home."[2] It was well he did, for Jung had several minor heart infarctions between March 20 and 30.

Hull's farewell visit occurred just before the onset of the March episodes, when Jung was well enough to express frustration at not being able to work on "an essay on symbols, in English."[3] He told Hull he was desperate to go to

Bollingen, where he could concentrate on it. Anxious and restless after the infarctions, he demanded that Fowler drive him there in April, when the weather was warm for the first time in more than a year and the sun shone every day.[4] Ruth stayed with him, and Fowler visited frequently until business called him to the United States.

Barbara Hannah developed the habit of coming every morning to help Ruth. If they were in Küsnacht, Hannah apportioned errands to the property's caretaker, old Müller; in Bollingen, she delegated chores to the handyman, Hans Kuhn.[5] Her daily visits were prompted by a dream Jung told her he had after the episode in Onnens, one he repeated later to Marie-Louise von Franz. In it, he saw "the other Bollingen" lit by gleaming light and heard a disembodied voice saying it was now ready for him to inhabit. Below the tower, he saw a mother wolverine teaching her cub to swim in the lake.[6] Hannah and von Franz interpreted the dream as one of impending death, with the wolverine cub representing adaptation to a new environment. Jung told Hannah he was not yet ready to die and would go to the temporal Bollingen instead. His doctor gave permission because Jung's determination to finish the essay was causing anxiety and elevating his normally high blood pressure to dangerous levels. Jung was frustrated by a body so weakened that it no longer fulfilled the commands his active mind issued, but his willpower remained strong, and he did finish the essay in the penultimate month of his life.[7]

It was published in the book that became *Man and His Symbols*, an outgrowth of the 1959 interviews John Freeman conducted for the BBC. Wolfgang Foges, managing director of Aldus Books, saw the telecasts and thought Jung's comments provided insights into his psychology that would interest an educated class of readers who were familiar with Freud's basic theory but knew little of Jung's. Foges asked Freeman to raise the possibility of Jung's writing such a book, for the generalist rather than the specialist.

"Jung listened to me in his garden for two hours almost without interruption — and then said no," Freeman recalled of the first of two meetings. "He said it in the nicest possible way, but with great firmness; he had never in the past tried to popularize his work, and he wasn't sure that he could successfully do so now; anyway, he was old and rather tired and not keen to take on such a long commitment about which he had so many doubts."[8] In addition — although Freeman knew nothing of it — Jung was embroiled in the ongoing controversies connected with the still floundering *Memories, Dreams, Reflections*.

Shortly after his refusal to Freeman, Jung had a dream that caused him to change his mind. He was speaking in a public forum to "a multitude of people who were listening to him with rapt attention and *understanding what he said*."[9] When Foges asked him to reconsider, Jung said he would do it under two conditions. First, he did not want the book to consist of his writing alone but to include essays by the "closest followers" to whom he entrusted the perpetuation of his psychology. His second condition was the more important of the two and was directly related to the textual quarrels over *MDR:* Jung wanted Freeman to serve as the book's general editor, to coordinate all the texts and deal with any problems that might arise between the authors and publishers.

Marie-Louise von Franz was the first person Jung selected, entrusting her with the cornerstone of his theory, "The Process of Individuation." As his prior collaborator on the alchemical manuscripts, she was keenly aware of his working methods and once again assumed an editorial prerogative. Indeed, after his death, she became not only Freeman's co-editor but also the final authority on the book's content.[10] Jung's next choice was Joseph L. Henderson (an American and the only non-Swiss), who was asked to write about his area of expertise, "Ancient Myths and Modern Man." Next, Jung chose Gerhard Adler to write about the analytic encounter. Adler accepted but withdrew shortly after for one of two reasons (according to who tells the tale): either he had too many other commitments or he was angry that all the contributors were to be paid less than Jung.[11] Jung asked Jolande Jacobi to replace him. She was hurt that he had not included her among the first choices, but she accepted because she never refused anything Jung asked her to do. Some time passed before he decided the book needed one more essay to round it out, on "Symbolism in the Visual Arts." Despite the frazzled, overburdened state he well knew Aniela Jaffé was in, he assigned her to write it. He reasoned that, as she had been secretary to the art historians Carola and Sigfried Giedion-Welcker, she could summarize the topic swiftly and easily.[12]

Jung was canny when he asked Freeman to coordinate the essays, for despite the sunny description Freeman recounted in his introduction, there were many stormy moments. Jacobi set one firm condition when she accepted, that she be permitted to read the other essays before writing hers. Jung, von Franz, and Henderson sent theirs, and when she read them, she told Jung they had covered everything important, leaving nothing for her to write about. He countered that this was the excuse of a lazy person, and she must be "helpful" and do it. Jacobi still refused, so Jung ordered von Franz to make a formal call and promise whatever was needed to persuade her. The two women despised each other, but probably more important in their personal dynamic, von Franz believed herself "far too elevated in intellectual stature" to stoop to petition anyone. To plead personally for Jacobi's cooperation was an event of unprecedented magnitude, but because Jung wanted it, von Franz made the call and Jacobi wrote an essay.[13]

Of them all, Jacobi's was the most controversial, for she used a single case to express the possibilities in conducting a Jungian analysis. Freeman wrote, "I puke on this," and he wanted to reject it outright. Von Franz, taking her cue from Freeman, urged Jung to reject it as well, but by this time, he had barely enough energy left for his own essay and was unable to give those of his colleagues the attention they probably merited. He told Freeman he approved of their basic content, so after Freeman and von Franz argued and edited, the book was subsequently published with most of what Jung's handpicked contributors originally wrote.

Jung's absorption in his essay was the reason he was so removed from the machinations of *MDR* during his last year of life. While everyone else quibbled over what he could or could not say in his "so-called autobiography," he was happily expressing his ideas directly in English for his essay. This was the kind of writing he liked best, to explain his theory in its purest form and with scant reference to himself as its originator. He believed that the English language was better suited to such explanations than German, as it offered the most precise, direct, and focused terminology with which he could reach the literate general reader. "I can get one word that explains my meaning in English whereas it would be a whole sentence in German," he told Ruth Bailey.[14]

This essay mattered so much to Jung that, although it has never been given the degree of scholarly attention it deserves, it is important to consider it as a counterbalance during the years in which he wrote *MDR*. Both texts are quasi-theory as well as quasi-biography, and they deserve attention for, if nothing else, the place they occupy in his life and work: they are the last.

The autobiography is a personal text: his explanation of how the young medical doctor, Carl Jung, gradually evolved into the respected mature psychologist, Professor C. G. Jung. The essay, on the other hand, is both the expression of the mature theorist's ideas and a guide for the individual who wishes to undertake Jung's particular approach to his or her subconscious. Jung wrote about his interpretation of symbols and signs and his views of organized religion, political movements, and national characteristics. He explained the usefulness of dreams and the differences between archetypes and instincts. With the always respectful nod he bestows upon Freud throughout his canon, he explains here how and why his ideas differed, especially those pertaining to the unconscious, the psyche, the religious, superstitious, and the irrational. What makes the essay especially remarkable is its tightly organized structure — more Freudian in style than Jungian — for he develops his ideas without the usual circularity but, rather, in a classical linear progression; each idea proceeds from the one before and leads naturally into the one that follows.

The essay is a tribute to his willpower, for he wrote it doggedly despite dangerously elevated blood pressure, lack of oxygen to his brain, inability to walk more than a few shuffling steps at a time, and even the need to recline and sleep more than to sit and think. By the end of April, he had so exhausted himself that Ruth packed up, closed the tower, and told him they were going home to Küsnacht. When she described how she did all this, she did not include what, if anything, Jung said or did when he left his beloved tower for what he must have presumed was the last time.

BECAUSE OF the dreams Jung told her about, Ruth thought his life was ending.[15] The first dream was of an enormous round stone elevated to an unspecified place. Jung said it bore the inscription "And this shall be a sign unto you of Wholeness and Oneness." He told Ruth it meant he would soon be dead. Trying to keep him jolly, she asked what she was supposed to do if he left her. He said he would be waiting to give her a fine welcome when she arrived on "the other side."[16] Back in Küsnacht, Jung dreamt of tall trees growing in a square, dominated by huge fibrous roots spilling out of the ground and enveloping him, all shot through with golden threads. Lying to the right side of this square were many large pottery vessels and vases. Ruth repeated the dream to Barbara Hannah, who thought it signified unity, wholeness, and closure.[17]

In early May, Jung's doctor thought it a good idea for him to go to the hospital for a thorough examination, and he spent several days there while tests were administered. For the week or so after he returned to Küsnacht, he was well enough to spend the mornings on the main floor, but once he went back upstairs for his afternoon nap, he stayed there, either in his bedroom or the library, where he took his evening meal. He usually wore a padded silk dressing gown of Oriental design and on his now-bald head one of his various skullcaps, his particular favorite made of velvet lined with fur. Sometimes when the sun was bright, he shuffled with aid to the balcony, where he could see the lake.

Marianne was always in the house, often confined to bed by her illness. Franz came frequently as well, and Ruth was grateful that the tension that had always existed between father and son was now entirely gone. Barbara Hannah tried to get Jung to go for short drives, as he loved riding in automobiles, but after May 6 he was too weak to leave the upper floor of his house. Aniela Jaffé saw him throughout the day in connection with her secretarial duties, but in Jung's last week of life, Franz asked her not to come to the house.[18] Marie-Louise von Franz usually spent half an hour in the late afternoon talking about *Man and His Symbols*, and she and Barbara Hannah were there daily until two days before Jung's death.

On May 17, Jung suffered another embolism, diagnosed as a blood clot that traveled to his brain, caused a stroke, and affected his speech. Some of his grandchildren were reduced to tears by the sight of the once-powerful head of their household now himself reduced to tears because he knew that gibberish, not speech, was pouring from his mouth.[19] If he did manage words, they were a mélange of all the languages he knew, plus an incomprehensible *Schwizertütsch*, but not in any order that made sense.[20] They believed that nothing in Jung's long life distressed him as much as this inability to communicate through language. Fortunately, he regained most of his speech, albeit slowly and in a whisper. He still had trouble formulating whole sentences, but he insisted that Aniela bring all his mail and read it to him. Now he actually looked forward to the daily packet of letters, for it assured him that there was still regard for him in the outside world. Even though he was asleep most of the time, he still wanted Aniela to sit beside him and read the daily letters.

On May 30, he had another physical collapse and was taken to bed. From then until the end, he did not leave his bedroom. He had another stroke several days later, after which he could not speak. Those who sat by his bedside reported that he would emerge occasionally from a comatose state and, obviously referring to a vision, say something that sounded like "how wonderful."

Marianne would not permit professional nurses, so she and Ruth were his primary attendants until early June. Even though she was very ill, Marianne wrapped herself in blankets and insisted on sitting in the chair next to her father's bed. Her children thought the bond between the dying father and the desperately ill daughter was eerie, and that the willpower of each held the other to life as if by a tenuous thread. One or the other had to let go in order for the other to die.

Jung's condition became so deteriorated that Marianne had to permit a professional nurse to be engaged for the last several days of his life. On the afternoon before he died, June 5, he regained a modicum of speech and consciousness. Franz sat beside him and they reminisced together. Jung asked Ruth to go down into the cellar and select an excellent bottle of wine for their dinner. She brought it up at once, as he had been mostly unable to eat for the past few days. Franz opened the bottle and he and Ruth toasted Jung, who enjoyed what little wine he could sip.

The next morning, Jung was coherent enough to sign papers needed for bank withdrawals to keep the household functioning. Marianne's son Rudolf helped her to get Jung's signature.[21] Sensing a grave change in Jung's condition, Marianne did not want to keep her routine doctor's appointment, but her son (himself a medical student) insisted. "When the beloved went away, then he could die," Dr. Niehus remembered, for Marianne was in her doctor's office when Jung's sleep gave way to a quiet death at 4:30 in the afternoon. After "a long slow sunset" with gradually "fading light,"[22] Carl Gustav Jung died on June 6, 1961.

THE NEXT day, while his children and grandchildren gathered downstairs, Marianne summoned Elsbeth Stoiber, curator of the Medizinhistorischen Museums of the University of Zürich and a specialist in the art of casting body parts, especially death masks.[23] The entire process of casting a death mask takes five hours or more, and Stoiber never permitted another person to be in the room while she worked. As the family members received visitors and tended to their private grief on the ground floor, Stoiber spent the long day alone with Jung's body, for Marianne asked her to make two separate casts.[24]

Stoiber remembered that the window in Jung's bedroom was open and the "fantastic air" of a clear summer day blew in through the curtains. "His body, lying on his bed, was so impressive," his visage resembling "something Asiatic, like Genghis Khan." On his forehead were three lines, "like a triton," a pattern similar to some she had seen in India on the faces of worshipers of Ra, the sun god.

Stoiber's technique was uniquely her own: an initial impression of plaster of Paris to ensure "a satisfactory image," followed by an infusion of wax because of its "certain meaning, immortality for example." She liked to use beeswax, "because the bee is the sign of culture and also the symbol of the pharaoh." Her mixture consisted of "certain resins, incense for symbolic reasons, and color." For Jung, whom she had never met and about whom she knew nothing except that he was a famous analyst, she chose "brown with lots of red," instinctively sensing that "he was a very earthy man besides his spirituality and he had a good relationship to stone."

Stoiber had never met anyone in the Jung family, and in all the years after she made the masks, she never found out how Marianne learned of her work or why she wanted two death masks. "Death masks were never a tradition in Switzerland," Stoiber recalled almost half a century after she made Jung's. "They were mainly a tradition in Catholic countries, and only the best sculptors were permitted to make them." The only contemporary ones she knew of in Switzerland were of Thomas Mann and Richard Wagner, "but then, they were Germans after all."

NEWS OF Jung's death spread immediately throughout the world. Telegrams arrived in a deluge, the telephone rang constantly, memorial services were scheduled in far-flung places, and many mourners convened for the Swiss services. Fowler McCormick heard the news of Jung's death in a tailor shop in Princeton, New Jersey, while being fitted for white trousers for his college reunion.[25] He booked a flight and was with the family during the mourning period. Tributes poured in from all over, from Jung's professional life (Paul Mellon, Helen and Kurt Wolff, and members of the Bollingen Foundation among them) to heads of state (among them Jawaharlal Nehru).[26] Obituaries were long and mainly respectful: the *New York Times* described Jung as "one of the great modern adventurers who sought to push back the dark frontiers of man's mind";[27] the British medical journal *The Lancet* rightfully noted that he was "the last survivor of the triad of pioneers in psychiatry" after Freud and Adler, but it also noted that "Jung's developed work is unique."[28] Hull was distressed that the *Manchester Guardian* ignored Jung's many contributions, choosing instead to bring up the old charges of collaboration with the Nazis.[29]

In Zürich, local officials wanted to honor Jung with burial ceremonies either in the Grossmünster or the Fraumünster, the two most historically significant churches. The family, still insisting that Jung's primary identification was as their father rather than as the world-respected psychiatrist, scheduled the services for the local Swiss Reformed Church of Küsnacht, after which Jung was quietly interred in his family's plot.

WHEN A memorial was held in New York six months later, an august group of speakers extolled Jung's contribution to his field.[30] Among them were his personal friends M. Esther Harding, Fowler McCormick, and Eleanor Bertine. Paul Mellon represented the Bollingen Foundation, and the field of psychology was represented by Edward F. Edinger, Henry A. Murray, and F. S. C.

Northrop. From theology came Paul J. Tillich and John M. Billinsky; and from literature and history, Arnold J. Toynbee. Edinger was the last speaker and the briefest. He described Jung as "the originator of a whole new era in man's understanding of himself," and added, "[Although] Jung the man is dead, the consequences of his creative genius are just beginning."[31]

Jung gave his own view of death in *Memories, Dreams, Reflections* as one of sharp contrasts, of "warmth and joy" juxtaposed against "terror and grief."[32] In his analytic terminology, the paradox of death was a "catastrophe" as seen by the ego, but also a "joyful event . . . a *mysterium coniunctionis*" as seen by the psyche. For Jung death was "indeed a fearful piece of brutality; there is no sense pretending otherwise." This brutality was not only physical but psychic, too: "A human being is torn away from us, and what remains is the icy stillness of death."

Certainly those to whom he had been important in life were inconsolable after his death in many different ways and for many years to come. But Jung was a scholar and thinker whose influence resonated in so many different ways. Dr. Hans Schär, one of the speakers at his memorial service, identified four decisive factors "in his character and life."[33] The first three, according to Schär, were his loyalty to himself and his self-discipline, his respect for reality, and his faith "in man and life." The fourth, he thought, was more difficult to define:

> Perhaps we come closest to it if we say: in his own mind as well as in his work and researches, Professor Jung always saw totality and the individual conjointly. He took the totality seriously but never to such an extent that he forgot or neglected the individual. Therefore, the fullness of reality was always present to his mind, while he was also able to keep his distance.

LEGEND HAS it that immediately after Jung died, a severe bolt of lightning destroyed the lakeside tree under which he liked to conduct analytic sessions in fine weather. "Just the sort of fantastic thing that *would* happen (no doubt legend will synchronize it with his [final] stroke)," Hull said when the tale reached him.[34] Actually, there was a storm, but it did not strike until much later that night; the tree was indeed split but lost only its bark and survived for many years afterward.[35] There was a second summer thunderstorm on the morning of the burial service, June 9. Thunder roiled as the four dignitaries who were chosen to speak praised Jung's lifetime achievements. Agathe Niehus-Jung, seated next to Ruth Bailey, leaned close and whispered, "That's Father grumbling."

Ruth thought to herself: "How he would have hated all that fuss."[36]

———∞∞∞———

The "So-called Autobiography"

"Jesus! What this book doesn't make us suffer! Jung must be having a belly laugh in his grave," Richard Hull told Gerry Gross two months after Jung's death.[1] Jung died with his professional affairs in a morass of confusion, and his heirs, who were forming the *Erbengemeinschaft C. G. Jung*, a committee of heirs, were planning a family conference in August to sort them out. Primary on their agenda was his "so-called autobiography."

Before Jung died, the family (primarily Walther and Marianne Niehus) insisted upon major changes and revisions and charged Aniela with conveying them to the Winstons.[2] The Winstons, confronted with the deluge and fearful of what might be published with their names on it, sent Gross "a cry of controlled anguish" and demanded that he use their original translation. From London, William Collins and Milton Waldman demanded immediate publication, not caring what the content was, just so long as Jung's name was on the cover and it did not exceed the length they agreed to pay to have it printed.

Meanwhile, Gross became as disgusted as Kurt Wolff had been with all the power plays. He was leaving Pantheon for another publishing position and wanted to leave full documentation for those who would inherit the "almost schizoid situation."[3] Gross enlisted Hull to try to compel the Zürichers to recognize and respect the realities of international publishing, and their correspondence provides a navigational chart of the many compromises that eventually resulted in the published text of *Memories, Dreams, Reflections* — two years after Jung's death, in 1963. Gross saw his most important task before leaving Pantheon as persuading Jaffé to stop revising, even though she had "final approval" and was determined not to surrender it.[4] All the publishers agreed to accept Jung's letter to her of October 21, 1957, as a binding contract that granted her "all rights" and authorized her to publish as she thought best her "notes of conversations with [Jung]."[5] A month before his death, on May 6, 1961, Jung wrote his last letter to Gerry Gross, and Jaffé enclosed one of her own with it. Jung's concluded with the sentence "In case of my incapacity, I entrusted her [Jaffé] with the responsibility for the final version of the whole manuscript."[6] Her letter asked Gross to acknowledge that he and all other publishers would honor Jung's decision. From that time on, the publishers were confused by Jaffé's autocratic enforcement of her authority over them, even as she constantly caved in to Jung's children and let them tinker with the text at will.[7]

A new problem occurred for Bollingen as well as Pantheon when an alarming number of Jung's descendants suddenly developed an interest that they had never before shown in his writings. They were insisting upon deletions and changes throughout the entire *Collected Works* as well as to *MDR*, with their main reason the typically cultural one: they could not conceive of Jung as a public figure and regarded him only as their father and grandfather; anything pertaining to his life and work belonged to the family and was subject to their concept of privacy.

Even though Jung named Walther Niehus his literary executor, his other children, their spouses, and his grandchildren were operating as a loose collective. When they found it impossible to arrive at decisions, a formal *Erbengemeinschaft* was legally established: each of the five Jung children elected one person from their branch of the family to represent their interest on a five-member executive board, where decisions were carried by a simple majority. However, this was not yet formalized in late summer 1961, when the publishers were having collective nightmares about how the heirs, none of whom worked in publishing or were educated in the law, might decide to tamper with the still unpublished writings of C. G. Jung.

Jaffé created a new alarm on August 9, when she sent Gross a cryptic cable: "Earnest reasons told later make publication urgent."[8] He had no idea what she meant, but shared her basic sentiment and hoped it would "make the lady easier to deal with."[9] Jaffé was referring to the imminent British publication of Bennet's quasi-biography, *C. G. Jung*.[10] As Rascher was trying to buy the rights for immediate German publication and planning to tout it as Jung's official biography, the Bollingen Foundation's board asked Kurt Wolff to determine what effect Bennet's book might have on *MDR*, not only if it appeared first but no matter when it was published. Kurt asked Jolande Jacobi for advice, and she told him he had several options but the best was to let Rascher publish whenever the firm pleased, for if he did not, another German publisher would certainly snap it up. She told him the only "positive" quality of Bennet's book was its "commercial value," and to prove her point, she told how Rascher gloated that he was buying it only because it would "sell well."

Jacobi scathingly critiqued Bennet's "apotheosis" as she pointed out its many errors.[11] She conceded that he had written "in good faith" but said he still made unforgivable mistakes because "he is friends only with Hannah and von Franz and doesn't listen to anyone else." Jacobi was perplexed about why the book was "composed of various ingredients" of Jung's life, for she remembered Jung telling her he gave Bennet permission to write about him only as a physician.[12] She objected to Bennet's lack of understanding of Jung's psychology, berating him for casting Jung as an "introverted-thinking" type, when he was "clearly an intuitive." Her major objection was Bennet's misreading of Jung's canon, particularly his thoughts about religion: she was horrified by his assertion that Jung described "Christ [as] a projection of the self."

Ultimately, Bennet's book was not widely reviewed, sold only modestly, and had little lasting influence upon later assessments of Jung's life and work. The book's one positive effect on Aniela Jaffé and the Jung heirs was to impress upon them — after so many years — that they needed to bring *MDR* to print swiftly, even if that sense of urgency did not last long. "The spinning does not diminish," Gross noted as no one honored or respected Jung's legacy or his wishes, and personal animosities impeded their professional responsibilities to his canon.[13]

In a letter written two weeks before his death, Jung pronounced the Winston translation "excellent," praised Hull for getting "into the spirit of the thing," and said he "quite agree[d] with most of [Hull's] changes."[14] Armed with such strong evidence, Gross thought all he needed to do was to ask Aniela to read the manuscript and impose strict deadlines so production could finally begin. He was to go to Zürich that same August as the heirs were meeting, and shortly before his departure, he sent Jaffé a newly retyped version of *MDR* that he considered "a workable manuscript in final form" based on the original Winston translation of Jung's handwritten German chapters I–III and IX–XII.[15] Gross deliberately gave Aniela short notice to read it because he did not want her to have time to show it to Walther and Marianne.

If there was an "ur-text," this typescript was it. In the earliest version, Hull made comments and suggestions on Winston's typescript, and Jung subsequently approved both by affixing his handwritten corrections and notations directly to it. Gross warned Jaffé that he could not leave Zürich without her "complete approval of the entire text."[16] To his great relief, she agreed with everything and did not once hint she would submit her copy to Jung's children after his departure. Even if she did, Gross felt confident that nothing untoward would happen because the Niehuses' lawyer, Bernhard Peyer, was "almost as upset by [the Niehuses'] machinations" as he was, and could be counted on to make them see reason.[17]

If the editorial meeting between Gross and Jaffé were evaluated on their compromises, it would be judged enormously successful. Gross succeeded in removing most of Aniela's "interventions" and returned Jung's writing and thinking to its earliest form. Both he and Jaffé signed a letter of full agreement "concerning the final version of the manuscript with the sole exception of Chapter II, 'School Years.'" No further changes were contemplated except for "proposals" that Hull might make to ensure scrupulous accuracy of small points in the translation. Publication was supposed to begin on September 15,[18] but the Zürichers stymied Gross yet again with problems that took the better part of a year to resolve.

One of the minor disputes revolved around the chapter entitled *"Begegnungen,"* the "Encounters" with famous persons. All those who tried to make it fit into the context of the book agreed with Jolande Jacobi that it was "flat and weak, and . . . Jung had no affinity whatsoever for it."[19] This was especially apparent when it was contrasted with the beginning and ending chapters he wrote unbidden with such fervor. While these emphasized the "inner" Jung and revealed the complexity of his intellectual development, the "Encounters" had an unexpected reverse effect, unintentionally emphasizing how Jung "neglect[ed] his relationship to the outside world entirely." It was "ice-cold and meaningless . . . like an alien element in the book," so Gross persuaded Aniela to eliminate most of it. She retained something of Flournoy, Wilhelm, and Zimmer for a German appendix, but only Wilhelm made it into the English.

Gross also persuaded Jaffé to put all Jung's references to other writings into "one long appendix, with accompanying notes at the back of the book," where it all "rightly belongs."[20] These consisted of letters between Jung and Freud, several of Jung's letters to unnamed correspondents, a genealogy of the Jung family,[21] and several other unspecified bits and pieces. It all appeared in the German edition, but only some of it was included in the English and in a different form. As for her textual interventions, Jaffé agreed to confine them to brief explanatory notes at the bottom of the pages of the corresponding text, clearly initialed as supplied by her.

When Gross told Hull of her agreement, he said, "[My] admiration for Jaffé's objectivity and insight continue to grow. . . . She is dead right when she writes to [Richard] Winston that this whole madly complicated and schizoid situation is a reflection in reality of Jung's own schizoid attitude toward the book from the very beginning. He wanted to write it and he did not want to write it."[22]

Hull said his own work was "affected by this dichotomy in Jung." When he finished revising the new chapters I–III, he had "an inexplicable hunch that there would be endless complications and misunderstandings" and he "did not want to be involved in them." He was uncannily prescient, as the next and most serious of all the machinations proved.

"No ONE will be able to top this," Gross wrote in an internal memo to his colleague Wolfgang Sauerlander days after he returned to New York. Far from being ready for publication, the book was threatened to be scuttled forever by a new rash of "Jung/Jaffé/Hull/Gross" exchanges.[23] The most serious of all the Zürich transgressions was abbreviated among the Pantheon editors and the Bollingen Foundation officials by its location in the typescript, "II: 58–70."[24]

Like a bolt from the blue, on August 30, Walther Niehus decreed that none of Jung's thoughts about religion, important because so much else in the text pivots upon them, could be printed.[25] Hull's view of the "doublecross" was succinct:

> A very astute move on Mr., or more probably Mrs., Niehus's part: by ruthlessly cutting the whole passage instead of tinkering about with it, they cannot strictly speaking be accused of "falsifying" the text. The fact that they have excised the emotional and intellectual backbone of the book appears not to bother them at all — or perhaps they are just too stupid to realize it.[26]

Jaffé was complaining about the "School Years" section of the translation even before Gross arrived in Zürich, so once there, both gave it their most intensive scrutiny.[27] Now Gross realized that Aniela's concerns had been mere echoes of Walther and Marianne's. Because Aniela insisted upon "final approval," Gross was understandably "*appalled*" by her telegram informing him that II: 58–70 had to be deleted.[28] He told Hull it made him feel "thoroughly 'beschissen'" (shit upon). Hull, in turn, told Aniela that when Gross read her telegram, he had "in fact used the English equivalent."[29]

In this portion of his second chapter, Jung explained the hollow emptiness he felt after receiving first Communion. II: 58–70 as he originally wrote it constitutes one of his most sophisticated and successful combinations of No. 1 reflecting upon and being refracted back by No. 2.[30] He wrote of this experience from the vantage point of an old man who pondered it repeatedly over time but whose primary aim was to explain how such thoughts first surfaced in his boyhood and then evolved throughout his life. Gross and Hull knew that if these pages were eliminated in their entirety, every philosophical argument that followed would be severely weakened, not only those about religion.

In these pages, Jung the boy asked himself: "What was the purpose of this wretched memorial service with the flat bread and sour wine?"[31] His thoughts coalesced into one of his first conceptions of God as an example of the *privatio boni*. Jung the old man recollected how his boyhood self asked why, if God was the "highest good," he had created a world that was "so imperfect, so corrupt, so pitiable." It left the boy "seized with pity" for his father, "who had fallen victim to this mumbo-jumbo."[32] His concluding thought as it appeared in his hand-corrected typescript became the focal point of the II: 58–70 disagreement, wherein he, the old man, reflected on the anguish of the boy he was when he decided he could no longer worship the Christian God of his father: "'Why, that is not religion at all,' I thought. 'It is an absence of God; the church is a place *one* should not go to. It is not life which is there, but death.'" Even before Aniela showed the typescript to Walther Niehus, she thought that if "such a short passage" were allowed to stand, it would "spoil the whole book," as "not only theologians but all [Jung's] enemies would tear it into pieces." Hull accused her of an "almost paranoiac" need to "protect" Jung and insisted she "had to be stopped, family pressure or no family pressure."[33] With an issue this vital at stake, he believed she could not be permitted to hide behind the authority to decide what constituted final manuscript: "It surely does not entitle her to bring Jung's way of expressing himself — and far more calamitous, his *thoughts* — into line with the thinking of his family, who are also a bunch of squares and bourgeois to the bone."

Jaffé won this point, however, as she "corrected" the second sentence (to her the most offensive) for the German version and insisted it had to read the same in *MDR*. She made Jung say, "*For me* it is an absence of God; the church is a place *I* should not go to."[34] Her reason was that, even though he was describing boyhood thoughts, "everybody knows that the book expresses Jung's real thinking of old age. And that Christianity *was* a religion for him is proved by his writings." Hull countered that this was still not a valid reason for her to "make [Jung] talk like one of his theologian uncles, when it is perfectly plain that both as a boy and an old man he regarded all theologians as a bunch of squares."[35]

Aniela became fixated on this point because it led ultimately to Jung's proposing an analogy with the incident of the Basel Cathedral. She tried to blame her stubborn objection on the Winston translation, asking if these "terribly clumsy" pages had been translated by "Mr. Hyde" (as opposed to Dr. Jekyll). Gross asked Hull to counter on Pantheon's behalf. Hull wrote:

> It is nonsense to imply that [Jung's] distrust of theologians and his views on churchgoing made him any the less of a "Christian" and "believer" in the Christian God (though actually the whole book is one long testimony to his *knowledge* and experience of God, as is evidenced by that "horrible business about the cathedral"). That too, I think you will find, is correctly translated.[36]

Hull accused Jaffé of not daring to let Jung "think his thoughts to an end." To attribute to Jung "all the proper views about theology and churchgoing" struck him as the most serious sort of blasphemy: "not only literary blasphemy but a sin against the Holy Spirit." Still, nothing budged and no one gave way. Telephone calls and telegrams to Walther went unanswered. Aniela did nothing except beg Gross to understand her "really bad situation."[37] Truly it was.

Aniela did not have a single ally with whom to discuss her plight now that Helen and Kurt Wolff were happily engaged in a new publishing venture, their own imprint with Harcourt Brace & Company. Aniela worked alone every day in Jung's nearly empty house, for Ruth had gone back to England and would return only to prepare it for Franz and Lilly Jung to occupy. Walther and Marianne were on an extended vacation, and the rest of Jung's children treated her coldly, furiously resenting that she stood to earn 50 percent of the royalties for *MDR*.

Just when it seemed that Pantheon would have to publish the book in the "vapid mélange favoured by the Swiss bourgeoisie,"[38] Hull found a way to save the day. He told Gross that his final and most important duty before leaving Pantheon should be to "call the aunts of both sexes to order, and to ask them what the hell they think they are doing." He was outraged that they should try to cut "a man of 'vision' in the truest sense . . . down to their own wretched size."

"How dare they do this," Hull raged. "You should ask them. It may be that only a feeling of shame will bring them to their senses."

Then he calmed down and plotted strategy. He told Gross that if Jung's corrected typescript was not proof enough of what he wanted *MDR* to be, Jaffé and the heirs should be confronted with Jung's handwritten manuscript. Every time Jaffé and the heirs deviated from Jung's original manuscript, Gross should demand that they make comparisons to both "the hand-corrected copy and the original." This, Hull thought, might provide the publishers with a legal "test case":

> that as responsible publishers you are acting with full understanding of Jung's position and desires. The text as it now stands is (with minor alterations) "correct and proper," and that is the book you intend to publish. If [Jaffé] and the family consider it an unfitting memorial, they are at liberty to bring out a more fitting one with another publisher. BUT — you regret that they will not be able to use Winston's translation, and will have to start again from the beginning. . . . I do not believe for one moment that they will call your bluff.

As the Pantheon contract represented an immediate cash cow for the Jung heirs, Hull thought it unlikely they would spend their own money on a new translation. Nor did he think they would risk the further expense of legal action if the English-language publishers printed the "non-bowdlerized text." He did, however, think they were canny enough to get Rascher to spend his money to sue for them, "on the ground that the English text was substantially different from the German."[39]

Hull conferred with Ximena Roelli at the Bollingen Press, and together they came up with another plan: to enlist Jack Barrett to throw the weight of the foundation into persuading the Zürichers to retain "the emotional and intellectual backbone of the book."[40] Because of what Hull called "internecine American politics," he reasoned that:

> [If] the bowdlerized text comes out and is later shown up to be such . . . the horrid question is going to be asked, "Why did the Foundation stand passively by while Jung's memoirs were falsified by the family?" . . . for as Ximena pointed out very cogently, these things are always "leaked." BOLLINGEN FOUNDATION SPONSORS FALSIFIED JUNG MEMOIRS would make just as uncomfortable a headline in *Time* magazine as BOLLINGEN FOUNDATION IN JUNG FAMILY EMBROGLIO [*sic*].

Hull suggested the wisest course was for Barrett to intervene with the heirs and for Gross to resist "the very understandable plea of [his] colleagues to publish the emasculated version on the ground that it is going to sell pretty well anyway." He added, "Give it this one last chance of life . . . if you are still of a mind with me."[41]

Hull then constructed a long, impassioned letter to Cary Baynes, presenting the history of what transpired throughout the troubled project. He included a capsule summary of every change that had been made to Jung's original text, starting with how the *Protocols* had been mined, refined, and ultimately "auntified." Drawing on his original 1960 report to Herbert Read, Hull summarized the evolution of the variant versions of manuscripts and typescripts. He also spoke of the Bennet book and others that were undoubtedly being written since Jung's death, cautioning that this forthcoming "spate of books" would reveal the falsity of *MDR,* for there was no way to ascertain how much of what the family considered "tabu" Jung had already told or given in some written form to "friends, visitors, or even strangers." Who knew, Hull pondered, the "unknown number of copies" of various versions of *MDR* that were already floating around? "Come to that," he chortled, "I have copies too, and I might deem it the task and pleasure of my serene old age to bring out a scholarly and well-documented study of the vicissitudes through which this remarkable book passed prior to its publication by Pantheon." To persuade Cary of the seriousness of his case, he added that "trunkfuls of notes, protocols, first, second, and third etc. versions of the text" were also "steadily piling up in Locarno." He said, "[It's] difficult to believe that Kurt is collecting this explosive material merely for sentimental reasons." Because of Kurt's own travails with Jaffé and the Niehuses, there was no telling what he might do with his archives.

Gross reviewed all the evidence Hull supplied but decided to present it to Pantheon's lawyers before taking action: "If we do not have a legal leg to stand on, there will be only the moral one. It behooves Pantheon to know whether we stand on one or two before making the plunge."[42] When the lawyers replied, Gross learned he had no leg upon which to stand: until publication, the author retains complete control over what is to appear in print bearing his or her name; because Jung had since died, "Jaffé [was] *the* author for all legal intents and purposes."[43]

Gross thought it unwise to enlist the Bollingen officials, so that line of attack was dropped in favor of Hull's sending Aniela his "superb letter" to force her to "face up to the terrible distortion" she "attempted to pass off" on them. Gross argued:

I can't see how she could avoid showing this letter to Mrs. Niehus, and I hope it will serve to shake that gracious lady to the very marrows. Whether or not the two ladies may then decide to show the letter to Niehus, we cannot say, but even if they do, I wonder, quite sadly, whether he is at all up to judging it properly.

Hull then sent Jaffé what has come to be known as the *"beschissen"* letter.[44] He asked her to ponder the question of why he would risk "meddling" with a book he had not officially translated. He presented his answer through a detailed description of Jung's distress over the *"tantifizierungen."* This was the first time Jaffé had heard the term and was the same time she learned that Hull's "Report" had gone to Herbert Read in 1960, after which it had been circulated to all the other publishers and many other interested parties (Kurt Wolff and Cary Baynes among them). Hull argued that removing II: 58–70 was *"censorship,"* a word he chose "very carefully." He cited the numerous times Aniela described herself as "no longer capable of being objective" and insisted that it was her *"duty"* to regain this ability: "It was into *your* hand, and nobody else's, that Jung entrusted the responsibility for the final version of his life's testimony." If Aniela did not restore the text, the old familiar charges of "family falsification" would be directed at her. Compared to such charges, he said, "attacks by theologians mean nothing . . . Jung was attacked by theologians most of his life; it did not discredit him and never caused him to turn a hair."

And so, Hull concluded, he had shot all his bolts and had done so without ulterior motive: "All my arguments pale and diminish beside the one dominant thought: why did that old man take the trouble to come to see me and talk so earnestly about the book, and why did he entrust it into your hands? I must leave it to you to find the answer."

Kurt Wolff's earlier letter led Aniela to change her behavior significantly, but Hull's shocked her to her very core. It was an embarrassment of epic proportion to learn that accusations of *tantifizierungen* had been floating about for well over a year. Eventually — but not quite yet — it led her to stand firm with Gross and Hull.[45] One week after receiving Hull's *"beschissen"* letter, she replied to Gerry Gross with a copy to Hull. Citing the effect Hull's letter had had on her, she wanted to "try to cross the bridge to [their] standpoint half-way or even more." She wrote: "I shall let you know the *very few* alterations I definitely want. I do so without consulting Mr. and Mrs. Niehus who are in [*sic*] vacations."[46] She thought it a great shame that "one loses one's freedom through fear of evil-minded people" but said she would do whatever was needed to avoid scandal or criticism. This last was a remark she repeated to anyone who tried to subvert Jung's original text from that time onward, for even the thought that she might be accused of *"suppressio veri"* gave her nightmares.[47]

"It appears that we have won the day," Hull said upon learning of her general agreement. "I can't tell you how glad I am that our nine months (!!) of plotting and scheming has come, so it would appear, to a successful end." Hull suggested a long-distance celebration: "Let us pat one another on the back as these embattled pages slide under the press — no one else will!"

"Please don't start celebrating just yet. I'm not," Gross replied as Walther Niehus struck back.[48] When Jaffé told Niehus she decided to retain II: 58–70, he rebutted that as Jung's literary executor, he had the right to refuse permission. Gross countered that if Niehus persisted, he would be forced to print a "Publisher's Note" stating that these pages were "omitted" because Jung's literary executor removed them, and he and not Pantheon was responsible for "falsify[ing] the evolution of this text as Jung wrote it." It would stir up "unfortunate repercussions," but the publisher's obligation was to tell readers the truth.[49]

Walther hid behind Rascher, as was his wont, and on Walther's behalf Rascher made the claim that Jaffé was illegally having the book retranslated. Gross had to explain that Hull merely served as "consultant" to all persons directly involved in preparing the manuscript, including the Winstons. Gross sent copies of this correspondence to Aniela, who by this time had worried herself into a state of near-nervous collapse. He asked her not to "fret," and promised to defuse the situation.[50] Soothing and conciliatory, Hull began to work diligently with Aniela to prepare the final manuscript.[51] He praised her for compromising "far more than halfway, in fact nearly all the way." The "long and wearisome preparations" of the text, coupled with the shock of Jung's death in mid-process, had affected everyone, he said, not just her; she was not the only one who had lost a certain degree of "objectivity, reading into innocent remarks sinister meanings which are not there at all!" He lauded her for agreeing to keep II: 58–70 basically intact and urged her to continue to "let the old man think his thoughts for now." It was his way of bolstering her resolve to ignore both Walther Niehus and Milton Waldman as well.

It was now November 1961, almost six months after Jung's death. Waldman seemed to have lost interest, but as soon as he learned that the book was ready for production, he became obsessed with cutting printing costs. He launched a series of demands for Jaffé to delete large chunks of text; these were in many cases arbitrary and vague, but in most others they were downright harmful.[52] Hull told her he now understood why "Waldman cannot serve *us* (and Jung). . . . The poor man seems absolutely out of his depth here."[53]

BY THE end of the year, Waldman appeared to have retreated, so everyone turned to the final text. Neither Jaffé nor Niehus would allow Jung to say God "shit" on the Basel Cathedral, but they did permit God to drop "an enormous turd" upon it.[54] Jung could still be the "poor parson's son" with "holes" in his shoes, but all his children insisted that he had to wear "socks."[55] There were other textual compromises of a more serious nature, dealing with Jung's thoughts on religion, but even if they were not his exact wording, Jaffé insisted that her rephrasing gave the gist, if not the actuality, of his intention. Gross and Hull decided she had given all the ground they were likely to gain and accepted her "pusillanimous" revisions without a fight.

Unfortunately, Waldman struck again, long enough to cause a serious delay. Because of the exigencies of American publishing, a book scheduled for spring publication had to be printer-ready by the previous autumn. In this case, with two conflicting publishers rather than a single one, Waldman's stubborn insistence upon cuts meant publication could not happen until fall 1962 at the earliest. Just as this date was agreed upon and Gross thought he could begin production, Waldman informed Jaffé that he was coming to Zürich in December 1961 to work with her on cuts.[56] She was in a panic, for Gross had been so preoccupied with preparing Pantheon's spring list that he had not replied to her several anguished letters asking for advice on what to do with Waldman.[57] Gross told Hull of this latest interference but asked him to restrain all "thunder," as it would only cause further delays.[58] He then asked Jaffé to join them in forming "a strong team" to circumvent Waldman, who, as usual, was evading or ignoring everyone's letters and telephone calls.[59]

Waldman showed his complete ignorance of Jung's writing style when he said Jung went "round and round the same topics, and would read better if reduced."[60] Jaffé was incensed and told Gross and Hull, who persuaded her it would be "deplorable" to let Waldman interfere, especially after all they had gone through to ensure the "purity" of the "School Years" chapter.[61] She remained steadfast, in solidarity with Gross and Hull, and Waldman retreated temporarily.

Ignoring Waldman, Hull sent Gross what he called "the absolutely 'final' changes," clarifications and refinements to the "sequence of the Jesuit experience and the phallus dream."[62] Aniela claimed to have found what Hull dryly called a "long extract from a fictive letter of 46 pp. which Jung had written to a fictive doctor in 1922, recently discovered in the Küsnacht cupboards."[63] Hull translated the text she provided and incorporated excerpts into the relevant portions of *MDR*, but he was worried because only Jung's heirs had the legal right to give permission to use documents that Jung had not specifically listed for use in *MDR*. To Hull's astonishment, Marianne Niehus said the extracts could appear exactly as he interpolated them.

Jung's letter related the Jesuit experience "much more vividly," and the phallus dream was much "less blurred." Each enhanced the other "in an entirely new way," demonstrating not only the significance of the two but, even more, "their far-reaching implications" and relationship to the experience of the Basel Cathedral. Everyone was so pleased, for this was the sort of "intervention" they had all been wanting for II: 58–70, rather than all the auntifications they had received instead.

WALDMAN CAUSED the last major disagreement that delayed publication when he decided at the last minute that the text everyone approved was too long and Collins would not pay for it.[64] Waldman wanted a minimum of 230 typed pages to be cut from the 916-page manuscript itself, as well as the entire text of the *Seven Sermons*, another 28 to 30 pages. He also sent Jaffé four pages of vague suggestions for further cuts that deprived what remained of meaning and intention. From the very beginning, Jung wanted the *Septem Sermones* (as all referred to the *Seven Sermons*) to be published as an appendix to *MDR*, and there had never been a word of disagreement because everyone took it for granted. Aniela wrote to Gross in some distress, and he sent her four pages of exceedingly careful and detailed responses.[65] In effect, his letter is an outline of what the book became, as he addressed each point she raised in response to Waldman's demands.

Gross assured her that Pantheon would go along with Waldman's request for cuts only if they did not conflict with "the text that Jung wrote himself as the expression of his religious or 'philosophical' thoughts [inner world]." He accepted Waldman's assertion that the general reader would not understand the Jungian terminology that appeared throughout the text and asked Jaffé to write "An Introduction to the Conceptual World of C. G. Jung," a short essay that could be printed at the beginning of the book. He quoted a long extract from Hull, which best expressed what they both thought:

> Jung detested hard-and-fast definitions because the psychological facts they referred to were still far from having been adequately investigated. This is an important point: there is definition-mania, or idolatry of the word, whose sole effect is to breed fanatical orthodoxies, deviations and heresies (cf. the history of Catholicism, Communism, and the Freudian movement!). To append anything of this sort to the *Vita* would seem to me highly inappropriate; and as for Jung's "conceptual world," he has made it plain enough on every page of the book.

Aniela proved herself equal to the task of writing such an essay but unequal to precision and brevity; deadlines came and went, her pages multiplied, and nothing was resolved. Gross eventually allowed Waldman to win this round: there was no essay, only Jaffé's concise glossary of terms.[66]

Gross's most surprising concession was to agree that the *Seven Sermons* could be eliminated from the English-language edition without otherwise harming the book. He agreed it would not only "improve the length," but would also "eliminate a difficult tract that is bound to confuse the average educated reader."[67] Aniela was dead set against it. "I bet you will regret it one day," she wrote. "I regret it because the whole story of its coming into being is told so that the reader gets very curious to see it and it is the only piece of poetry which Jung himself gave the permission to publish. If you leave it out an important side of Jung is missing." Perhaps hoping to change his mind, she said she would "keep it of course for the German edition."[68]

When Waldman insisted upon further cuts that showed complete disregard for the continuity of what remained, Jaffé felt she had to define her "standpoint (in general)": that it was much easier to eliminate entire rather than partial chapters. Eventually Waldman persuaded Gross to eliminate such passages as those about Jung's friendships with Vischer and Oeri, their sailing trips on the lake, and the detailed description of how he built the Bollingen Tower. Here again, Jaffé retained them in the German. Gross did not initially agree with Waldman to eliminate Jung's friendship with Richard Wilhelm or the pages of text taken from *The Red Book*, but later he allowed the Wilhelm text to be severely reduced, *The Red Book* to be eliminated entirely, and "Zimmer" and several other texts to be cut, all of which were retained in full in the German edition. These divergences between the texts in the two languages subsequently caused the exact sort of speculation about censorship and textual interference that everyone involved hoped to avoid. Scholars exchanged charges and countercharges from the moment both were published.[69]

This process dragged on and on, as Waldman blandly concentrated on reaching a six-hundred-page manuscript. Jaffé felt that Gross had betrayed and abandoned her, for he did appear to be giving in time after time. A major example (and a painful one for Jaffé) was the reduction to a capsule description Jung's experiences at the Taj Mahal and Sanchi, turning points in his life. She refused to accept Gross's excision until she learned they would appear in their full context within the year in a forthcoming volume of the *Collected Works*.[70]

At that moment, "the full irony" of the mess Waldman created struck Hull. Hull actually counted up the cuts Waldman demanded and found they came to a total of 96, not 230 pages. He had instigated negotiations that consumed everyone's energy for almost four months, and the only result was the "negative achievement" of delaying the book by a minimum of "six months." "I do rather wonder," Hull asked, if Waldman ever realized that "the 'Waldman mountain' has laboured and given birth to a mouse!"[71]

Waldman took advantage of Jaffé's nervousness and continued to play one party off against the other.[72] In a state of mental confusion and physical exhaustion, she resigned herself to powerlessness and told Gross to do whatever he wanted.[73] She also suggested that he allow Hull, who had been so kind and considerate when they shaped the text together, to become the final "objectifier." Hull told her he wished he could be a "catalyst," but he thought such a desire might be too optimistic, given the situation with Waldman.[74] Actually, Hull was all that and more. He told Gross he had been so moved by Aniela's plight that he sent her an immensely soothing letter full of suggestions for positive compromises she might make.

By the end of January 1962, Gross set a firm "dead end"[75] (as Aniela described his deadline for final text), with which she then complied. He urged everyone to ignore Waldman and to "cut the griping and simply move along with the very small amount of work that remain[ed] to be done."[76] Despite Gross's best efforts, negotiations continued for the better part of 1962, postponing publication until the spring of 1963.

In the end, Gross and Jaffé won out over Waldman, for they retained almost all of what they agreed was crucial. Compromises condensed Jung's travels into one chapter rather than five.[77] The account of how he built the Bollingen Tower was left mostly as he wrote it.[78] The troublesome "Encounters" chapter became a brief account of some friendships and assessments of personalities, either incorporated into other chapters or as separate appendices. They went to press with only one lasting disagreement: Aniela insisted on capitalizing the pronoun "He" for God or Christ, while they wanted it in lower case.

Jaffé asked Gross if he would pay for a trip to Mallorca so that she and Hull could save valuable time by copy-editing the final manuscript in person rather than by mail. He agreed, and told Hull his would be "the final stamp" on the book, adding, "But that is as the old man would have it, I am sure."[79]

GROSS LEFT Pantheon in September 1962, and his assistant, Sara (Golden) Blackburn, dealt even more firmly than he with all the others as she saw the book into print. In his last weeks with the firm, Gross had to deal with a hurdle that no one had envisioned. No one could resolve it, and it has done much in the years since *MDR* was published to fuel the many charges of textual interference. Aniela, through the lawyer Bernhard Peyer, asked for the return of all the manuscripts that had accumulated since 1957. She specifically asked for her handwritten notes of the *Protocols*, Jung's original manuscript, and the Winston typescript with his and Hull's notations. A flurry of correspondence ensued, as Gross contacted everyone from the Wolffs in Locarno and Wolfgang Sauerlander (now with the Bollingen Foundation) to Kyrill Schabert at Pantheon and everyone else who had worked on the book, down to the lowliest typesetter.

"I myself have heard about these papers, but I have never seen them," Gross eventually wrote to Peyer in early September.[80] He was sure none had been in Pantheon's offices during the years he was responsible for the book. By the end of the month, he had returned all the documents in his office to those who had claims of intellectual property rights upon them, and the only materials left were Jaffé's "corrected galleys,"[81] which he planned to send her as soon as the book was in print. Gross achieved his aim and Pantheon's offices were picked clean of Jungiana by the time he left, but questions remain about what happened to the many different versions of the manuscripts. Many of these documents were kept by private persons who may or may not have had the right to take them; others were deposited into private archives and scholarly libraries, here again by persons whose claims may have been dubious as well as by those whose ownership was legitimate. Full or partial copies surface from time to time, as did an almost-print-ready typescript, sold by an unnamed person to a private book dealer, who in turn sold it to a benefactor of the Countway Medical Library at Harvard, where it has since been used to fuel many scholarly fires.[82] All these versions add pieces to the ongoing puzzle of just exactly what Jung's "so-called autobiography" (to use his words) was, is, or should be.

MEMORIES, DREAMS, Reflections was a tremendous success when it was finally published six years after its inception. It has remained in print ever since and has been widely credited by many distinguished analysts as the inspiration for their careers, among them Anthony Stevens and Anthony Storr. Adam Phillips, Freud's "iconoclastic" editor, called it the book that inspired him to become an analyst.[83] There are so many others, ordinary citizens all, who never had a Jungian analysis and never read much, if any, of Jung's other writings, but who praise the beauty of this book and its influence on their lives in language that is lyrical and deeply moving.

Jung's term, however, that it is his "so-called autobiography," should not be interpreted as entirely self-deprecating. As Hull and the many others who worked on the book noted, Jung was of two minds about it. Great parts of it do depend on whether he was No. 1 or No. 2 when writing. Unfortunately, there were far too many others who wanted to "help" Jung write his book and thus did much to blur the line between the two aspects of his personality. Fortunately there were still others who fought to "let the old man say" what he wanted to say. From Kurt Wolff to Gerry Gross and Richard Hull, and — finally, yes — to Aniela Jaffé, all are entitled to the self-congratulatory pat on the back Hull suggested he and Gross give themselves because nobody else would do it for them.

"Strictly speaking," wrote Gerhard Adler when he read and reviewed *MDR*, "it is no autobiography at all but the report of his encounters with the inner world of the psyche."[84] Adler's review set the terms for the reviews and debates that followed, most of them concentrating on the "inner" versus the "outer," and what role each played in Jung's script.

In almost every version of a *Protocol*, manuscript, or typescript of what the book eventually became, Jung himself tried to explain what he intended this book to show, but one of the best descriptions comes from one of the earliest-known *Protocols*:[85]

I simply am someone who cannot be made to fit into the ordinary schema, and that is the meaning of my life. . . . What I am describing is a fact: it is me.[86]

He would not structure his story to satisfy an unknown reader, but only to satisfy himself, its creator. Whether his stories were true would not be a "problem" for him, because all he wanted, he wrote, was to tell "my fable, my truth."[87]

For Carl Gustav Jung, "life was something that had to be lived and not talked about."[88] This he did, and on his own terms and in his own time.

Appendix: The Honegger Papers

For many years, the paper Honegger delivered at the 1910 Nuremberg congress was assumed lost, so knowledge of its content came from the abstract printed in the 1910 *Jahrbuch*. With the release of the so-called Honegger Papers relating to the Schwyzer case, a fifteen-page paper bearing the same title as the abstract has been identified. As its form and content correspond to the abstract, the assumption is that it is a fairly final draft, if not the actual paper itself. Until or unless other examples of Honegger's writing are found, both the *Jahrbuch* abstract and the expanded paper must be considered Honegger's only contribution to the literature of psychoanalysis.

In 1911, Jung collected what have since come to be called the Honegger Papers,[1] but he never specified what he actually found or where he found them (whether, for example, they were at Honegger's mother's house, in his Klinik Rheinau rooms, or in Helene Widmer's possession). Jung also never explained how or why the persons legally entitled to possess the documents (the Honegger or Schwyzer heirs or the Burghölzli officials) surrendered them so easily, thus leaving what he chose to reveal of their content to his discretion. Jung kept the papers until the early 1930s, when he gave them to Dr. C. A. Meier, then a young physician on the Burghölzli staff who was treating Schwyzer and was interested in writing a book about his extraordinarily long case history (Schwyzer did not die until 1937).[2] Meier never wrote the book, but he kept the papers until 1981, when he gave them to the Swiss Federal Institute of Technology (ETH) in Zürich.[3]

In the early 1990s, William McGuire, executive editor of Jung's *Collected Works*, asked for and received a copy of the Honegger Papers from the ETH to use in connection with his work.[4] When McGuire was finished, he donated his copy to the Library of Congress. At this point controversy arose. The ETH papers had been sequestered ever since Meier donated them, primarily because of two unsettled issues: ownership of the physical document and, by extension, the copyright; and the question of the possible violation of doctor-patient confidentiality. When Dr. Beat Glaus, then director of the ETH Manuscript Division, became aware that a copy had been given to McGuire and was now outside his jurisdiction, he feared possible legal ramifications under Swiss law and ordered its return. Refusing to become involved in a question of disputed ownership, the Library of Congress surrendered its copy in compliance with Glaus's directive. The *Erbengemeinschaft C. G. Jung,* the committee of Jung's heirs, then claimed ownership and formally jricted the papers until all the legal issues were resolved.[5] Sometime in the 1990s, the Jung heirs engaged an "expert,"[6] about whom they refused to be more specific and whom they declined to identify. This person completed his findings in late 2001, when he declared that Schwyzer had no known heirs, and neither did Honegger, so "ownership" of the physical documents now resides with the Jung heirs. At the same time, officials representing the Burghölzli agreed that since Schwyzer died in 1937, the issue of patient confidentiality was moot. All parties agreed that final authority for the use of the papers rests with the current director of the ETH Research Library, Dr. Rudolf Mumenthaler, who declared them henceforth open and available to qualified scholars.

The "expert" left several crucial questions unanswered concerning the more than 350 pages of testimony by and about Emile Schwyzer.[7] The most important is who actually wrote them. He did not engage a handwriting expert, so the identities of the copyists can only be guessed at, even though some of the writing is similar to that of Maria Moltzer, Gertrud and Emma Jung, and Helene Widmer.[8]

The papers themselves fall into two distinct sections. The first is a long chronology of the patient's history, based on reports from his prior incarcerations and the daily assessments of various doctors in the Burghölzli. It also includes Schwyzer's dreams, fantasies, and hallucinations, plus six to eight pages of Swiss shorthand in at least two different hands. One may be Schwyzer's own record of his delusions, as he boasted of his shorthand prowess; the second shorthand scribe remains unidentified.[9] The second section of the papers is probably in Honegger's handwriting, for it resembles entries he made in Schwyzer's daily case history when he was on the Burghölzli staff. This section also includes Honegger's attempt toward a dissertation and the draft of his Nuremberg paper.

Dating the documents presents difficulties similar to determining the scribes. In the first section, some entries are preceded by dates, beginning with the last days of December 1909 and ending with February 1910 — the exact period when Honegger made his observations. After the approximately 200 pages of Schwyzer's history and commentary, the remaining 150 or so become mostly observations by one or more analysts. Honegger's handwriting is there, as is Jung's, thus raising the question of the degree of each man's involvement.[10]

The *Jahrbuch* abstract, which was probably written by Otto Rank, summarizes the Nuremberg paper's content in succinct, scholarly language that is very different from the paper itself. The abstract begins with the case of a former store clerk, unnamed but obviously Schwyzer, who was without formal education but who nevertheless envisioned a "whole series of ancient mythological and philosophical ideas."[11] Among these were:

> the idea of the rebirth of the world, the *aequivoca generatio*, the complete identification of the universe with God (i.e., with the patient), the idea of self-incubation (phoenix and scarab myth), the idea that the deity was originally feminine (Near Eastern mother cult), the moon as seed preserver (Asiatic mythology), the translation of the dead into stars in heaven, a variation of the transmigration of souls, a modification of the vampire legend.

Schwyzer is called "the patient" throughout the abstract as well as in the paper. Although he is aware that the earth is round, he insists upon reverting to the "Ptolemaic system: i.e., the earth is flat and surrounded by infinite seas."

The abstract lists two forms of the patient's thinking: "(1) the symbolic-mythological, the dream thinking; (2) the dialectical . . . understood as a mental exercise in compensation for symbolic thinking." It concludes that the patient's "autochthonous [i.e., indigenous] revival of ancient myths, philosophical ideas and theories of the world represents a regression that goes back not only to the individual's childhood but also to that of the whole human race." And because of the many correspondences between "the dream system and the delusional system," the abstract credits Honegger with an assertion that "even the apparently most unreasonable psychotic ideas are completely capable of analysis, if we do not wish value judgments to excuse us from the analytical work." The abstract ends by promising that "a detailed exposition of the case will soon appear in this yearbook." Whether it was to be by Honegger or Jung is not specified.

The actual paper differs greatly from the abstract. Honegger began his fifteen-page presentation with an obligatory homage to Bleuler for permitting him to spend two months concentrating on the Schwyzer case. Next, he thanked Jung, his "admired teacher," but crossed out the phrase, so it is not known if he spoke it. He explained that, for reasons of time, he would omit a detailed depiction of how paranoid dementia developed but would offer his own observations as a contribution to enrich the understanding of the illness's onset and progression. Honegger crossed out the following passage but still followed its methodology in his presentation:

> *I will try to fit together the fragments which I gathered here and there in the analysis, to collect everything that belongs to one theme, and thus present to you the entire delusional system if possible in the patient's own words, as if he himself*

had written them down as a unified whole so that it now stands before us like the work of a poet, like a coherent epic.[12]

He distinguished between the "fantastic creations" of hysterics, who "tend to tell us nicely composed, coherent stories in order to thereby gain our interest, our love," and dementia praecox, which "does not try to gain our favor: if it wants to reveal to us something of its inner beauty, this happens reluctantly, in broken-off sentences, incomprehensible chunks, with constant digressions from the subject." He struggled to give the patient's fragmentary, discursive ramblings "an order, to group them, in one word . . . to give the formations of dementia praecox the beauty of a hysterical fantasy." He vowed to "present . . . a quite coherent epic: *Of the Origin and the End of the World, of the Eternal Rebirth, of a God and of [word unclear] Devils, of one God's Omnipotence and Impotence, and of the Miracles of Heaven and Earth*" (Honegger's emphasis).

At this point, the paper shows a decided shift: Honegger glides into a first-person oration in which he speaks in the voice of the patient, occasionally veering into the third person to comment on the testimony he has just presented. In both voices, his medical objectivity is blurred and his arguments are specious. One example concerns the patient's actual delusion, which he recorded as "I am actually the Lord, I have the corpus, the basic semen-substance, the guiding semen, the ur-substance, through which everything has come into being and has life." Because Schwyzer's version "does not sound quite as poetic," he interjects the Gospel of John ("In the beginning was the word and the word was with God and God was the word").

This sort of internal dialectic continues for the next ten pages or so in a text that ranges from the lame and laconic to the obvious and only rarely astute. Then Honegger shifts the focus to those of Schwyzer's delusions relating to forms of transformation, such as "the notion of the transmigration of souls," or "when humans become animals." He argues that such delusions are frequently connected with "wish fulfillment, either as reward or punishment" and that these "degenerative progressions . . . serve the purpose of creating a compensation for the former life."

Using Schwyzer's self-appellation, "the Lord," Honegger describes how "the Lord also pleases himself in the enjoyment of his omnipotence," a veiled reference to the frequent masturbatory delusions that dot the text and culminate in various versions of the same one: "In his free time, he makes sun-experiments," and, by extension, "he makes the weather."

Honegger then melds all the many accounts Schwyzer told him during their two months of conversations into one description, relating it in a combination of his own words and Schwyzer's description of how he made these "sun-experiments" happen. As "the Lord," he had a duty to make the weather, and he described his technique for making the sun jump: he would close his right eye (the one unaffected by the shooting) and fix the left one (the strabismic eye) upon the sun. By using his "cosmic eye" (his term for the damaged left one), he could make the sun jump, become elongated, or pull apart. What Honegger found most important was Schwyzer's contention that he could "put an upward tail on it." Honegger does not specify whether he means to suggest Schwyzer's literal masturbation, but he describes how, whenever the patient moved this "upward tail" back and forth, especially in rhythm to music, he would conclude triumphantly, "that's how the wind is made." Honegger recorded that Schwyzer enjoyed making the sun "dance," for he thought it "a game that is very delightful with regular lights" and one in which he found the same satisfying image of the sun's "upward tail."

The delusions that Honegger recorded over the two months he concentrated on Emile Schwyzer's case were certainly the patient's, but the language in which he reported them to the audience in Nuremberg was his. Of the many times Schwyzer described how he "made the weather" or "made the sun dance," the one that comes closest to how Honegger reported it in Nuremberg occurred on February 17, 1910. On that day, Honegger recorded Schwyzer's testimony as follows:

> The brain must be squeezed together onto the eye. I have to sway my head back and forth for the shine to arise. I screw up my eye, but through the small opening I see the shine move back and forth. Sun, moon, and stars make the movement that I want.

Honegger then listed other references to parallel delusions, among which were some of Schreber's,[13] Wilhelm Busch's legend of the rays from which St. Anthony (in the desert) hangs his cap, and the children's fairy tales in which the sun is always a woman with golden hair. He followed these with several more pages of Schwyzer's delusions. They end abruptly with a brief, dismissive sentence in which he states his intention to prove all his theories "in a more detailed paper," but the section concludes with the incomplete remark that he "still has to consider another way of thinking, which constitutes a necessary supplement to the so far [word indecipherable] mytholog [*sic*]."[14] If he wrote such a paper, it has not yet been found.

True, hindsight is always perfect and a dangerous tool to use, but as the passages noted above deal with material that resonates with correspondences from Honegger's life, they cannot be ignored. "We know," Honegger begins one such, "from our psychoanalytical experience that a suicidal tendency doesn't always express itself consciously very often expresses itself unconsciously that it is rather those accidents that threaten our health or our life for which from a lack of causal thinking one . . ." This rambling, unpunctuated passage not only ends abruptly, but Honegger also strikes it out and follows it with a single sentence: "We learn that his [Schwyzer's] suicidal tendency already expressed itself earlier in a series of accidents." Honegger himself was, in the last several years of his life, prone to cuts, burns, and bruises that he laughed off as signs of clumsiness, or accidents that he insisted happened only because he was tired and over-worked.[15]

Honegger's mother disliked Helene Widmer intensely and supported his desire to end the engagement. A bit further down the page described above, he wrote:

> Our conjecture that the homosexual orientation of the libido came about because of a strong infatuation with the mother, as psychoanalytical experi-ence has shown in almost all cases so far, is confirmed when we learn that he was his mother's favorite son, still loves her tenderly now and that she plays an important role in his hallucinations and delusions as we will see.

Honegger allowed this passage to stand, but the remainder of the text drifts into a discussion of psychosis:

> In the beginning of the psychosis the normal self is overwhelmed but from now on tells the dominating self, that is reluctant to adjust, the un-varnished truth, it performs a direct analysis of it [several unclear refer-ents in German]. For example it tells it directly: you are too lazy to adjust, your whole psychosis is nothing but laziness. The deeper purpose of this direct introspection becomes [no punctuation or conclusion]. The same a similar degree of direct introspection can be perceived in himself by the person who knows psychoanalysis when he remembers his dream in the light half slumber before waking.

This passage, too, is crossed out and followed by a simple declarative sentence: "He then often succeeds surprisingly quickly at interpreting his dream." Several pages later, there is an attempt by someone other than Honegger (probably Jung) to organize what has just been described above into a coherent paper. These pages also end abruptly.

Honegger's role in formulating the collective unconscious sparked debate throughout Jung's life, even toward the end of it, in 1959 in a series of letters in the British magazine *The Listener.* Jung's British follower Dr. E. A. Bennet was prompted to rush to his defense. Bennet sent a number of his own questions to Jung and passed along some from R. F. C. Hull, who was then preparing En-glish translations for what became the *Collected Works.*[16] Bennet suggested that, as Jung had told him the Honegger Papers were in Hull's possession, Hull should check them for references to the solar phallus. Not knowing of the pro-fessional history between Jung and Honegger, Hull asked Jung if his references to Honegger might have been "a factual error, or that Honegger made use of [Jung's] observation." Jung was seriously ill at the time, and if he replied, his letter has not been found. Bennet's letter in *The Listener*[17] was directed to a reader who claimed Jung had appropriated Honegger's research as his own:

Nothing of the kind took place. Dr. Honegger, then a very young doctor and a pupil of Jung's, was told of the incident by Jung, who suggested, out of kindness, that he might investigate the matter further and publish a paper on the subject. Jung passed on to Honegger his own observations. Unfortunately, Dr. Honegger fell ill and died soon after and the paper was never completed.

Jung did not reply directly to Bennet, because he suffered another of the cardiac incidents that plagued the last decade of his life. On January 6, 1960, his secretary replied for him, saying Jung had read the published letter in *The Listener* and wanted her to tell Bennet, *"ja, in ordnung,"* that all was correct and quite okay. In retrospect, Bennet's letter solved nothing and became just another marker along the disputed boundary line of the argument.

Notes

Works frequently cited in the notes are identified by the following abbreviations:

CL   *C. G. Jung Letters*, selected and edited by Gerhard Adler in collaboration with Aniela Jaffé, trans. R. F. C. Hull, 2 vols. (vol. 1: 1906–1950; vol. 2: 1951–1961), Bollingen Series 95.1 and 95.2 (Princeton: Princeton Univ. Press, 1973 and 1991).

CW   *The Collected Works of C. G. Jung*, edited by Sir Herbert Read, Michael Fordham, Gerhard Adler, and William McGuire as executive editor, trans. R. F. C. Hull, 20 vols., Bollingen Series 20 (Princeton: Princeton Univ. Press).

ETG   *Erinnerungen, Träume, Gedanken von C. G. Jung*, aufgezeichnet und herausgegeben von Aniela Jaffé (Olten: Walter-Verlag, 1971).

F/Abraham   *The Letters of Sigmund Freud and Karl Abraham, 1907–1926*, ed. Hilda C. Abraham and Ernst L. Freud, trans. Bernard Marsh and Hilda C. Abraham (New York: Basic Books, 1965).

F/Ferenczi   *The Correspondence of Sigmund Freud and Sandor Ferenczi*, vol. 1, *1908–1914*, ed. Eva Brabant, Ernst Falzeder, and Patricia Giampieri-Deutsch, trans. Peter T. Hoffer (Cambridge, Mass., and London: The Belknap Press of Harvard Univ. Press, 1993).

F/J   *The Freud/Jung Letters: The Correspondence Between Sigmund Freud and C. G. Jung*, ed. William McGuire, trans. Ralph Manheim and R. F. C. Hull, Bollingen Series 94 (Princeton: Princeton Univ. Press, 1974).

F/Jones   *The Complete Correspondence of Sigmund Freud and Ernest Jones, 1908–1939*, ed. R. Andrew Paskauskas (Cambridge, Mass., and London: The Belknap Press of Harvard Univ. Press, 1993).

F/Pfister   *Psychoanalysis and Faith: The Letters of Sigmund Freud and Oskar Pfister,* ed. Heinrich Meng and Ernst L. Freud, trans. Eric Mosbacher (New York: Basic Books, 1963).

GW   *Die gesammelten Werke von C. G. Jung,* ed. Marianne Niehus-Jung, Lena Hurwitz-Eisner, Franz Riklin Jr., Lilly Jung-Merker, and Elisabeth Rüf (Zürich: Rascher Verlag, 1958–70; Olten: Walter Verlag, 1971–).

J/Pauli   *Atom and Archetype: The Pauli-Jung Letters, 1932–1958,* ed. C. A. Meier, trans. David Roscoe (Princeton: Princeton Univ. Press, 2001).

MDR   *Memories, Dreams, Reflections by C. G. Jung,* recorded and edited by Aniela Jaffé, trans. Richard and Clara Winston (New York: Vintage Books, 1989).

SE   *The Standard Edition of the Complete Psychological Works of Sigmund Freud,* 24 vols., ed. James Strachey et al. (New York: W. W. Norton, 2000).

Manuscript collections frequently cited are identified by the following abbreviations:

BA   Burghölzli Archives
ETH   Eidgenössische Technische Hochschule (Swiss Federal Institute of Technology)
HCL   Francis A. Countway Library, Harvard University
HE/STA   Henri Ellenberger, Institute Ste.-Anne, Paris
HW/BLY   Helen Wolff Archives, Beinecke Library, Yale University
KML   Kristine Mann Library, C. G. Jung Center of New York
LC   Library of Congress

INTRODUCTION: FAINT CLEWS AND INDIRECTIONS
1. *CL-2,* pp. 452–53.
2. See chapter 38 and the Epilogue for a full discussion of CGJ's autobiography.
3. CGJ to E. A. Bennet, September 15, 1956, ETH.
4. CGJ to E. A. Bennet, December 10, 1956, ETH.
5. *MDR,* Prologue, pp. 3–5.
6. CGJ to Kurt Wolff, June 17, 1958, in reply to Wolff's of June 3, HW/BLY.
7. All terms will be fully explained in their appropriate context within the biography.
8. These two were Drs. E. A. Bennet and H. L. Philp. Quote is CGJ to E. A. Bennet, October 10, 1956, ETH.
9. CGJ to Cary F. Baynes, August 4, 1954, ETH.
10. *MDR* retained this working title as late as October 1957, when Kurt Wolff wrote to Jung's eventual collaborator, Aniela Jaffé, setting out terms for a contract, HW/BLY.
11. E. A. Bennet to CGJ, December 7, 1956, ETH.

CHAPTER 1: HOW THE JUNGS BECAME SWISS
1. The Antistes, the approximate equivalent of a Protestant bishop, was elected by his peers.
2. German uses titles more precisely than English does, with multiple designations such as Dr. Med., Dr. Phil., or Dr. Jur. Carl Gustav I Jung's first name is spelled both Carl and Karl in the archival documents, but I follow the Jung family preference, Carl. CGJ was christened Karl Gustav II Jung, and he used the old spelling until he graduated from the University of Basel.
3. Recent German scholarship has paid no attention to either Carl Gustav I's or CGJ's contention of possible paternity. Professor Theodore Ziolkowski wrote in a letter to William McGuire, January 21, 1998: "In sum, I think it's safe to say that Goethe scholarship has not been at all interested in the paternity rumor, which seems to be

confined to the Jungian side of the equation." Professor Ziolkowski also provided the following references: *Das Goethebild des 20. Jahrhunderts* (1966), the standard biographies of Goethe by Karl Otto Conrady (German: 1982) and Nicholas Boyle (English: 1991), and K. R. Mandelkow's *Goethe in Deutschland*, vol. 2 (1919–82). Carl Gustav I Jung did have a lifelong friendship with Charlotte Kestner, niece of Goethe's "Lotte" (the Lotte of *Werther*), who settled in Basel in the last years of her life, reputedly because of this friendship.

4. In several family registers his first name is given as Simon, not Carl. CGJ gives his date of death as 1654 in *MDR* but 1645 in the *Protocols*. The genealogy of the Jung family can be traced only partially because the municipal archives of Mainz were destroyed by French siege in 1688. I have used interviews with CGJ's children and grandchildren and the following texts: the *Familienbuch* of the Jung family, a parchment-bound folio containing old letters and documents; *Historisch-Biographisches Lexicon der Schweiz*, vol. 4 (Neuenberg: Historisch-Biographischen Lexicons der Schweiz, 1927); *Aus den Tagebüchern meines Vaters* (Diary of C. G. I Jung), edited by his son Ernst Jung, O.J. (Winterthur, 1910); a Jung family genealogy commissioned by CGJ between 1928 and 1929; two articles by M. H. Koelbing, both in *Basler Nachrichten*, "How Carl Gustav [I] Jung Became a Professor in Basel," September 26, 1954, and "C. G. Jung's Ancestors from Basel," July 24, 1955; two articles by Aniela Jaffé, "Einiges über C. G. Jungs Familie von Aniela Jaffé," trans. as "Some Facts About the Family of C. G. Jung," found only in *ETG* (the German edition of *MDR*), pp. 399–407, and, in slightly different form, "Details About CGJ's Family," *Spring* (1984): 35–43; Aniela Jaffé, ed., *Word and Image*, Bollingen Series 97.2 (Princeton: Princeton Univ. Press, 1979); records relating to the Jung and Preiswerk families in the Staatsarchiv Des Kantons Basel-Stadt, the Schweizerische Eidgenossenschaft Kanton Basel-Stadt, the Psychiatrische Universitätsklinik Basel, the Gemeinderat Küsnacht (Zürich), and the Evangelisch-reformierte Kirchgemeinde Kleinhünigen; "Ein paar Jugenderinnerungen," by Albert Oeri, in *Festschrift zum 60. Geburtstag von C. G. J. herausgegeben vom Psychologischen Club Zürich* (Berlin: Springer Verlag, 1935), trans. and rev. as "Some Youthful Memories," in *CGJ Speaking*, ed. William McGuire and R. F. C. Hull, Bollingen Series 97 (Princeton: Princeton Univ. Press, 1977), and in *Spring* (1970); Henri Ellenberger, *The Discovery of the Unconscious: The History and Evolution of Dynamic Psychiatry* (New York: Basic Books, 1970), pp. 657–748; *CGJ's Medium: Die Geschichte der Helly Preiswerk*, by Stephanie Zumstein-Preiswerk (Munich: Kindler Verlag Gmbh, 1975); "Erinnerungen an Carl Gustav Jung aus der Studentenzeit," *Basler Stadtbuch* (1965): 117–63, by Gustav Steiner; and *Analytical Psychology: Notes on the Seminar Given in 1925*, ed. William McGuire, Bollingen Series 99 (Princeton: Princeton Univ. Press, 1989).

5. Swiss custom is to affix the woman's maiden name to her marital surname. She is called Maria Josepha Jung-Ziegler by Eduard His in *Basler gelehrte des 19. Jahrhunderts* (Basel: Benno Schwabe, 1941), pp. 69–76. His also writes of the "mystery of [Carl Gustav I's] origin: the date of his birth is contested. He himself claimed September 7, 1794; the *Basler Bürgerfamilienbuch* cites September 7, 1793, and official documents of a later date say September 7, 1795. The probable date is 1794" (author's translation).

6. Their descendants believe the marriage was an unhappy one. See CGJ's letters to his cousin, Dr. Med. Ewald Jung (M.D., psychiatrist in Bern, secretary of the psychoanalytical group founded on Jung's initiative in Zürich, 1910), *CL*-1 and 2, pp. 192–93 and 527–29 resp. CGJ also describes Sophie Ziegler and her sister as "lively artistic personalities" who were highly involved with the Mannheim Theatre. He posits

the possibility that Sophie has been confused in history with Marianne von Willemer, a friend of Goethe's whose maiden name was Jung but who was not related to his family (see *Marianne und Johann Jakob Willemer: Briefwechsel mit Goethe: Dokumente, Lebens-Chronik, Erläuterungen*, herausgegeben von Hans-J. Weitz [Frankfurt am Main: Insel-Verlag, 1965], esp. pp. 534, 540, and index, pp. 770–71). In one of the *Protocols* (private archive), CGJ says that Sophie Ziegler-Jung suffered from depression and it was generally assumed that her son, Carl Gustav, was by Goethe. He states that although his great-grandfather never mentioned it, "it was not impossible." However, Zumstein-Preiswerk, *CGJ's Medium*, pp. 116–17, notes that Marianne Jung was ten years old at the time of Carl Gustav I's birth. Zumstein-Preiswerk also provides a detailed appendix that is at times opinionated and sharply critical of CGJ: "Investigation of CGJ's Goethe Legend," pp. 113–19. Richard Friedenthal, in *Goethe: His Life and Times* (London: Weidenfeld and Nicholson, 1963), p. 436, writes that Marianne Jung's "origins are obscure; her father is unknown, the date of her birth doubtful, and even the name of Jung was a stage name taken by her mother." See also F. X. Charet, *Spiritualism and the Foundations of CGJ's Psychology* (Albany: State Univ. of New York Press, 1993), p. 85, n. 38; *F/J*, June 17, 1910, p. 329, n. 4; Ernest Jones, *The Life and Work of Sigmund Freud* (London: Hogarth Press, 1955), 2: 72, and *Free Associations: Memories of a Psychoanalyst* (London: Hogarth Press, 1959), p. 165.

7. See "The Story of Helene Preiswerk," in *Beyond the Unconscious: Essays of Henri Ellenberger*, ed. Mark S. Micale (Princeton: Princeton Univ. Press, 1993), esp. p. 299.

8. Hugo Kurz, *Carl Gustav Jung: Aus seinem Leben und über die Gründung des Anatomischen Museums Basel* (Basel: Anatomisches Institut der Universität Basel, 1994), 5: 27.

9. CGJ to M. H. Koelbing, October 27, 1954. Not in *CL*, original in Bibliothek Medizinhistorisches Institut und Museum, ETH. See also "C. G. Jungs Basler Verfahren," *Basler Nachrichten, Sonntagsblatt*, 49, no. 29, July 24, 1955.

10. Eduard His, *Basler gelehrte*.

11. CGJ describes Schleiermacher in the Koelbing letter as acting like his grandfather's "godfather" (October 27, 1954).

12. Henry Garland and Mary Garland, eds., *The Oxford Companion to German Literature* (Oxford and New York: Oxford Univ. Press, 1986), p. 799. In *CL-2*, p. 115, n. 2, editors describe his writings as being noted for their "combination of deep religiosity, clear intellect, and vivid sense of reality."

13. Sigismund von Jung (1745–1824) became a member of the nobility when he was chancellor of Bavaria.

14. In CGJ to M. H. Koelbing, October 27, 1954, CGJ says he retained his grandfather's "black-red-gold" banner *(schwarz-rot-goldenes Band)* denoting membership in this student group.

15. At the time of his death, von Kotzebue (1765–1819) was an agent in the Russian Foreign Service in Germany, a political informant to Tsar Alexander I. Karl Ludwig Sand (1795–1820), a theology student and member of the Burschenschaft at Jena and one of the founders of the Wartburgfest, was executed in Mannheim for the crime.

16. Jung languished in prison for thirteen months, during which the popular press described the hammer as a vicious pick-ax. In CGJ to M. H. Koelbing, October 27, 1954, he stresses that it was a "geological hammer."

17. CGJ to M. H. Koelbing, September 16, 1954, not in *CL*, original in Bibliothek Medizinhistorisches Institut und Museum, ETH.

18. For the role von Humboldt played in the reformation of Basel University, see Carl E. Schorske, "Burckhardt's Basel," in *Thinking with History: Explorations in the Passage to Modernism* (Princeton: Princeton Univ. Press, 1998), pp. 58–59.

19. Aniela Jaffé recorded it as such in the *Protocols.* CGJ repeated it in CGJ to M. H. Koelbing, October 27, 1954.

20. CGJ to M. H. Koelbing, October 27, 1954.

21. In CGJ to M. H. Koelbing, October 27, 1954, CGJ writes that he possessed von Humboldt's original letter of recommendation to Bürgermeister Wieland of Basel.

22. Hermann Reimer, German physician and psychiatrist and son of the Berlin book publisher in whose house Carl Gustav I lived as a student. Hermann became Carl Gustav I's son-in-law by marrying Anna, his surviving daughter by his first wife, Virginie de Lassaulx. CGJ visited Dr. Med. and Frau Dr. Reimer-Jung in Stuttgart in 1900, *ETG,* p. 118 and n. 402; *MDR,* p. 110.

23. Ernst Jung, *Aus den Tagebüchern,* gives her name as Virginie de l'Assault.

24. Kurz, *CGJ,* p. 8. Other letter writers were Gilbert Brechet, professor of anatomy and surgery in Paris; Leopold Gmelin, professor of chemistry in Heidelberg; and Franz Karl Naegele, a Heidelberg *Geburtshelfer* (obstetrician).

25. Schorske, "Burckhardt's Basel," p. 60, writes that "Basel fished in the troubled waters, winning a fine catch of front-rank academic talent" of liberal professors who fled government repression in the post-Napoleonic era, including Karl Follen, who later went to Harvard and founded German studies.

26. Schorske, "Burckhardt's Basel," p. 56.

27. "Basel," by Lionel Gossman, in *Geneva, Zurich, Basel: History, Culture and National Identity* (Princeton: Princeton Univ. Press, 1994), pp. 71–72. Gossman adds that Basel admitted so many political refugees from Germany and Austria that the city was considered by these respective governments "as a dangerous nest of liberals and revolutionaries." The most famous refugee at the time was the theologian Wilhelm de Wette, both disciple and friend of Schleiermacher and, later, of Carl Gustav I Jung.

28. Gossman, "Basel," pp. 73 and 89, quoting Heinrich Treitschke's *Briefe,* ed. Max Cornelius (Leipzig: S. Hirzel, 1914–20), letter to Overbeck, October 28, 1873, 3:375.

29. Daniel Burckhardt-Werthemann, *Bilder und Stimmen aus dem verschwundenen Basel* (Basel: Basel Reinhardt, 1946); *Hauser und Gestalten aus Basels Vergangenheit* (Basel: Basel Reinhardt, 1925); and *Vom alten Basel und seinen Gästen* (Basel: Basel Reinhardt, 1948); His, *Basler gelehrte;* Wilhelm His, "Zur Erinnerung an C. G. Jung," pp. 40–48 in *Zur Geschichte des anatomische Unterrichtes in Basel* (Sonderdruck aus: *Gedenkschrift zur Eröffnung des Versalianum*) (Leipzig: von Veit, 1985); H. Haupt, *Ein vergessener Dichter aus der Frühzeit der Burschenschaft, Carl Gustav Jung (1794–1864)* (n.p., n.d.); Ernst Jung, *Aus den Tagebüchern;* Kahlbaum, *Monographien a.d. Gesch. der Chemie,* HE/STA; and Kurz, *CGJ.*

30. His, *Basler gelehrte.*

31. A remark made by his colleague Rudolf Jhering as he departed for the law faculty of the University of Rostock. Jhering added that success in Basel required "more bowing and scraping than a simple North German like himself possessed" (Gossman, "Basel," p. 87, quoting a letter to J. J. Bachofen, June 22, 1846).

32. Fighting ended in 1833 when they became two separate cantons, Basel-Stadt (city) and Basel-Land (suburbs).

33. Schorske, "Burckhardt's Basel," p. 57, writes that "access to citizenship was tightly controlled, often requiring generations of family residence." Schorske also notes, p. 61, that "Basel had the reputation of giving refuge to maverick foreign professors" and "the leading families, normally known for the closed character of their society, welcomed such professors into their homes."

34. His gives 1828; Kurz, 1830.

35. In Basel, Virginie gave birth to either two other daughters (His) or four (Kurz). His believes the first of two died at three months, the second after a premature birth. Kurz believes there were four total, and three died of tuberculosis (as did Virginie). The sole surviving child was Anna, who later married Hermann Reimer and became Frau Dr. Anna Reimer-Jung of Stuttgart, Germany. W. His, "Zur Erinnerung an C. G. Jung," p. 48; and Kurz, *CGJ*.

36. Jacob Burckhardt, letter to Gottfried and Johanna Kinkel, September 11, 1846, *Briefe*, 3: 36.

37. Frau Sybille Willi-Niehus (CGJ's eldest granddaughter, daughter of Agathe Niehus-Jung), interview with the author, March 25, 1998, Baden.

38. The Jung family and most scholars agree on this version of the marriage. Zumstein-Preiswerk writes that Elisabeth Catherine married at eighteen, three years after entering the Jung household as a servant caring for "the children" of Carl Gustav's then-living first wife, Virginie.

39. CGJ to Aniela Jaffé, *ETG*, p. 404.

40. Ellenberger, "The Story of Helene Preiswerk," p. 300, creates this pastiche from observations and remarks made by Eduard His, Wilhelm His, and Ernst Jung (all cited above). See also Haupt, *Ein vergessener Dichter*; and Georges Schüler, "Der Basler Irrenarzt Friedrich Brenner (1809–1874)," (Med. diss., Univ. of Zürich, 1973).

41. His official title was *Grossmeister der vereinigten Schweizerlogen des Freimaurerordens*. Professor Claudio Bonvecchio, Grand Master of the Memphis Rite in Italy and Switzerland (Cavalieri Beneficenti della Città Santa, della Massoneria Rettificata Svizzera), in an e-mail of March 18, 2002, attests that "CGJ was a member of the Beneficent Knights of the Holy City, a distinct grade in Swiss Masonry corresponding to the 30th degree in the Memphis Rite." The CGJ heirs neither affirm nor deny this.

42. *ETG*, p. 404.

43. Born in 1812, she predeceased him in 1855. Of the fourteen children Carl Gustav fathered by his three wives, nine survived to adolescence or adulthood: Virginie had one, Anna; and Elisabeth Catherine had two, Karl and Karoline. Sophie had five sons and one daughter: Rudolf, who wrote poetry and died of tuberculosis at age twenty-one; Fritz, who played piano and studied medicine and died of tuberculosis at age twenty-four; Max, who became a secretary in a law office; Paul Achilles, CGJ's father and a priest; Ernst, an architect in Winterthur; and Sophie, a talented singer who married Dr. Robert Fiechter. "Karl" (as CGJ's name was then spelled) was very fond of Sophie and wrote letters to her during his student days that are still extant in family archives.

44. The first quotes are from Kurz, *CGJ*, p. 27; the latter are from Ernst Jung, *Aus meinem Leben*, a privately printed pamphlet of 60 pp. in the Jung family archives.

45. CGJ's account in *ETG*, p. 404, is contested by His and Kurz: in her brief three years of marriage, Elisabeth Catherine gave birth either to two sons who predeceased her (His) or to three children (Kurz). Kurz believes that one died as a child. A son named Karl either had an unhappy relationship with his father (His) or "abused his father's trust" (Kurz), but in either case he left for America and was never heard from again (His, Kurz, Zumstein-Preiswerk). Official documents in the CGJ archives at ETH support this latter view: the first Karl Gustav II Jung (the name later given to CGJ) was born on January 5, 1833, the day also given as Elisabeth Catherine's death. In 1853, when he was twenty, his father exiled him to "America," where relatives believe he became a medical doctor and father of four children. On July 4, 1888, in quest of this Karl Gustav's share of the family inheri-

tance, his surviving siblings went before the Swiss *Zivil Gericht* and declared under oath that they did not know his whereabouts. He was officially declared dead on January 20, 1873, in the *Verfallbuch*. The only point of agreement between His and Kurz is that Elisabeth Catherine's daughter, Karoline, was unhappy in the home of Carl Gustav I and Sophie, so she ran away to relatives in Darmstadt (His), where she soon died of typhus.

46. This exaggerated respect for the patriarch was a fairly common practice in several European cultures and countries. Simone de Beauvoir, among many others and a full generation later, remembered luncheons in her maternal grandfather's home ending this way. See D. Bair, *Simone de Beauvoir* (New York: Summit Books, 1990), p. 37.

47. As Carl Gustav's three wives and many of their children died of tuberculosis, it is quite likely that he, too, had the disease, even though the official cause of his death on June 12, 1864, was acute heart failure. He was buried on June 15 in a torch-lit mourning procession that moved from the Münsterplatz to the Kannenfeld-Gottesacker cemetery. Sophie and three of his sons are buried beside him.

48. Quoted by Gossman, "Basel," p. 85, from James Hastings Nichols's preface to J. Burckhardt, *Force and Freedom: Reflections on History* (New York: Pantheon Books, 1943), p. 17.

49. "Ueber des Karäers Jephet arabische Erklärung des Hohenlieder," von Paul Jung aus Basel (inaugural dissertation [. . .] der Georgia Auguste, Göttingen, 1862). Paul Jung wrote the dissertation in Arabic but with Hebrew letters. It consists of part of Ben Eli's commentary transcribed into Arabic script, part translated into German, and a brief conclusion of his own remarks.

50. E. Jung, *Aus den Tagebüchern*, and Zumstein-Preiswerk, *CGJ's Medium*. Frau Vischer was the mother of CGJ's friend, Dr. Med. Adolf L. Vischer. See also *CL*, note to p. 351. Col. Vischer-Preiswerk was married to a cousin of the same Preiswerk family into which Paul Jung later married.

51. Famed theologian and professor at the University of Basel, responsible for many of the "1820s University Reforms." See Schorske, "Burckhardt's Basel," p. 61.

52. CGJ to E. A. Bennet, in *CGJ: Einblick in Leben und Werk* (Zürich: Rascher Verlag, 1964), p. 23. CGJ does not specify that the legacy was left by Col. Vischer-Preiswerk, but documents in family archives verified it.

53. Karl Barth, *Protestant Theology in the Nineteenth Century* (London: S.C.M. Press, 1972), p. 145.

54. CGJ to Professor O. Schrenk, Paris, November 18, 1953, *CL-2*, p. 132.

55. *ETG*, p. 406; C. G. Jung, *Dream Analysis: Notes of the Seminar Given in 1928–30*, ed. William McGuire, Bollingen Series 99 (Princeton: Princeton Univ. Press, 1984), p. 518. In n. 6, McGuire says that Samuel Preiswerk thought he gave Hebrew names to all his children, but Emilie is actually of Latin origin. Zumstein-Preiswerk, *CGJ's Medium*, pp. 41–42, writes that he was fluent in French, Greek, and Latin, and his Hebrew grammar book, which went through three editions, was also published in French. She also quotes one of the "many" hymns he wrote.

56. Henri Ellenberger, in "The Story of Helene Preiswerk," p. 297, writes that Samuel Preiswerk's views resembled those held by many Swiss Protestant fundamentalists and pietists, and that "it was not by chance that the First International Zionist Congress took place in Basel in 1897." Ellenberger adds that Theodor Herzl, chairman of the congress, saluted the memory of Antistes Samuel as "one of the precursors of Zionism." See also "Carl Gustav Jung: His Historical Setting," in *Historical Explorations in Medicine and Psychiatry*, ed. Hertha Riese (New York: Springer, 1978), pp. 145ff.

57. James Mearns, "Preiswerk, Samuel," in J. Julian, ed., *A Dictionary of Hymnology*, rev. ed. 1907 (reprint, New York: Dover, 1957), 2: 907; and B. Pick, "Preiswerk, Samuel, Dr.," in J. McClintock et al., eds., *Cyclopedia of Biblical, Theological and Ecclesiastical Literature* (New York: Harper and Brothers, 1879), 8: 505. CGJ cites one of Samuel Preiswerk's hymns in *CW-5*, p. 344.

58. Samuel Gottlob (1825–1912), called Isemännli ("little iron man"), became a distinguished pastor at St. Alban. After Paul's death, he was the guardian of Emilie Jung-Preiswerk's children. He officiated at their confirmation in the Swiss Reformed Church.

59. CGJ and his descendants believe the name is a "Germanization of Favre du Faure" and that the family came originally from Tuttlingen. *CL-2*, p. 132.

60. The first quote is from Henri Ellenberger's miscellaneous notes from conversations with various members of the Preiswerk and Jung families about occult phenomena, HE/STA. The second is from *MDR*, pp. 48–49.

61. CGJ, *Aion*, *CW-9*, part 2, para. 12, p. 7.

62. *ETG*, p. 406; Hans A. Jenny, *Baslerisches — Allzubaslerisches* (Basel: Pharos-Verlag, Hansrudolf Schwabe AG, 1961).

63. This version is told by the current generation of Jungs. Works consulted include Aniela Jaffé, "Details About CGJ's Family," and *From the Life and Work of CGJ* (Einsiedeln: Daimon Verlag, 1989); Barbara Hannah, *Jung: His Life and Work, A Biographical Memoir* (Boston: Shambhala, 1991); F. X. Charet, *Spiritualism and the Foundations of CGJ's Psychology* (Albany: State Univ. of New York Press, 1993); and Zumstein-Preiswerk, *CGJ's Medium*. CGJ asks in his doctoral dissertation, "On the Psychology and Pathology of So-Called Occult Phenomena," if it might have been typhoid fever, adding that she did not awake until "the crown of her head was burnt with a red-hot iron" (*CW-1*, p. 17).

64. *CW-1*, p. 17; Zumstein-Preiswerk, *CGJ's Medium*, p. 17. In a book that is considered highly critical of CGJ and highly partisan toward his (and her) Preiswerk lineage, Zumstein-Preiswerk faults CGJ for distancing himself from the Preiswerk family and not mentioning here that both he and his sister were "genetically predisposed [to mediumistic impulses]." In a letter to Henri Ellenberger, January 28, 1975, HE/STA, Zumstein-Preiswerk defends her book as follows: "I'm documenting everything I say in the footnotes. I have not made up anything . . . I tried to be objective, to depict facts and not to criticize. My parents and my aunts Valerie, Ottilie, and Esther were all truthful and honest. . . . With the help of the Preiswerk family history I was able to put the séances in chronological order."

65. This diary was discussed in several instances by Aniela Jaffé: in an undated interview with Ellenberger, HE/STA; in a letter to Kurt Wolff, HW/BLY; and in *Life and Work*, p. 2. Its existence and content were both confirmed in my interview with Dr. Med. Peter Jung and Mr. Ulrich Hoerni, Zürich, March 7, 1998.

66. It is the German custom for a wife to be known by her husband's titles, so Emilie became "wife of the Dr. (Ph.D.) Preacher."

67. From her granddaughters: Agathe Niehus-Jung, interview with the author, and Gret Baumann-Jung, telephone conversation with the author.

68. A pastiche quote formed by Ellenberger for "The Story of Helene Preiswerk," p. 302, based on his undated interviews with C. A. Meier, Aniela Jaffé, Dr. K. von Sury (member of a Swiss medical committee founded in 1935), and Frau Charlotte Bertolf-Schulthess (the unnamed elderly woman from Kleinhüningen cited by Ellenberger in *Discovery of the Unconscious*, p. 661). All documents in HE/STA.

69. A stone set into the vicarage wall is inscribed "In this house was born Carl Gustav Jung, July 26, 1875–June 6, 1961, explorer of the human soul and its hidden depths."

CHAPTER 2: "PASTOR'S CARL"

1. *The Blue Guide to Switzerland*, p. 242. The Schloss is now a popular restaurant; Laufen is a frequently used German place-name for the rapids of a stream or river.

2. In *MDR*, p. 7, CGJ says an outing to Lake Constance when he was a child led to the decision that he had to live near a lake. Many of the dreams related throughout *CW* have distinguishing architectural features.

3. He oversaw three villages in this parish: Uhwiesen, Dachsen, and Flurlingen; in Kesswil, only one.

4. See Robert W. Brockway, *Young Carl Jung* (Wilmette, Ill.: Chiron Publications, 1996), pp. 62–63, for descriptions as it was in CGJ's time and as it is today.

5. *MDR*, pp. 7–9. Arna Davis, in "A Bridge Across a Fall: A Centenary," *Bulletin of the British Association of Psychotherapists* 18 (July 1987): 71–88, offers "a therapeutic view: a hundred years on" of CGJ's "personal myth as told by him [*MDR*]."

6. Dr. Robert Schneebeli says Jung's experience has parallels to three common legends specific to the region around Laufen, all found in the *Zürcher Sagen*, collected by K. W. Glaettli (Zürich: Verlag Hans Rohr, 1970). In particular, "Winterthur und Weinland," legends 31, 32, and 33, pp. 200–201.

7. The previous two quotations are from some original *Protocols* and are among the many passages that were omitted from *MDR*. References to this anecdote are in (among others) the uncatalogued Helen Wolff papers at BLY; the Bollingen Papers at LC; and in the several private German and English archives that their owners have made available to me. Official manuscripts of *MDR* known to date are three: the heavily copyedited English text in the CGJ oral archive at HCL; a full "protocol" in the Bollingen Collection at the LC; and an original German manuscript in the ETH (the last two restricted).

8. *MDR*, p. 8; private archival sources; interviews with Jung family members; HE/STA; and others.

9. Davis, "Bridge Across a Fall," p. 85, writes of "the confusion and collective oppression these parents carry," and of how CGJ "most likely" played the role of "stabiliser of the parents' marriage."

10. *MDR*, p. 8; Stephanie Zumstein-Preiswerk, *CGJ's Medium: Die Geschichte der Helly Preiswerk* (Munich: Kindler Verlag Gmbh, 1975); Jung family interviews; private sources. Auguste Dorothea (Aunt Gusteli) later married the "Widower Weiss." She had no children of her own but doted on Emilie's and was regarded as CGJ's "second mother."

11. CGJ also said (*Protocols*) that he revised this impression in his adult life because he had male friends who disappointed him, whereas the women friends he mistrusted never did. His meaning, in both English and German, is unclear and contradictory, but the inference is that he believed himself correct to mistrust women all his life.

12. *MDR*, p. 8.

13. *MDR*, p. 391.

14. Rumors have been handed down through several generations of families who knew both the Rauschenbachs and the Jungs that Bertha and Paul were lovers. It is strongly denied by the current generation of both the Jung and Homberger families (the descendants of Emma Jung-Rauschenbach's only sister), even though many do believe that Paul and Bertha were strongly attracted to each other.

15. *Protocols*, HW/BLY. On the folder containing this material, a note in Helen Wolff's hand reads: "revealing for changes 'toning down' Jung original — *bowdlerized version!* Highly interesting for what was done to keep out J's frank and true statements about himself." For a full discussion see chapter 38 and the Epilogue.

16. Henri Ellenberger, "CGJ: His Historical Setting," in *Historical Explorations in Med-*

icine and Psychiatry, ed. Hertha Riese (New York: Springer, 1978), p. 146. In her interview with HE/STA, Frau Charlotte Bertolf-Schulthess seemed puzzled by the way CGJ always played alone.

17. Jaffé, *Protocols*, quotes CGJ as aware of repeating himself, of considering things many times over and always from a different perspective. He found it congenial to "circle around questions repeatedly," describing his method as "a new kind of peripatetics."

18. For the Jesuit Order in nineteeth-century Swiss politics, see *A Short History of Switzerland*, by E. Bonjour et al. (Oxford: Clarendon Press, 1952), esp. chapter 10: "The Foundation of the Federal State," pp. 257ff. See also Gordon Craig, *The Triumph of Liberalism: Zürich in the Golden Age, 1830–69* (New York: Charles Scribner's Sons, 1988).

19. Eugène Sue, *The Wandering Jew*, 1844–45, quoted in Craig, *Triumph of Liberalism*, p. 69. Craig also cites the "perfervid rhetoric" of Gottfried Keller's "Jesuit Song," a popular poem denouncing the order for affiancing "Switzerland [the] beautiful bride . . . to the devil."

20. See Brockway, *Young Carl Jung*, p. 70, for a description of how CGJ may have confused the German *"Yayzoot"* (Jesuit) with *"Yayzoo"* (Jesus). Although CGJ was familiar with Renan's *Life of Jesus* (see chapter 3, p. 45), a wildly popular book much talked about in CGJ's youth was David Friedrich Strauss's 2-volume *Das Leben Jesu*, which treated the Gospel as historical record and marked a turning point in European biblical criticism. See Craig, *Triumph of Liberalism*, pp. 55–56.

21. *MDR*, p. 10. Brockway, *Young Carl Jung*, p. 69.

22. CGJ relates a dream in which he is surprised by his father's well-equipped zoological laboratory, *MDR*, p. 213.

23. Albert Oeri (1875–1950), Jung's contemporary in the Basel Gymnasium and at Basel University. Oeri got his Ph.D. in classical philology and history, was editor in chief of the *Basler Nachrichten*, and was elected to the Swiss National Council. During World War II, he was an outspoken critic of Nazi Germany. He remained a devoted friend to CGJ his entire life. His father was CGJ's Gymnasium teacher of grammar and rhetoric.

24. Albert Oeri, "Some Youthful Memories," in *CGJ Speaking*, ed. William McGuire and R. F. C. Hull, Bollingen Series 97 (Princeton: Princeton Univ. Press, 1977), p. 3.

25. Published version is *MDR*, pp. 11–15; the version here incorporates several unpublished *Protocols*.

26. Described as made of skin and flesh in *MDR*; neither word is used in any *Protocol*.

27. In *MDR* but not in *Protocols*.

28. Brian Feldman believes that, because this is such a "cognitively complex and highly structured dream," CGJ probably dreamed it later, "in the 5 to 6 age period" ("Jung's Infancy and Childhood," *Journal of Analytical Psychology* 37 [1992]: 265).

29. In one of the later *Protocols*, CGJ speaks of stone figures that he carved in England in 1920, calling them "a further development of that [quasi-sexual object from] fearful tree of my childhood-dream" (the phrase in square brackets was crossed out in the typescript by Aniela Jaffé). A heavily revised and much edited passage is *MDR*, p. 23. Among the most accessible and respected critical appraisals of this dream are Marie-Louise von Franz, *CGJ: His Myth in Our Time* (Toronto: Inner City Books, 1988), pp. 17ff.; Aniela Jaffé, "The Creative Phases in Jung's Life," *Spring* (1972); and Daniel Noel, "Veiled Kabir: CGJ's Phallic Self-Image," *Spring* (1974): 224–42. Brockway, in *Young Carl Jung*, pp. 70ff., offers interesting specula-

tion. Richard Noll, in "Jung the Leontocephalus," *Spring* 53 (1992): 43–44, n. 2, criticizes Jungian scholars and singles out James Hillman's *The Dream and the Underworld* (New York: Harper and Row, 1979) for neglecting the Mithras tradition and concentrating instead on the rites of Dionysius.

30. F. X. Charet, *Spiritualism and the Foundations of CGJ's Psychology* (Albany: State Univ. of New York Press, 1993), p. 73, citing *Aion, CW*-9, part 2, para. 357, p. 226. See also p. 73, n. 80.

31. *Protocols*, from a conversation dictated to Aniela Jaffé on September 30, 1957. By "initial life," he meant everything he had created intellectually, all of which was generated by "these initial sources of imagination and dreams."

32. He refers to Schreber, who was destroyed by such dreams and visions. CGJ added that the phallus of the dream could be interpreted "in a Freudian way because the phallus is an ur-experience. But it is not the penis. It is an enormous, mythological existence, just as among the people of India the Holy Phallus was worshipped underground. In the imaginations things came out in this form. I wrote them down the way they were passed on to me. It simply presented itself to me in this way. I didn't even know what my relationship to it was, for it simply fell upon me, and I wrote it down."

33. According to Swiss law, because Paul Jung was born in Basel, he was a citizen of Basel-Stadt and a foreign resident of Cantons Thurgau (Kesswil) and Zürich (Laufen). All his appointments came from the Consistory of Basel, to which he belonged both by birth and ordination. Although the name is often hyphenated, Kleinhüningen is correct.

34. Isaac Iselin was one of the leaders of the Basel Enlightenment in the seventeenth century. He left a manuscript known as the "Tagebuch Isaak Iselin," from which Werner Kaegi quotes extensively in his *Jacob Burckhardt: Eine Biographie* (Basel: Benno Schwabe and Co., 1947–77). Sources include a letter to Henri Ellenberger from the Evangelisch-reformierte Kirchgemeinde Kleinhüningen, Basel, October 12, 1963, HE/STA; P. Hugger, *Kleinhüningen* (Basel: Birkhauser Verlag, 1984); and Brockway, *Young Carl Jung*, pp. 81ff., who describes the house fully.

35. Henri Ellenberger, *The Discovery of the Unconscious: The History and Evolution of Dynamic Psychiatry* (New York: Basic Books, 1970), p. 664.

36. Usually the cheapest possible servant was an illegitimate girl, and the Jungs engaged one named Käterli. Frau Charlotte Bertolf-Schulthess, Ellenberger interview, HE/STA.

37. *MDR*, pp. 15–16.

38. Frau Charlotte Bertolf-Schulthess, Ellenberger interview, HE/STA.

39. Zumstein-Preiswerk, *CGJ's Medium*, pp. 20–22.

40. Zumstein-Preiswerk, *CGJ's Medium*, writes in a letter to Franz Jung, December 15, 1974: "Our fathers looked alike, they were friends until the age of about fifteen. My father was a bold 'pontonnier' [rider of pontoon boats] and was frequently in Kleinhüningen, and the two boys stoked a lot together back then with the fisherman Bürgin's family" (see the photograph in this book). Other views were held by Albert Oeri, in "Some Youthful Memories," originally *Die kulturelle Bedeutung der komplexen Psychologie* (Berlin, 1935), and *Spring* (1970), reprinted in *CGJ Speaking*, p. 4. Barbara Hannah, *Jung: His Life and Work, A Biographical Memoir* (Boston: Shambhala, 1991), p. 41, says that CGJ "detested" his cousin, as CGJ said himself in various *Protocols*.

41. *CW*-1, p. 18. Granted, he wrote this at the age of twenty-five or twenty-six, as part of Helly Preiswerk's case history and perhaps in an effort to disguise her identity

and the circumstances of her life. However, it is part of a pattern of behavior in which he took great care to distance himself from his mother's family.

42. Frau Charlotte Bertolf-Schulthess, Ellenberger interview, HE/STA. Repeated in Ellenberger interviews with Aniela Jaffé, C. A. Meier, and Dr. von Sury. Members of the Jung family made similar comments in interviews for this book.

43. *MDR*, p. 15. For general background see Paul Hugger, *Kleinhüningen* (Basel: Birkhauser Verlag, 1984).

44. *Protocols*. There is an extensive correspondence relating to this anecdote in HW/BLY, the Bollingen papers at the LC, and in several private archives.

45. In *Protocols*, CGJ compared pig sacrifice to the Great Mother (an act of appeasement to the Goddess) with "collective guilt." He used much the same reasoning as J. J. Bachofen (in *Myths, Religion and Motherright: Selected Writings of J. J. Bachofen*, Bollingen Series 84 [Princeton: Princeton Univ. Press, 1967], various citations pp. 69–207). Bachofen was the first to describe the pig as the symbol of the nourishing mother in various Mediterranean and Asiatic cultures. Pig sacrifice is part of the ritual killing of the instinctual mother and was widespread in many primitive tribes as a collective action that could right any number of wrongs. The adult CGJ was familiar with this and other symbolic interpretations of the pig as woman and mother, so it is interesting that he insisted upon the importance of this particular childhood memory and of keeping a revised portion of this anecdote in the published *MDR*, despite the wishes of his family that he remove it. Drs. Joseph Henderson and Thomas B. Kirsch offered helpful comments, and Steven O'Neill of the KML provided additional examples of pig symbolism. CGJ stressed the importance of Bachofen's *"Mutterrecht,"* especially the introduction, for a projected volume of his *CW* and in terms of general importance for his work in a memo from Kurt Wolff to John Barrett, February 10, 1954, HW/BLY.

46. *Protocols*. The phrase in square brackets was crossed out by CGJ and the subsequent phrase added. In what appears to be his hand, there is an exclamation point in the margin opposite this phrase.

47. *MDR*, p. 25, and various *Protocols*.

48. Von Franz, *His Myth in Our Time*, p. 27; *MDR*, pp. 90 and 359.

49. *MDR*, p. 25. CGJ equivocated over this passage. It was removed, then reinserted in several *Protocols*. It is not known if the final decision to include it was his or Aniela Jaffé's.

50. Information from members of the Jung family; various interviews in HCL; interviews in HE/STA.

51. See *MDR*, pp. 50–52, for CGJ's description of his mother's division into two personalities, numbers 1 and 2, and for other references to his own "Personalities 1 and 2."

52. *MDR*, pp. 18–19.

53. *MDR*, pp. 20ff. He deleted the following from the *Protocols*: "Later, when I read Greek mythology, I discovered that when Zeus was troubled in love he would sit down on a stone — he would sit on *his* stone in Euboea [?] or Crete. In my case it was not a question of troubled love, but of who 'I' really was" (square brackets are CGJ's). Anthony Stevens, *Jung* (Oxford and New York: Oxford Univ. Press, 1994), p. 4, discusses how this "childhood ritual prepared him for his later insights into the importance of *projection* in psychology," and how, "in this game we can trace the origins of Jung's mature insight into the mysteries of alchemy." Louise Erdrich, in "Two Languages in Mind, but Just One in the Heart," the Writers on Writing series, *New York Times*, May 22, 2000, p. E1, described stones in the Native American

Ojibwemowin language as "animate" and writes of their importance in Ojibwe philosophy: "Once I began to think of stones as animate, I started to wonder whether I was picking up a stone or it was putting itself into my hand. Stones are not the same as they were to me in English. I can't write about a stone without considering it in Ojibwe and acknowledging that the Anishinabe universe began with a conversation between stones."

54. *MDR*, pp. 20–22; recounted in all versions of the *Protocols*.

55. Feldman, "Infancy and Childhood," p. 269, discusses the development of CGJ's self-image.

56. In *MDR*, p. 33, CGJ says he lost "all memory" of the pencil case. In the *Protocols* he called "the whole story completely lost and forgotten. Perhaps the case is still lying there today."

57. Originally *Wandlungen und Symbole der Libido*, published 1912; rev. and retitled *Symbols of Transformation* (*CW*-5), 1956.

58. One such carving stood in his garden at Küsnacht until his death, when the family, fearing souvenir hunters or worse, removed it and several others to a safer haven.

59. Documents in the Humanistisches Gymnasium, Basel archives list CGJ as a student from 1886 to 1895, when he received his *Maturität*. Confirmed by letter from Dr. Hans Gutzwiller, Rektor, to HE/STA, February 15, 1967.

60. CGJ's daughter, Marianne Niehus-Jung, insisted that this be excised from *MDR*. See the Epilogue for full discussion.

61. *MDR*, pp. 64–66. In separate interviews, Drs. C. A. Meier and Marie-Louise von Franz cited CGJ's lifelong rage over this incident whenever someone accused him of dishonesty or alluded to the possibility that he had cheated. Both stressed how deeply it had affected him, and thus, how natural it was to include it among his most vivid memories.

62. CGJ wrote about him in the "friendships" section of the *Protocols*, but the chapter was omitted from *MDR*. Their friendship lasted through medical school, when Vischer left Switzerland to become director of the hospital at Urfa, Asia Minor, and they lost touch for many years.

63. Oeri, "Some Youthful Memories," p. 4.

64. *MDR*, p. 29, also pp. 64–66.

65. Hannah, *Life and Work*, p. 41, explains that drawing classes usually consisted of "soulless copying" and that CGJ could draw only when something stirred his imagination.

66. *MDR*, p. 30. A letter from Dr. Prof. P. Kleiholz, director, Psychiatrische Universitätsklinik Basel to Henri Ellenberger, February 26, 1960, HE/STA, provides details of Paul Jung's duties and states that he was a well-liked, productive member of the faculty/staff. Other notes among the Ellenberger papers cite comments of Paul Jung's evident pleasure in this aspect of his professional life.

67. In *MDR*, p. 94, CGJ writes that Paul Jung read Freud's translation of Bernheim's *Die Suggestion und ihre Heilwirkung*, but he does not place it in any particular context.

68. *MDR*, pp. 30ff.

69. In *MDR*, p. 76, CGJ gives an abbreviated version of this stay.

70. *MDR*, pp. 76–78; interviews with Marie-Louise von Franz and C. A. Meier.

71. Hannah, *Life and Work*, pp. 44 and 61, writes that Jung lost an entire year to this absence and was put into a new class whose boys had no knowledge of his earlier behavior and were thus more open to accepting him. Had he continued with his original class, he would have graduated from the Gymnasium at age eighteen, which was "unusually young," rather than at age twenty, which was fairly usual.

72. Oeri, "Some Youthful Memories," p. 4.
73. Bachofen was also Professor of Roman Law at the University of Basel. His major research was on the primacy of matrilineal descent, an idea later disregarded in academic circles.
74. In one *Protocol*, he talked about "the sow as an aspect of Demeter and . . . Isis," but said, "I didn't know that back then. It was an awful impression." There are many comparisons of Burckhardt and Bachofen, most of them refined and condensed for *MDR*.
75. It was also piqued because the parents of his friend Andreas Vischer were helping to support Nietzsche financially. Also, despite the fact that Albert Oeri's grandmother was Burckhardt's sister, CGJ said he still liked Oeri.
76. Hannah, *Life and Work*, p. 44; *MDR*, pp. 33ff.
77. Hannah, *Life and Work*, p. 48, believes that CGJ did not use these terms until he was "trying to make this curious phenomenon clear to the reader [of *MDR*]," although she heard him say them "many years earlier." D. W. Winnicott, reviewing *MDR* in *Psychoanalytic Explorations* (Cambridge, Mass.: Harvard Univ. Press, 1989), cites them among other examples as proof that CGJ suffered from "childhood schizophrenia." Helen Wolff, on p. 84 of her copy of the *Protocols*, HW/BLY, asks CGJ in a marginal note to delete the original passage and to insert instead a hitherto deleted paragraph from *ETG* in which he asserts that (in her words) "No. 2 is not a dissociated personality but a typical figure present in everyone." They agreed upon the passage published in *MDR* as para. 3, p. 45.
78. These quotes were eliminated from *MDR* (for the published version, see p. 36).
79. See *MDR*, pp. 38ff., for the edited account of CGJ's reasoning. See chapter 38 and the Epilogue for full discussion.
80. Official text is *MDR*, p. 53; quoted here from unpaginated *Protocols*. CGJ told Barbara Hannah (*Life and Work*, p. 51) that his father never forced him to go to church, but he always went before his confirmation because "one just did." Afterward, his attendance was sporadic.
81. Krug's four-volume *Allgemeines Handwörterbuch der philosophischen Wissenschaften, nebst ihrer Literatur und Geschichte, nach dem heutigen Standpuncte der Wissenschaft* was considered the "standard text" and was widely consulted throughout the nineteenth century.
82. *Christliche Dogmatik*. Biedermann (1819–85), a Protestant minister first in Basel, then in Zürich, was primarily interested in the unification of various factions of the Swiss Protestant religion. Biedermann's daughter married one of CGJ's uncles, but he did not specify which.
83. *MDR*, p. 69. On p. 61 he writes that there were no philosophers in his father's library: "They were suspect because they thought." CGJ does not specify where he read these books, but family members believe most came from Paul Jung's library.
84. Friedrich Theodor von Vischer (1807–87), best known for "his whimsical novel *Auch Einer* (2 vols., 1879), in which the hero wages unsuccessful war against a treacherous physical reality" (*The Oxford Companion to German Literature* [Oxford and New York: Oxford Univ. Press, 1986], p. 937).
85. In *MDR*, p. 68, he writes of Plato's "longwindedness of Socratic argumentation."
86. Friedrich Gerstäcker (1816–72), a novelist of adventure who toured and wrote about North and South America, Australia, Egypt, and Abyssinia. He made his reputation writing novels about exotic locales, among them Tahiti, Venezuela, Mexico, and Arkansas. He also wrote novels about German life and manners, but it was the adventure stories that appealed to CGJ. Family members believe he read them at home, for it is known that Emilie Jung shared his liking.

87. Because of Paul Jung's teaching, CGJ was able to read Latin for pleasure, a lifelong habit. His daughter Helene Hoerni-Jung remembered how he lay on the sofa on winter evenings engrossed in a Latin text while his five children played games, musical instruments, and generally caroused around him.

88. *MDR*, p. 73.

89. Hannah, *Life and Work*, p. 57; and author interviews with Marie-Louise von Franz, C. A. Meier, and members of the Jung family. Oeri, "Some Youthful Memories," p. 6, writes: "As far as I know, Jung never considered studying anything but medicine."

90. *MDR*, pp. 84–90; John Freeman, "Face to Face," BBC-TV interview, 1959. In a subsequent interview with Jean Nameche at HCL, Freeman said the subject matter of this interview was heavily edited for various reasons. This quote, however, in the original tapes now at the BBC Centre, London, was exactly as CGJ said it.

91. Interview with the author, June 1995. Her companion, Barbara Hannah, wrote of this in *Life and Work*, p. 57. The text is *CW*-12, p. 208.

92. In *MDR*, p. 86, he used this as yet another example of himself as an unlikable outsider, saying he was ashamed that the "top" people might be secretly against him and would reject Paul's petition. There are striking differences between the *Protocols* and the published text because he unifies and shapes the latter to reinforce the impression of himself as the outsider. His children and colleagues (Meier and von Franz) believed it a good example of his "literary license," as "it makes a better story this way."

93. Oeri, "Some Youthful Memories" (German text), p. 528.

94. The date is according to family records. The official registry from the Schweizerische Eidgenossenschaft Kanton Basel-Stadt gives it as January 23. CGJ calls it pancreatic in several of the *Protocols*, but in others he simply calls it "abdominal" or "stomach." His descendants are unsure as well.

95. In his middle age, CGJ commissioned a stone to be placed over Paul's grave. A letter from Rudolph Zürcher, deacon of the Evangelisch-reformierte Kirchgemeinde Kleinhüningen to Henri Ellenberger, October 12, 1963, HE/STA, says the graveyard is now in disrepair and the stone has been removed.

96. *MDR*, p. 96. Hannah, *Life and Work*, p. 63, writes, "He died just at the right time *for you*."

CHAPTER 3: UNCONVENTIONAL POSSIBILITIES

1. *MDR*, p. 95, and *Protocols*. CGJ was still signing his name as Karl, but university documents used the same spelling and form as his grandfather's.

2. Henri Ellenberger's notes of conversations with the Preiswerk family, HE/STA.

3. Stephanie Zumstein-Preiswerk, "The Genealogy of the Preiswerk-Faber Family," in *CGJ's Medium: Die Geschichte der Helly Preiswerk* (Munich: Kindler Verlag Gmbh, 1975), p. 134.

4. Zumstein-Preiswerk, *CGJ's Medium*, in a letter to Franz Jung, December 15, 1974, departed from the house's reality when she described it as "an Alsatian half-timbered construction, very beautiful, in a big old park." It has since been demolished.

5. Zumstein-Preiswerk, *CGJ's Medium*, p. 134.

6. This was an unusual thing for CGJ to do: according to Swiss custom, the widow's family was expected to provide for her and her children. The *Erbengemeinschaft CGJ* supports the view that Ernst Jung paid, but Zumstein-Preiswerk, *CGJ's Medium*, p. 125, n. 61, disagrees, saying that Eduard Preiswerk paid for CGJ's education. She describes CGJ's four paternal uncles as two who were dead, one who was not wealthy (Ernst), and one who disappeared after immigrating to the United States.

7. By the time he graduated, his debt was 3,000 Swiss francs, which he repaid shortly after his marriage to Emma Rauschenbach (author interviews with members of the Jung family).

8. Barbara Hannah, *Jung: His Life and Work, A Biographical Memoir* (Boston: Shambhala, 1991), p. 64, calls Emilie Jung impractical about money and relates several stories to support her contention. Members of the Jung family contest this, citing how well she managed the household accounts when her husband was alive.

9. *MDR*, p. 105. Members of the Jung family speak proudly of CGJ's financial ability but also of how he most happily and willingly surrendered all aspects of financial management to his wife after their marriage.

10. Information in the Basel Staatsarchiv, Eidgenössischen Medizinalprüfungen "Cassabuch" (Erziehung AA 28,2), shows that CGJ paid the required fee to take *Propädeuticum* no. 1 on October 7, 1896, and *Propädeuticum* no. 2 on October 7, 1897. He took the *Staatsexamen* for medical qualification on September 28, 1900. In a letter from the *Erbengemeinschaft CGJ*, June 29, 1998, Ulrich Hoerni of the Geschäftsfürender Ausschuss (executive committee) explained that the two required years of *Propädeuticum* are now three throughout the Swiss university system.

11. For a slanted, but nevertheless informative, account of CGJ's professor of zoology, Friedrich Zschokke, see Adolf Portmann, "Jung's Biology Professor: Some Recollections," *Spring* (1976): 148–54. This Professor Zschokke is not the Swiss author and historian mentioned by CGJ in *MDR*, p. 51, or by E. Bonjour et al. in *A Short History of Switzerland* (Oxford: Clarendon Press, 1952), pp. 255–56.

12. In *MDR*, pp. 100–101, CGJ calls himself simply a "junior assistant." In a *Lebenslauf* (résumé) written July 17, 1902, to accompany his doctoral dissertation, CGJ stated that he passed the exam in natural sciences on October 17, 1896, and the anatomical-physiological exam for physicians on November 2, 1897. He states that he held the position of "junior assistant for microscopic anatomy at the Anatomical Institute the previous semester." During the winter semester of 1897–98, he worked there as "junior assistant for macroscopic anatomy." From April 1, 1899, to September 30, 1899, he was "junior assistant at the Surgical Clinic at Citizens Hospital, Basel," and from October 1, 1899 to March 31, 1900, he worked in the medical clinic of the same hospital (from: "Lebenslauf CGJ med. pract. Burghölzli-Zürich, 27.IV.02 U 106 G.10," State Archive, Canton Zürich). In *Dream Analysis: Notes of the Seminar Given in 1928–30*, ed. William McGuire, Bollingen Series 99 (Princeton: Princeton Univ. Press, 1990), p. 387, CGJ described von Müller as most interested in correlating "the periodicity of menstruation with the tides and the time when all life was in the sea. . . . He always got into a bad mood when he was too closely pressed."

13. *MDR*, pp. 107–11.

14. *MDR*, p. 94. In the *Protocols*, CGJ provides more detail about how and when he came to choose psychiatry, but his language is curiously evasive and vague.

15. *Staatsexamen* information from the Basel Staatsarchiv (Erziehung AA 28,2); Krafft-Ebing from *MDR*, p. 108.

16. *MDR*, p. 105.

17. "Maid" is CGJ's term, but it was either Luggy or Helly Preiswerk, the cousins who worked without pay for Emilie Jung in the summers (Zumstein-Preiswerk, *CGJ's Medium*, p. 48; confirmed by members of the Jung family).

18. It belongs now to Frau Sybille Willi-Niehus, daughter of CGJ and Emma Jung's eldest daughter and their first grandchild.

19. See photo, *CL*-1, p. 181, with accompanying letter, CGJ to Professor J. B. Rhine, November 27, 1934.

20. It is now in the possession of descendants who live in the family home at 228 Seestrasse, Küsnacht. In his lifetime, CGJ liked to show it to people in order to illustrate anecdotes, make conversational points, or add further analysis.

21. For a full definition, see *A Critical Dictionary of Jungian Analysis*, ed. Andrew Samuels, Bani Shorter, and Fred Plaut (London and New York: Routledge, 1986), p. 146.

22. "Information from Frl. Dr. Gerda Walther for Prof. Henri Ellenberger," April 5, 1967, a "List of Sources" regarding CGJ and his interest in parapsychology, HE/STA. When CGJ participated in several 1925 sessions with two mediums, he was still citing its influence.

23. *MDR*, p. 99.

24. "From his early youth [CGJ] kept a watchful eye on parapsychological . . . phenomena, reading more on these subjects than is perhaps evident in his works" (Marie-Louise von Franz, "The Library of CGJ," *Spring* [1970]: 192). In *MDR*, p. 99, CGJ said he read seven volumes of Swedenborg's writings. For a related but somewhat discursive discussion of his reading at this time, see F. X. Charet, *Spiritualism and the Foundations of CGJ's Psychology* (Albany: State Univ. of New York Press, 1993), chapter 3, pp. 93–123.

25. Auguste Forel, *Rückblick auf meinem Leben* (Zürich: Europa Verlag, 1935), pp. 126–27.

26. Letter from Dr. W. Wackernagel to Henri Ellenberger, February 7, 1967, HE/STA. Wackernagel misspells the professor's name, calling him Dr. Willie.

27. The German terms are *"Spezielle Psychiatrie"* and *"Allgemeine Psychiatrie, Psychiatrische Klinik."*

28. Wackernagel to Ellenberger, HE/STA. Dr. Robert Schneebeli, fax to the author on June 24, 1998, writes that passing this exam qualified CGJ "to practice medicine in Basel as a general practitioner, but it did not entitle him to call himself Dr. Med. (although probably everyone would have called him 'Herr Doctor'). What gave him the right to carry the title or, in other words, conferred on him the dignity of a Medicinal Doctor, was the approval of a dissertation by the medical faculty of a university." In a fax of June 29, 1998, the *Erbengemeinschaft CGJ* confirmed that CGJ submitted such a dissertation to the University of Zürich in 1901/02, catalogued UNZ 1902.55. Discussion follows in chapter 4.

29. Hannah, *Life and Work*, p. 65; verified by the *Erbengemeinschaft CGJ*.

30. Quotes that follow are from Henri Ellenberger's notes from interviews with unnamed Zofingian classmates of CGJ, HE/STA; Albert Oeri, "Some Youthful Memories," in *CGJ Speaking*, ed. William McGuire and R. F. C. Hull, Bollingen Series 97 (Princeton: Princeton Univ. Press, 1977), p. 8. See also Charet, *Spiritualism*, chapter 4, "Spiritualism in Jung's Zofingia Lectures," pp. 125–48.

31. Passage eliminated from *MDR*, found in a typescript belonging to the translators of *MDR*, Richard and Clara Winston, 3: 26, now in a private archive.

32. Winston typescript, 3: 26.

33. Oeri, "Some Youthful Memories," p. 9. Gustav Steiner, "Erinnerungen an Carl Gustav Jung aus der Studentenzeit," *Basler Stadtbuch* (1965): 143, remembers that CGJ also spoke of Mesmer, Lombroso, Kerner, Jung-Stilling, and several others who were not named.

34. Published as *The Zofingia Lectures: Supplementary Volume A of the CW of CGJ*, Bollingen Series 20 (Princeton: Princeton Univ. Press, 1983). For the genesis of this volume, see Editorial Note by William McGuire, pp. v–vii, and Introduction by Marie-Louise von Franz, pp. xiii–xxv.

35. *Zofingia Lectures*, p. 3.
36. The *Zofingia Lectures*, like most of CGJ's early writing, have not been the subject of much scholarly inquiry. CGJ's Zofingia classmate Gustav Steiner's "Erinnerungen an CGJ" is a memoir written in response to *MDR*, dealing with student reaction to the lectures. Charet, *Spiritualism*, devotes chapter 4 to the lectures.
37. "German-speaking Switzerland . . . felt a kinship of race and culture . . . [and] imagined they could think and feel with the Germans without losing their peculiar national character or surrendering their own cultural ideal" (E. Bonjour et al., *A Short History of Switzerland*, pp. 344–45).
38. *Zofingia Lectures*, p. 36.
39. Information is from HS 1055, the first ms. in the CGJ archive, ETH. The *Erbengemeinschaft CGJ* believes it is what some scholars have called his "Preiswerk Diary."
40. This happened when CGJ was about to change the spelling of his first name to that of his grandfather's.
41. Zumstein-Preiswerk, *CGJ's Medium*, pp. 53 and 74, writes that they began in June 1895, when Emilie held one in the Kleinhüningen rectory, and that CGJ was the only male present. CGJ is generally believed to have blurred chronology in *MDR*, pp. 104–7, to make it appear the séances did not begin until 1898. He also gave this date in a letter to Professor J. B. Rhine, November 27, 1934, *CL*-1, pp. 180–82. Aniela Jaffé, in *Word and Image*, Bollingen Series 97.2 (Princeton: Princeton Univ. Press, 1979), pp. 29–32, accepts Zumstein-Preiswerk's chronology, as does Charet, *Spiritualism*, pp. 9–10 and nn. 47–55.
42. Zumstein-Preiswerk, *CGJ's Medium*, p. 51. Burckhardt wrote much about the Sforza family in his history of the Italian Renaissance, a book owned by the Preiswerk family and well known to CGJ.
43. In *CGJ's Medium*, n. 43, Zumstein-Preiswerk contradicts CGJ's version of how the séances came to be. As the book has not been translated into English and the only explication to date is a curious article by James Hillman ("Some Early Background to Jung's Ideas," *Spring* [1976]: 123–36), I have translated Zumstein-Preiswerk's text here: "CGJ describes the beginning of the séances completely differently in his dissertation as well as [*MDR*]. He claims that he hardly knew his medium, that he had been invited to the séances and met the girl there for the first time. He even says Helly had been active as a medium for quite some time before their acquaintance. He doesn't want to be seen as the initiator of the spiritist experiments. . . . On the other hand, the dedication in the spiritist books to Luggy [Helly's sister] in 1896–97, as well as his own statements that he was reading such books toward the end of the second semester [spring 1896] whenever he could get hold of them, prove that it was he who carried out the experiments and led them (in the spring of 1895 Helly Preiswerk was thirteen and a half years old!). This can also clearly be seen in the accounts of his friends Albert Oeri and Gustav Steiner."
44. Zumstein-Preiswerk to Henri Ellenberger, January 28, 1975, HE/STA.
45. Louise Preiswerk (1874–1957) was probably the cousin closest to CGJ throughout their childhood, but he deliberately distanced himself from her as an adult. In 1907, she married and moved to Küsnacht, near the homes of CGJ and Emma Jung and of Emilie and Gertrud Jung. She remained close to her aunt Emilie throughout her lifetime. Information from Zumstein-Preiswerk, "Descendants of Rudolf Preiswerk," in *CGJ's Medium*, and author interviews with members of the Jung family.
46. CGJ to Andreas Vischer, December 14, 1902, CGJ/ETH. Not in *CL*, copy in HE/STA.

47. Zumstein-Preiswerk to Ellenberger, January 28, 1975, HE/STA. CGJ's account is in *MDR*, p. 34.

48. Zumstein-Preiswerk recalled: "My German teacher reprimanded me with astonishment when I claimed that at school" (Zumstein-Preiswerk to Ellenberger, January 28, 1975, HE/STA).

49. Emily Zinsstag (1882–1962), Helly's school friend, became her sister-in-law when she married Wilhelm Preiswerk. They were the parents of Stephanie Zumstein-Preiswerk.

50. Miscellaneous notes taken by Henri Ellenberger, HE/STA, about interest in occult phenomena in the Preiswerk-Jung family. Ellenberger said all materials are now in the possession of a member of the Zinsstag family.

51. Zumstein-Preiswerk, *CGJ's Medium*, pp. 35–36, gives no documentation but states that CGJ had "conversations" about spiritualism with his mother and Luggy Preiswerk as early as 1890, thus predating the first séance by five years.

52. Miscellaneous notes by Henri Ellenberger, HE/STA; Zumstein-Preiswerk, *CGJ's Medium*, pp. 66ff. In a letter to Ellenberger, January 28, 1975, and in direct disagreement with the Jung family, Zumstein-Preiswerk insisted that both the table and the knife had belonged to Antistes Samuel: "The round table . . . (as well as the . . . knife) were from the 'trousseau' on the mother's side, that is, from the Antistes. . . . It was customary that the youngest daughter inherited the parents' furniture."

53. Celestine (1867–1917). Infected by a syphilitic husband, she gave birth to several deformed dead babies and died herself of the infection.

54. Zumstein-Preiswerk notes that CGJ did not write in his dissertation that Helly received the book as his gift. In letters to Ellenberger, HE/STA, she included photocopies of three books CGJ gave to Luggy Preiswerk. In *Das Rätsel des Menschen: Einleitung in das Studium der Geheimwissenschaften* (The Enigma of Man: Introduction to the Study of Secret Lore), by Dr. Karl duPrel (Leipzig: Philipp Reclam jun., n.d.), CGJ inscribed: "To his dear cousin Luggy a little booklet which deserves the thoughts of a beautiful soul, as a friendly supplement. New Year's 1897, K. G. Jung med." In *Das Leben Jesu*, by Ernest Renan, CGJ inscribed: "For his dear cousin, L. Preiswerk, as an expression of his admiration and deep respect. K. G. Jung med. in April of 1897." He used the initial "K" for his first name, which he did not do elsewhere.

55. CGJ reproduced it in *CW*-1.54, p. 30.

56. Zumstein-Preiswerk, *CGJ's Medium*, p. 71.

57. The first quote is from Oeri, "Some Youthful Memories," p. 7; the second is from CGJ to Andreas Vischer, December 14, 1902, ETH (not in *CL*). CGJ also wrote that even though Luggy participated in the séances, she did not believe in spirits; the implication is that her primary reason for taking part was to see him.

58. Camille Flammarion, *Astronomie Populaire* (Paris: Marpon and Flammarion, 1881).

59. The Preiswerks were related to Ottilie Wildermuth (1817–77) through Augusta Faber. Wildermuth was known as the happy housewife, who depicted domestic life with joy and pleasure.

60. Zumstein-Preiswerk, *CGJ's Medium*, p. 74.

61. Zumstein-Preiswerk, *CGJ's Medium*, p. 78.

62. Zumstein-Preiswerk, *CGJ's Medium*, p. 78.

63. Reproduced in Zumstein-Preiswerk, *CGJ's Medium*, pp. 81–82.

64. Paul Bishop describes this in *The Dionysian Self: CGJ's Reception of Friedrich Nietzsche* (Berlin and New York: W. de Bruyter, 1995), p. 86, as follows: "Sceptics will rejoice when they learn, as J's dissertation points out, that Samuel Preiswerk had

died too early to have read a word of Nietzsche. (If J's grandfather was indeed speaking from the Beyond, then it might be assumed that this problem could be ignored, of course.)"

65. On p. 37 of his dissertation, CGJ mentions an unnamed "gentleman who often took part in the séances"; Zumstein-Preiswerk, *CGJ's Medium*, p. 85, repeats this only to say the unnamed other man did not participate. The most likely candidate was one of the Preiswerk cousins, but as the males of that family were not known for either spiritualistic abilities or sympathies, CGJ was probably the only male present throughout.

66. Zumstein-Preiswerk to Ellenberger, April 22, 1976, HE/STA, described a paper on which CGJ stated that on August 18, 1897, he invited the following persons to a séance: Ernst Preiswerk (Helly's brother and a philosophy student), R. Gomser (medical student), and C. R. Staehelin (medical candidate). She added that the small notebooks where CGJ recorded details of all the séances were "most probably" destroyed by CGJ himself. Actually, it is extant as ms. HS 1055, ETH, believed by the *Erbengemeinschaft CGJ* to be the "Preiswerk Diary."

67. Ottilie Preiswerk told Ellenberger (miscellaneous notes, HE/STA) that she was not interested in this session and was sitting in a room on an upper floor of the mill when she heard "a loud confusion of voices and then silence," but she "never learned exactly what happened."

68. *CW*-1, pp. 3–88.

69. What follows is from conversations with the Jung family, among them Ulrich Hoerni, Dr. Med. Peter Jung, and Sybille Willi-Niehus.

70. *MDR*, 111.

71. Nietzsche to Franz Overbeck, postcard April 3, 1879, in *Briefwechsel*, Part 2, 5: 402; Burckhardt to Gottfried Kinkel, November 24, 1843, *Briefe*, 2: 51.

72. Burckhardt to Johanna Kinkel, September 11, 1846, *Briefe*, 3: 36. CGJ felt great affinity for Burckhardt; his library contains all of Burckhardt's major works, and his writings are peppered with references to the historian (*CGJ Bibliothek-Katalog*, compiled by his family in 1967, made available by *Erbengemeinschaft CGJ*).

73. *MDR*, p. 111.

74. Burckhardt to Gottfried Kinkel, August 20, 1843, *Briefe*, 2: 34–35.

75. The first quote is from two *Protocols*; the second is from *MDR*, p. 111.

76. *MDR*, p. 110; *Protocols*.

77. *MDR*, pp. 112–13.

CHAPTER 4: UNADMITTED DOUBT, UNADMITTED WORRY

1. *Protocols*; Manfred Bleuler, HCL interview and his articles "Eugen Bleuler," *Archives of Neurology and Psychiatry* 26 (1934): 610–28, and "My Father's Conception of Schizophrenia," *Bulletin of the New York State Asylum* 7 (1931): 1–16; Henri Ellenberger, *The Discovery of the Unconscious: The History and Evolution of Dynamic Psychiatry* (New York: Basic Books, 1970), pp. 666–67, and "The Scope of Swiss Psychology," in *Beyond the Unconscious: Essays of Henri Ellenberger in the History of Psychiatry*, ed. Mark S. Micale (Princeton: Princeton Univ. Press, 1993), pp. 177–79; and Peter Loewenberg, "The Creation of a Scientific Community: The Burghölzli, 1902–14," in *Fantasy and Reality in History* (New York and Oxford: Oxford Univ. Press, 1995), pp. 53ff.

2. James Hillman, "Jung's Daimonic Inheritance," *Sphinx, A Journal for Archetypal Psychology and the Arts* 1 (London: 1988): 9.

3. He uses this description of the hospital with what I interpret as his amazement even as an old man throughout the *Protocols* and, finally, in *MDR*, p. 112. Also, E. Bleuler to *Sanitätsdirektion*, Zürich, May 15, 1901, made official in the *Protokoll des Regierungsrates*, August 13, 1901. Copies in the BA. Also, CGJ's résumé, where he gives his title as *II Assistenzarztes an der Irrenheilanstalt Burghölzli* ("Lebenslauf CGJ med. pract. Burghölzli-Zürich, 27.IV.02 U 106 G.10," State Archive, Canton Zürich).

4. The account that follows is based upon the following: Franz Alexander and Sheldon T. Selesnick, "Freud-Bleuler Correspondence," *Archives of General Psychiatry* 12 (January 1965); Eugen Bleuler, *Dementia Praecox or the Group of Schizophrenias*, trans. Joseph Zinkin (New York: International Universities Press, 1950), and *Textbook of Psychiatry [1916]* (New York: Dover Publications, 1951); Hedwig Bleuler-Waser, *Aus meinem Leben* (Munich: Ernst Reinhardt Verlag, 1910); Manfred Bleuler, "Geschichte des Burghölzlis und der psychiatrischen Universitätsklinik," in *Züricher Spitalgeschichte* (Zürich: Regierungsrat des Kantons Zürich, 1951), and interview with Gene Nameche, HCL; and Ellenberger, "The Scope of Swiss Psychology," in *Beyond the Unconscious;* Auguste Forel, *Out of My Life and Work* (New York: W. W. Norton, 1937); Ernest Jones, *Free Associations: Memoirs of a Psycho-Analyst* (New York: Basic Books, 1959), and *The Life and Work of Sigmund Freud*, vols. 1–3 (London: Hogarth Press, 1953, 1955, 1957); Loewenberg, "Scientific Community"; Hans W. Maier, "Eugen Bleuler zur Feier seiner 25 jährigen Tätigkeit als Ordinarius der Psychiatrie und Direktor der Psychiatrischen Klinik in Zürich, April 1923," in *Zeitschrift für die gesamte Neurologie und Psychiatrie* 82 (Berlin: Julius Springer Verlag, 1923); Fritz Meerwein, *Hundert Jahre Kantonale Psychiatrische Universitätsklinik Burghölzli, Zürich, 1870–1970* (Zürich: Burghölzli staff, 1970); Regula Schnurrenberger, "Hedwig Bleuler-Waser (1869–1940), in *Ebenso Neu Als Kühn: 120 Jahre Frauenstudium an der Universität Zürich*, ed. Verein Feministische Wissenschaft (Zürich, 1988); Hans H. Walser, *Hundert Jahre Klinik Rheinau 1867–1967* (Aarau: Verlag Sauerländer, 1970), *Publications de la Société suisse d'histoire de la médicine et des sciences naturelles* 24 (1970); and Jacob Wyrsch, "Eugen Bleuler und sein Werk," *Schweizerische Rundschau* 39 (1939–40).

5. CGJ to Freud, February 20, 1908, in *F/J*, Bollingen Series 94 (Princeton: Princeton Univ. Press, 1994), p. 123.

6. Zollikon, now an elegant suburb on the "Gold Coast" of the lake, was then a small collection of farmhouses owned by peasants who were socially inferior (by legal decree until the 1830s) to the citizens of Zürich. In the early 1900s, there were still residual sentiments of this sort, and many persons who knew Bleuler believed they influenced his conduct and behavior.

7. E. Bonjour, H. S. Offler, and G. R. Potter, *A Short History of Switzerland* (Oxford: Clarendon Press, 1952), p. 207; Gordon A. Craig, *The Triumph of Liberalism: Zürich in the Golden Age, 1830–69* (New York: Charles Scribner's Sons, 1988), pp. 50–51; Ellenberger, *Discovery of the Unconscious*, p. 286.

8. Griesinger was the first director of the Burghölzli, which opened in 1860. Now considered a leading representative of dynamic psychiatry, he was best known in his time as the author of the standard textbook on psychiatry, *Pathologie und Therapie der psychischen Krankheiten* (Stuttgart: Adolph Krabbe, 1845). Von Gudden and Hitzig were famous neuroanatomists.

9. This is an important distinction, and it will be explored in chapter 13 in connection with the Honegger Papers. See also Bernard Minder re: "the staff situation," in "Sabina Spina Spielrein. Jungs Patientin am Burghölzli," *Luzifer-Amor, Zeitschrift*

zur Geschichte der Psychoanalyse 7, no. 14 (1994), trans. and reprinted as "Sabina Spielrein: Jung's Patient at the Burghölzli," in *JAP* 46, no. 1 (January 2001): 46ff.

10. This, too, is an important aspect of determining the authorship of the Honegger Papers discussed in chapter 13. In a letter to Freud, October 14, 1905 (LC Freud, B-4), Bleuler noted that he had begun to use a typewriter "close to a year ago" (i.e., 1904), when the Burghölzli first acquired several.

11. *Protocols*, part of a conversation with Aniela Jaffé, May 4, 1957. Complaints have been lodged against *MDR* (by, among many others, Ellenberger and Loewenberg) that the text is too internalized, and that CGJ never commented about any of the people, including Bleuler, whom he knew throughout his long life. The original text was actually filled with CGJ's observations and comments. For how they came to be excised, see chapter 38 and the Epilogue.

12. In his major work, *Dementia Praecox or the Group of Schizophrenias* (1911) (original title: *Dementia Praecox, oder Gruppe der Schizophrenien*, in Gustav Aschaffenburg, *Handbuch der Psychiatrie*, spezieller Teil, 4. Abt., I [Vienna: F. Deuticke, 1911]). The late date of this publication and the relative paucity of other writings is believed by many, including his son, Dr. Manfred Bleuler, to be due to his excessive devotion to his patients and his administrative duties. Loewenberg, "Scientific Community," p. 56, holds an opposing view: "Bleuler's creativity is remarkable in view of the burden of detail that he carried as an administrator."

13. Auguste Forel to "Herr Regierungsrath" (the senior civil servant on the selection board), November 27, 1887 [mistakenly dated; actually 1885], in Walser, *Klinik Rheinau*.

14. Auguste Forel, *Rückblick auf meinem Leben* (Zürich: Europa Verlag, 1935), and *Out of My Life*. Forel's letter about Bleuler is reproduced in Walser, *Klinik Rheinau*, pp. 27–28.

15. *Protocols; Zarathustra Seminar*, vol. 2.

16. However, when CGJ wrote about Bleuler in the *Protocols*, he called him "the best-known psychiatrist at the time."

17. *Seminar in Analytical Psychology: Notes of the Seminar Given in 1925*, ed. William McGuire, Bollingen Series 99 (Princeton: Princeton Univ. Press, 1989).

18. Ludwig von Muralt, chief assistant to Bleuler from 1901 to 1904. Besides his nickname, Ruedi, CGJ sometimes calls him "Alexander" in the *Protocols*. In an official "Aerzte zur Zeit CGJ's Tätigkeit am Burghölzli" (doctors on staff during CGJ's tenure), he is listed correctly as Ludwig von Muralt. He was also Bleuler's previous first assistant at the Klinik Rheinau, and he followed him to the Burghölzli in the same capacity.

19. In 1901, Jung's cousin by marriage, Franz Beda Riklin (usually called Sr. to distinguish him from his son, also Franz Riklin), joined the staff. This number dropped to five on October 31, 1904, when Riklin departed. The others on staff at that time (besides Bleuler, von Muralt, and CGJ) were Kurt Wehrlin, H. Preisig, Karl Abraham, Ernst Gebhard, N. Skliar, and Hans Maier.

20. The "old volumes" of unnamed journals in the *Protocols* are changed in *MDR*, p. 112, to "fifty volumes of the *Allgemeine Zeitschrift für Psychiatrie*."

21. The following account is from a letter from Jacob Wyrsch to Henri Ellenberger, February 13, 1967, HE/STA, parts of which Ellenberger used in *Discovery of the Unconscious*, p. 667, and from untitled lists of activities in the years 1900 to 1911, BA.

22. From a typescript entitled "On Dreams," dated June 25, 1901, ETH. See also *F/J* for full information concerning this manuscript.

23. Dr. Alphons Maeder, personal communication to Henri Ellenberger, n.d., in *Discovery of the Unconscious*, p. 667. Maeder did not actually join the staff until 1909, but if anything, the workload had intensified by that time.

24. BA. The medium is unidentified. Marie-Louise von Franz, *CGJ: His Myth in Our Time* (Toronto: Inner City Books, 1988), p. 56.

25. CGJ wrote in the *Protocols* that his friendship with von Muralt lasted until he married "a real American woman, a real animus-hound," who destroyed it through jealousy. In 1904, von Muralt contracted tuberculosis and left the Burghölzli to recuperate at Davos. Afterward he became a lung specialist.

26. Santiago Ramón y Cajal (1852–1934), physician and histologist noted for his work on the brain and nerves, isolating the neuron, and discovering how nerve impulses are transmitted to brain cells. In 1906, he shared the Nobel Prize for Physiology of Medicine.

27. James Hillman, "Some Early Background to Jung's Ideas: Notes on CGJ's Medium by Stephanie Zumstein-Preiswerk," *Spring* (1976): 134–35. See also Hillman's "The Fiction of Case History," in J. B. Wiggins, ed., *Religion as Story* (New York: Harper Colophon, 1975), pp. 123–73. George Hogenson read the dissertation as "metabiography" (with which I cannot agree) in *Jung's Struggle with Freud*, rev. ed. (Wilmette, Ill.: Chiron Publications, 1994), pp. 14–23. William Goodheart provides interesting conjecture in "CGJ's First 'Patient': On the Seminal Emergence of J's Thought," *JAP* 29 (1984): 1–34. See also Sabina Spielrein's account of CGJ's attitude toward Helly's trances in Aldo Carotenuto's *A Secret Symmetry: Sabina Spielrein Between Jung and Freud* (New York: Pantheon Books, 1982), pp. 104–6.

28. For further readings, see the section of Mark S. Micale's bibliographical essay dealing with the "medicohistorial study of the patient" in *Beyond the Unconscious*, pp. 397ff. See also George Mora and Jeanne Brand, eds., *Psychiatry and Its History: Methodological Problems in Research* (Springfield, Ill.: Charles C. Thomas, 1970).

29. *CW*-1, pp. 3–88, trans. from *Zur Psychologie und Pathologie sogenannter occulter Phänomene* (Leipzig, 1902), submitted to the Faculty of Medicine, University of Zürich. The title page for the 1902 book states that CGJ was then First Assistant Physician in the Burghölzli Clinic, where the dissertation was approved by Prof. Dr. Med. Eugen Bleuler. CGJ dedicated the book to his "wife," Emma Jung-Rauschenbach, whom he did not actually marry until February 14, 1903. Zumstein-Preiswerk, in a letter to Henri Ellenberger, January 28, 1975, stated: "Mother Emilie had always kept a journal of the parapsychological events that happened to her. These documents supposedly are at the Jung Institute [Küsnacht], as Frau Aniela Jaffé unwittingly confirmed to me. Protocols do not exist." The Jung family has confirmed that such a journal does exist but has chosen not to make it available to scholars. Ulrich Hoerni, speaking for the *Erbengemeinschaft CGJ* in 2000, said they will never be available for sustained scholarly study, because the family considers them "too private." Most likely, CGJ relied on it as well when he wrote his dissertation.

30. Richard von Krafft-Ebing, *Textbook of Insanity Based on Clinical Observations* (originally *Lehrbuch der Psychiatrie auf klinischer Grundlage* [Stuttgart, 1879]).

31. *CW*-1, pp. 17–92.

32. CGJ's diaries and his mother's are in the Jung family archives. CGJ apparently showed these entries to Sabina Spielrein (see Carotenuto, *Secret Symmetry*, pp. 104ff.).

33. It has been argued by (among many others) Charet, Goodheart, Hogenson, and Bishop that CGJ felt the need to elevate his Jung ancestors at the expense of the

Preiswerks, but I prefer the more intellectual reasons I elaborate here. There was, after all, a ritualistic, formulaic pattern that scholarly writing had to follow at the end of the nineteenth century.

34. Anthony Stevens, in *Jung* (Oxford and New York: Oxford Univ. Press, 1994), pp. 9–10, writes that Jung's dissertation was "greater than the doctorate it earned him. In it we can detect the origins of two ideas which were to become central to the practice of analytical psychology: (1) that part-personalities or 'complexes' existing in the unconscious psyche can 'personate' in trances, dreams, and hallucinations, and (2) that the real work of personality development proceeds at the unconscious level."

35. *CW*-18, p. 201. Frau Förster-Nietzsche sent CGJ a copy of Ernst Horneffer's *Nietzsches Lehre der ewigen Wiederkunft und deren bisherige Veröffentlichung* (Nietzsche's Doctrine of the Eternal Recurrence and Its Publication Hitherto) (Leipzig, 1900). The copy, inscribed "Erhalten in Dec. 1899 von Frau Dr. E. Förster-Nietzsche," is still in CGJ's library. Paul Bishop, *The Dionysian Self: CGJ's Reception of Friedrich Nietzsche* (Berlin and New York: W. de Bruyter, 1995), pp. 83–87, offers an explanation of CGJ's thinking about Nietzsche in this particular area. Bishop also writes (p. 20 and n. 1) that CGJ's son, Franz, told him Frau Förster-Nietzsche was "acquainted" with CGJ's parents.

36. *CW*-1, paras. 149–50, p. 88.

37. Officially catalogued in the Zentralbibliothek, Zürich, as UNZ 1902.55: Jung C(arl) G(ustav): (I. Assistenzarzt an der Heilanstalt Burghölzli): *Zur Psychologie und Pathologie sogenannter Occulter Phänomena*, Leipzig 1902. 121 Seiten 8. Zürich Med. Diss. 1901/02.

38. CGJ to Andreas Vischer, August 22, 1904, CGJ/ETH (not in *CL*), in which he complains of the family's narrow-minded reception of his dissertation.

39. The early papers are mostly collected in *CW*-1, pp. 89–224; the association experiments in *CW*-2.

40. For the principal publications of Franz Riklin Sr. (1878–1938), see *CW*-2, bibliography, pp. 624–25.

41. Aschaffenburg (1866–1944), professor of neurology and psychology at Heidelberg and Cologne, later in the United States. His publications on the "Experimentelle Studien über Assoziationen" are listed in *CW*-2, p. 618.

42. Sources include *Protocols;* Marie-Louise von Franz, *His Myth in Our Time*, pp. 56–57; Ellenberger, *Discovery of the Unconscious*, pp. 691ff.; and BA.

43. Barbara Hannah, *Jung: His Life and Work, A Biographical Memoir* (Boston: Shambhala, 1991), p. 80, writes that Franz Riklin Jr. told her this story.

44. Among those who participated in CGJ's and Riklin's work were Drs. Frederick W. Peterson and Charles Ricksher (with whom CGJ first published in English), J. B. Lang, Emma Fürst, and Ludwig Binswanger. To be able to communicate with the many French, English, and American doctors, CGJ took subscriptions to the newspapers *Le Matin* and the (British) *Independent*, both of which he read daily for several years and to which he gave credit for his fluent French and English vocabularies.

45. CGJ reduced the list from Bleuler's original 156 stimulus-words, changing some of them in the process. *CW*-2, p. 3; see also Part One, pp. 5ff., for the "General Experimental Procedure" that was followed.

46. *CW*-2, "On the Doctrine of Complexes," p. 598. This paper was written at the request of Dr. Andrew Davidson, Secretary of the Section of Psychological Medicine and Neurology, Australasian Medical Congress, and was read before that group's congress in Sydney, September 1911. It is primarily CGJ's explanation and justification of the word association test.

47. *CW*-2, p. 599.

48. For CGJ's own descriptions of how the association test was administered and interpreted, see *CW*-2, "The Association Method," pp. 439–65; also *CW*-18, the second
Tavistock Lecture, pp. 48–56. For a succinct and accessible history of the word association test, definition of terms, and description of Jung's contribution, see Ellenberger, *Discovery of the Unconscious*, pp. 691–96. See also *CW*-19, pp. 3–10, for a full
description of CGJ's publications relating to the association test during his
Burghölzli years.

49. "The Practical Use of Dream Analysis," *CW*-16, esp. paras. 319–20, pp. 148–49.

50. Quoted in Ellenberger, *Discovery of the Unconscious*, p. 692. Theodor Ziehen
(1862–1950) held the chair in psychiatry at Berlin.

51. Hannah, *Life and Work*, p. 81, gives a thorough layperson's description of CGJ's
definition of a complex. For a thorough professional definition, see Andrew
Samuels, Bani Shorter, and Fred Plaut, eds., *A Critical Dictionary of Jungian Analysis* (London and New York: Routledge, 1986), pp. 28–29; Elisabeth Roudinesco and
Michel Plon, *Dictionnaire de la psychanalyse* (Paris: Librairie Arthème Fayard, 1997),
pp. 185–86. For full references to the term throughout CGJ's writings, see also
CW-20, pp. 175–78. Anthony Storr, *The Essential Jung* (New York: MJF Books,
1983), p. 22, writes: "The word 'complex' is now seldom used; and most people associate the word with a kind of loose talk of 'having complexes' fashionable in the
nineteen-twenties and thirties, when psychoanalysis first entered the vocabulary of
the sophisticated."

52. In the Tavistock Lectures of 1935, *CW*-18, pp. 72–73, Jung personified the complex as "a little personality of itself."

53. *CW*-18, p. 71.

54. Von Franz, *His Myth in Our Time*, p. 57. Storr, *The Essential Jung*, p. 14, writes that
CGJ "continued to think of personality as being capable of dissociation into a number of subsidiary personalities, any of which could temporarily 'take over.'" Storr
also writes that even after CGJ became associated with Freud, he "continued to
think and write in terms of subsidiary, dissociated personalities, and it is important
to bear this in mind when approaching his work." Other scholars have stressed the
influence of Pierre Janet in this matter. Although Jung was certainly aware of
Janet's theory from his medical studies, it is important to note that he began this research in early 1901 and did not go to Paris until 1902. Although this work was not
published until 1906, extant manuscripts indicate that these portions were un-
changed from the earliest versions.

55. *CW*-2, p. 3.

56. *CW*-2, "On the Psychophysical Relations of the Association Experiment," pp.
483ff. His original is in the Burghölzli Museum, where Mr. Rolf Mosli, librarian,
called it to my attention.

57. Schnurrenberger, "Hedwig Bleuler-Waser," pp. 169–70; also Bleuler-Waser, *Aus
meinem Leben*.

58. *Protocols*, one in which a handwritten date is in the margin, June 14, 1957. Also,
ETG, pp. 378 and 379. A portion appears in English in CGJ's "Foreword:
Théodore Flournoy," in *From India to the Planet Mars* (Princeton: Princeton Univ.
Press, 1994), pp. ix–x.

59. *MDR*, p. 162.

60. Here, CGJ is referring to his dissertation and his work with Helly Preiswerk. For
CGJ's various uses of Flournoy, see the index to *CW*-2 and *CW*-20.

61. Alfred Binet and Théodore Simon, "Méthodes nouvelles pour le diagnostic du
niveau intellectual des anormaux," *L'Année psychologique* 11 (1905): 191–244.

62. Originally, there had been the *Société de Psychologie Physiologique* founded by Charcot and Charles Richet, but it began to decline after Charcot's death in 1893, and by 1900 it was defunct.

63. Henri Ellenberger writes about the paucity of biographical material on Pierre Janet in *Discovery of the Unconscious*, p. 580, but he still presents the most detailed account of his life and work to date. He writes that from November 1900, Janet's lectures at the Collège de France became the center of his activities, although he worked at the Hôpital Salpêtrière from 1893 to 1902. After Charcot's 1893 death, Janet took charge of the experimental psychology laboratory he founded. CGJ worked there, as well as attending Janet's lectures, which Ellenberger says were "mostly attended by foreign visitors, by non-specialists, and by very few students" (p. 343). These lectures were given once a week, the topics chosen for each academic year and announced well in advance. In 1902, Janet lectured on theoretical psychopathology.

64. CGJ to senior executives, July 23, 1902. Entered into the minutes of the meetings on that date, to become effective October 1, 1902. Documents now in Staadarchiv, Zürich.

65. Albert Oeri, "Some Youthful Memories," in *CGJ Speaking*, ed. William McGuire and R. F. C. Hull, Bollingen Series 97 (Princeton: Princeton Univ. Press, 1977), p. 9, tells how CGJ would offer his army-issued revolver to classmates who walked him home through "the sinister Nightingale Woods" during their student days. This is the same revolver he kept in his nightstand in *MDR*, p. 180. Letters to Henri Ellenberger (HE/STA) from Dr. H. R. Kurz, *Eidgenössisches Militaerdepartment*, Bern, January 24, 1964, and Franz Jung, February 4, 1966, both state that CGJ entered the Swiss Citizens' Army as a soldier in 1895, attending the *Infanterierekrutenschule* in Aarau. He became a lieutenant in 1901 and attended the *Sanitätsoffizierschule* in Basel. In 1907 he was *Beförderung zum Hauptmann der Sanität*; from 1914 to 1918, he was *Aktiver Dienst als Kommandant eines Sanitätszuges*. From 1917 to 1918, he was *Verwundetentransporte durch die Schweiz und Kommandant von Interniertenlagern englischer Offiziere*. He was discharged in 1923.

66. She became Emily Preiswerk-Zinsstag and the mother of Stephanie Zumstein-Preiswerk when she married Helly's brother Wilhelm. For a brief time, Emmy's brother Adolf was enamored of Helly, but when she spurned him, he turned his attentions to her younger sister Mathilde, whom he married in 1902. Zumstein-Preiswerk, *CGJ's Medium: Die Geschichte der Helly Preiswerk* (Munich: Kindler Verlag Gmbh, 1975), pp. 94–95.

67. Valerie Preiswerk (1883–1948) became a well-known Swiss actress and distinguished dressmaker in Basel.

CHAPTER 5: "TIMIDLY PROPER WITH WOMEN"

1. From several *Protocols*, one version dated June 7, 1957. He also described himself as an "absolutely reliable husband" for the first seven years or so of his marriage.

2. Albert Oeri, "Some Youthful Memories," in *CGJ Speaking*, ed. William McGuire and R. F. C. Hull, Bollingen Series 97 (Princeton: Princeton Univ. Press, 1977), p. 7, also gives a version of this.

3. *MDR*, pp. 79–80.

4. *F/J*, 49J, p. 95.

5. From personal interviews with the author and from Gene Nameche's interviews on behalf of the Frances Gillespy Wickes Foundation, now at HCL.

6. The separate sources who volunteered this particular information in individual interviews have asked not to be identified in any way other than as "members of the Jung family."

7. *MDR*, p. 76. Numerous persons in Zürich who were close to CGJ or his descendants have speculated greatly about the relationship between Paul Jung and his friend. I mention it because I frequently heard such talk during my research. This is not to say that such a relationship did not exist, only to say that I have found no documentary evidence to support the contention. CGJ's descendants, previously cited in n. 6, cite the passage in *MDR*, p. 52, where Emilie Jung told her eleven-year-old son about "a matter that concerned my father and alarmed me greatly" to support the possibility of a homosexual relationship. However, the entire anecdote is centered around CGJ's distrust of his mother's version of events from that moment on and should be read in that context. For a highly speculative view, see also Naomi R. Goldenberg, *Returning Words to Flesh: Feminism, Psychoanalysis, and the Resurrection of the Body* (Boston: Beacon Press, 1990), esp. chapter 8, p. 131, "Looking at Jung Looking at Himself," in which Goldenberg posits the possibility that "Carl was sexually assaulted by his father." I have found no evidence to support it.

8. *MDR*, p. 78.

9. *MDR*, p. 76.

10. Private archive, private source. Although I know this man's name, I have not identified him because of the uncertainty of the allegation. He is dead and I have been unable to locate any survivors.

11. In the *Protocols*, CGJ described how he sat down to rest and smoke a cigarette during a hike in the Val del Strias (Valley of the Witches). A goat appeared behind him and sniffed at the smoke. CGJ put the lit cigarette in the goat's mouth as a joke, then later gave him an unlit one, which he ate. CGJ explained that in this valley (also called Val del Strega), goats are considered to be witches, and strange accidents have befallen some who have encountered them there.

12. The following account is based on interviews with members of the Jung family; Gret Homberger-Rauschenbach's descendants, including Laurence Homberger and Marianne Homberger; Karin Beyeler-Hartmeier; Verena Müller; and personal interviews with persons who wish to remain private. Texts consulted include: Gertrud Henne-Bendel, *Jugend Erinnerungen: eine Grossmutter* (privately printed); Pfarrer Prof. Dr. Hans Schär, "Emma Jung-Rauschenbach," Funeral Sermon, Kirche Küsnacht, November 30, 1955; Gerhard Wehr, *CGJ: Bildbiographie* (Zürich: Schweizer Verlagshaus AG, 1989); Walter Henne, "Johannes Rauschenbach: ein Schaffhauser Industriepionier," in *Schaffhauser Mappe* (1988); Hans Wanner, "Johannes Rauschenbach," in *Schaffhauser Beiträge vaterländischen Geschichte* 34 (1957): 16–21; "Johannes Rauschenbach," Tageblatt für den Kanton Schaffhausen, March 3, 1905; "Riesige Schaffenskraft: Zweiter Schaffhauser Frauenpfad," in *SN* 2 (September 1991); "Johannes Rauschenbach," *Schaffhauser Biographien des 18. und 19. Jahrhunderts*, part 2, *vom Historischen Verein des Kantons Schaffhausen* (Thayngen Druck und Verlag Karl Augustin, 1957); "Die dritte und vierte Generation," *Journal of the IWC*, Schaffhausen, 1986; Alexander Pope, "CGJ and the IWC," *Leonardo*, a special edition of Watch International (Zürich: Haumesser Editions, 1997); Richard Traupel, "Die Industrielle Entwicklung des Kantons Schaffhausen" (diss., Univ. of Basel, 1942); Karin Beyeler-Hartmeier, "Emma Jung-Rauschenbach: 1882–1955," in *Frauenpfade: Auf den Spuren bekannter Schaffhauser Frauen* (Schaffhausen: Verlag am Platz, 1994); and Susanna Woodtli, *Du Féminisme à l'égalité politique: un siècle de luttes en Suisse, 1868–1971* (Lausanne: Editions Payot, 1977).

13. Obituary of J. Rauschenbach Jr., *Tageblatt für den Kanton Schaffhausen*, March 3, 1905 (date sometimes given as March 5).
14. Following Johannes Rauschenbach Jr.'s death in 1905, the firm was known as Uhrenfabrik von J. Rauschenbach's Erben (The Watch Factory of JR's Heirs), later Uhrenfabrik von Ernst Homberger-Rauschenbach, incorporating the name of the managing director, who was also the husband of Emma Jung's younger sister. It was later incorporated into the Georg Fischer AG, and the IWC was set up and remains today as a separate division of the international corporate giant. IWC's timepieces are no longer the cheap alternative to handmade Swiss watches. Advertisements for quality timepieces frequently appear in upscale publications such as *The New Yorker* and *Town & Country*.
15. Currently the site of the Kantonal Elektrizitätswerk.
16. *Schaffhauser Biographien des 18. und 19. Jahrhunderts*, p. 21.
17. Her descendants remember her as a woman of extreme privacy who would never play or sing when anyone else was around. If they were in the house when she practiced, they would take care to make her think they were far away from her, where she could not be heard.
18. Rauschenbach family memoir.
19. 86.485 acres. Laurence Homberger, interview with the author, March 1997.
20. Descendants of Ernst and Gret Homberger-Rauschenbach live there now. The house has been modernized only to the extent of adding an elevator; otherwise it is basically the same as when Emma Jung lived there. After Bertha Rauschenbach's death, the house went to the Homberger descendants, but the Jungs got first choice of the interior furnishings. The grounds were divided between the Jung and Homberger descendants, and members of both families have built new houses or live in existing dwellings on the property.
21. The first quote is from Franz Jung, interview with the author, November 1995. The last two are from Henne-Bendel's memoir of her grandmother, Barbara Rauschenbach-Vogel. Henne-Bendel was the daughter of Johannes Jr's. only surviving sister (of three born).
22. Obituary, *Tageblatt für den Kanton Schaffhausen*.
23. From separate interviews with private sources.
24. Beyeler-Hartmeier, "Emma Jung-Rauschenbach," p. 65.
25. For further information, see Gordon A. Craig, *The Triumph of Liberalism: Zürich in the Golden Age, 1830–69* (New York: Charles Scribner's Sons, 1988), pp. 157 and 213 ff.
26. Craig, *Triumph of Liberalism*, p. 156, cites a book by Dr. Seidler, *The Vocation of the Young Woman and Her Situation as Loved One and Betrothed: With Excellent Rules Concerning Propriety, Dignity, Family Feeling, Order, Cleanliness, Independence, Friendship, Love, Marriage, Economic Efficiency: Rules About Good Tone and Behavior in Society*. By 1900, the book had been reprinted in countless editions and was still the most highly recommended for "all young women, who will find in it their beautiful calling, to fulfill their natural and ethical vocation, to beautify family life, to appear attractive in society, as well as to prepare themselves to be worthy wives and governesses and good mistresses of the house."
27. Private sources. In *MDR*, p. 215, CGJ writes that Emma Jung had made the study of Grail legends "her life's task." After her death, he asked Marie-Louise von Franz to complete and edit Emma's text, published as *Die Grallslegend in psychologischer Sicht* (Olten: Walter Verlag AG, 1960). See also *The Grail Legend* (Princeton: Princeton Univ. Press, 1970).
28. Craig, *Triumph of Liberalism*, pp. 103–14.
29. Marie-Louise von Franz, *CGJ: His Myth in Our Time* (Toronto: Inner City Books,

1988), and interview with the author, estimated that CGJ and Emma exchanged more than a thousand letters, most during their courtship. Their grandchildren, Ulrich Hoerni and Dr. Med. Peter Jung, verified this estimate in an interview, March 7, 1998. Speaking on behalf of the Jung heirs, they stated that these letters are private papers housed in the family archives and will never be released to the public. However, they dangled the possibility that this policy might change when all of CGJ and Emma's children are deceased. Earlier, Vincent Brome, *Freud and His Early Circle* (New York: William Morrow, 1968), pp. 82 and 297, n. 4, wrote that Dr. Gerhard Adler had read the letters, which "will not be available for twenty years [1981]." Herr Hoerni and Dr. Jung insist that Adler never read the letters and Brome is mistaken.

30. CGJ uses this term in the *Protocols*. Barbara Hannah, *Jung: His Life and Work, A Biographical Memoir* (Boston: Shambhala, 1991), p. 84, confirms it. For fuller detail, see Henri Ellenberger, "The Scope of Swiss Psychology," in *Beyond the Unconscious: Essays of Henri Ellenberger in the History of Psychiatry*, ed. Mark S. Micale (Princeton: Princeton Univ. Press, 1993), pp. 176–91.

31. Private sources.

32. CGJ said the Grail legends belonged to his earliest memories, and a volume of them was one of his two favorite books (the other was Goethe's *Faust*). He never wrote of them because very early in their marriage he decided they belonged to Emma.

33. *Protocols*, in some versions as October 4, 1957. Also, William McGuire, in *Dream Analysis: Notes of the Seminar Given in 1928–30*, Bollingen Series 94 (Princeton: Princeton Univ. Press, 1984), p. xvi, cites information from Franz Jung that CGJ had already studied English in school, and that "during the early 1900s, he spent a summer in London." Franz Jung probably confused this "summer" with CGJ's trip to England from late December 1903 to early February 1904.

34. Information that follows is collated from four separate *Protocols*.

35. Arnold Böcklin was one of the most popular Swiss painters of the late nineteenth and early twentieth centuries. He, too, described himself as an exile from another place who chose to settle in Zürich, where his studio stands today on the Böcklinstrasse.

36. This is one of the many instances in the *Protocols* where CGJ uses an English word or phrase, frequently slightly off from the meaning he intends. In this case, he probably meant "sated."

37. Later, he had an unnamed painting by Franz Hals copied at the Louvre. Also later, in Florence, he had *The Madonna in the Woods* by Fra Lippo Lippi copied and "*Viellesse [sic] et jeunesse.*"

38. Zumstein-Preiswerk follows the general outline of CGJ's activities, i.e., the opera, theater, outings in the Bois de Boulogne, etc., but she is so eager to create an unrequited love relationship between CGJ and Helly Preiswerk that I have not relied upon this portion of her manuscript, entitled "The Last Years." I have generally followed information in several versions of the *Protocols* and interviews with private sources.

39. Zumstein-Preiswerk, letter to Ellenberger, HE/STA. In her book, *CGJ's Medium: Die Geschichte der Helly Preiswerk* (Munich: Kindler Verlag Gmbh, 1975), p. 107, she writes that the illness was not diagnosed until 1909, which, given the usual progress of the disease, seems more likely.

40. *MDR*, p. 296.

41. Because his health deteriorated so quickly, the marriage of the second daughter, Gret, to Ernst Homberger that same year on November 9 was a small and simple

family ceremony. Her descendants believe she always resented not having as elaborate a ceremony as Emma and CGJ did.

42. A previous biographer, Gerhard Wehr, in *An Illustrated Biography of CGJ* (Boston and Shaftesbury: Shambhala, 1989), reproduces the menu on p. 25 and adds the comment: "This shows the upward move in social status the marriage signified for the Swiss parson's son living in modest circumstances."

43. Vincent Brome, *Freud*, p. 297, n. 7, quotes an "English psychiatrist . . . who wishes to remain anonymous" as the source for his contention on p. 83 that CGJ and Emma argued over money on their honeymoon. As this has been repeated by other biographers and scholars, I think it is important to note that Brome's source, John Layard, was (in the most generous of terms) an unreliable witness, one to whom CGJ was unlikely to confide details of his personal life. A letter from Franz Jung to William McGuire, May 29, 1979, gives the following information about the honeymoon: they went first to Madeira, then, on March 22, 1903, to Las Palmas on Gran Canaria, then to Santa Cruz on Tenerife by April 3, 1903. They departed on April 6 or 7 for Barcelona, where they took the train to Zürich via Marseilles, Cannes, and Geneva, arriving April 16, 1903.

44. CGJ to Andreas Vischer, August 22, 1904, copy in the archives of HE/STA, Paris. Author's translation of the German; original in possession of S. Zumstein-Preiswerk (according to Angela Graf-Nold, "The Zürich School of Psychiatry in Theory and Practice," *JAP* 46, no. 1 [January 2001]: 102, n. 17).

45. The husband was head of the family by law, and it was his responsibility to make decisions for the couple about everything from the use and dispensation of money and property to the education and custody of the children. The husband became the sole administrator of the wife's property, so that any wealth accrued over and above what she brought to the marriage remained with him if they divorced. The Swiss had a legal saying for this: "Women's property doesn't grow, but it also doesn't decline." I am grateful to Dr. Jur. Margrith Bigler-Eggenberger for preparing a detailed report for this book pertaining to marital law in Switzerland from 1900 to the present, and also, to Dr. Jur. Vera Rottenberg-Liatowitsch and Dr. Jur. Othmar Schmidlin for conversations about the Swiss legal system.

46. CGJ to Andreas Vischer, August 22, 1904. Author's translation from the HE/STA German original.

47. In several of the *Protocols*, Jung expressed his aversion to anything that required him to listen. As he spent his professional life "listening intently," he did not wish to do so in his personal time. His children were musical, but he would not allow them (or his grandchildren) to listen to the radio in the evenings when he was present. His daughter Marianne enjoyed playing the piano, but Jung objected to her practicing after dinner when he could hear it (author interviews with Franz Jung, Dr. Med. Peter Jung, Dr. Rudolf Niehus, Frau Pfarrer Monica Walder-Niehus, Agathe Niehus-Jung, Frau Dr. Sybille Willi-Niehus, C. A. Meier, Marie-Louise von Franz, and others).

48. BA. When CGJ left the Burghölzli, Trudi did also. She and her mother lived in their own house in Küsnacht but frequently stayed in the Jung house to care for the children when CGJ and Emma were away. After Emilie's death in 1923, Trudi shared an apartment above the apothecary shop in Küsnacht with a friend, and the two women had sporadic employment as home health care aides. Dr. Med. Peter Jung, interview with the author, March 7, 1998, stated that unmarried women had to gain special permission from their closest male relative in order to live independently, and in this case, it was obviously given by CGJ, who also supported his sister financially until her death in 1935.

CHAPTER 6: "SOMETHING UNCONSCIOUSLY FATEFUL . . .
WAS BOUND TO HAPPEN"

1. Obituary of Johannes Rauschenbach, *Tageblatt für den Kanton Schaffhausen*, March 3, 1905 (date sometimes given as March 5). His descendants cite numerous causes, among them various cancers and/or complications from syphilis.

2. Laurence Homberger, interview with the author, February 27, 1997, Zürich, and Frau Marianne Homberger, September 4, 1995, Schaffhausen.

3. From "Die dritte und vierte Generation," *Journal of the IWC*, Schaffhausen, 1986, p. 47; Alexander Pope, "CGJ and the IWC," *Leonardo*, a special edition of *Watch International* (Zürich: Haumesser Edition, 1997), p. 36. CGJ's letter to Directors Haenggi and Vogel is dated February 8, 1911.

4. CGJ gave all his children, grandchildren, and god-children an IWC watch when they were confirmed in the Swiss Reformed Church, or when they reached the age of twelve or thirteen (the Jung children were not confirmed). CGJ's was a Lépine (a pocket watch without a spring lid), engraved with the letters CJ on the back of the case. It is owned today by his grandson René Baumann. Another grandson, Nicholas Baumann (both sons of Gret Baumann-Jung), is a serious collector of old IWC watches. Among those in his collection are Emma Jung's and her mother's.

5. From interviews with members of the Homberger and Jung families.

6. *Protocols*, in some versions dated September 23, 1957.

7. Dr. Thomas B. Kirsch, in personal communication, added that Freudians and other schools of psychoanalysis generally accept CGJ's work until approximately 1913, after which they fault him for deviating from scientific methodology.

8. *CW*-2, para. 924, p. 430.

9. See "Psychophysical Investigations with the Galvanometer and Pneumograph in Normal and Insane Individuals," *CW*-2, pp. 492–580. For a full list of Riklin's publications that resulted from his collaboration with CGJ, see *CW*-2, pp. 624–25.

10. For some of the ways in which CGJ changed Wilhelm Wundt's original methodology, see Sonu Shamdasani, "Spielrein's Associations: A Newly Identified Word Association Protocol," *Harvest* 39 (1993): 164–65.

11. An undated note in the BA from CGJ to Trudi Jung asks her to "be precise and observe exactly." From 1906 to 1908, Trudi worked directly with patients as a nurse and helped her brother on her own time. She left the Burghölzli shortly before CGJ did, in 1908, and until 1925 served occasionally as CGJ's secretary.

12. *Analytical Psychology: Notes of the Seminar Given in 1925*, ed. William McGuire, Bollingen Series 99 (Princeton: Princeton Univ. Press, 1989), p. 5. Andrew Samuels, Bani Shorter, and Fred Plaut, eds., *A Critical Dictionary of Jungian Analysis* (London and New York: Routledge, 1986), pp. 53–54, point out that whereas Freud used the term "libido" in "an exclusively sexual character," CGJ used it interchangeably with "energy" in a context that is "neutral in character." See also Marie-Louise von Franz, *CGJ: His Myth in Our Time* (Toronto: Inner City Books, 1988), pp. 57–59, for further explanation of CGJ's research from 1903 to 1906.

13. *Analytical Psychology: 1925 Seminar Notes*, p. 8.

14. *CW*-1, pp. 58 and 79.

15. *Analytical Psychology: 1925 Seminar Notes*, p. 14.

16. In "Answers to Questions on Freud," *Spring* (1968): 46, CGJ was asked to respond in writing to a series of questions submitted by a representative of the *New York Times* in Geneva. CGJ wrote: "The facts of repression, substitution, symbolization and systematic amnesia described by Freud coincided with the results of my association experiments (1902–04). Later on (1906) I discovered similar phenomena in schizophrenia. I accepted in those years all of Freud's views, but I could not make

up my mind to accept the sexual theory of neurosis and still less of psychosis, no matter how much I tried. I came to the conclusion (1910) that Freud's one-sided emphasis on sex must be a subjective prejudice."

17. The true correspondence was initiated by Jung in the early spring of 1906, when he sent Freud a copy of his *Diagnostic Association Studies*. CGJ's letter that accompanied his book is apparently lost, for it is not in *F/J*. Freud's first known reply to CGJ is dated April 11, 1906. CGJ sent *Diagnostische Assoziationsstudien: Beiträge zur experimentellen Psychopathologie*, vol. 1 (Leipzig, 1906). It consists of six studies by CGJ and other Burghölzli doctors, all edited by CGJ, who directed the research. Those by CGJ are reprinted in *CW-2*.

18. The only extant copy of this letter to date is in the BA. Bernard Minder, "Sabina Spielrein: Jungs Patientin am Burghölzli," *Luzifer-Amor, Zeitschrift zur Geschichte der Psychoanalyse* 7, no. 14 (1994), cites it to "prove" that CGJ was first of all trying to contact Freud, a remark that Zvi Lothane, "In Defense of Sabina Spielrein," *International Forum of Psychoanalysis* 5 (1996), accepts. This is speculative, as there is no evidence that Frau Spielrein ever sent her copy of the letter to Freud; nor did she try to contact him without it. As Aldo Carotenuto and Jeanne Moll (translator of excerpts from Spielrein's diary [*JAP* 46 (2001): 155–71]), citing the Sabina Spielrein papers found in the Claparède archives in Geneva, do not mention finding either a copy or any mention of this letter in Spielrein's files, the assumption is that the only extant copy is the one in the BA, cited here. The Burghölzli had begun to use typewriters by 1904. What appears to be an original typed letter (i.e., not a carbon copy) is in CGJ's case report and is found in two places: the original in the official BA and a copy in the files of the Burghölzli Museum.

19. A plaque indicating that she lived here is now on the apartment building. Her thesis was entitled "Uber den psychologischen Inhalt eines Falls von Schizophrenie" (Concerning the Psychological Content of a Case of Schizophrenia), *Jahrbuch* 3, no. 1 (1911). CGJ cites it frequently in *Symbols of Transformation*, *CW-5*, pp. 139ff.

20. I refer to the differences of opinion by (among many others) Aldo Carotenuto, *A Secret Symmetry: Sabina Spielrein Between Jung and Freud* (New York: Pantheon Books, 1982); John Kerr, *A Most Dangerous Method: The Story of Jung, Freud, and Sabina Spielrein* (New York: Alfred A. Knopf, 1993); Peter J. Swales, "What Jung Didn't Say," *Harvest* 38 (1992); Bernard Minder, "Jung an Freud 1905: Ein Bericht über Sabina Spielrein," *Gesnerus* 50 (1993), and *Jungs Patientin*; Zvi Lothane, "In Defense of Sabina Spielrein"; and Adeline van Waning, "The Works of Pioneering Psychoanalyst Sabina Spielrein: 'Destruction as a Cause of Coming into Being,'" *International Review of Psychoanalysis* (1992). Willy Holtzman's play "Sabina," a romanticized account of her relationship with Freud and Jung in which she is portrayed as a heroine, was staged Off Broadway in New York in 1996. Christopher Hampton's play *The Talking Cure* was staged at the National Theatre, London, in 2003. Elisabeth Márton's film, "Ich hiess Sabina Spielrein" (My Name Was Sabina Spielrein), produced by Idé Film Felixson AB, Sweden, and released in 2002, contains new information about her professional life. The *Journal of Analytical Psychology* 46, no. 1 (January 2001) devoted the articles section to the subject. And, of course, *F/J*.

21. The following account is based on CGJ's report, September 25, 1905; CGJ's clinical notes, 1904–05 (among which are notations by other doctors on the staff); the correspondence in the BA between Jung and Bleuler and Herr and Frau Spielrein; B. Minder's *Jungs Patientin*; and extracts from Spielrein's diary, quoted in Carotenuto, *Secret Symmetry*.

22. Friedrich Fröbel (1782–1852) specialized in the study of preschool-age children

through the use of toys designed to assess a child's inherent creativity. He promoted the creative spirit in the child as well as the parental consciousness of a child's mental and emotional needs. Fröbel was the inventor of kindergarten, and his model was widely copied throughout Europe and the United States.

23. *F/J*, 4J, October 23, 1906. CGJ added that Spielrein's first trauma occurred when she saw her father spanking her older brother when she was three or four. Between the ages of four and seven, she evinced "convulsive attempts to defecate on her own feet . . . tried to defecate and at the same time to prevent defecation."

24. Kerr, *A Most Dangerous Method*, pp. 32–34 and notes to pp. 515–16, compiles the history of such symptoms and those who also experienced them.

25. The translation into English is ambiguous: "The abusive acts of the boy aroused her, she also had to masturbate when seeing how he was punished." In "The Freudian Theory of Hysteria (1908)," *CW*-4, p. 20, CGJ writes that sexual excitement occurred when her younger brother was punished in the same way and adds that this gradually induced "a negative attitude towards her father." Karen Sophie Slaata, writing on behalf of the Spielrein estate in a 1996 letter to Burghölzli officials (in the BA), notes that Sabina Spielrein was probably sexually abused by her father, but she does not offer supporting evidence.

26. Bleuler to Frau Spielrein, August 27, 1904, BA.

27. Bleuler to *Sanitätsdirektion*, August 18, 1904, Zürich.

28. Bleuler to Herr Spielrein, September 14, 1904, BA.

29. Bleuler to Herr Spielrein, September 26, 1904, BA.

30. Bleuler to Herr Spielrein, October 25, 1904, BA.

31. CGJ to Frau Spielrein, February 13, 1905, BA.

32. The following account is from CGJ to Herr Spielrein, May 23 and 31, 1905, and June 7, 1905, all BA.

33. Sabina Spielrein, "Beiträge zur Kenntnis der kindlichen Seele," *Zentralblatt für Psychoanalyse und Psychotherapie* 3 (1912): 57 and 61.

34. CGJ to Freud, September 25, 1905, BA.

35. No evidence has yet been found to suggest that Freud ever saw CGJ's report. The first mention of Spielrein comes in *F/J*, 4J, October 23, 1906, pp. 6–7, in which CGJ tells Freud he is sending an offprint of "Association, Dreams, and Hysterical Symptoms," *CW*-2, pp. 353–407. Freud's reply (*F/J*, 5F, October 27, 1906) gives no indication that he had any prior knowledge of Spielrein's case history. She obviously saw the report, for in a draft letter for Freud, dated only June 13 (Carotenuto, *Secret Symmetry*, p. 101), she wrote that she possessed "a letter written on 25 November, 1905." One could surmise that she misremembered the date because the letter was in her mother's possession, not hers, as she claimed. This assumption gains credence because the report was not found among the papers consulted by Carotenuto or Moll.

36. *F/J*, 144J, June 4, 1909, pp. 228–29.

37. Gordon Craig, *The Triumph of Liberalism: Zürich in the Golden Age, 1830–69* (New York: Charles Scribner's Sons, 1988), p. 157, writes that "the surge in women's university education came later, and most women students were for a long time foreigners." The first woman student was a Russian, Maria Kniaschina, admitted to the medical school in 1863. A second Russian, Nadeschda Suslowa, was granted a doctoral degree in 1867.

38. Among them M. Cary Thomas, who later became the president of Bryn Mawr College.

39. Kerr, in *A Most Dangerous Method*, p. 13, describes Spielrein as "a woman with a predilection for insisting on her point of view at exactly those moments when his-

tory began moving in opposing directions." She appears to have done this from her first day at the Burghölzli.

40. CGJ ended the German text of the "Studies in Word Association" with "special thanks to Mrs. Emma Jung for her active assistance with the repeated revision of this voluminous material" (*GW-2*, p. 208, omitted in *CW-2*).

41. Private source, private archive.

42. "Aerzte zur Zeit C. G. Jungs Tätigkeit am Burghölzli, 1900–1909," BA.

43. Franz Jung, telephone conversation with the author, November 1995. According to Franz Jung, CGJ's diary gave no other specific details.

44. *CW-2*, para. 605, p. 235. The paper was originally published as "Über das Verhalten der Reaktionszeit beim Assoziationsexperimente," in *Journal für Psychologie und Neurologie* 6 (1905). See *CW-2*, p. 221, for full publishing details.

45. *CW-2*, para. 605, pp. 238–39.

46. From drafts of letters, c. 1909, in Carotenuto, *Secret Symmetry*, pp. 101–2.

47. "Die psychopathologische Bedeutung des Assoziationsexperimentes," *Archiv für Kriminalanthropologie und Kriminalistik* (Leipzig) 22 (1906): 2–3. *CW-2*, pp. 408ff.

48. *CW-2*, p. 420.

49. *CW-2*, p. 422.

50. "The Psychological Diagnosis of Evidence" (originally "Die psychologische Diagnose des Tatbestandes"). See *CW-2*, p. 318, for full publishing details.

51. This passage is in slightly different form in various *Protocols*.

CHAPTER 7: "WHO IS THE BOSS IN THIS HOSPITAL?"

1. Karl Abraham is an example of a doctor who had to wait four years (1901–1905) until the first vacancy occurred. Bleuler appointed him for the next three years.

2. *CW-19*, p. 61. CGJ's first two papers written in English were in conjunction with Drs. Frederick Peterson and Charles Ricksher, two Americans who were observing at the Burghölzli. In *MDR*, p. 120, CGJ credits these men with procuring his invitation to Clark University, adding, "simultaneously and independently of me, Freud was invited."

3. Information about Munsterberg is mainly from the book *Big Trouble* (New York: Touchstone Books, 1998), pp. 584–601, esp. p. 597, by the late J. Anthony Lukas, with whom I collaborated on this particular aspect of research. Munsterberg was born in Leipzig and studied with Wundt. Later, when working in his own laboratory at Freiburg University, he disavowed Wundt's work and proposed that all human behavior could be explained in materialistic or mechanistic terms. William James brought Munsterberg to Harvard in 1893 as his sabbatical replacement, describing him to his novelist brother Henry as "the Rudyard Kipling of psychology." CGJ cites Munsterberg throughout *CW-2* and elsewhere throughout *CW* (see *CW-19* and *CW-20* for full citations), but usually to point out the fallacies in his observations.

4. Letters are: CGJ to Charles W. Eliot, October 15, 1907; Eliot to Munsterberg, October 29, 1907; Munsterberg to Eliot, October 31, 1907, all Houghton Library, Harvard University. None are in *CL*. Jung held subscriptions to these newspapers for many years, claiming that reading them helped him to communicate with the many foreign doctors who came to the Burghölzli. In the *Protocols*, he said he began a subscription to the *Daily Telegraph* in 1904 because he was interested in the Russo-Japanese war.

5. Lukas, *Big Trouble*, p. 597.

6. Private source, private archive.

7. Most of these remarks are found throughout the BA, particularly in case reports I cannot cite because of doctor-patient confidentiality. For others, I am indebted to Herr Rolf Mösli and the Burghölzli Museum archives. There are a significant number of such remarks in HE/STA and in various correspondence between Freud and his followers. Others abound in Nameche interviews, HCL.

8. Many commentators have criticized CGJ for not having mentioned Bleuler in *MDR*. He wrote about Bleuler among the many others mentioned frequently throughout the *Protocols* but omitted from *MDR*. A typical reference is one in which CGJ describes Bleuler beginning around 1906 as "[making] fun of me for twenty years," before deigning to accept various constructs of Jung's psychology.

9. CGJ, *Promotionsakten*. Dokumente aus dem Staatsarchiv des Kantons Zürich. Two separate documents attest to Bleuler's statement.

10. Eugen Bleuler, *Dementia Praecox or the Group of Schizophrenias*, trans. Joseph Zinkin (New York: International University Press, 1950), p. 258. On p. 2 of this edition, Bleuler thanks CGJ "particularly."

11. Quoted material is from Ludwig Binswanger, *Sigmund Freud: Reminiscences of a Friendship* (New York and London: Grune and Stratton, 1957), p. 1. Much of the information that follows is from Dr. Kurt Binswanger's Nameche interview, February 3, 1970, HCL.

12. Dr. Hans Gunthardt, interview with the author, March 1997, said it was true even later during his student years at the ETH when CGJ lectured there. Dr. Kurt Binswanger confirmed it in his Nameche interview, HCL.

13. The woman gave me this information on the condition that she and her mother remain anonymous. She was one of a number who informed me of the history of women in Zürich and attitudes toward them in the late nineteenth and early twentieth centuries. Most chose to remain anonymous, but two granted thoughtful interviews: journalist and historian Verena Müller; and Susanna Woodtli, author of *Du Féminisme à l'égalité politique: un siècle de luttes en Suisse, 1868–1971* (Lausanne: Editions Payot, 1977).

14. *MDR*, pp. 118–19, gives the details of what CGJ called his "first real therapeutic experience . . . my first analysis [i.e., of a patient, not his own]." He gave this patient credit for bringing his first private patients to him, most of whom were wealthy women from Zürich and the surrounding towns.

15. Dr. Manfred Bleuler (son of Eugen Bleuler and director of the Burghölzli from 1942 to 1969), Nameche interview, December 8, 1969, HCL.

16. Previous sentence is a paraphrase of *MDR*, p. 114, and two versions of the *Protocols*. Quote is from *MDR*, p. 114.

17. Dr. Wolfgang Binswanger, Nameche interview, September 13, 1970, HCL.

18. Dr. Wolfgang Binswanger, Nameche interview, September 13, 1970, HCL.

19. One such example is Bleuler's letter approving Jung's request to resign: it would "pose no burdens at all to the institution" (Bleuler to the High Administration of Medical Services, Canton Zürich, March 7, 1909, BA).

20. An accurate dating of the commencement and duration of the Bleuler-Freud correspondence is not possible because the Bleuler heirs have refused permission to publish it (see Ilse Grubrich-Simitis, *Back to Freud's Texts* [New Haven and London: Yale Univ. Press, 1993], p. 59, n. 31). William McGuire, in the introduction to *F/J*, p. xx, n. 14, writes that Bleuler's son, Dr. Manfred Bleuler (in a personal communication), believes there was contact between Freud and his father as early as the 1890s, but McGuire gives the date of the first correspondence as 1904 and says it continued "sporadically" until 1925. McGuire also notes that the letters from Freud to Bleuler in Manfred Bleuler's possession are "barred" from publication.

Franz Alexander and Sheldon T. Selesnick, in "The Freud-Bleuler Correspondence," *Archives of General Psychiatry* 12 (January 1965): 6, agree with McGuire and give the date of Bleuler's first letter to Freud as September 21, 1904.

21. Leopold Löwenfeld's book contained Freud's revision of his thinking about the etiological significance of trauma and his most recent thoughts concerning his (Freud's) treatment methodology. Bleuler's review was published in the *Munich Medical Weekly*, April 1904. It is cited in Jeffrey Masson, ed., *The Complete Letters of Sigmund Freud to Wilhelm Fliess: 1887–1904* (Cambridge, Mass.: Harvard Univ. Press, 1985), p. 461, n. 3, and by John Kerr, *A Most Dangerous Method: The Story of Jung, Freud, and Sabina Spielrein* (New York: Alfred A. Knopf, 1993), p. 62, who notes that "one of the great curiosities of Freud's work during the period 1896–1904, noted by Löwenfeld and others, was that while he repeatedly based his claims on his new method of 'psychoanalysis,' he was forever begging off a detailed discussion of what exactly that method entailed." Kerr also notes, p. 65, that "Freud had not yet reported the method, which he had been using for at least four years, where the patient, and not the doctor, sets the day's agenda."

22. Several of Löwenfeld's writings are among the many others listed in the privately printed *Katalog: CGJ Bibliothek, Erbengemeinschaft CGJ,* 1967.

23. Ziehen and Hoch are quoted in Alexander and Selesnick, "The Freud-Bleuler Correspondence," p. 2.

24. Henri Ellenberger, *The Discovery of the Unconscious: The History and Evolution of Dynamic Psychiatry* (New York: Basic Books, 1970), p. 455.

25. *Analytical Psychology: Notes of the Seminar Given in 1925,* ed. William McGuire, Bollingen Series 99 (Princeton: Princeton Univ. Press, 1989), p. 15. On p. 16, n. 3, McGuire advises that CGJ's "recollections in this seminar, which of course were spoken off the cuff, sometimes diverge from what is recorded in the *Letters* and other documents."

26. *Protocols.* Similar passages with slight variants are in *Analytical Psychology: 1925 Seminar Notes,* pp. 15–16, and *MDR,* pp. 147–48.

27. *MDR,* p. 148. Variants in *Protocols.*

28. The first quote is from *MDR,* p. 148, and one *Protocol;* the second is from L. Binswanger's *Freud: Reminiscences,* p. 3. On p. 4 Binswanger notes that Freud's isolation began in 1895–96, following his split with Breuer, and ended in 1906–07, when he was taken up by "The Zürich School" (i.e., Jung).

29. Private documents written by E. Bleuler, from a source who wishes to remain anonymous.

30. The observation is mine; the quote is from Sarah Boxer, "Flogging Freud," *New York Times Book Review,* August 10, 1997, p. 12. Boxer's essay deals with recent negative criticism about Freud, but her citation of W. H. Auden's comment about Freud ("he is no more a person now but a whole climate of opinion") applies to CGJ.

31. In various *Protocols,* CGJ reads aloud to Aniela Jaffé some complete letters and portions of others to and from Freud because he believes they are important additions to comments he made about Freud, or because he wishes to clarify certain of their differences. William McGuire, editor of the Freud-Jung letters (*F/J*), assisted me in trying to locate these letters, but we were unable to do so. As McGuire was assured that he had been given the entire *extant* correspondence by the Freud and Jung heirs, it is evident that, for whatever the reason, some letters on both sides were not among them. A list of "Missing Items" is in *F/J* following Appendix 1 (p. 562). Vincent Brome, in *Freud and His Early Circle* (New York: William Morrow, 1968), p. 95, writes without further attribution that Freud destroyed letters

from CGJ, Abraham, and Ferenczi among "a mass of documents and letters" when he moved to his sister Frau Rosa Graf's apartment in 1908.

32. *F/J*, 1F, April 11, 1906, p. 3. A possible reason for Freud's eagerness to acquire CGJ's book may have been the lecture he was to give on the subject in June 1906, "Psycho-Analysis and the Establishment of the Facts in Legal Proceedings," in *SE*-9: 107ff.

33. Masson, *Complete Letters*, p. 461.

34. Ernest Jones, *The Life and Work of Sigmund Freud* (London: Hogarth Press, 1955), 2: 110, writes that until 1905, when the *Three Essays on Sexuality* appeared, Freud and his writings were either "quietly ignored" or "mentioned with a sentence or two of disdain." This changed to "a more active line," that if Freud's ideas "would not die by themselves they had to be killed."

35. *F/J*, 1F, April 11, 1906, p. 3.

36. Letter from one of the assistant doctors to his family. Author's translation. Private archive.

37. Gustav Aschaffenburg, "Die Beziehungen des sexuellen Lebens zur Entstehung von Nerven-und Geisterkrankheiten," *Münchener Medizinische Wochenschrift* (September 11, 1906): 173–98; quoted by Jones, *Life and Work*, 2: 111.

38. *F/J*, 2J, October 5, 1906, p. 4. McGuire notes that this correspondence is apparently lost.

39. "Die Hysterielehre Freud's. Eine Erwiderung auf die Aschaffenburg'sche Kritik," *Münchener Medizinische Wochenschrift* 53 (November 1906): 230–31; also in *CW*-4, pp. 3–9.

40. *F/J*, 6J, November 26, 1906, p. 9.

41. Jones, *Life and Work*, 2: 111. Jones was a Welsh psychoanalyst who, in the words of his biographer, Vincent Brome, was "a figure known internationally who not only manipulated many phases of psycho-analytical history but became the power behind the Freudian throne and actually made a great deal of that history. A close associate of Freud for thirty years, he contributed over two hundred theoretical papers, wrote eleven books and finally crowned his writing career with his three-volume biography of Freud described by the *New York Times* as 'one of the outstanding biographies of the age.' His enduring hostility and animosity toward CGJ cannot be emphasized strongly enough" (*Ernest Jones: A Biography* [New York: W. W. Norton, 1983], unpaginated preface).

42. *F/J*, 6J, November 26, 1906, p. 9.

43. *CW*-4, p. 4.

44. *F/J*, 2J, October 5, 1906, pp. 4–5; 3F, pp. 5–6.

45. The official translation is in *F/J*, 42F, September 2, 1907, p. 82. I have used Brome's *Freud*, p. 81.

46. Peter Gay, *Freud, A Life for Our Time* (New York and London: W. W. Norton, 1988), p. 157.

47. *F/J*, 3F, p. 6; *The Psychology of Dementia Praecox*, *CW*-3, pp. 1–5, originally published as *Diagnostische Assoziationsstudien: Beiträge zur experimentellen Psychopathologie*, ed. CGJ, with works wholly or in part by CGJ and with Franz Riklin.

48. At the Congress of Southwest German Psychiatrists, November 3–4, 1906. Jung is quoted in the *Zentralblatt für Nervenheilkunde und Psychiatrie*, n.s., 18 (March 1907): 185. See also *F/J*, 6J, November 26, 1906, p. 9.

49. That a letter from Freud is missing can be deduced from *F/J*, 7J, December 4, 1906, p. 10. See also *F/J*, 9J, December 29, 1906, p. 13, and "Missing Items," p. 562.

50. *F/J*, 11F, January 1, 1907, p. 17.

51. *F/J*, 9J, December 29, 1906, p. 14.
52. *CW*-3, pp. 57ff.; *F/J*, 9J, December 29, 1906, p. 14.
53. *F/J*, 9J, December 29, 1906, pp. 14–15.
54. *CW*-3, p. 58.
55. *F/J*, 9J, December 29, 1906, p. 15.
56. Manfred, b. 1903, who also became the director of the Burghölzli and a professor at Zürich University; Richard, b. 1905, who studied agriculture at the ETH and lived and worked in Morocco as a farmer and agricultural consultant.
57. *F/J*, 11F, January 1, 1907, pp. 17–19.
58. *F/J*, 12J, January 8, 1907, p. 20.
59. Private source and private archive.
60. Sidney L. Pomer, "Max Eitingon, 1881–1943," in *Psychoanalytic Pioneers*, ed. Franz Alexander, Samuel Eisenstein, and Martin Grotjahn (New York: Basic Books, 1966), p. 51. Eitingon received his medical degree in 1909 and moved to Berlin, where he worked with his friend Karl Abraham until he settled permanently in Palestine in September 1933.
61. Private archive, previously cited.
62. *F/J*, 46J, September 25, 1907, p. 90.
63. Sidney L. Pomer used the term "Vienna Psychoanalytic Society" in Alexander et al., *Psychoanalytic Pioneers*, p. 51. McGuire, *F/J*, n. 1, p. 23, citing H. Nunberg and E. Federn, eds., *Minutes of the Vienna Psychoanalytic Society*, I, Introduction, p. xviii, notes that Freud's followers were still meeting in his waiting room on Wednesday evenings, "the so-called 'Psychological Wednesday Evenings,'" and not until 1908 was the Vienna Psychoanalytic Society formed.
64. E. L. Freud, ed., *Letters of Sigmund Freud* (New York: Basic Books, 1960). Jones, *Life and Work*, 2: 32, described Eitingon's visit as "the first training analysis," as do Franz Alexander et al. in *The History of Psychiatry* (Northvale, N.J.: Jason Aronson, 1995), p. 211.
65. Alexander et al., *Psychoanalytic Pioneers*, p. 52, quoting M. Eitingon's "In the Dawn of Psychoanalysis," in M. Wulff, ed., *Max Eitingon, in Memoriam* (Jerusalem: Israel Psychoanalytic Society, 1950), p. 52.
66. Alexander et al., *Psychoanalytic Pioneers*, p. 51.
67. *F/J*, 12J, January 8, 1907, p. 20.

CHAPTER 8: DIVORCE/FORCE, CHOICE/PAIN

1. *F/J*, 4J, October 23, 1906, p. 7.
2. John Kerr, *A Most Dangerous Method: The Story of Jung, Freud, and Sabina Spielrein* (New York: Alfred A. Knopf, 1993), p. 122.
3. *F/J*, 5F, October 27, 1906, p. 8. Freud's general tenor strengthens the theory that Frau Spielrein never sent him CGJ's 1905 letter.
4. *F/J*, 35J, July 6, 1907, pp. 72–73. Sabina Spielrein is not named in this letter or in 135J, March 11, 1909, p. 211. Supporting evidence from Aldo Carotenuto, *A Secret Symmetry: Sabina Spielrein Between Jung and Freud* (New York: Pantheon Books, 1982), p. 140.
5. William McGuire, "Jung's Complex Reactions (1907): Word Association Experiments Performed by Binswanger," *Spring* (1984): 1–34. Ludwig Binswanger never identified CGJ as the subject, saying only that he performed the experiment on "twenty-three healthy persons." McGuire established that CGJ was one through the following sources: comments in Sabina Spielrein's letters to Freud, July 6, 1907, and June 13, 1909; Carotenuto, *Secret Symmetry*, p. 102; and Binswanger's own comment that CGJ helped him "even by letting me use him as a subject in ex-

periments" (*Sigmund Freud: Reminiscences of a Friendship* [New York and London: Grune and Stratton, 1957], p. 1); and *F/J*, F61, January 14, 1908, p. 109. Binswanger's paper was originally published as "Über das Verhalten des psychogalvanischen Phänomens beim Assoziationsexperiment," *Diagnostische Assoziationsstudien: Beiträge zur experimentellen Psychopathologie,* herausgegeben von Dr. CGJ, Zweiter Band (Leipzig: Barth, 1910) (English: *Studies in Word Association. Experiments in the Diagnosis of Psychopathological Conditions Carried Out at the Psychiatric Clinic of the U. of Zürich Under the Direction of CGJ,* trans. M. D. Eder [London: Routledge and Kegan Paul, 1969], pp. 446–530). In a letter to McGuire, January 11, 1984, Dr. Hilde Binswanger (Ludwig's daughter) said that neither she nor her brother, Wolfgang, ever heard their father identify CGJ as the subject of any tests, and that if McGuire came to such conclusions, he would have to make it clear that they were his own. Recent scholars find McGuire's conclusion convincing; they include Kerr, *A Most Dangerous Method,* pp. 124ff.; and Sonu Shamdasani, "Spielrein's Associations: A Newly Identified Word Association Protocol," *Harvest* 39 (1993): 164–68.

6. Shamdasani, "Spielrein's Associations," p. 165.
7. McGuire, "Jung's Complex Reactions," p. 2.
8. Binswanger's father, also Ludwig, was director of the sanatorium; his uncle Otto was a professor of psychiatry at the University of Jena. His son, Wolfgang, and daughter, Hilde, both became psychoanalysts.
9. Binswanger later became director of the Private Clinic for Nervous and Mental Patients in Kreuzlingen, and *not* the Kreuzlingen Mental Hospital, a distinction he takes care to make in *Freud: Reminiscences,* footnote on p. 2. He is noted for his development of existential analysis, most particularly the case of "Ellen West," published as "Der Fall Ellen West," *Schweizer Archiv für Neurologie und Psychiatrie* 53 (1944): 255–77 (English trans. in *Existence,* eds. Rollo May, Ernst Angel, and Henri Ellenberger [New York: Basic Books, 1958], pp. 237–364).
10. From three separate *Protocols.* Quotes are from one version marked "New Sheet, March 7, 1958" by Aniela Jaffé. See chapter 11, the case of "Babette S.," for elaboration.
11. William McGuire, in "Jung's Complex Reactions," p. 3, notes that this "'double image' quality is suggestive of certain stories by J. L. Borges." In a letter to Nelson Algren, Simone de Beauvoir referred to this as *"dédoublement,"* or "doubling," in which "the hero and the average man are the same — Clark Kent is also 'Superman'" (Deirdre Bair, *Simone de Beauvoir: A Biography* [New York: Summit Books, 1990], p. 365).
12. Binswanger, *Studies in Word Association,* p. 458.
13. Binswanger, *Studies in Word Association,* p. 464.
14. The Jung family never tired of telling Gret Baumann-Jung how strong this so-called resemblance was, and it plagued her for the rest of her life. Two of her sons and several of her nephews and nieces cited it as one of the reasons she and CGJ were in such frequent conflict.
15. Binswanger, *Studies in Word Association,* p. 459.
16. In the English translation prepared by Dr. M. D. Eder, the stimulus word is given as "all," the response as "ton," and the house's name as Alton. McGuire, "Jung's Complex Reactions," p. 4, notes that Ölberg translates as "Mount of Olives" and is unlikely to have worked as a test reaction.
17. He refers to this throughout the various *Protocols* as the only time in his life until he resigned from the Burghölzli when he was free to do so. His language is always loving and wistful.

18. This and personal information about CGJ and Emma, their children, and the Hombergers, are from private archives and private sources.

19. HarperCollins Dictionary provided definitions. I am grateful to Dr. Phil. Richard Merz and Ms. Ursula Schulte for this information, and also to Professor Theodore Ziolkowski for commentary.

20. Brahms set Goethe's popular verse to music as follows: "Eine Maus und eine Kröte / gingen eines abends spoete."

21. In the entire test, Binswanger identified "eleven different complexes, which constellate more than one reaction, and many lesser ones" (pp. 468–69).

22. This conclusion is based on my Zürich research. See also Binswanger, *Studies in Word Association*, p. 472; and McGuire, "Jung's Complex Reactions," p. 21. Several scholars (Peter Swales, "What Jung Didn't Say," *Harvest* 38 [1992], Shamdasani, "Spielrein's Associations," and Kerr, *A Most Dangerous Method*), have declared this to be proof of CGJ's marital infidelity. McGuire argues that it merely "would not rule out" that the reference was to Spielrein. Shamdasani argues that Sabina Spielrein is Binswanger's "Subject No. 15, Female Student" on p. 515. This is possible but still unproven; there were many female Russian medical students in Zürich at that time, among them several besides Spielrein who worked with Jung at the Burghölzli and participated in his testing.

23. What follows is from private archives and private sources that independently insisted this was the first of three separate instances when Emma Jung threatened to divorce her husband.

24. *F/J*, 16J, February 26, 1907, p. 24.

25. Binswanger's memoir, *Freud: Reminiscences*, pp. 2ff., gives his recollection of the visit.

26. The two men signed themselves as such, "Jung & Junger," in a postcard to Freud, reproduced in *F/J*, 73J, undated, p. 125. *"Junger"* also carries the meaning of "disciple" in German.

27. Binswanger, *Freud: Reminiscences*, p. 3. It should be noted that he wrote this much later in life.

28. Freud to Abraham, *F/Abraham*, March 5, 1908, p. 34.

29. CGJ, interview with Dr. Kurt Eissler, August 29, 1953. Manuscript Division, LC, Tape no. 74. Restricted until 2005 but generously made available for this book by Dr. Eissler and released to me by the LC at his request.

30. CGJ, interview with Kurt Eissler, LC. The German original reads as follows: *"Ich war natürlich, ich meine, natürlich, wenn man mit einem solchen Mann konfrontiert ist, dann ist man eben auch einbegriffen, nicht wahr, und ist Partei, nicht wahr, und das alles, all das, nicht wahr?!"*

31. *MDR*, p. 149.

32. Martin Freud, *Glory Reflected: Sigmund Freud — Man and Father* (London and Sydney: Angus and Robertson, 1957), pp. 108–9.

33. Among them, Ernest Jones, *The Life and Work of Sigmund Freud* (London: Hogarth Press, 1955), 2: 382–83; Peter Gay, *Freud, A Life for Our Time* (New York and London: W. W. Norton, 1988), p. 157; and Ronald W. Clark, *Freud: The Man and the Cause* (New York: Random House, 1980), p. 19.

34. Binswanger, in the German version, *Errinerungen an Sigmund Freud*, p. 11.

35. Jones, *Life and Work*, 2: 32. CGJ met Jones in Amsterdam in July 1907 at the International Congress of Neurology, where CGJ allegedly told him this account of the first meeting with Freud. The following November, Jones came to the Burghölzli as a visiting observer, and the two men renewed their acquaintance — or friendship at this time. As always, Jones's later animosity toward CGJ must be factored into his writings.

36. *Protocols*, in two versions under "October 24, 1957."
37. Jung's emphasis in CGJ's interview with Kurt Eissler, LC.
38. The first title is from Jones, *Life and Work*, 2: 32; the second is from Gay, *A Life for Our Time*, p. 173. In 1908, the group adopted its official name (Gay, p. 174). Gay, pp. 173–96, gives the most concise history to date of this group. See also Phyllis Grosskurth, *The Secret Ring: Freud's Inner Circle and the Politics of Psychoanalysis* (New York: Addison-Wesley, 1991).
39. Max Graf, "Reminiscences of Professor Sigmund Freud," *The Psychoanalytic Quarterly* 2 (1942): 472.
40. Jones, *Life and Work*, 2: 33.
41. Binswanger, *Sigmund Freud: Reminiscences*, p. 4.
42. Carl E. Schorske, *Fin-de-Siècle Vienna: Politics and Culture* (New York: Random House, 1981), pp. xxv–xxvi.
43. CGJ, interview with Kurt Eissler, LC.
44. N. G. Hale Jr., ed., *James Jackson Putnam and Psychoanalysis* (Cambridge, Mass.: Harvard Univ. Press, 1971), p. 189; and *F/J*, p. 308. Paul Roazen writes in *Freud and His Followers* (New York: Da Capo Press, 1992), p. 290: "Partly because of Freud's tendency to exaggerate opposition, it is hard to assess the anti-Semitism he complained of. . . . In private, Freud complained of Jung's 'lies, brutality, and anti-Semitic condescension towards [him].'" Roazen also observes: "Curiously enough, however, in Freud's correspondence with Jung, there is not a trace of any such accusation. . . . In a sense, Freud and his followers had to depict Jung as an anti-Semite, since Freud's enthusiasm for Jung in the first place had been essentially anti-Semitic in character."
45. CGJ, interview with Kurt Eissler, LC.
46. Jones, *Life and Work*, 2: 33. Roazen, *Freud and His Followers*, p. 10, makes an interesting observation about Jones: "History gets written by accident. Jones lived the longest of [Freud's devoted followers], and as a survivor had the last word. His pen was tireless, and his capacity to hate considerable."
47. Private source, private archive.
48. CGJ, interview with Kurt Eissler, LC. General information continues to be from the private source and archive quoted above as well as from this interview.
49. That is, until his daughter Anna became an adult and took her role. Elisabeth Young-Bruhl, *Anna Freud: A Biography* (New York: Summit Books, 1998), and Roazen, *Freud and His Followers*, offer the most satisfying explanations of the emotional complexities of the women in Freud's household.
50. CGJ, interview with Kurt Eissler, LC. CGJ stated the italicized words in English in an interview that was conducted in German.
51. Roazen, *Freud and His Followers*, pp. 59–63, makes a useful point: "The important matter is what Minna meant to Freud . . . and not so much the specifics of a possible sexual liaison between them. Freud seemed to have a split in his love life, his sexuality remaining with Martha and his spiritual involvement shifting to Minna."
52. This information is from *F/J*, "The Jungs in Vienna," p. 24. Fülöp (also known as Philip or Philippe) Stein (1867–1918) met Bleuler at the International Congress for Anti-Alcoholism in Budapest in 1905, after which he did research on the association experiment at the Burghölzli, but primarily with Bleuler.
53. Private archive.
54. *F/J*, 144J, June 4, 1909, pp. 228–29.
55. *F/J*, 19J, April 11, 1907, p. 32.
56. *F/J*, 26J, May 24, 1907, pp. 49–51.
57. *F/J*, 23F, April 21, 1907, pp. 40–43.

58. *F/J*, 26J, May 24, 1907, pp. 49–51.
59. In the *Protocols*, CGJ wrote that he never, ever met Janet. He seems not to have remembered that he attended receptions at Janet's apartment during his sabbatical in 1902, or that he spoke to Janet in Paris and was disappointed that he showed no interest in recent theory (*F/J*, 33J, June 28, 1907, p. 67). Nor did he mention Janet's presence at the Harvard Tercentenary, when they attended the same activities and social functions.
60. *F/J*, 29J, June 4, 1907, pp. 56–58; 30F, June 6, 1907, pp. 58–62. Although Schwyzer had been institutionalized in the Burghölzli since October 27, 1901, this is believed (to date) to be the first time Jung wrote about him.
61. *F/J*, 33J, June 28, 1907, p. 66.
62. *F/J*, 19J, April 11, 1907, p. 32.
63. *F/J*, 20F, April 14, 1907, pp. 32–35.
64. CGJ, interview with Kurt Eissler, LC.
65. *F/J*, 31J, June 12, 1907, p. 63.
66. *F/J*, 37J, August 12, 1907, p. 75.
67. *F/J*, 32F, June 14, 1907, p. 64.
68. *F/J*, 28J, May 30, 1907, p. 55.
69. From the BA, a private source, and several private archives.
70. *F/J*, 28J, May 30, 1907, p. 55; Bleuler's responses are from his letters in the BA to cantonal officials during CGJ's resignation, 1908–09.
71. *F/J*, 51J, November 8, 1907, p. 96; Vincent Brome, *Ernest Jones: A Biography* (New York: W. W. Norton, 1983), pp. 47ff. Roazen, *Freud and His Followers*, p. 10, describes Jones as follows: "Jones would not rank high in terms of the originality of his psychoanalytic contributions. His special talent lay in popularizing Freud's ideas and in helping the movement as an organization." CGJ recognized this quality and for a time considered Jones a rival.
72. *F/J*, 46J, September 25, 1907, p. 89.
73. *F/J*, 39J, August 19, 1907, p. 78.

Chapter 9: Vocatus atque non vocatus, Deus aderit

1. Fiechter was the grandson of CGJ's aunt Sophie Reimer, the first child of Carl I Gustav by his first wife, Virginie de Lassaulx. Fiechter was a respected architect and professor at the Technische Hochschule in Stuttgart. Franz Jung trained under his supervision.
2. Barbara Hannah, *Jung: His Life and Work, A Biographical Memoir* (Boston: Shambhala, 1991), p. 93.
3. The original house number was 1003, until 1915, when it was renumbered 228. For many years, the property was flanked on either side by vacant lots, until a public beach was built to its left and a large apartment house to its right. The main avenue, or entrance walkway, that led from the street to the house's front door had an unimpeded view for most of Jung's life, but in his last years a car dealership was built directly across the street, the first thing he saw when the door opened.
4. *Protocols*. He made this remark when discussing an offer to become a professor at Oxford University in 1913.
5. Dr. Med. Peter Jung most graciously gave a guided tour of the house and grounds, and other members of the Jung family provided further details about its construction, layout, and the use the family made of it.
6. All the children took music lessons, but Marianne (b. 1910) was considered by her siblings the most musically talented.

7. Hannah, *Life and Work*, p. 93.
8. Desiderius Erasmus (1466–1536), *Collectanea Adagiorum*. In the notes to *CL*-2, p. 611, the editors describe it as a collection of analects from classical authors and note that CGJ acquired a 1563 edition when he was nineteen.
9. CGJ to Eugene Rolfe, November 19, 1960, *CL*-2, p. 610.
10. Undated *Protocol* passages on the meaning of God. Also CGJ to E. Rolfe, November 19, 1960, *CL*-2, p. 610; CGJ to N. Roswitha, August 17, 1957, *CL*-2, p. 384.
11. *F/J*, 46J, September 25, 1907, p. 89.
12. *F/J*, 51J, November 8, 1907, p. 97; 59J, January 2, 1908, pp. 106–7.
13. *CW*-18, pp. 388–89.
14. *F/J*, 56J, December 16, 1907, p. 103. On December 8, 1907 (p. 102, 55F), Freud told CGJ he had little confidence that many French would become his followers, but said, "The Geneva people must be thought of as Swiss."
15. Miscellaneous archives, Burghölzli Hospital.
16. Ernest Jones, *The Life and Work of Sigmund Freud* (London: Hogarth Press, 1955), 2: 38. Brome, in *Jones*, p. 48, repeats the incident and gives Jones's interpretation of it by writing that Brill was "unaware of Jones's steadily growing psychoanalytic sophistication."
17. *F/J*, 54J, November 30, 1907, p. 101.
18. Brome, *Jones*, p. 47.
19. *F/J*, 55F, December 8, 1907, p. 102.
20. *F/J*, 56J, December 16, 1907, p. 104.
21. *F/J*, 75J, March 3, 1908, p. 128.
22. Part I, *CW*-2. Jones, *Life and Work*, 2: 49, writes that nothing came of CGJ's contact with Prince. In *F/J*, 69J, February 15, 1908, CGJ tells Freud that Prince made "unacceptable proposals."
23. *F/J*, 53F, November 24, 1907, p. 99; 54J, November 30, 1907, p. 101; and 55F, December 8, 1907, p. 102.
24. Bleuler's directive, "Answer this," is scrawled on several letters in the BA. Other letters are in miscellaneous folders at the ETH, and some few are in private archives in Zürich.
25. *F/J*, 81J, April 11, 1908, p. 136.
26. "Der Inhalt der Psychose" (trans. as "The Content of the Psychoses"), *CW*-3; also *CW*-19, p. 7. CGJ gave the lecture on January 16, 1908, to such a large list of subscribers that it had to be moved from the main lecture hall in the university to the larger auditorium in the *Rathaus*, or town hall.
27. See *F/J*, 62J, p. 110; also Appendix 4, pp. 571–72.
28. Brome, *Jones*, p. 49.
29. *F/J*, 65J, January 25, 1908, p. 114. CGJ's emphasis.
30. Jones, *Life and Work*, 2: 39–40.
31. *F/J*, 63J, January 22, 1908, p. 111.
32. *F/J*, 70F, February 17, 1908, p. 119. See also Peter Gay, *A Life for Our Time* (New York and London: W. W. Norton, 1988), pp. 213–15. Jones, *Life and Work*, 2: 34, writes that CGJ described Freud's Viennese followers as "a medley of artists, decadents and mediocrities," and that he "deplored" Freud's being surrounded by them. As Jones attributes this to CGJ's "'racial' prejudice," one should remember that he wrote this after World War II.
33. CGJ's views are from *F/J*, 39J, August 19, 1907, p. 78; Freud's are from 40F, August 27, 1907, p. 79.
34. *F/J*, 84F, April 19, 1908, p. 140.

35. "On Dementia Praecox," *Berliner Klinische Wochenschrift* 45, no. 22 (June 1, 1908): 1078ff.
36. *F/J*, 70F and 71F, February 17 and 18, 1908, pp. 119–22.
37. *F/J*, 72J, February 20, 1908, pp. 122–23.
38. Jones, *Life and Work*, 2: 40–43, says it took place on April 26. See also *F/J*, Appendix 4, pp. 571–72, where the date of the meeting is given as April 27 (guests arrived the previous evening, but no organized activity took place until the following day).
39. *F/J*, 87F, May 3, 1908, p. 144.
40. *F/J*, 86J, April 30, 1908, p. 143.
41. *F/J*, 87F, May 3, 1908, pp. 144–45.
42. Freud to Abraham, *F/Abraham*, May 3, 1908, pp. 33–34.
43. Freud to Abraham, *F/Abraham*, May 9, 1908, p. 35.
44. *F/J*, 91J, May 7, 1908, p. 149.
45. *F/J*, 92F, May 10, 1908, p. 150.

CHAPTER 10: ". . . LIKE MY TWIN BROTHER"
1. *F/J*, 92F, May 10, 1908, p. 150.
2. *F/J*, 50J, November 2, 1907, p. 96. Editor's note states that the society was located in New York and was then under the direction of James Hervey Hyslop, who most likely sponsored CGJ.
3. And, some would argue, still is. I was invited to several long-term, ongoing sessions held by different groups. My status was that of a private observer, and I was sworn to respect the groups' confidentiality.
4. In 1905, CGJ gave a lecture in Basel, "On Spiritualistic Phenomena," published then in the *Basler Nachrichten* and later in *CW*-18, *The Symbolic Life*, which contains other writings that show CGJ's lifelong interest. See also F. X. Charet's *Spiritualism and the Foundations of CGJ's Psychology* (Albany: State Univ. of New York Press, 1993), chapter 6, pp. 171ff.
5. Marie-Louise von Franz, *Jung: His Myth in Our Time* (Toronto: Inner City Books, 1988), p. 55, writes that CGJ "set up a kind of laboratory for parapsychology . . . in 1904/05, and . . . Eugen Bleuler supported him . . . wholeheartedly and generously."
6. Information about Emile Schwyzer is from his undated "Patient History," in his case records at the Burghölzli Mental Hospital. The history was recorded from his earliest years of hospitalization, and much of it is repeated verbatim in *F/J*, 29J, June 4, 1907, pp. 57–58. As these dates are prior to J. J. Honegger's joining the Burghölzli staff, it is quite likely that CGJ was the writer of this document, and if not he, an assistant who predated Honegger and took down the history at CGJ's request. For a full discussion of this controversial case, see chapter 13.
7. *F/J*, 29J, June 4, 1907, "Case of paranoia (paranoid D. pr.)," pp. 57–58. Freud analyzed the case in an enclosure to 30F, June 6, 1907, "The Paranoid," pp. 60–62.
8. This document is the first that gives Schwyzer's full history. It differs markedly from 29J, and also from the Honegger Papers, the final and (to date) definitive account of the case. The account here is given simply to introduce Schwyzer in the chronology of CGJ's life and work and to present the initial documentation that disputes claims made by (among others, none of whom consulted it) Richard Noll, Frank McLynn, and Ronald Hayman.
9. Bleuler-Jung correspondence with Hans Gross is in the BA. Bleuler's initial and lasting diagnosis was "addiction" complicated by "the constitution of psychopathology" (Bleuler to Hans Gross, July 10, 1902).
10. Freud's letter is May 6, 1908. Information that follows is from Burghölzli patient records. Some of these documents were provided by Richard Noll, others by

William McGuire and Gottfried Heuer. Information was also obtained in interviews with Dr. Bernhard Küchenhoff, director of the Burghölzli, and Dr. Emanuel Hurwitz, both November 19, 1999.

11. His name is sometimes given as Hanns, but I follow Martin Green's spelling in *Otto Gross: Freudian Psychoanalyst, 1877–1920* (Lewiston, Maine: The Edwin Mellen Press, 1999). Hans Gross was one of the leading authorities in the field of criminality and the originator of dactyloscopy, the science of interpreting and using fingerprints. The following biographical information about Hans and Otto Gross is from Janet Byrne, *A Genius for Living: The Life of Frieda Lawrence* (New York: HarperCollins, 1995); Leonhard Frank, *Links wo das Herz ist* (Munich: Nymphenburger Verlagshandlung, 1952); Martin Green, *The von Richtofen Sisters* (New York: Basic Books, 1974); Gottfried Heuer, "Jung's Twin Brother," reprinted from the Association of Jungian Analysts, London, 1977–98; Emanuel Hurwitz, *Otto Gross: Paradies-Sucher zwischen Freud und Jung* (Zürich: Suhrkamp, 1979); Jennifer E. Michaels, *Anarchy and Eros: Otto Gross' Impact on German Expressionist Writers* (New York: Peter Lang, 1983); Richard Noll, *The Aryan Christ* (New York: Random House, 1997); Michael Raub, *Opposition und Anpassung: Eine individualpsychologische Interpretation von Leben und Werd des frühen Psychoanalytikers Otto Gross* (Frankfurt am Main: Peter Lang, 1994); Richard Seewald, *Der Mann von gegenueber* (Munich: List, 1963); Michael Turnheim, "Otto Gross und die deutsche Psychiatrie," in *Freud und der Rest. Aufsätze zur Geschichte der Psychoanalyse* (Vienna: Verlag Turia und Kant, 1994); and Green's *Otto Gross*.

12. July 12, 1902, Bleuler to Freida Schloffer, who married Otto Gross later that year. Her name is spelled Freida in most of the unpublished archival records I have consulted, so I follow the custom here.

13. *F/J*, 94F, May 19, 1908, p. 152. Freud's emphasis. Green, *Otto Gross*, p. 46, disputes this, citing "alleged sadism . . . alleged by Otto," and deems the "alleged cruelty" as "psychological, and should be read as part of an ongoing struggle between . . . father and son."

14. By 1907, his published works included the following: "Zur Frage der socialen Hemmungsvorstellungen," in *Archiv für Kriminalanthropologie und Kriminalistik* 7, nos. 1 and 2 (August 1901): 123–31; *Die cerebrale Sekundärfunction* (Leipzig: F. C. W. Vogel, 1902); and *Das Freud'sche Ideogenitätsmoment und seine Bedeutung im manisch-depressiven Irresein Kraepelins* (Leipzig: F. C. W. Vogel, 1907).

15. Gross's contribution to the history of psychoanalysis has been subjected to serious and thoughtful reexamination, mostly notably in the work of Emanuel Hurwitz, Gottfried Heuer, and Martin Green. Although I differ with most of Richard Noll's conclusions, in both *The Jung Cult* (Princeton: Princeton Univ. Press, 1994) and *Aryan Christ*, he has amassed much biographical information about Gross that provides an excellent point of departure for further scholarship.

16. From the "Patient History," BA.

17. Heuer, "Jung's Twin Brother," p. 7. Heuer adds: "Those [analysts] who did paid the price of becoming ostracized as outcasts — Gross, Reich, Laing."

18. Frank, *Links wo das Herz ist*, p. 49.

19. Green, *Otto Gross*, p. 53, cites Gross's "1913/4 interviews with doctors," but gives no specific source.

20. I disagree with Emanuel Hurwitz that all of Gross's patient notes are in Jung's handwriting. None from 1902 or 1904 are; only those from 1908 are, which are consistent with his diagnoses as well. The account of these records that follows differs only slightly from Hurwitz's, *Otto Gross*, pp. 139–44; somewhat more so from Noll's, *Aryan Christ*, pp. 79–83.

21. *F/J*, 33J, June 28, 1907, pp. 65–66. CGJ was referring to Gross's *Das Freud'sche Ideogenitätsmoment und seine Bedeutung im manisch-depressiven Irresein Kraepelins*, written during his term at Kraepelin's Munich clinic and based mainly on Wernicke's *Sejunktionshypothese*, i.e., that mental or intellectual disorders, like dementia praecox, are caused by a process of loosening and separation of the cerebral association fibers. Gross posited an innate brain function that kept association fibers in such an order that thinking could follow, and this he called the "secondary function." CGJ believed that Gross was situating Freud "to be merely the mason working on the unfinished edifice of Wernicke's system." Freud thought the most interesting thing about the book was that it was written in "the clinic of the Super-Pope," Kraepelin, who was the most respected German academic psychiatrist at the time. *F/J*, 34F, July 1, 1907, p. 69.

22. *F/J*, 44J, September 11, 1907, p. 85.

23. *F/Jones*, 1J, May 13, 1908, p. 1.

24. *F/J*, 46J, September 25, 1907, p. 90.

25. Hurwitz, *Otto Gross*, pp. 170ff., describes Jung and Gross as "brothers." Freud, twenty or so years their elder, is the "father." He attributes CGJ's and Freud's differing views of Otto Gross in part to their father-son conflict with each other.

26. I disagree with Martin Green, *Otto Gross*, p. 113, who calls her "far from penniless" and cites her "60,000 krone" inheritance from her mother. The money was spent before she married Otto Gross on February 23, 1903, shortly after the end of his first hospitalization at the Burghölzli. It was probably dissipated by her father, whom Green calls "a not very successful lawyer."

27. "Blond Dionysius" was her term, according to the unnamed writers of these various documents. According to Heuer, "Jung's Twin Brother," pp. 20ff., Gross is known to have fathered two sons and two daughters by four different partners: Peter (by Freida Gross), a second Peter (by Else von Richtofen Jaffé), Camilla Ullmann (by Regina Ullmann), and Sophie Templer-Kuh (by Marianne Kuh).

28. *F/J*, 84F, April 19, 1908, p. 141.

29. Bleuler wrote a letter supporting Hans Gross's petition of November 21, 1913, describing Otto Gross as fulfilling "the Austrian Civil Law Book [definition] of madness." On December 23, 1913, two doctors at the Psychiatric Asylum in Tulln, Austria, declared Otto Gross insane after he was brought there under police escort from Berlin, where Hans Gross had him arrested as a dangerous anarchist. On January 9, 1914, Otto Gross was certified "insane according to the law" and incapable of managing his own affairs. The *Kaiserlich-königliches Landsgericht* (district court) finally granted Hans Gross full authority as his son's guardian. An unsuccessful campaign to reverse the decision was led by Erich Mühsam and supported by writers Franz Jung (not CGJ's son), Blaise Cendrars, Else Lasker-Schüler, and René Schickele. Hans Gross died in 1915, and Dr. Hermann Pfieffer replaced him as Otto's guardian.

30. CGJ noted in the patient history that Freida wanted to have a baby but wanted her husband detoxified before trying to conceive. There is no indication that either Hans or Freida told him that she gave birth to a son, Peter, in 1907, the same year that Otto fathered a second son by Else von Richtofen, the sister of Frieda von Richtofen Weekly Lawrence (with whom he also had a brief affair and who was later the wife of the writer D. H. Lawrence).

31. A close reading of the patient history from 1902 and 1907 shows that, as an unnamed commentator wrote in "Biographical Data," Gross probably resented how Bleuler treated him: "It is apparent that the patient met with little sympathy. His maladjustments and psychopathic symptoms take up relatively much space, while no attention is paid to his melancholy moods."

32. Bleuler to Hans Gross, April 19, 1908, BA.
33. *F/J*, 84F, April 19, 1908, p. 141.
34. *F/J*, 85J, April 24, 1908, p. 142.
35. The first quote is from *F/Jones*, F320, July 27, 1921, p. 434; the second is from Ricardo Steiner, *F/Jones* introduction, p. xxxi. Steiner speaks of Jones's "enormous, obsessive, and often authoritarian labor or control." The bulldozer analogy is from a private source.
36. Bleuler to Hans Gross, April 19, 1908, BA.
37. *F/J*, 87F, May 3, 1908, p. 146. Freud describes Freida Gross as "seriously smitten" with Jones, but most scholars and biographers share my view that this was another instance of Freud's reversal of circumstances in which he equivocated to the advantage of the man and denigration of the woman. In *F/Jones*, 1J, p. 1, Jones carefully tells Freud that his relation to Freida is "of course difficult" but adds that she is "deeply in love with another man."
38. Most scholars believe that Freud considered Otto Gross a "catch" he did not want to lose: Gross was not only one of his most brilliant supporters; he was also the son of a distinguished professor and (some say most important of all) a Christian.
39. My translation from the original German certificate, BA.
40. *F/J*, 90F, May 6, 1908, p. 147.
41. Bleuler-Jung correspondence with Hans Gross shows they had been charging him Sfr6 daily since mid-April to reserve a place for Otto.
42. Hurwitz, *Otto Gross*, p. 150, interprets CGJ's reliance upon Freida's version of Otto's illness as an indication that he (CGJ) identified fully with her to the detriment of Otto's treatment, which he terms "crude" and "hostile."
43. The following account draws on "Patient Notes," BA; a document entitled "Biographical Data" from a private source; information in Hurwitz, *Otto Gross*; and a separate private archive.
44. Jones, for example, used his association with Kraepelin to secure a position for himself in Canada.
45. From the "Biographical Data" and private sources. Richard Noll uses some of the same "Biographical Data" in *Aryan Christ*, chapter 5, pp. 70–89, but both his chronology and interpretations differ from mine, starting most particularly on p. 84.
46. From early childhood, Otto Gross had an aversion to meat because the smell disgusted him. As a medical student, he did not mind the dissecting room "because he didn't have to eat what smelled like that" (Green, *Otto Gross*, pp. 54–55).
47. CGJ wrote to Freida Gross in Munich on June 1, 1908: "[I am] very politely drawing your attention to the fact that Herr Dr. Gross doesn't have the necessary number of underwear. That is why we are asking you to send some."
48. Some scholars credit Gross for CGJ's idea of using patient drawings and other artistic creations in treatment. Martin Green, Gross's biographer (in a letter to the author, May 1, 1999), relates that Walter Benjamin, in a 1917 essay, "Painting and the Graphic Arts," compares children's drawings and paintings to Gross's. Green confirms that the only Gross drawings he knows of were those done for CGJ at the Burghölzli. As of 1999, Professor Green found none of these in the various archives he consulted; as of 2001, I found none in the archives of the Jung family, the Burghölzli, or the ETH.
49. Martin Green, *Otto Gross*, p. 52.
50. Jones (*F/Jones*, June 27, 1908) told Freud that Gross was back in Munich, euphoric and agitated, ingesting large quantities of cocaine, and planning to bring a lawsuit against Kraepelin that would prove the value of psychoanalysis to the world. Gross spent the remaining years of his life wandering throughout Europe (Munich,

Prague, Budapest, Vienna, Berlin) when he was not institutionalized in asylums in Italy, Austria, and Germany (Mendrisio, Tulln, Schlesien, Vienna, Temsvar, and others). He died in a sanatorium in Pankow (a Berlin suburb) of pneumonia and symptoms of withdrawal on February 13, 1920. "By mistake," he was buried there in the Jewish cemetery.

51. Heuer, "Jung's Twin Brother," p. 7.
52. *F/J*, 95J, May 25, 1908, p. 153.
53. *F/J*, 96F, May 29, 1908, p. 154.
54. *F/J*, 98J, June 19, 1908, pp. 155–57.
55. Bleuler echoed CGJ's diagnosis in his letter of June 30, 1908, to Hans Gross: "dementia praecox, a mental illness and in principle one that cannot be healed . . . the prognosis is quite dark." He said Otto should be separated from Freida and their son for their own good and "left alone as long as possible in freedom until fate constructs his situation in such a way that a stay in a closed institution can no longer be avoided."
56. CGJ to Fritz Wittels, January 4, 1935, original in ETH, not included in *CL*. Wittels (1880–1950), originally a psychoanalyst in Vienna, resigned from the Vienna Society in 1910. In 1924, he wrote a biography critical of Freud, *Sigmund Freud: His Personality, His Teachings, and His School* (London: Allen and Unwin), but in 1931 he published a second one, *Freud and His Time* (New York: Liveright), that was entirely favorable. He practiced in New York after 1928.
57. *Psychologische Typen* (Zürich: Rascher Verlag, 1912), reprinted as *Psychological Types* (1923) and as *CW*-6.
58. *F/J*, 252J, April 19, 1911, p. 415.
59. *F/J*, 108J, September 9, 1908, p. 171. Meyer (1866–1950) was considered "the dean of American psychiatrists." Born in Zürich, he studied under Forel and J. J. Honegger Sr. He went to America in 1892; in 1908 he was a professor of psychiatry at the Cornell University School of Medicine; in 1910 he was a professor of psychiatry at the Phipps Clinic, Johns Hopkins University.
60. The following is based upon several private archives.
61. *F/J*, 144J, June 4, 1909, p. 228. The other patient was Sabina Spielrein.

CHAPTER 11: POETRY

1. To cite one example, in her September 1910 diary (Aldo Carotenuto, *A Secret Symmetry: Sabina Spielrein Between Jung and Freud* [New York: Pantheon Books, 1982], p. 17), Spielrein describes Dr. Esther Aptekmann as "one of [CGJ's] many" and describes ambiguously what may have been a flirtatious or amorous relationship or simply a professional friendship. CGJ described Esther Aptekmann's research as "*very* scientific" (his emphasis) in *F/J*, 279J, November 6, 1911, p. 455. She wrote her thesis under Bleuler and returned to her native Russia to practice.
2. Unpublished Bleuler correspondence in a private archive.
3. Quotations are from Carotenuto, *Secret Symmetry*, p. 8; verified by Bleuler correspondence in the private archive previously cited.
4. Author's paraphrase and translation from the Bleuler correspondence in the private archive previously cited.
5. These letters are reproduced in the German edition of Carotenuto's *Secret Symmetry*, but not in the English. The German is entitled *Tagebuch Briefwechsel einer heimlichen Symmetrie: Sabina Spielrein zwischen Jung und Freud*, herausgegeben von A. Carotenuto (Freiburg: Kore, Verlag Traute Hensch, 1966). All quotations used here are unofficial translations and informal paraphrases by the author. Quote is from CGJ to Spielrein, June 20, 1908, Carotenuto, *Tagebuch*, p. 189.

6. See (among many others): Bruno Bettelheim, "Commentary" in Carotenuto, *Secret Symmetry*; John Kerr, *A Most Dangerous Method: The Story of Jung, Freud, and Sabina Spielrein* (New York: Alfred A. Knopf, 1983); and Zvi Lothane, "In Defense of Sabina Spielrein," *International Forum of Psychoanalysis* 5 (1996): 203–17.

7. CGJ to Speilrein, June 30, 1908, in Carotenuto, *Tagebuch*, pp. 189–90.

8. CGJ to Spielrein, July 22, 1908, in Carotenuto, *Tagebuch*, p. 191.

9. South of Appenzell, forty miles east of Zürich.

10. See *F/J*, p. 171, for a concise summary. Between July and September, he had been to Berchtesgaden, the Netherlands, England (Manchester, Blackpool, and other cities), Berlin, and then Zürich.

11. See Appendices 2 and 3 in *F/J*, pp. 563–70.

12. In a letter to Abraham, *F/Abraham*, May 15, 1908, p. 37, Freud said CGJ would write the Zürich/Swiss section, Maeder the French and French/Swiss, Jones the British, Abraham the Viennese and German, and "the purely negative and hostile literature" would be in a separate section.

13. Freud to Abraham, *F/Abraham*, July 23, 1908, p. 46.

14. Abraham to Freud, *F/Abraham*, July 16, 1908, pp. 44–45.

15. *F/Abraham*, July 23, 1908, p. 46.

16. *F/J*, 106F, August 13, 1908, pp. 167–68.

17. Freud to Abraham, *F/Abraham*, September 29, 1908, p. 51; *Protocols*, two unpaginated, incomplete versions; *MDR*, pp. 126–28; CGJ, interview with Dr. Kurt Eissler, August 29, 1953, Manuscript Division, LC, Tape no. 74.

18. Alphons Maeder, letter to Henri Ellenberger, February 15, 1964, HE/STA, writes: "Bleuler was jealous of our admiration for Freud. On his first visit to the clinic, Freud was introduced to no one. This was especially wounding because, at that time, everything in our clinic revolved around Freud."

19. Freud to Spielrein, September 28, 1908, in Carotenuto, *Secret Symmetry*, p. 194.

20. *MDR*, pp. 125ff.; *CW*-3, "The Psychology of Dementia Praecox" and "The Content of the Psychosis"; *Protocols;* and CGJ's interview with Kurt Eissler, LC.

21. *MDR*, pp. 128 and 126.

22. Word used throughout all the *Protocols* consulted, softened to "surprised" in *MDR*. In two *Protocols* he compares Babette S. to "those numerous *old spinsters* (he uses underlined English words throughout the German drafts) whom he counted among his "clientele" later and who "said touching and confused things out of their distress." He added: "Therapeutically, nothing happened with Babette S., she was too crazy for that."

23. CGJ's interview with Kurt Eissler, LC. CGJ was seventy-eight at the time.

24. Daniel Paul Schreber, *Memoirs of My Nervous Illness*, originally published as *Denkwürdigkeiten eines Nervenkranken*, 1903 (English trans. by Ida Macalpine and Richard A. Hunter, *Psychiatric Monograph Series* 1 [London, 1955]).

25. Quotes and information from CGJ's inteview with Kurt Eissler, LC. In *F/J*, 186J, p. 307, n. 1, McGuire posits that CGJ and Freud discussed Schreber "while together in Nuremberg or Rothenburg." In the Eissler LC interview, CGJ writes as if the first Schreber discussion took place at the Burghölzli in 1908. In a note to the 1952 *Symbols of Transformation* (originally *Wandlungun und Symbole der Libido*, 1912), *CW*-5, para. 458, n. 65, CGJ wrote: "The [Schreber] case was written up at the time by Freud in a very unsatisfactory way after I had drawn his attention to the book." Michael Vannoy Adams, in "Womanizing: Catastrophe, Creation, and the Mythopoeic Forces of Mankind" (unpublished thesis for the CGJ Institute of New York, 2000), pp. 12–13, also makes the interesting speculation that CGJ might have wanted to write about Schreber himself.

26. Bleuler's term for the meeting between Freud and CGJ. The information that follows is from the BA and the private archives previously cited.

27. Among them, Sabina Spielrein's, for he thanks her for money received in a letter of August 12, 1908 (Carotenuto, *Secret Symmetry*, p. 193).

28. Anne Harrington, *Reenchanted Science: Holism in German Culture from Wilhelm II to Hitler* (Princeton: Princeton Univ. Press, 1999), p. 75. The reference is to C. von Monakow, a contemporary of CGJ's in the Zürich academic community.

29. CGJ submitted his resignation as *privatdocent* in the medical faculty on April 30, 1914; it was accepted by cantonal authorities on June 3 (Archives of the University of Zürich, Staatsbibliotek, Zürich).

30. Alphons Maeder to Henri Ellenberger, February 15, 1964, HE/STA.

31. *CW*-4, pp. 301–23.

32. *CW*-4, para. 695, p. 304. The reference to Gross is in the original 1908 document but was removed from two subsequent revisions in 1926 and 1948 respectively.

33. From Gross's patient report, the "Biographical Data," and a private source.

34. *CW*-4, para. 727, p. 314.

35. *CW*-4, para. 729, p. 315.

36. Tentative title "Dreams and Myths." Abraham to Freud, *F/Abraham*, February 23, 1908, p. 27.

37. *F/J*, 106F, August 13, 1908, p. 169.

38. Alphons Maeder to Henri Ellenberger, February 15, 1964, HE/STA.

39. CGJ to Spielrein, December 4, 1908, Carotenuto, *Secret Symmetry*, p. 195.

40. *F/J*, 117J, December 3, 1908, p. 184.

41. *F/J*, 118F, December 11, 1908, p. 186.

42. *F/J*, 121J, December 21, 1908, p. 189.

43. CGJ to Spielrein, December 4, 1908, Carotenuto, *Secret Symmetry*, pp. 195–96.

44. Spielrein repeated these comments in a letter to Freud, June 13 [1909] (year not given, but his replies verify date) (Carotenuto, *Secret Symmetry*, p. 102).

45. Spielrein to Freud, June 11 [1909], Carotenuto, *Secret Symmetry*, p. 93.

46. *F/J*, 124J, January 7, 1909, pp. 192–93.

47. *F/Abraham*, January 17, 1909, p. 67.

48. *F/Ferenczi*, January 10, 1909, 1: 33.

49. *F/J*, 124J, January 7, 1909, p. 194.

50. *F/J*, 126J, January 19, 1909, p. 198.

51. Freud to Ferenczi, *F/Ferenczi*, January 18, 1909, 1: 38.

52. *F/J*, 127F, January 22, 1909, p. 201.

53. *F/J*, 128J, January 24, 1909, pp. 201–2.

54. *F/J*, 126J, January 19, 1909, p. 198.

55. Alphons Maeder to Henri Ellenberger, February 15, 1964, HE/STA. Maeder discussed Jung's career at the University of Zürich with several professors: "When they did not give him the title of professor, it was Jung himself who withdrew, wounded."

56. *F/J*, 124J, January 7, 1909, p. 195.

57. McGuire, ed., *F/J*, p. 206, n. 3, writes that the letter of invitation is missing.

58. *F/J*, 134F, March 9, 1909, p. 210.

59. *F/J*, 133J, March 7, 1909, p. 207.

60. *F/J*, 135J, March 11, 1909, p. 212.

61. Spielrein to Freud, June 11, [1909], in Carotenuto, *Secret Symmetry*, p. 93.

62. The extant correspondence is reprinted in Carotenuto, *Secret Symmetry*, pp. 91ff. Two other long fragments survive from 1909, but whether she actually sent them to Freud is not known.

63. Carotenuto, *Secret Symmetry*, pp. 113ff.

64. The telegrams are missing, according to McGuire, ed., *F/J*, 144J, June 4, 1909, p. 228, n. 1.

65. *F/J*, 147F, June 18, 1909, p. 234.

66. *F/J*, 145F, June 7, 1909, p. 231.

67. *F/J*, 146J, June 12, 1909, p. 232. The reference is to CGJ's March visit to Freud in Vienna, when Freud anointed him as his "successor and crown prince" (*F/J*, 139F, April 16, 1909, p. 218).

68. *F/J*, 148J, June 21, 1909, pp. 236–37.

69. Freud to Spielrein, June 24, 1909, in Carotenuto, *Secret Symmetry*, pp. 114–15.

70. The original address was simply "Im Feld, Küsnach bei Zürich," because it was in a rural area on the lake, about half a mile from what then constituted the village. Shortly after, the town became Küsnacht and the house 1003 Seestrasse. As the town grew, houses were renumbered and CGJ's became 228.

71. The entry is dated September 11, 1910, but the context shows clearly that Spielrein is referring to events of the previous year (Carotenuto, *Secret Symmetry*, p. 12).

72. Private source and private archive.

73. When the Jungs returned from a vacation in Vienna, Emma took the three children to Schaffhausen and remained there until the house was ready to receive her in June. In April, when he was released from the Burghölzli, Jung went on a ten-day bicycle trip to northern Italy, then camped out between the house, the hospital, and the Rauschenbach home in Schaffhausen.

74. Spielrein to Freud, June 13, 1909, in Carotenuto, *Secret Symmetry*, p. 103.

75. When CGJ resigned, Gertrud Jung left the Burghölzli as well. Members of the Jung family question whether she left willingly. From then until her 1935 death, she worked occasionally as a home health aide but mostly performed secretarial duties for CGJ and child care for Emma Jung. Agathe Niehus-Jung and Franz Jung, in separate interviews, spoke of how much they enjoyed going to their grandmother's house, and of the fun they had when "Aunt Trudi" and one of her friends stayed in the house during their parents' frequent absences.

76. This letter and Bleuler's that follows are in the BA.

77. Bleuler recommended Dr. Hans Meier for CGJ's position and Dr. Alphons Maeder to be second assistant. CGJ's salary had been Sfr4,000 per year; Bleuler recommended an increase to Sfr4,300 for Meier. It seems another of Bleuler's slights, as he made sure CGJ knew of it.

78. *F/J*, introduction, p. xix.

79. Barbara Hannah, *Jung: His Life and Work, A Biographical Memoir* (Boston: Shambhala, 1991), pp. 95–96.

80. *F/J*, 133J, March 7, 1909, p. 207.

81. Medill McCormick (1877–1925) was a Chicago newspaper man at the time he sought treatment from CGJ; later, he became a U.S. senator. Troubled by alcoholism all his life, he committed suicide in his Washington hotel suite. He is briefly mentioned by Richard Norton Smith, *The Colonel: The Life and Legend of Robert R. McCormick* (New York: Houghton Mifflin, 1997), pp. 125 and 127; Ron Chernow, *Titan: The Life of John D. Rockefeller, Sr.* (New York: Random House, 1998); and Clarice Szacz, *The Rockefeller Women* (New York: St. Martin's Press, 1995). The information that follows is primarily from undated *Protocols*.

82. CGJ's English expression in a German *Protocol*. He also added in this particular *Protocol* that Medill McCormick had "a rather delicate appearance" and was simply incapable of contradicting his mother. CGJ described his method of treating McCormick as a "kill-or-cure remedy."

83. Smith, *The Colonel*, note to p. 127.
84. CGJ's English expressions in a German *Protocol*.
85. The following is based on *F/J*; *F/Ferenczi*, vol. 1; and Saul Rosenzweig, *Freud, Jung, and Hall the King-Maker: The Historic Expedition to America, 1909* (St. Louis, Mo.: Rana House Press, 1992).
86. *F/J*, 146J, June 12, 1909, p. 233.
87. Rosenzweig, *Freud, Jung, and Hall*, p. 34.
88. *F/J*, 148J, June 21, 1909, p. 237. First-class passage was all that was left. Eventually, according to Rosenzweig, *Freud, Jung, and Hall*, p. 56, Freud and Ferenczi also booked first-class cabins.
89. *F/Ferenczi*, August 9, 1909, 1: 73.
90. *The New Yorker Staats-Zeitung*, Monday, August 30, 1909, p. 8.
91. Freud's hostility has generally been attributed to Stern's review of *The Interpretation of Dreams* in *Zeitschrift für Psychologie und Physiologie der Sinnesorgne* 26 (1901): 133, in which he called Freud's work "dubiously scientific" and full of "complete mysticism and chaotic arbitrariness."
92. I quote here the most oft-repeated version of the remark, told to me by Franz Jung. CGJ, interview with Kurt Eissler, LC, gives the same version; CGJ told Eissler he replied, "Oh well, we will see in a moment what the Americans do with it, right!?" Vincent Brome, in *Jung: Man and Myth* (New York: Macmillan, 1981), p. 117, quotes the remark told to him by E. A. Bennet (but does not specify in which of Bennet's three books about CGJ the quote appears): "Won't they be surprised when they hear what we have to say to them!"
93. *F/Ferenczi*, January 10, 1909, 1: 33.

CHAPTER 12: AMERICA

1. *Protocols*, one German and two English.
2. See also *F/J*, 33J, June 28, 1907, p. 65, and nn. 1 and 2; also following 321J, comment heading p. 514. In CGJ's interview with Dr. Kurt Eissler, August 29, 1953, Manuscript Division, LC, Tape no. 74, CGJ says it was he who told Freud to invite Ferenczi, but no extant evidence supports this.
3. Freud to Ferenczi, *F/Ferenczi*, January 17, 1909, 1: 36.
4. Alexander Freud lived in Vienna, where he was lecturer at the Consular Academy and employed by the Ministry of Freight, Transport, and Tariff Affairs. He died in exile in Canada after the Nazis occupied Austria.
5. Quoted in Saul Rosenzweig, *Freud, Jung, and Hall the King-Maker: The Historic Expedition to America, 1909* (St. Louis, Mo.: Rana House Press, 1992), pp. 52ff., from Freud's unpublished 1909 travel diary, "which exists in holograph in the restricted portion of the Freud Collection, L. of C." (p. 287, n. 1).
6. CGJ's version of Freud's faint is *MDR*, pp. 156–57. Jones, *The Life and Work of Sigmund Freud* (London: Hogarth Press, 1953 and 1955), 1: 316–17 and 2: 146–47, gives another version. Rosenzweig, *Freud, Jung, and Hall*, pp. 52–55, gives yet another.
7. The following is from *MDR*, pp. 156–57, two undated *Protocols*, and Rosenzweig, *Freud, Jung, and Hall* (with whom I differ), pp. 52–55.
8. See chapter 16 for the Munich 1912 incident. Quote is from *Protocols* and CGJ's interview with Kurt Eissler, LC. In CGJ to Ernest Jones, December 19, 1953, CGJ chided Jones for not having checked various facts before publishing his life of Freud. He insisted that his account of Freud's fainting was incorrect and advised Jones that the Munich attack was the second, the first having occurred in 1909 in

Bremen. CGJ said both happened "very much under the same psychological circumstances." For alternative views of Freud's fainting, see (among others) Bettelheim, introduction to Aldo Carotenuto's *A Secret Symmetry: Sabina Spielrein Between Jung and Freud* (New York: Pantheon Books, 1982), p. xxxii; Ludwig Binswanger, *Sigmund Freud: Reminiscences of a Friendship* (New York and London: Grune and Stratton, 1957), p. 49; Ronald W. Clark, *Freud: The Man and the Cause* (New York: Random House, 1980), p. 265; Jones, *Life and Work*, 1: 317, and *Free Associations: Memories of a Psychoanalyst* (London: Hogarth Press, 1959), p. 222; and Paul Roazen, *Freud and His Followers* (New York: Da Capo Press, 1992), pp. 246–50.

9. The impact this incident had on CGJ is great: it appears in these words in every *Protocol* that I have seen.

10. Freud's usual term for his psychoanalysis is *"die Sache,"* or "the cause."

11. CGJ's interview with Kurt Eissler, LC. CGJ added that he obeyed Freud's summons because "he would have been *terribly* hurt. He was so *tremendously* sensitive . . . also very *delicately* sensitive."

12. Freud's travel diary, quoted in Rosenzweig, *Freud, Jung, and Hall*, p. 57. Rosenzweig's interpretation of the American journey is so partisan that it is highly suspect and must be read with great care, but he does make the honorable comment that "one is struck by this unpleasant evidence of Freud's intolerance." I believe this incident offers both a parallel to and further corroboration of Freud's anti-Semitic comments in CGJ's interview with Kurt Eissler, LC.

13. Freud's letters, dated August 30 and August 31, are in the "restricted Freud Collection," LC, as quoted in Rosenzweig, *Freud, Jung, and Hall*, p. 59.

14. Freud's travel diary, Rosenzweig, *Freud, Jung, and Hall*, p. 66; *MDR*, CGJ to Emma Jung, September 6, 1909, Appendix 2, p. 365; one partial German *Protocol*; and CGJ to Emma Jung, August 31, 1909, reprinted in Aniela Jaffé, ed., *CGJ: Word and Image*, Bollingen Series 97.2 (Princeton: Princeton Univ. Press, 1979).

15. *Selected Papers on Hysteria and Other Psychoneuroses, Journal of Nervous and Mental Disease Monograph Series*, 4 (New York, 1909).

16. CGJ to Emma Jung, August 31, 1909, in Jaffé, *Word and Image*, p. 48. CGJ did not tell Emma that Rose Owen Brill was a medical doctor and a highly intelligent and erudite woman in her own right. In one partial *Protocol*, he described her as "pushy."

17. In *CW-5*, para. 272, p. 187, CGJ writes of the "strong maternal influence in the home and the social position of American women generally. The fact that more than half the capital in America is in women's hands gives one something to think about. As a result of this conditioning many American women develop their masculine side." Freud shared his thinking, decrying in *Civilization and Its Discontents* the "pettycoat [*sic*] government" that he believed ruled the United States and describing American women to a former patient, Joseph Wortis, as an "anti-cultural phenomenon" (Wortis, *Fragments of an Analysis with Freud* [Northvale, N.J.: Jason Aronson, 1984], p. 98).

18. According to Fritz Wittels, Freud told Brill: "Stay here, don't move from this spot; it is the nicest part of the city, so far as I can see" ("Brill," *Psychoanalytic Review* 35 [1948]: 398).

19. Swiss doctor and friend and colleague of Brill's, on whose behalf he escorted Freud and CGJ from the boat to their hotel.

20. In several versions of the *Protocols*. To the best of my knowledge, he did not elaborate further.

21. CGJ to Emma Jung, August 31, 1909, in Jaffé, *Word and Image*, p. 47.

22. Freud's travel diary, Rosenzweig, *Freud, Jung, and Hall*, p. 62.
23. What follows is based on Rosenzweig's account of his 1951 interview with CGJ (*Freud, Jung, and Hall*, pp. 64–67); CGJ's interview with Kurt Eissler, LC; two separate *Protocols*; and a private source.
24. CGJ's interview with Kurt Eissler, LC, the only mention known to date of correspondence relating to it. There are no letters in *F/J* postmarked from London during Freud's September 1–15, 1908, vacation.
25. CGJ's interview with Kurt Eissler, LC.
26. CGJ's interview with Kurt Eissler, LC. In the original German, Freud used an ambiguous form of address that could have been either simply "my dear Jung" or "my dear young boy" or a possible slur and means of putting CGJ in his place. Another version of this conversation appears in *F/J*, 330J, December 3, 1912, p. 526.
27. Anne Bernays, Freud's grandniece (letter to the author, May 8, 1999), said she remembered her mother saying, "Sigmund would never have slept with Minna; she was too unattractive." Bernays adds that her mother was "hung up on appearance," and her remark "demonstrated that she had no clue as to how love/lust works." As for her own opinion, Bernays holds "no strong convictions" either way. Anthony Storr gave me his correspondence with E. A. Bennet, November 23, 1971, and Godfrey Smith, editor of the *Sunday Times* (London), August 10, 1978, in regard to Dr. John Billinsky's claim that CGJ told him about the Freud/Minna Bernays affair. Storr thought it "very likely that Billinsky [had] drawn on his fairly active imagination."
28. *Protocols*. See also John Kerr's "America and the Core Complex," in *A Most Dangerous Method: The Story of Jung, Freud, and Sabina Spielrein* (New York: Alfred A. Knopf, 1993), pp. 235–62.
29. CGJ to Emma Jung, September 6, 1909, in *MDR*, Appendix 2, p. 366.
30. CGJ, "Your Negroid and Indian Behavior," *Forum* 83, no. 4 (April 1930): 194.
31. Until the 1930s or thereabouts, most American universities considered psychology a branch within another academic department: at Clark, for example, it was combined with pedagogy (the teaching of education) until 1949; at Harvard, William James held an appointment in the Department of Philosophy and Psychology (they became two separate departments in 1936).
32. His lecture dealt with issues of racial purity and the definition of race, topics he developed until the 1928 publication of *Anthropology and Modern Life*. He spoke at Clark in 1909 about the dangers inherent in a national policy that stressed racial purity.
33. Rosenzweig, *Freud, Jung, and Hall*, p. 120.
34. Jung's citation read: "Carl G. Jung of the University of Zürich, Switzerland, specialist in psychiatry, brilliant investigator by the *Diagnostische Assoziationmethode*, editor and fruitful contributor to the literature of psychotherapy: Doctor of Laws." CGJ gave great importance to the honorary degree, adding it to his letterhead. A facsimile is reproduced in *F/J* between pp. 324 and 325, wherein CGJ underlined the LL.D. and added an exclamation point after it.
35. Then loosely described as experimental pedagogy concerning children. His research concerned how children learned and developed memory. In 1905, he founded and edited the *Zeitschrift für experimentelle Pädagogik*.
36. Dr. Polly Young-Eisendrath, in private communication with the author, described Hall as one of the foremost eugenicists of his time and offered the possibility that Jung may have shared his interest.
37. All the participants' lectures were subsequently published in the *American Journal of Psychology* (April 1910), and in the *Lectures and Addresses Before the Departments of*

Psychology and Pedagogy, ed. G. S. Hall (1910). Freud's topics included: lecture 1: "Breuer as the Originator of Psychoanalysis and the Case of 'Anna O'" (in a 1924 edition of these lectures, Freud eliminated mention of Breuer and spoke of his own "unrestricted responsibility" for the discipline; in a curious coincidence, Bertha Pappenheim, the Anna O., who had become a social worker, was in the United States at the same time, giving lectures on prostitution and white slavery among Jews [see *Israelitisches Familienblatt*, 11, no. 31 (August 5, 1909): 11; and Marion Kaplan, *The Jewish Feminist Movement in Germany* (Greenwood, 1979), pp. 118–19]); lecture 2: "A Contradiction of Pierre Janet's Theory of Hysteria"; lecture 3: "Free Association and Its Use in Dream Analysis" (here he cited Bleuler and Jung for their work in word association tests); lecture 4: "Infant Sexuality" (here he discussed "Little Hans" and referred to Jung's paper on Agathe, "Little Anna"); lecture 5: "The Social and/or Cultural Aspects of Sexuality in Civilized Society."

38. *CW*-2, "The Association Method," the first of three lectures, delivered at Clark University on September 10, 1909, pp. 439–65.

39. "The Family Constellation," *CW*-2, pp. 466–79. Parts of the paper had been previously published as "Associations d'idées familiales," in the *Archives de psychologie* (Geneva) 7, no. 26 (October 1907): 160–68. Four of the graphs were later incorporated into lecture 3 of the Tavistock Lectures, 1935, appearing in the 1968 edition, pp. 83 ff.

40. "The Family Constellation," *CW*-2, para. 1009, p. 476.

41. *F/J*, 126J, January 19, 1909, pp. 197–200. Reprinted in *CW*-17 as "Psychic Conflicts in a Child," pp. 8–35. See pp. v–vi for the essay's publishing history.

42. *F/J*, 209F, August 18, 1910, p. 348.

43. *F/J*, 210J, August 31, 1910, p. 350.

44. From several of the earliest *Protocols*. For why this material was omitted from *MDR*, see chapter 38.

45. Freud gave an interview to Adelbert Albrecht in the *Boston Evening Transcript*, September 11, 1909, part 3, p. 3, in which he denigrated American religious therapy as "dangerous and unscientific." James supported pastoral counseling and faith healing, particularly the Emmanuel Movement in Boston, as a sound nonmedical usage of psychotherapy. James conveyed his denigration of Freud to Flournoy with the single word "Bah!" (*The Letters of William James and Théodore Flournoy*, ed. R. C. LeClair [Madison: Univ. of Wisconsin Press, 1966], p. 24; see also Rosenzweig, *Freud, Jung, and Hall*, chapter 9, pp. 313–14, n. 6).

46. *Protocols*. CGJ uses several French phrases to indicate that Freud was not born to "educated parents."

47. Repeated in slightly different language throughout all *Protocols* I have read: "I needed someone I could talk to, also about the problems that he and I were dealing with in our scientific work, e.g., somnambulism. I also took over the term '*imagination créatrice*,' and I took over the case of Miss [Frank] Miller . . . which I published in *Wandlungun und Symbole der Libido*."

48. CGJ used and emphasized the English word here in the original German *Protocol*.

49. CGJ's French in the original German *Protocol*.

50. CGJ's English in the original German *Protocol*.

51. See *CW*-19, p. 61, for full citations.

52. Putnam was an important figure in the development of psychoanalysis in America and instrumental in the establishment of the American Psychoanalytic Association, whose first president he became at its founding on May 9, 1910.

53. The following account is based in part on Jaffé, *Word and Image*, pp. 49–51, including CGJ's letter to Emma Jung of September 16, 1909; Rosenzweig, *Freud, Jung,*

and Hall, pp. 199–206; Nancy Lee, "Putnam Camp," *Adirondack Life* (November–December 1980): 42–46; G. E. Gifford, "Freud and the Porcupine," *Harvard Medical Alumni Bulletin* (March–April 1972): 28–31; and N. G. Hale Jr., ed., *James Jackson Putnam and Psychoanalysis* (Cambridge, Mass.: Harvard Univ. Press, 1971), including Freud's letter of September 16, 1909, to his family.

54. Jaffé, *Word and Image*, p. 51.
55. James sold his share to the Putnams around 1880 but continued his annual visits for many years afterward. According to one early *Protocol*, he had been invited to join the party in 1909, but his health did not permit.
56. CGJ to Emma Jung, September 18, 1909, in *MDR*, Appendix 2, p. 368.
57. *F/J*, 159J, November 8, 1909, p. 258.
58. CGJ to Emma Jung, September 22, 1909, in *MDR*, Appendix 2, p. 369.

CHAPTER 13: THE SOLAR PHALLUS MAN

1. *F/J*, 148J, June 21, 1909, p. 236; Freud to Pfarrer Oskar Pfister, *F/Pfister*, July 12, 1909, p. 26; and *F/J*, 177F, February 2, 1910, p. 291. Honegger's letter(s?) have not been found in any of his or Freud's archives and are presumed lost or destroyed.
2. Information about Honegger and his family is from *F/J*; *F/Ferenczi*; Hans H. Walser, "Johann Jakob Honegger (1885–1911): Ein Beitrag zur Geschichte der Psychoanalyse," *Schweizer Archiv für Neurochirugie und Psychiatrie* 112, no. 1 (1973): 107–13, and "An Early Psychoanalytical Tragedy: J. J. Honegger and the Beginnings of Training Analysis," *Spring* (1974): 243–55, and letter to the author; William McGuire, "Notes on the Honegger/Solar Phallus Case" (unpublished, 2 pp.), and letters to the author; and Richard Noll, *The Jung Cult* (Princeton: Princeton Univ. Press, 1994), *The Aryan Christ* (New York: Random House, 1997), and "Jung the Leontocephalus," *Spring* 53 (1992). Documents relating to the case of Emile Schwyzer are from the ETH archives, HS 1068: 10–15, HS 1068: 16–21. Patient documentation concerning Emile Schwyzer is in the BA. Private documentation is from personal archives concerning Honegger, Helene Widmer, and Emile Schwyzer; Dr. Med. Peter Jung and Mr. Ulrich Hoerni, on behalf of the *Erbengemeinschaft CGJ*; Dr. Beat Glaus, retired chief librarian at the *ETH-Bibliothek Wissenschafthistorische Sammlungen*, compiler of "Autographen und Manuskripten zur ETH-Bibliothek Zürich," *Gesnerus* 39 (1982): 4437–42; and Dr. Rudolf Mumenthaler, current ETH librarian, who authorized my reading of the official copy of the Honegger Papers in November 2001.
3. An advanced secondary school degree in Austria and Switzerland, called the *Abitur* in Germany and A Levels in Britain, similar in degree and content to that granted by an American junior college. Necessary for entrance to institutes of higher education.
4. Published in translation as *Comparative Anatomical Examinations of the Fornix and the Formations in the Human and Mammal Brain Connected to It* (Geneva, 1890), 233 pp., author listed as Jakob Honegger. Adolf Meyer, in *Collected Papers* 1: 229–30, admires Honegger Sr.'s work, which he describes as "representative of the old school of anatomical research. . . . He offers all the information which anatomy can give him; he leaves the solution of the physiological problems to the physiologist." Meyer also notes that Honegger Sr. "works quite independently of the other neurologists of Zürich" and praises his slide laboratory.
5. *August Forel: Letters/Correspondence* (Bern-Stuttgart, 1968).
6. Walser uses this term in "Ein Beitrag," p. 108. He does not cite official documents, but the term has been adopted by all other sources.

7. Jung initially asked Honegger to investigate the cases of several patients, all of whom invented various alternative realities involving *dopplegänger*, or doubles.

8. *F/J*, 148J, June 21, 1909, pp. 236–37.

9. The generally accepted time is early May, shortly after Jung resigned from the Burghölzli and returned from a short bicycle trip through northern Italy. In *F/J*, 138J, April 2, 1909, pp. 215–16, CGJ discusses a particular "madly interesting" case, ostensibly a woman; he speaks of wanting to get on with his "scientific work" and of unspecified accomplishments in his practice. Ferenczi to Freud, *F/Ferenczi*, 61, May 18, 1909, p. 63, interpreted CGJ's intention for his future work as wanting "to conclude the association work and immerse himself in the analysis of psychoses."

10. This is based on a reading of other case histories in the BA: some are signed by Jung, some have the notations "JJH" or "JH II," and some are unsigned. One handwriting is almost certainly CGJ's; the other (similar to portions of the Honegger Papers) is quite likely Honegger's.

11. Honegger describes the case of "Frl. Pfenninger" briefly in a section of the papers entitled "Some Theoretical Points Regarding Paranoia." There is also an approximately forty-page patient history at the conclusion of the various documents relating to Schwyzer that may or may not be a transcription of Frl. Pfenninger's verbatim account of her history.

12. CGJ first used this term in *Jahrbuch* 3, no. 1: 211. Mention of "an erect phallus on the sun" also appears in *CW*-5, para. 151, p. 101. Honegger is cited in the first instance but not in the second.

13. From the Honegger Papers, in a section giving the patient's background before his confinement and the chronology of his medical history afterward.

14. At this time, CGJ was also supervising independent research by Sabina Spielrein and Jan Nelken, which may have become part of their respective publications, "Die Destruktion als Ursache des Werdens" and "Analytische Beobachtungen über Phantasien eines Schizophrenen," both in *Jahrbuch* 4, no. 1 (1912). After completing his training at the Burghölzli and becoming a charter member of the Zürich society, Nelken moved to Paris and practiced psychiatry there. As another example, in *CW*-3, para. 390, p. 180, CGJ also mentions Drs. A. Maeder, S. Grebelskaja, and W. Itten, but there is no extant indication that he tried to recruit any of them for the Schwyzer research. Although he does speak here of the "powerful impression of the enormous symbolic activity in dementia praecox" that these doctors all found in their research, he does not include Honegger among them.

15. A reference to this way of working is in *F/J*, 33J, June 18, 1907, p. 66, in which CGJ tells Freud he is sending a paper "by a woman student of [his]" that will interest Freud. (See Dr. Emma Fürst, "Statistische Untersuchunger über Wortassoziationen und über familiäre Übereinstimmung im Reaktionstypus bei Ungebildeten," *Journal für Psychologie und Neurologie* 9 [1907].)

16. Information from the official patient history of Emile Schwyzer, BA. In the so-called Honegger Papers there exists another eleven-page history of the case that has slightly different information and contains contradictory statements, such as the unnamed author's assertion that Schwyzer was brought back to Switzerland by his family in 1884 to work again as a messenger from the ages of twenty-two to thirty-four (1896). The first clause of the next sentence states that Schwyzer was apparently normal until 1897; the second adds that Schwyzer was committed to the Mönchhof in March 1894.

17. Information about Emile Schwyzer from his undated "Patient History" folder containing his case records at the Burghölzli Mental Hospital. The history was recorded in the earliest years of his institutionalization, and much of it is repeated

in *F/J*, 29J, June 4, 1907. There is no documentation that makes it possible to date when or by whom these records were typed, but as they predate Honegger's staff appointment, CGJ is quite likely the holograph writer, and if not he, an assistant who predated Honegger and took down the history at CGJ's request.

18. The case history probably prepared by Honegger states that the paternal grandfather died of dementia senilis and that Schwyzer's father and mother were both alive and healthy, as were his two brothers and a sister. One of his mother's brothers suffered from a condition noted as *"encephalomalacie."*

19. How or where Schwyzer learned English is not known. In *CW*-8, para. 318, p. 150, "The Structure of the Psyche," CGJ writes that the unnamed patient (assumed to be Schwyzer) was "an ordinary clerk, employed in a consulate." There is no corroboration of this in any of the BA. In *CW*-9, para. 105, p. 50, "The Concept of the Collective Unconscious," CGJ writes that the same patient was educated "at a state school" and "employed as a clerk in an office." In the Honegger Papers, Schwyzer speaks of having been at various times a messenger, meatpacker, scribe and secretary of the English proconsul, and an employee of the Swiss Landesmuseum in Zürich. He also states (and Honegger accepts as true) that he lived and worked as a messenger in Paris for several years before he went to England. I have been unable to verify if any of the above is true.

20. Information that follows is from the Burghölzli case history, from incidental notations in the case histories of other patients, and from various miscellaneous papers that may have been notes presented by Jung and/or other doctors in 1906.

21. In October 2002, the *CBS Evening News* produced a segment based on photographs of the sun taken by space satellites showing how "little tails" upon the sun's surface were responsible for weather patterns on Earth. Throughout the segment, the commentator made many of the same observations as Schwyzer in his delusions.

22. *"dass er an einer unheilbaren Geisteskrankheit (Jugendverblödung) leidet"* (CGJ's emphasis).

23. Eugen Bleuler, "Die Prognose der Dementia Praecox–Schizophreniengruppe," in *Allgemeine Zeitschrift für Psychiatrie* 65 (1908): 436–64.

24. Although there is no direct evidence that Bleuler formulated this theory specifically because of Schwyzer's case, some of the correspondences between his arguments and CGJ's patient history are extremely close. Also, as Bleuler took pride in knowing the exact details of each patient's history and treating each personally from time to time, the parallels resonate strongly enough to bear further scholarly perusal.

25. In a draft copy of Honegger's paper for the Nuremberg congress, "On the Formation of Paranoid Delusions," he began by thanking Herr Prof. Bleuler for allowing him to spend two months on the sole study of Schwyzer's case of paranoid dementia. Honegger said his work was guided by the principles of Jung, his "admired teacher" (a phrase he immediately crossed out), before launching into a historical overview of dementia praecox by citing the research of Charcot and Kraepelin. Although the remarks that follow are inconsistently developed and have many cross-outs and revisions in phrasing, he concludes these several pages by saying that he intends his presentation to be a continuation of Jung's three papers, whose titles he gives as "On the Psychology of Dementia Praecox," "The Contents of Psychosis," and "The Meaning of the Father for the Fate of the Individual." Like Jung, he believed the doctor had to take the time and have the patience to follow a single case, and he repeats Jung's admonition that, above all, the doctor must "learn to listen."

26. At several places in the various versions of the case history attributed to Honegger, Schwyzer's maternal grandfather's profession is called tinsmith, coppersmith, or simply smith — an important distinction, because these were all specific divisions

within the Swiss metalworking professions. One of Schwyzer's repeated delusions is of having dropped an anvil from this grandfather's smithy onto his left ankle and piercing it when he was four years old. His account of what happened differed each time he told it.

27. From the official patient history. Honegger's history describes Schwyzer as having finished secondary school but gives no other detail. I was unable to find any evidence that Schwyzer either attended or graduated from secondary institutions in Canton Zürich.

28. In Honegger's various versions of Schwyzer's history, there are many references to literature and myth, from writers such as Mark Twain and Goethe to the Ahura Mazda and Eranian [*sic*] mythology. However, there is such confusion among the speaking voices, so many switches from first to third person and then back again, as well as from male to female to male, that I am reluctant to state conclusively in many instances whether the doctor or the patient is speaking. Where it can be verified, as in the marginal comments and notations added at a later date and sometimes in a different hand from the writer of the text, Honegger shows a formidable literary intelligence, particularly in nineteenth-century German literature (primarily in his knowledge of Goethe). Jung's comment about Honegger's slipshod research appears to be true, because there are no references to the mythological scholarship of the time that might support or explain some of Schwyzer's delusions.

29. Full bibliographic citations begin in *CW*-19, p. 12. See Appendix 1, n. 1, for William McGuire's "Notes on the Honegger/Solar Phallus Case."

30. *CL*-5, paras. 150 and 151, pp. 100–101.

31. Dieterich: (Leipzig: B. G. Teubner, 1903; 2d ed. Leipzig, 1910). Mead: (London: Theosophical Publishing Society, 1908). See *CL*-5, para. 223, pp. 159–60, for CGJ's explanation.

32. *CL*-5, para. 149, p. 100.

33. *CL*-5, para. 224, p. 158.

34. CGJ gives a partial explanation of this dream in a vague, nonchronological sequence in *MDR*, pp. 158–62. According to all versions of the *Protocols* where he discusses it, it is the one he tried to discuss with Freud in Central Park. This segment in some of the *Protocols* carries a heading handwritten and underlined by Aniela Jaffé: "Dreams about the inner history of the separation from Freud."

35. In CGJ's interview with Dr. Kurt Eissler, August 29, 1953, Manuscript Division, LC, Tape no. 74, CGJ says, "Finally he [Freud] proposed that it was probably . . . my wife. . . . Well, that simply doesn't fit the whole character of the dream at all."

36. CGJ's interview with Kurt Eissler, LC.

37. Some of these drawings are in the only known extant manuscripts, presumably written by Honegger and possibly transcribed by (among others) Maria Moltzer and Emma Jung.

38. At the conclusion of these various versions of the Schwyzer history, there is another document written in a Gothic script that differs from all of the several other handwritings. Approximately forty pages, it is a completely different patient history that may be that of "Frl. Pfenninger," whose case Honegger abandoned in order to concentrate on Schwyzer.

39. *F/J*, 170J, December 25, 1909, p. 279.

40. *F/J*, 158F, October 17, 1909, p. 255, and 160F, November 11, 1909, p. 260.

41. *F/J*, 160F, November 11, 1909, p. 259.

42. *F/J*, 162J, November 15, 1909, p. 262.

43. *F/J*, 165J, November 30–December 2, 1909, p. 270.

44. Emma Jung to Freud, November 24, 1911, in *F/J*, p. 465.

45. *F/J*, 155J, October 1, 1909, p. 247. CGJ's emphasis. This is also when Emma Jung began informal analysis with Dr. Leonard Seif of Munich, who came to the Burghölzli to observe both Jung and Bleuler and who returned repeatedly for the next several years, during which he became a loyal member of the "Zürich group," causing Freud to call him "their Munich appendage" (Freud to Abraham, *F/Abraham*, June 5, 1914, p. 179). E. A. Bennet, in *CGJ: Einblick in Leben und Werk* (Zürich, 1964), p. 36, chides Jones for his "minor lapse of memory," saying he "must have known Seif intimately" and would therefore have known that "he had joined Adler, and Jung confirmed this." According to Jones (*F/Jones*, 94J, September 18, 1912, p. 160), Seif was taking credit by 1911 for analyzing Emma and believed she took "a fairly objective view of her husband's failings."

46. Sabina Spielrein's diary, as cited in Aldo Carotenuto, *A Secret Symmetry: Sabina Spielrein Between Jung and Freud* (New York: Pantheon Books, 1982). I disagree with recent works (Zvi Lothane, "In Defense of Sabina Spielrein," *International Forum of Psychoanalysis* 5 [1996], and others) that equivocate in Jung's favor. In several instances during my interviews with the elderly daughters of the Zürichberg women who were among Jung's earliest patients, the women insisted that something between flirtation and actual affairs took place between CGJ and their mothers. When I said I could not report this without written documentation, some among them provided journals or diaries kept by their mothers. The descendants insist that these documents must remain private and permit me only to paraphrase the actual texts or the memories of what the descendants remember their mothers told them. I can state, however, that I believe what I have reported here to be both convincing and trustworthy.

47. *F/J*, 172J, postcard from Unterwasser, January 8, 1910, p. 284; 175J, January 30, 1910, p. 289. Emma gave birth to her fourth child and third daughter, Marianne, on September 20, 1910.

48. During the two years Trudi Jung worked at the Burghölzli, 1906 to 1908, she wrote a number of the entries on Jung's behalf into the Schwyzer patient history. She also assisted in preparing the Honegger Papers (see the Appendix). The Jung heirs describe her as CGJ's official full-time secretary until 1925–26, but my investigations indicate that she was more likely part-time or occasional, especially as she often worked full-time as a paid companion or home health attendant.

49. CGJ to Freud, *CL*-1, December 25, 1909, p. 13.

50. Here CGJ uses the Greek letters ΨA, his and Freud's shorthand version of the word "psychoanalysis." *F/J*, 159J, November 8, 1909, pp. 256–58. The quote about money is from 157J, October 14, 1909, p. 250; Freud's reply is from 158F, October 17, 1909, p. 254. The teaching quotes are from 165J, November 30–December 2, 1909, p. 269.

51. Dr. "Apothecary" Knapp in Bern invited CGJ and Freud to join the "I.O.," or International Fraternity for Ethics and Culture," of which Auguste Forel was president. Both declined. See CGJ to Freud in *CL*-1, February 11, 1910, p. 17; also *F/J*, 178J, February 11, 1910, p. 293, where the holograph reads *Internationaler Orden für Ethik und Kultur.*

52. A formal organization of approximately fifteen members, "several of them foreigners," was formed in June 1910. Among the Swiss were Franz Riklin Sr., Alphons Maeder, the Rev. Oskar Pfister, Ludwig Binswanger, and CGJ's psychiatrist cousin, Dr. Ewald Jung, who was elected secretary. Among the foreigners were Dr. Leonhard Seif, Trigant Burrow of Baltimore, Roberto Assagioli of Florence, and a Dr. Stockmayer of Tübingen (*F/J*, 198J, June 17, 1910, pp. 328–29; *CL*-1, pp. 19–20).

53. CGJ's emphasis. As these letters are filled with the gossip of politics, I will cite only

one example, *F/J*, November 22, 1909, pp. 267–68. See also Ernest Jones, *The Life and Work of Sigmund Freud* (New York: Hogarth Press, 1955), 2: 115ff., for a detailed but partisan account of the various dissensions surrounding Freud; and Peter Gay's chapter on "Psychoanalytic Politics," in *Freud, A Life for Our Time* (New York and London: W. W. Norton, 1988), pp. 213ff.

54. *F/J*, 163F, November 21, 1909, p. 266.

55. *F/J*, 169F, December 19, 1909, p. 276.

56. *F/J*, 170J, December 25 and 31, 1909, p. 279.

57. Perhaps there was more than one letter, but none addressed to Freud has yet been found among the few known surviving Honegger Papers in the ETH or the Freud Archives. The document entitled "Some Theoretical Points Regarding Paranoia" appears to be a letter that Honegger may or may not have written specifically to Freud.

58. *F/J*, 196J, June 2, 1910, p. 325.

59. *F/J*, 197F, June 9, 1910, p. 327.

60. *F/J*, 171F, January 2, 1910, p. 282. This was exactly what CGJ did when he wrote *Wandlungun und Symbole der Libido*.

61. *F/J*, 193J, May 24, 1910, pp. 318–19.

62. *F/Pfister*, March 17, 1910.

63. Richard Norton Smith, in *The Colonel: The Life and Legend of Robert R. McCormick* (New York: Houghton Mifflin, 1997), note on p. 127, describes what happened as follows: Jung diagnosed Medill's condition as "mental fatigue" brought on by the strain of business. The real strain, he concluded privately, was Kate [McCormick, his mother] herself, a "real power devil" whose possessiveness had crushed her son's spirit and defeated all his efforts at independence. Deciding on what he called "an act of *force majeure*, Jung — without consulting Medill — concocted a medical certificate declaring Medill to be a hopeless alcoholic incapable of carrying out his present job. The powers at the *Tribune* accepted this diagnosis, Kate reluctantly, the others with a sense of relief. Medill's life was thus spared through an act of mercy for which Jung earned his patient's lasting resentment.

64. *F/J*, 183J, March 9, 1910, p. 302. CGJ's emphasis.

65. Emma Jung to Freud, *F/J*, March 16, 1910, p. 303.

66. See the Appendix for a description of the paper and its abstract, published as *Jahrbuch f. psychoanalyt. u. psychopathol. Forschungen* 2 (1910): 734–35. A fifteen-page paper bearing the same title, "On the Formation of Paranoid Delusions," is in the Honegger Papers. Until or unless other examples of Honegger's writing are found, both the *Jahrbuch* abstract and the expanded paper are his only extant contribution to the literature of psychoanalysis.

67. Dinitia Smith, "Scholar Who Says Jung Lied Is at War with Descendants," the *New York Times*, June 3, 1995, p. 1. Smith's article concerns Richard Noll's charges against CGJ in *The Jung Cult* and the Princeton Univ. Press cancellation of his second book, *The Aryan Christ*.

68. Herman Nunberg among them, in *Memoirs, Recollections, Ideas, Reflections* (New York: The Psychoanalytic Research and Development Fund, 1969), p. 116.

69. *F/J*, 184J, April 6, 1910, pp. 304–5.

70. *F/J*, 196J, June 2, 1910, p. 325.

71. Honegger to Walter Gut, June 17, 1910, as quoted in *F/J*, p. 338, n. 6; also in Walser, "An Early Psychoanalytical Tragedy," *Spring* (1974): 246.

72. Information from Walser, "An Early Psychoanalytical Tragedy," p. 247; *F/J*, 219J, November 7, 1910, pp. 369–70; two interviews with private sources; and several letters in a private archive.

73. Walser, "An Early Psychoanalytical Tragedy," p. 247.
74. Dr. Karl Gehry, "unpublished autobiographical notes," as quoted by Walser, in "An Early Psychoanalytical Tragedy," pp. 247–48.
75. *F/J*, 247J, March 31, 1911, p. 412. The editors note: "*Minutes*, III, report no reference to JJH's death at the Vienna Society. It was, however, mentioned in the *Bulletin*, no. 5 (April 1911), p. 5."
76. *F/J*, 248F, April 2, 1911, p. 413.
77. See *F/J*, 245J–249J, pp. 410–14, for further details.
78. Private documents indicate that Emma Jung managed all of CGJ's professional affairs during this time, answering his correspondence and rescheduling patients, whom she did not see personally except to reassure them that their treatment would be resumed at CGJ's earliest opportunity. Her administrative skills thus enabled CGJ to concentrate on the many convolutions of the psychoanalytic politics of the period. Information about the Stuttgart meeting is from *F/J*, 252J, April 19, 1911, p. 415.
79. See the Appendix.
80. *F/J*, 159J, November 8, 1909, p. 258. There are similarities here to Honegger's avoidance of an explicit description of Schwyzer's masturbation.
81. Friedrich Creuzer, *Symbolik und Mythologie der alten Völker*, published between 1810 and 1823. Generally considered "the first truly comprehensive scholarly source in the German language for information about the spirituality of antiquity, especially about the ancient mystery cults of the Greco-Roman world . . . the foundation upon which successive generations of German scholars built their own ideas about Hellenic antiquity, whether they agreed with him or not" (Noll, *Jung Cult*, p. 179). For a partial account of the early evolution of CGJ's thinking about mythology, see also *F/J*, 162J, November 15, 1909, p. 263; 165J, December 2, 1909, p. 269; 170J, December 25, 1909, p. 279.
82. Originally published in German between 1890 and 1894 as *Psyche, Seelenkult und Unsterblichkeitsglaube der Griechen*.
83. Walser, "Ein Beitrag," p. 108.
84. Noll uses Dieterich as his source for the most sustained attack upon CGJ in his essay, "Jung the Leontocephalus."
85. John Freeman, "Face to Face," BBC-TV interview, 1959, reprinted in *CGJ Speaking*, ed. William McGuire and R. F. C. Hull, Bollingen Series 97 (Princeton: Princeton Univ. Press, 1997), pp. 424–39; partially published in a collection of Freeman's BBC-TV interviews.

CHAPTER 14: "THE FAMILY PHILOSOPHER"

1. From several private sources and analytic diaries in private archives. Members of the Jung family who do not wish to be identified also volunteered this information. Susanna Trüb-Wolff alludes to it in the Nameche interview at the HCL. Doris Straüli-Keller (daughter of Adolf and Tina Keller, goddaughter of Emma Jung) repeated it, along with a separate but related incident told to her by CGJ. Tina Keller deemed it "too personal" and removed it from a 1968 interview that she ordered Nameche to destroy. C. A. Meier, in interviews with the author, said Emma's comment was "one of the few things that came up in our three-way analysis." It was also repeated by many others not cited here because they heard it from the sources listed above.
2. Bruno Bettelheim, "Commentary" to Aldo Carotenuto's *A Secret Symmetry: Sabina Spielrein Between Jung and Freud* (New York: Pantheon Books, 1982), p. xxvi, gives the date as "sometime before March 1909."

3. Sabina Spielrein's diary entry for January 19, 1911, in Carotenuto, *Secret Symmetry*, p. 38. The English edition contains only one Spielrein letter from 1911, but in the German edition, *Tagebuch einer heimlichen Symmetrie*, pp. 188–225, Carotenuto has ten letters written by CGJ to Spielrein during 1911. From their content, they appear to be part of an ongoing dialogue concerning her dissertation and other exchanges of psychoanalytic theory, literature, and professional gossip. Personal matters are only rarely the subject, and then briefly and in connection with psychology and psychoanalysis. The natural assumption is that letters containing personal material have been withheld, as Thomas B. Kirsch posits in *Quadrant* 16 (1983): 89 (review of Carotenuto's *Secret Symmetry*). The entire correspondence (as published by Carotenuto in both languages) has been reprinted in *JAP* 46 (2001): 173–99, translated by Barbara Wharton.

4. "Die Destruktion als Ursache des Werdens," *Jahrbuch für psychoanalytische und psychopathologische Forschungen* 4 (1912): 494ff. Published in English as "Destruction as a Cause of Coming into Being," *JAP* 39 (1994): 155–86.

5. CGJ became her dissertation director by default because Bleuler, who had kept her manuscript for a year, had not yet read it. Bleuler had neither attended the Nuremberg conference of 1910 nor joined the International Psychoanalytic Association founded there, so Spielrein made the professional decision to throw in her lot with the organized group, of which CGJ had been elected president. Her dissertation was published as "Über den psychologischen Inhalt eines Falles von Schizophrenie (Dementia Praecox)" (trans. as "On the Psychological Content of a Case of Schizophrenia [Dementia Praecox]) in *Jahrbuch für psychoanalytische und psychopathologische Forschungen* 3 (1912): 400ff. For a discussion of its content, see John Kerr, *A Most Dangerous Method: The Story of Jung, Freud, and Sabina Spielrein* (New York: Alfred A. Knopf, 1993), pp. 296–98.

6. Carotenuto, *Tagebuch*, p. 199, dates the letter referring to Seif as "probably" July 1911; *JAP* accepts the date. The comment about Freud is from a letter of July 8, 1911, p. 199. In the same letter, CGJ describes Spielrein's "train of thought" as "bold, far-reaching and philosophical." He tells her she should try to make "an independent little book of it" because the *Jahrbuch* probably would not be the best place to publish it. He says he has not read far enough to make a preliminary overall judgment, but that he is "surprised by the wealth of splendid thoughts which anticipate various thoughts of my own." In his letter to Freud, *F/J*, 310J, April 1, 1912, p. 498, he describes this same paper with a Latin saying translated as "What at the top is a lovely woman ends below in a fish." He faults her "gross errors and, worse still, faulty, one-sided interpretations. She has read too little and has fallen flat . . . it is not thorough enough." Carotenuto, *Tagebuch*, prints letters CGJ wrote between November 1911 and March 25, 1912, in which he discusses Spielrein's work and replies to her comments and questions. In the March 25 letter, he writes that her work is "extraordinarily intelligent and contains excellent ideas, and I grant you their priority. You recognized the death tendency resp. death wish earlier than I did. . . . I express myself so very differently in my work than you that no one should even suspect that you borrowed from me. . . . Maybe it was I who borrowed from you. . . . What matters is what one makes of it. And you have made something good of it."

7. From an interview with the daughter of a woman who was Jung's patient and who wishes to remain private.

8. *F/J*, 265J, July 19, 1911, p. 435.

9. *Protocols*, undated passages in which CGJ describes at some length his strong physical attraction to Moltzer but stops short of admitting that it was ever consummated.

10. For CGJ's account of the "idiotic" proceedings, see *F/J*, 269J, August 29, 1911, pp. 439–40. For textual references, see *CW*-19, German 1912b, p. 13; 1913a, p. 14; English 1913b, p. 62; also *CW*-4.9. The case concerned a young girl first analyzed by Maria Moltzer and dealt with the patient's phobia about school, infatuation with her teacher, and her fantasies about reproduction and birth. CGJ reversed existing theory by arguing that the child's dreams resembled folk legends and tales because of unconscious evolutionary memories rather than their personal history.

11. *F/J*, 266F, July 21, 1911, p. 436.

12. There was a steady stream of wealthy Midwesterners during these years who either knew Medill McCormick or had heard of CGJ's treatment of him and as a result came to Zürich for varying periods of time. Among them was a woman with a keen memory who kept a detailed diary of her sessions that included CGJ's verbatim responses to everything she told him. She described this diary in several letters now held in private archives. In 1995, her daughter-in-law told me she destroyed the diary after the writer's death because in their family, social class, and city, it was still "scandalous" to have had analysis.

13. The first quote is from Ernest Jones, *The Life and Work of Sigmund Freud* (London: Hogarth Press, 1955), 2: 84; the second is from Kerr, *A Most Dangerous Method*, p. 343.

14. Jones, *Life and Work*, 2: 85.

15. Jan Nelken was the only junior physician who broke ranks with Bleuler, primarily because his research was supervised by CGJ.

16. Wilhelm Stekel (1868–1940) was one of the four original members of the Wednesday Evening Society (1902). Earlier, he was in analysis with Freud. Considered a brilliant writer and an intuitive psychoanalyst, he followed Adler by resigning from the Vienna Society in 1911 but continued to edit the *Zentralblatt* for a year, during which time Freud initially held some hope that he would return to the fold (he did not). He moved later to London, where he committed suicide.

17. Jones, *Life and Work*, 2: 85. The article was in reference to Otto Rank's paper, "The Motif of Nudity in Poetry and Legends."

18. About Seif, see *F/Jones*, 94, p. 160; about Putnam, see N. G. Hale Jr., ed., *James Jackson Putnam and Psychoanalysis* (Cambridge, Mass.: Harvard Univ. Press, 1971), pp. 39–40.

19. CGJ to Spielrein, probably August 17/18, 1911, in Carotenuto, *Tagebuch*, p. 200.

20. CGJ to Spielrein, probably September 21/22, 1911, in Carotenuto, *Tagebuch*, p. 201.

21. My interpretation differs from (among many) those such as Kerr's, *A Most Dangerous Method*, p. 349, that CGJ "most ungallantly declined to send her a letter of recommendation." The entire tone of this letter is one of mentor to pupil, filled with encouragement. His letters from then on attest to and support this interpretation. CGJ never saw Sabina Spielrein again. On June 14, 1912, she married Dr. Paul Scheftel. CGJ's only extant reference to the marriage is his letter of August 24, 1913, in which he sends best wishes to her and her new baby daughter, Renate. She allied herself with Freudian theory and became a member of the Viennese group and then worked for a time in Geneva, where her most famous analysand was Jean Piaget. She continued to publish in various journals and in 1923 returned (at Freud's urging) first to Moscow, then to Rostov, in her native Russia, where she and her two daughters were murdered by the Nazis in a local synagogue. For the fullest information about her life in Russia, see A. M. Etkind, "How Psychoanalysis Was Received in Russia, 1906–36," *JAP* 39 (1993): 191–202. See also Magnus Ljung-

gren, "Sabina mellan Jung och Freud," *Expressen* 15; Mireille Cifali, "Une femme dans la psychanalyse: Sabina Spielrein, un autre portrait," *Le Bloc-Notes de la psych-analyse* 8 (1988): 253–65; Peter J. Swales, "What Jung Didn't Say," *Harvest* 38 (1992): 30–37; Kenneth McCormick, "Sabina Spielrein: Biographical Note and Postscript," *JAP* 39 (1994): 187–90; and Fernando Vidal, "Sabina Spielrein, Jean Piaget — chacun pour soi," *L'Évolution Psychiatrique* 60, no. 1 (1995): 97–113.

22. *F/J*, 269J, August 29, 1911, p. 440.

23. The daughter of a wealthy distiller, she became a nurse to protest against the abuse of alcohol. She came to Zürich for psychiatric training with CGJ and began her own practice c. 1913. She is best remembered today as the analyst of Fanny Bowditch Katz, in whose archives at HCL was found a document purporting to be Jung's inaugural speech to the Psychological Club of Zürich. The basis for the ru-mor of an affair between Moltzer and CGJ is primarily Jolande Jacobi's interview with Gene Nameche, HCL: "Then I heard from others, about the time before he met Toni Wolff, that he had a love affair there in the Burghölzli with a girl — what was her name? Moltzer."

24. I mention the rumor about Moltzer and Böddinghaus because it has been written about so frequently by others who base their belief in an affair between CGJ and Moltzer on CGJ's comment to Freud in *F/J*, 211J, September 8, 1911, that be-tween Sister Moltzer and Frl. Martha Boeddinghaus (called Böddinghaus in Jones, *Life and Work*, 2: photo opposite p. 86) "there is naturally a loving jealousy over me." Martha Böddinghaus came to Zürich to study and analyze with CGJ. There, she married Hermann Sigg, a Swiss businessman from Küsnacht who often went with CGJ on cycling and mountain climbing excursions and who took him to Alge-ria and Tunisia in 1920. She became a friend of Emma's and under her married name, Sigg-Böddinghaus, published articles on Jungian psychology.

25. Beatrice Moses Hinkle (1872–1953), psychiatrist and analytic psychologist. Origi-nally from California, she was one of the leaders of the New York Jungian organi-zation for many years, during which time she was also director of a sanatorium in Washington, Connecticut. She studied with both CGJ and Freud and was the first English-language translator of *Wandlungun und Symbole der Libido* (see *CW*-19, German 1912a, p. 13; English 1916b, p. 65).

26. Her given name at birth was Toni, not Antonia. According to her nephew (inter-view with the author, July 9, 1998), Dr. Med. Georg Trüb, "there may be some of-ficial document somewhere in which her name is written as 'Antonia,' but she was named 'Toni' at her birth by her mother."

27. The family can be traced back to 1351 in Zürich, the year the city entered the orig-inal Swiss Confederation, and earlier in other parts of the country. Historians view the Wolff family as intellectuals, for among the family members are professors, ministers, engineers, architects, government officials, and wealthy merchants. One branch owns a grand château in Turbenthal and is known as Wolff von Turbenthal. Full genealogies can be found in (among other sources in the Zürich city library) *Zürich Bürger — Etat und Nieder — gelassene 1889*. Toni Wolff is listed in the *Lexi-con der Frau I–Z* (Zürich: Encyclios Verlag AG, 1954), 2: 1657. Information also comes from "Der Tyrann von Turbenthal," *Die Tat* 146 (June 23, 1972); "Die 'Wölfe' von Zürich," *Die Zürcher Woche* 39 (September 26, 1951): 3; "Altzürcher Familien," documents in Staadarchiv, Zürich, Wolff family file. I am grateful to Dr. Phil. Sonja Marjasch and Herr Hans Ulrich Herzog for additional information.

28. Dr. Med. Georg Trüb, son of Susi Trüb-Wolff, interview with the author, July 9, 1998, Zürich. I am grateful to the following members of the Wolff family who have

aided my research into the life and work of Toni Wolff: the children of Susi Trüb-Wolff: Dr. Med. Georg Trüb, Frau Ursula Cadorin-Trüb, Herr Wolf Trüb, and Frau Ursula Trüb-Offermann; and the son of Erna Naeff-Wolff, Dr. Chem. Paul Naeff.

29. Following the death of Frau Wolff-Sutz in 1947, the house was demolished and two apartment houses replaced it. The Naeff family, heirs of Erna Naeff-Wolff, own one, and the Trüb family, heirs of Susanna Trüb-Wolff, the other. Toni Wolff moved into an apartment in the Naeff building, now Freiestrasse 19.

30. Ursula Cadorin-Trüb, interview with the author, July 10, 1998, Zürich.

31. Konrad Wolff supported several of Toni's female cousins, all of whom either made successful careers or marriages, and sometimes both. Although they and their descendants remain grateful to Herr Wolff and fond of his memory, they have asked not to be identified here.

32. Toni Wolff's letter is believed lost or destroyed; Konrad Wolff's to her is dated September 20, 1905.

33. She did go to England for approximately four months when she was eighteen, when she became fluent in English and developed a lifelong passion for all things English, from tweeds to theater to tea. This affection did not carry over to American culture: although she spent frequent holidays in England, she found excuses to avoid her many invitations to visit the United States.

34. Family members and friends recall that this was "always a sore point for Toni. She was embarrassed that she did not have a formal education and had to be addressed as Fraulein Wolff because she had no degrees and thus, no titles."

35. In her adult life, both hung in her study. Her family members and analysands told me they felt she "somehow identified with these two gentlemen."

36. An elderly woman in Zürich whose father had been a student smitten with Toni Wolff and whose mother later became her patient said this was how both her parents described Toni in her student days. This same expression was used by several of her nieces and nephews in recounting what their parents told them.

37. It is not known why his first name is spelled William in the English fashion, but Wolfensberger is not well known today in Switzerland and his work is seldom read. He is briefly mentioned in Gustav Huonker's *Literaturszene Zürich: Menschen, Geschichten und Bilder 1914 bis 1945* (Zürich: Unionsverlag, 1985), p. 71. He is survived by a volume called *Ausgewählte Werke*, edited by his friend Robert Lejeune (Frauenfeld: Huber Verlag, 1964). Chiefly, he wrote in the genres of *Erzählungen und Gedichte*. Several small volumes were published in his lifetime: *Unseres Herrgotts Rebberg, Erzählungen* and *Religiöse Miniaturen, Weltliche Andachten*, both published in Heilbronn, Germany, 1916 and 1917 resp.; and *Lieder aus einer kleinen Stadt, Gedichte*, published in Zürich in 1918, the year he died of Spanish influenza. Dr. Phil. Robert Schneebeli provided bibliographical information.

38. His grandchildren ascribe it to "some sort of cancer," which he may have had as early as 1905, when he wrote the letter to Toni, quoted above.

39. The nephews and nieces of Toni Wolff.

40. Unless noted otherwise, information is from diaries and journals Toni Wolff wrote before meeting CGJ and that she kept faithfully afterward. Written on cheap paper in faint pencil, they are almost impossible to decipher. No one seems to have read all she wrote, because she tried to destroy them toward the end of her life. The few known to be extant are in the possession of one of her nephews.

41. *F/J*, 269J, August 29, 1911, p. 440.

42. *F/J*, 270F, September 1, 1911, p. 441.

Chapter 15: "Unsuited to the Position"

1. *F/J*, 270F, September 1, 1911, p. 441.
2. Jung's article appeared as "Wandlungen und Symbole der Libido," *Jahrbuch* 3 (1911–12): 120–227. It became the first part of his 1912 book *Wandlungen und Symbole der Libido* (Psychology of the Unconscious). The second part was published in *Jahrbuch* 4 (1912–13): 162–464.
3. Ferenczi to Freud, *F/Ferenczi*, 245, October 19, 1911, p. 304. The remark is from Ferenczi's letter; the editors note that Emma Jung's letter is "missing."
4. *F/Ferenczi*, pp. 304–5, Ferenczi's emphasis.
5. Freud to Ferenczi, *F/Ferenczi*, 246, October 21, 1911, p. 306.
6. *F/J*, 286F and 270F, pp. 438 and 441.
7. Ferenczi to Freud, *F/Ferenczi*, 247, October 23, 1911, pp. 307–8.
8. Freud to Ferenczi, *F/Ferenczi*, 248, October 25, 1911, p. 308.
9. Freud to Ferenczi, *F/Ferenczi*, 249, November 5, 1911, p. 309. Freud's Weimar congress lecture was entitled "Nachtrag zu dem autobiographisch beschriebenen Fall von Paranoia (Dementia paranoides)." The emphasis is his.
10. Emma's descendants and friends (among them Aniela Jaffé and Ruth Bailey) described how she destroyed her private archives before her death in 1955: if a correspondent was dead, she burned the letters; if living (as in the case of Cary F. Baynes), she returned the letters to the writer and asked that hers be returned to her. She then burned her side of the correspondence. The *Erbengemeinschaft CGJ* believes that her correspondence with Freud was among the many she burned. If she returned Freud's letters to anyone in the Freud family, they have not been identified or acknowledged by any of the Freud archives.
11. Emma Jung to Freud, *F/J*, November 6, 1911, pp. 455–57.
12. Even Jones cites Emma Jung's letter as his source for Freud's relationship with his wife in *The Life and Work of Sigmund Freud* (London: Hogarth Press, 1955), 2: 386, n. 6.
13. *F/J*, 280F, November 12, 1911. In 278F, November 2, 1911, Freud wrote that four publishers had declined to publish the new journal and he was about to contact a fifth, Hugo Heller, the Viennese bookseller and publisher, and a member of Freud's Vienna group, who eventually agreed to publish it (283F, November 14, 1911).
14. *F/J*, 279J, November 6, 1911, p. 454.
15. *F/J*, 276F, October 20, 1911, p. 451.
16. *F/J*, 273F, October 12, 1911, p. 447.
17. *F/J*, 280F, November 12, 1911, pp. 457–58.
18. *F/J*, 283F, November 14, 1911, p. 463. *Eros und Psyche* and commonly abbreviated as *Psyche* in correspondence and discussion; changed to *Imago* by the time of the first issue, March 28, 1912. The name originated in Carl Spitteler's 1906 novel, also called *Imago*, in which "the hero referred to his body as 'Konrad' because he was on such good terms with it" (*F/J*, 156F, October 4, 1909, p. 249, n. 5).
19. Hanns Sachs (1881–1947) was a lawyer (Dr. Jur.) and a psychoanalyst in Vienna, Zürich, and Berlin. A Jew, he left Germany and joined the faculty at Harvard University.
20. *F/J*, 283F, November 14, 1911, p. 463.
21. 284F, November 16, 1911, p. 464. Rank's paper was entitled "Die Lohengrinsage: Ein Beitrage zu ihrer Motivgestaltung und Deutung (Schriften zur angewandten Seelenkunde)."
22. *F/J*, 283F, November 14, 1911, p. 464.
23. Hirschfeld (1868–1935): Berlin sexologist and an original member of the Berlin Psychoanalytic Society, editor of the *Jahrbuch für sexuelle Zwischenstufen* and the

Zeitschrift für Sexualwissenschaft. Freud wrote CGJ that he was "no great loss" (*F/J*, 278F, November 2, 1911, p. 453). Freud wrote Abraham: "Hirschfeld's defection is really no loss to us, and for the work of our group it is rather a gain" (*F/Abraham*, October 29, 1911, p. 108).

24. Freud to Abraham, *F/Abraham*, January 2, 1912, p. 111. He refers to Morichau-Beauchant at Poitiers, and a pupil of Dr. Emanuel Régis, professor of psychiatry at Bordeaux.

25. He coined the name "paedanalysis" for this. Pfister (1873–1956) was the youngest of four sons of a Protestant pastor and a founding member of the Swiss Psychoanalytic Society in 1910. By 1914, he had disavowed CGJ and cast his lot with Freud, to whom he remained loyal throughout his life.

26. Published as *Sigmund Freud: Psychoanalysis and Faith, Dialogues with the Reverend Oskar Pfister* (New York: Basic Books, 1963), eds. Heinrich Meng and Ernst L. Freud, trans. Eric Mosbacher.

27. In the Introduction to *Psychoanalysis and Faith* by Heinrich Meng, p. 8, Pfister's marital history says nothing of divorce. He never got one, and he remained married to Erika Pfister-Wunderli until her death in 1929, when he married the widowed cousin, Martha Zuppinger-Urner.

28. References are *F/J*, 282J, November 14, 1911, p. 461; 284F, November 24, 1911, p. 465; 285J, November 24, 1911, p. 466; and 286F, November 30, 1911, p. 468. See also Freud to Ferenczi, *F/Ferenczi*, 294 and 307, pp. 366 and 386 resp.

29. Jones, *Life and Work*, 2: 141

30. *F/J*, 285J, November 24, 1911, p. 467.

31. *F/J*, 286F, November 30, 1911, p. 468.

32. *F/J*, 282J, November 14, 1911, p. 461.

33. Freud's letter appears not to be extant. Emma Jung's letters are in *F/J*, November 14 and 24, 1911, pp. 462–63 and 465–66 resp.

34. Information from the Jung children's interviews in HCL.

35. Jones, *Life and Work*, 2: 142.

36. *CW*-3, para. 75, p. 36. If not the first, CGJ was certainly one of the first to advance this possibility, a view he espoused for the rest of his life.

37. Alphons Maeder to Henri Ellenberger, February 15, 1964, Zürich, letter in HE/STA. Author's translation from the French.

38. *F/J*, 280F, November 12, 1911, p. 459.

39. Philip Rieff, in *The Triumph of the Therapeutic: Uses of Faith After Freud* (New York: Harper and Row, 1968), p. 43, discusses how CGJ "proposed to continue beyond the point where Freud felt any honest analyst must leave off," and how he "went about his self-appointed task of finding new 'meaning' for it all, and was paradoxical enough to be at once analytic and religious."

40. Freud's emphasis.

41. *F/J*, 282J, November 14, 1911, pp. 460–61.

42. Freud, *SE*-13: 1–162. Originally published as *Totem und Tabu: Über einige Übereinstimmungen im Seelenleben der Wilden und der Neurotiker* (1913).

43. George B. Hogenson, in *Jung's Struggle with Freud* (Wilmette, Ill.: Chiron Publications, 1994), p. xvii, makes the observation that Freud's "point of view is always retrospective; for Jung it is prospective, toward the future."

44. *F/J*, 288F, December 17, 1911, p. 472. Philip Rieff, in *Freud: The Mind of the Moralist* (Chicago: Univ. of Chicago Press, 1979), p. 24, writes that "Jung cannot help showing that he has read too much. He empties his notes into his books. Freud, however, does not disclose, at least publicly, his many connections with Ro-

mantic literature and philosophy. He is rigorous and searching in argument, elegant and precise in style."

45. To take *Wandlungen und Symbole der Libido* (*Psychology of the Unconscious*, retitled *Symbols of Transformation*) as just one example: completed in 1912 for its subsequent original publication, it was issued in a revised version in 1952 to include the views CGJ had developed in the intervening years. Aspects of these revisions are apparent in his seminars of the 1920s and 1930s and were subsequently included in the 1952 text.

46. This remark appeared repeatedly in personal interviews with the author, particularly with Marie-Louise von Franz and C. A. Meier; also in the Nameche HCL interviews and in various texts that are noted without attribution.

47. Andrew Samuels, Bani Shorter, and Fred Plaut, *A Critical Dictionary of Jungian Analysis* (London and New York: Routledge, 1986), point out that CGJ used the words "energy" and "libido" interchangeably (*CW*-6, para. 778). They define the dispute thus: "The exclusively sexual character which Freud assigned to libido or psychic energy. Jung's conception is closer to that of a form of life-energy, neutral in character. He pointed out that psychic energy in the pre-oedipal phases of development takes many forms: nutritional, alimentary, and so forth."

48. *F/J*, 293F, January 10, 1912, p. 480. Freud had supported Jung earlier at the Weimar congress, saying, "Jung had excellent grounds for his assertion that the mythopoeic forces of mankind are not extinct, but that to this very day they give rise in the neuroses to the same psychical products as in the remotest dark ages" (*SE*-12: 81). Hogenson, *Jung's Struggle*, p. xi, posits the theory that Jung's work with the association theory and the word association test "caused his initial, and continuing, skepticism about Freud's insistence that sexuality was the univocal source of psychic disturbance. The associative patterns that were evident in the responses of test subjects were simply too various to be reduced to a single causal factor."

49. Another example of how Freud worked appears in his letter to Ferenczi in which he discusses *Totem und Tabu*: "I am reading fat books without any real interest, since I know the conclusions already; my instinct tells me so" (*F/Ferenczi*, November 30, 1911, pp. 316–17).

50. *Protocols*. See also *MDR*, p. 150, for the highly polished version of his original comment.

51. In CGJ to Dr. Kurt Eissler, August 29, 1953, Manuscript Division, LC, Tape no. 74, CGJ described Freud as a "scientific positivist" who wanted to make sexuality a dogma "as a protection against the possibility that the black flood of shame descends [i.e., from the Catholic Church specifically, religion in general]. Yes, mysticism, you see?! That was his bête noire! Thus he called everything mysticism that was not yet understood at the time."

52. *F/J*, 287J, December 11, 1911, p. 471.

53. *F/J*, 286F, November 30, 1911, p. 469.

54. Herman Nunberg and Ernst Federn, eds., *Minutes of the Vienna Psychoanalytic Society*, vol. 3 (1910–11), trans. M. Nunberg (New York: International Universities Press, 1970), p. 335. For a discussion of how Freud and CGJ each interpreted the Book of Genesis, see Hogenson, *Jung's Struggle*, pp. 45–48.

55. *F/J*, 286F, November 30, 1911, p. 469.

56. *F/J*, 287J, December 11, 1911, p. 471.

57. Schreber's autobiography was originally published in 1903. CGJ discussed it in *CW*-3 (see Index, p. 301, for references). See also *F/J*, particularly 186J, p. 307,

n.1, and 187F, p. 311, n. 5. Freud's study appeared in 1911 as *Psychoanalytische Bemerkungen über einen autobiographisch beschriebenen Fall von Paranoia (Dementia paranoides)* (translated as *Psychoanalytic Notes on an Autobiographical Account of a Case of Paranoia [Dementia Paranoides]*), in *SE*-12.

58. He refers primarily to Ernst Haeckel's 1899 proposal for a phylogenetic psychology that would permit a scientific study of the phylogeny of the soul, more commonly described as his theory that "ontogeny recapitulates phylogeny." In a related parallel, CGJ's intention is to consider psychoanalysis as the science that will allow him to explore the historical development of the human species.

59. *F/J*, 288F, December 17, 1911, p. 472.

60. Miss Frank Miller has been "re-staged and re-dressed" by Sonu Shamdasani in a florid extended metaphor of women's clothing in *Spring* 50 (1990): 26–56. I employ only his biographical findings here.

61. For an interesting perspective on the CGJ-Flournoy relationship that deserves further scholarly consideration, see Richard Noll's "Jung the Leontocephalus," *Spring* 53 (1993): 57–59, n. 87.

62. *Protocols*. See chapter 38 and the Epilogue for how those who worked on the original text modified or refined his remarks about Flournoy and Freud that were published in the German *MDR* but eliminated from the English. I use CGJ's comments in the *Protocols* here because they are his most direct and immediate statements.

63. *Des Indes à la Planète Mars: Étude sur un cas de somnambulisme avec glossolalie*, originally published in 1899 (original English translation by Daniel B. Vermilye, published in abridged form by Harper and Brothers, New York, in 1900). Sonu Shamdasani changed Flournoy's subtitle to "A Case of Multiple Personality with Imaginary Languages" (*From India to the Planet Mars* [Princeton: Princeton Univ. Press, 1994]).

64. Shamdasani, *From India to Mars*, p. xxxii.

65. In 1911, Flournoy published his last work about mediums, a survey of mediumship entitled *Esprits et Médiums: Mélanges de Métapsychique et de psychologie* (Geneva: Kündig). In it, he expresses disappointment at his inconclusive results, but he did write an introduction to Frank Miller's "Quelques faits d'imagination créatrice subconsciente," originally published in *Archives de psychologie* (Geneva), 5 (1906), retranslated back into English by James H. Hyslop as "Some Instances of Subconscious Creative Imagination," *Journal of the American Society for Psychical Research* 1, no. 6 (1907) (reprinted as *Appendix: The Miller Fantasies, CW*-5, pp. 447–62). Shamdasani's article in *Spring* ([1990] 50: 42–43) must be taken advisedly, as he "unstitches" CGJ's use of this article, finds it in need of "retailoring," and offers alternative speculation about its writing and publication history.

66. The original English version has not been found to date. CGJ worked from Flournoy's French translation.

67. *CW*-5, para. 46, p. xxviii, and p. 485 describe it as such.

68. To date, no evidence has been found to indicate whether or not CGJ discussed Miss Miller with Ricksher then or in subsequent correspondence.

69. Elizabeth Lunbeck, "A New Generation of Women: Progressive Psychiatrists and the Hypersexual Female," *Feminist Studies* 13, no. 2 (fall 1987): 513–43.

70. In the 1916 English translation, p. 108, Honegger is credited with "discover[ing] the following hallucination in an insane man . . ." In *CW*-5, para. 151, p. 101, this has been changed to "I once came across the following hallucination in a schizophrenic patient . . ." Richard Noll has debated the veracity of Jung's involvement in this matter and posits differing views in *The Jung Cult* (Princeton: Princeton Univ.

Press, 1994) and *The Aryan Christ* (New York: Random House, 1997) and his article "Jung the Leontocephalus."

71. From the 1947 Dodd, Mead and Company reprinting of Beatrice Hinkle's 1916 translation, entitled *Psychology of the Unconscious: A Study of the Transformations and Symbolisms of the Libido: A Contribution to the History of the Evolution of Thought*, p. 41. Changed in *CW-5*, para. 46, p. 32, to "a series of fantasies, partly poetical in form."

72. Freud's undated comments to CGJ, cited as 199aF in *F/J*, pp. 332–33.

73. CGJ's initial knowledge of Mithraism came from Cumont and Dieterich. Noll, in *The Jung Cult*, pp. 123–29, provides a good basic interpretation of "Mithraism vs. Christianity," as Jung knew and possibly used both, but I differ with him over his subsequent analogy of "Aryans vs. Semites." Noll also offers citations for further readings that dispute Cumont's (and, by extension, Jung's) conclusions. For CGJ's response to both of Freud's criticisms, see *F/J*, 200J, June 26, 1910, pp. 335–37.

74. The contention is mine; the quotation is from Peter Homans, *Jung in Context: Modernity and the Making of a Psychology* (Chicago: Univ. of Chicago Press, 1979), pp. 63–64. John Kerr, *A Most Dangerous Method: The Story of Jung, Freud, and Sabina Spielrein* (New York: Alfred A. Knopf, 1993), pp. 277–78, makes a point of distinction that I also share.

75. Jones, *Life and Work*, 2: 143, referring to *F/Jones*, 91F, September 7, 1912, p. 157, and 95F, September 22, 1912, pp. 163–64.

76. In his first observation, Freud refers to CGJ's disagreement with his (Freud's) explanation of paranoia in the Schreber analysis. For further elucidation, see *F/Jones*, 95, p. 164, nn. 5 and 6.

77. *F/Jones*, 94J, September 18, 1912, pp. 160–61.

78. Bleuler to Jones, quoted in *F/Jones*, 97, October 30, 1912, pp. 167–68, n. 3.

CHAPTER 16: THE KREUZLINGEN GESTURE

1. Barbara Stephens, "An Affair to Remember . . . and Remember: Revisiting the Freud-Jung Correspondence," invited address at the 1996 Spring Conference of Jungian Analysts of Northern and Southern California, La Jolla, February 29–March 3, 1996, paper unpublished.

2. For information about Elfriede Hirschfeld, I am indebted to William McGuire and Dr. Phil. Ernst Falzeder for correspondence and Falzeder's article "My Grand-Patient, My Chief Tormentor: A Hitherto Unnoticed Case of Freud's and the Consequences," *Psychoanalytic Quarterly* 63 (1994): 297–331. Falzeder asserts that Hirschfeld is "one of the classical cases in the history of psychoanalysis, on a par with the cases of Anna O . . . Dora . . . etc." He alerts scholars that "this case plays a central role in the unpublished part of the Freud-Pfister correspondence (Freud Archives, LC)". Editors of Freud's letters did not use the same pseudonymous initials, so Hirschfeld is "Frau C" in *F/J*, "Frau H" in *F/Pfister*, "Frau A" in *F/Abraham*, and "Frau Gi" in Ludwig Binswanger, *Sigmund Freud: Reminiscences of a Friendship* (New York and London: Grune and Stratton, 1957).

3. Freud to Pfister, unpublished letter, May 28, 1911, LC, in Falzeder, pp. 300–301.

4. Falzeder, "My Grand-Patient," p. 303. Among those who treated her were Janet, Jung, Pfister, and Binswanger. Bleuler was a consultant.

5. Falzeder, "My Grand-Patient," p. 313.

6. *F/J*, 288F, December 17, 1911, p. 474.

7. *F/J*, 289F, December 18, 1911, p. 474. The editors note that a previous letter of CGJ's may be missing here.

8. *F/J*, 290F, December 31, 1911, pp. 475–76.
9. Falzeder, "My Grand-Patient," pp. 314–15, states that there are only two sources for what happened between CGJ and Frau Hirschfeld: "the Freud-Jung correspondence, and Freud's account of it ten years later" (when he spoke to the Secret Committee in 1921, and used the case to explain "its significance for his relationship with CGJ").
10. Carleton Smith, Nameche interview, HCL, March 18, 1970. Smith met CGJ around 1950 and later arranged for the publication of *The Undiscovered Self.*
11. *F/J*, 290F, December 31, 1911, p. 476.
12. He repeated this theme in his 1921 talk to the Secret Committee, when he described the case as "the first occasion on which CGJ betrayed his dubious character, for which his subsequent warped theories could not compensate me." He described CGJ's treatment of Frau Hirschfeld as follows:

> He expressed his amazement that she could endure being in an analysis with me without warmth and sympathy, and he recommended himself for a treatment in a higher temperature and with more verve. When she reminded him that she would have to report this statement to me, he was alarmed and asked her not to. The first and not yet sublimated attempt to compete with the father for the woman-object was a failure for the tender son.

See Ilse Grubrich-Simitis, *Back to Freud's Texts: Making Silent Documents Speak*, trans. P. Slotkin (New Haven: Yale Univ. Press, 1996), p. 209, also pp. 208–11.
13. *F/J*, 291J, January 2, 1912, p. 477.
14. Articles and letters in the *Neue Zürcher Zeitung*, January 2, 3, 10, 13, 15, 17, 27, 28, 31, and February 1, 1912; *Wissen und Leben* (now the *Neue Schweizer Rundschau*), February 15, 1912; and Henri Ellenberger, *The Discovery of the Unconscious: The History and Evolution of Dynamic Psychiatry* (New York: Basic Books, 1970), pp. 810–14. Kesselring is the unnamed doctor CGJ refers to in *F/J*, 285J, p. 467, when he accuses Bleuler of being "careless with certain remarks he made about a doctor here who has his knife into us anyway."
15. Founded in Frankfurt, 1907, by M. Eberhard Dennert (1861–1942) as an answer to the Monistenbund, founded by German biologist and philosopher Ernst Haeckel (1834–1919) in Jena, 1906, for the propagation of materialist monism. As has been noted previously, CGJ used some of Haeckel's ideas in *Wandlungen* but did not name him specifically. See also Ellenberger, *Discovery of the Unconscious*, p. 811.
16. Ellenberger, *Discovery of the Unconscious*, p. 811.
17. *F/J*, 295J, January 23, 1912, p. 482. CGJ's original English.
18. *F/J*, 293F, January 10, 1912, p. 481.
19. Ellenberger, *Discovery of the Unconscious*, p. 815, describes the differences: "In Vienna . . . the public [was conditioned] to accept Freud's sexual theories. In Zürich, another type of *genius loci* caused psychoanalysis to be accepted as a key to religious and educational problems, and to the understanding of myths and psychosis. It was inevitable that clashes should occur between these two diverging perspectives."
20. *F/J*, 295J, January 23, 1912, p. 483.
21. Two letters to Sabina Spielrein attest to this method of working: December 23, 1911 (Aldo Carotenuto, *Tagebuch einer heimlichen Symmetrie* [the German edition of *A Secret Symmetry: Sabina Spielrein Between Jung and Freud* (New York: Pantheon Books, 1982)], p. 206), in which CGJ tells her how he and she should proceed toward publication of her *Jahrbuch* 1912 article; and undated, probably beginning

of November 1911 (Carotenuto, *Tagebuch*, p. 203), in which he tells her that "apart from Freud, Rank, and Sachs (?)," there were no others in Vienna whose intelligence he valued.

22. From many Nameche interviews, HCL.

23. Published as "Die Destruktion als Ursache des Werdens," *Jahrbuch* 4, no. 1 (September 1912). CGJ to Speilrein, March 18, 1912, in Carotenuto, *Tagebuch*, pp. 206–7.

24. CGJ to Spielrein, March 25, 1912 (Carotenuto, *Tagebuch*, pp. 207–8).

25. *F/J*, 297J, c. February 15, 1912, pp. 483–84.

26. *F/J*, 299J, February 19, 1912, p. 486; 297J, c. February 15, 1912, pp. 483–84.

27. In *F/J*, 300J, February 25, 1912, he wrote of lecturing to "about 150 students . . . with great success."

28. CGJ to Spielrein, March 25, 1912 (Carotenuto, *Tagebuch*, pp. 207–8). Richard Noll and John Kerr are among the most prominent scholars who accuse CGJ of writing this work in haste and not bothering to edit it. Apparently, CGJ thought he was doing just that.

29. *F/J*, 297J, c. February 15, 1912, p. 484.

30. *F/J*, 300J, February 25, 1912, p. 487.

31. From interviews with (among many others) C. A. Meier, Mario Jacoby, Franz Jung, Hans Rudolf Wilhelm, Adolf Guggenbuhl-Craig; and telephone conversations with Gret Baumann-Jung and Dieter Baumann.

32. Riklin had become an object of professional derision by the time Abraham wrote this letter to Freud, *F/Abraham*, February 11, 1917, p. 247.

33. Ulrich Hoerni, letter to the author, December 15, 1999. She was the daughter of Sophie Fiechter-Jung, the youngest child of CGJ I and the sister of CGJ's father. Sophie Fiechter-Jung was the aunt with whom CGJ enjoyed a youthful correspondence and the mother of the architect, Ernst, who designed CGJ's Küsnacht house.

34. It is commonly believed by her descendants and others that she supported her family with her skilled needlework and other artistic endeavors during the periods when her husband earned no money, either through his analytic practice or his painting.

35. "Die Giacometti-Halle im Amsthaus I in Zürich," ed. the GSK Gesellschaft für Schweizerische Kunstgeschichte (2000), p. 16; also from research by Ursula Schulte, and her consultation with Dr. Phil. Fritz Hermann.

36. They are extant today. Giacometti later talked about how he could not teach Riklin the generally accepted fresco technique and how Riklin did it his own way, supposedly better.

37. *F/J*, 303J, March 3, 1912, pp. 490–92.

38. *F/J*, 304F, March 5, 1912, pp. 492–93.

39. *F/J*, 305J, March 10, 1912, p. 494; 310J, April 1, 1912, p. 498. Note 1 to 312J indicates that CGJ may have made his first visit to Ravenna at this time and corrects the 1913 date given in *MDR*, pp. 284–65.

40. *F/J*, 307J, March 22, 1912, p. 496.

41. *Protocols*. For a discussion of how and why he wrote this book, see William McGuire, ed., *Analytical Psychology: Notes of the Seminar Given in 1925*, Bollingen Series 99 (Princeton: Princeton Univ. Press, 1989), pp. 22–25.

42. *F/J*, 312J, April 27, 1912, p. 502.

43. *F/J*, 313J, May 8, 1912, pp. 502–3. Freud's reply to 312J, according to n. 1, is apparently missing.

44. *F/J*, 314F, May 14, 1912, p. 504.

45. *F/J*, 315J, May 17, 1912, pp. 505–6.

46. *F/J*, 316F, May 23, 1912, p. 507. In *CW*-4, p. 87, in connection with the Fordham lectures, "On the Theory of Psychoanalysis," CGJ writes that he became familiar with Adler's book *Über den nervosen Charakter* (The Nervous Constitution) "only after the preparation of these lectures, in the spring of 1912. . . . I recognize that he and I have reached similar conclusions on various points, but here is not the place to discuss the matter more thoroughly."

47. Binswanger, *Freud: Reminiscences*. On p. 39, he attributes his subsequent long life (d. 1966) to discovering the tumor at "an exceptionally early date."

48. Binswanger, *Freud: Reminiscences*, p. 39, quoting Freud's letter of April 14, 1912.

49. *F/J*, 315J, May 17, 1912, p. 505; and 317J, May 25, 1912, p. 508.

50. CGJ to Dr. Kurt Eissler, August 29, 1953, Manuscript Division, LC, Tape no. 74. CGJ elaborated:

> CGJ: Our professional relationship did not end immediately. He did not dismiss me, but I just said I could not go on anymore. I told him I would have to give up the editorship of the *Jahrbuch* if he insisted upon identifying the theory with the method, if he insisted . . . right from the start to prejudge everything, [that if he declares it as such] then it *must* be so! You asked me about his sensitivity, or his ambition, and so on: for example, I once had a discussion with him about some theoretical matter. And that's when I said in my opinion it wasn't so at all. He said, "Yes it is, it must be so!" and I asked why and he said, "Because after all I thought it!" When he thought something, then he was himself surprised by it and then it *had to* be right! Then it damn well had to be right! And that's what later made me think that he in his emotional life — he was delicately sensitive — was once disturbed somehow, severely disturbed. And that originally he wasn't a thinker at all, but began to think secondarily, and with difficulty.
>
> Eissler: Under the influence of a trauma?
>
> CGJ: No, you know, when feeling has been scared off, one escapes into thinking!

The emphasis is CGJ's, and the exclamation points are Eissler's, indicating (as he told me in conversation) great emotionalism on CGJ's part throughout the interview.

51. Ronald W. Clark, *Freud: The Man and the Cause* (New York: Random House, 1980), p. 311. He notes that when Adler dropped dead of a cerebral hemorrhage at a meeting of a British group in Aberdeen, Scotland, Freud wrote to Arnold Zweig that the "*Jew-boy* out of a Viennese suburb" had done well for himself. When Ernst Freud edited the correspondence for publication, he omitted the pejorative. I cite it here to show Freud's frequent use of anti-Semitic remarks and the ease with which he attributed such attitudes to others, most particularly CGJ.

52. Clark, *The Man and the Cause*, p. 317.

53. *F/J*, 319F, June 13, 1912, pp. 510–11.

54. According to Binswanger, *Freud: Reminiscences*, p. 9, he and Häberlin visited Freud in Vienna in April 1913. Häberlin asked Freud why "his most talented disciples, Jung and Adler, to give examples . . . had broken away from him." Freud replied: "Precisely because they too wanted to be Popes."

55. *F/J*, 320J, July 18, 1912, p. 511.

56. Emma Jung to Freud, *F/J*, September 10, 1912, p. 514.

57. Published in *SE*-14 as *On the History of the Psychoanalytic Movement (1914)*, pp. 3ff. According to James Strachey's editor's note: "The aim of the paper was to state

clearly the fundamental postulates and hypotheses of psychoanalysis, to show that
the theories of Adler and Jung were totally incompatible with them, and to draw
the inference that it would lead to nothing but general confusion if these contradictory sets of views were all given the same name."

58. Michael Balint to Ernest Jones, May 31, 1957; quoted in Clark, *The Man and the
Cause*, p. 337.
59. *F/J*, 321J, August 2, 1912, p. 512. Bleuler agreed; see also 328J, p. 523 and n. 2.
60. Letters now in the Jung family's private archive.
61. Jelliffe was clinical professor of mental diseases at Fordham Medical School; White
was superintendent of St. Elizabeths Hospital, Washington, D.C.
62. *The Fordham Monthly*, 31, no. 1 (November 1912).
63. *Protocols*, in some versions dictated to Aniela Jaffé, March 21, 1958. CGJ's emphasis.
64. In 1937, following the Terry Lectures at Yale, CGJ went to Boston to speak about
mandalas at Massachusetts General Hospital. A psychiatrist told him afterward that
he had described "scientific work." CGJ (*Protocols*, in some versions dictated to
Jaffé, March 21, 1958) responded that this was another example of the American
interest in technique rather than theory: "[The psychiatrist] only wanted to know
whether I had followed the *scientific* method. And I had to confirm to him that the
comparative method *is* scientific."
65. Reproduced in *CGJ Speaking*, ed. William McGuire and R. F. C. Hull, Bollingen
Series 97 (Princeton: Princeton Univ. Press, 1997), pp. 11–24. The interviewer's
introduction credited CGJ with bringing Freud "to the recognition of the older
school of psychology." The interviewer later acknowledged Freud as CGJ's precursor, adding that CGJ "has added to [this same theory] other scientific processes."
66. Jung to Jelliffe in John C. Burnham and William McGuire, eds., *Jelliffe's Correspondence with Sigmund Freud and CGJ* (Chicago: Univ. of Chicago Press, 1983), May
13, 1912, p. 190.
67. CGJ thanks "Dr. Gregory" of Bellevue Hospital for his assistance. McGuire, *CGJ
Speaking*, p. 11, describes his related professional activity.
68. "Versuch einer Darstellung der psychoanalytischen Theorie. Neun Vorlesungen,
gehalten in New York im September 1912," written in German but given in English, translated by Edith and M. D. Eder and Maria Moltzer. In *CW*-4 and 9.
69. *CW*-4, para. 252, p. 111. For an explanation of libido, see *CW*-5, *Symbols of Transformation*, paras. 185–89, pp. 128–31.
70. *CW*-4, paras. 340–52, pp. 151–56.
71. *CW*-4, para. 522, pp. 225–26.
72. Private sources and private archives.
73. Medill McCormick to President Theodore Roosevelt, October 3, 1912, LC. I cite
it here because McCormick's heady appraisal of CGJ as "the most distinguished
psychiatrist in Europe" was one that many other Americans shared. I thank Patricia O'Toole for the reference.
74. Medill McCormick was elected to the Senate from his home state of Illinois in
1918 and served one term. He was defeated for reelection in 1924. CGJ wrote this
account in several of the extant *Protocols* but did not include it in *MDR*. However,
he and Freud discussed Roosevelt in *F/J*, 311F; 312J, n. 3; and 316F.
75. Jones to Freud, *F/Jones*, 97, October 30, 1912, p. 165.
76. Jones to Freud, *F/Jones*, 102, November 14, 1912, p. 175.
77. Nathan G. Hale Jr., ed., *James Jackson Putnam and Psychoanalysis: Letters Between
Putnam and Sigmund Freud, Ernest Jones, William James, Sandor Ferenczi, and Morton Prince, 1877–1917* (Cambridge, Mass.: Harvard Univ. Press, 1971). It has not

been found in Putnam's extant archives; nor was it printed in his published correspondence with Freud. It is my contention that the language of this letter, when compared to the rest of Putnam's correspondence, is more similar to Jones's than to Putnam's.

78. *F/Jones*, 107J, December 5, 1912, p. 180; and Ernest Jones, *The Life and Work of Sigmund Freud* (New York: Basic Books, 1959), 2: 145.

79. CGJ to Jones, November 15, 1912, unpublished and in a private archive, where I consulted it along with fifteen other letters from CGJ to Jones dating from November 23, 1907, to December 19, 1953.

80. Letter in the Jung family private archives.

81. *F/Jones*, 107J, December 5, 1912, p. 180.

82. As does Phyllis Grosskurth (among many others), in *The Secret Ring: Freud's Inner Circle and the Politics of Psychoanalysis* (New York: Addison-Wesley, 1991), p. 46.

83. Jones, *Life and Work*, 2: 152–53.

84. For full explanation of the committee's origin and development, including Freud's complete response to Jones on August 1, 1912, see Grosskurth, *The Secret Ring*, pp. 47–48. Max Eitingon, Freud's first declared supporter, was not an original member but was added later, as was Otto Rank. Both received rings. Rank eventually disagreed with Freud and was ostracized. He moved to Paris, where he engaged in a torrid affair with Anaïs Nin, to whom he gave the secret ring. She, in turn, gave it to Henry Miller, another of her lovers. Miller didn't want it and gave it back to Nin, who claimed she returned it to Rank. See Deirdre Bair, *Anaïs Nin: A Biography* (New York: Penguin, 1996).

85. CGJ to Jones, November 15, 1912. This is the letter in which CGJ clearly wrote the date as November 25, leading Jones to charge that it was a deliberate act designed to make him miss the meeting. He was there, however, claiming to have heard the correct date from others.

86. Jones, *Life and Work*, 2: 146, writes that this was the occasion of Freud's second fainting spell in Munich. CGJ to Jones, December 19, 1953: "You got the story of Freud's fainting attack quite wrong."

87. Freud to Ferenzci, *F/Ferenczi*, 349, November 26, 1912, pp. 433–35.

88. *F/Jones*, 79J, July 22, 1912, writes that CGJ sent him a letter "which cannot but be construed into a formal disavowal of our hitherto friendly relations." The extant CGJ-Jones correspondence contains only the following letters for 1912: November 15 and 20. In his unpublished letter of the fifteenth, CGJ attempts to clear up "some mistakes or doubts about my attitude to you." There is no evidence in either letter of any animosity toward Jones, whom Freud described as "personally very attached recently" as he moved to ingratiate himself (Freud to Abraham, *F/Abraham*, October 21, 1912, p. 124).

89. In *F/J*, 133J, March 7, 1909, p. 208, CGJ described Häberlin as "a dazzlingly brainy fellow with an all-round education." He retained this view, even though they had theoretical divergences in years afterward.

90. CGJ, according to Freud, did not go sailing until "the weekend," which usually begins on Saturday (the twenty-fifth that year). The letter would have been delivered on Friday, the twenty-fourth, in one of the several daily mail deliveries. As noted earlier, Emma, who sorted the mail, would have recognized Freud's handwriting and would certainly have brought it to CGJ's attention. This, too, adds to the lack of credibility of Freud's account of CGJ's alleged sailing weekend.

91. In *MDR*, p. 157, CGJ writes of Amenophis IV (Ikhnaton). Jones, *Life and Work*, 2: 146–47, among those who have written about this incident, identifies the Egyptian pharaoh as Amenhotep; Clark does not name him; Frank McLynn calls him

Akhenaton in *CGJ: A Biography* (New York: Bantam Press, 1996). For recent developments in Egyptology about "Akhenaten" that correspond to CGJ's 1913 theories, see John Noble Wilford, "With Fresh Discoveries, Egyptology Flowers," *New York Times*, December 28, 1999, F1–2.

92. As the passage continues in the *Protocols*, CGJ veers onto the subject of Spielrein and her discovery of the death wish: "This idea comes from her. I already said it back then: life is not only geared toward life, but also toward death. Death is a goal. But for me that is not a death wish, but the facts of life and of death are simply givens. . . . I did not yet have the word archetype back then."

93. *F/Jones*, 108F, December 8, 1912, p. 182.

94. Freud to Ferenczi, *F/Ferenczi*, 349, November 26, 1912, p. 435.

95. Freud to Binswanger, December 16, 1912, in Binswanger, *Freud: Reminiscences*, pp. 48–49.

96. *F/J*, 335J, between December 11 and 14, 1912, p. 533. CGJ adds that the title was suggested by Zürich "theologians," but the local "pedagogues" were also voicing concerns. As noted earlier, these two groups jousted to prevail in how psychoanalysis was used in Switzerland.

97. *F/J*, 334F, December 9, 1912, pp. 532–33.

98. *F/J*, 335J, between December 11 and 14, 1912, p. 533.

99. *F/J*, 338J, December 18, 1912, pp. 534–35.

100. Author's emphasis. I believe this appellation was a rebuttal to Freud, who insisted that Jung had a "father complex" toward him.

101. *F/J*, 340F, December 22, 1912, p. 537.

102. I believe the more accurate translation is by Brabant et al. in Freud to Ferenczi, *F/Ferenczi*, 353, December 9, 1912, p. 440, rather than in *F/Jones*, 108F, December 8, 1912, p. 182, where the phrase is "changing from tenderness to overbearing insolence." In the latter, Freud calls CGJ "a perfect fool, he seems to be Christ himself." In this letter, Freud states that CGJ was analyzed by Sister Maria Moltzer and is now engaged in an affair with her. CGJ was consulting about mutual patients with Moltzer at this time, among them Fanny Bowditch Katz.

103. *F/J*, 342F, January 3, 1913, p. 539.

104. *F/J*, 343J, January 3, 1913, p. 539.

105. *F/J*, 344J, January 6, 1913, p. 540.

106. Jung wrote a long letter to Jones in Rome on November 20, immediately after the November 1912 meeting in Munich. Jones still made the accusations, and thus Jung replied in the letter quoted here, May 7, 1913, from the private archive cited previously. See also *F/Jones*, 109J, December 23, 1912, p. 184, in which he quotes from another letter allegedly written by Putnam but not found in Hale, *Putnam and Psychoanalysis*, and in which he accuses CGJ of not replying ("not a line") to his "two long conciliatory letters after Munich."

107. *CW*-4, para. 523, p. 229.

108. *CW*-4, paras. 567–68, pp. 247–48.

109. *CW*-4, para. 574, p. 250.

110. *F/Jones*, 133J, pp. 215–16. Ellenberger, *Discovery of the Unconscious*, pp. 817–19, gives an accurate, fact-based account that contradicts Jones's letter and his subsequent biography. Until otherwise noted, quotes here are from Jones's letter.

111. Freud to Ferenczi, *F/Ferenczi*, 414, August 5, 1913, p. 505.

112. From information about "The Munich Congress," *F/J*, p. 549.

113. Abraham to Freud, *F/Abraham*, July 20, 1913, pp. 143–44; Freud to Abraham, July 31, 1913, p. 145.

114. *SE*-12.

115. CGJ, unpublished postcard to Jones, November 25, 1913, private archive.
116. *CW*-6, Appendix 1, p. 499.
117. Lou Andreas-Salomé, *The Freud Journal* (London: Quartet Books, 1987), p. 168.
118. "A History of the Psycho-Analytic Movement," *SE*-14: 45.
119. Ferenczi to CGJ, November 13, 1913, unpublished letter from a private archive. Clark, *The Man and the Cause*, reprints part of this letter on p. 333, citing its earlier appearance in Vincent Brome's *Freud and His Early Circle* (New York: William Morrow and Co., 1968), p. 136, where provenance is not given.
120. *F/J*, 357J, 27 October 1913, p. 550. CGJ tells Freud that Maeder has told him his *bona fides* were in doubt, and an editorial note relates that Freud wrote the same in a letter to Maeder.
121. Jones, *Life and Work*, 2: 102; Jones's *Free Associations: Memoirs of a Psycho-Analyst* (New York: Basic Books, 1959), p. 224, has a different account; and unpublished letter, Freud to Maeder, private archive. CGJ reports unspecified persons making this charge in several *Protocols*.
122. Freud to Abraham, *F/Abraham*, July 31, 1913, p. 145.
123. *F/Jones*, 155F, November 17, 1913, p. 239.

CHAPTER 17: "MY SELF/MYSELF"

1. *F/J*, 11F, January 1, 1907, p. 18.
2. Freud to Lou Andreas-Salomé, January 12, 1914, p. 16, *Sigmund Freud and Lou Andreas-Salomé's Letters*, ed. Ernst Pfeiffer, trans. William Scott and Elaine Robson-Scott (London: Hogarth Press and Institute of Psychoanalysis, 1972).
3. Freud to Jones, *F/Jones*, May 17, 1914, p. 279.
4. *History of Psychoanalysis*, p. 7. In *The Jungians: A Comparative and Historical Perspective* (London and Philadelphia: Routledge, 2000), Thomas B. Kirsch describes Freud as "an autocratic, authoritarian figure who demanded complete personal loyalty" (pp. 248–49), one who insisted upon establishing himself as both the founder and owner of psychoanalysis.
5. One has only to read his letters to Freud during April 1913 for corroboration. Ronald Clark, *Freud: The Man and the Cause* (New York: Random House, 1980), p. 330, quotes from a letter Jones sent to Freud on April 25, 1913, from Colchester (not reprinted in *F/Jones*), in which Jones wrote that it was "a grand time to be alive . . . because it is fuller of fighting on which so much depends. . . . Yours enthusiastically, Jones."
6. A brief chronology of events: CGJ resigned as editor of the *Jahrbuch* "for reasons of a personal nature" on October 27, 1913, and Bleuler followed by resigning as director. Freud assumed the editorship, and the *Jahrbuch* continued to be published for one year. On April 20, 1914, CGJ submitted his resignation as president of the IPA (on April 30, he officially resigned from the University of Zürich teaching faculty). Freud persuaded the six European societies to elect Abraham provisional president until the next congress, scheduled for September 1914 but canceled due to war. On July 10, the Zürich group withdrew from the IPA. *F/J*, pp. 550–52, gives further detail, as does Clark, *The Man and the Cause*, chapter 14, "The Break with Jung," pp. 316–38.
7. CGJ to Jones, December 2, 1913. This is the last known letter CGJ wrote to Jones until December 19, 1953, when he replied to Jones's request to read letters Freud had written to him. Referring to the two episodes when Freud fainted in his presence, CGJ wrote: "Your biographical material is very interesting, although it would have been advisable to consult me for certain facts."

8. His emphasis, after which Aniela Jaffé or one of the editors affixed a question mark.

9. CGJ's spoken memories in the *Protocols* are given in slightly altered form in *MDR*, pp. 175–76.

10. CGJ describes this dream as his earliest attempt to explore the unconscious. Jaffé did not use what he actually said in *Protocols* in *MDR*, incorporating instead comments from the 1925 seminar. In the *Protocols*, CGJ equated any knowledge and insight gained at this time with "[falling] in love with women" and "say[ing] yes to it." He said it was the time when the "anima" was first manifested, but he did not yet understand its significance. On several *Protocol* typescripts, Jaffé made the following handwritten marginal notation to Cary Baynes, who was helping to edit the manuscript: "Carey [*sic*]: we should be careful with the English version."

11. The *Oxford-Duden German Dictionary* translates it as "cock-pigeon." CGJ remembered hearing an uncle say it when he was a boy.

12. CGJ's spelling in the *Protocols*. For the many references to Hermes Trismegistus, see *CW*-20, p. 30.

13. Jaffé presents an edited version of CGJ's dream of "Siegfried," taking enormous liberties to change what he actually said in the *Protocols*. This is verified by the typescripts with changes and corrections in CGJ's hand; pages prepared later by Jaffé bear no such markings. Also, in none of the extant typescripts with CGJ's markings does he date the dream, as she does, to December 18, 1913. She does not include his comment that he considered Siegfried "not an especially sympathetic figure" and thought Wagner's operatic character "exaggeratedly extraverted and at times actually ridiculous. I never liked him." CGJ adds that he could not understand why he felt such strong emotion in the dream and said he was only telling it to Jaffé because it connected to an earlier discussion about "art . . . and the change of values." This exchange ended with CGJ saying a great deluge of rain (in the dream) woke him, and he felt enormous relief. His interpretation of the dream is peaceful and almost euphoric; nowhere in any of the *Protocols* I read is there a description of panic it engendered — certainly not enough to cause him, as described in *MDR*, p. 180, to contemplate taking a loaded revolver from his nightstand and shooting himself. He summed up the meaning of the dream in the *Protocols* as follows: "The hero . . . is the symbol of the greatest value recognized by us. . . . So it appeared as if Siegfried were my hero. . . . I must then have had a hero I did not appreciate, and it was my ideal of force and efficiency I had killed. I had killed my intellect, helped on to the deed by a personification of the collective unconscious. . . . In other words I deposed my superior function. The rain that fell is a symbol of the release of tension, that is, the forces of the unconscious are loosed. When this happens, the feeling of relief is engendered. The crime is expiated because as soon as the main function is deposed, there is a chance for other sides of the personality to be born into life."

14. *CW*-19 belies this, as there are numerous publications for this period both in German and English.

15. Emma Helene, b. March 18, 1914.

16. Dr. Med. Peter Jung and Herr Ulrich Hoerni, interview with the author, November 5, 1999, Zürich.

17. Gene Nameche, "Jung and Persons," unpublished manuscript, University of Glasgow library, states that CGJ's psychiatric clientele was so diminished during these years that he was reduced to working as a general practitioner, "bandaging bones and bruises, treating colds, influenza, corns and the ordinary ailments of everyday life — what he called 'the whole stinking mess of human corporeality.'" I have

found no evidence to support this, neither in the many interviews Nameche conducted for the Wickes Foundation (now in HCL) nor in my own interviews, the ETH archives, or the personal documentation held by the *Erbengemeinschaft CGJ*. My research indicates that his analytic practice remained stable.

18. A fax from Ulrich Hoerni, August 15, 2001, describes *The Black Book* as six notebooks bound in black leather, 17.5 x 22.5 cm, with a thickness of about 2 cm. He further states that Jaffé's note in *MDR*, p. 188, is correct. In an interview with Hoerni and Dr. Med. Peter Jung, November 5, 1999, both stated that *The Black Book* comprises the family's "Sacred Cow." In a fax of September 7, 2001, Hoerni confirmed that there is no plan to publish the notebooks and they will remain in the private family archives.

19. For a fuller definition, see Andrew Samuels, Bani Shorter, and Fred Plaut, eds., *A Critical Dictionary of Jungian Analysis* (London and New York: Routledge, 1986), p. 140; also, *MDR*, Glossary, pp. 399–400. In a Q&A session following a meeting of the curatorium of the CGJ Institute in Küsnacht, June 22, 1957, CGJ answered Barbara Hannah's question (her actual words were not recorded) with a discussion of the *"Seelenbild,"* or "soul image," which he said he encountered for the first time in 1920 during the writing of *Psychological Types:* "The word 'soul' means: the living thing which we sense distinctly or indistinctly as the reason for our consciousness or as the atmosphere of our consciousness." He also compared "anima and animus" to the "personification of the soul."

20. *F/Jones*, p. 298, cited by William McGuire in "Firm Affinities: Jung's Relations with Britain and the United States," *JAP* 40 (1995): 312. McGuire also notes that CGJ was "feeling his way toward a terminology that would set his system apart from Freud's," and that for a time, he avoided naming it but called it the "Zürich School," as opposed to the "Vienna School." His first written use of the term "analytical psychology" (spoken to the British medical groups in London and Aberdeen) was in "On the Doctrine of Complexes" (paper presented to the Australasian Medical Congress, Sydney, Transactions of the Ninth session, 2: 835–39; reprinted in *CW*-2, 18, full citation *CW*-19, 1913a, p. 62).

21. *CW*-6.

22. *Jahrbuch* 6 (July 1, 1914), reprinted in *SE*-14. James Strachey's editor's note says that Freud's intention was "to show that the theories of Adler and Jung were totally incompatible" with "the fundamental postulates and hypotheses of psychoanalysis." Freud wrote to Lou Andreas-Salomé that his intention was to give Adler and Jung "a good clobbering" (Pfeiffer, *Freud and Andreas-Salomé's Letters*, June 29, 1914, p. 17).

23. "On the History of the Psychoanalytic Movement," part 3, in *The Basic Writings of Sigmund Freud*, trans. and ed. A. A. Brill (New York: Random House [Modern Library], 1983), pp. 959ff.

24. Paul Roazen's phrase, from *The Trauma of Freud: Controversies in Psychoanalysis* (New Brunswick, N.J.: Transaction Publishers, 2002). CGJ did, however, make comments about Freud's attack in various letters, among them the July 17, 1914, letter to Swedish analyst Poul Bjerre, in which he decried Freud's "break of medical discretion" for quoting the patient's letter, which he called "practices . . . characteristic of Viennese policies. Such an enemy is not worthy of the name." He entreated Bjerre to go to the (1914 canceled) Dresden congress and speak on behalf of himself and the Zürich group. In a note accompanying the letter, Freud unwittingly contributed to the controversy surrounding doctor-patient confidentiality when he explained why he had not asked the patient's permission: "I cannot admit that any psychoanalytical technique should claim the protection of discretion."

25. CGJ to Poul Bjerre, July 17, 1914, *CL-2*, p. xxix. Ludwig Binswanger claims to have been the sole dissenter in *Sigmund Freud: Reminiscences of a Friendship* (New York and London: Grune and Stratton, 1957), p. 55, saying he wrote to Freud on July 22, 1914, that he did not know whether the single dissenting vote was his but that he had written earlier to Chairman Maeder to say that he could not attend the meeting and wished to vote against the separation. However, documents in the Zürich Psychoanalytic Association archives, including the minutes of 1914, indicate that a Frau Professor Erismann actually cast the sole dissenting vote. William McGuire, ed., in *Analytical Psychology: Notes of the Seminar Given in 1925*, Bollingen Series 99 (Princeton: Princeton Univ. Press, 1989), p. 25, lists others who remained loyal to CGJ: J. B. Lang, Hans Schmid-Guisan, Martha Böddinghaus (later Sigg-Böddinghaus), J. Vodoz, C. Schneiter, Adolf Keller, Jan Nelken, and Maria Moltzer, who were all official members of the Zürich group. Also loyal to CGJ but not official voting members were Toni Wolff, Beatrice M. Hinkle, and (for a time) Smith Ely Jelliffe and Trigant Burrow. Jones, in a letter to Brill (Brill collection, LC), April 20 (prob. 1912), cites William Alanson White as among CGJ's supporters. I am grateful to Paul Roazen for pointing out this last to me.

26. In an earlier letter to Poul Bjerre, September 30, 1913, CGJ wrote that he was convinced Freud and the Viennese did not allow the break to occur during the Munich conference because "they did not want to endanger the existence of the newly founded [1912] *Internationale Zeitschrift für ärztliche Psychoanalyse*." Also in *CL-2*, p. xxix.

27. The first quotation is from *F/Abraham*, July 18, 1914, p. 184; the second is from *F/Abraham*, July 26, 1914, p. 186. Abraham was a cautionary voice throughout this time, alerting Freud to the inherent dangers of forcing CGJ out of the International Society. See especially his letter to Freud, *F/Abraham*, November 4, 1913, pp. 153–54.

28. Jones to Brill, April 1 (probably 1914), Brill collection, LC. Paul Roazen brought the Jones-Brill correspondence to my attention.

29. Riklin conducted an extensive correspondence with Freud in the years between 1909 and 1914, arguing frequently for the policies of the Zürich group and specifically for CGJ's so-called "deviations." Freud's replies are in possession of Franz Beda Riklin's surviving son, Peter Riklin, who has allegedly given full responsibility for them to Hans Rudolf Wilhelm, who refuses to make them available to other scholars. To the best of my knowledge, no other copies exist, either in the Freud or CGJ archives.

30. Jones particularly singled out Maeder for "behaving like an ass . . . writing that Jews can't understand lofty problems such as religion" (letter to Brill, June 1 [probably 1914], Brill collection, LC).

31. M(ontague) David Eder, "The Present Position of Psychoanalysis," *British Medical Journal* 2 (1913–15). Dr. Eder preferred to use his first initial and second name.

32. *F/Jones*, 192, June 2, 1914, pp. 285–86.

33. I asked the Jung heirs to search the family archives for information concerning this, and they found nothing as of 2003. To repeat, CGJ, Emma Jung, and Toni Wolff all destroyed their personal correspondence with one another, but Emma and CGJ both kept what might pass for diaries, and these still exist. The Jung heirs have not read them, nor do they intend to, and they state emphatically that none will ever be made public.

34. Described in *MDR*, chapter 9, sec. 5. In *F/J*, pp. 551–52, n. 2, the editors note that CGJ's dating of this trip was mistaken. Franz Jung used postcards in the family archive that CGJ sent to Emma to verify the correct date of his first (of three) vis-

its to Ravenna: April 1914. There appears to have been some muddle in CGJ's memory when he spoke of it to Aniela Jaffé for the *Protocols* (some of which are dated August 3, 1957; others are left undated and unpaginated). There he states that it happened in 1932, when he went with Toni Wolff, and that he had been in Ravenna once with "acquaintances" eight years earlier, so he knew the decorative art of the Arian baptistry. In a later *Protocol*, he says the acquaintance was Dr. Hans Schmid, with whom he bicycled from Switzerland to Ravenna.

35. Conversation with a member of the extended Wolff family who based her remarks on veiled allusions Toni made in a letter and in private written musings. The CGJ heirs are outraged over Morris West's depiction of intimacy between CGJ and Toni Wolff in his novel *The World Is Made of Glass* (New York: William Morrow, 1983), pointing out that the only horizontal surface in the Seestrasse boathouse, where the liaisons allegedly took place, is a narrow plank, not wide enough to support the body of a man as large as CGJ.

36. This idiom does not translate well from German into English, but it occurs in several instances in the *Protocols*. In a private archive, Barbara Hannah remembers it as a kind of showing off and cites examples of how CGJ used it to excuse his preening during several public lectures. It also occurs in some of the HCL interviews and individual films of *Matters of the Heart* (Los Angeles: CGJ Institute, 1990).

37. Interviews with Franz Jung, November 1995; HCL interviews with Franz and Lilly Jung-Merker; interviews with various members of the Jung family, 1995–99; interviews and correspondence with Dr. Med. Georg Trüb, 1998–99; private documents belonging to the Wolff/Trüb/Naeff families; conversations with Ursula Cadorin-Trüb, 1998; interviews with C. A. Meier, 1994–96, and Marie-Louise von Franz, 1995–96; private archives of associates and/or analysands of CGJ and Toni Wolff and others who wish not to be identified in any manner.

38. Toni shared her discomfort in the sun with Emma, who always shaded her clear, pale eyes with the darkest glasses. Emma gave the sun as the reason she avoided going to the Bollingen tower; because the structure was so dark, she had to spend much time outdoors, and she could not take that much light. Emma's bedroom and study were located on the north side of the house, the darkest rooms in it.

39. Reading between the lines in documentary evidence, I surmise that he permitted Emma to read portions of it in early 1915.

40. In Zürich I heard frequent criticism that a man who encouraged so many women to achieve individuation through education was adamant that his own four daughters should learn only those things that would prepare them to be wives and mothers. None of the Jung daughters went to a university, and all had what might best be described as "finishing school" training. In truth, this was Emma Jung's doing, for she directed their education and decided what would become of her daughters.

41. HCL interviews of Franz and Lilly Jung-Merker and Agathe Niehus-Jung; author's interviews with Agathe Niehus-Jung and Franz Jung; telephone conversation with Gret Baumann-Jung, all November 1995.

42. Agathe Niehus-Jung, in both HCL and personal interviews with the author, recalled with great emotion the happy times she and her husband spent lingering with their three children at the dinner table long after the meal was finished. She thought it sad that her own parents never knew such pleasure.

43. Franz Jung (conversation with the author, HCL interview, and in Linda Donn, *Freud and Jung: Years of Friendship, Years of Loss* [New York: Collier Books, 1990], p. 173) remembered how his father sometimes invited him into the library in the late afternoon and they sat at opposite sides of the table drawing, writing, and col-

oring. He said it was difficult "not to speak a word . . . hard to sit there in the chair opposite."

44. Their children believed that shortly after the birth of the last child, Emma and CGJ established separate bedroom and sitting rooms, not because of estrangement but because they did not want more children and because separate quarters were the custom in their social class.

45. From interviews and conversations with the Homberger family, grudgingly verified by Franz Jung. Also from a journal in a private archive.

46. Pastor of the Peterkirch, Zürich. One of CGJ's earliest friends and followers, along with his wife, Dr. Med. Tina Keller.

47. Conversation with the author, November 1995, Küsnacht. To Linda Donn, who based much of her book *Freud and Jung* on her friendship with Franz Jung and his interviews and conversations with her, he said (p. 174): "Think of my mother. . . . Can *you* imagine living with a man who slept with a gun by his bed and painted pictures of circles all day?" (his emphasis).

48. Donn, *Freud and Jung*, p. 173. I asked Franz Jung in 1995 if he had any idea of his father's response to this anecdote, or if Emma ever told it to CGJ. He said he remembered the anecdote being repeated when he and his sisters were adults, but he did not know if CGJ was aware of it: "I doubt that he would have wasted much time thinking about it. Things we did as children did not amuse him when we were adults."

49. A phrase, in one of its many variants, repeated during interviews with the author.

50. CGJ made the first remark in a *Protocol* describing his meeting H. G. Wells (see chapter 27), during an evening when the conversation was social and composed of "fragments of everything, everything mixed up." He made the second remark concerning why, when Thomas Mann came to live in the village of Kilchberg outside Zürich, he avoided socializing, not only with Mann but with others in general.

51. Einstein first visited the Jung home around 1911 and then again later, probably in 1912 or 1913. Mileva Marić came alone, probably around 1914 or 1915, inviting herself to tea once or twice with her two sons after she and Einstein separated in Berlin and she returned to live in Zürich. Franz Jung "vaguely remembered" that "a sad, divorced woman with two little boys" came to the house on several occasions, but that Emma had "nothing in common" with her and soon refused to see her. According to Andrea Gabor, *Einstein's Wife: Work and Marriage in the Lives of Five Great Twentieth-Century Women* (New York: Viking, 1995), p. 24, Marić left Einstein in Berlin and returned to Zürich in 1914.

52. *Protocols*: Einstein had a "somewhat shallow optimism and [was] a philanthropist of general kindness" in comparison to Freud, who was "bitter and resentful, hard, cynical. He also had a much stronger effect as a personality."

53. According to Susanna Wolff-Trüb, this never-named woman became a member of the Psychological Club when it was founded in 1916 and was still monopolizing CGJ to the annoyance of others as late as 1925.

54. Aline Valangin left her native Alsace before World War I. She married Vladimir Rosenbaum, a lawyer who for a brief time represented Jung on professional matters (see chapter 29). Both were Jung's patients for an indefinite period from the end of 1914 into early 1915.

55. Private Keller family papers from Doris Sträuli-Keller, August 30, 1998; and Tina Keller from a memoir in HCL.

56. Donn, *Freud and Jung*, quoting Franz Jung, p. 173; and interviews with Franz Jung, Frau Homberger, Laurence Homberger, and other members of the Jung and Homberger families.

57. This was a capsule description of Jung's activity from about 1915 to 1925, expressed by an elderly man who also described himself as "of the Zürich establishment." His description is representative of many I heard in interviews and conversations. The man quoted above was referring to the Hotel Sonne in Küsnacht, where many of Jung's foreign patients stayed during their analysis. The woman in the Baur au Lac was Mrs. Edith Rockefeller McCormick, and the club is the Psychological Club, all of which will be described fully in the chapters where they figure in the narrative of CGJ's life.

58. Dr. Med. Rudolf Niehus, interview with the author, November 24, 1994, Mönchaltorf.

59. CGJ told these anecdotes with seeming pleasure in the *Protocols*.

60. L. H. Davis, *Onward and Upward: A Biography of Katharine S. White* (New York: Harper and Row, 1979), p. 28; cited in McGuire, "Firm Affinities," p. 303, and in the Introduction to *Analytical Psychology: Notes of the 1925 Seminar*, p. x. Elizabeth (Elsie) Shepley Sergeant became a well-known writer and journalist in the United States (see her *Harper's* magazine article about CGJ, May 1931, reprinted in McGuire's *CGJ Speaking*, pp. 52–53; see also her own *Shadow Shapes: The Journal of a Wounded Woman* [Boston: Houghton Mifflin, 1920]). Sergeant was responsible for sending many notable Americans to Zürich to analyze with CGJ, among them Robert Edmond Jones and Mary Foote. Sergeant's younger sister was Katharine White, the *New Yorker* editor, wife of E. B. White, and mother of Roger Angell.

61. Dr. M. David Eder, his wife, Edith, and Maria Moltzer translated "The Theory of Psychoanalysis," which CGJ read in New York City in 1912. Edith Eder was among the first British subjects who went to Zürich for analysis.

62. Dr. Constance Long helped the American Dr. Beatrice M. Hinkle edit and translate the first English edition of CGJ's *Collected Papers on Analytical Psychology*. William McGuire, in the Introduction to *Analytical Psychology: Notes of the 1925 Seminar*, p. vii, described it as "a 520–page mélange of pre-Freudian, Freudian, and post-Freudian writings. . . . That volume and the major long works *Psychology of the Unconscious* and *Psychological Types* constituted in 1925 the English-language reading list for the student of Jungian psychology."

CHAPTER 18: "PSYCHOLOGICALLY MINDED" PERSONS

1. Henri Ellenberger interprets this tellingly in his article, "La Psychiatrie suisse III," *Évolution Psychiatrique* (1952): 154: "The most profound, the most subtle and sometimes the most paradoxical views follow one another with an incomparable ease and rapidity. One finds a reflection of this in his works, *above all in the published lectures*, in the measure to which the text does not move away too much from the original spontaneity" (author's emphasis).

2. William McGuire, ed., *Analytical Psychology: Notes of the Seminar Given in 1925*, Bollingen Series 99 (Princeton: Princeton Univ. Press, 1989), p. 25.

3. First published in German in 1921 as *Psychologische Typen* (Zürich: Rascher Verlag), later in *CW*-6.

4. Thomas B. Kirsch, *The Jungians: A Comparative and Historical Perspective* (London and Philadelphia: Routledge, 2000), p. 247, notes that CGJ "eschewed the word 'technique' but there was a general way in which he worked [using] dream analysis, active imagination, and amplification in face-to-face, relatively infrequent sessions, foster[ing] an active dialectic between himself and his patient."

5. To cite some of the better known: Richard Noll's *Jung Cult* (Princeton: Princeton Univ. Press, 1994) and *Aryan Christ* (New York: Random House, 1997); Sonu

Shamdasani's *Cult Fictions: CGJ and the Founding of Analytical Psychology* (London: Routledge, 1998); Henri Ellenberger's *Discovery of the Unconscious: The History and Evolution of Dynamic Psychiatry* (New York: Basic Books, 1970); and various biographies, from Barbara Hannah's to Frank McLynn's.

6. Ellenberger, *Discovery of the Unconscious*, p. 672.
7. William McGuire, "Firm Affinities: Jung's Relations with Britain and the United States," *JAP* 40 (1995): 315.
8. Kirsch, *The Jungians*, p. xxi.
9. The indices of Freud's correspondence with Ferenczi, Jones, and Abraham show how eagerly he and they exchanged tidbits that filtered through wartime restrictions between their countries and neutral Switzerland. Quotations are from Freud to Abraham, *F/Abraham*, December 30, 1914, p. 208, and Abraham to Freud, *F/Abraham*, February 28, 1915, p. 212.
10. *F/Jones*, 209, December 25, 1914, p. 309.
11. Nachmannsohn published "Freud's Libidotheorie verglichen mit der Eroslehre Platos" in the *Internationale Zeitschrift* 3 (1915). Quotation is from Freud to Abraham, *F/Abraham*, February 18, 1915, p. 211.
12. *F/Jones*, 209, December 25, 1914, p. 309.
13. *F/Jones*, 217J, October 31, 1916, p. 320.
14. *F/Abraham*, July 22, 1916, p. 238.
15. Texts consulted include: Sarah Barker, "The Club Problem" (unpublished essay); Ellenberger, "La Psychiatrie suisse III and VI"; the annual *Jahresbericht* publication of the Psychological Club of Zürich; *F/J*; Magnus Ljunggren, *The Russian Mephisto: A Study of the Life and Work of Emilii Medtner* (Stockholm: Stockholm Univ. Studies in Russian Literature, 1994); Emilii Medtner, "Bildnis der Persönlichkeit im Rahmen des gegenseitigen sich Kennenlernens," in *Die Kulturelle Bedeutung der Komplexen Psychologie*, ed. Psychological Club of Zürich; Friedel Muser, *Zur Geschichte der Psychologischen Clubs Zürich von den Anfangen bis 1928* (Zürich: Psychological Club, 1984); Noll, *The Jung Cult* and *The Aryan Christ*; Jane Cabot Reid, "History of the Psychological Club, Zürich" (unpublished pamphlet); Andrew Samuels, "A Jung Club Is Not Enough," *Harvest* 40 (1994): 155–67; Shamdasani, *Cult Fictions*; Anthony Storr, *Feet of Clay: A Study of Gurus* (New York: Free Press, 1996); Paul Stern, *CGJ: The Haunted Prophet* (George Braziller, 1976); private archives of the Wolff/Trüb/Naeff families; various HCL interviews (S. Trüb, Maeder, Keller, Heinrich Steiger, etc.); unpublished memoirs (Rosenbaum, Valangin, private sources); personal and private communications; and biographies of CGJ (Hannah, Wehr, etc.).
16. The *Zentralblatt für Psychoanalyse* 2 (1912): 480, gives February 13, 1912, as the official date of the first meeting, but various private documents and some of the HCL interviews give contradictory dates, so I give "early" 1912 as the closest approximation.
17. *F/J*, 300J, February 25, 1912, p. 487.
18. For CGJ's usage, see *CW*-6, paras. 757–62, pp. 448–50. Para. 757: "Individuation . . . is a process of *differentiation* (q.v.), having for its goal the development of the individual personality" (CGJ's emphasis). See also Andrew Samuels, Bani Shorter, and Fred Plaut, eds., *A Critical Dictionary of Jungian Analysis* (London and New York: Routledge, 1986), pp. 76–79, "Individuation."
19. Hans Rudolf Wilhelm, who describes himself as a scholar of Franz Beda Riklin's life and work, claims CGJ "organized his Mafia to destroy Riklin," campaigned actively to "marginalize" him, and caused him to leave psychoanalysis for art. Wil-

helm's comments were made during an interview with the author, November 4, 1999, Zürich. Wilhelm provided no documentation, and I have found none to support his charges.

20. Ursula Cadorin-Trüb, interviews with the author, July 9, 1998, and November 11, 1999. Susi Trüb's son Dr. Med. Georg Trüb, in interviews on the same dates, concurs, adding that his mother was "interested in women's way of life in general. . . . [Carl] Kerényi played a role in this thinking but was not central."

21. From a private document prepared by one of Moltzer's analysands who wrote minutely described accounts of sessions with her.

22. Shamdasani (*Cult Fictions* and "The Lost Contributions of Maria Moltzer" [*Spring* 64, pp. 103–6]) and Noll (*The Jung Cult* and *The Aryan Christ*) provide conflicting accounts. Her life has not been documented for the period after she left Zürich, other than in the Bowditch Katz archive at HCL, where Moltzer's last letter is dated 1934. In *The Aryan Christ*, p. 198, Noll writes correctly that "except for speculations about her possible affair with CGJ, her name never appears in the history books. Most Jungians have never heard of her."

23. The paraphrased quotation is, like other information, from Fanny Bowditch Katz's diary, c. 1913[?], HCL. In a 1916 entry, Bowditch Katz described the Zürich "resistances" to Moltzer, saying she had "a far harder adaptation to life. . . . Her life, solitude, not being protected by the law, etc., far harder than Dr. Jung. . . . I'm beginning to see more & more how positively heroic her life is — surrounded on all sides by opposition, and standing quite alone, fighting to the death for her belief. No wonder it has nearly killed her!"

24. In CGJ's archives at the ETH, there are occasional letters she handwrote on his letterhead. In one in a private archive to an otherwise unidentified "professor," Moltzer explains that she is attending to CGJ's correspondence while he is away and writing on his behalf. She must have known the recipient because she describes her apartment, her practice, and her life in general. I base my contention that Moltzer transcribed at least part of the Honegger Papers (see chapter 13 and the Appendix) on the handwriting in this and several other letters.

25. Her archives at the HCL give her dates as 1874–1967. Her father, Henry Pickering Bowditch (1840–1911), was professor of physiology at Harvard from 1871 to 1906. Her mother, Selma Knauth Bowditch, was of German origin, and Bowditch Katz was fluent in the language. Fanny married Dr. Rudolph Katz of Amsterdam in 1916.

26. From undated diary entries and references and allusions in letters to CGJ and Maria Moltzer, HCL. See also Noll, "Fanny Bowditch Katz — 'Analysis Is Religion,'" chapter 9 in *The Aryan Christ*.

27. As she addresses him in letters, HCL. Putnam, who referred her to CGJ for treatment in 1912, was the leading American neurologist and a staunch ally of CGJ until he transferred his primary allegiance to Freud around February 22, 1915. In a letter to Freud of that date, Putnam drew two hands clasped in friendship and greeted Freud as "Dear Friend." For further information, see Nathan Hale, ed., *James Jackson Putnam and Psychoanalysis: Letters Between Putnam and Sigmund Freud, Ernest Jones, William James, Sandor Ferenczi, and Morton Prince, 1877–1917* (Cambridge, Mass.: Harvard Univ. Press, 1971).

28. The words appear frequently in Moltzer's correspondence with CGJ, HCL. She apparently continued to correspond with CGJ, if not actually to analyze with him from time to time, for the reference here is taken from his letter of October 16, 1916.

29. Fanny Bowditch Katz papers, HCL. The rapport between Maria Moltzer and Fanny Bowditch Katz became so close and their collaboration so intense that scholars have been hard-pressed to figure out which ideas belong to whom.

30. William McGuire, "Jung's Seminars," *Quadrant* 16, no. 1 (1983): 30, states that Fanny Bowditch attended a "seminar" given by CGJ in summer 1913. He adds: "That her teacher was also her analyst may seem an unconventional psychoanalytic procedure, but Jung had already distanced himself from Freudian orthodoxy."

31. Maggy Anthony, *Jung's Circle of Women* (rev. ed. of *The Valkyries*) (York Beach, Maine: Nicholas-Hays, 1999), p. 20. Anthony also quotes Hugo Ball, who called Switzerland "a bird cage, surrounded by roaring lions."

32. Stern, *Haunted Prophet*, p. 145. I have changed the order of these clauses but not their meaning.

33. According to their daughter, Doris Sträuli-Keller, interview with the author, July 10, 1998, Adolf was forty-two and Tina twenty-four when they married. He wanted a young woman he could mold into the perfect clergyman's wife; she believed she was "not the perfect wife." After the birth of the third of her five children, she became depressed, and her husband sent her to CGJ, who told her, "You are not ill. You must go your own way. There is so much inside you." At his instigation, she went to medical school and became an analyst. She eventually left CGJ's analysis and went to Toni Wolff, who, she claimed, "gave [her], in a way, more than Jung ever gave [her]." CGJ became the godfather of her daughter Margit, and Toni became godmother to her son Pierre. Years later, Tina Keller cited Hans Trüb as her strongest analytic support and sided with him after his break with CGJ.

34. She later married a Dutch citizen, "Mr. Schoo," and moved to Denver, Colorado, where she died in 1993 at the age of 101.

35. Information about Valangin and Rosenbaum is primarily from his "Erinnerungen und Reflexionen," Aufnahme und Fragestellungen: Bernd H. Stappert, unpublished ms., Social Archives, Zürich, Ar. 115.1; interviews with Aline Valangin and Vladimir Rosenbaum by Gene Nameche, HCL.

36. Valangin, who alleges that "the many unfortunate women and girls in his practice had eroticized the man and precipitated his downfall." Oczeret's conduct became common gossip, and several parents of his young patients were on the verge of bringing charges, when the Zürich "chamber of physicians" urged him to leave the country. He returned to his home in northern Germany, where he made a living as a photographer until the ten-year statute of limitations expired in Switzerland. He returned to a small town and began to practice as a psychotherapist again. Valangin relates that one of his patients told her "he had completely changed, reversed his position on communal living as well as marriage and love relationships and had become very strict in his views." He died shortly after without making an impact on the history of psychotherapy.

37. Carola Giedion-Welcker, friend and sometimes patron of James Joyce, was among this latter group. An oft-repeated rumor in Zürich has the unnamed brother-in-law of Sophie Tauber, later the wife of Hans Arp, supposedly trying to enlist them and some of their artist friends for the *Verein*, but I have found no direct evidence that they ever attended meetings or joined. The same is true for the émigrés who formed the Dada movement and were unaware of CGJ (Hugo Ball and Tristan Tzara the most noticeable). Probably the two most famous refugees in Zürich during these years were James Joyce, who did not interact with Jung until later, and Lenin, who did not figure in CGJ's life or vice versa.

38. The most thorough and reliable study of Medtner is Ljunggren's *Russian Mephisto*.

39. Ljunggren, *Russian Mephisto*, p. 10, where he also writes that "in actual fact, this was one of the lies he [Emilii] lived," that his "aggressive dreams of power paralleled his sense of inadequacy." Emilii Medtner married Anna Batenshi in 1903, and they lived for fifteen years in a ménage à trois with Nicolai. During World War I, Anna

and Nicolai were marooned in Moscow, and from then on, she lived mostly with him. Emilii Medtner's letters to Anna are an invaluable archive, as he confided much of his daily life in Zürich in them.

40. Ljunggren, *Russian Mephisto*, p. 86.

41. Among those who said this were Alphons Maeder, quoted in the Nameche/Laing ms. as believing that CGJ was "far more interested in the 'science' of disturbed minds than he was in disturbed patients themselves"; Tina Keller in the HCL interview says much the same; Cary F. Baynes, according to her daughter, Ximena de Angulo Roelli, told CGJ he was "more interested in the ideas people brought him than in the people themselves." Baynes reported that CGJ "roared with laughter but he didn't disagree." Others such as Barbara Hannah, Marie-Louise von Franz, and Mary Bancroft reported anecdotes in which Emma Jung accused him of the same thing and received the same response as Baynes.

42. Ljunggren, *Russian Mephisto*, p. 89, quoting Medtner's "Bildnis," p. 574.

43. Ljunggren, *Russian Mephisto*, p. 89, quoting Medtner's "Bildnis," p. 565. As Medtner was an avowed anti-Semite who denounced both Freud and Adler because they were Jews, and as he later became a fervent supporter of Hitler, the question remains whether he was actually reporting CGJ's views or attributing his own. Medtner's language in the "Bildnis" is sometimes so vague that ascertaining responsibility for thoughts on any topic is difficult, if not impossible.

44. Ljunggren, *Russian Mephisto*, p. 90.

45. Ljunggren, *Russian Mephisto*, p. 92, citing Medtner's letter to his wife, Anna Medtner, November 6, 1914. He was repeating it as late as December 6, 1930, also in a letter to Anna.

46. The author of many books and articles on the subject of Jewish mysticism and responsible for imparting much knowledge to CGJ. His writings in CGJ's personal library are in the privately printed *CGJ Bibliothek Katalog*, p. 35. His wife, Lena Hurwitz-Eisner, was an editor of CGJ's *Gesammelte Werke*. His son, Dr. Emanuel Hurwitz, is an analyst and scholar of the life and work of Otto Gross.

47. Initially, CGJ sent Medtner to Maria Moltzer for therapy because he would be away on his annual month of military service, but he urged him to continue seeing her after he returned. However, his analysis with Moltzer was neither smooth nor long-lasting (Ljunggren, *Russian Mephisto*, pp. 101 and 107).

48. Rumors still circulate in Zürich that Medtner and Toni Wolff were attracted to each other and were lovers. There are letters c. 1923 in LC and the Music History Library, Washington, D.C., that convey varying degrees of eroticism in Medtner's comments, but there are no firm statements to support the actuality of an affair. No evidence in the Wolff family archives supports this rumor, which I address only because it has been so pervasive. Medtner did, however, have an affair with Susi Trüb-Wolff that lasted for several years and that (according to Trüb family documentation) Toni decried. When Ursula Cadorin-Trüb told me of Susi Trüb's relationship to Medtner, she described her mother as being "like Anaïs Nin. She had many 'friends.' Her character was very open, as was her behavior" (interview with the author, July 11, 1998, Erlenbach).

49. Susi Trüb, from Wolff family archives.

50. Destroyed by an arsonist on New Year's Eve 1922, but Steiner designed another, which was rebuilt after his death. It is now the headquarters of his society.

51. These were two among others whose families would not discuss them. For obvious reasons, the descendants of these men do not wish to make their identities known, but they have generously allowed me to consult the voluminous diaries (in one case) and journal entries of therapeutic encounters (in the other).

52. According to her children, these included Emil Durkheim and Henri Michel. Her daughter, Ursula Cadorin-Trüb, speculates that if she did not have a brief affair with CGJ during these years, "it was not because she did not try."

53. Professor of chemistry at ETH, scion of an old and rich Zürich family, and, according to his friend Heinrich Steiger (HCL interview), extremely conservative and "against socialists and communists."

54. Anthony, *Jung's Circle of Women*, p. 38. She quotes Fierz-David's son, Heinrich Fierz-Monnier. The same information came from Cornelia Brunner's and C. A. Meier's interviews with the author.

55. Anthony, *Jung's Circle of Women*, p. 39, who uses Fierz-David's expression "godlike animus."

56. This must be qualified: both women were repeatedly described in interviews by those who knew them well (Tina Keller, Cornelia Brunner, C. A. Meier among them) as cold, domineering, self-controlled, and self-involved. Heinrich Steiger (HCL) described Fierz-David as a "very studied and learned and prissy woman." Brunner said, "As far as each was able to give friendship to another, one could say these women gave it to each other." However, it must be noted that Toni Wolff was extremely close to her family, who always described her as "warm and loving," and that she took an active part in all their lives, which they very much appreciated. She kept this private side of her personality separate from her public persona.

57. Trüb family archives; HCL interview.

58. Susi Trüb, HCL interview; Doris Sträuli-Keller, personal interview; conversation with Ursula Cadorin-Trüb; interviews and conversations with Dr. Med. Georg Trüb.

59. Letters in the Trüb family archives. The *Erbengemeinschaft CGJ* has chosen not to make any documentation by or pertaining to Emma Jung available to scholars.

60. An expression used in separate interviews by Franz Jung and Agathe Niehus-Jung.

61. No matter the language, it was always pronounced as in German: "say gay."

62. HCL interview; interview with Ursula Cadorin-Trüb.

63. HCL interview; Doris Sträuli-Keller says she heard her mother repeat the story; in a personal interview with the author, C. A. Meier said Emma Jung told it to him; entries in diaries and journals in private archives.

64. *Protocols*; interviews with Franz Jung, Marie-Louise von Franz, and C. A. Meier; and private archives, including journal entries of one of the two male patients referred to earlier.

65. HCL interviews with Tina Keller and Heinrich Steiger; author interviews with C. A. Meier and Marie-Louise von Franz; and private archive.

66. Tina Keller described her in her HCL interview: "She had a very special quality beyond what can be taught. She had no academic qualifications, and her very efficient help is proof that there exist special qualities which can achieve results that are beyond psychology."

67. Letter written by Emma Jung in 1916, in a private archive.

68. Elizabeth B. Howes, "Memories of Emma Jung," in Ferne Jensen, ed., *CGJ, Emma Jung, and Toni Wolff: A Collection of Remembrances* (San Francisco: The Analytical Psychology Club of San Francisco, 1982), p. 34.

69. CGJ did not own a car until 1929. Until then, he took the train into Zürich on Wednesday mornings to give his seminars at the club. The ostensible reason he gave for spending the afternoon at the Wolff house was the difficulty of taking the train home to Küsnacht in time for lunch. Most people accepted it without comment or question.

70. Dr. Med. Georg Trüb, interview with the author, July 9, 1998.

71. These or similar phrases are found in many HCL interviews, as well as in personal interviews with the author.
72. Private archive.
73. Tina Keller, HCL interview. Dr. Joseph Henderson believes that "as nearly as possible in our monogamous society, Jung found two wives in these women and so provides no model for the rest of us to follow. It depended on a form of consciousness that totally transcended the ordinary worldly model — that of an important man who maintains a marriage and indulges himself on the side with a mistress" ("CGJ, Emma Jung, and Toni Wolff," in Jensen, ed., *CGJ, Emma Jung, and Toni Wolff*).
74. Tina Keller, HCL interview.
75. Smith Ely Jelliffe to CGJ, August 28, 1932, in *Jelliffe: American Psychoanalyst and Physician* and *His Correspondence with Sigmund Freud and CGJ*, part 1, ed. John C. Burnham; part 2, ed. William McGuire (Chicago: Univ. of Chicago Press, 1983), p. 245. McGuire, in a letter to Ron Chernow (copy to the author, September 1, 1996), wrote that he found "no Jung letter stating that Mrs. McCormick 'thought she could buy everything.'" Others, however, repeated this remark in interviews, among them Franz Jung, who said he frequently heard his father say it.
76. To be able to write about CGJ and the McCormicks, I am indebted to Richard Noll, who made vast archival materials available that he had collected to write *The Aryan Christ*; to Ron Chernow, with whom I enjoyed a cooperative exchange as he wrote *Titan: The Life of John D. Rockefeller* (New York: Random House, 1998); and to William McGuire, who made his personal and professional archives available and supplied me with various leads toward those held by others.
77. Chernow, *Titan*, p. 597.
78. Noll, *The Aryan Christ*, p. 201.
79. Nettie Fowler McCormick, B144 Mc, State Historical Society of Wisconsin, Archives Division. Harold McCormick enclosed six postcards on a sheet of Hotel Baur au Lac stationery on which he wrote: "My walking trip with Dr. Jung, August 1915."
80. Noll, *The Aryan Christ*, p. 201.
81. Noll, *The Aryan Christ*, p. 202 and p. 313, n. 1. Noll referred to his forthcoming article, "Styles of Psychiatric Practice, 1906–25: Clinical Evaluations of the Same Patient by James Jackson Putnam, Adolph Meyer, August Hoch, Emil Kraepelin, and Smith Ely Jelliffe," in *History of Psychiatry*, forthcoming.
82. Noll, *The Aryan Christ*, calls this an "unsubstantiated legend." Like Noll, I have found no written documentation to support it, but it is, however, widespread. Many of the persons I interviewed repeated it to me, including Franz Jung and several of the older Jung grandchildren, who all claimed they heard it from both CGJ and Emma.
83. CGJ, *Nietzsche's Zarathustra I* (Princeton: Princeton Univ. Press, 1998), p. 583.
84. Edith McCormick's chauffeur, Emile Ammann, in *Au service d'une milliardaire américaine* (1933), excerpted in *Spring* 52 (fall 1994): 1–19 as "Driving Miss Edith," alleges in a memoir more gossip than fact that CGJ had to hypnotize her to get her to board the ship. It is unlikely, as CGJ was neither a believer in the efficacy of nor a practitioner of hypnotism.
85. Harold McCormick to Laura Spelman Rockefeller, August 17, 1915.
86. Harold McCormick to Laura Spelman Rockefeller, January 16, 1915, and July 15, 1915.
87. Ammann also tells how CGJ tried to cure her agoraphobia by having her take the local train to Küsnacht while her car and driver sped from station to station down the line in case she needed to leave it for the privacy of her own vehicle.

88. Harold McCormick to Laura Spelman Rockefeller, August 31, 1915. He wrote again on September 6, 1915, describing Toni Wolff as "an analitiker and a protégé of [CGJ] — or rather a pupil, for she would not thank me for the term!"
89. Harold McCormick to John D. Rockefeller Sr., Box 32, Folder 250, Rockefeller family archives, Record group III 2-A.
90. Jolande Jacobi, *The Psychology of CGJ* (New Haven and London: Yale Univ. Press, 1973), p. 60.
91. Harold McCormick to Nettie Fowler McCormick, incoming 1916, Box 152, State Historical Society of Wisconsin, Archives Division. His emphasis.
92. Edith McCormick to Nettie Fowler McCormick, incoming 1916, Box 152, State Historical Society of Wisconsin, Archives Division.
93. Edith McCormick to John D. Rockefeller Sr., Box 32, Folder 251, Rockefeller family archives, January 31, 1916.
94. Which she founded after the death of her infant son John Rockefeller McCormick from scarlet fever. Harold was also a generous patron who gave considerable sums of his own money.
95. *F/Ferenczi*, 2 (1914–1919), p. 126.
96. The information that follows is from Muser, "Zur Geschichte des Psychologischen Clubs Zürich von den Anfängen bis 1928"; Jane Reid, "History of the Psychological Club, Zürich"; "Bemerkungen zu den Statuten für die Mitglieder" of the Psychological Club; "Statuten des Psychologischen Clubs Zürich, revidiert 1944"; various annual reports of the club, the "Jahresbericht"; various annual copies of the "Mitglieder-Verzeichnis"; "Bibliothekordnung" of the Psychological Club; correspondence of Hans Trüb, Toni Wolff, and Emma Jung; and documents and correspondence in private archives.
97. From the first bylaw, *The Purpose of the Club*.
98. This document has inspired the many rumors that CGJ "bilked" Mrs. McCormick or otherwise "seduced" or "hypnotized" her into giving him personally the $200,000, most of which he kept and used for private purposes. My research in the Swiss government archives in Bern and the archives of the Psychological Club in Zürich has uncovered only the legal document referred to here. There is one other official government document, signed by both Emma Jung and Toni Wolff, often referred to as "Amendment 7," and given the same negative interpretation, i.e., that the Jungs were funneling money into their own private coffers. It is actually an amendment to the original constitution of the club that allows Emma, as the president, and Toni, as the secretary (and/or any other officially elected president and secretary), to make decisions about how the endowment will be invested or spent and how club funds in general will be allocated.
99. These included some of the doctors who had worked with CGJ at the Burghölzli, among them Emma Fürst and L. von Muralt; CGJ's mother-in-law, Bertha Rauschenbach; his friend and fellow investigator of psychological types, Dr. Hans Schmid of Basel; and Helene Widmer, the former fiancée of J. J. Honegger, and her sister, Martha, with whom she made her home.
100. HCL interview.

CHAPTER 19: "THE WORK OF A SNOB AND A MYSTIC"

1. Barbara Hannah, *CGJ: His Life and Work, A Biographical Memoir* (Boston: Shambhala, 1991), p. 130. She adds that Toni Wolff told her it "started off on too luxurious lines, rather like an American club."
2. Harold McCormick's paper, "The Welfare of the Psychology Club," unpublished,

dated November 13, 1916, is in the McCormick Estate papers, State Historical Society of Wisconsin, Harold McCormick, Box 8, File 7. Additional copies are in the archives of the Psychological Club, Zürich, and still other copies are in the private archives of (among others I have seen) Franz Beda Riklin and Alphons Maeder. Eventually, when the club became CGJ's own private fief, "The School of Zürich" came to refer specifically to analytical psychology as he defined it.

3. The following is based on HCL interviews of Tina Keller, Alphons Maeder, Heinrich Steiger, and Susi Trüb; author interviews with C. A. Meier and Marie-Louise von Franz (both of whom independently related stories of the early years of the club told to them by others); and a diary of one member and the "journal" accounts of another.

4. From the private journal. Author's translations from the German.

5. Cornelia Brunner, interview with the author. Frau Brunner, a former president of the club, also said that "an invisible aura, a halo of flames, surrounded the head of Jung."

6. In his HCL interview Maeder repeats this in slightly different language than I have it here (as it appears in the journal and the diary).

7. Heinrich Steiger, HCL interview.

8. A professor at the University of Zürich whose best-known pupil was Marie-Louise von Franz. He soon became disillusioned with both groups, and though he did not resign for many years, he was relatively inactive.

9. All resided in Zürich except Schmid, who lived and practiced in Basel. Like all the others except Bleuler, Schmid was a member of the Psychological Club who attended most meetings and was considered from the beginning an authority on psychological types.

10. Many of these letters are in the files of the Psychological Club of Zürich; others are in possession of the *Erbengemeinschaft CGJ*; still others are in private archives. Fanny Bowditch Katz seems to have been the only member who declined. In a letter to Emma Jung, November 11, 1916, HCL, Bowditch Katz said she was unable to provide helpful suggestions but nevertheless was interested in the club's welfare. To her, analysis meant "more solitude than collectivity," so she felt "resistances to the atmosphere at the Club." She concluded: "I do not yet feel ready for analytical Club-life, and is this not perhaps the state of things with many others?"

11. From the paper she prepared in reply and rebuttal to Harold McCormick, an English-language copy ("The Zürich School and the Club") in the archives of the Analytical Psychology Club of New York; a version is reprinted in Sonu Shamdasani's *Cult Fictions: CGJ and the Founding of Analytic Psychology* (London: Routledge, 1998), pp. 90–105.

12. Moltzer's only specific reference to Riklin is a discussion of some of his paintings, which she says she does only for their "psychological value" to the exclusion of their "artistic merit." Her discussion of the "conflict between individuation and collectivity . . . the Libido-theory [and] transcendental Function" contains similarities to Riklin's. Information about Riklin is based on private archival materials held by the Riklin heirs and controlled by Hans Rudolf Wilhelm, and the private archives of others.

13. CGJ wrote to Jelliffe in late July 1915 (*Jelliffe's Correspondence with Sigmund Freud and CGJ*, ed. William McGuire [Chicago: Univ. of Chicago Press, 1983], p. 198) that Moltzer had begun to work "quite independently and quite efficiently. Financially she is quite independent."

14. See CGJ's "Prefaces to 'Collected Papers in Analytical Psychology,'" *CW*-4,

pp. 290–97. Versions of the actual paper are in the archives of the Psychological Club and the *Erbengemeinschaft CGJ.*

15. CGJ's letter is with the *Erbengemeinschaft CGJ.* All quotes from this until noted otherwise.

16. Maria Moltzer, "The Zürich School and the Club," English version, Analytical Psychology Club of New York. The original is in German in the Psychological Club archives.

17. I refer specifically to Richard Noll's *The Jung Cult* (Princeton: Princeton Univ. Press, 1994) and *The Aryan Christ* (New York: Random House, 1997) and Sonu Shamdasani's rebuttal in *Cult Fictions.* To a lesser extent, John Kerr is involved in the fracas, but I will confine myself to brief commentary on the points raised by Noll and Shamdasani. Noll's thesis is so submerged in bile and damnation-by-analogy that his considerable scholarship (for which I have great respect, and from which I have benefited) must be called into question. Shamdasani's argument is hampered by his insistence on using only those documents that support his contentions, rather than all available evidence. His single-minded intent on proving Noll wrong on every count leads to an equal equivocation-by-analogy. Each man's theory of authorship must therefore be considered plausible but not proven; one remains as valid as the other until or unless further documentation comes to light to prove who wrote this paper.

18. I refer here to documents in the Riklin archives, now in the control of Hans Rudolf Wilhelm and unavailable to scholars for detailed observation. Wilhelm insists that CGJ based his theory of types on Riklin's work, much of which he "stole," and that CGJ and "his Mafia" actively worked to subvert any acceptance of Riklin's thesis. It would behoove the Riklin heirs to make these documents available so that scholars could respond to these charges. Because of the close working relationship between Riklin and Moltzer, I find some validity in the argument that both he and she were responsible for the content of this paper, especially because some of the handwritten notations resemble samples of Riklin's writing. But there are other speculations: it could also be that he wrote these comments on CGJ's typed draft, or that he was the primary author of this text and a copy somehow ended up in Moltzer's files and, subsequently, in Fanny Bowditch Katz's HCL archives. Based on all the available evidence, there is, quite simply, no definitive answer.

19. Dr. Med. Hans Schmid-Guisan (1881–1932) was a psychotherapist who practiced in Basel but also took an active part in activities of the Zürich Psychological Club in its early years. He was the father of CGJ's secretary Marie-Jeanne Schmid, who worked for him from 1932 to 1952. For a detailed explanation of the correspondence between CGJ and Schmid, see *CL-1*, note to the letter of November 6, 1915, p. 30. All my quotations are from the translations prepared by R. F. C. Hull for a proposed appendix to *CW-6* that the editors decided not to include. They are published, however, in the original German in Hans Konrad Iselin's *Zur Entstehung von C. G. Jungs "Psychologischen Typen": Der Briefwechsel zwischen C. G. Jung und Hans Schmid-Guisan im Lichte ihrer Freundschaft,* Veröffentlichungen der Schweizerischen Gesellschaft für Geschichte der Medizin und der Naturwissenschaften, no. 38 (Aarau: Verlag Sauerländer, 1982). Iselin's book contains a short biography of Schmid and a shorter one of CGJ, facsimiles and transcriptions of the correspondence (five by CGJ, eight by Schmid), and a discussion of the evolution of the ideas of both men, in which Iselin makes claims for the primacy of Schmid's ideas. I am grateful to Dr. Med. Thomas Boni for calling this book to my attention.

20. This is still unusual, because in the Swiss Reformed Church, children are baptized

in their home parish, and godparents are generally chosen from family or friends in the home parish.

21. The earliest extant letter is dated April 4, 1915 (CGJ), and the last January 1, 1916 (Schmid).

22. Undated on Hull's copy, but internal evidence shows this was the letter of April 4, 1915, as Iselin has it. CGJ's emphasis. All quotes are from this letter until noted otherwise.

23. Schmid, July 6, 1915.

24. Marie-Jeanne Boller-Schmid, CGJ's personal secretary for twenty years and privy to the most intimate development of his thought, gives credit to Toni Wolff for identifying these two functions (HCL interview). However, Schmid-Guisan made the following marginal note in his copy of CGJ's 1917 essay "The Psychology of the Unconscious Processes" (discussed in chapter 20) opposite Jung's statement that the possibility of further types could not be ruled out: "*Intuition und Instinkt.*" But whether he ever showed CGJ his notations, discussed them personally, or wrote about them in letters cannot be definitively ascertained from the extant correspondence.

25. Marie-Jeanne Boller-Schmid made similar remarks in her HCL interview.

26. This and the quote above from Schmid, July 6, 1915.

27. CGJ, August 7, 1915.

28. CGJ, September 4, 1915.

29. Schmid, September 28, 1915. All quotes from this until noted otherwise. All emphases his.

30. Jung's part of the correspondence may not be extant. I am relying on internal evidence in Schmid's letters for the remarks that follow concerning Jung.

31. Schmid, December 1–7, 1915.

32. All quotes above from Schmid, December 11–14, 1915, until noted otherwise.

33. I am referring here to CGJ's differences with Father Victor White, chapter 35.

34. Without specificity, I simply refer the reader to Louis Breger's biography, *Freud: Darkness in the Midst of Vision* (New York: John Wiley, 2000), in which Freud's machinations are amply demonstrated, chapter by chapter.

35. Peter Homans, *Jung in Context: Modernity and the Making of a Psychology* (Chicago: Univ. of Chicago Press, 1979), p. 92. Preceding the 1921 book *Psychological Types* were *Two Essays on Analytical Psychology*, CW-7, and "The Transcendent Function," CW-8. For introductory definitions of these terms, see *A Critical Dictionary of Jungian Analysis*, ed. Andrew Samuels, Bani Shorter, and Fred Plaut (London and New York: Routledge, 1986), for entries on "Individuation," pp. 76–79, and "Transcendent Function," pp. 150–51. I wish to express my indebtedness for what follows to Peter Homans, Anthony Storr, and Anthony Stevens. Among their works I have consulted are Homans's *Jung in Context*; Storr's *Jung* (London: Routledge, 1991), *The Essential Jung* (New York: MJF Books, 1983), *Churchill's Black Dog* (London: Fontana/Collins, 1989), and *Feet of Clay: A Study of Gurus* (New York: Free Press, 1996); and Stevens's *Jung* (Oxford: Oxford Univ. Press, 1994), *On Jung* (Princeton: Princeton Univ. Press, 1999), *Private Myths: Dreams and Dreaming* (New York: Penguin, 1995), and *Archetype: A Natural History of the Self* (London: Routledge, 1982). I have also benefited from Jolande Jacobi's *The Psychology of CGJ* (New Haven: Yale Univ. Press, 1973).

36. For further information, see "Sabina Spielrein, Jean Piaget — chacun pour soi," by Fernando Vidal, in *L'Évolution Psychiatrique* 60, no. 1 (1995): 97–113. Spielrein and Piaget were initially drawn together by their interest in a proposed collaboration

concerning a theory of symbolism that never came into being. Her early letters, particularly those of late December 1917, contain questions on the subject that she put to CGJ.

37. CGJ to Spielrein, May 31, 1916, in Aldo Carotenuto, *A Secret Symmetry: Sabina Spielrein Between Jung and Freud* (New York: Pantheon Books, 1982). All quotes from this until noted otherwise.

38. If she replied before this date, the letters are either not extant or have been withheld by one or both estates.

39. Information is from CGJ to Spielrein, September 13, 1917, in Carotenuto, *Secret Symmetry*. CGJ's last letter to her is dated October 7, 1919. In her November 27, 1917, letter to CGJ she writes: "I would ask you, since it is very important for me, i.e., for my future research, that each time you send back my letter along with your reply" (p. 53). Apparently he did so, as her part of the correspondence is reprinted on pp. 50–90 of Carotenuto. In the last letter, dated January 28 (no year given), she again asks him to return her letter, "since it is one of the building blocks for my future development and I shall need it again."

40. Spielrein to CGJ, December 15, 1917 (Carotenuto, *Secret Symmetry*). Her emphasis.

41. Their letters are now focused upon the individuation process as CGJ formulated it in the three essays written between 1916 and 1917 and published as *Two Essays in Analytical Psychology* in *CW*-7 and "The Transcendent Function" in *CW*-8.

42. Both quotes are from Spielrein to CGJ, December 4, 1917 (Carotenuto, *Secret Symmetry*, pp. 56–57).

43. Thomas Kirsch, in *The Jungians: A Comparative and Historical Perspective* (London and Philadelphia: Routledge, 2000), pp. 206–7, notes that Medtner was in Château d'Oex with CGJ, where he had daily analytic sessions and worked on the translations. Medtner persuaded Edith McCormick to finance the translation and publication of CGJ's (then) three-volume *Collected Works* in Russian, which was printed and eventually published in Zürich in 1929. Only a small number of copies ever penetrated the Soviet Union, a few of which were found there after the 1989 collapse of the government. Ljunggren makes no comment about the quality of the translation; nor does Kirsch in his book, but in a personal communication with the author, Kirsch related the following: in his capacity as president of the IAAP, he visited the Soviet Union in 1990 and brought the first English *CW* to the Russian group. Most students had copies of Medtner's translations and found them "good," even though they had no basis for comparison. Those who could read English or German compared those versions with Medtner's and found that his "held up." Translation of the entire *CW* into Russian is an ongoing process.

44. See Spielrein's, pp. 59 and 65 in Carotenuto, *Secret Symmetry*; his are September 1 and October 7, 1919.

45. Spielrein, January 28 (no year given, prob. 1919, because of content of CGJ's September 1, 1919, letter, where he tells her he could not reply sooner because he was in England).

46. CGJ to Spielrein, September 1, 1919.

47. CGJ to Spielrein, October 7, 1919. All quotes from this until noted otherwise.

48. He also told her to reread the *Wandlungen* and *The Problems of Mysticism* by Silberer, "who picked up many of [CGJ's] ideas and continued to work on them independently."

49. Documents in the Hans Trüb archives.

50. Emanuel Hurwitz, interview with the author, November 19, 1999. Hurwitz recalled hearing his father, S. Hurwitz, who was a founding member, say: "In theory,

the club was originally founded so different schools could talk together. The expression we used was 'to put a roof on it [i.e., to incorporate all theories into one cohesive unity],' but in reality, it was from the beginning a purely Jungian club. In discussions, Jung always had to be shown to have gone beyond Freud; Freud had to be disvalued and only Jung to have either developed an entirely new idea or to have clarified Freud's idea much farther."

51. I have seen several of these notebooks, all of which vary widely in what the author thought he heard Jung say and how he wrote it down. The three I read (two English, one German, all private sources) were so contradictory that they were fairly useless in trying to arrive at a consistent interpretation of CGJ's talks.

52. To prepare this account, I have relied upon two journals/diaries of analytic experiences and several letters, all given to me by persons who do not wish the private archives of their family members to be identified. As they correspond so closely to Harold McCormick's letter of October 31, 1915, I use the letters primarily for quotations but rely upon the others to explain as fully as possible how CGJ's thought developed on this matter.

53. Edith's mother, Laura Spelman Rockefeller, died in March, and Edith chose not to return to the United States for the funeral; nor did she return for the wedding of Harold's brother Cyrus. John D. Rockefeller Sr.'s letter to Harold was in response to Edith's seeming inability to leave Zürich.

54. Harold McCormick to his mother, January 17, 1917, and August 29, 1917, Wisconsin Historical Archives. Most other writers, too numerous to list here, have written that CGJ encouraged Edith McCormick to become an analyst to keep her (and by extension, her money) in Zürich. I have found no written documentation to support this negative view in any of the archives I have consulted, either the *Erbengemeinschaft CGJ* or the private archives of others who were present to observe this period. What I have found are Edith's own comments on the success of her analysis; second-hand reports, such as those of Harold McCormick's, on how she came to thrive; and third-hand accounts from private journals and diaries, taking notice of the positive change in her personality and how much more she interacted with club members.

55. Freud to Jones, *F/Jones*, 310, May 19, 1921, p. 424.

56. Wilhelm Ostwald, author of a biography of great scientists (*Grosse Männer* [Leipzig: Akademische Verlagsgesellschaft, 1909]), in which he claimed their love lives had little influence upon their scientific contributions. He claimed they fell into two categories, which he equated with "classic" and "romantic," and which CGJ called introvert and extravert. See also Henri Ellenberger, *The Discovery of the Unconscious* (New York: Basic Books, 1981), pp. 302 and 700.

57. *Modern Man in Search of a Soul* (New York: Harvest, 1955 [rpt. of 1933 Harcourt Brace text]), pp. 75 and 86. This is a 1933 collection of essays written specifically for an American market in which CGJ attempted to explain his psychology to a literate general audience.

58. *CW*-6, para. 538, p. 319.

59. All quotes are from "General Criticism of James' Typology," *CW*-6, paras. 538–41, pp. 319–21.

60. Members of the Wolff/Trüb families told me that they recalled seeing a large number of papers written by Toni Wolff that appeared to be notes, diagrams, and passages of text that were based on *Psychological Types*. They are no longer in the family archives. An edition of Toni's few finished essays is forthcoming by Daimon Verlag, but nothing of this nature has been found by her publisher (Robert Hinshaw, personal communications and interviews with the author).

61. The phrase is from *Modern Man in Search of a Soul*, p. 88. The chapter "A Theory of Types" is his own explanation of the *Psychological Types*.
62. *Modern Man in Search of a Soul*, pp. 93–94.
63. *CW*-6, p. xiv, "Foreword to the Argentine Edition" (Buenos Aires, 1936). All quotes from this until noted otherwise.
64. Homans, *Jung in Context*, p. 91.
65. The first quote is from *CW*-8, para. 756, p. 391; the second is from *CW*-4, para. 265, p. 117; the third is from *CW*-8, para. 556, p. 292.
66. These same words were used by nearly everyone I interviewed and appear in most of the HCL interviews, so I cite no one specifically here.
67. The first quote is from the private analytic journal quoted earlier; the second is from Robert Edmond Jones, CGJ's patient in 1926, in a letter to Mary Foote (April 14, no year), BLY; the third is from *F/Jones*, 108F, p. 182; the last is Noll, *The Aryan Christ*, p. 121.

CHAPTER 20: A PRELUDE AND STARTING POINTS

1. *MDR*, p. 378. He had it printed "privately and pseudonymously" as a pamphlet in 1916, originally entitled "Basilides in Alexandria." See *CW*-19, 1916a, p. 15, and *CL*-1, pp. 33–34, n. 1, for the full publishing history.
2. Although published in the 1962 German *Erinnerungen*, it was omitted from the 1963 *MDR*. The 1925 English translation by H. G. Baynes was included in the 1966 *MDR* and has since been included in subsequent editions.
3. *Protocols*, in two separate versions under Aniela Jaffé's handwritten marginal notation "June [?] 28, 1957," undated in all others.
4. Because of its geographical location beyond the Rhine, CGJ always thought of Schaffhausen as the "spiritual borderline to Germany . . . a German enclave in Switzerland."
5. CGJ explained it in his fifth Tavistock lecture, London, 1935, in *CW*-18, paras. 39–40, pp. 169–76. See also the definition in Andrew Samuels, Bani Shorter, and Fred Plaut, eds., *A Critical Dictionary of Jungian Analysis* (London and New York: Routledge, 1986), p. 9.
6. See *MDR*, pp. 186 and 195; quote is from several *Protocols* in which he identifies Maria Moltzer by name as the voice he heard and the writer of the letter. To repeat: CGJ used the terms to define "the inner figure of woman held by a man and the figure of man at work in a woman's psyche" (Samuels et al., *Critical Dictionary*, p. 23). Both Emma Jung and Toni Wolff offered separate versions, Emma in *Animus and Anima: Two Essays* (Woodstock: *Spring* Publications, 1957), and Toni in numerous essays published as *Studien zu CGJs Psychologie* (Zürich: Rhein-Verlag, 1959; rpt. Daimon Verlag, 1981 [English translations forthcoming]). Robert Hinshaw of Daimon Verlag says titles will include (among others) "Thoughts on the Individuation Process in Women" and "Structural Forms of the Feminine Psyche."
7. In *MDR*, he is called Elijah. He is not named in the *Protocols*.
8. He is not named in the *Protocols*.
9. The *Erbengemeinschaft CGJ* describes *The Red Book* with all due respect but with the humorous expression "our family's 'Sacred Ox.'" In late 2001, the heirs reversed their long-held position that it would never be published and invited publishers to bid on their proposal for a facsimile edition. At the time of this biography's publication, the *Erbengemeinschaft CGJ* was still in negotiation with publishers, and none had been selected (fax from Ulrich Hoerni to the author, June 25, 2003). According to the official press release, *The Red Book* is "39 x 30 cm, approx. 180,000 words on 205 pages, 53 of images only, 71 containing both text and image, 81 pure (calli-

graphic) text pages." The heirs add that some portions have already appeared in print, among them a photo of the book itself and some of its pages in Aniela Jaffé's *CGJ: Word and Image*, Bollingen Series 97.2 (Princeton: Princeton Univ. Press, 1979), pp. 66–68; Gerhard Wehr's *Illustrated Biography of CGJ* (Boston and Shaftesbury: Shambhala, 1989), pp. 42–43. In a curious passage in CGJ to H. G. Baynes, January 22, 1944, *CL*-1, pp. 311–12, CGJ writes that he will "try to procure another copy of the Red Book" for Baynes. Ulrich Hoerni, on behalf of the *Erbengemeinschaft CGJ*, said he is unaware of the existence of any handmade copies (i.e., pre-photocopy) and does not know to what CGJ refers.

10. R. F. C. Hull to Jennifer Savary, June 20, 1961.
11. The painting no. 154 that Aniela Jaffé reproduces opposite p. 66 in *CGJ: Word and Image* is a later variant of the one described by CGJ in the *Protocols*, which was his first drawing of Philemon. Jaffé's reproduction also contains two circular drawings that were early mandalas, which CGJ began to draw in rudimentary and unnamed form sometime after 1914. He did not specifically define them until 1916, when he painted what he insisted was his "first mandala." It is reproduced opposite p. 77. CGJ gave the original to Jaffé as a gift toward the end of his life. At her death, she left it to Robert Hinshaw, who has it now. It has been at issue in numerous court cases in Switzerland, as the *Erbengemeinschaft CGJ* has contested Jaffé's possession and Hinshaw's ownership.
12. R. F. C. Hull to Jennifer Savary, June 20, 1961. At the time he wrote this, Hull had been CGJ's official translator for more than fifteen years.
13. The account that follows is taken from two *Protocols*, one German and one English.
14. In *MDR*, p. 190, CGJ gives Franz's age as nine. He was born November 28, 1908.
15. In *MDR*, p. 190, the "two maids" are in the kitchen. The published account there differs considerably from the version here, taken from the *Protocols*.
16. In a letter to Robert C. Smith, June 29, 1960, *CL*-2, p. 571, CGJ writes of a "poem in Gnostic style I made 44 years ago for a friend's birthday celebration."
17. Undated partial pages from a letter in a private archive. CGJ gave a copy of the privately printed pamphlet to Maeder, calling it "a fragment with far-reaching associations" for which he "deserve[d] no credit." He asks Maeder to find "a discreet resting place" for it (*CL*-1, January 19, 1917, pp. 33–34). On December 3, 1919, he sent "a small token of . . . great respect," probably a copy of the pamphlet, to Hermann Hesse, whom he analyzed for a time (*CL*-1, p. 574).
18. *MDR*, p. 378. For two diametrically opposed interpretations of the *Seven Sermons*, see Richard Noll, *The Aryan Christ* (New York: Random House, 1997), pp. 160–62; and Stephan A. Hoeller, *The Gnostic Jung and the Seven Sermons to the Dead* (Wheaton, Ill.: Theosophical Publishing House, 1982).
19. *Protocols*, in some versions dated October 23, 1957, in others left undated. The text is similar in all versions, where CGJ speaks of a personal correspondence with Mead, none of which is in *CL*. The *Katalog CGJ Bibliothek* lists all eighteen volumes of Mead's writings as being in CGJ's personal library. The quote is from Martin Seymour-Smith in *Gnosticism: The Path of Inner Knowledge* (San Francisco: Harper San Francisco, 1966), p. 12 (see pp. 14–15 for fuller discussion). See also *CW*-20, p. 152, for references to Mead in CGJ's writings. Mead, along with Dieterich, became a frequent reference for CGJ throughout the next decade, as his interest in Gnosticism gave way to alchemy.
20. Seymour-Smith, *Gnosticism*, describes the symbol of the hand as representing Abraxas, the most important god in Basilides' system. Ancient Greek had no numeral system, so each letter also represented a number. The letters in Abraxas's

name total 365, thus permitting him to represent both the solar year and eternity. Seymour-Smith writes: "In all probability his real name was a secret paraphrase of the Jewish God Yahweh, written in four (Hebrew) consonants" (p. 6).

21. In the *Protocols*, in connection with this sermon, CGJ describes Eros as "a power that stands in opposition to the logos, a function of relationships [that] creates and destroys relationships. . . . Eros binds facts together [and] creates oneness out of the many."

22. His English expression in a German passage in the *Protocols*.

CHAPTER 21: THE SECOND HALF OF LIFE

1. CGJ retired as a colonel. The first quote is from Vincent Brome, *Freud and His Early Circle* (New York: William Morrow, 1968), p. 107, without attribution; the source of the latter two is Maeder, quoted in Brome, p. 74.

2. From his correspondence throughout the 1920s and 1930s.

3. Cornelia Brunner, HCL interview, found also in many other HCL interviews.

4. Many letters attest to CGJ's propensity to change his schedule, among them those of Robert Edmond Jones, Mary Foote, and Leonard Bacon. Bacon, in a letter to Chauncey and Henriette Goodrich, May 10, 1925 (reprinted in *Spring* [1983]: 186), writes of a "mix-up in the mails," a subsequent telegram from CGJ to him in Rome, and of his immediate departure *"subito subito"* for Zürich.

5. A phrase used by many in interviews and conversations with the author, among them Frau Elisabeth Imboden, September 2, 1995; Cornelia Brunner, November 14, 1994; and Marie-Louise von Franz, June 10, 1994. The house at the conjunction of Theodor Brunner-Weg and Hornweg is now occupied by the C. G. Jung Institute. I am grateful to Phyllis and Thomas R. Hoehn, who made this peregrination on my behalf.

6. In an interview with the author, May 23, 1997, Dr. Joseph Henderson described some of these dinners and the friendships he formed.

7. Harold McCormick to Nettie Fowler McCormick, October 4, 1920, State Historical Society of Wisconsin, Archives Division. The difficulty for Americans to secure passports to travel to Europe can be seen in the many letters from Harold McCormick to various high-ranking U.S. government officials throughout 1919 and 1920, seeking a passport for his son, Fowler, then a student at Princeton University.

8. With homage to Robert Graves, whose title defined the sensibility of a generation.

9. *CW*-16, "The Aims of Psychotherapy," para. 83, p. 41.

10. A repeated charge leveled against CGJ is that his psychology neglects children and adolescents, attributed by his critics to a reaction against Freud's insistence upon the primacy of early memory. More likely, it has to do with CGJ's own intellectual interests and the fact that they could be shared only by intelligent adults who had attained a certain age and level of education. Sir Laurens van der Post, in *Jung and the Story of Our Time* (New York: Random House, 1977), p. 72, writes: CGJ's "concern for the child in life was as great as any of his contemporaries', but the problem of the child, he held in the main, had to be dealt with through the parents, so that whenever asked to help with disturbed children he would say, as he once told me, 'Bring me the parents and I will deal with the problems of the child through them.'"

11. This term occurs as early as Otto Gross's 1906 treatment and recurs from time to time throughout CGJ's patient records and correspondence. For related readings, see *CW*-15, particularly "On the Relation of Analytical Psychology to Poetry," paras. 97–132, pp. 65–83, a lecture originally delivered to the Society for German Language and Literature, Zürich, May 1922.

12. Jung's command of colloquial English was excellent by the 1920s. He particularly liked slang expressions because they offered exact meanings that were frequently elusive in German.

13. Information about Hesse is from *CL*-1, pp. 551–52 and 573–76; the Hermann Hesse archive at the Schiller-Nationalmuseum Deutsches Literaturarchiv, Marbach am Neckar; Ralph Freedman, *Hermann Hesse: Pilgrim of Crisis* (New York: Random House, 1978); Joseph Mileck, *Hermann Hesse: Life and Art* (Berkeley: Univ. of California Press, 1978); Emanuel Maier, "The Psychology of CGJ in the Works of Hermann Hesse," unpublished diss., now in the Hesse archive, Marbach; and Theodore Ziolkowski, *The Novels of Hermann Hesse* (Princeton: Princeton Univ. Press, 1965).

14. CGJ to Maier, March 24, 1950, *CL*-1, pp. 551–52, original in the Hesse archive, Marbach. Page 552, n. 2, states that Hesse modeled the character of Pistorius in *Demian* on Dr. Lang.

15. The Hesse situation was a major factor in the growing irritation and competition Lang felt toward CGJ. It resulted in Lang's eventual renunciation of Jung and closer adherence to Freudian theory.

16. CGJ to Maier, March 24, 1950.

17. I hold a different interpretation from Mileck's of why the Hesse-CGJ relationship ended in less than friendship (see *Hesse*, pp. 101–3). To prove that Hesse preferred Freud to CGJ, Mileck cites Hesse's cautious qualifications from 1928 and his 1934 reviews of CGJ's writings as evidence. I think the friendship, like so many of Jung's friendships with men, deteriorated after mutual jousting for intellectual supremacy. In support of my thesis, see CGJ to Hesse, *CL*-1, September 18, 1934, pp. 170–71; October 1, 1934, pp. 173–74; and October 27, 1936, p. 220. As CGJ's friendship with Dr. Lang ended in the same manner and over many similar theoretical differences, there is both precedent and parallel for what happened with Hesse.

18. The list here could be very long, but I will mention only Leonard Bacon, Elizabeth Shepley Sergeant, and Laurens van der Post.

19. Richard Ellmann, *James Joyce*, corrected and rev. (Oxford: Oxford Univ. Press, 1983 [paperback]), p. 386.

20. Stuart Gilbert, ed., *Letters of James Joyce*, vol. 1 (New York: Viking, 1966), James Joyce to Harriet Shaw Weaver, June 24, 1921. The sanatorium was the Brunner Sanatorium in Küsnacht, directed by Hans-Jorg Brunner and with which CGJ was also connected and where Lucia Joyce was installed in 1934. In Richard Ellmann's interview with CGJ for his biography of Joyce, August 8, 1953, Ellmann quotes CGJ as saying the Brunner Sanatorium was a reputable place but not the best one: the best was too expensive, and Joyce could not afford it.

21. Patricia Hutchins, *James Joyce's World* (London: Methuen and Company, 1957), p. 181. I have also consulted Richard Ellmann's *James Joyce* and the Ellmann archives at the University of Tulsa; William Walcott, "CGJ and James Joyce: Three Encounters," *Professional Reports, 1968*, 16th Annual Joint Conference of the Societies of Jungian Analysts of Northern and Southern California, March 1968 (copy in the KML); the archives of the James Joyce Stiftung, Zürich, particularly the Carola Giedion-Welcker papers; and Carol Loeb Schloss, "Joyce, Jung and Carola Giedion-Welcker: Ulysses in Zürich, 1928–32," *A Collideorscape of Joyce: Festschrift for Fritz Senn*, Ruth Frehner and Ursula Zeller, eds. (Dublin: Lilliput Press, 1998).

22. *Finnegans Wake*, p. 115.

23. To write this account, I have benefited from personal correspondence and conversations with Joan R. Acocella, editor of *The Diary of Vaslav Nijinsky* (New York: Farrar, Straus and Giroux, 1999). I have also consulted Romola Nijinsky, *Nijinsky* (New York: 1934; rpt. Telegraph Books, 1985); Tamara Nijinsky, *Nijinsky and Romola* (London: Bachman and Turner, 1991); Christian Dumais-Lvowski, *Cahiers: Le Sentiment/Nijinsky* (Paris: Editions Actes Sud, 1995); Peter Ostwald, *Nijinsky: A Leap into Madness* (New York: Lyle Stuart, 1991); and Alan Riding, "Nijinsky's Notebooks Are Published, Unexpurgated," *New York Times,* January 24, 1995, C13 and 16. The chronology of events in all these books is conflicting, and the account that follows is my estimation of when CGJ actually came in contact with Nijinsky. Tamara Nijinsky, p. 392, writes that Romola "had known Jung since back in 1919 . . . and had never lost contact with him." There is no documentation in the ETH or in the private archives of the *Erbengemeinschaft CGJ* to support this, although Romola did ask CGJ to write a preface for her 1936 edition of Nijinsky's notebooks. He apparently refused, but no documentation is extant. She also exchanged one letter with CGJ in May 1956 (see *CL-2*, pp. 299–300 for his reply).
24. Riding, "Nijinsky's Notebooks," p. C13.
25. Tamara Nijinsky, *Nijinsky and Romola*, p. 208, writes that Romola was "unable to get any satisfactory answers" in Zürich so she took Nijinsky to Vienna and consulted Julius Wagner-Jauregg and Freud, but "neither could offer any real help." Freud told Romola that psychoanalysis was "utterly useless" in treating schizophrenics. Romola Nijinsky, *Nijinsky*, p. 432, writes that among the many specialists she consulted were "Bleuler, Wagner Jauregg [*sic*], Kreplin [*sic*], Ferenczy [*sic*], Freud, Jung."
26. Nijinsky's confinement in Zürich coincided with Jung's extended trip to England, several short vacations with his family, the completion of *Psychological Types*, and his deep involvement with the politics of the Psychological Club.
27. I share this judgment with Noll, *The Aryan Christ* (New York: Random House, 1997), p. 236, as I do his appraisal of her as "one of the most prominent physicians in the British Empire [in the first decade of the twentieth century]" (p. 238). My interpretation of the professional relationship between Constance Long and CGJ differs in other respects, but I remain grateful to Noll for his extensive documentation concerning Long, Hinkle, and M. K. Bradby.
28. "Psycho-analysis," *Transactions of the Psycho-Medical Society*, vol. 4, pt. 2, pp. 19ff. Read August 5, 1913, London, probably translated from the original German by the Eders, published in a different translation in *CW-4*, 10.
29. Full citation in *CL-19*, 1916a, pp. 64–65. Long acted as translator and general editor, with some translations prepared by M. D. (David) Eder and Dora Hecht. By the time of publication, Long had stopped attending meetings of the London Psychoanalytic Society. There was an interesting exchange between Jones and Freud concerning the distinguished Dr. Long much earlier: Jones told Freud that Long was going to Zürich to consult CGJ (*F/Jones*, 156, November 19, 1913, p. 240). Freud replied: "*He* will be lost to you" (*F/Jones*, 157, November 22, 1913, p. 242). Jones answered: "Our member who goes . . . is a woman . . . a virgin of 40, hence in any case not too hopeful" (*F/Jones*, 159, November 29, 1913, p. 244).
30. *CL-19*, 1916b, pp. 65–66. Dr. Hinkle was then affiliated with the Neurological Department of Cornell University Medical School and the Post Graduate Medical School of New York. An ad in *The Masses* 5 (October 1913) carried two blurbs of note: G. Stanley Hall said the book "does for psychology what the theory of evolution did for biology; and promises an equally profound change in the thought of

mankind." The writer James Oppenheimer called it "that blend long sought for, the really modern ideal of the artist; namely the fusion of Science and Art — of truth presented in a quickening manner."

31. "International Conference of Women Physicians," in "Medical News," *Journal of the American Medical Association* (September 27, 1919): 996: "The Conference was assembled in response to new conditions created by the war under which good health became an asset to every women as never before."

32. Long and Hinkle may have met briefly once or twice in London or Zürich before this conference (Long's diary does not specify; nor does extant documentation concerning Hinkle), but their deep friendship developed only after it took place. Jung was deprived of one of his most staunch British supporters when Long died of pneumonia in New York on February 16, 1923, where she had been in "indifferent health" for some time and was "making a prolonged visit . . . as the guest of her friend and colleague, Dr. Beatrice Hinkle" (Long's obituary in the *British Medical Journal* [March 3, 1923]: 399). See also *The Lancet* (March 23, 1923): 463.

33. Beatrice Hinkle, "Pre-Archival Documents," KML.

34. Van der Post, *Jung and the Story of Our Time*, pp. 39–40.

35. "On the Problem of Psychogenesis," *CW*-3; "Instinct and the Unconscious," *CW*-8; and "The Psychological Foundation of a Belief in Spirits," *CW*-8.

36. Toni Wolff favored the first term and used it for many years, despite the fact that Jung had abandoned it in favor of analytical psychology. M. K. Bradby is credited with the first usage of the hyphenated term, which remained favored in British parlance for the next several decades.

37. Mostly recycled into *CW*-4 or found in earlier versions in Long's English edition.

38. The *Oxford English Dictionary* (1919) gives Bradby credit for first usage of the word "analyse": "I have had no nightmare . . . since I was analysed."

39. Noll, with the help of Graham Richards, is the first to identify Bradby as the "MKB" of Long's diaries. Noll generously conveyed the information to the author in a fax December 12, 1997. See also his *Aryan Christ*, pp. 242–46.

40. Accounts differ, depending on the source, so I have not been able to determine what were Bradby's actual encounters with Toni Wolff and Maria Moltzer, except to state that she considered them educational. Through Moltzer, whom she revered, Bradby met and befriended Fanny Bowditch Katz. References to Bradby's discussions and conversations with Moltzer, as well as to Moltzer's writings, occur in Long's diaries, as she tries to sort out the differences between CGJ's and Moltzer's theories through her own readings and translations of them and her versions of CGJ's as related to Long by Bradby. In her attempts to understand them all, Long resorts in her diary to diagrams, drawings, and other verbal charts and comparisons.

41. Long's diary for 1919–22 is in HCL. The pages are not numbered, but some are dated, as is the material quoted here from June 1919.

42. Bradby published the highly successful *Psycho-Analysis and Its Place in Life* (London: Henry Frowde and Hodder and Stoughton, 1919, reissued in 1922); *The Logic of the Unconscious Mind* (London: Henry Frowde and Hodder and Stoughton, 1920); and "Dreams in Psycho-Analysis and Its Place in Life," from a *Bibliography of Dream Research* (London: Henry Frowde and Hodder and Stoughton, 1919–22), 3: 81–151. After 1922, Bradby became less important to Jungian psychology as she emphasized her journalistic talents in the analysis of politics, particularly of Fabian causes. She assisted her sister and brother-in-law, Barbara and J. L. Hammond, with 1920 revisions to their 1911 book, *The Village Labourer 1760–1832: A Study in*

the Government of England Before the Reform Bill. In 1921, she was in Ireland to report on Irish independence for the *Daily News:* "What an Englishwoman Saw: An Appeal to Her Sisters," March 17, 1921, p. 4D.

43. Most were published posthumously in *Collected Papers on the Psychology of Phantasy* (New York: Dodd Mead, 1924).

44. I share Sir Laurens van der Post's assessment of these women as "one of the most remarkable groups of remarkably gifted women ever assembled round a single man, however great" (*Jung and the Story of Our Time,* p. 169).

45. I mention them here to place them within the chronology of Jung's life. Another mentioned only in passing was Joan Corrie, who met CGJ in London, attended some of his seminars, and had a correspondence with him. She originally intended to go to Zürich for analysis but for unspecified reasons never got there. Long thanks Corrie for correcting the proofs in 1920 of her *Collected Papers on the Psychology of Phantasy.*

46. "An Improvement on Psychoanalysis: The Psychology of the Unconscious — for Dinner-table Consumption," *Vanity Fair,* December 1916.

47. Walter Lippmann, *The New Republic,* May 6, 1916. A letter to the editor expressed surprise that Lippmann, whom he accused of taking "the Freudian stand," subsequently "omitted the most damning word of all [about Jung], namely 'mysticism.'"

48. Andrew Samuels, "The Professionalization of CGJ's Analytical Psychology Clubs," *Journal of the History of the Behavioral Sciences* 30 (April 1994): 140. Shaw and Wharton, and perhaps Bell as well, had also consulted Moltzer, but as in the case of Bradby, documentation from sources other than Samuels is unclear about whether or not they were actually in analysis with her.

49. Thomas Kirsch, *The Jungians: A Comparative and Historical Perspective* (London and Philadelphia: Routledge, 2000), p. 39.

50. Kirsch, *The Jungians,* p. 38, repeats this phrase that I heard throughout many interviews.

51. He translated the *Two Essays* with Cary Fink de Angulo, who became his third wife and as Cary F. Baynes, one of Jung's most trusted friends and translators.

52. Samuels, "The Professionalization of CGJ's Analytical Psychology Clubs," p. 140, places the membership at 25 in 1933, by 1957 at 100, and in 1994 at 250.

53. From a copy of the statement signed by "M. Esther Harding, Hon. Sec." on September 24, 1922, in the "pre-archival" collection of the papers of Beatrice M. Hinkle, KML.

54. Kirsch, in *The Jungians,* p. 39, notes that the club quickly grew from the original five members to twenty-five, and the requirement that all had to be analyzed "either by Jung or Toni Wolff" was quickly changed to "analysis and recommendation by any qualified Jungian analyst." Samuels, "The Professionalization of CGJ's Analytical Psychology Clubs," p. 140, n. 10, based on his reading of Baynes's documents in the Analytical Psychology Club (hereafter APC) papers, writes that he may have been "writing rather loosely, though prophetically here."

55. From the APC papers, as quoted in Samuels, "The Professionalization of CGJ's Analytical Psychology Clubs," p. 140. In 1922, Baynes gave a talk to the Psychological Club of Zürich in German, entitled "Analyse und menschliche Beziehung," stressing the closeness and collaboration of the London club with the parent organization (from the papers of the Zürich club archives, copy in KML).

56. I refer to (among others) the Oxford group, founded by Frank Buchman, and the various off-shoots of the original Jungian group. See also Samuels, "The Professionalization of CGJ's Analytical Psychology Clubs."

57. According to Jane C. Reid's unpublished pamphlet, "The History of the Psychological Club, Zürich," there were only chairpersons until 1926, when Frau L. Maeder (wife of Dr. Alphons) was elected the first club president. Besides Emma Wolf, chairperson from 1916 to 1920, others included Eugen Schlegel (1920–21), Hans Trüb (1921–24), and Hermann Sigg (1924–26). Toni Wolff became the second president in 1928 and served until 1945, after which she became honorary president until 1952. During her presidency, the 10 percent quota limiting Jewish membership was passed.

58. Cornelia Brunner, interview with the author, November 14, 1994. Frau Brunner did not become a member of the club until 1932, but she knew Herr Schlegel and said she was recounting his version of what happened in 1921.

59. Susi Trüb, HCL interview.

60. Hans Trüb to Harold McCormick, February 14, 1924, Trüb family archives. Hans Trüb explained: "In contrast to the [Zürich] club, we will maintain a new institution that works with only the small capital of 1,000 francs [Harold's gift] instead of 360,000 francs [the club's annual operating budget based on Edith's original gift]."

61. Among the many who offered differing opinions are Hans Rudolf Wilhelm, Mario Jacoby, Marie-Louise von Franz, C. A. Meier, Adolph Guggenbuhl-Craig, Peter Jung, Dieter Baumann, and Emanuel Hurwitz.

62. Maria Moltzer to Fanny Bowditch Katz, August 1, 1918[?], in the Fanny Bowditch Katz archives, HCL. Moltzer's resignation came after a long correspondence with CGJ in which she hoped to convince him at least to take her views into consideration before subjecting them to open ridicule at the club or speaking of them sarcastically in lectures or individual conversations. In a letter from Aniela Jaffé to William McGuire, dated only July 1976, Jaffé said without specifying that she knew "in whose hands the letters are." She was referring to Frau Gabrielle Kesser, widow of Moltzer's friend and analysand Armin Kesser, a Swiss critic of art and literature for the *Neue Zürcher Zeitung*. Frau Kesser refused to make them available for CGJ's *CL;* since her death, the correspondence remains sequestered and in the possession of the Kesser heirs.

63. Maeder, HCL interview.

64. The first two quotes are from Susi Trüb, HCL interview; the latter two are from Hans Trüb to Harold McCormick, February 14, 1924, copy in the Trüb family archives.

65. Susi Trüb, HCL interview.

66. Dr. Med. Georg Trüb, interview with the author, November 11, 1999, Zürich. Dr. Trüb described his father's friendship with CGJ as "a 'narrow' one," meaning that CGJ determined how it unfolded and Hans Trüb simply went along with him.

67. The first quote is Susi Trüb, HCL interview; the second is Hans Trüb to Harold McCormick, February 14, 1924.

68. Hans Trüb to Harold McCormick, February 14, 1924.

69. Private Trüb family archives.

70. From the announcements of the *Vergnügungskomittee Veranstaltet*, 1917–18, original documents in the Psychological Club, Zürich. They also include "Handicap Ping-Pong tournament[s]" and "Olympic Games."

71. Freud thought him "a serious fellow and undoubtedly a man to be reckoned with" (*F/J*, 234F, February 12, 1911, p. 390). Bjerre was then involved with Lou Andreas-Salomé, whom he introduced to Freud. She knew Buber earlier in Leipzig and was responsible for persuading him not to write the devastating attack on Freudian psychology he had planned. She introduced Buber to Bjerre, and for a time they became colleagues protesting World War I through the Forte Circle, founded in June

1910 in Potsdam. Around 1913, Bjerre told Freud he was sympathetic to CGJ, at which time he became anathema to Freud and the Viennese contingent. Noll, in *The Aryan Christ*, p. 113, writes: "Although Bjerre helped to found the first Swedish psychoanalytic society . . . today his works have been forgotten everywhere but in Sweden." Noll generously made available to me CGJ's letter to Bjerre of November 10, 1913 (not in *CL* but in the Poul Bjerre papers, Kungliga Biblioteket, Stockholm), which is frequently cited as proof of CGJ's anti-Semitism from an early date. The contested passage, which follows a lengthy discussion of Freud's and the Viennese contingent's opposition to his views is as follows: "Until now I was no anti-Semite, now I'll become one, I believe."

72. Grete Schaeder, "Martin Buber: A Biographical Sketch," in *The Letters of Martin Buber*, ed. Nahum N. Glatzer and Paul Mendes-Flohr (New York: Schocken Books, 1991), pp. 36–37.

73. Michel became one of Susi Trüb's longest-lasting lovers in a relationship known to her husband and children. He joined the Oxford Moral Rearmament Movement along with Spöeri and Brunner and many other dissatisfied club members when it came to Zürich in the 1930s.

74. Glatzer and Mendes-Flohr, *Buber Letters*, p. 37. The editors cite his "Writings on the Dialogical Principle" as their source.

75. For analysis of Trüb's friendship with Buber and his disagreement with CGJ, see Paul Bishop, "CGJ, Hans Trüb und die 'Psychosynthese,'" parts 1 and 2, *Analytische Psychologie* 27 (1996): 119–37 and 159–92.

76. Information from interviews with Ursula Cadorin-Trüb, Dr. Med. Georg Trüb, Wolf Trüb, and Ursula Trüb-Offermann in Zürich, Erlenbach, and Grindlewald, July 1998. Medtner joined the Trüb and Jung families on vacations at the Lauialp in the early 1920s. About Medtner they were in agreement: "[He was an] enigmatic figure who just came, to our family, to the club. He was a figure at the border of our life, and our parents thought he was neurotic and deserved pity."

77. The account that follows is based on papers in the archives of the Trüb family; Doris Sträuli-Keller's archives concerning her parents, Adolf and Tina Keller; Heinrich Steiger and Alphons Maeder interviews, HCL; interviews with Cornelia Brunner, C. A. Meier, Marie-Louise von Franz, and members of the CGJ family who do not wish to be specifically identified; and two private archives.

78. Cornelia Brunner, telephone conversation with the author, November 1994.

79. In the *Protocols*, CGJ attributes his joy in games such as this to *"schadenfroh,"* the enjoyment of others' troubles. In the German text, he uses English expressions: "pulling someone's leg," which was his "force" (he meant "pleasure"); he called it *"amusement"* and found it *"so dull"* (he means something between "boring" and "distressing") that others did not share his fun.

80. "Von der Verseelung der Welt," notes of an informal lecture delivered to the Psychological Club of Zürich, December 1923.

81. "Eine Szene im Sprechzimmer des Arztes" and "Aus einem Winkel meines Sprechzimmers," in *Die Kreatur* 3 (1929–30): 403–34. When Susi Trüb published her husband's major work posthumously, *Heilung aus der Begegnung* (Healing Through Meeting), Buber wrote the introduction.

82. Unpublished letters in the Trüb family archives.

83. Schmerzbergstrasse 28 was sold to the ETH some years ago and torn down to build a complex of offices and laboratories. Quote is from the Trüb family, Grindlewald interview, in which they also said that the interwar period in their grandmother's house was "an outgoing time, safe and optimistic, always the 'Wednesday' atmosphere," whereas in their own home, "there was cultural unrest

because [their] parents were more affected by the problems of society, the unrest, and then Hitler, and politics, and persecution."

84. Susi Trüb, HCL interview.

85. I first encountered this expression in the original diaries of Anaïs Nin at UCLA in letters of her cousin, Eduardo Sanchez. He wanted to consult CGJ to cure his homosexuality, she "to add another scalp to [her] belt." CGJ's son-in-law Fritz Baumann wrote an article in the *Zürichsee Zeitung* that he entitled "Der Alte weise von Küsnacht." His son Adrian Baumann uses the term in his HCL interview.

CHAPTER 22: BOLLINGEN

1. Agathe Niehus-Jung, interview with the author, November 28, 1994, Schaffhausen.

2. Helene Hoerni-Jung, "Memories of CGJ," *Küsnachter Jahrheft*, Herausgegeben von der Ortsgeschichtlichen Kommission der Kulturellen Vereinigung Küsnacht, 1999, p. 113.

3. Agathe Niehus-Jung, HCL interview.

4. When Emilie died, Agathe inherited the sideboard in which the knife cracked when CGJ was a boy. At her death on April 28, 1998, it went to her eldest daughter, Sybille Willi-Niehus. In the last several years of Agathe's life, the visions of her youth returned in full force. She told her children of the dead family members who came to her and what they had to say, in many instances stunning them with her revelations.

5. Sybille Willi-Niehus and Brigitte Merk-Niehus remembered their mother's stories of these occasions, HCL interviews. They and their mother repeated the same in interviews with the author. They also believed their mother sometimes resented having to be a second mother to her sisters.

6. Her first child was born a year later, 1924, making Emma and CGJ grandparents for the first time at the ages of forty-two and forty-nine respectively. Kurt Niehus was introduced to the Jung family by Max Preiswerk, who brought him to Grandmother Emilie's house. Kurt Niehus wanted to immigrate to the United States but did not, because the Swiss quotas were such that even with Harold McCormick's connections in Washington through his cousin Senator Medill McCormick, Kurt could not have taken his wife with him.

7. Gret Baumann-Jung, "Some Reflections on the Horoscope of CGJ," *Spring* (1975): 38.

8. Dr. Wolfgang Baumann (son of Gret), interview with the author, February 18, 1997, Basel.

9. Dr. Wolfgang Baumann, who added: "Our generation had it, too, but it was with our grandfather, not our own father." He added that his mother "was not only not encouraged by her father, she was even reproached by him [for wanting to become a psychoanalyst]. In later years, though, he had not much good feeling for the [CGJ] Institute [Küsnacht] when they would not recognize her as a lay analyst because she had no formal academic education."

10. Adrian Baumann, HCL interview: "Many things like this happened during her childhood which influenced her, so I can understand that she has some hard feelings."

11. Gret Baumann-Jung's sons Dr. Wolfgang Baumann and Dr. Dieter Baumann told me independently that she began to study astrology seriously around the age of sixteen. In her adult life, she was highly regarded for her skill.

12. Dr. Joseph Henderson, interview with the author, May 23, 1997, made the following observations about the Jung children: "They were brought up in a very conventional way. I always thought it was to Jung's and Emma's credit that they let

their society make of the children what was wanted, rather than what Jung and Emma would have wanted them to be."

13. Adrian Baumann, HCL interview: "I think my father had a tough time because my mother is so powerful, so he does not have an easy life." Dieter Baumann, in "My Grandfather CGJ: A Conversation," *Küsnachter Jahrheft*, 1999, p. 132, writes that his father was "in charge of the Raccords Suisses, a branch of Georg Fischer, Schaffhausen." This was in Paris, where four of the five sons were born. During the war, from 1939 to 1942, Gret and her sons lived in the Seestrasse house until Fritz Baumann found a job in Switzerland and they moved into their own Küsnacht home. When the CGJ Institute was founded, Gret Baumann-Jung was thwarted in her desire to play a major role within it because she did not have formal academic accreditation.

14. Agathe Niehus-Jung, interview with the author.

15. Franz Jung's wife, Lilly Jung-Merker, was Helene Hoerni-Jung's classmate at school. For Helene Hoerni-Jung's version of family life, some of which I have used here, see "Memories of CGJ," in *Küsnachter Jahrheft*, 1999, pp. 113–15.

16. CGJ to Joseph Henderson, HCL. Repeated in interviews with the author, April 6, 1995, and May 23, 1997.

17. Agathe Niehus-Jung, HCL interview.

18. The quotes here are from Wolfgang Baumann; Franz Jung and Agathe Niehus-Jung used only slightly different language in interviews with the author. All three, as well as Adrian Baumann and other members of the family, repeated the oft-heard story of how she picked too many chives in the garden at Bollingen and sprinkled the excess back over the ground "so they would grow again." They called her "intuitive, yes, but certainly not practical." A story repeated by more than a dozen of CGJ's descendants, both in interviews with the author and by most in their HCL interviews, concerned the time Fritz Baumann and Kurt Niehus threw Toni Wolff into the lake at Bollingen. Each person ended it with the comment "Our family liked that story."

19. A comment made by the children and grandchildren of Emma and CGJ in interviews, among them: Agathe Niehus-Jung and her children, Sybille Willi-Niehus, Brigitte Merk-Niehus, and Ludwig Niehus; Gret Baumann-Jung and her sons Wolfgang, Adrian, and Dieter; Franz Jung and his son, Dr. Peter Jung; Ulrich Hoerni, on behalf of himself and his mother, Helene Hoerni-Jung; the children of Marianne Niehus, Rudolf Niehus and Monica Walder-Niehus.

20. Adrian Baumann, HCL interview.

21. Dr. Joseph Henderson, interview with the author, May 23, 1997, said, "Jung once told me he was sorry he had not been able to direct their education better, but he was always too busy with his own work."

22. According to her daughters Agathe Niehus-Jung and Gret Baumann-Jung, Emma later branched out to paintings of original landscapes and flowers. She would spend long afternoons in her room painting contentedly alone, in what amounted to a kind of therapeutic meditation.

23. Many members of the Jung family told me this anecdote, including Agathe Niehus-Jung, Franz Jung, Dr. Peter Jung, Sybille Willi-Niehus, and Monica Walder-Niehus.

24. Werner Weick, "Carl Gustav Jung: Artist of the Soul," Mystic Fire video, 1997. Comment made by Agathe Niehus-Jung and her son Ludwig Niehus and by Gret Baumann-Jung.

25. The larger boat was a yawl with distinctive red sails that were strikingly visible on

the lake. It had a cabin large enough to sleep three. Besides the two sailboats, he had a rowboat and a canoe, which he used routinely for exercise.

26. Adrian Baumann, HCL interview.

27. Walther Niehus (husband of Marianne Jung), HCL interview.

28. Rudolf Niehus, interview with the author, November 24, 1994.

29. Agathe Niehus-Jung, HCL interview.

30. Repeated by Agathe Niehus-Jung in interview with the author; guarded references in her HCL interview; Rudolf Niehus said his mother and sister told him the same.

31. Agathe Niehus-Jung, HCL interview. She added that when she went to live in Augsberg, Germany, Frau Rauschenbach sent "Liebesgaben," or care packets of things that were difficult to find in postwar Germany, and wrote frequent letters, which Emma did not: "Mother hadn't much time. She wrote to me rather seldom because she really hadn't the time."

32. From separate interviews with Agathe Niehus-Jung and Franz Jung. Franz said, "It did seem contradictory that father would not want us to practice." When I asked him to explain, he added, "In light of his deep interest in the study of comparative religions and his insistence late in life that he believed in the existence of God."

33. Wolfgang Baumann's description, interview with the author. His comment came at the end of a discussion of the many women who clustered around CGJ. When I asked him to explain what he meant by the word, he was unwilling to be specific.

34. Rudolf Niehus; repeated in slightly different language by many of Emma's grand-children as well as others who knew her, among them Doris Sträuli-Keller, Tina Keller (in archival documents), and two private sources.

35. Marie-Louise von Franz, interview with the author; Jane Wheelwright, telephone conversation with the author, June 14, 2000. Mrs. Wheelwright added that CGJ was referring to the "inexperience" of such women who were "charmed by and attracted to him." He used this term, she said, in the sense that "they were a burden to him and not a delight. He simply did not know what to do with them. In the overall sense of this expression, he was fatherly with these women, certainly not seductive." I am also grateful to Lynda Wheelwright Schmidt for further discussion of this expression.

36. Private source, private archive.

37. Marie-Louise von Franz, interview with the author; Jane Wheelwright, interview with the author. (Von Franz discussed the Wolff-Jung rapport with Wheelwright when she was her houseguest in the 1950s.)

38. Agathe Niehus-Jung, HCL interview. Quotations by Rudolf Niehus, Ludwig and Luggi Niehus, and Walther and Sybille Willi-Niehus.

39. The Jung family translates *vas* as "vase," but the Latin dictionary includes the meanings of container, receptacle, or holder of any kind, which CGJ believed woman as anima or woman as wife was meant to represent.

40. Marie-Louise von Franz, interview with the author; Agathe Niehus-Jung, HCL interview and November 28, 1994, interview with the author; C. A. Meier, interview with the author. Agathe Niehus-Jung and Franz Jung, in interviews, said that if the family went exploring away from the campsite, someone always had to stay behind to guard it because the locals made them so uneasy.

41. Unless otherwise noted, what follows is from the question Aniela Jaffé asked on September 23, 1957, about the origins of the Bollingen property and dwelling. This dating occurs in two versions of the *Protocols* and is undated in others.

42. Theodore Ziolkowski, *The View from the Tower: Origins of an Antimodernist Image* (Princeton: Princeton Univ. Press, 1998), p. 133. Professor Ziolkowski adds: "Al-though the tower does not hold a privileged position among the images and arche-

types of his analytical psychology, it emerges in his personal life as the predominant site and symbol of his thought."

43. Walther Niehus, HCL interview.

44. Agathe Niehus-Jung, HCL interview: the English tent was "brought by [H. G.] Baynes or Jimmy Young."

45. Ursula Cadorin-Trüb, interview with the author, July 1997, believes that CGJ was staying in her parents' house, the one made possible by Harold McCormick's gift. A landscape painting done by CGJ dating from that time is still in the Trüb family's possession.

46. On a tour of Bollingen in February 1997, Sybille Willi-Niehus said that CGJ had collected many beautiful old brass candlesticks and oil lanterns, but they were stolen in one of several robberies in recent years.

47. His own carving is small and elegant, a stark contrast to the one made by the person who carved his death date.

48. CGJ to Alice Pearl Raphael [Eckstein], June 7, 1955, in the Mary Foote archives, BLY. Alice Raphael was an American writer, translator, and analyst who first consulted CGJ in 1928 and wrote and practiced under the name Raphael. She shared CGJ's interests in Goethe, Faust legends, and alchemy, and they exchanged an extensive correspondence, all of which she gave to Mary Foote. Only one letter from CGJ to Raphael is in *CL-1*, September 16, 1930, p. 76. In his 1955 letter quoted above, CGJ wrote the word "Philemon" in Greek and followed it by "= Kiss." He added that Philemon was "the complete opposite to the Superman Faust, the product of the devil." Also, the writing of the word *poenetentia* is not clear, and the "o" in the word may be under his cross-out.

49. *Protocols*. He connected this with the "significant dream" of Liverpool, related in *MDR*, pp. 197–98. Although it is undated in the *Protocols*, Aniela Jaffé supplies a date of 1957 and links it to the mandala done at about the same time and reproduced in *The Golden Flower*.

50. Gerhard Adler, in Introduction, in *In the Wake of Jung*, ed. Molly Tuby (London: Coventure Ltd., 1983), pp. 9–10, writes of seeing Jung at his desk several months before his 1961 death: "Looking out over the lake of Zürich but clearly looking out very much further and deeper, he sat, completely unaware of my presence, intensely still and absolutely concentrated, utterly alone with himself and engrossed in his inner images — the picture of a sage completely absorbed in a world of his own. . . . I shall never forget the image of the sage contained in his inner universe, or the immediate return to the reality of the actual human situation. Both were the same man, and the interplay reveals a great deal about the nature of his genius."

51. The older members of the Jung family describe this room with tongue-in-cheek playfulness as "the holy place," but it is still the one area of the Bollingen dwelling that they do not permit outsiders to see. This has given rise to all sorts of speculations about the uses to which CGJ put the room, most of them negative. However, the younger members of the family often hold parties in the compound, and they allow their guests to wander freely through it. I remember my astonishment on a Swissair flight to New York, when a young man sitting next to me, who was a friend of some of the younger Jungs, described this room in complete detail. He was surprised when I told him of the mystery and speculation attached to it, saying it was merely everyone's favorite place during parties to drink and have serious conversations.

52. In several *Protocols*, where Jaffé always strikes out the word "smaller." As it represents what CGJ thought of these talks, I include it here.

53. Agathe Niehus-Jung, interview with the author, November 28, 1994.

54. Agathe Niehus-Jung, HCL interview; repeated in interview with the author, November 28, 1994.
55. Agathe Niehus-Jung, HCL interview and interview with the author, November 1994; Gret Baumann-Jung, telephone conversation with the author, November 1994.
56. *Protocols*, repeated by family members in interviews. No one knew anything definite about him, except that many believed he may have been "a singer or musician of limited talent," and a man who was exceedingly refined and of high social standing. They think the relationship ended because he considered himself of a higher social class than Gertrud Jung.
57. Ulrich Hoerni and Dr. Peter Jung showed me the document CGJ had to provide to the Küsnacht city authorities, stating that he waived his rights to control how and where Gertrud Jung lived and worked.
58. I am struck by a description of the domestic arrangement of the architect Rem Koolhaas, his wife, Madelon Vriesendorp, and his "other female companion, Petra Blaisse," as described in Arthur Lubow's "The Architect's Architect in the Architect's Time," *The New York Times Magazine*, July 9, 2000, p. 34: "Koolhaas has manufactured a form for his life that radically rethinks convention to accommodate his requirements. The stress lines are visible."
59. Dr. Joseph Henderson, telephone interview with the author, July 30, 2000. Dr. Henderson said his observation was shared by "Dr. Eleanor Bertine and other members of the New York group who were able to observe Jung at that time."
60. A passage eliminated from *MDR* that was part of a longer discussion of the anima, whose understanding he believed was "damn hard to grasp."
61. From Wolff, Trüb, and Naeff family archives.
62. According to Jo Wheelwright, she liked Thackeray and George Eliot but found Virginia Woolf "confusing and perplexing." H. G. Wells and Arnold Toynbee were "interesting but mostly boring," and Wyndham Lewis was "crazy." In a letter to Henriette Blanding Goodrich (Mrs. Chauncey S.), July 22, 1924, Toni wrote: "Would it be unkind of me to remind you of your wish to send me the novel of Meredith, *Diana of the Crossways*? I feel as if I should like to read it very much. It sounds so symbolical" (Archives of the San Francisco Jung Institute Library).
63. Bertine was one of the first women physicians at Bellevue Hospital in New York and, with Harding and Kristine Mann, a founder of the New York Jung Society.
64. *MDR*, p. 228, a passage that has been taken out of context, edited, and revised, barely retaining CGJ's original meaning. In the *Protocols*, CGJ explained fully what Merlin meant to him; only the essence is given here:

> Merlin is an enormously important figure because he represents the actual solution of the problem of opposites. He is the son whom the devil begot with a pure virgin. He is a magician, but he is not really evil. His character represents the attempt of the unconscious of the time to bring out a figure parallel to Parsifal. . . . Something inside me always identified with that figure [i.e., the combination of Merlin/Parsifal]. My wife got stuck in this Merlin problem in her work on the Grail. It is a terribly difficult problem. Merlin is more important than Parsifal, infinitely more important. He is the actual figure, the great tragic figure in this whole epic.

In a lighter mood, CGJ added that he wanted to chisel "Le cri de Merlin" onto the back of the large square stone that stands before the original tower, for "Merlin disappears in the woods — He goes to Bollingen!"

65. Arthur J. Hubbard, M.D., "assisted by Mrs. Hubbard," *Authentic Dreams of Peter Blobbs and of Certain of His Relatives: Told by Himself with the Assistance of Mrs. Blobbs* (London: Longmans, Green, 1916). According to the *Katalog* of his library, CGJ owned a copy. Barbara Hannah, *Jung: His Life and Work, A Biographical Memoir* (Boston: Shambhala, 1991), writes that no written record of this seminar is extant. William McGuire, in *Dream Analysis: Notes of the Seminar Given in 1928–30*, Bollingen Series 99 (Princeton: Princeton Univ. Press, 1984), p. ix, writes: "There is no record, but this seminar . . . was kept in memory by several of the dozen who attended."

66. Fanny Moser, *Spuk: Irrglaube oder Wahrglaube* (Ghost: False Belief or True) (Baden bei Zürich: Gyr-Verlag, 1950), 1: 320; Foreword by CGJ, and "Jung's Contribution," pp. 253ff., reprinted in *CW*-18, pp. 317–26.

67. HE/STA: Letters to Henri Ellenberger from Karl E. Müller, April 16, 19[?], and June 7, 1967; Dr. Gerda Walther to Ellenberger, April 16, 1967.

68. See also E. Bleuler's "On Occultism and Its Critics," in *Zeitschrift für Parapsychologie* (1930): 654ff.

69. The sessions began on June 21, 1925, and were documented in Albert von Schrenck-Notzing, *The Phenomena of the Medium Rudi Schneider*. CGJ's library contained the following von Schrenck-Notzing publications: *Gesammelte Aufsätze zur Parapsychologie* (1929); and *Physikalische Phaenomene des Mediumismus* (1920); *Ueber Spaltung der Persönlichkeit, "sogenanntes Doppel-Ich"* (1896). In addition to CGJ, those who attended the June 21 session were H. and E. Bleuler, G. R. Heyer, Bernoulli, Dr. Oberholzer (no first name given, Burghölzli staff *Assistenzarzt*), and Dr. A. Reichel.

70. Note in the "protocol" of von Schrenck-Notzing's book.

71. Reported by Rudolf Bernoulli in *Zeitschrift für Parapsychologie* (July 1931): 313ff. Also verified by G. R. Heyer in a letter to Gerda Walther, April 17, 1967, copy in HE/STA.

72. G. R. Heyer to Gerda Walther, April 17, 1967, HE/STA. Heyer recalls that the baroness "had to sell" her palace on the Max Josefstrasse to the Nazis when they came to power. Of the dinner itself, he quotes Jung as saying some years later that he remembered the dinner "quite well. The food was just as splendid as the company, especially thanks to the conventional chatter of the Baroness — insipid!"

73. Heyer's opinion was that CGJ "wanted to fit the psi-phenomena *à tout prix* into his archetypology, thus for example the so-called synchronistic phenomenon."

CHAPTER 23: "THIS ANALYTICAL POWDER MAGAZINE"

1. William McGuire, *Dream Analysis: Notes of the Seminar Given in 1928–30*, Bollingen Series 99 (Princeton: Princeton Univ. Press, 1984), gives a history of CGJ's seminars; quote is from p. ix. The Harding/Mann unpublished thirty-eight-page transcript is in the archives of KML, Analytical Psychology Club of New York. Whether the title was CGJ's or their creation is not known. These and the later seminars were all distributed privately to the attendees but were not otherwise circulated until after CGJ's death, when his estate agreed to let them be published in edited versions.

2. *Protocols* and *MDR*, pp. 228–32.

3. To write the following I used William McGuire's private archives concerning the McCormick family and his articles "Jung in America, 1924–25," *Spring* (1978): 37–53, and "Firm Affinities: Jung's Relations with Britain and the United States," *JAP* 40 (1995): 301–26.

4. Ron Chernow, *Titan: The Life of John D. Rockefeller* (New York: Random House,

1998), p. 649. He gives her age as eighteen years older; *Time*, September 5, 1932, said the age difference was nineteen years.

5. *New York Times*, March 13, 1928, section 2, p. 3.
6. They had no children of their own, but according to documents in the State Historical Society of Wisconsin, they raised her four children from her previous marriage. Anne McCormick died in 1969, Fowler on January 6, 1972. Between her 1926 divorce and 1931 remarriage, Anne moved to Zürich to analyze with CGJ and Baynes. In a later interview she said, "My life was smashed like broken crockery. . . . Then Baynes and Jung took me in hand and taught me the real meaning of life" (quoted in McGuire, "Jung in America," p. 49).
7. *New York Times*, January 15, 1925, p. 21.
8. Franz Jung to William McGuire, May 10, 1977, and November 24, 1977.
9. Fowler McCormick to William McGuire, August 11, 1972.
10. Fowler McCormick to William McGuire, August 11, 1972.
11. George Porter (1881–1927) was the son of the builder of the Chicago & Eastern Illinois Railroad and Chicago's Dearborn Station. He graduated from Yale in 1903 and became a businessman, art collector, philanthropist, and important supporter of Theodore Roosevelt's Progressive Party in 1912. An army captain in World War I and after the war, he consulted CGJ in Zürich for "melancholia," then Dr. William A. White in Washington, D.C. He tried to arrange for CGJ to lecture at various American venues, including St. Elizabeths in D.C., but nothing came of it. Porter committed suicide on February 24, 1927, with a bullet to his head. He left $20,000 in stock to CGJ, but with the 1929 crash it became worthless. See McGuire, "Jung in America," pp. 49–51; also *Chicago Daily Tribune*, March 4, 1927, pp. 1ff. This account is also based on private correspondence generously made available by McGuire, conducted during his research for the article above.
12. McGuire documents this in "Jung in America" through private correspondence with Mrs. George F. Porter, p. 49 and p. 53, n. 39.
13. Gui de Angulo, *The Old Coyote of Big Sur: The Life of Jaime de Angulo* (Berkeley: Stone Garden Press, 1995), p. 69.
14. His income came from his wealthy Spanish family. Her mother was from a cultured and wealthy Louisville, Kentucky, family; her father was a German engineer who prospered while working for the Mexican government. (Cary was born in Mexico City.) She was a graduate of Vassar College and classmate and friend of Kristine Mann, who is credited with introducing her to the psychology of CGJ. Bilingual in German and English from childhood and fluent in several other languages as well, Cary Baynes became CGJ's most trusted consultant in the translation of his writings.
15. Among them Alfred Krober, Paul Radin, Paul-Louis Faye, and, later, Franz Boas and Ruth Benedict, when they were at Columbia University.
16. Private correspondence and chronology from Gui de Angulo, daughter of Jaime by his second marriage, to Lucy Freeland; also *Old Coyote*. Other sources include the Chauncey S. Goodrich papers, Bancroft Library, University of California at Berkeley; the Mabel Dodge Luhan archives, BLY; the Whitney/Goodrich/Chamberlain archives at the San Francisco Jung Institute Library; personal interviews with Ximena de Angulo Roelli (daughter of Cary and Jaime) and private documentation provided by her; interviews and correspondence with Elizabeth Whitney Chamberlain; correspondence between William McGuire and Peter D. Whitney and Chauncey S. Goodrich from McGuire's private archives; the archives of the Frances Gillespy Wickes Foundation, most of which are now in the San Francisco Jung Foundation Library and were graciously made available by George Hogel and

McGuire; Wendy Leeds-Hurwitz, "Jaime de Angulo: An Intellectual Biography" (unpublished Ph.D. diss., Univ. of Pennsylvania, 1983); Chauncey S. Goodrich, "Transatlantic Dispatches from and About Zürich," *Spring* (1983); and the archives of Leonard Bacon at Princeton University's Firestone Library.

17. Ximena de Angulo Roelli, interview with the author, September 22, 1995, Zürich. Although Cary and Jaime seldom saw each other after 1923, Gui de Angulo writes: "Cary was a couple of years older than Jaime, and very much of a contrast, very straightforward and direct with a strong sense of duty and responsibility. She brought out the best in him, and they found each other intellectually stimulating for as long as they were in contact, some twenty years" (*Old Coyote*, p. 71; on p. 150, she explains how Cary went to Zürich at Kristine Mann's instigation).

18. Gui de Angulo, *Old Coyote*, p. 96.

19. Cary Baynes to Jaime de Angulo, January 1922, in Gui de Angulo, *Old Coyote*, p. 164.

20. Lucy Freeland called herself Nancy because a clairvoyant she met on an ocean voyage told her that Nancy was her real inner and mystical name.

21. Gui de Angulo, *Old Coyote*, p. 169.

22. Gui de Angulo, *Old Coyote*, p. 173, quoting Jaime de Angulo to Cary Baynes, May (?) 1922. His emphasis.

23. Gui de Angulo, *Old Coyote*, pp. 176–77. She adds: "As I understand it [i.e., from the correspondence], Jung has the technique of trying to bring as many people as possible who were involved in a patient's case into analysis as well."

24. Gui de Angulo, *Old Coyote*, pp. 172–73, quoting Jaime de Angulo to Cary Baynes, April 15, 1922.

25. Gui de Angulo, *Old Coyote*, p. 204.

26. Gui de Angulo, *Old Coyote*, p. 213.

27. Quotations are from Gui de Angulo, *Old Coyote*, pp. 212–13 and 219–20, quoting Jaime de Angulo to Mabel Dodge Luhan, December 14, 1923, and January 21, 1924.

28. Gui de Angulo, *Old Coyote*, pp. 222–23, quoting Jaime de Angulo to Mabel Dodge Luhan, January 23, 1924, BLY, and Jaime de Angulo to Cary Baynes, January 26, 1924.

29. Jaime de Angulo to Mabel Dodge Luhan, January 16, 1925, BLY. Quoted at length in Gui de Angulo, *Old Coyote*, p. 246.

30. It was common for Pueblo Indians to have three names: Spanish, tribal, and an English translation of the tribal. I am grateful to Dr. Beat Glaus of the ETH, who found CGJ's correspondence with him under the name of Mirabal.

31. McGuire, "Jung in America," p. 42, notes that M. Esther Harding wrote of this friendship in her obituary of Frances Wickes, and that the poet Muriel Rukeyser, who was her executor and biographer, confirmed that Wickes met Mountain Lake before 1925. Correspondence between Henriette Blanding Goodrich and Frances Wickes dating from 1922 also mentions this friendship.

32. Gui de Angulo, *Old Coyote*, p. 226, quoting Jaime de Angulo to Cary Baynes, March 18, 1924.

33. Neither Mabel Dodge Luhan, Tony Luhan, nor D.H. Lawrence was in Taos during the winter of 1924–25, so CGJ did not meet them. Jaime de Angulo enlisted Tony Luhan's intercession through prior correspondence, much of which is in BLY and private archives of Ximena de Angulo Roelli.

34. Alcoholism verified by John Manchester, owner of the Manchester Gallery in El Prado, New Mexico, in a letter to William McGuire, July 22, 1976. Manchester also wrote that Tony Luhan spoke well of CGJ throughout his life. Luhan wrote of his meetings in "about 1967–68" with CGJ's grandson Dieter Baumann, who visited while touring the Southwest; Baumann set the date at 1964 in an undated let-

ter to McGuire (in telephone conversations with the author, November 1995, Baumann was unable to recall the exact date). Gret Baumann-Jung also went to Taos, in 1969, and met Mountain Lake on that visit.

35. Gui de Angulo, *Old Coyote*, p. 246; Jaime de Angulo to Mabel Dodge Luhan, January 24, 1925, BLY.

36. He was instrumental in 1933 in winning back the use of the land by the Blue Lake, source of the Taos River and most sacred shrine of the Pueblo religion. His efforts led to the July 1971 unconditional return of this land, when Richard Nixon signed a bill enacted previously by Congress.

37. Mountain Lake wrote to CGJ in 1932 to repeat that he had revealed nothing meaningful about Pueblo rituals, customs, and religion (ETH CGJ archives, but not in *CL*-1, although CGJ's reply to it is [October 21, 1932, pp. 101–2]; I am grateful to Dr. Beat Glaus for making an extensive search of uncatalogued archival material).

38. "Visits Taos Again," *Taos Valley News* 18, no. 2, Saturday, January 10, 1925, p. 1.

39. Gui de Angulo, *Old Coyote*, p. 406, quoting Jaime de Angulo to Ezra Pound, December 23, 1949 (Univ. of California at Santa Cruz special collections).

40. CGJ gives brief descriptions of his time with the Taos Pueblo in the *Protocols*. In none does he write anything that even vaguely approximates the description given by Aniela Jaffé in *MDR*, pp. 246–53. For her account, she has obviously culled everything else he wrote; for a full listing of these references, see *CW*-18, p. 45.

41. *Taos Pueblo* (General Series in Anthropology, 2; Menasha, Wisc., 1936).

42. Copies of Link's correspondence with CGJ are in the ETH; one letter is partially reprinted in *CL*-1, p. 320. Excised from the printed letter is CGJ's extreme exasperation that she continued for years, despite his firm protests to the contrary, to try to interest him in writing about, commenting on, and sharing her interest in the Navaho nation. His letters make it very clear that he had long ago lost interest in everything related to Native American cultures.

43. According to her daughter Elizabeth Goodrich Chamberlain (interview with the author, May 20, 1999), she was known by her various married names: Henriette Blanding Goodrich Durham Lehman.

44. They did so at the instigation of Cary Baynes and Jaime de Angulo. Upon returning to San Francisco, they set up dual practices as analytic psychologists. Their son, Dr. James Goodrich Whitney (1917–67), became the first Jungian analyst trained at the San Francisco Institute. See Thomas Kirsch, *The Jungians: A Comparative and Historical Perspective* (London and Philadelphia: Routledge, 2000), pp. 74–75. The other Goodrich sister, Frances Goodrich Léon, lived in New York with her attorney husband, the French national Maurice Léon. She went to Zürich in 1926 and spent the greater part of the next decade there.

45. See his autobiography, *Semi-Centennial: Some of the Life and Part of the Opinions of Leonard Bacon* (New York: Harper and Brothers, 1939), and also his poem "Analytical Dictionary," as reprinted in Chauncey S. Goodrich, "Transatlantic Dispatches," pp. 188–89.

46. L. H. Davis, *Onward and Upward: A Biography of Katharine S. White* (New York: Harper and Row, 1979), p. 28. See also McGuire, "Firm Affinities," p. 303. Others who were in this circle include Willard Durham (Henriette Blanding Goodrich's second husband) and a couple known only as "the Whipples."

47. Fowler McCormick to William McGuire, August 11, 1972.

48. Porter to White, December 16, 1925; White to Porter, December 18, 1925; Porter to White, January 1, 1925 (all from the McGuire archives, the first two misdated, as correct date is 1924).

49. There were already tensions in New York, as Wickes was not approved of by

Mann, Bertine, and Harding. Wickes remained a pillar of Jung's analytical psychology and a force in New York but was not welcomed by the official triumvirate formed by the other three.

50. CGJ to Frances Gillespy Wickes, January 1, 1925, on stationery of Fred Harvey's El Tovar Hotel, Grand Canyon National Park, Arizona. CGJ told Mrs. Wickes: "I *saw* the Canyon. But I say nothing about it." See also William McGuire, "From Esther Harding's Notebooks," *CGJ Speaking*, Bollingen Series 97 (Princeton: Princeton Univ. Press, 1977), pp. 30–31.

51. CGJ to Frances Gillespy Wickes, February 10, 1925, from Küsnacht (Frances Gillespy Wickes archives, San Francisco Jung Institute Library).

52. *New York Times*, untitled article, January 15, 1925, p. 2. The article also called CGJ "formerly a student of Sigmund Freud and later head of the Zürich Psychiatric Clinic."

53. Barbara Hannah, *Life and Work*, p. 164.

54. Barbara Hannah, *Life and Work*, p. 142.

55. Barbara Hannah, *Life and Work*, p. 142.

56. CGJ to Emma Jung, Monday, March 15, 1920, from Sousse. Reprinted as Appendix 3, *MDR*, pp. 371–72.

57. *MDR*, p. 273. Not in any *Protocols*.

Chapter 24: The Bugishu Psychological Expedition

1. From miscellaneous undated papers, State Historical Society of Wisconsin, Box 13; various folders, especially "Employee's Record Cards." The Princeton University alumni magazine, February 20, 1973, p. 16, in a "Memorial" for Fowler McCormick mistakenly states that he made the African journey.

2. George Porter to Kermit Roosevelt, March 16, 1925, Kermit Roosevelt papers, LC. Patricia O'Toole called this to my attention.

3. Information about Beckwith is from undated *Protocols* and a private archive containing documents by and about Toni Wolff.

4. Leonard Bacon, *Semi-Centennial: Some of the Life and Part of the Opinions of Leonard Bacon* (New York and London: Harper and Brothers, 1939), p. 184.

5. Ruth Bailey, HCL interview, says CGJ "loved Beckwith like a son." She is the only observer to make such a remark; all others correspond to the version given here.

6. According to Anne Baynes (H. G. Baynes's fourth wife), when Baynes's first wife decided to leave him for another man c. 1919, he sent her to Zürich to be analyzed by CGJ, but she would not consent to be analyzed, so Baynes went in her stead, and thus began his association with Jungian Depth Psychology. Information that follows is from Anne Baynes's HCL interview; Ximena de Angulo Roelli, interviews with the author; archival information from William McGuire, including his interviews and correspondence with Cary F. Baynes; and two private sources (the correspondence between CGJ, Peter Baynes, and a private source, and a second one, between CGJ and a private source).

7. In analytic terms, she had a transference, but as she was in her early twenties and Baynes was then a man approaching fifty, the term used by the private source seems more appropriate.

8. Anne Baynes, HCL interview.

9. Ruth Bailey, HCL interview, says Hilda Baynes threw herself off the roof of a mental hospital where she was institutionalized. Anne Baynes contradicts this, saying if she had been in a hospital, she would have been unable to gain free access to the roof. Bailey's version is that Hilda sent her nurse for a hot-water bottle and then made her escape and jumped.

10. Information about CGJ's, Emma Jung's, and Toni Wolff's responses is from the two private archives.
11. Anne Baynes, HCL interview.
12. The following account is based on Ruth Bailey's HCL interview; *Dr. H. G. Baynes's Files of CGJ's Expedition to Africa (1925);* a transcript of Ruth Bailey's commentary on his film, HCL (a copy of the film itself is in the C. G. Jung Biographical Archive of the San Francisco Jung Institute); CGJ and Ruth Bailey's correspondence, ETH; William McGuire's archives, including his interviews with Cary Baynes and Ximena de Angulo Roelli; Ximena de Angulo Roelli, interviews with the author; CGJ and H. G. Baynes's correspondence, ETH; and Dr. Joseph Henderson, interviews and telephone conversations with the author.
13. The first quotation is from Leonard Bacon, *Semi-Centennial,* p. 184; all others from Ruth Bailey's HCL interview.
14. Glin Bennet, "Domestic Life with CGJ," *Spring* (1986): 178.
15. The first description is from her friend, Dr. Joseph Henderson, telephone interview with the author, July 30, 2000; the second is from Bennett, p. 189.
16. Ruth Bailey, HCL interview. Nameche: "Was it sexual?" Ruth Bailey: "No, I didn't think so at all."
17. Ruth Bailey, HCL interview.
18. Ruth Bailey, HCL interview.
19. At this point, the stories of how Ruth Bailey joined the CGJ expedition differ, depending on who tells them. Bailey gave several versions to different interviewers toward the end of her life. The testimony with the most validity is the HCL interview, which coincides most closely to CGJ's testimony in the *Protocols* and other sources previously cited.
20. CGJ to Hans Kuhn, *CL-1,* January 1, 1926, pp. 42–43. Ruth Bailey, in commentary on the Baynes film, San Francisco Jung Institute archives, says they had approximately twenty native bearers while in Kenya, and when they left to go through Uganda and into Sudan and up the Nile, they had "between perhaps twelve and fifteen, no more."
21. Ruth Bailey, HCL interview.
22. Francis Daniel Hislop, "Dr. Jung, I Presume," *CGJ Speaking,* ed. William McGuire, Bollingen Series 97 (Princeton: Princeton Univ. Press, 1977), pp. 32–37.
23. Ruth Bailey, commentary on the Baynes film.
24. The following account is based primarily on Ruth Bailey's two conflicting testimonies: her HCL interview and the commentary on the Baynes film. It is also based on Anne Baynes's HCL interview; correspondence between CGJ and H. G. Baynes, ETH; the archives of Cary F. Baynes and Ximena de Angulo Roelli, William McGuire; and a private source. The account given by CGJ in *MDR,* pp. 260–61, seems unlikely in the face of all this other concurring evidence that contradicts his version. In none of the *Protocols* does he discuss how Ruth Bailey came to join them.
25. CGJ to Hans Kuhn, *CL-1,* January 1, 1926, pp. 42–43, says the camp was pitched at 2,100 meters and the actual climb was 2,900 meters. In her HCL interview, Ruth Bailey says they eventually climbed to 9,000 feet and that Mt. Elgon is 14,176 feet high.
26. Ruth Bailey, film commentary.
27. Ruth Bailey, HCL interview. Her emphasis.
28. He appears frequently throughout the first reel of Baynes's film. In the accompanying commentary, he is called by both names.
29. He also took the two *ruki* chairs in which he and Beckwith were carried by the natives.

30. *Protocols*, which are much closer to the raw emotion he felt than the beautifully polished and carefully constructed account in *MDR*.
31. Ruth Bailey's commentary on the Baynes film.
32. See *MDR*, pp. 260–61, for the final, polished version.
33. See also *MDR*, pp. 264–99.
34. Ruth Bailey's commentary on the Baynes film. CGJ gives a version in *MDR*, p. 259.
35. *MDR*, p. 269.
36. Ruth Bailey estimates the stay at two months, saying they went up in early November 1925 and did not come down until January 1926 (commentary on the Baynes film).
37. Ruth Bailey, HCL interview.
38. *MDR*, pp. 270–71; Bailey sets the date of this as their first night in Uganda in her commentary on the Baynes film.
39. From her commentary on the Baynes film. Her emphasis, her exclamation marks.
40. Ruth Bailey, HCL interview.
41. Ruth Bailey, HCL interview; she gives January 13 in the film commentary.
42. Sir Alan Cobham (1894–1973) was on his famous 1926 "Rochester to London [flight] by way of Australia" when CGJ met him in Africa. He was knighted by King George V immediately afterward, when he landed spectacularly on the Thames River in front of the Houses of Parliament.
43. Ruth Bailey's commentary on the Baynes film, which shows a small and guardedly filmed amount of fire in reel 2.
44. For a slightly different account, see Barbara Hannah, *Jung: His Life and Work, A Biographical Memoir* (Boston: Shambhala, 1991), p. 176, quoting Ruth Bailey's letter to her, undated.
45. Ruth Bailey, commentary on the Baynes film; undated passage in one partial *Protocol*. CGJ gives a different version of this anecdote in *Dream Analysis: Notes of the Seminar Given in 1928–30*, ed. William McGuire, Bollingen Series 99 (Princeton: Princeton Univ. Press, 1984), p. 649 and n. 9.
46. In the audio commentary cited above, Nameche presses Ruth Bailey to say what CGJ spoke about and who his audience was. She is vague and replies only that she thinks he spoke to "students," but she did not know if they were in the "medical faculty."
47. Ruth Bailey, HCL interview.
48. *Protocols*. CGJ does not explain why he cannot relate to Islamic culture, but he tries comparing it to different kinds of music: Arabic, Chinese, American tribal war chants, and the music of the Indian subcontinent: such sounds have meaning only within their own cultural contexts, and as he was not a member of those groups, he could not hope to understand them. Barbara Hannah, *Life and Work*, pp. 179–80, gives a contradictory version when she writes that he was "greatly struck . . . by the Islamic religion." I think she is confused, recalling only his interest in Islamic art and architecture and ignoring his antipathy toward the culture and society.
49. Ruth Bailey, HCL interview and commentary on the Baynes film.
50. *Protocols*. Also his letter to Frances G. Wickes, August 9, 1926, in *CL*-1, p. 44.
51. The italicized words are in English in all the German *Protocols*.
52. Ruth Bailey, HCL interview.
53. Hoyningen-Huene was a painter who later concentrated on photography. The work is now in the possession of Helene Hoerni-Jung. After my detailed exchanges from 2000 to 2002 with her son Ulrich Hoerni, the Jung heirs refused permission to reproduce it here because of unspecified complexities concerning copyright. Emma Jung's portrait was also painted by Baron Hass-Teichen. In what appears to

be a press release from an unidentified newspaper (clipping now in KML photo album), the baron states that CGJ also agreed to sit for a portrait "the next spring." No members of the *Erbengemeinschaft CGJ* know the location of Emma's portrait or if CGJ's was ever painted.

54. 1920 letter to Emma Jung, *MDR*, Appendix 3, p. 372.
55. He uses the expression "in Europe" in *MDR*; in some of the *Protocols* he says "at home" or "in Switzerland." This and all quotes until noted otherwise are from *MDR*. There is discussion of some of these issues in various *Protocols*, but they are diffuse and disorganized, and CGJ appears frustrated that he cannot convey his true meaning. CGJ's account in *MDR* most closely conveys the drama of this experience.
56. *MDR*, p. 272.

CHAPTER 25: "PROFESSOR" JUNG

1. CGJ to Jolande Jacobi, November 20, 1928, *CL*-1, p. 55.
2. Some of his advocates never got used to it. On February 21, 1946, Cary Baynes wrote to Marie-Jeanne Schmid to say she still could not bring herself to call him Professor, but would always use Doctor.
3. The word "seminars" first appears in the notebooks of Fanny Bowditch Katz around 1913, in her archives at the HCL. See also William McGuire, introduction to *Dream Analysis: Notes of the Seminar Given in 1928–30*, Bollingen Series 99 (Princeton: Princeton Univ. Press, 1984), pp. viiiff., for a capsule summary of CGJ's seminar history.
4. *Analytical Psychology: Notes of the Seminar Given in 1925*, ed. William McGuire Bollingen Series 99 (Princeton: Princeton Univ. Press, 1989).
5. The 1920 English talks at Polzeath were taken down in longhand by Kristine Mann and Esther Harding, who later melded their notes into a single document. Cary F. Baynes produced the first official transcript of CGJ's seminars, with his imprimatur.
6. Jung was given several free copies for his personal use. "Multigraph" was another word for mimeograph. The prices of the volumes varied over the years from 15 to 27 Swiss francs. As the seminars progressed and reproduction costs increased, some of the attendees donated funds to offset expenses. Among these were Alice Lewisohn Crowley, who made contributions of Sfr3,000 in 1933 and 1938. Paul Mellon provided (among other funds) Sfr963.55 in 1938 and Sfr6,500 in 1941. Complete lists of the names and addresses of those who attended each seminar as well as the amounts they paid are in the Mary Foote archives, BLY.
7. Jane Wheelwright is one of many who described "the gaggle of adoring females who ran after him." Cornelia Brunner described Emma's situation.
8. Ximena de Angulo Roelli speculated in interviews that CGJ may have had this marriage in mind when he wrote some of the more pessimistic passages in his essay for Keyserling's book on marriage.
9. Cary and Henri were family names of their mother's Kentucky ancestors and were given indiscriminately to sons or daughters.
10. Jane and Jo Wheelwright were among those who remembered fondly the warmth of Cary and Henri's hospitality. Joseph Henderson's English fiancée (and later his wife), Helena Cornford, stayed in their home when she visited from Cambridge, England, once for as long as three months.
11. Jo Wheelwright and Joseph Henderson are examples of CGJ's insistence upon men having medical training (but Dr. Henderson began his before CGJ suggested it). Both men got medical degrees in London before becoming analysts. Interestingly, CGJ never proposed medical education for women who wanted to become ana-

lysts, generally urging them to take doctorates in philosophy in fields in which he needed research assistance. Marie-Louise von Franz, for example, was urged to study classical languages and literature; Jolande Jacobi was steered toward comparative religion and mythology.

12. Dr. Joseph Henderson, in an interview with the author, October 4, 2000, described Cary Baynes and Henri Zinno as "having the same complex in different ways: having trained as a doctor, Cary could not practice; Henri, a talented painter, actually stopped painting for long periods of time, or else she destroyed her canvases as soon as they were finished."

13. See *CW-19*, 1928a and 1928b, pp. 69–70.

14. Mary Foote to Mabel Dodge Luhan, July 15, 1928, Mary Foote archives, BLY.

15. Elizabeth Goodrich Chamberlain, interview with the author, May 20, 1997.

16. Moon and Howes analyzed with Elizabeth Whitney, as well as with CGJ and Emma Jung in Zürich. In 1955, they formed the Guild for Psychological Studies, with Emma as a founding sponsor. The guild to this day maintains a deeply Christian orientation within its programs. See Thomas Kirsch, *The Jungians: A Comparative and Historical Perspective* (London and Philadelphia: Routledge, 2000), p. 76.

17. *Dream Analysis: Notes of the Seminar Given in 1928–30.*

18. See Maggy Anthony, *Jung's Circle of Women* (rev. ed. of *The Valkyries*) (York Beach, Maine: Nicholas-Hays, 1999), pp. 88–90.

19. Among his many credits were *The Green Pastures, The Emperor Jones,* and *Oedipus.*

20. M. Esther Harding, "Frances G. Wickes," in *Frances G. Wickes: A Memorial Meeting,* October 26, 1967, published by the Analytical Psychology Club of New York, New York Association for Analytical Psychology, and the CGJ Foundation for Analytical Psychology. Harding writes that Mrs. Wickes consulted CGJ in 1923–24 and then returned to New York to start her own practice in analytical psychology. At that time, she began regular meetings with Kristine Mann, Eleanor Bertine, Esther Harding, and several others. These meetings eventually resulted in the formation of the New York Analytical Psychology Club. Among Mrs. Wickes's patients were James Agee and Martha Graham, and it was she who introduced CGJ to her friend Mountain Lake.

21. According to Mary Bancroft, "Jung and His Circle," *Psychological Perspectives* (autumn 1975): 116, when Ann Bridge based a character in her novel *Peking Picnic* upon Foote, she was so shocked by the portrayal and her "sudden confrontation with the shadow" that she immediately sought help from CGJ. The expression quoted in the text is from Jones, who uses it throughout his letters to Mary Foote, specifically February 20, 1928, Robert Edmond Jones archives, BLY. On July 13, 1927, he tells her that CGJ and "his assistant, Miss Toni Wolff . . . know all about you from me. They are fond of me and will do all they can for you."

22. Mary Foote to Mabel Dodge Luhan, December 13, 1927, Mary Foote archives, BLY. The obituary is from the *Hartford Courant,* "Mary Foote, 95, dies: Secty. to Dr. Carl Jung," January 29, 1968. The actual number of years Mary Foote lived in Zürich is contested, but her lawyer, John A. Rand, Esq., said she was "well established in Salisbury [Conn.] in 1954."

23. Paul Mellon, interview with the author, October 31, 1995, New York.

24. See also Betsy Fahlman, "Women Art Students at Yale," *Women's Art Journal* 12, no. 1 (spring/summer 1991): 15–23.

25. The painting is now in the Richmond, Virginia, museum.

26. She painted him at Bollingen in 1937, and his portrait now hangs in the Beinecke Library, Yale University. See *CL-2*, p. xxxiv, for his letter of July 12, 1937.

27. March 10, 1919.
28. Edward J. Foote to Mary Foote Oppenheimer, June 22, 1977. He added that his mother [Mary Foote's sister] "burned some of her papers about unsavory connections during the mid-1930s." Referring to her years in Zürich, he wrote: "She should hang her head in shame for the discord she brought upon us."
29. Jones to Mary Foote, undated letter discussing his analysis, Robert Edmond Jones archives, BLY.
30. Jones to Mary Foote, 1927 (no month given; internal evidence suggests December), Robert Edmond Jones archives, BLY.
31. CGJ to Mary Foote, March 19, 1927, Mary Foote archives, BLY. CGJ wrote to her in care of the Trans-Siberian Railroad, Peking, while she was on a tour of China. Her letter differs slightly from the edited version in *CL-2*, p. xxxi.
32. Mary Foote to Mabel Dodge Luhan, December 13, 1927, Mary Foote archives, BLY.
33. Mary Foote to Mabel Dodge Luhan, July 15, 1928, and February 2, 1928 (internal evidence suggests misdate; it should be 1929), Mary Foote archives, BLY.
34. Mary Foote to Mabel Dodge Luhan, December 13, 1927, Mary Foote archives, BLY.
35. Mary Foote to Mabel Dodge Luhan, July 15, 1928, and September 7, 1928, Mary Foote archives, BLY.
36. I determined this in consultation with the *Erbengemeinschaft CGJ*, who consulted CGJ's appointment books on my behalf. Vincent Brome, *Jung* (New York: MacMillan, 1978), p. 226, writes: "Legend had it that [CGJ] grossly overworked, but Dr. [Liliane] Frey-Rohn made a study of his work-schedule for one year, only to discover that at least twenty-six weeks of that year were spent at Bollingen, where he went to relax." Cornelia Brunner, interview with the author, November 14, 1994 (and also in her HCL interview), said: "He held seminars on Wednesdays except during the holidays. From July to October he was in Bollingen. October to Christmas he worked. Then he had two to three weeks to a month of holiday. End January to end March he would give the seminar again. These very long holidays were only possible because he had a rich wife. Otherwise, he could not have done it."
37. Mary Foote to Leslie Field Emmet (no date, but internal evidence suggests 1927), Mary Foote archives, BLY.
38. Mary Foote to Mabel Dodge Luhan, July 15, 1928, Mary Foote archives, BLY. Her emphasis.
39. Marie-Louise von Franz, interview, who was told this by Barbara Hannah, who assisted Mary Foote from time to time during the 1930s. In interviews with the author, 1995 and 1996, C. A. Meier also quoted CGJ as saying this. The emphasis is von Franz's.
40. From unpublished documents provided by William McGuire, gathered during research for *Dream Analysis*.
41. For a list of the persons who attended this seminar and their countries of origin, see McGuire, *Dream Analysis*, pp. xviii–xix.
42. Paul Mellon admitted in an interview with the author that he and his first wife, Mary Conover Mellon, were among her "anonymous" supporters. Among the papers in the Mary Foote archives, BLY, pertaining to CGJ's seminars are various bills for "typing and retyping." On one dated March 22, 1938, she writes: "Due to me: 972 Fr." One of several indications that she frequently contributed her own money to offset printing costs is a note entitled "Stock of Zarathustra Notes on hand," where someone (probably the printer) has written that he was able to print more "with the help of 50 Fr. from Miss Foote." Her list of "Bad Debts" was often a long one.

43. Mary Foote to Mabel Dodge Luhan, from her apartment at 14 Hornweg, Küsnacht, January 6, 1931, BLY.
44. Letter from her brother William, October 25, 1941, saying he is also putting money into her "bond fund." When she died, she left an estate worth more than $200,000.
45. Tony Frey-Wehrlin, interview with the author, September 1996, Zürich. Dr. Frey lived on the Plattenstrasse, just behind Mary Foote's apartment on the Freiestrasse. He rescued as many paintings as he could before the trash collectors came.
46. Letter from Edward J. Foote to his "Uncle Norman," October 14, 1971, Mary Foote archives, BLY.
47. Mary Foote to Mabel Dodge Luhan (no date, but from 14 Hornweg, so it was probably after 1930).
48. CGJ to Mary Foote, August 7, 1931, Mary Foote archives, BLY.
49. Letter from Edward J. Foote to his "Uncle Norman," October 14, 1971. His mother, who destroyed the letters, "*thought*" they were from Hanfstängl (Mary Foote archives, BLY). Before World War I, Hanfstängl worked for Harold McCormick as a personal assistant and liaison to his International Harvester company. Some of their correspondence is in the State Historical Society of Wisconsin. Richard Noll called it to my attention.
50. Edward Foote to "Uncle Norman," October 14, 1971. A companion description came from Mary Foote's other brother, William, August 28, 1946, to Dorothy Bennett Foote, who wrote: "They — the Jungians — are the most incredible colony you ever saw. There is a Mrs. [Alice Lewisohn] Crowley . . . who looks and acts like a slightly decayed eagle. There is a Miss Hannah, a big hearty ho-ho-ho type, English and patronizing, who lives (I'm sure in sin) with a tiny little Austrian Miss von France [*sic*]. A few are strong — veddy strong — but most a sort of faint, perimeter people."
51. Donald Gallop, ed., *The Journals of Thornton Wilder* (New Haven: Yale Univ. Press, 1985), p. 144.
52. From a private archive given to the owner (not Marie-Louise von Franz) by Barbara Hannah herself and made available for this book.
53. The ever-caustic Mary Bancroft ("Jung and His Circle," p. 116) described Hannah as "a large English spinster of indeterminate age with a prominent nose that curved down to a chin that curved up to meet it [reminding] me of the witch . . . in *Hansel & Gretel*." See also Anthony, *Jung's Circle of Women*, pp. 87–88.
54. See Anthony, *Jung's Circle of Women*, p. 87, commenting on her pugnacious personality. Hannah was fond of English bulldogs, and in years to come, CGJ (among many others) often compared her stubborn aggressiveness to her dog's.
55. In the *Protocols*, CGJ responded to a question by Aniela Jaffé about his encounters by specifically naming Pauli. "Could I talk about that?" he asked. Apparently, she did not permit him to do so, because there is no further reference to the physicist in any version I have read. Discussing his friendships with men in general, from "Mountain Lake" to "an ordinary pandit in India," CGJ said he was not interested in the "foreground," or what successes they encountered in the world, but rather he was always in search of their "background," or their inner thoughts and emotions: "That's . . . what was crucial to me. And that's also where I found the people with whom I can have relationships. I have very many relationships."
56. Information about Pauli is from C. A. Meier, ed., *Atom and Archetype: The Pauli-Jung Letters 1932–58* (Princeton: Princeton Univ. Press, 2001); *Nobel Prize Winners Biographical Dictionary* (H. W. Wilson, 1987); C. P. Enz and K. von Meyenn, *Wolf-*

gang Pauli Das Gewissen der Physik (Braunschweig: Vieweg, 1988), pp. 518–19; and notes from William McGuire's private archives. Also, in a version slightly different from mine, CGJ describes Pauli's case in *The Tavistock Lectures*, *CW*-18, lecture 5, paras. 402–6, pp. 173–76.

57. C. A. Meier, ed. *(Atom and Archetype)*, comment made to him by CGJ, from manuscript p. 13, n. 7. Pauli's letter to Erna Rosenbaum is in the Pauli archive, ETH, Zürich. In *CW*-12, para. 45, p. 42, CGJ presents the history and evolution of his analysis of Pauli's dreams.

58. *Tavistock Lectures*, *CW*-18, lecture 5, para. 402, p. 174. C. A. Meier, ed., *Atom and Archetype*, p. 13, writes: "[CGJ] assigned Pauli to his young pupil Mrs. Erna Rosenbaum for analysis . . . on the grounds that Pauli had difficulties with women."

59. These essays, many originally given at the Eranos meetings in Ascona, were later collected in *Psychology and Alchemy*, *CW*-12, beginning with para. 45, pp. 41ff. In *CW*-18, para. 403, p. 174, CGJ states that Pauli produced "about thirteen hundred dreams." CGJ did not see Pauli throughout the treatment that produced the "first four hundred." Pauli spent five months under Rosenbaum's treatment, worked alone for the following three, and then returned to CGJ "for about two months . . . [for] a number of interviews" (para. 404, pp. 174–75).

60. Ruth Bailey, HCL interview.

61. Thomas B. Kirsch, in *The Jungians: A Comparative and Historical Perspective* (London and Philadelphia: Routledge, 2000), p. 9. Meier himself used the term — sarcastically — in his interviews with the author.

62. Interviews with the author, 1994–95.

63. Interviews with Marie-Louise von Franz, Cornelia Brunner, Mario Jacoby (no relation), Joseph Henderson, and some of her former patients who have asked to remain private. See also Anthony, *Jung's Circle of Women*, chapter 9, pp. 57–64.

64. This expression was used by many persons interviewed, not always in a complimentary fashion.

65. Anthony, *Jung's Circle of Women*, p. 64.

66. CGJ wrote about Zimmer in the German *MDR*, Appendix 8, "Heinrich Zimmer," pp. 385–86.

67. Freud to Jones, *F/Jones*, 518, February 18, 1928, p. 640. Jung's lecture was entitled "Struktur der Seele." See *CW*-19, 1928d, p. 19, for bibliographic details.

68. Information that follows, unless noted otherwise, is from interviews with Marie-Louise von Franz.

69. The first two quotes are from her interview with the author, June 1995; the third is one I read to her from Maggie Anthony's *Jung's Circle of Women* and asked her to comment upon in November 1995. She chose to interpret it positively, as a remark that proved her total and complete dedication to CGJ's doctrine. In her view, his psychology was final and fixed at his death, and no subsequent interpretation of theory could or should be either superimposed upon or incorporated within it.

70. His nickname because he was born and raised in Argentina; he only returned to Zürich for university studies. Some of the information that follows is from telephone conversations and correspondence with him; other information is from the Wolff family archives.

71. From interviews and conversations with members of the Jung and Trüb families; interviews with Cornelia Brunner and Joseph and Jane Wheelwright (among many others), and from Marie-Jeanne Boller-Schmid's HCL interview.

72. This expression was used by everyone from her nephews to her analysands and friends and all the persons named in the previous note.

73. CGJ's centenary celebration, BBC, 1975.

74. Joan Juliet Buck, "On Love, Maturity, and Happiness: An interview with Marie-Louise von Franz, Jung's Foremost Disciple," *Vogue*, November 1986, p. 206.

75. Anthony, *Jung's Circle of Women*; J. J. Buck's *Vogue* article; BBC CGJ centenary film, 1975; *A Matter of the Heart* and *Marie-Louise von Franz: Remembering Jung*, two films by Suzanne Wagner (Los Angeles: CGJ Institute, 1990); S. Segaller and M. Berger, *The Wisdom of the Dream*; HCL archives; and a private archive concerning Barbara Hannah and Marie-Louise von Franz.

76. Both Jo Wheelwright and Joseph Henderson, in separate interviews, agreed that Jung did categorize and separate into separate disciplines men and women who wished to become analysts. Wheelwright said: "I guess he figured men needed to make a good living and support families, and that they'd go off on their own anyway. Maybe he thought women didn't need as much [income], and maybe he thought of them as more dependent than men. But it sure is funny that he didn't send any of the women off to become doctors." Henderson thought the reason may have been that CGJ "feared the development of the animus" if these women became medical doctors.

77. Her comment from an interview in the private archive.

78. The concept of synchronicity is first mentioned on November 18, 1928, in the seminar on *Dream Analysis*, pp. 44–45. CGJ used the term in a letter to the physicist Pascual Jordan, November 10, 1934, *CL*-1, p. 176. The term was first published in CGJ's memorial address for Richard Wilhelm, *CW*-15, para. 81, p. 56.

79. From a private analytic diary of a male patient who told this to CGJ. He records CGJ's response as "something like a guffaw, a snicker."

80. Cornelia Brunner, Ximena de Angulo Roelli, and Marie-Louise von Franz were among the many who used a variant of this expression, which is also taken from the private analytic diary cited above.

81. Joseph Henderson, interview with the author; Catharine Rush Cabot, *Diary*, 1933, in Jane Cabot Reid, *Jung, My Mother, and I: The Analytic Diaries of Catharine Rush Cabot* (Einsiedeln: Daimon Verlag, 2000).

82. Cornelia Brunner, interview with the author. Brunner described herself as "a member of the younger or the second generation of Jung's women followers."

83. Cabot, *Diary*, 1941.

84. Now a Mövenpick restaurant directly opposite the Kunsthaus.

85. Cabot, *Diary*, 1933. She seldom went to these lunches, for the others disliked her for the snobbishness and derision with which she described them as "the flat-footed females of the seminar" (*Diary*, 1935).

86. Joseph Henderson, interview with the author, October 3, 2000.

87. Cabot, *Diary*, 1941.

88. Richard Wilhelm (1873–1930): best known for his translations of classical Chinese texts, particularly the *I Ching* (The Book of Changes). CGJ wrote a commentary for Wilhelm's *Das Geheimnis der goldenen Blüte*, in *CW*-13. His funeral oration, "Richard Wilhelm: in Memoriam," is in *CW*-15; a reminiscence is in *MDR*, Appendix 4. In the *Protocols*, in response to a question from Aniela Jaffé concerning CGJ's friendship with Heinrich Zimmer, CGJ replies that the friendship with Wilhelm mattered more and made the deeper impression.

89. Cabot, *Diary*, 1947.

90. From several long, detailed entries about Keyserling in various versions of the *Protocols*, some of which are dated June 28, 1957, or alternately "June [28?] 1957." Others are undated.

91. CGJ, *CW*-10, "The Rise of a New World," para. 933, p. 493.

92. Kurt Wolff, "Rabindranath Tagore," in *Kurt Wolff: A Portrait in Letters*, ed. Michael

Ermarth, trans. Deborah Lucas Schneider (Chicago: Univ. of Chicago Press, 1991), p. 122.

93. Wolff, "Rabindranath Tagore," p. 123.

94. See *MDR*, Appendix 4, pp. 373–77, for CGJ's memories of Wilhelm. Jaffé has culled many separate references from the *Protocols* to construct the published account.

95. *CW*-10, "The Swiss Line in the European Spectrum," para. 904, p. 479. This essay, written in 1928, provides interesting insights into CJG's biography as well as his thinking. See particularly para. 915, p. 485, for comparisons of the Swiss with Jews.

96. *Protocols*, two versions dated June 18, 1957, others undated. The expression "snowed under" is CGJ's English in all the German versions.

97. Quotations are from various *Protocols*. Ocampo went briefly to Zürich in the mid-1920s to be analyzed by CGJ, giving rise to the speculation that he incorporated various aspects of her personality into the composite case history of the mysterious unnamed woman in *MDR*, pp. 122–23, and with whom Morris West began his unflattering novel based loosely on CGJ's life, *The World Is Made of Glass* (New York: William Morrow, 1983). In *CGJ Speaking*, ed. William McGuire, Bollingen Series 97 (Princeton: Princeton Univ. Press, 1977), p. 82, McGuire gives the date of Ocampo's first meeting with CGJ as 1934, but he changed it in 2000 to agree with the information above in all reprinted editions and translations.

98. Olga Freun von Koenig-Fachsenfeld, "Memory of CGJ," in *CGJ, Emma Jung, and Toni Wolff: A Collection of Remembrances*, ed. Ferne Jensen (San Francisco: Analytical Psychology Club of San Francisco, 1982), p. 39.

99. Frobenius was part of the Frobenius-Dacqué circle in München, a group of writers, explorers, and ethnologists who studied primitive people and their cultures.

100. CGJ's English in all German versions of the *Protocols*.

101. Cabot mentions some of them in her diary, among them the Baron and Baroness Lüttichau, Baron and Baroness Boecklin.

102. Cabot, *Diary*, 1935, entry of December 5, 1935.

103. They and their daughter, Vita, figure throughout Cabot's diary. CGJ makes an occasional disapproving reference to them in the *Protocols*.

104. Cabot, *Diary*, 1935, her version of what CGJ told her.

105. In Cabot, *Diary*, 1935, CGJ speaks of the Archbishop of Salisbury; in her 1938 *Diary*, she has him making the same sort of observations about the Archbishop of York, who she also alleges consulted him "on matters of dogma." Neither *CW*-20 nor the *CL*-2 indices show entries for either name; nor can the *Erbengemeinschaft CGJ* verify any meetings between CGJ with either archbishop.

CHAPTER 26: UNCONVENTIONAL ANALYTIC HOURS

1. Joseph L. Henderson, "CGJ: A Reminiscent Picture of His Method," *JAP* 20 (1975): 117.

2. Aniela Jaffé, Preface, in *From the Life and Work of CGJ* (Einsiedeln: Daimon Verlag, 1989), p. vii.

3. Henderson, "A Reminiscent Picture," p. 117.

4. CGJ to Frances G. Wickes, August 9, 1926, *CL*-1, p. 44.

5. The first quote is Robert Jones to Mabel Dodge Luhan, dated only 1926; the second is dated December 31, 1936, both Robert Edmond Jones archives, BLY.

6. Jones continued to press CGJ, who continued to refuse to see Luhan. In another letter dated only 1926 (Robert Edmond Jones archive, BLY), Jones told her not to come to Zürich ("It is apparently not the right moment anymore"). Luhan never became CGJ's patient.

7. To write about Jung and AA, I have consulted CGJ to William G. Wilson (Bill W.), January 30, 1961, *CL-2*, pp. 623–25; "Bill W.–Carl Jung Letters," *AA Grapevine: The International Monthly Journal of Alcoholics Anonymous* 19, no. 8 (January 1963): 2–7; "Bill's Story," in *Alcoholics Anonymous* (New York: Works Publishing, 1939), pp. 10–26; Henri Ellenberger, *Discovery of the Unconscious: The History and Evolution of Dynamic Psychiatry* (New York: Basic Books, 1970), p. 733; and Matthew J. Raphael, *Bill W. and Mr. Wilson: The Legend and Life of AA's Cofounder* (Amherst: Univ. of Massachusetts Press, 2000). I am grateful to Mr. Raphael for personal correspondence about Jung and AA.

8. Dr. Joseph Henderson gives a variant version of this statement in "Jung's Research of the Past Ten Years," unpublished manuscript in KML, later reprinted in *Berkeley: A Journal of Modern Culture*, 6, no date.

9. In "The State of Psychotherapy Today," *CW*-10, para. 350, p. 163, CGJ defines the purpose of the training analysis as "to make [the analyst] not a human being but a correct applier of technique."

10. Kranefeldt did not have a Swiss work permit. Someone "who was jealous of his closeness to CGJ" reported him to the police, who then deported him to his native Germany. During World War II, even though he "played with the Nazis a bit," Emma Jung used him as a conduit to forward food packages to other non-Nazi Germans. She was furious when she learned that if Kranefeldt did not like the persons for whom she intended the packages, he would either keep them or give them to persons he did like (interview with Marie-Louise von Franz, who was told this by Barbara Hannah).

11. See also chapter 29. Rittmeister remained in Switzerland until 1937, when he was forced to leave because of political activity on behalf of German Communists. He joined the *Rote Kapelle* and was guillotined at Berlin-Plötzenzee on May 13, 1943. The quote is from Karen Brecht, Volker Friedrich, Ludger M. Herrmanns, Isidor J. Kaminer, and Dierk H. Juelich, eds., *"Here Life Goes On in a Most Peculiar Way . . ."*: *Psychoanalysis Before and After 1933*, English ed. by Hella Ehlers (London: Kellner Verlag, 1993), p. 186. Paul Roazen made this source available to me. Shareen Blair Brysac contributed further biographical information about Rittmeister in personal conversations and through her biography of Mildred Harnack. I have also consulted Regina Griebel, Marlies Coburger, Henrich Scheel, eds., *Erfast?: Gestapo Album of the Rote Kapelle* (Rendsburg, 1992).

12. Henderson, "A Reminiscent Picture," p. 117.

13. See Thomas B. Kirsch, *The Jungians: A Comparative and Historical Perspective* (London and Philadelphia: Routledge, 2000), for the role she, her husband, Dr. Joseph Wheelwright, and their friend, Dr. Joseph Henderson, played in Jungian activities in the San Francisco Bay area.

14. Jane Wheelwright, interviews and telephone conversations with the author.

15. Irene Champernowne was representative of the majority, although she did not actually consult Toni Wolff until the 1940s. See *A Memoir of Toni Wolff* (San Francisco: CGJ Institute of San Francisco, 1980). Tina Keller said much the same in her HCL interview. Jane Wheelwright, in conversations with the author, was reminded that her husband considered Toni Wolff "the very best" of all his analysts. Jane Wheelwright agreed that she was but insisted her husband's opinion only proved her point.

16. This account is based on personal interviews and telephone conversations with Dr. Henderson between 1995 and 2000, his HCL interview, and his own writings. These include "Jung's Research of the Past Ten Years" and "A Reminiscent Picture."

17. Henderson, "Carl Gustav Jung: 1875–1961," compiled and presented by Ean Begg, BBC Radio-3, July 27, 1975 (hereafter cited as Begg BBC-3).

18. CGJ sent a Swiss glass artisan to Bruges, Belgium, to copy the panes in a small church there. Information that follows is from Catharine Rush Cabot, *Diary*, 1935, in Jane Cabot Reid, *Jung, My Mother, and I: The Analytic Diaries of Catharine Rush Cabot* (Einsiedeln: Daimon Verlag, 2000).

19. Jaffé, "Alchemy," in *From the Life and Work of CGJ*, p. 55.

20. Jaffé, Begg BBC-3.

21. The descendants of this man made the journal available but asked that he not be otherwise identified.

22. Cabot, *Diary*, 1939.

23. Mary Briner-Ramsey, Begg BBC-3.

24. From the descendants of the woman, who wrote letters and left diaries in which she sometimes spoke of her analysis with Jung.

25. Jaffé, "From Jung's Last Years," in *From the Life and Work of CGJ*, p. 119.

26. Term used by Dr. Patricia Dunton in a 1976 interview with the author.

27. See, for example, Susanne Percheron's and Isabelle Hamilton Rey's excerpts from notes taken during or immediately after sessions from 1935 to 1961, in Ferne Jensen, ed., *CGJ, Emma Jung, and Toni Wolff* (San Francisco: Analytical Club of San Francisco, 1982), pp. 51–70 and 70–75 resp.

28. She claimed to be the second graduate of the CGJ Institute, Zürich, and was a member of the examining board until her eighty-fifth year. Her husband, Carl Gustav Briner, was on the Board of the Foundation of the Zürich Institute, then on the Board of Trustees until shortly before his death in 1973.

29. None of the fairly extensive correspondence between Mary Briner and CGJ was published in *CL*; only part is in the ETH. The letter that follows is filed in the CGJ to Mary Briner archive at the ETH, but it is listed as by CGJ to "anon." Although his is undated, Mary Briner's reply of November 28, 1958, clearly addresses it in all its relevant points. The ETH and the *Erbengemeinschaft CGJ* insist they were never given the actual manuscript of what Mary Briner wrote, which she describes as *"word for word what stands in my notes of each analytical hour and was written some twenty years ago* immediately after the hour, even to the 'he said,' and 'I said'" (her emphasis). Her son, Robin Briner, in an interview with the author, July 1997, said he went through his mother's remaining papers on my behalf, but he also could not find the document. He said: "I am sure my mother gave the only copy to Jung. If she did keep a carbon, she was probably so distressed by his reaction that she destroyed it."

30. CGJ's undated letter to "anon." described in the previous note.

31. Jane Cabot Reid, *Jung, My Mother, and I*. Mrs. Reid was long a pillar of the Zürich Psychological Club and practiced as a Jungian analyst there. The unpublished "Analysis Notebook 1926" kept by Christiana Councilman Morgan was widely quoted by her biographer, Claire Douglas, in *Translate This Darkness: The Life of Christiana Morgan* (New York: Simon and Schuster, 1993). The original manuscript is in the unsorted H. A. Murray papers, HCL.

32. From interviews with many persons who knew both her and CGJ, as well as those who worked collegially or analyzed with her. Mary Briner and CGJ's correspondence in the ETH as well as private documents in her archive also support my view.

33. Cabot has Jung making these comments about "English women" in general in *Diary*, 1940, and more specifically about Carol Sawyer Baumann, Mary Bancroft Rüfenacht, and Mary Briner (all American women who married Swiss men) in *Di-*

ary, 1941. It is, however, important to note that CGJ also made such remarks about Toni Wolff, Barbara Hannah, and Marie-Louise von Franz — his closest and most respected associates. I would tend to interpret such remarks in the light of his general attitude toward women rather than to specific representatives of their sex.

34. Cabot, *Diary,* 1941.
35. Among them her daughter, Jane Reid, Dr. Joseph Henderson, Jane and Jo Wheelwright, and others.
36. Cabot, *Diary,* 1937.
37. Cabot, *Diary,* 1940.
38. Cabot, *Diary,* 1938.
39. This is particularly evident during the years 1930 to 1934, when he gave the Vision Seminars, discussed below in connection with Christiana Morgan.
40. My main sources for what follows are: Claire Douglas, ed., *Visions: Notes of the Seminar Given in 1930–34,* Bollingen Series 99 (Princeton: Princeton Univ. Press, 1997), vols. 1 and 2, and *Translate This Darkness,* and *The Woman in the Mirror: Analytical Psychology and the Feminine* (Boston: Sigo Press, 1990); Forrest G. Robinson, *Love's Story Told: A Life of Henry Murray* (Cambridge, Mass.: Harvard Univ. Press, 1992); and the archives of Henry A. Murray and Christiana Morgan at HCL and LC.
41. I am grateful to Dr. Thomas B. Kirsch for these insights. In a personal communication, October 3, 2002, he added: "This happens to all of us therapists when we get more interested in the dream than the person. Always a danger."
42. CGJ to Christiana Morgan, December 28, 1927, *CL*-1, pp. 48–49.
43. Douglas, *Translate This Darkness,* p. 93.
44. Both Robinson, *Love's Story Told,* pp. 100–103, and Douglas, *Translate This Darkness,* p. 115, agree with this assessment.
45. Henry Murray, interview with Gene Nameche, November 4, 1968, HCL. Murray was seventy-six when he gave this interview, and his relationship with CGJ had undergone many different phases between 1926 and 1968. This should be factored in when interpreting his remarks.
46. Robinson, *Love's Story Told,* p. 120, writes that CGJ was "little engaged."
47. Henry Murray, HCL interview.
48. First published in both German and English in 1928. Full citations in *CW*-19, pp. 18–19 and 70–71.
49. Henry Murray, HCL interview.
50. Michael Fordham, in Begg BBC-3, described it as "Jung playing the great man. . . . He would give dissertations of a rather boring kind. I remember listening about LSD at least three or four times. He told it to me the same way each time and I got rather tired of it."
51. See especially *CW*-10, "Women in Europe," para. 253–55, and "Marriage as a Psychological Relationship," *CW*-17, paras. 331c–334. See also Henry Murray, HCL interview.
52. Each woman wrote her own version of women's psychology within Jungian typology: Toni wrote *Structural Forms of the Feminine Psyche,* 1934; Emma wrote *Animus and Anima,* reprinted in *Spring* Publications, 1957.
53. Paul Roazen, in *Freud and His Followers* (New York: Da Capo Press, 1992), p. 469, puts it more succinctly: "Western culture at the turn of the 20th century generally looked down on women, who were supposed to exist primarily for the sake of gratifying a man's needs, bearing his children, and running his house."
54. Claire Douglas, "Christiana Morgan's Visions Reconsidered: A Look Behind *The Vision Seminars,*" *The San Francisco Jung Institute Library Journal* 8, no. 4 (1989):

5–27. See also Demaris S. Wehr, *Jung and Feminism: Liberating Archetypes* (Boston: Beacon Press, 1989).

55. Douglas, "Christiana Morgan's Visions," p. 10.

56. She did not actually begin the so-called Vision Notebooks until July 9, 1926, ending on April 17, 1928. These consisted of more than one hundred versions of what CGJ discussed in the Vision Seminars from October 30, 1930, to March 21, 1934. Douglas writes: "For four years he explicated and elaborated her visions through a line-by-line discussion of some of them, giving them everything he had — quite often to their detriment" ("Christiana Morgan's Visions," p. 8).

57. Douglas, *Visions*, 1: 6.

58. William Morgan, unpublished notes on his analysis with CGJ and Toni Wolff, Henry Murray archives, HCL. Douglas also quotes them in "Christiana Morgan's Visions," p. 14.

59. My interpretation parallels Douglas's, *Translate This Darkness*, p. 149: "Though her admiration and Jung's propensity for projecting his anima ideal onto women of Christiana's type energized them both, it ultimately detracted from her therapeutic progress. Initially, however . . . Morgan [was] extremely receptive to all that Jung said, while his attraction for her made him willing to give her extra time and energy." See also CGJ, *Visions II*, lecture 11, March 21, 1934, p. 1366, in which he states: "You never see people exactly as they are, you always project something."

60. Douglas, *Translate This Darkness*, p. 147.

61. For a full description of "trancing" and active imagination as Jones practiced it, see Douglas, *Translate This Darkness*, pp. 155–56. Among the twenty or so patients who lived in the same pension besides Jones and the Morgans were Katy Cabot, Joseph L. Henderson, and Ruth Draper's brother, Dr. George Draper. Cabot and Draper began an affair that upset the dynamics of this group, which also included Barbara Hannah and an unnamed Australian woman physician. Henderson found their friendly eagerness to share analytic experiences so off-putting that he moved to another pension in search of "concentration and solitude." (His comments are from several interviews.) CGJ deplored the Cabot-Draper relationship, telling Katy Cabot that George Draper was "spiritually thin" (Cabot, *Diary*, November 20, 1933).

62. Morgan's transcription of CGJ's comments in her analytic notebook for July 8 and July 7, 1926.

63. Henry Murray, HCL interview.

64. C. A. Meier, interview with the author, November 11, 1994. Meier insisted that he was the director of these sessions, in effect becoming the analyst of the two women. Cryptic notations in Toni Wolff's archives do not support his contention. Her version has the two women talking at such cross-purposes that these sessions ended abruptly after only two (or possibly three — her notes are unclear) meetings. The meetings did, however, take place in Meier's office.

65. I share Douglas's view in *Visions*, Introduction, 1: xiv: "Morgan's material had elicited Jung's profound (and profoundly ambivalent) interest in the feminine imaginal realm, but, in the end, he subordinated her visions to his theory. . . . The subject matter of the darkly powerful feminine proved too potent for the Jung of the early 1930s." The Q & A after each seminar shows that no one argued against any of Jung's theory.

66. *CL-1*, December 28, 1927, pp. 47–48.

67. Douglas, *Woman in the Mirror*, quotes Henry Murray from a personal interview and from his postscript to *The Vision Seminars*: "Wouldn't you . . . guess that love was the key to it all?" Murray also stated about CGJ's December 28, 1927, letter to

Morgan, *CL*-1, pp. 48–49: "[When] measured in my scale of libidinous affection . . . [it] yields as high a rating as any letter written to any one of the more than 450 correspondents [in *CL*]." After Christiana Morgan's death, Henry Murray sent Christiana Morgan and CGJ's entire correspondence to Gerhard Adler, who was then preparing *CL* for publication. Adler deemed it all "inappropriate" and sent the letters to Franz Jung, who either sequestered or destroyed them. The *Erbengemeinschaft CGJ* claims they are extant but, as of 2003, has refused to make them available to scholars. This information is from 1994 and 1995 author interviews and conversations with Franz Jung, conversations with other members of the Jung family, and the archives of the Bollingen Foundation and Princeton University Press in connection with the preparation of *CL*. Douglas, *Translate This Darkness*, p. 167, writes what most scholars generally agree upon: "Until the Jung family releases the documents they own, there can only be suppositions about Jung's problems with his anima and with countertransference, and about that gossip that Jung . . . broke through a number of his patients' rings of fire by sexually exploiting them."

68. Douglas, *Translate This Darkness*, pp. 163–67.
69. Christiana Morgan's analytic diary, October 14, 1926, as quoted in Douglas, *Translate This Darkness*, pp. 164–65.
70. Cabot, *Diaries*, 1936 and 1937.
71. *Visions II*, p. 1379.
72. Full bibliographic detail is in *CW*-19 for publications that appeared between 1925 and 1930 in all languages. Most of these lectures are reprinted in very different form in *CW*-17. A number of fragmentary writings are still unpublished. These consist of notes in progress, early drafts of published articles, and a very small number of writings that, for whatever his reason, CGJ decided not to publish. Estimates of their total vary, but I estimate about thirty, with most in the ETH.
73. Originally written in French and delivered as a 1916 lecture, subsequently revised for 1928 publication in German. See the editorial commentary in *CW*-7, following para. 442, p. 269, for the currently known evolution of this text.
74. Henry Murray, HCL interview, cites Keyserling as "[CGJ's] greatest rival when I was there in 1925. . . . He [CGJ] made cracks about him all the time." Their published correspondence in *CL*-1 supports this.
75. "Women in Europe," *CW*-10, para. 260, p. 126.
76. Hermann Keyserling, ed., "Die Ehe als psychologische Beziehung," *Das Ehebuch* (Celle: Kampmann, 1925), pp. 294–307, and "Marriage as a Psychological Relationship," *The Book of Marriage*, trans. Theresa Duerr (New York: Harcourt Brace, 1925). A second translation was made by H. G. and Cary F. Baynes for *Contributions to Analytical Psychology* (New York: Harcourt Brace; and London: Kegan Paul, Trench, Trubner, 1928). The official translation by R. F. C. Hull is in *CW*-17, paras. 324–45, pp. 189–201.
77. In *CW*-10, para. 236, p. 113. See n. 1 for the publishing history of this article.
78. CGJ to Oskar A. H. Schmitz, May 26, 1923, *CL*-1, p. 39. Schmitz (1873–1931), a German writer, author of *Psychoanalyse und Yoga* (1923) and student of Jung's psychology, secured CGJ's first invitation to Keyserling's school.
79. Jung's irritation is fairly veiled in the few letters that are printed in *CL*-1 and quite evident in the extant correspondence at the ETH and in the Keyserling Archive, Darmstadt.
80. "Women in Europe," *CW*-10, para. 269, p. 130.
81. Dr. Joseph Henderson was among the first to notice this trend, in "Jung's Research of the Past Ten Years."
82. Henderson, "Jung's Research of the Past Ten Years."

83. For a capsule explanation of alchemy, how CGJ used it within his psychology, and for further references, see Andrew Samuels, Bani Shorter, and Fred Plaut, *A Critical Dictionary of Jungian Analysis* (London and New York: Routledge, 1986), pp. 12–15.

84. *MDR*, pp. 179–81.

85. The dream is in *MDR*, pp. 202ff.; the quote is from *Protocols*.

86. CGJ, Commentary to *The Secret of the Golden Flower*, *CW*-13, p. 87.

87. *Protocols*. I do not cite *MDR* here because of Aniela Jaffé's technique in presenting this information: she selected several brief passages from the *Protocols* and inserted them as topic sentences into *MDR* to explain the evolution of CGJ's thinking and the writing of his major works from that point on (*Psychology and Alchemy, Aion, Mysterium Coniunctionis, Answer to Job*). Unfortunately the several sentences she selects to introduce each topic do not fully convey his meaning and intention. Nor does what follows, much of which is simply taken out of context and appears to be a text that, to the best of my knowledge, is her creation and more her understanding of his thought than his thought itself.

88. Ruth Bailey and Cary F. Baynes were among the many who sent them faithfully.

89. Here he cited what he called the "Paracelsica," his 1929 and 1941 essays on Paracelsus, *CW*-15; and "Psychology and Religion," *CW*-11, the 1938 Terry Lectures at Yale University.

90. The following account is from interviews with Marie-Louise von Franz, Jo and Jane Wheelwright, Joseph Henderson, Cornelia Brunner, and others who did not wish to be identified.

CHAPTER 27: "DANGEROUSLY FAMOUS"

1. CGJ to Ruth Bailey, November 25, 1932, from CGJ and Ruth Bailey's correspondence, ETH.

2. Gustav Huonker, *Literaturszene Zürich: Menschen, Geschichten und Bilder 1914 bis 1945* (Zürich: Unionsverlag, 1985), pp. 68–70. Verena Müller provided information concerning Charlot Strasser, and Professor Robert Schneebeli conducted research on my behalf.

3. The first quote is from CGJ to H. Knoll, December 9, 1932; the others are from CGJ to "Mrs. N.," November 28, 1932; both *CL*-1, pp. 111 and 109, resp.

4. Elizabeth Shepley Sergeant, "Dr. Jung: A Portrait in 1931," *Harper's*, May 1931; abridged in *CGJ Speaking*, ed. William McGuire, Bollingen Series 97 (Princeton: Princeton Univ. Press, 1977), p. 51.

5. The first quote is from Charles Baudoin's 1934 *Journal*, p. 76; the second is from "Victoria Ocampo Pays Jung a Visit," p. 82, both in *CGJ Speaking*.

6. *CL*-1, CGJ to Hugh Walpole, August 15, 1930, p. 75.

7. E. A. Bennet, *What Jung Really Said* (London: Macdonald, 1966), p. 93, mistakenly claims that the Wells-Jung conversation resulted in "the theme of *Christina Alberta's Father*." In his "Note Before the Title Page" to the *Clissold* novel, Wells says CGJ's appearance in the novel is "very much as he talked in a London flat. He appears because certain original ideas of his have been taken and woven into the Clissold point of view."

8. CGJ, *Protocols*, appearing in several versions on typed p. 320, unpaginated in others. In *Civilization on Trial* (London and New York: Oxford Univ. Press, p. 11), Toynbee writes: "If I had been acquainted at the time with the works of CGJ, they would have given me the clue." In *CL*-1, p. 525, CGJ to Henri Flournoy, March 29, 1949, CGJ mentions Toynbee as having accepted "the existence of archetypes" in "History."

9. Catharine Rush Cabot, *Diary*, 1931, in Jane Cabot Reid, *Jung, My Mother, and I:*

The Analytic Diaries of Catharine Rush Cabot (Einsiedeln: Daimon Verlag, 2000); Nancy Milford, *Zelda: A Biography* (New York: Harper and Row, 1970); and documentation from the research of Marion Meade.

10. Information that follows is from F. Scott Fitzgerald to Judge and Mrs. A. D. Sayre [Anthony and Minnie], December 1, 1930, in *F. Scott Fitzgerald: A Life in Letters*, ed. Matthew Bruccoli (New York: Simon and Schuster, 1994), pp. 202–4. As the $500 figure has come down into popular history and is cited by many biographers of Scott and Zelda, among them Milford, *Zelda*, p. 179, I mention it here. All attribute it to "somewhere in the Princeton archives." There is no evidence that Fitzgerald ever contacted CGJ directly. I have been unable to confirm it, and the *Erbengemeinschaft CGJ* dismisses the $500, insisting that CGJ never charged such an amount for an initial consultation. Fitzgerald also claimed to have spent between $13,000 and $14,000 for Zelda's stay at Prangins, which lasted eighteen months. This does not correspond either to Forel's rates or to those of the Burghölzli. Fitzgerald told Catharine Cabot (*Diary*, 1931) that he spent "$4,000," so all his figures remain speculative. Fitzgerald's friend John Peale Bishop told Alan Tate that "he [Fitzgerald] lies" about his wife's condition and his account was "based only on Scott's drunken gossip" (Bishop, *The Republic of Letters in America: Correspondence of John Peale Bishop and Alan Tate* [Lexington, Ky.: Univ. Press of Kentucky, 1982]).

11. CGJ to Hugh Walpole, *CL*-1, August 15, 1930, p. 75.

12. "Picasso," *CW*-15, para. 204, p. 135.

13. The first quote is from *Visions II*, lecture 11, March 21, 1934, p. 1377; the second is from *CW*-15, para. 208, p. 137.

14. *CW*-15, n. 3, p. 137.

15. On June 17, 1952, CGJ was interviewed by the British art critic and historian J. P. Hodin, who published the account in his book *Modern Art and the Modern Mind* (Cleveland: Case Western Reserve Univ. Press, 1972), portions reprinted in *CGJ Speaking*, pp. 219–24. On September 3, 1955, CGJ replied to Hodin's letter asking him to comment on Oscar Kokoschka's art (*CGJ Speaking*, p. 221, n. 3; not in *CL*): "Nor do I pretend to have very much to say about modern art. Most of it is alien to me from the human point of view and too disagreeably reminiscent of what I have seen in my medical practice."

16. Information that follows is from *CW*-15, Appendix, pp. 132–33; the Richard Ellmann archives at the University of Tulsa; Ellmann's revised edition of his 1959 biography, *James Joyce* (New York: Oxford Univ. Press, 1983 [paperback]); *Letters of James Joyce*, vol. 1 ed. Stuart Gilbert, 1957; rpt. 1966; vols. 2 and 3 ed. Richard Ellmann, 1966 (New York: Viking Press and London: Faber and Faber); Thomas Faerber and Markus Luchsinger, *Joyce in Zürich* (Zürich: Unionsverlag, 1988); correspondence between CGJ and Cary Baynes, Richard Ellmann, and Ximena de Angulo Roelli; and Richard Ellmann and William McGuire (all from the Richard Ellmann archives, University of Tulsa). An account that differs from all those above is Carol Loeb Schloss, "Joyce, Jung and Carola Giedion-Welcker," *A Collideorscape of Joyce: Festschrift for Fritz Senn* (Dublin: Liliput Press, 1998), pp. 215–27.

17. It is not clear if this is the same journal or different from the one CGJ wrote about to J. Wilhelm Hauer, *CL*-1, November 14, 1932, p. 103.

18. In a letter to Richard Ellmann, October 19, 1962, now in the Richard Ellmann archives, University of Tulsa, Brody insisted that, although Joyce's account differed from the one he told Ellmann for the first edition of the James Joyce biography, he (Brody) stood behind this version because he heard it directly from Joyce. Brody added that he wrote an article on the "whole story" but asked Ellmann not to publish it. In Brody to Ellmann, November 12, 1962, Tulsa, Brody repeated that he did

not want Ellmann to publish his "article" in the *Kenyon Review*, as Ellmann had suggested. Brody wrote: "I would not like to make public the story of Ulysses and Jung as told by Joyce, as it is rather deprecating to the memory of Jung, a man whom I admire very much and who was a very good friend of mine." As of 2003, such a text has not yet been found among the documents Ellmann deposited in his archives in Tulsa. For conflicting accounts of how Brody may have chosen CGJ, see *CW*-15, "Psychology and Literature," p. 84, n. 1; Richard Ellmann, *James Joyce* (the first and rev. eds. differ), pp. 628–29 (rev. ed.); Patricia Hutchens, *James Joyce's World* (London: Methuen, 1957), p. 182; Schloss, *Joyce, CGJ and Carola Giedion-Welcker;* and William Walcott, "CGJ and James Joyce: Three Encounters," in *Professional Reports 1968*, Sixteenth Annual Joint Conference of the Societies of Jungian Analysts of Northern and Southern California, March 1968 (copy in the KML). Internal evidence in CGJ's essay "Ulysses: A Monologue," pp. 109ff., suggests that CGJ had been familiar with the novel since its original 1922 publication and probably read some or all of it from that date onward. However, the copy he owned was the tenth English-language printing (Paris, 1928), and this is the one he cited in his notes.

19. For full bibliographic information, see *CGJ Manuskripte-Katalog: Verzeichnis der im CGJ-Archiv der ETH-Bibliothek vorhandenen Manuskripte* (Zürich: Wissenschafts-historische Sammlungen der ETH-Bibliothek, 1995), pp. 27–28. Walcott, "CGJ and James Joyce," p. 92, offers a theory about which portions are original and which revised. The official version is in *CL*-15, paras. 163ff., p. 109.

20. Among her writings is the book *Schriften 1926–71* (Schauberg, Cologne: Verlag M. Dumont, 1973). Giedion-Welcker (1893–1979) met Joyce shortly after she published her own essay on *Ulysses* in the *Neue Schweizer Rundschau* in 1928. For further biographical detail, see Roman Bucheli, "Grenzüberschreitende Freundschaft: James Joyce and Carola Giedion-Welcker," *Neue Zürcher Zeitung*, no. 66, p. 81.

21. Kathleen McGrory and John Unterecker, eds., "Interview with Carola Giedion-Welcker, June 15, 1973, Burlington Hotel, Dublin," in *Yeats, Joyce, Beckett* (Lewisburg: Bucknell Univ. Press, 1976), pp. 110–17.

22. Notes from an interview between Carola Giedion-Welcker and Richard Ellmann, Richard Ellmann archives, University of Tulsa.

23. *transition: An International Quarterly for Creative Experiment*, 19/20 (June 1930). CGJ most likely came to Jolas's attention through Cary Baynes, who was a childhood friend of his wife, Maria, in Louisville, Kentucky. CGJ's publication in this prestigious avant-garde magazine is evidence of the growing interest by writers and artists in applying psychology to their genres.

24. N. 1 to *CW*-15, "Psychology and Literature," p. 84, posits the theory that CGJ read the essay but gives no further detail; nor does the *Katalog ETH*, p. 24. I have determined that he probably read it to one of the many literary "clubs" that proliferated in Zürich at the time: the Lesezirkel Hottingen, the Gesellschaft für deutsche Sprache und Literatur, or the Literarische Club Zürich.

25. *CW*-15, para. 143 and n. 7, p. 91.

26. Fritz Senn, director of the James Joyce Stiftung, Zürich, provided me with a copy of Giedion-Welcker's letter to CGJ, dated October 1930. It was reproduced in the *Neue Zürcher Zeitung*, March 18–19, 2000, no. 66, p. 81, in conjunction with the article by Roman Bucheli.

27. Richard Ellmann's notes, interview with Carola Giedion-Welcker, his p. 3, no date.

28. Ellmann, *James Joyce* (rev. ed.), p. 665. For further biographical information about Lucia Joyce, see Deirdre Bair, *Samuel Beckett: A Biography* (New York: Harcourt, Brace, Jovanovich, 1978), pp. 80–84.

29. In his August 8, 1953, interview with Richard Ellmann, CGJ states that the Brunner Sanatorium was "a reputable place, not the best, but the best was too expense [*sic:* expensive]." Joyce was not only paying for an expensive flat in Paris, but he and Nora lived in an expensive hotel in Zürich as well.

30. *Protocols*, undated, unpaginated, and part of a discussion about his reasons for wanting to concentrate on alchemical writings and archetypes. CGJ's refusal to deal with psychotics was widely known, as exemplified in F. Scott Fitzgerald's letter to Judge and Mrs. Sayre quoted above.

31. The source for Maria Jolas's involvement is Ximena de Angulo Roelli, letters to Richard Ellmann, February 27 and July 27, 1981, Richard Ellmann archives, University of Tulsa.

32. The account that follows is taken from notes made by Cary Baynes for her subsequent reports to CGJ, October 29 to November 24, 1934, Richard Ellmann archives, University of Tulsa. I am grateful to Ximena de Angulo Roelli for permission to use her mother's archive and for the several times she discussed the Joyce family during interviews with me. In Cary Baynes's written reports, she alludes to "Kristine," who was then having analytic sessions with CGJ. This was Kristine Mann, who was Cary's houseguest in her Kilchberg home, and with whom both she and CGJ discussed Lucia Joyce. Evidence suggests that both Mann and Cary Baynes had significant influence in CGJ's treatment of Lucia Joyce.

33. Cary Baynes, notes for November 20, 1934, Richard Ellmann archives, University of Tulsa.

34. James Joyce to CGJ, October 25, 1934, on stationery of the Carlton Elite Hotel, copy made available by William McGuire from his archives. Not in *CL*.

35. CGJ to Jack Hirschman, February 1, 1954. Original in the Manuscript Department of the Lilly Library, Indiana University, Bloomington; copy in KML. Not in *CL*.

36. Ellmann, *James Joyce* (rev. ed.), p. 679. These are Ellmann's words, not CGJ's. In his interview with CGJ, August 8, 1953, Ellmann writes: "latent schizo[phrenics] . . . it is like two men, who both get to bottom of river, but one falls and the other dives" (Richard Ellmann archives, University of Tulsa).

37. CGJ to Jack Hirschman, February 1, 1954.

38. CGJ to Patricia [Hutchins] Graecen, June 29, 1955, *CL*-2, p. 266.

39. Ellmann, *James Joyce* (rev. ed.), p. 680. *Finnegans Wake*, p. 115.

40. Ellmann, *James Joyce* (rev. ed.), p. 681.

41. CGJ's library, Küsnacht.

42. *Finnegans Wake*, p. 267.

43. *CW*-10, "After the Catastrophe," para. 430, p. 210.

44. *CW*-14, *Mysterium Coniunctionis*, para. 454, p. 324. CGJ cites Ernst R. Curtius, *James Joyce und sein Ulysses* (Zürich, 1929).

45. CGJ to Sir Herbert Read, September 5, 1960, ETH; internal evidence suggests in reply to a query by Sir Herbert Read to CGJ, not in ETH. Sir Herbert Read replied to CGJ with his own theories of modern art September 19, 1960, ETH.

46. Marie-Jeanne Boller-Schmid, HCL interview.

47. CGJ uses this expression in the *Protocols*. I am grateful to Ulrich Hoerni for devoting much time and energy to investigating the life and death of Gertrud Jung. Unfortunately, she kept her life so private that he was not able to ascertain the cause of death or contribute any biographical information other than what I have written.

48. *Protocols*, passage dated November 15, 1957. He describes a dream he had about his

parents and sister, expressing surprise that he had not recognized much earlier that Gertrud Jung was his anima.

49. Interviews with Franz Jung and Agathe Niehus-Jung. Marie-Jeanne Boller-Schmid tells the same story in her HCL interview.

50. Both Boller-Schmid and Jaffé say this in their HCL interviews.

CHAPTER 28: A "PRETTY GRUELING TIME"

1. William McGuire informed me that 1933 is the correct year and that *CL-1*, p. 251, n. 1, line 2, is in error: 1932 should be 1933, as I have it here.

2. Heinrich Fierz (one of the sons) HCL interview; the chariot/horse information is from Catharine Rush Cabot's diary, in Jane Cabot Reid, *Jung, My Mother, and I: The Analytic Diaries of Catharine Rush Cabot* (Einsiedeln: Daimon Verlag, 2000).

3. Heinrich Fierz, HCL interview.

4. H. E. Fierz-David, *Die Entwicklungsgeschichte der Chemie*, vol. 2 (Basel: Wissenschaft und Kultur, 1945). He dedicated it to CGJ.

5. Both comments can be found throughout Cabot's diaries and many HCL interviews.

6. James and Hilde Kirsch went to Palestine in November 1933. Information is from CGJ and James Kirsch's correspondence, ETH.

7. She died in April 1962 in Ascona but was cremated in Luzern because the local facility was in disrepair. Her ashes were returned to the Casa Gabriella.

8. H. Church, General Executive of Westinghouse Brake and Signal Co. Ltd., to William McGuire, June 14, 1978. From McGuire's private archives.

9. Information that follows is from William McGuire, *Bollingen: An Adventure in Collecting the Past*, Bollingen Series (Princeton: Princeton Univ. Press, 1982), and his articles from *Spring*: "Jung and Eranos in America" and "American Eranos Volume: Introduction" (both 1984), and "The Arcane Summer School" (1980): 146–56; Aniela Jaffé, "CGJ and the Eranos Conferences," *Spring* (1977): 201–12; Sybille Rosenbaum-Kroeber, "Was ist Eranos und wer wer Olga Fröbe-Kapteyn?" in *Monte Verità* (catalogue) (1978): 117–19; and Curt Riess, *Ascona: Geschichte des seltsamsten Dorfes der Welt* (Zürich: Europa Verlag, 1964), p. 110. Other sources I have consulted include Richard Noll, *The Jung Cult* (Princeton: Princeton Univ. Press, 1994), and *The Aryan Christ* (New York: Random House, 1997); Carl Kerényi, *Tagebuch;* Hermann Müller, *Der Dichter und sein Guru: Hermann Hesse, Gusto Graser, eine Freundschaft* (Wetzler: Gisela Lotz Verlag, 1978); and Robert Landmann, *Monte Verità: Die Geschichte eines Berges*, 3d ed. (Ascona: Pancaldi Verlag, 1934). Also, Jay Livernois, editor of the Eranos Yearbooks and Director of the Foundation, interviews and conversations with the author, 2002.

10. Riess says he was killed in the crash, as did Baroness Vera von der Heydt, interview with the author, 1995, London. Contemporary Eranos officials insist he was executed but provide no documentation in support.

11. They began to use it regularly from 1933 onward, Emma taking the large bedroom and CGJ sleeping in an alcove on a camp bed. Jaffé, in "CGJ and the Eranos Conferences," p. 201, mistakenly writes that the Jungs stayed in "Monte Verità (a villa on a nearby mountain)," the luxury hotel the Baron von der Heydt built and where others such as Toni Wolff and Barbara Hannah always stayed. McGuire, *Bollingen*, gives the most complete account of financing provided by the Bollingen Foundation for the continuation of the Eranos Foundation. See also McGuire's "The Arcane Summer School."

12. The title of an unpublished paper written by Olga Fröbe-Kapteyn, Ascona, De-

cember 1934, copy courtesy of William McGuire. Jay Livernois also provided a variant of this document, shorter, listing as supporters CGJ, Heinrich Zimmer, and Erwin Rousselle. The name J. W. Hauer was also typed, but his name was blacked out by Fröbe-Kapteyn.

13. The most informative article is McGuire's "Arcane Summer School."

14. Rosenbaum-Kroeber, *Monte Verità*, p. 118, writes that Buber lectured on the lawn: "Other course members recall that everyone reclined on the grass but Olga, for whom a chair was brought, on which she sat quite erect in the middle of the meadow."

15. The baron made an arranged marriage to the devoutly Catholic Baroness Vera von der Heydt, who separated from him and left Germany before World War II to move to England, where she became one of the most respected and well-beloved figures in analytical psychology. Earlier, she analyzed with CGJ and credited him with giving her the courage to make this enormous change in her life.

16. Riess, *Ascona*, pp. 92–93.

17. Bernard V. Bothmer found it and turned it over to local authorities, who discovered a photo of the baron wearing a Nazi emblem and his NSPD membership card. Information from William McGuire, private correspondence, January 4, 2002, giving details from his interview with Bothmer, May 20, 1979, New York. According to the diaries of Count Harry Kessler, *Berlin in Lights* (New York: Grove Press, 1999), pp. 407–8, the baron declared on December 9, 1931, that he was "no Nazi . . . certainly no anti-Semite, having far too many Jewish friends for that." As he saw no alternative but to deal with the Nazis, the baron suggested that he become a link between them in their dealings with the German government and private business and banking interests.

18. Riess, *Ascona*, p. 93.

19. Mary Bancroft, quoted in McGuire, *Bollingen*, pp. 27–28.

20. Ximena de Angulo Roelli, letter to William McGuire, March 5, 1979, graciously provided by both.

21. From a document entitled "Handwritten Notes by Olga Fröbe-Kapteyn, Probably 1958, from the Archives at Casa Gabriella." The copy was used by McGuire in his *Bollingen;* information within is also from Jay Livernois.

22. For a description of the "battle" that characterized their "relationship," see Jaffé, "Jung and Eranos," pp. 208ff.

23. Samuel Beckett to Thomas McGreevy, undated note, postmarked January 1935.

24. Mary de Rachewiltz (Pound's daughter), interview with the author, April 5, 1976. Cited in Deirdre Bair, *Samuel Beckett: A Biography* (New York: Harcourt, Brace, Jovanovich, 1978), p. 177.

25. Jung's lectures were originally published in book form as *Analytical Psychology: Its Theory and Practice; The Tavistock Lectures*, more commonly abbreviated as *The Tavistock Lectures*. Now in *CW*-18 as *The Tavistock Lectures: On the Theory and Practice of Analytical Psychology*. See the editorial note, pp. 3–4, for a capsule publishing history.

26. For further information about CGJ's important and lasting influence on Beckett, see Bair, *Samuel Beckett: A Biography*.

27. Bion attended all five of Jung's lectures and was among those who asked questions during the response period following lectures 1 (para. 55, p. 29) and 2 (paras. 135 and 137, pp. 65 and 66). He also became a leading influence in British Object Relations Theory, and to many scholars the most influential British analyst after Melanie Klein.

28. In *CW*-18, the lectures are untitled, but in para. 75, p. 36, CGJ states that these were the subjects of his first two lectures.
29. The first quote is from lecture 2, para. 97, p. 48; the rest are from lecture 3, para. 147, p. 71.
30. See Discussion following lecture 4, paras. 273–81, pp. 124–28.
31. Para. 275, p. 125.
32. Para. 276, p. 126.
33. Para. 277, p. 126.
34. Para. 279, p. 127.
35. Para 276, p. 126.
36. Lecture 5, para. 305, p. 135.
37. Para. 370, pp. 162–63. See also his letter to "N.," September 7, 1935, *CL*-1, pp. 197–98.
38. An outgrowth of "The Oxford Group," founded in 1908 by F. N. D. Buchman (hence called Buchmanites). He launched the "Moral Rearmament Movement" in 1938, whose international assemblies were held at Caux, near Montreux, Switzerland.
39. Lecture 5, para. 371, p. 163.
40. The following observations are based upon interviews with Dr. Joseph Henderson and Dr. Joseph Wheelwright, who were both in attendance; CGJ's correspondence with E. A. Bennet and H. G. Baynes, both in the Jung archives, ETH; private papers in the Toni Wolff family archives; the letters of Samuel Beckett to Thomas McGreevy, made available to me by the McGreevy estate in 1976; and a private correspondence with W. R. Bion, 1974 and 1976.
41. M. Esther Harding, "Seminar Dinner Speech," on the occasion of a dinner held in CGJ's honor by the Analytical Psychology Club of New York, October 25, 1937, unpublished, KML archives.
42. One person who took notes of his two sessions gave their time as 10 to 11 P.M.
43. Both Dr. Joseph Henderson and Dr. Joseph Wheelwright made the same observation in separate interviews. The private source in the previous note made a similar comment.
44. Cabot, *Diary*, 1940, quoting CGJ's description of Emma at age fifty-eight. He also said Emma had "a remarkable personality and extraordinary qualities, and was a great student." Also, in a diary entry for June 10, 1936, Cabot writes that she offered to accompany CGJ "and Miss Wolff to the U.S. on a ship." No other reference indicates that CGJ ever considered traveling with Toni to Yale and Harvard.
45. Kimball C. Elkins, Harvard University archivist to H. F. Ellenberger, January 31, 1967, HE/STA, wrote that Harvard conferred the honorary degree of Doctor of Science on "Karl [*sic*] Gustav Jung" on September 19, 1936. CGJ participated in the Tercentenary Conference of Arts and Sciences, and on September 7, in a symposium on the general subject of the factors determining human behavior, he delivered a paper entitled "Psychological Factors Determining Human Behavior." It was published with other papers in a book of the symposium's title by Harvard University Press in 1937. There, Jung is listed as "Charles Gustav Jung, Professor of Analytic Psychology, Technische Hochschule, Zürich."
46. CGJ to Henry Murray, September 10, 1935, *CL*-1, pp. 198–99.
47. CGJ to Jolande Jacobi, October 27, 1936, *CL*-1, p. 220. Reference was probably to *Psychologie und Alchemie*, not published until 1944 in book form, although a variety of material subsequently incorporated there appeared earlier as articles. No definitive study has yet been made to establish bibliographical chronology of some of the

still unpublished manuscripts in the ETH that appear to date from this time, so CGJ's reference remains vague.

48. Cabot, *Diary*, June 15, 1936.
49. Letters to Jerome D. Greene and W. G. Land of the Harvard Tercentenary Committee from (among others) Dr. W. Scott Polland of San Rafael, California; Mrs. Thomas L. (Isabel) Robinson of New York; Mrs. V. E. Kleven of Calgary, Canada; and Lt. Cmdr. John A. Gade, USN, Long Island, New York. Some of these persons communicated directly with CGJ.
50. For further information, see Henrietta Bancroft, "Bailey Island: The Contribution of a Place to Analytical Psychology," *Spring* (1983): 191–97; Alan Long, "Jung on Bailey Island," *The Times Record* (Brunswick, Maine), Friday, September 25, 1998; Claire Dewsnap, "A Tribute to Jung"; and miscellaneous documents pertaining to Esther Harding in the KML.
51. CGJ to Henry Murray, September 10, 1935, *CL*-1, pp. 198–99.
52. Cabot, *Diary*, June 15, 1936.
53. The "analyzed people" note is from Eleanor Bertine to CGJ, no date, ETH; his reply is February 23, 1936, also ETH.
54. Eventually, they sent him $1,500. The following year, when he lectured a second time, they sent him $3,200. These sums were in addition to payments made directly to him by patients with whom he had private analytic hours.
55. The quote is from Eleanor Bertine to CGJ, no date, ETH. Obviously he saw everyone privately who wanted to be treated, for Bertine wrote on November 2, 1937, to say she was sending a list of the people who had not yet paid and was writing to tell them to send their checks directly to him.
56. McGuire's introduction to "The 2,000,000-Year-Old Man," *CGJ Speaking*, Bollingen Series 97 (Princeton: Princeton Univ. Press, 1977), p. 88, says CGJ "prepared a press release, devoted chiefly to setting forth his political — or as he insisted, his nonpolitical — position." The text he alludes to is published in *CW*-18, paras. 1300–1304, pp. 564–65, and is quoted here below. The *New York Times* reporter later interviewed CGJ at the Hotel Ambassador for an article entitled "'Roosevelt Great,' Is Jung's Analysis," published Sunday, October 4, 1936.
57. Paul Roazen conducted archival sleuthing in the Harvard Tercentenary archives in Pusey Library on my behalf. Much that follows is based on his findings.
58. M. Léon to Jerome D. Greene, August 26, 1936, in the Harvard Tercentenary archives. Léon added that Dr. Frederick Peterson, professor of neurology at Columbia University School of Medicine and former colleague of CGJ at the Burghölzli, would be willing to verify his allegations against Jung. To date, there is no record that Peterson ever did, or that he expressed such views in private correspondence or a public forum.
59. Jerome D. Greene to Maurice Léon, August 31, 1936.
60. Maurice Léon to Jerome D. Greene, September 1, 1936.
61. *CGJ Speaking*, p. 88.
62. In a letter to Cary Baynes, April 15, 1937, ETH, CGJ commented on FDR's attempt to "diminish" the "unsurpassable grandeur" of the U.S. Supreme Court: "Roosevelt is, as I blasphemously said, an American edition of a dictator and as such, he never would stand an authority above himself." Here again, he compared FDR to Mussolini and Hitler, saying "the future is on his side" against the Supreme Court, as it was with Hitler in "the fight against the churches."
63. Cabot, *Diary*, December 14, 1936. CGJ's views were shared by another Harvard honoree, the Italian fascist Dr. Corrado Gini of the University of Rome, who said U.S. dictatorship was "almost inevitable" (interview by Richard O. Boyer, "U.S.

Dictator 'Almost Inevitable,' Fascist Tells Harvard Scholars," *Boston Herald*, September 10, 1936; Boyer noted that Gini echoed the remarks of Princeton professor Edward Samuel Corwin, who said much the same in his Tercentenary lecture).

64. These words may be Cabot's, but she attributes them to CGJ in *Diary*, December 14, 1936.

65. Dr. John Weir Perry, interview with the author, July 22, 1995, Larkspur, California.

66. Among Perry's publications is *The Self in Psychotic Process* (Dallas: *Spring* Publications, 1987), to which CGJ contributed the Preface.

67. Cabot, *Diary*, p. 135.

68. From the Tercentenary book (see n. 45, above).

69. See President James Bryant Conant, "The Day It Rained," in *College in a Yard*, ed. Brooks Atkinson (1957), in the Harvard Tercentenary archives, pp. 17–21.

70. George E. Gifford Jr., ed., *Psychoanalysis, Psychotherapy and the New England Medical Scene, 1894–1944* (New York: Science History Publications/USA, 1978), p. 391.

71. Paul Roazen, in conversation with the author and by fax, December 1, 2000, cited Helene Deutsche as the source of this anecdote. Deutsche was a close friend of the Cobb family, and apparently Cobb, who was extremely reserved and discreet, took uncharacteristic delight in telling this story for many years afterward.

72. Elizabeth Cobb to the Tercentenary Committee.

73. Of all the seminars presented, CGJ's drew the largest audience. The source is *Harvard Tercentenary Conference of Arts and Sciences, August 31–September 12, 1936*. CGJ lectured on Monday, September 7, in Sanders Theatre at 10:15 A.M., where his name was incorrectly given as "Charles" Gustav Jung. Professor Daniel Aaron, Harvard class of 1943, remembered how he and poet Charles Olson attended the lecture, and Olson "questioned Jung on the mandala figure in *Moby Dick* — a significant moment for me" (see "The Great Good Place," *Harvard Magazine*, September–October 2001, p. 49).

74. Roazen, *Freud and His Followers* (New York: Random House, 1975), p. 296, cites Henry Murray as his source for this anecdote. Murray apparently repeated it widely, as Joseph Wheelwright (who was then at St. Bartholomew's Hospital in London) and C. A. Meier (who was in Zürich) both told it to me during interviews for this book.

75. Roazen, in conversation with the author, December 1, 2000, repeated that the information in *Freud and His Followers*, p. 296, came in a letter to him from Henry Murray, September 1972. Roazen agreed with me that this account is highly speculative, as Erikson was then a very junior member of the faculty and unlikely to have such definitive influence on the committee. Dr. George E. Gardner, Ph.D., M.D., professor of psychiatry at Harvard Medical School and psychiatrist-in-chief at Children's Hospital Medical Center from 1947 to 1953, takes credit for Erikson's appointment: "[Erikson's] appointment at Harvard . . . was engineered by others, but initiated by me" (see Gifford, *Psychoanalysis*, p. 391). The Harvard Tercentenary archives that Paul Roazen and I consulted do not contain any information that might settle the matter one way or the other.

76. E. G. Boring to Jerome D. Greene, October 23, 1934. The others nominated were Karl S. Lashley of the University of Chicago and Wolfgang Köhler of Berlin, who was then the William James Lecturer at Harvard.

77. *The Tercentenary of Harvard College*, p. 96.

78. Fowler McCormick to CGJ, May 7, 1937, ETH. McCormick says he owed his invitation to "Professor Shapley."

79. Of the breakfast, Douglas, in *Translate This Darkness: The Life of Christiana Morgan* (New York: Simon and Schuster, 1993), p. 216, says Josephine Murray "left no record of her feelings [for CGJ], but it seems as if her discretion as well as her good manners and good heart made the meeting pass uneventfully."

80. From the Harvard Tercentenary archives.

81. Fowler McCormick, HCL interview.

82. Henrietta Bancroft, "Bailey Island," p. 196.

83. Fowler McCormick, HCL interview.

84. From Dr. Eleanor Bertine's "toast" to CGJ and Emma at the Plaza Hotel dinner, October 2, 1936, in the archives of the KML.

85. CGJ to Abraham Aaron Roback, September 29, 1936, *CL*-1, p. 219.

86. For Jane Pratt's introduction to the printed Bailey Island Seminars and CGJ's remarks following the Plaza Hotel dinner, see *CGJ Speaking*, "Is Analytical Psychology a Religion?," pp. 94–98.

87. Information about Paul and Mary Mellon is from the archives of Paul Mellon, specifically Paul Mellon's and Mary Mellon's correspondence with CGJ; the archives of William McGuire and Paul Mellon, both made available by their owners. Mary Mellon contacted CGJ on February 24, 1936, to ask for an appointment. He replied on March 2, 1936, to say that his schedule was full and she (they) would have to work with one of his assistants if they came to Zürich. They did not actually go to Zürich until the spring of 1938, when they both saw CGJ. Olivier Bernier provided information about Ann and Erlo van Waveren.

88. See Barbara Hannah, *Jung: His Life and Work, A Biographical Memoir* (Boston: Shambhala, 1991), pp. 237–38, for a version of their stay in London. Information about St. Bartholomew's is from interviews with J. Henderson and J. Wheelwright. Correspondence between CGJ and Peter Baynes, ETH, makes specific references to personal itineraries and professional engagements.

89. In interviews with both, Dr. Wheelwright credited CGJ with their enrollment in medical school, and Dr. Henderson stressed that his enrollment came from his dreams and that CGJ did not make this recommendation to him personally. Dr. Thomas B. Kirsch, in an e-mail of October 9, 2002, elaborated: Wheelwright told him that CGJ advised Wheelwright to go to medical school because he was "so undisciplined." Dr. Kirsch believes that it was "a much more individual thing" with CGJ, who "did not give very much advice." In Begg BBC-3, Wheelwright described an analytic session: "'You know, I've had a brainwave — I'd like to be an analyst or a therapist.' And [Jung] threw his hands up and he said, 'Oh, God, this happens all the time, it's just part of the transference.'"

90. See chapter 29 for full details. Internal evidence is from CGJ and Peter Baynes's correspondence, ETH.

91. October 18, 1936; reprinted in part in *CGJ Speaking*, "The Psychology of Dictatorship," pp. 91–93.

92. November 9, 1936, and December 1936.

93. CGJ to Jolande Jacobi, October 27, 1926, *CL*-1, p. 220.

94. CGJ was Yale's second choice; the invitation was first offered to Professor Norman Kaye Smith of the University of Edinburgh, who declined in a letter to President Charles Seymour on December 7, 1936 (presidential archives, Sterling Library, Yale).

95. From correspondence between William McGuire and The Hon. Dr. S. H. Senn, vice-chancellor of the University of Calcutta, June 1972 (from McGuire's private archives).

96. Information is from Esther Harding to CGJ, July 4, 1937, and September 8, 1937, CGJ archives, ETH. Philip Wylie's archives at Princeton University contain a 1937 mimeographed announcement that CGJ would give five lectures on "The Individuation Process as Shown in Dreams" on October 16, 17, 18, and 25 and 26.

97. McGuire, *Bollingen*, p. 18; See also *CL*-19 for full references to Dell's translations of CGJ's texts.

98. Wylie, in a letter March 11, 1967, to William McGuire (then managing editor of the Bollingen Series, at work on *CL*), Princeton University, said CGJ and Strong had probably corresponded extensively. By the time *CL* was under way, Strong was dead and his widow claimed to have no correspondence, saying it was apparently lost or destroyed. In Philip Wylie to William McGuire, September 7, 1971, Wylie repeats that CGJ and Strong had a "constant . . . irregular . . . but ongoing correspondence."

99. Eleanor Bertine was in charge of the schedule for private sessions. She set a fee of $20. Eleanor Bertine to Philip Wylie, September 8 and October 30, 1937; Wylie replied on January 2, 1938 (all in the Wylie archives, Princeton University), saying CGJ had been his houseguest, so he sent his check with a personal letter directly to CGJ.

100. CGJ to Philip Wylie, February 22, 1938, Wylie archives, Princeton University. In the same letter, CGJ thanks Wylie for his "friendly cheque." In subsequent correspondence, it appears they had, at minimum, analytic discussions, if not actual sessions of therapy.

101. Philip Wylie to William McGuire, December 24, 1966, Wylie archives, Princeton University.

102. McGuire expended a great deal of time and effort trying to verify this story but was unable to corroborate or disprove it. On April 10, 1967 (Philip Wylie archives, Princeton University), he wrote to Wylie to give the versions that appear in Barbara Hannah's *Life and Work*, pp. 211 and 289. Wylie claimed that CGJ had written about it in a letter to him, but no letter currently in the Philip Wylie archives contains mention of it.

103. Barbara Hannah among them, in *Life and Work*, p. 211 and n. c; and in interviews with Marie-Louise von Franz and C. A. Meier. Jung's grandchildren have never heard any version of this tale, nothing in Toni Wolff's archives indicates that she did, and Jolande Jacobi (who gave detailed reports of everything else about CGJ) never alluded to it.

104. Correspondence of Yale University Secretary of the Corporation Carl Lohmann, and unidentified pastor of the United Church, Lohmann papers, Sterling Library, Yale University.

105. From three press releases by the Yale University News Bureau: "'Voice' of Dreams Called Superior," October 20, 1937; "Jung Views Dreams as a Key to 'Isms,'" October 21, 1937; and "'Shadow' Carried by All, Says Jung," October 22, 1937. See also the editorial note in *CW*-11, *Psychology and Religion: West and East*.

106. Kenneth MacKenzie and Elaine Lewis provided information about CGJ at Yale.

107. Grinnell described CGJ's visit in "Jung at Yale," *Spring* (1976): 155–65. In his author's note, he is past president of the Italian Association for the Study of Analytical Psychology, former associate professor of philosophy at Stanford and of Medieval studies at Berkeley. He later published articles and a book about alchemy.

108. Most of the persons who told me the story cited Barbara Hannah as their source. But as Hannah conflates so many things about the two American universities (such as her description of a Harvard hostess who "dissolved in tears" [p. 236], when it was actually Mrs. French at Yale), I discount the anecdotes and rely on the evidence

of the Yale University archives. In this case, I cite three press releases from the News Bureau.

109. Cabot, *Diary*, 1938.

110. Among those who defended him in *The Saturday Review of Literature*.

111. The *Yale Daily News* printed only the News Bureau press releases. No reporter, either from Yale or the local or national press, interviewed him.

112. CGJ to Fowler McCormick, September 10, 1937, ETH. Here he invites McCormick to visit him at Yale, where he will be "less busy" than in New York.

113. Hannah, *Life and Work*, p. 241, is one source; a one-paragraph draft in the Wolff family archives that appears to be an unsent paragraph of a letter, probably written by Susi Trüb, is another. Hannah says Toni "was always convinced" that CGJ became ill because he was not inoculated prior to the trip; the draft states: "He left in such haste . . . so stubborn in his belief that nothing could assail him."

114. In several versions of the *Protocols*, CGJ writes that he wanted very much to go to India for an adjunct reason: the voyages out and back each took four weeks, for a total of eight, when no one could reach him.

115. As of 2003, their itinerary is still not definitely known. Varying accounts are given by the principal sources, among them Hannah's *Life and Work*; Jaffé's *Jung: Word and Image*, Bollingen Series 97.2 (Princeton: Princeton Univ. Press, 1979); *MDR*; Fowler McCormick's HCL interview; private archives of William McGuire; correspondence from contemporary officials of various Indian universities who were unable to find documentation in their files relating to CGJ's visit; various ETH correspondence, esp. to and from Fowler McCormick; and information provided by the *Erbengemeinschaft CGJ*.

116. In some *Protocols*, this passage is dated October 16, 1957, and is handwritten by CGJ. It is also crossed out with a line through it, but it is not clear if by CGJ or Aniela Jaffé, even though there is an unrelated marginal notation made by her. In other *Protocols*, this passage is absent.

117. Fowler McCormick had a different impression. In his HCL interview he said: "If one of the purposes of Jung's trip was to see to what extent he could come in contact with some of the wise men of India and gain an increased impression of what was meant by the wisdom of India, I think it must be said that on the whole that was not rewarded to any very large extent."

118. Fowler McCormick, HCL interview.

119. Helen Drutt English, fax from New Delhi to the author, January 3, 1997.

120. CGJ to Henry Murray, October 6, 1938, *CL-2*, p. xxxiv. See also F. Robinson, *Love's Story Told: A Life of Henry Murray* (Cambridge, Mass.: Harvard Univ. Press, 1992), p. 423, n. to p. 230.

121. Fowler McCormick, HCL interview.

122. *Protocols*, CGJ's English in the German, as well as his emphasis in all versions.

123. At this point in the *Protocols*, the passage ends abruptly and a marginal note reads "this page out?" It is not clear if Jung ever resumed speaking about this.

124. His emphasis, his English in all German versions of the *Protocols*.

CHAPTER 29: FALLING AFOUL OF HISTORY

1. To write the following account, I have consulted the following publications, documents, and archives: Michael Vannoy Adams, *The Multicultural Imagination: "Race," Color, and the Unconscious* (London and New York: Routledge, 1996); Pierre Ayçoberry, *The Social History of the Third Reich, 1933–45* (New York: New Press, 1999); K. Brecht, V. Friedrich, L. Hermanns, I. J. Kaminer, D. H. Juelich, eds., *Here Life Goes On in a Most Peculiar Way: Psychoanalysis Before and After 1933* (Ham-

burg: Michael Kellner Verlag, 1985); Geoffrey Cocks, "Psychoanalyse, Psychotherapie und Nationalsozialismus," *Psyche: Zeitschrift für Psychoanalyse und ihre Anwendungen* 37: 1057–1106, "Repressing, Remembering, Working Through: German Psychiatry, Psychotherapy, Psychoanalysis and the 'Missed Resistance' in the Third Reich," in *Resistance Against the Third Reich: Supplement, Journal of Modern History* 64: 204–16, *Psychotherapy in the Third Reich: The Göring Institute* (New Brunswick, N.J.: Transaction, 1997), and *Treating Mind and Body* (New Brunswick, N.J.: Transaction, 1998); Lucy S. Dawidowicz, *The War Against the Jews: 1933–45* (New York: Bantam Books, 1986), and *The Holocaust and the Historians* (Cambridge, Mass.: Harvard Univ. Press, 1993); Allen W. Dulles, *Germany's Underground: The Anti-Nazi Resistance* (New York: Da Capo Press, 2000); also private archives of the Dulles family and correspondence between Dulles and CGJ; Henri F. Ellenberger, *The Discovery of the Unconscious* (New York: Basic Books, 1981); Sanford Gifford, "Between Two Wars: Psychoanalysis in Europe, 1918–38," *History of Psychiatry* 17, no. 3 (1994): 649–65; Eileen B. Goggin and James E. Goggin, *Death of a "Jewish Science": Psychoanalysis in the Third Reich* (W. Lafayette, Ind.: Purdue Univ. Press, 2000); R. Haymond, "On CGJ: Psycho-social Basis of Morality During the Nazi Era," *Journal of Psychology and Judaism* 6, no. 2 (spring/summer 1982); Aniela Jaffé, "CGJ and National Socialism," in *From the Life and Work of CGJ* (Einsiedeln: Daimon Verlag, 1989); Marion A. Kaplan, *Between Dignity and Despair: Jewish Life in Nazi Germany* (New York: Oxford Univ. Press, 1998); Thomas B. Kirsch, *The Jungians: A Comparative and Historical Perspective* (London and Philadelphia: Routledge, 2000); Robert J. Lifton, *The Nazi Doctors: Medical Killing and the Psychology of Genocide* (New York: Basic Books, 1986); Regine Lockot, *Erinnern und Durcharbeiten: Zur Geschichte der Psychoanalyse und Psychotherapie im Nationalsozialismus* (Frankfurt: Fischer Verlag, 1985), and *Die Reinigung der Psychoanalyse: Die DPG im Spiegel von Dokumenten und Zeitzeugen (1933–45)* (Tübingen: edition diskord, 1994); A. Maidenbaum and S. Martin, eds., *Lingering Shadows: Jungians, Freudians, and Anti-Semitism* (Boston: Shambhala, 1991); Mary Ann Mattoon, ed., *Paris 89: Proceedings of the Eleventh International Congress for Analytical Psychology, August 28–September 2, 1989* (Einsiedeln: Daimon Verlag, 1991); Wilhelm Roepke, *The Solution of the German Problem* (New York: G. P. Putnam and Sons, 1946); and Andrew Samuels, *Jung and the Post Jungians* (1985), *Essays on Contemporary Events* (1988), and *The Political Psyche* (1993) (all London and New York: Routledge), "Jung and Anti-Semitism," *Continuum* 1, no. 1 (autumn 1990), "Jung's Birthday Greetings to Professor Göring: A *Zentralblatt* Piece Not in the *CW*," *JAP* 38, no. 4 (1993), "New Material Concerning Jung, Anti-Semitism, and the Nazis," *JAP* 38 (1993), (with John Allan) "There Is No Such Thing as a Liberal Dictatorship," *JAP* 37, no. 2 (1992), and "Reply to Farhad Dalal, 'Jung, a Racist,'" *British Journal of Psychotherapy* 4, no. 3 (1988).

2. CGJ to B. Cohen, March 26, 1934, *CL*-1, pp. 154–55. Cohen was the author of "Ist CGJ 'gleichgeschaltet'?" (Has CGJ Conformed to Nazi Ideology?), *Israelitisches Wochenblatt für die Schweiz* 35, no. 11 (March 16, 1934).

3. Samuels, *The Political Psyche*, p. 289.

4. In German, this English term "conformed" and the German *Gleichschaltung* are defined in different ways, some of them extreme. A typical usage is that given by E. B. and J. E. Goggin in *Death of a "Jewish Science"*: "The policy . . . or coordination of how individuals and institutions related to each other within National Socialist Germany. . . . In reality [it] meant bringing the people and institutions into line with Nazi rule." Barbara Hannah, in *Jung: His Life and Work, A Biographical Memoir* (Boston: Shambhala, 1991), p. 221, accepts the definition as given by Dr. Gustav Bally: a "reorganization" that results in "unification," that is, "the expulsion of all

members who are not pure German nationals and of all Jews." Pierre Ayçoberry, *Social History of the Third Reich*, pp. 106–7, translates it as "'falling into line,' . . . a current colloquialism, so we may as well stick with it." He adds that the term includes "the sense of discipline the new masters now imposed that was more or less willingly accepted by various preexisting groups," and "was achieved [with individuals] by terror, intimidation, or blandishments."

5. James Kirsch, "Carl Gustav Jung and the Jews: The Real Story," *Lingering Shadows* (Boston: Shambhala, 1991), p. 82. Kirsch is quoting from C. F. Meyer, *Homo sum* (Leipzig, 1872).

6. From a review of Jeremy Bernstein's *Power and Politics: The Psychology of Soviet-American Partnership* (Boston: Shambhala, 1989), by Russell Jacoby in the *Los Angeles Times;* quoted by Bernstein in "Opening Remarks," *Paris 89,* p. 465.

7. Its eminence was largely due to the clinical and organizational abilities of Karl Abraham and the initial financing of Max Eitingon. See Roazen, *Helene Deutsch: A Psychoanalyst's Life* (New Brunswick, N.J.: Transaction, 1992), pp. 183–84, and *Meeting Freud's Family* (Amherst: Univ. of Massachusetts Press, 1993), p. 109. Also, E. B. and J. E. Goggin, *Death of a "Jewish Science,"* pp. 9–10 and 13.

8. See CGJ to Oluf Brüel, March 19, 1934, *CL-1,* pp. 151–53, for CGJ's views.

9. Geoffrey Cocks, "CGJ and German Psychotherapy, 1933–40: A Research Note," *Spring* (1979): 221–31, notes that the German Medical Society for Psychotherapy refused to recognize the newly founded group.

10. Cocks, *Psychotherapy in the Third Reich,* p. 48, notes that the membership was diverse, ranging from "revisionists like the neo-Freudian Horney, [to] the almost indefinable Groddeck, the brilliant Reich, and the intensely intellectual rebel Schultz-Hencke." He posits that "there might well have been one or more genuine splits in, and even secessions from, the society during the process of attempting to resolve the powerful differences in theory, practice, and professionalization that dogged it before the Hitler era."

11. Kretschmer (b. 1888) directed the Universitätsnervenklinik in Marburg from 1926 to 1946 and held the same position from 1946 to 1959 in Tübingen. Lockot, *Erinnern und Durcharbeiten,* pp. 74ff., notes that Kretschmer posited a "rational system" of insights into psychological character traits and illnesses that he based on physiognomy. Kretschmer, in his *Gestalten und Gedanken* (Stuttgart: Georg Thieme, 1963), p. 157, writes that his theories were so far at variance with National Socialist racial theory that Goebbels, who found his entire book *Der geniale Mensch* "inappropriate," had it banned.

12. Lockot, *Erinnern und Durcharbeiten,* p. 74.

13. The CGJ Gesellschaft was registered as No. 95 VR 7.874 in the *Amstgericht* (district court) of Charlottenburg, Berlin. The chair was Frau Eva Moritz, and members of the governing council were Frau Kümmerlé (née Richter) and Herr Kranefeldt. General members were L. Boehm, H. Wertmann, A. Weizsäcker, L. Weizsäcker, M. Geitel, H. Kranefeldt, and a person who signed with an indecipherable signature. The group was still intact on November 19, 1939, when the governing council was composed of Moritz, Kümmerlé, L. Weizsäcker, and Brüning, and the membership included "Dubois Reymond, Delius, Krell, Hübner, Jungmann-Hermann, von Staehr, and Wünsche. Käthe Bügler's name was listed in some of the intervening minutes, but as a half-Jew, she quietly removed herself sometime in the mid-1930s, citing "unpleasant experiences in the Göringinstitut" (from the unpublished minutes of the Ausschuss [committee] für Psychotherapie, a small group of German Jungians that Bügler founded after the war). All the information given above is found in various archives of the Berlin Document Center and also in

Lockot, *Errinern und Durcharbeiten*, p. 51, where she lists other members as von König-Fachsenfeld, von Kujawa, Lindner, Lübbeke, May, von Prosch, and Stackmann. See also Kirsch, *The Jungians*, pp. 127–28.

14. For a thorough scholarly compilation of *völkisch* literature in nineteenth- and twentieth-century Germany as it concerns Jung, see Richard Noll's *The Aryan Christ* (New York: Random House, 1997) and, to a lesser extent, *The Jung Cult* (Princeton: Princeton Univ. Press, 1994). The preeminent historian on the subject is George L. Mosse in *The Crisis of German Ideology* (New York: Schocken Books, 1987) and *Masses and Man* (1980; rpt. Detroit: Wayne State Univ. Press, 1987). See also Petteri Pietikainen, "The Volk and Its Unconscious: Jung, Hauer and the 'German Revolution,'" *Journal of Contemporary History* 35, no. 4, pp. 523–39. Pietikainen, p. 524, defines "*völkisch* ideology" as "originally an ultra-nationalist reaction against the dominant social, political and cultural trends of the 1870s and 1880s." John Patrick Diggins called this last source to my attention.

15. Pietikainen, "Jung, Hauer, and the 'German Revolution,'" p. 528.

16. For further information about Hauer, see Margerete Dierks, *Jakob Wilhelm Hauer, 1881–1962* (Heidelberg, 1986), a biography that contains a full bibliography of his writings. See also Hauer, "Origin of the German Faith Movement," in Hauer, K. Heim, and K. Adam, *Germany's New Religion: The German Faith Movement*, trans. T. Scott-Craig and R. Davies (London, 1937); and Sonu Shamdasani, ed., *The Psychology of Kundalini Yoga: Notes of the Seminar Given in 1952 by CGJ*, Bollingen Series 99 (Princeton: Princeton Univ. Press, 1996).

17. Published as *The Psychology of Kundalini Yoga*.

18. Hauer, in *Germany's New Religion*, pp. 29–30.

19. Pietikainen, "Jung, Hauer, and the 'German Revolution,'" p. 527.

20. In her undated statement, c. 1933–34, Olga Fröbe struck Hauer's name from among her supporters for the founding of Eranos, leaving CGJ, Heinrich Zimmer, and Erwin Rousselle.

21. Originally published in *Schweizerland: Monatshefte für Schweizer Art und Arbeit* (Zürich) 4, no. 9 (1918): 464–72, and no. 11–12 (1918): 548–58; in *CW*-10, paras. 1–48, pp. 3–28.

22. *CW*-10, paras. 17–18, p. 13.

23. Catharine Rush Cabot, *Diaries*, in Jane Cabot Reid, *Jung, My Mother, and I: The Analytic Diaries of Catharine Rush Cabot* (Einsiedeln: Daimon Verlag, 2000).

24. Cabot, *Diaries*, p. 96.

25. Original source is Oswald Bumke, *Die Psychoanalyse und ihre Kinder. Eine Auseinandersetzung mit Freud, Adler und Jung*, 2d ed. (Berlin: Julius Springer, 1938), p. 123. Cited in Cocks, *Psychotherapy in the Third Reich*, p. 109; and Lockot, *Errinern*, pp. 74–75.

26. Such an exchange is alluded to in Cocks, *Psychotherapy in the Third Reich*; Martine Galland, "Jung's Attitude During the Second World War in the Light of the Historical and Professional Context," *JAP* 39 (1994); and Lockot, *Errinern*, but no specifics are given. No letters from 1933 are in *CL* or, at the present time, in the ETH archives. No letters have yet been found in archives pertaining either to the International Society or the *Zentralblatt*.

27. Ronald W. Clark, *Freud: The Man and the Cause* (New York: Random House, 1980), p. 489, who reports that Freud, when he learned about it, said, "I burn in the best of company."

28. Lifton, *The Nazi Doctors*, pp. 42–45. Lockot, *Errinern*, cites Kretschmer's students as "protecting" him by setting up a system in which he transferred authority to his assistant, Professor Dr. Mauz, while he worked only treating patients admitted to a

sanatorium by other doctors. Mauz was identified after the war as one of the seven psychiatrists who were early experts on how to kill the mentally insane. See F. K. Kaul, *Nazimordaktion T4: Volk und Gesundheit* (Berlin, 1973), p. 70.

29. K. Brecht et al., *Here Life Goes On*, p. 72.

30. The first quote is to Olüf Bruel from a letter of March 19, 1934, *CL*-1, p. 153; the second is to B. Cohen, March 26, 1934, p. 155.

31. Ernst Kretschmer, letter to H. Thomae, quoted in "Die Neo-Psychoanalyse Schultz-Henckes," *Psyche* 1 (1963–64): 63; also Lockot, *Erinnern*, p. 75.

32. Cocks discusses these procedures throughout *Psychotherapy in the Third Reich;* Lockot summarizes them succinctly in *Errinern*, pp. 8–9; and Gallard also elaborates on them in "Jung's Attitude," pp. 203–32. Eitingon moved to Palestine, where he lived for the rest of his life. After the war, Boehm wrote a personal (and some would say self-serving) history of psychoanalysis in Germany between 1933 and 1945, in which he insisted that every concession made to the Nazis by him or anyone else connected with the BPI was only after direct consultation with Freud and/or Jones ("Bericht über die Ereignisse von 1933 bis zum Amsterdamer Kongress im August 1951," *Schriften zur Psychoanalyse* [Munich, 1978]).

33. Letter quoted in Lockot, *Erinnern*, pp. 76–77.

34. Kretschmer was echoing the views of Wladimir Eliasberg, who left Germany in 1933 after warning that it was the duty and responsibility of his and other professions to impose their standards on the nation's policies, not the other way around (*Arzt und Propaganda: ein Stück medizinische Soziologie aus der ärtzlichen Wirklichkeit* [Vienna: Saturn-Verlag, 1936]).

35. To Olüf Bruel, March 19, 1934, *CL*-1, pp. 152–53.

36. Private archive, cited earlier (author's translation).

37. CGJ to Johann Heinrich Schulz, June 9, 1933, *CL*-1, p. 124.

38. Their joust continued until Göring was appointed chairman of the *Gleichschaltung* society on September 15, 1933. Lockot refers to "the power of [von Hattingberg's] family name" and says also that his nomination carried significant weight (*Errinern*, p. 80). See Cocks, *Psychotherapy in the Third Reich*, chapter 3, for biographical portraits of these and other analysts who figured during CGJ's presidency. Cocks describes von Hattingberg as "an enthusiastic and capable eclectic" and Schultz as "nothing less than an ecumenicist" (p. 72).

39. Lucy Heyer-Grote almost became CGJ's first biographer (see chapter 38). In her HCL interview, she cites G. R. Heyer's embrace of Nazism as the main reason for their postwar divorce. For further information, see also Lockot, *Die Reinigung der Psychoanalyse*, pp. 119–20; and Cocks, *Psychotherapy in the Third Reich*, pp. 60–62, and esp. n. 44, p. 262.

40. Cocks, *Psychotherapy in the Third Reich*, p. 61. Information from the Eranos archives provided by Jay Livernois shows that Heyer acted as a double agent: while openly espousing Nazi policies, he helped Jung and others funnel money into Germany for Jewish doctors. By 1938, when other Nazi sympathizers had been expressly disinvited to Eranos by the rabidly anti-Nazi Olga Fröbe, she still listed Heyer on the program.

41. See, for example, Cimbal to Göring, July 21, 1933, quoted in Lockot, *Erinnern*, p. 91. Some correspondence is in the ETH, other correspondence is in the papers of the *Zentralblatt*. Some is in the ETH among the C. A. Meier archives, and some is loosely filed in the Berlin Document Center. I am grateful to Gottfried Hauer, Andrew Samuels, and Thomas B. Kirsch, who assisted me with these materials.

42. A. von Muralt, "C. G. Jungs Stellung im Nationalsozialismus," *Schweizer Annalen*, Aarau (1946–47): 692 (author's translation).

43. Cimbal to Göring, July 21, 1933.
44. Cimbal to Göring, August 7, 1933, quoted in Lockot, *Erinnern*, p. 92.
45. Cimbal to CGJ, August 28, 1933. Quoted in Lockot, *Erinnern*, p. 92, not in *CL*.
46. Cimbal to Göring, August 26, 1933, quoted in Lockot, *Erinnern*, p. 92.
47. Cimbal to Göring, September 3, 1933, quoted in Lockot, *Erinnern*, p. 92.
48. Cimbal to Göring, September 3, 1933, quoted in Lockot, *Erinnern*, p. 93.
49. See Hannah, *Life and Work*, chapter 11. See also William McGuire, ed., *CGJ Speaking*, Bollingen Series 97 (Princeton: Princeton Univ. Press, 1977), "An Interview on Radio Berlin," Introduction and nn. 1 and 2, pp. 59–60.
50. Hannah, *Life and Work*, p. 210.
51. Hannah, *Life and Work*, pp. 210–11.
52. *Berliner Börsenzeitung*, May 14, 1933 (author's translation).
53. McGuire, *CGJ Speaking*, pp. 59–66. Lockot, *Erinnern*, pp. 91ff., writes that Jung adapted his answers completely to the aphorisms of the interviewer, leading "everyone [to be] under the impression that Jung supported his [von Weizäcker's] personal view. Those engaged in Nationalsocialism would read between the lines that he was sympathetic to Hitler; the opponents of the regime would happily extract Jung's remarks as a plea for a responsible autonomous leadership" (author's translation).
54. CGJ to Max Guggenheim, *CL*-1, March 28, 1934, p. 156.
55. CGJ to B. Cohen, March 26, 1934, *CL*-1, p. 154.
56. I refer to his letters to Guggenheim, *CL*-1, March 28, 1934, and to Mary Mellon, September 24, 1945, made available by Paul Mellon; not in *CL* but portions printed in Andrew Samuels, "Jung, Anti-Semitism, and the Nazis," pp. 463–70.
57. CGJ to Guggenheim, *CL*-1, March 28, 1934.
58. CGJ to Mary Conover Mellon, September 24, 1945. See also Andrew Samuels, "Jung, Anti-Semitism, and the Nazis," p. 466, for the full text of CGJ's letter; not in *CL*.
59. For differing interpretations of Göring's role, see Cocks, *Psychotheraphy in the Third Reich*, pp. 110–21; Lockot, *Erinnern*, pp. 93–94; and Goggin and Goggin, *Death of a "Jewish Science,"* pp. 27–29.
60. *Zentralblatt* 6 (1933).
61. From the "Report of the Recording Secretary [W. Cimbal] Concerning the Continuation of the General Medical Societies for Psychotherapy: The Preliminary Statement," *Zentralblatt für Psychotherapie und ihre Grenzgebiete* 6 (1933) (author's translation).
62. CGJ to Rudolf Allers, November 23, 1933, *CL*-1, pp. 131–32.
63. This description was provided by the editors of *CL*-1, p. 131.
64. Matthias Göring to C. A. Meier, November 30, 1935, from the general correspondence of the International Society, some of which is in the ETH, some in the Berlin Document Center, and some in other private archives. I am grateful to Gottfried Hauer, Andrew Samuels, and Thomas B. Kirsch for their help in amassing the collection I have used in this book.
65. CGJ to Rudolf Allers, November 23, 1933, *CL*-1, pp. 131–32.
66. CGJ to Poul Bjerre and CGJ to Alphons Maeder, both January 22, 1934, *CL*-1, pp. 135–38. Bjerre did found a Swedish chapter, but not until 1936; Maeder did not join (among others) CGJ, K. von Sury, C. A. Meier, K. Binswanger, and G. A. Farner, who organized the Schweizerische Gesellschaft für praktische Psychologie.
67. Freud to Max Eitingon, March 21, 1933, in Brecht et al., *Here Life Goes On*, p. 112.
68. The term "Freud's Rottweiler" is from a letter to the *Times Literary Supplement* by James Lieberman (December 15, 2000), referring to a review of Louis Breger's *Freud:*

Darkness in the Midst of Vision and Lesley Cha's *The Secret Artist: A Close Reading of Sigmund Freud* by Ritchie Robinson ("A Case of Pen Envy," October 27, 2000).

69. E. James Lieberman, *Acts of Will: The Life and Work of Otto Rank* (Amherst: Univ. of Massachusetts Press, 1993), p. 407. Lieberman is discussing Jones's "startling anti-Jewish bias" as shown throughout his 1945 essay "The Psychology of the Jewish Question"; reprinted in vol. 2 of E. Jones, *Essays in Applied Psycho-analysis* (London: Hogarth Press, 1951), and in *Psycho-myth, Psycho-history* (New York: Stonehill Books, 1974), 1: 284–300.

70. Jones to Benedeck, December 1, 1933, in Brecht et al., *Here Life Goes On*, p. 136.

71. Felix Boehm, memorandum of December 4, 1935, in Brecht et al., *Here Life Goes On*, p. 137.

72. By spring 1936, the DPG's headquarters at Wichmannstrasse 10 had been appropriated for headquarters of the Deutsche Institut für Psychologische Forschung und Psychotherapie, the official name of the Göring Institute.

73. See Goggin and Goggin, *Death of a "Jewish Science,"* pp. 154–56; Cocks, *Psychotherapy in the Third Reich*, p. 157; Lockot, *Erinnern*, pp. 151–53; and Brecht et al., *Here Life Goes On*, p. 115.

74. Ernest Jones, *The Life and Work of Sigmund Freud* (London: Hogarth Press, 1957), 3: 186. Jones wrote this in 1957, still intent on justifying his and Freud's action. P. Loewenberg, in his Foreword to Cocks's *Treating Mind and Body*, p. ix, writes: "Freud was clearly more interested in preserving the organization and presence of psychoanalysis in the Third Reich than he was in the dignity and esteem of his Jewish colleagues. . . . Ernest Jones, then president of the IPA, showed a callous insensitivity to the feelings and situation of Jewish colleagues whom he had advised to resign from the German group." Lewis Mumford compared CGJ's actions with Jones's and deemed them "a hardly less reprehensible Freudian parallel" (see "The Revolt of the Demons," *The New Yorker*, May 23, 1964, p. 175).

75. Martin Wangh, "The Working Through of the Nazi Experience in the German Psychoanalytic Community," paper presented at Frankfurt University, November 8, 1991, later incorporated into L. Rangell and R. Moses-Hvushovski, eds., *Psychoanalysis at the Political Border: Essays in Honor of Rafael Moses* (Madison, Wisc.: International Universities, Inc., 1996), pp. 283–302.

76. CGJ's actual letter has not been found. Evidence presented here is from Cimbal to Göring, February 20, 1934. See also CGJ to Oluf Brüel, March 19, 1934, p. 152.

77. Cimbal to Göring, March 10, 1934.

78. Although CGJ never accused Cimbal of direct responsibility, it was clear from his correspondence with others concerning the formation of new chapters of the International Society that Cimbal, as secretary-general, was the sole conduit for everything published in the *Zentralblatt*. See, for examples, CGJ to Poul Bjerre and CGJ to Alphons Maeder, both January 22, 1934, *CL-1*, pp. 135–38. See also CGJ to Heyer, April 20, 1934, *CL-1*, p. 158, where he accuses Cimbal of "motives . . . so obscure that an outsider like me cannot see through them." All translations from Göring's statement are unofficial and were prepared especially for this book; copies in similar prose were prepared in German for Ernest Harms, whose English translation is in KML.

79. "The Preliminary Statement," from the *Zentralblatt für Psychotherapie und ihre Grenzgebiete* 6 (1933). This English translation was either prepared by Jolande Jacobi or, more likely, by Ernest Harms, to whom it was sent. This copy is in the Harms archive, KML. A similar translation is in the HE/STA archives. Not in *CW* or *GW*. A separate translation based on the *Zentralblatt* text and both of the above has been prepared for this book.

80. In her commentary on this document, Jolande Jacobi writes: "That Jung specifically emphasized the fact that he did not intend any devaluation of the Semitic psychology was overlooked [by critics such as Roepke, Parelhoff, Muralt, etc.]. Only the statement that 'the long-known differences between the Germanic and the Jewish psychology . . .' was emphasized."

81. For one of the most pertinent critical exchanges on this subject, see John C. Burnham and William McGuire, eds., *Jelliffe's Correspondence with Sigmund Freud and CGJ* (Chicago: Univ. of Chicago Press, 1983), p. 263.

82. Barbara Hannah's impressions in *Life and Work*, p. 211. Quotes about "Nazi Leaders" are from *The Vision Seminars*, March 7, 1934, p. 1342.

83. Cimbal to Göring, March 11, 1934.

84. Göring to CGJ, March 12, 1934.

85. Meier to Göring, May 15, 1935.

86. Vladimir (spelled Wladimir in some sources) Rosenbaum attended most Eranos meetings in the 1930s but followed other Jews who took the precaution of not signing the official register (information from Jay Livernois).

87. In CGJ to Vladimir Rosenbaum, March 15, 1934, ETH, CGJ asks for an appointment of at least an hour on March 22 to discuss "certain legal and political questions of particular touchiness." Other sources include Wladimir Rosenbaum, *Erinnerungen und Reflexionen* (Remembrances and Reflections), conducted and recorded by Bernd H. Stappert. The original German manuscript is in the Sozialarchiv Schweiz, Zürich, Ar.115.1, nachlass Wladimir Rosenbaum. All quotes are from this until noted otherwise. See also Bernd H. Stappert, *Gespräche mit Aline Valangin*, Sozialarchiv Zürich, Ar.301.6; Peter Kamber, *Geschichte zweir Leben — Wladimir Rosenbaum und Aline Valangin* (Zürich: Limmat Verlag Genossenschaft, 1990); Zentralbibliothek Zürich, nachlass Rudolf Jakob Humm, 50.3: Handschriftenabteilung: Rosenbaumiania, 1933–34; Bundesarchiv Bern: EPD-Akten, E2001 (D), 1 BE73.e70: Rosenbaum und Konsorten; and Bundeswaltschaftsakten, E4320 (B) 1974/47, BD. 14. An important letter from Rosenbaum to CGJ is in the ETH, dated May 5, 1934, and filed as HS 1056: 2887. I am grateful to Peter Kamber for his assistance.

88. All passages of dialogue are those attributed to Rosenbaum in both the Stappert and HCL interviews.

89. In his HCL interview, Rosenbaum writes that he described the Nazification statutes as "*schweinerei*" (a dirty trick), whereas Jung insisted they were merely "*Fehler*" (a mistake). Otherwise, his interview parallels the documents in the Stappert interviews.

90. Vladimir Rosenbaum to CGJ, March 5, 1934, ETH. Peter Kamber called it to my attention.

91. Stappert and HCL interviews.

92. Cimbal to Göring, March 11, 1934.

93. These are informal translations prepared for use in this book. The official text is in *CW*-10, pp. 545–46.

94. I. Z. f. P., *Korrespondenzblatt*, 1936, p. 165. For a more detailed analysis of the roles played in this matter by Jones, Eitingon, and Freud, see Paul Roazen, "The Exclusion of Eric Fromm from the IPA," *Contemporary Psychoanalysis* 37, no. 1 (2001): 5–42.

95. The following account was provided by Christa Robinson, president of the Eranos Foundation and personal friend of Rosenbaum, now the keeper of a private archive he entrusted to her at his death. Telephone conversation with the author, February 24, 2002.

96. The German is *Auch das verwundete Tier verkriecht sich um zu verenden,* a much coarser and harsher formulation than the English translation (information from Christa Robinson).

97. Christa Robinson's phrases. Variations in wording but not thought were given by (among many others) Sonja Marjasch, Mario Jacoby, Andrew Samuels, Thomas B. Kirsch, Marie-Louise von Franz, Cornelia Brunner, and C. A. Meier. Quotes that follow, unless noted otherwise, are by Robinson.

98. Göring to W. Griesbeck, March 28, 1934.

99. For full bibliographic detail, see CGJ's "Rejoinder to Dr. Bally," *CL*-10, p. 535, n. 1, and pp. 543–44, no. 5. Author's translations of *Neue Zürcher Zeitung* texts.

100. Reprinted in *CW*-10, pp. 535–44.

101. CGJ was obliquely referring to the general Swiss attitude toward Jews. Edgar Bonjour et al., *A Short History of Switzerland* (Oxford: Clarendon Press, 1952), p. 302, points out that it was not until 1866, when an article to the constitution was adopted, that Jews in Switzerland were given "an equal footing with the rest of the population." Switzerland was the last country in central and Western Europe to do so.

102. Cabot, *Diaries,* February 9, 1945, p. 464.

103. B. Cohen, "Ist C. G. Jung 'gleichgeschaltet'?" The debate continued with both attack and defense by others, among them CGJ's supporter and friend Dr. Siegmund Hurwitz. See January 25, 1946, February 7 and 21, 1947, and March 7, 1947.

104. James Kirsch und Gerhard Adler, "C. G. Jungs Stellung zum Judentum," *Jüdische Rundschau* 62, no. 3.8 (1934), and James Kirsch, "Die Judenfrage in der Psychotherapie," *Jüdische Rundschau* 43, no. 29.5 (1934): 11.

105. *CL*-1, p. 161, n. 2. The following two key passages were omitted by the editors when the letter was published.

106. From CGJ's original typed letter to Kirsch, in the ETH; this passage was also omitted in the published text.

107. Winston Churchill, *Great Contemporaries* (New York: W. W. Norton, 1991), quoted in Dulles, *Germany's Underground,* p. 16. Dulles uses Churchill's remark as a precaution against the hindsight of "those who pass judgment on prewar Germany and express, as is often done, amazement that Hitler was not eliminated by the German people themselves long before 1939."

108. CGJ to Göring, October 31, 1935.

109. Göring to Meier, November 30, 1935.

110. CGJ to Göring, December 21, 1935. See also CGJ to J. H. van der Hoop, January 3, 1936, *CL*-1, pp. 207–8.

111. See, for example, Forrest G. Robinson, *Love's Story Told,* pp. 225–28, particularly note to p. 230, p. 423; also CGJ to Henry Murray, October 6 and December 19, 1938, *CL*-2, pp. xxxiv–xxxv.

112. The joint conference took place in October in Bern. C. A. Meier assured Göring that there would be "no emigrants [i.e., Jews]" among the speakers (Meier to Göring, June 3, 1937).

113. CGJ to Göring, January 10, 1936.

114. "Wotan" was first published in the *Neue Schweizer Rundschau,* Zürich, n.s. 3 (March 1936): 657–69; now in *CW*-10, paras. 371–99, pp. 179–93. Portions were reprinted in *The Saturday Review of Literature,* October 16, 1937, at the time of his Terry Lectures at Yale.

115. "Wotan," para. 388, p. 185.

116. "Wotan," para. 389, p. 186.

117. "Wotan," para. 390, pp. 186–87.

118. Von Muralt made these arguments verbally in the latter half of the 1930s, as personal interviews with the author and some in HCL attest. The essay that summed up all his earlier criticisms was not published until 1946–47 in the *Schweizer Annalen,* Aarau (1946–47): 192 and 194.
119. CGJ to Göring, February 22, 1938.
120. Meier to Göring, May 15, 1937.
121. Curtius to Göring, February 17, 1937.
122. Curtius to Göring, March 3, 1937.
123. CGJ to Oluf Brüel, December 12, 1936, *CL*-1, p. 221. For a related discussion, see CGJ to Hauer, June 7, 1937, *CL*-1, p. 233.
124. Göring to Meier, May 17, 1937, Göring to CGJ, February 26, 1938.
125. Hannah, *Life and Work,* p. 211, tells of a meeting between CGJ and Goebbels that she includes in the events of 1933. Others believe it occurred in 1937. The only evidence for such a meeting is heresay, much of it in interviews at HCL. To date, I have found no direct evidence to prove that such a meeting ever took place. For CGJ's thoughts about Mussolini and Hitler, see McGuire, *CGJ Speaking,* "Diagnosing the Dictators," pp. 115–35.
126. Regine Lockot, personal interview with Frau Strauss-Klöbe, August 5, 1980; quoted in *Erinnern,* p. 104.
127. On February 21, 1938, CGJ told Jolande Jacobi that he was still debilitated from the Indian illness and could not partake of any activity that required him to exert himself (CGJ to Jolande Jacobi, ETH).
128. C. A. Meier, interview with the author, March 1995. Although Meier would not discuss the details of his final break with CGJ, he did say resentment at "being treated like a lackey" during these years contributed to it.
129. For an account of their friendship, see CGJ's Foreword to *Hugh Crichton-Miller, 1877–1959: A Personal Memoir by His Friends and Family* (Dorchester: Longmans, Ltd., 1961); revised version in *CW*-18, pp. 639–41.
130. CGJ to Peter Baynes, December 12, 1938, ETH.
131. Peter Baynes to CGJ (Marie-Jeanne Schmid), November 4 (no year given, but probably 1937), ETH. See letters that follow between Baynes and CGJ through March 1938, also ETH, regarding plans for the congress.
132. From a letter filled with recriminations and self-serving recapitulations of the society's history as seen from his point of view; Göring to Meier, December 11, 1940.
133. CGJ to Göring, March 26, 1938. See also CGJ to Eric B. Strauss, March 26, 1938, *CL*-1, p. 242.
134. CGJ to Eric B. Strauss, March 26, 1938, *CL*-1, p. 242.
135. One example is from Göring to Meier, April 20, 1938: "Neugarten . . . would like to give a lecture in Oxford. . . . Since he is Jewish, what he does and says is beyond our control. The same for Stransky. . . . For him it is very hard because his wife is Aryan."
136. Peter Baynes to CGJ, July 20, 1938, ETH.
137. Barbara Hannah is one of many who recounts this story, in *Life and Work,* p. 254. Robert McCully says he tells Franz Riklin Jr.'s version in "Remarks on the Last Contact Between Freud and Jung," *Quadrant* 20, no. 2 (1987): 73–74. I have been unable to locate any evidence that the event actually took place.
138. This story may have been conflated with another that is true: Jung was quietly assisting others in Zürich to raise money for German Jews. He was assisted in this by (among others) the parents of Dr. Christa Robinson, the current president of the Eranos Foundation.

139. For various conflicting and contradictory accounts of this event, none of which provide any sort of documentation, see (among many others) van der Post, *Jung and the Story of Our Time*, p. 148; Frank McLynn, *Jung* (New York: St. Martin's Press, 1997), pp. 416–18; Hannah, *Life and Work*, pp. 254–55; and McCully, "Remarks on the Last Contact," p. xxx.

140. CGJ's presidential address is in *CW*-10, paras. 1064–68, pp. 561–63.

141. Göring to CGJ, February 26, 1938.

142. The letter is to Meier and signed only "Baumann," January 14, 1939.

143. Personal interview with Meier, November 1995.

144. Curtius to Göring, March 9, 1939.

145. *Zentralblatt für Psychotherapie* 2 (1939): 193–94. A modified version is reprinted in "Jung's Birthday Greetings to Professor Göring," *JAP* 38 (1993): 471–74.

146. McGuire, *Bollingen*, p. 21. Further detail was provided by Jay Livernois. Correspondence is in a private archive concerning Olga Fröbe-Kapteyn, CGJ, and others who wish not to be identified. Olga Fröbe's second-born twin daughter, Inge, suffered brain damage at birth and had been institutionalized in Germany since the 1920s. When she went to visit her, Frau Fröbe learned her daughter had been put to death. This marked the beginning of her outspoken anti-Nazi activism, which she ceased after the Nazi invasion of Holland, where her other daughter, Bettina, lived. Frau Fröbe received notice to desist or Bettina would be imprisoned. Independently, I have verified that Jung was aware of these developments as they happened, for he discussed them in several letters in a private archive.

147. J. Stüssi-Lauterburg, librarian of the Swiss Federal Military Library and head of the Swiss Military Historical Service, Bern; letter to the editor of the *International Herald Tribune*, August 23, 1995.

148. Although a total of 295,381 "foreigners" were eventually admitted, historians generally agree that approximately 20,000 of this number were Jewish. For the most thorough account to date, see Jean Ziegler, *The Swiss, the Gold, and the Dead: How Swiss Bankers Helped Finance the Nazi War Machine* (New York and San Diego: Harcourt Brace, 1998).

149. The Cahan letters date from April 16, 1937, to August 14, 1943; the Jacobi *Attest* is dated October 31, 1938. See also CGJ's offer to write one for "Frau N.," October 5, 1939, *CL*-1, pp. 277–78.

150. Jaffé, "CGJ and National Socialism," *Life and Work*, p. 86, n. 17.

151. CGJ to Heinrich Zimmer, *CL*-1, December 14, 1936, pp. 222–23.

152. Examples are found in (among many others) the letters of Esther Harding and H. G. Baynes, whom he entreated to assist Grete Adler (Gerhard Adler's first wife), April 1, 1939; Julius Spier, a Berlin palm reader, December 16, 1938; and Dr. Fritz Meyer, also a German Jew, March 4, 1938; all CGJ to Peter Baynes, ETH.

153. Erich Neumann to CGJ, December 15, 1938, in *Lingering Shadows*, p. 282.

154. CGJ to Erich Neumann, in *Lingering Shadows*, p. 283. The ellipses in the letter itself were made by Mischa Neumann, who did not print the text entirely as Jung wrote it.

155. CGJ to Hugh Crichton-Miller, June 28, 1939, *CL*-1, pp. 271–72.

156. CGJ to Peter Baynes, March 27, 1937, ETH. CGJ expresses condolences in this letter that Baynes's house was burned to the ground.

157. The constraints of biographical narrative require that much of the political maneuvering that took place from this date until CGJ's final resignation in 1940 be summarized. For the most complete and objective account to date, see Lockot, *Erinnern*, chapter 6, section 5, pp. 261–81.

158. Meier to Göring, July 21, 1939 (author's emphasis).
159. Interview with the author, March 1995.
160. Lockot, *Erinnern*, pp. 104 and 106.
161. Meier interview, March 1995; CGJ to J. H. van der Hoop, October 26, 1940, *CL*-1, pp. 286–88.
162. Göring to Hugh Crichton-Miller, October 14, 1938.
163. Curtius to Göring, August 18, 1939.
164. Göring to CGJ, July 4, 1940.
165. Originally in *Hearst's International Cosmopolitan*, January 1939; reprinted in *CGJ Speaking*, pp. 115–35. There is no evidence that Göring actually read Jung's lectures or saw the original interview. Curtius sent it to him in the heavily censored form that was permitted in Germany. The importance CGJ attributed to this article can be seen in CGJ to Peter Baynes, August 12, 1940, ETH, where he wrote that he "often complained that Mr. Chamberlain has not read my interview with Knickerbocker."
166. Two letters (September 26, 1942, and May 23, 1943) from L. Fernau, the Leipzig book distributor for Rascher Verlag of Zürich, describe how Jung's writings could no longer be sold in Germany, as he was one of several of their authors who had been placed on the *Schwarze Liste*. A letter to CGJ of June 7, 1948, from Editions Stock, publisher of *Essais de Psychologie Analytique*, told him that his work had been placed upon the *Otto Liste* (named after Otto Abetz, and the French equivalent of the *Schwarze Liste*) immediately after the 1940 German occupation of Paris. The letter said CGJ was one of "two or three other writers, Vicki Baum and Stefan Zweig," whose books the German occupiers insisted had to be destroyed. Lockot, *Erinnern*, p. 108, also corroborates CGJ's place upon the *Schwarze Liste*.
167. CGJ to Göring, July 12, 1940.
168. CGJ to E. Beit von Speyer, April 13, 1934, *CL*-1, p. 157. See also CGJ to A. Pupato, March 2, 1934, *CL*-1, pp. 147–49.

CHAPTER 30: ROOTED IN OUR SOIL
1. Toni Wolff wrote briefly about it in "A Few Words on the Psychological Club Zürich and on Professor Jung's Work since 1939," *Harvest* 36 (1990): 113–20. Texts consulted for information about Switzerland at the outbreak of war and after include Edgar Bonjour, *Swiss Neutrality: Its History and Meaning* (London: Allen and Unwin, 1946); E. Bonjour, H. S. Offler, and G. R. Potter, *A Short History of Switzerland* (Oxford: Clarendon Press, 1952); N. Bouvier, G. A. Craig, and L. Gossman, *Geneva, Zürich, Basel: History, Culture, and National Identity* (Princeton: Princeton Univ. Press, 1994); Dieter Fahrni, *An Outline History of Switzerland* (Zürich: Pro-Helvetia Arts Council of Switzerland, 1994); *Fortune*, "Switzerland Sits Tight," September 1941; Gordon Craig, "How to Think About the Swiss," *The New York Review of Books*, June 11, 1998; J. Christopher Herold, *The Swiss Without Halos* (New York: Columbia Univ. Press, 1948); Donald P. Hilty, ed., *Retrospectives on Switzerland in World War II* (Rockport, Maine: Picton Press, 2001); Georg Kreis, "La Suisse Pendant la Guerre: État Démocratique en État de Siège?," *Revue d'Histoire de la Deuxième Guerre Mondiale* (1981); Lydia Lehmann, ed., *Switzerland Inside Out* (Zürich: Swiss Japanese Chamber of Commerce, 1998); Ernst Leisi, *Freispruch für die Schweiz* (Frauenfeld: Huber Verlag, 1997); René Levy, *The Social Structure of Switzerland* (Zürich: Pro-Helvetia Arts Council of Switzerland, 1998); John McPhee, *La Place de la Concorde Suisse* (New York: Farrar, Straus and Giroux, 1983); Kenneth D. McRae, *Switzerland, Example of Cultural Coexistence* (Toronto: Cana-

dian Institute of International Affairs, 1964); Mitya New, *Switzerland Unwrapped: Exposing the Myths* (London and New York: Tauris Publishers, 1997); Jerrold M. Packard, *Neither Friend nor Foe: The European Neutrals in World War II* (New York: Charles Scribner's Sons, 1992); Werner Richter, "The War Pattern of Swiss Life," *Foreign Affairs* (July 1944); D. de Rougemont and C. Muret, *The Heart of Europe* (New York: Duell, Sloan and Pearce, 1941); Roland Ruffieux, "La Suisse Pendant la Guerre: De l'Ordre Nouveau à la Nouvelles Préoccupations," *Revue d'Histoire de la Deuxième Guerre Mondiale* (1981); Leo Schelbert, ed., *Switzerland Under Siege 1939–45: A Neutral Nation's Struggle for Survival* (Rockport, Maine: Picton Press, 2000); Jonathan Steinberg, *Why Switzerland?* (Cambridge: Cambridge Univ. Press, 1976); and Jean Ziegler, *The Swiss, the Gold, and the Dead: How Swiss Bankers Helped Finance the Nazi War Machine* (New York: Harcourt Brace, 1998).

2. Jane Cabot Reid's observation in *Jung, My Mother, and I: The Analytic Diaries of Catharine Rush Cabot* (Einsiedeln: Daimon Verlag, 2000), p. 205.

3. Reid, in *Jung, My Mother, and I*, p. 205, tells an anecdote of how CGJ and Toni Wolff enjoyed clowning and joking. Barbara Hannah, in a private archive, repeats other anecdotes along these same lines.

4. Wolff, "A Few Words," p. 113.

5. Packard, *Neither Friend nor Foe*, pp. 7 and 10, is among the many who cite this.

6. See Fahrni, *An Outline History*, photo opposite p. 113; and Ziegler, *The Swiss, the Gold, and the Dead*, p. 50.

7. Agathe Niehus-Jung, Franz Jung, and Cornelia Brunner (among others), interviews with the author; Barbara Hannah private archive; and an analytic diary kept by a man who was a Nazi sympathizer and objected to CGJ's comments.

8. Ziegler, *The Swiss, the Gold, and the Dead*, pp. 13–14, quotes from Hans Ulrich Jost's essay "Menace et repliement," *Nouvelle Histoire de la Suisse et des Suisses* (Lausanne), 3 (1983): pp. 90ff., as follows: "Switzerland was [in 1940] integrated de facto into the Reichsdeutsch economic area. . . . [Between] 1941–42, sixty percent of the Swiss munitions industry, fifty percent of the optical industry, and forty percent of the engineering industry were working for the Reich."

9. President of the Swiss Confederation, Pilat-Golaz made this remark in a radio address on June 25, 1940. See also Ziegler, *The Swiss, the Gold, and the Dead*, p. 77.

10. Alfred Häsler, *Das Boot ist voll* (Zürich: Pendo Verlag, 1992), p. 122. Häsler's title came from a 1942 speech by Swiss Minister of Justice Eduard von Steiger, in which he declared the "Swiss lifeboat" was unable to hold any more refugees.

11. First told by C. A. Meier, interview with the author, November, 1994; repeated and confirmed in various conversations since that date; a version reprinted by Jane Cabot Reid in *Jung, My Mother, and I*, p. 408, n. 1. Klaus Urner, "Neutrality and Economic Warfare," in *Retrospectives*, ed. Hilty, p. 16, writes of this "malicious saying."

12. Hans Senn, "Defending Switzerland: The Impact of Armed Neutrality in World War II," in *Switzerland Under Siege*, ed. Schelbert, pp. 6–7, writes that Hitler planned to invade Switzerland on June 23, 1940, because he was angry for three reasons: Germany could neither "bring the Swiss press into line" nor "impose a 'neutrality of conscience' on the Swiss people"; Swiss pilots shot down eleven German planes on their return from bombing France when they violated Swiss airspace (the Swiss lost only three); and Hitler's goal of completely sealing off the country early in the war had failed.

13. HCL interviews with survivors of Albert Oeri; and the archives of Albert Oeri and CGJ, ETH. Ziegler, *The Swiss, the Gold, and the Dead*, p. 60, also mentions that in

defiance of censors, Oeri was regularly reelected to the Swiss federal parliament by his fellow citizens of Basel.

14. HCL interviews with Oeri's surviving children; verified in interviews and conversations with Franz Jung.

15. Guisan's remarks were made on July 25, 1940. See also Hans Senn, "Reasons Germany Dropped 'Operation Switzerland,'" in *Retrospectives*, ed. Hilty, p. 70.

16. Walter Lüem and Andreas Steigmeier, *Die Limmatstellung im Zweiten Weltkreig* (Baden: Baden Verlag, 1997).

17. CGJ to Mary Mellon, August 21, 1940, original in ETH; not in *CL-1*.

18. Jelliffe, for example, wrote to Jones after he saw CGJ at Harvard: "He was distinctly his age" (William McGuire, ed., *Jelliffe's Correspondence with Sigmund Freud and CGJ* [Chicago: Univ. of Chicago Press, 1988], p. 270). Barbara Hannah, *Jung: His Life and Work, A Biographical Memoir* (Boston: Shambhala, 1991), pp. 255–56, touches upon his illness.

19. Not in *CW*, but CGJ referred to them in his other writings. See *CW-20*, p. 344, for full citations.

20. See Thomas Maissen, "Women in Switzerland's Mobilization," in *Switzerland Under Siege*, ed. Schelbert, pp. 39–43. Officially the *Frauenhilfsdienst* was assigned to medical service, administration, communication, transportation, care-taking of refugees, carrier pigeons, and dogs; and to the "Intellectual Auxiliary Service," preparing news bulletins and aircraft observation.

21. Photos of Toni Wolff and information were generously provided by Dr. Georg Trüb; Barbara Hannah has a version of Toni Wolff's wartime service on p. 274 of *Life and Work*.

22. Personal interviews and telephone conversations with Franz Jung and his son, Peter Jung; Agathe Niehus-Jung and her children, Ludwig Niehus, Sybille Willi-Niehus, and Brigitte Merk-Niehus; the sons of Gret Baumann-Jung, Wolfgang Baumann and Dieter Baumann; Ulrich Hoerni; and the children of Marianne Niehus-Jung, Rudolf Niehus and Monica Walder-Niehus.

23. Cabot, *Diary*, February 1940, p. 253.

24. Friedrich T. Wahlen, "Das schweizerische Anbauwerk im Zweiten Weltkrieg," in *Innen- und Aussenpolitik: Primat oder Interdependenz? Festschrift zum 60. Geburstag von Walther Hofer*, Urs Altermatt and J. Garamvölgyi, eds. (Bern, 1980), pp. 353–65. See also Urner, "Neutrality and Economic Warfare," p. 20; and Edgar Bonjour, "Swiss Neutrality During Two World Wars," in *Under Siege*, ed. Schelbert, p. 125. Dr. Peter Jung took me on a tour of the house and grounds and explained how the land was farmed during the war.

25. CGJ's correspondence with H. G. Baynes refers occasionally to Baynes's gifts as well as those of others.

26. CGJ to Mary Mellon, August 21, 1940; these passages are missing from the partially reprinted letter in *CL-1*, p. 283 (courtesy of Paul Mellon).

27. Dieter Baumann, telephone conversation with the author.

28. Hannah, *Life and Work*, p. 269, and Regine Lockot, *Erinnern und Durcharbeiten: Zur Geschichte der Psychoanalyse und Psychotherapie im Nationalsozialismus* (Frankfurt: Fischer Verlag, 1985), p. 108. As noted, CGJ's name was also on the French *Otto Liste* and his books were banned in that country.

29. CGJ to Merrill Moore, September 23, 1940, not in *CL*; CGJ sent similar letters to (among others) Paul and Mary Mellon, particularly CGJ to Mary Mellon, August 21, 1940, of which only one short paragraph is reprinted in *CL-1*, p. 283, and Henriette Goodrich, May 20, 1940, again, only partially reprinted in *CL-1*, p. 282.

30. These occurred on March 4, 1945. For further detail, see James H. Hutson, "The

Allied Bombing of the Sister Republic," in *Switzerland Under Siege*, ed. Schelbert, p. 97.

31. Marie-Louise von Franz, interview with the author, June 1995.
32. Paul Mellon, interview with the author, October 31, 1995, New York.
33. CGJ to Paul Mellon, June 10, 1940; correspondence in the Paul Mellon archives. Not in CGJ's correspondence with Mary and Paul Mellon in the ETH.
34. Cabot, *Diaries*, p. 371.
35. Quoted in Margerete Dierks, *Jakob Wilhelm Hauer, 1881–1962* (Heidelberg, 1986), p. 297; and Petteri Pietikainen, "The Volk and Its Unconscious: Jung, Hauer, and the 'German Revolution,'" *Journal of Contemporary History* 35, no. 4 (2000): 53.
36. From the private diary of a club member, quoted previously (author's translation).
37. Document in the Archives of the Psychological Club, Zürich. The phrase "if possible" was a substitution for the original "under no circumstances." For a thorough discussion, see Thomas B. Kirsch, *The Jungians: A Comparative and Historical Perspective* (London and Philadelphia: Routledge, 2000), pp. 32–35. See also Ariah Maidenbaum, "Report from New York," in Mary Ann Matoon, ed., *Paris 89: Proceedings of the Eleventh International Congress for Analytical Psychology, August 28–September 2, 1989* (Einsiedeln: Daimon Verlag, 1991), pp. 468–69; A. Maidenbaum and Stephen A. Martin, eds., *Lingering Shadows: Jungians, Freudians, and Anti-Semitism* (Boston: Shambhala, 1991); and Jay Sherry, "Instead of Heat, Light," *San Francisco Jung Institute Library Journal* 8, no. 4 (1989): 36–37.
38. It was just as secretly removed from the statutes in 1950, but neither action was publicly disclosed until approximately 1988 or 1989. See Maidenbaum, "Report from New York," pp. 468–69.
39. Maidenbaum, "Report from New York," p. 469, writes: "Almost every person interviewed [for his article] acknowledged that Jung was aware of the quota then in effect." I find it interesting that none of the persons who were members of the Psychological Club referred to this in their HCL interviews; nor did Nameche discuss it in his unpublished manuscript in the Glasgow University Library. In my own interviews, I asked nearly everyone about CGJ and Emma's knowledge of the quota, and none could give me concrete evidence one way or the other; they could only offer speculation or secondhand commentary that I could not verify.
40. This observation is based on documents in the Wolff family archives; letters written to two persons by Linda Fierz-David; and diary entries made by these two persons.
41. Cabot, *Diaries*, p. 374; similar language is found in HCL interviews with (among others) Cornelia Brunner and Susi Trüb-Wolff; also Ximena de Angulo Roelli, interview with author; Barbara Hannah private archive; two private analytic diaries kept by men; Mary Bancroft in *Matters of the Heart: The Extraordinary Journey of CGJ* (film; 107 min.); and correspondence between CGJ and Mary Mellon (Paul Mellon archives) and CGJ to Jolande Jacobi (ETH).
42. For CGJ's working methodology, see also William McGuire, *Bollingen: An Adventure in Collecting the Past*, Bollingen Series (Princeton: Princeton Univ. Press, 1982), pp. 14–15.
43. Hannah, *Life and Work*, mentions the Swiss professors in passing on p. 272; in a private archive she made the comments I have used in the text. Her views were verified by Ximena de Angulo Roelli in conversation, and by Cary F. Baynes in correspondence with CGJ, and in other private documentation made available for this book. See also Toni Wolff, "A Few Words," for further insights into lecturers and their topics.
44. Peter Baynes to CGJ, August 22, 1936, ETH. Ashton-Gwatkin was at the time head of the Economic Department of the Foreign Office. He was a specialist in the

affairs of Eastern Europe and had been a member of the Runciman group in the Czecko-Slovakian mission.

45. *CW*-10, paras. 1–48, pp. 3–28.

46. CGJ to Peter Baynes, August 12, 1940, ETH. Partially reprinted in *CL*-1, p. 285.

47. Allen W. Dulles, *Germany's Underground: The Anti-Nazi Resistance* (New York: Da Capo Press, 2000), p. 16.

48. Most of this correspondence is Peter Baynes to CGJ, ETH, beginning around March 6, 1937, CGJ to Peter Baynes, and particularly the letter of Baynes to CGJ, September 7, 1938. They continued to discuss Fordham's case through the early years of the war, even though he had stopped being Baynes's patient by then.

49. See also Fordham's *The Making of an Analyst: A Memoir* (London: Free Association Books, 1993), pp. 70ff., "Memories and Thoughts About CGJ," *JAP* 20 (1975): 102–13, and his HCL interview. James Astor, in his critical/biographical study of Fordham (*Michael Fordham: Innovations in Analytical Psychology* [London and New York: Routledge, 1995], pp. 106–7), alludes to the Baynes book but does not cite it in his bibliography or otherwise identify it or discuss Fordham's reaction to it.

50. Peter Baynes to CGJ, January 11, 1940, ETH. *Germany Possessed*, introduction by Hermann Rauschning, published by Jonathan Cape, 1941.

51. Olga Fröbe wrote to Paul and Mary Mellon on August 18, 1938, to thank them for their sponsorship of several "winter research journeys" of "about 1000 dollars a winter." She also thanked them for subsidizing the Farrar and Rinehart American edition of CGJ's Eranos lectures of 1933, '34, '35, and '36. Paul Mellon made a copy available to me via William McGuire.

52. Baynes's daughter, Ximena de Angulo Roelli, was also beginning to work as an editor on both CGJ's writings and the Eranos publications. CGJ to Mary Mellon, November 18, 1941, tells her how Barbara Hannah, who also worked on some texts, complained about changes made by X. Roelli. He also asks her to contribute an additional $150 to Frau Fröbe for a collection of pictures of Hermes and tells her he contributes $250 toward Eranos publications yearly. See also McGuire, *Bollingen*, p. 35.

53. Cary Baynes to CGJ, December 14, 1938, ETH.

54. CGJ to Cary Baynes, June 11, 1939, ETH.

55. Cary Baynes to CGJ, January 16, 1939, ETH.

56. Peter Baynes to CGJ, September 10, 1940. Translated by W. Stanley Dell and published as *The Integration of the Personality* (New York: Farrar and Rinehart; London: Kegan Paul, 1940). For prior publishing history, see *CW*-19, 1939a (English), p. 75. William McGuire, letter to the author, March 30, 2001, states his belief that Mary Mellon paid for the simultaneous publication of this book in England and the United States. Olga Fröbe, letter to Paul Mellon, August 18, 1938, asks Paul and Mary Mellon to do so, and it is generally accepted that they did.

57. Marie-Louise von Franz, *Alchemy: An Introduction to the Symbolism and the Psychology* (Toronto: Inner City Books, 1980), p. 13.

58. For a relatively full account of Jung's intellectual activity, see CGJ to Peter Baynes, May 27, 1941, ETH, also *CL*-1, pp. 299–301. See also CGJ to Peter Baynes, August 12, 1940, ETH, *CL*-1, pp. 285–86, for prior remarks on some of these same subjects.

59. Emma Jung, letter to Catharine Rush Cabot, September 25, 1941, in Reid, *Jung, My Mother, and I*, p. 384.

60. For CGJ's own summation of the subjects of his ETH lectures to that date, see his letter to Peter Baynes, May 27, 1941, *CL*-1, pp. 299–301.

61. B. 1493 in Einsiedeln, d. 1541 in Salzburg. For a biographical summary, see Diana

Fernando,"Paracelsus," in *Alchemy: An Illustrated A to Z* (London: Blandford Books/ Cassell, 1998), pp. 123–24.

62. *CW*-13, para. 146, p. 111. See also Jolande Jacobi, ed., *Paracelsus: Lebendiges Erbe* (Zürich: Rascher Verlag, 1942).

63. Full publication history in *CW*-19, pp. 32–33.

64. *CW*-13, para. 149, p. 115.

65. *See CW*-13, index, pp. 422–23, for partial listing; *CGJ Bibliothek Katalog*, p. 56, for a list of the works CGJ owned; and CGJ to B. Milt, June 8, 1942, *CL*-1, pp. 316–18 (esp. Paracelsus references on p. 318).

66. *Mysterium Coniunctionis*, *CW*-14, para. 518a, p. vii. This appears in chapter 4, "Rex and Regina," and needs to be read in the context of the chapter's subheading, "The Religious Problem of the King's Renewal," most particularly after para. 518.

67. Scholastic theologian and philosopher (1096–1141) whom he quotes infrequently in *CW*-5, p. 97, and *CW*-14, p. 550, but to whom there are numerous references in the unpublished ETH lectures, particularly to the *De laude Caritatus* and the text best known by the Anglo-Saxon title *Sawles Worde*. From the latter, CGJ expounded upon the ritualized meditations that resulted in the soul's ascent to communion with God: *cogitatio, meditatio*, and *contemplatio*.

68. *CL*-1, p. 300, n. 7; *CW*-11, p. 203. CGJ speaks of their collaboration in his letter to Mary Mellon, April 10, 1942, courtesy of Paul Mellon, not in *CL* or ETH.

69. In CGJ's April 10, 1942, letter to Mary Mellon, he says he revised his own essay on the symbolism of the mass to make it "independent of Dr. Jud's lectures."

70. Von Franz, *Alchemy*, p. 20.

71. Writings mainly in *CW*, vols. 9a and b, 11, 12, 13, and 14.

72. Von Franz, *Alchemy*, p. 156.

73. Marie-Louise von Franz, interview with the author, June, 1994; *Alchemy*, p. 38.

74. The indispensable text for the history of the undertaking is McGuire's *Bollingen*. For the history of the Bollingen Foundation, officially incorporated on January 6, 1942, see pp. 45ff. I am also grateful to William McGuire and the late Paul Mellon for their generous cooperation through personal interviews and archival contributions. Mail service between the United States and Switzerland was not cut off until March 1943. In July, Alphonse Hättenschwiler, a Swiss diplomat, volunteered to take correspondence between Mary Mellon and CGJ in his diplomatic pouch, which allowed them to correspond from time to time (from letter of Mary Mellon to CGJ [undated] in the Paul Mellon archives; also in McGuire's *Bollingen*, p. 72).

75. Edgar Wind was an art historian and refugee from Germany; Stringfellow Barr was the president of St. John's College, Annapolis. Ximena de Angulo Roelli was a recent graduate of Bennington College, and the Bollingen Foundation was her first job.

76. CGJ to Mary Mellon, April 10, 1942, courtesy of Paul Mellon; not in *CL* or ETH.

77. Published posthumously as Marie-Louise von Franz, Historical Introduction and Psychological Comment to *Muhammad Ibn Umail's Hall Ar-Rumuz* (*Clearing of Enigmas*) (Egg, Switzerland: Fotorotar AG, 1999).

78. Carl Kerényi: Hungarian philologist and mythologist, resident in Ascona after 1943, author of many works on Greek mythology. *CL*-1, note to p. 284, offers a capsule biography of his relationship to CGJ.

79. CGJ's entire correspondence with Roland Cahan in ETH supports this contention.

80. McGuire, *Bollingen*, p. 48.

81. The first expression is from Barbara Hannah, private archive; the second was used by Marie-Louise von Franz and Ximena de Angulo Roelli in separate interviews with the author.

82. Francis Carmody to Mary Mellon, *Bollingen*, pp. 49ff.

83. McGuire, *Bollingen*, p. 51; unpaginated description in FBI file 100–21061, consisting of numbered pp. 1–30.
84. Archives of the State Department, December 23, 1940, and January 11, 1941, document number 811.0158/449.
85. Signed by "Secretary to Mrs. Roosevelt," dated November 8, 1940, copy in the FDR Library, Hyde Park, New York.
86. Mary Mellon to Olga Fröbe-Kapteyn, November 10, 1941, Eranos archives.
87. Unpaginated FBI file.
88. McGuire, *Bollingen*, pp. 51–52.
89. McGuire, *Bollingen*, p. 54.

CHAPTER 31: AGENT 488
1. CGJ to Mary Mellon, April 10, 1942, Paul Mellon archives, not in ETH.
2. Heinz K. Meier, "Between Hammer and Anvil," *Switzerland Under Siege 1939–45: A Neutral Nation's Struggle for Survival*, ed. Leo Schelbert (Rockport, Maine: Picton Press, 2000), p. 132.
3. Josef Rosen, *Wartime Food Developments in Switzerland*, War-Peace Pamphlets, no. 9 (Stanford: Stanford Univ. Food Research Institute, 1947), esp. chapter 5.
4. CGJ to Catharine Rush Cabot, August 19, 1942, in Jane Cabot Reid, *Jung, My Mother, and I: The Analytic Diaries of Catharine Rush Cabot* (Einsiedeln: Daimon Verlag, 2000), p. 415.
5. CGJ was referring to to a revised version of the essay "The Unconscious in the Normal and Pathological Mind." CGJ to Mary Mellon, April 10, 1942, courtesy of Paul Mellon archives.
6. Mary Bancroft, *Autobiography of a Spy* (New York: William Morrow, 1983), p. 172.
7. Mary Bancroft, "Original of Reports from Mary Bancroft to Allen W. Dulles," February 9, 1943. This is one of the frequent routine reports Bancroft prepared for Dulles, now in her archives and made available (along with her correspondence with CGJ) by her grandson Hugh Taft-Morales.
8. Bancroft, *Autobiography of a Spy*, pp. 171–73, gives a version of this story. C. A. Meier confirmed it in a telephone conversation with the author, August 1996. In her February 9, 1943, report to Dulles, Bancroft gives another version of the rumor: "He [CGJ] says the rumor about his flying to the Ostfront is at the moment very current, or if he doesn't actually, it is that Sauerbruch comes here, goes to see Jung, and then takes bracing messages back to the Führer. . . . We had a good laugh about that." Much of the text of this report has been integrated into *Autobiography of a Spy*, chapter 20, pp. 171ff.
9. Although the doctor has never been identified, it was quite likely either Dr. Werner Zabel, who was a great admirer of CGJ, or the psychotherapist Erika Hantel, who worked for Zabel at his "biological sanatorium" in Berchtesgaden. See Geoffrey Cocks, *Psychotherapy in the Third Reich: The Göring Institute* (New Brunswick, N.J.: Transaction, 1997), p. 214. There is no solid documentation to determine exactly when this event occurred. Cocks is alone in dating it to 1939. Barbara Hannah, *Jung: His Life and Work, A Biographical Memoir* (Boston, Shambhala, 1991), p. 405, places it in the summer of 1942. CGJ to J. H. van der Hoop, January 14, 1946, *CL-1*, pp. 404–6, writes of it, and p. 405, n. 5, obliquely corroborates the 1942 date. Laurens van der Post, personal interview with the author, May 1995, London, said CGJ told him this happened in the summer of 1942. C. A. Meier said the same in a telephone conversation with the author, August 1995. Marie-Louise von Franz said she believed it happened during the time Barbara Hannah placed it, as she remembered Hannah confiding it to her after it had come to naught. The involvement of

Wilhelm Bitter, a German psychiatrist who practiced analytical psychology, makes the 1942 date most likely.

10. Mary Bancroft to Allen W. Dulles, "Report," February 9, 1943, quotes "reliable sources" as having told CGJ this. She added that CGJ thought "this would be a very likely thing for him to do, seeing as he has never drunk much and has never ceased to call Churchill, who probably drinks less than many of the Nazi leaders, a 'drunkard.' . . . Jung says every time he has read Hitler's remarks on this point he has thought them psychologically significant — and as soon as he heard Hitler was drinking it somehow fitted in."

11. In a letter to Allen W. Dulles, February 25, 1950, CGJ described Bitter as a lawyer in Stuttgart who studied medicine in order to become a psychotherapist. He founded the Institute for Psychoanalysis there but was persecuted by the Nazis and took refuge in Switzerland. Afterward, American authorities refused him permission to return because they thought he was a Communist. CGJ "secured a certain financial help for [Bitter's] Institute through the aid of the Minister for Finances for [the state of] Würtemberg" and asked Dulles for assistance to let Bitter return. Dulles replied on March 14, 1950, that he "warmly endorsed" CGJ's recommendation and had sent his letter to Shepard Stone, formerly of the *New York Times* and now "our High Commissioner in Germany." Dulles's letter to Stone, also dated March 14, 1950, is in his archives at Princeton University (as is his to CGJ). Through the offices of CGJ and Dulles, Bitter returned to Stuttgart. See also Wilhelm Bitter, HCL interview, recorded in Stuttgart, September 10, 1970. The interview is valuable for many other insights and perspectives on CGJ, not only for his participation in this wartime plot.

12. In his HCL interview, Bitter describes how Lambert became physically ill and was given permission to leave Germany for Switzerland. He states that CGJ "esteemed her highly and she was the only person he accepted for this [his personal] analytic training [during the war years]." See also Regine Lockot, *Erinnern und Durcharbeiten: Zur Geschichte der Psychoanalyse und Psychotherapie im Nationalsozialismus* (Frankfurt: Fischer Verlag, 1985), and Thomas B. Kirsch, *The Jungians: A Comparative and Historical Perspective* (London and Philadelphia: Routledge, 2000), for further detail about Bügler and Lambert.

13. Bitter, HCL interview.

14. William McGuire ed., *CGJ Speaking*, Bollingen Series 97 (Princeton: Princeton Univ. Press, 1977), p. 132.

15. Jung gave an interview to the *Schweizer Illustrierte*, "The *Schweizer Illustrierte* interviews the well-known Psychiatrist, Prof. Dr. C. G. Jung," August 12, 1942, German original in KML archives, English translation by Charles Boyd, edited by Werner Meier, *JAP* 46, no. 2 (April 2001): 355–59. In this interview, CGJ repeated that he had advocated Germany's eastward expansion since the Knickerbocker interview.

16. CGJ was instrumental in setting it up in 1938. He was president, Gustav Bally was secretary, and members included (among others) Medard Boss, Kurt Binswanger, and Alphons Maeder. See *CL*-1, pp. 404–5, n. 1, for further detail. It is interesting that Bally, one of Jung's most severe critics, not only joined the organization as late as 1938 but was still a member after the war ended.

17. Bitter, HCL interview.

18. One who is strongly suspected of contributing both money and advice to the plot is Gottlieb Duttweiler, founder of Migros, the first Swiss co-operative trading society and the "Landesring der Unabhängigen," the Political Party of the National Group of Independents. Duttweiler asked CGJ to stand as a candidate for Parliament, but he was not elected. See *CL*-1, p. 277, to "Anonymous," and pp. 279–80,

to G. Duttweiler, and n. 2. The son of a prominent Swiss banker, now deceased, spoke to me on the condition that I not identify him or his father. He insisted that his father was a major player in this intrigue, but he was unable to provide documentation to support his claim. This man also insisted that Duttweiler was among the leaders of the group. Mary Bancroft, in some of her undated "reports" for Allen Dulles, conveys information given to her by wives of "big bankers in Credit Suisse" that alludes to this and several other plots against Hitler that came to naught.

19. In her report to Dulles of December 14, 1943, Mary Bancroft said that CGJ told her "some man" was "communicating through him with the Archbishop of Canterbury." She told him he must tell this to Dulles himself, and he said he already had done so. William Temple, who became Archbishop of Canterbury in 1942, is considered one of the most significant Anglican churchmen of the twentieth century and the most renowned Primate in the Church of England since the English Reformation.

20. Mary Bancroft to Allen W. Dulles, "Report," August 21, 1944.

21. Hannah's version of the story is in *Life and Work*, pp. 273–74; quote is from Marie-Louise von Franz, interview with the author. See also Bitter, HCL interview, for further detail.

22. Cocks, *Psychotherapy in the Third Reich*, pp. 214–15, gives an accurate version of these events.

23. CGJ to Mary Mellon, April 10, 1942, Paul Mellon archives.

24. Undated, on her personal stationery, but internal evidence suggests sometime in the summer of 1943, because she refers to Heinrich Zimmer's death (from pneumonia), which occurred on March 22, 1943.

25. Mary Bancroft, telephone conversations with the author, 1995.

26. See Peter Grose, *Gentleman Spy* (Boston and New York: Houghton Mifflin, 1994), p. 151, for the dramatic details of Dulles's entry into Switzerland. For a thorough overview of Dulles's work, see also Neal H. Peterson, *From Hitler's Doorstep: The Wartime Intelligence Reports of Allen Dulles, 1942–45* (University Park, Penn.: Pennsylvania State Univ. Press, 1996); and James Srodes, *Allen Dulles: Master of Spies* (Washington, D.C.: Regnery Publishing, 1999).

27. Grose, *Gentleman Spy*, pp. 148ff.

28. Grose, *Gentleman Spy*, p. 92.

29. Grose, *Gentleman Spy*, p. 154.

30. Allen Walsh Dulles, *The Craft of Intelligence* (New York: Harper and Row, 1963), p. 48; quoted in Grose, *Gentleman Spy*, p. 154.

31. Reid, *Jung, My Mother, and I*, pp. 421–23, has a version of this incident. The late Robin Briner, in a 1995 telephone conversation with the author, told a different version. Marcus Fierz, also in a telephone conversation, August 1995, gave yet a third version concerning his mother, Linda Fierz-David, and Toni Wolff, who both allegedly objected to Mary Briner's "elevation" by Dulles over other "more suitable" Americans. The account herein is a synthesis of information based on the printed sources cited previously, correspondence from several private archives, documents in the U.S. National Archives (courtesy of John Taylor), the Bancroft and Dulles archives cited previously, and other private archives.

32. Mary Bancroft's son by her first marriage to Sherman Badger lived with his father and stepmother in the United States. Her daughter, Mary Jane Badger, lived in Zürich. She later married Horace Taft, Dean of Yale College and son of Senator Robert Taft and grandson of President of the United States Robert Taft.

33. Reid, *Jung, My Mother, and I*, pp. 374–75, is but one example of such accounts. Cabot attributes comments to CGJ that I have been unable to document through other

archival materials. Based upon my close reading of other diaries, journals, and letters, I find it unlikely that he would have said many of them to Cabot or anyone else.

34. Mary Bancroft, *Autobiography of a Spy*, p. 94. Information about Linda Fierz-David is from a telephone conversation with Marcus Fierz, August 1995.

35. I owe several meetings with Mary Bancroft to the good offices of the late Mary Perot Nichols, who told me we both owed them to arrangements on our behalf by Charles Kinsolving, whom I never met. Much of what is written here is based on personal conversations with Bancroft as well as her book, *The Autobiography of a Spy*, and the filmed interview she gave to Suzanne Wagner in connection with *Matters of the Heart*. I am also grateful to Bancroft's daughter, Mary Jane Taft, and her son, Hugh Taft-Morales, for correspondence between Mary Bancroft and CGJ and other family archives. I am also relying on documents kept by the late Mary Briner and provided by her late son, Robin Briner, as well as materials from private archives that will be cited specifically where appropriate. All quotes until noted otherwise are from Mary Bancroft.

36. Bancroft, *Autobiography of a Spy*, pp. 128–29. These pages are examples of the considerable intelligence Bancroft generally hid beneath her "flighty extravert persona" (her own description in a conversation).

37. Grose, *Gentleman Spy*, p. 163.

38. Grose, *Gentleman Spy*, pp. 22ff.

39. Their daughter, Joan Dulles Buresh, who graciously provided information through telephone interviews and archival documentation, also trained in Zürich and became a prominent Jungian analyst in the United States. Clover Dulles analyzed with Jolande Jacobi for seven years after the war. Jacobi stayed in the Dulles home when she visited Washington, D.C. In her HCL interview, Jacobi said Dulles told her CGJ "must be a good politician because he knows the souls."

40. Bancroft, *Autobiography of a Spy*, p. 129.

41. Besides the Bancroft memoir and Grose's biography of Dulles, see also Reid, *Jung, My Mother, and I*, pp. 419–22. Jane Reid's husband, P. R. Reid, wrote *Escape from Colditz* (London: Hodder and Stoughton, 1952).

42. A. W. Dulles, *Germany's Underground: The Anti-Nazi Resistance* (New York: Da Capo Press, 2000), chapter 10, "Contacts in Foreign Countries," pp. 125ff.; see also Grose, *Gentleman Spy*, pp. 176ff.; Hans-Bernd Gisevius, *To the Bitter End* (Boston: Houghton Mifflin, 1947); Bancroft, *Autobiography of a Spy*; Fabian von Schlabrendorff, *The Secret War Against Hitler* (New York: Pitman Press, 1965); and Neal H. Peterson, *From Hitler's Doorstep*.

43. Dulles, *Germany's Underground*, chapter 6, "The Abwehr," pp. 70ff.

44. Gisevius, *To the Bitter End*.

45. Bancroft, *Autobiography of a Spy*, p. 137.

46. Mary Bancroft, conversations with the author.

47. I am grateful to John Taylor of the National Archives and Records Administration, who brought this information to my attention. Neal Peterson also reports it, in *From Hitler's Doorstep*.

48. Jane Cabot Reid gives the impression in her book (p. 421) that Bancroft first asked her mother, Catharine Rush Cabot, to assist her. Private documents in the Briner archives (other than correspondence between Bancroft and Briner) support the interpretion offered here.

49. Mary Bancroft, conversations with the author; Robin Briner, who remembered his mother "alluding" to this, "because she never really confided details, she always kept secrets."

50. Bancroft, *Autobiography of a Spy*, p. 140. The first quotation is CGJ's, the rest are hers.

51. Her remarks in a telephone conversation; see also *Autobiography of a Spy*, pp. 140–41, for some of the innocent but important kinds of information she imparted.

52. The expressions are by Jocelyn Rochat, "CGJ: Profileur de Hitler," *L'Hebdo*, December 28, 2000, p. 43. Elisabeth Roudinesco and Thomas Höehn called this article to my attention.

53. Copy in the Allen W. Dulles archives, Princeton University; portions reprinted in *L'Hebdo*, p. 47.

54. Ulrich Hoerni, on behalf of the *Erbengemeinschaft CGJ*, told Jocelyn Rochat: "Family members knew that Jung had known Dulles, but he never spoke openly of it to them. You must understand, this sort of subject was highly secret." According to Hoerni, Dr. Peter Jung, Herr Ludwig Niehus, Frau Sybille Willi-Niehus, and other members of the family consortium, none of CGJ's patient records are extant.

55. Bancroft's word in a telephone conversation with the author.

56. CGJ's emphasis. For information about Pilet-Golaz, see *Switzerland Under Siege*, ed. Schelbert. CGJ's views and all quotes until noted otherwise are from Mary Bancroft to Allen W. Dulles, "Report," December 14, 1943.

57. Mary Bancroft, telephone conversation with the author. She referred to CGJ's early 1900s appearances in criminal court cases as an expert witness.

58. Allen Dulles to Paul Mellon, February 17, 1950, Allen W. Dulles archives, Princeton University. In a letter of May 18, 1964, to William McGuire, then editor of the Bollingen Series, and in response to McGuire's request for correspondence to include in *CL*, Dulles wrote that he "often journeyed to Jung's house on the Lake. I greatly profited from my conversations with Jung during those days." Dulles said the talks "covered chiefly the psychological reactions of Hitler, Mussolini and one or two others of the Nazi-Fascist leaders in the face of the events as they developed toward the close of World War II" (copy in the Allen W. Dulles archives, Princeton University).

59. Bancroft, telephone conversation with the author.

60. William Kennedy, HCL interview, June 21, 1972. He was also director of the CGJ Foundation, New York.

61. CGJ to Allen Dulles, February 1, 1945, ETH.

62. CGJ's emphasis. Dulles replied on February 3, 1945, saying he would take the letter to Eisenhower and also pass on messages to Paul Mellon.

63. Mary Bancroft to Allen W. Dulles, "Report," October 29, 1943.

64. William Kennedy, HCL interview. Kennedy met Gisevius after the war when Kennedy was Officer in Charge of Films, Theater, and Music for Bavaria. When he asked Gisevius if the rumor was true that he consulted CGJ, he "professed great admiration for Jung but said he did not know him." Kennedy added that unnamed Americans resident in Zürich during the war "who were in a position to know said Gisevius consulted CGJ a number of times over a period of years."

65. Bancroft, telephone conversation with the author.

66. Mary Bancroft to Allen W. Dulles, "Report," December 14, 1943.

67. Bancroft, *Autobiography of a Spy*, pp. 171ff.

68. Mary Bancroft to Allen W. Dulles, "Report," October 29, 1943.

69. Here, CGJ referred to Gisevius's analysis of the Fritsch-Blomberg crisis, the section entitled "Caulaincourts," the Gestapo infiltration of all branches of the German government, and the Canaris *Abwehr*. Bancroft gives her usual slangy appraisal of what Jung said, but her comments indicate his deep knowledge of all the situations mentioned above and hint that he had detailed information from other contacts (patients?) that he wished her to convey to Dulles.

70. Jung had always been interested in extrasensory perception and began a correspon-

dence in 1934 with Prof. J. B. Rhine, then a professor of psychology at Duke University. Their exchanges were ongoing for the rest of CGJ's life. CGJ also knew the Swiss graphologist Max Pulver, but he was more reserved about Pulver's research. See listings in *CL*-1 for further detail.

CHAPTER 32: THE VISIONS OF 1944

1. Information that follows is based primarily on the HCL interviews of Barbara Hannah, Jolande Jacobi, and Marie-Louise von Franz (among others); personal interviews with von Franz, C. A. Meier, members of the CGJ family; telephone conversation with Professor Marcus Fierz; documents in the Wolff-Trüb family archives; CGJ's correspondence with Mary Bancroft, Mary Briner, Mrs. Ann Baynes, and others (some ETH, some private archives); *MDR*, chapter 10, "Visions," pp. 289ff.; and *Protocols*, mostly undated.

2. Drs. Jakob Stahel Sr. and Jr.

3. "Dr. H." in *MDR*, he is identified in some versions of the *Protocols* dated October 16 and 18, 1957; in others undated. Unless noted otherwise, material that follows is from *Protocols*. The content of these accounts closely follows the version in chapter 10 of *MDR*, but the language is much more earthy and direct. The language of *MDR* has been not only refined but also interlaced with elaborations and clarifications that are not found in the *Protocols* or in any supporting documentation I have consulted. Jane Cabot Reid, *Jung, My Mother, and I: The Analytic Diaries of Catharine Rush Cabot* (Einsiedeln: Daimon Verlag, 2000), p. 460, n. 1, distinguishes between two doctors named Haemmerli who treated CGJ at different times: Dr. Hammerli-Schindler (who died durng CGJ's illness) and Dr. Hammerli-Steiner.

4. *Protocols*. In *MDR*, p. 189, he describes the treatment as "oxygen and camphor injections." Dr. Thomas B. Kirsch has provided the following interpretation of CGJ's treatment: "The Swiss have always used some naturalistic remedies along with high-quality, high-technology modern medicine. Camphor was one of those old-time remedies. However, the fact that it was wartime may have meant that not many medications were readily available. Basically the treatment for myocardial infarct is oxygen, morphine to reduce the pain, and other medications to make the patient comfortable. If there is congestive heart failure, medications are used to remove excess fluid. My sense from reading CGJ's description is that he had a massive heart attack but did not go into congestive heart failure. Therefore, the camphor was used to make him more comfortable."

5. In both the *Protocols* and *MDR*, he describes Haemmerli as a "Basileus from Kos," a "king" or "revered holy man" from the ancient city that was the site of the temple of Asklepios and the birthplace of Hippocrates. He had a premonition that seeing the doctor as such was an announcement of his imminent death. CGJ was Dr. Haemmerli's last patient, as he died of septicemia in April 1944 (*MDR*, p. 293; undated *Protocols*).

6. Barbara Hannah, *Jung: His Life and Work, A Biographical Memoir* (Boston: Shambhala, 1991), pp. 283–84. Not in *MDR* or *Protocols*.

7. Mary Bancroft (telephone conversation with the author) was not permitted to visit Jung in the hospital. She was shocked to hear this when the news made the rounds of the Psychological Club.

8. *Protocols*, which are quite similar here to *MDR*, pp. 293–95.

9. In the *Protocols*, CGJ confuses the genders of Malchuth and Tifereth, whom he calls "Malchut und Tiferet," and for whom he interchanges masculine and feminine articles. See also *MDR*, p. 294, n. 2.

10. For references to "hierosgamos" (sacred marriage), see listings in *CW*-19, p. 327. The *Protocols* differ from *MDR*, p. 294, and I have relied on them for the account that follows.

11. In some *Protocols*, dated October 1, 1957, under the heading "Bollingen with Kurt Wolff," a conversation in which the two men discuss the difference in style between the published works and the informal observations of the material Aniela Jaffé converted into *MDR*.

12. At this point, there is a handwritten addition to the manuscript in Aniela Jaffé's hand: "Allusion to his scientific accuracy."

13. Several *Protocols*, where Jaffé has added the following questions to herself: "Q. 7 Sermones — perh. in appendix? If those notes from *The Red Book* are supposed to be considered, it would probably go into the course of events, as it, too, is one of the events."

14. He told this to Jolande Jacobi and Barbara Hannah (both HCL interviews) and Marie-Louise von Franz (interview with the author). Later, in a letter to Jacobi, August 8, 1946, he wrote (because of a dream he had nineteen years previously): "It appears to me that I will die at the age of 73, so in 1948. But the other day I had a dream that made me less certain. It appeared as though I might be granted a few years beyond that."

15. See Hannah, *Life and Work*, p. 279, for further explanation of this custom.

16. Hannah mentions this in *Life and Work*, p. 284. Von Franz spoke of it in interviews with the author, June 1994.

17. He makes occasional references to "dreams of Emma" in various sections of the *Protocols*, but in all the versions I have consulted, Toni is noticeably absent from passages connected to his 1944 illness.

18. Examples of her letters are in Jane Reid Cabot, *Jung, My Mother, and I*, pp. 452–54; others are in the archives of (among others) Paul and Mary Mellon, Allen Dulles, Esther Harding, Cary F. Baynes, H. G. Baynes, and James and Hilde Kirsch.

19. Mary Bancroft to Allen W. Dulles, "Report," August 21, 1944.

CHAPTER 33: "CARL JUNG, RE: SUBVERSIVE ACTIVITIES"

1. Kennedy HCL interview; interview with Vernon Brooks, Cambridge, December 1996.

2. Information that follows is from a "Medical Report" written by CGJ in conjunction with Prof. Dr. Med. W. Löffler, dean of the University of Zürich Medical School and "Direktor der mediz. Universitäts-Klinik," March 6, 1945. Also, Handschriften-abteilung Dossier: MS Briefe, Zentralbibliothek, Zürich: correspondence between CGJ and Löffler and Löffler and Furtwangler. Alexis Schwarzenbach, Eva Koralnik, Ursula Schulte, and Dr. Phil. Richard Merz provided assistance and information.

3. "Medical Report," p. 1.

4. Stenographic notes about the consultation dated March 5, 1945, Zentralbibliothek, Zürich. "Medical Report," copy in the Furtwängler private archives, originally prepared for Dr. Paul Niehaus, director of the clinic La Prairie, Clarens-Montreux, who requested it.

5. Furtwängler to Löffler, May 3, 1945, Clarens; Zentralbibliothek, Zürich.

6. Anne Baynes, HCL interview.

7. John D. "Jack" Barrett is described by William McGuire, *Bollingen: An Adventure in Collecting the Past*, Bollingen Series (Princeton: Princeton Univ. Press, 1982), p. xvi, as "a youngish man whose elegance, calm, and kindness made an immediate impression."

8. Cary's daughter, Ximena de Angulo Roelli, described her this way in an interview

with the author, 1995. Dr. Joseph Henderson said: "Cary never made a decision unless compelled to do so; she hated to finish anything, disliked conclusions, and preferred to maintain a status quo — whatever it may have been." Information about Cary that follows is also taken from Mary Mellon and Cary Baynes's correspondence and memoranda in the Bollingen archives, Manuscript Division, LC, among them Cary Baynes to Mary Mellon, February 18, 1946.

9. Not in ETH; her reply is dated June 23, 1945.
10. Ruth Bailey to CGJ, February 10, 1947, ETH.
11. Aniela Jaffé to Ruth Bailey, May 10, 1958, in the Ruth Bailey archives, ETH. The letter here is typical of how much Ruth Bailey's ongoing cheerfulness meant to CGJ.
12. Information from Trüb and Naeff family heirs.
13. Barbara Hannah, *Jung: His Life and Work, A Biographical Memoir* (Boston: Shambhala, 1991), p. 289, n. b, says Heyer and Curtius were the only persons who were expelled. Heyer's ex-wife, Lucy Heyer-Grote, was not expelled. She remained fairly close to CGJ as she tried to become his first biographer (see chapter 38). Jay Livernois believes the reason Richard Heyer was not expelled from Eranos was that he was a "double agent" who assisted Olga Fröbe in helping German Jews. The writer of one of the private analytic journals wrote that the situation within the club was made so unpleasant for him because of his "patriotic German sympathies" that he had no option but to resign. He does not name them, but he wrote that "others" did the same in solidarity with him. I have been unable to ascertain whether his version is correct or whether they were actually stripped of membership. In a letter to Jolande Jacobi, August 8, 1946, CGJ writes of a possible third expulsion: "Seiffert has made a fool of himself with me. Heyer has been expelled and Curtius is unfortunate."
14. Hannah, *Life and Work*, p. 286.
15. A Festschrift volume of the *Eranos Jahrbuch* was dedicated to him on his seventieth birthday: Bände XXX, 1945, *Studien zum Problem des Archetypischen*. Festgabe für C. G. Jung zum 70. Geburtstag, 26 Juli, 1945. Jay Livernois made a copy available to me. Another was dedicated to CGJ on his seventy-fifth: Bände XVIII, 1950, *Aus der Welt der Urbilder*. Sonderband für C. G. Jung zum 75. Geburtstag, 26 Juli, 1950.
16. Jolande Jacobi, third HCL interview.
17. Franz Jung, telephone conversation with the author, November 1995, in the context of releasing information to scholars. He used the remark to express his "resentment of all forms of scholarship" that impinged on his family's privacy. Many of the Jung grandchildren told me they agreed with their parents on the issue of personal privacy and were only reluctantly acceding to contemporary attitudes.
18. Eventually published as *CGJ: Psychological Reflections: A New Anthology of His Writings, 1905–61* (with R. F. C. Hull), Bollingen Series 31 (Princeton: Princeton Univ. Press, 1970).
19. Mary Bancroft, "Carl Gustav Jung on His 70th Birthday," from the original article she wrote late July 1945 and submitted to the Associated Press. There, it was heavily "revised" (her description) by unnamed editor(s). On the revised copy sent to her by the AP, Bancroft added marginal comments, most of which consist of "He never said it! M.B." or "There is absolutely nothing here that Jung said to me. Part of it is made up. Some phrases have been taken from articles or other interviews." At the end of the version the AP published, she has written: "After this appeared, Dr. Jung asked me the meaning of it. I decided not to work anymore for AP. I could understand their changing or rejecting my stuff — but not paying me when they didn't use a word of it!" A copy is in the Mary Bancroft archives; she sent a second to CGJ (not in the ETH), and another has gone with her papers to the Schlesinger

Library at Harvard. She also writes extensively about it in slightly different form in chapter 32 of *Autobiography of a Spy* (New York: William Morrow, 1983), pp. 252–54.

20. The others, in order of presentation, were Clark University, Harvard, Oxford, and the universities of Benares, Allahabad, and Calcutta.

21. "Nach der Katastrophe," *Neue Schweizer Rundschau*, n.s. 13, no 2 (June 1945): 67–68; "After the Catastrophe," *CW*-10.

22. He actually used this phrase in "After the Catastrophe," *CW*-10, para. 419, p. 203. In para. 420, p. 205, he calls Göring a "bon vivant type of cheat." The German expression is not repeated in the English text.

23. Paul Mellon had excerpts dated May 10, 1945, translated from the Zürich weekly, of "Werden die Seelen Frieden finden?," *Die Weltwoche*, 13:600, May 11, 1945, as "The Postwar Psychic Problems of the Germans," in *CGJ Speaking*, Bollingen Series 97 (Princeton: Princeton Univ. Press, 1977), pp. 149–55.

24. *AJP* 102, no. 2 (September 1945).

25. "Zur Gegenwärtigen Lage der Psychotherapie" (The Present State of Psychotherapy), *Zentralblatt* 7, no. 1 and 2 (1934): 8–10. I used the word "alleged" advisedly here because I cannot find the passages Feldman said he was quoting, either in the original German or in two different English translations: one prepared by Jolande Jacobi for Ernest Harms (a Jung defender), copy in the Harms archives, KML; and another translated from the original and prepared specifically for this book.

26. Jacobi translation, Harms archives, KML.

27. S. S. Feldman, "Dr. CGJ and National Socialism," *AJP* 102, no. 2 (September 1945): 263.

28. Sir Laurens van der Post, interview with the author, May 1995, London. Sir Laurens said CGJ described the two women's "constant quarreling" as akin to "two irritated swans pecking at each other." He also said CGJ told him this was "quite typical" behavior of many of his same-sex patients and friends. See also Hannah, *Life and Work*, pp. 293–94.

29. The Bollingen files, LC, and private archives attest to the grave concern felt by all the editors who feared this would come to pass. Cary Baynes wrote to Mary Mellon on August 24, 1945: "You must be *very* cautious in dealing with the problem of Barbara Hannah, for *all* of her ambition is locked up in this [and] a veritable hornet's nest will be released if she thinks we are trying to take it away from her." Mary Mellon, in undated notes prepared for J. D. Barrett prior to his first visit to Zürich, wrote that Hannah's translations "are not good and will constitute a certain cause of dissention, I am afraid, here [New York] and there [Zürich]." Later in the same report she added: "I would not let her get one inch within the organization of Jung's edition, as she will undoubtedly try to take many miles."

30. Jolande Jacobi to CGJ, October 1, 1945, ETH.

31. See *CW*-19, 1946a, p. 35, and 1947a, p. 78, for full citations.

32. Jacobi and von Muralt letters dated September 17 and 25, 1945, are in CGJ and Jolande Jacobi's archive, ETH.

33. CGJ to Jolande Jacobi, August 8, 1946, ETH.

34. Paul Mellon to C. Halliwell Duell, November 23, 1948, in the Paul Mellon private archives, also in the Bollingen Foundation archives, LC.

35. Carol Baumann, November 19, 1945; Eleanor Bertine and M. Esther Harding (who signed the same letter), December 5, 1945.

36. Geoffrey Parsons to Allen Dulles, December 21, 1945, in the Allen Dulles archives, Princeton University Library.

37. Allen Dulles to Geoffrey Parsons, December 28, 1945, Allen Dulles archives, Princeton University Library. Cary Baynes to Mary Mellon, February 19, 1946, cites a 1945 conversation with Violet de Laszlo in which a pupil of de Laszlo's who was going to Zürich to study with CGJ asked Dulles to intercede with the U.S. embassy there to help him find work. The unidentified student said, according to Baynes, that Dulles "showed little or no interest, and said that though he had liked Jung, perhaps he might have been taken in and that there might be something in these rumors after all. This represents a complete right about-face, for Dulles had told [another] friend that he liked Jung *very* much and that he understood all about the smear campaign."

38. Bancroft, *Autobiography of a Spy*, chapter 31, pp. 241ff.

39. CGJ to Mary Bancroft, January 25, 1946, copy in her archives, Schlesinger Library, Harvard, and in CGJ to Mary Bancroft, ETH archives. CGJ's statement may well have been taken from the proposed preface for the Rascher book. It was not published there; nor is it filed among his unpublished writings in the ETH.

40. Adler's article was published in *The New Statesman* on May 24, 1946, following a second attack by Parelhoff that appeared on May 17.

41. Marie-Jeanne Boller-Schmid to Cary Baynes, January 29, 1946, copy in CGJ and Cary Baynes's archives, ETH.

42. CGJ to Mary Bancroft, January 25, 1946, copy in her archives, also in ETH.

43. CGJ, statement prepared for Mary Bancroft, in her archives but not in his at the ETH.

44. Ernest Harms, "CGJ: Defender of Freud and the Jews," *The Psychiatric Quarterly* (April 1946).

45. McGuire, *Bollingen*, p. 213.

46. *The Protestant*: part 1, June–July 1946, pp. 22–28; part 2, August–September 1946, pp. 26–31; part 3, February–March 1947, pp. 17–20.

47. CGJ to Philip Wylie, June 27, 1947, Philip Wylie archives, Princeton University. CGJ is referring to *When Worlds Collide, After Worlds Collide, Gladiator,* and *Finnley Wren*, all published by Farrar and Rinehart. He added: "I was under the impression that it was their initiative and not yours."

48. Although his published correspondence does not include many such letters, there are many in the ETH archives as well as in the private archives of his friends and associates. Among those I have seen are letters to Alan W. Dulles, Mary Bancroft, Mary Briner, Cary F. Baynes, Gerhard Adler, and James Kirsch.

49. The heirs who possess this journal did not give permission to quote these passages, only to express their content.

50. One of the letters is dated March 12, 1947; the others are all March 13, 1947. It is not clear which he actually sent, but all are in his archives, Princeton University Library.

51. Philip Wylie to CGJ, March 13, 1947; CGJ to Philip Wylie, March 30, 1947.

52. Quote is the headline of Wylie's column, June 14, 1947. Thompson was then executive director of the New York division of the William A. White Institute of Psychiatry. She charged that CGJ, as a Swiss citizen "who did not have to live in Germany did not have to accept [the presidency of the International Society] under any pressure or threats. It must have been an expression of his own interests."

53. *The Saturday Review of Literature*, August 2, 1947. Parelhoff's letter was published in the September 6, 1947, issue.

54. Wylie's letters appeared in *The Saturday Review* July 12, 1947, and in *Life* on July 14, 1947.

55. CGJ to Philip Wylie, July 30, 1947, Philip Wylie archives, Princeton University Library.
56. Both Marie-Jeanne Boller-Schmid, HCL interview, and later, Aniela Jaffé, *From the Life and Work of CGJ*, described this in much the same language.
57. CGJ to Philip Wylie, July 5, 1949, Philip Wylie archives, Princeton University Library.
58. For a full history of the prize and of this particular episode, see McGuire, *Bollingen*, pp. 208–17. To write this account I have relied on McGuire as well as the Ernest Harms archives at the KML, the Philip Wylie archives at Princeton University Library, the Mary Bancroft archives at the Schlesinger Library, Harvard University, and CGJ and Cary F. Baynes's correspondence, ETH.
59. CGJ to Philip Wylie, July 5, 1949, Philip Wylie archives, Princeton University Library.
60. This is attested to in correspondence, among them, from Barbara Hannah and Marie-Louise von Franz to Toni Wolff and Linda Fierz-David. Mary Foote was particularly affected, as documents in her archives at BLY show.
61. McGuire, *Bollingen*, p. 210.
62. McGuire, *Bollingen*, pp. 213–14.
63. Robert Hillyer, "Treason's Strange Fruit: The Case of Ezra Pound and the Bollingen Award," *The Saturday Review*, pp. 9–11 and 23.
64. CGJ to Philip Wylie, July 5, 1949, Philip Wylie archives, Princeton University Library.
65. *The Saturday Review*, July 30, 1949, pp. 6, 7, and 36.
66. Edel wrote in the *New York Daily Compass*; citation is McGuire, *Bollingen*, p. 214.
67. Cowley's article appeared on October 3, 1949; citation is McGuire, *Bollingen*, p. 216.
68. J. D. Barrett to Ernest Brooks Jr., president of the Old Dominion Foundation, August 26, 1949. Original letter in "Barrett, Europe 1949" Bollingen archives, Manuscript Division, LC; copies extant in various private archives, not among Jacobi archives at ETH; nor is the report she actually prepared. As I was not permitted to read Gerhard Adler's archives, I cannot ascertain whether the copy she sent him is extant. All quotes are from the Barrett letter until noted otherwise.
69. The political ramifications of CGJ's invitation to meet Churchill were noted by E. A. Bennet to Emma Jung, September 16, 1946, ETH: "It is a very pleasant compliment to Dr. Jung and the significance of it will not be missed."
70. Not exactly true: CGJ's writings were prominent on the *Otto Liste* prepared by Otto Abetz, the chief German representative in Paris, but whether they were actually burned was a matter of local choice.
71. The retired government official in Bern who was privy to the uses of this dossier has asked not to be identified.
72. Malcolm Cowley to Allen Tate, October 21, 1949; McGuire, *Bollingen*, p. 218, gives its provenance as having "turned up in the Bollingen files."
73. A copy of this document plus related correspondence is in the National Archives and Records Administration, College Park, Maryland. For assistance in locating them, I thank John Taylor for his intrepid archival assistance, Dr. Milton O. Gustafson, senior archivist, and Fred Romanski, archivist. Ann Casement, chair of the UK Council for Psychotherapy, very kindly made another copy available, along with related correspondence from Léon to Baron Robert Gilbert Vansittart, then of the British Foreign Office, and P. H. Dean, Esq., then with the British War Crimes Executive, Nuremberg. Andrew Samuels provided various clues I followed,

and Thomas Hoehn introduced me to Professor William Schoenl, who most generously made a copy of CGJ's FBI file available during the several years I waited for the Bureau to honor my FOIA request.

74. Maurice Léon to Benedict English, February 18, 1946, copy in the National Archives.

75. *The New Columbia Encyclopedia* (1975) gives the following credentials for Vansittart (1881–1957): undersecretary for Foreign Affairs 1930 and consistently anti-German; 1938–41, chief diplomatic adviser to the Foreign Secretary; advocate of a hard peace for Germany.

76. Vansittart to F. F. Garner, March 6, 1946; Garner to P. H. Dean, March 25, 1946, copies provided by Ann Casement, UK Council for Psychotherapy archives.

77. F. F. Garner to P. H. Dean, March 25, 1946.

78. Letter from S. K. McKee, special agent in charge, Pittsburgh, Pennsylvania, to W. V. Wiggins, Divisional Director of the INS, Pittsburgh. Information that follows is from CGJ's FBI dossier, FOIA. William McGuire received a copy of Olga Fröbe's FBI file while writing his *Bollingen* history and made it available to me.

79. FBI, CGJ File, September 13, 1944, New York office; also October 28, 1944, report conducted in New York City.

80. Seventeen pages were sent to Professor Schoenl; four years after I made my initial request, only fourteen were sent to me.

81. Told to me by both Mary Bancroft and Ximena de Angulo Roelli. Bancroft also interceded on Olga Fröbe's behalf. In Ximena Roelli's letters to Mary Mellon, among them March 9, 1945 (Bollingen archives, LC), she writes of a "friend in New Haven [Conn.]," i.e., Mary Bancroft's son-in-law, who discussed Oga Fröbe's plight with "an American high up in Bern," who then spoke with Frau Fröbe and was satisfied with her innocence. He assured Mary Bancroft and the other women that "the case is closed."

82. Ximena de Angulo Roelli, telephone conversation with the author, February 27, 1997, Cavigliano-Zürich.

83. I refer to A. Maidenbaum and S. Martin, eds., *Lingering Shadows: Jungians, Freudians, and Anti-Semitism* (Boston: Shambhala, 1991), as well as to the many articles, lectures, and conferences that routinely address the subject. In November 2001, I spoke at one such, the Société internationale d'histoire de la psychiatrie et de la psychanalyse's symposium in Paris, where my topic was "Jung, the Nazis, and Anti-Semitism."

84. Rascher published the *Eranos Jahrbuch* under its auspices. This was "Aus der Welt der Urbilder," cited earlier.

85. J. D. Barrett to Ernest Brooks, August 26, 1949. Brooks was director of the Old Dominion Foundation, another of the Mellon family foundations and "sister" to Bollingen (information from William McGuire, February 27, 2002).

CHAPTER 34: THE JUNGIAN UNIVERSITY

1. CGJ to Philip Wylie, February 19, 1947, Philip Wylie archives, Princeton University Library, in *CL-2*, pp. xxxvii–xxxviii.

2. Barbara Hannah, *Jung: His Life and Work, A Biographical Memoir* (Boston: Shambhala, 1991), pp. 292–95, gives a somewhat contradictory account, some of which I summarize; Franz Jung, interview with the author, November 1994, insisted that this second "episode" was not really serious but was an illness typical of an old man in his seventies. Cary Baynes gave Mary Mellon information from Olga Fröbe-Kapteyn and Marie-Jeanne Boller-Schmid, December 10, 1946 (Bollingen archives, Manuscript Division, LC), the account I follow most closely.

3. Hannah, *Life and Work*, p. 294, citing *MDR*, p. 297, conflates the first and second illnesses by attributing CGJ's comment about the first, that his "attitude" was responsible for the second. Ann Conrad Lammers, *In God's Shadow: The Collaboration of CGJ and Victor White* (New York and Mahwah, N.J.: Paulist Press, 1994), p. 302, n. 17, cites Franz Jung's comment that the second illness was "partly psychosomatic in origin." My unofficial conclusion based on conversations with several physicians, is that CGJ suffered a second infarct, less damaging than the first, that may or may not have been brought on by overwork.

4. *Protocols*, which conveys the directness and vibrancy of CGJ's language. *MDR*, last paragraph p. 199 and chapter 7, pp. 200ff., presents CGJ's comments as arranged by Aniela Jaffé.

5. Aniela Jaffé, "The Influence of Alchemy on the Work of CGJ," *Spring* (1967): 7.

6. *Psychology and Alchemy*, *CW*-12, paras. 1–3, pp. 3–4.

7. Andrew Samuels, Bani Shorter, and Fred Plaut, *A Critical Dictionary of Jungian Analysis* (London and New York: Routledge, 1986), p. 14.

8. Jaffé, "The Influence of Alchemy," p. 9, quoting *MDR*, p. 189.

9. Lammers, *In God's Shadow*, p. 12, points out that CGJ and Father Victor White used the word as a metaphor to express both the hopes and frustrations of their theological-psychological collaboration.

10. See Samuels et al., *A Critical Dictionary*, p. 14, for the full definition of this term.

11. Jaffé, "The Influence of Alchemy," p. 11.

12. In *The Practice of Psychotherapy*, *CW*-16, "The Psychology of the Transference."

13. He states this in various ways throughout the *Protocols*, all of which convey his frustration at the inability to find the precise language he needs to describe it. I use Jaffé's refinement of them all, as it appears in *MDR*, p. 221.

14. CGJ to Victor White, *CL*-1, December 19, 1947, pp. 479–81.

15. CGJ to Adolf Keller, *CL*-2, March 20, 1951, p. 10.

16. CGJ to Victor White, *CL*-1, December 19, 1947, pp. 479–81.

17. *Protocols*, some dated January 25, 1957, as conversation with Aniela Jaffé; others undated and melded into a general discussion of alchemy.

18. *The Vision Seminars*, 2:870. "Zur Psychologie der Trinitätsidee," *Eranos Jahrbuch 1940/41*, ed. Olga Fröbe-Kapteyn (Zürich: Rhein-Verlag, 1942), p. 53. The concept of *privatio boni* is linked to CGJ's friendship with the English Dominican Father Victor White, discussed in chapter 35. Translation by Lammers, *In God's Shadow*, p. 172.

19. CGJ, *Aion*, *CW*-9, part 2, para. 79, p. 45.

20. *Protocols*, January 25, 1957.

21. Jolande Jacobi, first HCL interview, December 23, 1969.

22. Hannah, *Life and Work*, p. 297, states that he saw four patients daily. Franz Jung checked several of CGJ's appointment books from this period (I was not permitted to see them myself) and said the description I offer here is more typical.

23. Jolande Jacobi, third HCL interview, December 30, 1969.

24. Michael Fordham's version, HCL interview: CGJ thought he was "never big enough. He was bitterly disappointed at his reception." Fordham then quoted a letter from CGJ to Montgomery Watt (not in *CL*) in which CGJ was "resentful and depressed" because "he was not recognized, nobody appreciated him." Fordham said it was "so like a senile depression . . . Jung was a narcissistic personality and had a lot of paranoia to deal with. Such people are never satisfied, you know."

25. HCL interviews with Marie-Jeanne Boller-Schmid, Jolande Jacobi, Aniela Jaffé, and Liliane Frey-Rohn; and two private sources.

26. She alludes to this in *Life and Work*, p. 289, and describes the driving on p. 292.

27. To write the following account, I have consulted all the HCL interviews of persons who were involved with the founding of the CGJ Institute; the most valuable were Jolande Jacobi, Barbara Hannah, Marie-Louise von Franz, Cornelia Brunner, Liliane Frey-Rohn, and C. A. Meier. I have also relied upon author interviews with Meier, von Franz, Mario Jacoby, Joseph Henderson, and Jo and Jane Wheelwright. Thomas B. Kirsch was an invaluable source, as is his *The Jungians: A Comparative and Historical Perspective* (London and Philadelphia: Routledge, 2000). Barbara Hannah presents a highly sanitized version of the institute's founding in *Life and Work*, pp. 295ff. Franz Jung offered personal observations in telephone conversations during November 1994. Jane Cabot Reid consented to multiple interviews concerning the Psychological Club's participation in the early days of the institute.

28. A private source confirmed that Fierz-David was the executive committee's first choice. Hannah, *Life and Work*, p. 295, does not mention her by name but alludes to her again in her HCL interview.

29. Hannah, *Life and Work*, pp. 295–96.

30. In her HCL interview, Jacobi disputed Meier's claim that he alone wrote the statutes for the institute, even though he was in consultation with CGJ. She insisted that Meier worked from the first draft of her 1939 proposal, "which then disappeared." Meier, in a telephone conversation in 1995, denied this, calling it "a dream Jacobi cooked up." Hannah, *Life and Work*, p. 297, says Toni Wolff participated: "This was the only administrative activity which Jung allowed Toni to take."

31. The most thorough factual account is in Kirsch, *The Jungians*, pp. 17ff.

32. CGJ to Victor White, *CL*-1, December 27, 1947, pp. 481–82. See also Kirsch, *The Jungians*, p. 17. In a private communication, July 14, 2001, Kirsch said that among those with whom he discussed how the institute was named were his parents, James and Hilde Kirsch, and also Jo Wheelwright, C. A. Meier, and Liliane Frey-Rohn. For additional sources and information, see Paul Bishop, "CGJ, Hans Trüb und die 'Psychosynthese,'" *Analytische Psychologie* 27 (1996): 119–37, part 1, p. 122, with reference to p. 135, n. 10.

33. In 1955, when K. Basch and Franz Riklin Jr. were appointed to the expanded board.

34. Private source. Hannah, *Life and Work*, pp. 297–98, gives a different account, but I believe the one here is more reliable.

35. Hannah, *Life and Work*, p. 297. Her passage that follows is contradictory and equivocal.

36. Michael Fordham, HCL interview, said Jo Wheelwright told him that when he told CGJ he wanted to found an institute in San Francisco, CGJ replied: "I'm not interested in that. I don't know why you did it." Fordham added that CGJ was against societies because "it goes against individuation. If you get a group, you immediately lower the status of the individual." In an interview with Jo Wheelwright, he denied ever having had this conversation with Fordham, saying "it never happened." Also in his HCL interview, referring to the founding of the London group, Fordham said he wrote to ask CGJ if they could use his name in the title. He said CGJ replied that "he hoped to God we would not get the money to start it." Fordham said he wrote again to say "it was not a question of getting the money, it was to be a clinic to make money from." He said CGJ told him to go ahead and found it. To date, I have found no corroboration for this anecdote.

37. For full detail, see CGJ to Victor White, *CL*-1, December 27, 1947, pp. 481–82. Pauli accepted in a letter to CGJ, *J/Pauli*, 33P, December 23, 1947, p. 32.

38. Jolande Jacobi, third HCL interview.

39. Jolande Jacobi, third HCL interview. Found in slightly different language in interviews with Cornelia Brunner, Hanni Binder, Mario Jacoby, and several private
sources.
40. Kirsch, *The Jungians*, p. 19.
41. Sybille Willi-Niehus, CGJ's first grandchild, also became the first woman to be
president of the *Erbengemeinschaft CGJ*, or commitee of his heirs; Ludwig Niehus
held the same office later; Brigette Merk-Niehus has participated as well.
42. *CW*-18, "Address on the Occasion of the Founding of the CGJ Institute, Zürich,
24 April, 1948," paras. 1129ff., pp. 471–76.
43. With Pauli, see *CW*-19, p. 84, for full bibliographic information.
44. *CL*-1, pp. 180–82.
45. *CW*-18, p. 474, notes.

CHAPTER 35: "WHY MEN HAD TO QUARREL AND LEAVE"
1. Mario Jacoby, interview with the author, November 12, 1994, Zollikon. Jacoby's
descriptions were repeated by other students in interviews and conversations.
Among those whose insights are represented in this chapter are Vernon Brooks,
Hanni Binder, Patricia Dunton, David Hart, Peter Lynn, Sonja Marjasch, James
Hillman, Thomas B. Kirsch, Murray Stein, Adolf Guggenbuhl-Craig, Robert Hin-
shaw, Paul Brutsche, and Marie-Louise von Franz. Maggy Anthony provides an ac-
count of what the first class was like in "A Forum Is Created," *The Valkyries: The
Women Around Jung* (Longmead, Shaftesbury: Element Books, 1990), pp. 1–7.
Thomas Kirsch, *The Jungians: A Comparative and Historical Perspective* (London and
Philadelphia: Routledge, 2000), is a valuable resource. Dr. Peter Lynn, "CGJ,
Emma Jung, and Toni Wolff," in Ferne Jensen, ed., *CGJ, Emma Jung, and Toni
Wolff: A Collection of Remembrances* (San Francisco: The Analytical Psychology
Club, 1982), pp. 41–42, describes his experiences as a student from 1950 to 1953.
2. The distinguished graduate of the institute who showed me student notebooks and
described the gestures of these persons has asked not to be identified.
3. Fowler McCormick made a large donation to the fledgling institute that paid most
of the rent for the first five years of its existence. Quarters were shared until 1970,
when the former home of the Swiss writer Conrad Ferdinand Meyer, within walking distance of the Jung home in Küsnacht, became available for long-term rental.
It remains the home of the institute today.
4. Jane Cabot Reid most graciously took me through the club in November 2001 to
show me Jung's tapestry and all the photographs and paintings that were there in
the years I write about. She does not remember the photographs being hung as
Lewis Mumford wrote about them in "Reflections: European Diary," *The New
Yorker*, July 6, 1968. In the same article, Mumford discussed Jung's attitude toward
Nazi Germany in connection with A. J. P. Taylor's biography of Hitler and concludes that "alongside this seemingly equable but insidious reworking of the evidence of a trained scholar, Jung's political sins during the overheated thirties seem
venial."
5. Richard Noll, *The Jung Cult* (Princeton: Princeton Univ. Press, 1994), p. 289.
6. Dr. Peter Lynn and Dr. David Hart, in individual interviews, both confirmed that
they went to the American embassy in Paris to persuade officials there to put the
institute on the list of approved places where GIs could study in Europe. Dr. Lynn
said, "[Emma Jung was] so proud of us for doing this. She would say, 'Even the
U.S. government now recognizes us!'"
7. M. I. Rix Weaver, "An Interview with CGJ," in Jensen, ed. *CGJ, Emma Jung, and
Toni Wolff*, pp. 90–95. Weaver was the first Australian to study at the institute.

8. Several *Protocols* contain large segments of such Q & A sessions: one with institute students, another with members of the Psychological Club, and another with a group of Catholic priests who convened a seminar of their own in Zürich. Aniela Jaffé appears not to have used any of it directly in *MDR* but has incorporated the occasional remark into, to give one example, chapter 7, "The Work."

9. "Comments on a Doctoral Thesis by CGJ," *CGJ Speaking*, ed. William McGuire, Bollingen Series 97 (Princeton: Princeton Univ. Press, 1977), pp. 212–13. The thesis was written by Ira Progoff.

10. Mario Jacoby, November 12, 1994; the sentiment was shared by most others cited in n. 1, above.

11. I refer to biographies, memoirs, and critical studies that present this view at face value, among them Vincent Brome, Michael Fordham, Ronald Haymann, Frank McLynn, Richard Noll, Paul J. Stern, and numerous others.

12. *CL*-1, pp. 404–5, n. 1. In his HCL interview, March 21, 1970, Boss stated that Jung originally invited "four psychotherapists who he thought were the most promising," and he listed himself, Bally, Meier, and Maeder. He does not explain why or when the group was enlarged to seven, with Jung making the eighth member.

13. Meier interview with the author, November 1995.

14. Medard Boss, HCL interview.

15. In the HCL interview, Nameche questions Boss as follows:

Nameche: Did he intend to?
Boss: Yes, he said so, too. He intended to make us his followers in order to have his teachings brought about or spread out.
Nameche: He said that directly?
Boss: Yes, well, that is good, right.
Nameche: Yes, but it seems strange to me.

In the HCL interviews of others in the group, Maeder and Binswanger among them, no one else describes the meetings as Boss does, but none later experienced the profound disagreement with Jung that Boss did.

16. Bern, 1947 (German); New York, 1949 (English: heavily revised, with many changes following those suggested by CGJ to Mary Bancroft, *CL*-2, June 27, 1947, and August 5, 1947). The book *Psychoanalysis and Daseinanalysis* appeared in 1963.

17. Boss, HCL interview.

18. CGJ to Mary Bancroft, *CL*-2, June 27, 1947 (quote is from n. 4); also August 5, 1947.

19. June 27, 1947, *CL*-2, p. xl.

20. Mary Bancroft to CGJ, not published in *CL*-2 but listed in n. 1, p. xliii, as July 17, 1947. Mary Bancroft and CGJ's correspondence is listed in the ETH archives but was not available for this book. In a private conversation, a Swiss physician and former student of Boss's told me that he read an extensive exchange between Boss and Jung that, in his view, was "informative and well worth publishing; of great value to those in the healing professions." At the time of our 1997 conversation, he did not know what had become of the letters.

21. CGJ to Mary Bancroft, *CL*-2, August 5, 1947, p. xliii.

22. Boss, HCL interview.

23. Published posthumously in 1951 by Ernst Klett Verlag, Stuttgart. To date, there is no English translation.

24. The lecture took place on May 17, 1936, and was followed by Jung's dissenting response. Trüb wrote his own dissent in the form of a letter to Martin Buber and

Rudolf Pannwitz. All three documents are in the Martin Buber archive, Jewish National and University Library, Jerusalem. Some of the works I have consulted include: J. B. Agassi, ed., *Martin Buber on Psychology and Psychotherapy* (Syracuse: Syracuse Univ. Press, 1999); Paul Bishop, "C. G. Jung, Hans Trüb und die 'Psychosynthese,'" *Analytische Psychologie* 27 (1996): 119–37 (part 1) and 159–92 (part 2); Henri Ellenberger, *Discovery of the Unconscious* (New York: Basic Books, 1981), pp. 732ff.; Nahum N. Glatzer and Paul Mendes-Flohr, eds., *The Letters of Martin Buber: A Life of Dialogue* (New York: Schocken Books, 1991); CGJ, "Religion and Psychology: A Reply to Martin Buber," *CW*-18, paras. 1499ff., pp. 663ff.; Robert C. Smith, "A Critical Analysis of Religious and Philosophic Issues Between Buber and Jung" (unpublished Ph.D. diss., Temple Univ., 1961); and Barbara D. Stephens, "The Martin Buber–CGJ Disputations: Protecting the Sacred in the Battle for the Boundaries of Analytical Psychology," *JAP* 46 (2001): 455–91. Copies of the following works of Hans Trüb were made available by his estate: *Über Aufmerksamkeit und Auffassungstähigkeit bei Gesunden und Kranken* (unter Besonderer Berücksichtigung des Stupors) (Berlin: Verlagsbuchhandlung von Julius Springer, 1917); *Aus Einem Winkel Meines Sprechzimmers: Meinen Patienten Gewidmet* (Berlin: Verlag Lambert Schneider, 1930); *Psychosynthese: Als Seelisch-Geistiger Heilungsprozess* (Leipzig-Z.: Max Niehaus Verlag, 1936); "Vom Selbst zur Welt," in *Sonderdruck aus der Zeitschrift Psyche*, 1 folge (Leipzig-Z.: Speer Verlag, 1947); *Heilung aus der Begegnung* (Stuttgart: Ernst Klett Verlag, 1951 [posthumous: Trüb died in Zürich on October 8, 1949]).

25. Bezzola's (1868–1936) capsule biography is *CL*-18, para. 935, p. 398.
26. Dr. Med. Georg Trüb said an exact English meaning is still lacking, and perhaps a better way to express it is as "being 'a' self."
27. Hans Trüb's emphasis, from "Randbemerkung," marginal notes or comments written by Trüb on a copy of a letter he received from Gustav Bally, June 26, 1941, original written by Bally to CGJ (not in *CL*). Provided by the Hans Trüb estate.
28. Trüb, *Aus Einem Winkel.*
29. Trüb quotes von Weizäcker's *Kreaturheft.*
30. The following is based on interviews with Dr. Med. Georg Trüb and Ursula Cadorin-Trüb; CGJ's unpublished correspondence with Hans Trüb and Susanna Trüb in the Trüb family archives; author interviews with Cornelia Brunner, Marie-Louise von Franz, Franz Jung, Vernon Brooks (who provided information from William Kennedy), and Mario Jacoby; HCL interviews of Jolande Jacobi, Cornelia Brunner, Medard Boss, Wilhelm Bitter, Marie-Louise von Franz, Barbara Hannah, and Marcus Fierz; Liliane Frey-Rohn; and several private sources.
31. Trüb family archives.
32. Gustav Bally to CGJ, June 26, 1941, not in *CL*, copy in the Trüb family archives, annotated in Trüb's "Randbemerkung."
33. He refers to his essay "Individuation, Guilt, and Decision: On the Boundaries of Psychology," originally published as "Individuation, Schuld und Entscheidung: Über die Grenzen der Psychologie," in *Die Kulturelle Bedeutung der komplexen Psychologie* (Berlin, 1935), Festschrift for CGJ's sixtieth birthday, ed. Emilii Medtner.
34. CGJ to Theodor Bovet, *CL*-2, pp. 276–78.
35. See Trüb's letters to Buber in Glatzer and Mendes-Flohr, eds., *The Letters of Martin Buber*, nos. 334 and 350, pp. 332 and 345.
36. Dr. Med Georg Trüb, interview with the author, November 11, 1999; documents in the Wolff-Trüb-Naeff archives.
37. Glatzer and Mendes-Flohr, eds., *The Letters of Martin Buber*, p. 455, n. 5, Rudolf Pannwitz's two letters, December 2 and 5, 1936, paraphrased but not quoted di-

rectly. The editors write that Pannwitz believed that "as a pragmatist Trüb would not be able to accomplish the attempted theoretical-systematic elaboration of his thought that was intended to go beyond the psychoanalysis of CGJ, vis-à-vis whom Trüb had a sort of Oedipus complex."

38. Toni Wolff reminded Susi Trüb of this in her letter of July 17, 1952, which became a critique of the book. The letter is the source for quotes until noted otherwise.

39. "Dialogue": F. X. Charet, "A Dialogue Between Psychology and Theology: The Correspondence of CGJ and Victor White," *JAP* 35 (1990): 421–41. "Dispute": Adrian Cunningham, "Victor White, John Layard, and CGJ," *Harvest* 38 (1992): 44–57; see also Adrian Cunningham, "Victor White and CGJ: The Fateful Encounter of the White Raven and the Gnostic," *New Blackfriars* 62 (1981). "Wall": Franz Jung, quoted in Ann Conrad Lammers, *In God's Shadow: The Collaboration of CGJ and Victor White* (New York and Mahwah, N.J.: Paulist Press, 1994), p. 260. "Failure": Lammers, *In God's Shadow*, p. 12.

40. Two titles representative of White's interests are "The Frontiers of Theology and Psychology" and "St. Thomas Aquinas and Jung's Psychology." For a full listing of the articles originally sent by White to CGJ, see *CL-1*, p. 382, n. 1.

41. Layard and his wife, Doris, went to Zürich in the late 1930s for sessions with CGJ, Emma Jung, and Toni Wolff. For information about their stay, see Adrian Cunningham, "Victor White, John Layard, and CGJ," pp. 48–50. See also John Layard's interview, HCL. I agree with Nameche that it "should be handled with several grains of salt" because of "Layard's feeling of being unloved and unwanted" by CGJ. Layard said CGJ's rapport with White was similar to his own: "He didn't want to talk about me. He wanted to pick my brains about anthropology, as he later picked Victor White's brains about theology and sent him pretty batty."

42. CGJ to Victor White, *CL-1*, September 26, 1945, p. 382.

43. CGJ to Victor White, *CL-1*, October 5, 1945, p. 383.

44. Lammers, *In God's Shadow*, p. 278, n. 29.

45. Lammers, *In God's Shadow*, p. 35.

46. Barbara Hannah, private archive.

47. Lammers tells why the total correspondence is not and will not be available (*In God's Shadow*, Appendix A).

48. Among them Adrian Cunningham, Ann Conrad Lammers, F. X. Charet, Barbara Hannah, all cited above, and Aelred Squire, in Lammers, Appendix C, whose views Lammers cites. Murray Stein provides sound observation in his introduction to *Jung on Christianity* (Princeton: Princeton Univ. Press, 1999). Also, interviews with Marie-Louise von Franz, C. A. Meier, Mario Jacoby, Cornelia Brunner, Baroness Vera von der Heydt, Molly Tuby, Anthony Stevens, Anthony Storr, and Sir Laurens van der Post, and private archives made available for this book.

49. I agree with John P. Dourley's reading of the published letters that he cites in "Jung and the White, Buber Exchanges," *A Strategy for a Loss of Faith* (Toronto: Inner City Books, 1992), p. 37 and nn. 85 and 86. For the most complete history of CGJ and Victor White's correspondence to date, see Lammers, *In God's Shadow*, Appendix A, pp. 257–62.

50. CGJ to Victor White, April 2, 1955, *CL-2*, pp. 238–43, and May 6, 1955, p. 251.

51. Charet, "A Dialogue," p. 422.

52. CGJ "To the Mother Prioress of a Contemplative Order," February 6, 1960, *CL-2*, p. 536. She has since been identified by Lammers, *In God's Shadow*, p. 278, n. 29, as Mother Michael of the Blessed Trinity.

53. Charet, "A Dialogue," p. 421.

54. Published in *Dominican Studies* (Oxford) 2, no. 4 (October 1949).

55. Lammers, *In God's Shadow*, pp. 98ff.
56. CGJ to Victor White, January 19, 1955, *CL-2*, pp. 212–14, esp. nn. 1 and 2, April 2, 1955, p. 239, n. 2.
57. CGJ to Victor White, April 2, 1955, *CL-2*, pp. 238–43, esp. nn. 1 and 7.
58. "Jung on Job," *Blackfriars* 36, 3/55 (Oxford: Blackfriars Publications); also in *God and the Unconscious* (Dallas: *Spring* Publications, 1982). See also Lammers, *In God's Shadow*, pp. 101ff.
59. Lammers, *In God's Shadow*, p. 101.
60. CGJ to Victor White, April 2, 1955, *CL-2*, p. 241.
61. White was not the only scholar to hold this view. Walter Kaufmann, in *Discovering the Mind: Goethe, Kant, and Hegel* (New York: McGraw-Hill, 1980), p. 414, calls *Job* "a long delayed adolescent rebellion against the Bible stories on which he had been raised." On p. 421 he compares CGJ to "a man who never managed to resolve his Oedipus-complex."
62. Marilyn Nagy writes in *Philosophical Issues in the Psychology of CGJ* (New York: State Univ. of New York Press, 1991), p. 146, that CGJ "is angry at God in a way no unbeliever could ever be."
63. CGJ to Victor White, December 31, 1949, *CL-1*, pp. 539–41, esp. n. 2. For full bibliographic citations see *CW-19*, 1949b, p. 39.
64. To give one example of how his irritation clouded his explanation, see "Religion and Psychology: A Reply to Martin Buber," *CW-18*, paras. 1499–1513, pp. 663–70.
65. CGJ to Victor White, December 31, 1949.
66. CGJ to Victor White, May 6, 1955, *CL-2*, p. 251.
67. Originally posed by Ann Conrad Lammers, the only scholar who, to date, has read the letters in their entirety.
68. Lammers, *In God's Shadow*, p. 105.
69. *Soul and Psyche: An Enquiry into the Relationship of Psychotherapy and Religion* (New York: Harper and Brothers, 1960).
70. Victor White to CGJ, May 21, 1955, quoted in Lammers, *In God's Shadow*, pp. 106–7. She calls it White's "final letter."
71. Victor White to CGJ, May 19, 1955, in Lammers, *In God's Shadow*, p. 107.
72. CGJ to Victor White, April 30, 1960, *CL-2*, pp. 554–55.
73. Victor White to CGJ, May 8, 1960, in Lammers, *In God's Shadow*, p. 111.
74. Many references abound in *CL-2*, c. 1951ff.
75. CGJ's writings on synchronicity appear in *CW-8*, 7, "Synchronicity: An Acausal Connecting Principle," paras. 816ff., pp. 419ff.
76. Hannah, *Jung: Life and Work, A Biographical Memoir* (Boston: Shambhala, 1991), p. 305, who gives the credit for this definition to Marie-Louise von Franz. Hannah follows the definition with the incident of the scarab beetle, which CGJ uses in *CW-8*, para. 843, p. 438. For the most thorough paraphrase of CGJ's essay and the most orthodox explanation (i.e., of which CGJ would have approved), see von Franz's *Psyche and Matter* (Einsiedeln: Daimon Verlag, 1988), particularly the chapters on synchronicity, pp. 203ff.
77. *CW-8*, para. 866, p. 452.
78. *CW-8*, para. 867, pp. 453–54.
79. *CW-8*, para. 868, p. 454.
80. Hanni Binder, from an interview with the author, April 23, 1996, Zürich. Mary Elliot was one of a group of Englishwomen who lived in the Sonne Hotel and who diligently provided whatever secretarial service CGJ needed. Along with Mary Foote and Elizabeth Welsh, she transcribed most of his seminars and lectures. To write this account I have also made use of a telephone conversation with Gret

Baumann-Jung, several with her son Dieter Baumann, and an interview with another son, Wolf Baumann.

81. Hanni Binder, interview, April 23, 1996. Throughout, Binder repeated: "You must tell everyone that Jung *never* gave a formal seminar on the Tarot, Jung *never* wrote anything on the Tarot." Anthony Storr sent me by fax, July 3, 1995, a copy of a letter written by Edgar Wind to Professor Jack Good, about CGJ and astrology. Wind had a conversation with CGJ in the mid-1930s in London that was "confined to one subject — astrology." CGJ told Wind that he had cast his own horoscope and it taught him much about himself. He often recommended it to patients. Wind asked whether CGJ meant that astrology was a science that enables one to predict future events or whether it was "merely . . . a schematic substratum . . . to arouse the imagination and project into the schema certain images that unconsciously occupy your mind." Wind said CGJ "burst out laughing" and said "of course he meant the second, but . . . if he told that to his patients it would not work. . . . He believed that his schemata were *effective* [Wind's emphasis], and that was all that interested him about them . . . the calculation of a horoscope can have a cathartic effect. Therefore he recommends horoscopes and that is all." Wind called CGJ "the only psychoanalyst of any school whom I ever found to have a sense of humor."

82. Gret Baumann-Jung alluded to this with discretion in a telephone conversation; Hanni Binder was more blunt in an interview: "We did all this work for three years, and then Jung got ill and he gave it all to Mrs. Fierz. Her son who was the analyst took it when she died, and now he is dead and his old widow has it in her house, and she is ill now, too. I don't know what will happen to it, because she does not want anyone to see it." Dr. Markus Fierz and Frau Minga Fierz, in letters and telephone conversations in 1995 and 1996, declined to discuss this matter.

83. CGJ to Dr. H., *CL*-2, March 17, 1951, pp. 7–9.

84. CGJ to Adolf Keller, *CL*-2, March 20, 1951, pp. 9–10. This and CGJ's previous letter to Dr. H. are typical of the many comments he made on the subject. Another important letter is CGJ to Victor White, *CL*-1, November 25, 1950, pp. 566–68.

85. *CW*-12, "The Symbolism of the Mandala," para. 210, p. 162. For CGJ's discussion of the Dogma, see *CW*-12, "Answer to Job," paras. 743–44, pp. 457–59, and paras. 748–57, pp. 461–69.

86. CGJ to Philip Wylie, partial handwritten letter, undated; in the Philip Wylie archives, Princeton University Library.

87. Philip Wylie to CGJ, July 9, 1949, Princeton University Library.

88. CGJ to Philip Wylie, December 22, 1957, *CL*-2, pp. 404–5.

89. Wylie's claim is made in his letter to McGuire, who replied on April 5, 1967, that Adler was in possession of a letter from CGJ dated June 1960. It is not in *CL*, nor is it in the Princeton University Library archives. As Wylie was scrupulous about preserving CGJ's letters, I tend to take him at his word.

90. Philip Wylie to William McGuire, December 24, 1966, Philip Wylie archives, Princeton University Library. McGuire was then seeking letters on behalf of Gerhard Adler, who was editing *CL*. Only the first page of this letter is extant.

91. McGuire, *CGJ Speaking*, introduction to "Comments on a Doctoral Thesis," pp. 205–6. It became his first book: *Jung's Psychology and Its Social Meaning* (New York: Dialogue House Library, 1953).

92. "Comments on a Doctoral Thesis," pp. 205–18.

93. CGJ's "secretary" (probably Una Thomas or Doris Gautschy, replacements for the newly married Marie-Jeanne Boller-Schmid) wrote to Ira Progoff, asking him to return missing sections of the text.

94. Ira Progoff to CGJ, August 24, 1954, ETH.

95. CGJ to Ira Progoff, March 22, 1955, ETH. CGJ put the phrase "advanced ideas" in quotation marks in the original typed letter.
96. In a letter to Michael Fordham, June 20, 1955, CGJ called Progoff "merely a Dr. Phil," ETH archives but not in *CL*.
97. *CW*-8, para. 963, p. 514.
98. CGJ to Ira Progoff, January 30, 1954, copy in ETH, not in *CL*.
99. This assessment, with which I disagree, is C. A. Meier's in his Foreword to *Atom and Archetype: The Pauli-Jung Letters 1932–58* (Princeton: Princeton Univ. Press, 2001), p. lviii. Meier considers this relationship valid throughout their life; I believe it changed when Pauli returned to Zürich after World War II.
100. Pauli to CGJ, *J/Pauli*, December 23, 1947, pp. 32–33.
101. "Synchronicity," *CW*-8, para. 828, p. 427.
102. Pauli to CGJ, *J/Pauli*, June 28, 1949, pp. 36–42. Pauli gave a long and thoughtful critique of the entire essay, and it is obvious from *CW*-8 that Jung followed all his advice and incorporated much of it. Dr. Elisabeth Rüf, one of the textual editors of the German *Gesammelte Werke*, told me in a telephone conversation (August 17, 1995) that the most difficult editorial task she faced was to ensure two things: (1) that CGJ's quotations were correct and accurate; and (2) that what he claimed was his own writing and thinking "really was his, not the actual words or a paraphrase of someone else." Dr. Sonja Marjasch, in a separate telephone conversation, August 19, 1995, also discussed how Jung "was like a magpie, picking everything up and taking it home." Her comments were made in connection with examples of the kind of work CGJ required of von Franz and Barbara Hannah as well as of Rüf's editing concerns. Ximena de Angulo Roelli described in an interview how "every statement he attributed to someone else as well as every fact he claimed as his own had to be checked and double-checked to make sure he was right."
103. The first quote is *CW*-8, para. 827, p. 426; the second is para. 827, p. 427.
104. Two lectures, given at the Psychological Club, Zürich, February 28 and March 6, 1948: "Der Einfluss archetypischer Vorstellungen auf die Bildung naturwissenschaftlicher Theorien bei Kepler," reprinted as Appendix 6, *J/Pauli*, pp. 203–9; later revised and published as Pauli's contribution to *Naturerklärung und Psyche (The Interpretation of Nature and the Psyche)*, 1952 (German), 1955 (English); CGJ's essay republished in *CW*-8. For full bibliographic citations, see *CW*-19, 1952b (German), p. 43; 1955a (English), p. 84.
105. Pauli to CGJ, *J/Pauli*, November 7, 1948, pp. 34–35.
106. CGJ to Pauli, *J/Pauli*, p. 36. C. A. Meier's editorial note on p. 38 refers the reader to the evolving drafts at the ETH for changes that occurred because of CGJ's ongoing talks and correspondence with Pauli.
107. For example, CGJ's conciliatory reply in *J/Pauli*, pp. 59–63, to Pauli's letter, pp. 53–59.
108. For example, see J. D. F. Jones, *Storyteller: The Many Lives of Laurens van der Post* (London: John Murray, 2001).
109. *Jung and the Problem of Evil* (London: Rockliff, Salisbury Square, 1958). See also their correspondence at the ETH.
110. *Conversations with Carl Jung* (New York: Van Nostrand Reinhold, 1964).
111. *CGJ* (London: Barrie and Rockliff, 1961); *What Jung Really Said* (London: MacDonald and Jane's, 1966); and *Meetings with Jung* (Zürich: Daimon Verlag, 1985).
112. See the preface to *CGJ*, p. vii, for one of the many insertions of privileged access to CGJ that color E. A. Bennet's writing.

Chapter 36: "The Memory of a Vanishing World"

1. Emma Jung to Catharine Cabot, in Jane Cabot Reid, *Jung, My Mother, and I: The Analytic Diaries of Catharine Rush Cabot* (Einsiedeln: Daimon Verlag, 2000), pp. 564–65.
2. Interviews with Rudolf Niehus and Monica Walder, 1995.
3. Agathe Niehus-Jung, interview with the author, 1995.
4. To write this account I have consulted the following: Gerhard Adler, "Reflections on Chance and Fate," in *The Shaman from Elko* (San Francisco: CGJ Institute of San Francisco, 1978); Maggy Anthony, *The Valkyries: The Women Around Jung* (Longmead, Shaftesbury: Element Books, 1990); Irene Champernowne, *A Memoir of Toni Wolff*, Foreword by Joseph L. Henderson, privately printed by the CGJ Institute of San Francisco, 1980; Ferne Jensen, ed., *CGJ, Emma Jung, and Toni Wolff: A Collection of Remembrances* (San Francisco: The Analytical Psychology Club, 1982); R. Lane, "Recollections of Toni Wolff," *A Well of Living Water*, Festschrift privately printed for Hilde Kirsch's 75th birthday (Los Angeles: CGJ Institute, 1977); and Jane Reid, *Jung, My Mother, and I*. Also, author interviews with Joseph Henderson, Jane and Jo Wheelwright, Mario Jacoby, Thomas B. Kirsch, Baroness Vera von der Heydt, Ursula Cadorin-Trüb, Georg Trüb, Adrian Baumann, Franz Jung, Barbara Hannah, and Marie-Louise von Franz. Also HCL interviews, including Ruth Bailey, archives from two sources who wish to remain private, and the Barbara Hannah private archive.
5. Ruth Bailey returns to this several times in her HCL interview; she speaks of it again in the Glin Bennet interview in *Spring* ("Domestic Life with CGJ: Tape-recorded Conversations with Ruth Bailey" [1986]).
6. Ruth Bailey, HCL interview.
7. Vincent Brome, *Jung: Man and Myth* (New York: Macmillan, 1981), p. 238, quotes Barbara Hannah as saying that CGJ "disliked funerals on principle and never went to them." I find this unlikely, especially since CGJ's presence was recorded at many funerals, both of persons close to him and of those he hardly knew but to whom he felt he owed the respect of being there. Also, in her private archive, Hannah spoke of CGJ's "extreme emotional distress" over Toni's death. CGJ's letters to Susi Trüb support this interpretation.
8. *Protocols.* Barbara Hannah, *Jung: His Life and Work, A Biographical Memoir* (Boston: Shambhala, 1991), p. 313, gives a somewhat different account of this dream.
9. Dr. Peter Jung, on a guided tour in 1998, said that like many other artifacts that had graced the property in CGJ's lifetime, the stone had been removed to safer quarters to protect it from souvenir hunters and thieves.
10. In a private archive, read to me by the owner, who did not permit me to read them myself.
11. I asked nearly all the persons interviewed for this book if they or their acquaintances had ever heard Emma make such a remark. No one could confirm or corroborate Barbara Hannah's statement. This is not to say that Emma did not say it but merely to state my reservation that I find it unlikely; the rapport between Emma Jung and Barbara Hannah was "too formal" to support the intimacy this remark implies. An aside: Sallie Nichols, in Jensen, *CGJ, Emma Jung, and Toni Wolff*, p. 48, tells how Toni urged her to invite her husband's mistress to lunch and spoke of what a mistress could do for a marriage in terms that paralleled hers with CGJ and Emma.
12. Joseph L. Henderson, "CGJ, Emma Jung, and Toni Wolff," in Jensen, *CGJ, Emma Jung, and Toni Wolff*, p. 33.

13. CGJ to Catharine Rush Cabot, March 31, 1953, in Reid, *Jung: My Mother, and I,* p. 566.
14. Emma Jung to Catharine Rush Cabot, 1953, in Reid, *Jung, My Mother, and I,* p. 568.
15. CGJ to Catharine Rush Cabot, November 6, 1953, in Reid, *Jung, My Mother, and I,* p. 570.
16. CGJ to Gerhard Adler, November 25, 1955, ETH.
17. The first mention of Emma's illness in writing appears to be E. A. Bennet's reply to CGJ, September 26, 1952, ETH. CGJ's letter to Bennet is missing from the archive.
18. Werner Engel, "Memory of Emma Jung," in Jensen, *CGJ, Emma Jung, and Toni Wolff,* p. 14; Elizabeth Howes ("Memory of Emma Jung," p. 34) had therapy for several months in 1955 but did not notice anything untoward.
19. Heinrich K. Fierz, "Memory of CGJ," in Jensen, *CGJ, Emma Jung, and Toni Wolff,* pp. 21–22.
20. CGJ to E. A. Bennet, July 4, 1955, ETH.
21. CGJ to E. A. Bennet, July 14, 1955, ETH. Bennet, in his HCL interview, confirms that he and Ruth Bailey were "the only outsiders" at the celebration who were also houseguests.
22. The account that follows is from E. A. Bennet's HCL interview.
23. CGJ to Cary Baynes, March 24, 1955, ETH. The recording was done in Ascona, with van der Post, CGJ said, "getting my melodious voice for the BBC."
24. CGJ singled out the American Gerald Sykes, "the author of the 'Nice American,' who is not nice at all, but I am afraid true" (CGJ to Cary Baynes, March 24, 1955, ETH).
25. Originally printed in two volumes in German. Aniela Jaffé, "The Creative Phases in Jung's Life," p. 181, states that he began writing this book in 1941 when he was sixty-six and finished it sixteen years later in 1957.
26. Cary Baynes to CGJ, July 21, 1955, ETH. CGJ's letter to her is missing from the archive.
27. The quote is from the author's bio on her book, *Reserve du Patron: Im Gespräch mit K* (Stäfa: Rothenhausler Verlag, 1989); see particularly pp. 209–11. Attenhofer was an actress and writer celebrated for her talent, her vocal anti-Semitism, and her marriage to the distinguished professor of literature at the ETH (and Jung's friend) Karl Schmid. Ursula Schulte called this book to my attention.
28. Jolande Jacobi, HCL interview: "I am not sure that he felt flattered. It was an unusual compliment."
29. Ruth Bailey, HCL interview.
30. Discussed with (among others) E. A. Bennet, in letters of December 15, 1949, and December 20, 1949.
31. Ruth Bailey's expression in her HCL interview.
32. Bennet, "Domestic Life," pp. 177ff.
33. Aniela Jaffé (for CGJ) to Jacquetta Hawkes, November 1, 1955; Aniela Jaffé to J. B. Priestley, December 9, 1955; not in *CL* but both in ETH. According to Jaffé, it was the last book Emma read.
34. M. I. Rix Weaver, in Jensen, *CGJ, Emma Jung, and Toni Wolff,* pp. 90–95. CGJ usually tried to give to each student a personal interview at some point during his or her study. The patients' waiting room was also the room in which the household linens were stored; after CGJ's death, Franz Jung converted it into his kitchen and dining room.

35. Weaver, in Jensen, *CGJ, Emma Jung, and Toni Wolff;* HCL interviews of Ruth Bailey and Adrian Baumann; van der Post and Niehus family interviews with the author; and Barbara Hannah private archive.

36. Adrian Baumann, HCL interview. He added: "I don't know if she said good-bye to my grandfather, too. I can't remember that now."

37. Other biographers, Vincent Brome among them (*Jung*, p. 258), write that Emma had a stroke and was unconscious in the last week of her life. Family members deny it. CGJ wrote to Erich Neumann, *CL-2*, December 15, 1955, that Emma was "mostly in a coma," but Franz Jung said she was "mostly asleep because of the medication."

38. Ruth Bailey, personal interview with Brome, quoted in *Jung*, p. 260. She gives a similar account in her HCL interview.

39. Frieda and Michael Fordham were prominent among those who claimed to be with CGJ after Emma's funeral. In interviews with C. A. Meier and Marie-Louise von Franz, both insisted that no one but family saw CGJ. Franz Jung said he was so grief-stricken he did not remember clearly but thought it unlikely that outsiders were taken upstairs. However, in the months that followed Emma's death, many persons attested to hearing CGJ call her "a queen."

40. Ruth Bailey, HCL interview.

41. After CGJ's death, she returned to her family's home in Cheshire, where she died in 1981.

42. Laurens van der Post, *Jung and the Story of Our Time* (New York: Random House, 1977), p. 254. I corroborate after a tour generously provided by Dr. and Mrs. Willi-Niehus.

43. Aniela Jaffé, describing the dreams recorded in *MDR*, in "Remembering Jung," an interview with Suzanne Wagner, *Psychological Perspectives* 26 (1992): 108.

44. Adrian Baumann, HCL interview.

45. According to private banking officials in Zürich who spoke on the condition of anonymity, Emma Jung was the second-richest woman in Switzerland, but they could not reveal the actual amount of her fortune. According to Ulrich Hoerni and Dr. Peter Jung, who spoke officially for the *Erbengemeinschaft CGJ*, Emma Jung-Rauschenbach made a private will that, once it was officially ajudicated according to cantonal law, was returned to the privacy of her attorney's archives and now remains within the private archives of her descendants. I am grateful to Dr. Jur. Vera Rottenberg Liatowitsch, active justice of the Swiss Supreme Court, and Dr. Jur. Margrith Bigler-Eggenberger, retired justice of the Swiss Supreme Court, for assisting me with an understanding of Swiss matrimonial law. Dr. Jur. Othmar Schmidlin was my informal consultant about general Swiss law.

46. Emma Jung to Sigmund Freud, *F/J*, November 6, 1911, p. 456.

47. The account that follows is based on Adrian Baumann, Ruth Bailey, Walther Niehus, Ludwig (Lutz) and Luggi Niehus, all HCL interviews; my interviews with Sir Laurens van der Post and Marie-Louise von Franz; and Barbara Hannah's private archive. Dr. Peter Jung, in a guided tour of the Küsnacht house, discreetly pointed out some of the interesting places in the grounds and the former gardens. Ulrich Hoerni conducted research in answer to other questions.

48. Bennet, "Domestic Life," p. 186.

49. Among them: Sir Laurens van der Post; J. B. Priestley and his then wife, Jacquetta Hawkes; Chilean diplomat Miguel Serrano; French analyst Charles Baudouin; Swiss-French journalist Georges Duplain; British television presenter John Freeman; and American scholar Richard Evans. Many of these persons published or

presented their work individually; McGuire presents excerpts from many in *CGJ Speaking*, Bollingen Series 97 (Princeton: Princeton Univ. Press, 1977).

50. Aniela Jaffé, "From Jung's Last Years," in *From the Life and Work of CGJ* (Einsiedeln: Daimon Verlag, 1989), p. 118, describes this archive as books, technical writings, photographs, news clips, letters, reports of dreams, and CGJ's own notes, which "rapidly filled several bookshelves and five or six large files." See also references to published correspondence in *CL*-1 and 2 and ETH archives such as Priestley/Hawkes letters. See also chapter 38 for his shared interest in UFOs with R. F. C. Hull.

51. The person who provided this description and who was close to Barbara Hannah and "liked her very much, but . . ." has asked to remain anonymous here. Mary Mellon prepared undated detailed notes for John D. Barrett before his first visit to Zürich. Of Hannah she wrote: "She has a most difficult character and has used her position with Dr. Jung as translator to the hilt. She is passionately fond of Dr. Jung and has dedicated her life to his work. This makes her very hard to deal with, as she takes it upon herself to know all there is to know about Jung — his private life, his professional life, his comings and goings, and his books. . . . She has always irritated a great many people, including myself, but I do not hold this against her." Cary Baynes, in a letter to Mary Mellon, August 24, 1945 (Bollingen archives, LC), described Hannah as "activated *au fond* by ambition."

52. Information about Una Thomas is from her HCL interview and those of others.

53. CGJ to Eugen Böhler, *CL*-2, March 25, 1957, p. 353.

54. Aniela Jaffé, HCL interview. Nameche notes that Jaffé rewrote her interview after he conducted it and that she asked him to destroy the original transcript and the tape. He described the final product as "friendly non-cooperation."

55. "Bilder und Symbole aus E. T. A. Hoffmanns Märchen *Der goldene Topf*," in *Gestaltungen des Unbewussten*. See *CW*-19, 1950a, p. 40.

56. Jaffé, "From Jung's Last Years," p. 117.

57. Although archival access has been limited by the Jung heirs and the constraints of the ETH staff, there is evidence from partial manuscripts and various jottings that he continued to think and refine his psychology until the end. Many of these coincide with passages in the *Protocols*. Most bear no dates or titles.

58. The relevant texts on schizophrenia appear in *CW*-3: "Recent Thoughts on Schizophrenia," paras. 542ff., p. 250; "Schizophrenia," paras. 553ff., p. 236; and Appendix 9, p. 272. "A Psychological View of Conscience" is in *CW*-10, paras. 825ff., p. 437.

59. *CW*-3, paras. 549 and 548, pp. 254 and 253. CGJ's emphasis. As early as July 7, 1949 (E. A. Bennet to CGJ, ETH), Bennet was arranging for CGJ to meet "Dr. Rosen of New York" and "Dr. Campbell of San Francisco" to discuss their research on schizophrenic and catatonic patients.

60. *CW*-3, para. 548, pp. 253–54. Van der Post, *Jung and the Story of Our Time*, p. 261, gives CGJ's ultimate attitude toward drug therapy: "Jung viewed [it] with total distrust as a source of enlightenment."

61. He cites 1946 as the beginning of his interest, in the "letter to *Weltwoche* (Zürich), JHG 22, no. 1078, July 9, 1954; in *CW*-18, paras. 1431–51, pp. 626–33. Archival evidence supports c. 1950.

62. CGJ to Beatrice Hinkle, *CL*-2, February 6, 1951, pp. 3–4.

63. CGJ to Fowler McCormick, *CL*-2, February 22, 1951, pp. 5–6.

64. *CW*-18, para. 1431, p. 626.

65. CGJ to Fowler McCormick, *CL*-2, March 20, 1956, pp. 294–95.

66. *Ein moderner Mythus. Von Dingen, die am Himmel gesehen werden* (1958); *Flying*

Saucers: A Modern Myth of Things Seen in the Skies (1959). See *CW*-19, G1958a, p. 51, and E1959b, p. 90. "On Flying Saucers," *CW*-10, beginning pp. 307ff. CGJ dedicated this book to his son-in-law Walther Niehus, who shared his interest and provided much of the research and documentation for it.

67. Several letters are published in *CL*-2, to J. E. Schulte, pp. 440–41, and to Walter Schaffner, pp. 627–28; many more still unpublished are in ETH archives, and others are in private collections.

68. CGJ, "On Flying Saucers," *CW*-10, p. 309.

69. CGJ to E. A. Bennet, February 7, 1959, ETH, not in *CL*.

70. *CW*-10, para. 590, p. 312.

71. Charles Lindbergh to Helen Wolff, December 11, 1968. The letter was written at her request, as a report of his encounter with Jung. Lindbergh transferred all rights for every form of reproduction to Helen Wolff in a second letter, January 11, 1969. Used here through the courtesy of a private source.

72. A partial bibliography for Böhler is in *CL*-2, pp. 282–83. See also *CGJ und Eugen Böhler: Eine Begegnung in Briefen* (mit einer Einleitung von Gerhard Wehr) (Zürich: v/dlf, Hochschulverlag AG an der ETH, 1996). Dr. Med. Thomas Boni and Verena Müller called this book to my attention.

73. See Thomas Kirsch, *The Jungians: A Comparative and Historical Perspective* (London and Philadelphia: Routledge, 2000), pp. 24–25.

74. Cary Baynes to CGJ, July 21, 1955, ETH.

75. Ruth Bailey and Jolande Jacobi, HCL interviews; Violet de Laszlo, unpublished correspondence in a private archive.

76. CGJ to E. A. Bennet, November 21, 1953, ETH, not in *CL*.

CHAPTER 37: GATHERING JUNG FOR THE FUTURE

1. The first two quotes are from William McGuire, *Bollingen: An Adventure in Collecting the Past*, Bollingen Series (Princeton: Princeton Univ. Press, 1982), p. 108; the first is his description, the second CGJ's. The last is from p. 114.

2. McGuire, *Bollingen*, p. 62.

3. See McGuire, *Bollingen*, for the full series of publications. When Kurt Wolff left Pantheon Books, the Bollingen Series moved to Princeton University Press, Jung's U.S. publisher to the present time. For additional publishing information, see also McGuire's "Firm Affinities: Jung's Relations with Britain and the United States," *JAP* 40 (1995): 301–26; and Paul Mellon (with John Baskett), *Reflections in a Silver Spoon* (New York: William Morrow and Co., 1992), chapter 9, "CGJ, Zürich, and Bollingen Foundation," and Appendices C–E.

4. Michael Ermarth, ed., *Kurt Wolff: A Portrait in Essays and Letters*, trans. Deborah Lucas Schneider (Chicago: Univ. of Chicago Press, 1991). Quotations are from, respectively, jacket copy and the Foreword, p. xi.

5. The harrowing journey from Germany to New York is depicted in Herbert Mitgang's profile of Helen Wolff in *The New Yorker*, August 2, 1982, pp. 41–73. John Ferrone called it to my attention.

6. The original is in the Manuscript Division, LC.

7. Mitgang profile, p. 55; McGuire, *Bollingen*, pp. 60–61.

8. Hellmut Lehmann-Haupt in *The Book in America*, quoted in McGuire, *Bollingen*, p. 61. For a full account of the Wolffs' publishing experience as it concerns CGJ, see pp. 60–62.

9. Mitgang profile, McGuire's *Bollingen*, and Ermarth's "Biographical Sketch," in *Kurt Wolff*.

10. Essential sources are Mellon's *Reflections in a Silver Spoon;* McGuire's *Bollingen;* Bollingen archives, LC; and the Helen Wolff archives, BLY. I have also consulted the private archives of persons who were involved at one time or another in bringing CGJ's *Collected Works* and *Gesammelte Werke* to fruition.

11. Extract of a letter by A. Hättenschwiller, Swiss Legation, Washington, D.C., to Mary Mellon "on behalf of CGJ." Original in LC, copy provided by Paul Mellon.

12. In *Bollingen,* p. 106, McGuire cites the March 1945 letter and names the publisher as Kegan Paul. On p. 108, he explains: "The firm was actually two interlocking old houses, George Routledge & Sons and Kegan Paul, Trench, Trübner. Jung's works appeared [since 1916, with *Psychology of the Unconscious*] under the Kegan Paul imprint, but the business was transacted on the Routledge letterhead. In December, 1947, the two firms became one: Routledge & Kegan Paul."

13. CGJ to Mary Mellon, letter of April 10, 1945, Paul Mellon archives.

14. See McGuire, *Bollingen,* p. 108, for possible reasons why the "volatile and enthusiastic style" of the "extraverted intuitive" Mary Mellon might have given CGJ pause about entrusting his writings to her. See also Mellon, *Reflections in a Silver Spoon,* pp. 222–24, for a description of Mary Mellon's personality.

15. Stanley Young, then managing editor of Bollingen, to Cecil Franklin, July 30, 1945. Cecil Franklin to Stanley Young, August 14, 1945, said an examination of his files showed, "much to our surprise, that Harcourt Brace have no option at all." Both letters are in the Bollingen archives, LC.

16. One of McGuire's sources is the letter quoted above. In an interview with John D. Barrett, June 10, 1976, McGuire recorded the following dialogue:

> Barrett: But all that arrangement Routledge had from Rascher. All the rights in the English language. So if we in America wanted anything, we had to get it from Routledge. And to make it very simple, although it wasn't as simple as I'm going to make it, what we did, was for nothing take over the American rights from Routledge in return for paying for the translation.
>
> McGuire: And everything, and so much more.
>
> Barrett: And so much more if you will. And obviously Rascher had to come into it.
>
> McGuire: Sure, except no money was paid to Rascher, or to the present owners? It was all paid directly to Jung.
>
> Barrett: To Jung.
>
> McGuire: Routledge and Bollingen pay separately.
>
> Barrett: But Rascher had to approve of whatever Routledge did.
>
> McGuire: Yes, that's quite a contract.

17. McGuire, *Bollingen,* p. 107.

18. McGuire, interview with John D. Barrett, June 10, 1976. See *Bollingen,* p. 126.

19. Mellon, *Reflections in a Silver Spoon,* p. 173. Paul Mellon knew Barrett, his and Mary's personal friend, from Yale. He transformed himself, in a very short time, "from a well-read and well-traveled amateur into a highly competent foundation executive and professional editor."

20. Among them, descriptions of Toni Wolff, Jolande Jacobi, Barbara Hannah, Marie-Louise von Franz, and Mary Foote (copy provided by McGuire from his *Bollingen* archives; original in the Bollingen archives, LC).

21. A letter outlining details of the contract that was eventually effected was written by

John D. Barrett to Herbert Read, June 20, 1946. A second document prepared by Marie-Jeanne Boller-Schmid indicates there was a second meeting: "Notes on the Meeting between Prof. C. G. Jung, Mr. Herbert Read, Mr. J. D. Barrett, and Dr. Michael Fordham, held at Ascona on September 2nd, 1946." Both are in the Bollingen archives, LC.

22. John D. Barrett, interview with William McGuire, June 10, 1976.

23. McGuire, *Bollingen*, pp. 123–24, credits Paul Mellon with honoring all his late wife's commitments and moving swiftly after her October 1946 death to put them into effect.

24. Originally published in 1935. See CGJ's reaction to it in *CL*-1, pp. 509–10.

25. Mary Mellon to CGJ, May 29, 1946, ETH. John Barrett (McGuire interview, June 10, 1976) described de Laszlo as a woman who did not express herself clearly in conversation but who did slow, careful, and thorough work on any project with which she was connected. He said, "She was never a *Jungfrauen* [*sic*]. She kept out of that."

26. The first quote is from McGuire, *Bollingen*, p. 109, the second from Cary Baynes to CGJ (addressed to Marie-Jeanne Boller-Schmid), February 21, 1946. In a letter to Mary Mellon, August 24, 1945, Cary Baynes wrote that her only "merit as a translator is the fact of understanding the text," but when it came to "the ability to get the product out of translator's English, there I am a complete flop."

27. Mary Mellon wrote a long letter to CGJ on May 10, 1946, outlining possible procedures, Bollingen archives, LC, Manuscript Division (copies in ETH and Paul Mellon private archive).

28. Herbert Read to CGJ, May 23, 1946, Bollingen archives, LC; not in ETH. Read presented Michael Fordham as a fait accompli even before he discussed the appointment with CGJ.

29. CGJ to Mary Mellon, May 21, 1946, ETH.

30. Read was acquiescing to CGJ's suggestion for "an editorial committee of three," in "Notes for the September 2nd, 1946, meeting in Ascona."

31. McGuire, *Bollingen*, p. 109.

32. R. F. C. Hull, HCL interview.

33. Michael Fordham, quoted in McGuire, *Bollingen*, p. 111. For a full biographical portrait, see McGuire, "R. F. C. Hull: Recollections," *Spring* (1975): 68–75.

34. McGuire, *Bollingen*, p. 124. CGJ received 15 percent of the first five thousand copies sold by each publisher; 20 percent subsequently.

35. McGuire, *Bollingen*, p. 125; not in ETH.

36. R. F. C. Hull to John D. Barrett, October 18, 1949, Bollingen archives, LC. McGuire, "Reflections," p. 71, also writes that he used "one and a half hands" to become "fantastically glib" on the IBM. When he reread the corrected manuscript, Hull wrote: "I thought I could never bear to look at this book again on account of the miseries it cost me to type the original draft; but I found myself enjoying it quite a lot" (letter to John D. Barrett, October 18, 1949).

37. Cary Baynes to Mary Mellon, August 24, 1945, Bollingen archives, LC.

38. John D. Barrett to Mary Mellon, January 25, 1946, Bollingen archives, LC.

39. Mary Mellon, capsule biography prepared for John D. Barrett, Bollingen archives, LC.

40. Mary Mellon to John D. Barrett, January 29, 1946, Bollingen archives, LC.

41. CGJ, quoted in "Notes on the Editorial Conference held at Küsnacht-Zch, August 25, 1948," Bollingen archives, LC. Present were: CGJ, Herbert Read, John D. Barrett, Michael Fordham, and Gerhard Adler, with Marie-Jeanne Boller-Schmid taking notes. McGuire, *Bollingen*, p. 125, also writes of this meeting.

42. "Notes on the meeting between Professor Jung, Herbert Read, and John D. Barrett, August 19, Küsnacht," prepared by Marie-Jeanne Boller-Schmid. Bollingen archives, LC.

43. R. F. C. Hull to John D. Barrett, October 18, 1949, Bollingen archives, LC. See Barbara Hannah, *Jung: His Life and Work, A Biographical Memoir* (Boston: Shambhala, 1991), pp. 334–35, for her version of events concerning Hull. William McGuire, e-mail to the author, September 16, 2001, described Hannah as "surely a source of Jungian wisdom for Richard [Hull], who was new to analytical psychology."

44. Cecil Franklin to Stanley Young, August 14, 1945, Bollingen archives, LC.

45. See Thomas Kirsch, *The Jungians: A Comparative and Historical Perspective* (London and Philadelphia: Routledge, 2000), pp. 15–16, for a capsule biography of his achievements.

46. Their son, Dr. Emanuel Hurwitz, became a respected Jungian analyst in Zürich.

47. These phrases were repeated by many persons in interviews with the author, among them C. A. Meier, Marie-Louise von Franz, Sir Laurens van der Post, Emanuel Hurwitz, and members of the Jung family. These descriptions are also found in many of the HCL interviews, among them Ruth Bailey and Jolande Jacobi, and also in a private archive relating to Barbara Hannah.

48. In interviews, her two surviving children (of three; a son, Franz, died in 1991), Monica Walder and Rudolf Niehus, described their mother's dedication to preparing the *Gesammelte Werke* as the supreme passion of the last part of her life. Both believed it contributed to her resolve to live.

49. Emanuel Hurwitz, interview with the author, November 19, 1999.

50. CGJ to R. F. C. Hull, May 2, 1955, ETH. CGJ added that he still had "the first drafts of almost anything I have written, but usually I don't let them out of my hands." See also McGuire, "Recollections," p. 74, for further information about the process.

51. In an e-mail to the author, September 16, 2001, William McGuire (who joined the Bollingen staff in 1948 as a free-lance editor and rose during the next twenty-one years to become executive editor of the *Collected Works* and the unparalleled authority on the published texts) recalled that mostly "the Swiss editors and I exchanged news of corrections, etc."

52. CGJ to R. F. C. Hull, December 27, 1958, *CL*-2, pp. 469–71.

53. The following account relies upon correspondence in the ETH, the Bollingen archives in the LC, the private archives of Paul Mellon, William McGuire, and Birthe-Lena Hull, and several members of the Jung family and others who wish to remain private.

54. CGJ to R. F. C. Hull, February 9, 1951, copies in ETH; Bollingen archives, LC; McGuire and Paul Mellon archives. CGJ's emphasis.

55. Although Hull did not use CGJ's exact phrasing, his intent pervades all translations in which this term appears.

56. CGJ to R. F. C. Hull, July 6, 1953, ETH.

57. CGJ to R. F. C. Hull, May 22, 1953, ETH; Bollingen archives, LC. The essay is in *CW*-8, paras. 816–968.

58. CGJ to R. F. C. Hull, July 6, 1953, ETH.

59. CGJ to R. F. C. Hull, November 25, 1953, ETH.

60. CGJ to R. F. C. Hull, May 5, 1954, ETH. After CGJ's death, his heirs appointed various persons to oversee editions of some of the seminars.

61. CGJ to R. F. C. Hull, January 24, 1955, ETH. CGJ continued to sign his letters "CG Jung." See Adler's Introduction to *CL*-2, p. xvii, for a discussion of how CGJ addressed his correspondents.

62. CGJ to R. F. C. Hull, December 27, 1958, *CL*-2, pp. 469–71.
63. Gerald Gross to R. F. C. Hull, September 26, 1961, Bollingen archives, LC, Manuscript Division. Hull's letter to Gross is not in this file.
64. Requests such as these are in CGJ to R. F. C. Hull, May 2, 1955, and April 11, 1956, ETH. They are among many others dating from c. 1953.
65. CGJ to R. F. C. Hull, January 24, 1955, ETH.
66. Parts were to be published in *The New Republic*, according to CGJ to R. F. C. Hull, May 2, 1955, ETH. CGJ's correspondence with Upton Sinclair begins October 28, 1952, and ends (with a letter from Aniela Jaffé on CGJ's behalf) July 1, 1960. Originals are in the Manuscripts Department of the Lilly Library, Indiana University, Bloomington; some copies are in the ETH; others are in KML.
67. CGJ to R. F. C. Hull, January 6, 1961, ETH, *Protocols*.

CHAPTER 38: "I AM AS I AM, AN UNGRATEFUL AUTOBIOGRAPHER!"
1. Kurt Wolff to CGJ, January 26, 1958, HW/BLY.
2. Cary Baynes to CGJ, November 19, 1953, ETH.
3. Lucy Heyer-Grote to CGJ, February 7, 1936, ETH. "Inhaltsübersicht" in the Lucy Heyer-Grote file, CGJ archives, ETH.
4. HCL interview, where she describes her ex-husband as "a low-level Nazi." Among the journals she wrote for were *Merkur* and *La Revue de Culture Européene*.
5. This happened prior to November 1953, when CGJ discussed it with Cary Baynes (ETH archives); on July 24, 1954, CGJ asked Lucy Heyer-Grote to return all that he had loaned her (ETH).
6. Cary Baynes to CGJ, November 19, 1953, ETH. In the Icelandic Siegfried saga, Fafnir is the guardian dragon of the Nibelungs.
7. Lucy Heyer-Grote, HCL interview.
8. Cary Baynes to CGJ, August 4, 1954, ETH. She wrote: "Quotes are from your letter of May 4th." The letter is not in the ETH. Nor are several others that internal evidence in this letter suggests should be extant.
9. Paul Mellon, in an interview with the author, said this was an arrangement through his private funds; she never held an official Bollingen fellowship or grant.
10. CGJ to Cary Baynes, September 10, 1954, ETH.
11. CGJ to Cary Baynes, September 10, 1954, ETH.
12. CGJ to Lucy Heyer-Grote, February 2, 1955, ETH.
13. H. L. Philp's first book was *Freud and Religious Belief* (London: Rockliff Publishing Corp., 1956). The quotation is from *Jung and the Problem of Evil* (London: Rockliff Publishing Corp., 1958), p. xi.
14. Philp included most of their discussions in his book *Jung and the Problem of Evil*, which Jung initially described as the best explication of his views about religion (CGJ to H. L. Philp, October 26, 1956, *CL*-2, pp. 334–35; see also n. 2, p. 335). Three of their exchanges are in *CL*-2, but many more form Appendices 1–3 of Philp's book, pp. 209ff.
15. E. A. Bennet to CGJ, March 18, 1958, ETH, ultimately damns Philp's book with faint praise, describing it as written with a "typical Capricorn outlook."
16. Jo and Jane Wheelwright, interview with the author. Dr. Joseph Henderson separately confirmed this as an accurate description.
17. The several letters between CGJ and E. A. Bennet in *CL*-2 do not do justice to the wide range of their mutual intellectual interests. Most of their large correspondence is in the CGJ archive, ETH. To cite several examples: February 1 (Bennet) and 8 (CGJ), 1937, discuss the best way to deal with Göring and the German Society during an upcoming conference; on October 20, 1936, CGJ asks Bennet to help

Dr. Erna Rosenbaum relocate after she fled Berlin and settled in London; in his HCL interview, Bennet cites CGJ's letter of February 8, 1937, in which he urges the British delegation to attend the Copenhagen conference because it will be "truly international."

18. Prominent among them was *The New Statesman*, whose refusal they discussed in letters of June 27 (Bennet) and July 7 (CGJ), 1958.

19. Information gleaned from CGJ to E. A. Bennet, February 22, 1952; CGJ to E. A. Bennet, November 23, 1953; E. A. Bennet to CGJ, January 11, 1955; E. A. Bennet to CGJ, June 14, 1955; and E. A. Bennet to CGJ, June 19, 1955, all ETH.

20. A version of CGJ to E. A. Bennet, November 21, 1953, appears in *CL-2*, p. 133. The vitality of the ETH original has been muted and formalized by the editors.

21. E. A. Bennet to CGJ, February 6, 1951; Anthony Storr, interview with the author, Oxford, England, May 1995.

22. See McGuire, *Bollingen: An Adventure in Collecting the Past*, Bollingen Series (Princeton: Princeton Univ. Press, 1982), pp. 173–74. The book was published as *Myth, Religion, and Mother Right* as vol. 84 in 1967, one of the first publications of the Bollingen Series through the auspices of Princeton University Press.

23. CGJ to Cary Baynes, February 20, 1954, ETH.

24. Cary Baynes to CGJ, April 19, 1954, ETH.

25. In Kurt Wolff to Aniela Jaffé, November 1, 1957, Wolff states that he first met CGJ in Munich "in the early 1920s."

26. Undated "Notes from JDB [Barrett]," LC, state that Barrett and Paul Mellon sailed on the *America* for Europe to meet with CGJ at Casa Gabriella and attend the Eranos meeting, after which the three met to discuss publishing contracts. In an interview with William McGuire, June 10, 1976, Barrett said his first trip to meet CGJ and discuss contracts happened in 1946, which other documentation verifies. McGuire accepts 1946 as the date in his *Bollingen*, p. 148.

27. Jolande Jacobi, HCL interview; correspondence between Jacobi and Kurt Wolff, HW/BLY; correspondence between Jacobi and CGJ, ETH; Bollingen archives, LC; and private archives.

28. From "Memo from KW to JB [Barrett], February 10, 1954 — cc. to [William] McGuire," HW/BLY. The conversation was mainly between Kurt Wolff and CGJ; Helen Wolff was present but said little. Herbert Mitgang, in a profile of Helen Wolff for *The New Yorker*, August 2, 1982, described such occasions by quoting her: "I never felt that I was in my husband's shadow; I always felt that I was in his light." Background information about Kurt and Helen Wolff was provided by John Ferrone, William McGuire, Paula van Doren McGuire, and the late Paul Mellon.

29. One of the Gnostic papyri discovered in Chenoboskion, Upper Egypt, known as the *Codex Jung* and published as *Evangelium Veritatis*, eds. M. Malinine (expert in the philology of "the little known Upper Egyptian idiom" in which the codex was written), H. C. Puech (specialist in Oriental philosophy), and G. Quispel (scholar of theological implications), Studien aus dem C. G. Jung Institut, 6 (Zürich: Rascher Verlag, 1956). Funds to buy the codex were donated by George H. Page, "a rich American [living in Switzerland] who was a friend of C. A. Meier" (E. A. Bennet, HCL interview). Page purchased it from the estate of Albert Eid, a Belgian dealer in antiquities who acquired it in Egypt. Given by bequest to the Coptic Museum, Cairo, where it is today. For further detail and CGJ's address at the presentation, see *CW-18*, paras. 1514–17, pp. 671–72; and paras. 1826–34, pp. 826–29.

30. CGJ to E. A. Bennet, November 21, 1953, ETH.

31. On April 15, 1953, Herbert Read wrote to Gerhard Adler and Michael Fordham (his co-editors of the British edition of *CW*) that CGJ "expressed in the strongest

possible terms his dissatisfaction with the progress in the publication of the *CW*, accusing his publishers of the virtual suppression of his work over a period of several years" (quoted in William McGuire, undated memo for *Bollingen*). Similar remarks also appear in CGJ's letters to Bennet and Cary Baynes (among many others) and are found in internal memos and correspondence of the Bollingen archives, LC, and in private archives. See also *CL*, particularly vol. 2, for letters such as CGJ to J. B. Rhine, February 18, 1953, pp. 106–7.

32. February 11, 1954, Bollingen archives, LC, Manuscript Division.

33. Cary Baynes to CGJ, June 17, 1958. She told him how his letter to Vaun Gillmor praising the Bollingen Books was received: "You will never know what delight it caused her — and will cause Jack and Paul."

34. Jolande Jacobi to Kurt Wolff, July 28, 1960, HW/BLY. The exact meaning is "uterus," but Jacobi is using it in the sense explained in the text.

35. Jolande Jacobi, HCL interview.

36. CGJ alludes to this project in his letter to Henri Flournoy, February 12, 1953, *CL*-2, p. 106. William McGuire, in an e-mail to the author, September 26, 2001, wrote that he did not remember any other interviewer and believed the rumor undoubtedly arose because of Kurt Wolff's negotiations with Aniela Jaffé.

37. CGJ to J. M. Thorburn, February 6, 1952, *CL*-2, pp. 38–39. See also CGJ to Gerald Sykes, November 21, 1955, *CL*-2, pp. 279–80. Author of *The Hidden Remnant*, a collection of essays on psychology, Sykes was an American writer who also wished to write a biography of CGJ. Aniela Jaffé refers to the possible appearance of such a book in a letter to Gerald Gross, but Sykes never wrote one.

38. This is the earliest date in any of the *Protocols* I have read. Kurt Wolff said interviews began in "the summer of 1956," but there is no dated passage reflecting this.

39. This date is consistent in all *Protocols* I have read.

40. *CW*-4, "A Critical Review of Morton Prince," paras. 163–65; also, a description of a "young Jewess" that appears to be cobbled together from memories of the case history of Sabina Spielrein.

41. Aniela Jaffé to Kurt Wolff, November 6, 1957, but nearly all her correspondence with Kurt Wolff begins with her apologies for delays in *MDR* because of such duties.

42. Context is Ruth Bailey, HCL interview. Quote is Aniela Jaffé to Kurt Wolff, October 21, 1957.

43. CGJ to Kurt Wolff, March 4, 1958, original in a private archive.

44. E. A. Bennet to CGJ, September 15, 1956.

45. CGJ to E. A. Bennet, October 10, 1956, ETH.

46. E. A. Bennet to CGJ, December 7, 1956, ETH.

47. CGJ to E. A. Bennet, December 10, 1956, ETH.

48. E. A. Bennet, *C. G. Jung* (London: Barrie and Rockliff, 1961) and *What Jung Really Said* (London: MacDonald and Jane's, 1966).

49. Rascher believed their contract entitled them to publish anything Jung wrote in German. They only became involved on April 1, 1959, with a telegram to Kurt Wolff, ordering him to cease negotiations with Fischer Verlag, as "German and world rights" were theirs. Whether that was true or not, Rascher published the hardcover *MDR* only, and Kurt Wolff arranged for Fischer to publish the first paperback edition.

50. In letters to John D. Barrett, October 3 and November 6, 1957, HW/BLY, CGJ explains why *MDR* should not be part of *CW*.

51. Terms appear in correspondence among the principals of Routledge, Bollingen, and Rascher, with Kurt Wolff at Pantheon and with the editors of *CW* and Aniela

Jaffé; and in internal memos and messages (many undated) among all the principals above.

52. Publishing contract between Kurt Wolff (Pantheon Books), CGJ, and Aniela Jaffé, dated October 25, 1957, HW/BLY.

53. With the exception of the 1925 seminars, all these are listed, along with capsule descriptions of each, in Aniela Jaffé to Kurt Wolff, October 19, 1957, HW/BLY. The seminars are discussed in Aniela Jaffé to Jolande Jacobi, May 15, 1958, where Jaffé writes that Pantheon Books holds a "ten year *exclusive* copyright" for the 1925 seminars (her emphasis).

54. E. A. Bennet to CGJ, January 14, 1957, ETH.

55. Cary Baynes to Helen Wolff, November 18, 1958, HW/BLY.

56. References to Bennet color Jaffé's correspondence with Kurt Wolff from 1957 to CGJ's death in 1961, HW/BLY.

57. "Publishing contract, dated 25 October, 1957," HW/BLY.

58. "Memo: Kurt Wolff to Aniela Jaffé: Some Preliminary questions re: notes from the time between January 18 to October 24, 1957," HW/BLY.

59. *F/J*, 260F, pp. 428–30. The important discussion centers around Schwyzer's solar phallus delusion and Honegger's participation in the research.

60. Aniela Jaffé to Kurt Wolff, October 13, 1957, HW/BLY.

61. Whether she sent them is not known. Neither she nor Kurt Wolff ever commented about these notes, which appear either to have been restricted by persons unknown or to have disappeared from any archive connected with CGJ or Jaffé. They are also missing from HW/BLY. In the *Protocols* I consulted, there is nothing except the occasional reference to "Miss [Toni] Wolff" and no discussion of Toni Wolff's relationship with CGJ.

62. R. F. C. Hull, in his HCL interview, said, "There was a story going round that Jung did write a chapter about Toni Wolff," and he remembered Ximena de Angulo Roelli telling him that she thought it had been "suppressed or possibly burned" (which implies that he himself never saw such a chapter). In a 1996 telephone conversation with the author, Ximena de Angulo Roelli said she did not remember having such a conversation with Hull. In his interview, Hull said, "I can't imagine the Jung family burning a potentially very valuable document. It might be sitting in the vault of a bank." In Aniela Jaffé to Gerald Gross, September 23, 1961, after telling of her trip to London, Jaffé describes the many rumors then circulating, of "the famous Toni Wolff chapter, which I left out, or which was left out." There is no further explanation. R. F. C. Hull to Gerald Gross, October 8, 1961, alludes to "the 'non-existent' Toni Wolff chapter" in such a way that makes it seem that at one time there was such a chapter. Alan Elms, *Uncovering Lives* (Oxford and New York: Oxford Univ. Press, 1994), p. 66, writes that Jaffé "gleefully announced that there was a whole chapter about Toni, which she was planning to publish over the Jung family's strenuous objections. (Alas, Frau Jaffé died before she could see that chapter into print.)" Helen Wolff, in her HCL interview, said CGJ "would have talked about it and there might have been passages, but they were all deleted. He mentioned her but this was taken out."

63. Aniela Jaffé to Kurt Wolff, January 10, 1958, HW/BLY.

64. CGJ to Kurt Wolff, February 1, 1958, private archive.

65. Aniela Jaffé to Kurt Wolff, January 23, 1958, HW/BLY.

66. In Kurt Wolff to William Collins (the British publisher that eventually published *MDR*), September 21, 1960, HW/BLY, Wolff repeated CGJ's assurance that "no British publisher has any rights to new books of his other than the ones to form

part of *CW.*" There was no question "of inclusion of the Memoirs into the *CW.*" Kurt Wolff's agreement with both CGJ and Aniela Jaffé was that CGJ, in a "formal declaration . . . consider[ed] the book excluded from the *CW.*" He had informed Routledge of this, but Cecil Franklin was nevertheless challenging Collins's right to publish. Franklin never explained "on what he base[d] his claim."

67. Correspondence between Aniela Jaffé (September 23, 1961) and Gerald Gross (September 26, 1961), Bollingen archives, LC, Manuscript Division, shows that Jaffé was disputing various versions of the title. Gross informed her that it had been agreed upon by Kurt Wolff and CGJ in the original agreement of August 27, 1957. She made no further attempt to change it.

68. Aniela Jaffé to Kurt Wolff, January 23, 1958, HW/BLY.

69. Entitled "From the Earliest Experiences of My Life," portions of which were incorporated into *Protocols.* Quote is Cary Baynes to Helen Wolff, November 18, 1958, HW/BLY.

70. Cary Baynes to Helen Wolff, August 4, 1960, HW/BLY. The statement was repeated by Franz Jung and expressed in similar language by some of his grandsons in interviews with the author.

71. This comes at the end of a long undated passage in all *Protocols* I have read, but the entry that follows bears the date in several versions as April 11, 1958.

72. *Protocols*, undated, but the one following is April 30, 1958.

73. CGJ to Kurt Wolff, June 17, 1958, in reply to Kurt Wolff's of June 3, HW/BLY.

74. One of the earliest examples of Aniela Jaffé's interference with CGJ's text occurs in Kurt Wolff to Aniela Jaffé, June 19, 1958, HW/BLY. Kurt Wolff refers to William James as the subject of Jaffé's June 16 letter, which included a carbon of CGJ's of June 17. Noting that CGJ was "in a way declining my request for a few pages on William James and a substantial piece on the psychotherapist's experiences," he thanks Jaffé for "see[ing] a way to do both." He was "optimistically looking forward to [her] happy solution." This and subsequent textual study show how likely it is that all the writings about William James were Jaffé's and not CGJ's.

75. Aniela Jaffé to Kurt Wolff, June 5, 1958, HW/BLY.

76. CGJ to Kurt Wolff, June 4, 1958, HW/BLY. Many of the statements from CGJ's letter eventually became part of his appraisal of Hugh Crichton-Miller that was originally intended to become an appendix discussing his influence and that of Flournoy, Wilhelm, Zimmer, and possibly others as well. The passage devoted to Crichton-Miller was elminated from all editions; those pertaining to Flournoy, Wilhelm, and Zimmer were retained in *ETG* but eliminated from *MDR.* Copies of CGJ's Crichton-Miller statement are in HW/BLY and the Bollingen archives, LC Manuscript Division.

77. Aniela Jaffé to Kurt Wolff, June 5, 1958, HW/BLY. She continued to belabor this subject on May 16 and 18, June 2, and October 19, all 1958.

78. Kurt Wolff to Cary Baynes, May 21, 1958, HW/BLY. Kurt Wolff thought there was a perfect place for it within the text, following an anecdote Jung told about the origins and history of the swastika symbol at a 1933 dinner party he attended in Berlin at the home of Frau von Schnitzler. CGJ's retelling of the anecdote is unclear and incomplete, which is probably why it appeared only in one early *Protocol* and was not included in the published text.

79. Kurt Wolff to Cary Baynes, September 18, 1959, HW/BLY.

80. R. F. C. Hull, HCL interview.

81. Kurt Wolff to Cary Baynes, September 18, 1959, HW/BLY.

82. Kurt Wolff appears to contradict himself in a letter to Cary Baynes, September 18,

1959: he wrote that he left Zürich in October 1958 with the book "as good as finished, except for the last chapters." His correspondence throughout 1959, not only with Cary Baynes but also with others, proves just the opposite.

83. See Thomas Kirsch, *The Jungians: A Comparative and Historical Perspective* (London and Philadelphia: Routledge, 2000), pp. 178–82.

84. Aniela Jaffé to Kurt Wolff, October 28, 1958, HW/BLY.

85. Helen Wolff to CGJ, November 14, 1958, HW/BLY.

86. CGJ to Kurt Wolff, March 18, 1958, private archive.

87. CGJ to Helen Wolff, November 11, 1958, HW/BLY.

88. Kurt Wolff to CGJ, May 30, 1959, HW/BLY.

89. CGJ to Kurt Wolff, May 30, 1959, private archive. He did not specify the content of the dream.

90. Aniela Jaffé to Kurt Wolff, July 22, 1959, HW/BLY.

91. These remain the private property of the *Erbengemeinschaft CGJ*.

92. This was the only one among all these documents that Jaffé included in several of the earlier *Protocols*; not included in *MDR*.

93. Kurt Wolff to CGJ, August 17, 1959, HW/BLY.

94. Kurt Wolff to CGJ, August 27, 1959, HW/BLY.

95. Ruth Bailey's HCL interview and many letters among the principals.

96. Kurt Wolff to CGJ, August 27, 1959, HW/BLY.

97. "Memo first day of work: Helen Wolff with Aniela Jaffé, Zürich 15.XI.59," HW/BLY.

98. Kurt Wolff to Cary Baynes, September 18, 1959, HW/BLY.

99. Quoted by Kurt Wolff to Cary Baynes, September 18, 1959. He cites Jaffé's letter to him of September 4, 1959, and claims to be quoting exactly, HW/BLY.

100. Kurt Wolff to CGJ, August 27, 1959, HW/BLY.

101. Cary Baynes to Helen Wolff, November 18, 1958, HW/BLY.

102. Helen Wolff's "Memo first day of work."

103. Helen Wolff to CGJ, no date on first page; second and variant version dated November 18, 1959; both HW/BLY.

104. Jolande Jacobi, HCL interview; also undated memo to Kurt Wolff, probably 1959 or 1960.

105. Documentation concerning the civil actions is available from Aniela Jaffé's executor, Robert Hinshaw. The *Erbengemeinschaft CGJ* has chosen to keep it private. As this happened after CGJ's death and does not fall within the purview of a biography, I do not discuss it.

106. Helen Wolff to CGJ, first copy undated, second dated December 18, 1959, third dated December 19, 1959; all HW/BLY.

107. CGJ to Kurt Wolff, December 19, 1959, HW/BLY.

108. On June 22, 1961, Gerald Gross and other editors at Pantheon were still worried that Rascher would do so. Gross told Hull they were forced to credit Jaffé with co-authorship, for, without her, "Rascher could claim copyright as part of his exclusive agreement with Jung" (correspondence files of Wolfgang Sauerlander, Bollingen archives, LC).

109. CGJ to Kurt Wolff, June 2, 1960, HW/BLY. Cary Baynes was correct about Emma's will.

110. Term coined by R. F. C. Hull in a letter to Gerald Gross, April 27, 1962; repeated by him and Gross in subsequent correspondence, Bollingen archives, LC, Manuscript Division.

111. CGJ to Walther and Marianne Niehus-Jung, January 3, 1960, *CL-2*, p. 530.

112. The children who told me this asked that I not identify them by name.

113. CGJ to Walther Niehus, April 5, 1960, *CL-2*, p. 550.

114. Kurt Wolff to William Collins, October 31, 1960, HW/BLY.

115. Cary Baynes first used this expression in a letter to Kurt Wolff, November 18, 1958, HW/BLY. It was repeated by both many times afterward.

116. Recurring phrases in letters to Kurt Wolff, Helen Wolff, R. F. C. Hull, and, after 1960, Gerald Gross, Wolfgang Sauerlander, and others at Pantheon Books.

117. A young German refugee who began as Pantheon's stock boy and bookkeeper but who became one of the Wolffs' most trusted and valued associates. He played a significant role in preparing *MDR* for publication.

118. Cary Baynes to Kurt Wolff, June 19, 1960, HW/BLY. Peter Jung, in an interview with the author in November 2001, said his mother called Aniela Jaffé "a liar to her face." Jaffé replied that this was true, but she was "an honest liar."

119. Helen Wolff to William Collins, November 26, 1950, HW/BLY.

120. Aniela Jaffé to Kurt Wolff, April 1, 1960, HW/BLY.

121. Kurt Wolff to Aniela Jaffé, August 1, 1960, HW/BLY.

122. Kurt Wolff to F. W. Beidler, April 1, 1959. Beidler represented the Swiss Society of Authors, the Société des Écrivains Suisse.

123. Aniela Jaffé to Kurt Wolff, March 8, 1960; Kurt Wolff to William Collins, October 31, 1960, both HW/BLY.

124. Walther Niehus to Cecil Franklin, April 12, 1960, HW/BLY.

125. Helen Wolff to Cary Baynes, July 13, 1960, HW/BLY.

126. Cecil Franklin to Walther Niehus, April 20, 1960, HW/BLY.

127. Kurt Wolff to William Collins, November 26, 1960, HW/BLY.

128. In Kurt Wolff to William Collins, September 21, 1960, Wolff says Franklin will "get an injunction the moment Collins announces [separate] publication of *MDR*"; also inferred in Kurt Wolff to John D. Barrett, December 23, 1959, both HW/BLY. Confirmed by William McGuire, e-mail to the author, October 15, 2001.

129. Helen Wolff to William Collins, November 26, 1960, HW/BLY. They had learned of an earlier meeting between "Dr. Jung, the Bollingen people and Herbert Read" in which Read suggested co-publishing as a viable alternative.

130. Kurt Wolff explained it to Collins in a letter of September 21, 1960; Helen Wolff further explained it in a letter to Collins of November 26, 1960; both HW/BLY.

131. Kurt Wolff to William Collins, September 21, 1960, HW/BLY.

132. McGuire, *Bollingen*, pp. 273–75.

133. Nikolaus Wolff, telephone interview with the author, October 23, 2001. See also Mitgang's *New Yorker* profile of Helen Wolff, pp. 61–62. The firm was sold to Random House by the remaining directors, Schabert and Jacques Schiffrin, whose health was also poor; his son, André, took over management of Pantheon and launched his own distinguished career in publishing. Pantheon retained its separate imprint while benefiting from the larger firm's distribution system.

134. Aniela Jaffé to "Beidler," September 19, 1958: "Jung wants S. Fischer"; also "Table of Contents of the Jung file," memo by Wolfgang Sauerlander to Kurt Wolff, attached to letter of October 14, 1960, HW/BLY.

135. R. F. C. Hull, phrases first used in his letter to Kurt Wolff, May 22, 1960, HW/BLY, repeated frequently thereafter.

136. Kurt Wolff, "Some General Remarks," notes about *MDR* written for Aniela Jaffé, May 28, 1958.

137. R. F. C. Hull to Kurt Wolff, July 8, 1960, HW/BLY. These works were Neumann's

Origins and History of Consciousness, The Archetypal World of Henry Moore, and "the three little books by the Herrigels."

138. Kurt Wolff to R. F. C. Hull, July 6, 1960, HW/BLY.

139. Aniela Jaffé to Vaun Gillmor "re: Dr. Jung's final days," June 14, 1961, Bollingen archives, LC, Manuscript Division; copy in KML, File J. Fowler McCormick, typed note appended to correspondence card from CGJ, January 14, 1960, from the McCormick family papers, State Historical Society of Wisconsin, Archives Division.

140. The first quote is Cary Baynes to Kurt Wolff, March 1960; the second is Aniela Jaffé to Kurt Wolff, October 3, 1960; both HW/BLY.

141. CGJ to Kurt Wolff, December 24, 1959, private archive.

142. Kurt Wolff to John D. Barrett, HW/BLY.

143. "International Touring and Culinary Research Association."

144. R. F. C. Hull to Kurt Wolff, May 22, 1960, HW/BLY; R. F. C. Hull to Aniela Jaffé (copy to Gerald Gross, in private archive).

145. R. F. C. Hull, "A Record of Events Preceding the Publication of Jung's Autobiography, as seen by R. F. C. Hull," dated July 27, 1960, Bollingen archives, LC, Manuscript Division. In letters to Gerald Gross, August 11 and 14, 1961, Hull describes it as a "Report" prepared for Herbert Read at Routledge and Kegan Paul. He adds that it was *not* addressed to Jack Barrett (as Vaun Gillmor thought) but says that a copy might have been sent to him by Read. All quotes from R. F. C. Hull's private archives and correspondence are through permission of his widow, Birthe-Lena Hull.

146. Hull surmises that this is what happened in his letter to Aniela Jaffé, August 26, 1961 (copy to Gerald Gross, private archive).

147. In R. F. C. Hull to Aniela Jaffé, September 26, 1961 (partial copy to Gerald Gross, in private archive), Hull quotes CGJ as having said, "'I have written it and I want it — a bit blunt and crude, but that's the way I am.' (Words to this effect)."

148. R. F. C. Hull to Aniela Jaffé (copy to Gerald Gross), partial letter accompanying Gerald Gross to Wolfgang Sauerlander, September 26, 1961, private archive.

149. R. F. C. Hull to Kurt Wolff, May 9, 1960, HW/BLY.

150. "*MDR* mss. translation, etc.," black binder containing file folder, pp. 1–109 of an early Winston translation, HW/BLY.

151. Hull's "Report" for Herbert Read.

152. R. F. C. Hull to Kurt Wolff, May 22, 1960, HW/BLY. See also R. F. C. Hull to Wolfgang Sauerlander, February 18, 1961, Bollingen archives, LC, Manuscript Division. Hull explains that Jaffé deleted these passages, and with CGJ's approval he restored them, only to have her delete them again.

153. Aniela Jaffé and R. F. C. Hull to Gerald Gross, April 27, 1962.

154. From the "*MDR* mss. translation, etc." folder; also R. F. C. Hull to Kurt Wolff, May 9, 1960; both HW/BLY.

155. Helen Wolff, HCL interview.

156. This discussion dominated much of 1960 and 1961 and appears frequently in the correspondence between Hull, Gerald Gross, and Wolfgang Sauerlander, Bollingen archives, LC. In her HCL interview, Helen Wolff blamed CGJ's "children" and "also the in-laws" [i.e., spouses of the children] for the "considerable problems: one had the material and it was taken away again and reworked and the spontaneity was taken from it. For this reason . . . work was quite tense and difficult, and it became more tense and difficult as time went on."

157. R. F. C. Hull to Gerald Gross, August 11, 1961. Hull adds: "Don't quote this without checking Jung's words with Cary. That was No. 2 speaking and he [No. 2]

speaks at least half the time in this book." Cary Baynes's letter to CGJ discussing this is not in the ETH; hers to Kurt Wolff, August 6, 1960, is in HW/BLY. The Ravenna passage appears in *MDR*, chapter 9, "Travels."

158. Ruth Bailey to R. F. C. Hull, May 3, 1960, HW/BLY.
159. Aniela Jaffé to Kurt Wolff, October 19, 1960, HW/BLY.
160. Wolfgang Sauerlander "Memo" for Kurt Wolff, October 14, 1960, citing Rascher letters of March 31, 1959, to Kurt Wolff and S. Fischer Verlag.
161. R. F. C. Hull to Kurt Wolff, May 9, 1960, HW/BLY.
162. Cary Baynes to Kurt Wolff, August 6, 1960, HW/BLY.
163. Aniela Jaffé to Gerald Gross, August 4, 1961, private archive.
164. Both dated January 13, 1961, both HW/BLY.
165. Kurt Wolff to Cary Baynes, January 19, 1961, HW/BLY.
166. CGJ to Kurt Wolff, January 18, 1961, HW/BLY.
167. From a "resume of correspondence prepared for the use of Gerald Gross and other Pantheon people" by Paula van Doren (later McGuire), cited with her permission; also the archives of William McGuire.
168. Nikolaus Wolff, interview, October 23, 2001. In her HCL interview, Helen Wolff described how CGJ allowed such a situation to arise: "He did, in a sense, contradict himself in order to avoid tensions and to avoid quarrels, dissensions. This was in the last years of his life, when he might just have wanted not to waste his strength on dissensions within the family."
169. In letters throughout 1961 and 1962, Jaffé frequently declines to meet, because the Niehuses are "on vacation" or "holiday." In the next letters, she admits, "they have not yet gone," or "they did not go as intended, but remain here." All in HW/BLY and Bollingen archives, LC, Manuscript Division.
170. Gross went to Macmillan Publishers at the end of 1966, and Sara (Golden) Blackburn, his assistant, saw the book to publication.
171. R. F. C. Hull to Jennifer Savary, June 20, 1961.

CHAPTER 39: "THE ICY STILLNESS OF DEATH"

1. HCL interviews of Ruth Bailey, Fowler McCormick, and Barbara Hannah; and Monica Walder, Rudolf Niehus, Franz Jung, and Agathe Niehus-Jung, interviews with the author.
2. CGJ to Cary Baynes, February 9, 1960.
3. R. F. C. Hull to Jennifer Savary, June 20, 1961.
4. Aniela Jaffé to Vaun Gillmor, "re: Dr. Jung's final days," June 14, 1961, Bollingen archives, LC, Manuscript Division; copy in KML, File J.
5. Barbara Hannah, *Jung: His Life and Work, A Biographical Memoir* (Boston: Shambhala, 1991), pp. 342–43.
6. Hannah, *Life and Work*, p. 344.
7. "Approaching the Unconscious," in *Man and His Symbols*, ed. CGJ and Marie-Louise von Franz (New York: Doubleday Anchor Books, 1964).
8. John Freeman, Introduction, *Man and His Symbols*, p. 9.
9. Freeman's emphasis, Introduction, *Man and His Symbols*, p. 10.
10. See Hannah, *Life and Work*, p. 342, for an account heavily influenced by her relationship with von Franz.
11. Jolande Jacobi, fourth HCL interview, January 6, 1970. Confirmed also by a private source who showed me a letter written by Jaffé to a family member of the source.
12. In Jaffé's letter cited above, n. 11, she also confirmed that she was a late addition to the book and was offended when CGJ did not ask her to be an original contributor.

13. From the private source cited in the two previous notes; also confirmed by Jolande Jacobi's fourth HCL interview.

14. Glin Bennet, "Domestic Life with CGJ: Tape-recorded Conversations with Ruth Bailey," *Spring* (1986): 188.

15. Ruth Bailey gives an account of CGJ's dreams in Bennet's tape-recorded conversations in *Spring* and in her HCL interview that differs from the one Barbara Hannah gives in *Life and Work*, p. 347. As it was such an emotional time for both women, and as Ruth Bailey was not noted for the precision of her memories, I simply give the details of the dreams without comment.

16. Miguel Serrano, in *CGJ and Hermann Hesse* (London: Routledge and Kegan Paul, 1966), p. 97, recounts a conversation with Ruth Bailey about this. In her HCL interview, Bailey is angry that he used this information without her permission, as he did her letter of June 16, 1961, reproduced on pp. 104–5. She is especially upset that he invented a self-aggrandizing compliment that she never said (p. 98).

17. See Hannah, *Life and Work*, pp. 347–48, for interpretations and references to *MDR*.

18. Aniela Jaffé to Gerald Gross, August 4, 1961, private archive.

19. These four persons, interviewed separately, have asked not to be identified.

20. Aniela Jaffé to Vaun Gillmor, "re: Dr. Jung's final days."

21. Dr. Rudolf Niehus, interview with the author, November 24, 1994.

22. Aniela Jaffé to Kyrill Shabert and Gerald Gross, June 14, 1961, private archive.

23. Elsbeth Stoiber, interview with the author, April 17, 1996.

24. Marianne Niehus-Jung kept one, which has since "disappeared." Stoiber kept the second, and in 1995, she mounted an exhibition at the museum, featuring it. In a second interview, April 24, 1996, she described an unpleasant encounter with Franz Jung, who she said forced her to sign an agreement giving him the second mask and everything pertaining to it.

25. Fowler McCormick, HCL interview.

26. Ruth Bailey to Miguel Serrano, June 16, 1961, reprinted (without her permission) in *CGJ and Hermann Hesse*, pp. 104–5.

27. "Dr. CGJ is dead at 85; Pioneer in Analytic Psychology," by the Associated Press, *New York Times*, June 7, 1961.

28. "Obituary: CGJ," *The Lancet* (June 17, 1961): 1356–57.

29. R. F. C. Hull to Aniela Jaffé (partial copy to Gerald Gross), private Bollingen archive.

30. Jointly sponsored by the New York Association for Analytical Psychology and the Analytical Psychology Club of New York, December 1, 1961. Booklet privately printed, copy in KML.

31. Memorial booklet, p. 46.

32. *MDR*, p. 314.

33. Professor Hans Schär, D.D., Bern, "Address," from the funeral service program, *In Memory of CGJ*, Friday, June 9, 1961, Reformed Church, Küsnacht.

34. R. F. C. Hull to Jennifer Savary, June 20, 1961.

35. The tree was still alive in February 1998, when Dr. Peter Jung gave me a guided tour of the Küsnacht house and grounds.

36. Bennet, "Domestic Life with CGJ," p. 189.

EPILOGUE: THE "SO-CALLED AUTOBIOGRAPHY"

1. R. F. C. Hull to Gerald Gross, August 4, 1961, private Bollingen archive.

2. Gerald Gross sent letters to Jaffé and Hull, both dated July 21, 1961, restating the

previously agreed-upon procedures; and to Richard Winston, July 31 and August 10, 1961 (acknowledging his of August 1, 3, and 5). All copies in private Bollingen archive.

3. R. F. C. Hull to Gerald Gross, August 4, 1961.

4. Gerald Gross to Milton Waldman, August 10, 1961.

5. His letter further stipulated the writings Jaffé could reproduce or quote from, provided she paid him or his heirs the agreed-upon 50 percent royalty, and that the book never became part of the *Collected Works*. Shortly before CGJ's death, all the publishers agreed to accept this "letter of contract."

6. Gerald Gross to R. F. C. Hull, June 16, 1961.

7. Aniela Jaffé to Gerald Gross, July 24, 1961, private Bollingen archive.

8. Aniela Jaffé to Gerald Gross, August 9, 1961.

9. Gerald Gross to Milton Waldman, August 10, 1961.

10. E. A. Bennet, *CGJ* (London: Barrie and Rockliff, 1961). At the time, Gerald Sykes was reported to be writing a biography of CGJ.

11. Jolande Jacobi to Kurt Wolff, July 17, 1961, HW/BLY.

12. Jolande Jacobi to Kurt Wolff, July 20, 1961, HW/BLY.

13. Gerald Gross to Richard Winston, August 10, 1961, private Bollingen archive.

14. CGJ to R. F. C. Hull, May 27, 1960, original in Hull archives, copies in the Bollingen Foundation archives, LC, Manuscript Division, and private Bollingen archives.

15. When changes were made to CGJ's original in the various typescripts, the abbreviation "GMS" (German manuscript) was written in the margin beside them. Thus, by the 1961 typescripts, many of the major violations to what CGJ actually wrote can be clearly established. I was granted access to several of these typescripts from private archives, and I compared them with other full and partial typescripts, among them those in the Bollingen Foundation archives, LC; HCL; and HW/BLY.

16. Gerald Gross to Aniela Jaffé, July 28, 1961, Bollingen private archive.

17. Gerald Gross to R. F. C. Hull, September 15, 1961.

18. Letter signed by Gerald Gross and Aniela Jaffé, dated August 26, 1961, copy in the Sauerlander correspondence file, Bollingen Foundation archives.

19. Jolande Jacobi to Kurt Wolff, HW/BLY.

20. Gerald Gross to Aniela Jaffé, June 16, 1961, private Bollingen archive.

21. Although this has always been attributed to Jaffé, in a letter to Gerald Gross, dated September 6, 1961, R. F. C. Hull wrote: "The section about the ancestors, purportedly written by Jaffé, was actually dictated by Jung, though in less complete form."

22. R. F. C. Hull to Gerald Gross, August 11, 1961.

23. Gerald Gross to Wolfgang Sauerlander, September 26, 1961, private Bollingen archive.

24. Jaffé sometimes referred to these pages as "II: 61–70" (as she did in a letter to Gerald Gross, August 4, 1961, private Bollingen archive); others mostly used the version quoted here.

25. From Jaffé's telegram to Gerald Gross of that date.

26. R. F. C. Hull to Cary Baynes, September 7, 1961.

27. Aniela Jaffé to Gerald Gross, August 4, 1961.

28. R. F. C. Hull to Aniela Jaffé, September 26, 1961. His emphasis in a partial letter enclosed with Gerald Gross's to Wolfgang Sauerlander of that date.

29. R. F. C. Hull to Gerald Gross, September 26, 1961, with a partial copy of Hull's to Jaffé enclosed.

30. R. F. C. Hull to Cary Baynes, September 7, 1961, describes this passage as "written with considerable cunning and artistry."

31. This passage appears in the typescript Gross took to Zürich, in II: 55, private Bollingen archive. In *MDR*, it appears in a slightly different context and a rewritten paragraph on p. 55.

32. Gerald Gross typescript, II: 63, private Bollingen archive. Some of this is in *MDR*, pp. 58–59.

33. R. F. C. Hull to Gerald Gross, August 11, 1961. In his letter to Cary Baynes, September 7, 1961, he discusses it in greater detail.

34. Aniela Jaffé to Gerald Gross, August 4, 1961. The printed passage, *MDR*, p. 55, does not begin with "for me." The phrase occurs several sentences earlier, when CGJ explains: "Communion had been a fatal experience *for me*."

35. R. F. C. Hull to Gerald Gross, August 11, 1961.

36. R. F. C. Hull to Gerald Gross, August 11, 1961.

37. Aniela Jaffé to Gerald Gross, expression first used August 4, 1961, and repeated for the next several months. On September 7, 1961, Hull wrote to Cary Baynes: "From the emotional and at times disoriented tone of her letters we gathered that she must be under some kind of pressure — and the likeliest source of pressure would be the Niehuses. This inference proved to be correct, as was made abundantly plain to Gerry while he was in Zürich."

38. R. F. C. Hull to Gerald Gross, August 11, 1961.

39. R. F. C. Hull to Gerald Gross, September 6, 1961.

40. This phrase became one Hull used repeatedly in letters to all the principals as he urged them to keep the disputed passage, "II: 58–70."

41. The decision to publish bowdlerized text if there was no other recourse was arrived at in Paris, when Gross met William Collins at the conclusion of his Zürich meetings. The Hull letter quoted here is vital for scholars who will seek to reconstruct the unexpurgated text of *MDR*, which the biographical form does not permit me to do in detail. I point out this one important passage: "Our key passage (II: 58–70) is there in germinal form, and . . . the words 'Gott Scheisst auf den Münster' occur at least five times. It is made absolutely clear that the Cathedral experience was the most shattering in Jung's life."

42. Gerald Gross to R. F. C. Hull, September 15, 1961.

43. Gerald Gross to R. F. C. Hull, September 22, 1961.

44. Dated September 9, referred to by Gross in his letter to Hull, September 15, 1961, and in partial copy to Gross of September 26, 1961.

45. Based on Jaffé's correspondence with publishers and private individuals. Two of the most important are Aniela Jaffé to Milton Waldman, September 20 and 29, 1961, in which she insists she will not be a party to the falsification of Jung's words or assent to "family-censorship." She says she is "terribly afraid of any scandal — this word is always used and had not failed to impress me."

46. Aniela Jaffé to Gerald Gross, September 19, 1961.

47. Aniela Jaffé to Milton Waldman, September 20, 1961, is only one example of the many that show her anguish over this charge.

48. Gerald Gross to R. F. C. Hull, September 27, 1961.

49. Gerald Gross to R. F. C. Hull, the second of four letters dated September 26, 1961.

50. Gerald Gross to Aniela Jaffé, September 28, 1961.

51. A very important exchange is R. F. C. Hull to Aniela Jaffé, September 30, 1961.

52. Milton Waldman to Aniela Jaffé, September 18, 1961.

53. R. F. C. Hull to Gerald Gross, October 8, 1961.

54. *MDR*, p. 39.

55. *MDR*, p. 24.

56. Aniela Jaffé to Gerald Gross, November 23, 1961.

57. Gerald Gross to Aniela Jaffé, November 14, 1961, in which he explains why *MDR* would not be on that list.

58. Gerald Gross to R. F. C. Hull, November 29, 1961.

59. Gerald Gross to Aniela Jaffé, November 28, 1961.

60. Milton Waldman to Aniela Jaffé, dated only October 1961.

61. R. F. C. Hull to Gerald Gross, October 8, 1961.

62. As they appear in *MDR*, pp. 10–15. R. F. C. Hull to Gerald Gross, November 2, 1961.

63. The letter is not in *CL* or in the ETH; the Jung heirs claim not to know of anything resembling it.

64. Milton Waldman to Aniela Jaffé, October 2, 1961.

65. Gerald Gross to Aniela Jaffé, December 1, 1961.

66. There was ongoing disagreement over this until the last moment before publication. On February 27, 1962, there was still the question of whether to use her glossary at all, as it was too "abstruse" (Gerald Gross to R. F. C. Hull).

67. In Gerald Gross to Milton Waldman, December 1, 1961, Gross repeats that he agrees to eliminate *Seven Sermons* "for the sake of overall length." It did not appear in the first Pantheon edition but was included in all subsequent editions and remains in the Vintage paperback that is in widest use today.

68. Aniela Jaffé to Gerald Gross, December 5, 1961.

69. Most prominent among them Sonu Shamdasani and Alan C. Elms (*Uncovered Lives: The Uneasy Alliance of Biography and Psychology* [New York: Oxford Univ. Press, 1994]), who base many of their charges on incomplete evidence and nonobjective speculation.

70. R. F. C. Hull to Aniela Jaffé, December 8, 1961. They appear in *CW*-10.

71. R. F. C. Hull to Gerald Gross, December 9, 1961.

72. Gerald Gross to R. F. C. Hull, December 11, 1961, spells out Waldman's "shenanigans" and expresses Gross's annoyance.

73. See, for example, her perplexity in Aniela Jaffé to Gerald Gross, December 5, 1961.

74. R. F. C. Hull to Aniela Jaffé, December 8, 1961. Everything changed within the week, when Jaffé became angry that Hull might serve as "final judge . . . and be in a position to overrule her and the Niehuses" (R. F. C. Hull to Gerald Gross, December 14, 1961).

75. Aniela Jaffé to R. F. C. Hull, December 11, 1961.

76. Gerald Gross to R. F. C. Hull, January 5, 1962.

77. R. F. C. Hull to Gerald Gross, December 14, 1961.

78. In Aniela Jaffé to Gerald Gross, January 22, 1962, she writes cryptically of "the new beginning of Tower, rewritten by Richard Hull, with which I fully agree."

79. Gerald Gross to R. F. C. Hull, March 13, 1962. Many more changes in content and structure were negotiated until the end of August 1962.

80. Gerald Gross to Bernhard Peyer, September 6, 1962.

81. Gerald Gross to R. F. C. Hull, September 18, 1962.

82. This account is a synopsis of a detailed letter sent to me by one of the persons, on behalf of the others, who were involved in collecting, saving, and eventually dispersing the many pages of writing that eventually became *MDR*. The letter writer wanted me to convey the facts without revealing names or details and has given me permission to divulge the letter at a future date I am not at liberty to specify.

83. Robert S. Boynton, "The Other Freud (The Wild One)," *New York Times*, Saturday, June 10, 2000, p. B9. Phillips makes an interesting comment about analysts in

general that I find applicable to Jung: "The craving for academic respectability has made analysts want to be recognized either as real scientists or real artists. They aren't comfortable sustaining the ambiguity that comes with being neither."

84. Gerhard Adler, "The Memoirs of CGJ," *Spring* (1964): 139.

85. In the English but not the German; the date is May 20, 1958.

86. The ellipsis signifies a note in one version of the *Protocols* where Jaffe's handwriting indicates "deletion."

87. CGJ, *MDR*, rev. ed. (New York: Vintage Books, 1989), p. 3.

88. CGJ to Kurt Wolff, June 17, 1958, HW/BLY.

APPENDIX: THE HONEGGER PAPERS

1. Because this case deals with one of the several most controversial aspects of CGJ's life and work, I include here portions of an unpublished chronology, "Notes on the Honegger/Solar Phallus Case," compiled by and generously made available to me by William McGuire.

The case first appears in Jung's writings in 1912, in part 2 of:

(A) *Wandlungen u. Symbole der Libido*, p. 94:

"Honegger hat bei einem Geisteskranken (paranoide Demens) folgende Wahnidee entdeckt: Der Kranke sieht an der Sonne einen sogennanten "Aufwärte Schwans" (d. h. soviel wie erigierten Penis).

(B) Translated by Hinkle (pp. 95–96 in new PUP edn. of *Psychology of the Unconscious*): "Honegger discovered the following hallucination in an insane man (paranoid dement.): The patient sees in the sun an "upright tail" similar to an erected [*sic*] penis."

McGuire adds: However, cf. the comment on Jung's copies of Dieterich and Creuzer at the end of these notes.

(C) In Jung's revisions entered (around 1946) in the 1938 edn. of *Wandlungen und Symbole der Libido*, he changed A to:

Ich habe bei einem Geisteskranken folgende Wahnidee beobachtet: Der Kranke sieht an der Sonne ein membrum erectum.

(D) Version C appeared in *Symbole und Wandlungen*, 1952 edn., p. 169, and 1973 edn. (*Gesam. Werke*), p. 133. There is no mention of Honegger.

(E) In *Symbols of Transformation*, par. 151, Hull translates C as:

I once came across the following hallucination in a schizophrenic patient: he told me he could see an erect phallus on the sun.

The text from here on is McGuire's commentary: Hull's translation isn't exact. Surely Jung wrote: "I have observed the following hallucination in an insane patient: the patient sees an erect phallus on the sun."

Together with all that, there's the confusion over Jung's citation of the 1910 edn. of Dieterich, *Mithrasliturgie*, ignoring (or being unaware of) the original edn. of 1903, several years before Honegger's patient presumably saw the solar phallus. In *Symbole u. Wandlungen* 1952, only the 1910 edn. is cited; in the 1973 (*GW*) edn., the Swiss editors (after Jung's death) cite in the Bibliographie "2 Aufl. Berlin 1910," but do not mention the 1903 edn.

Jung cites the solar phallus case as his own, without reference to Honegger, in "The Structure of the Psyche," *CW*-8, pars. 318–19, and "The Concept of the Collective Unconscious," *CW*-9i, par. 105. (The London editors inserted a footnote in both instances exculpating Jung for the 1910 Dieterich citation, and the *GW* editors translated the same footnote.)

How early did Jung take credit for the solar phallus case? According to the General Bibliography (*CW*-19), the first publication of what was later called "The Structure of the Psyche" was as a part of G.1927a, "Die Erdbedingtheit der Psyche," in Keyserling's *Mensche und Erde*. According to *CW*-19 and the editorial note in *CW*-8, par. 318, the first part was then published as G.1928d, "Die Struktur der Seele," *Europaische Revue* IV, 1 & 2. . . . The solar phallus case is not in it. The text varies far from the next and final version, G.1931,7, "Die Struktur der Seele," in *Seelenprobleme der Gegenwart*, where Jung reports the case as his own. That version is translated as "The Structure of the Psyche" in *CW*-8.

Accordingly, it appears that Jung first took credit for the solar phallus case in 1930, the date of his foreword to *Seelenprobleme der Gegenwart*.

In "The Tavistock Lectures," which Jung delivered in London in Sept./Oct. 1935, Jung referred obliquely to the case — cf. *CW*-18, par. 85: "I saw a patient with schizophrenia who had a peculiar vision . . . and later I came on a book by Dieterich." The next year he cited it as his own in a lecture, "The Concept of the Collective Unconscious," given in New York and London and published in local journals. See E.1936a and d and *CW*-8, par. 105.

The *Katalog of the C. G. Jung Bibliothek (Küsnacht)* lists Creuzer, 4 vols. 1810–1821, and Dieterich, *Eine Mithrasliturgie* (1910). Jung did not write the dates of acquisition in any of the volumes. The *F/J letters*, 160J, n. 7, suggest that Jung could have owned Creuzer by November 8, 1909; 201F, n. 8, suggests that in early 1910 he intended to buy Dieterich; and 210J, n. 1, suggests that by August 31, 1910, he had acquired it and was reading it. The 1910 edition [of Dieterich] indicates on the title page of Jung's copy that it is the 2nd edn. and that the first was published in 1903. There are many annotations in Jung's hand but no indication of when he purchased the book.

2. From interviews and telephone conversations with C. A. Meier. For further corroboration, see his *Jung and Analytical Psychology*, lectures given to Andover Newton Theological School and published by the Department of Psychology, Newton Centre, Massachusetts, 1959, pp. 18–19. In interviews, Meier said CGJ gave him the Honegger Papers "sometime in early or mid-1930s because he would never get around to writing them up and he thought [Meier] should make a book of them."

3. The contents are listed on two cards in the ETH catalogue: HS 1068: 10–15, and HS 1068: 16–21.

Card 1: 10–15: Schwyzer, Emil (1862– : mentally deranged; confined at Burghölzli*)
Analysis of Emil Schwyzer, by Dr. J. J. Honegger

10. Schwyzer's map of the world. 2 sheets.
Manuscripts of the Analysis
11. The dreams . . . records of analysis, Jan./Feb. 1910, 100 sheets / 186 pages (with insertions)
12. About spinning. Sister Bertha. Opéra comique . . . 2 sh./3 p.

13. The brain-semen theory. The toad that Scherer brings along. Why the shot was a shot by God . . . 4 sh./7 p.
14. (. . . childhood). Bertha Bosshardt. Doctor's title. Why it was that the semen-body became male. Freemasons. How did the world begin? Explanation of the earthquake of Messina . . . 14 sh. (a–h)/25 p. w. enclosure: newspaper clipping w. picture of young Queen Victoria.
15. The Chinese. Text in shorthand (on Schwyzer's analysis?) 2 sh./4 p.

---

* According to Prof. C. A. Meier, C. G. Jung owes essential ideas of his archetype theory to this medical history. Schwyzer's "upward tail" of the sun was already found in a Parisian papyrus . . . cf. Jung *CW*-5 (1973), p. 200.

Card 2: 16–21: Various (partly fragmentary) handwritten evaluations
16. Some theoretical aspects concerning paranoia. 11 sh./p.
17. On the formation of paranoid delusions (lecture). 7 sh./14 p.
18. Medical history: Excerpt. Preliminary remark. Chronological overview of the psyches. Case E. S. 6 sh./11 p.
19. Chronological overview of the psyches. The Scherers' role as psyches, as all-animating demon. 6 sh./11 p.
20. Analysis of a case of paranoid dementia; fragments. 11sh./13 p. + 5 sh. (in small format)/6 p.
21. It was during the summer of 1901 that I became acquainted with spiritism (ms. by Dr. Honegger?). 22 sh./44 p.

4. Correspondence with William McGuire, March 23 and May 21, 1966; Dr. Beat Glaus (former director of the Manuscript Division of the ETH), interviews and conversations during research there November 1994–April 1998; Dr. Peter Jung and Herr Ulrich Hoerni, interviews, conversations, correspondence 1995–2002. The current director, Dr. Rudolf Mumenthaler, granted an interview November 28, 2001, and made the official Honegger Papers available then.
5. It was at this point that Richard Noll was refused permission to read the papers and he made the accusations in the *New York Times*, previously cited (see page 711, n. 67).
6. The phrase was used by Dr. Peter Jung and Herr Ulrich Hoerni, March 7, 1998, interview with the author.
7. The "expert's" official report is not available for consultation. The following observations are based upon my own unofficial English translation (which must be regarded as paraphrase) of the German originals.
8. These are my own unofficial comparisons.
9. Swiss shorthand differs from German. Ms. Ursula Schulte and Dr. Phil. Richard Merz prepared a German transcription for my use. The English translation is my own and unofficial. I offer the possibility that Schwyzer wrote some of the shorthand because he was an office clerk before his hospitalization, at a time when all Swiss clerks were expected to know shorthand. The several analysts who have read these passages think some of the first-person stream-of-consciousness narration could well be dictation taken down as Schwyzer spoke it, which raises the question of who did so. I have been unable to verify that Honegger knew shorthand, and I know that Jung did not.
10. Dr. Meier said CGJ and Honegger had similar handwriting and that sometimes he was unable to distinguish them when he studied these papers. He said he could not persuade Jung to identify who wrote which sections: "After [Jung] entrusted them

to my keeping, he never once looked at them, no matter how many times I asked him to do so."

11. English quotations from Honegger's original German abstract are by A. K. Donoghue, in Walser, *Spring* (1974): 253–54. References to Honegger's actual paper are my unofficial translation of the original German in the ETH's Honegger Papers and the private archival copies.

12. The passage in the original is underlined, most likely Honegger's method of emphasis.

13. Daniel Paul Schreber, *Memoirs of My Nervous Illness*, originally published as *Denkwürdigkeiten eines Nervenkranken* in 1903, written about by Freud and much discussed by him and CGJ in their correspondence. See *F/J* for full citations.

14. Earlier, Honegger identified the two forms of thinking, the "symbolic-mythological, the dream thinking; (2) the dialectical . . . understood as mental exercise in compensation for symbolic thinking." As the Nuremberg paper concentrates only on the former, perhaps he intended to discuss the latter in the next one.

15. This and the following statement is based upon information held by a private source, who also holds a copy of the Honegger Papers.

16. Hull was referring to what became *CW*-5, paras. 150ff., pp. 100ff.; *CW*-8, paras. 228 and 313, pp. 111 and 149; and *CW*-9/1, para. 105, p. 50. Bennet's letter is E. A. Bennet to CGJ, December 15, 1959, ETH, not in *CL*.

17. A draft of Bennet's letter to a "Mr. Hetherington" via the *Listener* is dated November 12, 1959, ETH; the draft of Bennet's letter to CGJ is undated.

Acknowledgments

A biographer requires the cooperation and assistance of a great many people during the long years it takes to write about someone's life. So many helped with this one that I would like to write mini-biographies about their contributions, but space dictates that I express my gratitude by listing their names alphabetically and in some cases their affiliations.

I owe special thanks to those who were with me every step of the way: John Ferrone, Jean and Thomas B. Kirsch, Herbert and Virginia Lust, William McGuire and Paula van Doren McGuire, Paul Roazen, Andrew Samuels, and Aileen Ward.

I thank the *Erbengemeinschaft C. G. Jung*, the children and grandchildren of C. G. and Emma Jung, who granted interviews or telephone conversations, hosted me on numerous social occasions, and gave me guided tours of the Bollingen Tower and the Küsnacht house, and whose unfailing generosity went far beyond the usual scholarly courtesy: the children, Agathe Niehus-Jung, Gret Baumann-Jung, and Franz Jung; the grandchildren, Adrian Baumann, Dieter Baumann, Wolfgang Baumann, Ulrich Hoerni, Peter Jung, Brigitte Merk-Niehus, Ludwig Niehus, Rudolf Niehus, Monica Walder, and Sybille Willi-Niehus; also, the children and grandchildren of Gret Homberger-Rauschenbach (Emma Jung's sister), Marianne Homberger and Laurence Homberger.

In Switzerland, so many people offered professional assistance and personal friendship that I take the liberty of listing them without their many distinguished titles: Olga and Robert Betschart, Cordelia and Rudolf Bettschart, Karin Beyeler-Hartmeier, Margrith Bigler-Eggenberger, Hanni Binder, Frances and Thomas Boni, Robert Briner, Cornelia Brunner, Paul Brutsche, Ursula Cadorin-Trüb, Barbara Davies, Ernst Falzeder, Trudy Fredericks, Toni Frei-Wehrlin, Marianne Frisch, Adolf Guggenbuhl-Craig, Marjorie and Hans Gunthardt, Regine Heim, Katherine Herter, Gertrude Hess, Robert Hinshaw, Thomas and Phyllis Hoehn, Emanuel Hurwitz, Theodor Itten, Felix Jaffé, Mario Jacoby, Peter Kamber, Daniel and Anna Keel, Emmanuel Kennedy, Eva and Pierre Koralnik, Leonardo La Rosa, Lydia Lehmann, Hans-P. and Anita Margulies, Sonja Marjasch, C. A. Meier, Richard Merz, Gabrielle Merzbacher, Yvette Mottier, Verena Müller, Paul Naeff, Gerda Neideck, Mischa Neumann, Jane Cabot Reid, Alfred Ribi, Christa Robinson, Ximena de Angulo Roelli, Vera Rottenberg-Liatowitsch, Sally Schaffer, Othmar and Lissa Schmidlin, Robert Schneebeli, Ursula Schulte, Alexis Schwarzenbach, Fritz Senn, Elsbeth Stoiber, Doris Sträuli-Keller, Elisabeth Stumm, Georg and Maja Trüb, Wolf and Ursula Trüb-Offermann, Marie-Louise von Franz,

Ruth Weibel, Elsbeth Wernli, Sigmund Widmer, Fatma Turkkan Wille, Susanna Woodtli, and Stephanie Zuellig.

In Paris: Claude Courchay; Christian Gaillard, and Elisabeth Roudinesco. In England: Ann Casement, Mary Clemmy, Gottfried Heuer, Jean Knox, Renos Papadopoulos, Molly Tuby, Anthony Stevens, Anthony Storr, Sir Laurens van der Post, and Vera von der Heydt. In Norway and Sweden: Bjorn Lindahl and Nina and Sebastian Kjølass. In Spain, Birthe-Lena Hull and Edward McGuire. In Australia: Mary Beasley, Robert Boynes, Robert Hamilton, Mandy Martin, Susan Mitchell, Christina Slade, Ghillian Sullivan, and James and Robyn Walter.

In the United States and Canada: Michael Vannoy Adams, Charles Amerkhanian, Joyce Ashley, Mary Bancroft, Mali Bé Lé, Stephen J. Bergman, Hélène de Billy, Barbara and Louis Breger, Peggy Brooks, Vernon Brooks, Shareen Blair Brysac, Joan Dulles Buresh, Joseph Cambray, Linda Carter, Kenneth Catandella, Diana Cavallo, Ron Chernow, D. Gerard Condon, Jane Kinney Denning, John Patrick Diggins, Muriel Dimen, Kurt Eissler, Grace Ferrar, Marianne Gilbert Finnegan, Donald and Patricia Freed, Bruce and Karolyn Gould, Ronald Grant, Phyllis Grosskurth, Karl Hagedorn, David Hart, Joseph Henderson, Judith Hennessee, James Hillman, Peter Homans, Ann and George Hogel, Lucy Kachele, Carol Law, Elaine Lewis, E. James Lieberman, Jay Livernois, Patricia Louis, Peter Lynn, Kenneth MacKenzie, Marion Meade, Paul Mellon, Karl Meyer, Roberta Nesheim, Nancy and Donald Newlove, Richard Noll, Patricia O'Toole, Louis and Lynn Prosek, Wayne and Ricki Rush, Stacy Schiff, Linda W. Schmidt, William Schoenl, Thomas Singer, Murray Stein, Barbara Stephens, Sydney Stern, Allison Stokes, Rosemary Sullivan, Hugh Taft-Morales, Deborah Tegarden, Amanda Vaill, George and Suzanne Wagner, Carl Walker, Demaris S. Wehr, Anika Weiss, Barry and Beverly Wellman, Joseph and Jane Wheelwright, Edward C. Whitmont, Nikolaus Wolff, Polly Young-Eisendrath, and Beverly Zabriskie.

I thank the following libraries and their ever-resourceful and cordial staffs. At the Kristine Mann Library, C. G. Jung Center of New York (my home away from home): Michele McKee, Steven O'Neill, David Ward, and Arnold de Vera. At the ETH's Wissenschafthistorische Sammlungen: Drs. Beat Glaus, Rudolf Mumenthaler, and Yvonne Voegeli. At the Burghölzli Mental Hospital: Dr. Prof. Hell, Dr. Prof. Bernhard Kuecherhoff, and Rolf Mösli. At the Medizinhistorisches Institut und Museum: Dr. Walther Fuchs. At the National Archives: Dr. John Taylor, Dr. Milton O. Gustafson, and Fred Romanski. At the Library of Congress: Dr. Marvin Kranz. I thank also the special collections departments of the libraries of the University of Tulsa and Princeton University; the Beinecke Library of Yale University; the Francis A. Countway Library of Medicine at Harvard University; the Wisconsin State Historical Society; and the Social Archiv, the Staatsanwaltschaft, the Staatsarchiv, and the Zentralbibliothek, all of Canton Zürich.

For grants-in-aid, I thank Oliver Bernier and the board members of the Anne and Erlo van Waveren Foundation; Dr. Soren Ekstron and the board members of the C. G. Jung Institute of New York: the Hartog Fellowship, School of the Arts, Columbia University. For residencies, I wish to thank the Rockefeller Foundation Bellagio Study and Conference Center and the Bogliasco Foundation Liguria Study Center for the Arts and Humanities.

My professional family has supported me above and beyond with this book: I thank my agent and friend, Elaine Markson, her associates Geri Thoma and Gary Johnson; and my former publisher, the visionary James B. Silberman. My editor, William D. Phillips, was truly *il miglior fabbro*, the better maker, who made the shaping of this book an incredibly enriching experience for me. I also thank Michael Pietsch, Asya Muchnick, and Zainab Zakari for unfailing editorial support. Pamela Marshall copyedited the manuscript with infinite patience and care, turning what could have been an overwhelmingly daunting task (for me, that is) into a positive and pleasant experience. I also thank Heather Rizzo, Alison Vandenberg, and Tracy Williams.

My family has been consistently sustaining. This book is for the Wizzerbel, who put her little hand on her hip and asked, "Just who is this Jung guy anyway, Gamma? Does he live in your [com]pooter?" My children, Vonn Scott and Katney Bair and Niko Courtelis, were always there; as were my sister, Linda B. Rankin, and John and Kim Rankin; my mother, Helen; my brother, Vincent, and sister-in-law, Judith; and all the Bartolottas, Aldo and Joan, Armand and Lorayne, Bruce and Camera, Toni Jo and Archy, Dora, Robin, B. G., and Andrea; Leah Balliard; and especially Catherine Montecarlo and the memory of Christopher Montecarlo.

Finally, I salute the dear friends who were with me at the start but not at the end: Sara Golden Blackburn, Pamela Fox Emory, Carole H. Klein, Winnifred S. Pasternack, and Mary Perot Nichols.

Once more, I wish to thank all those persons I named, those who helped but did not want to be identified, and those whom I may have inadvertently omitted.

Index

Deidre Bair is the author of the National Book Award–winning *Samuel Beckett: A Biography*, as well as the acclaimed biographies *Simone de Beauvoir* and *Anaïs Nin*. She has been a literary journalist and university professor of comparative literature and culture and has held fellowships from the Guggenheim and Rockefeller Foundations, the Bunting Institute of Radcliffe College, and the C. G. Jung Center of New York. She lives in Connecticut.